AMERICAN NATURE WRITERS

AMERICAN NATURE WRITERS

JOHN ELDER
Editor

VOLUME I

Edward Abbey
to
John McPhee

CHARLES SCRIBNER'S SONS
Macmillan Library Reference USA
Simon & Schuster Macmillan
NEW YORK

SIMON & SCHUSTER AND PRENTICE HALL INTERNATIONAL
LONDON   MEXICO CITY   NEW DELHI   SINGAPORE   SYDNEY   TORONTO

Library of Congress Cataloging-in-Publication Data

American nature writers / John Elder, editor.
   2 vols.   cm.
   Includes bibliographical references and index.
   Contents: v. 1 Edward Abbey to John McPhee—v. 2 Peter Matthiessen to Western Geologists and Explorers.
   ISBN 0-684-19692-1 (2-vol. set :alk. paper)
   1. American literature—Dictionaries.   2. Nature in literature—Dictionaries.   3. Authors, American—Biography—Dictionaries. 4. American literature—Bio-bibliography—Dictionaries.   5. Nature in literature—Bio-bibliography—Dictionaries.   6. Natural history—United States—Historiography—Dictionaries.   7. Natural history—United States—Bio-bibliography—Dictionaries.   I. Elder, John, 1947–
PS163.A6   1996
810.9'36—dc20   96-31237
                                                                      CIP

10 9 8 7 6 5 4 3 2 1

PRINTED IN THE UNITED STATES OF AMERICA

The paper used in this publication meets the minimum requirements of the American National Standard for Information Sciences—Permanence of Paper for Printed Library Materials, ANSI Z39.48-1984.

ACKNOWLEDGMENTS

Acknowledgment is gratefully made to those publishers and individuals who permitted the use of the following texts in copyright. (Illustration credits are printed before the Index in Volume II.)

DIANE ACKERMAN. Quotations from *A Natural History of the Senses* by Diane Ackerman, © 1990 by Diane Ackerman, and *The Moon by Whale Light* by Diane Ackerman, © 1991 by Diane Ackerman. Reprinted by permission of Random House, Inc.

ANNIE DILLARD. Extracts of fewer than 500 words each from *The Living* by Annie Dillard (Copyright © 1992 by Annie Dillard); *Teaching a Stone to Talk* by Annie Dillard (Copyright © 1982 by Annie Dillard); *Pilgrim at Tinker Creek* by Annie Dillard (Copyright © 1974 by Annie Dillard); *Holy the Firm* by Annie Dillard (Copyright © 1977 by Annie Dillard); *The Writing Life* by Annie Dillard (Copyright © 1989 by Annie Dillard); *An American Childhood* by Annie Dillard (Copyright © 1987 by Annie Dillard); and *Living by Fiction* by Annie Dillard (Copyright © 1982 by Annie Dillard). Reprinted by permission of HarperCollins Publishers, Inc., and the Blanche Gregory Agency.

ROBERT FINCH. Excerpts reprinted from *The Primal Place* by Robert Finch, by permission of W. W. Norton & Company, Inc. Copyright © 1983 by Robert Finch. Text excerpts reprinted from *The Cape Itself*, Text by Robert Finch, Photographs by Ralph MacKenzie, by permission of W. W. Norton & Company, Inc. Text Copyright © 1991 by Robert Finch. Photographs Copyright © 1991 by Ralph MacKenzie.

SUE HUBBELL. Excerpt totaling 4 pages from *A Book of Bees . . . and How to Keep Them* by Sue Hubbell. Copyright © 1988 by Sue Hubbell. Reprinted by permission of Random House, Inc. Excerpt totaling 2 pages from *A Country Year* by Sue Hubbell. Copyright © 1983, 1984, 1985, 1986 by Sue Hubbell. Reprinted by permission of Random House, Inc., and Darhansoff and Verrill.

THE FORMS OF AMERICAN NATURE POETRY. The lines from "Corson Inlet" are reprinted from *The Selected Poems: 1951–1977* by A. R. Ammons, by permission of W. W. Norton & Company, Inc. Copyright © 1977, 1975, 1974, 1972, 1971, 1970, 1966, 1965, 1964, 1955 by A. R. Ammons. "At the Fishhouses" from *The Complete Poems:*

1927–1979 by Elizabeth Bishop. Copyright © 1979, 1983 by Alice Helen Methfessel. Reprinted by permission of Farrar, Straus & Giroux, Inc. "I was sleeping where the Black Oaks Move" from *Jacklight* by Louise Erdrich. Copyright © 1984 by Louise Erdrich. Reprinted by permission of Henry Holt and Co., Inc., "Canticle to the Waterbirds" Copyright © 1978 by William Everson. Reprinted from *The Veritable Years: 1949–1966* with the permission of Black Sparrow Press. Nine lines from "West-Running Brook" from *The Poetry of Robert Frost.* Copyright © 1956 by Robert Frost. Copyright © 1928, 1969 by Henry Holt and Co., Inc. Reprinted by permission of Henry Holt and Co., Inc., and Jonathan Cape.

Twelve lines from "Directive" from *The Poetry of Robert Frost.* Copyright © 1975 by Leslie Frost Ballantine. Copyright © 1947, 1969 by Henry Holt and Co., Inc. Reprinted by permission of Henry Holt and Co., Inc., and Jonathan Cape. Brewster Ghiselin, "Rattlesnake" and lines from "Sea." From *Windrose: Poems, 1929–1979.* Copyright © 1980 by Brewster Ghiselin. Reprinted by permission of the author. Nine lines from "The Purse-Seine" from *The Selected Poetry of Robinson Jeffers* by Robinson Jeffers. Copyright © 1937 and renewed 1965 by Donnan Jeffers and Garth Jeffers. Reprinted by permission of Random House, Inc. "O Taste and See" from *O Taste and See* by Denise Levertov. Copyright © 1966 by Denise Levertov Goodman. Reprinted by permission of New Directions Publishing Corporation and Bloodaxe Books. "Snail Garden" from *Poems Old and New* by Janet Lewis. Copyright © 1981 by Janet Lewis. Reprinted with the permission of the Ohio University Press/Swallow Press, Athens.

Three lines from "Learning a Dead Language" from *Selected Poems* by W. S. Merwin. Copyright © 1988 by W. S. Merwin. Reprinted with permission of the author. Four lines from "After the Alphabets" and three lines from "Witness" from *Rain in the Trees* by W. S. Merwin. Copyright © 1988 by W. S. Merwin. Reprinted with permission of the author. "The Fish" reprinted with permission of Faber and Faber, Ltd., and Simon & Schuster, Inc., from *Collected Poems of Marianne Moore.* Copyright © 1935 by Marianne Moore, renewed 1963 by Marianne Moore and T. S. Eliot. Six lines each from "The Shape of the Fire" and "Four for Sir John Davies" from *The Collected Poems of Theodore Roethke* by Theodore Roethke. Copyright © 1966 by Theodore Roethke. Reprinted by permission of Bantam Doubleday Dell Publishing Group, Inc. "Second Witness" was published in *Firekeeper: New and Selected Poems* by Pattiann Rogers (Milkweed Editions, 1994). Copyright © 1994 by Pattiann Rogers. Used with permission from Milkweed Editions.

"For All" from *Axe Handles* by Gary Snyder. Copyright © 1983 by Gary Snyder. Reprinted by permission of North Point Press, a division of Farrar, Straus & Giroux, Inc. "Anecdote of the Jar" from *Collected Poems* by Wallace Stevens. Copyright © 1923 and renewed 1951 by Wallace Stevens. Reprinted by permission of Alfred A. Knopf, Inc. Fifteen lines from "The Idea of Order at Key West" from *Collected Poems* by Wallace Stevens. Copyright © 1936 by Wallace Stevens and renewed 1964 by Holly Stevens. Reprinted by permission of Alfred A. Knopf, Inc., and Faber and Faber, Ltd. Excerpts from "The Lilacs" in *Walking to Sleep: New Poems and Translations*, copyright © 1963 and renewed 1991 by Richard Wilbur, reprinted by permission of Harcourt Brace & Company and Faber and Faber, Ltd. "Spring and All" from *Collected Poems 1909–1939*, vol. 1, by William Carlos Williams. Copyright © 1938 by New Directions Publishing Corporation. Reprinted by permission of New Directions Publishing Corporation and Carcanet Press, Ltd. "A Sort of a Song" from *Collected Poems 1939–1962*, vol. 2, by William Carlos Williams. Copyright ©. 1944, 1948 by William Carlos Williams. Reprinted by permission of New Directions Publishing Corporation and Carcanet Press, Ltd.

EDITORIAL STAFF

CONTENTS

Volume I

CONTENTS

Volume II

CONTENTS

INTRODUCTION

ECOLOGISTS SPEAK OF THE "EDGE-EFFECT" created where two ecosystems meet. The joining of marine and terrestrial environments along a rocky shoreline and the brushy margin between a meadow and a forest are examples of such edges or "ecotones." These mixed, dynamic habitats are particularly rich in a couple of ways. They contain more species than are found in either constituent ecosystem, and they have a greater density of organisms within a given species. The special interest and importance of nature writing come from the ways in which it too represents a vivid edge—between literature and science, between the imagination and the physical process of observation, and between humanity and the many other forms of life with which we share this earth.

The term "nature writing" has generally been used to describe a particular form of prose that is closely associated in American literature with the work of Henry David Thoreau. One basic definition of the genre might be as follows: personal, reflective essays grounded in appreciation of the natural world and of science, but also open to the spiritual meaning and value of the physical creation. Many venerable forms of literary engagement with nature are obviously outside this category, and I will come back to this issue of exclusion. Even so, the nature essay as designated above has had its own remarkable power and importance in our tradition.

The authors discussed in this collection present an impressive continuity in American literature. The field of nature writing was already well established in the late eighteenth century, as exemplified by a figure like William Bartram. And it is a form of literature that enjoys an unprecedented flowering today. More than a third of the essays here are devoted to contemporary authors. The achievements of recent writers certainly account, at east in part, for the growing popularity of this literature and for its increasingly frequent inclusion in college syllabi. But another source of current interest in the genre is surely the widespread concern about our global environment. Readers are hungry for books that address with artistic authority the complex balance, the integrity, and the intrinsic value of nature. Nature writing is, in this sense, a testimonial literature.

Conventionally, the study of literature has been divided into poetry, fiction, and drama. Nonfiction, or "the essay," has until lately been emphasized much less in departments of English, and then often in the context of classes on composition. Over the last half-century, though, there has been a growing interest in nature writing, not merely as a subcategory of a secondary field, but as an original, significant, and popular American genre in its own right. Such a development might be tracked through anthologies that have sketched the outlines of a tradition. Among the most important were William Beebe's *The Book of Naturalists* (1944), Joseph Wood Krutch's *Great American Nature Writing* (1950), John Kiernan's *Treasury of Great Nature Writing* (1957), and Frank Bergon's *The Wilderness Reader* (1980). These collections began to identify lineages within the genre. They illuminated, in particular, the direct influence exercised by Thoreau on such successors as John Burroughs and John Muir, and through them, on the modern environmental movement.

Three more recent anthologies have also played a large role in disclosing the tradition of nature writing. Thomas Lyon's *This Incomperable Lande* (1989), with its comprehensive, introductory "History," draws attention at once to the continuities and the distinct varieties within the "taxonomy" of America's literature of nature. *The Norton Book of Nature Writing* (1990, coedited by Robert Finch and John Elder) emphasizes an Anglo-American progression, in which such figures as Thoreau were both anticipated and strongly influenced by the English parson Gilbert White and other amateur naturalists of the Linnaean age. Lorraine Anderson's *Sisters of the Earth* (1991) highlights the central contributions of women writers, as well as the connection between the nature essay per se and other literary forms.

The influx of nature writing into literary culture and education has offered three particular gifts. Most immediately, there has been a surge of inspiration from the powerful, engaged voices of contemporary American writers who practice this genre. When one starts to make a list of the many outstanding proponents of nature writing now working on the national scene—including but by no means limited to Annie Dillard, Barry Lopez, Scott Russell Sanders, Wendell Berry, Terry Tempest Williams, Gary Snyder, Edward Hoagland, Gretel Ehrlich, Ann Zwinger, Rick Bass, and Richard Nelson—one quickly notes what a large proportion of our most original literary authors it includes.

There is often also a *qualitative* difference between the idealism and ambition of today's nature writers and the temper of much contemporary fiction and poetry. While there are many wonderful exceptions, the sorts of short stories and lyrics now mastered in MFA programs and published in literary magazines can be rather dreary. The dysfunctionality of human relationships is frequently mirrored in the depressed speaker's isolation and confinement within an apparently viewless room. By contrast, even when a storm of grief for despoiled beauty fills their pages, nature writers bring a characteristic vividness to their engagements with this world and its possibilities.

The ambitious, inspiring character of contemporary nature writing is epitomized by the following passage from Annie Dillard's *Pilgrim at Tinker Creek*, published in 1974. This celebrated paragraph from her chapter on "Seeing" might be taken as an update of Thoreau's exhortation in *Walden* (1854) to "live in infinite expectation of the dawn":

> One day I was walking along Tinker Creek thinking of nothing at all and I saw the tree with the lights in it. I saw the backyard cedar where the mourning doves roost charged and transfigured, each cell buzzing with flame. I stood on the grass with the lights in it, grass that was wholly fire, utterly focused and utterly dreamed. It was less like seeing than like being for the first time seen, knocked breathless by a powerful glance. The flood of fire abated, but I'm still spending the power. Gradually the lights went out in the cedar, the colors died, the cells unflamed and disappeared. I was still ringing. I had been my whole life a bell, and never knew it until at that moment I was lifted and struck.

Such literature simultaneously affirms the possibility for human life to be a spiritual quest and the central value of literature in focusing our attention on the world's meaningfulness. It inspires students as well as their teachers, helping all to remember that the stakes in our reading, writing, and discussion are high indeed—and that such activities are fundamentally in the service of life more abundant.

The literary scholarship inspired by and complementary to contemporary nature writing has also offered a gift of its own, by disclosing a tradition of attentiveness to the earth that spans more than two centuries. It has been vital to establish that the eloquent writers of our own day are not simply reacting to environmental abuses or, for that matter, articulating values derived from the modern environmental movement. Such a perspective would allow them only a contingent, and perhaps evanescent, interest. In fact, though, this tradition has been central to American literature almost from its beginning and has included a large number of distinctive and impressive authors. Nature writing is a much more powerful resource for environmentalism because of these deep roots. The most effective activism always draws sustenance from a lineage of affirmation—it is ultimately activism on behalf of, rather than merely against. Knowledge of this literary tradition assures those who care deeply about the land that we have ancestors in our own culture and in the land alike.

When we are considering the existence of a tradition of nature writing, however, the word "construction" is also definitely to the point. Filling in the gaps has been an ongoing process. Particularly in the period separating Muir and Austin from writers of the mid-twentieth century, there were a number of important women nature writers who have fallen mostly out of print. As a group, they have also not yet been adequately represented in anthologies. Now, thanks to the work of editors and scholars such as Lorraine Anderson, Vera Norwood, and Lawrence Buell, there is a renewed recognition of authors like Anna Botsford Comstock, Josephine Johnson, and Gene Stratton Porter, as well as of earlier figures like Susan Fenimore Cooper and Celia Thaxter. There is also a prospect for their works to become more widely available and more frequently taught. The present collection of critical essays attempts to build upon such recent expansions in our understanding of the tradition. Accordingly, this work's table of contents includes not just the long-recognized mainstays of the Thoreauvian tradition but also the many neglected but important figures such as Comstock, Johnson, and Stratton Porter, as well as a rich sampling of the writers now at work.

A third gift of nature writing to the college curriculum, specifically, has been in fostering connections between literature and the natural sciences. On how many of our campuses has the division between the "two cultures" been ratified by the physical separation of lab buildings from those that house humanities classrooms? But because the authors we call nature writers are themselves often quite interested in the sciences, and sometimes possess academic credentials in these fields, they have provided openings for scholars in literature to co-teach courses with their scientific colleagues. English teachers have thus found it possible and profitable to study John McPhee in a class with a geologist; to read Dillard in a joint venture with a botanist, while investigating changing patterns of flora in their local landscape; and to introduce the work of Terry Tempest Williams when considering the sense of place in a collaboration with a geographer. Through facilitating such interactions, nature writing has conveyed its richness of "edge-effect" into our educational institutions.

In addition to the variety of species and the abundance of organisms that are typical of ecotones, such environments are also marked by their dynamic character. Dynamic and, from the perspective of creatures venturing into such a zone, precarious. New possibilities for nourishment draw individual plants and animals in from each side but along with such augmented resources comes the chance that a given pioneer may end up itself as a meal for a fellow opportunist venturing in from the facing ecosystem. This risky, shifting aspect of edge-effect is as pertinent to nature writing as is its biological richness. Several drawbacks in the way the genre has been defined account for an edgy skittishness among the field's contemporary writers and scholars.

"Nature writing" is an awkward term, for one thing, with one noun modifying another. The second of those words, "writing," also has the effect of marginalizing this species of literature. "Poetry," "fiction," and "drama" are recognized as literature without such appendages. There is a similarly equivocal effect in the title of a closely associated, and also rapidly growing, field of study. "Nature *writing*" and "Environmental *Studies*" have the same self-deprecatory ring as the disclaimer in the labeling of certain startlingly yellow grocery items: "cheese-*food*." If one were invited to a party promising wine-drink and cheese-food, the edge of one's anticipation would surely be dulled. It is scarcely surprising that a number of today's outstanding nature writers are eager not to be restricted by that term. Gary Nabhan, for example, has fun proposing that everything on the increasingly distinguished and diverse shelf of "nature writing" be called simply "literature," while other contemporary books be categorized as "urban dysfunctional writing."

Another serious problem with the term "nature writing" is that it may seem to claim too much — especially to those who are not familiar with the Thoreauvian tradition to which it implicitly refers. It can sound as if it pertains to all literature about nature, while its range is actually circumscribed in specific and important ways. This particular form of the personal essay seems to have been especially favored by writers in English, for one thing — a correlation that reflects the scientific, economic, and political history of Britain and America since the eighteenth century. The Swedish scientist Linnaeus, who developed his biological nomenclature early in that century, had many followers in England. The wealth associated with English manufacturing, as well as with the growth of empire, created a large class with the leisure to become ardent amateur naturalists. These amateurs, and the museums and collections associated with them, in turn supported the work of early American explorers and writers. In fact, clear up through the accounts of late-nineteenth-century writers like Clarence King and John Wesley Powell, one hears the voice of naturalist-adventurers reporting on the grandeur of American wilderness for an affluent, scientifically educated, urban readership.

This genre has also been the province of white authors to a greater degree than has been true in the other major American genres. In earlier periods, this fact was correlated with the racial identities of England's well-to-do amateur naturalists, of the federally commissioned explorers and scientists of the new American Republic, and of the first generation of environmentalists. More recently, it has reflected the constituency of the major environmental organizations. The wilderness movement has been one major inspiration for much contemporary nature writing, as well as for environmentalism in general. And it has also been associated primarily with a specific upper-middle-class, white population both able and inclined to afford lengthy excursions in the mountains and other landscapes far from the cities. One certainly does not need to see anything either pernicious or intentionally exclusive in these connections. Still, they do represent a limitation in the range of human and social experience covered by the genre of nature writing.

In order to acknowledge how much vital literature of the earth is left out of the usual definition of "nature writing," and to encourage attention to a wider variety of ethnic, linguistic, and generic approaches, this book thus includes a section of "General Subject Essays." Rather than looking for the traditional nature essay where it has simply not been the preferred form, the pieces in this section take a broader perspective on topics such as "African-American Writers and Nature" and "Nature in Native

American Literatures." Essays on "The Forms of American Nature Poetry," "Literary Theory and Nature Writing," "Bioregionalism in Nature Writing," and "Contemporary Ecofiction" similarly both blur and enrich the bounds of this collection.

Another limiting tendency in the Thoreauvian tradition of American nature writing has been a greater emphasis placed upon solitary experiences of natural revelation than upon social experience. Such an emphasis has sometimes seemed to ratify the conventional but dangerous distinction between nature and culture. When Edward Hoagland wrote a tribute to Edward Abbey in the *New York Times Book Review*, following Abbey's death in 1989, he especially praised Abbey's unstinting rage in the face of environmental holocaust. We need such passionate and politically engaged defenders of the earth, Hoagland wrote, instead of "mystic Transcendentalists" purveying "Emersonian optimism." Addressing his own contemporaries whose natural reveries seemed to leave them disengaged from the realities of environmental destruction, he continued, "Emerson would be roaring with heartbreak and Thoreau would be raging with grief in these 1980's. *Where were you when the world burned? Get mad, for a change, for heaven's sake!*" In the increasing attention of some nature writers to social justice and ecological crises, we can find one response to Hoagland's cry from the heart.

Recognizing limitations in the genre as we have understood it until now is by no means intended to disparage this form of writing. On the contrary, nature writing remains a distinctive and prophetic voice in our American tradition, and one of the chief antagonists of the materialism that continually threatens our national soul. Acknowledgment that it is still not a comprehensive literature of the earth offers a way to begin opening up and extending this vital cultural resource. Just as the largely white wilderness movement is called upon today to address the condition of our cities, and to enter into closer collaboration with Americans of color, so too the nature writing so closely associated with it must now be redefined more inclusively.

Recent anthologies and textbooks that attempt to link nature writing in its conventional sense with grounded poetry and fiction, as well as to acknowledge the rich oral traditions of nature-centered peoples around the globe, are helping to extend the benefits of the Thoreauvian genre. A major aid in this last, tricky business of appreciating indigenous peoples' experience of nature has been the contemporary writing in English by authors who are themselves rooted in such traditions. One essay that has been enormously helpful is Leslie Marmon Silko's often-reprinted "Landscape, History, and the Pueblo Imagination." At the same time, contemporary non-Indian writers like Richard Nelson and Gary Snyder are trying to forge their own connections between Western culture and indigenous lifeways. Through attending to these new authors, we may also gain an enhanced appreciation of certain earlier nature writers who felt the power of indigenous history and stories in the land. Bartram, Thoreau, and Austin are especially interesting and admirable in this regard. Powerful new voices thus call attention to their own direct predecessors, and make the entire tradition newly available.

Appreciation of Native American perspectives accords with a growing emphasis in nature writing on the life and the value of human communities. A number of current writers lead the way in their insistence that culture is always an important element of a concrete sense of place. Wendell Berry, for example, explores farming as a practice of natural awareness and relationship within his native Kentucky. Scott Russell Sanders reveals the ways in which mindful work and a dedication to marriage and parenthood may both benefit from and enhance the seasons of his Ohio River Valley. Terry Tempest Williams connects her fidelities as writer, daughter and wife, teacher, naturalist, and activist to the ebbing and flowing of life in the Great Basin.

Nature writing, then, has been one vital way to think about humanity's place in, and identification with, the world. As we try now to stretch our understanding of the term, however, it becomes harder to keep thinking of it as a separate genre. We will be struggling to find the right language for this field of literature for years to come. And that's good. The unsatisfactory nature of our terms leaves no choice but to turn back, yet again, to the bewilderment and fecundity of the actual world. Vitality comes when the brushy edge of literature tangles with the world, and writer and reader alike ask, "What have we *here*?" This question frames the beginning of the nature writing tradition in English, and it also marks a transition, now, to as-yet-undiscovered modes of writing and reading. New categories of literature will follow from our new natural perceptions, as surely as theology succeeds revelation and, for a while at least, renders it more widely accessible. But again and again, we will also return to the surprising presentness of the world, and to the joy of uncategorical regard.

JOHN ELDER
MIDDLEBURY COLLEGE

CONTRIBUTORS

Lorraine Anderson. Davis California. TERRY TEMPEST WILLIAMS and NEW VOICES IN AMERICAN NATURE WRITING

Ralph W. Black. Davidson College. JOHN BURROUGHS

Marcia Myers Bonta. Tyrone, Pennsylvania. ANNA BOTSFORD COMSTOCK and THEODORA COPE STANWELL-FLETCHER

Michael P. Branch. University of Nevada, Reno. RALPH WALDO EMERSON and EARLY ROMANTIC NATURAL HISTORY LITERATURE

Stuart C. Brown. New Mexico State University. JOSEPH WOOD KRUTCH

Paul T. Bryant. Radford, Virginia. H. L. DAVIS

Lawrence Buell. Harvard University. HENRY DAVID THOREAU

Mark Busby. Center for the Study of the Southwest, Southwest Texas State University. JOHN GRAVES

Alison R. Byerly. Middlebury College. CATHY JOHNSON and LEWIS THOMAS

Neil B. Carmony. Tucson, Arizona. WALLACE STEGNER

Michael P. Cohen. Southern Utah University. LITERARY THEORY AND NATURE WRITING

John Cooley. Western Michigan University. SIGURD F. OLSON

Kathleen Danker. South Dakota State University. LINDA HASSELSTROM

Thomas K. Dean. Michigan State University and Cardinal Stritch College. LESLIE MARMON SILKO

Terrell F. Dixon. University of Houston. RICK BASS and JOHN HANSON MITCHELL

John Dotson. Monterey, California, ENOS MILLS

John Elder. Middlebury College. EDITOR

Nancy Freehafer. Visiting Faculty, DePaul University School for New Learning. HELEN HOOVER

Peter A. Fritzell. Lawrence University. ALDO LEOPOLD

Deborah Strom Gibbons. Hopewell, New Jersey. MODERN BIRDWATCHING LITERATURE

Cheryll Glotfelty. University of Nevada. RACHEL CARSON

Betsy S. Hilbert. Miami-Dade Community College. MARJORIE KINNAN RAWLINGS

J. Parker Huber. Brattleboro, Vermont. ROBERT FINCH

Cynthia Huntington. Dartmouth College. JOHN HAY and NOEL PERRIN

Zita Ingham. Arkansas State University. EDWARD ABBEY

CONTRIBUTORS

Stephanie Kaza. University of Vermont. GRETEL EHRLICH

Lisa Knopp. Southern Illinois University at Carbondale. BRENDA PETERSON and ERNEST THOMPSON SETON

Karen Knowles. Western Michigan University. VIRGINIA EIFERT and DIANA KAPPEL-SMITH

Harriet Kofalk. Eugene, Oregon. FLORENCE MERRIAM BAILEY

Michael Kowalewski. Carleton College. DAVID RAINS WALLACE

Gale Lawrence. University of Vermont. SALLY CARRIGHAR

Thomas J. Lyon. Utah State University. JOHN MUIR

Marilyn Chandler McEntyre. Trenton State College. SUE HUBBELL and DAVID QUAMMEN

Lucy B. Maddox. Georgetown University. SUSAN FENIMORE COOPER

Christopher Merrill. College of the Holy Cross. THE FORMS OF AMERICAN NATURE POETRY

Patrick D. Murphy. Indiana University of Pennsylvania. GARY SNYDER

Herman Nibbelink. Pleasant Hill, Missouri. WENDELL BERRY

William Nichols. Denison University. SCOTT RUSSELL SANDERS

Aina Niemela. *Orion Magazine*. FAITH McNULTY

Vera Norwood. University of New Mexico. JOSEPHINE JOHNSON and CELIA THAXTER

Nicholas O'Connell. University of Washington. CONTEMPORARY ECOFICTION

John P. O'Grady. Boise State University. MARY HUNTER AUSTIN

Daniel G. Payne. Honeoye, New York. HENRY BESTON and PETER MATTHIESSEN

Michael Pearson. Old Dominion University. JOHN McPHEE and ROBERT MICHAEL PYLE

Sydney Landon Plum. Storrs, Connecticut. HOPE RYDEN and GENE STRATTON PORTER

Rebecca Raglon. University of British Columbia. CANADIAN NATURE WRITING IN ENGLISH

Hilda Raz. University of Nebraska-Lincoln. MAXINE KUMIN

David Robertson. University of California, Davis. BIOREGIONALISM IN NATURE WRITING

David M. Robinson. Oregon State University. DIANE ACKERMAN

Don Scheese. Gustavus Adolphus College. ANNIE DILLARD

Sara L. St. Antoine. Washingon, D.C. GARY PAUL NABHAN

Matthias Schubnell. Incarnate Word College. N. SCOTT MOMADAY

Steven B. Shively. University of Nebraska-Lincoln. JOHN JANOVY, JR.

David Lionel Smith. Williams College. AFRICAN AMERICANS, WRITING, AND NATURE

Stan Tag. Albertson College of Idaho. EDWIN WAY TEALE

John Tallmadge. Union Institute, Graduate School. BARRY LOPEZ, RICHARD K. NELSON, and WESTERN GEOLOGISTS AND EXPLORERS

Fred Taylor. Antioch New England Graduate School. LOREN EISELEY and CHET RAYMO

David W. Teague. University of Delaware. EDWARD HOAGLAND and WILLIAM LEAST HEAT-MOON

CONTRIBUTORS

Philip G. Terrie. Bowling Green State University. WILLIAM BARTRAM

Mikel Vause. Weber State Unversity. LITERATURE OF MOUNTAINEERING

Melissa Walker. Decatur, Georgia. MARJORY STONEMAN DOUGLAS

Peter Wild. University of Arizona. JOHN C. VAN DYKE and ANN ZWINGER

Kate H. Winter. University at Albany, State University of New York. ANNE LaBASTILLE

Hertha D. Wong. University of California, Berkeley. LINDA HOGAN and NATURE IN NATIVE AMERICAN LITERATURES

EDWARD ABBEY
(1927–1989)

ZITA INGHAM

I N MARCH 1989, when Edward Abbey knew the internal bleeding of which he was dying would very soon finish its work, he left the hospital, went into the desert near Tucson, Arizona, with three friends and his wife, Clarke, and with their help settled in. He died at his home on 14 March. Abbey's written instructions for burial, as recounted by Edward Hoagland in "Edward Abbey: Standing Tough in the Desert," asked that his desert grave—unmarked and officially unsanctioned, but not unsanctified by close friends and relatives—be piled with rocks to keep coyotes away. Hoagland writes that since this final act of resistance, "false rockpiles at ideal gravesites throughout the Southwest" have appeared, through the efforts of his friends to confound the legend hunters (p. 45).

In the weeks after Abbey's death, obituaries and celebratory essays appeared widely, from a hometown newspaper, *The Tucson Weekly*, to the *New York Times Book Review*. Edward Hoagland, a nature writer, wrote that Abbey's "rarest strength was in being concise, because he really knew what he thought and cared for" (p. 44); "his ambitions were confined to truth-telling, rhapsody and the lambasting of villains" (p. 45). Peter Wild, in *Sierra* magazine, celebrated "Abbey at his flashing best: absurd, sarcastic, and funny all at once, but often speaking the truth that lay in our own hearts... combining the rapier of Thoreau and the large-

souled righteousness of John Muir" (p. 100). James R. Hepworth, writing in the scholarly journal *Western American Literature*, proclaimed that "no one has written more ardently or more passionately in defense of the American West than Abbey did" (p. 150).

The Tucson Weekly (5–11 April 1989) collected ten pages of reminiscences, tributes, and last letters from Abbey's friends and fellow writers, odes of sorrow and celebration. Prominent Western writers catalogued his personal and literary traits: Barry Lopez wrote of Abbey's "caustic accusations and droll humor"; Barbara Kingsolver recalled him as "wonderfully guileless"; John Nichols praised his writing as having a "lyricism that sang, and an outrage that was full-bore, no-nonsense and straight as a desert highway headed south." The poet Gary Snyder, with whom Abbey had quarreled about ecological politics, noted, "He was so smart that even when he was (I thought) wrong he was damned near right." Friends and colleagues documented hikes, conversations, campfires, and readings shared with him. Fellow writer and colleague in the University of Arizona's creative writing program, Robert Houston, acknowledged Abbey's lack of national critical success, citing "Ed's old enemy, the Eastern press." Others, such as Ray Ring and Gregory McNamee, proposed ways of celebrating Abbey: getting outside, shooting the TV, reading his books, carrying on in the struggle to protect the wilderness, naming a scrap of desert after him. Some remembered his words to them: "One brave deed is worth a thousand books"; "Those mountains, that land—you don't get religion from them. They ARE religion." As Abbey met his passing as conscientiously as possible, so did his personal and his literary communities.

In "The Author's Preface to His Own Book" (*Slumgullion Stew: An Edward Abbey Reader*, 1984), Abbey provides an assessment of his own. He cites the foolishness of writing about his own writing, advising the reader to skip the rest of the preface, but ends with as clear and straightforward a statement of purpose as he ever gave:

> In such a world, why write? . . . I write to entertain my friends and exasperate our enemies. I write to record the truth of our time, as best as I can see it. To investigate the comedy and tragedy of human relationships. To resist and sabotage the contemporary drift toward a technocratic, militaristic totalitarianism, whatever its ideological coloration. To oppose injustice, defy the powerful, and speak for the voiceless.
>   I write to make a difference. . . . Distrusting all answers, to raise more questions. To give pleasure and promote esthetic bliss. To honor life and praise the divine beauty of the world. For the joy and exultation of writing itself. To tell my story. (pp. xiv–xv)

To these ends, Abbey wrote eight novels, one nonfiction work, numerous essays and articles (collected in five books), and commentary to accompany five books of photography. He aspired first and foremost, always, to be a novelist, producing *Jonathan Troy* (1954), *The Brave Cowboy: An Old Tale in a New Time* (1956), *Fire on the Mountain* (1962), *Black Sun* (1971), *The Monkey Wrench Gang* (1975), *Good News* (1980), *The Fool's Progress: An Honest Novel* (1988), and, appearing posthumously, *Hayduke Lives!* (1990). His most famous work, *Desert Solitaire: A Season in the Wilderness*, appeared in 1968. He published essays in such magazines as *Audubon, Harper's, Penthouse, Outside, Play-*

boy, Pioneer Conservationists of America, Backpacker, Rolling Stone, Rocky Mountain Magazine, High Country News, National Geographic, and the *New York Times.* The best of these pieces are collected in *The Journey Home: Some Words in Defense of the American West* (1977), *Abbey's Road* (1979), *Down the River with Henry David Thoreau and Friends* (1982), *Beyond the Wall: Essays from the Outside* (1984), and *One Life at a Time, Please* (1988). *Slumgullion Stew: An Edward Abbey Reader* (1984; republished as *The Best of Edward Abbey*, 1988) contains selections of Abbey's fiction and nonfiction from 1954 to 1984. A slim volume of gleanings from Abbey's copious and yet-to-be-published volumes of journals, *A Voice Crying in the Wilderness: Notes from a Secret Journal,* appeared in 1989. The "coffee-table" books, each focused on a particular place or region, are *Appalachian Wilderness: The Great Smoky Mountains* (1970), *Slickrock: The Canyon Country of Southeast Utah* (1971), *Cactus Country* (1973), *The Hidden Canyon: A River Journey* (1977), and *Desert Images: An American Landscape* (1979).

Early Life / Early Novels

Born on 29 January 1927, the son of Paul Revere Abbey and Mildred Postlewaite Abbey, Edward Abbey grew up in the Allegheny Mountains near Home, Pennsylvania. He graduated from high school there, in 1945. The summer before his senior year, he hitchhiked to Seattle and then to Arizona. In "Hallelujah on the Bum," reprinted in *The Journey Home* (1977), Abbey chronicles some of the adventures of this trip. After serving in Italy as a U.S. Army rifleman (1945–1946), he returned to the West and enrolled at the University of New Mexico, from which he received a B.A. in 1951.

As an undergraduate, Abbey continued his explorations of the Southwest and began his writing career. He wrote regularly in his private journal (a practice he began in 1946 and continued until his death, accumulating more than

Edward Abbey

From 1951 to 1952, Abbey was a Fulbright fellow based in Edinburgh, Scotland, and traveled throughout Europe. He enrolled as a graduate student in philosophy at Yale University in 1952, but left after two weeks — "scared off," he later said, by a course in symbolic logic. He married Rita Deanan in late 1952 (this marriage lasted until 1965 and produced two sons, Joshua and Aaron) and worked in a factory in New Jersey for a while. In 1954 he returned to the West and received his M.A. in philosophy at the University of New Mexico in 1956.

Jonathan Troy appeared in 1954, to very little acclaim. The quest by many of Abbey's characters for a balanced existence — between wilderness and civilization, between anarchy and culture, between freedom and the restraints of community — destined to culminate in a mythical West, begins with Jonathan. As a bildungsroman, the novel traces the transformation of Jonathan — burdened by an eccentric father, subject to ill-timed desires, suffocating in his depressing Eastern surroundings — into a man headed for the West, bound for a better future. In the "Literature of the Southwest Student Interview," Abbey recalls the book as "a teenage drama... a very poor book, I think" (*Resist Much*, p. 110). The critic Ann Ronald, in *The New West of Edward Abbey*, notes its "ill-designed plot, its unbelievable characters, and its foolish eccentricities" (p. 15), but commends the novel for its "early glimpse" of "Abbey's greatest strength — the power of his prose," its identification of the future themes of Abbey's work (including anarchy and ecology), and its vision of a mythical, metaphorical West, the foundation of all of Abbey's work (p. 5).

The Brave Cowboy (1956) also was generally ignored by critics, although a movie based on it, *Lonely Are the Brave*, with screenplay by Dalton Trumbo and starring Kirk Douglas and Walter Matthau, appeared in 1962. Traditional themes and patterns of the Western novel overlie what Ronald sees as a "formal romance," a work wherein the writer exposes the problems of his society in terms of the world he creates, rather than providing with that world merely a vehicle for his reader's escape. The protagonist, Jack

twenty chronological notebooks), began drafting *Jonathan Troy*, published a couple of stories, and edited *The Thunderbird*, the university literary magazine. His story "Some Implications of Anarchy" appeared in the March 1951 issue, on the cover of which he placed an epigram from Voltaire: "Man will never be free until the last king is strangled with the entrails of the last priest." With a flash of the ironic humor that was one of his best qualities, he ascribed the quotation to Louisa May Alcott. The epigram enraged local civic and religious authorities and ended his term as editor. During this period, Abbey was briefly married.

3

Burns, rides his horse across freeways and past strip malls to rescue a friend jailed for draft resistance. Burns is a chivalric figure, a knight-errant on an old crusade in a new world. The first edition of the book ends with Burns's death after he is hit by a truck while riding across a highway; the University of New Mexico Press edition (1977) omits the paragraph at the end of the book assuring the reader of his death to allow for Burns's reappearance in *The Monkey Wrench Gang* (1975) and *Good News* (1980). The change in the ending leaves Abbey's central philosophical and political question—Can the old survive the new?—unresolved.

Fire on the Mountain (1962) presents a slightly different version of the question: the elderly hero, John Vogelin, refuses to surrender his land, which was taken by his forebears from the Apaches a hundred years earlier and coveted later by the railroad and the big cattle companies, to the U.S. Air Force for inclusion in the White Sands Missile Range. Vogelin joins Jack Burns as the earliest in Abbey's Don Quixote–like protagonists, who fight progress—the government and developers—in morally determined, sometimes violent, and often comical ways. The critic Paul Bryant sees the quest for the preservation of wilderness as a theme throughout Abbey's work; like the desire for anarchy, it serves to counterbalance the technological oppression and totalitarian tendencies of industrialized society. Bryant argues, "Abbey sought a balanced environment that includes the urban and the rural as well as the primeval, and a balanced polity that includes freedom and order. . . . Abbey sees extreme environmentalism as quixotic and destined only for failure" (1989, pp. 42–43). The fates of Abbey's quixotic extremists support Bryant's argument: Burns in *The Brave Cowboy* and (resurrected) in *Good News*, Vogelin in *Fire on the Mountain*, Hayduke in *The Monkey Wrench Gang* and in *Hayduke Lives!*—die or just barely survive.

Although his heroes never prevail—Vogelin does not keep his land, the Monkey Wrench Gang never blows up Glen Canyon Dam—they are never obliterated; if they fight to the death, they are resurrected in one form or another. Bryant suggests that Abbey values these doomed, morally driven extremists as a response to the imbalance of the technological, antinatural world. The valorization of such heroes in his books determined Abbey's leadership as an environmentalist. Ann Ronald argues that *Fire on the Mountain* is, like the novels written before and after it, a romance and that it is the first work in which Abbey clearly identifies the elements that compose his mature vision: the fate of the land, the freedom of individuals, the power of government and monied interests, the initiation into manhood—or even into wisdom—as aspects of the struggle between individuals and society.

Desert Solitaire

Critics and readers agree that *Desert Solitaire* is Abbey's best, most moving, and most unified work. Ann Ronald sees the book as the fullest expression of both Abbey's celebration of the Southwestern landscape and his argument against its degradation. As the "cornerstone of Abbey's reputation," *Desert Solitaire* is, in Ronald's view, "a nonfiction examination of selfhood, of wilderness, of progress, of desecration" (1987, p. 605). Don Scheese notes that with this book Abbey follows in the nature writing tradition of John Wesley Powell, John C. Van Dyke, Mary Austin, and Joseph Wood Krutch by popularizing a celebratory aesthetic of the desert, as well as by proposing new arguments for wilderness preservation and advocating political activism.

Abbey grouped the book with his collections of essays as "personal history," which he labeled "informal, personal (sometimes highly personal) accounts of travel, ideas, people, nature, places, adventures" (*Slumgullion*, p. x). But in contrast with Abbey's essays, *Desert Solitaire* draws heavily on the characterization of the narrator, use of anecdote, unities of space and time, imagery. In her discussion of the book, Ronald (1988) explicitly differentiates the author from the narrator, "Ed Abbey," and the critic Richard Shelton attributes much of the book's success to the compelling nature of the narrator's character, its embodiment of opposites in tension: "the soaring romantic and the cynically realistic, high places and the sudden descent" (p. 69). Paul Bryant suggests, in "Structure and Unity," that despite the appearance of a loose, journal-like form similar to Thoreau's *Walden*, the structure of the book is not casual at all; he notes its seasonal arrangement and the ways in which Abbey interrupts this arrangement in his quest to resolve the paradoxes that are key to experiences of the desert.

The narrator's sensibility—described by Edwin Way Teale as "a voice crying in the wilderness, *for* the wilderness" in his contemporary review of the book—determines the polemical aspects of the book, worked out in his argument, for instance, against permitting cars in national parks: "We have agreed not to drive our automobiles into cathedrals, concert halls, art museums, legislative assemblies, private bedrooms and the other sanctums of our culture; we should treat our national parks with the same deference, for they, too, are holy places" (1971 ed., p. 60). The narrator's argument for the preservation of wilderness "as a refuge from authoritarian government" (p. 149) culminates in a radical act, the careful removal of five miles of survey stakes; because Abbey's arguments arise from a passion that is seductive, we end up sharing his sense of loss.

Desert Solitaire is, at first glance, an impressionistic collection of observations, arguments, ramblings, stories, people, and events drawn from two summers Abbey spent working as a park ranger in Arches National Monument (now Park), near Moab, Utah, in 1956 and 1957. For the readers who count this book as one of their favorites, the achievement of *Desert Solitaire* is its portrayal of someone in love with a landscape. Shelton writes that the book "was written by an arch-romantic trying desperately not to be romantic. . . . Much of *Desert Solitaire* is a love lyric" (p. 68). Ronald identifies Abbey's success, in this more mature period of his career, as the negotiation of a "three-step transfiguration of the land, from the literal to the metaphoric to the mythic": from the literal West of *The Brave Cowboy*, to the metaphoric struggles of good and evil in *Fire on the Mountain*, to the mythical arena of this "Season in the Wilderness" (1988, p. 79). Abbey here begins to map a region of borderland where we can glimpse the possibility of humans and nature in balance. Scheese defines Abbey's "eco-vision" as including both an unrelenting critique of misguided technology and a passionate celebration of meditative solitude in wild places. Others, such as Diane Wakoski and David E. Gamble, would add Abbey's version of "inhumanism," a term coined by the poet Robinson Jeffers for the rejection of Western civilization's tradition of seeing nature as peripheral and relative to human life and activity. Wakoski sees Abbey's vision as Dionysian, an understanding of all life as part of a cycle, with both death and birth required, and all life as interdependent.

As nonfiction that draws heavily on techniques of fiction, *Desert Solitaire* (published one year before Jacques Derrida's first major work of poststructuralist theory) displays features of modern, even postmodern, literature: the individual isolated from others, language as reality, knowledge as relative to individual experience, the reliance on irony. Abbey's vision of the desert is nostalgic: the desert is one of memory, despite his suggestion of an overriding immortality. He describes the book as "not a travel guide but an elegy. A memorial" (p. xii) to a land that was, even in 1968, irrevocably changed. He suggests a quite literal way of using the book: "You're holding a tombstone in your hands. A bloody rock. Don't drop it on your foot—throw it at something big and glassy. What do you have to lose?" (p. xii) An ultimate paradox, an ultimate rhetorical device: the book as rock, piece of desert—immovable, eternal—and also as protest, action. To realize his emphasis on surfaces, Abbey proposes that the book itself become a literal medium, one solid object. This suggestion illustrates Abbey's superior ability to tie the physical to the metaphorical, to evoke experience, as a narrator and as an author, with a particular gesture.

For all of Abbey's later work, the key literary figure underlying both form and content is paradox. For example, one of the qualities Abbey bestows on the desert is immortality, so that the landscape becomes an emblem of immortality even as he decries its loss. In one of his most "inhumanist" moments, Abbey strikes a note of cynicism triumphant in his vision of the beauty of a world without humans:

> Let men in their madness blast every city on earth into black rubble and envelope [*sic*] the entire planet in a cloud of lethal gas—the canyons and hills, the springs and rocks will still be here, the sunlight will filter through, water will form and warmth shall be upon the land and after sufficient time, no matter how long, somewhere, living things will emerge and join and stand once again, this time perhaps to take a different and better course. (p. 301)

The suggestion, even assumption, of annihilation has, paradoxically, the rhetorical effect of being the ultimate argument for preservation.

As a writer of the postmodern era, whose subjects are the postmodern conflicts of individual, society, and a devolved nature, Abbey uses the desert quite consciously as "medium," as a language itself. In the context of contemporary literary movements, language, as abstraction, can only lead to abstraction; texts refer to themselves as texts. Abbey treats this awareness of language very directly in the 1968 edition's "Author's Introduction": "Since you cannot get the desert into a book any more than a fisherman can haul up the sea with his nets, I have tried to create a world of words in which the desert figures more as medium than as material. Not imitation but evocation has been the goal" (p. x).

In the quest to overcome abstraction, Abbey gives us the first representation of the desert that takes into account detailed experiences of the body. In the introduction, he directs the reader: "In the first place you can't see *anything* from a car; you've got to get out of the goddamned contraption and walk, better yet crawl, on hands and knees, over the sandstone and through the thornbush and cactus. When traces of blood begin to mark your trail you'll see something, maybe" (p. xii). If "language makes a mighty loose net with which to go fishing for simple facts," Abbey maintains, "I have striven above all for accuracy, since I believe that there is a kind of poetry, even a kind of truth, in simple fact. . . . For my own part I am pleased enough with surfaces—in fact they alone seem to me to be of much importance. Such things for example as the grasp of a child's hand in your own, the flavor of an apple, the embrace of friend or lover; the silk of a girl's thigh . . .—what else is there? What else do we need?" (pp. x–xi). For Abbey, close examination of surfaces, even of this text itself as a surface, is the key to understanding this world. His passionate regard for all of the surfaces of the natural world, including language, drive his fiction and nonfiction polemics.

In the preface, Abbey confesses, "I know nothing whatever about true underlying reality, having never met any" (p. xi). Yet, ultimately he asserts an intractable "truth" of the desert, that its "finest quality" is its indifference to human life (pp. 300–301). He directly addresses the issue of abstraction, of making metaphors from what we see, when discussing Delicate Arch: "Depending on your preconceptions you may see the eroded remnant of a sandstone fin, a giant engagement ring cemented in rock, a bow-legged pair of petrified cowboy chaps, a triumphal arch for a procession of angels. . . . You may therefore find proof for or against His existence. Suit yourself" (p. 41). For Abbey, the "meaning" of the desert, by definition, lies beyond metaphor: "If Delicate Arch has any significance it lies, I will venture, in the power of the odd and unexpected to startle the senses and surprise the mind out of their ruts of habit, to compel us into a reawakened awareness of the wonderful. . . . The shock of the real. For a little while we are again able to see, as the child sees, a world of marvels" (pp. 41–42). Meaning resides only in the thing itself. Abbey suggests that appreciation requires limiting the mind in favor of the senses, while paradoxically acknowledging (in the book *Desert Images*) that "all deserts begin in the mind" (p. 13): "What does the desert mean? It means what it is. It is there; it will be there when we are gone. But for awhile we living things—men, women, birds, coyotes howling far off on yonder stony ridge—we were a part of it all. That should be enough" (p. 224).

But it is not, especially for Abbey, who made a living of composing a desert for his readers. In his lengthiest discussion of "what the desert means," near the end of *Desert Solitaire*, Abbey goes beyond what is "enough" to ascribe some qualities, even as he recognizes the danger "of confusing the thing observed with the mind of the observer," as well as of "separating too deeply the observer and the thing observed" (p. 270). Attempting to answer the question "What is the peculiar quality or character of the desert that distinguishes it, in spiritual appeal, from other forms of landscape?" (p. 270) he identifies paradoxes while invoking the romantic metaphor of veiled mystery:

The desert says nothing. Completely passive, acted upon but never acting, the desert lies there like the bare skeleton of Being, spare, sparse, austere, utterly worthless, inviting not love but contemplation. . . . Despite its clarity and simplicity, however, the desert wears at the same time, paradoxically, a veil of mystery. Motionless and silent it evokes in us an elusive hint of something unknown, unknowable, about to be revealed. Since the desert does not act it seems to be waiting—but waiting for what? . . . There is something about the desert that the human sensibility cannot assimilate. . . . Even after years of intimate contact and search this quality of strangeness in the desert remains undiminished. . . . Where is the heart of the desert? I used to think that somewhere in the American Southwest, impossible to say exactly where, all of these wonders which intrigue the spirit would converge upon a climax—and resolution. . . . I am convinced now that the desert has no heart, that it presents a riddle which has no answer, and that the riddle itself is an illusion created by some limitation or exaggeration of the displaced human consciousness. . . . I find myself in the end returning to the beginning, and can only

say, as I said in the first place: There is something about the desert. (pp. 270–273)

Simplicity and mystery, silence and revelation—Abbey names paradoxes that continue to draw people to this landscape. He describes a desert that "seems to be waiting"; but it is we who are waiting, of course, not the desert—awaiting revelation, paradoxically indifferent to its manifestations.

The Pictorial Essays

In 1970, Abbey's first "book of place" appeared. *Appalachian Wilderness, Slickrock* (1971), *Cactus Country* (1973), *The Hidden Canyon* (1977), and *Desert Images* (1979) are collaborative works, documented by lush photography in "coffee-table book" format, with Abbey providing essays and commentary. In these books, he provides distilled and muted versions of his polemics and a simplified version of his reverence for wild landscape. For instance, in *Appalachian Wilderness*, he compares traveling in the Smoky Mountains of North Carolina, eastern Kentucky, and eastern Tennessee to his boyhood home in Pennsylvania's Allegheny Mountains: "the town set in the cup of green hills. . . . beyond the town were the fields, the zigzag rail fences, the old gray barns and gaunt Gothic farmhouses, the webwork of winding roads, the sulfurous creeks and the black coal mines and—scattered everywhere—the woods. . . . Land of the breathing trees, the big woods, the rainy forests" (pp. 9, 12). And then, describing the small town as it is now—polluted, dirty, crowded—in comparison with how it once was, he relinquishes Appalachia as his home forever. Because these books are meant for a particular audience, one that enjoys displaying large, expensive books rather than reading them, Abbey merely touches on the personal history, the arguments, and the vision that comprise his other nonfiction work.

Black Sun

Black Sun (1971), in Abbey's judgment his best novel, skillfully combines elements from *Desert*

Solitaire and from his earlier novels: we can see his traditional Western themes here illuminated by the introspection of the novel's protagonist, a fire lookout living alone in his cabin by the lookout tower in a Western forest. The novel is a love story, too, Abbey's only novel of romance — of love found and lost in the wilderness, the sting of memory, a lonely man's dream of a girl against a forest and canyon backdrop. The setting is paradise, the girl — Sandy — seems to arise from the wilderness and to disappear back into the earth, leaving behind Will Gatlin, modern man, lost and wandering. The book, a fable of a descent into hell after a brief ascent into heaven, is dedicated to Abbey's third wife, Judy, whom he had married in 1965 and who died of leukemia in 1970. Abbey had one daughter, Susie, by this marriage.

The book is modern in its form, in its lack of a linear time frame. Abbey plays with the narrative line, for instance, by dropping a scene of Sandy and Will together into the book long after she has gone, and not as a memory but as an isolated fragment, floating. Abbey does unify the fragmented scenes of Sandy and Will together by writing them in the past tense, as opposed to the scenes occurring after her disappearance, which are written in the present tense. A version of the traditional quest motif, with an investigation of loss as its center, *Black Sun* is another of Abbey's journeys in the wilderness, another foray toward "the discovery of the self in its proud sufficiency which is not isolation but an irreplaceable part of the mystery of the whole" (*Journey Home*, p. 98).

Essays

Abbey's nonfiction career began before the publication of *Desert Solitaire* as his first major work of nonfiction. His essays appeared in a range of sources: intellectual, such as *Harper's*; popular, such as *Reader's Digest*, *National Geographic*, *Rolling Stone*, and *Playboy*; environmentalist, such as *Sierra* and *Audubon* Magazine; outdoor enthusiast, such as *Outside* and *Backpacker*; and regional, such as *High Country News* and the *Mountain Gazette*. Periodically, beginning with *The Journey Home* (1977) and including *Abbey's Road* (1979), *Down the River* (1982), *Beyond the Wall* (1984), and *One Life at a Time, Please* (1988), Abbey produced loosely organized collections of his articles and essays. These collected essays contribute most to his acclaim as a cultural critic and compelling autobiographer.

In *The Journey Home*, Abbey proposes that the book is "in part the story of how I discovered my home, in part a description of it, and in its emphasis an effort to defend that home against alien invaders" and likens it to a stew — "redneck slumgullion" (p. xiv). Here he covers his arrival in the West in 1944, details the histories and environs of Telluride (Colorado), Yosemite and Big Bend national parks, and the north rim of the Grand Canyon, among other places. He justifies in "The Great American Desert," as he did in *Desert Solitaire*, his obsession with the arid West. In *Abbey's Road*, the personal history continues, with the map traced somewhat larger: he documents travels to Australia and to islands and mountains of Mexico, as well as to his familiar desert haunts, the Grand Canyon, Canyonlands National Park, the Rio Grande, and Lake Powell. In the section "Polemics and Sermons," he argues that "science in our time is the whore of industry and war," that "scientific technology has become the instrument of a potential planetary slavery" (p. 125); and he calls for a return to "Reason . . . intelligence informed by sympathy, knowledge in the arms of love" (p. 127). The essay "Science with a Human Face" is a tour de force of allusions; Abbey cites C. P. Snow, Einstein, Nietzsche, H. G. Wells, Hannah Arendt, and the work of a host of twentieth-century scientists to argue that

the orthodox scientific view reduces the world to measurable and predictable units, to that which can be charted, graphed, statistically analyzed; the traditional religious or mystical view reduces the world to a reflection of human, anthropomorphic desires and intuitions. . . .

They are wrong. Even a rock is a being, a thing with character and a kind of spirit, an existence worthy of our love. To disparage the world we know for the sake of grand verbal abstractions, whether they are called mesons and electrons or the vibrations of an endlessly slumbering and reawakening Brahma, is to be false to the mother who sustains us. The highest treason, the meanest treason, is to disavow and deny this lone but gracious planet on which we voyage through the cold void of space. . . .

For what do we really know? I think of a lightning-blasted but still living shagbark hickory in the pasture back home on my father's farm in Pennsylvania; I think of a twisted juniper on a ledge of sandstone at Cape Solitude, far above the Colorado River; I think of the pelicans that sail along the shores of the Sea of Cortez; I think of a thousand other places I have known and loved, east and west, in North America and Australia and Europe, and all the creatures great and small that live there—each a part of a greater whole, but each an individual as well, one and unique, never to be known again, here or anywhere, each as precious as the vivid moment in which it first appeared on earth. . . .

I know where I belong. Heaven is home. (pp. 128–129)

In this polemic, as in many other places in his fiction and nonfiction, Abbey is arguing first for a reverent vision of the world as home. In other essays in this collection, he ruminates on gun control, the future of America, Christmas, Winnebago motor homes. It is in the essays that Abbey seems most at home, speaking as himself, with fewer fictional veilings between him and his readers, ranging from one subject to another as his mind and his travels carry him.

His humor is most evident here, too, and his play with language. In the "Preliminary Notes" to Down the River, he announces, "This book is about some recent boat trips and about related things now going, going—sold!—down the river. . . . None of the essays in this book requires elucidation, other than to say, as in everything I write, they are meant to serve as antidotes to despair. Despair leads to boredom, electronic games, computer hacking, poetry, and other bad habits" (pp. 2–3). He chronicles river

trips on the Tatshenshini in the Canadian Yukon, on the Colorado in the Grand Canyon, and down the San Juan in southern Utah. He reviews books, sketches friends, and questions the proposed MX missile system to be located in the West. His nonfiction collections proceed eclectically, unified by Abbey's singular voice. The themes, arguments, and images first seen in Desert Solitaire can be traced through these books, culminating in, as in that first nonfiction, a vision of the earth and the cultures that seem bent on destroying it.

The Journey Home ends with the short "Dust; A Movie," a cinematic treatment complete with camera directions of a desert ghost town—day and night, heat, storm, flood, lovers alive and dead—that resolves to a vision, in the depths of a passing mountain lion's eyes, of "the cliffs, the clouds, the sky, the earth, the human mind, the world beyond this world we love and hardly know at all." The screenplay concludes, "DISSOLVE. This film goes on, it has no end. . . . DISSOLVE . . . " (p. 242). In form and in content, the collections show the balance that Abbey strived for, driven by a vision of the land as sacred. In the last essay in Abbey's Road, he clarifies the nature of this vision by comparing it against an otherworldly "mysticism," which displays a

poverty of the imagination. As any honest magician knows, true magic inheres in the ordinary, the commonplace, the everyday, the mystery of the obvious. Only petty minds and trivial souls yearn for supernatural events, incapable of perceiving that everything—everything—within and around them is pure miracle.

Or so I say. So I have always thought. But I am willing to see my whole world splintered by a sword of light, if such can happen. (pp. 195–196)

The balance always struggled for, the opposites always present, held in tension—these compel the reader. In this section, the resolution is the same as in others: "The silent desert makes no reply." The voice, the vision, and the elements held in tension in Abbey's work are multitudinous and are always ultimately subordinated to the landscape.

It's not that Abbey doesn't believe in God; it's that "the term seems insufficient" (p. 120). Abbey's "sacrality" (as proposed by William T. Pilkington), his reverence for the land as Mother, as source, as energy, are everywhere in his work; all of his finest descriptions arise from that. In a 1987 interview, Abbey stated, "Writing is a form of piety or worship. I try to write prose psalms that praise the divine beauty of the natural world. . . . If I have a religion, it's pantheism, the belief that everything is in some sense holy, or divine, or sacred. Everything—even human life" (Jimerson, p. 55). His reverence for human life is qualified in that it does not take precedence over all other existence.

In the same interview, he suggested that all of his work, including the polemical, "is meant as literary art." In the essays, social and political arguments are given free, even exaggerated, rein. In *The Journey Home*'s "The Second Rape of the West," an investigation of the growth of stripmining, and again in *One Life at a Time, Please*, in "Arizona: How Big is Big Enough?," we find the oft-quoted sentence adopted from Abbey by an entire faction of environmental activists: "Growth for the sake of growth *is* the ideology of the cancer cell" (*Journey Home*, p. 183). But ultimately, Abbey's argument is simply for balance in the context of contemporary life: "I believe it is possible to find and live a balanced way of life somewhere halfway between all-out industrialism on the one hand and a make-believe pastoral idyll on the other" (p. 234).

Using the form of the Western novel, such as in *The Brave Cowboy*, Abbey critiques two extremes of our culture: our homage to and dependence on technology and progress, and our belief in and dependence on a romantic view of "Nature" and the rural. What he wishes for is simple and sane: "Good beer, good fresh healthy food for all," comfortable homes, urban transit and continental passenger train service, clean air, clean water, "and now and then, when we want it, some space and solitude and silence" (*Journey Home*, p. 187). The Western novel has always been about finding a new life: in the words of a character after the gunfight at the end of the classic Western film *Shane*, "there must be some better way to live." Abbey echoed those words in a 1980 interview: "I'm a practical romantic. . . . I still think it's possible to find some better way to live, both as an individual and as a society" (Solheim and Levin, p. 91). Abbey's work is very much in the tradition of the Western, and for him, "the westering myth is the nearest thing to a national myth we can ever create in the country" (Hepworth and McNamee, p. 41). How the myth determines the implementation of his own vision for the future, Abbey states, "will be the job of another generation of thinkers and doers . . . to bring it closer to reality" (*Abbey's Road*, p. 137).

Abbey's voice, through his actions as well as his nonfiction and fiction, supported the growth of some of those thinkers and doers, especially in the formation of the environmental group Earth First! On 21 March 1981, a feeling of general failure of progress on the part of traditional environmental groups led to a demonstration by the newly formed environmental group Earth First! at Glen Canyon Dam, with Abbey as a featured speaker. A group of activists, including Dave Foreman, who documented the formation and purposes of the group in *Confessions of an Eco-Warrior* (1991), unfurled three hundred feet of black plastic down the front of the dam, as a symbol of its breaching. In his speech to eighty members of the group, Abbey described the "green and living wilderness" that was once Glen Canyon (his essay "Damnation of a Canyon" does this, too), its theft from the public by politicians and developers for the sake of power, growth, and profit, and the appropriate course of action: to "Oppose. . . . And if opposition is not enough, we must resist. And if resistance is not enough, then subvert" (Foreman, p. 22).

But one must be careful in identifying Abbey exclusively as an "environmental writer," if only because he did not see himself that way. In a 1977 interview, he suggested that the popularity of *Desert Solitaire* led to his categorization as a "Western environmental writer," which was counter to his desire to be regarded as a novelist. He admitted to not trying very hard to dispel the image, because with it came the lucrative sideline of commissioned articles. He begins his introduction to *The Journey Home* by proclaiming that he is not a naturalist, as some reviewers and librarians have suggested. Perhaps what is closest to the truth about Edward Abbey as a writer is his statement in this interview:

> It sometimes seems to me that the Edward Abbey who writes these articles and books and so on is just another fictional creation, not much resemblance to the real one, to the one *I* think I know. The real Edward Abbey — whoever the hell that is — is a real shy, timid fellow, but the character I create in my journalism is perhaps a person I would like to be: bold, brash, daring. I created this character, and I gave him my name. I guess some people mistake the creation for the author, but that's their problem. (Hepworth and McNamee, p. 42)

Abbey is as unlikely to reveal anything more than this deflection of a central truth about him as the desert is to yield up its truth, its center.

We should also keep in mind Abbey's cautionary assessment of the literary interview, given in "A Writer's Credo," which appears in his fifth and final book of collected essays, *One Life at a Time, Please* (1988). He defines the literary interview as "a popular device through which the supercilious author provides facetious answers to superficial questions from skeptical reporters for the momentary entertainment of the bored and indifferent. In general the serious writer should avoid interviews and the serious reader should avoid reading them" (p. 167). "A Writer's Credo" provides Abbey's most elaborate summation of his reasons for and intentions in writing, versions of which are scattered throughout his prefaces and interviews. As a freelance writer, he states, it is his responsibility to critique his society, to "be of use" to his community, to "Speak out: or take up a different trade" (p. 164): "The task of the honest writer — the writer as potential hero — is to seek out, write down, and publish forth those truths which are *not* self-

evident, not universally agreed upon, not allowed to determine public feeling and official policy" (p. 166). He quotes Samuel Johnson, as he does elsewhere: " 'It is always a writer's duty to make the world better' " (p. 178). And this encapsulates what he did best.

Wendell Berry celebrates Abbey as being, in essence, "an autobiographer. . . . Mr. Abbey understands that to defend and conserve oneself as a human being in the fullest, truest sense, one must defend and conserve many others and much else. . . . [H]e speaks insistently as himself" (pp. 12, 14). Berry likens Abbey to Thoreau in his independence of spirit, in "his great effort to conserve himself as a human being in the best and fullest sense" (p. 13). Berry, himself a novelist, essayist, and "nature writer," admires Abbey as "a cultivated man"; he admires his ability "to stand aside from himself" and write about his failings with hilarity, his use of humor to temper outrage, his devotion to the "idea of property" as well as the "speed and activity of his pages."

> But the quality in him that I most prize, the one that removes him from the company of the writers I respect and puts him in the company, the smaller company, of the writers I love, is that he sees the gravity, the great danger, of the predicament we are now in, he tells it unswervingly, and he defends unflinchingly the heritage and the qualities that may preserve us. I read him, that is to say, for consolation, for the comfort of being told the truth. There is no longer any honest way to deny that a way of living that our leaders continue to praise is destroying all that our country is and all the best that it means. We are living even now among punishment and ruins. For those who know this, Edward Abbey's books will remain an indispensable solace. (p. 19)

A few readers have been angered, rather than consoled, by Abbey's work. His female characters, of whom there are only a very few — good sport Bonnie Abbzug of *The Monkey Wrench Gang*, the elusive Sandy of *Black Sun*, the dissatisfied or dead wives of *The Fool's Progress* — are seen most often offstage, merely drifting through the male characters' emotional landscape. Abbey's novels and nonfiction are peppered with jabs at feminism, *Ms.* magazine, and Gloria Steinem. In the essay "The Future of Sex," he celebrates femininity and his own "involuntary reaction" as a "male primate" to divide "all females . . . at once, emphatically and radically, into two distinct classes: those he desires and those he can ignore" (*One Life*, p. 200). In this discussion, as in all of his nonfiction, Abbey relies on allusions to and quotations from contemporary and historical writers and thinkers; here he calls on Doris Lessing, who agreed that " 'feminism is a trivial cause,' " and Margaret Mead, who wrote, " 'Each sex should do the kind of work it is best suited for' " (p. 205). But Abbey does try to temper his reactionary arguments with this statement: "There *is* a revolutionary potency in feminism because the apparent future, the general drift of technological society, is toward that androgynous world I have sketched above, a world where unisexual, interchangeable, replaceable units of desexed semihumanity carry on the subjugation of nature and human nature in a universe dominated by interlocking, embracing, copulating machines" (p. 205). Feminism, in so far as it furthers the revolution against technology and social oppression, can be useful.

In a less rhetorically aggressive setting of the argument—Henry Lightcap's comic analysis of his disastrous marriage to Elaine (*The Fool's Progress*)—Abbey calls up a list of aphorisms on marriage from male philosophers, including one he ascribes to Nietzsche, " 'The married philosopher is a figure out of a stage farce,' " and George Santayana's pronouncement, " 'It takes patience to appreciate domestic bliss' " (p. 37). Lightcap concludes, though, that what Elaine really needed, which he could not give her, was

what humans need: a sense of community. Interesting, dignified and essential work to do. (Like finding food or raising a baby.) She needed connection with the past and future of family, clan, kinfolk and tribe. And most of all she needed ownership of a piece of earth, possession of enough land to guarantee the

pride and dignity and freedom that only economic independence can bestow. Without that, what are we? Dependents, that's what. Employees. Personnel. Peasants. Serfs. Slaves. Less than men, less than women. (p. 38)

Abbey artfully deflects Elaine's complaints against Lightcap onto the panorama of modern life, and skillfully uses the words and authority of other writers to frame his arguments. Whatever complaints feminist readers and critics might have, the power of Abbey's overriding argument—that modern men and women both exist in a state of debilitating, unconscious dispossession—overwhelms his failings.

This is not to say that even his more straightforward arguments about the oppression of classes of men and women, which Abbey deems more important than the oppression of women by men, do not invite controversy. In "Immigration and Liberal Taboos," he proposes that

it might be wise for us as American citizens to consider calling a halt to the mass influx of even more millions of hungry, ignorant, unskilled, and culturally–morally–genetically impoverished people. At least until we have brought our own affairs into order. Especially when these uninvited millions bring with them an alien mode of life which—let us be honest about this—is not appealing to the majority of Americans. Why not? Because we prefer democratic government, for one thing; because we still hope for an open, spacious, uncrowded, and beautiful—yes, beautiful!— society, for another. The alternative, in the squalor, cruelty, and corruption of Latin America, is plain for all to see. (*One Life*, p. 43)

But Abbey is not entirely unsympathetic to the plight of the huddled masses. He suggests that "if we must meddle, as we have always done, let us meddle for a change in a constructive way. Stop every *campesino* at our southern border, give him a handgun, a good rifle, and a case of ammunition, and send him home. He will know what to do with our gifts and good wishes. The people know who their enemies are" (p. 44).

This is Abbey at his anarchical, ornery best—honest, ironic, tough, and imaginative, even visionary, if unrealistic.

Abbey's master's thesis, "Anarchism and the Morality of Violence," concludes that although acts of political violence are not desirable or ultimately justifiable, they are understandable under certain conditions. His novels bear out this early conclusion. In a much later discussion, "Theory of Anarchy," Abbey clarifies his stance. He postulates that one solution to the civil wars that plague the world is

> partition of territory, a devolution into self-governing, independent regions and societies. This is the natural tendency . . . and it should not be restrained. The tendency runs counter, however, to the love of power, which is why centralized governments always attempt to crush separatist movements.
>
> Government is a social machine whose function is coercion through monopoly of power. . . . The purpose of anarchism is to dismantle such institutions and to prevent their reconstruction. Ten thousand years of human history demonstrate that our freedoms cannot be entrusted to those ambitious few who are drawn to power; we must learn—again—to govern ourselves. Anarchism does not mean "no rule"; it means "no rulers." (*One Life*, p. 27)

In his nonfiction, Abbey's solutions for world peace do not move beyond these general, allusion-laden arguments, but the plots of his novels are driven by characters who think about and act on such ideas.

Later Fiction

In 1975, Abbey's most popular novel appeared: *The Monkey Wrench Gang*, a rollicking adventure novel of the camaraderie of environmental saboteurs in the face of government- and socially sanctioned ecological destruction. Mostly unnoticed by the literary establishment, the book became an underground classic, selling well over half a million copies. The book's subversive stance is clear even from the epigrams that preface it, including a line from a poem by Richard Shelton—"but oh my desert/yours is the only death I cannot bear"—a line from Walt Whitman—"Resist much. Obey little"—and a line attributed to Thoreau ("Now. Or never"), and a dictionary etymology of the word "sabotage." The content of the epigrams progresses from grief to unfocused resistance to decision to action, following the logic underlying radical environmental activism.

The book begins with "Prologue: The Aftermath," a scene, written in the present tense, of the dedication of a bridge across Glen Canyon, during which the bridge explodes. The four protagonists, Doc Sarvis and his girlfriend, Bonnie Abbzug, Seldom Seen Smith, and George Washington Hayduke, meet to make a river raft trip through Glen Canyon. Seizing on the idea of blowing up Glen Canyon Dam, they prepare themselves by making war on billboards and bulldozers, generally undoing as much of the work of roadbuilders and developers as they can by pulling up survey stakes, cutting fences and wires, pouring Karo Syrup into gas tanks of large equipment, and dropping pipe wrenches into oil drilling rigs. The gang is smart, crude, crudely funny, and dedicated. Along with these Western adventures, Abbey includes sections detailing acts of "monkeywrenching," informing the reader on how to drain the oil from the crankcase of an Allis-Chalmers HD-41 tractor and what basic supplies are necessary for exploding a forty-foot bridge. Abbey's characters, with their motto "Keep it like it was," are driven by their need for freedom and wilderness; he adapts the frontier ethic of self-reliance and moral action to their modern war against progress and technology. The book reads well as a new Western, as a manifesto for eco-terrorists, and as an "antidote to despair" for the disappearing Western landscape. Abbey said of the book, "I think of it primarily as an adventure story with an environmental theme. I guess you could say there is also a strong element of wish fulfilment. Everyone will read it in their own way, but I intended it to be mock-heroic, or perhaps a little more than that. But above all I wanted it to be entertaining" (Baker, p. 6).

A note on the cover of the 1975 paperback edition, attributed to *The National Observer*, labels the book as "a sad, hilarious, exuberant, vulgar fairy tale . . . it'll make you want to go out and blow up a dam." Ann Ronald cites other reviewers' classifications—"ecological caper" and "propaganda novel"—but argues that it is principally a romance, with stylized figures, a mythic landscape, and picaresque action. The book precipitated and continues to inspire one of the public images of radical environmentalism.

In 1980, with the appearance of *Good News*, eco-war in the Southwest continues, expanded into an apocalyptic, darker vision. Set in and around a destroyed Phoenix, Arizona, *Good News* is almost all bad news. The city lies in ruins; society has disintegrated into civil war. Abbey's protagonist, Jack Burns, the brave cowboy resurrected, travels through the rubble of civilization to find his long-lost son. The book ends in irresolution: the son perhaps found; the father dead, we think; and the battle to be carried on, probably. Critics Ann Ronald and Jay Dougherty view this work as driven by irony, rather than romance, in its dystopian vision. Ronald states, "its theme is chaos," not at all the freewheeling and free-loving anarchy espoused by characters in *The Monkey Wrench Gang* (1988, p. 228). Ronald attributes some of its failings—"abrupt tonal shifts, its disconnected scenes, and its one-dimensional characters" (p. 183)—to the form of the novel, which is determined by irony, a subversion of expectations, an undercutting of any pattern. Abbey still uses traces of the romantic forms that structure his other fiction—the quest myth, battles of good and evil—but now his fictional world and everyone in it are paralyzed or robotized by paradoxes, and whatever optimism the reader can glean from this dark vision is only suggested.

We get something like relief from this dark vision in Abbey's next novel, *The Fool's Progress: An Honest Novel* (1988). This novel chronicles a trip home: after his wife leaves him, the narrator, Henry Lightcap, travels from Arizona to his boyhood home in West Virginia, accompanied by the memories he recounts, his dying dog, and his irascible and incorrigible nature.

A version of the first chapter of *The Fool's Progress*, "In Medias Reas, Arizona," appeared in 1986, in a chapbook edition entitled *Confessions of a Barbarian*. In the "Editor's Preface" that introduces this piece, Edward Abbey the wily effete editor recounts the tall tale of receiving the manuscript from Henry Lightcap, a wily redneck, who has since disappeared. Abbey the editor labels Lightcap's manuscript a "novel in the form of a memoir, or memoir in the form of a novel. . . . If a novel, it is the baggiest sort" (p. 14). Abbey sets up these straw men for the sake of amusement, as a way of promoting the book in an apology for it, and to give one persona the chance to comment on the other. Abbey the editor writes,

> Has Lightcap's book any literary merit whatsoever? No; none whatsoever. Why then publish such rubbish? The chief reason has been alluded to above: commercial greed. But one further and less than merely incidental apology may be suggested: this "novel" has a certain antiquarian value, or if not value then interest, in that in its pages we can contemplate, in the person of this Henry H. Lightcap, an American type now totally anachronistic. . . . There is no place for such awkward, abrasive and non-productive anarchs as Lightcap. . . . The Henry Lightcaps of America, like the redskinned buffalo-hunting horsemen of the West, had their day—a century ago! They are the final incarnations of the Vanishing Americans. Let us let them vanish. It is the one sole merit of Lightcap's *Confessions* that it enables us to grasp, between thumb and forefinger as it were, how little our loss entails. (pp. 15–16)

Abbey's ironical strategies include undercutting his work in order to advance it in complicated ways, by directing attention to a fictionalized version of himself (the author) and to his fictionalization of himself (his narrator). In this preface we see a version of the process of a writer's fictionalizing of himself as author, as Abbey suggested occurs in his case: "the Edward Abbey who writes these articles and books and so on is just another fictional creation" (Hepworth and McNamee, p. 42). This dissembling emphasizes the modesty, evidence of a higher morality, of the Western hero as seen in popular novels, movies, and television and of this late twentieth-century version of Western hero as writer.

Abbey's final work of fiction was *Hayduke Lives!*, which appeared posthumously in 1990. The theme of this book is resurrection, perhaps not an ironic choice for the dying author. Not only does the presumed-dead Hayduke reappear, but so does Jack Burns, who could have been considered dead in both *The Brave Cowboy* and *Good News*, with the effect of unifying Abbey's work of the previous twenty-five years. The book begins with a desert tortoise's view of the destruction of wilderness by human development, as the tortoise is crushed under a giant yellow earth mover. The book ends with the miraculous reemergence of the tortoise from the earth, under the salutary gaze of a lone horseman, "not far from a certain half-dead juniper tree that lifts a twisted silvergray limb toward the sky—a gesture of static assertion, the affirmation of an embattled but undefeated existence" (p. 307). Intervening events include the reunion and continued work of the Monkey Wrench Gang, but this version turns murderous; Abbey suggests that the resurrection of the natural, wild landscape from its apparent destruction might require that such a price be paid.

Paul Bryant maintains that despite the triumph of environmental radicalism in *Hayduke Lives!*, the measure of Abbey's moderate stance is shown by the flaws he gives the radical character Hayduke: "Only non-human nature—i.e. the tortoise—and Jack Burns, the scout, remain and endure. Only non-human nature remains unambiguous, unironic, in Edward Abbey's writing" (1991, p. 321). As Abbey warns us on the very first page of the book, even before we read its title page, "Anyone who takes this book seriously will be shot. Anyone who does not take this book seriously will be buried alive by a Mitsubishi bulldozer." As he has echoed in his interviews, a better way of life is approachable only through a maze of paradoxes.

Abbey's search for that way was, in part, a communal one. He had five wives, five children, and many lovers, friends, comrades in arms. *Hayduke Lives!*, surprisingly, does not begin with his usual "Author's Preface" or "Preliminary Notes." This last book, completed as he knew he was dying, lists those to whom he feels indebted and gives thanks "for the affection and good times and adventures in the world that we shared, that I will never forget, that can never be lost" (n.p.).

Personas and Influences

Among Abbey's fictional, nonfictional, and real-life personas was that of creative writing professor. During most of the 1980s, Abbey taught one semester each year in the creative writing program at the University of Arizona. One of his students, the essayist Nancy Mairs, describes Abbey the teacher in "597ax." Mairs notes his rugged handsomeness, the magazines, essayists, and books he recommended, her discomfort when he addressed her formally ("Ms. Mairs"), as he did all of his students, and the difficulties of the writing workshop. She quotes his written comment on a "dreary, static reminiscence" she turned in:

> I can understand that your reminiscences seem precious to you, as mine do to me, but somehow you've got to find a way, a device, a meaning, to make these memoirs readable to an ordinary bored, busy, hard-nosed, cynical, weary, cigar-smoking, whisky-drinking, fornicating old fart like—not me!—but your typical magazine or book editor. In its present form it will not sell. Maybe you don't care about that, and that's okay, but still, your primary obligation as a writer is to give pleasure, to entertain, or at least to instruct. (p. 47)

Mairs remembers the end-of-semester party at Abbey's home, a fire on the patio and evening stars, in an atmosphere belying the formality of the early weeks of the semester. His advice to her plays on this contradiction as well: Abbey as himself but not. It seems a matter of persona.

The disdain that Abbey felt for people in large groups in general—the thread of which runs through all of his polemics—surfaced in his public persona of famous writer. That disdain even extended to his listeners on occasion. Anyone who attended one of Abbey's readings in the late 1970s and early 1980s might suspect he did not think much of his audience, because he seemed to take a certain pleasure in annoying it; his ways of handling his acclaim were not always comfortable. Once he read what one reviewer called "low-class erotic poetry, boring letters from his fans and his now-trite works condemning urban sprawl and smelter pollution" (Hepworth and McNamee, p. 34). On another occasion he merely stupefied the audience with some tedious, most definitely in-progress writing. In her contribution to the special issue of the *Tucson Weekly*, the author Barbara Kingsolver remembers asking Abbey, " 'Do you just do the Old-Bastard image so people will leave you alone?' He gave me an absolutely radiant smile and said, 'Yep' " (quoted in Biggers, p. 6). Creating characters, even the character of Ed Abbey, was something he enjoyed.

Part of Abbey's persona as writer was his capacity as a reader. He drew heavily on the writing of others—writers, thinkers, philosophers—and incorporated it into his work. Any of his essays reveals quotations ascribed, most often correctly, to philosophers, statesmen, and writers of the past. When we drift down a river with Abbey, he is as likely to bring along references to Huck Finn or Longfellow's *Hiawatha* as he is to quote from Thoreau, which he does with such skill in his journal-like essay "Down the River with Henry Thoreau." In "Watching the Birds: The Windhover," for example, he quotes or refers to Einstein, Francis Bacon, Elinor Wylie, Ernest Hemingway, and Robinson Jeffers, all in the space of six pages. Paul Bryant, investigating literary allusions in Abbey's last novel, finds references to Epicurus, William Butler Yeats, Gertrude Stein, Rudyard Kipling, Stephen Crane, Emily Dickinson, John Steinbeck, Henry James, and contemporary writers (1991, pp. 314–318). In his work on *Desert Solitaire*, Bryant lists Abbey's "allusions [to] and echoes" of Heraclitus, Hegel, Plato, Robert Frost, Shakespeare, Wordsworth, Raleigh, Robinson

Jeffers, Homer, Spinoza, Donne, and others (1993, p. 14). In her study, Ann Ronald (1988) documents Abbey's debts to the explorer John Wesley Powell, the nature writer Joseph Wood Krutch, Everett Ruess, and Thoreau. Richard Shelton, in "Creeping up on *Desert Solitaire*," proposes John C. Van Dyke's *The Desert* (1901)—a book Abbey called "unjustly forgotten"—as "the direct literary antecedent" of parts of Abbey's most popular nonfiction work, particularly the narrator's stance as a lover of the desert (p. 73). Clearly, Abbey knows well the culture he critiques.

Appraisal

As much as Abbey is revered by environmentalists, writers, and fellow lovers of what remains of the wild places of the Southwest, their high regard is not without, on occasion, some critical distance. He himself named flaws in his writing: "I tend to be self-indulgent. I ramble on and on. I write too much about myself. . . . My main difficulty in fiction, especially in novel form, is plotting. . . . I just don't understand how you construct a plot. . . . I think I write fast, but carelessly, but always pretty damn spontaneously, which may be both a strength and a weakness" (Solheim and Levin, p. 89). The critic Peter Wild has faulted the tenuousness of his plots, the flatness of his characters, and the inconsistency of his arguments. In "Edward Abbey: The Middle-Class Maverick," Wild is especially critical of Abbey's very American, very middle-class "teenage mind," characterized by "revolt against authority; celebration of the common man and misfits; the hero as rebel; nature as a refuge from the nastiness and responsibilities of civilization; the joys of escape and of quest; adoration of women, that is, unpossessable women; and lastly . . . elevation of the ego above all other concerns" (p. 19). The historian Patricia Limerick joins Wild in his criticism of Abbey's arguments as being weakened by their underlying conventionality, superficiality, and lack of clarity, stemming from contradictions that Limerick maintains Abbey never resolves and only dresses up as paradoxes: how to encourage a love for wilderness without encouraging more visitors to it, how to throw off government restraints while ensuring that land is protected for future generations.

Limerick sees a larger concern for Abbey, as a writer in the Romantic tradition, in meeting contemporary nature writing's major challenge: "How was he to make repeated declarations of wonder without sacrificing the conviction and freshness that supposedly characterized his faith?" (p. 160). Limerick argues that, in spite of his failings, Abbey meets this challenge successfully, through the compelling intensity of his prose descriptions, the energy and novelty of his arguments in defense of the land, a playful, bawdy, clever humor that tempers those arguments, his use of popular and intellectual references and allusions. Abbey's work seduces the reader's appreciation not only of desert wilderness but also of a sort of ecology of the writer's mind.

Wild states that one of Abbey's most important contributions was that he "gave us permission to speak of a snaggy tree as simply gone mad, to guffaw at bureaucracy when necessary, and yes, guffaw at ourselves on occasion" (1989, p. 100). In his assessment of Abbey's work, Edward Hoagland notes that whatever his failures to "surpass himself," Abbey's "ambitions were confined to truth-telling, rhapsody and the lambasting of villains" (1989, p. 45), at which he certainly succeeded. With *Desert Solitaire*, Abbey popularized the genre of contemporary American nature writing.

Abbey's most important contribution is his delineation and demonstration of a passion for wilderness, the desert in particular. The most successful of his writing conveys a recognition of the paradoxes such a passion entails, probably unsurpassable lyric descriptions of the land, and the engaging intellect he brought to bear in argument and action. He was most comfortable working on the borders of things — for instance, places where the desert meets the city, where the desert meets the sea, and those places where the Western novel meets nature writing, where romance meets environmentalism, where sexual

comedy meets reverence for creation. Edward Abbey shaped a literary place, a terrain formed by his work and play with language, for us to stand together, if only momentarily and ridiculously but ever full of heart, in the contemporary landscape.

Selected Bibliography

WORKS OF EDWARD ABBEY

NOVELS

Jonathan Troy (New York: Dodd, Mead, 1954); *The Brave Cowboy: An Old Tale in a New Time* (New York: Dodd, Mead, 1956; repr., Albuquerque: Univ. of New Mexico Press, 1977); *Fire on the Mountain* (New York: Dial, 1962; repr., Albuquerque: Univ. of New Mexico Press, 1978); *Black Sun* (New York: Simon and Schuster, 1971; repr., New York: Avon, 1982); *The Monkey Wrench Gang* (Philadelphia: Lippincott, 1975; repr., New York: Avon, 1976, 1992); *Good News* (New York: E. P. Dutton, 1980; repr., 1991); *The Fool's Progress: An Honest Novel* (New York: Henry Holt, 1988); *Hayduke Lives!* (Boston: Little, Brown, 1990).

NONFICTION

Desert Solitaire: A Season in the Wilderness (New York: Simon and Schuster, 1968; repr., 1990; New York: Ballantine, 1971); *In Praise of Mountain Lions* (Albuquerque: Albuquerque Sierra Club, 1984), with John Nichols; *Confessions of a Barbarian* (Santa Barbara, Calif., 1986); *A Voice Crying in the Wilderness: Notes from a Secret Journal* (New York: St. Martin's, 1989).

PHOTOGRAPHIC ESSAYS

Appalachian Wilderness: The Great Smoky Mountains (New York: E. P. Dutton, 1970), with Eliot Porter; *Slickrock: The Canyon Country of Southeast Utah* (New York: Sierra Club/Charles Scribner's Sons, 1971), with Philip Hyde; *Cactus Country* (New York: Time-Life Books, 1973); *The Hidden Canyon: A River Journey* (New York: Viking, 1977), with John Blaustein; *Desert Images: An American Landscape* (New York: Harcourt Brace Jovanovich, 1979), with David Muench.

COLLECTIONS

The Journey Home: Some Words in Defense of the American West (New York: E. P. Dutton, 1977); *Abbey's Road* (New York: E. P. Dutton, 1979); *Down the River with Henry David Thoreau and Friends*

(New York: E. P. Dutton, 1982); *Beyond the Wall: Essays from the Outside* (New York: Holt, Rinehart and Winston, 1984); *Slumgullion Stew: An Edward Abbey Reader* (New York: E. P. Dutton, 1984), repr. as *The Best of Edward Abbey* (San Francisco: Sierra Club, 1988); *One Life at a Time, Please* (New York: Henry Holt, 1988).

SELECTED ARTICLES

"On Nature, the Modern Temper, and the Southwest: An Interview with Joseph Wood Krutch," in *Sage* 2 (spring 1968); "Living on the Last Whole Earth," in *Natural History* 80 (November 1971); "On the Need for a Wilderness to Get Lost in," in *New York Times*, 29 August 1972; "The Second Rape of the West," in *Playboy* 22 (December 1975).

BIOGRAPHICAL AND CRITICAL STUDIES

John F. Baker, "Edward Abbey," in *Publishers Weekly* (8 September 1975); Joseph Barbat, "Review of Abbey's Road," in *Smithsonian* (October 1979); Wendell Berry, "A Few Words in Favor of Edward Abbey," in *Resist Much, Obey Little: Some Notes on Edward Abbey*, ed. by James Hepworth and Gregory McNamee (Salt Lake City, Utah: Dream Garden, 1985; repr., Tucson, Ariz.: Harbinger House, 1989); Douglas Biggers, ed., "A Celebration of the Life and Work of Edward Abbey," in *Tucson Weekly* 6 (5–11 April 1989); James Bishop, Jr., *Epitaph for a Desert Anarchist: The Life and Legacy of Edward Abbey* (New York: Atheneum, 1994); Paul T. Bryant, "Edward Abbey and Environmental Quixoticism," in *Western American Literature* 24 (May 1989), "Echoes, Allusions and 'Reality' in *Hayduke Lives!*," in *Western American Literature* 25 (February 1991), and "The Structure and Unity of *Desert Solitaire*," in *Western American Literature* 28 (May 1993).

Walter Clemons, "Endangered Air: Review of *The Monkey Wrench Gang*," in *Newsweek* (5 January 1976); Carl L. Davis, "Thoughts on a Vulture: Edward Abbey, 1927–1989," in *RE arts and letters: REAL* 15 (fall 1989); Terrell Dixon, "Abbey's Biocentric Epiphany: *Desert Solitaire* and the Teaching of Environmental Literature," in *CEA Critic* 54 (fall 1991); Jay Dougherty, " 'Once more, and once again': Edward Abbey's Cyclical View of Past and Present in *Good News*," in *Critique: Studies in Contemporary Fiction* 30 (summer 1988); Fred Erisman, "A Variant Text of *The Monkey Wrench Gang*," in *Western American Literature* 14 (fall 1979); Dave Foreman, *Confessions of an Eco-Warrior* (New York: Harmony Books, 1991); David E. Gamble, "Into the Maze with Edward Abbey," in *South Dakota Review* 26 (1988); Gerald Haslam, Introduction to *Fire on the Mountain*, by Edward Abbey (Albuquerque: Univ. of New Mexico Press, 1978).

James Hepworth, "Edward Abbey, 1927–1989," in *Western American Literature* 24 (August 1989); James Hepworth and Gregory McNamee, eds., *Resist Much, Obey Little: Some Notes on Edward Abbey* (Salt Lake City, Utah: Dream Garden, 1985; repr., Tucson, Ariz.: Harbinger-House, 1989); Jerry Herndon, " 'Moderate Extremism': Edward Abbey and 'The Moon-Eyed Horse,' " in *Western American Literature* 16 (August 1981); Edward Hoagland, "Review of *Black Sun*," in *New York Times Book Review* (13 June 1971), and "Edward Abbey: Standing Tough in the Desert," in *New York Times Book Review* (7 May 1989); Kay Jimerson, "Edward Abbey: Interview," in *This Is About Vision: Interviews with Southwestern Writers*, ed. by William Balassi, John F. Crawford, and Annie O. Eysturoy (Albuquerque: Univ. of New Mexico Press, 1990); M. Jimmie Killingsworth, "Realism, Human Action, and Instrumental Discourse," in *Journal of Advanced Composition* 12 (1992).

Neal E. Lambert, Introduction to *The Brave Cowboy*, by Edward Abbey (Albuquerque: Univ. of New Mexico Press, 1977); Patricia Nelson Limerick, "Edward Abbey," in *Desert Passages: Encounters with the American Deserts* (Albuquerque: Univ. of New Mexico Press, 1985); Jack Loeffler, "Edward Abbey, Anarchism and the Environment," in *Western American Literature* 28 (May 1993); Thomas J. Lyon, "Review of *Black Sun*," in *Western American Literature* 6 (summer 1971); Nancy Mairs, "597ax," in *Resist Much, Obey Little*, ed. by James Hepworth and Gregory McNamee (Salt Lake City, Utah: Dream Garden, 1985; repr., Tucson, Ariz.: Harbinger House, 1989); Garth McCann, *Edward Abbey* (Boise, Idaho: Boise State Univ., 1977); James I. McClintock, "Edward Abbey's 'Antidotes to Despair,' " in *Critique: Studies in Contemporary Fiction* 31 (fall 1989); Bill McKibben, "The Gleam of Open Sky: Review of *Hayduke Lives!*," in *Hungry Mind Review* 14 (May/June 1990); David Miller, "Paeans to the Desert," in *Progressive* (January 1978); Tom Miller, "*Abbey's Road*," in *New West* (23 October 1978); John G. Mitchell, "The Howling Last Stand," in *Rocky Mountain Magazine* (May/June 1981); Ted Morgan, "Subvert and Conserve: Review of *The Journey Home*," in *New York Times Book Review* (31 July 1977); David Copland Morris, "Celebration and Irony: The Polyphonic Voice of Edward Abbey's *Desert Solitaire*," in *Western American Literature* 28 (May 1993); John A. Murray, "The Hill Beyond the City: Elements of the Jeremiad in Edward Abbey's 'Down the River with Henry David Thoreau,' " in *Western American Literature* 22 (February 1988).

Gilbert Neiman, "Review of *The Brave Cowboy*," in *New Mexico Quarterly* 26 (autumn 1956); David Petersen, "Cactus Ed's Moveable Feast: A Preview of *Confessions of a Barbarian: Pages from the Journals of*

Edward Abbey," in *Western American Literature* 28 (May 1993); William T. Pilkington, "Edward Abbey: Southwestern Anarchist," in *Western Review* 3 (winter 1966), and "Edward Abbey: Western Philosopher, or How to Be a 'Happy Hopi Hippie,'" in *Western American Literature* 9 (May 1974): 17–34 (as Tom Pilkington); Lawrence C. Powell, "A Singular Ranger," in *Westways* (March 1974): 32–35, 64–65; Donn Rawlings, "Abbey's Essays: One Man's Quest for Solid Ground," in *Living Wilderness* 44 (June 1980); Paul W. Rea, "Abbey's Country," in *Journal of the Southwest* 31 (summer 1989); "Review of *Abbey's Road,*" in *New Republic* (25 August 1979); Ann Ronald, "Edward Abbey," in *A Literary History of the American West* (Fort Worth: Texas Christian Univ. Press, 1987), and *The New West of Edward Abbey* (Reno: Univ. of Nevada Press, 1988).

Don Scheese, "*Desert Solitaire:* Counter-Friction to the Machine in the Garden," in *North Dakota Quarterly* 59 (spring 1991); Richard Shelton, "Creeping Up on *Desert Solitaire,*" in *Resist Much, Obey Little,* ed. by James Hepworth and Gregory McNamee (Salt Lake City, Utah: Dream Garden, 1985; repr., Tucson, Ariz.: Harbinger House, 1989); Scott Slovic, "'Rudolf the Red knows rain, dear': The Aestheticism of Edward Abbey," in *Seeking Awareness in American Nature Writing* (Salt Lake City, Utah: Univ. of Utah Press, 1992); Dave Solheim and Rob Levin, "The *Bloomsbury Review* Interview," in *Resist Much, Obey Little,* ed. by James Hepworth and Gregory McNamee (Salt Lake City, Utah: Dream Garden, 1985; repr., Tucson, Ariz.: Harbinger House, 1989); Les Standiford, "Desert Places: An Exchange with Edward Abbey," in *Western Humanities Review* 24 (autumn 1970).

Stephen Tatum, "Closing and Opening Western American Fiction: The Reader in *The Brave Cowboy,*" in *Western American Literature* 19 (November 1984); Edwin W. Teale, "Making the Wild Scene," in *New York Times Book Review* (28 January 1968); Eric Temple, producer and director, *Edward Abbey: A Voice in the Wilderness* (South Burlington, Vt., 1993), a video; Diane Wakoski, "Edward Abbey: Joining the Visionary 'Inhumanists,'" in *Resist Much, Obey Little,* ed. by James Hepworth and Gregory McNamee (Salt Lake City, Utah: Dream Garden, 1985; repr., Tucson, Ariz.: Harbinger House, 1989); Peter Wild, "Edward Abbey: The Middle-Class Maverick," in *New Mexico Humanities Review* 6 (summer 1983), and "Into the Heart's Wild Places: Edward Abbey (1927–1989)," in *Sierra* 74 (May 1989); Delbert E. Wylder, "Edward Abbey and the 'Power Elite,'" in *Western Review* 6 (winter 1969).

DIANE ACKERMAN
(b. 1948)

DAVID M. ROBINSON

DIANE ACKERMAN'S emergence in the early 1990s as one of the most widely read and admired of America's natural history essayists can be viewed as both an enlightening narrative of the development of a versatile and original writer, and an indication of the broadening appeal and increasing social impact of nature writing in contemporary American culture. Ackerman won her current place within the tradition of American nature writing with her 1990 study of the biological and cultural evolution of the five human senses, *A Natural History of the Senses*, and her 1991 collection of essays on animals, *The Moon by Whale Light*. These volumes, however, were preceded by some two decades of work in poetry and two quite different volumes of prose. What may at first have seemed to be the rather sudden emergence of a new observer of natural history was, in fact, the result of a long auctorial evolution coinciding with the development of a readership with a thirst for fresh and detailed representations of the natural world. Ackerman's nature writing is a rich amalgam of the factual and the intuitive, of empirical observation, precise description, faithful reportage of information, and uninhibited cosmological speculation.

Education and Early Work

Ackerman was born on 7 October 1948 in Waukegan, Illinois, to Sam Fink and Marsha Tishler Fink. She attended Boston University from 1966 to 1967 and earned her B.A. from Pennsylvania State University in 1970. She then entered the M.F.A. program in creative writing at Cornell University, beginning there the first phase of her career as a poet and a teacher of English and creative writing. Ackerman completed her M.F.A. in 1973 and started work on her Ph.D. in English at Cornell. She served as a teaching assistant and then as a lecturer at Cornell until she finished her dissertation and received her degree in 1979. Ackerman then held academic positions at the University of Pittsburgh (1980–1983) and Washington University (1984–1986) and accepted several shorter appointments at other universities in the 1980s as writer-in-residence. During the late 1970s and 1980s, Ackerman gradually established herself as a poet of stature, publishing a verse drama and three volumes of poetry, and collaborating on another volume of poetry. Her 1991 collection, *Jaguar of Sweet Laughter: New and Selected Poems*, appearing just as her two volumes of natural history writings, *A Natural History of the Senses* and *The Moon by Whale Light*, were propelling her into national prominence as a nature writer, reflects her growing interest in natural history and also constitutes a summation of the first two decades of her poetic career.

These volumes on natural history mark a second phase in Ackerman's career, which began when she joined the *New Yorker* as a staff writer in 1988. She established herself through that influential magazine as an astute chronicler of the contemporary desire for a more direct and profound experience of the natural world. In particular, Ackerman brought to her writing a capacity to blend scientific information, cultural history, and personal experience; her decriptions of the processes of the human senses, or the characters of familiar yet exotic animals, are engaging, informative, and philosophically suggestive.

Ackerman's later achievement in nature writing is of course connected with her earlier development as a poet, but a review of her poetry reveals that she can by no means be pigeonholed into the category of nature poet, if that category is taken in any restrictive sense. *The Planets: A Cosmic Pastoral* (1976), *Wife of Light* (1978), and *Lady Faustus* (1983) are varied in subject matter, and the variety of her concerns is further demonstrated by her 1988 volume, *Reverse Thunder*, a verse dramatization based on the life of Juana Inés de la Cruz. But many of the poems, despite their variety in tone and subject matter, contain a characteristic dynamic of probing curiosity, perceptual discovery, and celebration, an enactment of the ever-renewing process of the world's disclosure of itself.

In this respect, Ackerman can claim a place in the American literary tradition originating with Ralph Waldo Emerson and including Henry David Thoreau and Walt Whitman. A desire for the renewal of the powers of perception and a more profound engagement with experience, expressed in Emerson's *Nature* as hunger for an "original relation with the universe," is perhaps the hallmark of a literary tradition that continues to take new forms and directions in contemporary America, as suggested by the poetry of A. R. Ammons and Mary Oliver and the prose of Gary Snyder, Wendell Berry, and Annie Dillard. Thoreau's crusade for renewal and reawakening at Walden Pond and Whitman's attitude of passionate curiosity about the life being lived all around him, both of which arise from an urge to take fuller account of our capabilities of awareness, are defining and influential intellectual gestures of this tradition. This literary sensibility,

in part mediated to Ackerman through the work of Ammons, the central figure in Cornell's creative writing program, is one of the subjects of her doctoral dissertation on the contemporary forms of the "metaphysical mind."

Something of the originality of Ackerman's approach to the genre of nature writing is suggested in her 1976 poetry collection, *The Planets: A Cosmic Pastoral*, a book in which nature is defined in terms not only of the organic processes of living organisms on the earth but also of the enormity and splendor of the solar system and, by implication, the entire cosmos. The volume, illustrated with NASA photographs of the planets and replete with astronomical information about them, suggests Ackerman's determination to join poetic imagination and scientific observation, with the ultimate goal of giving adequate expression to a sense of amazement at matter's overwhelming permutations. *The Planets* exemplifies how a consciousness attuned to the physical vastness of space nourishes an open and speculative frame of mind, poetry's fertile ground.

A later collection, *Lady Faustus* (1983), contains poems that anticipate some of the themes Ackerman would pursue in her nature-oriented prose. But it is important to note that her poems are most directly concerned with the human. Her poetry is resolutely observant of human appearance, emotion, and interaction, and the focus on the natural world that typifies her recent prose depends on a working assumption that the fully human can be seen only as part of what we have somewhat falsely isolated and categorized as "nature." Ackerman's work constitutes a repudiation of this dichotomy.

Ackerman did not enter nonfiction prose as a natural history writer, however, but as an autobiographical chronicler of different ways of life or activity. In her chronicles of the West and learning to fly, she establishes the persona of a curious and adventuresome observer and learner of the new and unfamiliar. In *Twilight of the Tenderfoot: A Western Memoir* (1980) Ackerman recounts her stay at a cattle ranch in New Mexico, relating the rhythm of the cattleman's year and describing her own attempts to know

Diane Ackerman

and live the life she found there. Ackerman understood her narrative role well: she was a non-Westerner come to a kind of quintessential West, a woman observing and learning work that had been traditionally defined as male, and a modern individual confronting a way of life that had changed little for several decades. The book is thus the exploration of a new and somewhat exotic way of life, informed by a deep respect for that life and its people, and a recognition of the drama and comedy in an outsider's attempts to become part of a well-established social environment.

In *On Extended Wings* (1985), Ackerman recounts her experience of learning to fly an airplane, a process through which she satisfied a deep and long-standing personal desire. Ackerman demonstrates here the blend of the poetic and the technical that characterizes her later books on natural history. Her dazzlement at the visual beauty and physical sensation of flight is evident in several highly charged descriptive passages, but most of her narrative attention is devoted to her attempt to master the knowledge, language, and technique of piloting, a process that is more severe and painful than she expected. In one sense, *On Extended Wings* is an investigation of the process of education, or the mastery of an art, in which Ackerman, a teacher of the craft of writing, observes herself as a learner of another craft and the student of other teachers.

A Natural History of the Senses

While it is possible to trace an author's development by using the record of the past, noting elements of the earlier writings that help account for later developments, it must be recognized that an author's growth and changes are by no means predictable. Literary innovation is a phenomenon more easily acknowledged and celebrated than explained. *A Natural History of the*

23

Senses (1990) was such an innovation, an unusual and appealing book that established Ackerman as a capable translator of the enormous recent accumulation of scientific information about the human body and as an acute interpreter of that data in the light of cultural history. Ackerman's title alludes to one of the historically most important genres in scientific writing, natural history, as a tool for explaining and categorizing botanical and zoological specimens and their habitats. Ackerman approaches the subject of the evolution and nature of the five senses with a similar mission of discovery and explanatory analysis, adding to it a zeal to correct the loss of sensuous experience in contemporary culture. "We need to return to feeling the textures of life," she writes. "Much of our experience in twentieth-century America is an effort to get away from those textures, to fade into a stark, simple, solemn, puritanical, all-business routine that doesn't have anything so unseemly as sensuous zest" (p. xviii). Ackerman explains the functioning of the senses with an eye to celebrating them, dramatizing human experience, including her own, in ways that emphasize the joy of their exercise.

Ackerman divides the book into five sections, each devoted to one of the senses, beginning with smell and proceeding through touch, taste, hearing, and vision. She follows these analyses with a chapter titled "Synthesia," the combination or harmony of the senses, and a "Postscript" that with renewed vigor and interest calls our attention to the "astonishment" and "mystery" of our life in the senses, a plea for the renewal of wonder not unlike Thoreau's charge to be fully "awake" to our experience.

Although her discussion of each particular sense does not develop in any rigidly sequential way, thus preserving a sense of spontaneity and dialogue, Ackerman's treatment of each sense encompasses four broad themes: information about the evolution of the sense, emphasizing aspects that gave it biological survival value for the individual or for the species; a description of the physiological mechanism of the sense within the context of the processes of the body and mind that it helps to sustain; numerous

allusions and, in some cases, sustained analyses of the function of the sense in literary and cultural history, linking the reader's personal experience of that sense to a larger context of social and artistic development; and vignettes of her own personal experience—impressions or remembered moments that help to bring the more factual elements of her analysis into the dimension of contemporary experience. Ackerman is in this sense a guide or mentor to the reader in quest of a more profound awareness of the value of the senses.

The categories of discussion listed here are of course overlapping and intertwined. In describing the physiology of each sense organ, Ackerman sometimes places its function and development within the framework of human evolution, repeatedly reminding us that whatever pleasures we now take in the exercise of a particular sense, it developed through the strict discipline of biological survival, providing our distant ancestors with some fundamental advantage that helped assure their survival. But evolution has also been continued by what we might call cultural means, as Ackerman's many artistic and historical allusions remind us. We exercise our senses within a context of cultural norms and taboos of which we are often only dimly aware, and this context conditions our sense experience in crucial ways. Our senses also form the basis for the exercise of artistic creativity. Ackerman's structural method, an interlaced series of brief, topically focused sections within each chapter, helps to emphasize the interrelationship and indivisibility of scientific and cultural modes of explanation for human development and experience. The senses, she writes, are "an extension of the genetic chain that connects us to everyone who has ever lived; they bind us to other people and to animals, across time and country and happenstance" (p. 308).

"Of Violets and Neurons," an early section of slightly more than two pages in the opening section on smell, offers a representative example of the effectiveness of this synthetic literary procedure. Ackerman begins with an attempt to describe the smell of violets ("burnt sugar cubes that have been dipped in lemon and velvet"), a linguistic exercise that demonstrates our propensity for "defining one smell by another smell or another sense" (p. 9). Ackerman then recounts Napoleon and Josephine's mutual love of the smell of violets, expressed through her characteristic perfume and his planting of the flowers on her grave. She mentions Ralph Vaughan Williams' symphonic description of the cry of a London flower girl and offers Shakespeare's description of the fleeting smell of the flower, before explaining, "Violets contain ionone, which short-circuits our sense of smell" (p. 9).

After further elaboration on the nature of the scent, Ackerman explains in detail the actual process of smelling, in which "receptor cells bearing microscopic hairs called cilia" (p. 10) absorb molecules of odor that have been taken into the nasal cavity. The precision and detail of the description account for its impact; like a number of other technical descriptions throughout the book, it portrays the intricate mechanisms that make possible even the most seemingly ordinary experiences. Ackerman then provides a visual description of the human olfactory areas, comparing their light yellow color with the darker yellow found in the fox and the cat, whose sense of smell is acute. She ends by reminding us of the psychological impact of smell, noting the work of one researcher who had established the fact that smell could contribute to memory retention.

This technique of writing has been referred to here as a synthesis for the way that it brings together disparate fields of knowledge and linguistic systems to illuminate a single process. But the technique, in effect, is expansive, a barrage of information and impressions that continually pushes the reader into new intellectual and experiential territory. Ackerman is especially effective in interspersing the informational and analytical elements of the book with personal anecdotes, as when she illustrates the idea that "we each have our own aromatic memories" through her recollection of "deeply fragrant" groves of eucalyptus in California, where she participated in a study of monarch butterflies that inhabit the groves (p. 18). The special nature of this area is in large part attributable to the

distinctive fragrance of the eucalyptus, a smell that returns her to her childhood, "feeling my mother massage my chest with Vicks VapoRub" (p. 19). The description of the eucalyptus groves and the monarch butterflies is itself impressive; her linking of this shrine of nature with the more domestic experience of childhood adds another dimension to the passage, etching it more deeply into our own memories of the book, and keeps a genial and accessible narrator before us.

This strategy of open and uninterrupted presence of the narrator helps keep the text securely anchored in the present, but the nature of Ackerman's material also contains a contrary impulse, a pull toward the past. Ackerman writes, indeed, as a natural *historian*, placing her descriptions of the human senses in the wide perspective of both biological evolution and human cultural development. The breadth of literary reference of course attests to Ackerman's professional roots in university departments of English and creative writing and to her literary identity as a poet. But her perspective is also conditioned by an awareness of the prehistoric human past; she uses evolutionary history as a key explanatory category in elucidating the nature of the senses. Ackerman continually reminds readers of their mammalian lineage, of the creatureliness that they share with other animals with whom they have struggled for survival and dominance. The sense of smell was crucial, she explains, to the capacity of early humans to hunt for food. Although in the modern era it has become "the least necessary of our senses" (p. 37), it is vitally connected with a period of our origins when our direct dependence on nature was necessarily extremely close. Tracing the history of smell further to the evolution of the brain, Ackerman explains, "Our cerebral hemispheres were originally buds from the olfactory stalks. We *think* because we *smelled*" (p. 20).

The importance of sense development in the early struggle for survival is well-illustrated. Ackerman notes that touch, manifesting itself as pain, serves "to warn the body about possible injury" (p. 106), and she also reports Desmond Morris' theory that a more pleasurable manifestation of touch, deeply erotic kissing, is tied to the necessary practice of the mother's mouth-to-mouth feeding of her infant in early human cultures, the pleasure of which was enhanced by the extreme sensitivity of the lips and tongue (p. 112). But touch is perhaps most crucial in the nurture and stabilization it provides in early childhood development, the foundation of adult psychological health. Recounting her experience helping to massage premature babies at a Miami hospital, Ackerman explains how this therapeutic technique enhances their development: "Touch reassures an infant that it's safe; it seems to give the body a go-ahead to develop normally" (p. 75). Touching and caressing a baby re-creates the comfort and security of the womb, thereby cushioning the shock of birth. Moreover, it is through touch that we learn "the difference between *I* and *other*" (p. 79), the fundamental paradox of our simultaneous autonomy as individuals and dependence on others.

Taste also has played a role in our survival history, adding, like touch, elements of pleasure and displeasure to help guide our necessary consumption of food. Cravings for particular tastes or kinds of food are sometimes connected, Ackerman explains, to some specific nutritional need; and the uses of certain foods in particular regions and cultures have corresponded to needs and opportunities arising from the geography and climate of the area. Ackerman also reports the remarkable powers of hearing in many animals whose evolution has been dependent on ranges of hearing far beyond the human, such as the use of echolocation by bats. The human sense of hearing has evolved differently, in part because the placement of the larynx and tongue has made complex acts of speech possible. The development of language and of complex social organizations is thus in part based on a sense of hearing, and connected with the ability to process language in the brain. The ability to communicate intricately has been the basis for the development of complex social organizations. And Ackerman offers a fascinating account of the development of vision in all animals: "In the ancient seas, life-forms developed faint patches of skin that were sensitive to light" (p. 231). From this primitive capacity to judge light from dark developed the ability to "judge motion, then form, and finally a dazzling array of details and colors" (p. 231).

Ackerman's commentary on the evolutionary basis of the functioning of the senses supports a larger explanation of their physiological dynamics, one of the most fascinating and informative components of the book. We learn, for instance, that odors are based in the correspondence of molecular shapes with odor receptor sites in the olfactory regions of humans and other animals, and that mating behavior in many animals is controlled by odor secretions called pheromones. Ackerman describes the layered structure of the skin, explaining that touch receptors are located not on the surface but in a second layer. We also learn the four basic kinds of touch receptors, which respond to sensations of heat, cold, pressure, and pain, and find descriptions of other specialized receptors such as Meissner's corpuscles, located in erogenous zones, and Pacinian corpuscles, which relay information to the brain about changing pressures on the body. This presentation of technical detail is informative, but it also plays a larger function in the book by inculcating in the reader a sense of amazement at the body's intricate mechanisms, at the complex physiology behind the most ordinary capabilities and responses.

Ackerman offers a similar level of detail in describing the structure of a taste bud, noting the number and placement of the taste buds on the tongue and comparing human taste buds with those of other animals. She relays the information that after we reach age forty-five, taste buds are replaced more slowly, and the intensity of taste correspondingly deteriorates. She explains the connection between our hearing at various pitches and the frequency of the vibration of air molecules, and she describes the broad range of our peak hearing capacity. In a discussion of the physiology of vision, which makes use of the metaphor of the eye as a camera, Ackerman details the eye's ability to capture and record light and follows her technical explanation with a description of the overwhelming glare of the ice and water in Antarctica, a landscape that at points "seemed like pure color" (p. 234).

While Ackerman's capacity to convey factual information about the senses and their modes of interaction with the environment is central to the appeal of *A Natural History of the Senses*, the impact of that information is greatly enhanced by the web of literary and historical allusions that she builds into the text. We not only learn of the structure of the taste bud but also are provided with an account of the feasting by the upper class in ancient Rome, where participants "amused themselves with the lavishness of a people completely untainted by annoying notions of guilt" (p. 144). The discussion of hearing includes an account of the unique sound quality of the Stradivarius violin, which is enhanced through playing. The repeated vibration "could make microscopic changes in the wood; we perceive those cellular changes as enriched tone" (p. 204). The inescapable impression of Ackerman's assemblage of information is that the "scientific" and "cultural" realms of knowledge overlap and interpenetrate as categories of explanation and that a complete perspective on human development must include both.

These complementary perspectives are enhanced by Ackerman's use of her personal experience to ground the text in an identifiable and engaging narrative voice. Though the book is, on one level, organized with a rigorous logic, it is marked in other respects by the play of free association, conditioned by memory. The section "Kissing" in the chapter "Touch," which also appears in *A Natural History of Love* (1994), centers on Ackerman's memory of the "tough, soul-steeling rigor" of high-school kissing in the 1960s. She also describes her attempts to use scents to repel deer from her roses, relates the experience of having her palm read, declares her passion for chocolate, and recounts a moment of poetic reverie occasioned by a view of the sky over the Pacific Ocean. Such personal memories, anecdotes, and testimonials form the unifying texture of the book, binding its wide range of analytical and informational elements into a distinct narrative sensibility marked by curiosity, intensity of engagement, and catholicity of taste and appreciation.

Ackerman's *A Natural History of Love*, a sequel to *A Natural History of the Senses*, builds on the structure of the earlier book in its treatment of the cultural history and physiological foundations of human love. Like its predecessor, *A Natural History of Love* combines disparate modes of knowledge, including, for example, an extended account of various philosophical and psychological theories of love, as well as information on the evolution of human sexuality. Using material that ranges from medieval codes of chivalry and courtly love to the manners and mores of the battle of the sexes in contemporary America, Ackerman attempts to inculcate a broadened awareness in her readers of the biological drives and cultural conventions that have governed, and continue to govern, human love and sexuality.

The Moon by Whale Light

The Moon by Whale Light is a series of essays on animals and the human attempt to know and preserve them. This collection and several related pieces, such as her 1991 essay "Golden Monkeys" in the *New Yorker*, constitute Ackerman's most direct and influential contribution to "nature writing," combining a descriptive and reportorial power with a persuasive call to ecological commitment and action.

The subject of each of the essays in *The Moon by Whale Light* is an animal species — bats in the first essay, "In Praise of Bats," crocodilians in "The Eyelids of Morning," whales in "The Moon by Whale Light," and penguins in "White Lanterns." Each of these animals holds a special place in the human imagination and has, as an object of repulsion (bats), awe and fascination (whales), fear (crocodilians), or comic and sentimental tenderness (penguins), become very deeply entwined in the development of human culture. Each essay depicts the human thirst for kinship in the world and is an information-laden tribute to the beauty, grace, and dignity of the animal under study. "There is no animal that isn't fascinating if viewed up close and in detail," Ackerman declares, and to study them teaches us not only about nature but also about "the human condition" as it has evolved in nature (p. xv).

The book bears constant witness to the beauty and fascination of the animals, even those like the bat and the alligator which in conventional terms have not been regarded in a positive light. As in *A Natural History of the Senses*, where Ackerman's strategy of reacquainting us with our sensory lives depends in part on the array of information that she has assembled about the complex functions of the sense organs, these essays describe bats or penguins in such detail that we are inclined to alter our view of them completely as we become sensitized to their unique and remarkable capacity to thrive in the earth's demanding and competitive environment. These species are survivors of the evolutionary process, but, as Ackerman makes startlingly clear, their continued survival is by no means assured. And, like the survival of every species, including the human, their survival is a delicate miracle.

Ackerman builds this implicit ecological argument with an assemblage and juxtaposition of information and description, offering facts that, as Thoreau said, "flower into truths." Thus we find within the space of a few pages that, though bats "eat 150 tons of insects every night" (p. 5), they are frequent objects of both intended and wantonly thoughtless destruction by humans, and their nesting environment is extremely vulnerable to damage. Alligators, which are "a hundred times more ancient than human beings" (p. 60), are also, we learn, subject to intense environmental pressure in their tropical habitat, due to economic and population growth in areas that had been relatively undeveloped. We are given strikingly vivid descriptions of the austere beauty of the Antarctic, "one of the last wildernesses" (p. 198), and also are brought to recognize the dependence of huge populations of penguins on its waters and nesting areas. Ackerman describes the haunting beauty of whale songs, the mystery of which is enhanced by the fact that we have not yet come to a complete understanding of what the purpose of the songs is, or exactly how they contribute to the survival of the whales.

Much of the information of each of the essays, and much of their rhetorical power, originates in Ackerman's interest not only in the animal that is the subject of the essay but also in particular researchers and scientists whose work has been devoted to the study and preservation of that species. The essays develop in part as personality profiles, in which Ackerman gives concerned and learned scientists an effective forum both for advocating the virtues of the animals and for warning of their fragility. The hero of "In Praise of Bats" is Merlin D. Tuttle, whose care for bats as unjustly maligned but beautiful and beneficial animals is combined with an impressive sense of adventure as he pursues bats to study them in their habitat. Similar roles in the other essays are played by Kent Vliet, a zoologist whom Ackerman observes working in Florida at the St. Augustine Alligator Farm; George Campbell, an alligator expert who once kept a large alligator collection in his Detroit basement; Roger Payne, a whale researcher with a particular interest in whale song; and several researchers whom Ackerman accompanies during penguin studies in the Antarctic.

Ackerman's essays offer a glimpse of the physically demanding and intellectually exacting nature of zoological field research, and they highlight the intensity of concern that helps motivate such work, a concern arising from the researchers' conviction of the vulnerability of many kinds of animals in the modern world. The combination of these scientists' deep knowledge and profound concern results at points in plain speech with a striking eloquence. Tuttle, for example, tells Ackerman and her readers of the relatively slow reproduction rate of bats and of their extreme vulnerability in their nesting places. "I personally know of caves where people have wiped out millions of bats in one day," he says (p. 7). Payne notes the intricate, cooperative basis of the social networks of whales, a sign of their highly developed intelligence: " 'This is not the sort of animal you should turn into fat and oil and lipstick and margarine and cat food and corset stays' " (p. 163).

The essays in *The Moon by Whale Light* are in part narratives of Ackerman's excursions with scientists and field researchers. Her ventures into such wild and little-known places as the Big Bend country of Texas and the Antarctic become stories of exploration and geographical discovery. Central to the essays are moments of actual encounter with animals, in which Ackerman brings herself as close as she can to pushing through the barriers that divide us from other species. After Tuttle captures a free-tailed bat, he demonstrates to her its gentle harmlessness, a "frightened and fragile" creature. " 'Want to touch?' " he asks her, and she strokes its fur and the "thin rubbery membrane" of its wings (p. 9). She assists the Florida researchers in determining the sex of alligators, something that can only be done by climbing onto the animal and feeling for the sexual organs. She reaches out of a boat to touch a curious young whale and notes that his entire body flinches, sensitive to the contact. She feeds and caresses a penguin chick at San Diego's Sea World and later observes penguins closely in the Antarctic wilds.

Each of these acts of kindly curiosity bespeak Ackerman's belief that humans must break their ordinary pattern of noninteraction with animals and with the natural world in general, that we must push beyond conventional limits. Payne tells her that people who swim close to whales usually lose their nerve within the last ten feet. "But that's what life's all about," Ackerman replies. "That's where you find all the intimate details. How awful it would feel, at the end of your life, to look back and know that if you had just stayed in there a few more feet, you would have witnessed something truly astonishing" (p. 166).

Ackerman's essays ultimately center on the tension between our feeling of kinship with other species and our tendency to regard them with fear or as some exotic creature utterly strange to us. There are grounds for both of these attitudes, as Ackerman makes clear. While she justifies our desire for a creaturely bond by articulating the familial and domestic qualities that she finds in the animals, she also clearly describes their enormous power and the wildness of the places that are home to them. At times the animals are presented in human terms; at other times they are shown to be superior in many ways to the humans who threaten them. And, as in *A Natural History of the Senses*, we are inevitably reminded of our own animal nature. Our complex bodies, intricate minds, and elaborate social arrangements represent only one such variety in the myriad species of nature. "Mind is such an odd predicament for matter to get into," Ackerman comments during a discussion of the mental lives of whales (p. 131). Her meditation on the nature of mind in another creature of course raises the question about the nature of our own mental existence and how it came to be: "Why did automatic, hand-me-down mammals like our ancestors somehow evolve brains with the ability to consider, imagine, project, compare, abstract, think of the future?" (p. 131).

Such questions are of course versions of the fundamental questions of philosophy, and they represent an openness to philosophical speculation that characterizes Ackerman's work. To see the human being as another natural species only sharpens the questions we have traditionally raised under the categories of metaphysics, ethics, and speculative philosophy. Ackerman's concern with factual detail, accurate description, and open-minded observation of the phenomena before her, all virtues of the scientific mind, is never entirely separate from a strand of philosophical wonderment, the kind of deep and curious speculation that arises from seeing the world new.

Selected Bibliography

WORKS OF DIANE ACKERMAN

POETRY

Poems (Ithaca, N.Y.: Stone Marrow, 1973), with Jody Bolz and Nancy Steele; *The Planets: A Cosmic Pastoral* (New York: William Morrow, 1976); *Wife of Light* (New York: William Morrow, 1978); *Lady Faustus* (New York: William Morrow, 1983); *Reverse Thunder* (New York: Lumen, 1988), verse drama;

Jaguar of Sweet Laughter: New and Selected Poems (New York: Random House, 1991).

PROSE

Twilight of the Tenderfoot: A Western Memoir (New York: William Morrow, 1980); *On Extended Wings* (New York: Atheneum, 1985); "Albatrosses," in *New Yorker* 66 (24 September 1990); *A Natural History of the Senses* (New York: Random House, 1990); "Golden Monkeys," in *New Yorker* 67 (24 June 1991); *The Moon by Whale Light, and Other Adventures Among Bats, Penguins, Crocodilians, and Whales* (New York: Random House, 1991); "Insect Love," in *New Yorker* 68 (17 August 1992); "Last Refuge of the Monk Seal," in *National Geographic* 181 (January 1992); *A Natural History of Love* (New York: Random House, 1994); *The Rarest of the Rare* (New York: Random House, 1996).

MANUSCRIPTS AND PAPERS

A collection of manuscripts, proofs, and other material relating to several of Ackerman's works is held at the library of Boston University.

BIOGRAPHICAL AND CRITICAL STUDIES

Julie Gleason Alford, "Diane Ackerman," in *Dictionary of Literary Biography*, vol. 120 (Detroit: Gale, 1992); Franklin Burroughs, "De Rerum Natura," in *Southern Review* 28 (autumn 1992); R. H. W. Dillard, "Diane Ackerman," in *Contemporary Poets*, 4th ed., ed. by James Vinson and D. L. Kirkpatrick (New York: St. Martin's, 1985).

MARY HUNTER AUSTIN
(1868–1934)

JOHN P. O'GRADY

SOMETIME IN THE 1920s, noted professor and literary editor Carl Van Doren suggested that Mary Austin have a new degree conferred upon her: "M.A.E., Master of the American Environment." Though one might suspect Van Doren of some tongue in cheek here, he could not have chosen more accurate words to honor the life and work of his friend Mary Austin. In her autobiography, *Earth Horizon* (1932), Austin writes of herself: "She wanted to write books that you could walk around in" (p. 73). Yet of all her books—more than thirty published in her lifetime—the one that readers have most preferred to walk around in is her first, *The Land of Little Rain* (1903).

The attention that this book has enjoyed as a classic in the canon of American nature writing is not unwarranted. By developing a style that rejected the sentimentalism of her times—a sentimentalism inspired largely by the success of Helen Hunt Jackson's *Ramona*—Austin achieved immediate critical acclaim. She succeeded where her literary contemporaries in the American West—among them Owen Wister and Zane Grey—had not: her writing conveyed something of the spirit inherent in the land itself. In referring to the power of Austin's first book, Van Doren praised her words, "which have the authority of something curiously first-hand. She speaks as if she had just come back from the desert with fresh truth. But the desert

from which she has come is not in California; it is the clear country of the mind" (p. 10). Perhaps she succeeded too well, too early. Often in her later years, she would complain that her readers and critics—less enamored of her social causes and sibylline pronouncements than she herself was—were always clamoring for another *Land of Little Rain*.

Austin's anxiety over being pigeonholed was justified. The critical commonplace remains that her first book was her best, that she never quite rose to this standard again. Reviewers tended to focus on and celebrate her style, and when they turned to the substance of the book, they usually chirped over its writer's fine eye for detail. Ambrose Bierce, who knew Austin, is representative. He wrote an effusive letter to the California poet George Sterling about *The Land of Little Rain:* "But the best of her is her style. That is delicious. It has a slight 'tang' of archaism—just enough to suggest 'lucent sirups tint with cinnamon,' or the 'spice and balm' of Miller's seawinds. And what a knack for observation she has! Nothing escapes her eye. Tell me about her" (p. 114). By directing attention to style, however, what Bierce and the reviewers—almost exclusively male—tended to ignore was the book's theme of human relationships in dissolution, or, as Karen Langlois expressed it in her essay "A Fresh Voice from the West," in Austin's "treacherous desert country men are lost, children die, [and] women who wish to become wives and mothers live wasted lives" (p. 33). Compared with other American nature writers at the turn of the century, Austin is alone in her extraordinary attention to issues of race, class, and gender.

From early in her career, Austin aspired to be a social novelist, and a large portion of her literary production during the period 1907–1920 focused on social issues of her day, most notably feminism. Her writings on women's issues are very often infused with the same potent mysticism that enlivened her earlier "desert books." Although her books were never best-sellers, they did enjoy a substantial readership. But Austin herself was continually disappointed with the reception of her work, frequently charging her publishers with inadequate marketing effort. In this sense, Ambrose Bierce was prophetic when, in the same letter to Sterling, he concluded: "But she'll have to hammer and hammer again and again before the world will hear and heed" (p. 114).

Mary Hunter Austin certainly did "hammer and hammer again," not only at her writing but also at the American public, particularly its intellectuals, with whom she not so much conducted debate as beleaguered them with oracular criticism, via the premier journals of her day — *The Forum, The Century, The New Republic, The Nation*. Altogether she wrote nearly two hundred articles, appearing in some sixty-five periodicals, mostly during the last twenty years of her life. Austin was a commanding and paradoxical presence among the intelligentsia of the time, right up to her death on 13 August 1934. She was both admired and belittled, but the general response is perhaps best captured in her friend Adam Adamic's reminiscence in Helen MacKnight Doyle's biography: "She was a strange, grand woman. I did not understand her in my mind for she was full of contradictions. She was at once extremely fine and perilously near to being bombastic; all sound common sense then a vague folk-cultist" (p. 263). Lest one believe that only men were perplexed by this woman they referred to as "God's mother-in-law," there is Anne Martin, prominent feminist

and first woman to run for the Senate (to represent Nevada), who, despite her deep admiration for Austin, made this observation to biographer Helen MacKnight Doyle: "Mary Austin was a lonely, disappointed woman with an empress complex. She thought she was so important!" (p. 229). And her close friend Mabel Dodge Luhan wrote in memoriam: "She never knew her woman's ego was running away with her so she never checked it. . . . Mary was the innocent uninhibited Eve all her life in the garden. She was often ridiculous" (Houghland, p. 19).

How can one account for this wide latitude of response? Or for the variable tenor of Austin's writing, which ranges — especially in later years — from the glorious to the foolish, often within the same sentence? Austin herself, with some regularity, offers the best explanation. "The creative writer," she explains in *Experiences Facing Death* (a book that is, in fact, more about creative writing and its processes than it is about death), "is beset by a mysterious compulsory honesty" (p. 35). This "compulsory honesty" is but another way of referring to her mysticism. In *Earth Horizon* she phrases it this way: "There is something in Mary which comes out of the land; something in its rhythms, its living compulsions, which dominates over her French, Scotch, Irish, Dutch, English, even the far-off traditional aboriginal strain, governing her own progressions, coloring her most intimate expression" (p. 15). More than one critic has remarked that central to an understanding of Mary Austin is the recognition that her work is charged with mystical awareness, though these same critics often chastise her for what they say is the mystic's profound lack of humor. Austin's gravity, on the other hand, is amply compensated by the invigorating swings of her uninhibited mind, by the joy generated in covering vast distances between each intuitive perception. Mystics do have a wild comic sense, albeit one best appreciated by those who themselves laugh along the margins.

Nevertheless, it behooves all readers of Austin's work to make the sympathetic leap in regard to her mysticism, so that one might, if not understand, at least appreciate the remarkable gesture she made again and again, from her first writings to *Earth Horizon*, in which she reports on the America she saw emerging, "the America which is the expression of the life activities of the environment, aesthetics as a natural mode of expression" (p. 368).

Early Years in Illinois: The Roots of a Naturist

Mary Hunter was born on 9 September 1868 in Carlinville, Illinois. Her mother, Susan Savilla Graham, belonged to a family of pioneer stock that—as Austin was fond of pointing out—traced its American lineage deep into colonial times and even contained some Indian blood. The relationship between mother and daughter was always strained, one of Austin's greatest sources of sorrow and most recurring literary themes. She rendered this pain with poignant understatement in her autobiography: "Mary and her mother missed each other" (p. 221). Her father was George Hunter, an English immigrant who fought on the Union side during the Civil War, then afterward settled into a successful law practice in Carlinville. Hunter was a man with a profound literary sensibility, which he shared readily with his daughter Mary. The Hunter family was rounded out with three other children: James, two years older than Mary, and the younger Jennie and George. For various reasons, Mary's relationship with her brothers suffered strain over the course of their lives; she and Jennie, however, were very close.

Tragedy struck the Hunter family in 1878, when Mary's father died of a malarial illness contracted during his years as a soldier. His death was devastating to his oldest daughter: "The appalling thing that had happened to Mary by the loss of her father was that she was also deprived of most of the items that, out of the place you stay, make home" (p. 91). As if this were not misfortune enough, two months later Mary's sister died of diphtheria. "The loss of her is never cold in me, tears start freshly at the mere mention of her name. . . . She is the only

one who ever unselflessly loved me" (p. 87). For the rest of their respective lives, Mary's relationship with the surviving members of her family would always be tense, and often outright contemptuous. In the end, she outlived them all.

Until her father's death, Mary's life had not been particularly unhappy; in fact, it was rather congenial in its middle-class, midwestern, and Methodist ways. Her upbringing was most conventional, beset by the strident morality of the Victorian era. Around the age of six, however, Mary had the first of what would prove to be a lifetime of unconventional experiences. She did not write about this initial mystical experience until 1931, when she included it in *Experiences Facing Death*:

> It was a summer morning, and the child I was had walked down through the orchard alone and come out on the row of a sloping hill where there was grass and a wind blowing and one tall tree reaching into infinite immensities of blueness. Quite suddenly, after a moment of quietness there, earth and sky and tree and wind-blown grass and the child in the midst of them came alive together with a pulsing light of consciousness. There was a wild foxglove at the child's feet and a bee dozing about it, and to this day I can recall the swift inclusive awareness of each for the whole—I in them and they in me and all of us enclosed in a warm lucent bubble of livingness. I remember the child looking everywhere for the source of this happy wonder, and at last she questioned—"God?"—because it was the only awesome word she knew. Deep inside, like the murmurous swinging of a bell, she heard the answer, "God, God. . . ." (pp. 24–25)

Austin was quick to point out that by "God" she meant "the experienceable quality in the universe," not a person in the Christian sense of the word. God was a presence but "only faintly descried in the inknowing core of perception as Being" (p. 24).

Even if this incident in the orchard is to some degree self-fashioned apocrypha (as some critics have been fond of suggesting), it nevertheless is representative of the perspective Austin brought to bear on *all* her subjects, whether the land, women's issues, the study of indigenous cultures, or her theories about "genius." She never tired of reminding her readers of this mystical coloring to her experience. "In admitting so much," she writes in *Earth Horizon*, "I realize that practically all my books have been done in this fashion; they come out of the arc of the Earth Horizon"—which is to say, her work is deeply intuitive. "That is why my books have no sequence other than the continuity of the search for the norm of moral and spiritual adjustments which I have tried herein to describe" (p. 367). Thus if Mary Austin claims that her understanding of the "Earth Horizon" first came to her in that long-ago Illinois orchard, perhaps we might—in the interest of sympathetic understanding—best take her at her word.

When she was twelve years old, Austin attended a series of Chautauqua lectures on geology, where she discovered Hugh Miller's classic of natural history, *Old Red Sandstone:* "I remember the very look of the pages, the easy, illustrative charts, the feel of the author behind the book, the feel of the purposeful earth" (p. 104). Later this was the first book she purchased with her own money. In 1884 she enrolled in Blackburn College in her hometown, where she received formal training in science and pursued studies in art. From the very start, it seems that Austin was committed to bridging the gap between what C. P. Snow has called "the two cultures," the sciences and the humanities. This gap, however, is one that many find daunting and would prefer to leave alone. Years later, in an essay titled "Science for the Unscientific" (1922), Austin argued that "a new type of writer will have to be evolved, writers whose approach is purely literary but who are capable of immersing themselves in the data of science to the point of saturation" (p. 565). In making her distinction between "writing which aims merely at producing an effect, and writing which is affective" (p. 565), Austin proved a precursor of a host of writers who would follow later in the century, among them Loren Eiseley, Aldo Leopold, Rachel Carson, and Ann Zwinger. For her efforts to link

the sciences and the humanities, Austin met frequent rebuke from members of both "cultures" (though there were some notable exceptions). This pattern of rejection might very well have contributed to the nervous breakdowns she suffered, the first of which occurred in 1885, after she transferred to the State Normal School in Bloomington, Illinois. After she recovered, she returned to Blackburn and graduated in 1888.

Shortly after this, Susanna Hunter decided that the family would migrate to California, where Mary's older brother, George, was looking into homesteading possibilities in the southern San Joaquin Valley. The move would prove momentous in the life of Mary Hunter, for in the West she would quickly find her voice as a writer.

Early Years in California and Marriage

The impact of the arid West upon the sensibilities of twenty-year-old Mary Hunter was immediate and profound. In language similar to that she used to describe her encounter with God in the orchard, she recounts in her autobiography the view she had from the train window on the way from Illinois to California, a journey that also symbolized her transition from childhood to adulthood: "All that long stretch between Salt Lake and Sacramento Pass [Donner Pass], the realization of presence which the desert was ever after to have for her, grew upon her mind; not the warm tingling presence of wooded hills and winding creeks, but something brooding and aloof, charged with a dire indifference, of which she was never for an instant afraid" (p. 182).

After continuing on to Los Angeles for a brief stopover in Pasadena, the Hunters made the final and most arduous leg of their journey. Over rough roads through the wild but by no means unpopulated San Francisquito Canyon, they came at last to the vicinity of Rancho Tejon, where her brother George was staking claims to land. Although Austin gives an account of this journey in *Earth Horizon*, rendered in the characteristic oracular style of her later years, she wrote an earlier version shortly after arriving in California, and submitted it to her alma mater's magazine *The Blackburnian*.

Published in 1889 and entitled "One Hundred Miles on Horse Back," the account has lately received effusive praise, including some from her biographer Esther Lanigan Stineman, who argues in her *Mary Austin: Song of a Maverick* that this essay "limns a journey of liberation encompassing body and spirit" (p. 31). Although such a reading shackles the piece with a meaning more critic's than author's, "One Hundred Miles on Horse Back" does contain some vivid passsages of description of a southern California now long lost. The essay is particularly noteworthy for its lack of any mention of what Austin would later call the "Spirit of the Arroyos," a description of which she belabored in *Earth Horizon*: "There was something else there besides what you find in the books; a lurking, evasive Something, wistful, cruel, ardent; something that rustled and ran, that hung half-remotely, insistent on being noticed, fled from pursuit, and when you turned from it, leaped and suddenly fastened on your vitals. This is no mere figure of speech, but the true movement of experience" (p. 187). Compare this with what she wrote about the same locale in 1889: "It is not possible for the mind to conceive of a force that could throw the elements of the solid earth into such confusion as is here displayed." There is no mention of spirits in "One Hundred Miles on Horse Back"; indeed, its author seems to avoid figures of speech as much as possible.

If anything, the essay is notable for its plainness of style, especially when compared with *The Land of Little Rain*, written more than a decade later. Several conclusions can be drawn from this. Either the later Mary Austin—the established woman of letters and renowned authority on matters mystical—embellished her memory of that distant journey with a few exotic flourishes of rhetoric; or the twenty-year-old Mary Hunter feared that her rather conservative Christian audience back in Illinois might take umbrage at any mention of spirits in the arroyos;

or perhaps this young writer simply lacked the vocabulary and writerly skills necessary to make her perceptions clear to those readers unfamiliar with such things. As is so often the case when considering Mary Austin, no single answer can be proffered with any certainty. We might best accept them all.

Unfortunately for the homesteading Hunters, they arrived in the midst of periodic drought that characterizes the California climate. Their efforts to establish themselves on the land failed, and Mary found herself having to teach wherever in the area she could find work. Nevertheless, what amounted to agricultural failure for the family proved to be a literary boon for young Mary Hunter, who established a friendship with General Edward Fitzgerald Beale, owner of the vast Rancho Tejon and former associate of Kit Carson. Beale regaled her with stories of the region, of the Indians, of the early settlers, and he encouraged her literary aspirations. A substantial amount of material that later appeared in her earliest books—*The Land of Little Rain*, *The Flock*, and *Lost Borders*—came from Beale and his majordomo, José Jesús López. López later recalled to Helen MacKnight Doyle that he never saw Mary Austin "without a pad or pencil in her hands. Sometimes she would sit watching everything that went on around the Ranchos, other times she would go into the canyons or washes and be gone all day" (p. 94).

During her days in the southern end of the San Joaquin Valley, Austin was witness to a vicious battle for irrigation rights, a drama that, much to her dismay, was replayed for her in the Owens Valley and again along the Colorado River. Water and its scarcity haunt the works of Mary Austin just as they do the West itself. Elizabeth Ammons has perceptively noted that the desert springs encountered in *The Land of Little Rain* are rendered in sexually charged language suggesting they are female. Ammons goes on to write, "All of life—trails/tracks/language—gathers around the simple principle of thirst being relieved" (p. 93). Thirst becomes a symbol related to gender, and it can be traced to what Austin always regarded as the particular pain of womanhood and its sensitivity, a pain that she first observed in her mother and later suffered herself.

She laments in *Earth Horizon* that much of her adolescence was spent brooding "about what widowhood might mean to a woman like Mary's mother." Upon realizing that widowhood was in fact a social stigma—just one of the ways in which a woman could find herself without a man—Austin detected in herself "the earliest social resentment, the first conscious criticism of the organization of the adult life" (p. 98). Despite the profound problems that Austin and her mother had with one another, the daughter did recognize that neither she nor her mother was to blame for their failed relationship; instead it was the turn-of-the-century American society that she held culpable, with—as she expressed it in the preface to her play *The Arrow-Maker*—its "enormous and stupid waste of the gifts of women" (p. xii). Austin devoted a substantial portion of her life's energy to women's causes.

In the summer of 1890, Mary Hunter met Stafford Wallace Austin, a "rather tall, slender, quite young man [who] appealed to Mary because he bore the mark of a gentleman and a scholar." They were married the following May. Helen MacKnight Doyle, a doctor in Bishop, California, who befriended Mary a few years later, writes: "Had circumstances been different, Mary might not have responded as she did to the wooing of Wallace Austin" (p. 127). Which is to say, had there been more eligible men available, or had her mother offered counsel instead of silence ("there was always the consideration that a daughter married was a problem settled, a responsibility ridded"), Austin's life might have taken a different course altogether (*Earth Horizon*, p. 221). Although most of her biographers attempt to explain in one way or another the marriage as one of convenience, the courtship was not altogether without passion. "I think Mary Hunter was in love with Mr. Austin in her own modest way," said one who knew them to Doyle. "Mr. Austin was persistent and as ardent as an absent-minded professor could be" (p. 128).

The first year of their marriage was spent near Bakersfield, where Wallace Austin pursued a scheme to establish himself as a vineyardist. Mary applied herself with vigor to her writing. Over the next year, Wallace's agricultural scheme failed, resulting in the couple's having to move to the Owens Valley on the east side of the Sierra Nevada, where he found work on an irrigation project. Mary's creative endeavors, however, met with success, and she published her first story, "The Mother of Felipe," in the *Overland Monthly*, "the first literary magazine that had sprung into national prominence in the new world of the West" (*Earth Horizon*, p. 229). This brought her immediate literary attention, most notably from the Oakland poet Ina Coolbrith.

The Austins' marriage was already having its problems—and these were compounded by Mary's discovery that she was pregnant. One of the problems was what she called her husband's "lack of foresight." He was simply unable to provide for his family. More troublesome, however, was a fundamental incompatibility in their personalities. From her perspective, he failed in "the most venerable of the fidelities of marriage, the common fronting of man and woman to the wilderness" (p. 243). As Austin expresses it in *Earth Horizon*, she and Wallace never saw the world from the same vantage. "Once he had given himself to me, my husband never looked at another woman; but also he never looked with me at any single thing. He never, any more than he could help, afforded me a clue as to where he himself might be looking" (p. 243). In the face of this emotional desertion, Mary looked at the land and tried to write her way to resolution.

The move to the Owens Valley brought Mary Austin to the place that is still known by the name she gave it: "the Land of Little Rain." Throughout the years spent in the sparsely populated rain shadow of the Sierra Nevada, she suffered a painful childbirth and then the devastating revelation that her child, Ruth, was mentally handicapped. In the face of these challenges, Austin applied herself ever more intensely to her writing, in the hope that she would make enough money to provide care for Ruth and that she might move her family to a location more congenial to literary endeavors.

During this difficult period, something of the land did in fact soak into Mary Austin's consciousness, which focused her vision and transformed her style. Her immersion in this spectacular mountain and desert landscape coincided with her own spectacular loneliness, all of which served to clarify her sense of herself as a woman benighted by the restrictions of a male-dominated society. She discovered that the desert had essentially different effects upon men and women. Using her husband as an example, she wrote:

> There was the promise of the land; its rich and alluring possibility; there was the residue of the romantic mining experience; also something must be allowed to the allure of the desertness. Men of my husband's type of mentality, once they had exposed themselves to it, spent their lives going around and around in it, always keyed to the expected, the releasing discovery. They felt themselves enchanted by its longer eye-reach, its rainbow horizons; but in fact it was the timeless space that held them. With the women, it was not so; they felt, as they hung there suspended between hopes that refused to eventuate, life slipping away from them. For women have "times"; the short recurrent rhythm of well-being, the not-to-be-evaded times of birth, the climaxes of their racial function, the effacing hand of Time across their charm, which points inescapably the periods within which experience is available. (pp. 284–285)

In short, Austin perceived that men could afford to be romantic in their attitude toward life, whereas women could not.

It was also during these years, as she and Wallace struggled to make a living by drifting between teaching positions up and down the Owens Valley, that Mary had the opportunity to visit Oakland, where she met and talked with William James. In 1899 she moved with Ruth for a time to Los Angeles, where she became friends with Charles Lummis, founder and editor of *Land of Sunshine* (later *Out West* magazine). It was to Eve, the second of Lummis' wives, that Austin dedicated her first book, referring to her as "the comfortess of unsuccess." In 1903, ten years after Austin first came to the Owens Valley, Houghton Mifflin published *The Land of Little Rain*, illustrated with line drawings by the well-known artist E. Boyd Smith.

The Land of Little Rain

Captured in Austin's rhythmic and piquant prose is not only an austere sense of the Mojave desert and its various human tragedies but something, too, of the vast loneliness and stoicism of the book's author. In the volume's title chapter, Austin writes:

> If one is inclined to wonder at first how so many dwellers came to be in the loneliest land that ever came out of God's hands, what they do there and why stay, one does not wonder so much after having lived there. None other than this long brown land lays such a hold on the affections. The rainbow hills, the tender bluish mists, the luminous radiance of the spring, have the lotus charm. They trick the sense of time, so that once inhabiting there you always mean to go away without quite realizing that you have not done it. Men who have lived there, miners and cattle-men, will tell you this, not so fluently, but emphatically, cursing the land and going back to it. For one thing there is the divinest, cleanest air to be breathed anywhere in God's world. Some day the world will understand that, and the little oases on the windy tops of hills will harbor for healing its ailing, house-weary broods. There is promise there of great wealth in ores and earths, which is no wealth by reason of being so far removed from water and workable conditions, but men are bewitched by it and tempted to try the impossible. (p. 15)[1]

While avoiding sentimentalism, Austin nevertheless persistently anthropomorphizes the desert in ways that often startle. For instance, of the coyote she writes that he is "your true water-witch, one who snuffs and paws, snuffs and paws

---

1. All citations from *The Land of Little Rain* and *Lost Borders* are drawn from the combined reprint of the two books: *Stories from the Country of Lost Borders*, edited by Marjorie Pryse (1987).

again at the smallest spot of moisture-scented earth until he has freed the blind water from the soil. Many water-holes are no more than this detected by the lean hobo of the hills in localities where not even an Indian would look for it" (p. 22). William Scheick has found fault with this narrative strategy, which runs counter to what he claims is Austin's intention of providing her readers with a mystical fusion with the landscape: "The language of anthropomorphism and autobiography confiscates the land through a rhetorical figuration that amounts to a dis-figurement of what is Other" (p. 43). What Scheick fails to acknowledge, however, is that this is the very problem faced by every mystic who attempts to write about the mystical experience: language by its very nature is a re-presentation, and thereby cannot help but "dis-figure" what it represents. Austin makes no claims that her book is a "fusion," mystical or otherwise; in fact, she laments its failure to convey more effectively her real intention, which is to alert her readers to their multifarious world—one of great beauty but at the same time of great pain. She is merely offering an account of her own experience, or, as she phrases it in the book's preface: "you shall have such news of the land, of its trails and what is astir in them, as one lover of it can give to another" (p. 4).

Critical reception of the book, however, was overwhelmingly positive, and has remained so. In many ways, *The Land of Little Rain* represented a stylistic revolution, employing a strategy Axel Carl Bredahl has labeled "divided narrative," a pattern that was not brought to fruition again until Sherwood Anderson's *Winesburg, Ohio*. "With few guides before her," Bredahl writes, "excepting the journals of the previous century or the puncturing prose of Twain, Austin recognizes that focusing on the life of the land requires new use of language and form" (p. 53). Elizabeth Ammons claims that *The Land of Little Rain* is Austin's "most innovative work," and that it "radically relocates us (by 'us' I mean western-educated consumers)" (p. 88). Certainly it was Austin's intention to "relocate" her readers, though perhaps a more appropriate word would be *"dislocate."* In *Lost*

Borders (1909) she made this clear: "Out there where the borders of conscience break down, where there is no convention, and behavior is of little account except as it gets you your desire, almost anything might happen; does happen, in fact, though I shall have trouble making you believe it" (p. 156). For more than ninety years now, readers seem to be in agreement that *The Land of Little Rain* is Mary Austin's best book, even if many have not bothered to test this judgment by applying themselves to any of her other work. Still, one would not be too far astray if this were the only book of Austin one knew.

Lost Borders is a collection of short fiction, yet the desert setting is the same and the style is congruous with that of Austin's first book, suggesting that this volume is an extension or even a sequel. Indeed, this perception has been reinforced by the fact that Marjorie Pryse brought the two books together and Rutgers University published them in one volume under the title *Stories from the Country of Lost Borders* (1987). In response to questions concerning her stories, Austin once explained in a letter that her method very much had its roots in the oral tradition: "they are in reality, each one of them, openings of a window through which you are to see the desert as I see it. You are to suppose that I have sat down before the fire with you and . . . [have begun] to talk about the desert" (Langlois, "Fresh Voice," p. 32).

Although there are a handful of human characters in *The Land of Little Rain* — most notably Seyavi "the Basket Maker" and the man known simply as "the Pocket Hunter" — the book's main players are a host of animals, including the coyote, quail, and vulture. One could say that the main character in this first book about the Owens Valley was the land itself. The same land makes a repeat performance in *Lost Borders*, but added now are several human characters, all of whom interact with the land. The author's approach here to her subject matter corresponds to the fictional theory she later described in an essay titled "Regionalism in American Fiction" (1932): "The first of the indispensable conditions is that the region must enter constructively into the story, as another character, as the instigator of plot. A natural scene can never be safely assumed to be the region of the story when it is used merely as a back drop" (p. 105). In Austin's most engaging work, the land is never a backdrop. The opening story in *Lost Borders*, titled "The Land," is her most pointed portrayal of this character that so dominates her early books set in the California desert. Here again we find that startling use of anthropomorphism:

If the desert were a woman, I know well what like she would be: deep-breasted, broad in the hips, tawny, with tawny hair, great masses of it lying smooth along her perfect curves, full lipped like a sphinx, but not heavy-lidded like one, eyes sane and steady as the polished jewel of her skies, such a countenance as should make men serve without desiring her, such a largeness to her mind as should make their sins of no account, passionate, but not necessitous, patient—and you could not move her, no, not if you had all the earth to give, so much as one tawny hair's-breadth beyond her own desires. If you cut very deeply into any soul that has the mark of the land upon it, you find such qualities as these—as I shall presently prove to you. (p. 160)

Throughout her work, Austin ascribes female gender to the land, but in a very different fashion from that of the men described by Annette Kolodny in *The Lay of the Land*. Even at the end of her career, Austin was still working with this idea; in *Earth Horizon*, she writes of her years in the desert: "There was a spell of the land over all the men who had in any degree given themselves to it, a spell of its lofty and intricate charm, which worked on men like the beauty of women" (p. 270). Austin attributed a female essence to the land, and for this reason she believed that females were closer to nature than males—a notion that Kolodny and the majority in the mainstream of feminist thought would strongly refute. Nevertheless, this was Austin's belief, and it informed not only her understanding of the natural world but her feminism as well.

The land, in Mary Austin's work, is always something more than its aggregate physical features, more than a mere knowledge of its geology, its climate, its plant and animal life, or its human life. These phenomena are but textures in a conditioned reality, manifestations of what Austin calls "spirit." Her work is sometimes referred to as "natural history," but this designation is misleading. She knew natural history, and by all accounts was a fairly proficient amateur botanist. But the scientific "facts" alone were not enough for her; to these facts she always brought her intuition, her creative understanding, which immediately invalidates her work in the eyes of the professional scientist. Austin, in fact, could at times be quite contemptuous of the whole discipline of science, which she frequently referred to as the "male ritual of rationalization." Thus, rather than as a "naturalist," Mary Austin should be referred to by the term she preferred, "naturist"—one who, to use her own words, is "taken with the land, with the spirit trying to be evoked out of it" (*Earth Horizon*, p. 188).

The publication of *The Land of Little Rain* inaugurated one of the most prolific writing careers in American literary history; Austin followed her first effort with *The Basket Woman* (1904), *Isidro* (1905), and *The Flock* (1906), all in quick succession, all drawn from her experience of the American West. From this point on, there were very few years in which Mary Austin did not bring out a new book—no mean feat, especially when one considers her voluminous contribution to the periodicals in the last fifteen years of her life, fugitive pieces that have yet to be collected in book form.

Carmel to Europe

Following the success of *The Land of Little Rain*, Austin found herself in a position, both financially and emotionally, to begin extricating herself from the social environment she found so stifling in the Owens Valley. In 1904, while in the area doing research for her novel *Isidro*, she visited Carmel, on the central coast of California, the same region Robinson Jeffers soon celebrated in his poetry. Austin was enchanted by the intimidating beauty she encountered there. She returned the following summer, attracted by the growing colony of artists and writers gathered around the poet George Sterling. Here, in addition to Sterling, she found Jack London, Nora May French, and James Hopper, all of whom became her friends.

It was also in 1905 that, after several years of boarding her daughter in various homes in the Owens Valley, Austin formally committed Ruth to an institution for the mentally retarded in Santa Clara, California. Wallace Austin objected to this action, convinced that "the child should remain in the home even though all of the mother's time and strength was devoted to her care" (quoted in Stineman, p. 68). Wallace himself never participated significantly in the parenting responsibilities; this burden fell to Mary entirely. Her choosing to engage others to carry out the child-care duties had long since roused the ire of people in the various Owens Valley communities, who labeled her selfish and irresponsible, whereas Wallace escaped such castigation. Austin herself took these events as indicative of a culture that saddled the mother with complete responsibility for the children while permitting the father his gadabout ways. In any case, Ruth's institutionalization—ending only with her death from influenza in 1918— freed her mother to pursue a literary career. However, for the rest of her life Austin remained deeply affected by what she regarded as her failure as a mother.

In 1906, Austin sold the house that she and Wallace had built in Independence in 1900, the house in which she had written *The Land of Little Rain*. She bought land in Carmel and joined the artists' colony, building her own house there the following year. During the next few years, she completed two novels, *Santa Lucia* (1908) and *Outland* (1910), and composed the stories that would constitute *Lost Borders* (1909). Throughout this time she was plagued by financial worry, particularly in regard to paying for Ruth's care. Her husband, who chose not to join her in Carmel, charged her with desertion; their divorce, however, was not finalized until 1914. Although having achieved her long-

sought liberation from the restrictions of family life, free now to devote herself entirely to her writing, Austin was confronted with yet another challenge: in 1907 she was diagnosed with breast cancer and given nine months to live. She decided to go to Europe. "Mary had wanted to see Rome," she writes in *Earth Horizon*, and then adds in lugubrious simplicity: "she thought it a place to die in" (p. 308).

Austin departed for Europe in 1908. Shortly after arriving in Rome, she discovered that the pain she had been feeling had disappeared, cured miraculously, as she explained much later in her short book *Can Prayer Be Answered?* (1934): "Feeling cautiously for the place where the pain used to be I realized that, somewhere in the business of achieving complete detachment for the furtherance of my prayer project, I had left my ailment behind me" (p. 24). Whatever the source of her cure, Austin remained in Europe, mostly in Italy and England, for the next two years. In London, while she was staying with her friends Herbert and Lou Hoover, she met such literary and political luminaries as H. G. Wells, George Bernard Shaw, Henry James, Joseph Conrad, and Anne Martin. She also arranged to have an "Indian play" she had written, *The Arrow-Maker*, produced on the stage in New York. She returned in 1910 and saw it open in February 1911. The play received mixed reviews and ran for only eight performances. Austin intended this work to be "a folk play, written in the poetic rhythms of Indian verse; formalistic, and climbing up and up to ritual" (*Earth Horizon*, p. 315). Reviewers did not quite see it this way; most faulted it for what seemed to them an unauthentic portrayal. As Stineman reports in her biography, one critic ridiculed it: "Not American Indians, but Anglo-American Indians they seem in great part." Another wrote: "Mrs. Austin's Indians seem very sophisticated in their speech; and they talk a great deal" (p. 114).

Although *The Arrow-Maker* is of debatable literary merit, it does stand as a key text in understanding Austin and her work as a whole, for in it we find "The Chisera," or "witch-woman," a figure many critics have taken as an emblem for Mary Austin herself. In her preface to the published version of the play, she explains: "The Chisera is simply the Genius, one of those singular and powerful characters whom we are still, with all our learning, unable to account for without falling back on the primitive conception of gift as arising from direct communication with the gods" (p. x). Austin believed she herself was endowed with vatic gifts; thus the words in this introduction imply that what we make of the figure of the Chisera is what we should also make of the writer Mary Austin. "The whole question then becomes one of how the tribe shall work the Chisera to their best advantage" (pp. xi). American literary history has yet to answer the question of how to work Mary Austin to its best advantage.

The Arrow-Maker is also a milestone in the career of its author. It marks the close of her first period of writing, the one in which she drew exclusively upon materials she gathered in the American West. Although she would still return to her Western source materials, the next twelve years of her attention were largely directed toward other concerns, particularly feminist issues. Yet *The Arrow-Maker* also points ahead, to the theme that would preoccupy Austin during the last decade of her life: the role of the creative artist in the shaping of her society.

New York, Feminism, and Genius

Although Austin was immensely productive during the years when her primary residence was New York City, there is less here to interest a reader specifically concerned with her nature writing. Nevertheless, other themes that first emerged in *The Land of Little Rain* and inform all of her nature writing—particularly feminism and mysticism—do predominate in this middle period. Austin was not only a highly productive writer, she was facile as well, refusing to accept any limiting designation that people—especially critics—were wont to impose on her.

From 1912 to 1923 her vast literary output included four social novels, *A Woman of Genius* (1912), *The Lovely Lady* (1913), *The Ford* (1917), and *No. 26 Jayne Street* (1920); a travelogue, *Christ in Italy* (1912); a sort of landscape reminiscence, *California, Land of the Sun* (1914); a biography, *The Man Jesus* (1915); a book of theological and philosophical meditations, *Love and the Soul Maker* (1914); a collection of stories, *The Trail Book* (1918); a feminist-informed handbook of political science, *The Young Woman Citizen* (1918); plus numerous poems, stories, and essays contributed to periodicals.

Although not in the genre of "nature writing," *A Woman of Genius* is valuable to readers interested in Austin's variety of feminism or in fictionalized details of her life. The book is important in that it provides an understanding of the problems Austin faced as a woman and an artist who constantly confronted a society that refused to accord her the respect it so readily bestowed upon males doing the same thing and often not as well. Austin faced the same difficulty in her family while growing up in Carlinville, again when she moved to California, then again from her censuring neighbors in the Owens Valley. Once she established herself in a position to be heard—among the literati in the publishing capital of the United States—she never relinquished her voice. As might be expected, male critics were often harsh in their judgments of her work, but surprisingly many feminists of the day were also taken aback by what they considered a feminism that was *too* radical. For example, in an essay that appeared in *Harper's Weekly*, titled "The Failure of Free Love" (1914), Austin made a stab at one of society's most revered institutions, advising that "it is time to stop sentimentalizing about the home, and fairly recognize the fact that the conduct of married life today is more largely conditioned by affairs outside the house than within it" (p. 27). In this assault on the traditional home and its values, Austin was perhaps ahead of her time. She frequently complained that she lived in a world "densely populated with conformists and conservatives."

If there is one trait in the personality of Mary Austin that rises above all others, it is that of being a maverick. Her primary mode of perception was intuition, a style of consciousness that inevitably strikes others as quirky or uncanny. Austin herself liked to call this her "genius." Although she granted that all people have at least some capacity for genius, she believed that in an increasingly technological society most never develop it. She also insisted that there was a fundamental difference between the genius of men and that of women, a belief she brought to her feminism.

Her book *The Young Woman Citizen* to some degree reflects Austin's involvement with Herbert Hoover's World War I propaganda corps, yet it remains one of her more fascinating works. Published by the YWCA and directed toward the millions of women who were on the threshold of political life, the book still makes lively reading. In its skepticism of the Cult of Bigness, it touches upon ideas that today might be called "bioregional." She cautions her female audience: "Cease to know how the water and lighting of your community are handled, how your milk comes in and your garbage goes out, and you very shortly hear the blue flies of political profiteering buzzing in the obscurity" (p. 80). More important, the book shows that Austin could direct her intuitive ideals toward practical ends. It also reflects her essentialist views of gender: "This capacity for intuitive judgment is the best thing women have to bring to their new undertaking, this and the things that grow out of it. This is what women have to stand on squarely; not their ability to see the world in the way men see it, but the importance and validity of their seeing it some other way" (p. 19). From the perspective of many feminist theories today, there are problematic elements in Austin's view, but a full consideration of these matters is not possible until one reads the entirety of her writings on this subject, most of which are out of print or in the disintegrating pages of difficult-to-find magazines buried in research libraries.

In regard to Austin's "nature writing" during this period, a handful of her works are worthy of note. The first is *California, Land of the Sun* (1914), a book first published in England and later republished under the title *The Lands of the Sun* (1927). The volume is a hodgepodge of pieces, including some of her most beautiful descriptive passages; however, the collection as a whole lacks the strong, purposeful unity of her previous California books. If anything, the book serves as an elegy to the California that Austin knew — or imagined — before chamber of commerce boosterism began to transform significant portions of it into a vast urban tangle. In 1918, she published *The Trail Book*, a collection of stories for children illustrated by Milo Winter, which is of interest not only because the pieces are set in the West but also because they were written in conjunction with the development of her theories of storytelling and the folk tale.

Finally, there is *The Ford*, published in 1917, set in California. This novel does have its moments in which the affective qualities of the land suddenly stand forth, reminiscent of Austin's earliest work: "Lands, waters, and minerals, he took them up and laid them down again, wholly uninformed of the severances and readjustments made necessary by that temporary possession. The most he knew of mortgages, overdue installments, foreclosures, were their legal limitations; he did not know that men are warped by these things out of all manhood and that women died of them" (p. 176). But, as this passage suggests, the novel concentrates on social interaction and its effects rather than on affective qualities of the land itself; thus the land seems less a character and more a backdrop than in most of Austin's work set in the West. Missing, too — as is the case with all of her novels of this period — is the poetic economy of style that characterizes *The Land of Little Rain*, *The Flock*, and *Lost Borders*, an estimation that might bother some contemporary critics interested in resuscitating Austin's social novels. It distressed Austin herself. Nevertheless, it must be acknowledged that reading these novels is more a chore than a pleasure.

Return to the West and Journey's End

During her years in New York, Austin became an intimate friend of Mabel Dodge (later Mabel

Dodge Luhan), a wealthy, eccentric patron of artists and radical intellectuals known for the salon she conducted: it drew Lincoln Steffens, Emma Goldman, John Reed, Walter Lippmann, and Max Eastman, among others. When Dodge moved to Taos, New Mexico, in 1917, she attracted numerous artists to her vicinity, including D. H. Lawrence, Gerald Cassidy, Ina Sizer Cassidy, and Witter Bynner. Austin, who had been planning to travel to New Mexico to conduct research on the Native American and Hispanic cultures, accepted an invitation to visit in 1918. This marked the first of many extended visits she made over the next several years, culminating in her building a house in Santa Fe and settling there permanently in 1924. The New Mexico landscape also directed her creative attention back to the American West. "I liked the feel of roots," she writes in *Earth Horizon*, "of ordered growth and progression, continuity, all of which I found in the Southwest" (p. 349).

Almost everything that Mary Austin produced in the last ten years of her life should interest those concerned with her "nature writing." Yet before considering this work, we need to acknowledge that her predilection for essentialism shaped her views of the Native American and Hispanic cultures she encountered in the Southwest. If nothing else, this acknowledgment offers opportunity to consider Austin's work as an oeuvre, which reveals that her so-called nature writing and regional writing are very much interconnected with her social novels, her feminism, and her political activism.

The origins of Austin's essentialist perspective can be located in her earliest writings about the land, as *The Land of Little Rain* makes apparent in what is perhaps its most famous line: "Not the law, but the land sets the limit" (p. 9). Austin's perplexing notion of the "landscape line," articulated in *The American Rhythm* (1923), is but a theoretical expression of her primary essential: the land itself. "Better than I knew any Indian," she admits in *The American Rhythm*, "I knew the land they lived in. This I hold to be a prime requisite for understanding originals of whatever description" (p. 38). It

bears repeating that this essentialism, at least according to Austin herself, is the result of her own experience—heightened by her intuitive perceptions—and *not* derived from psychological or sociological theories found in books. If there is fault in her perspective, it is very much her own and not somebody else's.

In her essay "Indian Arts for the Indians" (1928), Austin characterizes the Native Americans she encountered in New Mexico as living in creative community: "The Puebleños are also all of the temperament which is called 'artistic,' which means that they are highly susceptible to natural beauty, deeply interested in the inner meaning of the world they live in, and happy in the human expression of these things, in music and in poetry, in the dance and mimetic representation, and especially in expressional design" (p. 382). Regarding Hispanic culture in the region, Austin was prone to make the curious claim that although Hispanics do represent a society adapted to the land, their spiritual source is not located in the Southwest but in history, in what she calls "Old Spain." If one expects consistency from Mary Austin, disappointment will inevitably follow. She did, however, believe that these various cultures—Hispanic as well as Native American—were rooted in folk tradition and lived in environmental harmony; thus they had much to teach the dominant American culture, which she believed was becoming increasingly addicted to the "California Cult of Bigness." She made the preservation of these Southwest cultures the priority project of her last decade, and she played no small role in establishing a constituency and even a market for cultural goods produced in the Southwest.

These attempts at cultural preservation are not without critics. The Chicano scholar Genaro Padilla finds great fault with what he calls the "extracultural intercessions" of Mary Austin and other publicists, all non-Hispanic, who came to New Mexico—particularly to Taos and Santa Fe—from elsewhere. He charges that these "artists" did not so much preserve culture as *invent* it. These comments are significant; the issue is complex, one that has been all but

Mary Hunter Austin

back at least to Thomas Cole and the Hudson River School, it was already a century old when she was promulgating it. Austin, however, gave the idea a new twist: she encouraged artists to study American Indian and other "true" folk arts, claiming these were deeply connected to the natural environment. She insisted that such study would aid contemporary artists in absorbing a sense of the land and thereby reinvigorate American culture.

The best expression of Austin's ideas on this subject can be found in *The American Rhythm* (1923). Subtitled *Studies and Reëxpressions of Amerindian Songs* in the revised (1930) edition, the book elaborates her poetics, opening with a long essay, followed by a collection of her "reëxpressions" of Native American poetry. The essay's tone is dull and scholarly, but its thesis is intriguing and her approach is deeply personal. Although the book evinces her thorough familiarity with the methods of ethnology and its literature, she prefers to draw her authority from having "lived with aboriginals." The poetry of the American Indian, she claims, has an experiential basis in the land; likewise, her own work is based upon experience and not upon book-derived knowledge. By the time she published the first edition of *The American Rhythm*, Austin did command respect on matters Native American. That she was an acknowledged expert is demonstrated by the fact that she was asked to contribute the chapter "Non-English Writings, Aboriginal" to the 1917 edition of the *Cambridge History of American Literature*.

Although *The American Rhythm* retains some historical interest for today's scholars in Native American studies, it is probably of greatest value to those interested in tracing the development of twentieth-century American poetics. Although vague, her concept of the "landscape line"— which she defined as the "disposition of the aboriginal poet to arrange his words along . . . the line shaped by its own inner necessities" (p. 54)—points in a direction traced again by poets attempting to explain the principles behind the New American Poetry. Neither William Carlos Williams with his notion of the "variable

ignored in the Austin scholarship. Padilla, however, entirely ignores any consideration of the possible value of Austin's shamanistic role, a role very much valued in both traditional Hispanic and Native American cultures. And as is the case with Austin's views on feminism, many of her primary writings on this subject are difficult to obtain. Despite the obstacles, this aspect of her work needs more thorough scholarly investigation.

A recurring theme in Austin's later work was her desire to make Americans—especially artists—see how the landscape profoundly influences their art. The idea was not new; tracing foot," nor Charles Olson with his talk about the "breath" as the guiding principle in modern American poetry, came any closer to demonstrable success in their theories than did Mary Austin. The notable difference is that Austin claims place-specificity: "It is this leap of the running stream of poetic inspiration from level to level, whose course cannot be determined by anything except the nature of the ground traversed, which I have called the landscape line" (p. 55). Given her efforts to instill respect for the Native American traditions, Austin may, as James Ruppert has argued in his essay "Discovering America," prove to be a "pivotal figure in understanding the relation between American Indian literature and modern American literature" (p. 250).

Closely related to Austin's concern with Native American poetics is her interest in the folk story and folk traditions. Unfortunately, most of her writing on this subject was done for the periodicals and never collected in book form. Perhaps the best entrée into this aspect of Austin's work is an essay titled "The Folk Story in America." Published in the *South Atlantic Quarterly* in 1934, it very well could have served as the preface to her *One-Smoke Stories* (1934), a collection of short, short stories, the literary form that Austin believed was "the true Indian genre." The essay begins: "Now that I can look back on the whole scale of my story interests, I can see that I had always liked the folk story better than any other" (p. 10).

Over the course of the piece, Austin distinguishes for her reader the difference between the "exoteric" and "esoteric" varieties of Indian tales, a distinction that she felt scholars had failed to grasp, and she chastises them accordingly. To those who would better understand Austin's nature writing—especially books like *The Land of Little Rain, The Flock,* and *Lost Borders*—her comments on style and craft are of particular interest:

What annoyed me excessively in my first volume of short stories [i.e., *Lost Borders*] was the insistence of the publishers that they should be each introduced by explanatory comment growing out of their occasions. Among aboriginals this sort of thing is never done. By making the story too intimately the possession of the teller, something of the possessiveness of the hearer is lost, and it is indispensable to the primitive teller that the story should stand to the hearer in place of an experience, which is the primary reason why it should be told at all. (p. 17)

What attracted Austin to the folktale—and what she often borrowed from it in her own work—is the fact that in these stories, the term "reality" encompasses vast realms hardly imagined in modern American culture. She cautions her reader that in the folk tradition, much occurs in the "borderland" between "palpable existence" and those things that have "only a psychic reality."

Published in 1924, *The Land of Journey's Ending*—its very title echoing Austin's first book—marks a return to the source of her poetic inspiration. The book received high praise when it was published, perhaps because this was the type of book critics and readers wanted Mary Austin to write. The style is reminiscent of the earlier work, but it is clear that the book is the result of a several-week vacation and historical research rather than of extended living in that landscape; thus lacking is the quality of intimacy that vitalizes every page of *The Land of Little Rain.* Nevertheless, many readers share Lawrence Clark Powell's assessment that *The Land of Journey's Ending* is "the book that best embodies the essences of the region whose heartland is Arizona and New Mexico" (*Southwest Classics,* p. 95).

The Land of Journey's Ending is valuable for the light it sheds on a little-understood aspect of Mary Austin's vision of the human relationship to the land. She is often celebrated by those critics with an environmentalist perspective for her assertion "Not the law but the land sets the limit," as if this were to suggest that Austin was somehow a precursor to what has come to be known as Deep Ecology, a philosophy that seeks a "nonanthropocentric" vision of reality. Certainly many things that Austin wrote can, at least on a certain level, be interpreted as nonanthropocentric. On the opening page of *The Land of Journey's Ending* she writes of joys of "the traveler who gives himself up" to the southwestern landscape. Such a "giving up" would seem prerequisite to a Deep Ecology perspective. However, Austin then continues, "Go far enough on any of its trails, and you begin to see how the world was made." Her train of thought concludes: "What man in some measure understands, he is no longer afraid of; the next step is mastery" (pp. 3–4). No understanding of Austin's vision of the land is complete without full appreciation of this notion of environmental "mastery."

Although Austin felt that the land was the primary factor in shaping not only the individual artist's work but also the dominant qualities of the culture at large, she did not believe this meant humans should just throw up their hands and allow the land to have its way with them. On the contrary, she insisted that humans need to enter into a working relationship with the powers that imbue the land, and, once connecting with and understanding those powers, use them for the benefit of humankind. She derived this understanding from her observations of Native Americans, and it can be traced back to *Land of Little Rain:* "It is the proper destiny of every considerable stream in the West to become an irrigation ditch. It would seem the streams are willing" (p. 123). This is not the vision of a radical environmentalist, but rather of a mystical steward. This vision, however, becomes problematized for contemporary readers if they recall that Austin consistently eroticized water, ascribing female gender to it.

In regard to this vision of the human relationship to the indwelling power of the land, Austin is perhaps best understood in the context of what she called "prayer," a subject to which she devoted considerable attention over the course of her life. In her short book *Can Prayer Be Answered?*, she writes: "Prayer, to the aboriginal, is an explicit motion of the inner self which puts you in touch with the living principle which controls the existing emergency, whether it be of sickness or the need of rain to make crops grow"

(p. 7). Similarly, in *Earth Horizon* she explains: "Prayer . . . had nothing to do with emotion; it was an act; an outgoing act of the inner self toward something, not a god, toward a responsive activity in the world about you, designated as The-Friend-of-the-Soul-of-Man; Wakonda, to use a term adopted by the ethnologists—the effective principle of the created universe" (p. 276). Prayer is an effective human gesture capable of enlisting this life force, this "Wakonda," into human service. Shamanistic belief of this sort colors every word Mary Austin wrote, forcing one to reconsider Carl Van Doren's suggestion that she be awarded a "Masters in the American Environment." Might we not be confronted here with a pun?

One needs to remember Austin's notion of animistic engineering when considering what is often referred to as her "environmental activism." The best and most thoroughly researched consideration of Austin's role in the Colorado River controversy is an essay by Benay Blend titled "Mary Austin and the Western Conservation Movement: 1900–1927." Blend, however, failing to take into account Austin's animistic beliefs, comes to the conclusion that the author of *The Land of Little Rain* "never knew quite where she stood, recognizing both the pull of wilderness and civilization on the American landscape" (p. 29). Just the opposite is the case: Austin knew exactly where she stood; unfortunately for her, very few others were standing in the same vicinity. Blend accurately points out that Austin had little interest in the growing movement toward wilderness preservation. Like Native American people, she had no desire to reserve land that would, in the words of the 1964 Wilderness Act, be "untrammeled by man, where man himself is a visitor who does not remain."

In the water rights battle over the Colorado River—a battle that extended over several decades—Austin took an active role, arguing against building a dam in Boulder Canyon (a dam eventually built and named for her friend Herbert Hoover). She did not have a problem with dams per se, but rather with who would control the water and power derived from them.

In the Boulder Canyon controversy, she opposed the fact that California would be the great beneficiary, a state already well embarked on a course of unhindered urban expansion. For California to appropriate resources to which it had no legitimate claim would deny states like Arizona and New Mexico, not yet in a position to exploit those resources. Thus Austin's objection to damming the Colorado was not that a beautiful river and canyon would be lost, but that the California Cult of Bigness would triumph. Although Austin sided with the interests representing Arizona and New Mexico—she was even appointed a delegate to the Second Colorado River Conference in 1927—few people on this side of the battle could understand her motives. As one person quoted in Benay's essay expresses it:

> Never in my life have I seen anything so funny as that speech she made. There were all these men armed to the teeth with facts, and Mary Austin stood up and made a speech that—well the kind of speech Mary would make. Oh, I don't mean that they weren't interested and that it wasn't a good speech. But those hard headed, hardboiled men didn't care how beautiful Arizona is or what folk-lore and Indians it has. (p. 22)

Austin's efforts did not halt the construction of Hoover Dam, but she did articulate a countercultural sentiment that became more prevalent over the next four decades.

The baffling effect Austin had on the policymakers of her day is not unlike the effect her work can still have on readers today. Whether it be in environmental activism, feminism, poetics, Native American studies, or her autobiography, Austin was ever responsive to what she regarded as the land's challenge. Many dismissed her as an eccentric, not to mention a crank. Yet she was well aware of the effect she had on people. In a 27 March 1930 letter to the poet Arthur Ficke, Austin defends herself against the charges that her methods were not "scholarly," and therefore not "serious." The letter is remarkable, too, in that it reflects the unrepentant egotism and elitism that people found so bothersome:

> I see myself, primarily, as a creative thinker—or creative writer, whichever term suits you best—which I feel to entail a higher obligation than that of stodgy and meticulous demonstration for the uninitiated, of what has come to me through the regular channels of scholarly experience. I felt that I couldn't be faithful to my primary obligation if I must go dragging after me all the fructifying sources, as a queen bee trails the entrails of her mate.

Although Austin eventually washed her hands of environmental "activism," she remained committed to politics on the local level in Santa Fe, doing whatever she could to aid the preservation and even development of the cultures she knew there. She bequeathed her house to the Indian Arts Fund.

Earth Horizon and Beyond

In many ways, Austin's autobiography, a book she called *Earth Horizon* (1932), is both the best and the worst place to begin one's acquaintance with a woman who is one of twentieth-century America's most interesting and still overlooked writers. Reading this long story of her life provides an extensive survey of her interests and career. Its tone is vintage Mary Austin, and it remains the most important source of information to biographers. Yet one must be careful about taking her too literally. There is enough fictional distortion of the "facts" to recommend that one approach the text more like a novel than an accurate historical record of her life. In constructing my own presentation of Austin and her work, I have drawn extensively upon this book, but having done so leaves me unsettled.

In addition to its problems of accuracy, the text of *Earth Horizon* regularly assumes its audience's familiarity with ideas that Austin may have developed elsewhere; this is particularly true of her notions about folk culture. Thus, without tracking down these extraneous and often difficult-to-locate sources, a reader confronted with certain passages in *Earth Horizon* might feel that the writing is more obscure than is actually the case. In any event, it is a book that rewards subsequent readings, especially after one has become more thoroughly acquainted with Austin's other work.

One of the most engaging aspects of *Earth Horizon* as autobiography is its use of perspective. Shifting between the third and first persons, the narrative seems presented by two different people. Austin designated these voices "I-Mary" and "Mary-by-herself," the former being the part of herself that draws its power from the "Wakonda" and the latter being that part deprived of these superpersonal ministrations. In light of recent developments in literary theory pertaining to autobiography—plus the fact that *Earth Horizon* has been brought back into print—this text may soon attract more sophisticated critical treatment than has been the case until now.

Critical assessment of Austin's work is likely to remain varied because many readers will not be sympathetic to the mysticism and wild flights of mind that are her trademarks as a writer. She will likely elude all attempts to inscribe her. In *Earth Horizon* she bemoans the fact that "deeply rooted in the American consciousness [is] a disposition to take offense at what is strange, because being strange it implies a criticism of the familiar of which we lack any criterion of authenticity other than that it is ours" (p. 230). Mary Austin stings in response to being stung. Despite whatever harsh judgments are likely to befall her, it is certain that she was exploring territory more and more Americans seem interested in visiting.

Above all, Mary Hunter Austin was concerned with how Americans—most of whom are recent arrivals—will meet the challenge presented to them by the land they inhabit. That we are up to the challenge was not at all clear in Austin's day, nor is it in ours. We might ponder this in the words of Dr. Caldwell, a character from her early novel *Santa Lucia*: "[I]t is my belief that here in the West, perhaps in all America, we do not take enough account of the power of our inanimate surroundings to take on the spiritual quality of the life that is lived in them, and give it off again like an exhalation, and not pains enough, when we have made such a place, to preserve it for those who come after from generation to generation."

Selected Bibliography

WORKS OF MARY HUNTER AUSTIN

BOOKS

One Hundred Miles on Horse Back (Los Angeles: Dawson's Book Shop, 1963), first published in *The Blackburnian* (January 1889); *The Land of Little Rain* (Boston: Houghton Mifflin, 1903), repr., with intro. by Edward Abbey (New York: Penguin, 1988); *The Basket Women* (Boston: Houghton Mifflin, 1904; repr., New York: AMS Press, 1969); *Isidro* (Boston: Houghton Mifflin, 1905; repr., New York: AMS Press, 1973); *The Flock* (Boston: Houghton Mifflin, 1906; repr., Santa Fe, N.Mex.: William Gannon, 1973); *Santa Lucia* (New York: Harper and Brothers, 1908); *Lost Borders* (New York: Harper and Brothers, 1909); *Outland* (London: J. Murray, 1910), under pseudonym Gordon Stairs, and, as Mary Austin (New York: Boni and Liveright, 1919); *The Arrow-Maker* (New York: Duffield, 1911; rev. ed., Boston: Houghton Mifflin, 1915; repr., New York: AMS, 1969); *Christ in Italy* (New York: Duffield, 1912); *A Woman of Genius* (Garden City, N.Y.: Doubleday Page, 1912), repr., with afterword by Nancy Porter (Old Westbury, N.Y.: Feminist Press, 1985); *The Green Bough* (Garden City, N.Y.: Doubleday Page, 1913); *The Lovely Lady* (Garden City, N.Y.: Doubleday Page, 1913); *California, Land of the Sun* (New York: Macmillan, 1914), rev. ed. titled *Lands of the Sun* (Boston and New York: Houghton Mifflin, 1927); *Love and the Soul Maker* (New York: Appleton, 1914); *The Man Jesus* (New York: Harper and Brothers, 1915), rev. ed. titled *A Small Town Man* (New York: Harper and Brothers, 1925); *The Ford* (Boston: Houghton Mifflin, 1917); *The Trail Book* (Boston: Houghton Mifflin, 1918); *The Young Woman Citizen* (New York: Woman's Press, 1918; repr., Fullerton, Calif.: Designs Three, 1976).

No. 26 Jayne Street (Boston; Houghton Mifflin, 1920); *The American Rhythm* (New York: Harcourt Brace, 1923; enl. ed. Boston: Houghton Mifflin, 1930; repr., New York: Cooper Square, 1970); *The Land of Journey's Ending* (New York: Century, 1924; repr., Tucson, Ariz.: Univ. of Arizona Press, 1983); *Everyman's Genius* (Indianapolis: Bobbs-Merrill, 1925); *The Children Sing in the Far West* (Boston: Houghton

Mifflin, 1928); *Taos Pueblo* (San Francisco: Grabhorn Press, 1930; repr., New York: New York Graphic Society, 1977), photographs by Ansel Adams; *Experiences Facing Death* (Indianapolis: Bobbs-Merrill, 1931; repr., New York: Arno, 1977); *Starry Adventure* (Boston: Houghton Mifflin, 1931); *Earth Horizon: An Autobiography* (Boston: Houghton Mifflin, 1932; repr., Albuquerque, N.Mex.: Univ. of New Mexico Press, 1991); *Can Prayer Be Answered?* (New York: Farrar and Rinehart, 1934); *One-Smoke Stories* (Boston: Houghton Mifflin, 1934); *The Mother of San Felipe and Other Early Stories*, ed. by Franklin Walker (Los Angeles: Book Club of California, 1950); *Literary America, 1903–1934: The Mary Austin Letters*, ed. and with intro. by T. M. Pearce (Westport, Conn.: Greenwood, 1979); *Stories from the Country of Lost Borders*, ed. by and with intro. by Marjorie Pryse (New Brunswick, N.J.: Rutgers Univ. Press, 1987), combined repr. of *The Land of Little Rain* and *Lost Borders*; *Western Trails: A Collection of Short Stories*, ed. by Melody Graulich (Reno, Nev.: Univ. of Nevada Press, 1987); *Cactus Thorn*, foreword and afterword by Melody Graulich (Reno, Nev.: Univ. of Nevada Press, 1988); *Writing the Western Landscape*, ed. by Ann H. Zwinger (Boston: Beacon, 1994), with John Muir.

ESSAYS AND OTHER SHORT PIECES

"The Temblor," in *The California Earthquake of 1906*, ed. by David Starr Jordan (San Francisco: A. M. Robertson, 1907); "The Failure of Free Love," in *Harper's Weekly* 58 (21 March 1914); "Sex Emancipation Through War," in *Forum* 59 (May 1918); "Automatism in Writing," in *Unpartisan Review* 14 (October/December 1920); "American Women and The Intellectual Life," in *Bookman* 53 (August 1921); "Non-English Writings: Aboriginal," in *The Cambridge History of American Literature*, ed. by William Peterfield Trent, John Erskine, Stuart P. Sherman, and Carl Van Doren (New York: G. P. Putnam, 1921), vol. 4, chap. 32; "Religion in the United States," in *Century* 104 (August 1922); "Science for the Unscientific," in *Bookman* 55 (August 1922); "Women as Audience," in *Bookman* 55 (March 1922); "Greatness in Women," in *North American Review* 217 (February 1923); "Sex in American Literature," in *Bookman* 57 (June 1923); "The Sense of Humor in Women," in *New Republic* 41 (26 November 1924); "The Colorado River Controversy," in *Nation* 125 (November 1927); "The Colorado River Project and the Culture of the Southwest," in *Southwest Review* 13 (October 1927); "The Forward Turn," in *Nation* 125 (July 1927); "George Sterling at Carmel," in *American Mercury* 11 (May 1927); "Woman Alone," in *Nation* 124 (2 March 1927).

"Indian Arts for the Indians," in *Survey* no. 7 (1 July 1928); "Folk Literature," in *Saturday Review of Literature* 5 (11 August 1928); "Hunt of Arizona," in *Nation* 127 (28 November 1928); "The Lost Garden" (1928), MS in Mary Austin Collection, AU 318, Henry Huntington Library; "Aboriginal Fiction," in *Saturday Review of Literature* 6 (28 December 1929); "How I Found the Thing Worth Waiting For," in *Survey* no. 61 (1 January 1929); "Regional Culture in the Southwest," in *Southwest Review* 14 (July 1929); "Why Americanize the Indian?" in *Forum* 82 (September 1929); "American Indian Dance Drama," in *Yale Review* 19 (summer 1930); "Aboriginal American Literature," in *American Writers on American Literature* (New York, 1931); "Mexicans and New Mexico," in *Survey* no. 66 (1 May 1931); "Life in Santa Fe," in *South Atlantic Quarterly* 31 (July 1932); "Regionalism in American Fiction," in *English Journal* 21 (February 1932); "Sources of Poetic Influence in the Southwest," in *Poetry* 43 (December 1933); "The Folk Story in America," in *South Atlantic Quarterly* 33 (January 1934); "How I Learned to Read and Write," in *My First Publication*, ed. by James D. Hart (San Francisco: Book Club of California, 1961), reprint of "My Maiden Effort"; "The Friend in the Wood," in *Wind's Trail: The Early Life of Mary Austin*, by Peggy Pond Church, ed. by Shelley Armitage (Santa Fe, N.Mex.: Museum of New Mexico Press, 1990).

MANUSCRIPTS AND PAPERS

Mary Austin Collection, Henry E. Huntington Library, San Marino, Calif., by far the most extensive collection of Austin MSS, photographs, letters, and other memorabilia; the Ina Sizer Cassidy Collection, Bancroft Library, University of California at Berkeley; the T. M. Pearce papers and the Peggy Pond Church Papers, Special Collections, University of New Mexico; the Bender Collection, Mills College, Oakland, Calif.

BIBLIOGRAPHY

Joseph Gaer, ed., *Mary Austin: Bibliography and Biographical Data* (Berkeley, Calif.: California Library Research Digest, 1934).

BIOGRAPHICAL AND CRITICAL STUDIES

BOOKS

Morely Baer, *Room and Time Enough: The Land of Mary Austin* (Flagstaff, Ariz.: Northland, 1979); Ambrose Bierce, *The Letters of Ambrose Bierce*, ed. by Bertha Clark Pope (New York: Gordian, 1967); Peggy Pond Church, *Wind's Trail: The Early Life of Mary*

Austin, ed. by Shelley Armitage (Santa Fe, N.Mex.: Museum of New Mexico Press, 1990); Richard Dillon, *Impressions of Bohemia* (Carmel, Calif.: Pacific Rim Galleries, 1986), a good description of Carmel and its artists in Austin's day; Helen MacKnight Doyle, *Mary Austin: Woman of Genius* (New York: Gotham House, 1939); Augusta Fink, *I Mary: A Biography of Mary Austin* (Tucson, Ariz.: Univ. of Arizona Press, 1983); Willard Houghland, ed., *Mary Austin: A Memorial* (Santa Fe, N.Mex.: Laboratory of Anthropology, 1944); Annette Kolodny, *The Lay of the Land* (Chapel Hill, N.C.: Univ. of North Carolina Press, 1975); Jo W. Lyday, *Mary Austin: The Southwest Works* (Austin, Tex.: Steck-Vaughan Co., 1968); T. M. Pearce, *The Beloved House* (Caldwell, Idaho: Caxton Printers, 1940) and *Mary Hunter Austin* (New York: Twayne, 1956); Esther Lanigan Stineman, *Mary Austin: Song of a Maverick* (New Haven: Yale Univ. Press, 1989).

ARTICLES AND SHORT WORKS

Elizabeth Ammons, "Form and Difference: Gertrude Stein and Mary Austin," in her *Conflicting Stories: American Women Writers at the Turn into the Twentieth Century* (New York: Oxford Univ. Press, 1991); Benay Blend, "Mary Austin and the Western Conservation Movement: 1900–1927," in *Journal of the Southwest* 30 (spring 1988); Axel Carl Bredahl, "Divided Narrative: Mary Austin and Sherwood Anderson," in his *New Ground: Western American Narrative and the Literary Canon* (Chapel Hill, N.C.: Univ. of North Carolina Press, 1989); Ina Sizer Cassidy, "I-Mary and Me: The Chronicle of a Friendship," in *New Mexico Quarterly* 9 (November 1939).

Richard Drinnon, "*The American Rhythm:* Mary Austin," in his *Facing West: The Metaphysics of Indian-Hating and Empire-Building* (Minneapolis, Minn.: Univ. of Minnesota Press, 1980); Thomas W. Ford, "*The American Rhythm:* Mary Austin's Poetic Principle," in *Western American Literature* 5 (spring 1970); Faith Jaycox, "Regeneration Through Liberation: Mary Austin's 'The Walking Woman' and Western Narrative Formula," in *Legacy* 6 (spring 1989); Karen S. Langlois, "Mary Austin and Houghton Mifflin Company: A Case Study in the Marketing of a Western Writer," in *Western American Literature* 23 (May 1988), "A Fresh Voice from the West: Mary Austin, California, and American Literary Magazines, 1892–1910," in *California History* 69 (spring 1990), and "Mary Austin's *A Woman of Genius*: The Text, the Novel and the Problem of Male Publishers and Critics and Female Authors," in *Journal of American Culture* 15 (summer 1992); "The Literary Spotlight: Mary Austin," in *Bookman* 58 (September 1923).

Anne Martin, "A Tribute to Mary Austin," in *Nation* 139 (10 October 1934); "Mary Austin," in *Nation* 139 (29 August 1934); *Mary Hunter Austin: Author, Poet, Lecturer, Naturalist* (Independence, Calif.: The Mary Austin Home, 1968), pamphlet that includes a partial bibliography and short tributes by Ansel Adams and others; Vera L. Norwood, "The Photographer and the Naturalist: Laura Gilpin and Mary Austin in the Southwest," in *Journal of American Culture* 5 (summer 1982), and "Heroines of Nature: Four Women Respond to the American Landscape," in *Environmental Review* 8 (spring 1984); John P. O'Grady, "Mary Austin's Gleanings of the Wild," in his *Pilgrims to the Wild* (Salt Lake City, Utah: Univ. of Utah Press, 1993); Genaro Padilla, "Lies, Secrets, and Silence," in his *My History, Not Yours* (Madison, Wis.: Univ. of Wisconsin Press, 1993).

Donald P. Ringler, "Mary Austin: Kern County Days, 1888–1892," in *Southern California Quarterly* 45 (March 1963); Lois Rudnick, "Re-Naming the Land: Anglo Expatriate Women in the Southwest," in *The Desert Is No Lady*, ed. by Vera Norwood and Janice Monk (New Haven: Yale Univ. Press, 1987); James Ruppert, "Discovering America: Mary Austin and Imagism," in *Studies in American Indian Literature*, ed. by Paula Gunn Allen (New York, 1983), and "Mary Austin's Landscape Line in Native American Literature," in *Southwest Review* 68 (autumn 1983), two works that provide the best studies of Austin's poetics; William J. Scheick, "Mary Austin's Disfigurement of the Southwest in *The Land of Little Rain*," in *Western American Literature* 27 (spring 1992); Henry Smith, "The Feel of the Purposeful Earth: Mary Austin's Prophecy," in *New Mexico Quarterly* 1 (February 1931).

Esther Lanigan Stineman, "Mary Austin Rediscovered," in *Journal of the Southwest* 30 (winter 1988); Carl Van Doren, "*The American Rhythm:* Mary Austin," in his *Many Minds* (New York: Knopf, 1924); James C. Work, "The Moral in Austin's *The Land of Little Rain*," in *Women and Western American Literature*, ed. by Helen Winter Stauffer and Susan J. Rosowski (New York: Whitson, 1982); David Wyatt, "Mary Austin: Nature and Nurturance," in his *The Fall into Eden: Landscape and Imagination in California* (New York: Cambridge Univ. Press, 1986); Dudley Taylor Wynn, "Mary Austin, Woman Alone," in *Virginia Quarterly Review* 13 (April 1937); Elémire Zolla, *The Writer and the Shaman: A Morphology of the American Indian*, trans. by Raymond Rosenthal (New York: Harcourt Brace Jovanovich, 1973).

DISSERTATIONS AND THESES

Mark Hoyer, "Dancing Ghosts: Mary Austin's Synthesis of Biblical and Indigenous Mythologies" (Ph.D.

diss., University of California at Davis, 1995); Fanny Alice Mayer, "A Study of the Conception of Land in the Writings of Mary Hunter Austin" (M.A. thesis, University of Southern California, 1947); Inez Tingley Thoroughgood, "Mary Austin: Interpreter of the Western Scene, 1888–1906" (M.A. thesis, University of California at Los Angeles, 1950); Dudley Taylor Wynn, "A Critical Study of the Writings of Mary Hunter Austin, 1868–1934" (Ph.D. diss., New York University, 1940).

FLORENCE MERRIAM BAILEY
(1863–1948)

HARRIET KOFALK

AWAKING ONE MORNING to the song of a robin, New York City businessman Clinton Merriam was so reminded of the peace and deep satisfaction of country life, he determined that very day to return to the hills of northern New York State, where his family had homesteaded at the beginning of the nineteenth century and where his parents still lived. Like his own father, he treasured the wilderness and resolved to instill in his own children an appreciation for the natural world. The Civil War was then being fought, and Merriam felt the weight of its ravages even while he reaped the benefits of its commerce.

Merriam's daughter Florence heard her father tell this story many times, and it made a deep impression on her. In her later years, she referred to it as the first influence on her own interest in studying birds — live birds, not those that had been killed, as was in scientific vogue at the time.

Thus it was that Florence Merriam Bailey was born on 8 August 1863 at Homewood, the expansive home her father built on the hill above his parents' home near Leyden, New York. Her birth name was Florence Augusta Merriam. Florence's sister, Gertrude, then five, died the day before she was born. Gertrude's absence had a lasting effect on the budding naturalist, who treasured the pink spring beauty flowers that grew profusely around Homewood and that re-

minded her father of the daughter he had lost. A year after Florence's birth, Merriam retired from business at the age of forty to manage the family farm and care for his aging parents. He later served two terms in the U.S. Congress.

In the Merriam household, knowledge of all aspects of nature was highly valued. Each member of the family had a specialty; together they learned from one another. Florence's mother, Caroline Hart Merriam, loved astronomy and often took her young daughter to the cupola on the rooftop to watch a special display in the night sky. Clinton Merriam shared his wife's enthusiasm for the stars, writing later to his daughter that "everyone should become acquainted with all visible constellations, so that when the soul takes wings and flies into illimitable space it would know the roads and not get lost." Merriam's interest in natural history had led him to develop a correspondence with the naturalist John Muir, who had developed a theory of how glacial activity had created the Yosemite valley. One of Muir's earliest explications of his theory is contained in a letter to Clinton Merriam, who traveled to California to meet with Muir in 1870.

Merriam's sister Helen Bagg lived nearby and was the family botanist, encouraging her own children as well as her brother's to explore the woods for specimens she could collect in her growing herbarium. One of Florence's uncles taught paleontology; another farmed and raised bees in southern California. She had two older brothers, Collins, who pursued a business career, and Clinton Hart (called Hart to distinguish him from his father), who was a renowned ornithologist before he was out of his teens. Hart trained to become a physician, and developed a lifelong love of mammals, especially bears.

It's little wonder that Florence Merriam Bailey became a naturalist, given this environment and her family's enthusiasm for the world of nature. She received her early schooling at home, both by family preference and for health reasons — a respiratory ailment that was probably tuberculosis. She later described her early education as coming mainly from the woods and fields where, like Thoreau, she found Shakespeare's "books in trees, sermons in stones, and good in everything." The family often spent part of the winter in New York City because of the harsh weather in Lewis County, where heavy snowfall could isolate the family for weeks. In an unpublished memoir written for her nieces, Florence Merriam told the story of one evening drive home in a sleigh, when she was "unceremoniously tipped over into a snowdrift." But she enjoyed strapping on snowshoes and taking nature walks in the Homewood environs with her father and brother, the ever-present dogs "bringing up the rear in dignified silence."

Hart Merriam was eight years older than his sister, and she followed him everywhere. He taught her how to identify the local birds, in which Florence took special delight. Hart would preserve the skins of the small mammals and birds he collected, and soon had so many specimens that his father built a three-story museum to house them. From her brother's experience, Florence decided that her own interest was in *live* birds. In a letter to her brother she described her vision of a firm of "Merriam and Sister," but such a joint venture was not to be. After completing his training as a physician, Hart served his home community briefly before being tapped to head a newly created division of the U.S. Department of Agriculture that later became the U.S. Biological Survey. His marriage in 1886 would mark the beginning of Florence Merriam's

coming into her own power. She continued to study the birds, and sent Hart reports on all her findings. But in the woods around Homewood, Florence was developing an authority all her own.

College Life and Bird Advocacy

Florence Merriam entered Smith College, considered the best women's college in the country, in 1882. Because she did not meet Smith's prerequisites for formal education, she was admitted as a "special" student, and had the option of choosing those upper-level subjects that most interested her. Science was not yet a formal course, so she worked mainly in writing, English literature, geology, ethics, comparative religions, and philosophy. Her favorite teacher, a cousin of the naturalist David Starr Jordan, then in California studying the effects of Darwin's theory of evolution, put a strong emphasis on rhetoric. Miss Jordan was also well grounded in science and encouraged Florence to believe that she could succeed in all her endeavors. She became a mentor to Florence in her passion to serve society.

Meanwhile, Hart Merriam helped to found the American Ornithologists' Union (AOU), and soon prominent professionals became more frequent guests at Homewood. One was Henry Henshaw, who once described the surroundings of the Merriam estate as affording "unlimited opportunities to the naturalist." In 1885, while still in college, Bailey became the first woman associate member of the AOU. It had been organized, among other reasons, to protect birds from extinction. One threat to species survival was the demand for millinery feathers. It was estimated that five million birds a year were being killed to produce women's hats. Bailey rallied the young women at Smith College to protest the destruction of birds for fashion, and the small club she started soon counted a third of the campus among its membership. So many girls took their hats to be retrimmed that a milliner in town inquired if the college had banned the use of birds. The following spring brought help from the naturalist-sage John Burroughs, who responded to Bailey's request to conduct nature walks for the Smith women, so they could appreciate birds in their natural habitats. In the flush of success with her project, she soon extended her work to writing articles for newspapers about the plight of her "bird friends."

The organization of Smith women became the first official chapter of the fledgling Audubon Society, which Bailey's brother's friend George Bird Grinnell had founded. In order to keep up with the society's growing membership, Grinnell started the *Audubon Magazine*, and Florence undertook what would become her life's work as she began to compose a series titled "Hints to Audubon Workers: Fifty Common Birds and How to Know Them."

In an exchange of correspondence with her brother in 1886 — a lifelong pleasure for them both — Florence refined her earlier Thoreauvian philosophy. "Fundamentally we all believe the same things though we call them by different names. . . . Infinite goodness is the underlying thought in every case." She described her concerns about whether she could write sufficiently well to pursue a career as an author even as she determined to succeed. She concluded, " 'To ease the burden of the world,' and help others to the truer higher living . . . this is my aim and to leave the world better for my having lived, and I feel that I can fulfill it better through my pen than in any other way." When she left Smith in 1886, Florence undertook to achieve this goal.

With her brother's encouragement, Florence Merriam turned her work for the Audubon Society into her first book, a small handbook titled *Birds Through an Opera Glass* (1889). She directed it toward women and young people, the first bird book that did not presuppose shooting. It brought accolades from professionals, one of whom compared her work favorably with that of Thoreau and Burroughs in a review in *Auk* that October. Her father pasted copies of the reviews into his copy of the book. The *Atlantic Monthly* called her book a "collection of bird portraits tossed off with a deft and vivid touch."

Her brother edited the manuscript for scientific accuracy, a service he provided throughout her life — objecting at times to her choice of words. Florence was at heart a Victorian, and when she traveled to Utah among the Mormons practicing polygamy in 1893 and wrote about the journey (her only non-birding book), he sputtered, "I'll never be able to show my face in Utah again if you publish this!" The toned-down manuscript became another way to introduce young Easterners to the grandeurs of the West, and to encourage them to get off their sofas and take to the outdoors. The manuscript was published as *My Summer in a Mormon Village* (1894).

Florence's traveling companion on the trip to Utah was Harriet Mann Miller, who wrote under the pen name of Olive Thorne Miller. With Bailey, she was one of the four most important woman authors of bird books in the nineteenth century, according to historian Robert Welker. She was criticized by the scientific community for publishing in nonscholarly publications, but Miller defended her work in an article published in *Auk* in January 1894. It can be seen as a defense of Florence Merriam Bailey's work as well:

> There is, first, my great desire to bring into the lives of others the delights to be found in the study of Nature, which necessitates the using of an unscientific publication. . . . Let those who will spend their days killing, dissecting and classifying; I choose rather to give my time to the study of life, and to doing my small best toward preserving the tribes of the air from the utter extinction with which they are threatened. (pp. 85–86)

Florence Merriam spent the winter of 1893–1894 at Stanford University. She studied partly under the tutelage of Miss Jordan's cousin, David Starr Jordan, whom she described to her Smith classmates as teaching a "strong course . . . on Evolution." In the spring, she traveled southward on a visit to her uncle Gustavus Merriam, who had moved to northern San Diego county after the Civil War, in search of a better climate for his ailing wife. They were the first Anglo homesteaders in that part of California, and the fifth generation of the family still lives on the property, now surrounded by suburban houses. At the ranch he called Twin Oaks, Gustavus Merriam tried a succession of crops, including fruit trees and wine grapes. A profusion of wildflowers on the land attracted bees, and he shipped honey to the gold country in beeswax-lined barrels. Wildflowers also attract birds, and these were of more than passing interest to his visiting niece. Hummingbirds, especially, abounded; their beauty made Florence lament reports of the commerce in their skins—four hundred thousand of them had sold in London in just one week, according to Robert Ridgway.

At Twin Oaks, Bailey wrote one of her most popular books, *A-Birding on a Bronco* (1896). Her mount, Old Billy, was hardly a "bronco," to judge by the pictures in her book, but the young naturalist soon discovered that she was virtually invisible to birds while on horseback, whereas they would scatter if she was on foot. So she rode daily across the back country to check the nests of her friends and to write about their activities "at home."

> Every morning, right after breakfast, my horse was brought to the door and I set out to make the rounds of the valley. I rode till dinnertime. . . . After dinner I would take my camp-stool and stroll through the oaks at the head of the valley, for a quiet study of the nearer nests. Then once more my horse would be brought up for me to take a run before sunset; and at night I would identify my new birds and write up the notes of the day. What more could observer crave? The world was mine. I never spent a happier spring. (pp. 1–2)

She had first visited her uncle before, and time had already wrought its changes on the California landscape. The place where a shrike had once nested under her patient watching was now "converted into a well kept prune orchard." The phoebes who had made their home in an abandoned adobe vacated when her uncle built a schoolhouse nearby.

Florence returned east via the dry, high country of northern Arizona, a mecca for those with "lungs," the euphemism of the day for respir-atory ailments. Her own health was much improved by the long hours she spent riding and walking into the high country. Her brother Hart came west to travel with her by wagon to the Grand Canyon, but urged her not to publish the article she had written about Arizona, filled, he felt, with "all the infernal lies you've been stuffed with" about western mythology. She followed his advice. Back in Washington, D.C., she moved in with her brother and his family, which now included two young daughters.

Professional Life and Marriage

In addition to assisting Hart Merriam with his work, Florence was active in the Women's National Science Club, the largest organization of its kind. One of the few outlets available to women in science, it planned to open chapters across the country and met annually in Washington, so that members could report on their research.

Florence Merriam's organizational affiliations continued to grow. She served on the AOU Committee on the Protection of North American Birds, as did her friend Olive Thorne Miller. In 1897 she helped found a local chapter, the Audubon Society of the District of Columbia. One of the goals of the newly constituted Audubon Society was to educate schoolchildren, and Florence took up the task of training teachers, so bird study could be introduced into the schools. "Field work, of course, should be the basis in every possible case," she concluded her letter read to the AOU annual meeting in 1898 as part of the "Report of Committee on Bird Protection." In 1900, the society opened its bird study classes to the public. Bailey was the only woman instructor; fifteen students were initially enrolled. Enrollment doubled the following year, and by the end of the decade numbered more than 200, according to a 1912 historical report on the classes authored by Bailey and published by the society.

In addition to contributing various articles to magazines, in 1898 she also completed her next book, *Birds of Village and Field*, a handbook for beginners. In its review, *Osprey* (April 1898) praised her work, while crediting her family connections as a "favored person in this field being a sister of Dr. C. Hart Merriam." The reviewer acknowledged that the book would benefit not only new students of birds, but was "one which the ornithologist will lay down with the satisfaction of time well spent."

By 1899 a longtime friendship Florence had developed with Vernon Bailey, the chief naturalist at the U.S. Biological Survey under her brother Hart, had grown into long-term commitment. They were married on 16 December of that year, and made their home in Washington, D.C. Vernon Bailey had spent the previous twelve years traveling mostly by himself, and Florence had a similar history. She now wanted to travel more in the West she had grown to love, and he was commissioned to do likewise by his work at the survey. She wrote to her brother the following spring, as the newlyweds headed by train to the Southwest for the summer field season, "How thankful I am not to be coming back to it alone! But all the years of loneliness and wandering, which have been brought back so vividly by the misery of the poor 'lungers' alone on the train, seem now a part of another existence, for all the pain and weariness of my life have gone, and it is filled with peace and happiness. It seems almost wicked to be so happy when the world is so full of sorrow."

One of Bailey's most popular magazine articles came into initial form that summer as she and her husband traveled across Texas. "Meeting Spring Half Way" was serialized in the bird journal *Condor* in 1916. In it she described the Texas landscape—and the birds thereof—in enthusiastic detail. "As the train passed through a stand of pine we breathed the velvety air of sulphuring pineries—nature was full of rich promise. . . . Through the open windows came the spring songs of Tomtits, Cardinals, and Mockingbirds. . . . The handsome red horse-chestnut blooming in the woods recalled Audubon's famous painting of the Carolina Wren."

The Baileys returned to the Southwest in the summer of 1901 to continue their fieldwork.

Louis Agassiz Fuertes, whom many today consider equal to Audubon as a bird artist, joined them to work on illustrations for Biological Survey publications. The Baileys were unsuccessful in their attempts to start their own family, and Fuertes became like a son to them. The couple went on to nurture many other young people who came across their path in the scientific world.

Late in the summer of 1901 they traveled on to California, where Bailey introduced her husband to her uncle Gustavus and his family. At Lake Tahoe they joined her brother Hart and his friend John Muir. Sitting around the campfire they listened to stories about Muir's childhood, which were later published in his book *Boyhood and Youth*. Muir also traced for them his theory on Yosemite glaciation that Florence Bailey's father had corresponded with him about more than twenty years earlier.

The pattern that developed in the Baileys' married life was summers spent in the field and winters in Washington, D.C., writing up their field notes. In Florence Bailey's case, these notes resulted in books or magazine articles; her husband's notes for the most part became government documents. Over the course of their forty-plus years together, she published (and contributed chapters to) thirteen books and more than a hundred magazine articles. Throughout her publications on birds she supported the work of the Biological Survey in "economic ornithology," helping farmers identify the insect-eating benefits of bird species.

In his work for the Biological Survey, Vernon Bailey published the official *Fauna* of several Western states, which meant that they spent extensive time in each, surveying the wildlife. This work took them to North Dakota, Texas, New Mexico, and Oregon, with adventures in between as well. Help for ranchers and farmers (the Biological Survey being under the Department of Agriculture) also called her husband to many other areas, and Florence Bailey traveled with him whenever she could, though her health—or book-proofing deadlines—sometimes intervened. She studied the birds; he studied the mammals. They collaborated on a few books, but primarily wrote separately, although in close proximity. At their home in Washington, D.C., they had back-to-back desks in their study, and in the formal dining room they entertained visiting scientists or staff friends from the Biological Survey. In 1942, the Baileys' personal and professional relationship was characterized by Edward Preble in *Nature Magazine* as one which was "governed by the principle of 'working together,' and working for others, whether in natural-history studies, or in any field—social, educational, or humane—that called for cooperative effort."

Handbook of Birds of the Western United States

By 1900 Bailey was deeply involved in her first major writing project, *Handbook of Birds of the Western United States*. She received her brother's special help on this work, for he saw not only the need for such a text, but also her expertise as well as the lack of time for such an endeavor among his own staff at the Biological Survey. When not conducting her observations in the field she spent months studying the bird skins collected in the "cramped but delightful old bird gallery of the Smithsonian" Institution in Washington, as she described it to her Smith classmates. Her book complemented the study on birds of the eastern United States published a half-dozen years earlier by Frank Chapman.

As a handbook, Bailey's followed the pattern of the times in extensive prose descriptions of nesting and food habits, her particular specialty. Birders today—and readers—focus much less on this kind of explication, and field guides have changed accordingly. Gone are the descriptions; in are the color maps of distribution. In its day, her *Handbook* was hailed widely by the knowledgeable press. Her friend Chapman reviewed it in *Bird-Lore* (November–December 1902), calling it "the most complete text-book of regional ornithology which has ever been published." In *Auk* (January 1903), J. A. Allen not only credited it as "thoroughly scientific yet not unduly technical," but acknowledged the author for so bene-

ficially using her "rare opportunities for personal observation of the birds in life." The handbook was referenced in many other bird books of the day, guiding later writers including Roger Tory Peterson, who credited her in early editions of his popular field guides.

Her book also served in the wider context of natural history, gratefully acknowledged by leaders such as William Temple Hornaday of the New York Zoological Society. The *Handbook* went through numerous editions, each greeted with praise for its expansion, as more people became interested in birds and travel to the West became more accessible. Her book also helped to lead more naturalists to the Baileys' door in Washington, D.C., where they continued to entertain the scientific community, alternating that with summers in the field among the winged and four-footed communities.

Bailey's writing about live birds would bring her many accolades, including a formal portrait published in the September 1904 issue of *Condor*, which contained this acknowledgment:

> There are probably few writers who have exerted a more wholesome influence on the trend of popular ornithology than Mrs. Florence Merriam Bailey, whose "Birds Through an Opera Glass" (1889) has been one of the most successful and effective books of its class. Mrs. Bailey has had the advantage of a wide and varied field experience throughout the West, as well as in the eastern states, and her "A-Birding on a Bronco," like all of her works, reflects an intimate acquaintance with the live bird. (p. 137)

Birds of New Mexico

Florence Merriam Bailey's major work, *Birds of New Mexico* (1928), stands today as a monument to her abilities to synthesize and enlarge upon the work of earlier writers. New Mexico is an especially significant state for bird study since, as Bailey points out in her book, birds were first recorded by white men there in 1540, "eighty-two years before the first recorded birds

Florence Merriam Bailey with her husband, Vernon, at the Grand Canyon, 1929

were seen in New England" (p. 1). More than eight hundred pages detail historic accounts of the known birds in the state, starting with reports by the Spanish explorers; no other work on this subject equals hers in scope. In fact, only one other comprehensive book on New Mexico birds has even been attempted. When J. Stokley Ligon published his *New Mexico Birds and Where to Find Them* in 1961, he commented that although Bailey had not been a contemporary of the pioneering ornithologists of the Southwest, she "warrants the title of greatest American woman ornithologist" (p. 11).

In writing her book, Bailey worked from the notes of Dr. Wells W. Cooke, who had died in 1916 before completing a study of New Mexico's birds for the U.S. Biological Survey. She expanded on Cooke's research with "a study of complete range, descriptions of the birds, their nests, eggs and food, together with accounts of their general habits," as she states in the introduction. The artwork throughout the text called on the skills of the best artists of the day. Louis Agassiz Fuertes was commissioned to provide all of the colored plates, but he was killed in an accident after having completed only one of the illustrations. His close friend—and a friend of the Baileys as well—Canadian artist Major Allan Brooks, completed the rest.

When *Birds of New Mexico* came out late in 1928, all of the birding magazines hastened to review it. *Auk* editor Witmer Stone noted its value as the first "adequate ornithology" of a noncoastal state (January 1929). As the *Condor* review (March 1929) pointed out, the book's influence went beyond New Mexico, encompassing birds of the Southwest, most of which were largely unknown before publication of her book. The reviewer, H. S. Swarth, appreciated the thoroughness of Bailey's field work, which allowed "the author to depict in her usual happy vein her reactions to the actual presence and companionship of the birds she loves so well."

Birds of New Mexico earned Bailey election as the first woman fellow of the AOU in 1932, "the highest honor to which an American ornithologist can attain," as Elliott Coues, another fellow of the AOU, had noted. Other women ornithologists were both surprised and delighted by the appointment. "No, man's nature must change before a woman is a Fellow," Althea Sherman had written to Margaret Morse Nice shortly before hearing the news about their coworker.

The same year, the AOU awarded Bailey the coveted Brewster Medal, given biennially for the most important book on birds of the western hemisphere. Not only was she the first woman to receive it, but it was the first time the award went to a book about a particular state. In 1933 she was also awarded an honorary doctorate from the University of New Mexico.

Later Field Studies

In 1918 the Baileys had collaborated on *Wild Animals of Glacier National Park: The Mammals by Vernon Bailey, The Birds by Florence Merriam Bailey*. Commissioned to do a similar publication for the Grand Canyon, the Baileys spent the 1929 field season exploring their beloved Southwest, completing notes of previous excursions. The following summer the Baileys returned to the Grand Canyon for further fieldwork. Florence Bailey enjoyed the simple life in camp, where as she wrote in *Among the Birds in the Grand Canyon Country* (1939), "the sincere uplifted notes of the hermit thrush rang out through the stillness, seeming to interpret the far view in terms of human life—free of all belittling earthly influence, urging a far, serene view of life" (p. 180). This book was Florence Bailey's last. In the introduction, Bailey encouraged her readers as she always had:

> Whatever one's especial or scientific interest may be in the birds of the canyon country, there is much more. In telling the story of our enriching summer, my hope has been not only that old interests be quickened and the pleasures of the way be enhanced but that to those with seeing eyes and listening ears may come the deeper satisfactions underlying bird study in the inspiring setting of the Grand Canyon.

The following excerpt, which provides an example of Bailey's way of "telling the story," is from the Canyon book:

> Behind a row of tent houses, two of which became ours, on a stony mesquite and cactus slope lived a number of those companionable birds of the desert region, the Gambel's quail, which was good to find again. When treated with respect, not intruded upon suddenly, they afforded many a delightful picture as they went about their own pleasant affairs. Close behind our tent house my first Gambel was seen. A handsome cock with black topknot curved forward over his black face, he was walking carefully up the stony slope calling softly *where, where*, and as he crossed a patch of sunshine his rufous cap glowed brightly. Another time, when discovered by his soft call, the rotund father of the family was seen perched on top of a round boulder. Here he made not only a most attractive picture but an enlightening one to the student of protective

coloration, for the contrasting horizontal sections of his color pattern—black face, gray chest, buffy breast, and black belly patch—at a little distance by "secant coloration" cut his bird form disguisingly. On this stony slope, he was sometimes seen picking silently about in the sun under a bare thorn bush. Under the shadow of a leafy mesquite, where his white-streaked rufous side patches doubtless served their own protective purpose, he kept up his conservational *quare, quare,* whether I answered him or not. (p. 25)

As they crossed the country for the last few times, the Baileys took time to visit relatives along the way. A cousin and her family lived in Taos, New Mexico, near the pueblo whose sacred Blue Lake the Baileys had helped in 1903 to protect. One of her grandnieces aspired to a career in writing.

That year for Christmas, she sent her young niece a diary in which to preserve the "beautiful thoughts and eager enthusiasms" she had seen in the girl's eyes. "It would be a pity to lose them. Something suggested by your studies, some fine or heroic trait that appealed to you. . . . You get the idea. Be putting down the foundation for your future stories and books. Live and work with a purpose. And keep in your heart the purpose to make the world sweeter and better and stronger for your having lived" (unpublished letter).

After Vernon Bailey retired from the Biological Survey in 1933, they had a home built next to the homestead land of Florence Bailey's Uncle Gustavus in southern California. Its wide "veranda" was to be a viewing place for the "starry heavens," with a long view of the Merriam Valley her uncle had now planted in grapes. Here she would continue to watch her bird friends "in their homes," while her husband continued to work to develop more humane traps that would minimize the suffering of animals caught in them. These were sold under the name VerBail traps. But within a year the Baileys returned to their longtime home in Washington, D.C., where they spent the rest of their days.

Vernon Bailey died in 1942, the same year as Florence Bailey's beloved brother Hart. She lived quietly until her death on 22 September 1948. An era had ended, and with the end of World War II, a new scientific era of bird study had begun.

Florence Merriam Bailey's reputation in her era was well deserved and respected. Yet, as with so many of our pioneers—not only in the natural sciences—little is known of her today or of the groundbreaking work she did that so many of us have used in times since. Her books are no longer in print, as the scientific approach to birding has become the standard. However, through people like her we can know the difference one person can make, who lives with determination to "uplift" and a passion to bring new light to the world. Throughout her life she retained the mission she had described in the preface to *Birds Through an Opera Glass,* her first book: "it is not merely those who can go to see for themselves I would tell of my walks; it is above all the careworn indoor workers to whom I would bring a breath of the woods, pictures of sunlit fields, and a hint of the simple, childlike gladness, the peace and comfort that is offered us every day by these blessed winged messengers of nature." Her work was her life, and she wrote of birds, not of her own ways. She knew them as friends, and wrote of them with that respect, mirroring the respect for all nature that she had learned so well at home—in the field.

Selected Bibliography

WORKS OF FLORENCE MERRIAM BAILEY

BOOKS

Birds Through an Opera Glass (Boston: Houghton Mifflin, 1890); *My Summer in a Mormon Village* (Boston: Houghton Mifflin, 1894); *A-Birding on a Bronco* (Boston: Houghton Mifflin, 1896); *Birds of Village and Field* (Boston: Houghton Mifflin, 1898); *Handbook of Birds of the Western United States* (Boston: Houghton Mifflin, 1902); *Bird Classes of the Audubon Society of the District of Columbia, 1898–1912* (Washington, D.C., ASDC, 1912); *Wild Animals of Glacier National Park: The Mammals by Vernon Bailey, The Birds by Florence Merriam Bailey* (Washington, D.C.: Government Printing Office,

1918); *Bird Classes of the Audubon Society of the District of Columbia, 1913–1922* (Washington, D.C.: ASDC, 1922); *Birds Recorded from the Santa Rita Mountains in Southern Arizona* (Berkeley, Calif.: Cooper Ornithological Club, 1923); *Birds of New Mexico* (Santa Fe, N.Mex.: New Mexico Department of Game and Fish, 1928); *Among the Birds of the Grand Canyon Country* (Washington, D.C.: Government Printing Office, 1939).

CONTRIBUTIONS

Biographical Sketches, in Frank M. Chapman, *Handbook of Birds of Eastern North America* (1895) pp. 245, 304, 314, 317, 324, 382; "Birds," in Vernon Bailey, *Cave Life of Kentucky Mainly in the Mammoth Cave Region* (Notre Dame, Ind.: Notre Dame Univ. Press, 1933).

SELECTED ARTICLES

"Our Smith College Audubon Society," in *Audubon Magazine* 1 (1887), signed "From Behind the Scenes"; "Orie," in *St. Nicholas* 17 (June 1890); "How Birds Affect the Farm and Garden," in *Forest and Stream* 47 (8, 15, 22 August 1896); "Notes on Some of the Birds of Southern California," in *Auk* 13 (April 1896); "A True Observer (Mrs. Olive Thorne Miller)," in *Observer* 7 (1896); "How Our Birds Protect Our Trees," in *Arbor Day Annual* (New York State Department of Public Education, 6 May 1898); Report in William Dutcher, "Report of Committee on Bird Protection," in *Auk* 15 (January 1898); "Bird Study," in *Chautauquan* (Chautauqua Literary and Scientific Circle Round Table, 1900), ch. 30, ch. 31; "How to Conduct Field Classes," in *Bird-Lore* 2 (June 1900); "Meeting Spring Half Way," in *Condor* 18 (July 1916, September 1916, November 1916); "Koo," in *Bird-Lore* 24 (September/October 1922); "Red Willow People of the Pueblos," in *Travel* 45 (September 1925).

UNPUBLISHED LETTERS AND PAPERS

Florence Merriam Bailey Papers (82/46), in Bancroft Library, University of California at Berkeley; Letters, Class of 1886, 1886–1947, in Smith College, Northampton, Mass.; "Pages from the Merriam Family History for the Children of Lyman Lyon Merriam," Merriam family private collection.

BIOGRAPHICAL AND CRITICAL STUDIES

Marianne Ainley, "The Involvement of Women in the American Ornithologists' Union," in Keir B. Sterling and M. G. Ainley, *A History of the American Ornithologists Union* (in press); J. A. Allen, "Mrs. Bailey's 'Handbook of Birds of the Western United States,'" in *Auk* (January 1903); Paul Brooks, "Birds and Women," in *Audubon* (September 1980), and *Speaking for Nature* (Boston: Houghton Mifflin, 1980); Frank Chapman, "Handbook of Birds of the Western United States," review in *Bird-Lore* (November/December 1902); "Florence Merriam Bailey," *Town and Country Life* (n.p., c. 1930s); Henry Wetherbee Henshaw, "Autobiographical Notes," in *Condor* (March 1920); Elizabeth Horner and Keir B. Sterling, "Feathers and Feminism in the Eighties," in *Smith College Alumnae Quarterly* (April 1975); Harriet Kofalk, *No Woman Tenderfoot: Florence Merriam Bailey, Pioneer Naturalist* (College Station, Tex. A&M Univ. Press, 1989), as Harriet Kimbro, "The Birds and Bees in Twin Oaks: Visit of a Naturalist in 1889," in *Journal of San Diego History* (spring 1985), and "Roger Tory Peterson and Florence Merriam Bailey," in *Bird Watcher's Digest* (July/August 1984); J. Stokley Ligon, *New Mexico Birds and Where to Find Them* (Albuquerque, N.Mex.: Univ. of New Mexico Press, 1961); Olive Thorne Miller, "Popular vs. Scientific Ornithology" (letter to editor responding to William Brewster's "Two Corrections," October, 1893), in *Auk* (January 1894); Obituary (of Florence Merriam Bailey), in *Audubon Magazine* (January/February 1949); Paul H. Oehser, "Florence Augusta Merriam Bailey," in *Notable American Women*, ed. by Edward T. James (Cambridge, Mass.: Harvard Univ. Press, 1971), "In Memoriam: Florence Merriam Bailey," in *Auk* (January 1952); "Florence Merriam Bailey: Friend of Birds," in *Nature Magazine* (March 1950); "Official Circular No. 12," *Memorabilia of Smith College, 1874–1888* (Northampton, Mass.: Smith College, October 1985); Robert Ridgway, *The Hummingbirds* (Washington, D.C.: Smithsonian Institution, 1892); Margaret W. Rossiter, *Women Scientists in America* (Baltimore, Md.: Johns Hopkins Univ. Press, 1982); Althea Sherman, letter to Margaret Morse Nice, 30 May 1932 (Margaret Morse Nice Papers, Archives of the Cornell University Libraries); Keir B. Sterling, *Last of the Naturalists: The Career of C. Hart Merriam* (New York: Arno, 1977); Witmer Stone, "Mrs. Bailey's 'Birds of New Mexico,'" in *Auk* (January 1929); Deborah Strom, ed., *Birdwatching with American Women* (New York: W. W. Norton, 1986); H. S. Swarth, "The Birds of New Mexico," review in *Condor* (March 1929); Robert Henry Welker, *Birds and Men: American Birds in Science, Art, Literature, and Conservation, 1800–1900* (Cambridge, Mass.: Harvard Univ. Press, 1955); Howard Zahniser, "In August, Florence Merriam Bailey," in *Nature Magazine* (August 1936).

WILLIAM BARTRAM
(1739–1823)

PHILIP G. TERRIE

WILLIAM BARTRAM SPENT four years (1773–1777) wandering through the wild and sparsely settled territory of southeastern North America. His travels in Florida, Georgia, and South Carolina and his more distant forays into southern Appalachia and west to the Mississippi resulted in one of the earliest accounts in English of a beautiful, richly endowed land and its native peoples. First published in 1791, Bartram's *Travels* constitutes, suggested N. Bryllion Fagin, an early biographer of Bartram, the "first genuine and artistic interpretation of the American landscape" (p. 10).

More than a nature book, the *Travels* is a lyrical statement of intense personal religious faith, an important examination of the customs and travails of American Indians, and a defense of Indian rights against the predations of corrupt white traders and land-hungry settlers. With an eye sensitive to the details of both nature and human societies, Bartram left an invaluable record of the wilderness and people of the Southeast. The significance of Bartram's work was quickly recognized: reprints in England and Ireland and translations in German, Dutch, and French fed the European appetite for depictions of the American wilderness. It was an inspiration to Wordsworth and Chateaubriand, and Coleridge declared it "a work of high merit every way," while the English philosopher Thomas Carlyle wrote to Ralph Waldo Emerson to rec-

ommend it, asking, "Do you know Bartram's 'Travels'? Treats of Florida chiefly, has a wonderful kind of floundering eloquence in it; and has grown immeasurably old. All American libraries ought to provide theselves with that kind of book" (as quoted by Mark Van Doren in his edition of *The Travels of William Bartram*, 1928). Its literary quality and far-ranging scope have established the *Travels* as one of the most important books written by an American in the eighteenth century. In the *Columbia Literary History of the United States*, William Hedges praised it as "the most astounding verbal artifact of the early republic" (p. 190).

Bartram's discipline was what the eighteenth century called natural history, a broad domain that included the modern sciences of geology, botany, and zoology. It was devoted to examining, collecting, and cataloging the observable data of the physical world. In the areas of botany and zoology the preeminent figure was the Swedish naturalist Carolus Linnaeus, who established the system of classification by genus and species that is still used today.

Before Bartram, no American had written about nature in a spirit of appreciation combined with sensitive, close observation. Various European-American writers, engaged in exploration, surveying, or speculation, had composed descriptions of the North American landscape, and Puritans dragged unwillingly into the wilderness

William Bartram

preciatively cataloged the plants and animals he encountered there. He was eager to find classifiable, familiar patterns in his surroundings and ever hopeful of making useful discoveries in the wilderness. Bartram's attitudes toward nature straddled the watershed between the Enlightenment and romanticism and displayed elements of both. From the Enlightenment, Bartram absorbed a predisposition for the orderly, symmetrical, and coherent: the best index of his inclination to see nature as rationally organized is his enthusiastic subscription to the Linnean system of taxonomy with its rigidly hierarchical classification scheme. To Bartram and other scientists of his day, the systematic organization of nature reflected the supreme rationality of the deity behind it. To these ideas about the divine orderliness of nature Bartram added an emotional and warm appreciation. Bartram's nature, like that of the Romantics of the next generation, was itself vibrant with divinity, feeling, and spirituality.

John Seelye has noted that William Bartram's response to nature is a departure from that of the previous generation, which had been relentlessly utilitarian in its approach. While Bartram did indeed see the landscape as exploitable, he is a paradigmatic figure, illustrating the emergence of proto-Romantic values and responses from the often mechanical register of the Enlightenment. In all its effervescence, the *Travels*, along with such representative works as Crèvecoeur's *Letters from an American Farmer*, falls into the mode Seelye labels the "hyperpastoral," combining the emphasis on close observation characteristic of the Enlightenment with the idealistic lyricism of the early Romantics.

by Indian captors had offered accounts of the dense forests of New England. Thus while the natural environment had been written about in one way or another from the onset of European contact with the New World, it may fairly be said that American nature writing as a distinct genre began with Bartram.

Always enthusiastic about the abundance of the natural world, Bartram studiously and ap-

Life

The son of Philadelphia botanist John Bartram (1699–1777) and Ann Mendenhall, William was born on 9 February 1739. His father had been an orphan with few opportunities who had forged his own way. John Bartram educated himself in Latin, science, and mathematics and in 1730 founded a botanical garden, the first in America, at his home on the Schuylkill River at Kingsessing, Pennsylvania, near Philadelphia. From there he profitably sold seeds for American plants to an eager English market; he became known as the "king's botanist." Both a merchant and a scholar, he carried on a busy correspondence with notable continental scientists such as Linnaeus, who identified him as "the greatest natural botanist in the world," and with the Englishman Peter Collinson, who collected exotic plants for his vast gardens in Surrey. John Bartram supplied Collinson with seeds and cuttings for over three decades. Along with Benjamin Franklin, John Bartram was part of a group of American intellectuals who established the American Philosophical Society.

By the time of William's birth, the Bartram household was a place where the educated elite of the day, including Franklin, called to visit. Raised a Quaker, William Bartram learned Greek and Latin at the Philadelphia Academy (which later became the University of Pennsylvania). There his teacher of classical languages was Charles Thomson, an early advocate of Indian rights.

Not inclined to adopt the life of a leisured gentleman, Bartram considered printing, engraving, surveying, and trade. But botany was his love, though the opportunities for making a living as a collector and systematizer of plants were limited. As his father wrote to Collinson about William's interests: "Botany and drawing are his . . . delight; am afraid he can't settle to any business else" (quoted in Meyers, p. 12). William accompanied his father on a trip into the Catskills when he was fourteen, and, after a time of trying his hand at trade, acted as his father's assistant on a royally subsidized expedition to the wilderness of Florida in 1765–1766. Here William first encountered the country, including the wild St. Johns River, that he later described so eloquently in his *Travels*.

Before undertaking his own expedition, however, William endured several years of financial uncertainty, from which he was rescued by the intervention of the English Quaker John Fothergill, an associate of John Bartram's. Fothergill had seen some of William's botanical drawings

and agreed to underwrite further explorations in Florida. A physician with a lucrative London practice, Fothergill had laid out extensive gardens on his estate in Essex, where he cultivated rare plants gathered from around the world. He employed Bartram to search out interesting and useful plants, particularly those that might survive transplanting to England. Thus began the sponsorship that would lead to the *Travels*.

The *Travels* was Bartram's only book, and the expedition it recounted was never replicated. After returning to Philadelphia from the Southeast, Bartram lived peacefully around the city, where he worked on converting his field notes into a publishable manuscript and where he and his brother John ran a nursery on the site of the botanical garden begun by their father. After the *Travels* was published, in 1791, it sold well in Europe and attracted a healthy readership among American intellectuals. The *Travels* established Bartram as a leading authority on botanical and ornithological matters, and his opinions were often sought by contemporary scientists. Thomas Jefferson offered him a position on the Lewis and Clark expedition to the Pacific Northwest, but he preferred to stay near home.

One reason Bartram elected to live quietly in Philadelphia was declining health. On his travels he contracted a fever in Alabama, and this appeared later to have affected his eyesight and to have weakened his constitution. Throughout the first two decades of the nineteenth century, he continued to work and study on the family property. On 22 July 1823 he died suddenly while walking in his garden.

Travels

"At the request of Dr. Fothergill, of London, to search the Floridas, and the Western parts of Carolina and Georgia, for the discovery of rare and useful productions of nature, chiefly in the vegetable kingdom; in April, 1773, I embarked for Charleston, South Carolina" (p. 29).[1] The opening of Bartram's *Travels* describes the first

---

1. All quotations from Bartram are from the 1988 edition of the *Travels*, published by Viking Penguin.

leg of a journey that would cover thousands of miles—including six thousand by horseback and many hundreds by small sailboat or canoe—comprising nearly four years of travel in Georgia, Florida, the Carolinas, Alabama, and Louisiana. During these years Bartram spent many weeks alone in the wilderness, ranged as far west as the Mississippi River, encountered a variety of Native Americans, investigated alligators and other exotic forms of wildlife, and explored parts of the Southeast unknown to all but a handful of whites.

Most early commentators emphasized, as had Carlyle, the joy with which Bartram embraced the wilderness. Mark Van Doren was struck by Bartram's "gentle and passionate love of nature," while Hans Huth found his devotion "unrestrained." Donald Worster wrote that Bartram "shared [Linnaeus'] love of the Creator's handiwork" as revealed in nature, and Roderick Nash similarly remarked that Bartram's appreciation of the sublime reflected a "love of the wild." David Rains Wallace, a late-twentieth-century nature writer, was drawn to Bartram's delight in the wilderness and partly modeled his own book about the Florida environment, *Bulow Hammock* (1988), on Bartram's *Travels*. The figure of Bartram "wandering in a sort of rapture, as though in an earthly paradise" struck Wallace as emblematic of the appreciation elicited by the lush landscape of Florida before it was changed forever by suburbs and shopping malls.

But other critics discerned, in addition to Bartram's genuine appreciation for the beauty and bounty of nature, a pervasive anxiety about nature's unpredictability and violence. Amy R. Weinstein Meyers remarked in a 1985 dissertation that Bartram was capable of presenting a "grim picture of Creation," while Douglas Anderson noted that Bartram's use of metaphors of warfare in describing nature is suggestive of his anxiety about the human world.

In fact, Bartram describes a wilderness that is at one moment serene and inviting, at the next, violent and inhospitable. Bartram's benign and orderly world can quickly become chaotic and threatening. This alternating view of nature develops in the context of Bartram's profound skepticism concerning the character of human affairs, and reflects a projection of Bartram's anxieties about human nature and human history onto the natural world.

While Bartram's picture of nature does indeed become hellish at times, his account of day-to-day life in the wilderness is richly appreciative and amazingly diverse. Consider, for example, the variety of his activities and interests during a few characteristic days in August of 1777 (pp. 324–330), when he was exploring the rivers and lowlands near the Gulf coast village of Mobile. Paddling a light canoe, he set off up the Pearl River, where he spotted "artificial mounds of earth and other ruins" indicating "the site of an ancient town of a tribe of Indians." As always, he was on the lookout for "curious vegetable productions," and was therefore pleased to identify a certain species of shrub (called by him *Myrica inodora*); this "beautiful evergreen" particularly interested him because the French settlers of the area made long-lasting candles from its waxy berries and Bartram was ever concerned with the utilitarian features of the natural world. A few days later he "was struck with surprize [sic] at the appearance of a blooming plant, gilded with the richest golden yellow: stepping on shore, I discovered it to be a new species of the Oenothera . . . perhaps the most pompous and brilliant herbaceous plant yet known to exist"; along with a lengthy technical Latinate description, he added that it formed "a pyramid in figure."

Passing vestiges of "ancient French plantations," he encountered "Canes and Cypress trees of an astonishing magnitude" and "stately columns of the Magnolia grandiflora." Awed by the grandeur of the forest, he exclaimed, "What a sylvan scene is here! the pompous Magnolia reigns sovereign of the forests; how sweet the aromatic Illicum groves! how gaily flutter the radiated wings of the Magnolia auriculata, each branch supporting an expanded umbrella, superbly crested with a silver plume, fragrant blossom, or crimson studded strobile and fruits!" After spying alligators sunning on the shore and swimming, he spent a peaceful night. The next morning, ascending the Tombigbe River, he

66

noticed extensive specimens of a lovely yellow flower, the "seed vessel" of which provided "sweet and pleasant eating." Bartram "fed freely on them without any injury, but found them laxative." After remarking on the fertility of the soil and the abundant, enormous trees, he found a "well cultivated plantation" where he spent the night. On the following day, he was discomfited by a fever, but a search for a local plant known for "extraordinary medical virtues" proved successful; this plant, a "diuretic and carminative, and esteemed a powerful febrifuge," appeared to cure Bartram, allowing him to continue his explorations, from which he returned to Mobile "fully satisfied with the day's excursion, from the discovery of many curious and beautiful vegetables."

This account illustrates the delight with which Bartram responded to so much of nature. Usually traveling alone, Bartram experienced profound isolation in the primeval forest. On many occasions, he expresses awe at the glories of raw nature. Outside the village of Wrightsborough, Georgia, for example, he encountered an untouched stand of huge oaks, the "most magnificent forest I had ever seen." Here were ancient giants with breast-height diameters of ten or eleven feet. "To keep within the bounds of truth and reality, in describing the magnitude and grandeur of these trees, would, I fear, fail of credibility" (p. 56). As a literate eighteenth-century traveler, moreover, he keenly appreciated what that age called the sublime, which, in terms of landscape, usually involved rough, precipitous mountainous terrain that underscored human insignificance compared with the omnipotence of God. In the rugged territory of Appalachia, reaching a high promontory, Bartram beheld "with rapture and astonishment a sublimely awful scene of power and magnificence, a world of mountains piled upon mountains . . . [an] amazing prospect of grandeur" (p. 293).

Just as sublimity is seen as manifesting God's omnipotence, all of nature is taken to be evidence of God's handiwork and design. "This world," Bartram wrote in his introduction, "as a glorious apartment of the boundless palace of the sovereign Creator, is furnished with an infinite variety of animated scenes, inexpressibly beautiful and pleasing, equally free to the inspection and enjoyment of all his creatures" (p. 15). The *Travels* is full of similar statements of Bartram's conviction that the perfection of nature demonstrates the existence, benevolence, and omniscience of the deity behind it: "O thou Creator supreme, almighty! how infinite and incomprehensible thy works! most perfect, and every way astonishing!" (p. 72). The various plants and trees, he declared, "excite love, gratitude, and adoration to the great Creator, who was pleased to endow them with such eminent qualities, and reveal them to us for our sustenance, amusement, and delight." The animal world, too, "excites our admiration, and equally manifests the almighty power, wisdom, and beneficence of the Supreme Creator and Sovereign Lord of the universe" (pp. 20–21).

Bartram's nature displays a wonderfully complex precision. One evening on the St. John's River he encountered millions of tiny insects he called "Ephemera," which are "delicious food for birds, frogs, and fish." Watching fish and other creatures feeding on these insects (devoured while the insects are mating), Bartram meditated on their incredible numbers and the complexity of nature and the food chain: the insects, "whose frame and organization are equally wonderful, more delicate, and perhaps as complicated as those of the most perfect human being," seemed "created merely for the food of fish and other animals" (pp. 88–89). The insects themselves were viewed as marvelous creations; their place in what we would now see as the ecological dynamic equally marvelous.

In his routine insistence that nature reflects the divinity behind it, Bartram usually discovered a landscape that fit his age's sense of the divine. He imposed a sense of the symmetrical, orderly, and mechanical on the natural world, in keeping with his belief in a rational plan underlying all creation. In discussing the arrangement and variety of the animal kingdom, he declared "how wonderful is the mechanism of these finely formed self-moving beings, how complicated their system, yet what unerring uniformity prevails through every tribe and particular species!"

(p. 21). The machine metaphor especially suited his need to see nature rationally organized and constructed. He compared the intricacy of nature to the "mechanism of a watch" and repeated his awe at how "beautiful [and] harmonious" was the working of these "inimitable machines" (p. 21). Later, describing the beauty of a Florida dawn, he combined organic and mechanical imagery: "At the return of the mornings by the powerful influence of light, the pulse of nature becomes active, and the universal vibration of life insensibly and irresistibly moves the wondrous machine" (p. 159).

But most of Bartram's paeans employ the vocabulary of utility. Bartram shared the characteristically eighteenth-century assumption that the earth and its creatures were designed to serve mankind. His travels, research, and reflections consistently reveal his conviction that nature—however lovely in its unaltered state—exists to be used and that his own mission in discovering and describing nature was to hasten the process of exploitation: "My chief happiness consisted in tracing and admiring the infinite power, majesty, and perfection of the great Almighty Creator, and in the contemplation, that through divine aid and permission, I might be instrumental in discovering, and introducing into my native country, some original productions of nature, which might become useful to society" (p. 82).

Like many other eighteenth-century commentators on the function of nature, Bartram often extended his utilitarianism to classifying and valuing land in terms of its agricultural potential. He returned repeatedly to speculations on the fertility of the soil. He described the cane swamps outside Savannah, for example, as "incredibly fertile" (p. 60), and at a small lake on the St. Johns he mused on the "high ridges fit for the culture of corn, indigo, cotton, bananas, &c. and of low swamps and marshes, which when properly drained and tilled, would be suitable for rice" (p. 134). Bartram's subscription to the popular notion that all land should be judged in terms of its usefulness to man located him squarely in the physiocratic tradition of Thomas Jefferson and Crèvecoeur, to whom the "middle

landscape," that area neither urban nor completely wild, constituted the ideal. The urban environment, believed Jefferson and many of his fellow Americans, was corrupt with excessive civilization, overcrowding, and pollution, while the untouched wilderness lacked the charm added by cultivation or other putatively benign improvements. Despite his obvious affection for the uncultivated wilderness, Bartram found it deficient compared with the georgic charms of the farmscape that might replace it. Inspired by the potential of a plain in west Florida, he contemplated what improvements hardworking yeomen might effect:

This vast plain, together with the forests contiguous to it, if permitted (by the Siminoles [sic] who are sovereigns of these realms) to be in possession and under the culture of industrious planters and mechanics, would in a little time exhibit other scenes than it does at present, delightful as it is; for by the arts of agriculture and commerce, almost every desirable thing in life might be produced and made plentiful here, and thereby establish a rich, populous, and delightful region; as this soil and climate appears to be of a nature favourable for the production of almost all the fruits of the earth. (p. 199)

This preference for the middle landscape over the wilderness is but one illustration of how Bartram's appreciation for nature is not exactly the unqualified embrace that earlier critics found. When we consider how Bartram's account of the actual wilderness encountered is full of predation, unpredictability, and obvious threats to his existence, we begin to see that his encomia to nature as evidence of divine perfection are often little more than formulaic invocations of eighteenth-century convention. Bartram's wilderness is not a consistently benign place, despite his occasionally boilerplate declarations to the contrary.

One way that Bartram tried to resolve the conflicting pulls on his response to wilderness was in his repeated and routine employment of classical imagery. To be sure, when Bartram described the wilderness as an Elysium or a paradise, he was honestly searching for some way to express his genuine sense of awe or appreciation. Of an isolated campsite on the St. Johns River he wrote, "How happily situated is this retired spot of earth! What an elysium it is!" (p. 107). Passing another attractive spot on the same river he determined "not to pass this Elysium without a visit" (p. 135). In a particularly striking example Bartram described his encounter with a group of young Cherokee women in the mountains near what would become the North Carolina–Tennessee line; the "young, innocent Cherokee virgins" were "hamadryades," "sylvan nymphs," and Bartram longingly admitted that the entire episode suggested "Elysian fields" (pp. 289–290).

While Bartram sincerely wanted to believe that nature was indeed the paradise of classical mythology, his own experience often suggested otherwise. One important hint of this is the way his accounts of bliss in the wilderness are nearly always shattered by sudden disruptions. Early in his travels, for example, Bartram, having ridden past the line of white settlement, expressed feeling at peace with his solitude and the wilderness around him:

> It was drawing on towards the close of day, the skies serene and calm, the air temperately cool, and gentle zephyrs breathing through the fragrant pines; the prospect around enchantingly varied and beautiful; endless green savannas, chequered with coppices of fragrant shrubs, filled the air with the richest perfume. . . . Nature seemed silent, and nothing appeared to ruffle the happy moments of evening contemplation." (p. 44)

But then the sudden appearance of an armed and apparently hostile Indian is described. The blissful moment evaporates, and Bartram's communion with nature turns into fear for his life. Bartram manages to avoid harm, though he later learns that this Indian has a reputation for violence, has been shunned by his own relatives, and had been heard to say earlier that day that he would "kill the first white man he met." After the Indian and Bartram part, Bartram finds himself in the midst of what he explicitly labeled a "dreary wilderness." The character of nature, in other words, depends on the psychological circumstances of the perceiver.

The pattern of peace followed by violence, which is in turn followed by peace, recurs through Bartram's *Travels*. Typically, an event of violence or disruption or danger is resolved or succeeded by a respite of calm. Bartram established this pattern early on in the narrative: on a ship to Charleston he observed how "sublime, awful, and majestic [were] the seas themselves, in a tempest" and how equally sublime was the "encircling horizon, after the turbulent winds have taken their flight, and the lately agitated bosom of the deep has again become calm and pacific" (p. 30). Many similar scenes are described in the *Travels*; thunderstorms and other dramatic events often give way to irenic resolution.

Shortly after setting out on his land explorations, he tells of a violent thunderstorm: "the tempest, the fulgour and rapidity of the streams of lightning, passing from cloud to cloud, and from the clouds to the earth, exhibited a very awful scene." He saw a large pine tree set afire by lightning. But soon, "the tempest being over . . . the air was now cool and salubrious" (p. 39). On another occasion he reveals with particular clarity the anxiety with which he responded to natural disruptions in his description of a wild storm and its end: "All seemed a frightful chaos. When the wind and rain abated, I was overjoyed to see the face of nature again appear" (p. 133) — as if the storm were somehow an aberration.

Bartram's decided insecurity about human affairs and human nature chiefly determined his response to and account of physical nature, the actual wilderness of forest and swamp, alligators and fish. The connection in Bartram's mind between the human realm and the natural environment is clear in the way he routinely anthropomorphized nature, bestowing all sorts of human characteristics on plants and animals. We see a persistent urge to present nature as intelligible on the basis of certain analogies with human affairs. In a typically florid passage, he insists that "birds are in general social and benevolent creatures; intelligent, ingenious, volatile, active beings." He pursues this line, claiming that birdsong is "performed only by the males, about the time of incubation, in part to divert and amuse the female, entertaining her with melody, &c. This harmony, with the tender solicitude of the male, alleviates the toils, cares, and distress of the female, consoles her in solitary retirement whilst sitting, and animates her with affection and attachment to himself in preference to any other" (p. 25). Later he recalls listening gratefully to the "divine hymns of the feathered songsters of the grove." This sort of anthropomorphism illustrates Bartram's tendency to attribute to nonhuman creatures the kind of behavior he wishes obtained in the human world.

In his descriptions of nature as fearfully predatory, he imposed a different mode of anthropomorphism. Early in the *Travels* Bartram constructed an elaborate metaphor comparing a carnivorous spider with a human hunter: "This cunning intrepid hunter conducted his subtle approaches with the circumspection and perseverance of a Siminole when hunting a deer"; he described the spider catching and eating a bumblebee in great detail and noted dispassionately that "perhaps before night, [the spider] became himself the delicious evening repast of a bird or lizard" (pp. 24–25). Nature is an eat-and-be-eaten place. Bartram's interest here is more or less that of neutral observation, an admiration of nature's economy, but it is telling, particularly in the eighteenth-century context, that he chose to make explicit the similarity between the human hunter and the spider.

On another occasion Bartram described an occasion when he and a companion spent a few moments in rapt study of a similarly predatory scene. On the bed of a small, calm creek, they spotted "a number of gravelly pyramidal hills . . . constructed by a species of small crayfish." These mounds were the "citadel or place of retreat" where the crayfish found escape from the "attacks and ravages of their enemy," a certain species of fish. Between the crayfish and their foes "the war seemed to be continual," the predators usually on the attack except when "small detachments of veteran cray-fish sallied out upon them," whereupon "a brilliant fight ensued" (p. 61). As with the description of the spider, Bartram is drawn both to the violence in nature and to the use of anthropomorphic rhetoric to convey his response to it. Later in western Florida, he wonders at the fish in the Little St. Juan River (now called the Suwannee); in some spots they seemed at peace, while at others he saw "eternal war, or rather slaughter." How, he asked himself, do they manage, even sporadically, to control their predatory impulses? "Do they agree on a truce, a suspension of hostilities?" (p. 195).

Yet another account of piscine life viewed from above provides a useful gloss on the scene of crayfish and their "enemies." One of the passages of the *Travels* that has struck nearly every reader and that was the inspiration for a passage in Coleridge's "Kubla Khan" describes a remarkable spring or fountain feeding into Lake George. This "inchanting [*sic*] and amazing crystal fountain" bubbles up from deep caverns and spews out "tons of water every minute." In the perfectly transparent waters of this remarkable fountain lived many species of fish which, incredibly, manifested "no signs of enmity, no attempt to devour each other." But on further inspection what seemed to be a "paradise of fish," exhibiting "a just representation of the peaceful and happy state of nature which existed before the fall, yet in reality . . . is a mere representation" (pp. 149–151). These fish, Bartram concluded, are just like all other fish. They are predatory and carnivorous, but the conditions in the spring are such that to the passing observer, their subtle stratagems can go undetected. This fountain, too, Bartram calls "Elysian," indicating how illusory is the notion of paradise in a postlapsarian world.

The question of whether animals—including birds, fish, reptiles, and mammals—are "at war" with one another is one to which Bartram returned obsessively. The specter of conflict haunted him. He insisted endlessly, as with the "social and benevolent birds," that wild creatures live in "harmony"—because he so wanted to think they do. But he just as often discovered animals "at war" with one another, as he imposed his fears about the human tendency toward violence on the natural events of predation and survival.

Behind all of Bartram's eloquent descriptions of the wilderness and his undeniably marvelous adventures in it is his unstated fear that the world is fallen, shown especially in his frequent return to two persistent issues. First is the ubiquitous evidence of human failure and transience that Bartram found in numerous ancient Indian ruins, monuments, abandoned fields, and other indications of vanished civilizations. Coupled with the occasional vestige of failed European plantations, these sites of former Indian occupation served to remind Bartram of the transience and unpredictability of human accomplishments. This is a common eighteenth- and nineteenth-century preoccupation, of course, epitomized perhaps by Shelley's "Ozymandias."

A second theme coloring Bartram's narrative of adventures in the wilderness is the constant threat of hostilities breaking out between whites and Indians. Bartram's refusal to blame all such conflicts on Indians and his willingness to accept the Indians as human beings similar to whites in all important respects is refreshing. But it is important to note that he saw the Indians as no better than whites; while he insisted that Indians were not the bloodthirsty savages of popular stereotypes, he also admitted that they could be as warlike as whites and for the same reasons. The possibility that an Indian war is about to occur lurks on nearly every page of the *Travels*, as Bartram routinely checks with local authorities on current Indian relations. The omnipresent specter of human conflict provides the background of Bartram's explorations of the physical world. By emphasizing warfare and other difficulties with Indians, Bartram continually suggests how volatile and even chaotic are human nature and human affairs.

Bartram encountered Indian ruins early on in his travels. Along the Alatamaha River in Georgia, only a few days into his journey, he came upon "evident vestiges of an ancient Indian town . . . old extensive fields, and conical mounds,

or artificial heaps of earth" (p. 41). Near Augusta, he found "many very magnificent monuments of the power and industry of the ancient inhabitants of these lands." A "conical pyramid," "vast tetragon terraces," and "a large sunken area, of a cubical form" were all "traces of a larger Indian town, the work of a powerful nation, whose period of grandeur perhaps long preceded the discovery of this continent" (pp. 56–57). Similar encounters occur throughout the *Travels*. Nor were the ruins all Indian; on more than one occasion he describes the ravaged site of an abandoned English or French plantation. On St. Simon Island he found extensive traces of a failed English settlement: "A very large part of the island had formerly been cleared and planted by the English, as appeared evidently to me, by vestiges of plantations, ruins of costly buildings, highways, &c. but it is now overgrown with forests" (p. 73). That overgrowth of forest reminded him of the fragility and transience of human achievements.

More important than the signs of human failure are those of human malice. The inevitably violent, cruel, even evil inner nature of his fellow humans—and by logical extension, perhaps, of himself—troubled Bartram profoundly, even though he was reluctant to confront openly his implicit fears. At times he tried to excuse apparently vicious behavior by invoking the explanation of acculturation. When one of his temporary traveling companions kills a female bear and is about to kill its cub, Bartram regrets his participation in what seems a crime: "I was moved with compassion, and charging myself as if accessory to what now appeared to be a cruel murder, endeavored to prevail on the hunter to save its life, but to no effect! for by habit he had become insensible to compassion toward the brute creation" (p. 22).

Mostly Bartram feared warfare between whites and Indians. This possibility continually arises in the narrative but is nearly always averted by a fortuitously reached treaty or other understanding. At one point, when describing the resolution of a conflict that threatened to prevent him from exploring west of Augusta, Georgia, he wrote hopefully, "The treaty concluded in unanimity,

AMERICAN NATURE WRITERS

peace, and good order" (p. 54). "Peace" and "order" are precisely what Bartram most wanted to believe are the controlling forces in both nature and human history. But his narrative suggests their elusiveness. After a particularly fulsome account of the peaceful ways of the Cherokee has led him to label their valley "Elysian fields," he shatters the mood with mention of the conflict between the "Overhill Indians" and some Virginia settlers who had abused them—another potential war in need of a diplomatic solution.

Treaties, anticipated rhetorically by the peaceful outcome of the encounter with the armed Indian described at the beginning of the *Travels*, are the precise human parallel for the calm following thunderstorms and other natural disruptions contained in the narrative. Bartram explicitly noted the parallel between natural and human events after the recounting of one of the many storms that punctuate his narrative. "The tempest now relaxed, its impetus being spent, and a calm serenity gradually took place"; as he watched the sky brighten and the waves on the river subside, Bartram insisted that human history, though equally interrupted by periods of violence and strife, always returns to an ostensibly normal state of harmony and that this pattern reflects the benevolence of God. "So is it with the varied and mutable scenes of human events on the stream of life." Do not despair, he declared, but "wait and rely on our God, who in due time will shine forth in brightness [and] dissipate the envious cloud" (pp. 66–67). The adjective "envious" used to describe a cloud emphasizes Bartram's sense of the source of human conflict, his need to explain natural phenomena in anthropomorphic terms, and his hope that peaceful resolutions of natural crises mirror what can occur in the human realm.

Burdened by doubts about the capacity of his own species to live in harmony, Bartram, like many a twentieth-century backpacker, responded appreciatively to the absence of civilized vices in the wilderness. Along the St. Johns, he gloried in the fact that he was "under no controul [sic], but what reason and ordinate passions dictate, far removed from the seats of strife" (p. 110). He located the absence of reason, the triumph of unbridled passion, and every manifestation of strife, in the city, the place where human beings congregate. He goes on to insist that he and his companions enjoyed a "situation . . . like that of the primitive state of man, peaceful, contented and sociable. The simple and necessary calls of nature being satisfied, we were altogether as brethren of one family, strangers to envy, malice, and rapine" (p. 110). As we might expect, Bartram found that certain Indians, especially those uncorrupted by whites, also lived in a state of prelapsarian harmony. Among the Cherokees of western Carolina he found "divine simplicity and truth, friendship without fallacy or guile, hospitality disinterested, native, undefiled, unmodified [sic] by artificial refinements!" (p. 284). But this condition is understood to be fragile; Bartram was only too aware that most traders cheated the Indians with whom they dealt and that warfare almost inevitably resulted.

The suggestion that overcivilization leads to corruption and savagery while a life close to nature breeds wholesome independence and virtue was an eighteenth-century commonplace, of course, and Bartram's subscription to this conviction should come as no surprise. The point here is to see how Bartram's doubts about human nature colored his responses to the wilderness. Studies have questioned the conventional depiction of the Enlightenment as an era of unmitigated optimism, democracy, rationalism, and progress. Robert A. Ferguson has argued that one of the chief characteristics of the Enlightenment was the quest to dominate external nature while simultaneously repressing an ambiguous and possibly threatening inner nature. One episode in the *Travels* illustrates especially well how this paradigm of conquest and repression functions and how it accounts for some of Bartram's most interesting descriptions of nature.

Among the most often anthologized parts of the *Travels* is a fascinating and exciting encounter with alligators on the St. Johns River. Sailing up the river, Bartram, aware that he is entering territory populated by alligators, fears their "subtle attacks"; in the river, teal are eaten by the "voracious trout; and he, in turn, as often by the subtle greedy alligator." The combat of alligators is described with language Bartram could just as easily apply to a description of warfare between members of his own species: here, tails instead of swords are "brandished," and the action is "horrid," "dreadful," the victor of the conflict "exulting" (pp. 114–115). He describes two alligators as fighting like dragons, belching smoke and unleashing thunder. Far from being the benign paradise depicted in Bartram's more formulaic moments, nature is here a place of conflict, strife, and violence, requiring momentous efforts toward self-preservation. The alligators attack Bartram, who beats them with a club and kills one with his gun; he ingeniously sets up a camp where he is the resolute, self-reliant individual defending himself against a malevolent force. He witnesses an amazing display of alligators devouring thousands of fish. Later he compares sailing through a throng of alligators to "running the gauntlet betwixt two rows of Indians armed with knives and firebrands" (p. 120).

Just as moments of serenity follow the menacing sublimity of the thunderstorm, the episode with the alligators leads to another characteristic moment of peace, even though the dormant threat of violence persists: "The noise of the crocodiles kept me awake the greater part of the night; but when I arose in the morning, contrary to my expectations, there was perfect peace. . . . Yet I was not able to suppress my fears and apprehensions of being attacked by them in future" (p. 120). Pursuing his course up the river, Bartram experiences repeatedly the pattern of threat and respite, commotion and calm. One night, drawn to the breaking point by his sense of peril, he finally falls asleep, but "this happy temporary release from cares and troubles" is quickly interrupted by screech owls, whose "dreadful peals vibrating through the dark extensive forests" remind him of his "extreme misery" (p. 127). The very next day, however, the sense of being at ease in nature returns: a noontime nap is a "blissful tranquil repose" from which he awakes "refreshed and strengthened." His mood is one of cheer, the day "cool and pleasant" (p. 129).

The episode with the alligators provides the most telling example of Bartram's primary organizing device—the violent interlude followed by the anxiously desired peaceful resolution. To Bartram the Florida alligator represents all he suspects about his own species. His alligator is fierce, unpredictable, greedy. Deeply anxious about his own potential for violence, Bartram projects his nervousness about human nature onto a natural avatar. Faced with the threat offered to his physical safety by the alligator, Bartram deflects it with ingenuity, resolution, and—most important—his own use of violence. Beating the alligators with a club, blowing out the brains of one of them "by lodging the contents of my gun in his head" (p. 117), Bartram is figuratively at war with himself. He appears to emerge triumphant from this battle—the alligators retreat and he passes safely by them.

But the chief (and mostly hidden) source of conflict is not resolved; this is the conflict between Bartram's genuine desire for the wilderness to be an Elysium, a place where the individual is peacefully integrated with nature, and his equally powerful suspicion that nature is grimly threatening. As long as he remained in doubt about human society and history, his understanding and appreciation of nature could be nothing but ambivalent.

Perhaps because the journey into nature reminded him too much of this inner conflict, Bartram never again undertook such an extensive exploration of the American wilderness. The legacy of this trip, the *Travels*, remains a classic, in many ways the defining archetype of American nature writing. Like all the best examples of the genre, it is both a record of the encounter of a perceptive consciousness with the natural world and a lyrical account of the impact of that encounter on the mind and soul of the traveler.

Selected Bibliography

WORKS OF WILLIAM BARTRAM

BOOKS

Travels through North and South Carolina, Georgia, East and West Florida, the Cherokee Country, the Extensive Territories of the Muscogulges, or Creek Confederacy, and the Country of the Choctaws (Philadelphia: James & Johnson, 1791; repr., with intro. by Mark Van Doren, New York: Dover, 1928; repr., with intro. by James Dickey, New York: Viking Penguin, 1988); *Travels in Georgia and Florida, 1773–74: A Report to Dr. John Fothergill*, ed. by Francis Harper, in *Transactions of the American Philosophical Society* 33 (November 1943); *William Bartram: Botanical and Zoological Drawings, 1756–1788*, ed. by Joseph Ewan (Philadelphia: American Philosophical Society, 1968).

BIBLIOGRAPHY

Rose Marie Cutting, *John and William Bartram, William Byrd II, and St. John de Crèvecoeur: A Reference Guide* (Boston: G. K. Hall, 1976).

BIOGRAPHICAL AND CRITICAL STUDIES

Douglas Anderson, "Bartram's *Travels* and the Politics of Nature," in *Early American Literature* 25 (1990); Lester Cappon, "Retracing and Mapping the Bartrams' Southern Travels," in *Proceedings of the American Philosophical Society* 118 (December 1974); Larry R. Clarke, "The Quaker Background of William Bartram's View of Nature," in *Journal of the History of Ideas* 46 (July/September 1985); Ernest Earnest, *John and William Bartram: Botanists and Explorers. 1699–1777, 1739–1823* (Philadelphia: Univ. of Pennsylvania Press, 1940); Joseph Ewan, "Early History," in *A Short History of Botany in the United States*, ed. by Joseph Ewan (New York: Hafner, 1969); N. Bryllion Fagin, *William Bartram: Interpreter of the American Landscape* (Baltimore: Johns Hopkins Univ. Press, 1933); Robert A. Ferguson, "What Is Enlightenment?: Some American Answers," in *American Literary History* 1 (summer 1989); William Hedges, "Toward a National Literature," in *Columbia Literary History of the United States*, ed. by Emory Elliott (New York: Columbia Univ. Press, 1988); Hans Huth, *Nature and the American: Three Centuries of Changing Attitudes* (Berkeley, Calif.: Univ. of California Press, 1957); Christopher Looby, "The Constitution of Nature: Taxonomy as Politics in Jefferson, Peale, and Bartram," in *Early American Literature* 22 (1987).

Amy R. Weinstein Meyers, "Sketches from the Wilderness: Changing Conceptions of Nature in American Natural History Illustration, 1680–1880" (Ph.D. diss., Yale Univ., 1985); Charles A. Miller, *Jefferson and Nature: An Interpretation* (Baltimore, Md.: Johns Hopkins Univ. Press, 1988); Roderick Nash, *Wilderness and the American Mind*, 3d ed. (New Haven, Conn.: Yale Univ. Press, 1982); Pamela Regis, *Describing Early America: Bartram, Jefferson, Crèvecoeur, and the Rhetoric of Natural History* (DeKalb, Ill.: Northern Illinois Univ. Press, 1992); John Seelye, "Beauty Bare: William Bartram and His Triangulated Wilderness," in *Prospects* 6 (1981); Bruce Silver, "William Bartram's and Other Eighteenth-Century Accounts of Nature," in *Journal of the History of Ideas* 39 (October/December 1978); Mark Van Doren, Editor's Note, in *Travels of William Bartram* (New York: Dover, 1928); David Rains Wallace, *Bulow Hammock: Mind in a Forest* (San Francisco: Sierra Club Books, 1988); Donald Worster, *Nature's Economy* (San Francisco: Sierra Club Books, 1977).

RICK BASS
(b. 1958)

TERRELL F. DIXON

SINCE 1985, Rick Bass has published four works of nonfiction, one collection of essays, two short story collections, and a collection of three novellas. These eight books cover a range of subjects: his family's deer lease in the hill country of central Texas; his white-water canoe adventures on the rivers of the South; the declining grizzly bear population in the West; an old man who seeks to escape his boring life and live as a wild man in a nearby swamp; his work as a petroleum geologist; the rigor and beauty of winter in the mountains; the efforts of wolves to move back into Montana; a retired Alaskan evangelist who turns Montana river valley land into a huge vegetable garden; and the life of a young couple living in a part of the Mississippi landscape that is returning to the wild.

What unifies this diverse body of work is Rick Bass's preoccupation with place and, more specifically, his ongoing fascination with the wild landcapes of the Rocky Mountain West and the Pacific Northwest.

Born on 7 March 1958 in Fort Worth, Texas, the son of C. R. Bass, a geologist, and Lucy Robson, Rick Bass has deep ties to Texas, especially to the land of the Texas hill country where his grandfather maintained a deer lease that was an important gathering place for the men of the Bass family. Bass went away for his university work, however, and during the years spent studying for his B.S. degree at Utah State University, he fell in love with the landscapes of the Rocky Mountain West. After his degree, he returned to the South and worked in Mississippi. Even during those years, his writing is shaped by his view of the mountains as a place where he can find what he loves most: wildness. His early writing, in many ways, prepared him for his later decision to move to the Yaak Valley in far northern Montana, and his writing underwent significant changes once he found a home there.

The Importance of Place

"River People," an early and deeply personal essay that appeared in *Wild to the Heart* (1987), describes Bass's wrestling with the question of where to live. At the time he wrote this piece, Bass was living in Jackson, Mississippi, where he made a good salary as a petroleum geologist. Over a long Memorial Day weekend, he decided not to make his usual hurried trip to the high country of the West. He chose, instead, to take a canoe trip with the "river people," adventurers who live to run the white waters of the South. The group included his friends, the brothers Lucian and Winfred E. Hill from Yazoo, Mississippi, who own "seven canoes, six kayaks, and a beagle. No car" (p. 135).

Because there is no white water in Yazoo City, this absence of an automobile has special significance. The brothers routinely hitchhiked with their canoes to whatever rivers in Georgia, Tennessee, and the Carolinas were getting rain. At the time of Bass's trip with them, Winfred, who later moved to Kentucky, had no furniture in his house because the canoes and kayaks took up all the space. He could not bear to be away from rivers for long; after a five- or six-day absence, he went to bed with all the faucets running, soothed by the sound of running water.

As "River People" recounts, Bass runs three rivers on this weekend, experiencing "the wild joy of going down, down the river, hard out, all the way to the end" (p. 143). He tells himself that he can live like his friends, finding wildness in encounters with the white water of southern rivers, and so he decides that he will remain in Jackson for a while, and confront the task of city living with renewed resolve. However, to the question he asks himself—"does one no longer love the aspen and the glaciers with all his heart and all his soul?"—he must answer, "I think not" (p. 153). As part of this debate, Bass first formulates the credo that underlies his writing: "If it's wild to your own heart, protect it. Preserve it. Love it. And fight for it, and dedicate yourself to it" (p. 158). He thinks of other men who loved the mountains, such storied explorers of the West as John Colter and Jed Smith, and he reminds himself that they too left for a while, but came back. As for himself, for now, he resolves that he will study on it some more, though it is clear both to himself and to his readers where his own heart lies.

The Deer Pasture and Wild to the Heart

Rick Bass's love for the country, especially the high country, was fostered in the central Texas hill country on the deer lease where three generations of his family have hunted. His first book, *The Deer Pasture* (1985), chronicles his love for that place. It was there that Bass learned how to hunt, and in this book, as elsewhere, Bass reveals himself to be a thoughtful, unapologetic hunter. His discussion of hunting, placed precisely in the center of the book, begins with a careful review of the explanations that hunters often give for what they do.

These "near-reasons"—rationales that Bass believes have lost their validity—include the phrase, usually said defensively and disingenuously, "I hunt for the meat" (p. 157). Since few families today really need the meat to sustain themselves, as opposed to merely making use of the meat once they have it, this is not a legitimate reason. Neither is the other most frequently offered explanation, the claim that hunting keeps animal populations in balance. Bass believes that though many hunters do attempt to cull older or less healthy animals, this, too, is ultimately just an excuse for hunting deer. Bass concludes with what he sees as a valid reason for hunting:

> The reaffirmation of survival skills, the confidence obtained by deciding to try to go out and do something and then actually doing it—discovering a deer that does not want to be discovered, doing better than he at his own game in his own environment on his own home ground—winning—there is appeal to some in doing this and this is why they hunt. (p. 59)

Bass broadens this into "a hunt for the hunter inside—a tracking of his own self" (p. 60). Although most deer hunters do not realize this consciously, "the buck in the middle of the path at the end of the trail" (p. 61) is not the end of their search. The real reason to hunt is "the unrolling of the path itself" (p. 60), and the self-discovery made possible by that process.

This chapter, entitled "Why We Do It," also features a second section—a hunting story that balances and supplements this analytical argument. The story is Bass's personal narrative about his first, and most significant, hunt in the deer pasture, one where he met "the first deer that ever beat me, in Gillespie County, in the Texas Hill Country" (p. 69). As the story unfolds, this giant deer takes on some of the symbolic significance of the animal hunted in

William Faulkner's story "The Bear." It lives somewhere in the mysterious east side of the lease, among bluffs that are "as dark as twilight" (p. 62). This area is farthest away from the little bit of civilization that is the camp cabin, located "in the depths of a cataclysmic, exploded, twisted, contorted mass of boulders and tilted-vertical rock formations called Hell's Half-Acre" (p. 63).

After the young Rick Bass has hunted this terrain unsuccessfully for two seasons, he comes to view this deer in mythic terms. He argues that this great and beautiful animal, with its huge horns and sleek, butter-tan coat should remain nameless. Because this big buck is unattainable, it would be wrong to designate it with any of the names—such as Old Mossy Horns or the Big Twelve Point—that hunters have traditionally given to such special quarry.

Unlike Faulkner's bear, this deer cannot be killed or even really known; the *attempt* to know the animal, however, is still crucial. Hunting him, the young hunter learns the land; he becomes a careful, dedicated student of the east pasture area, "paying intense and minute attention to every detail" (p. 65). When the deer mysteriously disappears from a perfect stalk (during which Bass, ironically, has worried that he might come upon the animal too close to make the kill), the conclusion suggests an outlook on wild land and wild animals that marks another difference from the Faulkner story. The bear kill portends the end of wilderness, but Bass's hunting story suggests that wildness can survive. The giant deer's escape also offers a possible counterbalance to the view of hunting as a test of self and confidence described in the analytic first half of the chapter. Two important lessons emerge from Bass's experience in the wildest part of the deer lease: the first is that hunting can be a way of knowing nature as well as self, and the second, actually a complicating corollary to the first, is that wild nature, even the wild nature that we begin to know somewhat, still possesses an abiding elusiveness, mystery, and power.

The Deer Pasture also records Bass's observations on men and nature. The young writer's

Rick Bass

stories about the Texas hill country fit naturally into three categories covering the stages of men's lives: boyhood, middle age, and old age. Most prominent among the first group are Bass's anecdotes about his cousin Randy, an early family version of the wild man eccentrics who inhabit much of Bass's prose. C. R. is the kind of young man who takes his girlfriend on a two-hour duck-hunting expedition before their 8:30 A.M. class, and then strides into the classroom dressed in hunting clothes, with feathers peeking out of his pockets. He once persuaded Bass to run through the deer lease waving a white handkerchief in the hope that the white-tailed deer would mistake him for one of their own and follow him.

Uncle Jimmy, Cousin Randy's father, represents the outdoorsman at midlife. He is a fifty-eight-year-old executive who wears a suit and manages a large office, but he has hunted the deer pasture for forty-seven seasons and has been known to depart early from business meetings halfway around the globe to join the Bass men at their annual November gathering. He has been seen running through a herd of deer grazing in the pasture, not to shoot at them but just because he felt like it. Bass's father, who has made forty-five trips of his own to the deer pasture, is proud at his son's high spirits. When Rick recklessly turns over the family jeep, he responds not with anger but with pride in how closely his son's jeep spill replicates an earlier accident of his own.

The old men of the hill country and their way of life also occupy much of the writer's attention. Bass notes carefully, for example, the activities of the seventy-five-year-old German emigrant Werner Schnappauf, especially his obvious enjoyment in fixing such things as the starter on the family jeep. From Mr. Edgar Gold, an old man from a pioneer hill country family who knew the habits of the deer, wild turkey, and bream, he learns the world of nature. Mr. Gold could tell a genuine Indian arrowhead from an unfinished scraper, and he could call an armadillo into camp by rubbing pebbles against leaves, imitating the sound of the bugs the armadillos liked to eat. Bass learned to see in the hill country old-timers the durable value of a life lived in nature and to feel that such lives "are stronger and more basic than lives in the city, and they stand the eroding tests of time better" (p. 110).

Most prominent among the outdoorsmen honored in this narrative is the man Bass calls Granddaddy; indeed, *The Deer Pasture* is in many ways a valediction to him. It was Bass's grandfather who first found the deer lease and who enabled two subsequent generations of Bass men to hunt that land. The brief closing chapter of this first book, titled "Autumn," chronicles Granddaddy's stroke, his weakness, and his grandson's sadness that his own children will not be able to hunt the deer pasture with him.

This loss is balanced by the author's delight in the ongoing physical beauty of the area—the sounds of the Pedernales River and the polished surface of the dome of Big Granite Mountain

under the light of the stars and the moon—and by the beginnings of an ecological perspective. Bass reads the cycles of Texas hill country life as "a balancing act: people, calves, owls, grass, and rabbits. Deer and foxes, coyotes and hawks" (p. 15). In this context, Bass's recounting of a youthful fantasy developed by himself and C. R. also points to a larger vision. The boys plan, on the one-hundredth anniversary of the deer lease, to turn loose a hundred or so black bears of all sizes and ages, males and females, thus restoring their wild presence to this country. This early ability to envision ecological connections and possibilities for restoration inaugurates an important and consistent theme in Bass's work, one that becomes amplified in his writing about the West.

In *Wild to the Heart*, the celebrations of landscape and family develop into more complex considerations and relationships. While *The Deer Pasture* presents some of the tension Bass feels between wildness and urban life (the preface, for example, describes how he plants and tends a hill-country cedar in downtown Jackson), that tension becomes a central conflict here. Bass tries to be open and tolerant, accepting of the wilderness provided by the nearby forests of Mississippi and the rivers of the South. On the other hand, the divide between his wage-earning city life and his love and longing for wild country has grown more pronounced. Because the love of wild landscape first nurtured by the Texas hill country has begun to locate itself further afield in the Rocky Mountain West, his efforts to reconcile his diverse impulses grow more difficult.

Most of the essays collected here fall into two major groups: those that deal with aspects of his life in the South, and those that chart his growing fascination with and commitment to the West. Such boundaries are never absolute, however: the essays set in the South are often laced with longing for or memories of the Rockies, and Bass's experiences in the Rockies include his questions about continuing to live in the South. There is also a smaller, third category of essays with an environmental orientation, one set in the South and one in the West.

Many of the essays set in Mississippi exhibit Bass's efforts to carry out the vow made at the end of "River People" to immerse himself in the wildness that the South affords rather than to focus on his dissatisfactions and a possible move to the West. This state of mind informs "Good Day at Black Creek" and "Sipsey in the Rain." In the first, he describes a hike he took with the chairman of the Central Mississippi Sierra Club to look at land that would, if approval were granted, become Mississippi's first national wilderness area. He sees this trip as an opportunity to expand his sense of what constitutes a wilderness area, to see that wilderness possibilities exist apart from the mountains. Bass views the Black Creek area as a "buffered" sort of wilderness, one that has remained very much like it was in the 1800s and even in hunter-gatherer times. It is not wilderness in the sense that it is five hundred miles from a telephone, but wilderness in that it is a sparsely settled area that has undergone little change over time.

"Sipsey in the Rain" chronicles another southern backpacking trip, with passages like the following expressing Bass's delight in the outdoor life as vividly as any of his writings:

> Suddenly we are in a canyon. I am beside myself with joy. Slick rock walls, sheer faces wet with leaking springs, tall cliffs, like out West! There are dogwoods everywhere. The blossoms hang motionless over the canyon, and our boots fall silently on the thick carpet of fern and moss. There are huge leafy trees everywhere: it is like a drizzling rain forest. Thompson Creek sounds wild. There are felt-covered green boulders everywhere, the smallest ones as big as refrigerators, and we pick our way around them. (p. 70)

One characteristic feature of Bass's wilderness essays is the engaging field notes he includes on the various styles of his fellow hikers. From observations of southerners with their long, loping strides, for example, Bass speculates that the flatter southern trails require a different body type than the steeper Rockies, which call for short and squatty backpackers built like tanks.

Bass also provides a humorous study of backpacking food-preparation styles. There is what he calls the glamorous style, practiced by his friends. It involves mulling over possible menus, shopping for food, carefully preparing eggplant pizza, and then cleaning up: total time, two hours and forty-eight minutes. In distinct contrast, there is his own decidedly non-gourmet but practical alternative of cramming a pack with blueberry energy bars and Vienna sausages: total time, twelve minutes.

The last part of the book's final essay, "Strawberries," testifies to the felt sweetness of these southern wilderness trips. Bass describes the conclusion of a trip he took with friends down the Buffalo River in Arkansas. During the car trip home, they are all, himself included, tired and happy as they forage in a plastic bag for sugar-dusted strawberries.

Much of Bass's outdoor experience in the South is not in wilderness, however, and two essays serve to illustrate the range of his attitudes. "Fish Fry," set during a lazy afternoon on a lake fifteen miles out of Jackson, shows Bass resting on a dock, drinking Chablis, watching his friends fish unsuccessfully for dinner, and wondering if he will have to use the three-pound piece of venison that he brought as backup provisions. The evening, complete with its magnificent sunset, is saved by his friend Chuck, the one person on the lake who knows enough about the habits of fish to catch them for supper.

"Burrisizing" serves as a kind of companion piece to "Fish Fry," balancing its sense of satisfaction with a different view of the same life. Set in Jackson in what is apparently late summer or early fall with a group gathered around an apartment pool, it features Bass's friend, Jackson Burris, telling acquaintances about the horrors of a Utah camping trip the two took together. Jackson is embellishing or, as Bass phrases it, "Burrisizing" about the dangers that they faced and the hardships that they endured. In Burris' account lightning that had been in the vicinity becomes lightning that struck their camp, and the horned toad they saw becomes a gila monster. Frost on their sleeping bags becomes an August snowstorm.

The story is interrupted by a sudden very strong wind that has the feel of an early norther. The group—led by a fully clothed city girl—begins to jump into the pool. Bass recalls the Utah Polar Bear Club (a hardy group that defies the cold winter weather by jumping into icy cold water) as he follows his friends into the pool. This norther is a false front, however, and Bass sadly climbs out of the pool, posing for himself a rhetorical question: "What in the world am I doing in Jackson, Mississippi, at this time of year?" He first answers, "Because Jackson is the best place to do what I do." This explanation is quickly followed, however, by a sardonic, one-word commentary on his own attempts at self-deception: "Burrisizing" (p. 82).

It is not surprising then that the least conflicted and most exuberant essays in his *Wild to the Heart* collection are the western pieces, "Shortest Route to the Mountains," "On Camp Robbers, Rock Swifts, and Other Things Wild to the Heart," "Magic at Ruth Lake," and "First Snow." "Shortest Route to the Mountains," which opens the book, is Bass's journal of an accelerated, blue-highways trip out from Jackson through the fields and small towns of the South into what he calls "the state of my rebirth" (p. 17). It features two sentiments common in his writing, the joy of movement through landscape and the unique exhilaration of approaching and being in wild country.

"On Camp Robbers, Rock Swifts, and Other Things Wild to the Heart" begins with another car journey out from Jackson, this one to the Pecos Wilderness of New Mexico. This essay deals with Bass's brief stay, another long weekend, in the Pecos Country, where he feels like a man escaped from prison, and his hike up Hermit Peak, where he exults in having the mountain to himself. "Magic at Ruth Lake" pays tribute to the beauty and power of the mountains near Utah State University, where he attended college (after learning that it was the university closest to where the movie *Jeremiah Johnson* was filmed) and to Rob, the friend with whom he first camped there.

A final travel-to-the-mountains essay, "First Snow," also charts a drive west. This one occurs in late September; his companions are two hound dog puppies. Bass's plan is to drive until he meets the snow. In the Rockies of Utah, Bass and the puppies sit by a fire and watch the snow fall "until the woods are whitened, reborn, begun again" (p. 165).

Two other essays in this book look at conservation from a personal and then a national perspective, asking how one can best go about paying one's ecological dues in serving the country's needs for the preservation and restoration of wildlife. "Paying Dues" is set on the Mississippi Gulf Coast near Biloxi, where the narrator accompanies a friend to a Sierra Club banquet. Though he chooses to spend the evening out on the golf course looking for alligators rather than indoors dancing, the trip shows the narrator considering and perhaps beginning to correct a tendency to view such conservation organizations in stereotyped and suspicious ways. "The Grizzly Cowboys" describes a journalistic assignment Bass undertook in the West, during which he looked for grizzlies in a huge wilderness of two million acres where only six grizzlies, at most, remained. He also relates the shameful history of grizzly study in this region and in nearby Yellowstone National Park, and his fear that the grizzly bear will disappear entirely from the lower forty-eight states.

The Watch and Oil Notes

The Watch: Stories published in 1989, is Rick Bass's first book of fiction; like *Wild to the Heart* it is informed by his concern for wildness and his desire to explore wild landscapes. These collected stories, set mostly in the familiar Bass environs of Mississippi, Texas, and Utah, employ a wide range of literary skills and fictional modes, demonstrating early in his career that Bass is one of those rare writers who can achieve excellence in both fiction and literary nonfiction. This collection is notable, too, for its thematic treatment of the natural world; it adds to the growing body of significant contemporary ecofiction.

Three stories in this collection suggest a bleaker view of the possibilities for wildness in the southern landscape than do the essays in *Wild to the Heart*. "Wild Horses" echoes D. H. Lawrence in its heavily symbolic narrative about how a man who breaks wild horses finally breaks through grief to win the love of his dead friend's fiancée. "The Government Bears" and "The Watch" are companion stories that continue Bass's interest in linking old men, nature, and wildness. In the former, Pitts, an eccentric Mississippian, laments the lack of healthy wildness in Mississippi. As Pitts takes care of a sick son and helps care for his grandsons, he complains about the decline of the state. Its population of degraded, resident black bears symbolizes the absence of wildness around him. These are definitely "not Faulkner's bears, but postdepression government bears, little thirty- and forty-pound dwarf things the government put in there, genetically trapped in their sorrowful size forever" (p. 173).

The title story develops some of these key themes in a narrative that employs the techniques of magical realism. Buzbee, the seventy-seven-year-old protagonist of this story, lives in a ghost town where he and his mad, talkative son run an almost deserted country store. When Buzbee moves into the remains of an old settlement in the nearby swamps, he becomes Bass's version of a septuagenarian wild man, catching and smoking small alligators and large fish for winter food and perching naked in a tree where he watches for interlopers from the town. Buzbee also steals chickens, turning them loose so that they can locate quinine berries for him to fend off the yellow fever that killed the earlier settlers. Several black women, beaten and abused by their husbands in the town, join his settlement and share his hut. In one passage, they watch Buzbee leap into the water after alligators:

That first time they thought he had lost his mind: he had rolled around and around in the thick gray-white slick mud, down by the bank, jabbing the young alligator with his pocketknife again and again, perforating and muttering savage dog noises, until they could

no longer tell which was which, except for the jets of blood that spurted out of the alligator's fat belly. (p. 77)

Buzbee's son, Hollingsworth, meanwhile forms an alliance with a former bicycle racer, and the two of them plot various ways to capture Buzbee and bring him back to town. They finally trap him with dogs. The story ends with the former wild man chained to the front porch of his former home, plotting his next escape while forced to listen to his son's meaningless chatter.

The two stories that frame the collection continue this bleak depiction of the South by focusing on the ills of urban life. Both show the young male protagonist and his buddy, Kirby, trying to find ways to get by in what they see as the big and unlivable city of Houston: "Hell will come here first, when it opens. Everyone here's already dead. The heat killed them or something. People don't even fall in love here anymore: it's just the pelvic thrust, and occasionally children as the result. There's no love, and that's the surest sign of death" (p. 13).

They turn to nature as a possible source for connection with life. In "Mexico," the story that opens the collection, Kirby, newly rich with oil money, has bought a big house, "like a tabernacle, a state capitol" (p. 21), in a good neighborhood, and built a deep pool to go with it. The suburbanization stops here, however; the pool is placed in the front yard, not the back, and Kirby seeks to turn it into a bass pond. He fills it with stumps, gravel, old trees, an old Volkswagen, and then starts to raise a bass he calls Shack, one he hopes will grow into a trophy fish. When the men are on a trip to the Mexican bullfights, the big bass is caught by neighborhood boys and dies.

In "Redfish," the narrator and Kirby again try fishing as an attempt to get beyond the deadness of contemporary urban life. This time they try for redfish on the Texas gulf coast. Their preparations are extensive. They've read about redfish and speckled trout fishing; they've bought the necessary fishing equipment; they even bring a used couch to sit on while they fish. They stoke themselves with Cuba Libres and with the thought that they are "braving the elements, tackling nature, fishing for the mighty red drum" (p. 184). Their connection with nature comes not through a heroic hookup with a big fish, however, but through an unexpected natural occurrence that is a rare event on the gulf coast: a snowstorm.

The two stories set in the West also feature young men. In "In Ruth's country," nature serves primarily as a setting that reinforces character and story line rather than as a subject of the fiction; the desert landscape outside of Moab, Utah, reflects the progress and complications of the love affair between Ruth, a young Mormon woman, and the narrator, a young man who runs wild cattle on the high country desert with his uncle. As their attraction turns into a sexual relationship, the desert blooms with a wild profusion of flowers; the desert lightning storms echo the electricity and danger of their illicit relationship. When they wade the river, Ruth's reluctance to risk pulling the narrator out of the dangerous fast water foreshadows her final unwillingness to step outside her community to be with him.

"Choteau" treats the western landscape as fictional theme. Galena Jim Ontz, the wild-man protagonist of this story, set in the isolated Yaak Valley of northern Montana, "has two girlfriends and a key to Canada" (p. 34). Though nearly forty years old, Ontz is imprisoned in the attitudes of boyhood, acting as if he had all his choices still before him and unwilling to decide between a woman his own age in Yaak and a teenage girlfriend down the road in Libby, Montana. Buck, Ontz's son from an early marriage, is serving a life sentence for murder in the state prison at Choteau. When Ontz, the onetime rodeo rider, injures himself trying to ride a huge moose as if it were a rodeo animal, the young narrator slowly drives him home, hoping all the while that a heart ailment he knows Ontz has will not act up.

The highway into Yaak sparkles with the "pure glittering space-blue slick and shiny heavy-as-lead galena" (p. 36) that Ontz, ten years earlier, had stolen and added to the ore for the road. For all its glitter, however, the paved road has made access to the wilderness easier and more permanent, and thus it has begun the process of transforming the wild. "Choteau" thus adds an important dimension to *The Watch*, linking Bass's fears about the survival of the wilder landscapes of the West with his pessimism about the survival of wildness in the older, more settled southland.

Oil Notes, Bass's fourth book and the last thus far in his career to focus on the land and people of the South, was also published in 1989. This literary nonfiction in the form of field notes concentrates on his work as an oil-field geologist and his unfolding personal history, especially his courtship of Elizabeth Hughes, the artist whose drawings illustrate this and other books by Rick Bass and the woman whom he later marries. In this work Bass comments on the discursiveness of his own literary method: "I am a geologist, and these are going to be notes that I write in little journal books that I carry around . . . and a whole lot of them are going to lack any structure at all, but if you know a geologist, you know that is the way he expresses things" (p. 3). Remembering the novelist Jim Harrison's quote from Franz Kafka about "freeing the frozen sea within us" (p. 1), Bass begins by confiding to his readers that he knows how to find oil, but that getting it out, conveying to us what he knows, "is the frozen sea within him" (p. 2).

Despite this concern, Bass provides an engaging introduction to earth science as practiced by a petroleum geologist and nature writer who is able to see both the technical process of the oil business and its awe-inspiring results. An important unifying thread throughout these journals, for example, is an extended glossary of industry terms, each one explaining at length some aspect of the oil business by tying it to Bass's personal experience. A development geologist, for example, is one who, like Bass, goes into an area where there is already a producing well and figures out how much oil is there, where it is, and how and when to drill other wells. An exploratory geologist, on the other hand, seeks wildcat wells, wells drilled in an area where nothing has been found before.

"Creekology," called surficial geology in the college catalog listings, is a form of historical natural history in which the geologist looks at the surface of the ground to speculate on what went on in the geological past. To the person who knows the land, for example, a map showing early settlements or railroads can help show where to drill for oil. The process goes like this: The early settlements occurred at those places where it was easiest to drill water wells, and those often occurred where water might have escaped from a sub-surface fault. Thus the oil, which might also be in such areas, could be found by looking at the old settlement maps or even the old railway maps showing the rail lines that linked up these settlements. Such landscape detective work could thereby help locate an area of geological activity, a possible drilling hotspot.

As he describes the oil business and what it means to him, Bass weaves in some material from his domestic life. By this time, Bass has moved out of Jackson to a farm twenty-four miles away from town, a beautiful area of ferns and oaks, dragonflies and jays and mourning doves. He has adopted two hounds, Ann and Homer, who first appeared in "First Snow," and his protective feelings for them lead to thoughts of marriage and children. Elizabeth lives in a different part of the area, but his relationship with her involves driving through beautiful country. Bass tells us that the Trace, "the federal parkway between her house in the country and the town of Jackson, Mississippi, site of my office, is perhaps the prettiest drive downhill of the Rockies" (pp. 3–4). Both his growing love for Elizabeth and the search for oil make him increasingly aware of time and mutability, and *Oil Notes* contains some of Bass's most meditative writing.

Bass makes it clear that he succeeds as a geologist because he is a passionate "student of the earth" (p. 33), one who knows how to read the land, woods, rivers, and trees. Such study succeeds not by detachment, but because he has fallen in love with underground geology. If he were forced to tell someone, in one sentence, how to find oil, it would go like this: "The closest I can come to that sentence, beyond 'Listen to the earth,' is that you have to get down under and beyond the mere occupational greed and look into the simplicity, the purity, the sacred part of it—the act, not the results, and yourself—and be aware that it is history, buried" (p. 13).

The technical and the personal, awe-inspiring aspects of his work come together most tellingly in the climax of *Oil Notes*, when Bass talks about how oil people often keep on their desk a sample two-ounce jar of oil they have found. The importance of such jars cannot be overestimated. It is, admittedly, partially based on achievement (he keeps on his desk a sample from the first well his father ever drilled), but Bass argues that the oil bottle, more than an olympic medal or a world series photo, has life. It is captured energy, from deep within the earth, that can be smelled and touched. When the cap is off and the bottle held to the ear, it evokes an ancient seashore, "a world so different from the one we are in now it is frightening" (p. 109).

The Move West

In 1987, Rick Bass and Elizabeth Hughes made their long-awaited move west. After an extended search for a place to call home, they took up residence on the Fix Ranch near Yaak, Montana, very near the Canadian border. Three books he has published since that move—*Winter: Notes from Montana* (1991), *The Ninemile Wolves: An Essay* (1992), and *Platte River* (1994)—embody substantial changes over his earlier work. Bass has entered a new life, more fully and truly in place in the kind of wild landscape where he has always wanted to live. In this new stage of his career, the focus falls less on travel and where to live and more on how to live. There is more joy and less longing, more space for reflection, more time to describe the landscape and its inhabitants in depth, and more attention also to environmental issues.

The exuberance, however, is at first mixed with apprehension. Winter follows soon upon their September move, and Bass must learn quickly how to ready his family for it; much of

Winter: Notes from Montana is about what and how he learns. He works frantically to get in enough fuel (forty cords of wood) for him and Elizabeth to make it through the winter. Although he works with felled trees, there are still substantial dangers. He wears a hard hat, goggles, earplugs, steel-toed boots, and leather gloves. He learns to wear baggy pants so that if a branch does run up his cuff he can get free from it rather than tripping with a running chain saw in hand.

Through all the adventures of adjustment, his delight in the remote northern location of Yaak remains constant. He exults in the absence of shopping malls, television, and phones, and he takes comfort in an estimate that it would cost eighty-thousand dollars to bring electricity to the lodge; such a price means it will never happen. Above all, there is his continued fascination with winter, its newness, its power, and its meaning. Fear of the extreme cold leads to a frantic push to get in enough wood for the winter, but when the first snow finally arrives he finds that it solidifies the sense of peace he has found in the new place. The more snow that falls, the richer he feels. Winter teaches him that nature has its own rules; it is bigger than he is. Winter protects the wildness of the country, so that "if you *really* love the country—then you may find yourself able to love it in winter most of all" (p. 131). To yearn for spring is sometimes tempting, but to do so would be to betray winter, which is the heart of wildness.

Learning this new land, northern Montana in winter, elicits Bass's very best work as a nature writer. *Winter* is composed of dated journal entries that amply accommodate his observations of and reflections on the natural world. Bass describes in detail, for example, how the four-foot-tall great gray owl and the playful coyote hunt for mice in the fields near the lodge. He observes also how the great snowshoe hares, which are the size of large cats, have evolved so that with the approach of winter their coats turn white, lending them protection from predators in the snow. Bass notes that what Edward Hoagland has designated the courage of turtles could also, in this north country, be described as the

wisdom of rabbits; he hopes that he, like them, can learn his own survival skills.

Such ecological and literary reflection is characteristic of the mature accomplishment that marks *Winter*. More than in previous books, Bass contemplates his predecessors and his contemporaries in nature writing. *Winter* shows that in finding his geographical place, Bass found his identity as a writer, and his place in the tradition of American nature writing. The 25 September entry, for example, describes a walk Bass took up Vinal Creek, where he watched an ouzel on a waterfall. Bass describes the area and his own responses to its beauty, but this walk is also an occasion for him to begin sorting out his literary heritage and his own place as a nature writer; the waterfall and the ouzel led him to discuss how various predecessors ranging from the English Romantic poets to John Muir to Raymond Carver have dealt with similar subjects. This increasing knowledge of literary natural history enriches and sharpens his own work.

An incident that occurred toward the end of Bass's first winter in Montana illustrates how deeply the move west anchored his and his wife's identification with nature. Bass describes a February night when he and Elizabeth had dinner in the nearby town of Libby. A winter storm made the roads dangerous, but instead of checking into a hotel for the night, they decide to head home in their car, through a tunnel of snow, drawn always further into the wilderness. As they cross the summit of a major pass, caught up in the race of wind and ice crystals alongside them, Elizabeth exclaims, "It's like *we're* the wind" (p. 153). Their city ways are peeling off; they are moving more deeply into the world of the woods, into a sense of oneness with the natural world.

Bass's second book after the move, *The Ninemile Wolves*, illustrates how his environmental concerns became amplified after his settlement in the Northwest. In *Winter*, he talked about those "names on the old maps of this area that break my heart, names like Caribou Creek and Caribou Mountain" (p. 37), names that speak of a time when there were herds of caribou in an area where now there are none. This disappearance of the "glory species" (p. 36) of large wild animals is a subject that Bass also pursued in numerous magazine articles about grizzlies, but it receives its fullest development thus far in his writing about wolves. In *The Ninemile Wolves*, he devotes the entire book to the wolf, emphasizing the efforts of wolves to reenter the Ninemile valley of Montana after six decades of absence.

His journalistic narrative begins in 1989, when the appearance of a two-year-old female wolf near Marion, Montana, between the nearby town of Libby and Glacier National Park, triggers a flurry of activity and observation in the state, and it sets in motion as well Bass's own narrative tracking of both the wolves and the human responses to their return. As Bass tells the history of her mating and offspring (a three-generation genealogy of the Ninemile wolves is also presented in chart form in an appendix) and the points of intersection between the human species and these wolves, he explores the larger history, the myth, the mystery, and the biology of the wolf in America. All of these elements are woven into a complex narrative that makes an eloquent plea for recognition of the wolf's importance.

The history of wolves has both tragic and hopeful elements. There were, for example, an estimated seven hundred thousand wolves killed in Montana between 1870 and 1877; they were shot, trapped, poisoned, and even dynamited. Over a century later, the spirit of extirpation survives in the form of such present-day figures as Dick Mader of the Common Man Institute, who urges people to "SAY NO TO WOLVES" (p. 84) and who warns us that we can go either man's way or the ways of nature. Balancing such uncompromising outbursts are the human efforts on behalf of the wolf. People such as the Thisted brothers, the ranchers on whose land the Marion wolf and her pups found sanctuary, and Mike Jimenez, the wildlife biologist who works tirelessly for the protection and survival of the Ninemile wolves, are also featured. Their efforts, coupled with the wolves' own strength and survival skills, offer hope.

Bass also addresses the differences among groups who work for wolf restoration. He begins this book, for example, by describing and then rejecting an admonition from the scientific community:

> They say not to anthropomorphize—not to think of them as having feelings, not to think of them as being able to think—but late at night I like to imagine that they are killing: that another deer has gone down in a tangle of legs, tackled in deep snow; and that, once again, the wolves are feeding. That they have saved themselves, once again. . . . All they've got is teeth, long legs, and—I have to say this—great hearts. (p. 3)

This tension between the detachment associated with scientific and governmental bureaucracies, and the sympathy associated with naturalists is a central, persistent theme of this book.

The best scientists are those who do not, cannot, avoid attachment, those driven by a strong involvement with the orphaned wolf pups and their efforts to survive. Bass's models are men like Mike Jimenez, who celebrated the Ninemile orphans' developing aptitude for hunting "as if it were his child's first lost tooth" (p. 74). The reliance on technological devices such as radio tracking collars and isotopic scat reading machines become aligned with an unwholesome preference for bureaucratic "management" as opposed to daily, personal involvement. When Jimenez is reassigned away from the Ninemile Valley, so that the Fish and Wildlife bureaucracy can gain a computer and a new office employee, Bass feels that such action betrays the best that can be done for the wolves. Such actions are probably not fatal, but only because the nearly magical ability of the wolves to maintain the species defies the muddled efforts of the bureaucracy.

In a history filled with many moving stories about the wolves and human interaction with them, perhaps the most powerful is the one with which Bass ends the book. The setting is a bar in Fairbanks, Alaska, where a friend relates to Bass how a man he knew, a dentist, talked about hunting wolves from a plane. As the plane flew low, cruising along behind the wolves, "riding right on the pack's back," the man was not only physically close to the pack but frustratingly close to the kind of sympathetic understanding that Bass feels we all need. The man said to Bass's friend, "I tell you, Joe, it was like nothing I've ever seen or done — Joe, for a few seconds there, we were right in with them, following right behind them — and the big leader looked back, and for a minute, Joe, following along behind them like that, it was like *we* were one of the pack" (p. 161).

What this man almost saw, but finally, tragically, could not quite grasp is what Bass says implicitly and explicitly throughout *The Ninemile Wolves*: all species are part of one another's history and destiny. For Bass, destruction of the wolf signs the death warrant of the human soul as well as that of the wolves, and it signs also "the death warrant of the earth, of our respect for our place on it" (p. 161).

In 1994 Bass published a collection of three novellas entitled *Platte River*, which features his most experimental fiction thus far. Each of the three stories — "Mahatma Joe," "Field Events," and "Platte River" — presents a male protagonist working through some critical life stage or problem. The first two stories continue and expand the magical realism of "The Watch" in narratives that incorporate elements of the tall tale, fable, and myth; the title story is a more traditional, Hemingway-like tale of men and women and steelhead fishing in Michigan.

In "Mahatma Joe," an evangelist comes from Alaska to a valley much like the Yaak and tries to clean it up by putting an end to the traditional "Naked Days" celebration, during which the locals go without clothes during the warm Chinook wind season. Despite achieving his aim, he worries that he is getting old without having accomplished enough. His solution is to plant a huge vegetable garden on the banks of the river and to send the vegetables out to an African village, though it is uncertain how much of the produce reaches its destination. "Field Events" features three young men of exceptional physical strength. Two brothers, John and Jerry, first see the giant-like A. C. swimming upriver, dragging a canoe from a rope held by his teeth. The

brothers want to make this strongman into a world champion discus thrower, and they all practice in a giant shed through a rough winter in upstate New York. All three men fall in love during this time, and their respective subsequent marriages promise to heal former sadness.

Harley, the main character in "Platte River," is a former football player now living in an enormous lodge in the wilds of the Pacific Northwest. Harley physically restrains his lover from leaving him by chasing her through the woods and bringing her back, even though he knows that she will inevitably find a way to leave him for good. A long middle section involves his visit to a small college in Michigan, where his old college football buddy Willis teaches English. The two men go fishing for steelhead with Nick, a depressed colleague of Willis' who also teaches at the school. Along the Platte River late at night Harley experiences a sense of community with these other men: "He had the feeling that not only was his secret being read, but that those men had gone through the very same thing" (p. 126). He loses a fish, swearing that he can feel it, a part of himself now, running out to the lake; he is sorry to lose the fish, but he is also learning how to release rather than just to hold on tightly, to relinquish easily what he cannot own. Five years later, when another woman comments on how nice it would be to jump on a passing ship and just keep going, Harley doesn't argue with her; he simply answers, "yes."

The range and the importance of Bass's work is underscored also by the excellent 1995 short story collection *In the Loyal Mountains*. This group of ten short stories, more traditional in style than the novellas collected in *Platte River*, continues to explore his fascination with place and with wildness. This is evident in such stories as "The Valley" and "Days of Heaven" that express both his love for and his fears for the Yaak Valley. There are also Houston stories, "Swamp Boy" and "The Wait," that explore the city and nearby Galveston Bay as both remembered and possible future sites for a subject that Bass has left unexplored in much of his earlier work: urban wildlands.

The two most compelling stories, however, are "In the Loyal Mountains" and "The History of Rodney." "In the Loyal Mountains" closes the collection with a tale of conflicting family and landscape loyalties. The narrator recalls his early years when he favored the renegade outdoorsman life of his bachelor uncle Zorey over the life that his professional golfer father lived on "manicured greens." The highlights of his youth were the excursions to the Loyal Mountains of the Texas hill country with his uncle Zorey; these were wild trips where he drank Jim Beam and had sex with Spanda, his uncle's employee. Later, after he has married and become a father himself, the narrator looks back both at those days and at his uncle's subsequent suicide with a different eye. His loyalty shifts from the excesses of Uncle Zorey to the domestic calm that he desires for his own wife and baby son.

"The History of Rodney," the opening story in this collection, explores a new possibility for the long-settled lands of the South—the hope that wilderness can be restored. Rodney is a former port town in Mississippi whose bustling commercial life was lost when an oxbow bend of the Mississippi River broke, leaving the town stranded some seven miles from the river. The young couple featured in this story delight in living on a land where a diminishing population lets the land restore itself to the wild. Their huge old house features a tree growing through the floor and an owl that lives in the attic, and they seek a life that features support of the reemerging wilderness, not destruction of it.

These recent fiction collections thus emphasize that in just a very few years Bass has produced a remarkably diverse body of writing about the natural world and the human place in it. From *The Deer Pasture* through *In the Loyal Mountains*, his dedication to place and his search for wild landscapes have led him to create engaging, passionate, and important essays and fiction. As his list of literary achievements has grown, Bass has expanded also his vision of what constitutes wilderness and his commitment to the belief that wildness once found needs to be fought for and protected. Even though he is still a relatively young writer, Rick Bass has already earned a place as one of our most important advocates for the natural world.

Selected Bibliography

WORKS OF RICK BASS

LITERARY NONFICTION

The Deer Pasture (College Station, Tex.: Texas A&M Univ. Press, 1985; repr., New York: Norton, 1989); *Wild to the Heart* (Harrisburg, Pa.: Stackpole 1987; repr., New York: Norton, 1989); *Oil Notes* (Boston: Houghton Mifflin/Seymour Lawrence, 1989); *Winter: Notes from Montana* (Boston: Houghton Mifflin/Seymour Lawrence, 1991); *The Ninemile Wolves: An Essay* (Livingston, Mont.: Clark City Press, 1992; repr., New York: Ballantine, 1993).

FICTION

The Watch: Stories (New York: Norton, 1989; repr., 1994); *Platte River* (Boston: Houghton Mifflin/Seymour Lawrence, 1994); *In the Loyal Mountains* (Boston: Houghton Mifflin, 1995).

UNCOLLECTED ESSAYS

"The Afterlife," in *Witness* 3 (winter 1989); "Valley of the Crows," in *Witness* 3 (winter 1989); "Why I Hunt," in *Esquire* (October 1990); "Crossing Over," in *Petroglyph: A Journal of Creative Natural History Writing* 4 (1992); "Beloit," in *Mississippi Review* 22 (1993); "Grizzlies: Are They Out There?" in *Audubon* (September/October 1993); "Creatures of the Dictator," in *Men's Journal* (April 1994); "Out on the Wild Fringe," in *Audubon* (January/February 1994).

UNCOLLECTED SHORT STORIES

"Mississippi," in *Cimarron Review* (summer 1987); "Where the Sea Used to Be," in *Paris Review* 102 (spring 1987); "Dilution," in *Kansas Quarterly* 20 (fall 1988); "Penetration," in *Story* 37 (fall 1989); "Ironwood," in *Antioch Review* 50 (fall 1992); "The Earth Divers," in *Weber Studies: An Interdisciplinary Humanities Journal* 11 (fall 1994).

INTERVIEW

Scott Slovic, "A Paint Brush in One Hand and a Bucket of Water in the Other: Nature Writing and the Politics of Wilderness: An Interview with Rick Bass," in *Weber Studies: An Interdisciplinary Humanities Journal* 11 (fall 1994).

BIOGRAPHICAL AND CRITICAL STUDIES

Robert Buffington, "Tolerating the Short Story," in *Sewanee Review* 102 (fall 1994), review of *Platte River* and collections by other writers; Terrell Dixon, essay-review of *In the Loyal Mountains*, in *Western American Literature* 30 (spring 1995); Ursula Hegi, "Splendid Isolation," in *New York Times Book Review* (10 February 1991), review of *Winter: Notes from Montana*; Rhoda Koenig, "The Long and Winding Road," in *New York Times Book Review* (17 July 1989), review of *Oil Notes*; Susan Lowell, "Country Love and Naked Laundresses," in *New York Times Book Review* (5 March 1989), review of *The Watch*.

WENDELL BERRY
(b. 1934)

HERMAN NIBBELINK

IN HIS ESSAY "The Long-Legged House," Wendell Berry declares that "whereas most American writers—and even most Americans—of my time are displaced persons, I am a placed person" (*Recollected Essays 1965–1980*, p. 42). His place is the hilly country of north central Kentucky, in the vicinity of Port Royal, once a thriving little agricultural center, now a village struggling to survive. "For longer than they remember," Berry says, "both sides of my family have lived within five or six miles of this riverbank" on the Kentucky River. Berry acknowledges his enduring affection for this place and says, "As a writer, then, I have had this place as my fate" (p. 42).

Born to John M. and Virginia Berry on 5 August 1934 in Henry County, Kentucky, Wendell Berry lived as a youth in New Castle, the county seat, where his father practiced law and served prominently in the Burley Tobacco Growers Association. Berry and his younger brother John spent much time in their formative years on family farms near Port Royal and at "the Camp," a family-owned property on the riverbank. Berry attended the University of Kentucky, receiving his B.A. in 1956 and M.A. in 1957. In the summer of 1957, before assuming his first teaching position at nearby Georgetown College, Berry and his bride, Tanya Amyx, lived at the Camp. In "The Long-Legged House" Berry recalls the summer that began his mar-

riage and his dedication as a writer to this place. But he occupied it only intermittently over the next several years.

After a year at Georgetown the Berrys moved to California, where Berry attended Stanford University on a Wallace Stegner Writing Fellowship. In 1961–1962, a Guggenheim Fellowship provided the opportunity for an extended stay in Europe. From 1962 to 1964, Berry taught English at New York University; in 1964 he joined the English Department at the University of Kentucky in Lexington, and the Berry family returned to Kentucky for good. In 1965 they purchased Lanes Landing Farm, a property adjacent to the Camp. Here they have lived and reared their children, Mary Dee and Pryor Clifford (Den).

As husband and father, farmer and writer, Wendell Berry has tended his place on earth. His fiction, essays, and poetry explore the rightful habitation of humanity in nature.

Fiction

In his novels and collections of stories, Berry has richly imagined a community much like the one in which he lives. Some of his fictional characters bear a passing resemblance to the relatives, friends, and neighbors he writes about by name in his essays and poems. In his essay "Nick and

Aunt Georgie," Berry acknowledges that "the character of Aunt Fanny in my book *A Place on Earth* is to some extent modeled on Aunt Georgie." However, his intent "is not to represent Aunt Georgie, and [Aunt Fanny] comes off as a much simpler character" (*Recollected Essays*, pp. 126–127). Outlines of the Berry family also carry over into the stories, especially in the fictional Feltner and Catlett families. Mat and Margaret Feltner, who farm on the outskirts of Port William—as Berry's maternal grandparents farmed near Port Royal—are central characters in *A Place on Earth*, *The Memory of Old Jack*, and some of the short stories. Their daughter Bess is married to the lawyer Wheeler Catlett, and Bess and Wheeler have two sons, Andy and Henry. Like Berry himself, Andy grows up to be a writer and farmer; his adult life appears in several of the stories and in *Remembering*. Andy's brother Henry, like Wendell's brother John, becomes a partner in his father's law firm.

While these superficial resemblances do not make Berry's fiction autobiographical, the correspondence of reality and fiction in his writing is complicated. "Pray Without Ceasing," a story narrated by Andy Catlett about the murder of a Feltner ancestor, is based on an incident in Berry's family history. In a contributor's note accompanying the appearance of the story in *The Best American Short Stories 1993* (edited by Louise Erdrich), Berry says, "I am always comforted to know that a story I have imagined is validated by a real story somewhere behind it." But he adds, "Nobody knows the whole of any real story. For a story, even a real one, to become whole, it has to be imagined" (p. 359).

Berry's first novel, *Nathan Coulter* (1960, revised in 1985), is an episodic story of boyhood experiences including pranks, hunting and fishing expeditions, work in the tobacco fields, and a Fourth of July carnival; it shares with many first novels a youthful, first-person narrator. Themes that become familiar in Berry's later fiction already emerge here: the importance of work; marriage and family; community; the cycle of the seasons and the corresponding cycle of human lives and deaths. In this story, however, these

themes are recognized more in loss and failure than in any realization of their success.

After their mother's death, which occurs near the beginning of the novel, young Nathan Coulter and his brother live with their grandparents and their uncle Burley on an adjoining farm. The boys are never far from their father—here, as in all of Berry's fiction, neighboring farmers work together much of the time—but the grandparents take over the parenting as the grieving father lives on alone, driven by his work, aiming "to own his farm without having to say please or thank you to a living soul" (rev. ed., p. 8). Life with their grandparents is not much better: "Grandma said you didn't live with a man like Grandpa; you lived around him" (p. 54).

In this novel marriages turn cold and mean (the grandparents') or end in a spouse's early death (the parents'). Work seems largely a curse; Nathan's father says, "you work on this damned old dirt and sweat over it and worry about it, and then one day they'll shovel it in your face, and that'll be the end of it" (p. 139). Burley aims to live without commitments. "He said land was worse than a wife," Nathan says; "it tied you down" (p. 8). Ironically, it is their uncle Burley who mainly nurtures the boys. When their father is angry, Burley consoles them: "That's just his way. . . . He loves you boys" (p. 21). Burley teaches Nathan to hunt and fish and to be silent and observant in the presence of the wild. From his teaching, Nathan learns to read nature and accept its mysteries, and to find comfort there in the face of life's mystery and loss.

In an author's note prefacing the revised edition of *Nathan Coulter*, Berry says of this early work, "I did not know that I had begun an interest in these characters that would still be productive twenty-five years later." Indeed, most of the characters reappear often in Berry's later fiction, their places secure in the Port William community that also remains a favorite setting in Berry's fiction. Berry's incipient themes in this novel—of the importance of work and commitment, of respect for others and for the land, of accepting the cycles of nature's seasons and of human life and death—point the way to their fuller realization in his later fiction and their corresponding development in his essays and poetry.

Berry's second novel, *A Place on Earth* (1967, revised in 1985), remains his most ambitious and satisfying work of fiction. With its focus on the Port William community in the last months of World War II, this novel interweaves the narratives of a number of Port William's residents and neighbors, with Mat Feltner emerging as the central figure, or, in Jack Hicks's words, "the ideal husband" (Merchant, p. 124) and farmer of the novel.

Incessant rainfall and the gloomy war news dominate the end-of-winter atmosphere in which this novel begins, and the tragedy of war comes home to the Feltner family when Virgil is declared missing in action. An only son, and Mat's farming partner, young Virgil married during the war; his pregnant wife, Hannah, makes her home with the Feltners. Virgil's loss is poignantly rendered in Mat's response to the news. On the following Sunday he takes out pen and paper as usual for his weekly letter to Virgil, but all he can think to say is, "My dear boy, today we have had grievous news" (rev. ed., p. 58).

The Feltners are not the only members of the Port William community to suffer from tragedy. Nathan Coulter's brother Tom was killed two years earlier; and Nathan, after a brief furlough, has just returned to the war. Several of the most engaging vignettes in the novel come in the form of Burley's letters to Nathan, full of news about the weather and work in the fields, laced with gossip and rumors about the neighborhood.

Other tragedies occur closer to home. Gideon and Ida Crop, tenant farmers on a run-down farm owned by Mat's alcoholic cousin, lose their only child to a spring flood that also washes out a bridge and damages their barn. Unable to face life at home, Gideon leaves, taking his grief with him to unknown places, and Ida copes as best she can by staying home to tend the animals. Burley Coulter organizes the neighbors to help Ida with the crops, and Mat Feltner has his son-in-law, Wheeler Catlett, draw up the papers that give Mat guardianship over his incompetent cousin's property. Now Mat can see to the repair and improvement of Gideon and Ida's farm. He arranges for Ernest Finley, the local carpenter, to repair the bridge and barn. In this way, Burley and Mat, both struggling to heal their own war-torn, grieving lives, become healers in the community.

Ernest Finley is Margaret Feltner's brother, and he, too, bears the scars of war. Crippled by his wounds in World War I, Ernest has never married. He lives with the Feltners and has learned to do well what he still can do. Now he painstakingly repairs the material damage caused by the flood. The lonely Ida invites him to eat with her when he works there, and against his better judgment Ernest is drawn to her, daring to imagine a life he never thought to have. When Ida finally hears from Gideon, she joyfully shares her news with Ernest. That evening, back in his shop in Port William, Ernest commits suicide.

Mat's healing from the tragedies in this novel occurs, Jack Hicks says, through "the most dominant concerns of the husband's life: work, history, marriage" (Merchant, p. 126). It begins in the acts of work. During the lambing season in late January, Mat passes a dark night in the sheep barn, assisting in the births of lambs: "He holds himself and his thoughts near to these things that his work and care have made familiar again" (p. 85).

Mat has learned farming from his father, who learned it from his father before him. And Virgil has learned from Mat. Mat tells Hannah, "We've been slow to have enough sense to farm this kind of land, and lack plenty yet" (p. 176). In a brief portrait of Port William's history near the beginning of the novel, Berry says that the early settlers made grievous mistakes. "In two or three generations the country was imponderably changed. . . . Whoever wanted to make a beginning, then, had to begin with something already half-finished. And scarcely known" (p. 25). Mat tells Hannah what he has learned and passed on to Virgil: "I told him that a man's life is always dealing with permanence—that the most dangerous kind of irresponsibility is to think of your doings as temporary. . . . What you do on the earth, the earth makes permanent" (p. 176).

Mat's work and sense of history and responsibility are not enough; he also needs his marriage. Margaret is more able than Mat to speak directly about the loss of Virgil. "From the day he was born I knew he would die," she says. "I was familar with the pain. I'd had it in me all his life." She tells Mat that when Virgil's "death is subtracted from his life . . . what it leaves is his life." Then she adds, "We belong to each other. After all these years. Doesn't that mean something?" Mat responds, "I don't know what it means [but] I know what it's worth" (pp. 257–258).

When news of the war's end reaches Port William by radio, the town celebrates. For Burley Coulter and some of his friends, the celebration turns into an all-night drinking bout. They cap their escapades with a mock funeral, carrying Whacker Spradlin, who has passed out, to the newly dug grave intended for Ernest Finley. Mat Feltner hears their irreverent dirge as the drunks go by his house, where he sits before Ernest's coffin. At first upset, Mat then recognizes that "the peaceful sleep of the town should be broken, not by any song of victory or thanksgiving, but by voices singing a dirge—that seemed to him to be fitting" (p. 299). Mat senses a change now; he has begun to heal.

In the final section of the novel, Mat walks out beyond the pasture, into a wood, to search for a cow that has left the herd to bear her calf in the wilderness. He sits down to rest, and "there comes to [him] the sense of a lost and dead past, a past perfect . . . and . . . it does not sadden him" (p. 316–317). Mat feels the "great restfulness" of this wild place "where death can only give into life" (p. 317). Once again, as Jack Hicks points out, Mat Feltner knows his place on earth.

Berry's third novel, *The Memory of Old Jack* (1974), continues the delineation of the Port William community, this time focusing on the last day of old Jack Beechum's life, in September of 1952, and the memories through which Jack recalls much of his past.

Since the beginning of World War II, the widowed, elderly farmer has resided at the old hotel in Port William. Jack is Mat Feltner's uncle, and as his nearest local kin, the Feltners have assumed the family responsibilities for their aged relative. Their son-in-law Wheeler Catlett serves Jack as lawyer, adviser, and friend, especially in regard to Jack's farm, now occupied by hardworking, faithful tenants, Elton and Mary Penn.

Much healing has taken place in Port William in the seven years since the war. Nathan Coulter is back home on the farm, married to Virgil Feltner's widow, Hannah, who "has learned by loss what it is she has" (p. 94). Mat Feltner is sixty-eight, still a leading farmer, though some of his land is now sharecropped by the Coulters; and on the day of Jack Beechum's death, young Andy Catlett, Mat's grandson, is spending his last day on the farm before going off to the state university, fearful that "to be what he might become he would have to cease to be what he had been" (p. 143).

From early on, Jack has known sorrow, loss, and failure. By the time he was six, his two older brothers had been killed in the Civil War and his mother had died of grief. Though Jack would live most of his life on the family farm, his "mind had already learned what would be one of its characteristic motions, turning away from the house, from the losses and failures and confinements of his history, to the land, the woods and fields of the old farm" (p. 24).

In his youth Jack had indulged in the vanities available to handsome and reckless young men, and then he married Ruth Lightwood, an elegant young woman who thought she could change him, and thus fulfill her family's ambitions for her: wealth, refinement, the city. It was not to be. Jack was married to his farm. After the birth of Clara, their only surviving child, Ruth never again shared the marriage bed with Jack. For a time Jack carried on an affair with Rose McInnis, a youthful widow. By the time Rose perished in a house fire, Jack had realized that their love "could lead to nothing." In his marriage, "his work had led to no good love. With Rose, his love led to no work" (p. 134).

Jack's work, too, had suffered. Greedy for more land, he bought a second farm and hired as tenant a black man, Will Wells. Wells worked hard and faithfully, but Jack was not easily satisfied. A disagreement over work led to a fight, and Wells packed up his family and left without reconciliation, for he and Jack were "far off in history from the terms and the vision of such a peace" (p. 84). The experience taught Jack "the difference between hopeful and hopeless work" (p. 84), and he knew "that he could not ask another man to work without hope" (p. 164). Eventually, Jack "became again the true husband of his land" (p. 165), but "he had not united farm and household and marriage bed, and he could not" (pp. 165–166).

On the last evening of his life, Jack retires as usual to his room in the hotel and sits before the window that looks out on the town and the fields beyond. The next day Mat Feltner finds him there, dead in his chair. In an epilogue, set a few months later, the neighboring farmers work together in Elton Penn's tobacco barn. Their talk turns to Old Jack as they remember his sayings and turn them to the work at hand. Thus Jack is remembered, doubling the meaning of the book's title.

In two collections of short stories, *The Wild Birds: Six Stories of the Port William Membership* (1986) and *Fidelity: Five Stories* (1992), Berry has filled in gaps and extended the Port William saga. In *The Wild Birds*, Wheeler Catlett helps Elton and Mary Penn secure the farm Jack Beechum wanted them to have, Mat Feltner takes his last walk into the woods on his property, and Burley Coulter acknowledges that Danny Branch, a young man of previously uncertain fatherhood, is his son and rightful heir. The title story in *Fidelity* involves several neighbors and friends in the defiant kidnapping of the dying Burley from a Louisville hospital so that they can fulfill Burley's wish to die where he has lived—on his land.

Remembering (1988) is Berry's fourth novel and the only one where the present time and action are largely set outside of the Port William community. It opens with Andy Catlett suffering a wakeful night in a San Francisco hotel, where he recalls the events of the past few days. An agricultural journalist and farmer who deplores the trends of American farming toward agribusi-

ness, Andy had been a speaker at a midwestern agricultural conference where he denounced the enthusiasm of the conferees for scientific and agricultural practices that ignore the plight of the farmer and his way of life. From there he flew to San Francisco to speak at a college. However, he evaded this appointment, going directly to the hotel where he spends his fitful night. Tormented by the recent loss of his right hand in a cornpicker accident, by an unfinished argument with his wife just before he left home, and by his behavior of the past few days, Andy knows he is "out of control" (p. 33).

Before dawn he walks the streets of the city, encountering along the way various representatives of urban life who occupy the nearly deserted streets. Andy "is a man fated to be charmed by cities" (p. 71), and he muses about what his life might have been had he remained in this spectacular city where he began his journalistic career. He recalls his second job, in Chicago; here a dispute with his editor spurred the decision to move back home to Port William, where he and his wife purchased a run-down farm. The dispute centered on an assignment to interview a successful agribusinessman whose solitary farmstead stood among thousands of acres of corn. "Debt is a permanent part of an operation like this" (p. 75), Bill Meikelberger had said as he popped pills to soothe his ulcer.

Later, Andy had driven through an Amish community dotted with neighboring farmsteads among diversified fields of grain and pasture, where families and neighbors all worked together. Andy stopped to visit one of these Amish farms and concluded, "Twenty-five families like Isaac Troyer's could have farmed and thrived—could have made a healthy, comely, independent community—on the two thousand acres where Bill Meikelberger lived virtually alone with his ulcer" (p. 84).

Though the lure of the city is strong, Andy turns away, knowing he must return to the life he has chosen. Within hours he is back in Kentucky; and once he is at home, he takes another walk—out across his fields to the woods. On a journey that parallels his own urban walk in San Francisco and the healing walk to the woods taken by his grandfather Mat Feltner in *A Place on Earth*, Andy relocates himself in his place, envisioning among the trees the dead who have gone before him: "Their names singing in his mind, he lifts toward them the restored right hand of his joy" (p. 124).

Remembering is both a polemical treatise on the evils of agribusiness and a tribute to a way of life still practiced only by the Amish and a few others. Andy's absent right hand is a glaring symbol of the loss suffered by one literally committed, as farmer and writer, to manual labor. What there is of plot is largely the conflict in the protagonist's mind. However, Carl D. Esbjornson has demonstrated that *Remembering* "draws on epic tradition rather than the conventions of the modern novel" (Merchant, p. 161). It is, he says, "a retelling of Dante's epic of spiritual dismemberment and healing" (p. 156). Having lost his right hand and descended into urban darkness, Andy nevertheless emerges and returns, "to gain re-membership," Esbjornson says, "in the communal order of Port William" (p. 161).

As in all of Berry's fiction, the ideology expressed in *Remembering* is grounded in his practice as a writer and farmer in Port Royal, Kentucky. His characterization of the agribusinessman's economic slavery, which contrasts sharply with the spiritually centered lives of the Amish, draws upon Berry's firsthand experience of farming and upon facts he has garnered as an agricultural reporter. In his essay "Does Community Have a Value?" Berry notes that in the mid 1980s "midwestern industrial farmers have often found it impossible to net 10 percent of gross" (*Home Economics*, p. 189), while the small Amish farm of David Kline in hilly eastern Ohio, "in addition to the family's subsistence...has been grossing about $50,000 a year and netting $25,000 to $30,000" (p. 188).

Essays

The most direct record of Berry's thought is gathered in his volumes of collected essays; portions of his first five books reappear in *Recollected Essays 1965–1980* (1981), and this volume serves as a convenient introduction. The first three essays, taken from *The Long-Legged House*, and the final essay, "The Making of a Marginal Farm," first published in *Smithsonian* in 1980, frame the book and establish Berry's home ground and his affinity for this place where he grew up and to which he returned as an adult to restore a ruined farm. Between these essays are key chapters from *The Hidden Wound* (1970), *A Continuous Harmony: Essays Cultural and Agricultural* (1972), *The Unforeseen Wilderness: An Essay on Kentucky's Red River Gorge* (1971), and *The Unsettling of America: Culture and Agriculture* (1977).

The selections from *The Long-Legged House* make clear Berry's affection for his home and people; however, Berry also laments the largely ruinous history of the white man's settlement here — from inattentive farming that eroded hillsides and depleted soil to the destruction by modern developers whose bulldozers clear the countryside to profit from urban sprawl. In contrast, Berry says, "the American Indian...knew how to live in the country without making violence the invariable mode of his relation to it" (*Recollected Essays*, p. 84). Like the "Old World peasants," these people "belonged deeply and intricately to their places." The Kentucky road builders and settlers were "*placeless* people" (p. 85) who assumed "that what was good for us would be good for the world." For Berry, "the tragic understanding of hindsight" teaches us "the contrary assumption that what is good for the world will be good for us" (p. 98).

Berry's family history also carries the ruinous social and economic relationships that accompanied the ruination of the land. In "Nick and Aunt Georgie," Berry acknowledges "something large and implacable and rigid that I had been born into, and lived in — something I have been trying to get out of ever since" (p. 142). He is speaking of racism. Remembering Nick, his grandfather's hired hand, a man Berry loved and learned from as a child, he says, "He had lived from childhood with the knowledge that his fate was to do the hardest of work for the smallest of wages, and that there was no hope of living any other way" (p. 118).

Wendell Berry

In "Discipline and Hope," the major essay in *A Continuous Harmony* and the longest selection in *Recollected Essays*, Berry explains the cultural disorder of our time as a failure of discipline. Discipline for Berry entails caring work that is informed by the past, engaged in with reverence, and attentive to its long-term consequences. It is ecological work that considers its place in the community of man and nature. Such work is complex and difficult and must therefore be enacted on a small scale, locally. In our time the old standards of such discipline are threatened by, among other things, specialization, which brings fragmentation of knowledge as well as its increase, and "requires not discipline, not a mastery of means, but rather a carelessness of means, . . . subjection of means to immediate ends" (p. 157). Such "short-term vision," Berry says, brings about "ecological and social disaster" (p. 160), in part by the creation of waste, which does not exist in a natural state.

The discipline of agriculture—husbandry, the marriage of person to land—establishes a right relation between nature and culture, the wild and the domestic. Enacted as ceremony, as marriage, agriculture is thus critical to culture; without it, there is no healthy culture.

"Discipline and Hope" is followed in *Recollected Essays* by three essays from *The Unforeseen Wilderness*, an account of a personal journey on foot through Kentucky's Red River Gorge, a wilderness area threatened by modern development. This journey reminds Berry that "wilderness is the element in which we live encased in civilization, as a mollusk lives in his shell in the sea" (p. 236). And yet, this small segment of wilderness "is an island surrounded by the machinery and the workings of an insane greed, hungering for the world's end" (p. 240).

Berry's fullest conceptualization of the relation of nature, culture, and agriculture is found in his book *The Unsettling of America*, represented in *Recollected Essays* by its longest chapter, "The Body and the Earth." While this selection fairly represents Berry's understanding of these relationships, its argument is clearer if one understands the crises in American society as Berry describes them in the first four chapters of *The Unsettling of America*. What keeps America unsettled in Berry's view is the predicament of our history, "that we are divided between exploitation and nurture." Berry describes "these opposite kinds of mind" as follows:

> I conceive a strip-miner to be a model exploiter, and as a model nurturer I take the old-fashioned idea or ideal of a farmer. The exploiter is a specialist, an expert; the nurturer is not. The standard of the exploiter is

efficiency; the standard of the nurturer is care. The exploiter's goal is money, profit; the nurturer's goal is health — his land's health, his own, his family's, his community's, his country's. (*The Unsettling of America*, p. 7)

The ecological necessity of a nurturing agriculture is threatened by the division of producer and consumer in our exploiter-driven society, a situation that for Berry represents an ecological and agricultural crisis: "The producer no longer sees himself as intermediary between people and land . . . and becomes interested only in production. The consumer eats worse, and the producer farms worse. And, in their estrangement, waste is institutionalized" (pp. 37–38). These crises bring about a crisis of culture in a society where "we now have more people using the land (that is, living from it) and fewer thinking about it than ever before" (p. 38). Berry concludes, "We can build one system only within another. We can have agriculture only within nature, and culture only within agriculture" (p 47).

In "The Body and the Earth," Berry raises "the question of human limits, of the proper definition and place of human beings," which, he says, "finally rests upon our attitude toward our biological existence." This view entails a number of questions about the value and uses of the body, and the relations between body and earth, body and mind, body and soul — questions that are fundamentally religious but also fundamentally agricultural, "for no mattter how urban our life, our bodies live by farming; we come from the earth and return to it, and so we live in agriculture as we live in flesh" (*Recollected Essays*, p. 269).

The rise of urban life and industry allowed us to forget, Berry says, "that wilderness still circumscribed civilization and persisted in domesticity" (p. 273). He turns to Chinese landscape paintings and Shakespeare's *King Lear* to show that only "by understanding accurately his proper place in Creation, a man may be made whole" (p. 271). Wholeness, in Berry's ecological view, is at the root of the concept of health, the one value, he said in *A Continuous Harmony*, that even in a relativistic age we should all be

able to agree on. Health and wholeness depend on right relations that are rooted in our biology and protected, for human beings, by moral disciplines that are essentially connective and cannot be practiced in isolation or in ignorance of our dependence on nature. Hence specialization, extreme individualism, and exploitation are destructive, while agriculture, marriage, and the maintenance of local culture are connective, nurturing, healthy.

Berry's ecological view of the essential connectives between nature and culture — often expressed in sexual terms — also has direct implications for human sexuality. The health of the body and of the community both depend on a healthy affirmation of natural sexual energy, Berry says, but "at the root of culture must be the realization that . . . in nature all energies move in forms; that, therefore, in a human order energies must be *given* forms" (p. 302). The responsible discipline of sexual energy is marital fidelity:

The forsaking of all others is a keeping of faith, not just with the chosen one, but with the ones forsaken. The marriage vow unites not just a woman and a man with each other; it unites each of them with the community in a vow of sexual responsibility toward all others. The whole community is married, realizes its essential unity, in each of its marriages. (p. 302)

Berry claims that "if one is to have the power and delight of one's sexuality, then the generality of instinct must be resolved in a responsible relationship to a particular person." A corollary implication is that one cannot love the world in a generalized way, as is suggested by expressions about the "world citizen" and the "global village." Berry says, "No matter how much one may love the world as a whole, one can live fully in it only by living responsibly in some small part of it" (p. 303). That love and care are nevertheless universal values is clear from Berry's conclusion: "It is impossible to care for each other more or differently than we care for the earth" (p. 304).

The Gift of Good Land: Further Essays Cultural and Agricultural (1981) extends the thought developed in *A Continuous Harmony* and *The Unsettling of America.* Its twenty-four short essays provide numerous examples of good farming to counteract the industrial agriculture Berry has decried in the earlier books and to demonstrate the kind of agricultural connection between nature and culture that Berry deems necessary to a healthy society. He examines Peruvian hillside farms, where tradition and need have combined to ensure that the skills required to practice sustainable agriculture are maintained. He finds similar practices among the Papago in the Sonora Desert; these contrast with the "squandering of Arizona's land and water" (p. 67) by modern industrial society. In other essays Berry evaluates horse- and hand-powered tools that offer appropriate technology for small farms. Six essays describe Amish and other viable small farms in the United States farm belt.

The title essay in *The Gift of Good Land* is Berry's most overt attempt to construct "a biblical argument for ecological and agricultural responsibility" (p. 267). Berry's insistence on using language that honors the Western Christian heritage has brought discomfort to some of his readers who hold this tradition responsible for many of the ills of modern industrial society, but his argument brings no less discomfort to those satisfied with conventional expressions of Christianity. "I wish to deal directly," Berry says, "with my own long held belief that Christianity, as usually presented by its organizations, is not *earthly* enough—that a valid spiritual life, in this world, must have a practice and a practicality . . . a material result" (p. 267). However, Berry's determination to find support for his ecological philosophy in the Judeo-Christian heritage has also garnered favorable attention. In a 1991 article, William Merrill Decker speaks of Berry's "insistently religious understanding of ecology" as "one of the great contributions to ecological thought made in the last three decades" (p. 244).

In "The Gift of Good Land," Berry confronts the view that the Christian tradition is respon-sible for the ecological crisis of modern industrial societies. The argument is best known through Lynn White, Jr.'s, widely published essay, "The Historical Roots of Our Ecologic Crisis," which traces the Western penchant for exploitation of land and other resources to the biblical injunction to "subdue" the earth. Berry points out that since this instruction was given to Adam and Eve before the Fall it could hardly offer a license to violate the Creation. He supports this contention with other evidence of the care for the earth that God demanded of his people, for example, the requirement that the Israelites let their land lie fallow every seventh year and that they return it to the original settlers every fiftieth year, "as if to free it," Berry says, "of the taint of trade and the conceit of human ownership" (p. 271).

The fallow laws for Berry are reminders to the Israelites "that the land is theirs only by gift; it exists in its own right, and does not begin or end with any human purpose" (p. 271). The people may hold the land in trust, that is, as long as they faithfully practice stewardship of it—a discipline requiring practical acts of charity that depend on practical skills. "How can you love your neighbor," Berry asks, "if you don't know how to build or mend a fence, how to keep your filth out of his water supply and your poison out of his air . . . ?" (p. 275). To love one's neighbor, in other words, one must love the earth.

Since his three major books on culture and agriculture, Berry has published four more essay collections, *Standing by Words* (1983), *Home Economics* (1987), *What Are People For?* (1990), and *Sex, Economy, Freedom and Community* (1993). As Paul Merchant has observed in his introduction to *Wendell Berry*, Berry's later essays "continue with increasing sharpness and penetration to investigate the concerns of the earlier volumes" (p. 3).

The title essay in *Standing by Words* asserts the need for accountability and fidelity in our use of language. The disintegration of language accompanies, for Berry, the "disintegration of communities and the disintegration of persons," which, he says, are "two epidemic illnesses of our time" (p. 24). He cites examples from a wide range of sources: freshman English textbooks, transcripts of the Nuclear Regulatory Commission, and an article about animal agriculture, among others. Throughout the essays of this book, Berry calls upon the great poets of the Western tradition—Homer, Dante, Shakespeare, Milton—for expressions of the right relations with others and with our place on earth. "This word-keeping," he says in "Poetry and Marriage," "standing by one's word, is a double fidelity: to the community and to oneself," whereas "to break one's word in order to be 'free' of it," as Berry finds in the modern quest for poetic freedom and originality, "is to make and enforce a damning equation between freedom and loneliness" (p. 208).

The essays in *Home Economics* range widely in their subject matter: a visit to Ireland, higher education, patriotism, wilderness preservation. His aim in all of them, Berry says in his preface, is to continue "an argument that I began twenty or so years ago . . . that things connect—that we are wholly dependent on a pattern, an all-inclusive form, that we partly understand" (p. ix).

A similar aim informs *What Are People For?*, a book that opens with two meditative and epigrammatic essays on damaging and healing work. The next several essays pay tribute to writers Berry admires—from Nate Shaw, a black farmer whose oral autobiography was published as *All God's Dangers*, to Wallace Stegner, Berry's teacher at Stanford. There follow several essays on a variety of topics. In the title essay, Berry examines the displacement of small farmers to the city and the problems of urban unemployment. "The great question that hovers over this issue," he says, "is the question of what people are *for*."

For Berry, our society's "absolute premium on labor-saving measures, short workdays, and retirement" suggests that "unemployment and welfare dependency . . . are only different names for our national ambitions." While "the obsolescence of human beings" seems to have become "our social goal," Berry reminds his readers of much "necessary work" that remains to be done: "restoring and caring for our farms, forests, and rural towns and communities"

(p. 125). In "Nature as Measure," the last essay in *What Are People For?*, Berry argues that nature is the only appropriate measure to find "an atonement between ourselves and our world, between economy and ecology, between the domestic and the wild" (p. 208).

In *Sex, Economy, Freedom and Community*, Berry extends the idea of "nature as measure," arguing that the absence of such a standard in our pursuit of productivity and self-liberation has brought us far down the path of destruction and disintegration of healthy human communities. Berry finds such disintegration in issues as diverse as the General Agreement on Tariffs and Trade (GATT), the war against Iraq, and the U.S. Senate hearing on Clarence Thomas' nomination to the Supreme Court, where conflicts between public and private life and between local and national or international concerns are irresolvable by our present standards and goals. For Berry the only "indispensable form that can intervene between public and private interests is that of community . . . a locally understood interdependence of local people, local culture, local economy, and local nature" (pp. 119–120). This idea, for which nature is the measure, may "extend itself beyond the local, but it only does so metaphorically. The idea of a national or global community is meaningless apart from the realization of local communities" (p. 120).

One of Berry's nonfiction prose works is a biography, *Harlan Hubbard: Life and Work* (1990), an affectionate tribute to the Kentucky painter who for Berry embodied the ecological ideals Berry has sought in his own life and work. For more than forty years Harlan and Anna Hubbard lived in a house they built themselves at Payne Hollow on the Kentucky River in Trimble County, Kentucky. Here they grew most of their own food and bartered their produce for goods they could not provide themselves. The marriage of the solitary Harlan and the refined Anna "is best understood," Berry says, "as a harmony between the two seemingly opposite themes of domesticity and wildness" (p. 8).

Hubbard's early farm-landscape paintings, Berry says, reveal an artist who "has been admitted intimately into the presence of the country"

(p. 50) to present, in Hubbard's own words, "the life of man in harmony with nature; a brief flowering between the primeval wilderness that was gone and the urban blight that was to come" (p. 52). Lest anyone think this work nostalgic, Berry immediately qualifies what Hubbard meant by "a brief flowering." Hubbard's paintings of "preindustrial hill farms," Berry says, offer "a proper kind of human artifice. . . . They are perceptions and celebrations of a decent way of living on the earth," a way that is "inescapably economic as well as aesthetic and spiritual" (p. 52).

Of the Hubbards' settlement at Payne Hollow, Berry says that their particular knowledge of and love for this place distinguished them from most American settlers whose "plans . . . have not included what was already there." He continues, "I can think of no one else who has so purposefully, so fully, and for so long a time immersed himself in any American place. . . . This is his revolution and his rare Americanism, and this is why his life is as important to us as his work" (pp. 89–90).

That Harlan Hubbard "made no . . . division" between his life and work aligns him in Berry's view with John Milton's thought that the artist "ought him selfe to bee a true Poem" (p. 56). Berry approvingly quotes Hubbard's *Journals* about our "perishable . . . relation with the earth" which "must be constantly renewed"—an obligation that is endangered by seeing "with the intellect alone, instead of the intellect through the senses" (p. 41). The perception is that of the artist, the poet, one who like Milton seeks to make of his life on earth an art, aware of—though never fully achieving—a sense of the wholeness and connectedness of things. It is a perception that is ecological; it is also spiritual, and it enlightens Berry's work, especially his poetry.

Poetry

In addition to chapbooks and limited editions, Berry has published ten volumes of poetry. His *Collected Poems, 1957–1982* (1985) contains selections from the first seven of these and from *Findings*, a small press publication long out of print. Two later books have appeared, *Sabbaths* (1987) and *Entries* (1994).

Wallace Stegner has written in an open letter to Berry that upon first meeting Berry in 1958 at Stanford, "I recognized you as one who knew where he was from and who he was" (Merchant, p. 50). While Berry's poems show ample evidence of humility and awe in the face of mystery, they also reveal a writer who, in addition to knowing his place, knows what he is about. The titles of his books hint at Berry's uncommonly clear sense of who he is at each stage of his development as a poet: there is a young man's awareness of setting out on a tentative exploration (*The Broken Ground*, 1964; *Openings*, 1968; *Findings*, 1969); a grown man's assurance of achievement (*Farming: A Hand Book*, 1970; *The Country of Marriage*, 1973; *Clearing*, 1977); a mature man's recognition of how much his vocation has both set him apart and yet joined him to all that is in the cycle of birth, growth, death, and rebirth (*A Part*, 1980; *The Wheel*, 1982); and an older man's acknowledgment of his need for rest from his labors and renewal of his spirit (*Sabbaths*, 1987).

Although Berry's poems frequently turn on the nuances of a farmer's work and observations, a quality that Donald Hall praises as Berry's "dailyness" (Merchant, p. 171), no form has been as congenial for his art as the elegy and its subject, death. "Though the green fields are my delight," Berry says in the first of three elegiac poems about the death of his friend Owen Flood, "elegy is my fate" (*Collected Poems*, p. 233). Berry's first widespread recognition as a poet came with the publication in the *Nation* (21 December 1963) of "November 26, 1963," an elegy for President John F. Kennedy. An elegy for his paternal grandfather appeared in *Openings*, and "Three Elegiac Poems" for his maternal grandfather in *Findings*. Reviewing Berry's *Collected Poems* in the *New York Times Book Review*, David Ray said this volume contains "poems . . . as fine as any written in our time," but it "will probably be valued most of all for its 'Elegy' on the farmer Owen Flood."

For a poet who honors the traditions of his elders and who, as a farmer, measures life by nature and the cycles of its seasons, the pastoral tradition, the seasonal or cyclical form, and the honorific mode of the elegy are indeed fitting. Berry begins his elegy on President Kennedy with a grieving reference to "the winter earth." Following the traditional sequences of the elegy (grief and mourning, the funeral procession, the interment, and an apotheosis), Berry then notes "the mourners standing in the rain," "the mouth of the grave waiting," and "the young dead body carried in the earth into the first deep night of its absence." Then he looks ahead to "the long approach of summers toward the healed ground where he will be waiting." The repetitive form and long lines are reminiscent of Walt Whitman and of the biblical psalms; day and night, winter and summer, lend nature's measure to the cadence and sense of the verse.

Another early elegy is the one for Berry's paternal grandfather, Pryor Thomas Berry. For obvious reasons, the poem represents a more personal experience; however, a sense of distance marks the poem (the grandfather died in the poet's youth) and contributes a mood of dignity. Again, the measure of the poem may be taken in terms of daylight and darkness, winter and spring. Winter and night dominate the opening sections: "A flood of snow" accompanies the grandfather's death, and "His shadow... / Moves the dark to wholeness." In the third section, the poet recognizes that "the numb dead know / No fitfulness of wind" (*Collected Poems*, p. 3), and in the final section there is a sense of the coming spring: "Spring tangles shadow and light, / Branches of trees / Knit vision and wind" (p. 5).

In "Three Elegiac Poems" for Harry Erdman Perry, Berry's maternal grandfather, who died in 1965, the more mature poet has found a way to merge the high seriousness of the elegiac form with the mundane, the commonness of death's setting. The first poem is a formal supplication: "Let him escape hospital and doctor. / ... Let him go free of tubes and needles. / ... Let him die in one of the old rooms / of his living" (*Collected*

Poems, pp. 49–50). In the second poem, the poet "stand[s] at the cistern in front of the old barn / in the darkness, in the dead of winter." He drinks from the cold cistern while in the farmhouse "An old man I've loved all my life is dying / in his bed there" (p. 50). Having made plain the ordinary places and acts upon which the mystery of death intrudes, the poet in the third poem speaks of a kind of transcendence that nevertheless remains rooted in the ordinary reality of nature's cycles. The dead man "goes free of the earth," and "The earth recovers from his dying." The word "recovers" is aptly chosen, for the mound of broken earth that is the grave heals over, nourished—as is nature's way—by decay. In the end, the poet's dead grandfather is "hidden among all that is, / and cannot be lost" (p. 51).

Berry's most remarkable achievement in the elegiac mode, and surely one of his finest poems, is the elegy for Owen Flood. Here the marriage of high seriousness and everyday reality is complete. The poem begins with the poet's recognition that "To be at home on its native ground / the mind must go down below its horizon / ... to receive the lives of the dead." Like Dante, the poet descends "as through a furrow, and the dead / gathered to meet me" (*Collected Poems*, p. 234). He sees his long dead grandparents. "Those were my teachers," he says. Then he meets Owen, another teacher, and hands him a clod of earth that he has brought. Owen takes the clod and says, "Wendell, this is not a place / for you and me." The poet responds, "The crops are in the barn ... / and I have turned back to accept, / if I can, what none of us could prevent" (p. 235).

Owen leads Wendell across the hills and valleys of their lives, teaching him that "Our way is endless," and "We are what we have lost." As his friend speaks, the poet hears a Creation song: "That moment, earth and song and mind, / the living and the dead, were one" (p. 240). His teaching mission completed, Owen drops the clod of "beloved earth" and releases the poet from his company. "And I," the poet says, "inheritor of what I mourned, / went back toward the light of day" (p. 241).

What Berry is seeking in the elegies is a sense of atonement, or as he puts it in *A Continuous Harmony*, "at-one-ment." His capacity for finding atonement in the ordinary is demonstrated by a modest poem in *Sabbaths* in which he mourns a dog's death with a sense of decorum wholly free of the humor or sentimentality one might expect. "The eager dog lies strange and still / Who roamed the woods with me" (p. 28), he begins this poem written in ballad stanzas, noting the loss of his dog's company on a Sunday morning walk through the woods. The silence of the loss is met by a quiet that brings the poet face to face with a deer on this "morning of God's mercy" (p. 29). In a note Berry cites Lamentations 3 : 22–23 as the source of this line ("It is of the Lord's mercies that we are not consumed, because his compassions fail not. They are new every morning.").

At times Berry does confront death—his own—with appealing humor. In "Testament" he asks his "relatives and friends" to say when he has died "that I have found / A good solution, and am on my way / To the roots" (*Collected Poems*, p. 163). He reminds them "that the Heavenly soil / Need not be too rich to please / One who was happy in Port Royal," and he proposes an epitaph: "Beneath this stone a Berry is planted / In his home land, as he wanted" (p. 164).

The range of Berry's humor—including satire, jest, and sarcasm—may be seen in his "mad farmer" poems. "The Mad Farmer Revolution" is a bawdy narrative poem of drunkenness and debauchery—a counterpoint to Berry's usual reverence for marriage and fidelity—in which the mad farmer "plowed" the parson's wife, and together

> they sowed and reaped till all
> the countryside was filled
> with farmers and their brides sowing
> and reaping.
> (*Collected Poems*, p. 120)

In "The Contrariness of the Mad Farmer," the speaker mocks Berry's veneration of the dead by saying he laughs at funerals "because / I knew the dead were already . . . / preparing a comeback." Later in the same poem, the speaker raises a sarcastic question that echoes Berry's moral indignation about war: "Did you finish killing / everybody who was against peace?"

In sayings, prayers, and manifestos, the mad farmer speaks out, sometimes to voice Berry's deepest concerns with biting wit, sometimes to parody Berry's own sacred cows. The mad farmer also epigrammatically addresses Berry's insistence on seeing a spiritual dimension to life and his equal insistence that the spiritual is rooted in the earthly. "What I know of spirit is astir / in the world," he says (*Collected Poems*, p. 134), and

> The world
> is a holy vision, had we clarity
> to see it—a clarity that men
> depend on men to make
> (p. 154)

The search for clarity of vision, to find the spiritual in the earthly, motivates much of Berry's poetry and may be the most significant achievement in the poems of the mature farmer in *Farming: A Handbook* and *Clearing*. The incipient farmer is already to be found in Berry's earlier poetry, in the title poem of *The Broken Ground*, for example. The image is that of the plowman faithfully imagining what is to come from his work:

> the breaking
> through which the new
> comes [. . .]
> bud opening to flower
> opening to fruit opening
> to the sweet marrow
> of the seed
> (*Collected Poems*, p. 25)

While the imagery aptly demonstrates Berry's poetic tendencies, it lacks the keen particularity that the experience of farming gives to his later poetry.

Farming: A Handbook, whose title makes the outrageous claim that poetry is practical, that farming and poetry are instructive, opens with

101

"The Man Born to Farming," a poem that immediately establishes the particular imagery that yields the farmer's knowledge:

> The man born to farming
> [. . .] enters into death
> yearly, and comes back rejoicing. He has
>   seen the light lie down
> in the dung heap, and rise again in the corn
> (*Collected Poems*, p. 103)

This handbook is not so much about how to farm—though it is that—as about how to live.

Written during the Vietnam War, *Farming: A Handbook* contains a number of poems that register Berry's protest against that war. "The Morning's News" brings to mind the grisly killing that is claimed "to moralize the state." The poet says he can understand animal savagery, "But to kill by design, . . . / that is the sullen labor that perfects Hell." His son's innocent eyes and his "fields now turning/green with the young grass of April" lead him to "purge my mind of the airy claims/of church and state. I will serve the earth/and not pretend my life could better serve" (*Collected Poems*, pp. 109–110).

Farm and family teach the poet about choices to make, higher laws to obey. Such a choice governs the poet's thought in "February 2, 1968," a poem whose title marks the date of the Tet Offensive. In a world full of danger, death, and war, the poet "walk[s] the rocky hillside, sowing clover." A superficial reading might suggest the poet has chosen to avoid the unpleasant reality of the world's news. In fact, he has made a careful choice, grounded in knowledge and faith, to help the earth itself survive while nations are at war. The farmer-poet knows that clover provides excellent cover to heal an eroding "rocky hillside," and he has the faith to plant it there "in flying snow, in the dead of winter." With the mad farmer, his task is to "practice resurrection" (*Collected Poems*, p. 152).

Clearing is Berry's *Walden*, a poetic account of the purchase and restoration of Lanes Landing Farm. The range and integral relation of the seven long poems that constitute *Clearing* are not fully rendered in the five poems, some of them shortened versions of those included in *Collected Poems*. Understandably omitted are lengthy passages of fact, an accumulation of names, dates, tract sizes, and other land records that honor Berry's subject by their clarity and detail but seem prosaic out of context. More significant omissions are two passages on the subject Berry calls "reverdure." The first is "Returning to the Beloved," a section of "Work Song," where reverdure is claimed for the act of hauling manure with a team of horses in the fall of the year, "rebuilding promise/In the ground" (*Clearing*, p. 36). The second is the final poem of the book, entitled "Reverdure." "Reverdure is my calling," the poet says here, "to make these scars grow grass" (p. 50). The word names the essential act of the farmer, ecologist, and poet—to unite farmer with farm, nature with culture, and flesh with mind.

In spite of these and other omissions, the five poems from *Clearing* that reappear in the *Collected Poems* demonstrate Berry's ecologically minded, farm-based poetry. The first poem, "History," locates the subject in time, at the end of a long line of explorers, hunters, and settlers. The speaker is all of these:

> I have arrived here
> many times. I have come
> on foot, on horseback, by boat,
> and by machine
> (p. 174)

Midway through the poem, the speaker becomes Berry himself:

> Through my history's despite
> and ruin, I have come
> to its remainder, and here
> have made the beginning
> of a farm
> (pp. 174–175)

In "Where" the poet mediates upon the land he has purchased, hoping for a song to heal

> the scars
> of minds whose history
> was imprinted by no example
> of a forebearing mind
> (p. 178)

"The Clearing" evokes work, and the purposes of work. "Vision must have severity/at its edge," the poet says. After cataloging the "trees / that follow man's neglect," he takes a chain saw to the overgrown land: "sing, steel, the hard song/of vision cutting in." "Married /to his place" the poet returns to feed the animals: "Fidelity /reaches through the night" to "Feed / the lives that feed/lives." This is the hard vision of the farmer, whose work is a necessary, nurturing link that marries nature and culture.

In "Work Song" Berry says that "If we will have the wisdom . . . / to stand like slow-growing trees/on a ruined place, renewing, enriching it," then one day "Families will be singing in the fields." This vision "is no paradisal dream./Its hardship is its possibility."

The selections from *Clearing* in the *Collected Poems* end with "From the Crest," a musing, dreamlike poem in which "The thought of work becomes/a friend of the thought of rest." These lines, which bring to mind both renewal and finality, express the theme of Berry's next book of poems, *Sabbaths*.

The poems of *Sabbaths* are organized in eight sections, by their years of composition between 1979 and 1986. Within each section the poems are numbered but not titled, though the table of contents identifies each poem by its first line. Although Berry has written formal verse before, and has always honored Western poetic traditions, such verse dominates the poems of *Sabbaths*. Many are structured in simple, rhymed tetrameter reminiscent of traditional Protestant hymns. Elsewhere, pentameter and more challenging forms, such as terza rima, lend their order to Berry's verse. Most notable, perhaps, is the extent to which in *Sabbaths* Berry depends on the language of Christian worship to express mysteries comprehended only dimly by a mind temporarily at rest from labor. These poems register the full extent of Berry's attempt to make art that (as he noted of Harlan Hubbard's landscape paintings) acknowledges mystery and grace beyond the pale of human understanding.

Berry muses on these things in the second poem in *Sabbaths*, where his Sabbath musing takes place in the woods, not in church. It is a place where

> Resurrection
> Is in the way each maple leaf
> Commemorates its kind, by connection
> Outreaching understanding
>
> (p. 7)

Thus, the poet sees that "The mind that comes to rest is tended/In ways that it cannot intend," and he concludes, "Your Sabbath, Lord, thus keeps us by/Your will, not ours" (p. 8).

Berry does not come to such conclusions lightly, and his expression of Christian faith remains unconventional. In a poem beginning "Whatever is foreseen in joy," Berry notes that "Harvest will fill the barn; for that/The hand must ache, the face must sweat." But once "the field is tilled," it is "left to grace," for "Great work is done while we're asleep" (p. 19). It is the thought of labor that brings such recognition, and for Berry it is not achieved in church. In a poem beginning "The bell calls in the town," Berry says, "I hear, but understand/Contrarily, and walk into the woods." Even in the woods, "Projects, plans unfulfilled/Waylay and snatch at me like briars" (p. 10). Later in the poem he relinquishes the "hopes and plans/that no toil can perfect" (p. 11). Resurrection for Berry lies not in some distant hereafter but in the continual cycle of ruin and renewal in the earth:

> Ruin is in place here:
> The dead leaves rotting on the ground,
> The live leaves in the air
> Are gathered in a single dance
> That turns them round and round.
>
> (p. 12)

While the Christian sabbath is weekly occurrence, and Berry does observe it, nature's sabbath is yearly. Its coming in the fall is an inevitable reminder of the fall of man, the death of the body, and the limits of intellect. "The intellect so ravenous to know," Berry says, "Must finally know the dark" (p. 35). By nature's measure—labor and rest, light and dark, ruin and renewal—the poet reaches a small clearing of the mind. "Who makes a clearing makes a work of art," Berry begins still another poem, and he concludes, "Bewildered in our timely dwelling place,/Where we arrive by work, we stay by grace" (p. 67). Such graceful clearings are Berry's sabbath dwelling places.

Berry's *Entries* (1994) is an "eclectic gathering," as Berry has said, of poems written during the preceding fifteen years. "A Marriage Song" commemorates the marriage of the Berrys' daughter Mary. Other poems are meditations on aging, on the endurance of marital love, or varied remembrances—William Carlos Williams, the poet's mother, the deaths of neighbors. The final section recalls the last days and death of Berry's father.

Unlike the formal elegies, these poems about Berry's father are informal, though moving—anecdotal remembrances in free verse. Here Berry recalls an argument with his father over the Vietnam War; it ends in a terse dialogue of reconciliation:

> "Do you know who has been, by God,
> the truest teacher in my life
> from the beginning until now?"
> "*Who*, by God"
>   "*You*, by God!"
> He wept and said, "By God, I'm proud."
>   (*Entries*, p. 66)

In another poem Berry remembers his father as "the most demanding man/I have ever known"—demanding because he was always afraid of loss. "I know his fear now by my own," the poet says. "Precious things are being lost" (p. 67). Another affords a glimpse of the son caring for his dying father: "At night I help him to lie down upon/ That verge we reach by generation and by day" (p. 69).

What unites the poems of this book is the sense in all of them of the poet at home, a member of a household, a family, a community. These are the poems of "a placed person."

Conclusion

In the years since Wendell and Tanya Berry bought the twelve acres of Lanes Landing Farm on the bank of the Kentucky River, the Berry land has expanded to 125 acres of woods, pasture, and cropland. Their daughter Mary and son Den have both married and settled on nearby farms where they are now rearing their children. Wendell Berry has farmed, lectured, written, and also taught intermittently at the University of Kentucky at Lexington. He has received honorary doctorates from a half-dozen colleges and universities, and numerous other awards.

While reviewers have occasionally glossed his ideas as nostalgic or complained that his lyrics do not sing, Berry's essays, short stories, and poetry have been well received in such diverse publications as *Organic Gardening*, the *Draft Horse Journal*, *Harper's Magazine*, the *Atlantic Monthly*, and the *Hudson Review*. His books are receiving increased and favorable critical attention in academic journals. Most extraordinary, perhaps, are the tributes Berry has received from fellow thinkers and writers. Agronomist Wes Jackson has said that Berry "is truly an authentic source for our time" (Merchant, p. 69). Naturalist Terry Tempest Williams has called him "our nation's conscience" (p. 67). In a long poem, Hayden Carruth says Berry's

> fields [. . .] are secure, right with the world,
> proper, and full of meaning, which is love
> in action, as your poems are. And what
> a blessing this has become for us all.
>   (p. 74)

Such praise is uncommon for any writer or thinker in our time. That Wendell Berry's name is not yet a household word may best be explained in an essay by Scott Russell Sanders, entitled "Speaking a Word for Nature." Sanders places Berry among our eloquent contemporary nature writers, including Annie Dillard, John McPhee, Barry Lopez, and others, most of whom "work outside the braided literary currents that critics, reviewers, and publishers regard as the 'mainstream.'" It is a current from which "a deep awareness of nature has been largely excluded," says Sanders, who would have Berry at the center of what is most important: "For Berry, no matter how much the land has been neglected or abused, no matter how ignorant of their environment people may have become, nature is the medium in which life transpires, a prime source of values and meaning and purpose" (Sanders, pp. 221–222).

Contrary as the mad farmer of his poems, faithful in marriage and in land stewardship, rich in the conviction of his ideals, Wendell Berry has become a significant figure among the ecologically minded thinkers of our time.

Selected Bibliography

WORKS OF WENDELL BERRY

FICTION

Nathan Coulter (Boston: Houghton Mifflin, 1960; rev. ed. San Francisco: North Point, 1985); *A Place on Earth* (New York: Harcourt, Brace and World, 1967; rev. ed., San Francisco: North Point, 1985); *The Memory of Old Jack* (New York: Harcourt Brace Jovanovich, 1974); *The Wild Birds: Six Stories of the Port William Membership* (San Francisco: North Point, 1986); *Remembering* (San Francisco: North Point, 1988); *Fidelity: Five Stories* (New York: Pantheon, 1992); "Pray Without Ceasing," in *The Best American Short Stories 1993*, ed. by Louise Erdrich (Boston: Houghton Mifflin, 1993).

ESSAYS

The Long-Legged House (New York: Harcourt Brace Jovanovich, 1969); *The Hidden Wound* (Boston: Houghton Mifflin, 1970); *The Unforeseen Wilderness: An Essay on Kentucky's Red River Gorge* (Lexington: Univ. Press of Kentucky, 1971); *A Continuous Harmony: Essays Cultural and Agricultural* (New York: Harcourt Brace Jovanovich, 1972); *The Unsettling of America: Culture and Agriculture* (San Francisco: Sierra Club, 1977); *The Gift of Good Land: Further Essays Cultural and Agricultural* (San Francisco: North Point, 1981); *Recollected Essays 1965–1980* (San Francisco: North Point, 1981); *Standing by Words* (San Francisco: North Point, 1983); *Home Economics* (San Francisco: North Point, 1987); *What Are People For?* (San Francisco: North Point, 1990); *Harlan Hubbard: Life and Work* (Lexington: Univ. Press of Kentucky, 1990); *Sex, Economy, Freedom and Community* (New York: Pantheon, 1993).

POETRY

"November 26, 1963," in *Nation* 197 (21 December 1963); *The Broken Ground* (New York: Harcourt, Brace and World, 1964); *Openings* (New York: Harcourt, Brace and World, 1968); *Farming: A Handbook* (New York: Harcourt Brace Jovanovich, 1970); *The Country of Marriage* (New York: Harcourt Brace Jovanovich, 1973); *Clearing* (New York: Harcourt Brace Jovanovich, 1977); *A Part* (San Francisco: North Point, 1980); *The Wheel* (San Francisco: North Point, 1982); *Collected Poems, 1957–1982* (San Francisco: North Point, 1985); *Sabbaths* (San Francisco: North Point, 1987); *Entries* (New York: Pantheon, 1994).

BIOGRAPHICAL AND CRITICAL STUDIES

Hayden Carruth, "Essays for Wendell," in *Wendell Berry*, ed by Paul Merchant (Lewiston, Idaho: Confluence, 1991); William Decker, " 'Practice Resurrection': The Poesis of Wendell Berry," in *North Dakota Quarterly* 55:4 (fall 1987); William Merrill Decker, "The Wild, the Divine, and the Human Word: Rereading Wendell Berry," in *North Dakota Quarterly* 59:2 (spring 1991); Carl D. Esbjornson, "Remembering and Home Defense," in *Wendell Berry*, ed. by Paul Merchant (Lewiston, Idaho: Confluence, 1991); Donald Hall, "His Dailyness," in *Wendell Berry*, ed. by Paul Merchant (Lewiston, Idaho: Confluence, 1991); Jack Hicks, "Wendell Berry's Husband to the World: *A Place on Earth*," in *American Literature* 51 (May 1979), repr. in Paul Merchant, ed., *Wendell Berry* (1991); Wes Jackson, "On Cultural Capacity," in *Wendell Berry*, ed. by Paul Merchant (Lewiston, Idaho: Confluence, 1991); Paul Merchant, ed., *Wendell Berry* (Lewiston, Idaho: Confluence, 1991); Speer Morgan, "Wendell Berry: A Fatal Singing," in *Southern Review* 10:4 (fall 1974): 865–877; Herman Nibbelink, "Thoreau and Wendell Berry: Bachelor and Husband of Nature," in *South Atlantic Quarterly* 84:2 (spring 1985): 127–140, rcpr. in Paul Merchant, ed., *Wendell Berry* (1991); David Ray, "Heroic, Mock-Heroic," in *New York Times Book Review* (24 November 1985), sec. 7, 28–29; Scott Russell Sanders, *Secrets of the Universe* (Boston: Beacon, 1991); Wallace Stegner, "A Letter to Wendell Berry," in *Wendell Berry*, ed. by Paul Merchant (Lewiston, Idaho: Confluence, 1991); Jeffery Alan Triggs, "Moving the Dark to Wholeness: The Elegies of Wendell Berry" in *Literary Review* 31:3 (spring 1988), "A Kinship of the Fields: Farming in the Poetry of R. S. Thomas and Wendell Berry," in *North Dakota Quarterly* 57:2 (spring 1989), and "Farm as Form: Wendell Berry's *Sabbaths*," in *Wendell Berry*, ed. by Paul Merchant (Lewiston, Idaho: Confluence, 1991); Terry Tempest Williams, "A Full Moon in May," in *Wendell Berry*, ed. by Paul Merchant (Lewiston, Idaho: Confluence, 1991).

HENRY BESTON
(1888–1968)

DANIEL G. PAYNE

WHEN *The Outermost House*, Henry Beston's account of a year spent living alone in a small cottage on the great beach of Cape Cod, was published in 1928, Beston was forty years old, a writer and editor at the midpoint of an accomplished if rather obscure literary career. Up to that point, Beston had written almost nothing that gave any indication that he was particularly interested in nature or in writing about nature. *The Outermost House* was almost immediately recognized as a work of remarkable insight and power, and was frequently compared—much to Beston's displeasure—to Henry David Thoreau's *Cape Cod* and *Walden*. Beston's cottage on Cape Cod was designated a national literary landmark in 1964, and a plaque celebrating the "Outermost House" was erected at a ceremony which Beston attended in that year. In February 1978, exactly fifty years after *The Outermost House* was published, a great storm blowing in from the Atlantic demolished the house; the irony of such an event would no doubt have been appreciated by the man who had written of Cape Cod, "To understand this great outer beach, to appreciate its atmosphere, its 'feel,' one must have a sense of it as the scene of wreck and elemental drama" (p. 95).[1]

<hr />

1. All page numbers from *The Outermost House* refer to the 1971 Ballantine edition.

Early Life

Although he usually wrote in the first person, Beston rarely discussed the details of his own life; much of what we do know is provided by his wife, Elizabeth Coatsworth, in works such as *Especially Maine: The Natural World of Henry Beston from Cape Cod to the St. Lawrence* (1970). What little Henry Beston wrote about his childhood often concerned his mother, Marie Louise Sheahan, who had been born in Paris, France. It was there that she met and married Beston's father, Joseph Maurice Sheahan, a Quincy, Massachusetts, physician of Irish ancestry who had been studying medicine in France.

Beston was born in Quincy on 1 June 1888, and he spent most of his young life in that busy municipality on the outskirts of Boston. (Christened Henry Beston Sheahan, Beston ceased using the surname Sheahan in the early 1920s for reasons that—like much of his early life—remain somewhat hazy.) Beston claimed that the two greatest influences in his life were the sea and his French upbringing (Lorenz, p. 108). He often cited his bilingual education as a vital element in the development of his writing style. Beston appears to have had little early exposure to outdoor life; with the exception of summers spent with his mother rooming in farm boardinghouses, nature in Quincy was limited to that found in a suburban setting. Of these childhood years Beston would later write, "There was no *poetry*. Fugitive glimpses, perhaps, but no deep, underlying mood" (*Especially Maine*, p. 48).

From the standpoint of formal education, however, Beston's was a relatively privileged lot. He attended Adams Academy and from there went on to Harvard University. At Harvard he majored in English, receiving his bachelor's degree in 1909 and a master's degree in 1911. Following his graduation from Harvard, Beston went to France for a year, during which time he traveled extensively and taught English at the University of Lyons. While in France, Beston spent a considerable amount of time in Ste. Catherine-sous-Rivière, a rural village in the Monts Lyonnais, about twenty miles from the Rhône. This period was significant, Beston would later write, because Ste. Catherine was "the first place in which I encountered and knew and loved the earth" (*Especially Maine*, p. 48). From France, Beston returned to Harvard, where he taught English for the next two years.

The outbreak of war in Europe in 1914 profoundly affected Beston, as it did many Americans with personal and cultural ties to France. In 1915, he enlisted as an ambulance driver in the American Field Service, along with many other idealistic young Americans including his literary peer, Ernest Hemingway. Two of the articles that Beston wrote about what he saw at the front, "Verdun" and "The Vineyard of Red Wine," were published in the *Atlantic Monthly* in 1916. His first book (published under the name Henry Sheahan), *A Volunteer Poilu* (1916), included these and other essays about his experiences as an ambulance driver in wartime France. When the United States entered the war in 1917, Beston took a position as a naval correspondent, serving in the submarine corps. A number of the dispatches that Beston wrote in this capacity were published (under the name of Henry B. Beston) in periodicals as disparate as *Outlook, The North American Review, Country Life*, and *Ladies' Home Journal*. They would later be collected in *Full Speed Ahead: Tales from the Log of a Correspondent with Our Navy* (1919).

Although for the most part Beston's wartime essays were simply straightforward reporting—Beston always referred to them somewhat disparagingly as "journalism"—his fine eye for detail and talent for description are already evident. The carnage that Beston saw firsthand during the war also had an inestimable effect in forming the opinions on the links between modern industrial society and violence that are central to his later works. In "Vineyard of Red Wine," for instance, he describes an instance where he was en route to a field hospital to deliver a wagonload of convalescents when the convoy of ambulances is hit by artillery: "a few seconds later, there sounded the terrifying scream of an air-bomb, a roar, and I found myself in a bitter swirl of smoke. . . . Something sailed swiftly over my head and landed just behind the ambulance. It was a chunk of the skull of one of the horses" (p. 247). Despite Beston's tendency to use phrases such as the "Great Cause" in referring to the war ("With the American Submarines"), the senseless destruction of the conflict contributed to his pessimism about the effect of industrial civilization on the human spirit.

In part as a tonic for his experiences in the war, Beston took to writing children's stories, an interest he pursued enthusiastically throughout the 1920s and returned to occasionally thereafter. His first such effort was *The Firelight Fairy Book* (1919), a collection of original fairy tales. He followed this work with another book of fairy tales, *The Starlight Wonder Book* (1923). Although Beston felt that some of these tales were weak—he later revised several (leaving others out entirely) for *Henry Beston's Fairy Tales* (1952)—Elizabeth Coatsworth writes in *Especially Maine* that he always "had some affection" for these therapeutic children's stories (p. 1). Beston went on to write a number of other books for young people, including *The Book of Gallant Vagabonds* (1925), a series of six historical narratives relating the lives and adventures of the monk Belzoni, Arthur Rimbaud, Edward John Trelawny, John Ledyard, James Bruce, and Thomas Morton of Merrymount; *The Sons of Kai: The Story the Indian Told* (1926); and later several collaborations with his wife, a noted children's author in her own right. As was the case with his journalistic endeavors, however, these works were little more than a pleasant diversion, and, said Coatsworth, "none . . . came up to Henry's exacting standards" (*Especially Maine*, p. 2).

From 1919 to 1923, Beston was editor of *The Living Age*, a monthly magazine published by the Atlantic Monthly Press. *The Living Age* was primarily a collection of articles reprinted from various European periodicals, but Beston also wrote a number of reviews and commentaries (both signed and unsigned) for the magazine. During this period, and for several years thereafter, Beston wrote prolifically for the magazines, producing a diverse body of work that was published in an equally diverse range of periodicals; almost none of this work, however, had anything to do with natural history. Although his magazine work during this period undoubtedly did much to hone his precise, straightforward prose style, it failed to satisfy Beston in either a personal or a literary sense. As he later wrote, "after reading billions of other magazines for two years in the office of *The Atlantic Monthly*, I asked myself, can I write? Then what the deuce am I doing here?" (Lorenz, p. 108).

The Outermost House

In the mid 1920s Beston bought a small plot of dune land on the eastern shore of Cape Cod, overlooking the Atlantic. He drew up plans and hired a local carpenter to build a small house, which he christened the "Fo'castle," and which he intended to use as a summer residence. This house, Elizabeth Coatsworth recalls in *Especially Maine*, "was small, strong and exactly what he wanted. Others might call it a cottage, a cabin or even a shack. Henry called it a house" (p. 13). It consisted of just two rooms, a bedroom and a combined kitchen and living room, with a fireplace set between the two rooms. In his "amateur enthusiasm for windows" Beston had the builder install ten, including seven in the main room (*Outermost House*, p. 5). Beston's nearest neighbors were the coastguardsmen stationed at Nauset, some two miles away, which afforded Beston the distance from the affairs of men that he desired: "South lay the farther dunes and a few far-away and lonely gunning camps; the floor of marsh and tide parted me on the west from the village and its distant cottages; the ocean besieged my door. North, and north alone, had I touch with human beings. On its solitary dune my house faced the four walls of the world" (p. 7).

Beston traveled to his house on the Cape for a two-week vacation in September 1926. Little if anything is known about Beston's state of mind during this period (Wild, p. 192), but Winfield Townley Scott suggests that Beston, a middle-aged bachelor, was feeling pressured to marry and that *The Outermost House* works on the level of an "anti-domestic" work (cited in Paul, p. 95). As a man with literary talent who had, thus far, relatively little to show for it, Beston may have been suffering from some professional anxiety. Others have argued that at some point Beston may have been beset by both problems — Elizabeth Coatsworth may have made Beston's completion of *The Outermost House* a virtual prerequisite of their marriage (Paul, p. 95). As mentioned previously, it also seems evident that ever since the war, Beston had felt increasingly alienated from what he saw as a soul-less, violent, modern society. In any event, as Beston wrote in *The Outermost House*, something compelled him to remain at his isolated house on the Cape far longer than his vacation plans had originally called for:

> The fortnight ending, I lingered on, and as the year lengthened into autumn, the beauty and mystery of this earth and outer sea so possessed and held me that I could not go. The world to-day is sick to its thin blood for lack of elemental things, for fire before the hands, for water welling from the earth, for air, for the dear earth itself underfoot. In my world of beach and dune these elemental presences lived and had their being, and under their arch there moved an incomparable pageant of nature and the year. . . . The longer I stayed, the more eager was I to know this coast and to share its mysterious and elemental life; I

found myself free to do so, I had no fear of being alone, I had something of a field naturalist's inclination; presently I made up my mind to remain and try living for a year on Eastham Beach. (p. 8)

Whatever unstated personal reasons may have formed Beston's decision to live on the great beach for a year, they were soon subsumed by larger issues. As with *Walden*, much of the brilliance of *The Outermost House* lies in the fact that it not only studies the natural history of a particular place (athough that is certainly part of it), but it also considers that most fundamental of questions: What is our place — both as individuals and as a species — in nature?

In his record of this year on the great beach, Beston reveled in the sights, sounds, and smells of a world free from the "stench" of industrialized society. Modern civilization had produced a "new synthetic man," Beston said, who was no longer able to experience nature as he had in the ages before he had dulled his senses in smoke-filled cities. "We ought to keep all senses vibrant and alive," he writes. "Had we done so, we should never have built a civilization which outrages them" (p. 150) — and it is his own awareness of the world all about him that makes his descriptive passages so vivid. At times Beston's writing is almost achingly beautiful, as in his description of a flight of geese that passed overhead while he was out walking on the dunes one night:

> As I approached the shadow of the dune, I heard from behind it, and ever so faint and high and far away, a sound in the night. The sound began to approach and to increase in its wild music, and after what seemed a long minute, I heard it again from somewhere overhead and a little out to sea. . . . Over the elbow of the Cape came the flights, crossing Eastham marsh and the dunes on their way to the immensity of space above the waters. There were little flights and great flights, there were times when the sky seemed empty, there were times when it was filled with an immense clamour which died away slowly over ocean. Not unfrequently I heard the sound of

The Outermost House, Cape Cod, in 1976

> wings, and once in a while I could see the birds — they were flying fast — but scarce had I marked them ere they dwindled into a dot of moonlit sky. (pp. 112–113)

Beston's descriptive powers were all the more remarkable since he was extremely nearsighted and somewhat hard of hearing; however, these deficiencies seem to have been rendered inconsequential by an intensity of concentration that more than compensated for them.

Beston believed that industrial civilization, in addition to dulling our physical senses, had distorted humankind's understanding of our own relation to nature. Not the least of these misconceptions was the notion that humanity was somehow set apart from and superior to the rest of the natural world. As he observed the flights of shorebirds that inexplicably flew in cohesive groups as though guided by a single intelligence, he mused, "Are we to believe that these birds, all of them, are *machina*, as Descartes long ago insisted . . . or is there some psychic relation between these creatures?" (p. 19). Beston rejected any mechanistic explanation for the mysterious interplay between individual members of the flock, suggesting instead that our understanding of such phenomena is limited by the anthropocentric and narrowly analytical way in which we view our fellow creatures:

> We need another and a wiser and perhaps a more mystical concept of animals. Remote from universal nature, and living by complicated artifice, man in civilization surveys the creature through the glass of his knowledge and sees thereby a feather magnified and the whole image in distortion. We patronize them for their incompleteness, for their tragic fate of having taken form so far below ourselves. And therein we err, and greatly err. For the animal shall not be measured by man. In a world older and more complete than ours they move finished and complete, gifted with extensions of the senses we have lost or never attained, living by voices we shall never hear. They are not brethren, they are not underlings; they are other nations, caught with ourselves in the net of life and time, fellow prisoners of the splendour and travail of the earth. (pp. 19–20)

As was the case with John Muir (and to a certain extent other early nature writers such as Thoreau and John Burroughs), Beston rejected the traditionally anthropocentric worldview of western civilization and replaced it with a biocentric one that extended a respectful sympathy for other species. When Beston finds three seabirds that have become covered with oil discharged from a passing tanker, he takes them home and attempts to wash them off and nurse them back to health. He is forced to abandon this symbolic act of contrition when he finds that the captive birds will not eat; he releases them, "just as soon as I saw that I could not possibly help them and that Nature had best deal with the problem in her own way" (p. 81).

Not only had industrial civilization distanced humanity from an understanding of our fellow creatures, so too had it obscured our understanding of our own vital connection with the earth. Beston would often return to this theme in later works, but his statements about the healing power of the earth seem to have a personal significance in *The Outermost House*. As he is out beachcombing one day shortly after his arrival on the Cape, he sees—for the first and only time in his life, he says—a flight of swans traveling south over the ocean: "Glorious white birds in the blue October heights over the solemn unrest of ocean—their passing was more than music, and from their wings descended the old loveliness of earth which both affirms and heals" (p. 28). Although Beston's comments regarding himself are characteristically restrained, it appears that part of the healing process was the rediscovery of the ability to live in the present rather than—as is so common in modern life—the past or the future. The most important thing he had learned from his year on the Cape, Beston wrote, "is a sense that the creation is still going on, that the creative forces are as great and as active to-day as they have ever been, and that to-morrow's morning will be as heroic as any of the world. *Creation is here and now*" (p. 173). As the circle of the seasons closed and Beston prepared to return to a more conventional life, "time gathered again like a cloud, and presently the stars began to pale over an ocean still dark with remembered night" (p. 173).

The solitary nature of Beston's life on the Cape, his emphasis on nature, and the fact that he wrote about a place that Thoreau had also written extensively about all contribute to inevitable comparisons. In fact, what little critical attention has been devoted to Beston inevitably plays on the Thoreauvian influence in his writing, but Beston disapproved of the equation, complaining that Thoreau "had very little heart" (*Especially Maine*, p. 2). In what may have been an effort to put some distance between his year on Cape Cod from Thoreau's at Walden Pond, Beston played down the solitary aspect of his stay, stating that, with his weekly trips for groceries and his frequent visits from the coast-guardsmen stationed nearby, "a medieval anchorite would have probably regarded me as a dweller in the market place" (p. 74), and confessing that without the solicitude of the Coast Guard crew at Nauset "my experiment might well have been both over-solitary and difficult" (p. 104). In private, he spoke disparagingly about

Henry Beston in 1963

puts it in the same class as *Walden* and Edward Abbey's *Desert Solitaire* (1968), calling it a "talismanic book of solitude" (p. 83). Although sales were initially somewhat disappointing, due in part to the onset of the Great Depression, they were steady, and the book went through numerous editions. The effect that the book had on many of his fellow naturalists through the years must have been particularly gratifying to Beston; in a letter to David McCord, he sends greetings to Rachel Carson, proudly making reference to her statement that *The Outermost House* was the only book that had influenced her (*Especially Maine*, p. 146).

A Farmer-Naturalist

In June 1929, Beston married Elizabeth Coatsworth, who had been working on her own book, *The Cat Who Went to Heaven* (for which she was awarded the 1931 Newbery Medal for children's literature). After a honeymoon spent at the Fo'castle, the Bestons moved into a home in Hingham, Massachusetts, a suburb of Boston overlooking the harbor. In *Personal Geography: Almost an Autobiography* (1976), Elizabeth Coatsworth writes: "I was thirty-six years old when I married and Henry was five years older, so that for both of us it was very much of an adventure and we embarked upon it gaily and warmly. At the same time, writing remained of great importance to us both" (p. 110). After the revelatory experience of his year spent close to nature on Cape Cod, however, Beston found a return to suburban life difficult. Coatsworth writes in the foreword to *Especially Maine* that her husband "did not like this life with its grind of passing cars and its quality of an old South Shore village slowly turning into a suburb" (p. 5). In this atmosphere there was little of the poetry of the earth, and brief visits to the Cape failed to provide Beston with what he needed for either his writing or his spiritual well-being. He abandoned plans to write a book on the inner Cape, perhaps because he realized that he would have a difficult time adding to what he had already said about the Cape in *The Outermost House*. It

Thoreau's own pretensions to solitude, stating that "Thoreau used to chop wood for his mother every day, and in bringing it he always picked up a pie or chocolate cake" (Lorenz, p. 109). It may be that Beston was sensitive about the comparison with Thoreau (as was John Burroughs, another nature writer frequently likened to Thoreau) because it hit too close to home—Sherman Paul speaks of the "anxiety of influence" in this connection—but there are also stark differences between the two writers, as Paul and other critics such as Donald Federman have pointed out.

Beston was certain that *The Outermost House* was far better than anything he had written before, and Elizabeth Coatsworth states that he immediately knew that it was a classic (*Especially Maine*, p. 5). Contemporary reviewers and modern critics alike have confirmed Beston's self-appraisal of the work: Thomas Lyon, the editor of one of the many anthologies that has included a selection from *The Outermost House*, was soon obvious that life in suburban Boston would provide him with little of the inspiration that life on the Cape had. As Beston remarked caustically in a letter to a friend, in Hingham "There is no nature for a naturalist to see, there are no birds save 'the Spotted Chevrolet and the Greater and Lesser Buick'" (*Especially Maine*, p. 72).

While visiting friends in Maine, Beston heard of a farm for sale near the small town of Damariscotta. "He who might hesitate for hours on the choice of a few words, could make up his mind on the future course of his life in an instant," recalls Elizabeth Coatsworth in *Especially Maine* (p. 6). A few weeks later, the Bestons were the owners of a home in Maine they called Chimney Farm. Beston describes it in *Herbs and the Earth*: "The house was old and country-like and painted a farmhouse red. It stands in the midst of fields on a hillside sloping east, with a lake below lying blue . . . and a far country of woods" (p. 21). The move to Chimney Farm was a gradual one, as the Bestons now had two young daughters in school: Margaret, born June 1930, and Catherine, born April 1932. They would not make a complete break with Hingham until 1944, although they spent every summer in Maine and returned to the farm as often as possible.

Beston enthusiastically embraced rural life, finding the seasonal course of farm work to be in tune with what he had learned about nature on Cape Cod. "From the beginning," wrote Coatsworth, "Henry was happy at Chimney Farm" (*Especially Maine*, p. 41). Beston's tendency toward a nostalgic brand of pastoralism became increasingly pronounced following the move to Maine and is most evident in *Herbs and the Earth* (1935) and *Northern Farm: A Chronicle of Maine* (1948). Overall, Beston's work probably has more in common with that of farmer-naturalists such as John Burroughs, Wendell Berry, and Edwin Way Teale than it does with the flinty transcendentalism of Thoreau. For Beston, it was not necessary to seek a self-imposed isolation from human contact or a retreat to the primeval wilderness in order to return to a life grounded in the natural rhythms of the earth; for

him, life in a farming community was as far from the perceived sterility of modern industrial civilization as he needed to get.

Despite Beston's fondness for country life, however, the emphasis at Chimney Farm was always more on writing than on farming. The farming that was done at the Beston place was, more often than not, performed by hands hired from neighboring farms. Still, as he wrote in *Herbs and the Earth*, in farm life there was "the poignant and poetic recognition of the long continuity of man" (p. 5) that he had found modern urban life to be lacking. Farm life was free from the spiritual malaise he felt was characteristic of an industrial civilization that was "without a truly human past and may be without a human future" (p. 5). As he had noted in *The Outermost House*, "A year indoors is a journey along a paper calendar; a year in outer nature is the accomplishment of a tremendous ritual" (p. 47), and an agricultural lifestyle, tied to the ebb and flow of the seasons, was a means of fulfilling this ritual.

Herbs and the Earth

Beston's study at the farmhouse was a large herb attic where he installed bookshelves, a small woodstove, and a cot. On stormy nights he would sometimes sleep up in the study so that he could listen to the rain on the roof. The herb attic may well have served as the inspiration for Beston's first gardening project at Chimney Farm, the small herb garden about which he writes in *Herbs and the Earth*. Beston approached gardening from a decidedly metaphysical standpoint:

When the bed was planted, Henry, dressed in his oldest working clothes, would go out to sit beside the border staring down at it. At long intervals he might crumble a piece of earth between his fingers, or pull up a weed. But mostly he was just staring and staring. When he came in, he would say, "I've been working in the herb garden all morning." It might indeed be the man-of-all-work who had spaded and planted and weeded, but in a truer sense Henry *would* have been working even harder in the herb garden, pondering the meaning of the earth between his fingers and the fragrant leaves about him. (*Especially Maine*, p. 7)

To enter the herb garden and to work with "the oldest group of plants known to gardeners" (*Herbs and the Earth*, p. xvii) was for Beston a symbolic act of renewal, a return to a time when man's connection with the earth had not yet been obscured by the apparatus of industrial civilization. In the herb garden, he wrote, "the earth underfoot is the earth of poetry and the human spirit; in this small sun and shade flourishes a whole tradition of mankind" (1990 ed., p. 6).

Beston described *Herbs and the Earth* as "part garden book, part musing study of our relation to Nature" (p. xvii). The book contains a wealth of information about herbs, their history and uses, and their cultivation, but Beston was far more interested in the poetry of the earth than he was in the science of agriculture. Beston's inclusion of practical advice on the planting of an herb garden seems almost to be a grudging afterthought: "There are plenty of books and pamphlets concerned with the making of borders and beds, plenty of leaflets about composts and manures and other hearty matters, and I do not intend to go into the elementary side of garden-making" (p. 120). The aspect of gardening that most interested him was how this participation in nature's continuing act of creation was so deeply ingrained in the human spirit:

It is only when we are aware of the earth and of the earth as poetry that we truly live. . . . It is this earth which is the true inheritance of man, his link with his human past, the source of his religion, ritual and song, the kingdom without whose splendor he lapses from his mysterious state of man to a baser world which is without the other virtue and the other integrity of the animal. (pp. 4–5)

Beston suggested that gardening was one of the ways by which one could narrow the gap be-

tween man and the earth that had been opened up by the artificiality of modern life. This gap, which he believed had been increasing ever since the commencement of the industrial age in the nineteenth century, had resulted in an age in which mankind had "lost the earth, but found (since the comfortable century of philosophers in dressing gowns) a something which it calls 'nature,' and of which it speaks with enthusiasm and embalms in photographs" (p. 5). As was the case in *The Outermost House*, the question of time surfaces in *Herbs and the Earth*. Once again, the narrative structure of the book is based on the passage of the seasons, and there is a patient acceptance of the passage of time that has more in common with eastern philosophy than with the linear, western sense of chronology. He also felt that the act of tending a garden had a humanizing effect on the gardener himself:

Impatience does not beset [gardeners], for their herbs are of interest from the moment they appear in spring, lifting their fragrance and beauty of leaf out of still another winter; they are willing that their plants shall take their time, well aware that here any flower is but a part of the cycle of beauty. It is from this equable temper of gardener and garden that the living relation between them which can be so subtle and profound can best arise. Only by some such imponderable bond may the response which certain plants make to certain people be explained, the debt on the other side being even more intangible but no less real. When the bond is truly living, both shall be sustained, and in return for the human cherishing, something of earth's patience and instinct of life, something of the peace of gardens, shall find its way into the flowing of the blood. (p. 53)

As was the case on Cape Cod, where Beston had felt "a secret and sustaining energy" that flowed from the natural world all around him, gardening was a means by which one could have contact with a life force that was universal in nature. And, unlike the solitary life of an ascetic, it was a means of spiritual fulfillment compatible with family life.

114

While Beston's thoughtful musings on man and nature give *Herbs and the Earth* much of its depth, it is his clear and graceful prose that gives the work its poetry. Beston considered the final chapter, "Epilogue to Spring," to be the finest thing he had ever written (*Especially Maine*, p. 8), and in *Herbs and the Earth* there is a lyrical quality to his prose that is on a par with *The Outermost House*. For instance, in a passage that describes the end of a hot summer day, he writes:

When the heat of some long summer day has followed the sun behind the pasture hill, when the glare has gone and the hour of the garden hose and the watering pot approaches with the dusk, when the whole of nature surrounding the gardener as he works is vibrating with a heavy-laden summer immediacy and profusion of life and there is a moment's flutter of birds in the apple tree, when the lake, the garden, and the hill are each released from the weight and splendor of day, how pleasant it is to be busy with the earth in this place of green! Here the first coolness comes, welling from the earth and fragrant with herbs, the odors mingling and strengthening as the gardener stirs the beautiful and timeless leaves, here gathers the first quiet of the coming evening, that quiet of summer and the beginning night which overlies the fruitful tension of the earth. (p. 50)

The long first sentence of this paragraph, with its series of contingent phrases each beginning with "when," draws out the sentence in a manner that suggests the length of the long hot day itself. The rhythmic cadences of Beston's sentences suggest that, like the sermons of a Baptist minister, this is language that is meant to be spoken. Beston never used a typewriter when he wrote because he felt that the noise of the machine would interfere with the "rhythm of his sentences" (*Especially Maine*, p. 4); he would sometimes spend an entire morning on a single sentence, "unable to go on until he was completely satisfied with both words and cadence, which he considered equally important" (*Especially Maine*, p. 4). To craft language that conveyed the right sound as well as the intended

meaning was a laborious process, but, Elizabeth Coatsworth says in *Especially Maine*, "his writing always seemed inevitable when it was finished. He kept it fresh, however long he might work upon it" (p 8).

"The Earth Which Men Have Loved"

Beston would explore the poetic link between man and the earth again in his last major work, *Northern Farm: A Chronicle of Maine* (1948), but even in those works that did not directly deal with nature, there was a recurring strain of nostalgia for the preindustrial past. In *American Memory: Being a Mirror of the Stirring and Picturesque Past of Americans and the American Nation...* (1937), an anthology of colonial and early American writings that Beston compiled and edited, he relates "the adventure of the Republic" from the time of the first European settlements to the close of the nineteenth century. Beston begins the anthology with a section that describes the most "irreplaceable quality" of the North American Indians as "their religious relation to the beauty and mystery of the American earth" (p. 4), and significantly, he ends with the passage from *The Education of Henry Adams* (written in 1905) that deals with the dynamo and the steam engine, the inventions that signaled the beginning of the industrial era in American history. While Adams and Beston may have differed somewhat in their analysis of exactly what was lost as a result of industrialism, like Adams, Beston believed that the material prosperity of an industrial society was a poor substitute for what was lost.

During the 1930s and early 1940s the Bestons were not particularly hard hit by the Great Depression, finding the time and the means to travel extensively. They made frequent trips to Canada for a book on the Saint Lawrence River that Beston was working on for the Rivers of America Series, as well as journeys to Mexico and the western United States. In between their individual writing projects, the Bestons collaborated on several children's books, including

Five Bears and Miranda (1939) and *The Tree That Ran Away* (1941). Despite their insulation from the worst effects of the depression, Beston saw the displacement and economic hardship of the period as yet another symptom of a society that had lost its bearings. In a letter to the Reverend J. Luther Neff, he wrote: "I see no future for this form of civilization with its brutal egotism, its absence of poetic relation to the earth, and its failure to give the meagerest life religious significance" (*Especially Maine*, p. 60).

In a sense, *The St. Lawrence* (1942) was Beston's most ambitious literary project; Sherman Paul writes, "It is at once a guide book, a children's book (when historical events, Indian captivities, and legends are recounted), and a nature-book" (p. 109). Beston divided the book into three parts, the first dealing with the history of the region, the second with present-day life in Laurentian Canada, and the third with "the almost timeless forces of nature neighboring the river and its coasts" (p. ix). Beston traveled extensively in the area to get a feel for the history of the region and the lives of those who lived along its banks, but, he advises in the preface, "I have tried first and foremost to keep my eyes on the river itself" (p. ix). Beston seems to have intended to write an ecological history of the Saint Lawrence that included man as one of the forces affecting and affected by the river, but he was only partially successful in achieving this ambitious goal. While human activity might be one of the most noticeable and at times the most destructive force affecting the river, it was not the only one. *The St. Lawrence* is nevertheless an engaging work that often transcends genre entirely.

As he did in *American Memory*, Beston in *The St. Lawrence* pointedly contrasts the Native Americans' relationship with nature with that of the European settlers who supplanted them in the Saint Lawrence region: "[The Indians] were at peace with the tense American earth. The white civilization of their inheritance was at war with the earth; an occupation beginning as a conquest, a clearing, and a killing had fastened on the land without a moment's pause of means or mood. The Indians made no such war"

(p. 44). Particularly in the final section of the book, Beston writes with great feeling about "The mightiest of all pageants of nature and the earth . . . the wilderness miracle of ancient North America" (p. 202), and how that pageant was irrevocably altered during the relatively short period of time since European settlement of the continent. While acknowledging the destructive excesses of the early fur trade, Beston pointed to the nineteenth century as the era that "ended the pageant almost as if it had a purpose to empty the forests and the air" (p. 203). Using religious imagery reminiscent of John Muir's condemnation of the "money changers" who had nearly destroyed the Yosemite, Beston railed against those who "decended on the animal world to make a devil's emptiness on earth. . . . At the end of the happy period, North America was no more. Like a great church whose windows have been stoned out and whose beauty sacked, it had become something else and something less" (p. 203).

Despite the profligacy of the industrial age, the region still offered a few vestiges of the wilderness miracle of North America, such as the annual migratory passage of the snow geese through Cap Tourmente, a spectacle that Beston traveled to see and describe. A human link to the past was represented by the Ursuline community of Quebec, a French-Catholic sect dating back to the seventeenth century and the founding of Quebec. Like the herb garden of *Herbs and the Earth*, the Ursulines served as a living and symbolic link to the past, representing "the very soul of old French Canada" (p. 23). For Beston this sense of continuity with the French-Canadian past had a personal significance as well as a historical one. As he traveled around the French-speaking communities bordering the Saint Lawrence and delved into the history of the region, in a sense he was making a pilgrimage back into his own French-Catholic ancestry as well. We hear a certain self-conscious pride, perhaps, when Beston states that "for all his redoubtable prowess with the ax, [the French-Canadian] was at peace with his earth and his fields" (p. 107), in a way that the Anglo-American was not.

Despite his identification with the French-Canadians, however, Beston conceded that "an honest observer must set down that the people of the river are extraordinarily careless of their physical past" (p. 169). He described the destruction caused by *le pulp*, the "savage business" of pulpwood logging, as "a commerce of pure destruction thoroughly bad in the long run for the psyche of any people" (p. 155). In yet another passage that has a striking resemblance to the near-religious rhetoric of John Muir, Beston drew a sharp distinction between the types of destruction that he saw during his travels:

> There is one destruction which is of God, and that is the destruction inherent in the renewal of life; the dead leaf must wither and crumble in the cold, the flower give way to the relentless pressure of the seed below. Opposed to this is another destruction which is of the Devil, a destruction without necessity and without creative future, a destruction only conceivable in an age of the emptiness of the human spirit, and working itself out in brutality and the ruin of the heritage of men. Of this the earth is full, the smoke of the torment ascending, and it will need all the trumpets of Revelation to restore to us the earth which men have loved. (p. 172)

With what seems to be more wistful hope than empirical conviction, Beston wrote that this kind of profligacy was a historical anachronism, and that, "Sooner or later, guided by its own intelligence or by bitter necessity, a civilization will again remember that visible nature is not the immediate spoil of an age or its generations, but the timeless inheritance of man, the ancient mystery to be forever shared with those who forever are to come" (p. 155).

The outbreak of war in Europe once again in 1939 seemed to confirm all of Beston's worst suspicions about the spiritual decay and violence spawned by modern industrial civilization. More and more, Beston came to see farm life in Maine not simply as a retreat from the world but as a way to counteract the effects of a modern society where " 'comfort' and 'violence' are indeed the pillars of our time" (*Especially Maine*, p. 147). In addition to numerous essays on nature and farm life written for various periodicals, Beston wrote several letters denouncing some of the more brutal aspects of the Allied war effort, including the saturation bombing of Berlin in 1945 and the use of the atomic bomb against Japan. Beston realized, however, that such protests were ineffectual, and there is a note of resignation in the new foreword he wrote for the 1949 edition of *The Outermost House*, where he states that it is one of the privileges of a naturalist "to concern himself with a world whose greater manifestations remain above and beyond the violences of men."

Northern Farm

Shortly after moving to Maine for good in 1944, Beston was invited by Morris Rubin to write a weekly feature called "Country Chronicle" for Robert La Follette's *Progressive.* These essays were collected and published in 1948 as *Northern Farm: A Chronicle of Maine*, Beston's last major work. In these essays Beston described farm life in Maine and expanded on his familiar theme of modern life being at odds with the poetry of the earth. Each chapter is divided into three parts: observations and descriptions of farm life; selections from Beston's farm diary; and a concluding section usually comprising thoughts on the complicated relation between humankind and the earth or a comparison of city life with country life. As was the case with Beston's two earlier books dealing primarily with nature, *The Outermost House* and *Herbs and the Earth*, the simple narrative structure of *Northern Farm* follows the passage of the seasons through the course of a year on the farm. Although there is nothing particularly original or striking about this as a literary device, the issue of mechanical time versus earth time is central to Beston's worldview. In the artificial time of cities, he wrote in *Northern Farm*, "one is bulwarked against the seasons and the year, time, so to speak, having no natural landmarks, tends to stand still" (p. 7). The consequence is that human affairs devolve into an "endless and unnatural present" (p. 7) that all too often results in alienation and violence. Beston includes in his denunciation the "great show and carnival of death" of the recent war; he sternly warns, "Our strength and intelligence have been used to counter the very will and purpose of the earth. We had better begin considering not what our governments want but what the earth imposes" (p. 238).

The nostalgic tinge to Beston's writing that was apparent in works such as *Herbs and the Earth* and *The St. Lawrence* is even more pronounced in *Northern Farm*. The book opens with the description of a train ride home to Maine that serves also as the symbol for a return to an earth-centered way of living. As he observes the Maine countryside and muses about "what had gone out of American life as one sees it in the city and the suburb" (p. 4), he concludes each paragraph with the mantra-like refrain, "Home. Going home." Much of the book is a celebration of the simple homely virtues of country life: the sense of community, the pleasant and fulfilling duties of the farm, and the quiet joys of a life spent close to nature. To live happily in the country, Beston writes, "[one] must be wisely prepared to take great pleasure in little things" (p. 185), a dictum that is reflected throughout the book. *Northern Farm* contains some of Beston's finest descriptive writing, and whether he is describing the early-morning sounds of the farm, a spring rain, or the snow shadows of a winter's day, Beston gracefully conveys a sense of the near-religious joy he takes in such small miracles.

According to Elizabeth Coatsworth, *Northern Farm* was the "companion piece" to *The Outermost House*, and both in its narrative structure and main themes there is considerable support for this assertion. *Northern Farm* is certainly Beston's most fully considered statement on man and nature since *The Outermost House*, and if its tone is more tranquil and domestic than in the earlier work, that is probably to be expected; in farming Beston had found the vital link with the earth that he had sought on Cape Cod, the "secret and sustaining energy" (p. 74) first described in *The Outermost House*. In *Northern Farm*, Beston restated his familiar po-

sition on the link between man and nature in the clearest terms:

> I muse again on the dogmatic assertion which I often make that the countryman's relation to Nature must never be anything else but an alliance. . . . When we begin to consider Nature as something to be robbed greedily like an unguarded treasure, or used as an enemy, we put ourselves in thought outside of Nature of which we are inescapably a part. Be it storm and flood, hail and fire, or the yielding furrow and the fruitful plain, an alliance it is, and that alliance is a cornerstone of our true humanity. (p. 36)

This alliance between man and nature was one that had been celebrated in former times by wiser civilizations "who never lost sight of the religious significance of the earth" (p. 44). The poetry, ritual, and awe traditionally associated with mankind's relation to the earth was in danger of being lost, Beston feared, and with this loss the human spirit itself was diminished and "man has almost ceased to be man" (p. 245). A letter to the Reverend Neff suggests that Beston had some affinity for the old pagan rituals celebrating the earth and the seasons: "All our various Christian religions are altogether too much out of relation to the living year—they inhabit a sort of ethical vacuum removed from the norm of natural experience. I'm all for Harvest festivals and things of that kind. They are both emotionally and religiously right" (*Especially Maine*, p. 113).

After *Northern Farm*, Beston's productivity slackened—largely because of his deteriorating health—although he continued to work on revisions of earlier works and also edited a new anthology of essays on Maine entitled *White Pine and Blue Water* (1950). He also gave frequent lectures on nature writing and was a regular speaker at seminars in Cooperstown and Dartmouth. A steady stream of academic and literary honors came his way, including the Emerson-Thoreau Award in 1960 and the designation of the Fo'castle as a National Literary Landmark in 1964. Perhaps most gratifying was the continued success of *The Outermost House*, which went through a number of editions, including a French paperback; Beston delightedly exclaimed that the book was even better in French than it was in English (*Especially Maine*, p. 14). For several years the Bestons went to California in the spring to avoid "mud time" in Maine, but in the last four years of his life Beston's health was so poor (owing to hardening of the arteries) that he was essentially an invalid until his death on 15 April 1968.

Although *The Outermost House* is widely considered a classic in American literature, Beston's life and work have been much neglected by modern literary scholars. There is as yet no major biography of his life, and what little critical attention has been accorded to his work almost invariably considers *The Outermost House* alone. Given the accomplishment that work represents, to a certain extent this is understandable; however, as Sherman Paul (one of the few critics to consider Beston's work at some length) has written, "Beston should figure for us as a writer of several works, not just *The Outermost House*" (p. 97). Beston's fine descriptions of nature are sufficient in themselves to recommend his work to many readers, but there is also a philosophical underpinning to his work — such as his biocentric worldview and his search for spirituality in nature — that warrants greater study than it has thus far received.

Selected Bibliography

WORKS OF HENRY BESTON

NONFICTION

A Volunteer Poilu (Boston and New York: Houghton, 1916); *Full Speed Ahead: Tales from the Log of a Correspondent with Our Navy* (Garden City, N.Y.: Doubleday, 1919); *The Outermost House: A Year of Life on the Great Beach of Cape Cod* (Garden City, N.Y.: Doubleday, Doran, and Company, 1928; New York: Ballantine, 1971); *Herbs and the Earth* (Garden City, N.Y.: Doubleday, 1935), with intro. by Roger Swain (Boston: David R. Godine, 1990); *American Memory: Being a Mirror of the Stirring and Picturesque Past of Americans and the American Nation: Together with Loving Studies and First Accounts of*

Many Things Uniquely American: Set Down in the Vigorous Prose of Those Who Saw and Experienced These Things (New York: Farrar & Rinehart, 1937), anthology ed. and with intro. by Henry Beston; *The St. Lawrence* (New York: Farrar & Rinehart, 1942), part of the Rivers of America Series; *A Glimpse of the Indian Past* (Cohasset, Mass.: South Shore Nature Club, 1946); *Northern Farm: A Chronicle of Maine* (New York: Rinehart, 1948); *White Pine and Blue Water: A State of Maine Reader* (New York: Farrar, Strauss, 1950), anthology ed. and with intro. by Henry Beston; *Especially Maine: The Natural World of Henry Beston from Cape Cod to the St. Lawrence* (Brattleboro, Vt.; Stephen Green, 1970), anthology of Beston's writing selected and with intro. by Elizabeth Coatsworth.

CHILDREN'S BOOKS

The Firelight Fairy Book (Boston: Atlantic Monthly Press, 1919); *The Starlight Wonder Book* (Boston: Atlantic Monthly Press, 1923); *The Book of Gallant Vagabonds* (New York: George H. Doran Co., 1925); *The Sons of Kai: The Story the Indian Told* (New York: Macmillan, 1926); *Five Bears and Miranda* (New York: Macmillan, 1939), collab. with Elizabeth Coatsworth; *The Tree That Ran Away* (New York: Macmillan, 1941), collab. with Elizabeth Coatsworth; *Henry Beston's Fairy Tales* (New York: Aladdin Books, 1952); *Chimney Farm Bedtime Stories* (New York: Holt, Rinehart, and Winston, 1966), with Elizabeth Coatsworth.

MANUSCRIPTS AND PAPERS

The Dartmouth College Library, Hanover, New Hampshire holds the papers of Henry Beston dating 1933–1956. The collection contains holographs, typescript, printed matter, letters to H. F. West, H. G. Rugg, and F. M. Smith, and also includes a 1966 letter from Mrs. Beston to Dartmouth College Library, manuscript of *The Outermost House* (1928), introductory sections of *American Memory* (1937), and Beston's notes for a lecture to H. F. West's class "Nature Writers" (1954). Additional papers are contained in the Special Collections at the Bowdoin College Library and at the Harvard University Widener Library.

SELECTED ARTICLES

"Verdun," in *Atlantic Monthly* 118 (July 1916); "Vineyard of Red Wine" in *Atlantic Monthly* 118 (August 1916); "With the American Submarines," in *Atlantic Monthly* 122 (November 1918); "The Wardens of Cape Cod," in *World's Work* 47 (December 1923); "Night on a Great Beach," in *Atlantic Monthly* 141 (June 1928); "Sound and Life," in *Atlantic Monthly* 151 (January 1933); "Garden Escapes," in

House Beautiful 78 (November 1936); "Some Birds of a Maine Lake," in *Audubon Magazine* 45 (September 1943); "Sistcr Swallow, Beloved Bird of Europe," in *Audubon Magazine* 46 (July 1944); "The Need of Belief as a Factor in Reconstruction," in *Human Events* 4 (29 October 1947); "Spring Comes to the Farm," in *Progressive* 12 (May 1948); "End of a Farm Summer," in *Progressive* 12 (October 1948); "Bestons Tell a Maine Story," in *Christian Science Monitor Magazine* (31 December 1948); "The Farm Remembers," in *Progressive* 13 (January 1949); "Summer Regained," in *Progressive* 14 (June 1950); "Season of Splendor," in *Progressive* 14 (November 1950); "Sound and Surf. Excerpt from *The Outermost House*," in *Reader's Digest* 59 (August 1951); "Comment on 'Is America a Civilization?'," in *Shenandoah* 10 (Autumn 1958).

BIBLIOGRAPHY

Maryellen Spencer, "Henry Beston (1888–1968): A Primary Checklist," in *Resources for American Literary Study* 12 (spring 1982): 1, 49–63.

BIOGRAPHICAL AND CRITICAL STUDIES

Elizabeth Coatsworth, *Personal Geography: Almost an Autobiography* (Brattleboro, Vt.: S. Greene, 1976), contains passages pertaining to marriage with Henry Beston; Donald Federman, "Toward an Ecology of Place: Three Views of Cape Cod," in *Colby Library Quarterly* 13 (1977); Frank Graham, Jr., "Earthlog," in *Audubon Magazine* 80 (May 1978); Clarissa M. Lorenz, "Henry Beston: The Outermost Man," in *Atlantic Monthly* 242 (October 1978); Thomas Lyon, *This Incomparable Lande: A Book of American Nature Writing* (Boston: Houghton Mifflin, 1989); Sherman Paul, "Coming Home to the World: Another Journal for Henry Beston," in *North Dakota Quarterly* 59 (spring 1991), essay also contained in Paul's *For Love of the World: Essays on Nature Writers* (Iowa City: Univ. of Iowa Press, 1992); Nan Turner Waldron, *Journey to Outermost House* (Bethlehem, Conn.: Butterfly and Wheel, 1991); Peter Wild, "Henry Beston's *The Outermost House*," in *North Dakota Quarterly* 55 (winter 1987).

JOHN BURROUGHS
(1837–1921)

RALPH W. BLACK

IN THE EARLY spring of 1921, eighty-three-year-old John Burroughs, renowned naturalist and nature writer, friend to presidents, industrialists, poets, and scientists, died on a New York–bound train that had left southern California only days before. He had been ill for some time and had, in recent years, taken to spending the winter months in places warmer than his wind-whipped Catskill Mountains farm. His last words, spoken to Clara Barrus, his longtime companion, secretary, and first biographer, took the form of a simple question: "How far are we from home?"

Riverby

Burroughs' last words provide as useful an epigraph as they do an epitaph in any estimation of his life and work. "Home," in its many derivations, was his prime artistic and ideological directive. Home was the subject he wrote most about, and the interpretive lens through which he invariably peered when he was writing about matters farther afield. Home was Riverby, the old farmstead he had built himself on the banks of the Hudson River, a hundred miles north of Grand Central Terminal. It was the land he had cleared and worked for years, the stone walls he had built and mended, the grapevines and apple trees he had planted and tended. Home, too, was Slabsides, the hemlock- and chestnut-covered, Walden-on-Hudson cabin he had built in 1895 a mile back behind Riverby. Slabsides was his study, the place he entertained such invited guests as John Muir and Theodore Roosevelt, and such uninvited guests as the hundreds of girls who came up from Vassar to catch a glimpse of the "Sage of Slabsides." In his last years, Burroughs fought diligently to keep Slabsides as his retreat from the seemingly constant invasion of well-wishers and autograph seekers. His successes were, at best, intermittent.

In a larger sense, however, home was the reach and roll of the mid-Hudson valley, the pastureland giving way to the trout streams and birch thickets tucked up in the surrounding hills; it was what he called "the blue curve of the Catskills," the lineaments and praises of which he would sing for nearly sixty years.

In his later years, Burroughs wrote fondly of his family's farm near Roxbury, New York, which he called the "Old Home." Such remembrances, collected in *The Life and Letters of John Burroughs* (1925), are thick with nostalgia: "I was the Child that went forth," he wrote, echoing Whitman for neither the first nor the last time, "and every object that I looked upon, with pity or love or dread, that object I became, and that object became a part of me" (vol. 1, p. 19). The farm chores and the daily, familiar contact with nature were remembered romantically as the most significant of his early years. In one rather worship-laden estimation, Clara Barrus tries to pinpoint what she saw as the connection between his writing and the local landscape in which he was raised: "His environment clothed him as a mantle," she wrote. "His sentences flow with the same large simplicity as do the lines of his native landscape; seem as spontaneous as the springs; yield the quiet and privacy of the woods; and are as limpid, musical, and varied as a mountain brook" (*Letters*, vol. 1, p. 3).

But we do Burroughs a disservice to think of him as merely a regional writer. In the heat of a literary scuffle to define a modernist poetic, T. S. Eliot said that he found William Carlos Williams "a writer of some local importance, perhaps." The same misreading could be, and has been, applied to Burroughs. But it is important to recognize that for Burroughs, as for Williams, the local gave way to the universal. He records in his journal how his knowledge of the birds and animals led to a knowledge of all things: "There are so many ways by which Nature may be come at; so many sides to her . . . —when one thing is really known, you can no longer be deceived; you possess a key, a standard; you effect an entrance, and everything else links on and follows" (quoted in Bergon, *A Sharp Lookout*, p. 22).

His interest in relating the regionally specific detail with the universal context in which that detail thrives places him squarely in the fold of his American romanticist forebears. In the essay "Before Beauty," Burroughs places himself as the essential mediator between the beauty of the natural world and any sense of the universal, of the divine, that that beauty might reveal. "When I go to the woods or the fields," he writes, "I do not seem to be gazing upon beauty at all, but to be breathing it like the air. . . . What I enjoy is commensurate with the earth and sky itself. It clings to the rocks and trees; it is kindred to the roughness and savagery; it rises from every tangle and chasm; it perches on the dry oak-stubs with the hawks and buzzards. . . . I am not

a spectator of, but a participator in it. It is not an adornment; its roots strike to the centre of the earth" (*Birds and Poets*, pp. 169–170). In *Signs and Seasons* (1886), his admonition to stay at home and know thoroughly "one's own spot of earth" is part of his developing poetic of natural history. The naturalist whose work is firmly rooted in the local has access to a range of subjects because eventually "nearly everything of interest will come round to him. . . . The great globe swings around . . . like a revolving showcase" ("A Sharp Lookout").

More important, knowing the close-at-hand with intimacy is a great source of power for the naturalist, one of the sources of the charm he attributes to Gilbert White and Henry David Thoreau: "One's own landscape comes in time to be a sort of outlying part of himself; he has sowed himself broadcast upon it, and it reflects his own moods and feelings ("A Sharp Lookout"). It is not just the flora and fauna of the landscape that is to be the subject for the naturalist, but the moods and feelings the naturalist brings to that landscape: "This home feeling, this domestication of nature, is important to the observer. . . . The place to observe nature is where you are; the walk you take to-day is the walk you took yesterday. You will not find just the same things: both the observed and the observer have changed; the ship is on another tack in both cases."

The agricultural metaphor which he employs here is itself quite telling, illustrating just how immersed Burroughs was in the topography of his native land. The simple, agrarian life is not disparaged here as it was by Thoreau—absent, for instance, is the farmer from *Walden* who ploughs into the soil the best years of his life. Perhaps it was the hardworking Calvinist tendencies of his Baptist parents that allowed Burroughs to celebrate the kinship he had long observed between a farmer and the abundant land. In most cases, his regional poetic served him well, though, as we will see, there were times when he could not seem to muster a language to depict the actual topography he found himself in.

Beginnings

Burroughs was more than just a product of his geographical place, or of the agrarian lifestyle that place gave rise to. He was born on his parents' three-hundred-acre dairy farm just outside of Roxbury, New York. It was April third of 1837, just seven months after the publication of Emerson's *Nature*, and the same year that Thoreau graduated from Harvard and wrote the first entry in what would become his monumental journal of nearly two million words. The seventh of ten children, Burroughs was the only one to make a name for himself outside the insular communities of Delaware County. None of his siblings read beyond a rudimentary level, and his biographers report that no one in his family ever read his books. His father Chauncey and his mother Amy Kelly were both devoutly religious people. Though his father had received some schooling, and had even taught school locally for a time, his reading was limited, according to Burroughs, to a Bible, a hymnbook, and a monthly religious newspaper, *The Spirit of the Times*.

A young man during the Civil War and an old one during World War I, Burroughs lived during one of the most dynamic periods in American history. In "An Egotistical Chapter," written at the request of a magazine editor, Burroughs reflects on the various influences that formed and informed his life. It is a generous, reflective essay, with appreciative nods to Wordsworth, Coleridge, Carlyle, Emerson, Arnold, Thoreau, and, of course, Whitman. He was far from blind to the stroke of providence that placed him in his particular intellectual stratum:

> I was not born out of time, but in good time. The men I seemed to need most were nearly all my contemporaries; the ideas and influences which address themselves to me the most . . . forcibly have been abundantly current in my time. . . . I have lived in the present time, in the present hour, and have invested myself in the objects nearest at hand. (*Indoor Studies*)

In the spring of 1854, hoping to earn enough money to attend the Ashland Collegiate Institute in nearby Greene County, Burroughs worked as an itinerant school teacher in the town of Tongore, just over the mountain from his Delaware County home. Seventeen years old, earning eleven dollars a month, Burroughs found himself practicing a trade that his three most influential mentors—Emerson, Whitman, and Thoreau—had also practiced in their respective youths. Burroughs used the time to further his education, reading everything from Gibbon's *Decline and Fall of the Roman Empire* to a handbook on phrenology, the *Rambler* essays of Dr. Johnson, and the philosophy of John Locke. In a small notebook, dated 1855 (the year Walt Whitman inaugurated modern American poetry by self-publishing a little green book called *Leaves of Grass*), seventy-nine books are listed under the emphatic heading, "Books I *will* read." The list is an ambitious one, whatever the reader's age, and includes such items as histories of Rome, Greece, India, and England. In addition to the writings of Plato, Plutarch, and Hume are encyclopedias and studies of oratory. There are compendiums of literature representing the classical and modern traditions, Spanish, British, and American literature, and collections of Poe, Hawthorne, Byron, and Emerson. There is little, beside Emerson, to suggest the literary direction that the young Burroughs would follow, except for Saint-Pierre's *Studies in Nature*.

His journal entries for this period, as cited by Clara Barrus, are full of a young man's enthusiasm for new ideas, quotations from and responses to the books he was reading. The flyleaf of a journal from the mid-1850s bears the inscription "A Book of Solitude, Sentiment, and Study." In another, from 1859, he inscribes this helplessly romantic heading: "A Notebook containing a few smooth pebbles which the waves of Thought leave, from time to time, upon my Shores." A subsequent inscription mentions his "apprenticeship to Truth," and sports a carefully drawn (perhaps Emersonian?) eye (Barrus, ed., *Journals*, pp. 14–15).

123

Burroughs' first published essays were, by his own estimation, weak Johnsonian reiterations. The short essays he wrote for the *New York Saturday Press*, which appeared during the spring and summer of 1860 under the title "Fragments from the Table of an Intellectual Epicure" under the name All Souls, sported such tellingly abstract and quasi-philosophical titles as "Deep," "Theory and Practice," and "Some of the Ways of Power." A passage from his first published essay, "Vagaries viz. Spiritualism" (1856), argues against a proponent of supernatural phenomena. It suggests, if nothing else, the stilted and rhetorical tenor that many of his youthful essays would take: "And how consistent it is with every notion we ought to entertain of those celestial beings, to suppose they would leave the bright shores of immortality and descend to this obscure corner of creation for the mere purpose of satisfying the idle curiosity of particular individuals!" (*Letters*, vol. 1, p. 39). Burroughs would later remark to Barrus that these essays represented little more than "second-hand truths"; they were "chaff—chaff—no wheat there" (p. 42).

The wheat would begin to flourish for Burroughs when he exchanged Johnson's *Rambler* and *Idler* essays for the works of Emerson. In the spring of 1856, having completed another term as a teacher at Tongore, he enrolled for a semester at the Cooperstown Seminary. Though he had come across Emerson before, it was at Cooperstown that he read Emerson "in a sort of ecstasy." Years before, Whitman had written that while he had long been "simmering, simmering," it was Emerson who had "set [him] to boil." Burroughs' reaction was similar: "I got [Emerson] in my blood, and he colored my whole intellectual outlook. His words were like the sunlight on my pale and tender genius which had fed on Johnson and Addison and poor Whipple. His boldness and unconventionality took a deep hold upon me" (*Journals*, 30 April 1882).

Just how deep that hold was is evident in his essay "Expression," published in the *Atlantic Monthly* in November 1860. The ideas of analogy, of nature as wholly dependent on the cultural prospect of the observer, rather than as an objective fact, echo the tone and style of Emerson's *Nature* (1836). A morsel of early Burroughs lore has it that James Russell Lowell, then editor of the *Atlantic*, held up publication of the essay so he could check through the works of Emerson to assure himself that the essay was not plagiarized. As *Atlantic* articles were published in those days without a byline, many readers assumed the essay was in fact Emerson's; both *Poole's Index* and *Hill's Rhetoric* credited the essay to Emerson for many years after its publication.

If "Expression" lacks originality, it is at least suggestive of the intellectual climate that surrounded Burroughs. The essay may rely heavily on an abstract construction and intellectualization of the world—"We can behold nothing pure," he writes. "Nature stands related to us at a certain angle, and at a little remove either way"—but it does not stop there. Natural images are scattered throughout the essay, and they move it beyond a reductive, imitative Emersonian vision. They suggest just how much the natural world and, specifically, the landscape of the mid-Hudson valley were already finding their way into his work. Human thoughts lie in us "like the granite rock in the earth, whole and continuous, without break or rupture." Spoken thoughts are "only foam from the surface, with more or less sediment in it." The images themselves are far from notable, but their placement in this early work suggests that the seeds of natural history were already planted in the young writer.

Fortunately for the young Burroughs, friends and editors were glad to point out to him how little prepared the world was for another Emerson, particularly a second-rate one. Shortly after the publication of "Expression," no doubt realizing that such imitation had more to do with mediocrity than with flattery, Burroughs began writing about the rural life he knew best. An occasional column called "From the Back Country" began appearing in the New York *Leader* in 1860. These essays were about making butter and maple sugar, the construction of stone walls, and other rural and farm-based topics.

Though a reflective quality remained in his work for some time to come, his decision to leave behind the philosophical essay was a conscious one: "It was mainly to break the spell of Emerson's influence and get upon ground of my own that I took to writing upon outdoor themes," he wrote. "The woods, the soil, the waters, helped to draw out the pungent Emersonian flavor and restore me to my proper atmosphere" ("An Egotistical Chapter," *Indoor Studies*). It was with the hope of finding a voice and subject of his own that Burroughs had "gone home," back to the familiar, back to Roxbury and West Park and the farmland and mountains of the mid-Hudson valley he knew so well. He stopped looking for "sermons in stones," and focused instead on the rock-solid facts of the familiar world, "the great, shaggy, barbarian earth" (quoted in Bergon, *Sharp Lookout*, p. 13).

In an early genre-based study, *The Development of the Natural History Essay in American Literature* (1924), Philip Marshall Hicks underscores the irony of how differently two of the most prominent literary naturalists of the nineteenth century, Thoreau and Burroughs, responded to Emerson's work. For Thoreau, Emerson's philosophy impelled him toward the natural world. For Burroughs, nature—as place as well as subject—offered an escape from a stylistic influence he could not seem to otherwise avoid. In the late 1960s, Perry Westbrook wrote convincingly of Burroughs' ability to reconcile literary romanticism and scientific (or Darwinian) determinism—positions that for many had proven mutually exclusive. Emerson's vision of the natural world, and the place of the human dweller in that world, gave Burroughs a way to persevere, compelling him to challenge and strengthen his own literary efforts.

Burroughs and Whitman

Though Burroughs was best known during his lifetime as a writer of natural history essays, his first published book was not a collection of essays on "out-door themes," but a study of (and homage to) Walt Whitman. The two first met in Washington, D.C., in the fall of 1863. Burroughs had married Ursula North in 1857 and his sporadic and itinerant teaching career provided insufficient means to support a new wife and home. He moved to the capital and eventually found a position with the Currency Bureau of the Treasury Department.

Notes on Walt Whitman as Poet and Person was self-published in the spring of 1867. It is an assessment and defense of a poet whose work was being dismissed as "obscene" by a public that had grown up with formal, artifice-laden verse. One hears the voice of Whitman himself in Burroughs' assertion that Whitman was a different sort of poet altogether and demanded a different sort of reading. He was a bard of and for the nation, whose work was not just about knowing and saying the truths of the world, but about doing them as well. Whitman's life and work were inseparable, Burroughs wrote, and the fiery conviction with which he approached both demanded something new on the part of the reader. Knowing Whitman's propensity at this time to ghostwrite reviews of his own work, it is hardly a surprise to find Burroughs admitting years later that Whitman had read and revised much of the book himself, supplying the book's title and a complete chapter, "Standards of the Natural Universal."

Burroughs' friendship with Whitman was lifelong, and the influence the elder poet had on his work was significant. It was Whitman who supplied the title to Burroughs' first book of nature essays, *Wake-Robin* (1871)—"Capital title. Capital title!" Burroughs remembered hearing from Emerson (*Letters*, vol. 1, p. 143). And Whitman was instrumental in urging the young writer to stick with the material he knew best. One can imagine the two men walking the busy streets of the capital or visiting the field hospitals along the Potomac, talking about Emerson or Lincoln. Burroughs took Whitman birding in Washington's Rock Creek Park, and his description of the song of the hermit thrush provided Whitman with a central figure for his Lincoln elegy, "When Lilacs Last in the Dooryard Bloom'd" (1865).

Invariably, when Burroughs' prose is pitched at a level of excitement or exuberance, it is Whitman's ebullient cadences that are most detectable. In the opening to his later book on the poet, *Whitman: A Study* (1896), Burroughs tells how he came to call the landscape surrounding Slabsides "Whitman Land":

> I call this place Whitman Land, because in many ways it is typical of my poet, — an amphitheatre of precipitous rock, slightly veiled with a delicate growth of verdure, enclosing a few acres of prairielike land, once the site of an ancient lake, now a garden of unknown depth and fertility. Elemental ruggedness, savageness, and grandeur, combined with wonderful tenderness, modernness, and geniality.

Just as the natural world reminded Burroughs of Whitman's poetry, so did the poetry, as well as the man, remind him of "the sanity and repose of nature." It is not just that the poet "contained multitudes," or was elemental and physical in his sensibilities. He wrote about the immediate, the soil or pavement under his feet, the recognizable "stuff" of the world.

The contrasting images of the wild and the civilized in his description of Whitman suggest the importance Burroughs placed on finding a balance between the natural and human worlds. He had been raised among people who demonstrated the necessity of maintaining close ties with the land. Burroughs' rural and agrarian roots had given him a deeper sense than most people have of what it meant to have one's survival depend on such a relationship, and his landscapes tend, far more than those of Thoreau or John Muir, to be populated. For all the times he regards with pleasure those unpopulated landscapes of breadth and scope, he is likely to include one that the human has moved onto, claimed and domesticated: "Last summer I saw [a farmer] take enough stones and rocks from a three-acre field to build quite a fortress, and land whose slumbers had never been disturbed with the plough was soon knee-high with Hungarian grass. How one likes to see a permanent betterment of the land like that!—piles of renegade

stone and rock. It is such things that make the country richer" (quoted in McKibben, p. 33).

Edward J. Renehan, Jr., tells a story in his biography that suggests just how much Burroughs owed to Whitman. In answer to his wife's seemingly constant complaints about the piles of papers and books that "littered" their home, Burroughs gathered together the numerous unsold copies of his *Notes on Whitman* and stacked them into columns. A board placed across the top provided him a makeshift, but significantly supported, writing table.

Wake-Robin

Most of the essays published in *Wake-Robin* (1871) and in *Winter Sunshine* (1875) were written during Burroughs' stay in Washington. In an introduction appended to an 1895 edition of *Wake-Robin*, Burroughs tells a curious story of how his governmental post enabled him to write about the natural world beyond the edge of the city:

> I wrote the book sitting at a desk in front of an iron wall. I was the keeper of a vault in which many millions of bank-notes were stored. During my long periods of leisure I took refuge in my pen. How my mind reacted from the iron wall in front of me, and sought solace in memories of the birds and of summer fields and woods!

In Washington as elsewhere, memory and solace were closely associated in Burroughs' mind. However diligently he studied the natural occurrences of his immediate surroundings, he would often cast those occurrences in a retrospective, nostalgic light.

The first essay in *Wake-Robin*, "The Return of the Birds," is a seasonal calendar of bird lore, a romantic and often anthropomorphic litany of ornithological identification. While Burroughs the Victorian writes sentimentally of one of the "songsters," a bobolink, as "a lithe, merry-hearted beau," he displays a perceptive and lyrical gift in his description of the song of the field sparrow. "Go," he advises, "to those broad, smooth, uplying fields where the cattle and sheep are grazing, and sit down in the twilight . . . and listen to this song." The song he describes validates the praise he received later in life as a master of birdsong:

> On every side, near and remote, from out the short grass which the herds are cropping, the strain rises. Two or three long, silver notes of peace and rest, ending in some subdued trills and quavers, constitute each separate song. . . . The grass, the stones, the stubble, the furrow, the quiet herds, and the warm twilight among the hills, are all subtly expressed in this song; this is what they are at last capable of. (p. 15)

In "The Invitation," the last essay in *Wake-Robin*, Burroughs makes explicit the encouragement that his other work had implied. "The satisfaction is in learning [ornithology] from nature," he wrote. "One must have an original experience with the birds. The books are only the guide, the invitation."

The numerous guns and bird "skins" that figure in these first essays seem peculiar given the emotional attachment the rest of his ornithology seems to suggest. If nothing else, they call into question just what Burroughs means by "an original experience with the birds." But in advocating the collection of bird "specimens," Burroughs is only showing himself to be a product of his time, part of the Victorian belief in nature's unlimited abundance. He also shows himself to be a faithful student of John James Audubon, who was famous, or infamous, for the prodigious number of specimens he took from the wild to facilitate his bird study. In Burroughs' view, there is no substitute for close, exacting observation: "First find your bird; observe its ways, its song, its calls, its flights, its haunts; then shoot it (not ogle it with a glass), and compare with Audubon." Today, one marvels at his inability to hear the ironic turn of his final sentence: "In this way the feathered kingdom may soon be conquered."

In later essays like "Bird Enemies" (*Signs and Seasons*) and "The Ways of Sportsmen" (*Riverby*, 1904), Burroughs will passionately de-nounce the destructive habits of "professional collectors," but at this stage a specimen bag is an integral part of his ornithologist's role. A journal entry from this period calls his own habits into question for philosophical rather than moral or ethical reasons:

> I confess my excursions to the woods are often spoiled, or at least vitiated, by taking my gun and making it a specialty to obtain a bird. I am too much preoccupied and miss everything but the bird. . . . The full fruition of enjoyment and delight comes when I go out without any purpose except to get nearer the earth and sky, and accept the whole. . . . A more intimate and harmonious relation is established between me and Nature. I do not outrage the woods; I do not hunt down a bird. (*Journals*, 26 May 1865)

It was during these years that Burroughs was struggling to define and practice a particular kind of natural history. From his reading of Charles Darwin and Gilbert White he developed an interest in clear, uncluttered scientific observation. From his earlier study of Emerson he obtained an abiding interest in philosophy, in the human truth that is always lurking within the natural one. And yet striking a balance between the two sometimes opposing modes of observation—science and literature—was not always so easily achieved.

The Art of Seeing Things

When Burroughs' second book of nature essays, *Winter Sunshine*, was published in 1875, Henry James said that it showed "originality" and "vividness," "a style . . . capable of remarkable felicity," "a real genius for the observation of natural things." But James, much to Burroughs' chagrin, did not stop there: "Mr. Burroughs is a sort of reduced, but also more humorous, more available, and more sociable Thoreau (quoted in Bergon, *A Sharp Lookout*, p. 24).

Burroughs was more than a little miffed at what became for him "that Thoreau business," finding it a pronouncement difficult to live down. And though at the time his familiarity with Thoreau's work was somewhat limited, he later became a voracious, though extremely ambivalent, reader of Thoreau. It was from these readings that he began to compile critical journal entries delineating some of the marked differences he saw between his own work and Thoreau's.

Though Burroughs wrote that reading Thoreau's books was like "eating onions — one must look out or the flavor will reach his own page," he would admit to little more than the occasional "whiff of him" as being detectable in his own work. The differences he sets out tell us a great deal about the priorities Burroughs held as a writer of natural history: "Thoreau preaches and teaches always. I never preach or teach. I simply see and describe. I must have a pure result. I paint the bird for its own sake, and for the pleasure it affords me, and am annoyed at any lesson or moral twist" (*Journals*, 26 February 1878).

Much of Burroughs' criticism of Thoreau was based on what he saw as the slipshod nature of the latter's "field work." Though he recognized a singular originality in Thoreau's philosophy and admired his keen interest in natural history, Burroughs found him ultimately more interested in "the natural history of his own thought over that of a bird." Burroughs saw Thoreau as a student of "supernatural history," and disparaged his need to find "the bird behind the bird, — for a mythology to shine through his ornithology" (*Indoor Studies*, 1889, p. 35). Other essays on Thoreau appeared throughout Burroughs' career, and in "Thoreau's Wildness," published when Burroughs was sixty-five, he strikes a more conciliatory tone. He has come to realize how different Thoreau's motives are from his own: "What Thoreau was finally after in nature was something ulterior to science, something ulterior to poetry, something ulterior to philosophy. . . . He went to Nature as to an oracle; and though he sometimes . . . questioned her as a naturalist and a poet, yet there was always another question in his mind" (*Literary Values*, 1902).

As Burroughs' assessments of Thoreau would suggest, he was as dedicated a student of the rapidly changing scientific discourse of his day as he was of the literary and philosophical climate. The writings of various naturalists, particularly the ornithology of John James Audubon, Thomas Nuttall, and Alexander Wilson, are frequently cited in his work to correct or confirm his own observations. His discovery of Audubon's *Birds of America* at the West Point Library was a crucial step in his lifelong passion for ornithology. "It was like bringing together fire and powder," he wrote of that first encounter (*Letters*, vol. 1, p. 74).

In *Wake-Robin* he refers to the three ornithologists to settle an ongoing dispute about the merits of the songs of the wood and hermit thrushes:

> Both the great ornithologists, Wilson and Audubon, are lavish in their praises of the former, but have little or nothing to say of the song of the latter. Audubon says it is sometimes agreeable, but evidently has never heard it. Nuttall, I am glad to find, is more discriminating, and does the bird fuller justice. ("The Return of the Birds")

When Burroughs read Darwin during the spring and summer of 1883, he found in his books a map of creation far more suitable than the one his father, drenched in his old-world Baptist views, had professed. Emerson's philosophy was the first to instill in him a religious vision of the tangible, physical world; now Darwin amplified and clarified that vision. He found confirmation in Darwin that as a species, humans were not separate from the rest of creation; man, he writes with delight in his journal, is inextricably linked to "the system of things," his appearance in the world "not arbitrary, or accidental, but a vital and inevitable result." One cannot help but hear in the journal passages that accompany his reading of Darwin an implicit response to his father's religious fervor:

Who has not felt what a mechanical, inartistic view of creation that which the churches have so long held is? But that all these vast, complex results and forms of life were enfolded in the first germ—*that* view makes the universe alive, the veritable body of God, the organism of a vast, mysterious, all-embracing, eternal power. (*Journals*, 17 August 1883)

Darwin's books were a touchstone for Burroughs for the authoritative support they provided to his practice of natural history. They confirmed his belief (inherited from Emerson) that the natural world offered religious as well as scientific truths. "Here," he wrote of *The Descent of Man*, "is my testament of faith" (quoted in Renehan, pp. 154–155). As these literary and scientific figures continue to appear, however peripherally, in Burroughs' essays, one has the sense of the young naturalist striving to stake a claim for himself in their fold. To invoke a cartographic metaphor, it is as if Burroughs was working to triangulate his own position as a writer and observer of the natural world by taking frequent readings off the always-visible high points that these predecessors represented.

Birds and Poets

Writers such as Darwin and Audubon offered Burroughs far more than a simple template for the practice of accurate scientific observation. Their merits as scientists were amplified by the literary power he found in their work. Sounding a note he explored throughout his career, Burroughs begins his essay "Birds and Poets" with an appreciation of the literary achievements of the ornithologists. Of Audubon, he says, "if he had not the tongue or pen of the poet, [he] certainly had the eye and ear and heart . . . and the singleness of purpose, . . . the love, that characterize the true and divine race of bards." And of Audubon's predecessor: "So had Wilson, though perhaps not in as large a measure; yet he took fire as only a poet can" (*Birds and Poets*).

Darwin's theories offered more than just fuel for Burroughs' practice of good science. However

adamant Burroughs was about the importance of having scientific fact as the basis of engaging natural history, he was also unyielding in his charge that sound natural history was finally a literary enterprise. He found in Darwin a singular model for these convictions, a writer who located and explored the essential intersection of science and poetry. In Burroughs' essay "Science and Literature," Darwin's work is lavishly praised for its ability to make faithful and lasting art out of faithful and lasting science:

Darwin's interest in nature is strongly scientific, but our interest in him is largely literary; he is tracking a principle, the principle of organic life, following it through all its windings and turnings and doublings and redoublings upon itself, in the air, in the earth, in the water, in the vegetable, and in all the branches of the animal world. . . . He is said to have lost his taste for poetry, and to have cared little for what is called religion. His sympathies were so large and comprehensive; the mere science in him is so perpetually overarched by that which is not science, but faith, insight, imagination, prophesy, inspiration. (*Indoor Studies*)

The science of Gilbert White, Audubon, and Darwin helped to strengthen Burroughs' resolve to provide accurate information about the physical and biological environment. Such information became the foundation upon which his essays were built. To name the land and its organisms is to know it, and knowing it intimately leads to an ecological worldview as the relationships among those organisms become clearer and more familiar. But however avid a student of science Burroughs was—of biology, geology, ornithology—he finally aligns himself with Emerson's associative view of nature: the facts of natural history become truly meaningful only when their connections to human nature are made explicit. It is not insignificant that Burroughs refers to himself as a nature writer or a literary naturalist, but never as a proper natural scientist. However essential the scientific impulse, it finally plays a subordinate role to the literary. "The poet's pursuit of Nature is the only true one," he writes in his journal (*Journals*, 17 January 1866). Lines from "A Sharp Lookout" echo many of the precepts that Emerson outlines in *Nature*:

> The gold of nature does not look like gold at the first glance. It must be smelted and refined in the mind of the observer. . . . One goes to Nature only for hints and half truths. Her facts are crude until you have absorbed them or translated them. Then the ideal steals in and lends a charm in spite of one. It is not so much what we see as what the thing seen suggests. (*Signs and Seasons*)

Burroughs seems to be moving back toward his transcendental forebears here, instead of away from them, as we might expect when remembering his early struggles with Emerson and his critical assessments of Thoreau. But what Burroughs' vision as a nature writer requires is a balance between poetic and scientific mode and discourse. Demanding a lyrical as well as a scientific allegiance to the natural world, he comes to realize that only when the scientist's "fact" is clearly established as a foundation can the poet's more interpretive act begin.

Burroughs' reading of the early naturalists and of Darwin, his farmboy background and his friendship with Whitman, had all made clear to him the connection between the human and natural worlds. In his essay "Touches of Nature," he is unwavering in his placement of "man" not at the top of an evolutionary stair, but in the midst of an ecological web of interconnectedness. The human, he says, is not so much the adapter of the natural world as, like all living things, adapted by it: "Man," he writes, "is the outcome of Nature and not the reverse. . . . The physical cosmos is the mould, and man is the molten metal that is poured into it" (*Birds and Poets*).

His early essays do occasionally tend to romanticize or sentimentalize nature—birds are "songsters" and "feathered tribes," foxes are known by their folktale name, "Reynard"— but

he worked hard against the impulse, recognizing it as a conceit likely to obscure the intrinsic power of the natural fact. Natural selection and adaptation are not, according to Burroughs, a sign of nature's wisdom, but rather a sign of her impartiality. "[Nature] does not care a fig more for one creature than for another, . . . whether the hunter slay the beast or the beast the hunter; she will make good compost of them both" ("Touches of Nature," *Birds and Poets*). The strength of his conviction fires his prose to a lyrical, Whitman-tempered pitch:

> The geological ages, the convulsions and parturition throes of the globe, were to bring [humans] forth no more than the beetles. Is not all this wealth of the seasons, these solar and sidereal influences, this depth and vitality and internal fire, these seas, and rivers, and oceans, and atmospheric currents, as necessary to the life of the ants and worms we tread under foot as to our own?

The Nature-Fakers

Unlike his contemporary John Muir, Burroughs' work rarely engages in or initiates a political debate. He was an eternal optimist, and the evenhandedness of his essays seems to eschew criticism—whether of people, customs, or institutions. The one notable exception is the so-called nature-faker controversy that sprang up at the turn of the century with the publication, in March 1903, of Burroughs' "Real and Sham Natural History" in the *Atlantic Monthly*.

The one area of confrontation from which Burroughs rarely shied was the province of natural history. In his private journals and published essays alike he seems to have criticized as inept the natural history practices of everyone from Virgil to Pliny the Elder, from Wordsworth to Thoreau—though he had no quarrel with nature books or animal stories, like those of Rudyard Kipling and Jack London, that took imaginative or fictional leaps with the facts of nature. Science fiction, as it were, was not his concern. It was only when writers tried to pass their fiction off as science that Burroughs became

John Burroughs seated in front of the fireplace, 1910

testy. The criticism he levels at Ernest Thompson Seton's *Wild Animals I Have Known* (1898) and Reverend William J. Long's children's books, *Ways of the Wood Folk* (1899) and *School of the Woods* (1902), is not so much about the fantastic and heroic feats performed by foxes and orioles as it is about the authors' unwillingness to label their stories as fiction.

In Seton's *Wild Animals*, a particularly wily fox lures a group of pursuing hounds to a train trestle where he "knows" they will be struck down by a passing train. In his *Atlantic* article, Burroughs points out the unlikely presumption that Seton's fox has access to both a watch and a train schedule. Burroughs is no less dubious about Reverend Long's belief that instinct plays no role in the animal world, and that animal parents "teach" their young the ways of nature. Long tells of a kingfisher "kindergarten" he had observed where the older birds catch minnows in a large stream, release them in a shallow pool near the nest, round up their young and then demonstrate for their edification the art of catching fish. The story would be just as believable, says Burroughs, if Long had seen "the parent birds fishing with hook and line, or dragging a net of their own knitting. . . . Why," he asks, "should anyone palm off such stuff on an unsuspecting public as veritable natural history?" (quoted in Renehan, p. 234).

There is a sense in all this that Burroughs is defending not only the artistic territory he has worked so hard to define for himself, but his readers' positions within that territory. His criticism of Seton is applicable to any who would "defraud" his public:

> Mr. Seton says in capital letters that his stories are true, and it is this emphatic assertion that makes the judicious grieve. . . . Are we to believe that Mr. Seton, in his few years of roaming the West, has penetrated farther into the secrets of animal life than all the observers who have gone before him? . . .

131

Darwin, Jeffries, and others in England; . . . Bates in South America, Audubon roaming the whole country, Thoreau in New England, John Muir in the mountains of California and in the wilds of Alaska have nothing to report that comes within gunshot of what appear to be Mr. Seton's daily experiences. Such dogs, wolves, foxes, rabbits, mustangs, crows, as he has known, it is safe to say, no other person in the world has ever known. (quoted in Renehan, p. 232)

The nature-faker controversy drew considerable attention. Burroughs received a letter of support from President Roosevelt and went on to write other essays criticizing practitioners of unchecked anthropomorphism, collecting many of them in *Ways of Nature* (1905). Roosevelt, who was a friend of both men, encouraged Seton to move away from his fanciful "animal tales," and Seton went on to publish several scientifically adept nature studies. Reverend Long, however, held fast, responding to the charges with justifications of his scientific methodology. In 1907, Roosevelt, no doubt hoping to silence once and for all the opposition, convened a symposium for *Everybody's Magazine* called "Real Naturalists on Nature Faking." Preeminent scientists and field naturalists from around the country joined in to discredit the work of writers like Long. Renehan quotes a short letter that Jack London wrote to Upton Sinclair when the whole controversy had finally died down:

Only rich hobbyists like Roosevelt and his aristocratic band of happy hunters could bother to spend so much time and energy debunking what was already fourth rate literature to begin with. Men beg for bread in the streets—and Roosevelt and Burroughs confine their muckraking to the defense of accuracy in nature writing! (quoted in Renehan, p. 239)

Sinclair forwarded the letter on to Burroughs, with his comment, "He's right, you know!" written in the margin. Burroughs, in a comment addressed more to himself than to Sinclair, wrote, "Yes, I know," then stuck the letter into his copy of London's *The Call of the Wild*. With the wake of the industrial revolution and the Progressive Era clearly in the minds of Burroughs' colleagues, he might have just as well, and more poignantly, tucked the letter into a copy of Sinclair's *The Jungle* (1906).

Time and Change

London's criticism raises an important question about what some critics have seen as Burroughs' unwillingness or inability to engage some of the more crucial social, political, and even environmental issues that arose at the end of the century. Of the numerous movements and influences that shaped Burroughs' life, few challenge our reading of his literary work more than his lifelong friendship with some of the most powerful and environmentally destructive robber barons of Mark Twain's "gilded age."

In an 1866 journal entry, Burroughs decries the toll exacted by the industries that ushered in the post–Civil War expansion: "We are removed from nature and life by the whole distance of our wealth and refinement. . . . A man may live now and travel without hardly coming in contact with the earth or air. He can go around the world in a parlor. Life is intensely artificial" (quoted in Renehan, p. 3). But such remarks are rare in Burroughs' writing; and one wonders whether his close association with such figures as Jay Gould, a friend from childhood, Thomas Edison, Henry Ford, Andrew Carnegie, and E. H. Harriman compromised what might have become a more overt environmental ethos.

The particulars of these friendships suggest that these steel, lumber, and railroad magnates were far from blind to the publicity their association with the famous naturalist could buy them. In 1913, Ford sent Burroughs a gift of a new Model T after reading his nature books, and the following year he bought the original Roxbury farm, which the extended Burroughs family had mortgaged and remortgaged in their efforts to run it successfully. Ford presented Burroughs with the deed to the "Old Home," enabling the naturalist to concentrate on other, less worri-

Burroughs with Theodore Roosevelt (center) during their 1903 expedition to Yellowstone

some things. Carnegie and Harriman also became benefactors, knowing that photographs associating the renowned naturalist with their work could only be positive. Though the potential for political gain from these associations should not be overlooked, neither should it suggest that these men could not more simply have been fond of each other's company. They traveled and camped together numerous times, and Burroughs' writing reveals a man who is nothing if not affable.

When word got out that President Roosevelt had written a letter to the superintendent of Yellowstone National Park expressing an interest in hunting cougar during his forthcoming trip there, the New York press had a field day with the image of the President "thundering through a wilderness preserve with shotgun in his hand." Roosevelt was quick to invite Burroughs along on the journey, savvy enough to know that having the mild-mannered poet of nature by his side would be, as he wrote his son, like "the town's prize burglar attended by the Methodist parson" (quoted in Renehan, p. 243).

If such stories work to undermine our conception of Burroughs' environmental work, we should not let them completely obscure the conservation ethic that does appear in his essays. A comparison to the tireless and lyrical activism of John Muir is perhaps inevitable, but the naturalists' differing sensibilities led them to quite different, but equally effective, methods.

133

John Muir and the West

John Burroughs and John Muir first met briefly in the mid-1880s, when each was coming into his own as naturalist and writer—they later came to be known as "the two Johns": "John o'Birds" and "John o'Mountains," respectively. When Muir came to visit Burroughs (at Burroughs' invitation) at the newly completed Slabsides in 1896, Burroughs was immediately struck by what might well be called Muir's "range"—in both the intellectual and topographical senses of the word. Though both men cared deeply for and wrote passionately about the natural world, their senses of place, nurtured and honed in such vastly different geographies and bioregions, at times seemed irreconcilable. Where Burroughs found the woods and farms of the Hudson valley to be an ample enough territory for his life and work, Muir had a larger, more sublime image, and topography, in mind. Burroughs writes with humor of Muir's inclination to tell the story of his dog, Stickeen, and weave into it "the whole theory of glaciation," or of his inability to "sit down in a corner of a landscape, as Thoreau did; he must have a continent for his playground" (*Letters*, vol. 2, p. 360). But Burroughs' response to the landscapes Muir knew and loved reveals much about the limits imposed by his own regionalist tendencies.

During the several trips that Burroughs took west—to Alaska as a member of the Harriman expedition in 1899, to Yellowstone with Roosevelt in 1903, and to California with Muir in 1909—he wrote continually about the things that reminded him of his Catskill home. Descriptions of robins or apple trees occur where we might otherwise expect the grandeur and sublimity of the mountains. He engaged Muir in heated debates about geological theory and glaciation, but this was familiar to him from his reading of Darwin, among others. The geysers and hot pools of Yellowstone he had found "unearthly," suggesting "the traditional infernal regions" (*Camping and Tramping with Roosevelt*, 1907, p. 28). His brief journal entry describing Yosemite relies not just on a descriptive vocabulary imported from agrarian New York, but on a need to domesticate a wilderness he cannot otherwise seem to appreciate:

> It is like a great house in which one could find a nook where he could make his nest, looked down upon by the gods of the granite ages. The floor of the Valley really has a domestic, habitable look, with its orchards and ploughed lands, its superb trees, and its limpid, silently gliding river. . . . The ethereal beauty of the waterfalls, and the genial look of the pure streams, make almost any place habitable. (*Journals*, 1 May 1909)

Houses, nests, orchards, and ploughed lands—we are a long way from Muir's Yosemite, his description of windstorms and snowstorms, or of his climb up behind Yosemite Falls.

Clara Barrus (1914) emphasizes the divergent sensibilities in her narrative of a trip Burroughs took to an even more distant, biologically distinct land: "On Hawaii, where we saw the world's greatest active volcano throwing up its fountains of molten lava sixty or more feet high, the masses falling with a roar like that of the 'husky-voiced sea,' Mr. Burroughs found it difficult to understand why some of us were so fascinated that we wanted to stay all night, willing to endure the discomforts of a resting-place on lava rocks, occasionally stifling gusts of sulfur fumes, dripping rain, and heat that scorched our veiled faces, so long as we could gaze on that boiling, tumbling, heaving, ever-changing lake of fire. Such wild, terrible, unfamiliar beauty could not long hold him under its spell" (pp. 238–239).

When Burroughs traveled to Alaska as part of the Harriman expedition, he was able to depict something of that grand, heroic landscape. His narrative of the expedition, in *Far and Near* (1904), includes the occasional foray into the sublime: "How elemental and cataclysmal it all looked! I felt as if I were seeing for the first time the real granite ribs of the earth. . . . All I had seen before were but scales and warts on the surface by comparison; here were the primal rocks, sweeping up into the clouds and plunging down into the abyss, that held the planet together" ("In Green Alaska: White Pass"). Unfamiliar terrain tended to stifle rather than to fire Burroughs' imagination. In such places he is unable to maintain for very long his epistemological footing. His usual tendency, as he writes in *Far and Near* (1904), is to be wary of such picturesque locales:

> Scenery may be too fine or too grand and imposing for one's daily and hourly view. It tires after a while. It demands a mood that comes to you only at intervals. Hence it is never wise to build your house on the most ambitious spot in the landscape. Rather seek out a more humble and secluded nook or corner, which you can fill and warm with your domestic and home instincts. . . . In some things the half is often more satisfying than the whole. ("Wild Life About My Cabin")

These differing senses of place, the disparity between the rural and the wild, the domestic and the sublime, help distinguish the work of "the two Johns." Much of Muir's work was fired by his political sensibility, a literary activism (in response particularly to the flooding of Yosemite's Hetch Hetchy Valley) that became the modern conservationist movement. Burroughs' conservation ethic is not as focused as Muir's, and is of course far more localized and personal, but one might argue that his essays were finally instrumental in the development of an environmental consciousness during the first two decades of the century.

By establishing a genre for and popularizing the nature essay, Burroughs helped to foster a widespread interest in natural history. His books were responsible for urging thousands of Americans across the country to consider the importance of the natural world they were most familiar with—the landscapes that rolled away from their front doors. As Bill McKibben has argued, his essays gave them a language with which to recognize and appreciate the small but glorious wonders of that world. His journals are filled with notes of the visitors who would come up the Hudson to see him: "One hundred and ten Vassar girls yesterday at Slabsides," goes one

such passage, "and a dozen High School girls from Poughkeepsie. . . . Rare April days" (*Journals*, 25 April 1915).

When he traveled west with Roosevelt, it was often difficult for chroniclers to determine who among the gathered throngs had come to welcome the president, and who the naturalist. His books were read and discussed in schoolrooms across the country, and John Burroughs societies and nature-study groups were cropping up from Maine to the Dakotas. In 1887, Houghton Mifflin, Burroughs' publisher, hired a Chicago school teacher to select and edit essays by Burroughs specifically for classroom use. His impact on this audience, and its impact on the formative years of the conservation movement, should not be overlooked.

"The Grist of the Gods"

As we have seen, Burroughs recognized early on the philosophical if not the ethical dilemma in his reliance on a rifle to facilitate his study of ornithology. Later essays would take a far more political turn. In *Far and Near*, he writes of a collector of bald eagle eggs that "he had only proved himself a superior human weasel. . . . What would it profit me," he asks, "could I find and plunder my eagle's nest, or strip his skin from his dead carcass? Should I know him better? I do not want to know him that way. I want rather to feel the inspiration of his presence and noble bearing" ("Wild Life About My Cabin"). In his essay "Bird Enemies," he is more indignant: "The professional nest-robber and skin-collector should be put down, either by legislation or with dogs and shotguns" (*Signs and Seasons*).

In "The Grist of the Gods," an essay purporting to be a meditation on geology, Burroughs takes a much wider, more holistic view of things ecological. We catch a glimpse in it of what might be called his "ecological imagination" as he uses various disciplines to explore the complex relationships among the geological and biological matter of the earth. The science of geology becomes a philosophical lens through which the natural and human histories of the earth can be explored. "This story of the soil appeals to the imagination," he writes. "The trembling gold of the pond-lily's heart, and its petals like carved snow, are no more a transformation of a little black muck and ooze by the chemistry of the sunbeam than our bodies and minds, too, are a transformation of the soil underfoot." The pastoral and the universal conjoin: "The rocks turn to herbage, the fetid gases to the breath of flowers. The mountain melts down into a harvest field; volcanic scoria changes into garden mould. . . . Your lawn and your meadow are built up of the ruins of the foreworld." As history and nature intersect with culture in this expansive overview, Burroughs' vantage point becomes more explicitly, and prophetically, ecological:

> One cannot but reflect what a sucked orange the earth will be in the course of a few more centuries. Our civilization is terribly expensive to all its natural resources; one hundred years of modern life doubtless exhausts its stores more than a millennium of the life of antiquity. Its coal and oil will be about used up, all its mineral wealth greatly depleted, the fertility of its soil will have been washed into the sea, . . . its wild game will be nearly extinct, its primitive forests gone, and soon how nearly bankrupt the planet will be! ("The Grist of the Gods, " in *Leaf and Tendril*)

"The Grist of the Gods" is one of Burroughs' most captivating and visionary essays; its examination of and reflection on the chemical, geological, and spiritual processes of the earth are charged with a decidedly Whitmanesque exuberance. Here, prefiguring some of the theories of "Deep Ecology," the planet is seen as a living organism, its organic and inorganic components fundamentally interrelated. The physical characteristics of the landscape are rendered with the careful scrutiny of the practiced naturalist, and on that landscape, and as part of that landscape, the human figure is fully revealed as integral, as, in Emerson's lexicon, "part and particle" of the world: "The doors and windows of the universe are all open; the screens are all transparent. We are not barred or shut off; there is nothing foreign or unlike; we find our own in the stars as in the ground underfoot; this clod may become a man; yon shooting star may redden his blood." This is Burroughs integrating fully his strengths as a natural philosopher, as a writer of the local and the physical, but also of the universal and the metaphysical. It is the theory as well as the practice of natural history brought to rare fruition.

Accepting the Universe

Burroughs' last essays return in many ways to the metaphysical territory with which his writing career began. But this work is far from the exercise in intellectual overindulgence that some of those apprenticeship pieces seem to be. Essays like "A Hay-Barn Idyl" and "The Circuit of the Summer Hills," both published in *The Summit of the Years* (1913), have about them a quiet, reflective quality. If nostalgia overshadows the exuberance of earlier years, the naturalist's eye that surveys the fields and forests around Riverby has not dimmed in the slightest. *Accepting the Universe* (1920) addresses some of the large theological questions from his youth. Again, he tries to find a balance between the scriptures he knew from his parents and those he found in Darwin and Emerson, and knew from his own many years in the natural world: "I shall not be imprisoned in that grave where you are to bury my body," he wrote. "I shall be diffused in great Nature. . . . My elements and my forces go back into the original sources out of which they came, and these sources are perennial in this vast, wonderful, divine cosmos" (quoted in Renehan, p. 300).

During more than sixty years of writing nature essays, Burroughs codified and popularized a literary genre that Audubon and Thoreau had inaugurated in America. But he did much more. As a product of a diverse range of intellectual ideas and factions, Burroughs' essays raise as many questions as they answer. As Frank Bergon has pointed out, Burroughs' essays (and life) are filled with inconsistencies and contradictions. While he dedicated himself to ferreting out the anthropomorphizing of the nature-fakers, he continued his own practice of personifying birds. One essay claims that nature must not be reduced to a cluster of symbols illuminating human truths, and another that it is in fact a text that the properly attuned observer will decipher. At times he states that science highlights one's knowledge of the world; at other times, that science obscures and sterilizes the world. His long friendship with Whitman no doubt taught him to disregard, if not embrace, such contradictions.

An understanding of these contradictions, and of the complexity of Burroughs' life, is essential to any real appreciation of his place in the tradition of American nature writing. Though strongly influenced by the intellectual debates of his day, his relationships with his diverse and strong-willed predecessors were never marked by passive acquiescence. He persisted almost heroically in his explorations of both natural and philosophical fields, struggling to make personal sense of them. Emerson, Thoreau, and Darwin were, among them, the recipients of dozens of articles by Burroughs, and his last, posthumously published book, *The Last Harvest* (1922), includes assessments of all three. The last thing he wrote was, in fact, the concluding paragraph of an essay on Emerson's journals.

If he seemed impressed at one time with Muir's range, it was perhaps because he had not completely grasped how far-reaching his own had become. The volumes that make up his published work include essays on landscape, literature, animal behavior, politics, natural science, and religion. He wrote eloquent essays about cows and strawberries as well as about birdsong and trout fishing. He did more than accommodate the demands of Emersonian nature worship and of modern science: he honed and occasionally perfected an interdisciplinary literary genre that meshes personal narrative, metaphysical reflection, poetry, and exacting scientific observation. At his hand they became interdependent and equally powerful ways of knowing the world.

What Burroughs finally wanted was to uncover and illuminate for his readership the mysteries of nature, not dissect them into a lifeless collec-

tion of figures and measurements. As he says in the preface to *Wake-Robin*, he wants his essays to provide "a live bird,—a bird in the woods or the fields,—with the atmosphere and associations of the place, and not merely a stuffed specimen" (1908 ed., p. vi). When he gave a talk in 1913 to a group of schoolchildren at New York's Museum of Natural History, he told them that museums, and nature books, were not the places to look for nature. "A bird shot and stuffed and botanized is no bird at all," he said. "And a bird described...in cold print is something less than you deserve" (quoted in Renehan, p. 9). He hoped that his books piqued a curiosity that only a long walk in the woods with a decent pair of field glasses could satisfy.

In 1926, Burroughs' legacy was assured by the founding of the John Burroughs Association at the Museum of Natural History in New York. Since that time, nearly sixty natural history writers have received the Association's annual Burroughs Medal for nature writing. Though the work of many of the award's recipients has been forgotten, others—Rachel Carson, Joseph Wood Krutch, John Hay, Loren Eiseley, and Aldo Leopold among them—have worked diligently in the Burroughs tradition, challenging, amplifying, and promulgating the aesthetic and scientific precepts of the nature essay. With Burroughs' decisive push, the genre continues to be a vital and lasting part of our cultural and literary heritage.

Selected Bibliography

WORKS OF JOHN BURROUGHS

BOOKS

Notes on Walt Whitman as Poet and Person (New York: American News Company, 1867; rev. ed., New York: J. S. Redfield, 1871); *Wake-Robin* (Boston: Houghton Mifflin, 1871); *Winter Sunshine* (Boston: Houghton Mifflin, 1875); *Birds and Poets* (Boston: Houghton Mifflin, 1877); *Locusts and Wild Honey* (Boston: Houghton Mifflin, 1879); *Pepacton* (Boston: Houghton Mifflin, 1881); *Fresh Fields* (Boston: Houghton Mifflin, 1884); *Signs and Seasons* (Boston: Houghton Mifflin, 1886); *Indoor Studies* (Boston: Houghton Mifflin, 1889); *Riverby* (Boston:

Houghton Mifflin, 1894); *Whitman: A Study* (Boston: Houghton Mifflin, 1896); *The Light of Day* (Boston: Houghton Mifflin, 1900); *Alaska: The Harriman Expedition, 1899* (New York: Doubleday, Page, 1901; repr., New York: Dover, 1986), as ed., with John Muir et al.; *The Life of Audubon* (New York: n.p., 1902); *Literary Values* (Boston: Houghton Mifflin, 1902); *Far and Near* (Boston: Houghton Mifflin, 1904); *Ways of Nature* (Boston: Houghton Mifflin, 1905); *Bird and Bough* (Boston: Houghton Mifflin, 1906); *Camping and Tramping with Roosevelt* (Boston: Houghton Mifflin, 1907); *Leaf and Tendril* (Boston: Houghton Mifflin, 1908); *Time and Change* (Boston: Houghton Mifflin, 1912); *The Summit of the Years* (Boston: Houghton Mifflin, 1913); *The Breath of Life* (Boston: Houghton Mifflin, 1915); *Under the Apple-Trees* (Boston: Houghton Mifflin, 1916); *Field and Study* (Boston: Houghton Mifflin, 1919); *Accepting the Universe* (Boston: Houghton Mifflin, 1920); *Our Vacation Days of 1918* (privately printed, circa 1920); *Under the Maples* (Boston: Houghton Mifflin, 1921); *My Boyhood*, with a conclusion by Julian Burroughs (Garden City, N.Y.: Doubleday, Page, 1922); *The Last Harvest* (Boston: Houghton Mifflin, 1922).

COLLECTED WORKS

The Writings of John Burroughs, 23 vols. (Boston: Houghton Mifflin, 1904; repr., New York: William H. Wise, 1924; New York: Russell and Russell, 1968); *The Life and Letters of John Burroughs*, 2 vols., ed. by Clara Barrus (Boston: Houghton Mifflin, 1925; repr., New York: Russell and Russell, 1968); *The Heart of John Burroughs's Journals*, ed. by Clara Barrus (Boston: Houghton Mifflin, 1928).

MANUSCRIPTS AND PAPERS

Berg Collection of the New York Public Library (New York, N.Y.); Special Collections Division, Vassar College Library (Poughkeepsie, N.Y.); The John Burroughs Collection, Clifton Waller Barrett Library, University of Virginia (Charlottesville, Va.).

BIOGRAPHICAL AND CRITICAL STUDIES

Justin Askins, " 'Thankfully, the Center Cannot Hold': John Burroughs," in *North Dakota Quarterly* 59 (spring 1991); Clara Barrus, *Our Friend John Burroughs* (Boston: Houghton Mifflin, 1914), and *Whitman and Burroughs, Comrades* (Boston: Houghton Mifflin, 1931); Frank Bergon, "Burroughs, Literature, and Science in the Hudson Valley," in *The John Burroughs Review* 1:1 (3 April 1987), and introduction to his *A Sharp Lookout: Selected Natural History Essays of John Burroughs* (Washington, D.C.: Smithsonian Institution, 1987); Ralph W. Black, "The Imperative of Seeing: John Burroughs and the Poetics of Natural History," in *The CEA Critic* 55:2 (spring 1993); Sarah K. Bolton, "John Burroughs," in her *Famous American Authors* (New York, 1887; repr., New York: Crowell, 1924); Paul Brooks, "The Two Johns," in his *Speaking for Nature: How Literary Naturalists from Henry Thoreau to Rachel Carson Have Shaped America* (Boston: Houghton Mifflin, 1980); R. J. H. De Loach, *Rambles with John Burroughs* (Boston: Gorham, 1912); Robert Elman, "John Burroughs and the Literary Publicists," in his *First in the Field: America's Pioneering Naturalists* (New York: Mason/Charter, 1977); Norman Foerster, *Nature in American Literature* (New York: Macmillan, 1923); Philip Marshall Hicks, "John Burroughs," in his *The Development of the Natural History Essay in American Literature* (Philadelphia: Univ. of Pennsylvania Press, 1924); Hans Huth, *Nature and the American: Three Centuries of Changing Attitudes* (Berkeley, Calif.: Univ. of California Press, 1957); Clifton Johnson, *John Burroughs Talks: His Reminiscences and Comments* (Boston: Houghton Mifflin, 1922); Elizabeth Burroughs Kelley, *John Burroughs: Naturalist, the Story of His Work and Family* (New York, 1959; repr., West Park, N.Y.: Riverby, 1986), and *John Burroughs's Slabsides* (Rhinebeck, N.Y.: Moran, 1974); Edward Kanze, *The World of John Burroughs* (New York: Abrams, 1993); Jack Kligerman, ed., *The Birds of John Burroughs: Keeping a Sharp Lookout* (New York: Hawthorne Books, 1976); Bill McKibben, "The Call of the Not So Wild," in *New York Review of Books* (14 May 1992); William Perkins, *Indexes to the Collected Works of John Burroughs*, ed. by Frank Bergon and Frank Knight (New York: The John Burroughs Association, Inc., 1995); Bliss Perry, "John Burroughs," in his *The Praise of Folly and Other Papers* (Boston, Houghton Mifflin, 1923); Edward J. Renehan, Jr., *John Burroughs: An American Naturalist* (Post Mills, Vt.: Chelsea Green, 1992); George D. Richards, "John Burroughs: An Emersonian Naturalist in the Age of Darwin," in *Perspectives on Nineteenth Century Heroism*, ed. by David C. Leonard (Madrid: Porrua Turanzas, 1982); Harriet B. Shatraw, *John Burroughs: Famous Naturalist* (Charlotteville, N.Y.: SamHar House, 1972); H. R. Stoneback, "John Burroughs: Regionalist," in *The Literature of the Mid-Hudson Valley*, ed. by Alfred H. Marks (New Paltz, N.Y.: SUNY at New Paltz, 1973); Henry Chester Tracy, "John Burroughs," in his *American Naturalists* (New York: Dutton, 1930); Robert Henry Welker, *Birds and Men: American Birds in Science, Art, Literature, and Conservation, 1800–1900* (Cambridge: Harvard Univ. Press, 1955); Perry Westbrook, *John Burroughs* (New York: Twayne, 1974), and "John Burroughs and the Transcendentalists," in *Emerson Society Quarterly* 55 (April 1969); Farida A. Wiley, ed., *John Burroughs' America* (New York: Doubleday, 1951).

SALLY CARRIGHAR

(1898–1985)

GALE LAWRENCE

IN 1933, during the darkest days of the Great Depression, Sally Carrighar tried to commit suicide. She was thirty-five years old, out of work, and starving. In her autobiography, *Home to the Wilderness* (1973), she says, "To this desperate near-end I had come by the determination to write my own truth, to explore what would be found in obscure depths" (p. 232). What she discovered in the aftermath of her suicide attempt was that her own "obscure depths" were not the best place to be looking for her subject matter. It was not until she turned to nature that she discovered a different kind of truth in a different kind of place.

Ironically, her journey "home to the wilderness" began with a mouse singing from inside her radio in her downtown San Francisco apartment. She was trying to find words to describe the mouse's song when she was seized with the thought: "*This* is what I should write about! Birds and animals! I could after all be a writer, a nature writer. Of course!" (p. 274). After several failed attempts at fiction, she had given up on ever becoming a serious or significant writer. But after hearing the mouse sing, her response was, "My whole future life burst open that night like some great and beautiful flower, blossoming in the span of a thought" (p. 275).

Between this sudden conversion and her death at age eighty-seven, Sally Carrighar wrote six nature books, a collection of essays on Alaska, a Civil War novel, and an autobiography. To understand how she approached nature and why she chose to write about it as she did, it is necessary to backtrack to her childhood — to her birth, in fact — when her first nature book was still half a lifetime away.

Early Life

On 10 February 1898 Sally Carrighar was born to Perle Avis Harden and George Thomas Beard Wagner. Her birth name was Dorothy Wagner, but because "Sally Carrighar" is the name she assumed as a writer, it seems unnecessarily confusing to refer to her birth name beyond acknowledging it.

The birth was a difficult one for both mother and child, resulting in an almost total rejection of the child by the mother and a heightened nervousness and excitability in the child. Needless to say, Sally Carrighar did not have a happy childhood. But she survived, and she developed some significant behaviors, attitudes, and feelings that would serve her well much later when she became a nature writer. Most notably, she learned to be silent, observant, intuitive, and psychically receptive to nonverbal communications.

Carrighar's troubled mother managed to convince her small daughter that she should talk as little as possible, especially when her mother was around. In *Home to the Wilderness*, Carrighar comments on the long-term effects of not being able to talk about anything she was experiencing: "Stored away, it can become a sort of personality capital, giving an inner sense of having accumulated significance as an individual. ... The storing is not a comfortable process, but it may not be entirely unfortunate" (p. 6).

Given that Sally Carrighar did eventually become a nature writer, it would be convenient to think that this child, rejected by her mother and deprived of words, would turn instantly to nature for solace and companionship, but in truth Carrighar was not an especially outdoorsy child. Her earliest memories of the outdoors include walks with her father around the industrial parts of Cleveland and formal horse and buggy rides with her very proper maternal grandmother, who lived in the riverside town of Painesville, Ohio.

Before nature came music. When Carrighar was six years old, her parents took her to a violin concert that changed her young life. The words Carrighar uses to describe this early experience reflect the intensity and receptiveness that would eventually play a role in her nature writing. In explaining her response to the music, she says, "I seemed to receive this magnificent sound not through my ears alone but through the skin all over my body" (p. 37). Much later, in describing animal sensations, she would write about such total body feelings as "shelter-touch," "ear view," and "skin-feeling," all of which seem related to the way she herself had learned to perceive things as a child.

She goes on to explain that music would become her own special way of talking without words—and Carrighar's deep sensitivity to sound shows itself later in the strong sound-imagery in her nature books and in the rhythmic quality of her prose. Music, specifically the piano, was her passion until she was seventeen. Over the course of her childhood the outdoors became more important to her, but it is difficult to see a serious naturalist developing in the little girl who liked to wander in John D. Rockefeller's Cleveland rose garden and later, when her family moved to Kansas City, Missouri, to play with chipmunks in a city park.

Carrighar's first real exposure to the outdoors, beyond frequent and comforting visits to her grandparents' riverside home in Painesville and to an uncle's farm outside Cleveland, was a summer vacation on an island in Canada. She was fifteen, and still very serious about her music, but at the island resort she met a young man, the son of the owners, who was a champion canoeist and competent outdoorsman. He took an interest in her, taught her how to paddle a canoe, and invited her to come along to various special places he knew. Before Carrighar met this young man she had been afraid of the Canadian woods, afraid of getting lost, afraid of everything that was different from the gardens, pastures, and city parks she knew. But in her new friend's company she began to enjoy the wilderness.

She had her first taste of how powerfully nature could affect her that summer. In describing how it felt to sit in a place where the trees were full of birds and squirrels, she says it "began to seem almost the same experience as making music, as the way, when I played the piano, I *was* the music, my physical body feeling as if it dissolved in the sounds" (p. 96). She goes on to explain the selfless, out-of-body sensation that music induced in her: "I could say my dimensions then were those of the melodies and the harmony that spread out from the piano in all directions. I had no consciousness of my individual self." She describes as well the unique ability she would eventually bring to her nature writing. Her strange, intense, nonverbal childhood had helped her develop the sense "of losing myself ... by becoming identified with whatever I was especially aware of."

Not long after the summer in Canada, Carrighar developed an interest in writing. She read voraciously from books she found around her house and decided that writing was a skill much like music. She thought if she could master words as she had notes, perhaps she could have as much pleasure from writing as she did from music. It was fortunate that she was beginning to develop a second interest, because when she was seventeen she realized that she had neither the physical strength nor the talent to become a professional concert pianist. In a pattern that would repeat itself throughout her life, she responded to this crisis by becoming sick. By the time she recuperated and went off to college at Wellesley in the fall of 1918, she had let go of music and opened herself to new possibilities.

At Wellesley, Carrighar discovered that she indeed had an aptitude for writing. Her English professors built her confidence in this new talent to the point that, even though she had to leave Wellesley after two years because her health was failing again, she was already thinking of herself as a writer. But nature writing was still many years in the future. After leaving Wellesley, she worked at a resort in the Ozarks as a fishing guide, and considered writing a novel about the people she met there. But her job ended before she had enough time to observe her subjects very deeply. Next she traveled to Emporia, Kansas, where she presented herself to William Allen White as a promising young journalist. He did not need her. When she finally returned to Kansas City and started working as her father's secretary at the headquarters of a paint manufacturing company, her distressed mother arranged for her to move to Hollywood to live with an uncle, whose family would introduce her around.

Carrighar still wanted to be a writer, but the more urgent business of earning a living forced her to learn a new set of skills. Her first job in Hollywood was with a play and casting agent. She served as his receptionist and was also expected to read plays, make summaries of their plots, and give her boss ideas about how to pitch them to the movie studios. From this experience she learned the importance of visible action. She also met some of the stars of the silent film era, and flirted briefly with the prospect of becoming a professional dancer. When she discovered that her employer was moonlighting as a pimp, however, she found another job.

This job took her to Cecil B. DeMille's Metropolitan Studio, where she worked as an assistant to the studio manager, met more movie people, watched movies being made, and learned the importance of making every scene dramatically effective. It was here that she had the first of her recurring psychic experiences with animals. She was watching the filming of a scene that involved a trained lion, and found herself imagining the now captive and degraded lion as it had been in the wild. Suddenly the lion jumped off the couch it was supposed to be lying on, pushed through the studio crowd, and stopped two feet from Carrighar, where it stared intently into her eyes: "How long did he hold his gaze? Two minutes, three? Long enough for a blaze of light to come streaming into my mind. For that length of time I saw nature's truth, much more overpowering than even the clearest of human truth. From the lion's eyes I partook of wildness, so that now his truth was mine too" (p. 194). Twice more during the filming of that movie the lion approached Carrighar, and the experience convinced her that it was time to leave: "What I had thought of as human truth had always made it disturbing to live in the false atmosphere of Hollywood, but the glimpses of nature's much deeper truth had made it impossible to stay" (p. 196).

She moved to San Francisco, where she acquired more skills that she would eventually bring to her nature writing. She learned to write magazine articles by writing for a financial monthly. She wrote so well that she soon became the editor, but the job did not pay her enough to promise a secure future, so she moved on to the advertising office of a building and loan association. Here she learned how to write advertising copy; she learned as well that her bosses were dishonest. She decided to quit commercial writing and write fiction—honest, truthful fiction of the type she had dreamed of writing at Wellesley. But when she tried, she was alarmed by the dark and violent stories that emerged from her troubled imagination. Eventually what little money she had saved from her various jobs ran out, and she lost all hope of a better future for herself as a person or as a writer. It was at this low point in her life, which happened to coincide with the dark days before the newly elected U.S. president, Franklin Delano Roosevelt, could institute his public works programs, that she decided to commit suicide.

Sally Carrighar's attempted suicide was a clear turning point, but her career as a nature writer did not begin immediately upon her recovery. As if to see how many different kinds of writing she could try, she next found a job writing radio advertisements. She was very successful at creating short dramas that promoted various products, and supported herself during two years of psychoanalysis and two more of experimenting with disappointing fiction before the singing mouse finally provided her with more fruitful subject matter.

Once she had established the clear goal of writing about animals rather than about herself or other human beings, she quit her radio job and addressed herself to a rigorous program of self-education. She was thirty-nine years old, with only a high school background in botany and a college course in zoology, and writing experiences about as far removed from nature writing as anyone could imagine. Carrighar set out to find work that would enable her to be a freelance student. She hired out as a temporary office worker until she had enough money to subsidize a block of study time, studied until her money ran out, then worked as an office temporary again.

She educated herself by asking questions of the scientists she met at the University of California and the California Academy of Sciences, by doing research in natural history libraries, and by making her own observations. As it turned out, the scientists she gravitated toward were field biologists fascinated by the behavior of wild animals in their natural environments. Carrighar was working with an early generation of American ethologists—animal behaviorists—and their approach to animals would influence her profoundly. One of her new mentors, a National Park Service naturalist named Joseph Dixon, suggested that Beetle Rock in Sequoia National Park would be a good place to observe animals living and interacting naturally in the wild. And so began the writing of Sally Carrighar's first nature book, *One Day on Beetle Rock*, which would be published in 1944 to considerable acclaim.

One Day on Beetle Rock

One Day on Beetle Rock was seven years—plus a whole lifetime—in the making. It reflects various influences from Carrighar's complex past. Her silent childhood had taught her to observe closely and infer meaning from gesture, attitude, and movement. Her passion for music had taught her to perceive, interpret, and express strong emotions that were not spoken and not necessarily her own. Wellesley had taught her to write truthfully; Hollywood to write visually, actively, and dramatically; advertising to write engagingly; her scientific mentors taught her to write factually.

The result of this unusual combination of influences—none of them other nature writers—is a strangely psychic style of nature writing that defies easy categorization. Carrighar imagines her way deeply into the experiences of each animal she focuses on and describes in great sensory detail exactly what it feels like to be that animal. She does not so much humanize her animals (as some later critics have felt) as "animalize" her human readers.

Her goal in this first book was to dramatize biological, ecological, and ethological facts by portraying one specific day in the lives of nine different animals. In her autobiography she says she had no role model for what she was trying to do, though she might have found kindred spirits in the English naturalist Henry Williamson, who wrote *Tarka the Otter* (1927) and *Salar the Salmon* (1935), and also in the early Rachel Carson, whose first book, *Under the Sea Wind* (1941), experimented with a similar, if less psychic, approach.

Working in relative isolation, with scientists rather than nature writers as her mentors and her own creative impulses drawing her toward the techniques of drama and fiction, Carrighar produced what might be called a collection of dramatic nature stories, or even a nature novel. Her carefully connected narratives are unified in time by one June day, in place by Beetle Rock, in theme by the shared tension of surviving, and in point of view by Carrighar's omniscience.

She begins the book by introducing the nine animals in an anticipatory scene designed to frame the ensuing narratives and establish Carrighar's main theme: "The willing tension that keeps a wilderness society stable" (p. 9). Then she takes us into the world of her first animal, the weasel, with a paragraph that shows Carrighar's rhythmic, poetic, exquisitely descriptive language at work:

> Night's end had come, with its interlude of peace, on the animal trails. The scents that lay like vines across the forest floor were faded now, and uninteresting. Hungry eyes had ceased their watch of the moonlight splashes and the plumy, shimmering treetops. No heart caught with fear when a twig fell or a pebble rolled. For most of the nocturnal hunters had returned to their dens, or ignored one another in a truce of weariness. (p. 12)

This is the prose that contemporary reviewers called "intense and subtle" and "scrupulous," that had won her a contract from Alfred A. Knopf and sold the chapter to the *Saturday Evening Post.*

A few sentences later Carrighar takes us inside the mind of an animal, a female weasel: "On the hillside where she hunted with her young she suddenly pulled herself up, sweeping the slope with her nose and eyes, trying to cup the forest in her ears for the sound of a chirp, a breath, or an earth-plug being pushed into a burrow" (pp. 12–13). As she describes the weasel physically she invites us not just to see the weasel, but to feel what it feels like to be a weasel: "She was a squirrel's length stripped to a mouse's width, and was no glutton. But was driven by insatiable hungers of the nerves" (p. 13).

After describing the weasel's intense and highly dramatic day, which includes killing a chipmunk and a squirrel for her young to eat and losing two of her young to a coyote with cubs of his own to feed, Carrighar concludes with an image designed to fix the essence of the weasel in our minds. The weasel is hunting a mouse: "On the end of the log she waited, with her eyes fixed on the grass. Poised for a leap, erect, she was as sharp as a small, arrested flame" (p. 28). Carrighar uses the same strategy throughout the book: eight more intense, descriptive, and dramatic narratives covering the same day, the same place, and the same events, with the same animals moving in and out of each other's stories. One after another, she takes us inside the experience of a Sierra grouse, a chickaree, a black

Sally Carrighar with a lodgepole chipmunk at Beetle Rock

bear, a lizard, a coyote, a deer mouse, a Steller's jay, and a mule deer.

By ending with the mule deer, who has played a key role in the anticipatory scene, Carrighar shows her thematic and narrative control. The book begins with the mature mule deer buck, the leader of his herd, arriving on Beetle Rock for another summer; in the final scene he relinquishes leadership to a younger, more aggressive male. The mule deer's experience both frames the other narratives and relieves the thematic tension that Carrighar has established at the

143

outset. The final paragraph offers readers a sense of closure: "For ten years, he had not relaxed completely—his muscles often, but never his alertness. He had poised himself on the forest movements, scents, and sounds as tirelessly as if he had been a bird, born in the air, who must soar through all its life. But finally he would be able to alight. Did he know that now?" (p. 196). That final question brings us back to the human perspective and leaves us with the central mystery that Carrighar spent the rest of her life exploring.

Carrighar's ability to describe animals accurately, poetically, and dramatically from the inside out won her highly favorable reviews. Edwin Way Teale called *One Day at Beetle Rock* "an event in nature-literature publishing" (p. 5). Other reviewers called it "a book of rare distinction" and commented on her "deep feeling," "subtle perception," and "great intensity." In the *Saturday Review of Literature*, Alan Devoe summarizes the struggle that had been going on in nature writing since the turn-of-the-century "nature fakers" controversy and the later separation of professional scientists from traditional nature writers. He points to the two extremes that writing about animals had taken—popular anthropomorphism and the cold method of science—and then posits a third type: "imaginative participance . . . by an instructed and passionate empathy." He places Carrighar in this third category and credits her with "an uncommon and peculiar genius" (Devoe, 1945, p. 29).

Even if *One Day on Beetle Rock* has not totally withstood the critical tests of the second half of the twentieth century, it remains a significant experiment. Carrighar's approach to nature writing combines serious science with sympathetic imagination to communicate geological, ecological, and ethological facts in a manner designed to change human perceptions of animals.

One Day at Teton Marsh

After her success with the day-in-the-life formula at Beetle Rock, Sally Carrighar moved to a new location and addressed a new ecosystem. But she did not merely repeat the same formula. She had paid her dues and was ready to stretch a bit. Her life circumstances had also changed. The success of *One Day on Beetle Rock* had brought her a contract and advance before she even began her research at Teton Marsh. She was now able to sell everything she wrote to national magazines. The only blight on her success was the termination of an eight-year relationship with a man she had met at her radio job. He had been her lover, friend, and editor throughout the crucial years when she was launching her new career. The relationship ended just as she was beginning to succeed.

Carrighar went to the Tetons ready to consolidate and build on her success—and to continue her exploration of the natural world, which had already served as her healer and was now increasingly serving as her alternative to the human world. *One Day at Teton Marsh* (1947) is set in a large beaver pond and marsh along the Snake River near Jackson Hole, Wyoming. The location marks a shift from the relatively stable terrestrial environment of Beetle Rock to a dramatically changing aquatic environment. The boundaries here are altogether less certain, and the ecosystem itself undergoes a major change during the day Carrighar describes: a severe storm topples a tree, breaks the beaver dam, and drains the pond.

The setting changes from a pleasant summer day in the woods, when mating and family life are primary, to an ominous fall day in the marsh, when families are breaking up, young are dispersing, birds are migrating, and the entire community is threatened by winter. Some of the animals of Teton Marsh are also less visible than those of Beetle Rock, their experiences further removed from the experiences of humans, who are asked to empathize with such animals as a trout, a mosquito, a shrimplike creature called a scud, a leech, a frog, and a snail.

Once again, Carrighar performs the feats of language and imagination that impressed her contemporaries, but two elements begin to detract from her artistry. One is the tone of her protests against such human practices as killing trumpeter swans for their down, using lead shot to kill ducks, and trapping beavers. In *One Day on Beetle Rock*, she attempted to dramatize the effects of human interference by showing the reactions of a coyote who had been pushed out of his home range by the predator control programs operating around the lower elevation ranches. In *One Day at Teton Marsh*, by contrast, she has descended to lecturing.

The second bothersome element might be brushed off as occasional lapses into anthropomorphism in an otherwise accurate book, but the problem is more complicated. Because Carrighar is trying to dramatize animals in crisis and transition, she needs them to make choices. If she were writing a novel about human beings, she could motivate her characters with such familiar plot drivers as love, anger, fear, grief, or loneliness. Her scientific mentors had made it clear that she could not do that with her animals, so she is forced to fall back repeatedly on "instinct" and "inherited memory"—to the point that these words begin to distract from the drama and draw attention to themselves. She wrestled with the same issue in *One Day on Beetle Rock*, but managed to keep it under control, perhaps because she was still being extremely cautious in trying out her new nature writing strategy. The actions on Beetle Rock were also perhaps easier to explain because the animals were not stressed by a draining pond and changing season.

Despite the increasing tension between Carrighar's science and her art, her reviews remained basically positive. William Beebe, who had published his anthology *The Book of Naturalists* in the same year Sally Carrighar published *One Day at Beetle Rock*, comments, "For a minimum of anthropomorphism, and in faithful representation of activities possible in a day in the life of each of these creatures, Miss Carrighar's book deserves a place near the top of fictional natural history" (Beebe, p. 10). Other reviewers continued to refer to her with such superlatives as "exceptional," "like no one else who has ever written about animals, birds and insects" (Jackson, p. 18), and "the most imaginative and poetic nature writer in this country" (McCord, 1947, p. 178).

Alaska

Sally Carrighar's success with her one-day books won her a Guggenheim Fellowship (the first of two she would receive) to support her next project, and she planned to do research in San Francisco and then go to Alaska for a year to observe the wildlife. From the outset, she intended to produce something broader in scope than her previous books, but she had no idea just how much broader until she got to Alaska in the summer of 1948. She spent nearly nine years in Alaska, bought a house in Nome, conducted some original scientific research on lemmings, acquired a Siberian husky, and wrote not just one but three books.

The book that took her to Alaska was *Icebound Summer*, which was published in 1953. During this same period another nature writer, Rachel Carson, was following her own 1951 bestseller, *The Sea Around Us*, with a close study of an intertidal zone — the part of the coast that is exposed at low tide and covered with water at high tide. It was published in 1955 as *Edge of the Sea*. Carrighar's project addressed a somewhat similar but more massive zone: the part of Alaska that is briefly exposed during the summer and covered by snow and ice during the winter. In her introduction to *Icebound Summer*, she describes the area in characteristically poetic language as "the limit of summer, the narrow strip that the seasons dispute. There the sea ice has only withdrawn from the shore for as long as the winds permit, and the permafrost in the soil will not thaw down as deep as a dozen inches. This is an icebound summer, lovely if never lush" (p. ix).

The one-day, one-place formula had clearly become too confining for her. With her time frame expanded to a whole summer and her study area to vast arctic spaces, her animals, too, become bigger. This time she includes whales, walruses, and seals, as well as lemmings, loons, foxes, terns, and golden plovers. Human beings also have a place among her characters, not as evildoers, this time, but as members of the ecological community. She devotes an entire chapter to an Eskimo family that has traveled to their summer campsite south of Point Barrow to hunt and fish near Icy Cape. They come dangerously close to becoming part of the food chain themselves, suggesting that in an environment like the one Carrighar now describes, human beings still belong to the eat-or-be-eaten ecosystems that surround them.

As in her one-day books, Carrighar's descriptions of the scenes and animals are exquisite, but she is once again haunted by the need to motivate and explain animal behavior to keep her individual narratives—and the whole book— moving at a dramatic pace. And once again "instinct" works to keep the animals in motion. As poetic and informative as her language is, even the staunchest supporters among her reviewers begin to sound a bit defensive in their efforts to downplay her anthropomorphism. *Atlantic* reviewer Phoebe Lou Adams, for instance, qualifies: "While she sometimes describes what she saw in suspiciously emotional terms, she has on the whole steered a straight course between sentimentalizing her wild subjects and dissecting them" (p. 88). The *New Yorker*, too, acknowledges "moments when Miss Carrighar's determination to sound the deeps of animal fears and delights carries her perilously close to anthropomorphism," before going on to declare *Icebound Summer* "admirable" (pp. 86–87).

The three books Carrighar derived from her almost nine years in Alaska are related to and make reference to each other. Together they give us a fairly detailed account of that period of her life. *Icebound Summer* was her main project, and was published first, but she had already started writing magazine articles that would find their way into the following two books.

The second to be published was *Moonlight at Midday* (1958), which is a departure from her nature narratives. It includes some of her popular magazine writings of the period, plus essays on Alaskan history, sociology, and economics, and commentary about Alaska's impending statehood. The least appealing essays are the ones in which she appears to be writing for the Alaska Chamber of Commerce; the most appealing are the profiles of various Eskimos, bush

pilots, and non-native Alaskans she met during her extended stay, and the autobiographical chapters that show her living in the Eskimo village of Unalakleet, going off on lemming hunts, and living the life of a serious nature writer in circumstances that would have discouraged a less committed person.

The third Alaska book is another departure from the nature narratives, but is more closely related to her early books than *Moonlight at Midday*. After she bought her house in Nome, she took in a Siberian husky who had belonged to neighbors who were moving away. This dog was a major part of her life for seven years, and *Wild Voice of the North* (1959) is a biography, ethological study, and celebration of this dog. She had first made him famous in 1953 by writing an article about him titled "The Dog That Trained Me" for the *Saturday Evening Post*.

After Alaska

After nine years and three books, Sally Carrighar decided to leave Alaska. She had contracted undulant fever from drinking unpasteurized milk, and could not recover easily. At first she considered returning to San Francisco, but her mother (who remained unfriendly) had settled there, so she decided to live in the East for a while. She moved to the Hanover, New Hampshire, area. Her next book, *The Glass Dove* (1962), was a novel based on family history. Ancestors on her mother's side had been involved with the Underground Railroad, and Carrighar reconstructs enough Civil War history to tell her fictionalized version of their story. The novel got lukewarm reviews, but Carrighar was on to other things anyway.

In 1964, Walt Disney introduced her to a new generation by making a television movie of *One Day at Teton Marsh*, which aired on 8 November 1964, and by then she was finishing the most academic of her nature books: *Wild Heritage*, published by Houghton Mifflin in 1965. In *Wild Heritage*, Carrighar shifts from dramatizing animal behavior to explaining ethology itself, defending the relatively new science and presenting what ethologists had learned so far about four key animal behaviors: parenthood, sex, aggressiveness, and play. The book is a readable summary of ethological research, and Carrighar is in her element explaining the science she had studied for so long and worked so hard to dramatize in her nature narratives. *Wild Heritage* might be viewed as an extended statement of Carrighar's credo, and also as a defense of her chosen way of writing, with a twenty-page bibliography to back it up.

Autobiography

Sally Carrighar's mother died in the mid 1960s at the age of ninety-two. Perhaps as a way of laying that complicated relationship to rest, Carrighar's next book was her autobiography, which is as much about her mother as it is about herself. In *Home to the Wilderness* (1973), Carrighar finally explores the "obscure depths" she could not work with in her early attempts at fiction. She revisits the darkest days of her childhood, including a recovered memory of her mother's attempt to strangle her when she was six. She also speculates that her mother may have attempted to starve her when she was a teenager and then to poison her with arsenic when she was struggling with anemia. She remembers clearly that when she was seventeen her mother suggested she commit suicide because her health problems were costing the family so much money.

The first two-thirds of the book covers the long, mother-haunted, mother-controlled part of her life, culminating in her suicide attempt at age thirty-five. The last third takes us through her psychoanalysis, her discovery of what she calls "nature's healing art" and the writing of *One Day on Beetle Rock.* It is in this autobiography, published thirty-six years after Carrighar committed herself to writing about nature, that she articulates her beliefs about nature and nature writing. Nature offered Carrighar a healthy alternative to the painful, half-mad world of human beings. She explains that in the natural world she found a "code of behavior so well understood and so well respected that the laws could be depended on not to be broken" (*Home to the Wilderness*, p. 321). Wilderness was a healing place where she could spend the rest of her life seeking mental and emotional health.

Home to the Wilderness also articulates her personal philosophy of nature writing. Carrighar's early scientific mentors had taught her about ecology and its emphasis on nature as a network, but she wanted her own emphasis to be different: "to portray the pattern but devote most attention to individual creatures in it. I wanted to tell how these animals were related to one another but to show chiefly what was interesting to the creatures themselves. They did not see themselves as strands in a net" (p. 278).

In her nature writing, accuracy would always be essential. She says, "whatever I wrote about animals must be right. The facts must be accurate and one must not make any statements about what the animals feel beyond what can be safely assumed from the way that they act" (p. 279). She also explains the particular strategy she chose for her nature books:

> They would be narratives, stories, but with the animals not doing anything they don't do in real life. The hardest thing, as I was beginning to recognize, would be to create suspense, for the dramatic events in a wilderness happen suddenly and are over quickly. Only in rare circumstances do they build to a climax. Those were problems that I would have to work out. (p. 297)

These problems were considerable and ultimately limited her enduring appeal. Because she needed clearly motivated action to dramatize her narratives, she relied heavily on "instinct" and "inherited memory" to explain why her animals did what they did. Because the instincts and inherited memories cropped up where emotions would have in human dramas, they began to sound increasingly like human emotions, and Carrighar eventually fell victim to the dreaded accusation of anthropomorphism. Although she spent her entire career researching animal behavior, the narrative form she had chosen to make her facts accessible to a popular audience eventually doomed her. She did indeed reach a wide popular audience with both her books and magazine articles, but her popularity was brief and her books are no longer widely read.

The Twilight Seas

In her last book, Sally Carrighar returns to the narrative strategy that had served her so well earlier in her career. She had begun with one day on a rock, expanded to a longer, less determinate day at a marsh, and then to a whole summer in Alaska. *The Twilight Seas* (1975) goes even farther. It covers four years and moves around much of the Southern Hemisphere. Instead of focusing on numerous small- and medium-sized animals, she has chosen to focus on just one, a member of the largest species on earth: a blue whale. It is as if she has stretched imagination to its absolute capacity to take us inside the experience of a huge marine mammal that most of us will never see, except perhaps for fleeting glimpses as it surfaces to breathe before returning to its underwater world.

Carrighar's familiar techniques are still evident: her exquisite, multisensory descriptions, her musical prose, her extensive research—and her dangerously emotionlike, thoughtlike "instincts" that motivate the whale's actions, choices, and decisions. The narrative, however, has taken a definite turn toward melodramatic protest, with human whale hunters serving as the agents of evil. The reviewers this time were less forgiving of Carrighar's choices. Peter Benchley of the *New York Times Book Review* was her severest critic, calling her "one of the most egregious anthropomorphizers" (p. 28). He goes on to attack the central problem in her nature writing: the conflict between her science and her thinking, feeling whale.

The Twilight Seas was Sally Carrighar's last book, and she had abandoned magazine work a decade earlier. In 1974, before this final book was published, she moved to Carmel, California, to live near her brother and his family. In 1981, she moved into the Ave Maria Convalescent Hospital, where she lived for the last four years of her life. On 9 October 1985, at the age of eighty-seven, she died in relative obscurity, her only obituaries in the *Monterey Peninsula Herald* and the *San Jose Mercury News*.

Selected Bibliography

WORKS OF SALLY CARRIGHAR

BOOKS

One Day on Beetle Rock (New York: Knopf, 1944; repr., Lincoln: Univ. of Nebraska Press, 1978); *One Day at Teton Marsh* (New York: Knopf, 1947; repr., New York: Ballantine, 1972; Lincoln: Univ. of Nebraska Press, 1979); *Icebound Summer* (New York: Knopf, 1953; repr., Lincoln: Univ. of Nebraska Press, 1991); *Moonlight at Midday* (New York: Knopf, 1958); *Wild Voice of the North* (Garden City, N.Y.: Doubleday, 1959; repr., Lincoln: Univ. of Nebraska Press, 1991); published in England as *A Husky in the House* (London: M. Joseph, 1959); *The Glass Dove* (Garden City, N.Y.: Doubleday, 1962); *Wild Heritage* (Boston: Houghton Mifflin, 1965; New York: Ballantine, 1965, 1971, 1976); *The Twilight Seas* (New York: Weybright and Talley, 1975), published in England as *Blue Whale* (London: Gollanz, 1975).

PRIVATE PRINTINGS

Exploring Marin: Sir Francis Drake Highway (San Anselmo, Calif.: Marin Conservation League, 1941, 1948); *As Far as They Could Go* (Fairbanks, Alaska: 1956).

AUTOBIOGRAPHY

Home to the Wilderness: A Personal Journey (Boston: Houghton Mifflin, 1973; repr., New York: Penguin, 1974).

SELECTED ARTICLES

"Forest Buccaneer," in the *Saturday Evening Post* (18 December 1943); "Spinster of Beetle Rock," in *Saturday Evening Post* (4 December 1943); "Buck on the Rock," in *Saturday Evening Post* (29 July 1944); "He Flew into Sunlight," in *Harper's* (October 1945); "Trout in the Quickening River," in *Harper's* (May 1946); "Call to a Trumpeter," in *Saturday Evening Post* (29 March 1947); "World of the Leopard Frog," in *Audubon* (July 1947); "San Francisco Festival of Modern Poetry," in *Poetry* (September 1947); "Reds Are Rapping at Our Arctic Door," in *Saturday Evening Post* (4 February 1950); "I Flew with an Arctic Bush

Pilot," in *Saturday Evening Post* (17 June 1950); "Cities of America," in *Saturday Evening Post* (27 January 1951); "Prey of the Arctic," in *Saturday Evening Post* (31 March 1951); "Alaska Needs Her Bush Pilots: Why Drive Them Out?" in *Saturday Evening Post* (16 June 1951); "Foolhardy Fox," in *Saturday Evening Post* (1 September 1951); "Captive of the North," in *Saturday Evening Post* (22 December 1951); "Unalakleet, Alaska," in *Saturday Evening Post* (19 January 1952); "Honorable Death of a Rogue," in *Colliers* (24 January 1953); "Flight of the Golden Plover," in *Colliers* (28 February 1953); "Marooned Children," in *Saturday Evening Post* (7 March 1953); "Day at the Beach," in *Mademoiselle* (May 1953); "Ordeal of the White Whale," in *Colliers* (16 May 1953); "The Dog That Trained Me," in *Saturday Evening Post* (5 December 1953); "Gold Rush Isn't Over Yet!" in *Saturday Evening Post* (16 January 1954); "Party Is Over for the Eskimos," in *Saturday Evening Post* (20 February 1954); "Best-Mannered Children in the World," in *Saturday Evening Post* (4 December 1954); "How to Make Friends with Animals," in *Saturday Evening Post* (12 March 1955); "I Tried to Outwit the Arctic," in *Saturday Evening Post* (29 October 1955); "Try Housekeeping at the Arctic Edge," in *Reader's Digest* (February 1956); "Why Live in Alaska?" in *Reader's Digest* (September 1956); "Murder in the Schoolroom," in *Harper's* (June 1957); "Gift Well Given," in *Mademoiselle* (October 1957); "Bad Ape-Man Seed," in *Saturday Review* (16 December 1961); "Some Waspish Words for Bats," in *Saturday Review* (17 March 1962); "To Him the Unknown Was Home," in *Saturday Review* (20 June 1964); "Sex: The Silent Bell," in *Atlantic* (March 1965); "Culture of Animals: A Lesson in Evolution," in *Saturday Review* (1 May 1965); "War Is Not in Our Genes," in *UNESCO Courier* (August 1970).

MANUSCRIPTS AND PAPERS

The Baker Special Collections of Dartmouth College Library includes original typescripts with printer's notations and author's corrections; signed holographs; various photographs; and letters.

BIOGRAPHICAL AND CRITICAL STUDIES

SELECTED REVIEWS

Phoebe Lou Adams, "Reader's Choice," review of *Icebound Summer*, in *Atlantic* (August 1953); "Arctic Life Histories," review of *Icebound Summer*, in *Nation* (1 August 1953); Marston Bates, "It's a Wild Life," review of *Wild Heritage*, in *New York Times Book Review* (28 March 1965); William Beebe, review

of *One Day at Teton Marsh*, in *New York Herald-Tribune Book Review* (28 September 1947); Peter Benchley, "All the Families in the Order Cetacea," in *New York Times Book Review* (10 November 1975); Robert Gorham Davis, "Deep-tangled Wildwood," review of *One Day at Teton Marsh*, in *New York Times Book Review* (19 October 1947); Alan Devoe, "Sally Carrighar's Animal Alley," review of *One Day on Beetle Rock*, in *Saturday Review of Literature* (24 February 1945) and review of *Icebound Summer*, in *New York Herald-Tribune Book Review* (19 July 1953); Peter Farb, "Myths of Man and Beast," review of *Wild Heritage*, in *Saturday Review* (20 March 1965); J. H. Jackson, review of *One Day at Teton Marsh*, in *San Francisco Chronicle* (25 September 1947); Martin Levin, "A Reader's Report on Current Fiction," review of *The Glass Dove*, in *New York Times Book Review* (11 March 1962); David McCord, review of *One Day on Beetle Rock*, in *Atlantic* (February 1945), review of *One Day at Teton Marsh*, in *Atlantic* (November 1947), and review of *Moonlight at Midday*, in *New York Herald-Tribune Book Review* (26 October 1958); Anita Moffett, "Sequoia Vignettes," review of *One Day on Beetle Rock*, in *New York Times Book Review* (10 December 1944); Richard L. Neuberger, "Lovely, Cold, and Lonely," review of *Moonlight at Midday*, in *New York Times Book Review* (26 October 1958); Review of *Icebound Summer*, in *New Yorker* (15 September 1953); Lillian Smith, "Underground Railroad," review of *The Glass Dove*, in *Saturday Review* (31 March 1962); Edwin Way Teale, review of *One Day on Beetle Rock*, in *Weekly Book Review* (26 November 1944); Walter Magnes Teller, "In a Spell of Sunlight," review of *Icebound Summer*, in *New York Times Book Review* (19 July 1953); Edward Weeks, "The Peripatetic Reviewer," review of *Wild Heritage*, in *Atlantic* (April 1965).

CRITICAL STUDIES

Mary F. Tobin, "Nature Writers as Dissenting Moderns: Modernization and the Development of American Beliefs About Nature," Ph.D. diss. (University of Maryland, 1981); Gregg W. Wentzell, "Wildness and the American Mind: The Social Construction of Nature in Environmental Romanticism from Thoreau to Dillard," Ph.D. diss. (Miami University, 1993).

OBITUARIES

"Naturalist, Wildlife Author Sally Carrighar Dies at 87," in *Monterey Peninsula Herald* (12 October 1985); "Sally Carrighar, 87, Writer on Wildlife," in *San Jose Mercury News* (13 October 1985).

RACHEL CARSON
(1907–1964)

CHERYLL GLOTFELTY

It is Miss Carson's particular gift to be able to blend scientific knowledge with the spirit of poetic awareness, thus restoring to us a true sense of the world.

—Henry Beston

She did her homework, she minded her English, and she cared.

—David Brower

TODAY, RACHEL CARSON'S fame rests upon her classic indictment of modern pesticide use, *Silent Spring*: "A few thousand words from her, and the world took a new direction," proclaimed one newspaper editorial (quoted in Brooks, 1980, p. 140). While *Silent Spring* is often credited with launching the modern environmental movement, it is easy to forget that Carson wrote three other, quieter, books about the sea, books that were also best-sellers in their day. Behind all of Carson's work, whether polemic or poetic, lies an abiding love of nature that extends back as far as she could recall.

"I can remember no time when I wasn't interested in the out-of-doors and the whole world of nature," Rachel Carson once said. "I was rather a solitary child and spent a great deal of time in woods and beside streams, learning the birds and the insects and flowers" (quoted in Brooks, 1972, p. 16). Rachel Louise Carson was born 27 May 1907, in Springdale, Pennsylvania, a rural, wooded town outside of Pittsburgh. Her father was Robert Warden Carson, and she had a sister (Marian) and a brother (Robert)—but Carson's mother, Maria (McLean) Carson, remained the strongest influence throughout Rachel's life, teaching her to love nature, books, and music. Carson later observed that more than anyone else she knew, her mother "embodied Albert Schweitzer's 'reverence for life'" (quoted in Brooks, 1972, p. 242).

From the time she was a young girl Carson aspired to be a writer. When she was only ten, one of her stories appeared in *St. Nicholas* magazine, a popular children's periodical of the time that published the juvenile writing of other subsequently well-known modern writers including William Faulkner, F. Scott Fitzgerald, E. E. Cummings, Eudora Welty, Edna St. Vincent Millay, and E. B. White. With her goal set on a writing career, Carson entered Pennsylvania College for Women (now Chatham College) as an English major, where she is remembered as having been a quiet, serious, and gifted student. Although Carson had never seen the sea, somehow she knew that her destiny was linked to it. She recalls having read Alfred, Lord Tennyson's poem "Locksley Hall" and feeling an intense emotional response to its final line, "For the mighty wind arises, roaring seaward, and I go."

In her junior year, having taken a biology class

that captivated her, Carson shocked everyone by changing majors from English to biology. At that time, women were discouraged from becoming scientists, and job opportunities for female biologists were scarce. Initially, Carson thought that she would have to abandon her goal of being a writer, but then she realized that science and writing might be combined. As she confided to a college friend,

> I have always wanted to write, but I know I don't have much imagination. Biology has given me something to write about. I will try in my writing to make animals in the woods and waters where they live as alive and as meaningful to others as they are to me. (quoted in Brooks, 1980, p. 139)

After graduating magna cum laude in 1929, Carson won a scholarship to the master's program in zoology at Johns Hopkins University. During successive summers she worked and studied at the Marine Biological Laboratory at Woods Hole, Massachusetts. The title of her master's thesis attests to her commitment to science, but gives little indication that she would later become a best-selling author: "The Development of the Pronephros During the Embryonic and Early Larval Life of the Catfish (*Inctalurus punctatus*)."

Life for Carson was not easy after earning her M.S. from Johns Hopkins in 1932. The Great Depression meant that jobs of any kind were hard to find, and Carson's financial worries were exacerbated because she was the principal breadwinner for her parents, who had moved to Maryland to live with her. For a few years, Carson pieced together teaching and laboratory-assistant jobs at the University of Maryland and at Johns Hopkins. Carson's situation became even more strained when her father died in 1935 and her married sister died a year later, leaving behind two young daughters who were taken in by Carson and her mother.

Carson's lucky break came in 1935 when she was hired on a temporary basis by the Bureau of Fisheries (which later became the U.S. Fish and Wildlife Service) to write the scripts for seven-minute radio spots on sea life, broadcast in a series called "Romance Under the Waters." When a permanent position for a junior aquatic biologist was announced, Carson took the civil service exam and scored higher than anyone else, becoming one of only two women to be hired by the bureau in other than a clerical capacity. In her sixteen years of government service, Carson rose through the ranks to become biologist and editor-in-chief of Fish and Wildlife Service publications. Throughout her government career and despite family demands on her time, Carson doggedly worked on her own writing at night, placing her earliest pieces in the *Baltimore Sun*.

"Undersea"

Carson's first major literary success came about as a result of her government work. Her boss, Elmer Higgins, asked her to write a general introduction for a published version of the "Romance Under the Waters" radio series. When Carson showed Higgins her piece, he suggested that she submit it to a literary magazine, such as the prestigious *Atlantic Monthly*. *Atlantic*'s acceptance of the piece, published in September 1937 and titled "Undersea," represented an official endorsement of her abilities and put wind in Carson's literary sails. Furthermore, "Undersea" was noticed by respected naturalists and writers, who encouraged her to write something longer. Reflecting on her accomplishments years later, Carson observed that from "Undersea" "everything else followed."

"Undersea" begins with the question, "Who has known the ocean?" Conceding that human beings cannot know the ocean world through their "earth-bound senses," Carson helps her readers know the ocean vicariously, through imagination stoked with the findings of science. In Carson's writing, scientific facts are never dull or dry, for the alchemy of her prose transforms technical information into images of fascinating beauty. Via her poetic descriptions, the reader, like a space explorer venturing wide-eyed into the unknown, is transported downward into the world beneath the sea.

Carson's lyrical style imbues the object of her description—the undersea world—with loveliness. A radiolarian shell, for example, appears as a "miracle of ephemeral beauty that might be the work of a fairy glass-blower with a snowflake as his pattern." In the bluish twilight a hundred feet below the surface, "swarms of diminutive fish twinkle through the dusk like a silver rain of meteors." Carson's poetic style transforms even ordinary sea slugs into creatures of magical beauty, "spots of brilliant rose and bronze, spreading arborescent gills to the waters."

While Carson's lyricism encourages readers to see the beauty in unfamiliar creatures, her frequent use of metaphor helps readers to understand the undersea world in terms of the familiar terrestrial one. Thus, she compares ebb tide to nightfall, a time when some creatures retreat to safety while others emerge to hunt; she describes the surface waters of the ocean as analogous to "boundless pastures" on land; and she depicts "the ravenous bluefish" as "roving buccaneers" who "take their booty where they find it."

In "Undersea," as in all of Carson's later writing, the lessons of ecology are conveyed even though the word "ecology" may never be mentioned:

> Thus we see the parts of the plan fall into place: the water receiving from earth and air the simple materials, storing them up until the gathering energy of the spring sun wakens the sleeping plants to a burst of dynamic activity, hungry swarms of planktonic animals growing and multiplying upon the abundant plants, and themselves falling prey to the shoals of fish; all, in the end, to be redissolved into their component substances when the inexorable laws of the sea demand it. (reprinted in Brooks, 1972, p. 29)

This intricate tapestry of life preying on life creates, for Carson, an almost mystical vision of creation, in which "individual elements are lost to view, only to reappear again and again in different incarnations in a kind of material immortality."

"Undersea" not only marks Carson's debut as a writer, but also establishes the poetic voice, the scientific grounding, the ecological vision, and the steadfast love of nature that would characterize her writing for the next twenty-five years.

Under the Sea-Wind

While "Undersea" provides tantalizing but fleeting glimpses of a multitude of creatures, Carson's first book, *Under the Sea-Wind* (1941), follows the lives of many of those creatures of the eastern seaboard in much closer detail, so that the reader comes to know them intimately, even to see the world through their eyes. The book is divided into three major sections, the first focusing on birds, the second on mackerel, and the third on eels. In each section Carson features several protagonists, whom she names and whose lives she chronicles.

Section 1 introduces the reader to Rynchops, a black skimmer, who flies about the tidewaters at sunset, taking minnows and surveying the island below him. We also meet two sanderlings named Blackfoot and Silverbar, and we accompany them as they hunt crabs and make their annual spring migration to the Arctic tundra, where they will mate and rear their young. In the Arctic, Ookpick, a snowy owl, searches for lemming and ptarmigan and rescues his mate from an unseasonably heavy blizzard. Back in New England, we watch Pandion the osprey dive for fish while White Tip the bald eagle initiates an aerial battle in which he pirates away Pandion's fish.

In section 2 Scomber the mackerel is the leading character. The narrative begins with a spring mackerel spawn in the waters southeast of Long Island. In this spawn Scomber comes into being, "a tiny globule no larger than a poppy seed, drifting in the surface layers of pale-green water" (p. 113). Scomber enters a world "filled with small hunters, each of which must live at the expense of its neighbors" (p. 115). The odds that Scomber will reach maturity are very slim, but luck is with him as he narrowly escapes a succession of ravenous predators, including jellyfish, glassworms, anchovies, bluefish, nereids, squid, sea bass, a conger eel, tuna, dogfish, killer whales, and the seine nets of man.

The final section, "River and Sea," traces the five-hundred-mile autumn journey of Anguilla the eel, who, after having reached adulthood in a freshwater pond, instinctively makes her way downstream to the coast, far out into the ocean, over the continental shelf, and down into the deepest abyss of the Atlantic, "the primeval bed of the sea" (p. 259), south of Bermuda, where she will spawn, grow old, and eventually die, to "become sea again" (p. 255). Like Scomber's, Anguilla's survival depends upon both finding food and escaping from others who regard her as food.

Perhaps the most striking aspect of *Under the Sea-Wind* is its point of view. The book resembles a novel in which the actions of the story are refracted through the eyes of each of the principal characters. In this case, however, the characters are marine birds and fish, and the drama concerns their interactions with one another as they go about the business of survival and reproduction. Whereas much of the interest in a traditional novel hinges upon unraveling the complex tangle of motives behind characters' actions, in *Under the Sea-Wind* the universal single motive is instinct, and interest derives from beholding the intricacy of the pattern that is created by the intersecting instincts of myriad life forms. Whereas "Undersea" helps readers to imagine what life might be like underwater by taking them on a submarine tour, *Under the Sea-Wind* goes a step further in extending our vantage point by encouraging readers not just to look at but imaginatively to *become* a fish or a bird or an eel or a drifting plankton.

If the "Undersea" view from the submarine is one of marvelous beauty, the view in *Under the Sea-Wind* is from the perspective of lives fraught with peril. The phrase "it's a jungle out there" aptly characterizes how the world appears to a fish like Scomber. Indeed, the most common verb in the book is "to seize," closely followed by "to devour," "to attack," "to lunge," "to crush," "to slash," "to gorge," "to feast," "to pursue," "to snap at," "to capture," "to thrash," "to struggle," and "to hunt." Typical nouns

include "carnage," "terror," and "monster." Given the prevalence of such violent diction, it is surprising that the overall tone of the book conveys a sense of harmony. This philosophical calm results from Carson's awareness that every death makes another life possible, that even in death a creature does not vanish from the earth, but rather becomes converted into another form of life in a process of endless reincarnation.

Although Carson's vision of nature in *Under the Sea-Wind* is undeniably "red in tooth and claw," it is not so much a Darwinian world as it is a world of chance, for survival depends less upon strength and cunning as it does upon sheer luck and coincidence. Scomber, for example, manages to survive not because he is the fittest fish, but because as a hatchling he happens to be carried by the current into an area rich in plankton, and because each time he is about to be seized by a predator, it just so happens that a bigger predator comes along and devours the fish that was about to devour him.

Ironically, the fate of Carson's first book, like the fate of the mackerel Scomber, was likewise dictated by luck and coincidence. *Under the Sea-Wind* had the good fortune to fall into the hands of a first-rate publisher (Simon and Schuster) and to receive favorable notice from both scientists and literary critics. Unfortunately, however, the book had the bad luck to be issued one month before the Japanese bombing of Pearl Harbor and America's entrance into World War II. *Under the Sea-Wind* was lost in the melee of wartime, selling fewer than 1,600 copies in six years (Brooks, 1972, p. 69). It was not until ten years later, when Carson's second book—*The Sea Around Us* (1951)—became a runaway bestseller, that *Under the Sea-Wind* resurfaced to be reprinted and become a belated success.

Government Publications and *The Sea Around Us*

Although a decade elapsed between Carson's first and second books, it would be wrong to infer that there was a hiatus in her writing. On the contrary, between 1941 and 1951 Carson saw more than 300 pages of her work published, consisting of government publications and magazine articles. During World War II, while still employed by the U.S. Fish and Wildlife Service, Carson wrote four U.S. Government Conservation Bulletins about the fish resources of New England, the Middle West, the South Atlantic, and the Middle Atlantic, respectively. Because meat was scarce during the war, the government urged citizens to eat more fish. Carson's bulletins were designed to educate Americans about little-known or underutilized fish species in order to avoid overexploiting common seafood staples such as cod and haddock.

For each geographic region, Carson's bulletins present the history of the fisheries in the area and provide "biographies" of local fish species, including information on seasonal availability, flavor, food values, and preparation techniques. The bulletins also describe the fishes' habits, migrations, and relations to the varied sea environment. In total, the four bulletins profile nearly one hundred different species of fish and shellfish. As is characteristic of all of Carson's work, the bulletins are meticulously accurate, a product of extensive research; factual information is presented clearly and engagingly; and a special effort is made to elucidate the ecological principles that underlie the delicate balance of nature.

After the war, Carson directed the production of a series of twelve "Conservation in Action" booklets, authoring four of them herself and coauthoring a fifth. These booklets, most of which were guides to individual national wildlife refuges, acquainted the American people with a variety of different government efforts to protect wildlife from the pressures of modernity. Carson's eloquent mission statement prefaced each booklet:

> Wild creatures, like men, must have a place to live. As civilization creates cities, builds highways, and drains marshes, it takes away, little by little, the land that is suitable for wildlife. And as their space for living dwindles, the wildlife populations themselves decline. Refuges resist this trend by saving some areas from encroachment, and by preserving in

them, or restoring where necessary, the conditions that wild things need in order to live.

Carson's refuge guides focus primarily on birds, educating the public about migration, feeding, and reproduction patterns and introducing refuge visitors to some of the species they might encounter. Occasional flashes of eloquence, such as the following passage about Canada geese at Mattamuskeet refuge, distinguish these guides from standard government fare: "Underlying all the other sounds of the refuge is their wild music, rising at times to a great, tumultuous crescendo, and dying away again to a throbbing undercurrent" (p. 5).

Even as Carson worked by day on the "Conservation in Action" booklets and served as chief editor of publications, she labored after hours on her next book, *The Sea Around Us* (1951), which she conceived of as a multifaceted profile of the sea for nontechnical readers. The book, epic in scale and worldwide in scope, is a monumental synthesis of old and new, of ancient legends of the sea and the latest scientific discoveries in oceanography. Scientific study of the ocean had accelerated during World War II to help the Allied powers compete with the Germans in submarine warfare and naval communications. Taking advantage of this new research, Carson consulted more than one thousand different sources and corresponded with dozens of authorities all over the world in order to produce a book that would answer all the questions her readers might have about the ocean and countless others they had never thought to ask.

The individual essays that comprise *The Sea Around Us* are divided into three parts. Part 1, "Mother Sea," consists of eight captivating chapters that cover ambitious topics such as the history of the earth, the different zones of the sea and the life that inhabits them, the harsh conditions of the abyssal deeps, the information contained in deep-sea sediments, the birth and unique life forms of volcanic islands, and the changing sea levels throughout geologic time. The three chapters of part 2, "The Restless Sea," explain water movement: the physics of waves, the nature of ocean currents, and the different kinds of tides. Part 3, "Man and the Sea About Him," teaches how the oceans regulate climate, inventories the mineral wealth dissolved in ocean waters, and, finally, chronicles man's daring sea voyages.

In point of view, *The Sea Around Us* is closer to Carson's government publications than it is to her earlier book, *Under the Sea-Wind*, for whereas *Under the Sea-Wind* tells a story of marine creatures as seen subjectively from their point of view, *The Sea Around Us* interprets natural phenomena from the objective perspective of a scientist. Like the government booklets, *The Sea Around Us* claims the reader's attention by appealing directly to "you," the reader: "If you could be close to the surface waters..." (p. 17); "If you took a map of the world..." (p. 21); "The next time you wonder why the water is so cold at certain coastal resorts of the eastern United States, remember that the water of the Labrador Current is between you and the Gulf Stream" (p. 142). This rhetorical device of direct address helps to make Carson's popular science much more readable than the tedious scientific reports upon which the book is based.

Even though *The Sea Around Us* resembles Carson's government publications in stance, it strikes a relatively more personal tone through occasional first-person revelations: "The events of which I write..." (p. 4); "When I think of the floor of the deep sea, the single, overwhelming fact that possesses my imagination is the accumulation of sediments" (p. 74); "But the link between tide and living creature I like best to remember..." (p. 165). Such revelations are rare, but they do reveal an intimate glimpse of Carson's love for the sea, a love that the reader is encouraged to share.

Just as Carson employs science to help the reader mentally grasp the ocean's physical properties, she draws upon literature to fathom the ocean imaginatively. Each chapter thus begins with an epigraph from literary figures like Milton, Arnold, Shelley, Swinburne, and Shakespeare. Furthermore, Carson quotes liberally from a variety of sea authors, including Thor Heyerdahl and Joseph Conrad, and alludes to a treasury of sea legends, such as the lost island of Atlantis, "gloomy hulks of vessels doomed to endless drifting" in the Sargasso Sea (p. 27), Samuel Taylor Coleridge's *The Rime of the Ancient Mariner*, Homer's *Odyssey*, and Edgar Allan Poe's "Descent into the Maelstrom." Carson uses science to substantiate some legends and to discredit others, yet she sounds a repeated refrain that there are many things we do not know: "We can only sense that in the deep and turbulent recesses of the sea are hidden mysteries far greater than any we have solved" (p. 133).

The Sea Around Us, portions of which were serialized in the *New Yorker* prior to publication, was a meteoric success. It was a Book-of-the-Month Club alternate selection; it remained on the *New York Times* best-seller list for a record-breaking eighty-six weeks, and the *Times* Christmas poll voted it "the outstanding book of the year" (Brooks, 1972, p. 127). Reviewers praised Carson for being one of the rare scientists possessed of a literary gift, a true scientist-poet. A chapter of the book that appeared in the *Yale Review* won the George Westinghouse Science Writing Award of the American Association for the Advancement of Science. The book itself, published by Oxford University Press, won the John Burroughs Medal for natural history writing, the National Book Award for the best nonfiction book of 1951, and the Henry G. Bryant Medal of the Philadelphia Geographical Society. The book was eventually translated into thirty-two different languages. Carson was voted "woman of the year in literature" by the women's-page editors of the nation's newspapers. RKO purchased motion-picture rights to the book, and in 1953 *The Sea Around Us* won an Oscar for the year's best feature-length documentary film.

Thanks to the popularity of *The Sea Around Us*, *Under the Sea-Wind* was reissued and also became a best-seller. Overnight, Carson found herself catapulted into fame, and at age forty-four, for the first time in her life, she did not have to worry about money; in fact, sales of the book enabled Carson to purchase a coveted binocular-microscope and to realize her long-cherished dream of buying some land on the

Maine coast, where she had a cottage built that overlooked the sea. Most important, the success of *The Sea Around Us* had allowed Carson to quit her job with the Fish and Wildlife Service in order to devote herself full time to writing.

The Edge of the Sea and "Help Your Child to Wonder"

After completing *The Sea Around Us*, Carson agreed to write a layman's handbook to seashore life for Houghton Mifflin's nature guide series. *The Edge of the Sea* (1955), Carson's answer to Houghton Mifflin's invitation, is nothing short of radical, a book written against the grain of the typical nature guide. Most nature guides are intended to help the reader to identify the flora and fauna he or she may encounter in the wild. Accordingly, such guides generally consist of illustrations of each plant and animal species, accompanied by a verbal description of the species, including Latin nomenclature, field marks, behavior, habitat, and range. Plant and animal species are normally arranged taxonomically or by appearance, such that all owls appear on adjacent pages, for example, or all pink flowers are grouped in the same section. While such an arrangement facilitates identification, it tends to represent species as discrete entities, recognizable by outward appearance, but independent of environmental context and isolated from ecological communities.

Carson's preface specifically warns her readers that correct identification of a species is insufficient:

> To understand the shore, it is not enough to catalogue its life. . . . It is not enough to pick up an empty shell and say "This is a murex," or "That is an angel wing." True understanding demands intuitive comprehension of the whole life of the creature that once inhabited this empty shell: how it survived amid surf and storms, what were its enemies, how it found food and reproduced its kind, what were its relations to the particular sea world in which it lived. (pp. vii–viii)

With the larger goal of true understanding of shore life in mind, Carson organizes *The Edge of the Sea* not by taxonomy or by classification schemes based on physical appearance, but by shore types and life zones. Furthermore, as if to underscore the point that no species exists in isolation, chapters rarely contain subsections, nor are the names of species printed in boldface. Instead, the narrative runs continuously, with transitions between species based on their relationships to one another—predator and prey, host and parasite, friend and enemy—all interwoven into a seamless prose picture in which no single species predominates.

The three principal shore types to which Carson devotes individual chapters are rocky coasts, sandy beaches, and coral reefs. Carson's examples are drawn from the Atlantic coast of the United States, one of the few coastlines in the world that displays fine examples of all three types. Each of these basic shore types exhibits a distinctive geological history, a unique dynamic between water and land, and a characteristic host of life. Within each of the three shore types, Carson delineates a variety of life zones, based on the intensity of the surf, the temperature of the water, and the percentage of time a given area is underwater. Areas high on shore, underwater only during the highest tides, support a community of life much different from low areas that are infrequently exposed to air.

Each intertidal life zone is depicted as a miniature world, a world apart, inhabited by a multitude of life forms, each one exquisitely adapted to the unique conditions and forces of that particular zone, each linked in an intricate network of relationships with the other plants and animals of its world. Although Carson does enable identification by describing the physical appearance of nearly three hundred different species, and although the book contains more than 160 illustrations by Bob Hines, Carson's emphasis remains insistently ecological and holistic as she probes into the very nature of life itself.

The three main chapters of *The Edge of the Sea* on shore types are introduced by a chapter entitled "Patterns of Shore Life," which reviews material presented in *The Sea Around Us*, including a geologic history of the sea, the origin and evolution of life in the sea, and the sea's basic forces — waves, currents, and tides — that combine to mold and determine shore life. Carson thus establishes the larger historical and geophysical context in which present-day shore life should be understood. These core informational chapters are framed by brief introductory and concluding chapters that are at once more poetic, more personal, and more philosophical than the core chapters of exposition. These brief framing chapters serve to create a mood in which the facts presented in the book intimate a deeper significance and evoke a heightened sense of wonder. Thus, the structure of the book embeds descriptions of life forms in a broader ecological and geophysical context, which is in turn embedded in the still-broader metaphysical context of the ultimate mystery of life.

Chapter 1, "The Marginal World," might well be titled "The Magical World," as Carson recollects a series "of places that have stirred me deeply, . . . and . . . that make the sea's edge, for me, a place of exceeding beauty and fascination" (p. viii). Mirroring the shape of the book as a whole, "The Marginal World" recalls treasured personal memories associated with the three different shore types of rocky coast, sandy beach, and coastal reef. In each "enchanted place," Carson reveals personal moments of epiphany in which she is dazzled by beauty or struck by a sudden flash of insight. Recalling one "mysterious" night on a Georgia beach, Carson senses "the darkness of an older world, before Man" (p. 5) as she observes a lone ghost crab near the sea:

> Suddenly I was filled with the odd sensation that for the first time I knew the creature in its own world — that I understood, as never before, the essence of its being. In that moment time was suspended; the world to which I belonged did not exist and I might have been an onlooker from outer space. The little crab alone with the sea became a symbol that stood for life itself — for the delicate, destructible, yet incredibly vital force that somehow holds its place amid the harsh realities of the inorganic world. (p. 5)

Never before in her public writing had Carson been so personal in her revelations. This willingness to share her intimate insights and her experiences in the natural world, coupled with the tacit assurance that her readers would care to read about them, suggests that Carson's self-confidence was by now at high tide and that since the phenomenal success of *The Sea Around Us* she had become an authority whose opinions were quoted, rather than an unknown writer who quoted authorities.

As the encounter with the crab on the beach illustrates, the unifying theme of *The Edge of the Sea* is the drama of life, not just human life, but all life. Behind every individual creature lurks some hidden truth about "the ultimate mystery of Life itself" (p. 250). Throughout the book, from the first page to the last, Carson returns to this preoccupation like a curious child to an unopened Christmas gift, always striving to grasp the "inner meaning" of life and to apprehend its deeper significance. Her fascination is with life in the abstract, life as manifest concretely in the "endlessly varied stream of living things that has surged through time and space to occupy the earth" (p. vii). She discovers that life displays "enormous toughness and vitality" (p. 1); that life expresses "the need . . . to reach out and occupy all habitable parts of the earth" (p. 27); that life "exists on other life, or within it, or under it, or above it" (p. 95); that the "life force" is an "intense, blind, unconscious will to survive, to push on, to expand" (p. 189); that life "flow[s] as inexorably as any ocean current, from past to unknown future" (p. 250); and, finally, that life constitutes "a force as tangible as any of the physical realities of the sea, a force strong and purposeful, as incapable of being crushed or diverted from its end as the rising tide" (p. 250).

Like *The Sea Around Us*, *The Edge of the Sea* earned excellent reviews and was immensely popular, remaining on the *New York Times* best-seller list for twenty-three weeks. The book reviewer for the *Christian Science Monitor* expressed the prevailing opinion of critics, writing, "Miss Carson's pen is as poetic as ever and the knowledge she imparts is profound. *The Edge of the Sea* finds a worthy place beside Miss Carson's masterpiece of 1951" (quoted in Sterling, p. 142). In addition to the book's positive reviews and healthy sales, Carson accrued two more honors: the Achievement Award of the American Association of University Women and a citation for authoring "the outstanding book of the year" from the National Council of Women of the United States.

That Carson would write another book after *The Edge of the Sea* was never in question; the question was what book. While casting about for her next major project, Carson completed two smaller projects, both by invitation. One of these assignments may have reminded Carson of her first job with the U.S. Bureau of Fisheries, when she wrote the script for radio broadcasts on marine life. This time, however, Carson's task was to write the script for a television documentary on clouds, sponsored by *Omnibus* magazine. Carson privately expressed indifference to television, but she realized that "it is probably the medium that reaches the largest audience" (quoted in Brooks, p. 198), so she fulfilled her commitment with characteristic eloquence:

> Hidden in the beauty of the moving clouds is a story that is as old as the earth itself. The clouds are the writing of the wind on the sky. They carry the signature of masses of air drifting across sea and land. . . . But most of all they are cosmic symbols, representing an age-old process that is linked with life itself. (quoted in Brooks, pp. 198–199)

The fascination with life that Carson disclosed in *The Edge of the Sea* persists, conceived now in terms of life's relationship to the "ocean of air."

The second assignment that Carson undertook after publication of *The Edge of the Sea* was a magazine article commissioned by the *Woman's Home Companion* about teaching children to be aware of nature. For this assignment Carson drew upon her own experience in sharing nature with her young grandnephew Roger Christie. The article, titled "Help Your Child to Wonder" (published in July 1956), is a charming evocation of the freshness with which children view nature, implying that adults have much to learn from children:

> A child's world is fresh and new and beautiful, full of wonder and excitement. It is our misfortune that for most of us that clear-eyed vision, that true instinct for what is beautiful and awe-inspiring, is dimmed and even lost before we reach adulthood. If I had influence with the good fairy who is supposed to preside over the christening of all children I should ask that her gift to each child in the world be a sense of wonder so indestructible that it would last throughout life. (*The Sense of Wonder*, pp. 42–43)

Although Carson planned to expand this piece into a book, other projects and responsibilities intervened, and she never found the time to do so. The article was published posthumously in book form, however, with Carson's text gracing a collection of photographs by Charles Pratt and others. Dedicated to Roger, the book was titled *The Sense of Wonder* (1965). In retrospect, "Help Your Child to Wonder" may have been the last time that Carson herself could look upon nature with unclouded joy. The end of innocence was near.

Silent Spring

In January 1958, Carson received a letter that would change her life and ultimately alter the course of history. The letter was from her friend Olga Owens Huckins, who with her husband maintained a private bird sanctuary in Duxbury, Massachusetts. In the summer of 1957, without the Huckins' permission, their property had been sprayed with the insecticide DDT in a state mosquito-control program. Aerial spraying was a common practice at that time and was widely assumed to be harmless to humans and wildlife. The Huckinses were dismayed to find the bodies of many dead songbirds littered about their property after the spraying. Olga Huckins wrote a letter to the Boston *Herald* protesting the spraying and describing the pitiful deaths of the birds. Upon learning that another mass spraying was

Carson refilling her bird feeder near her house in West Southport, Maine

being planned, Olga Huckins sent a copy of the *Herald* letter to Carson, along with a personal letter requesting the names of people in Washington who might be consulted for help. Carson recalled years later that "it was in the source of finding that 'someone' that I realized I must write the book" (quoted in Brooks, 1972, p. 233).

More than a decade earlier, from her vantage point in the Fish and Wildlife Service, Carson had seen evidence of DDT's toll on wildlife, and in 1945 she proposed to write an article on the subject for *Reader's Digest*, but was apparently turned down. Between 1945 and 1958, use of chemical pesticides in the United States increased fivefold and showed no signs of abating. In making inquiries for Huckins, Carson discovered the extent of this chemical poisoning of the earth, a discovery which, coupled with her growing awareness of the damage done by radioactive fallout, forced her to jettison her long-cherished faith that life was "incapable of being crushed or diverted." This "sea change" in outlook is powerfully expressed in Carson's correspondence:

It was pleasant to believe...that much of nature was forever beyond the tampering reach of man. . . . It was comforting to suppose that the stream of life would flow on through time...without interference by one of the drops of that stream, Man. And to suppose that, however the physical environment might mold Life, that Life could never assume the power to change drastically—or even destroy—the physical world.

These beliefs have been part of me for as long as I have thought about such things. To have them even vaguely threatened was so shocking that I shut my mind—refused to acknowledge what I couldn't help seeing. But that does no good, and I have now opened my eyes and my mind. (quoted in Graham, 1970, pp. 13–14)

Perhaps Carson's own reluctance to face the reality of a world fundamentally threatened by man helped her to anticipate the mind-set of her readers: they, too, would resist this upsetting truth about the world. Moreover, DDT was heralded as a wonder of modern science, the "atomic bomb of insecticides," having protected millions of lives during World War II from the deadly insect-borne diseases of typhus and malaria. Its inventor had won a Nobel Prize. By making a case against DDT, Carson would be bringing people the unwelcome news that their ally was in reality their enemy. As she wrote to her editor, "It is a great problem to know how to penetrate the barrier of public indifference and unwillingness to look at unpleasant facts that might have to be dealt with if one recognized their existence" (quoted in Brooks, 1972, p. 258). She would have to tell the story of chemical pesticides in such a way that readers could not help but be moved. But, as historian Frank Graham, Jr., asks, "How could she make chlorinated hydrocarbons compelling?" (1970, p. 47).

Writing *Silent Spring* proved to be a monumental task, taking several years longer than Carson anticipated. In addition to the challenge of amassing, organizing, synthesizing, and translating boxes upon boxes of technical information into a clear, concise, and cogent argument, Carson faced considerable personal challenges during these years. In 1957, at the age of fifty, she adopted her five-year-old grandnephew Roger Christie, whose mother had died. In 1958, Carson's own mother died; she had lived with Carson most of her life. Rachel herself was beset with a host of illnesses, which eventually included sinus infections, flu, an ulcer, an intestinal virus, a staphylococcus infection in the knees which immobilized her for three weeks, arthritis, iritis, and cancer, which necessitated a mastectomy and for which she received radiation treatments that drained her of energy and caused her to lose hair, obliging her to wear a wig. That Carson persisted with her work testifies to the depth of her commitment and the strength of her character.

From cover to cover, *Silent Spring* is a model of effective rhetoric. The title itself, suggested by Carson's editor Paul Brooks, is simple and potent, catching the reader's interest and arousing curiosity. Carson's dedication—"To Albert Schweitzer who said, 'Man has lost the capacity to foresee and to forestall. He will end by destroying the earth'"—further captures attention by linking the name of a world-revered figure to a terrifying forecast. Carson was by this time a beloved author and trusted figure in her own right, famous for her three scientifically informed yet poetically evocative books on the sea. When Carson's tune suddenly changed from one of gentle appreciation to one of grim alarm, people listened.

A fundamental principle of rhetoric states, "Begin strong," for it is often the first chapter that lures or loses readers. To introduce a topic as potentially dull as pesticides, Carson begins her fact-laden book with a little fable: "There was once a town in the heart of America where all life seemed to live in harmony with its surroundings" (p. 1). Carson conjures the popular image of America as an agrarian Eden, embellishing this pastoral canvas with "prosperous farms," "green fields," "countless birds," and "shady pools where trout lay."

By the third paragraph, however, something is terribly wrong with the picture:

> Then a strange blight crept over the area and everything began to change. Some evil spell had settled on the community: mysterious maladies swept the flocks of chickens; the cattle and sheep sickened and died. Everywhere was a shadow of death. (p. 2)

Doctors report new sicknesses appearing in townspeople, birds no longer sing, spring is eerily silent, apple trees bear no fruit because there are no bees to pollinate them, streams are choked with dead fish. Lest readers be tempted to relegate this nightmarish scene to dim recesses of the imagination or to some remote dystopian future, Carson warns that every one of the disasters she describes "has actually happened somewhere, and many real communities have already suffered a substantial number of them" (p. 3). She continues, "A grim specter has crept upon us almost unnoticed, and this imagined tragedy may easily become a stark reality we all shall know" (p. 3).

Having lodged this disturbing image of a lifeless world firmly in the reader's mind, Carson reviews the history of pesticide use in America, explaining how the nation got itself into the predicament of dependency on deadly poisons. She then provides a who's who of chemical pesticides, introducing the two major families of modern insecticides: the chlorinated hydrocarbons like DDT, dieldrin, and chlordane, and the organic phosphorous insecticides like malathion and parathion. Both types of modern insecticides are nonselective, killing "friendly" species like bees as well as so-called "pest" species like mosquitoes. As opposed to earlier pesticides like arsenic, which were naturally derived and inorganic, both families of modern insecticides are man-made and organic, having the unique property of entering into the vital processes of the body, often causing irreversible change at the subcellular level.

Once Carson's readers have a basic understanding of pesticides, the chapters progress up the food chain, documenting pesticide contamination in groundwater and soils and pesticide poisoning in plants, birds, fish, and, climactically, humans. Believing that the public must now understand issues formerly reserved for specialists, Carson strives to give her readers not just the facts but the scientific grounding necessary to understand those facts and to see how all the pieces fit together. Thus, *Silent Spring* is an amalgam of science lessons, whose readers get an armchair education in organic chemistry, toxicology, hydrology, soil science, ecology, cell physiology, pathology, genetics, and entomology. Together, these chapters build up a compelling argument that pesticides pervade the modern world and that they disrupt a delicate ecological balance upon which human survival depends.

To strengthen her case against the indiscriminate use of chemical pesticides, Carson employs a range of different strategies, including the use of quantitative data (tons of DDT sprayed, numbers of bird deaths, miles of denuded roadside); presentation of case studies (the fire ant

"eradication" program in Alabama, gypsy-moth spraying in Long Island, the Japanese beetle campaign in the Midwest); testimony of experts (scientists, doctors, and government officials); and eyewitness accounts from average Americans (residents whose pets died after aerial spraying, fishermen reporting fish die-offs, a housewife nauseated by household insecticide). Although Carson does not belabor the reading with distracting footnotes, her credibility is amply substantiated by fifty-five pages of endnotes, meticulously documenting her sources. Even a cursory glance at the endnotes, which contain hundreds of technical references with intimidating titles like "Isolation of an Epoxide Metabolite from Fat Tissues of Dogs Fed Heptachlor," is enough to impress one with Carson's expertise as a translator.

That we persist in broadcasting hundreds of thousands of tons of chemical poisons into the environment despite known evidence of their harmful effects begins to strike the reader of *Silent Spring* as insane. Indeed, the sense of craziness is tinged with irony as Carson goes on to demonstrate that for all the risks we have incurred, chemical pesticides have not even been effective. First, modern insecticides such as DDT lower environmental resistance to pest species by killing off the natural predators that would normally keep these problem species in check. And second, some insects develop an immunity to DDT; when these resistant insects multiply, a new "super race" of insect is born against which the sprays have no effect.

Having proved DDT and its chemical kin to be both harmful and futile in solving our insect problems, Carson takes a more positive approach in the final chapter, suggesting that there is another road, a road of biological controls based upon an understanding of ecology. Several options show promise, including male sterilization by X rays, chemical sex attractants, ultrasonic sound, introduction of insect diseases, and importation of natural predators. All of these methods are scientifically sophisticated, depending on a knowledge of "the whole fabric of life" (p. 278), and all show a "reverence [for life] even where we have to struggle against it" (p. 275).

The book ends on a revolutionary note by condemning the reigning anthropocentric worldview itself, a utilitarian paradigm that has for too long (mis)guided our treatment of nature:

> The "control of nature" is a phrase conceived in arrogance, born of the Neanderthal age of biology and philosophy, when it was supposed that nature exists for the convenience of man. The concepts and practices of applied entomology for the most part date from that Stone Age of science. It is our alarming misfortune that so primitive a science has armed itself with the most modern and terrible weapons, and that in turning them against the insects it has also turned them against the earth. (p. 297)

Here, in a clever coup de grâce, Carson subverts the commonly held view that applied entomology is on the cutting edge of modern science, and instead she insinuates that the concepts of applied entomology are old-fashioned and that its weaponry ought to be decommissioned. It is the power of this cultural critique that turned what could have been a topical book on pesticides into an enduring classic of the environmental movement. Biographer Paul Brooks reflects, "The really scary thing was that she was questioning the whole attitude of industrial society toward the natural world" (in Marco, et al., eds., p. 6).

While *Silent Spring* shares with Carson's earlier works a deep respect for life, an appreciation for the beauty of nature, and an ecological orientation, it stands out boldly in its engagement with contemporary issues and in its political analysis. Whereas Carson's sea books celebrate geologic time, eternal forces, and the cyclical processes of nature, *Silent Spring* concerns the post–World War II, industrialized present, "the modern world" in which "there is no time" (p. 6). Furthermore, Carson displays unprecedented authority in defining her time, issuing blanket statements about the modern age: for example, "Along with the possibility of the extinction of mankind by nuclear war, the central problem of our age has...become the contamination of man's total environment" (p. 8). Later, she observes, "This is an era of

specialists, each of whom sees his own problem and is unaware of or intolerant of the larger frame into which it fits. It is also an era dominated by industry, in which the right to make a dollar at whatever cost is seldom challenged" (p. 13). Never before has Carson sounded so angry.

Not only does *Silent Spring* chronicle the adverse effects of pesticide use, it analyzes the economics of the problem as well. Like an investigative journalist, Carson exposes university entomology departments as being underwritten by the corporate chemical industry. She asks, "Can we then expect [entomologists] to bite the hand that literally feeds them?" (p. 259). She reveals the sinister partnerships between science, industry, and even government in promoting pesticides for immediate profit, heedless of the long-term costs to the environment and the hidden costs to public health.

In a sense, just as *The Edge of the Sea* illuminates the intricate ecology of tide pools, *Silent Spring* examines what might be termed "the ecology of modernity." Carson characterizes the capitalist "environment" in which pesticide use thrives and identifies the forces — economic, political, and ideological — that sustain it. In this "environment," science and industry enjoy a symbiotic relationship as mutually advantageous as any found in nature. Carson's task is to expose the way this "ecosystem" works so that a new force of public opinion will arise to create an environment hostile to pesticide survival.

As rhetoric, *Silent Spring* is unsurpassed. In its effort to goad readers to action, it appeals to all dimensions of human experience: emotional, intellectual, aesthetic, imaginative, and moral. Perhaps most powerfully, *Silent Spring* evokes fear in its readers, a fear that if they do not do something *now* to halt the poisoning of the environment, they may "join the dinosaurs as an obsolete form of life" (p. 188).

Carson's rhetoric worked. Before *Silent Spring* appeared in book form on 27 September 1962, a three-part condensation of the book ran in the weekly *New Yorker*, beginning 16 June 1962, in the column "Reporter at Large." The series caused such a storm of public outcry that the

New York Times ran an article on the controversy entitled "*Silent Spring* Is Now Noisy Summer," and *Life* magazine referred to the storm as "Hurricane Rachel." Based on the explosive response to the *New Yorker* series, chemical companies attempted to block publication of the book. When Velsicol Chemical Corporation threatened Carson's publisher with a libel suit, Houghton Mifflin purchased extra insurance from Lloyds of London but refused to halt publication (Lear, 1993, p. 46). The book became an overnight sensation, selling 500,000 copies in hardcover before being published in paperback; it remained on the *New York Times* best-seller list for thirty-one weeks. In April 1963, CBS Reports did a special program titled "The *Silent Spring* of Rachel Carson," hosted by Eric Sevareid, in which a calm Carson faced her agitated critics.

Meanwhile, viewing the furor as a public-relations problem, chemical trade groups such as the National Agricultural Chemicals Association earmarked a quarter of a million dollars to improve their image. Their attacks on Carson were vicious. She was called sentimental, hysterical, impractical, a crackpot, a "priestess of nature," "a devotee of a mystical cult," a "bird and bunny lover," a "Nervous Nellie," a "Cassandra in the cornfields." Carson was accused of being avaricious, greedily piling up royalties by frightening the public. Alternately, it was suggested that she was part of a communist plot to destroy the American economy. One government official is reputed to have said, "I thought she was a spinster. What's she so worried about genetics for?" (Graham, 1970, p. 50).

While some critics slandered the author, others attacked the book. *Time* magazine branded *Silent Spring* an "emotional and inaccurate outburst" that would "do harm by alarming the nontechnical public" (quoted in Brooks, 1972, p. 297). A spokesman for the chemical industry, Dr. Robert White-Stevens of the American Cyanamid Company, charged that "the book's major claims...are gross distortions of the actual evidence" (quoted in Downs, p. 266).

Other tactics included attempts to scare the public with the specter of a world without pesticides. *Croplife: A Businesspaper for the Farm Chemical Industry*, for example, warned, "If man were to faithfully follow the teachings of Miss Carson, we would return to the Dark Ages, and the insects and diseases and vermin would once again inherit the earth" (quoted in Brooks, 1972, p. 298). The Monsanto Chemical Company did a parody of *Silent Spring* in *Monsanto Magazine* entitled "The Desolate Year," likewise predicting that famine and plague would devastate a world without pesticides, accompanied by massive crop losses and soaring prices. Although Carson had explicitly stated that "it is not my contention that chemical insecticides must never be used" (p. 12), here and elsewhere her critics chose to misread *Silent Spring* or, worse, not to read the book at all, castigating Carson for things she never said.

The chemical industry's aggressive campaign against the book unwittingly promoted sales as no advertising scheme could have hoped to do. Carson's fame skyrocketed. She was given more awards than she had the time or energy to accept (by 1963 she was suffering badly from cancer). Among the most deeply satisfying awards were the Albert Schweitzer Medal from the Animal Welfare Institute and election to the American Academy of Arts and Letters, which cited her as "a scientist in the grand literary style of Galileo and Buffon" who had "used her scientific knowledge and moral feeling to deepen our consciousness of living nature and to alert us to the calamitous possibility that our short-sighted technological conquests might destroy the very sources of our being" (quoted in Brooks, p. 323).

In *Silent Spring*, Carson had asked, "When will the public become sufficiently aware of the facts to demand...action?" (p. 152). The answer proved to be "in the summer of 1962." Letters flooded in to newspapers, magazines, senators, and the president from citizens demanding immediate action. As a result of public pressure, the federal government began an investigation of its pesticide-control programs. A special panel of President John F. Kennedy's Science Advisory Committee formed to investigate the matter, issuing a report in May 1963 entitled *Use of Pesticides*. This report corroborated Carson's claims and became an important step in revising the federal government's pesticide policy. The Senate established a committee on environmental hazards, headed by Connecticut senator Abraham Ribicoff. Carson was called to testify, and despite failing health she appeared. Her testimony, reprinted in the July 1963 issues of *American Forests*, is thoughtful and pragmatic, offering a concrete plan for a series of legislative actions.

Historians have credited *Silent Spring* with providing the impetus for a host of environmental laws and actions. Within a year of publication of the *New Yorker* series, pesticide bills were introduced in forty state legislatures. At the federal level, the 1963 Clean Air Act, the 1965 Water Quality Act, the 1969 National Environmental Policy Act, and important amendments to the Insecticide, Fungicide, and Rodenticide Act in 1972 have all been chalked up to Carson's influence. In 1970 the Environmental Protection Agency (EPA) was created in the executive branch, a recommendation Carson had made in her proposals to the Ribicoff committee. In 1972, the EPA banned the use of DDT. Aldrin and dieldrin were banned in 1974, chlordane in 1988. In 1990 the National Environmental Education Act mandated a new EPA award named the Rachel Carson Award.

Silent Spring—translated into twenty-two languages—set off international reverberations. The book quickly became well known in Britain, where the British Ministry of Agriculture, Fisheries, and Food placed severe restrictions on the use of DDT-related insecticides. In a darkly humorous statement to the House of Lords, Lord Shackleton alluded to "the story of the cannibal in Polynesia who now no longer allows his tribe to eat Americans because their fat is contaminated with chlorinated hydrocarbons" (quoted in Brooks, p. 312). The United Nations called a world conference of the Food and Agriculture Organization, which met in Rome to study how pesticides can be used effectively without harming people. Despite such measures, worldwide pesticide use has risen dramatically since *Silent Spring*. Although banned in the United States, DDT continues to be manufactured in huge quantities by U.S. companies for export to other countries. One pesticide-information group estimated that by 1990, worldwide pesticide use totaled six billion pounds per year (Briggs, 1990).

Considering the fact that both in the United States and overseas chemical pesticide use has increased since 1962, it would seem that the lasting significance of *Silent Spring* is to be found in attitudes more than in actions. As biographer Paul Brooks writes, "*Silent Spring* has been recognized throughout the world as one of those rare books that change the course of history—not through incitement to war or violent revolution, but by altering the direction of man's thinking" (Brooks, 1972, p. 227). *Silent Spring* started the modern environmental movement. It made "ecology" a household word, along with related terms like "interconnection," "interrelationship," "interdependency," "balance of nature," "web of life." It popularized the notion that humans are part of nature and that we cannot harm nature without also harming ourselves. Before *Silent Spring*, conservationists had focused on resource use and park protection; since *Silent Spring*, pollution has been added to the environmental agenda. *Silent Spring* taught Americans to question authority, to question the experts, to question government, even to question technology and progress itself.

Perhaps the greatest as well as the most ambivalent legacy of *Silent Spring* is that it inaugurated the idea of what historian Donald Worster has called "ecological apocalypse" (1985 ed., p. 23). In 1958, Carson's peace of mind had been shattered by the realization that humans possessed the power to destroy the physical world. Together, *Silent Spring* and the atom bomb mark the end of innocence for us all.

Literary Tradition and Scholarship

Carol Gartner, the first literary critic to study Rachel Carson's writing, argues that Carson "belongs not only in history, but in literary history as well" (1983, p. 136). The artistry and craftsmanship that distinguish Carson's work certainly earn her a place in the literary canon; however, the striking differences among her books defy simple categorization.

Under the Sea-Wind might be shelved alongside the British writer Henry Williamson's animal sagas *Tarka the Otter* and *Salar the Salmon*, tales told from the point of view of animals while remaining factual in natural-history detail. Indeed, Williamson was one of Carson's favorite writers. Many children's books about nature also adopt an animal's point of view. Carson, however, knows more science than most authors of children's books, and she avoids the anthropomorphism typical of them. Although Carson's animal protagonists do have names, they do not speak English nor do they display a human range of emotion.

The Sea Around Us deserves an honored place among other classic books on the sea. Carson lists some of her favorites in the "Outstanding Sea Prose" section at the end of the book. She loved Henry Beston's *The Outermost House*, a lyrical, personal account of a year of solitude on a pristine Cape Cod beach. In newspaper articles carrying headlines such as "A Treasure Chest of Sea Books" and "Sea Leaves Its Mark on World Poets," Carson recommends Melville's novel *Moby-Dick* for its unparalleled rendition of "the timeless, unhurried spirit of the sea" (quoted in Gartner, 1983, p. 129). Other favorites were Joseph Conrad's *The Mirror of the Sea* and H. M. Tomlinson's *The Sea and the Jungle*. In a different medium, the television specials of Jacques Cousteau carry on this tradition of expressive voyages beneath the sea.

In addition to its place on "Neptune's bookshelf," *The Sea Around Us* stands as a progenitor of popular science writing. The essence of Carson's art in this book lies in sharing with the public the exciting findings and current debates of modern science. Later works in this vein include Stephen Jay Gould on evolutionary biology, Lewis Thomas on medicine, Carl Sagan on astronomy and on the evolution of human intelligence, Fritjof Capra on quantum physics, James Gleick on chaos theory, Stephen Hawking on the nature of time, and Gary Nabhan on ethnobotany.

Of all Carson's books, *The Edge of the Sea* belongs most squarely within the classic nature-writing tradition. Nature writing—usually nonfiction prose that blends science and art—has been characterized by scholar Thomas J. Lyon as having three main dimensions: "natural history information, personal responses to nature, and philosophical interpretation of nature" (Lyon, p. 3). Well-known early nature writers in America whose work may have influenced Carson were William Bartram, Henry Thoreau (whose journals Carson enjoyed), John Burroughs, and John Muir. Carson's contemporaries in the genre, most of whom were her friends or correspondents, include William Beebe, Robert Cushman Murphy, Henry Beston, Aldo Leopold, Joseph Wood Krutch, Lois Crisler, Olaus Murie, and Edwin Way Teale. In the nature writing tradition, Carson is notable for her personal reserve; unlike other writers in the Thoreauvian tradition, Carson rarely reveals her own inner landscape. Of today's nature writers, two women in particular, Ann Zwinger and Terry Tempest Williams, acknowledge Carson as a literary foremother.

Silent Spring has frequently been compared to Harriet Beecher Stowe's *Uncle Tom's Cabin* as an intellectually explosive book that "blew American society apart at the seams" (Nash, p. 78). Just as President Abraham Lincoln had described Stowe as the lady who caused the Civil War, President John Kennedy cited Carson's work as the catalyst that led to his staff's investigation into pesticides. Historian Roderick Nash observes that Carson "challenged the right of humans to own and abuse nature just as Harriet Beecher Stowe . . . challenged that right with regard to black people" (p. 82). In *Books That Changed America*, cultural historian Robert Downs places *Silent Spring* in the company of Thomas Paine's *Common Sense*, Stowe's *Uncle Tom's Cabin*, and Upton Sinclair's *The Jungle*, all of which demanded instant action and which had an enormous impact on public consciousness.

Donald Worster has called *Silent Spring* the first book in the new literary tradition of ecological apocalypse. Such books incite fear by predicting imminent global disaster—"ecological meltdown"—if we do not change our ways now. Latter-day environmental prophets of doom include Paul Ehrlich (*The Population Bomb*, 1968), Donella Meadows, et al. (*The Limits to Growth*, 1972), Jonathan Schell (*The Fate of the Earth*, 1982), Stephen Schneider (*Global Warming: Are We Entering the Greenhouse Century?*, 1989), Bill McKibben (*The End of Nature*, 1989), and Albert Gore (*Earth in the Balance: Ecology and the Human Spirit*, 1992). Like *Silent Spring*, these successors urge humanity to take "the other fork of the road—the one 'less traveled by,'" which, Carson says, "offers our last, our only chance to reach a destination that assures preservation of our earth" (p. 278).

Despite the difficulty in pigeonholing Carson's work, there are several characteristic traits of style and outlook that unify her oeuvre. Carson wrote slowly and made many revisions, striving for clarity of sense and harmony of sound. Although she understood scientific jargon, she did not use it. She never forgot her audience, and that audience was always the general public. From beginning to end, Carson's work embodies the spirit of Albert Schweitzer's "reverence for life." Throughout her work, she advocates an attitude of humility instead of arrogance before the natural world. The precision of her facts and extent of her research enhance rather than diminish the mystery of life. Key phrases that recur throughout Carson's work exemplify her philosophy: "material immortality," "continuing creation," "drama of life," "flowing stream of time," "balance of nature," "sense of wonder," "flash of insight," "exquisite beauty," and "the understanding eye." Always, Carson's vision was ecological: a life can be understood only in the context of its environment and in relation to other life.

For twenty years after the publication of *Silent Spring*, scholarship on Carson tended to be historical and biographical rather than critical. In 1970 a volume by Frank Graham, Jr., titled *Since Silent Spring* briefly reviewed the background of Carson's life, traced the genesis of *Silent Spring*, described the controversy it caused, and reported on the progress made since 1962 in pesticide reform. The first biography of Carson also appeared in 1970, Philip Sterling's *Sea and Earth: The Life of Rachel Carson*, a book written for high-school-age readers. In 1972, Carson's editor and friend Paul Brooks published *The House of Life: Rachel Carson at Work*, a compilation of selected letters, essays, and chapters from Carson's literary career, accompanied by well-documented background information on her life. Brooks's work remains the definitive biography.

After Brooks's *The House of Life*, Carson suffered benign neglect from scholars for more than a decade. While the academic world continued to cite her name and to acknowledge her importance, no books were written about her. In 1983, Carol Gartner broke the silence with the first literary study of Carson's work, arguing that Carson had yet to be recognized as "a significant literary figure" and attempting to win Carson her rightful place "in the pantheon of American writers with Henry David Thoreau" (p. 122). In 1985 Ralph Lutts published an essay arguing that the enormous impact of *Silent Spring* was generated by its ability to draw parallels between chemical pesticides and the known dangers of radioactive fallout from nuclear testing. In 1984 a symposium of scientists, chemical engineers, pesticide experts, and government officials was held in Philadelphia to address topics that Carson had raised in *Silent Spring*. In a curious twist of fate, the proceedings were published by the American Chemical Society (Marco, et al., eds., *Silent Spring Revisited*, 1987).

The late 1980s and early 1990s have witnessed a resurgence of scholarly activity around Carson's work, some of it quite sophisticated and much of it informed by feminism. In a 1987 essay in the women's studies journal *Signs*, Vera Norwood joins Carol Gartner's earlier effort to restore Carson's reputation, this time as a thinker, contending that "Carson's work reveals a much more conflicted and complicated approach to nature than her reputation gives her credit for" (p. 747). H. Patricia Hynes's *The Recurring Silent Spring* (1989) is an ecofeminist critique of science, which argues that pesticides, like the atom bomb, are a product of patriarchy, that Carson's work was belittled by the misogynistic scientific establishment, and that genetic engineering and new reproductive technologies are the latest manifestations in the recurring pattern of male domination of both nature and women. Vera Norwood's chapter on Carson in *Made From This Earth: American Women and Nature* (1993) situates Carson within a distinctive female culture of nature study.

Carson's status as a literary figure was confirmed in 1993 when the Twayne United States Authors Series brought out Mary A. McCay's overview of Carson's life and work, which concludes that *Silent Spring* is not an exception in Carson's canon, but is a natural outgrowth of her sea books. The same year also saw renewed public interest in Carson's legacy with the airing on PBS of Neil Goodwin's documentary film *Rachel Carson's "Silent Spring,"* which contains memorable footage of children frolicking in clouds of DDT spray and noteworthy interviews with Carson's closest friends and associates. Linda J. Lear's 1993 essay of the same title in *Environmental History Review*, an earlier version of which was consulted to make the documentary film, provides a detailed analysis of the historical context and lasting significance of *Silent Spring*.

The future of Carson scholarship looks bright. Martha Freeman recently edited a collection of letters between Carson and her close friend Dorothy Freeman. Ann Cottrell Free is working on a book on the influence of Albert Schweitzer and Rachel Carson on the environmental and animal protection movements. Linda J. Lear is writing the first full-length biography of Carson, drawing from materials hitherto unavailable and highlighting Carson's stature as a scientist. An anthology of original scholarly essays on Carson is also being planned. With all four of Carson's books still in print, it is likely that her words will continue to reach not just scholars but the general public for whom she wrote.

Conclusion

The last years of Carson's life might be described as an extended crusade on many fronts, relieved by summer retreats to her cottage on the coast of Maine. A less-dedicated person might have withdrawn from the political fray, letting *Silent Spring* speak for itself. But Carson recognized that the book had put her in a position of considerable influence, and in spite of deteriorating health she somehow mustered the stamina to make many public appearances across the nation and even to do a bit more writing, using her influence to advance causes that she felt were important.

In 1962, Carson flew to California to address the graduating class of Scripps College. Her commencement address, titled "Of Man and the Stream of Time," traces humankind's changing attitudes toward nature, from the fear and superstition of primitive times, to modern-day arrogance, expressed in the language of conquest and exemplified by the atom bomb. She argues that "man's attitude toward nature is today critically important, simply because of his new-found power to destroy it" (p. 8). In closing, she regrets past mistakes that have darkened the present and calls upon the graduates to work toward a brighter future:

> I wish I could stand before you and say that my own generation had brought strength and meaning to man's relation to nature, that we had looked upon the majesty and beauty and terror of the earth we inhabit and learned wisdom and humility. Alas, this cannot be said, for it is we who have brought into being a fateful and destructive power.
>
> But the stream of time moves forward and mankind moves with it. Your generation must come to terms with the environment. . . . You go out into a world where mankind is challenged, as it has never been challenged before, to prove its maturity and its mastery—not of nature, but of itself. (p. 11)

Another cause on Carson's agenda in her final years was that of animal welfare. As early as 1959 Carson joined others in a successful effort to stop the Food and Drug Administration from caging hundreds of beagle hounds for life in a basement laboratory. In 1962 Carson sent a message to Congress urging proper care and treatment of laboratory animals and avoidance of cruel experiments. She lent her support to campaigns to stop steel-jaw leghold trapping and poisoning of wildlife. She wrote a preface for an Animal Welfare Institute publication entitled *Humane Biology Projects*, which offered substitutes for dissection and invasive experiments. And in 1964, the last year of her life, Carson wrote a foreword to Ruth Harrison's *Animal Machines: The New Factory Farming Industry*, published in England. Carson's praise of Harrison can well be applied to herself:

> The modern world worships the gods of speed and quantity, and of the quick and easy profit, and out of this idolatry monstrous evils have arisen. Yet the evils go long unrecognised. Even those who create them manage by some devious rationalising to blind themselves to the harm they have done society. As for the general public, the vast majority rest secure in a childlike faith that "someone" is looking after things — a faith unbroken until some public-spirited person, with patient scholarship and steadfast courage, presents facts that can no longer be ignored. (p. vii)

The tenor of Carson's message had varied little since *Silent Spring*. She had become outraged by the "conquest" mentality, echoing "an unqualified no" (p. viii) to the question of whether humanity has a moral right to dominate other forms of life. Her mission in these final years was to "shock the complacency" (p. vii) out of the public so that they would rise up to protest all cruelty to life and further destruction of the environment.

Carson died at home of cancer and heart failure on 14 April 1964. Her funeral took place in Washington's National Cathedral and was attended by friends, colleagues, scientists, conservationists, and government officials. Secretary of the Interior Stewart L. Udall and Senator Abraham Ribicoff were among her pallbearers. Even after her death, work in her name continued and formal recognition of her achievements grew. In 1965 a group of Carson's friends created the Rachel Carson Trust for the Living Environment (now the Rachel Carson Council)

to monitor pesticide use and to serve as a public clearinghouse of pesticide information. Under the aegis of the National Audubon Society, a Rachel Carson Memorial Fund was established to review government and industry pesticide activities and to promote safer pest-control methods. In 1969, the U.S. Department of the Interior christened the Rachel Carson National Wildlife Refuge on the coast of Maine.

One of Carson's greatest honors was conferred upon her posthumously in 1980, when President Jimmy Carter awarded her the Presidential Medal of Freedom, the highest honor a United States civilian can attain. The citation is a fitting memorial to Rachel Carson's life and work:

> Never silent herself in the face of destructive trends, Rachel Carson fed a spring of awareness across America and beyond. A biologist with a gentle, clear voice, she welcomed her audiences to her love of the sea, while with an equally clear determined voice she warned Americans of the dangers human beings themselves pose for their own environment. Always concerned, always eloquent, she created a tide of environmental consciousness that has not ebbed. (quoted in Gartner, 1983, p. 28)

Selected Bibliography

WORKS OF RACHEL CARSON

BOOKS

Under the Sea-Wind: A Naturalist's Picture of Ocean Life (New York: Simon and Schuster, 1941); *The Sea Around Us* (New York: Oxford Univ. Press, 1951; rev. ed., New York: Oxford Univ. Press, 1961); *The Edge of the Sea* (Boston: Houghton Mifflin, 1955), with illustrations by Bob Hines; *Silent Spring* (Boston: Houghton Mifflin, 1962), with drawings by Lois and Louis Darling, and 25th anniv. ed. (Boston: Houghton Mifflin, 1987), with foreword by Paul Brooks; *The Sense of Wonder* (New York: Harper & Row, 1965), book version of "Help Your Child to Wonder," with photographs by Charles Pratt and others; *The Rocky Coast* (New York: McCall, 1971), text of section 3 from *The Edge of the Sea*, with photographs by Charles Pratt, drawings by Bob Hines.

SELECTED ARTICLES AND PUBLIC ADDRESSES

"Undersea," in *Atlantic Monthly* (September 1937), reprinted in Brooks (1972); "How About Citizenship Papers for the Starling?" in *Nature Magazine* 32, no. 6 (June/July 1939); "The Bat Knew It First," in *Collier's* 114, no. 21 (18 November 1944); "Ocean Wonderland," in *Transatlantic* (April 1945); "The Great Red Tide Mystery," in *Field and Stream* (February 1948); "Lost Worlds: The Challenge of the Islands," in *The Wood Thrush* (May/June 1949); "The Sea," in *New Yorker* (2 June, 9 June, and 16 June 1951), three-part series in "Profiles"; "Help Your Child to Wonder," in *Woman's Home Companion* (July 1956); Preface to *Humane Biology Projects* (New York: Animal Welfare Institute, 1960), repr. in *Atlantic Naturalist* 15 (October/December 1960); "Of Man and the Stream of Time," in *Scripps College Bulletin* 36, no. 4 (July 1962), graduation address to Scripps College; "Rachel Carson Answers Her Critics," in *Audubon Magazine* 65, no. 5 (September/October 1963); "Miss Carson Goes to Congress," in *American Forests* 69, no. 7 (July 1963); Foreword to *Animal Machines: The New Factory Farming Industry*, by Ruth Harrison (London: Vincent Stuart, 1964).

GOVERNMENT PUBLICATIONS

"Food from the Sea: Fish and Shellfish of New England," U.S. Dept. of the Interior, Fish and Wildlife Service, Conservation Bulletin 33 (1943); "Fishes of the Middle West," U.S. Dept. of the Interior, Fish and Wildlife Service, Conservation Bulletin 34 (1943); "Fish and Shellfish of the South Atlantic and Gulf Coasts," U.S. Dept. of the Interior, Office of the Coordinator of Fisheries, Conservation Bulletin 37 (1944); "Fish and Shellfish of the Middle Atlantic Coast," U.S. Dept. of the Interior, Office of the Coordinator of Fisheries, Conservation Bulletin 38 (1945); "Chincoteague, a National Wildlife Refuge," U.S. Dept. of the Interior, Fish and Wildlife Service, Conservation in Action 1 (1947); "Parker River, a National Wildlife Refuge," U.S. Dept. of the Interior, Fish and Wildlife Service, Conservation in Action 2 (1947); "Mattamuskeet, a National Wildlife Refuge," U.S. Dept. of the Interior, Fish and Wildlife Service, Conservation in Action 4 (1947); "Guarding Our Wildlife Resources," U.S. Dept. of the Interior, Fish and Wildlife Service, Conservation in Action 5 (1948); "Bear River, a National Wildlife Refuge," U.S. Dept. of the Interior, Fish and Wildlife Service, Conservation in Action 8 (1950), coauthored with Vanez T. Wilson.

PUBLISHED LETTERS

Always, Rachel: The Letters of Rachel Carson and Dorothy Freeman, 1952–1964, ed. by Martha Freeman (Boston: Beacon, 1994).

MANUSCRIPTS AND PAPERS

Most of Carson's unpublished writings, along with reviews of her books and articles about her, are housed in the Rachel Carson Collection, Beinecke Rare Book and Manuscript Library, Yale University, New Haven, Conn. Other papers and unpublished letters are stored in the Rachel Carson Council Library, Chevy Chase, Md.; Executive Director Shirley A. Briggs was a close friend and colleague of Carson's.

BIOGRAPHICAL AND CRITICAL STUDIES

Elizabeth Anticaglia, "Rachel Carson," in *Twelve American Women* (Chicago: Nelson-Hall, 1975); Marcia Myers Bonta, *Women in the Field: America's Pioneering Women Naturalists* (College Station: Texas A&M Univ. Press, 1991); Shirley A. Briggs, "Remembering Rachel Carson," in *American Forests* 76 (July 1970), and "*Silent Spring*: The View from 1990," in *The Ecologist* 20, no. 2 (March/April 1990); Paul Brooks, *The House of Life: Rachel Carson at Work* (Boston: Houghton Mifflin, 1972), illus., "Carson, Rachel Louise," in *Notable American Women: The Modern Period: A Biographical Dictionary*, ed. by Barbara Sicherman and Carol Hurd Green (Cambridge, Mass.: Belknap/Harvard Univ. Press, 1980), *Speaking for Nature: How Literary Naturalists from Henry Thoreau to Rachel Carson Have Shaped America* (Boston: Houghton Mifflin, 1980), and "The Courage of Rachel Carson," in *Audubon* 89 (January 1987); Robert B. Downs, "Upsetting the Balance of Nature," in *Books that Changed America* (London: Macmillan, 1970).

Sean Duffy, "*Silent Spring* and *A Sand County Almanac*: The Two Most Significant Environmental Books of the 20th Century," in *Nature Study* 44, nos. 2–3 (February 1991); Thomas R. Dunlap, *DDT: Scientists, Citizens, and Public Policy* (Princeton, N.J.: Princeton Univ. Press, 1981); Paul R. Ehrlich, "Paul R. Ehrlich Reconsiders *Silent Spring*," in *Bulletin of the Atomic Scientists* 35 (October 1979); Donald Fleming, "Roots of the New Conservation Movement," in *Perspectives in American History* 6 (1972); Stephen Fox, *The American Conservation Movement: John Muir and His Legacy* (Madison: Univ. of Wisconsin Press, 1981); Ann Cottrell Free, "Since *Silent Spring*: Our Debt to Albert Schweitzer and Rachel Carson" (Washington, D.C.: Flying Fox, 1992); Carol B. Gartner, "The Gentle Storm Center," in *Life* 53, no. 15 (2 October 1962), and *Rachel Carson* (New York: Frederick Ungar, 1983); Frank Graham, Jr., *Since Silent Spring* (Boston: Houghton Mifflin, 1970), and "Neptune's Bookshelf," in *Audubon* 91, no. 2 (March 1989); Wayne Hanley, *Natural History in America: From Mark Catesby to Rachel Carson* (New York: Quadrangle, 1977).

Bob Hines, "Remembering Rachel," in *Yankee Magazine* 55, no. 6 (June 1991); H. Patricia Hynes, "Catalysts of the American Environmental Movement," in *Women of Power* 9 (spring 1988), and *The Recurring Silent Spring* (New York: Pergamon, 1989); G. Kass-Simon and Patricia Farnes, eds., *Women of Science: Righting the Record* (Bloomington: Indiana Univ. Press, 1990); Linda J. Lear, "Bombshell in Beltsville: The USDA and the Challenge of *Silent Spring*," in *Agricultural History* 66, no. 2 (spring 1992), and "Rachel Carson's *Silent Spring*," in *Environmental History Review* 17, no. 2 (summer 1993); Jack Lewis, "Titans in Conservation: Rachel Carson," in *EPA Journal* 18, no. 2 (May/June 1992); Jennifer Wilder Logan, "A Scientist's Reverence for Life," in *Chrysalis* 7 (spring 1992); Ralph H. Lutts, "Chemical Fallout: Rachel Carson's *Silent Spring*, Radioactive Fallout, and the Environmental Movement," in *Environmental Review* 9, no. 3 (fall 1985).

Thomas J. Lyon, *This Incomperable Lande: A Book of American Nature Writing* (Boston: Houghton Mifflin, 1989); Gino J. Marco, Robert M. Hollingworth, and William Durham, eds., *Silent Spring Revisited* (Washington, D.C.: American Chemical Society, 1987); Mary A. McCay, *Rachel Carson* (New York: Twayne, 1993); Roderick Frazier Nash, *The Rights of Nature: A History of Environmental Ethics* (Madison: Univ. of Wisconsin Press, 1989); Geoffrey Norman, "The Flight of Rachel Carson," in *Recorder: The Chatham Alumnae Magazine* 54, no. 2 (spring 1985); Vera L. Norwood, "Heroines of Nature: Four Women Respond to the American Landscape," in *Environmental Review* 8, no. 1 (spring 1984), "The Nature of Knowing: Rachel Carson and the American Environment," in *Signs* 12, no. 4 (summer 1987), and *Made from This Earth: American Women and Nature* (Chapel Hill: Univ. of North Carolina Press, 1993); Obituary, in *New York Times* (15 April 1964); John H. Perkins, *Insects, Experts, and the Insecticide Crisis: A Quest for New Pest Management Strategies* (New York: Plenum, 1982); Margaret W. Rossiter, *Women Scientists in America: Struggles and Strategies to 1940* (Baltimore: Johns Hopkins Univ. Press, 1982).

Dorothy Thompson Seif, "How I Remember Rachel," in *Recorder: The Chatham Alumnae Magazine* 54, no. 2 (spring 1985); Philip Sterling, *Sea and Earth: The Life of Rachel Carson* (New York: Thomas Y. Crowell, 1970); Fred D. White, "Rachel Carson: Encounters with the Primal Mother," in *North Dakota Quarterly* (spring 1991); James Whorton, *Before Silent Spring: Pesticides and Public Health in Pre-DDT America* (Princeton, N.J.: Princeton Univ. Press, 1974); Peter Wild, "Elder of the Tribe, Rachel Carson," in *Backpacker 30* 6 (December 1978/January 1979); Terry Tempest Williams, "The Spirit of Rachel Carson," in *Audubon* 94, no. 4 (July/August 1992); Donald Worster, *Nature's Economy: A History of Ecological Ideas* (San Francisco: Sierra Club, 1977; repr., Cambridge, Mass., 1985).

ANNA BOTSFORD COMSTOCK
(1854–1930)

MARCIA MYERS BONTA

BEFORE THERE WAS ecology, there was nature study. "Nature-study," wrote its chief proponent, Anna Botsford Comstock, in her *Handbook of Nature-Study* (1911), "is, despite all discussions and perversions, a study of nature; it consists of simple, truthful observations that may, like beads on a string, finally be threaded upon the understanding and thus held together as a logical and harmonious whole" (p. 1). To Comstock, it was essential that children be given a "sense of companionship with life out-of-doors and an abiding love of nature" (p. 2). Such children, she reasoned, would attain "that serene peace and hopeful faith that is the sure inheritance of all those who realize fully that they are working units of this wonderful universe" (p. 2).

Such peace and faith was inculcated in Comstock as a small child by her gentle Quaker mother, who had a passionate love for the beauties of nature. She spent her happiest hours afield with her mother, who taught her the names of more than sixty wildflowers and a dozen constellations. The only child of Phoebe Irish and Marvin S. Botsford, Anna was born on 1 September 1854, in southwestern New York state, in her parents' modest log house. Her father had come as a child to Otto, in Cattaraugus County, with his strongly Methodist family. He, like his wife, rejected rigid thinking and encouraged reading and discussion in their home.

It was obvious, from Comstock's posthumously published autobiography, *The Comstocks of Cornell* (1953), that while she respected her well-educated, thoughtful, generous, and prosperous farmer father, she adored her radiant, good-hearted mother and emulated her. In fact, her description of her mother as "strong of body, blithe of spirit, courageous, capable, fearless, peace-loving, and self-sacrificing" (p. 57) was an accurate description of herself as an adult. In addition, her parents' habit of opening their home and hearts to relatives and friends in need so influenced Comstock that she and her husband did the same when they owned their own home.

Still another gift from her mother was her love of poetry, nurtured as a small child when she nightly fell asleep to the sound of her mother reciting poetry instead of singing, a skill Mrs. Botsford had never acquired during her Hicksite Quaker upbringing. Instead, she had cultivated a love for the music in words.

Early Education

The other great influence on Comstock's younger years was her educated female neighbor, Mrs. Ann French Allen, a teacher who had married a wealthy widower and who filled her home with books, paintings, comfortable furniture, and a piano. She often stayed with the Allens, listening eagerly as husband and wife read poetry, essays, political speeches, and magazine articles aloud to each other. According to Comstock, "Mrs. Ann French Allen was the one who aroused my ambition for a higher education and implanted in me a desire to make my work in the world count to the utmost of my ability" (p. 69). Apparently, although her father built a succession of larger homes for his family as his farm improved, Anna's parents remained plain country people without the cultural refinements of the Allens. But they saw to it that their precocious daughter attended a good private boarding school—the Chamberlain Institute and Female College in Randolph, eighteen miles from her home—after she completed her elementary education at the village school. She particularly enjoyed debating in the literary society and won first prize one year. Although she respected her teachers, all male graduates of Wesleyan University, she did not like the religious regimentation of this Methodist school and refused to embrace the religious dogma everyone tried to force on her. She had been taught by her parents to respect but not necessarily adopt the religious beliefs of others, and she could not accept the image of a jealous, vengeful God that the Methodists preached. In later years Anna attended the Unitarian Church, but she was proud of the fact that her intimate friends included people of every creed and no creed.

Anna graduated from high school in 1873 and a year later entered Cornell University. Her neighbor Mrs. Allen had originally suggested that she attend the University of Michigan, the nearest university that admitted women, but by then Cornell, founded by philanthropist Ezra Cornell in 1868, had opened its doors to women students, the first coeducational college in the eastern United States.

The temptation to attend school closer to home than Ann Arbor, Michigan, led Anna to choose Cornell even though there was, at that time, no on-campus housing for women. In addition, the male students initially resented the thirty-seven women students, a situation she took in stride because she was more interested in learning than socializing with men. But the men soon came calling at her boarding house, including William Berry, her first serious beau. After an engagement in 1875, the "affair fell by its own weight. It was too emotional to meet the realities of life," Anna later explained in her autobiography (p. 78). According to her, Berry was emotionally unstable, brilliant but erratic, and mentally ill during the last years of his life.

Her next beau was quite the opposite. John Henry Comstock—instructor in entomology and five years Anna's senior—"felt so keenly the wonder of creation that he carried the classes along with him on the tide of his own earnest enthusiasm" (*The Comstocks of Cornell*, p. 52). In fact, their courtship was not recognized by either of them as anything more than friendship based on a mutual love of the natural world.

Although Anna majored in modern literature, she did take Comstock's zoology course. Once, sensing a receptive mind, he gave her a tour of his laboratory and showed her his thousands of insects. When she described him and his laboratory to her mother in a letter, she emphasized his kind and pleasant personality. They spent many happy hours together outside, walking and talking, becoming the best of friends. But he had an understanding with Jennie Bartlett, a friend of Anna's who contracted tuberculosis. While visiting her at a sanitarium in Florida, however, he wrote a steady succession of letters to Anna, mostly about the entomological work he was doing—for instance, collecting fifteen grasshopper species in one day.

Finally, Bartlett decided against marriage because of her failing health. Comstock returned to Ithaca bitterly disappointed, and spent the rest of the spring walking and talking with Anna, the only person who had known of the relationship with Bartlett and his real reason for visiting Florida. Anna then left school, without a degree, returning home to live with her parents. Comstock continued his work and research at Cornell, all the while writing long letters to her about his discoveries and, finally, his advancement to assistant professor of entomology in December 1876.

In one letter he described his visit to the Centennial Exposition in Philadelphia, where he paid particular attention to work displayed by the American Entomological Society. He commented that he hoped entomologists would soon learn the importance of knowing what the insects do as well as their names, an idea Anna later repeated time and again in her nature books and articles.

Immediately after his promotion, Comstock visited Anna and her family over the Christmas holidays. An enthusiastic, energetic, practical young man, he never sat still, not even when he was reading. The ambitious, hardworking professor made a favorable impression on her parents. Sensing latent artistic talent in Anna, he sent her drawing materials and instructions in January 1877, so that she could try to draw insects. Later, in the spring, he also applied for a building lot on campus with a view of Cayuga Lake in the distance, confidently planning his future home with Anna as his future wife. The Botsfords and their home had become the parents and the home the orphaned Comstock had never had. Raised a foster child in a succession of families, his father dead, his mother far away, trying to earn enough money to support her son, he had begun to make his own hard living by the time he was fifteen, as a cook on a succession of Great Lakes steamers. So the Botsfords' stable home meant a great deal to him, and when his health failed briefly, it was there that he went to recover.

By then Comstock and Anna were engaged. After he had spent a summer studying the cotton worms in Alabama, during which he contracted recurrent malaria and escaped a yellow fever epidemic, they were married on 7 October 1878.

No one has ever suggested that their marriage was other than the proverbial "marriage made in heaven," except for their childlessness, which both of them regretted. According to one close friend, they were lifelong friends with congenial and complementary tastes. Comstock herself mentioned close companionship as their marriage basis, and after a year she wrote to a friend planning to be married that marriage had brought her undreamed-of riches, even though she sometimes had to struggle to see her husband's side of an issue. Frankness and unselfishness were the most important traits partners could bring to a marriage, she concluded. At first Comstock did all the housework because she felt it to be her duty. But even then she helped her husband by writing his business letters and making illustrations for his lectures; he helped her wash the dishes.

Then, as they were settling into the social and intellectual milieu of Cornell, an entomologist friend, Leland Howard, notified John Comstock that Dr. Charles Valentine Riley, chief entomologist, had had a falling out with General William G. Le Duc, the commissioner of agriculture. Howard suggested that John Comstock apply for the position. Because of his work with the cotton worm, the thirty-year-old professor was appointed chief entomologist, and the Comstocks moved to Washington, D.C., after he had secured a two-year leave of absence from Cornell.

As always, Anna Comstock served willingly as an unpaid assistant until Le Duc decided to appoint her a clerk and pay her a salary, something she had never expected but that made her very happy. In her husband's name she wrote letters and entomological notes, and answered queries for agricultural papers that he read and verified before signing.

Once he finished the cotton worm work, John Comstock settled on a study of scale insects that were wreaking havoc in the citrus groves of Florida and California. Anna worked in the Washington office, studying and caring for the specimens her husband sent almost daily from Florida; when he went to California, she accompanied him to take care of the laboratory while he conducted his fieldwork. Taking care of the laboratory consisted of caring for the live insects her husband brought back, noting their habits, and drawing those that could not be preserved.

When they returned to Washington, John Comstock embarked on painstaking microscopic study of the pygidia (tail-like structures) of female insects, which often provided the only distinguishing characteristic of different species. After Anna worked out on paper the anatomy of each insect under the microscope, John classified the drawings and used them as a foundation for classifying the scale insects of America.

Collaborative Work

To help them in their work, the Comstocks used a book by the well-known French scientist V. A. Signoret. When John Comstock sent him one of Anna's drawings of a male scale insect, Signoret was lavish in his praise. "The drawing of the male is magnificent. It was made by the hand of a master," Comstock reported in her autobiography. "I think," she added, "this commendation did much to start me on my career as an artist in natural history" (p. 130).

With a change of administration, Le Duc was out and a champion of C. V. Riley was in. Despite letters of support from scientists all over the country, John Comstock was replaced by Riley, and he and Anna returned to Cornell, chastened by their experience in the political world. In a letter that John wrote to Anna about his future, he devoted an entire paragraph to what "we" will do, including original scientific work. To free her for such work, they hired a maid. He also encouraged her to return to Cornell and get a degree in science. Together they decided that she should learn wood engraving so she could illustrate a textbook, *An Introduction to Entomology,* that he planned to write. "With my usual daring on untried paths I went at it," she wrote in her autobiography (p. 144). At the New Orleans Exposition of 1885 her scientific drawings won first honorable mention. She also worked on her degree, writing a thesis on the dobsonfly, and received her Bachelor of Science degree in 1885.

Then Comstock took up wood engraving more seriously, going to New York City and studying under gifted teacher and artist John P. Davis for six weeks. But she did engravings of insects only so they could be used in her husband's book. On two more occasions she went back for still more instruction. Eventually she was elected to the prestigious American Society of Wood-Engravers, specifically because of her skill in

representing the texture of butterfly wings, only the third woman to be so honored.

John Comstock's belief in studying live insects was particularly bolstered when he received funds for what he called the Insectary—a greenhouse for growing plants attractive to injurious insects where he could study their life histories and habits. In it Anna found a north window where she could do her engraving.

Finally, in November 1888, *An Introduction to Entomology* by John Henry Comstock, filled with many of Anna's illustrations, was published. With that, their sometimes joint, sometimes separate, writing careers were launched; for both of them, "Our writing was the thread on which our days were strung," Anna wrote in *The Comstocks of Cornell* (p. 274). One month later she was one of the first four women to be initiated into Sigma Xi, a national honor society for scientists and engineers that had been founded in 1886.

Instead of writing Part II of his textbook, as he had originally planned, John Comstock decided to write a whole new work—*A Manual for the Study of Insects*—with Anna. He wrote in the early mornings, and she worked on the engravings from eight in the morning until six in the evening. Because he wanted a reasonable price for the book so it could be used as a class text, the Comstocks decided to publish the book themselves. Joining with their friend and colleague Simon H. Gage, they established the Comstock Publishing Company (forerunner of Cornell University Press) in 1893. As for the book itself, it "fulfilled all and more of our dreams of its usefulness. It was the means of bringing knowledge of insects to the general public: it was placed in school and public libraries, besides serving as a textbook in colleges and universities" (*The Comstocks of Cornell,* p. 188).

A Manual for the Study of Insects is a substantial tome of nearly 700 pages. In the preface John Comstock acknowledges Anna as "Junior Author." Not only had she contributed all the engravings, most of which had been done from nature, but she had also written a substantial part of the text. Although there is no indication of who wrote which sections, it is easy to distinguish Anna Comstock's lucid prose from the more pedantic portions of the text. For instance, the opening of Chapter III, "Class Hexapoda, The Insects," states the same philosophy she later espoused in her *Handbook of Nature-Study*, that "all life is linked together in such a way that no part of the chain is unimportant" (p. 48). Furthermore, she insists that one's intellectual growth can be positively affected by a study of insects because of the pleasure one can derive from original investigation. After all, one need not be a scientist to study insects: "Any one can find out something new regarding insect architecture" (p. 49) if he or she is a careful observer, another recurrent theme of Comstock's.

John Comstock admitted in his introduction that at first they had intended to make the book much more elementary than it became in its final form. "It has seemed best, however, to leave these parts as written [by Anna] in order that the work may be of interest to a wider range of readers than it would be were it restricted to a uniform style of treatment" (p. vi). For instance, the click beetle story is consistent with Comstock's contribution to the book.

> We remember well carrying these creatures into the old district schoolhouse, where all lessons had to be learned from books, and where Nature was never given a chance to teach us anything. Here, with one eye on the teacher and one on this interesting jumper laid on our book behind the desk, we found a most fascinating occupation for the tedious moments. But the end was always the same: the beetle jumped so high that it betrayed us and was liberated, and we were disgraced. (pp. 544–545)

Such anecdotes are skillfully interwoven with more substantial scientific information throughout *A Manual for the Study of Insects*. The kinds of illustrations by Comstock are also diverse. There are several full-page, artistic engravings; many smaller, scientifically accurate, but pleasing engravings of bugs, butterflies, caterpillars, and insect nests; and strictly technical diagrams of insect wings.

The book even has touches of humor, most notably the section on tree-hoppers. "Nature must have been in a joking mood when tree-hoppers were developed," Comstock writes, "for these little creatures are most comically grotesque in appearance. In general outline they resemble beech-nuts, except that many have humps on their backs. . . . If the young entomologist wishes to laugh, let him look at the faces of tree-hoppers through a lens" (pp. 154–155). To illustrate her point, she has arranged on a horizontal cornstalk leaf four tree-hoppers that are, indeed, laughable.

> Their eyes always have a keen, droll look, and the line that separates the head from the prothorax gives them the appearance of wearing glasses. In some cases the prothorax is elevated above the head, so that it looks like a peaked nightcap; in others it is shaped like a Tam-o'-Shanter; and sometimes it has horns, one on each side, which have given one species the name of the Buffalo Tree-hopper. (p. 155)

After reading her description and laughing aloud at her illustration, the individuality of tree-hoppers is indelibly stamped in the reader's mind. Because of such images, modern readers can still derive pleasure from leafing through this attractive, well-written melding of scientific treatise and nature book.

The same year *A Manual for the Study of Insects* was published, Comstock was swept up in the incipient nature study movement. Utilizing her talents as a writer, artist, teacher, and speaker, it provided a perfect career for the childless woman who loved children and nature. With one exception, all of her books were written in some way to encourage nature study and an interest in nature, and most were aimed at children.

Because of the agricultural depression of 1891–1893, droves of rural youth headed to New York City for work. To keep them on the farm, philanthropists and state officials decided to introduce nature study into rural schools. They thought that if youth learned to appreciate their natural surroundings, they would be content to stay in the country. After Comstock helped to lauch a pilot study in Westchester County schools, the New York state legislature voted to fund the teaching of nature study in rural New York schools by the State College of Agriculture at Cornell. Then Comstock, along with Professor Liberty Hyde Bailey, head of the Department of Horticulture, and others started writing nature leaflets for teachers. Out of those came the germ of Comstock's *Handbook of Nature-Study*.

In 1897 Bailey was appointed head of the nature study movement, but it was Comstock who did the bulk of the work. In acknowledgment of her position, she was appointed an assistant professor of nature study in the Cornell University Extension Division in 1899, followed by a demotion in 1900 to lecturer in nature study after several Cornell trustees objected to having a woman professor. Her nature study propaganda work, as Comstock called it, upset all her drawing and engraving plans. She believed it to be important, however, so she plunged into a hectic schedule of teaching Nature Study School during summer sessions, and lecturing to Teachers' Institutes and teaching college courses on nature study the rest of the year. She also became a staple in the Chautauqua lecture series.

Nature Writer and Advocate

Comstock and Bailey worked well together, and as editor of the periodical *Country Life in America*, he asked her to edit poetry for the journal. In addition, she wrote *Trees at Leisure* in 1901, which was later republished as a small book by the Comstock Publishing Company in 1916, "as good a bit of writing as I ever did" (*The Comstocks of Cornell*, p. 197). Unlike most of Comstock's nature writing, *Trees at Leisure* makes no attempt to teach the reader anything. Instead, it is an extended prose poem praising the beauty of trees, especially in winter. She believes that identifying trees in winter cannot be learned from a book. It is a matter of feeling and empathy for individual trees. She also equates humanity's growing sense of beauty with growing mental stature:

> Ages must have passed before man gained sufficient mental stature to pay admiring tribute to the tree standing in all the glory of its full leafage, shimmering in the sunlight, making its myriad bows to the restless winds; but eons must have lapsed before the human eye grew keen enough and the human soul large enough to give sympathetic comprehension to the beauty of bare branches laced across changing skies, which is the tree-lover's full heritage. (p. 11)

Furthermore, she contends that "The mortal who has never enjoyed a speaking acquaintance with some individual tree is to be pitied; for such an acquaintance, once established, naturally ripens into a friendliness that brings serene comfort to the human heart, whatever the heart of the tree may or may not experience" (p. 21).

From this beginning Comtock goes on to characterize numerous Eastern America tree species. The American elm has "benignant and inviting curves" (p. 19), whereas the isolated sugar maple is "self-centered" in contrast to one that grows in a woodland, "a living pillar... [possessing] a certain majesty of mien [that] proclaim at once its identity and its place as a peer in the forest realm." She then contrasts the sugar maple to the red maple: "each of its bud-laden twigs a ruddy dreamer of scarlet past and crimson future" (pp. 19–21).

Never have trees been described as well as Comstock does in this small jewel of a book. Had she had no sense of duty to educate, had she not been overburdened with work all her life, it is probably fair to say that she would have written more nature books such as *Trees at Leisure*, instead of tucking beautifully descriptive passages among her more pedantic works. More than any other book she wrote, *Trees at Leisure* reveals Comstock's poetic soul.

She followed that book with a collection of several of her periodical articles written about insects in *Saint Nicholas, Chautauquan, Observer,* and *Cornell Nature-Study Bulletin*, supplemented by other material, which she titled

Ways of the Six-Footed, published by Ginn & Company in 1903. Although it was intended as a book for children, Comstock does not write down to them, using words such as "anti-cannibalistic" without explanation. She combines her passion for scientific observation and accuracy with snatches of poetic allusions and makes frequent use of entertaining anecdotes. And once again her descriptive passages sing, especially in her chapter on insect music, "Pipers and Minnesingers": "few of us comprehend the debt of gratitude that we owe to the little fiddlers in the grass, the drummers in the trees, and the pipers in the air. There is cheer in their music, as well as restfulness. Their fugues afford companionship, and at the same time inspire in us a comfortable sense of isolation and peace" (pp. 3–4).

Although Comstock believed that all her scientific information for children should be accurate, she insisted that her nature study materials should be romantic, poetic, artistic, and anthropomorphic, so as to nurture children's interest in and love of nature. For example, her section on katydids includes a detailed description of their singing apparatus complete with a technical drawing, yet, like her description of tree-hoppers in *A Manual for the Study of Insects*, she also "humanizes" them: "His face wears a very solemn expression, but somewhere in it is a suggestion of drollery, as if he could appreciate a joke; he keeps his long silken antennae waving in an inquiring way that suggests curiosity rather than fear" (pp. 19–20).

A careful reading of *Ways of the Six-Footed* provides some insight into Comstock's feelings about her life that she does not reveal in her autobiography—for instance, when she mentions in "A Little Nomad" how she went to the woods to be alone, away from "a world of work and care" (p. 29). She "was tired of a world that lectured and talked and argued and did many other noisy things that wore on one's nerves" (p. 30). In "The Perfect Socialism," her chapter on bees, wasps, ants, and termites, she favorably compares the apparent altruism in social insects to the acquisitiveness and competitiveness in mankind, concluding that "the generosity of these insect citizens toward each other is an ideal which still lies beyond the horizon of accomplishment in the human world" (p. 71).

Regarding women's rights, a cause she believed in but did not actively campaign for, Comstock comments facetiously in "Two Mother Masons": "It is safe to assert that in the insect world the question of 'woman's rights' is settled permanently in the affirmative" (p. 97). And her answer to those who routinely shoot predators because of sympathy for the prey is that "in studying the histories of animals we had best start out with the cheerful theory that a 'square meal' is due to any creature that is strong enough or cunning enough to get it; and that it is a futile waste of sensibilities to sympathize with the meal" (p. 105). To Comstock, nature had its own rhythms that were to be observed but not interfered with. She always appreciated nature as it is, not as she thought it should be.

Her next book, *How to Know the Butterflies*, was again written with her husband, this time at her request so she could use it in her Chautauqua lectures. Even though John Comstock fretted that her summer lecturing was too hard on her health, he agreed to help her after she signed a contract with Appleton Publishing Company. The book was published in 1904 with thirty-five colored plates and written in the usual anecdotal Comstock style with snatches of poetry juxtaposed with scientifically accurate descriptions. For example, after a table titled "Geographical Distribution in the East of the Forms of the Spring Azure," she writes, "In the early spring when we are weary of winter this butterfly appears in our path like a fleck of the welcome blue sky above. It flits above on uncertain wing or loafs about damp places or hovers about the forest mantle" (p. 253). What a delightful contrast to the dry, fact-filled field guides of present day, which lack even a hint of poetry or appreciation for the subject.

Comstock followed that book with *How to Keep Bees: A Handbook for the Use of Beginners* in 1905. Although it contains pertinent beekeeping information, based on the many years she and her husband were part-time beekeepers, it also contains elegant nature writing—for instance, she describes the queen bee, surrounded by her attendants, as "a sight that makes men feel how very limited is their knowledge of any other world than their own to see the queen bee, surrounded by her ring of attendants, each with head toward her, as if she were the centre of a many-rayed star" (p. 28). She hopes that the beginning beekeeper has a sense of beauty in the placement of the hives, and she thinks that a love of natural science is the best reason for keeping bees.

As in *Ways of the Six-Footed*, Comstock comments favorably on the bees' "perfect" socialism, writing in regard to the queen bees' production of drones, "If our poor human queens possessed this power of producing male heirs at will, much trouble would have been saved to many of them and, to some of them, their heads. However, the perfect socialists do most things better than we" (p. 33). She also thinks the queen is "wise" because she "has in mind the dangers of overpopulation... it is certain that Malthusian doctrines are rigorously and successfully practised by the perfect socialists of the hive" (p. 34). Furthermore, "the individual is nothing in the perfect socialism, and the colony is everything; the treatment is Spartan, with none of the weakness which makes us keep alive the hopelessly insane, the idiotic, and the criminal" (p. 44).

Finally, she concludes that "Any bit of comb-building seems to be the result of a consensus of public opinion and not of individual skill and enterprise. There is a oneness in bee enterprises which harmonises capital and labor, and which precludes strikes and lockouts" (pp. 56–57). Once again, nature's ways seem to make more sense than humanity's in Comstock's social commentary. On the other hand, when discussing the deceitful ways of robber bees, she characterizes such scientific facts as "not always beautiful, however interesting they may be" (p. 194). Thus the reader is left with the vision of Comstock as interested nature observer, awed by what she sees but sometimes tempted to make unflattering comparisons with humanity's ways.

Comstock's next book, *Confessions to a Heathen Idol*, published in 1906 by Doubleday, Page & Company, was a novel she had worked on for several years during bouts of insomnia. Because of her reputation as a scientific woman, she decided to use a pseudonym—Marian Lee, who was also the narrator of the story. But nearly everyone guessed who the author was, so the second edition was issued under her name. Although it is not a particularly good novel, it is a thinly veiled account of Comstock's inner life and, as such, makes interesting reading. By taking on the persona of Marian Lee, Comstock was free to say what she thought about a good many things, something she never did in her autobiography.

Lee, like Comstock, derives great pleasure from wood-engraving in her "cosy, chip-littered room...where I could always find peace and comfort" (*Confessions to a Heathen Idol*, p. 16). But, as a longtime widow close to forty years old (Comstock was then fifty-two), she still has familial obligations—to her professor father, her much younger brother, and her mother-in-law. Her chief fault "is that I give too much of my life away, and to too many people, I suspect. I often feel as if I were a sort of social lunch-counter, always so crowded that no one ever gets a square meal from it" (p. 90), a wonderful metaphor that aptly portrays Comstock's situation.

Nature is Lee's refuge from the busy world, just as it is Comstock's. "I must give myself to her without any reservations if I would experience the blessing of her companionship. Nature is no moralist; she does not care whether I am good or bad; all she asks is that I be happy and sympathetic" (p. 44). And when she is badly hurt, she escapes by going to visit her restful Quaker relatives in the country, something that Comstock often did. "It is my way...when I am hit, not to stay and waste myself in further struggle, but to flee from the battlefield, turn my face to green fields and sunny skies; and by keeping my thoughts thoroughly antiseptic, let the hurts heal through Nature's own kindly treatment" (p. 296).

The best passages of this little romance are those that describe the natural world. During a twilight sleigh ride with the man she has secretly loved for many years, Lee, a self-proclaimed tree lover, like Comstock, writes elegiac words about the pine woods:

> On either side dimly visible were innumerable columns holding aloft the black canopy, which was broken in a tasseled fresco above our heads, against a sky beset with stars which had been invisible to us until then. Almost imperceptibly we became conscious of a faint, far, mysterious sound—a sibilant breathing somewhere aloft which grew louder as it came nearer, until, like a great surf on a rocky shore, it seemed to break above our heads, and then recede, leaving us again in silence. . . . Again and again as we passed on, came that all-pervading, mysterious flood and ebb of sound. It was overwhelming to the spirit; I felt awed, as if I had unwittingly shared a service in some vast, secret temple of the gods. (pp. 214–215)

She also writes excellent descriptions of beautiful birdsongs, giving herself "over to the beguilement of the meadow-larks' refrain. There are no words to express what their song means to me" (p. 298). Another favorite field bird is the bobolink: "Ever since I was a child the bobolink song has tinkled itself joyously into the uttermost parts of my being...I am proud to be in any world that has in it a bobolink" (p. 299).

Best of all, though, is when she goes into the "great woods on the 'templed hills,'" where she listens to a bird concert: "and now and then a hermit thrush sent his heavenly voice echoing through the twilight spaces, music so exquisite that we might not bear more than a single phrase" (p. 295).

Lee also discusses her feelings about aging and retaining her girlish innocence. She is "a girl who would not learn to grow old when the gray hairs came creeping into her black locks; a girl who boldly declares the whole world is rose-color because she deliberately chooses to wear pink spectacles...a girl stunted in growth by rank optimism and kept in eternal girlhood thereby" (p. 29).

Anna Botsford Comstock

Yet, she (and Comstock) were growing older, and she knew it: "I look upon a year lived as a year earned;—and that each year earned means greater treasure of experience and power laid up against time of need. It is only when growing old means cessation of development that it is to be feared" (p. 4).

Certainly Comstock continued to "earn" each year, working harder than ever. In addition to teaching a steady string of nature study courses at Cornell, she served as a trustee of William Smith College in Geneva, New York, which she had helped the founder to develop in 1903.

Handbook of Nature-Study

In the winter of 1909, Comstock decided to write her *Handbook of Nature-Study*. But she could not interest any commercial publisher in the project. Even Liberty Hyde Bailey and her husband thought it would be a financial disaster. Comstock, on the other hand, disagreed: "I went at my task with defiant courage. I knew that my husband would help me financially with my book, even if it would be a total loss..." (*The Comstocks of Cornell*, p. 229). And so he did. In addition to helping her gather material for the book, when it was finished he published it under the Comstock Publishing Company imprint even though he thought it would lose $5,000.

Instead, it became the all-time best-seller among books published by Cornell University, going through twenty-five editions and being translated into eight languages. With its publication, the nature study movement spread throughout the nation, and the book became the standard text for public school teachers' summer school courses.

Comstock dedicated the book to Liberty Hyde Bailey, who, she explained in her introduction, "has been the inspiring leader of the movement, as well as the official head" (p. x), and fruit grower John W. Spencer, who had realized the importance of helping teachers through simply written leaflets. Based on a home nature study course she had written between 1903 and 1911, the leaflets had been rewritten for consistency and she had added new lessons "to bridge gaps and make a coherent whole" (p. x). She also aimed to make the lessons useful for fieldwork.

It is an enormous book—more than 900 pages—filled with information on every subject from birds and insects to trees and wildflowers. It was almost immediately dubbed the "Nature Bible," because it contains all the information teachers needed to teach youngsters about every aspect of the outdoors, along with 232 carefully planned lessons for teachers to follow, complete with suggested field trips, experiments, and questions to ask students. It also includes an excellent bibliography. Although there is less of Comstock's usual anecdotal style, there is poetry by a wide variety of poets interspersed throughout the text, as well as an abundance of photographs and illustrations. Many of the latter are Comstock's, including a reprint of her droll tree-hopper portrait on a corn stalk.

Part I, "The Teaching of Nature-Study," sets the stage for the format and philosophy of the book. In it Comstock defines nature study and explains what it should do for children. Most important, it should give them practical and helpful knowledge so they are not helpless during natural disasters. It should also cultivate their imaginations, as fairy tales do, while it gives them a regard for what is true and the ability to express it. In addition, nature study should encourage a love of beauty and nature in children.

Furthermore, Comstock believed that any adult who loves nature should be able to inculcate such love in children. No doubt she was thinking of her mother's ability to inspire her. When she was eighty, her mother turned to Anna with a radiant face after watching a sunset and said, "Anna, heaven may be a happier place than the earth, but it cannot be more beautiful" (*The Comstocks of Cornell*, p. 57).

Another lesson children should learn from nature study is that "nature's laws are not to be evaded. Wherever he looks, he discovers that attempts at such evasion result in suffering and death" (p. 2), a lesson humanity continues to evade at its own peril but one that nature writers continue to emphasize.

Comstock equates mental health in later life with love of nature, writing, "Out in this, God's beautiful world, there is everything waiting to heal lacerated nerves, to strengthen tired muscles, to please and content the soul that is torn to shreds with duty and care" (p. 3), surely a commentary on her own life. But she regrets that for most men to enjoy the outdoors, "they must go out and try to kill some unfortunate creature"—what she calls "sacrificial blood." Her hope is that "through properly training the child [in nature study] the man shall be enabled to enjoy nature through seeing how creatures live rather than watching them die" (p. 2). On the other hand, she cautions teachers "never [to] magnify the terrors of death. Death is as natural as life and is the inevitable end of physical life on our globe. . . . a circumstance common to all" (p. 12).

Comstock also clearly distinguishes between nature study and biological science, declaring that science "begins with the simplest animals and plants and progresses logically through to the highest forms . . . [in order] to give the pupils an outlook over all the forms of life and their relation one to another." Nature study, on the other hand, "begins with any plant or creature which chances to interest the pupil" (p. 5)—for instance, those click beetles Comstock smuggled into school when she was a child. "Nature-study is science brought home. It is a knowledge of botany, zoology, and geology as illustrated in the dooryard, the cornfield or the woods back of the house" (p. 21).

Comstock wants teachers to encourage children to be close observers of living creatures and to realize that they have the chance to "see things never yet recorded in scientific books" (p. 11). She also hopes teachers can inculcate in children a "reverence for life. . . . exemplifying and encouraging the humane attitude toward the lesser creatures, and repressing cruelty which wantonly causes suffering" (p. 12).

Finally, Comstock reiterates another of her favorite themes, asking teachers to go beyond the naming of species by emphasizing the "why," instead of the "what," an idea that has been embraced by generations of nature study teachers. She also illustrates ways nature study can be integrated with the standard school subjects—geography, history, English, arithmetic and art—practical, creative advice that, for the most part, still has not penetrated the standard school curriculum. She concludes by italicizing the following statement: *"The chief aim of this*

volume is to encourage investigation rather than to give information" (p. 24), which summarizes her own style in all the books she wrote about nature.

The best-seller status of the *Handbook of Nature-Study* was the crowning point of Comstock's life. Two years after its publication, she was finally made an assistant professor at Cornell. In 1914 her husband retired, but she continued teaching and writing, publishing *The Pet Book* that same year under the Comstock Publishing Company imprint. The pets she discusses are both domestic—cats (which she was particularly fond of), dogs, bantams, pigeons, canaries—and wild—porcupines, alligators, crayfish, turtles, owls, for instance. She claims that teachers and Scout groups had asked for such information so they could make nature study more interesting. She also wants to save from death the many wild creatures children take home as pets, by providing proper food and care information. Such a book had never been written before, so she had called on curators at the New York Zoological Gardens for advice. As usual, in addition to specific how-to instructions followed by bibliographical information at the end of each chapter, she includes natural history, anecdotes, and poems (most of which are unsigned and seem to have been written by her). She illustrates the book with a wide selection of black and white photographs from friends, colleagues, and popular periodicals.

Much information from the *Handbook of Nature-Study* and some of the anecdotal material is reworked and reused in *The Pet Book*, specifically "The Pet Note-book," which Comstock footnotes as "from the Author's *Handbook of Nature-Study*" (p. 79). The notebook includes a day-by-day account of her attempt to raise a baby red squirrel she named "Furry." By reprinting her account she hopes to encourage children who have pets to keep their own notebooks.

As in *The Ways of the Six-Footed*, Comstock refuses to write down to children, and she painlessly imparts a good deal of information to young readers. Even snakes get an enthusiastic endorsement from her as "absorbingly interesting" pets that are "wonderfully constructed"

(p. 267). She includes a photograph of a small child holding one snake in her lap while another curls about her neck and captions it: "The Little Child Loves Living Playthings" (p. 268). Subtle propaganda indeed for what are still nature's most despised creatures, even by many who profess themselves to be nature lovers.

In *The Pet Book*, as in all her other nature books, Comstock writes matter-of-factly about all aspects of nature and of nature's creatures as part of the intricate web of life that is to be respected, instead of being judged by human moral standards. Such an attitude was not always present in nature writers of the period, especially those who wrote for children.

Honors and Awards

The Pet Book was Comstock's last book, although she continued writing nature study leaflets for schoolchildren. In 1917 she assumed the editorship of the *Nature Study Review,* for which she had been writing ever since its founding in 1905. In July 1919, Cornell made Comstock a full professor, a tribute to her long service to the university as well as to the Department of Nature Study she had developed. But despite being of retirement age, she continued formal teaching for two more years, conducting her last official class in the now-old Insectary in January 1921.

Comstock continued her classes in the Cornell University summer sessions, as well as her public speaking. She also was persuaded to run for Cornell alumni trustee in 1922 and 1923, in an attempt by alumnae to elect a woman; she lost both times despite endorsements from Cornell Women's Clubs. Although the male graduates of the College of Agriculture supported her, most alumni would not vote for a woman.

One honor Comstock received that pleased her very much was her initiation into the Phi Kappa Phi honorary society in 1922. She was flabbergasted when she picked up the *New York Times* on 6 May 1923 and learned that she had been named by the League of Women Voters as one of the twelve greatest living women in America. At first she thought they had made a mis-

take, but she was finally persuaded that she was the personage—chosen in the field of natural history—and furthermore, as her husband reassured her, that she deserved the honor. After all, her *Handbook of Nature-Study* had sold over 40,000 copies and had affected the lives of many children.

"Harry [as she called her husband] always comforted me in my perplexities and crises" (*The Comstocks of Cornell*, p. 264). He had, in fact, been the center of her life and she had been his, so much so that she could write, "For Harry and me, November 4, 1924, was one of the great days in our lives, for on that day his book of 1,064 pages, *An Introduction to Entomology,* was published" (*The Comstocks of Cornell,* p. 265). He was called the greatest teacher of natural history that America has known, but his best pupil had been his wife who, even after her novel was finished, would not send it to a publisher before he read it and gave it his stamp of approval.

Two years after their great day came the "calamity which, for us, ended life. All that came after was merely existence." On that sad note, Comstock concluded *The Comstocks of Cornell* (p. 267) after her husband had a series of strokes that left him speechless and helpless. For four years Comstock struggled on, caring for her "precious invalid" even as she ignored her own health problems and continued her exhausting schedule of lectures and classes.

In 1930 Comstock traveled to Geneva, New York, to receive an honorary Doctor of Humane Letters from Hobart College. Two weeks after teaching her last summer class in her home, she died of cancer on 24 August 1930. Her husband died seven months later.

The lengthy obituary for Comstock in the *Ithaca Journal News* the day following her death was a paean of praise to her from friends who mentioned her "breadth of human sympathy" and her pioneer work in nature study. It was her colleague Liberty Hyde Bailey who best summed up Comstock's life. She "blessed us all," he said. "She leaves a fragment memory of high achievement, noble service, unselfish co-operation, constructive counsel, inspired teaching, loving kindness and unforgettable companionship. Her life was a poem" (Bonta, *Women in the Field,* p. 166).

Selected Bibliography

WORKS OF ANNA BOTSFORD COMSTOCK

BOOKS

A Manual for the Study of Insects (Ithaca, N.Y.: Comstock, 1895), written with John Henry Comstock; *Ways of the Six-Footed* (Boston: Ginn, 1903), repr. with a foreword by Edward H. Smith (Ithaca, N.Y.: Cornell Univ. Press, 1977); *How to Know the Butterflies: A Manual of the Butterflies of the Eastern United States* (New York: Appleton, 1904), written with John Henry Comstock; *How to Keep Bees: A Handbook for the Use of Beginners* (New York: Doubleday, Page, 1905); *Confessions to a Heathen Idol* (New York: Doubleday, Page, 1906), written under the pseudonym Marian Lee; *Handbook of Nature-Study* (Ithaca, N.Y.: Comstock, 1911; 25th ed., Ithaca, N.Y.: Cornell Univ. Press, 1986); *The Pet Book* (Ithaca, N.Y.: Comstock, 1914); *Trees at Leisure* (Ithaca, N.Y.: Comstock, 1916); *The Comstocks of Cornell: John Henry Comstock and Anna Botsford Comstock,* ed. by Glenn W. Herrick and Ruby Green Smith (Ithaca, N.Y.: Cornell Univ. Press, 1953).

PAPERS

The papers of Anna Botsford Comstock are housed in the Department of Manuscripts and University Archives, Cornell Univ. Libraries.

BIOGRAPHICAL AND CRITICAL STUDIES

Marcia Myers Bonta, *Women in the Field: America's Pioneering Women Naturalists* (College Station: Texas A&M Univ. Press, 1991) and, as ed., *American Women Afield: Writings by Pioneering Women Naturalists* (College Station: Texas A&M University Press, 1995); Audrey B. Champagne and Leopold E. Klopfer, "Pioneers of Elementary-School Science: II Anna Botsford Comstock," *Science Education* 63 (1979), which includes a bibliography; Kathleen Jacklin, "Comstock, Anna Botsford," in *Notable American Women, 1607—1950,* vol. 1, ed. by Edward T. James (Cambridge, Mass.: Belknap, 1971); Arnold Mallis, *American Entomologists* (New Brunswick, N.J.: Rutgers Univ. Press, 1971); James G. Needham, "The Lengthened Shadow of a Man and His Wife," in *Scientific Monthly* 62 (February 1946 and March 1946); Ruth Sawyer, "What Makes Mrs. Comstock Great?" in *Woman Citizen* 28 (20 September 1924); Edward H. Smith, "The Comstocks and Cornell: In the People's Service," in *Annual Review of Entomology* 21 (1976) and "Anna Botsford Comstock: Artist, Author, and Teacher," in *American Entomologist* 2 (summer 1990); Deborah Strom, ed., *Birdwatching with American Women: A Selection of Nature Writings* (New York: Norton, 1986); William G. Vinal, "The Science Janus," in *School Science and Mathematics* 53 (May 1953); Bill Vogt, "National Wildlife Federation's Conservation Hall of Fame: Anna Botsford Comstock," in *National Wildlife* 26 (October/ November 1988).

SUSAN FENIMORE COOPER
(1813–1894)

LUCY B. MADDOX

WHEN RALPH BIRDSALL published the *Story of Cooperstown* in 1917, he devoted one page of his history of the small New York town to recalling the life and work of Susan Fenimore Cooper, a member of the town's most famous family. Birdsall noted briefly that Cooper, whom he identified as "a daughter of the novelist," had gained some distinction within Cooperstown for her "knowledge of the birds and flowers of [the] Otsego hills" and some recognition beyond Cooperstown as a "graceful writer." But he made it clear that, from his point of view as a local historian, the work for which she would best be remembered was her activity on behalf of two civic institutions: the Orphan House of the Holy Saviour, founded by Cooper in 1873, and the Thanksgiving Hospital, which, according to Birdsall, "originated in Miss Cooper's heart and mind." Although this brief testimonial to Cooper's accomplishments may have accurately reflected the local estimation of the "somewhat prim" eldest surviving daughter of Cooperstown's best-known resident, James Fenimore Cooper, it underestimated both the success she achieved as a writer during her lifetime and the attention that some of her writing would continue to attract long after her death. For contemporary readers, Susan Fenimore Cooper is best known not as a doer of charitable deeds but as a writer, and especially as the author of *Rural Hours* (1850), a book that is coming to be seen as a small classic of American nature writing.

Rural Hours is the journal of a year, composed of Cooper's sharp observations of plant, animal, and human activity through the course of the four seasons as she walked, rode, and rowed around Cooperstown and its environs. In recording her observations and her responses, Cooper generally avoids using the pronoun "I," preferring instead the more self-effacing "we." Whatever her reasons for this choice (she may have had one or more companions on most of her forays, and was therefore simply being accurate), the plural pronoun affects the reader as a reminder of Cooper's strong ties, through her family, to the place she describes. When she calls Cooperstown "our village" or speaks of "our trees," Cooper's language locates her within the community that is her subject; at the same time, it locates her within the family that had more reason than most to think of Cooperstown as its own.

The village was founded in 1789 by Susan's paternal grandfather, William Cooper, who rose to prominence (and some notoriety) in the area as a land developer and an active and outspoken Federalist politician. It was this Judge Cooper, as he later became known, for whom the village was named; it was also Judge Cooper who wrote the first of the books about the Cooperstown area that were to issue from the family. His book, *A Guide in the Wilderness; or, The History of the First Settlement in the Western Counties of New York with Useful Instructions to Future Settlers*, was published in 1810; his son, James Fenimore Cooper, set his novel *The Pioneers* (1823) in the area that became the site of Cooperstown; when James's daughter Susan published *Rural Hours* in 1850, she extended into the third generation the family practice of writing about the town that carried their name.

Early Life

Although Cooper spent virtually all of her adult life in Cooperstown—from the age of twenty-three until her death there on 31 December 1894, at the age of eighty-one—most of her youth was spent elsewhere. She was born at Mamaroneck, New York, on 17 April 1813 and given her mother's name, Susan Augusta (she added Fenimore to her name later, in 1826). Her parents returned to the family home at Cooperstown before Susan was a year old. In 1817, Fenimore Cooper moved to Scarsdale, New York, with his growing family and established a farm there, which he named "Angevine." It was here that he wrote his first novel, *Precaution* (1820), and that Susan was given her first schooling, with her mother as her teacher. The proper education of his children was always a priority for Fenimore Cooper, and it was largely for this reason that in 1822 he once again moved his family, this time to New York City. They rented a house on Beach Street, next door to a boarding school for girls to which Susan and her younger sister were sent. Susan later recalled that she was punished for disobedience at this school by having to wear a pig's foot around her neck and that she appalled her father by reporting that she was required to write a composition on the differences between the characters of Washington and Franklin.

In part because the Coopers despaired of finding a school in the United States where their daughters could be properly educated and "finished," they moved the family to Europe in 1826, settling in Paris. The girls were estab-

lished in a school there, where they were taught—evidently to the satisfaction of their parents—music, drawing, and dancing as well as literature, history, and languages (Susan eventually became proficient in four languages and sometimes wrote letters to her friends in an elegant French). The family remained in Europe until 1833, using Paris as their primary residence and taking extended trips to Switzerland and Italy. Susan's recollections of these European travels later found their way into *Rural Hours* in her frequent comparisons between country life in the United States and in various parts of Europe.

Susan's relationship to her novelist father, which had always been close, took a new turn during their European stay: in the winter of 1831–1832, when Susan was eighteen, she began serving as Fenimore Cooper's copyist and general secretary, a service she continued to perform until his death in 1851. In return, her father (who was still calling her "so dear a child" when she was nearing forty) was strongly protective of his daughter, discouraging any suitors—including, if rumor may be trusted, Samuel F. B. Morse, who subsequently acquired wealth and fame as the inventor of the telegraph. He expressed his concern about her future in a letter written shortly before his death: "I am horribly afraid for [Susan]. She is so pretty, and good, and engaging, and all that, I fear some fellow will be after her." Her father prevailed, and Susan never married.

If Fenimore Cooper's solicitude for his oldest surviving daughter seems in some ways repressive, it is also the case that he encouraged her intellectual growth and independence by actively supporting her efforts and ambitions as a writer. Without his confidence in her and his wish to please her, it is possible, perhaps even likely, that *Rural Hours* would never have been published. When Susan gave him the manuscript of her book to read, he responded in a letter to her by praising the "purity of mind, the simplicity, elegance, and knowledge" in her writing, and expressed his conviction that the book would be successful. To help ensure that success, Fenimore Cooper personally negotiated with the publisher, Putnam, on behalf of his daughter, encouraging the publication of a "fine" edition to follow the first printing; he also located a second publisher in London whom he persuaded to bring out an English edition.

The Coopers' European stay ended in November 1833. The family returned to New York City and, three years later, to Cooperstown, where they took up residence in the remodeled Otsego Hall, the family home originally built by Judge William Cooper. Susan was to remain in Cooperstown for the rest of her life, living in Otsego Hall until it was destroyed by fire in 1852, when she and one of her sisters moved into the much smaller Byberry Cottage, which they never left. Those who remembered Susan (or stories about her) in her later years spoke of her as "a noble woman" or even "a saint," describing her as slightly built, going about her charitable work in the village in spite of her deafness, wearing her trademark bonnet and paisley shawl. Ralph Birdsall's portrait of the older "Miss Cooper," although admiring, suggests that she may have gained a reputation as something of an eccentric local character:

> She would best be represented in the midst of orphan children whom she catechises for the benefit of some visiting dignitary, while the little rascals, taking advantage of her growing deafness, titter forth the most palpable absurdities in reply, sure of her benignant smile and commendatory "Very good; very good indeed!" (p. 305)

Her nephew (also named James Fenimore Cooper) reinforced the image of Cooper's eccentricity by reporting, in his *Legends and Traditions of a Northern County* (1921), that his Aunt Susan achieved considerable local fame as a psychic who demonstrated her powers for family and friends by moving heavy objects through the power of concentration. (According to this nephew, on more than one occasion she succeeded in moving a dining table on which a man was seated atop a pile of books.)

The years of Susan Fenimore Cooper's life between her return from Europe as a young woman and her philanthropic and psychic activities as an older woman are difficult to reconstruct, although we do know that she remained her father's amanuensis until 1851. The best evidence we have of what the rest of her life must have been like comes from the record of her own writing. The local knowledge she displays in *Rural Hours* suggests that much of her time was given to exploratory excursions in and around Cooperstown; and the general knowledge displayed there, including her familiarity with a range of works of literature, history, travel, theology, zoology, and botany, suggests that she spent much time reading. Perhaps more important, the record provides evidence that Cooper was actively writing, editing, and publishing during most of her years in Cooperstown.

Elinor Wyllys

Her first published book was a novel, *Elinor Wyllys; or, The Young Folks of Longbridge*, published in 1846, which she signed with the name "Amabel Penfeather." Because the name is so obviously a whimsical invention, and because the editor of the novel was identified on the title page as James Fenimore Cooper, it was long assumed that the father, rather than the daughter, was the real author, disguising himself as editor. Susan's authorship was not established until 1934, when Robert E. Spiller (in *A Descriptive Bibliography of the Writings of James Fenimore Cooper*) produced evidence from the Cooper correspondence that settled the question persuasively.

The novel is set in a small community in upstate New York that bears considerable resemblance to Cooperstown. The plot of the novel focuses on the title character, an orphaned young woman whose most distinguishing characteristics are quiet intelligence, moral sturdiness, and physical plainness. Although Cooper clearly sees these qualities as appropriate for a true American heroine, they make the character almost invisible in the fictional community of Longbridge: she was "too modest for her intelligence to be generally known or cared for; while her personal appearance exposed her to be entirely overlooked and neglected by strangers" (vol. 1, p. 41). Elinor changes little, if at all, in the course of the novel, maintaining her quiet, simple dignity in the face of the changing fashions—material and intellectual—that consume the energy of her peers.

Elinor is both the product and embodiment of the values Cooper sees in the simple life of rural America, and the greatest threat to her comfort and self-confidence comes from her acquaintances who have become convinced, through their reading of "foreign" novels, that aristocratic Europe offers women a richer, freer, more exciting life than they can have in America. Elinor's constancy is eventually rewarded by the love of her cousin Harry Hazlehurst, who has tasted the delights of European life and almost makes the disastrous mistake of marrying a woman who attracts him by her sophistication and physical beauty. Virtue ultimately triumphs, however; more specifically, the distinctively American virtues of plainness and simplicity triumph over the attractions—here identified as European— of artificial beauty and moral complexity.

By naming foreign novels as one of the sources of the frivolousness of many of the young women who surround Elinor in Longbridge, Cooper establishes a theme that underlies all her subsequent writing: American readers, especially female readers, need to be provided with American books that will lead them to respect and appreciate their homeplaces and be content to remain in them. With *Elinor Wyllys* and the works that followed, Cooper offered her contributions to a library of appropriate books for American readers.

Rural Hours

There is evidence from Fenimore Cooper's letters that in 1848 Susan had finished another work of fiction, titled "The Lumley Autograph," that her father attempted to place in the London publication *Miscellany*. "Depend on it," he wrote to the publisher, Richard Bentley, "it is clever, and will do your magazine credit." Apparently Bentley refused the manuscript, and it never appeared in print.

Cooper's next publication was *Rural Hours*, a book whose commercial success seems to have surprised even her most enthusiastic supporter, her father. Fenimore Cooper had assured his daughter that her book would be ultimately well received, although he cautioned her that "at first the American world will hesitate to decide." The first American edition, published by Putnam in 1850, was followed later in the same year by a two-volume British edition, and then by a "fine" illustrated edition from Putnam in 1851, with twenty-one color plates. The illustrated edition was reprinted by a different publisher in 1854, and a second British edition appeared in 1855, under the title *Journal of a Naturalist in the United States*. Two more American editions were to follow. In the 1868 edition, Cooper added a new preface in which she mentioned the changes that had occurred in Cooperstown in the eighteen years since the book first appeared. Noting the coming of the telegraph, the addition of gaslight, and the near approach of the railroad, Cooper wrote equivocally: "One scarcely knows, whether to mourn or to rejoice over this event in our history. Progress, alas, is not always improvement."

A final American edition of *Rural Hours* appeared in 1887, with the original preface restored and with a significant reduction in the amount of text: this version is nearly 200 pages shorter than the original, with most of the brief notations on the weather omitted, as well as some of the longer and more didactic passages, most of them explorations of biblical themes. Cooper's only addition to the preface of this edition is a brief note: "The present edition is a revised one, and some passages not needed to-day have been omitted." By this point, Cooper must have realized that her readers would not need to have it pointed out to them in a prefatory note that rural life in upstate New York had changed dramatically between 1850 and 1887; her text would speak for itself, as a record of a life that used to be.

The most significant of Cooper's publications after *Rural Hours* were editions of the work of others. In 1853 there appeared an edition of the English naturalist John Leonard Knapp's *Country Rambles in England; or, Journal of a Naturalist*. In her introduction, Cooper praised Knapp (along with Gilbert White) as one of those writers whose work seems artless, as if it "opened spontaneously, one might almost say unconsciously, from the author's mind." Knapp's artlessness, she implies, comes from his comfortable familiarity with the local landscape and from his access to a language, a system of naming, that brings words and things into easy conformity. She took the occasion of this introduction to reiterate her concerns — already expressed in *Rural Hours* — about the absence of an indigenous naming system in the United States and the problems that created for the project of consolidating a national identity. Americans are, she argued in the introduction to Knapp, "half aliens to the country Providence has given us"; because Americans are given to reading English books while living in an American landscape, the "forms of one continent and the names and characters of another, are strangely blended in most American minds." As a result, she continued, in language that anticipates Thoreau's in *Walden*, most Americans are content to live their lives in a "dream-like phantasmagoria," where daily language and daily experiences are constantly at variance (pp. 16–17).

The edition of Knapp was followed in 1854 by an anthology of nature poetry by various writers, entitled *The Rhyme and Reason of Country Life; or, Selections from Fields Old and New*, in which Cooper provided a long introduction to a collection of poems, arranged by subjects that vary from "The Bee" and "The Butterfly" to "The Forest" and "Evening and Night." In this introduction Cooper expresses her uneasiness about the growth of cities in the United States, with their attendant distractions: commercial speculation, political contentions, the growth of science, and especially a "spirit of personal ambition and emulation." The fevered life of the cities is exciting and attractive to Americans, she notes; this attraction is balanced, however, by an instinctive love of nature that Cooper identifies as part of the national character and therefore

Susan Fenimore Cooper

part of the national literature: "Probably if an experienced critic were called upon to point out some general characteristic of American poetry, more marked than any other, he would, without hesitation, declare it be a deeply-felt appreciation of the beauty of the natural world" (p. 31).

This affinity for natural beauty, instinctive though it may be, still requires encouragement and cultivation; hence her anthology, kept to a size that would make it easily portable, in which the work of poets from various ages and countries is offered as a reminder to American readers of their special advantage in being able to retreat so easily to those rural places that have always been the poet's greatest source of inspiration. The volume was dedicated to the American poet William Cullen Bryant, who had been one of the first to praise Cooper's own work in *Rural Hours*.

The anthology was followed in 1858 by *Mount Vernon: A Letter to the Children of America* — a patriotic celebration of the life of George

Washington that ends with an appeal for funds to aid in the preservation of Mount Vernon — and, in 1861, by her first edition of her father's work: *Pages and Pictures, from the Writings of James Fenimore Cooper, with Notes by Susan Fenimore Cooper*. This volume consists of a biographical sketch of Fenimore Cooper and excerpts from twenty-five of his novels, with Susan's notes and comments on each. These notes Cooper later revised and expanded into introductions to a new edition of Fenimore Cooper's novels, commissioned by Houghton Mifflin in 1876.

As this partial record indicates, Cooper devoted much of her energy to compiling, editing, and promoting the work of others, especially that of her father; yet contemporary readers are coming to know her primarily as the author of *Rural Hours* — the work that her father had praised so highly for its simplicity and sweetness. When the book was first issued, *Harper's Magazine* (June–November 1850) offered a brief favorable review, echoing Fenimore Cooper in calling *Rural Hours* charming and unpretentious, characterized by an "intellectual honesty and simplicity" that "a more ambitious style of composition would never have been able to command." Her simple style allows the reader to see things as they actually are, the review continues, without any "artificial gloss." Noting that the author (identified on the title page only as "A Lady") was reported to be the daughter of the distinguished Fenimore Cooper, the *Harper's* reviewer complimented Susan's accurate observation and vigorous description by declaring them "not unworthy of her eminent parentage."

Susan Cooper surely must have been pleased by this review, both for its emphasis on the simplicity and honesty of her writing and for its favorable comparison between her literary skills and those of her father. She had dedicated the volume to "the author of *The Deerslayer*," withholding her own name and disclaiming any literary ambitions for herself by declaring in the preface that hers was only a "simple record of . . . little events" that was done purely "for the writer's amusement." The text itself, however, constantly gives evidence of a strong authorial presence; Susan Cooper writes intelligently, knowingly, and with a firm authority, shaping her material carefully and frequently using her observations of Cooperstown life as the occasion for small, sometimes didactic essays on subjects that are apparently close to her heart. The position she assumes is one that might now be called that of the participant observer; she speaks both for and about the rural community of Cooperstown, placing herself within the collective "we" that represents the community and yet able to view the life around her with the critical and analytical eye of the ethnographer.

One of the earliest entries in the book, that for 22 March, describes the "joy of the whole community" at the return of the robins to the vicinity. "It is one of the great events of the year for us . . . we have been on the watch for them these ten days." The book thus opens with mention of two spring rituals: the annual reappearance of the robins, and the watch kept by the citizens of Cooperstown for a first sight of the returning migrants. This passage about the robins establishes a general pattern that characterizes the book as a whole. Through the course of a year of observations, arranged chronologically, Cooper follows the seasonal cycles of human and nonhuman life in the country, noting the interdependence of the two, as well as the predictability of certain occurrences among the human population and the plants and animals.

The appearance of the robins, for example, presages two other events that are as predictable as the return of the birds, and both of which Cooper describes in detail: the gathering of maple sap and the processing of maple sugar on the farms, and the annual flurry of spring housecleaning in the village. These accounts of ritualized human behavior, prompted by seasonal changes in nature, suggest why Cooper uses the word "rural" in her title: hers is a book about the inhabited countryside rather than the wilderness, about the happy fit between the simple, ordered lives of rural people and the ordered patterns of the natural world. Like the wild flowers they live among, which Cooper finds far superior to cultivated flowers, her country people have "freedom and a simple modest grace." In the landscape she surveys, both literally and figuratively, Cooperstown and its people occupy a prominent place:

The little town, though an important feature in the prospect, is not an obtrusive one, but quite in proportion with surrounding objects. It has a cheerful, flourishing aspect, yet rural and unambitious, not aping the bustle and ferment of cities; and certainly one may travel many a mile without finding a village more prettily set down by the water-side. (9 June)

The opening section of the book, "Spring," includes much more than accounts of village activity, however. Cooper keeps the reader posted on the gradual warming of the weather and the breaking up of the ice on the lake; the first appearances of many wildflowers—all of whose names she knows; the opening of the springs in the area; the return of the swallows and other migratory birds—all of whose names she also knows. She pauses in her observations occasionally to pursue some thought to which she has been led, as when she speculates about whether the trees on which the Israelites hung their harps in the biblical account were weeping willows or some other kind of willow (she hopes they were the weeping kind), or when she compares the natural beauty of a spring day to the illustrations that monks once added to manuscripts of the Bible.

In the process of recording her observations and comments, while never intruding directly into the narrative, Cooper gives the reader small glimpses into the life of this woman who drives about in a sleigh until the snow melts, then walks and rows on the lake until the winter closes in again, expresses her mild dislike for spiders and European weeds, measures a fallen tree with her parasol, patiently stands in one spot until she has counted ten different species of birds—"all varieties peculiar to America"—and even more patiently counts the seed-pods on a mullein spike, reporting the total to be 570.

The method and the content of the "Spring" section are reflected in the remaining three sections of the book: careful, detailed observation of

natural processes and phenomena is combined with ethnographic information on life in a rural New York village (which she describes at one point as "this school-going, lecture-hearing, newspaper-reading, speech-making community"), occasional forays into history and the natural history of other parts of the world, and frequent reminders—some of them homiletic in tone—that the beauty and harmony of nature are signs of the goodness of God in providing for his creatures. Even the excursive passages, however, are carefully situated in the text and tied to her observations of nature.

In the "Summer" section, for example, she muses skeptically on a line from a Mr. Tupper's *Proverbial Philosophy* that includes the image of a hummingbird feeding on a tulip, noting that she has watched hummingbirds for several seasons without ever seeing one visit a tulip. In the "Summer" section, she takes up the strange history of theories of swallow migration, recalling that swallows were for a time thought to lie torpid through the winter in caves or hollow trees, or to burrow in the mud at the bottom of rivers and lakes. These theories, she contends, must actually be of fairly recent origin, since ancient writers, including the prophet Jeremiah, include swallows among other migratory birds. Her conclusion is that the migration of swallows "seems only to have been doubted during a century or so; and among the achievements of our own age may be numbered that of a return to the simple truth on this point of ornithology" (23 August). The "Winter" section contains a disquisition on the rituals of Christmas and their importance to Christians; a celebration of the pleasures of an open wood fire; and a lengthy description of a typical country store, with an accompanying discussion of theories she has encountered that the word "store" is an Americanism and, therefore, a barbarism. Cooper staunchly defends both the institution of the store and its name: "The store, in fact, has taken its peculiar character, as well as its name, from the condition of the country; and the word itself, in this application of it, might bear a much better defence than many others which have found their way into books" (27 January).

Cooper almost never informs the reader of news that reaches her village from outside. She makes one exception in the case of reports of the gold finds in California, which she calls the "California gold mania," remarking that a group is forming in the county to head west, "and the notices are posted up on the village trees in every direction." A second exception is made for reports from around the state of sightings of a panther, an animal that Cooper says has not been seen in the vicinity for more than forty years. She is clearly intrigued by these reports and suspicious of them at the same time, wondering if wildcats are not being mistaken for the rare panther When a panther is ultimately reported very near Cooperstown, in an area where Cooper had walked only a few days before, she acknowledges that she would "have liked to have caught a glimpse of it—just near enough to decide the point, and to boast for the rest of one's days of having met a real live panther in our own woods!" (14 December).

The panther stories are anomalous among the entries in *Rural Hours* because of the surprise Cooper registers in hearing of the possible presence of the animal near Cooperstown. She is curious, she is skeptical, and she would like to see for herself—to discover the truth about the reports. Most of Cooper's entries in *Rural Hours*, on the other hand, give the impression—and they seem to do so deliberately—that she is not setting out to make discoveries or to test theories (the hummingbird–tulip conundrum is an exception in this case); instead, her journeyings outdoors most often lead her to see what she expects to see. Her method is not that of the scientist who is looking, through a process of experimentation, to add something new to the general store of knowledge. Her business is confirmation rather than discovery; for her, the natural world is like a familiar, sacred text that one rereads even though one already knows most of it by heart, and the disclosures of that world are most available to those who, like Cooper herself, are "content to await the natural order of things." Her entry for 15 May is typical of many:

Flowers are unfolding on all sides—in the fields, along the roadside, by the fences, and in the silent forest. One cannot go far, on any path, without finding some fresh blossoms. This is a delightful moment everywhere, but, in the woods the awakening of spring must ever be especially fine. . . .

Violets are found everywhere; the moose-flowers are increasing in numbers; young strawberry blossoms promise a fine crop of fruit; the whortleberry-cups are hanging thickly on their low branches, and the early elders are showing their dark, chocolate flower-buds, which we should never expect to open white. The ferns are also unrolling their long, colored fans. We gathered some ground laurel, but the squirrel-cups are forming their seeds.

What Cooper sees around Cooperstown often sends her back to her books for information, so that many of her entries include mini-lessons on the habits, life cycles, and geographical distribution of plant and animal species. The sources she cites are naturalists and travelers rather than scientists, and many of their names are familiar: Charles Buonaparte, Alexander Wilson, Alexander von Humboldt, Edward Jesse, Thomas Nuttall, John James Audubon. The entries in *Rural Hours* also include many references to other kinds of texts in which Cooper finds relevant information or references—especially the work of the British poets and the Bible. In the "Autumn" section she includes a long meditation on the representation of the season by "the poets of our mother-speech," noting with impatience that, until recently, autumn was invariably described in English poetry only as a melancholy season, with no attention given to its beauty. The poets who memorialized autumn did so, she contends, without paying much attention to what actually *happened* at that time of year; both Spenser and Thomson, for example, committed the error of setting the grain harvest in September in their poems, when "in truth the wheat-sheaf belongs especially to August, in England" (11 October).

This pattern of sentimentalizing autumn without regard to the facts has changed in the nineteenth century, she continues, as all descriptive writing has become less vague and general. She offers several reasons for the change: the influence of landscape painting, the preference for a less artificial style in gardening, and, especially, the example of American writers, who have helped to open the eyes of their more gloomy European contemporaries to the natural splendors of the season. The results have been entirely salubrious, for the European poets, following the American example, "learned at length to look at nature by the light of the sun, and not by the glimmerings of the poet's lamp. And a great step this was, not only in art, but in moral and intellectual progress" (11 October).

Cooper's references to the Bible are frequent, and they function consistently to reinforce her expressed belief that a study of nature not only is completely compatible with the Christian life; it is in fact an inducement to faith in the wisdom and beneficence of the Christian God and in the veracity of the Bible. Nature provides, she notes, "great and worthy illuminations of the written Word of God." At times she uses biblical texts as supplements, as when her note on the absence of gleaners in American wheat fields leads her to the book of Ruth for its account of gleaning, which in turn leads her to a lengthy commemoration of Ruth as a model of a life led simply, without artifice or ambition. At other times she turns to the Bible as a source of arcane information, which she is inclined to accept without question. For example, citing two Old Testament passages that include images of an eagle bearing its young on its wings, Cooper concludes that the "Eastern eagle" obviously was able to perform this astonishing feat, although she is characteristically cautious about taking the evidence too far: "whether the eagles in this part of the world resort to the same practice one cannot say."

The reviewer who originally praised *Rural Hours* for its simplicity and modesty was referring to the straightforward style, the accuracy of description, and the self-effacing stance of the author. However, simplicity and modesty are also subjects in Cooper's book; one could even

say that the most complex aspect of *Rural Hours* is its defense of simplicity—which Cooper sees as the quality that not only distinguishes life in America from that in Europe but makes it superior as well. Americans can learn a lesson from the excesses of Europe, which have left Europeans with little space that has not been cultivated or developed, and help to preserve the natural beauty of their own national place by learning the lessons of simplicity, best exemplified in the patterns of rural life. "Closer observation will reveal to us the beauty and excellence of simplicity," she writes, "a quality as yet too little valued or understood in this country. And when we have made this farther progress, then we shall take better care of our trees" (28 July).

In *Elinor Wyllys*, Cooper had written of the country-dwelling Elinor that "her whole manner . . . was always natural; its simplicity was its great charm, for one felt confident that her grace and sweetness, her ease and quiet dignity, flowed readily from her character itself." The equation suggested in this description is implicit throughout *Rural Hours*: because nature itself is simple, simplicity in human beings is therefore a sign of naturalness and integrity of character. Americans have the opportunity to learn the lessons of simplicity, and therefore to shape the moral character of their communities and their nation, by observing life in the abundant rural towns and villages of the country. Those rural places Cooper sees as having reached, in the middle of the nineteenth century, exactly the condition in which they best represent the industry, the restraint, and the interdependence of man and nature that characterize the country as a whole:

This general fertility, this blending of the fields of man and his tillage with the woods, the great husbandry of Providence, gives a fine character to the country, which it could not claim when the lonely savage roamed through wooded valleys, and which it must lose if ever cupidity, and the haste to grow rich, shall destroy the forest entirely, and leave these hills to posterity, bald and bare, as those of many older lands. (2 August)

The preservation of the American landscape, and with it the preservation of the moral qualities that set the young country apart from the countries of the Old World, depends on the ability of its citizens to live according to the rules of nature, especially the cardinal rule of simplicity.

Cooper explores a number of subjects that come under the general rubric of the need for simplicity. She expresses her concern at times, as in the passage cited above, that in their haste to push forward too quickly rather than awaiting "the natural order of things," Americans will fall into the pattern of exploitation that has left the hills of the Old World denuded and its rural villages too "close and confined." She notes with some anxiety the signs of European encroachment on the American scene, often betraying a clear distaste for whatever is "foreign" in the local landscape. Of introduced European plants, for example, she observes that "these foreign intruders are a bold and hardy race, driving away the prettier natives." On 6 June she complains of the number of weeds springing up that "do not belong here"; she goes on to list the names of fifty-four of these nuisance plants that "are now choking up all our way-sides, forming the vast throng of foreign weeds."

Her concern for preserving what is natural, indigenous, and therefore pleasing in the American rural landscape leads Cooper to protest the removal of churchyards to make room for roads and buildings; the trend toward more ornate architectural styles; the reckless extermination of game birds and animals, which she speculates may be "without a precedent in the history of the world"; the indiscriminate cutting of trees, especially old-growth forests; and even the disturbing changes in fashions and manners she sees taking place around her. The new trend toward cropped hair on women she sees as "all but unnatural," and she clearly disapproves of the "wildly extravagant dress" that has begun appearing on some of the young women of Cooperstown. An autumn visit to the school in the nearby community of Red Brook leads Cooper to a small dissertation on problems in the direction of American education. The two great principles of education, she pronounces, are impulse and restraint; whereas the former is being given ample room to flourish, the principle of restraint "seems to receive less consideration than it deserves." Her notion of a proper American education is inflexible: children should be taught "plain, sound, earnest lessons of piety, truth, honesty, justice, and self-discipline."

The subject that probably receives the most sustained attention from Cooper in *Rural Hours* is the inadequacy of American names for plants and places, which she describes as at best unsatisfactory and at worst in a deplorable state. In both cases the root of the problem is the persistence of Americans in imitating European — and especially English — practices. Her preference in naming plants is to use the terms by which they are known locally — "Indian turnip" is preferable to "dragon arum," for example — but the indigenous names are hard to come by, since so many of the country people are surprisingly ignorant of the names of the plants they live among. Without a local stock of names, Cooper finds the matter of naming plants not only problematic but personally frustrating to her as a writer who is concerned to be accurate. Some plants are called by several different names, some are erroneously called by the names of European plants they may or may not resemble, and some have only Latin names. "What has a dead language to do on every-day occasions," she asks, "with the living blossoms of the hour? Why should a strange tongue sputter its uncouth, compound syllables upon the simple weeds by the wayside?" (23 June). Cooper's frustration with the lack of American names for American plants leads her to one of the few genuinely comic moments in *Rural Hours*, as she speculates about what would have been the result if Shakespeare had not been able to name English plants with common, English names: "Fancy poor Ophelia prattling to Laertes about the wreath she had woven; instead of her 'rosemary,' and 'pansies,' and 'herb-o'grace,' hear her discourse about 'Plantanthera Blepheroglottis, or Psycodes, Ageratum, Syntheris, Houghtoniana, Banksia, and Jeffersonia'" (23 June).

The question of plant names is a matter of more than linguistic fussiness on Cooper's part. The need to find a fit between names and things is part of the larger need she sees for an American language that is organic, native, an outgrowth of the experience of the American environment, and therefore a language in which the names of things may sometimes be "thoroughly homely and rustic," even showing at times "a touch of quaint humor." An indigenous naming system would be an encouragement for future generations to take more interest—and more pleasure—in the natural environment, because it would allow children to learn the names of plants as easily as they learned the names of other common objects, without having to memorize the Latin terms in their botany lessons at school. In addition, and perhaps just as important for Cooper, a system of American names would allow American poets to "sing" their flowers as "sweetly" as Chaucer, Herrick, Burns, and Wordsworth sang theirs. In this matter of names, therefore, Cooper acknowledges, with great regret, the superiority of the English to the Americans.

This superiority also obtains, in her opinion, when it comes to the names of places. "Was there ever a region more deplorably affected with ill-judged names, than these United States?" she asks (7 February). With some exceptions, American place-names lack "fitness and propriety," once again reflecting Americans' resistance to adapting their language to their local experience.

> The passing traveller admires some cheerful American village, and inquires what he shall call so pretty a spot; an inhabitant of the place tells him, with a flush of mortification, that he is approaching Nebuchadnezzarville, or South-West-Cato, or Hottentopolis, or some other monstrously absurd combination of syllables and ideas. (7 February)

The names she most approves of are Indian names, because they reflect what she sees as the Indian propensity to give names that are descriptive of the particular characteristics of the place named. The Indian names are a legacy very much worth preserving and imitating, both as a way of inscribing the Indian presence on the American landscape—like many of her contemporaries, Cooper sees the Indians as rapidly becoming extinct—and because "the Indian," unlike his Yankee successors, "never gives an unfitting name to any object whatever." Although Cooper never comments on the name of her own village, named for her grandfather, she does provide lists of names she sees as appropriate for American places, and none of them are personal names. She offers a list of possible names that reflect the Indian habit of fitting a name to the physical characteristics of the place (Broadmeadows, Rivermead, Oldoaks); names that incorporate old Saxon place terms (rise, wick, burn, shire); and names that include terms reflecting the origins of the settlers of the place (heim, feld, champ, lock). In this case, as in the case of the names of plants, Cooper's concern is to domesticate the system of naming, to make language coterminus with the experience of the American place.

Cooper's obvious annoyance with the American system of naming is the result of her commitment in *Rural Hours* to giving readers a thoroughly American text that will attach them to their place and give them reasons for understanding the opportunities they have to demonstrate to the rest of the world the possibilities for living the good, simple life, a life in which experience, language, belief, and instinct come together into an organic whole. Her own directness and simplicity, her consistently optimistic tone, her conviction that the precepts of Christianity and the demands of rural life are ideally suited, her fascination with the shifting but predictable patterns of nature are also part of that same commitment. Rural America is, in her eyes, the place where human life can best be lived as it was meant to be lived, in harmony with the processes of the natural world. She offers her book as "a sort of rustic primer," as she puts it, a guide to the rudiments of rural life. Her optimism about the future of America is tinged with some anxieties that have in fact been borne out by subsequent events—her fear, for example, that the abundant woods of the country, especially the old-growth forests, would not survive, and her concern that with no restraints on hunting, many North American quadrupeds would disappear in the course of the next century. (Interestingly, this remark appears only a few pages after Cooper's statement that two varieties of wolf, the black and the gray, are quite common in New York state.)

Conclusion

Susan Fenimore Cooper has, thus far, received little scholarly attention; contemporary readers and critics have been slow to discover her work in spite of a reprinting of the shorter edition of *Rural Hours* in 1968. At first blush, the book may seem interesting primarily as an artifact, as an ethnographic document, or even as a utopian vision of a placid rural America that never really existed except in the mind of a patriotic Christian who loved her rather leisurely life in the country. It is surely worth reading for any of these reasons. But it is also very much worth reading for other reasons: as the work of a woman writer who believed strongly that women, whose occupations made them familiar with the small details of daily life, were appropriate interpreters and chroniclers of the cycles of nature; as the observations of an amateur naturalist who saw nature not as a rebuke or a corrective to human failings but as a confirmation of what is best and most promising in human nature; and, especially, as the notes of an observer with a keen eye, an abundant store of knowledge, a genuine love of the place she inhabited, and an indefatigable curiosity about what was happening outdoors. Reading *Rural Hours* makes one want to grab a walking stick (or a parasol), perhaps a pencil and paper, and set out to see what one can see.

Selected Bibliography

WORKS OF SUSAN FENIMORE COOPER

BOOKS

Elinor Wyllys; or, The Young Folks of Longbridge, 2 vols. (Philadelphia: Carey and Hart, 1846), written under the pseudonym Amabel Penfeather; *Rural Hours. By a Lady* (New York: Putnam, 1850; repr., 1868), repr. as new and rev. ed. (New York: Riverside, 1887), repr. with intro. by David Jones (Syracuse, N.Y.: Syracuse Univ. Press, 1968); *Mount Vernon: A Letter to the Children of America* (New York: Appleton, 1858); *Rear-Admiral William Branford Shubrick. A Sketch* (New York: n.p., 1877); *William West Skiles: A Sketch of Missionary Life at Valle Crucis in Western North Carolina, 1842–1862* (New York: James Pott, 1890).

WORKS EDITED BY COOPER

John Leonard Knapp, *Country Rambles in England; or, Journal of a Naturalist* (Buffalo, N.Y.: Phinney, 1853); *The Rhyme and Reason of Country Life; or, Selections from Fields Old and New* (New York: Putnam, 1854); *Pages and Pictures, from the Writings of James Fenimore Cooper* (New York: W. A. Townsend, 1861), repr. as *The Cooper Gallery* (New York: James Miller, 1865); *The Works of James Fenimore Cooper, with Introductions and Notes by Susan Fenimore Cooper*, 32 vols. (Boston: Houghton Mifflin, 1876–1884).

BIOGRAPHICAL AND CRITICAL STUDIES

Ralph Birdsall, *The Story of Cooperstown* (Cooperstown, N.Y.: Arthur H. Crist, 1917); James Franklin Beard, ed., *The Letters and Journals of James Fenimore Cooper*, 6 vols. (Cambridge, Mass.: Harvard Univ. Press, 1960–1968); Susan Levin, "Romantic Prose and Feminine Romanticism," in *Prose Studies: History, Theory, Criticism* 19 (September 1987); Lucy B. Maddox, "Susan Fenimore Cooper and the Plain Daughters of America," in *American Quarterly* 40 (June 1988).

H. L. DAVIS
(1894–1960)

PAUL T. BRYANT

AS POET, short-story writer, novelist, nature essayist, and critic, H. L. Davis situated his best work in the natural landscape of the American West, exploring the interaction of the people with that landscape. He came specifically to the nature essay only in the last decade of his life, but nature was a central and informing presence from the beginning. This construction of the Western landscape as a primary element in his work became both an artistic/aesthetic strength and a political/cultural hindrance for Davis' career as a writer.

Harold Lenoir Davis was born 18 October 1894 at Rone's Mill, an ephemeral sawmill camp near Nonpareil in Douglas County, Oregon. His father, James Alexander Davis, was a country schoolteacher who also trained draft horses and was a skilled marksman with firearms. These accomplishments were made more notable by the fact that he had lost a leg in a sawmill accident. Harold's mother, Ruth Bridges Davis, was the daughter of a Hard-Shell Baptist preacher. A strong woman, she held the family together—eventually there were four sons—under the strain of the frequent moves required of country teachers as schools opened and closed in temporary logging communities.

Harold's maternal and paternal grandparents had migrated to Oregon from Tennessee. The Bridges followed the Oregon Trail to the Umpqua Valley in 1852. Harold's paternal grandfather, Alexander Davis, was killed fighting for the Confederacy in the Vicksburg Campaign in 1863. His stepgrandfather Moser, sent to inform Davis' widow, returned to marry her after the war and moved the family, including young James Davis, to Oregon. This family history provided Harold with both a pioneering and a Southern/Tennessean heritage significant in the imaginative life from which his writing developed. It gave him his first sense of a people drawing their living from a land recently settled, bounded by remaining wilderness.

Until Harold was twelve, his family's moves—every two or three years—kept them in the valleys between the Cascade Mountains and the Coast Range of Oregon, a region of mild temperatures, plentiful rainfall, low mountain ridges covered with heavy timber, and rich valleys. As Davis later observed in his fiction, it was easy to gain a living there, but no one could get rich.

In 1906 the family made a longer move, to the town of Antelope, east of the Cascades in the high, dry plateau country. Instead of heavy timber and fertile, well-watered bottomlands, there were sagebrush plateaus supporting large cattle and sheep ranches, dryland wheat farming, and irrigation from the mountains to the west. Davis lived in Antelope only from 1906 to 1908, but the impression it made upon him is frequently reflected in the settings of his fiction. In the summer of 1907 he gained his first writing experience working for the local newspaper, the *Antelope Herald*, a job that gave him insight into community ways and foibles in the sagebrush country.

The Davises finally ended their peripatetic existence in 1908, when James became principal of the high school in The Dalles, on the Columbia River. This was the last move they were to make as a family. Harold regarded The Dalles as his home for twenty years. This river town in a sense completed his range of experience in Oregon. The Dalles was a trading center that handled river commerce, railroading, the movement of agricultural products to markets and of harvest hands, supplies, and equipment to orchards, farms, and ranches. A crossroads, it gave young Harold a microcosmic insight into the life of the whole region.

Davis graduated from high school in The Dalles in 1912, and soon thereafter became a deputy tax assessor for Wasco County, of which The Dalles was the county seat. In Wasco County the authority for collecting taxes was vested in the sheriff's office, and for that reason Harold was made a deputy sheriff. His responsibilities never actually included law enforcement, other than tax collection, but again the work helped him become more familiar with a broad spectrum of the people and the landscape in his region. In 1916 or 1917, he took a job with the U.S. General Land Office, surveying in the Mount Adams area of Washington, work that required long pack trips into the Cascade Mountains.

By the fall of 1917, Davis had saved $1,500. With this as a stake, he traveled to Palo Alto, California, intending to enroll in Stanford University to study engineering. When he arrived on the Stanford campus, he quickly discovered that his funds were not sufficient for a college education there. Although he returned to The Dalles without enrolling, he later claimed to have studied at Stanford.

On 23 September 1918, well after the United States had entered World War I, Davis was drafted into the army and sent to Fort McDowell, California, where he served as a clerk until his discharge, after less than three months of service, on 10 December. He later referred obliquely to serving in the cavalry, pursuing Pancho Villa in northern Mexico, but this was fiction. Indeed, much of the biographical information Davis provided in his years as a writer was more fiction than fact. In particular he offered various birth dates, from 1894 to 1904 (1894 is correct), various birthplaces, and a remarkable range of military experiences more exciting than a clerkship at Fort McDowell.

The Poetry

Davis' real accomplishment during three months in the army was sending a group of poems, collectively called "Primapara," to Harriet Monroe for publication in *Poetry*. Monroe enthusiastically accepted them for the April 1919 issue of the magazine, thereby beginning Davis' career as a published writer. The poems won the Levinson Prize for poetry in 1919. For the next decade Davis was primarily a poet, publishing a total of thirty-nine poems between 1919 and 1933.

Davis was astonished at the success of his first submission for publication. With the "Primapara" poems, Harriet Monroe announced the advent of a major new poet, whose "long lines and slow rhythms sounded a new music, a strain original and noble." To which Davis responded, in a letter to Monroe: "I was surprised to learn that you have found the poems of such merit. . . . There seems something suspicious about their turning out so well" (Monroe, *A Poet's Life*, 1938, p. 423). Monroe's enthusiasm was shared by others in the literary community. Carl Sandburg said that Davis was the "only poet" in the Pacific Northwest. Robinson Jeffers noted that although Davis' lack of interest in current trends in literary fashion might keep his work from gaining wider recognition, no other modern poet presented the countryside with such "Virgilian sweetness."

Much of the strength of Davis' poetry derives from this "Virgilian sweetness," the vivid, sometimes lyric, often elegiac presentation of the natural landscape that dominates most of the poems, leaving the human figures vague and indistinct. Jeffers wondered if this failure of clarity was reticence, haughtiness, or evasion that "blurs the composition a little." Whatever the reason, Davis' effective presentation of the natural landscape in his early poetry adumbrates the centrality of nature in all of his writing—short stories, sketches, novels, and essays as well as poetry.

Even in the earliest poems Davis uses a technique that might be called "praising by naming." Reminiscent of Walt Whitman's technique of cataloging, Davis involves the natural scene by naming elements within it— lists of flowers, types of forests, natural features on the land: "Wild bunches of blue lupin, rock roses, short wild hollyhocks/Belled close with red-orange, over fox-gloves and striped irises" ("Of the Dead of a Forsaken Country"). Such lists carry on through his prose, leading concrete specificity to his presentation of nature.

In the poetry, the cycles of the seasons, as well as the responses of the land to the efforts of the people to gain their living from it, become metaphorical parallels to the inner lives of those people. The moods of the characters, albeit presented indistinctly, even ambiguously, seem to be a reflection of the season, the weather, the vegetation. Sometimes it is farmland—the "old men" who have "put the hills in foal" ("The Old Are Sleepy")—and sometimes it is the margin between farmland and wild land, stubble and "the flood margin which they feared" ("A Field by the River").

This metaphoric correspondence between internal and external landscape, however, does not produce an idealized, abstract, or surrealistic nature. Davis' landscapes are real, concrete, vivid, detailed presentations drawn from close observation and intimate knowledge. Thomas Hornsby Ferril, himself a poet accomplished in presenting the Western landscape, has written that nature is never used in Davis' writing as

H. L. Davis

decorative stage setting: "I can open his poems at random and find luminous transfusions of life into nature and nature into life recalling primitive metamorphosis" (p. iv). Davis' landscapes are alive, Ferril concludes, but "you'll look in vain for pathetic fallacy" (p. iv). Davis' knowledge of plants and animals, "winds and waters," Ferril says, distinguishes him as "a superb ecologist" and a "naturalist of transitoriness," a quality of special significance for a writer of the West (p. iv).

By 1927 Davis' poetry had begun to include longer narrative works, and by 1928 he was writing prose sketches and short stories. With the publication of "New Birds" and "In Argos" (a long narrative poem) in *Poetry* in May 1933, his writing of poetry appeared to have ended. *Proud Riders and Other Poems,* published by

Harper in 1942, included only two short poems, "Mountain Autumns" and "Brynhild," and one longer, narrative poem, "The Deaf and Dumb Girl," that had not been published previously. However, in 1978 Ahsahta Press published *The Selected Poems of H. L. Davis*, a volume that included not only selections from *Proud Riders* but also fourteen previously unpublished works found in Davis' papers. Not all of these poems showed a date of composition, but of those that were dated, many were written as late as 1959, the year before his death.

Some of these late poems are little more than commentary on contemporary political and social situations, but some have substantial artistic merit. These more successful poems retain the vivid presentation of nature that so distinguishes Davis' earlier poetry, but they add a dimension lacking in his earlier work: the human voice, the human consciousness in the poem is presented more clearly, directly, vividly. The reserve—whether from haughtiness or shyness—that so troubled Jeffers has been overcome. Emotional response to the landscape by the persona of the poem is at last presented less ambiguously, more clearly and directly.

In one of these late poems, "A Stock-Taking," Davis articulates his theory of developing poetry through nature. Poetry, he writes, must come from the experience of the senses, "Of stones, earth, light, colors, running water, wind,/Reflections of light on blowing grass...," on hawks' wings and "red bushes in old snow." Such perceptions of the senses, he says, should lift the poem to some truth. For Davis that truth would not be abstracted metaphorically from the physical world of nature but would grow directly out of it.

These perceptions of the senses were brilliantly present in Davis' earliest work, always well grounded in nature. What was lacking early, but emerged in the late poems, is the clarity of the perceiver. Had Davis continued to write and publish poetry, rather than shifting to prose, he might have become an important twentieth-century American poet. As it was, the poetry clearly set the pattern for his use of nature as a central element in all of his writing.

The Sketches and Short Stories

By 1927 Davis had become friends with James Stevens, a proletarian poet, essayist, and novelist who gained wide recognition through his novels and Paul Bunyan stories. Davis' interest was moving toward prose rather than poetry, and he was characteristically keeping himself outside of the literary "establishment" in the Pacific Northwest. This maverick tendency was intensified in 1927 when he and Stevens published a small pamphlet attacking the Northwest's more prominent arbiters of literature, including editors and teachers of creative writing. This blast, ponderously titled *Status Rerum: A Manifesto, upon the Present Condition of Northwestern Literature, Containing Several Near-Libelous Utterances, upon Persons in the Public Eye,* provoked immediate outrage among the literary community, and marked Davis as the "outsider" that he remained throughout his career. It also shows the influence of H. L. Mencken, who had begun publishing work by both Stevens and Davis, and who was encouraging Davis to turn to prose. Glen Love has detailed the influence of Mencken on the development of the styles of both Stevens and Davis. Love concludes that *Status Rerum* "served to further establish the early literary personae of Stevens and Davis as it appears in their essays and fiction for Mencken's *Mercury* in the 1920s." These personae, Love says, were tough but ironic, "with a broad streak of humor and plenty of experience in the real world" (p. 333).

This assertion of independence in *Status Rerum* came at a crucial juncture in Davis' life. On 25 May 1928, Davis married Marion Lay, an aspiring writer. That same year, the political group in Wasco County with which his father had been allied was voted out of office, reducing his father's ability to help Harold gain employment. As a result, Harold and Marion left The Dalles and moved to Bainbridge Island, Washington, intending to earn their livelihood from writing. Also in 1928 Davis collaborated with Stevens on two short stories published in *Adventure* magazine. In Washington, Davis also worked with Stevens on a local radio program of

202

folk music, for which they composed the now widely known "folk" song "The Frozen Logger" ("I see you are a logger,/And not a common bum,/For no one but a logger/Stirs his coffee with his thumb"). Davis was an accomplished guitarist and knew hundreds of genuine folk songs in several languages. From that time he became primarily a writer of sketches, short stories, novels, and, late in his life, nature essays.

Making a distinction between Davis' sketches and his short stories may seem arbitrary, but such a division can be based both on formal grounds and, to some extent, on the dates of composition. The sketches are anecdotal, telling about a person, group, custom, place, or event, but without the clear plot line and dramatic development of a short story. Characterization through dramatic development does not appear in the sketches to the extent expected in a successful short story. For example, the sketch "Team Bells Woke Me" presents a picture of the latter days of wagon freighting but does not focus on the development of an individual character. In contrast, the short story "Old Man Isbell's Wife" is a unified presentation of a plotted series of related events that round out and show the significance of the life of a specific, three-dimensional pioneer character.

The works that can most clearly be classified as sketches were published between 1929 ("The Old Fashioned Land—Eastern Oregon") and 1933 ("American Apostle"). The short stories, on the other hand, were published between 1929 ("Old Man Isbell's Wife") and 1941 ("A Sorrel Horse Don't Have White Hoofs"), except for "The Kettle of Fire," a fable published in 1959.

As their titles suggest, Davis' sketches were drawn from his intimate knowledge of the land, the people, and their history on the land. James Potts has observed that Davis' "varied, numerous uses of nature and landscape, the element of place, link him with the Romantic and transcendental writers" (p. 120). Yet his presentation of the people in his sketches is not in the least romantic. The people—Indians, pioneers, descendants of the pioneers—he presents with a wry, ironic vision in the tradition of the frontier humor of Mark Twain and the Old Southwest. He does not romanticize the Native Americans as noble children of nature, but instead presents them as "a hard-riding, good-natured set of berry-peddlers who embarrassed townspeople by nursing papooses and settling family rows in the middle of the business district," or an old Piute with "a bunch of cavernous-gutted grown sons" who stayed with their father because he supported them, but who "weren't worth killing" ("Team Bells Woke Me"). Nor does he show the white settlers and their descendants as either villainous or heroic. Latter-day homesteaders are "dirty, sallow and starved," beating their horses savagely in the mud and looking "glary and scared." Their wagons contained "cold, half-naked children who sat and bawled monotonously, without opening their mouths" ("Back to the Land—Oregon, 1907"). They all have their full share of common human flaws and foolishness, selfishness and shortsightedness, ignorance of the past and false dreams for the future. This wry realism, particularly in such sketches as "A Town in Eastern Oregon," a thinly veiled caricature of The Dalles, earned Davis further resentment from his native region's boosters.

The land itself, on the other hand, is presented with unironic brilliance, a constant base of nature that endures under the burden of humans who draw their sustenance from it, or try to do so. At times the beauty and harmony of nature, and the strength and endurance of wild creatures, provide a contrast with the blindness of the humans who live surrounded by wild nature but learn nothing from it. Waves of settlement sweep over it and recede; nature covers the scars and returns. The land abides. The humor in Davis' sketches is always in the people. The beauty is most often in nature.

In contrast, the fictional characters in Davis' short stories do sometimes learn from nature and rise above their foibles and foolishness. Old Man Isbell, a senile survivor of pioneer times, and his fat, homely young wife, both initially comic figures, gain stature and dignity from old Isbell's deathbed reliving of his youthful adventures in the wilderness. In "The Homestead Orchard," one of Davis' best initiation stories, young Linus Ollivant learns from the beauty of blossoms in an abandoned orchard about endurance and the values of a close relationship with the land. The basic context of the lesson from the blooming of an abandoned orchard is a reworking of a theme initially explored in Davis' earlier poem, "Of the Dead of a Forsaken Country" (1926).

In another of Davis' initiation stories, "Open Winter," young Beech Cartwright learns courage and endurance on the drought-ridden grasslands, and survives the experience by his ability to find water for his horses. In effect, on the verge of giving up, Beech achieves sufficient insight into the ways of nature to know that water in a seep below cottonwood trees will come to the surface at night, when the trees are not drawing it up so rapidly. By living in nature, depending directly upon it, and learning from it, Beech gains greater understanding of himself and of the land. Similar patterns of growth through greater understanding of, and harmony with, the processes of nature can be found in many of Davis' stories.

The contrast between the sketches and the fiction—novels as well as short stories—becomes clear in comparison. The sketches present the too frequent historical reality of human failure to achieve harmony with the land. The fiction allows Davis to develop a character who learns to understand nature more clearly, and who grows as a result.

During the years in which Davis depended upon the sale of short stories for his income, he produced a number of potboilers, entertaining pieces that spun a good tale but had no particular depth or significance. Most of these were published in *Collier's* and the *Saturday Evening Post*, popular magazines with large circulations that paid good rates. Some of his short fiction, however, has the artistic richness and depth that merits continued attention. These include "Old Man Isbell's Wife" (1929), "Shiloh's Waters" (1930), "Beach Squatter" (1936), "Open Winter" (1939), "The Homestead Orchard" (1939), "Stubborn Spearmen" (first published in 1941 as "A Flock of Trouble"), and "The Kettle of Fire" (1959).

The theme of achieving understanding and harmony with the land is developed, in some of Davis' best stories, with traditional Christian symbolism. The Christian pattern of death and resurrection fits well, of course, with the cycle of the seasons and of the alternation of drought with life-giving rain. The fall of Adam and Eve and their expulsion from the Garden of Eden (their homestead orchard), followed by the redemption by Christ, the Second Adam, provides a symbolic background for initial alienation from, and disharmony with, nature, followed by new understanding and reconciliation with the processes of nature. Thus philosophical/religious insights come together with ecological concerns in some of Davis' best short fiction.

Davis' last published short fiction, "The Kettle of Fire," is a fable rather than a story with any pretensions to realism. In it he draws on Greek mythology, using both Oedipal and Promethean patterns. In the treatment of nature this fable is reminiscent of *Gulliver's Travels*: the young protagonist, in his quest for and return with fire for the wagon train, encounters a series of natural communities, each suffering from a particular vice or excess. Antelope make themselves vulnerable nuisances because of their curiosity. Sage rats create a wasteland in their self-absorbed conviction that only their own affairs are of any significance in the world. Owls are so blinded by daylight that they cannot perceive the reality around them. Jackrabbits procreate themselves into overpopulation, making their lives a diseased agony in which they continue to procreate. Geese emulate Swift's Yahoos by flying up in indignation, spattering young Capron with their filth. Mormon crickets become little more than unbridled appetites, denuding the countryside. Presented as natural phenomena in the fable, all of these excesses can be seen as parallels of environmentally destructive human behavior.

The story is fraught with error and foolishness and suffering: young Capron mistakenly kills his adopted father; he risks his life and suffers injury and privation; the settlers of the wagon train fail to find their own salvation and yet ignore Capron's service to them. Yet Davis, ill and soon to die when he wrote this fable, can conclude that humans can, and must always, find the need to bring home the fire, "through the same hardships and doubts and adversities of one's life that make up the triumph of having lived it" (*Kettle of Fire*, p. 189).

The Novels

Having left The Dalles and begun depending on his writing for a livelihood, Davis' finances were precarious at best. He and Marion moved to Arizona in 1930. There he applied for a Guggenheim Fellowship to Spain, where he proposed to work on a long poem. The initial application was not granted, and the Davises moved back to Washington. Then in 1932 the Guggenheim Foundation belatedly offered Harold an exchange fellowship to Mexico, which he accepted. The Davises moved first to Mexico City, then to Oaxaca, which was their home at various times for the rest of Harold's life.

There is no evidence that Davis ever worked seriously on the projected long poem. Instead, he continued to produce short stories and began serious work on his first novel, for which he had started making notes in 1930.

Although the Guggenheim grant had run out in a year, the Davises were still living in Oaxaca when Harold's first novel, *Honey in the Horn*, was published in 1935. A picaresque story of rural life in Oregon in the first decade of the twentieth century, *Honey* ranges from the Oregon coast through the central valleys to the arid eastern slope of the Cascades. In a prefatory note Davis claims that he tried to include "a representative of every calling that existed in the State of Oregon during the homesteading period—1906–1908," but had to give up the attempt for lack of space.

The structure of the novel might at first glance lend some credence to such a purpose. The protagonist, Clay Calvert, travels around various parts of Oregon, doing a variety of work and encountering others working at a wide range of occupations, but a closer look suggests that Davis' statement is another of his misdirection

jokes about his work. The story is more tightly structured than a loose catalog of occupations. It is an initiation story about a young man who has to learn about the nature of good and evil in human society, and the inevitable intertwining of the two. Clay, whose name suggests his Adamic quality, has to learn not only humanity's general capacity for evil as well as good, but also the inseparable mixture of good and evil in his own nature. The woman he loves, Luce (Spanish *luz*, light), serves as both Eve and Lilith in his initiation, and helps him come to terms with himself and with society. As John Lauber has pointed out, Clay is like Huck Finn, although Clay becomes reconciled to society rather than "lighting out for the Territories." The land, though, continues to be Edenic. The settlers achieve some level of social harmony among themselves, but they repeatedly misunderstand and fail to come to terms with the natural landscape.

When *Honey* won the Harper's Novel Prize for 1935, the Davises used a portion of the $7,500 prize money to purchase a car and set out for a visit to New York. In Tennessee, Marion became seriously ill with paratyphoid, and they were forced to remain at Horn Springs, near Nashville, through the winter while she convalesced. During this time Davis began work on another novel, which was to become *Beulah Land*. They were still at Horn Springs in the spring of 1936 when Davis was notified that *Honey in the Horn* had won the Pulitzer Prize for 1936.

With two prestigious literary prizes in hand, Davis moved to California, where he had bought a small "ranch" near Napa by the spring of 1937. At work on an early version of *Beulah Land*, he continued to publish short stories through 1941. From 1941 to 1947, at a time when Davis' rising reputation as a fiction writer might be expected to foster high output, Davis published no new fiction. In 1942 Harper's produced *Proud Riders*, a collection of already published poetry.

This six-year gap apparently was a result of two major difficulties in Davis' life, one personal and one professional. At the personal level, his marriage, often on uncertain ground, was in serious trouble. Its problems led to a final separation in February 1942, and formal divorce later that year. The professional problem was a dispute with Harper and Brothers over royalties for *Honey* and publication rights for subsequent work. Davis finally initiated legal action, and in June 1947 the matter was settled out of court.

In the meantime, Davis had become friends with Thayer Hobson, chief editor at William Morrow and Company, who expressed interest in his work. When the dispute with Harper's was settled, publication rights to Davis' writing were assigned to Morrow. By this time, he had two novels in manuscript. *Harp of a Thousand Strings* was published almost immediately (1947), and *Beulah Land*, on which Davis had been at work since 1936, appeared in 1949.

Critical reception of *Honey in the Horn* had been mixed, despite the prestigious prizes it earned. Critics in the Eastern literary establishment often were condescending toward books set in the American West, and in this case, even when they praised the novel, they tended to focus on local color. *Harp of a Thousand Strings*, on the other hand, presented a geographical range from Paris to Tripoli to the prairies of the American West. Whereas *Honey* seemed superficially to present a loosely connected series of picaresque adventures, the interwoven lives of a larger cast of characters in *Harp* were clearly a patterned illustration of a set of principles about the nature of human affairs. Critics accordingly were more willing to examine *Harp* as a serious, carefully crafted novel.

In the late 1940s and early 1950s, from his ranch near Napa and from Oaxaca, Davis was working as a researcher and writer for various motion picture studios. During this time he began to experience health problems, apparently involving arteriosclerosis and related heart disorders. Nevertheless, he continued to revise the manuscript for *Beulah Land*.

Beulah Land is both a chronicle of American westering in the nineteenth century and a study of white and Native American attitudes toward the land and human society. It follows the search of a half-white, half-Cherokee girl, and a white boy adopted by the Cherokees, for a place where love is possible without becoming destructive. The search begins in the Cherokee lands of the Carolinas, moves through the Midwest to the new Cherokee Nation in the Oklahoma Territory, and finally ends in the Pacific Northwest. Late in his life, Davis liked this novel best of the five he produced. The critics received it favorably, noting again that Davis presents the landscape more positively than the people in it.

Winds of Morning, published in 1952, was Davis' most successful novel. In it, he returned to the themes and patterns of *Honey in the Horn*, but with greater complexity. The setting is the back country of eastern Oregon. The plot involves a journey through the awakening spring landscape and presents an awakening—a double initiation—for a boy becoming a man and for an old man coming to terms with his past. As in "Open Winter" and "Homestead Orchard," the novel combines the turning of the season in a luminous spring landscape with the symbolic stories of Adam, Eve, Lilith, and Christ. Again humans struggle, err, and learn, while the land abides.

The success of *Winds* was followed in 1953 by publication of *Team Bells Woke Me*, a collection of previously published sketches and short stories. Davis' writing was going well, gaining recognition, and keeping him busy. He was still doing assignments for films, working on his next novel, and beginning work on a series of essays for *Holiday* magazine.

On 2 June 1953, Davis married Elizabeth Tonkin Martin del Campo, in San Antonio, Texas. This marriage was happier than his first, and his writing continued to go well until his health began to present serious problems. Acute arteriosclerosis required amputation of Davis' left leg in October 1956, while he was living in Mexico. Although he was not expected to survive for long, he lived and continued to write for four years. During that time he was never out of pain.

These were the conditions under which Davis completed and saw to publication his fifth novel, *The Distant Music* (1957). In many ways this novel is the inverse of Davis' previous four. Rather than the life of one or two central characters, it presents the history of a family through three generations. Rather than showing the central characters journeying through a changing landscape, this novel centers on a single piece of homesteaded land, showing how commitment to that land affects successive generations who own it, or are owned by it. Thus the landscape finally becomes not only the setting but also the center of the story.

James Potts has concluded that each Davis novel "contributes to our understanding of the ways in which people developed physical, emotional, and spiritual bonds with their land—what may be called Davis' conception of an American land ethic" (p. 119). This is especially important in his final novel.

Davis received early recognition for his poetry, and his sketches and short stories are still occasionally anthologized, but his novels have received the greatest sustained critical and popular attention. In particular, *Honey in the Horn* and *Winds of Morning* seem destined to survive as significant works of American literature.

The Nature Essays

Early in the 1950s, when Davis' career was at its height, he began a series of eleven articles for *Holiday* magazine. Nine focus primarily on the Pacific Northwest. The two that stay outside of that region are "The Wilds of Mexico" and "Palm Springs." These eleven might now be considered nature essays, although such a designation was not generally recognized at that time. Environmental concerns that Davis touches upon in these essays were only beginning to come into popular awareness at that time, helped along by such writers as Aldo Leopold, Rachel Carson, and Wallace Stegner, and by renewed interest in John Muir, John Burroughs, and Henry Thoreau.

Holiday was a large-format, widely circulated, expensively produced magazine on travel. It was able to command the work of some of the finest writers of the period, including A. B. Guthrie, Jr., Jack Schaefer, Donald Culross Peattie, Wright Morris, Rachel Carson, Jacques Barzun, and Arthur C. Clark, as well as Davis. That Davis was

a regular contributor in such company is an indication of his national recognition as a writer of the first rank.

In his introduction to Davis' *Collected Essays and Short Stories* (1986), Robert Bain notes that the tone of these essays is "a curious mixture of the voices of Thoreau and Mark Twain" (p. 10), and he is correct. The voice of Thoreau can be heard in the presentation of the landscape; the quite different voice of Twain enters with the presentation of the people in that landscape. Bain concludes, however, that "the voice that emerges from these small gems is Davis' own" (p. 10).

The first essay in this series, "Oregon," published in 1953, presents a broad view of the varied landscapes and human history in Davis' native state. He begins in the area where he was born, "the greentimbered valley country" between the Cascade Mountains and the Coast Range, "where people sometimes lived all their lives without having any idea what the naked earth looked like." His most detailed and graphic descriptions are reserved for the coast, with its clash of ocean against high headlands and its dense, rich vegetation. There, as in his poetry, he catalogs the trees in the forest, the wildflowers, the berries, and the wild animals. The vividness of his descriptions arises not from evaluative adjectives of "purple prose" but from the profusion of objective detail.

As Davis turns his attention to the country west of the Cascades, he places more emphasis on topography and weather than on wild flowers and fruits. The animals—mallards, snow geese, gulls, trumpeter swans, mule deer, antelope—also get greater attention. Except for the journey through Santiam Pass, the mountains are seen only from the distance of the eastern plateau. This is consistent with Davis' own experience. The mountains were a presence in his life in Oregon, but only as barriers that changed the climate or as sources of water for the crops.

The contrast in Davis' fiction between the lyric presentation of the beauty of the landscape and the wry, ironic view of the people who live there is quickly evident in these essays. The country was filling up with newcomers who built new roads and cottages and shacks, piled garbage in the creeks, and "fixed everything around to suit themselves." They want to experience wilderness, so they build a highway into it. This, Davis concludes, is like driving a red hot poker into a living tree, and then expecting the tree sap to begin circulating in the poker. But the people who do these things do not stay.

Because the people come and go, they know little of the true history of the country, seeing what is old as new, because it is new to them, and imagining a past that did not occur. Here Davis plays one of his Western humor tricks. While debunking a newcomer's idea of wild times at an old stage-stop hotel, he offers as the truth an even less probable tall tale about his grandfather shooting himself out of a third-floor hotel window by accidentally stuffing the tail of his nightshirt into a muzzle-loading shotgun. The humor is irresistible, but the physics are impossible. The newcomer's conventional expectations of a "wild West" history is illusion, Davis says, whereas his story of his grandfather is a tradition. Illusion is brought in from outside, but tradition grows up within the country. Both, the reader must observe, are pure fiction.

The movers, Davis says, come to Oregon and settle for a generation. The children then move away, and the first generation often follows. In this pattern, he finds a reversal of what the movers expected when they first came. They see it as new country, although it is not. They set out to change it to suit themselves, but the country changes them. They become "civilized" by the country rather than the reverse. As they learn to live with the land, rather than trying to remake it, they become more civil, more in harmony with their surroundings. The next generation, born into this newly developed civilization, leave, taking it with them to other places. The land civilizes the people by teaching them how to live.

Oregon, Davis says, has no complete stories of its own. They are all stories that have begun somewhere else and concluded in Oregon, or that began in Oregon and moved elsewhere. In this he returns to the thesis of *Harp of a Thousand Strings*. The West does not have its own,

isolated, special history. It is merely part of stories that began elsewhere and that never end.

As the people move on and leave the country, nature moves in again. The lands abides and, given the chance, will finally heal itself from human intrusion.

"Fishing Fever," Davis' second essay in the series, also was published in 1953. Although it ranges briefly into California and Mexico, this essay again focuses primarily on the Pacific Northwest. Typically, it contrasts the foibles (this time sympathetically presented) of those who fish with the beauty, endurance, and mystery of the natural world. Gentle scorn is reserved for the practice of stocking easily accessible streams with nearly tame hatchery trout to be caught almost immediately by crowds of tourists who stand so close they tangle each other's lines. Contrasted with these are the "true" anglers who seek out more remote sites where they can fish for "wild" trout with "silence and passion."

"The Puget Sound Country," published in the May 1954 issue of *Holiday*, presents a summary tour of that part of the state of Washington, again focusing on how the people interact with the setting—the climate, the landscape, the sea. Like Oregon, it is an area where people can gain the minimum requirements of survival very easily. He notes that before white settlement, the local Indian tribes did no hunting although they lived in an area rich with game. The fact that some of the tribes hunted whales in the open sea from canoes suggests that their reluctance to hunt on land was "hardly a sign of lackadaisical temperament." Rather, the sea and the wild fruits provided enough food with less effort. That, Davis says, is still available, although seldom used. Here he takes a view echoed later by Edward Abbey in *Desert Solitaire*: "Living close to Nature for a few weeks every year or so is an excellent restorative, but having to depend on Nature for a livelihood year in and year out takes the fun out of it." Still, even the cities are affected by the natural countryside. It adds something to a city, Davis says, to be able to look from its streets directly into "real forests and canyons and mountains and expanses of water." Landscape, he concludes, counts in the character of a place, as do the people. In this he echoes Thoreau, in "Walking": "A town is saved, not more by the righteous men in it than by the woods and swamps that surround it."

The title of "A Walk in the Woods" (published November 1954) suggests echoes of Thoreau's "Walking," even more. Thoreau speaks of returning to his senses, of being fully aware of the immediate natural world on his walks. Davis uses an account of a great-uncle and of his own encounter with a deer to make the same point. "Nothing knocks the color out of walking in the woods like forcing some purpose into it," Davis says. Carrying a camera or a gun makes the walk a failure. Thoreau would concur.

Thoreau speaks of a wood as a "hall" in which "some ancient and altogether admirable and shining family had settled." They are not troubled by the farmer's cart path through the middle of their hall, "as the muddy bottom of a pool is sometimes seen through the reflected skies." Davis says such an image might provide "a parable of some kind." At a distance, he says, a pool reflects its surroundings—trees, sky—but when you get closer over the water, you see instead your own reflection. Closer still and you see "down past all the reflections to the reality of underwater life," including bugs, worms, weeds. The water, the context, which provides "both reflections and reality," is itself invisible, yet is the medium by which we see. For both Thoreau and Davis, walking in the natural landscape, with no purpose other than direct experience of the natural world, can provide both reflection of the sky and direct vision of reality.

"The Wilds of Mexico" appeared in May 1957, only a few months after Davis' leg was amputated. Although he was living in Mexico at the time, this essay must have been drawn from recollection and research. For some time before its publication his health would not have allowed him to make the journeys he describes. The Mexico essay is perhaps as purely descriptive nature writing as anything Davis produced, yet he couches it in a largely narrative format,

describing a journey and then relating a series of anecdotes. He reminds us that both the beauties and the dangers of the wilderness then still existing in Mexico had once been present in the United States—wild parrots in the Ohio Valley, ivory-billed woodpeckers in the South, wild peccaries in Kansas.

After Davis' leg was amputated in October 1956, his health was a constant concern. After six months in the hospital, he returned to his home in Oaxaca and continued to write. His work does not show any change of vision or vigor. He continued to produce the essays for *Holiday* and to work on his novels. *The Distant Music* appeared the following year, and in 1959 he published *Kettle of Fire*, a collection of *Holiday* essays plus "The Kettle of Fire," his last short story.

"The Pleasures of the Brook," later collected in *Kettle of Fire* simply as "The Brook," appeared in the July 1957 issue of *Holiday*. In this essay Davis returned to the Oregon landscape. As usual in his essays, he uses a series of anecdotal narratives, but his theme is the essential unity of the natural landscape. To know a brook at any point is to be in contact with all of the course of that stream, and with all the land in its watershed. "To know the brook was to live in a big section of country instead of a small one." He then begins near the brook's mouth, in a town, and traces it upward through its course to the high, cold mountain spring headwaters, giving us sketches not only of the land, vegetation, fish and wildlife, but also of the human history along its entire course. The concept of the unity from flowing water parallels a similar vision by Loren Eiseley in *The Immense Journey* (1957). Just as Eiseley, floating on the Platte River on the Great Plains, "felt the cold needles of the alpine springs at my fingertips," so Davis felt the silence of the cold, high mountain springs where the brook flowed through town, "through the big culvert under the railroad tracks where it spread out into the river and vanished."

"Palm Springs," published in October 1957, is the other essay, besides "The Wilds of Mexico," to move exclusively outside the Pacific Northwest. It has Davis' typical pattern of vivid description of the desert and desert mountains of the region, contrasted with wryly humorous accounts of the behavior of the people. The humor is not so boisterous, and there are positive descriptions of some of the accommodations for visitors. In all, this essay most clearly shows the restraint that might have been expected from the *Holiday* editors, who were, after all, publishing a magazine designed to promote travel.

"Our Resourceful Forests," reprinted in *Kettle of Fire* as "The Forests," is almost purely descriptive. This contrasts with Davis' usual method of anecdotal narrative as a basic structure for his essays. This essay appeared in the July 1958 *Holiday*, an issue devoted to surveying the natural resources of the United States. In the same issue A. B. Guthrie, Jr., wrote about the mountains, Jack Schaefer wrote about the deserts, Donald Culross Peattie wrote about the birds, Wright Morris about the plains, and Rachel Carson about the seashores.

Because of the national focus of the issue, Davis briefly presents the forests of New England and the old Northwest, devotes somewhat more space to the forests of the South, and finally settles with obvious relish into a detailed description of the Oregon Cascade Mountains, traversing them from the Umpqua Valley eastward to the sagebrush desert. As in his earliest poetry, he creates the sense of the beauty of the region by cataloging in rich detail the flowers, fruits, shrubs and vines, and forest trees. His adjectives are primarily objective, with very few value-laden words. The profusion of sense detail—colors, sounds, light, movement—carries the description that creates rather than merely telling about the beauties of the forests.

Davis returns to his anecdotal narrative technique in "The Best Time for Camping" (reprinted as "The Camp" in *Kettle*). This essay, published in September 1958, is about camping in the Pacific Northwest, and is built primarily around experiences—some of them possibly true—of camping in that country. Using the narrative structure again, Davis is able to introduce his characteristic humor, which is missing in his purely descriptive writing.

The May 1959 issue of *Holiday* carried "Sheepherders: The Quiet Westerners" ("Sheep Herding" in *Kettle*). It presents the "other" livestock workers (other than cowboys) in the open western rangelands. Again it is primarily anecdotal narrative in which Davis embodies the essence of the Western landscape and the people who draw their living from it. In poor health, in pain from his amputated leg, Davis draws upon his recollection and invention to tell folktales, and make up tales of his own, about sheepdogs and the trials of the herder in wild country, most of them presented as if they had happened to him. His concluding scene, of striking camp in a heavy autumn snowfall in the high mountains, draws directly from a scene in *Honey in the Horn*. In both, the final impression is of the snow covering and finally obliterating all signs of the sheep camp. The human life in the place is only transitory. Nature abides and returns; humans are only ephemeral incidents in the infinite endurance of the natural world.

In October 1960 the Davises set out from their home in Oaxaca for a visit to San Antonio, Texas. They experienced difficulty crossing the border and had to call upon Thomas Hornsby Ferril, in Denver, to verify to U.S. emigration authorities that there was such a person as Harold Lenoir Davis and that he had been born a U.S. citizen, in Oregon. One of the country's premier living writers had to prove to its government that he really existed. While in San Antonio, Davis suffered a heart attack on 18 October, his sixty-sixth birthday, and was hospitalized. On 30 October, still in the hospital, he suffered a second heart attack, and died the following day.

Davis' final *Holiday* essay, perhaps appropriately titled "Oregon Autumn," was published posthumously, in the November 1961 issue. There is an autumnal tone to the essay, as its subject would suggest, but it is not the valedictory tone of one near the end of his life. Again the anecdotal narrative technique recalls illustrative incidents, many of them likely only imagined or embellished; but the joy of being in wild country, the keen consciousness of the sounds, the colors, the light, and life of the wild land-scape is undiminished.

Early in his writing career, H. L. Davis' poetry often had an autumnal tone. As he moved into fiction, the emphasis moved more to spring and the renewal of life. At the close of his career, and his life, he returned to the sense of ending of the autumnal landscape, looking back on the rich seasons of life fully lived.

In all the varied forms of Davis' work—poetry, sketches, short stories, novels, nature essays—there is a unity of view and of purpose. As James Potts has noted, his work is "a coming to terms with the world around us by examining our roots, our heritage, our land and our responses to that land" (p. 119). Davis' response to the land was a search for harmony and understanding.

Selected Bibliography

WORKS OF H. L. DAVIS

COLLECTIONS

Proud Riders and Other Poems (New York: Harper & Bros., 1942); *Team Bells Woke Me and Other Stories* (New York: Morrow, 1953); *Kettle of Fire* (New York: Morrow, 1959); *The Selected Poems of H. L. Davis* (Boise, Idaho: Ahsahta, 1978); *H. L. Davis Collected Essays and Short Stories* (Moscow: Univ. of Idaho Press, 1986), intro. by Robert Bain.

NOVELS

Honey in the Horn (New York: Harper & Bros., 1935); *Harp of a Thousand Strings* (New York: Morrow, 1947); *Beulah Land* (New York: Morrow, 1949); *Winds of Morning* (New York: Morrow, 1952); *The Distant Music* (New York: Morrow, 1957).

MANUSCRIPTS AND PAPERS

The largest collection of Davis' letters, journals, manuscripts, and other papers is held by the Humanities Research Center at the University of Texas, Austin. Other collections are in the University of Oregon Library, the Tennessee State Library and Archives, the Harriet Monroe collection of the Joseph Regenstein Library at the University of Chicago, and the Douglas County Museum in Roseberg, Oregon.

BIOGRAPHICAL AND CRITICAL STUDIES

Robert Bain, *H. L. Davis* (Boise, Idaho: Boise State University, 1974); Paul T. Bryant, *H. L. Davis* (Boston: Twayne, 1978); Thomas Hornsby Ferril, preface to *The Selected Poems of H. L. Davis* (Boise, Idaho: Ahsahta, 1978); John Lauber, "A Western Classic: H. L. Davis's *Honey in the Horn,*" in *Western Humanities Review* 16 (winter 1962); Glen A. Love, "Stemming the Avalanche of Tripe," in *H. L. Davis Collected Essays and Short Stories* (Moscow: Univ. of Idaho Press, 1986); James T. Potts, "H. L. Davis' View: Reclaiming and Recovering the Land," in *Oregon Historical Quarterly* 82 (summer 1981).

ANNIE DILLARD
(b. 1945)

DON SCHEESE

"WHAT DOES IT feel like to be alive?" asks Annie Dillard in *An American Childhood* (1987). She raises this question as she describes her visit to a friend's house in the country when she was twelve years old. The weekends at the farmhouse are so precious to Dillard—walking barefoot through pastures, pumping water from a stone well, storytelling around a fireplace after dinner—and she so precocious and sensitive, that she begins to imagine herself in the distant future remembering her lost childhood. She realizes that awareness—of her surroundings, her actions, her joy—can actually inhibit her happiness, as well as her perceptions. "How much noticing could I permit myself without driving myself around the bend? Too much noticing and I was too self-conscious to live. . . . Too little noticing, though—I would risk much to avoid this—and I would miss the whole show" (p. 155).

As many critics have observed, consciousness—awareness, alertness, being awake—is perhaps Annie Dillard's greatest concern. In her best-known book, *Pilgrim at Tinker Creek* (1974), she spends a good deal of time on activities she variously calls seeing, noticing, stalking: "It's all a matter of keeping my eyes open" (p. 18).[1] In *Holy the Firm* (1977), she writes that during her stay on an island off the Washington coast her purpose is "to study hard things" (p. 19)—meaning complex philosophical issues and the tangible world out of which they spring. In *Teaching a Stone to Talk* (1982) she writes in the title essay that "we are here to witness" (p. 72). In *Living by Fiction* (1982) she examines the relationship between artistic awareness and the world. In *The Writing Life* (1989) she declares, perhaps in jest, that the act of writing results in amputating oneself from the rest of the world: "the life of the writer—such as it is—is colorless to the point of sensory deprivation" (p. 44). Even in *The Living* (1992), a novel about nineteenth-century settlement on the Washington coast, the infinitesimal details noted by the omniscient narrator testify to Dillard's lifelong habit of attention.

But consciousness alone is not the subject of her work. The question becomes, once it is established, where does consciousness lead? What does one become aware of? For Annie Dillard, consciousness is a means to an end, a methodology. Awareness of the self and the physical world, the world inside as well as outside one's mind, ultimately stimulates her to raise questions of autobiography, metaphysics, and religion. Who am I? What events have shaped my life? Is knowledge possible? If so, how do we acquire it? Does the world have meaning, or do we make it up? Does God exist, and in

---

1. All page numbers for *Pilgrim at Tinker Creek* refer to the 1975 Bantam Books edition.

what form? If God exists, then why all the suffering?

To examine the work of Annie Dillard is to reveal both the power and the limitations of the term "nature writer." The genre has traditionally been defined as a first-person nonfiction narrative based on an appreciative aesthetic response to a scientific view of nature. Much of Dillard's writing meets this criterion. Other elements generally considered important to a definition of nature writing include a celebration of a particular place, an elegy to a lost or diminished wilderness, a polemic directed at despoilers of nature, and an argument for biocentrism over anthropocentrism. These other criteria, however, have not been a central concern of Dillard's, leading some critics to wonder whether she should rightly be considered a nature writer.

The problem with defining the genre of nature writing recapitulates the problem nineteenth-century American transcendentalists had with natural history, nature writing's predecessor: neat categorization, they discovered, is ultimately limiting rather than enhancing. To label the work of Annie Dillard "nature writing" does her a disservice. She is a nature writer, in the narrow sense of the term; but she is much more. Ultimately she addresses a much more important issue: the nature of nature itself. Like Ralph Waldo Emerson, she asks: *What* is Nature?

Early Life

Born Meta Ann Doak on 30 April 1945, Annie Dillard (she has retained the surname of her first husband) was the oldest of Frank and Pam Doak's three children, all daughters. The formative events of her first sixteen years are told in *An American Childhood*. The origins of her imaginative capacity, her interests in the natural world, her religiosity, are all well documented in this autobiography, this story of coming-to-consciousness.

Frank Doak was an executive of American Standard Corporation, the family business, and the Doak family lived among well-heeled neighbors in Pittsburgh. The first personal event that Dillard reveals in *American Childhood* occurred when she was ten years old. Her father, inspired by many readings of Mark Twain's *Life on the Mississippi*, decided to quit his job and float down the Ohio and Mississippi Rivers to New Orleans on a twenty-four-foot cabin cruiser. With his family's encouragement he set off, but after six weeks on the river he grew lonely, sold his boat, and returned home. Though the trip was cut short, its inception indicates how important reading and books were to the family and how the Doaks saw literature as a guide to life.

It was around this time in her life, Dillard reports, that the scales of unconsciousness and consciousness were tipped in the latter's favor, and she became more awake than not. Her mother, Pam, also contributed substantially to her intellectual and spiritual development. She encouraged her daughters to read extensively and eclectically, to practice their storytelling, and to pursue their own interests wherever they might lead. As an adolescent Dillard read *Mad* magazine, *Native Son*, *Walden*, Augustine's *Confessions*, *The Little Shepherd of Kingdom Come*. In general she was encouraged to be a nonconformist.

Her grandparents had a summer home on Lake Erie, where she took up birdwatching. At the local public library she discovered *The Field Book of Ponds and Streams*, a work on how to study and collect flora and fauna, which she reread every year of her childhood. In a statement that reflects the movement of *Pilgrim at Tinker Creek*, she writes that "the visible world turned me curious to books; the books propelled me reeling back to the world" (p. 160). She acquired a microscope and for the first time saw an amoeba; confirming its existence thrilled her to no end, causing her to declare, "I had a life" (p. 149).

After she enrolled in private school in 1955, an incident occurred that symbolized her increasingly fine sensitivity to the world around her. Her biology teacher released a freshly hatched Polyphemus moth from a mason jar. Dillard became horrified as it emerged from its container. Since the jar was too small, the moth had not been able to spread and dry its wings;

they had congealed unopened on its back. As the teacher let the deformed creature escape outside, Dillard records the impact of the event on her consciousness:

> I knew that this particular moth . . . could not travel more than a few more yards before a bird or a cat began to eat it, or a car ran over it. Nevertheless, it was crawling with what seemed wonderful vigor, as if . . . it was still excited from being born. I watched it go till the bell rang and I had to go in. I have told this story before [in *Pilgrim at Tinker Creek*], and may yet tell it again, to lay the moth's ghost, for I still see it crawl down the broad black driveway, and I still see its golden wing clumps heave. (p. 161)

Her spiritual growth and education continued with "getting religion" at a Presbyterian church camp. As she grew older, she became familiar with the Bible but grew to hate the church itself and what she perceived as its worshipers' hypocrisy. At age sixteen she left over the issue of Job, writing in one of her school papers, "If the all-powerful creator directs the world, then why all this suffering?" (p. 228). Her parents were aghast; her minister, to whom she wrote a nasty letter of resignation from the church, loaned her several works by C. S. Lewis and offered the hope that she would soon return to the flock.

She would—by way of Emerson, who, she reports, excited her tremendously, because, in part, his writing consisted of "philosophy minus the Bible" (p. 238). She had essentially already been living a key tenet of his Transcendental faith: that through a deep immersion in the natural world one can gain religious insight by establishing a connection between natural facts and spiritual truths. Emerson's call for an original relationship with the universe, as well as his nonconformity, were of particular appeal to Dillard during her rebellious teenage years, and struck a fundamental chord in the writer that has sounded ever since.

Upon graduating from private school she attended Hollins College in Virginia, where the headmistress sent all her "problem students" (Dillard had been suspended from school for smoking and had to appear in juvenile court once for drag racing). There she enrolled in creative writing courses and also took a number of courses in theology. At the end of her sophomore year she married her creative-writing teacher, Richard Dillard, a poet, critic, novelist, and specialist in horror films. She went on to receive a bachelor's degree, then a master's degree, in English, writing a master's thesis, "Walden Pond and Thoreau." Finishing her formal study in 1968, she continued to live near the Blue Ridge Mountains of Virginia for the next seven years. In 1970 she began to keep a journal, and at the same time she undertook daily excursions in her natural environs near Tinker Creek. A near-fatal bout with pneumonia in 1971 left her determined to live life more fully, to heighten her awareness of the world outside the mind.

Pilgrim at Tinker Creek

In *The Writing Life*, Dillard describes in some detail the composition of *Pilgrim at Tinker Creek*. The book is based on the four seasons she observed at Tinker Creek in 1972; Dillard wrote the first half at home in early 1973, the remainder at a study carrel in the Hollins College library the rest of the summer. "Appealing workplaces are to be avoided," she advises in *The Writing Life*. "One wants a room with no view, so imagination can meet memory in the dark" (p. 26). After a while she shut the blinds of her carrel for good and proceeded to craft a narrative about life at the creek based on her journals, which had expanded to twenty volumes, the significant contents of which she then transferred to 1,100 index cards. One night she was distracted by the sound of frequent thumps outside her window. Thinking it was a persistent June bug, she opened the blinds to witness the flashing and explosion of fireworks. "It was the Fourth of July, and I had forgotten all of wide space and all of historical time" (p. 31).

The irony, of course, is that the narrator of *Pilgrim* is acutely conscious of her physical world—as well as of herself. These two themes, consciousness and self-consciousness, complement and contradict each other throughout the book, functioning as a kind of dialectic from which Dillard ultimately synthesizes a number of important topics: spiritual autobiography, American transcendentalism, natural history (including scientific and popular Darwinism), and theology.

Early on she refers to herself as an anchorite, one whose vocation is seclusion for religious reasons. Her meticulous and microscopic examination of nature, and her careful and voluminous reading of natural history, cause her to contemplate issues of ontology, epistemology, and theodicy. The narrative is organized around a series of paradigmatic moments that ultimately lead to a deeper understanding of the self, nature, and the relationship between the two.

Although the book ostensibly is an almanac, progressing through the year from January to December, Dillard (quoting Thoreau) describes it as a "meteorological journal of the mind" (p. 12). This narrative strategy gives her license to move back and forth through time to report significant events. One of the most (in)famous images in *Pilgrim*, of a frog being sucked lifeless by a giant water bug, actually occurred several summers earlier. After recalling the event, Dillard comments:

> That it's rough [out there] and chancy is no surprise. Every living thing is a survivor on a kind of extended emergency bivouac. But at the same time we are also created. In the Koran, Allah asks, "The heaven and the earth and all in between, thinkest thou I made them *in jest*?" It's a good question. What do we think of the created universe, spanning an unthinkable void with an unthinkable profusion of forms? . . . If the giant water bug was not made in jest, was it then made in earnest? (1975 ed., p. 7)

The issue she raises here has to do with the nature of the creator. Why does there appear to be horror and brutality in the world? Like Emerson and Thoreau (whom she occasionally invokes), she seeks to transcend the natural historian's traditionally narrow emphasis on taxonomy by asking larger questions concerning spiritual and metaphysical aspects of nature. Dillard follows Emerson's lead in *Nature*, the bible of American transcendentalism, when he critiqued contemporary natural history for its "tyrannizing unity . . . which evermore separates and classifies things, endeavouring to reduce the most diverse to one form. . . . I cannot greatly honor minuteness in details, so long as there is no hint to explain the relation between things and thoughts."

American transcendentalists generally held a positive, affirmative view of nature and the human place within it. This is also true of Dillard at times; to counter her appalling vision of the frog's death she recalls a mockingbird's straight vertical descent from a four-story building and is reassured that there "seems to be such a thing as beauty, a grace wholly gratuitous" (p. 8). But her vision of nature is dominated by the macabre, the horrific, the sense that we as humans are a species inherently separate from the rest of the universe. She observes a pregnant praying mantis slobbering over its egg case, and then recollects from reading the entomologist J. Henri Fabre the horror of the mating ritual as the female devours the male part by part. In her occasionally colloquial style she observes that insects "gotta do one horrible thing after another" and describes the entire natural world as one "horrible nature movie" (pp. 65–66). Her view of nature has been darkened by a Darwinian shadow: life is a struggle for existence.

She seeks to immerse herself in nature, to become one with the natural world, as Emerson does in the famous "transparent eyeball" passage of *Nature*, in order to know God. But in a key moment—at, of all places, a near-deserted gas station along an interstate highway—Dillard achieves transcendence only at the expense of alienation from nature. She pats the belly of a hot-skinned puppy and gazes at a nearby mountain. "And the second I verbalize this awareness in my brain, I cease to see the mountain or feel the puppy. I am opaque, so much black asphalt. But at the same second, the second I know I've lost it, I also realize that the puppy is still squirming on his back under my hand. Nothing has changed for him." She comes to the realization that "the one thing that all religions recognize as separating us from our creator — our very self-consciousness — is also the one thing that divides us from our fellow creatures. It was a bitter birthday present from evolution, cutting us off at both ends" (p. 80).

Here she confronts the dilemma faced by many nature writers. How does one become one with nature, that is, lose one's self-consciousness, and at the same time maintain a sense of self or other-ness in order to record and re-create the experience? How, in other words, can one truly become as well as write nature? Dillard's self-consciousness, her egocentrism — which she blames on culture, the urbanization of the human species — seem to prohibit, or at least severely inhibit, a Transcendental perspective in which nature and the self merge.

Nature writing, as a form of autobiography, celebrates the self. In a pivotal chapter entitled "Fecundity," this tendency is placed in tension with the apparent waste, not economy, of nature. She ponders the fate of species produced en masse. Reading accounts of Thor Heyerdahl's Atlantic expedition, she is fascinated by the report of barnacle larvae that manage to survive and grow by clinging to gobs of tar floating in the ocean. "How many gooseneck barnacle larvae must be dying out there in the middle of vast oceans for every one that finds a glob of tar to fasten to?" (p. 177). Her speculation calls to mind a statement from Darwin's *The Origin of Species*: "with all beings there must be much fortuitous destruction." Is there a better way to run a universe? Dillard concludes gloomily: "Evolution loves death more than it loves you or me." Culture "value[s] the individual supremely, and nature values him not a whit" (pp. 179–180).

This deeply troubling realization causes Dillard to consider abandoning her life at Tinker Creek, but after further contemplation she arrives at two alternatives: either nature — God — is a monster, intentionally indifferent to our plight as morally sensitive individuals; or nature is blameless and our morality makes us freaks, moral creatures in an amoral world. She opts for the Judeo-Christian interpretation: we are exceptional for our morality. Upon returning to the creek, the natural world thus becomes a sanctuary for her, a refuge, in the pastoral tradition of nature writing. She is no longer brutalized by nature's fecundity, for she now knows that through her consciousness and morality she brings humanism to nature, providing solace in the face of its ubiquitous struggle and death. This is a crucial moment in Dillard's pilgrimage, her spiritual conversion or transformation.

Dillard has referred to herself as a "Christian mystic"; she places great emphasis on direct, unmediated awareness of the presence of God, and it is through nature that she experiences His presence. Some critics have labeled her a panentheist; she holds, according to their interpretation, that not only is the natural world contained within God but that God extends beyond the natural world. Not "all is God" (pantheism); rather, "all in God" (panentheism): God is both immanent and transcendent. Part of the title poem of *Tickets for a Prayer Wheel*, a short collection of Dillard's verse published the same year as *Pilgrim*, illustrates this theological view:

> He has no edges,
> and the holes in him spin.
> He alone is real,
> and all things lie in him
> as fossil shells
> curl in solid shale.
> My sister dreamed of God
> who moves around
> the spanding, spattered holes
> of solar systems hollowed in his side.

While it is not accurate to describe Dillard as a traditional Christian, she employs centuries-old techniques of Christian mystics. In an interview she once explained that she organized *Pilgrim* around the two mystic ways to experience God: the *via positiva*, or positive way, and the *via negativa*, or negative way. The former focuses on the intricacy and beauty of creation and the possibility of its comprehension by humans; the latter, on all that is not God, on God's essential unknowableness. Only when she decides to remain at the creek, when she recognizes the virtue of morality in an amoral world, does she continue on her spiritual ascent.

Yet much of her understanding is seemingly undercut in "Stalking," an oft-anthologized chapter. Here she once again loses track of herself, sheds her self-consciousness, as she follows the tracks of a muskrat. For forty minutes she is able to observe, from less than an arm's length away, a muskrat foraging. She comes to feel that "even a few minutes of this self-forgetfulness is tremendously invigorating" (p. 202). Anthropocentrism appears to have been sacrificed in favor of biocentrism: seeing the world from a nonhuman perspective. She gains, it would seem, some ecological humility.

Or does she? For shortly thereafter Dillard cites Heisenberg's Principle of Indeterminacy, which basically holds that you cannot know both a particle's velocity and its position. Its larger implications are that everything becomes metaphysical; we cannot study nature itself—since nature cannot be fixed, it remains unknowable—we can only study our investigations of nature. "I find in quantum mechanics a world symbolically similar to my world at the creek" (p. 205). She does not stalk muskrats; she stalks herself. There can be no knowledge of nature, since she has determined that humans are distinct and "unnatural" because of their self-consciousness. There is no Tinker Creek; there is only her mental and verbal construct of it.

Remember that she opens *An American Childhood* in this way: "When everything else has gone from my brain...what will be left, I believe, is topology: the dreaming memory of land as it lay this way and that." She refers not to the land itself but to its memory; a landscape of the mind. Which is why, perhaps, pilgrims have never flocked to Tinker Creek in the way that they have to, say, Walden Pond. It is not on the American roster of sacred places to visit, because it is not the place that Dillard celebrates so much as a state of mind, a heightened awareness of place. Tinker Creek exists, is numinous, largely because Dillard notices its existence.

Rather than be troubled by her anthropocentrism, Dillard seems to revel in it. She accounts for the coexistence of beauty and death in a similarly anthropocentric way. "Northing," a chapter that marks the turn toward fall, describes a literal fall—autumn—as well as a figurative rise, toward further revelations. Through a cabin window Dillard watches a goldfinch land on the head of a purple thistle and proceed to empty the flower's seed case, sowing the air with down, seeds of new life. This perfectly ordinary event becomes the catalyst for another epiphany. In Transcendental fashion—the invariable mark of wisdom, said Emerson, is the ability to transform the common into the miraculous—Dillard has created a fable of dissemination and renewal. The deflowering of the thistle, through the agency of the finch, will lead to rebirth. As Wallace Stevens writes in "Sunday Morning" (a poem to which Dillard has referred more than once), "Death is the mother of beauty."

The penultimate chapter of *Pilgrim at Tinker Creek* recalls "the tree with lights in it," a reference to a scene recorded early in *Pilgrim*. One day, thinking of nothing at all, she looked at a cedar tree in her backyard and watched it "buzzing with flame." "I had been my whole life a bell," she writes, "and never knew it until at that moment I was lifted and struck" (p. 35). What she sees is a vision of God, a way to reconcile science and theology through capturing for a moment the shimmering force of the transcendent. Dillard wonders afterward whether the twigs of the cedar were bloated with galls, stricken by parasitism—as so much of the natural world is—and whether because the tree was a flawed work of creation her vision was flawed as well. It does not matter: corruption is one of beauty's deep-blue speckles" (p. 247).

In the tradition of spiritual autobiography represented by Augustine's *Confessions* and carried on in America by writers from Jonathan Edwards to Thoreau and other nature writers, Dillard's narrative moves toward a grand conversion experience. Death, horror, *is* the mother of beauty. It must occur for species to evolve. A falling maple key provides the book's final epiphany: seizing it, she throws it into the wind. "Bristling with animate purpose, not like a thing dropped or windblown...but like a creature muscled and vigorous" (p. 275), the maple key carries out its function. It does what it has been designed through evolution to do: spread its seed, procreate. There is beauty, and design, after all.

In arriving at many of her metaphysical insights, Dillard relies on the Book of Nature, in both the primary and secondary senses of the phrase. Dillard's fascination is with meta-nature: In *Pilgrim* she studies and writes about the natural world itself, and she continually cites natural historians from Pliny to Edwin Way Teale. To the discipline of natural history she has added her acute, postmodern self-consciousness, her openly acknowledged uncertainty over scientific positivism, and her moments of spiritual despair. Readers seeking a more straightforward natural-history narrative have sometimes been disappointed and confused as a result of their encounters with this pilgrim.

So why is the book so highly regarded, so frequently anthologized in collections of nature writing, so often taught in courses on nature writing? Many critics have seen *Pilgrim* as a twentieth-century version of *Walden*, and indeed the two texts share important similarities. Both works condense years of experience into the fiction of a single year, and both are arranged organically, around the cycle of the seasons; both are based on "the simple life," confronting the essential facts of life by clarifying one's vision and insight through voluntary material poverty; both employ science and natural history for higher ends; both advocate a close study of nature as the best possible means of self-culture. But Dillard is different from Thoreau in two key ways. One is that she hews to the Christian tradition (she is a self-described "old-fashioned churchgoer"); the other is that she is a child of the twentieth century and therefore much less affirmative about what we can know and do with our knowledge. Whereas Thoreau left the church following college and turned to a kind of Transcendental pantheism, Dillard stubbornly maintains her debt to Christianity. Whereas Thoreau was an amateur scientist and believed in science's empirical truths (though he felt science did not go far enough in questing for the spiritual significance of natural facts), Dillard declares

outright she is no scientist. Yet she is a veritable encyclopedia of scientific facts and statistics and expresses no qualms over the practice of science.

Like Thoreau, however, Dillard is a superb stylist. A sampling of choice metaphors should suffice to demonstrate the verbal pyrotechnics of *Pilgrim*: the frog sucked dry by the water bug collapses "like a kicked tent" (p. 6); describing her method of nature study, she writes "I am the arrow shaft . . . and this book is the straying trail of blood" (p. 13); the praying mantis tending its egg case looks like "a hideous harried mother slicking up a fat daughter for a beauty pageant" (p. 59). In a recent interview Dillard confessed embarrassment over her early "show-off tendencies."

The style of *Pilgrim* is probably a good way to account, at least in part, for the book's fame. It became a Book-of-the-Month Club selection and won the Pulitzer Prize for nonfiction in 1975. Since its publication nearly a million copies have been sold. The author became a notable literary commodity, inundated by requests to write books, scripts for Hollywood films, lyrics for songs, to speak and lecture, to appear on television. Life suddenly became more complex for the young writer. Her first marriage ended in divorce, and, experiencing a kind of spiritual crisis, she fled the East Coast to rededicate herself to the pursuit of writing. She accepted a position as a scholar-in-residence at Western Washington University in Bellingham, Washington, where she taught poetry and prose writing from 1975 to 1979 and again in 1981. Living for a time in a one-room cabin on an island, she continued writing on some of the same themes addressed in her first book—and continued to defy expectations about traditional genres and boundaries of traditional disciplines.

Holy the Firm

In *The Writing Life*, Dillard declares *Holy the Firm* to be her favorite book of all her own work, and she describes its subjects as "the relation of eternity to time and the problem of suffering innocents." Initially, she says, much of it was

Annie Dillard

written as poetry. When she decided to transform the poetry into prose, the language "was so intense and accented, and the world it described was so charged with meaning, that the very thought of writing a word or two further made me tired. How could I add a sentence, or a paragraph, every day to this work I myself could barely understand?" (p. 47).

Holy the Firm is a difficult book. Because it is only seventy-six pages in length, and because it takes on cosmic themes, its texture is dense and compressed. Dillard spent fifteen months writing it, and its literary craft is obvious. Ostensibly it is about three consecutive days on an island off the Washington coast. For the first time in her life, Dillard later reflected, she was truly on her own, without the security of family or husband. Perhaps her personal isolation during the time of composition explains in part the book's emphasis on the themes of loneliness and sacrifice.

Holy the Firm consists of three sections. It begins on the morning of the first day, moves through the second day, and ends on the morning of the third day. In an interview Dillard explained that she patterned the structure after the Creation, the Fall, and the Redemption. The number three—so significant in Christian cosmology—also figures if one reads the work as moving from faith to doubt to renewal of faith.

What has all this to do with nature writing? First of all, like *Pilgrim*, this is a work of spiritual autobiography, and nature becomes the basis, the groundwork, of speculations about the relationship between humans and the rest of the world. Locale is very important to this work; observing and writing at the edge of the continent, the rim of the world, the *ultima thule*, Dillard underscores her own isolation, physical and emotional, which becomes a way to clarify her vision and contemplate ultimate issues.

These ultimate issues are introduced by way of observations that occur in the physical realm outside her mind. Dillard interprets facts in light of their spiritual significance, which is to say she employs once again Emerson's theory of correspondence: particular natural facts are symbols of particular spiritual facts. As in *Walden* and other classics of nature writing, the author is fundamentally engaged with matters of metaphysics.

Furthermore, as in *Pilgrim*, there is an unmistakable Darwinian theme which runs through the work. Horror and death occur often and seemingly at random; tragedy is a fact of life. This time, all the more painfully, human tragedy is involved, and Dillard's grieving leads her to raise once more the issue of theodicy: to attempt to reconcile suffering with the concept of a benevolent Creator.

"Nothing is going to happen in this book," she writes in part 1. "There is only a little violence here and there in the language, at the corner where eternity clips time" (p. 24). Eternity, perhaps, is represented by the mountains, the Cascade Range to the east, to which she pays significant attention, especially Mount Baker, a ten-thousand-foot volcano that she can see clearly from her island. The Cascades form "the western rim of the real" (p. 20), and she lies just west of reality, on the perimeter of the imagination.

220

She reflects on the spiderweb in her bathroom and the empty corpses of insects scattered on the floor, including those of moths. The carcasses of moths trigger a memory of a camping trip two summers before, when a moth extinguished itself by flying into a candle as she read a novel entitled *The Day on Fire* (about the symbolist poet Arthur Rimbaud, whom she greatly admired as a teenager). The moth, acting as a wick, burned for two hours, "like a hollow saint, like a flame-faced virgin gone to God" (p. 17), while she read by its light—the light of illumination. For like the tree with lights in it, fire can enlighten. The difference here is that even as she is reborn, renewed by the light, another creature perishes; her enlightenment comes at the expense of another.

Dillard does not grieve for the moth: just as its hollowness allows it to burn, the emptiness of the mystic and artist allows divine creativity to operate. Overall, the tone of part 1 is affirmative, optimistic. She opens with Emersonian echoes—"Every day is a god. . . . I worship each god" (Emerson once wrote, "No one suspects the days to be gods"). She feels the world is, intellectually speaking, at her feet: "the world through the window, is an illuminated manuscript" (p. 24). The Book of Nature is open, there for her to read, write, and interpret. It is comprehensible. And it has positive truths to offer.

Part 2 shatters this sense of serenity and positivism. It opens with the observation, "Into this world falls a plane" (p. 35). On her second day on the island, a plane crash occurs in which a man and his daughter, whom Dillard knew, both survive. But in escaping the wreck, the seven-year-old girl, Julie Norwich (a pseudonym), has her face burned off by a gob of fiery plane fuel. "Little Julie mute in some room at St. Joe's now, drugs dissolving into the sheets. Little Julie with her eyes naked and spherical, baffled. Can you scream without lips? Yes. But do children in long pain scream?" (p. 36).

Now, on this day, the day "*was* a god" (p. 42, emphasis mine). Unlike in *Pilgrim*, Dillard does not here invoke Heisenberg's Principle of Indeterminacy and play games of metaphysics, hypothesizing that events and places may only be creatures of the mind, mental constructs. This tragedy, the pain that Julie Norwich suffers, is real. It is all the more poignant and personal because Dillard and the girl look alike; it could have been Dillard in that wreck; it *was* she, in a sense. Like the moth drawn to the light of the candle, she is drawn to the fire of this tragedy. Like a soul drawn to the light of God? Is this what happens when one is drawn to God?

It is at this point that issues of theodicy are specifically raised.

> Has God a hand in this? Then it is a good hand. But has he a hand at all? Or is he a holy fire burning self-contained for power's sake alone? Then he knows himself blissfully as flame unconsuming, as all brilliance and beauty and power, and the rest of us can go hang. Then the accidental universe spins mute, obedient only to its own gross terms, meaningless, out of mind, and alone. The universe is neither contingent upon nor participant in the holy, in being itself, the real, the power play of fire. (p. 48)

Dillard seems burned by her enlightenment. Part 2 concludes with a loss of faith: "If days are gods, then gods are dead, and artists pyrotechnic fools" (p. 50).

Part 3 opens, "I know only enough of God to want to worship him, by any means ready to hand." One thinks of the speaker's vacillation in Wallace Stevens' poem "Sunday Morning" over her religious beliefs, as she metaphorically wanders through religious landscapes of Christianity, pantheism, agnosticism, paganism. In fact, in *The Writing Life*, Dillard reveals that while composing a scene from Part 3—"A wildish passage in which the narrator, I, came upon the baptism of Christ in the water of the bay in front of the house" (p. 76)—she had been repeating to herself for hours a line from the poem: "It is the grave of Jesus, where he lay." How does she resolve her spiritual crisis?

She tries to get word on Julie's condition, but cannot. She recalls a passage from the New Testament in which Christ gives sight to a blind man and says, "Neither hath this man sinned, nor his parents: but that the works of God should be made manifest in him." The passage infuriates her. "Do we really need more victims to remind us that we're all victims? . . . Do we need blind men stumbling about, and little flamefaced children, to remind us what God can—and will—do?" (p. 61). She has returned to the issue of Job, the problem of evil that had caused her to leave the church, temporarily, when she was a teenager.

Spiritually emptied, the narrator is now ready, once again, to receive God. "Who are we to demand explanations of God?" It comes back to alertness, attention. "We are most deeply asleep at the switch when we fancy we control any switches at all. . . . we wake, if we ever wake, to the silence of God" (p. 62). And what has she awakened to? To the knowledge that what is real is holiness. She has burrowed to the base and found holy the firm. God is in the world; God is above the world. "Matter and spirit are of a piece but distinguishable; God has a stake guaranteed in all the world. And the universe is real and not a dream, not a manufacture of the senses; subject may know object, knowledge may proceed, and Holy the Firm is in short the philosopher's stone" (p. 71). The philosopher's stone: a mystical substance that has the power to redeem us, to effect spiritual regeneration. Holiness is her philosopher's stone, and she has located it in the world of the senses.

Holy the Firm concludes with a hopeful vision of Julie Norwich's future. We are reminded of Julian of Norwich: a fourteenth-century English mystic, a Benedictine nun who wrote a work describing her visions during a serious illness, who believed in God's unfathomable love. Julie is seven, the mystic number believed in the Middle Ages to represent the cosmos, as the sum of the earthly four and the spiritual three. Seven is also the age designated in the Middle Ages to represent one's last year of innocence. Earlier Dillard had written that Julie might as well become a nun. Now, as Dillard imagines the girl being restored by surgery, getting married, having children, she thinks, "I'll be the nun for you. I am now" (p. 76). Dillard is both the nun and the artist, and both vocations—the nun as art-

ist, the artist as a nun, of nature—require sacrifice and single-minded vision.

Reading *Holy the Firm*, one realizes how fluid the boundaries of nature writing are, how vast and varied its topography can be. There is no plea here to save an endangered species; what is endangered is Dillard's, and our own, faith. She helps restore it, through her attention to the world. She reminds us that everything around us is "nature," not just national parks or wilderness areas. In leading us through the wilderness of her mind we come to recognize that virtually all writing is, can be considered, nature writing, in the broadest sense of the term: imaginative writing that engages our thinking about events in the physical world.

Teaching a Stone to Talk

Dillard's next book-length work, a collection of essays, was published in 1982. It appeared following her appointment as visiting professor of creative writing at Wesleyan University in Middletown, Connecticut (initially in 1979, then again in 1981, where she has since remained). *Teaching a Stone to Talk* breaks new ground for Dillard in that it marks a movement from the isolatto of *Pilgrim* and *Holy the Firm* to a more social animal. She makes an imaginative journey with a church group to the North Pole; she travels with scientists to the Amazon rain forest and the Galapagos; and she and her husband, along with many other pilgrims, travel to eastern Washington to view a total eclipse. But a few essays hearken back to her mostly solitary years as a resident at Tinker Creek. Isolated while stationary, more gregarious while on the move: in "Sojourner" she characterizes the patterns of movement of her life and writing in this way: "I alternate between thinking of the planet as home—dear and familiar stone hearth and garden—and as a hard land of exile in which we are all sojourners." The earth itself, she goes on to point out, "is a sojourner in airless space, a wet ball flung across nowhere" (pp. 150–151).

Whether she writes of life at Tinker Creek or of a journey to South America, her themes remain the same: a heightened sense of awareness of our physical surroundings; the maintaining of faith in a world of suffering and doubt; the roles of science and religion in the acquisition of knowledge; and the transforming of a preoccupation with consciousness into art.

A number of essays testify to her role as witness to Creation. "Living Like Weasels," the opening piece (first published in 1973, before *Pilgrim*), ostensibly a tribute to the animal's tenacious hold of its prey, transforms the weasel into a symbol of the artist's and the mystic's dedication to purity. She encounters one at a pond near Tinker Creek, and then follows a prolonged period of mindlessness, a momentary stay of consciousness as she watches this "muscled ribbon." Their eyes lock, "and someone [throws] away the key" (pp. 13–14). She insists that she was in the weasel's brain for a minute, he in hers, and that this mental exchange was mutually beneficial.

> I would like to learn, or remember, how to live. I come to Hollins Pond not so much to learn how to live as, frankly, to forget about it. That is, I don't think I can learn from a wild animal how to live in particular... but I might learn something of mindlessness, something of the purity of living in the physical senses and the dignity of living without bias or motive. . . . And I suspect that for me the way is like the weasel's: open to time and death painlessly, noticing everything, remembering nothing, choosing the given with a fierce and pointed will. (p. 15)

What she most admires about the weasel is its instinctual lunge for the jugular vein and its elemental commitment not to let go of what it seizes. She would like to live her own life in this way.

"Total Eclipse" carries a similar message. In much of her work Dillard seems intent on finding the miraculous in the commonplace; here she focuses on one of nature's extravagant and rare occurrences. These events are necessary, she explains, because they remind us to awaken to the world. "We teach our children one thing only, as we were taught: to wake up. . . . As adults we are almost all adept at waking up. We have so mastered the transition we have forgotten we ever learned it. . . . We live half our waking lives and all of our sleeping lives in some private, useless, and insensible waters we never mention or recall" (pp. 97–98). On a hilltop in the Yakima Valley of eastern Washington, a crowd of onlookers, looking like they had gathered to pray at the onset of the apocalypse, shrieks and screams as the eclipse occurs and a dark shadow comes hurtling toward them. It is the shadow of the moon, traveling 1,800 miles per hour. Dillard then makes a remarkable statement, given her vocation as wordsmith: "Language can give no sense of this sort of speed" (p. 100). For all her epiphanies in nature, this is one of the few times that she admits she cannot write the Book of Nature.

Two essays focus on her travels to the Galapagos: "Teaching a Stone to Talk" and "Life on the Rocks." In the first she observes that the world is in short supply of sacred groves, and goes off in search of one, finding the Galapagos "a kind of metaphysics laboratory" (p. 73). Here she can be a perfect witness and watch nature unfold with little human intervention or cultural history; the islands remain a kind of prelapsarian Eden. A neighbor in Washington was trying to teach a stone to talk, in hopes of communicating with God; she is at the Galapagos for the same reason, to witness. "What is the difference between a cathedral and a physics lab?" she asks. "Are not they both saying: Hello?" (p. 71).

The second essay directly engages a writer whose work has exerted an enormous influence on her writing: Charles Darwin. It was on the Galapagos, of course, during his worldwide voyage aboard the *Beagle* from 1831 to 1836, that Darwin observed a natural phenomenon that proved to be a catalyst in his formulation of a theory of evolution. He noticed that subspecies of finches had developed different-sized beaks, and later hypothesized that they had evolved in response to varying environmental conditions on the islands. After summarizing his discoveries and the subsequent adoptions and distortions of Darwin's thought by scientists and social thinkers, she gets to the heart of what Darwin discovered when he noticed the difference between the finches' beaks: "Geography is the key, the crucial accident of birth. . . . Geography is life's limiting factor" (pp. 126–127).

Other essays focus on less spectacular or storied landscapes, and are more personal, revealing. "Aces and Eights," the concluding piece, is perhaps the finest of this lot. It recounts a summer visit to a cottage in the Appalachian Mountains with a nine-year-old girl. Perhaps the girl is Dillard's daughter, because, with her fantastic recollections (she remembers being born, the light hurt her eyes so), the girl seems a double of the precocious author of *American Childhood*. At any rate they encounter an old man who lives in the area, Noah Very, a direct descendant of the nineteenth-century transcendentalist Jones Very (who taught Thoreau at Harvard). As in much of her writing, Dillard is preoccupied with time. The essay strikes a poignant tone as she fixes a lunch for the girl and sends her off to play in the woods. She reflects on the fact that she is now thirty-five years old, in the middle of the journey. She talks with Noah Very about remembering this scene in the future and reflecting back on the time when her child was little. Finally, at the end of the weekend stay at the cottage, as she walks with the child in a meadow, a cool breeze out of the north washes over them. "Who authorized this intrusion?" she wants to know. The breeze reminds her of the coming fall—and of something else. "It is an entirely misplaced air—fall, that I have utterly forgotten, that could be here again, *another* fall, and here it is only July. I thought I was younger, and would have more time" (p. 177). Like the father in E. B. White's "Once More to the Lake," who feels the chill in his groin as he watches his young son don a wet swimsuit, Dillard confronts, through her offspring (imagined or real), her eventual mortality.

Other essays address religion, and Christianity, explicitly. A tour de force in this regard is "An Expedition to the Pole." Here the author implicitly compares the inadequate preparation of polar explorers in the nineteenth century with the inadequate preparation of today's church-

goers for their encounters with God. Dillard refers to "The Pole of Relative Inaccessibility," " 'that imaginary point on the Arctic Ocean farthest from land in any direction'" (p. 18). Its analogue in the religious realm, of course, is God. She attends mass at a Catholic church during Advent and considers the church's innovations as [of] various means to get closer to God: guitars and the "passing of the peace" (shaking hands or exchanging ritual pleasantries with neighbors in a pew). Polar explorers at first resisted innovations. Members of Sir John Franklin's 1845 expedition, for example, included no special clothing to accommodate the extreme cold of the North; but during meals the officers dined with cut-glass wine goblets and heavy, ornately designed silverware. When the expedition disappeared and search parties were sent out, they discovered officers frozen on the ice floes clutching the useless Victorian artifacts that symbolized their lack of preparation. Not until explorers like Roald Amundsen and Robert E. Peary went native—that is, used Eskimo technology and travel techniques—was the North Pole reached.

So how does one "go native" in the spiritual sense? Dillard provides an answer by stating, "Wherever we go, there seems to be only one business at hand—that of finding workable compromises between the sublimity of our ideas and the absurdity of the fact of us" (p. 30). It is not that she fully ridicules the early explorers; she does admire them for their dedication, their sense of purpose. Inadequately prepared as they were, suffering frostbite and (if they did survive) amputations of digits and limbs, they were committed. They believed in something. Dillard comes to believe the same is true of her fellow churchgoers. Though at one point she decides, "On the whole, I do not find Christians, outside of the catacombs, sufficiently sensible of conditions. Does anyone have the foggiest idea what sort of power we so blithely invoke? Or, as I suspect, does no one believe a word of it?" (p. 40), ultimately Dillard sheds her feelings of superiority and joins them in the search for God. Just as she is attracted to the polar explorers because they dared to venture to the terrestrial equivalent of *via negativa*, where God appears to be silent and utterly hostile, so she gathers with the worshipers.

"An Expedition to the Pole" concludes on a communal, and surreal, note. The narrator imagines herself exploring the polar ice alone, until she encounters a priest from her past, figures from previous Arctic expeditions—and clowns passing out Girl Scout cookies. A pianist plays "The Sound of Music," then "On Top of Old Smoky." "Christ, under the illusion that we are all penguins, is crouched down posing for snapshots." She bangs a tambourine and joins in song. The essay concludes: "For we are nearing the Pole" (p. 52). She cannot search for God by herself. While the quest for God and the Pole may seem absurd and futile, it cannot be done alone. There is no such thing as a solitary explorer.

In melding natural history, spiritual autobiography, careful observation of the natural world, and postmodern surrealistic techniques, Annie Dillard represents an avant-garde force in nature writing. Ironically, she accomplishes this while she takes the genre back to its roots. Seventeenth-century natural historians such as John Ray and William Paley engaged in their discipline in order to confirm the Argument from Design and prove God's existence; natural history and natural theology, we are reminded, were once synonymous. Dillard may not always reach the same comforting conclusions as her predecessors, but simply by the virtue and persistence of her quest she has revived religious faith in many of her readers, even during a time that has been described as a "postreligious" age.

The same year that *Teaching a Stone to Talk* appeared, *Living by Fiction*, a work that has been classified as literary criticism, was also published. These works were followed by *Encounters with Chinese Writers* in 1984, a "purified nonfiction narrative" based on her participation in a State Department cultural exchange with the People's Republic of China. The work on the book was supported by a grant from the National Endowment for the Arts. She then won a John Simon Guggenheim Foundation grant in 1986 to work on *An American Childhood*. A year after

that memoir was published, in 1988, she divorced her second husband (Gary Clevidence, a professor of anthropology and a writer whom she had married in Washington in 1980) and married Robert Richardson, a scholar who had just written *Henry Thoreau: A Life of the Mind*, which she greatly admired. He moved to Connecticut and they both now teach at Wesleyan as adjunct professors. In 1989 *The Writing Life* was published.

The Living

In 1978 Dillard published a short story in *Harper's* magazine entitled "The Living." Set in northwest Washington in the fictional town of Whatcom, its plot centers on a gratuitous death threat made by Beal Obenchain, a shadowy, evil scholar right out of a Hawthorne novel, to Clare Fishburn, one of the town's leading citizens. The story is about the power of ideas and language; how one can be made a prisoner, so to speak, by words.

Dillard came back to the story in the early 1990s and transformed it into an epic, nineteenth-century novel told through an omniscient narrator. It traces the settlement, rise, and fall of Whatcom from 1855 to 1897. Why a historical novel, after years of writing nonfiction? In an interview Dillard offered several reasons. One had to do with her disenchantment with modern fiction, its self-indulgent self-referentiality (documented in *Living by Fiction*); she wanted to write fiction that, in contrast, dealt with the world outside the mind. Another concerned her fondness for historical research; *An American Childhood*, for example, began as an epic frontier history of Pittsburgh, but after writing two hundred pages of such material she discarded this approach because she could not integrate history and autobiography.

She also explains that she wanted to write about "little-bitty people in a great big landscape." This last justification relates to two relevant questions concerning the novel and its place in the nature-writing canon. Are nature writing and fiction compatible? Is *The Call of the*

Wild nature writing? *The Grapes of Wrath?* *The Monkey Wrench Gang?* What all these works have in common is the land's looming presence; it functions as a major character, almost dwarfing human individuals.

Likewise, while *The Living* focuses on three or four families during the latter half of the nineteenth century, the novel's human characters are nearly lost amidst the towering Douglas firs, the overarching sky, and the dominating mountains—especially Mount Baker, to which Dillard continually refers (as in *Holy the Firm*). At one point a character looks to the east from his home on the bay and observes the mountain, thinking, "Its mineral significance brooked no argument, admitted no sentiment" (p. 297). Another character interprets the Cascade Mountains (of which Mount Baker is a part) as "imperturbable, frank in their cruelty" (p. 251). And at the end of the novel, as a party of settlers tries to climb an unnamed peak in the Cascades, the narrator reflects back on the first climb of Mount Baker, in 1868, when, upon ascending the mountain, the group broke out into the Doxology: "Praise God from whom all blessings flow" (p. 387).

As in all her works, Dillard uses nature as a basis from which she examines philosophical issues. A litany of random deaths occurs throughout the novel: two settlers digging a well are poisoned to death when they strike a gas pocket; a boy watches his father drown in a logjam; a New Jersey woman on the Overland Trail loses her mind and brains her baby with a rock, sets fire to her family's wagon, then sets off across the desert alone. Dillard is still obviously preoccupied with the problem of evil and its ontological implications. As in *Pilgrim*, the individual seems to matter "not a whit." A key difference between this novel and her previous works, however, is that here, through the third-person omniscient narrator, Dillard becomes a kind of Old Testament God in that she assumes the persona of a capricious Creator whom she had alternately questioned, criticized, and worshiped in her nonfiction.

Even if this development represents a reaffirmation of her Judeo-Christian heritage, her theology continues to resist neat and easy classification. Though many reviewers were apprehensive over her shift from the essay to fiction because it meant she would be leaving out her best character—herself—a close reading of *The Living* suggests that she is very much present in the novel, expressing herself through the pieties and religious doubts uttered by her characters. A mother who questions why her infant died in a fire is offered "this morsel of theology: that God swept up early into heaven those children who were too pure for this spotted world" (p. 131). On another occasion a Methodist minister tells a senator he is happy in his new land, but that he cannot understand "why God pressed down on them so hardly on earth" (p. 129). Finally, near the end of the novel a character reflects on the widespread death and suffering of the town and asks, "How was it possible to endure the losses one accumulated just by living?" (p. 376).

This ironically titled novel thus perpetuates the author's Darwinian concerns, this time applied to the human species en masse. Not only are the characters victim to random natural disasters, their fates are also controlled by larger historical and economic forces. Their main impetus for transforming the landscape from forest to farmland is of course pecuniary. Spurred by Manifest Destiny, the pioneers unthinkingly migrate westward with little regard for differences of geography and climate between their old and new homes. As they arrive and begin settling the Washington coast, their actions are dictated by market forces outside the region.

In the middle of the novel, the narration shifts temporarily to Saint Paul, Minnesota, where the robber barons James Hill, owner of the Great Northern Railway, and Frederick Weyerhauser, a major lumber-company owner, conspire to harvest the timber of the Pacific Northwest and ship it back East on Hill's railroad. It was Hill who once declared that "the fortunes of railroad companies are determined by the survival of the fittest," and his Darwinian social philosophy rationalizes the economic deaths of entire towns such as Whatcom. Its citizens hoped it would become the western terminus of the northwestern branch of the transcontinental railroad, but Whatcom loses out to Tacoma in the ensuing competition. Over the years the town suffers a series of boom-and-bust cycles, owing to economic vicissitudes such as the panics of 1873 and 1893. At the novel's end, rumors fly of a gold rush in the Klondike, so the townspeople are left hoping they can capitalize on Whatcom's geographical proximity to the North and become a stepping-stone to Canada.

The Living, with its deterministic themes, bears more than a slight resemblance to the naturalistic fiction written by Jack London, Theodore Dreiser, and others at the turn of the century. The biological and social Darwinism that propels this novel, however, is muted by the keen sensibilities and religious faith of some of the main characters; Dillard herself does not endorse the philosophy of social Darwinism. Ada Fishburn, the grand dame of the novel whose presence spans the entire course of its telling, remains resolute in her faith despite numerous spiritual and economic losses. Her son Clare reminds one of Dillard in his acute awareness of and appreciation for his surroundings. Our first introduction to him comes when he is young: "Clare was an exuberant, bony boy who loved his world. He often woke exalted, his heart busting in its rib cage, thinking 'Today is the day!'" (p. 28). By the end of the novel he is much more sober, having witnessed many deaths and tragedies, and his worldview is summarized in this way: "Here is a solid planet...stocked with mountains and cliffs, where stone banks jut and deeply rooted trees hang on. Among these fixed and enduring features wander the flimsy people. The earth rolls down and the people die; their survivors derive solace from clinging, not to the rocks, not to the cliffs, not to the trees, but to each other" (p. 351). Dillard's previous work had largely presented the protagonist living in a society of one; here she seems to take a wider view of the world, emphasizing the importance of community in the face of the universe's indifference.

With its thorough documentation of the settlers' relationship to nature and their transformation of the landscape—the work reads at times like an environmental history of the Pacific Northwest—and with its metaphysical meditations on encounters with the natural world, a strong case can be made that *The Living* qualifies as a work of nature writing. What does the author herself have to say about being classified within this genre?

"There's usually a bit of nature in what I write," she remarked in an interview in 1981,

> but I don't consider myself a nature writer either. Weirdly, I would consider myself a fiction writer who's dealt mostly with nonfiction. The idea of nonfiction as an art form interests me more than anything else. The idea of the nonfictional essay's having the abstract intellectual structures of poetry interests me. Its content is the world. Its content isn't the poet's brain and it isn't the words. Its content is the structure itself and that which is stretched over the structure. The fabric of the surface is the world itself with its data, even, as well as such sensory pleasures as the world's days afford.

A couple of important points emerge from this self-assessment. First, Dillard is interested in experimenting with forms, pushing the boundaries of traditional literary genres. (It is interesting, and revealing, that a number of her works have been written on either edge of the continent—islands off the coast of western Washington or Cape Cod—because they serve as a metaphor for her desire to fashion art that is on the creative brink.) Second, she is a craftsperson, a stylist, a *writer* first, trying to give shape and structure to the world she perceives.

Finally, she is interested in the world and all its data. Dillard is not a nature writer so much as she is a *world* writer; she creates worlds through her art. If one considers all the world "nature" then she is of course a "nature writer," in the broadest sense of the term: nature being everything that exists and occurs in the universe, the world inside as well as outside the mind.

One can count on reading more provocative work by this woman of remarkable powers of consciousness and articulation. In a review of *Pilgrim at Tinker Creek*, Eudora Welty confessed that she did not always know what Annie Dillard was talking about. This did not trouble Welty, though, because she felt it better to be blessed with too much imagination than to have too little. Nor need one be concerned with Dillard running out of imagination; as she concludes in *An American Childhood*, "And still I break up through the skin of awareness a thousand times a day..." (p. 250).

Selected Bibliography

WORKS OF ANNIE DILLARD

NONFICTION

Pilgrim at Tinker Creek (New York: Harper's Magazine Press, 1974; repr., New York: Bantam, 1975); *Holy the Firm* (New York: Harper & Row, 1977); *Teaching a Stone to Talk: Expeditions and Encounters* (New York: Harper & Row, 1982); *Living by Fiction* (New York: Harper & Row, 1982); *Encounters with Chinese Writers* (Middletown, Conn.: Wesleyan Univ. Press, 1984); *An American Childhood* (New York: Harper & Row, 1987); *The Writing Life* (New York: Harper & Row, 1989).

POETRY

Tickets for a Prayer Wheel (Columbia, Mo.: Univ. of Missouri Press, 1974); *Mornings Like This: Found Poems* (New York: HarperCollins, 1995).

NOVEL

The Living (New York: HarperCollins, 1992).

COLLECTED WORKS

The Annie Dillard Reader (New York: HarperCollins, 1994).

UNCOLLECTED ESSAYS

"Thinking About Language," in *The Living Wilderness* 37 (autumn 1974); "Winter Melons," in *Harper's* 248 (January 1974); "Some Notes on the Uncertainty Principle," in *New Lazarus Review* 1 (1978); Foreword to Pinions, *Wind on the Sand: The Hidden Life of an Anchoress* (Ramsey, N.J.: Paulist, 1981); "Island Reflections," in *Science* 81 (April 1981); "First Taste of America," in *American Heritage* (December 1984); "The Purification of Poetry— Right out of the Ballpark," in *Parnassus* 11 (fall/winter 1984); "Why I Live Where I Live," in *Esquire* 101 (March 1984); "Memories of the Season," in *Pittsburgh Magazine* (December 1985); "Singing with the Fundamentalists," in *Yale Review* 74 (winter 1985); "Galapagos Revisited," in *Signature* 21 (August 1986); "How I Wrote the Moth Essay—and Why," in *The Norton Sampler*, ed. by Thomas Cooley (New York: Norton 1986); "Natural History: An Annotated Booklist," in *Antaeus* 57 (Autumn 1986); "The French and Indian War: A Memoir," in *American Heritage* 38 (July/August 1987); "Making Contact," in *Yale Review* 72 (October 1988).

UNCOLLECTED POETRY

"The Affluent Beatnik," in *The Girl in the Black Raincoat*, ed. by George Garrett (New York: Duell, Sloan, and Pearce, 1966); "Conifers," in *Field* 11 (autumn 1974); "The Sign of Your Father," in *Field* 11 (autumn 1974); "The Weighing of Daleville," in *New Orleans Review* 4 (1974); "A Natural History of Getting Through the Year," in *Poetry* 125 (February 1975); "Quatrain of the Body's Sleep," in *Poetry* 125 (February 1975); "The Heart," in *Poetry* 125 (February 1975); "The Blind Spot," in *Concerning Poetry* 9 (1976); "Monarchs in the Field," in *Harper's* (October 1976); "Metaphysical Model with Feathers," in *Atlantic* (October 1978); "Soft Coral," in *Antigonish Review* 48 (1982); "The Windy Planet," in *Songs from Unsung Worlds: Science in Poetry*, ed. by Donnie B. Gordon (Boston: Birkhauser, 1985); "Language for Everyone," in *Southwest Review* 71 (1986); "Found Poems: Observations," in *Kenyon Review* 12, no. 2 (spring 1990); "Light in the Open Air," in *Antaeus* 64–65 (spring/autumn 1990); "Observations and Experiments," in *Harper's* (August 1990); "Mornings Like This," in *Georgia Review* 47, no. 3 (fall 1993); "Index of First Lines," in *New Republic* 1 (November 1993); "Mayakovsky in New York: A Found Poem," in *Atlantic* (September 1994).

UNCOLLECTED SHORT STORIES

"Life Class," in *Carolina Quarterly* 24 (spring 1972); "Ethiopian Monastery," *The Hollins Critic* 10 (August 1973); "Five Sketches," in *North American Review* 263 (summer 1975); "Some Easy Pieces," in *Antioch Review* 33 (1975); "The Stone," *Chicago Review* 26 (1975); "The Doughnut," in *Antioch Review* 34 (fall/winter 1975–1976); "A Christmas Story," in *Harper's* 252:58 (January 1976); "Stone Doctor," in *Epoch* 26 (fall 1976); "Utah," in *TriQuarterly* 35 (spring 1976); "At Home with Gastropods," in *North American Review* 263 (spring 1978); "The Living," in *Harper's* 257 (November 1978); "Notes on a Voyage," in *Wesleyan Review* 4 (winter 1980); "Forest and Shore," in *Harper's* 265 (January 1985); "Ship in a Bottle," in *Harper's* 269 (September 1989); "A Trip to the Mountains," in *Harper's* 271 (August 1991).

BIOGRAPHICAL AND CRITICAL STUDIES

Catherine Albanese, *Nature Religion in America: From the Algonkian Indians to the New Age* (Chicago: Univ. of Chicago Press, 1990); Craig Albin, "In Search of 'The Spirit's One Home': A Reading of Annie Dillard's Pilgrim at Tinker Creek," in *Journal of the American Studies Association of Texas* 20 (October 1989) and "A Ray of Relation: Transcendental Echoes in Annie Dillard's Pilgrim at Tinker Creek," in *Journal of the American Studies Association of Texas* 23 (October 1992); Judy Schaaf Anhorn, "Annie Dillard's 'Purified Nonfiction,'" in *Cross-Cultural Studies: American, Canadian and European Literature 1945–1985*, ed. by Mirko Jurak (Ljubljana, Yugoslavia: Filozofska Fakulteta, 1988); John E. Becker, "Science and the Sacred: From Walden to Tinker Creek," in *Thought* 62 (December 1987); Joan Bischoff, "Fellow Rebels: Annie Dillard and Maxine Hong Kingston," in *The English Journal* 78 (December 1989); Douglas Burton-Christie, " 'A Feeling for the Natural World': Spirituality and Contemporary Nature Writing," in *Continuum* 2 (February 1992).

Mary Cantwell, "A Pilgrim's Progress," in *New York Times Magazine* (26 April 1992); Marc Chenetier, "Tinkering, Extravagance: Thoreau, Melville, and Annie Dillard," in *Critique* 31 (spring 1990); Suzanne Clarke, "The Woman in Nature and the Subject of Nonfiction," in *Literary Nonfiction: Theory, Criticism, Pedagogy*, ed. by Chris Anderson (Carbondale: Southern Illinois Univ. Press, 1989); Robert Paul Dunn, "The Artist as Nun: Theme, Tones, and Vision in the Writing of Annie Dillard," in *Studia Mystica* 1 (winter 1978); John Elder, *Imagining the Earth: Poetry and the Vision of Nature* (Urbana: Univ. of Illinois Press, 1985); Susan M. Felch, "Annie Dillard: Modern Physics in a Contemporary Mystic," in *Mosaic* 22 (spring 1989); Peter Fritzell, *Nature Writing and America: Essays upon a Cultural Type* (Ames: Iowa State Univ. Press, 1990); Jacob C. Gaskins, " 'Julie Norwich' and Julian of Norwich: Notes and a Query," in *Fourteenth Century English Mystics Newsletter* (1980).

Stan Goldman, "Sacrifices to the Hidden God: Annie Dillard's *Pilgrim at Tinker Creek* and Leviticus," in *Soundings* 74 (spring/summer 1991); Karla M. Hammond, "Drawing the Curtains: An Interview with Annie Dillard," in *Bennington Review* 10 (April 1981); Sandra Humble Johnson, *The Space Between: Literary Epiphany in the Work of Annie Dillard* (Kent, Ohio: Kent State Univ. Press, 1992); Joseph Keller, "The Function of Paradox in Mystical Discourse," in *Studia Mystica* 6 (fall 1983); Belden Lane, *Landscapes of the Sacred: Geography and Narrative in American Spirituality* (New York: Paulist, 1988); David Lavery,

"Noticer: The Visionary Art of Annie Dillard," in *Massachusetts Review* 21 (summer 1980); Thomas J. Lyon, *This Incomperable Lande: A Book of American Nature Writing* (Boston: Houghton Mifflin, 1989); Rosalind S. Mayberry, "Voice in the Wilderness," in *CEA Critic* 54 (fall 1991); James I. McClintock, *Nature's Kindred Spirits: Aldo Leopold, Joseph Wood Krutch, Edward Abbey, Annie Dillard, and Gary Snyder* (Madison: Univ. of Wisconsin Press, 1994).

Mary Davidson McConahay, "Into the Bladelike Arms of God: The Quest for Meaning Through Symbolic Language in Thoreau and Annie Dillard," in *Denver Quarterly* 20 (fall 1985); Margaret McFadden, "The I in Nature: Nature Writing as Self-Discovery," in *Teaching Environmental Literature: Materials, Methods, Resources*, ed. by Frederick O. Waage (New York: Modern Language Association of America, 1985); Gary McIlroy, "*Pilgrim at Tinker Creek* and the Burden of Science," in *American Literature* 59 (March 1987), "*Pilgrim at Tinker Creek* and the Social Legacy of Walden," in *South Atlantic Quarterly* 85 (spring 1986), " 'The Sparer Climate for Which I Longed': *Pilgrim at Tinker Creek* and the Spiritual Imperatives of Fall," in *Thoreau Quarterly* 16 (summer/fall 1986) and "Transcendental Prey: Stalking the Loon and the Coot," in *Thoreau Society Bulletin* 176 (summer 1986); Richard E. Messer, "The Spiritual Quest in Two Works by Annie Dillard," in *Journal of Evolutionary Psychology* 9 (August 1988).

Vera Norwood, "Heroines of Nature: Four Women Respond to the American Landscape," in *Environmental Review* 8 (spring 1984) and *Made from This Earth: American Women and Nature* (Chapel Hill: Univ. of North Carolina Press, 1993); Virginia Stem Owens, "Truth Through Testimony: The Fierce Voice of Annie Dillard," in *Reformed Journal* 33 (April 1983); Eugene H. Pattison, "The Great Lakes Childhood: The Experience of William Dean Howells and Annie Dillard," in *The Old Northwest* 14 (winter 1989–1990); Eugene H. Peterson, "Annie Dillard: Praying with Her Eyes Open," in *Theology Today* 43 (1986–1987); Margaret Loewen Reimer, "The Dialectical Vision of Annie Dillard's *Pilgrim at Tinker Creek*," in *Critique* 24 (spring 1983); Bruce Ronda, "Annie Dillard and the Fire of God," in *Christian Century* 100 (May 1983) and "Annie Dillard's Fictions to Live By," in *Christian Century* 14 (November 1984); Linda Ross-Bryant, "The Silence of Nature," in *Religion and Literature* 22 (spring 1990); Don Scheese, review of *The Living*, in *Georgia Review* 47 (spring 1993).

Ronald Schleifer, "Annie Dillard—Narrative Fringe," in *Contemporary American Women Writers: Narrative Strategies*, ed. by Catherine Rainwater and William Schiek (Lexington: Univ. Press of Kentucky, 1985); Scott Slovic, *Seeking Awareness in American*

Nature Writing: Henry Thoreau, Annie Dillard, Edward Abbey, Wendell Berry, Barry Lopez (Salt Lake City: Univ. of Utah Press, 1992); Linda Smith, *Annie Dillard* (Boston: Twayne, 1991); Albert E. Stone, *Autobiographical Occasions and Original Acts: Versions of American Identity from Henry Adams to Nate Shaw* (Philadelphia: Univ. of Pennsylvania Press, 1982), and "Modern American Autobiography: Texts and Transactions," in *American Autobiography: Retrospect and Prospect*, ed. by Paul John Eakin (Madison: Univ. of Wisconsin Press, 1991); Elaine Tietjen, "Perceptions of Nature: Annie Dillard's *Pilgrim at Tinker Creek*," in *North Dakota Quarterly* 56 (summer 1988); Patricia Ward, "Annie Dillard's Way of Seeing," in *Christianity Today* (May 1978); Eudora Welty, "Meditation on Seeing," in *New York Times Book Review* (24 March 1974); Eleanor B. Wymard, "A New Existential Voice," in *Commonwealth* 24 (October 1975).

MARJORY STONEMAN DOUGLAS
(b. 1890)

MELISSA WALKER

ON THE FIRST day of March 1994, I waited in the living room of Marjory Stoneman Douglas' cottage in Coconut Grove, one of the oldest sections of Miami, Florida. Just five weeks short of her 104th birthday, Douglas had agreed to meet with me to talk about her writing and her life, particularly her seven decades of struggle to save the Florida Everglades. I had never met anyone more than a century old, and I was somewhat uneasy about interviewing someone whose conscious memory stretched back a hundred years. When Douglas was born in 1890, Herman Melville and Walt Whitman were in their early seventies, Mark Twain was fifty-five, Edith Wharton was twenty-eight, and T. S. Eliot was two years old. Douglas was nine when Ernest Hemingway was born and seventy-one when he died in 1961. She began publishing short fiction in the *Saturday Evening Post* about the same time he did, but her first book came out in 1947, long after his major novels were published. She has lived more than thirty years since his death, and during those years she has achieved some of her most important work as an activist and public figure.

As I waited for Douglas to emerge from the tiny bedroom where she had been napping, I looked around at the large room that has been her work and living space since she moved into this simple house she had built in 1926 with money she earned writing short stories. The walls were lined with books, and scattered about on desk- and tabletops were plaques, carved birds, and other examples of the many awards that she had received over the past few decades. There were overstuffed chairs and straight-backed chairs, lamps on tables and standing lamps. On a nearby table was an album of photographs taken on Douglas' visit to the White House in 1993. When Douglas entered this cluttered, comfortable, lived-in room, it was clear that she was blind, but with a little help she was able to make her way to the chair she has used for decades to receive visitors.

I had done my homework, and I did not waste time telling her what I had learned by reading *Voice of the River*, her autobiography dictated to and compiled by John Rothchild. I knew that she was born in Minneapolis on 7 April 1890; that at the age of three she moved with her parents to Providence, Rhode Island; and that about three years after that, her parents separated and she went with her mother, Florence Lillian Trefethen, to live with her maternal grandparents in Taunton, Massachusetts, until she entered Wellesley College in 1908. After graduating with a degree in English composition in 1912, she worked in various department stores. In 1913 she married Kenneth Douglas, thirty years her senior, a man she hardly knew. In 1915 she left him and moved to Florida to live with her father, Frank Bryant Stoneman, whom she had not seen since 1896. She worked two years as a reporter for the *Miami Herald*, then served for about a year in the U.S. Naval Reserves during World War I. In September 1918, she went to Europe to work for the American Red Cross, then returned to Miami to stay in 1920. As we settled into our two hours together, I mainly asked her questions about the Everglades and about her life as a writer.

When I asked Douglas about the ongoing fight to stop the damage done to the Everglades by sugar growers in south Florida, she observed that there are others who know more about these issues than she does: "I'm old and I'm blind. I can't see to read. So I am not so useful as I used to be." What is particularly inspiring about this comment is what it does not say. At 104 she does not say, or apparently believe, that she is useless. To Marjory Stoneman Douglas, to be useful is among the highest virtues. In her short story "A Flight of Ibis," published in 1935, a female character who is trying to impress a man

is determined to "show him she wasn't useless" (p. 70).

Douglas acknowledges that her blindness and hearing impairment limit her, but she does so without complaint, and she continues to make the most of her days. She listens to recorded books and has people come in to read to her. She gives interviews, makes statements to the press, and encourages others in the ongoing struggle to preserve and restore the complex ecosystem called the Everglades. During her husband's presidential campaign, Hillary Rodham Clinton privately visited Douglas at her home in Coconut Grove. In 1993 Douglas traveled to Washington; there she stayed in the White House and received the Medal of Freedom on 30 November. Even in her 104th year, a public pronouncement from her lips made front-page headlines in the *Miami Herald*.

When I asked Douglas what can be done to stop the environmental damage caused by sugar-cane growers, she responded that we can pass

Marjory Stoneman Douglas

232

laws against them. All of her professional life she has recognized the necessity of political action to preserve the natural world. In her first book, *The Everglades: River of Grass* (1947), she combined her skills as a journalist and writer of short fiction with her power to persuade others to get involved in the political process to prevent continued destruction of the already seriously damaged watery world she loved.

South Florida and the Everglades

To appreciate the life and work of Marjory Stoneman Douglas requires some understanding of the region that she has given so much of her life to preserve. Few people are so intimately associated with a place as she is connected with the Everglades. To mention Marjory Stoneman Douglas is to evoke the glades, and to mention that amazing place is to call forth her name.

The southern half of the Florida peninsula in the last years of the twentieth century is a very different place from the one Douglas saw when she arrived in Miami in 1915. At that time the seas bordering Florida were clean and teeming with fish and other sea life, as were the shallow pristine waters of Florida Bay at the bottom of the peninsula. The hundreds of mangrove islands of the bay provided homes for thousands of birds, and its many sandbars were their feeding ground. North of the bay were the vast reaches of saw grasses dotted with tree islands. North and to the west were the ancient trees of the Big Cypress Swamp; to the northeast lay the pine flats. Still farther north, in the middle of the peninsula, was a cluster of pure lakes from which a beautiful tree-lined river meandered south and flowed into the 730 square miles of Lake Okeechobee.

During the wet season water spilled continuously from this shallow lake, sending a spreading sheet of water through the marshes that slope gradually to Florida Bay. There were no roads or canals to break the flow of water. The clean water was the home of many plants, fish, shellfish, and other creatures that provided food for a great variety of animals and birds—great egrets, white ibis, herons, wood storks, and pelicans. On the raised areas of land throughout the saw grass marshes, known as islands, grew various kinds of vegetation, depending on the elevation from the water. The waters that moved through the marshes flowed slowly southward and eventually passed through the mangrove thickets that bordered much of the peninsula and spilled into the estuaries of Florida Bay and the Gulf of Mexico. There were significant populations of crocodiles, bears, and Florida panthers.

Except for drainage projects north of Lake Okeechobee and in and around Miami, this pristine world was mostly intact in 1915. But that was then. Now the bird population is less than 10 percent of what it was in the 1930s. There are fewer than 200 bears and 30 Florida panthers. The drainage projects begun in the 1910s and the completion in 1926 of the Tamiami Trail, connecting Tampa on the west coast with Miami on the east, began a process that has continued to this day and has resulted in numerous threats to the waters and life forms of Everglades National Park. The massive development and rapid population growth of south Florida, the extensive canal and levee system, and the agricultural runoff are among the causes of unnatural and damaging levels of water flow through the glades, the increased salinization of the waters of Florida Bay, the dangerous levels of mercury and other pollutants in the once sweet fresh waters of the glades, and the decline of animal and bird populations. Fish populations have fallen considerably, and many fish caught in the waters of the Everglades National Park are not safe to eat.

The population of Miami was approximately 3,500 people when Douglas arrived there and began writing a social column for the *Miami Herald*, the paper her father helped to found. In the process of covering the social scene she came to know the movers and shakers in this small community that only a few years later would become one of the fastest-growing boom towns in America. From the early days in Miami and throughout her life, Douglas has had strong ties to the most influential citizens there. In the spring of 1916, for example, Mrs. William Jennings Bryan invited her to go to Tallahassee to lobby for women's suffrage before the state legislature.

Except for her two years with the Red Cross in Europe after World War I, Douglas has made Miami her home since 1915. By staying in one place and remaining ever alert to the swirling and changing life of that place, she gradually became one of the most influential people ever to live in the state of Florida. In 1928 Ernest Coe founded the Tropical Everglades Park Association, which became the host organization for the national commission set up about the same time to investigate the possibilities of a national park. Douglas was one of two women appointed to the commission. From that day to the present, the Everglades have been a primary concern for her. She does not, however, take credit for the existence of the park. That distinction, she insists in "The Forgotten Man Who Saved the Everglades," belongs to Coe alone.

Overview of Douglas' Work

At the time she became involved in the movement to establish an Everglades National Park, Douglas was mainly writing short stories. Some of them were set in the glades, but she was just as likely to write about real estate speculators as plume hunters. As a journalist in the 1910s and early 1920s, Douglas recorded her observations of a largely frontier land dominated by outlaws and entrepreneurs. As a writer of short fiction in the 1920s and 1930s, she observed the wide range of social types taking hold in booming Florida and told their stories in the *Saturday Evening Post* and other popular magazines. As a student of the unique ecosystem known as the Everglades, she spent much of the 1940s learning about the human and natural history of that threatened place and producing the still unrivaled book *The Everglades: River of Grass.* In the 1950s Douglas used her extensive knowledge of the history of Florida to produce an adult novel, *Road to the Sun* (1951); two novels for young

people, *Freedom River* (1953) and *Alligator Crossing* (1959); and *Hurricane* (1958), an extensive treatment of the nature and history of the powerful storms that have had such an impact on life in Florida. In the 1960s, while working as director of the University of Miami Press and president of Hurricane House Publishers, she continued to deepen her understanding of the region she chose as her home. During those years she wrote *Florida: The Long Frontier* (1967), a history of the state from its geological formation to the middle of the twentieth century.

When *Florida* was published, Douglas was seventy-seven years old and already losing her eyesight, but she was far from finished with her work. In 1970 she founded and became president of Friends of the Everglades. Originally started to halt the building of a jetport inside the Everglades, the organization continues to be a significant force opposing harmful development and seeking restoration of the still-threatened glades. Throughout the 1970s and 1980s, Douglas gave much of her energy to this effort. Though she has not published a book on her own since *Florida*, she worked for many years on a biography to be titled "W. H. Hudson: Environmentalist." Almost finished, the manuscript is housed with many of her papers in the Special Collections of the University of Miami Library.

A cursory look at Douglas' bibliography might lead to the incorrect conclusion that she is something of a dilettante because she has moved from one genre to another, writing newspaper and magazine articles, a play, short stories, history, novels, and biography. But anyone who takes the time to read carefully through her canon will discover a mind that is intensely focused. From her earliest writing to her last, there is a concern with the relationship of humans to the natural world, an insistent consideration of the historical context of contemporary problems, and an interest in all aspects of life in southern Florida, the small part of the world to which she has given her intellectual and creative energy.

Douglas' first publication was a three-paragraph piece published by the *Boston Herald* on 23 June 1907, when she was seventeen years old. A winner of a competition sponsored by the paper, "An Early Morning Paddle" tells of a boy crawling from a tent that he shares with a chum to paddle his canoe out into the lake to watch the sun rise. Moving across the water through cold air and darkness, he waits for the singing of "countless birds" and for the "deluge of sunshine" bringing a new beginning, possibility, and light. Then he feels hunger pangs and paddles back to camp for breakfast.

Written in Taunton, Massachusetts, long before Douglas was concerned about the impact of human activity on water quality, "An Early Morning Paddle" focuses on the birds, the water, the light, and finally the need for food, four elements featured in her many writings about Florida. No matter how preoccupied she has become with the devastation of the natural world caused by human activity, Douglas has never lost touch with the wonder of that world; and no matter how dark the prospects for change may have seemed, she has never given up fighting for the future health of the watery world she loves. When I asked Douglas what her favorite bird is, she responded with the characteristic impatience she reserves for anything she thinks is trivial or irrelevant, letting me know that she thought I had asked a silly question.

After a brief pause, however, she closed her sightless eyes and said, "The most interesting birds are the white ibis. The nuptial flight of the white ibis is a sight to see. It's a great wheel of white birds floating over the country. It's an amazing thing." In the same interview she spoke of her first sight of the Everglades. She had gone one morning in 1925 with friends to the then unfinished eastern side of the Tamiami Trail to watch the sun rise, look out over the untouched river of grass, see the birds, and cook breakfast. Birds, water, light, food. In *Voice of the River*, she tells of the time she was driving along the Tamiami Trail and saw the ibis in nuptial flight: "We looked out at a great wheel of white birds slowly drifting over the land. . . . Birds seemed to leap into the air and then swing around in a huge circle. As soon as one group landed on the ground, another would lift off and fly" (p. 136).

JOURNALISM

After returning from Europe, Douglas resumed working for the *Miami Herald* in 1920. From 7 March through 9 June of that year she wrote a column, "The Galley Proof." From 10 June 1920 to 30 June 1923 the column was called "The Galley." A typical column began with poetry, followed by a string of short items such as book reviews, comments on local or national politics, diatribes against various social injustices, and musings on various social attitudes and values.

Readers of the column encountered topics ranging from evolution and prohibition to gardening and fashion. They learned about the advantages of the new one-piece dress introduced in 1922, reasons people resist the theory of evolution, inadequate nutrition among the poor, and the evils of prohibition. Interspersed throughout the whole run of the column was a preoccupation with what Douglas called in one column "the living beauties of South Florida." She wrote about the destruction of the native Caribbean pine, the beauty of the sea grape and the mahogany trees (22 August, 22 September), and the folly of building cities without adequate provision for parks. There is little in the column to suggest that in the early 1920s Douglas was particularly concerned about the Everglades, but she does mention them as the central feature of the south Florida landscape. Arguing for the importance of recognizing and preserving the unique qualities of every bioregion, she described south Florida on 22 December 1922 as a "region, flat, bordered by sea and gulf, centered with Everglades."

SHORT STORIES

From 1925 to 1943, Douglas published approximately fifty short stories, the majority of them in the *Saturday Evening Post*. Scenes set in the Everglades appear periodically in these stories. The subject matter of the stories is as varied as that of her column in the *Miami Herald*. There are adventure tales about aviators, rumrunners, and kidnappers; disaster stories of plane crashes, shipwrecks, hurricanes, and floods; social satires that expose the recklessness of the leisure class;

and realistic tales of the hardships of the working poor. Many include a love story as part of some larger drama. More than half are set in Florida and deal with subjects that she later treated in longer works. For all this variety, however, Douglas returned to some subjects over and over again. One is the conflict between the people and the creatures that live in the Everglades.

A typical story featuring the Everglades is "A Flight of Ibis," published in the *Saturday Evening Post* on 21 December 1935. Joe Harper, a photographer trying to salvage his failing career, finds the rookery of one of the last great flocks of white ibis, most of which had been killed off by hunters who sold them for meat. Determined to salvage his reputation with photographs of these amazing birds, Joe sits up all night, waiting for dawn, when he can make the perfect pictures he will show to the "man from Washington," a representative of the Audubon Society. Confident that he has taken good shots, Joe walks out of this remote Everglades wilderness back to the Tamiami Trail, where a girl named Mary Sue Martin is pumping gas.

Smitten by the girl, Joe stays for supper at her father's invitation, and in her presence he talks about the wonderful birds and the pictures he has made. Mary Sue goes out that night with Leroy Pennock, whose father, a plume hunter, was murdered in a shootout between two rival gangs of hunters. After carelessly telling Leroy the whereabouts of Joe's birds, Mary Sue confesses to Joe what she has done. Afraid that Leroy will find and kill the birds, they go back to the lake and wait for him and his cronies to arrive. Leroy's gang arrives and starts killing the birds with clubs. Shots are exchanged, and in the end, Joe and Mary Sue scare them away with flash cartridges that illuminate the whole lake with "a ghastly crackling light." In the process, Joe succeeds in getting the evidence that the Audubon Society has sent him to get—pictures of every man, complete with clubs and dead birds. The happy ending is typical of Douglas' stories. As Joe and Mary Sue kiss, she knows that he loves her and "that loving him was the best thing she could ever do" (p. 72).

"A Flight of Ibis" is more than the story of Joe Harper's recovery of his career and two people falling in love. Merged into the plot is a detailed description of the glades. The opening paragraph includes a brief sketch of the mangroves, saw grass, and dwarf cypress that Joe passed through to find the hidden stronghold. Douglas describes the journey back to the lake that he makes with Mary Sue in much more detail. They pass through the edge of the pineland "among the waist-high palmetto"; they thread "an open swale of saw grass" that is often more than head high; fight their way through an "almost impenetrable" cypress jungle; and crawl through the great arched roots of the mangroves in the darkness created by their "interlaced boughs" (pp. 70, 72). "A Flight of Ibis" may have been the best source of information about the nature of the Everglades that was available to general readers in 1935.

RIVER OF GRASS

People who know little else about *River of Grass* know the first line: "There are no other Everglades in the world." There is also only one Marjory Stoneman Douglas, and her most famous book, *The Everglades: River of Grass*, is one of a kind. It does not fit in a genre, and it combines elements of several disciplines: natural science, geology, agriculture, economics, hydrology, and politics. But more than anything else, this remarkable book is history, the story of what has happened to alter and threaten what Douglas calls in the final words of the book the "beauty, the vast, magnificent, subtle and unique region of the Everglades."

Except for her novel *Road to the Sun*, all of Douglas' book-length works were written at the suggestion of a publisher or editor. In *Voice of the River* she explains that she always thought it was a good idea to take on books that publishers wanted done rather than having to sell them on a project. The idea for her first book came when an editor at Rinehart approached her about writing a book on the Miami River for a series on American rivers. After explaining that there was not much to that spoiled river, Douglas proposed to write a book about the Everglades, which she concluded was really a river rather than a swamp, because its waters flowed in one direction.

The Everglades: River of Grass (1947) treats a wide range of topics in its fifteen chapters. Chapter 1, "The Nature of the Everglades," describes the geology, the geography, the water systems, and the living things of the region before people invaded it. There is no human presence in the scenes she describes. The second chapter, "The People of the Glades," tells of the early Indian tribes, the Calusas, the Tekestas, and the Mayaimi people. Chapters 3 through 7 relate the exploits of the early explorers, conquerors, and settlers of south Florida; and Chapter 8 focuses on the influx of Seminoles, Mikasukis, and runaway slaves into southern Florida. The next three chapters tell about the Indian wars and the Civil War.

In the last four chapters of the book Douglas turns to the activities that have devastated the complex ecosystem of the Everglades: the slaughter of hundreds of thousands of birds for the plume trade, the near extermination of alligators, the landgrab by the railroads, the introduction of cattle and farming, the extensive drainage projects, and the real estate boom and bust. The first chapter and the last three chapters of the original edition contain much of what Douglas had to say in 1947 about the nature of the glades and the human activities that have nearly destroyed them. The rest of the book constructs the historical context in which she places every subject she considers.

Douglas typically relates history through the stories of individuals. The index of *River of Grass* includes the names of more than 400 people: explorers, Indian chiefs, military leaders, politicians, railroad magnates, real estate speculators, settlers, socialites, and dreamers. The prose is dense and packed with dates, details of animal and plant species, figures, place names, and government agencies in addition to the numerous characters who have developed, drained, farmed, or worked to restore the once pristine Everglades. The bibliography in both the first edition and the revised edition of 1988 suggests the extensive research that went into the preparation of the book.

To explain the forces that threaten the Everglades, Douglas moves back in time to the earliest inhabitants, who lived in harmony with their environment; she looks anew at the colonial enterprise that was the beginning of the destruction of a singular environment; and she explores the steps by which the Indian ways were replaced by European ways. Small numbers of Indians were able to live in harmony in the seemingly hostile region; moderate numbers of Europeans, bent on changing it, led to its near destruction. Year after year, decade after decade, century after century, the Indians succeeded in obstructing the European efforts to conquer south Florida; eventually, however, the descendants of the explorers won out and initiated the process that eventually interrupted the predictable flow of water through the Everglades.

Chapter 13 of *River of Grass*, "Drainage and the Frontier," is an account of the efforts of settlers and developers to make money in the Everglades at the beginning of the twentieth century. The first drainage project, sponsored by Governor Napoleon Bonaparte Broward, was begun in 1905. In the next several years settlers bought the newly drained land; with little understanding of the rhythms of flood and drought in the area, they attempted to grow vegetables. Many failed and left. Desperate and ruined, others resorted to illegal activities. Violence often erupted.

In "The Eleventh Hour," the last chapter of the 1947 edition of *The Everglades: River of Grass*, Douglas brings her readers up to 1946, when "the Everglades were dying" as a consequence of drought and fires brought on by drainage of the glades. The structure of this chapter is similar to the one Douglas uses in much of her writing. She begins with an isolated situation—in this case a fire in the Everglades—and then steps back from the scene to the larger context. As in other writings, she contrasts the mind of the Indian with that of the city dweller. Faced with the destruction of their watery home, the Indians felt "a sense of evil abroad . . . that one passing rainfall could not change" (1974 ed., p. 270). Inhabitants of the rapidly growing nearby cities—Miami, Fort Lauderdale, Fort Myers—failed to perceive the threat to the ecosystem that in the long run could determine their future.

As "The Eleventh Hour" progresses, Douglas fills in more and more details—about development in the cities, the lives of farm workers, and the growth and decline of the cattle industry. Then she circles back to the drought that turned a river of grass and sweet water into "a river of fire." In the end, as in almost everything she has written, Douglas veers away from despair to point out the hopeful signs for the future. In 1947 she saw hope in the public outcry for action, in the formation of the Everglades National Park, and in the possibility that enough people would finally turn away from narrow self-interest "to consider the truth of the whole situation" (p. 297). As a writer and as an activist, Douglas has continually worked to help her readers see things whole. Never does she look through a narrow lens at a small part of a problem and conclude that the part she sees is indicative of the whole. Rather, as if she were using a wide-angle lens, she takes a sweeping view of southern Florida and focuses on one spot after another until her panorama is rich with detail.

A contemporary edition of *The Everglades: River of Grass* (1988) included a new chapter, "Forty More Years of Crisis," written by journalist Randy Lee Loftis in consultation with Douglas when she was in her ninety-eighth year. Shortly after the first edition of Douglas' most famous book went to press in 1947, south Florida was hit by two hurricanes. The result was massive water control projects that have made it possible to move water from lakes and agricultual areas in a number of complicated ways. A new set of environmental problems has been the result. Wildlife has continued to decline as water has been withheld from habitats or brought into them at inauspicious times, depriving wading birds of feeding ground at one time, flooding alligator nests at another. Aggravating the damage to the environment has been the rapid influx of more and more people, the growth of the sugarcane industry, the decline of the soil, the pollution of Lake Okeechobee, and the diversion of contaminated agricultural waters into the Everglades. Consistent with Douglas' method of ending with the positive, the chapter concludes with a description of the various plans to restore the natural conditions that once prevailed in this irreplaceable area: "If the people will it, if they enforce their will on the managers of Florida's future, the Everglades can be restored to nature's design" (p. 427).

ROAD TO THE SUN

Road to the Sun, Douglas' first novel and second book, begins shortly after the early drainage projects opened up new farmland in the second decade of the twentieth century. It focuses on a young couple who have left far more civilized lives to homestead in the glades and traces their progress through the turbulent times of the early twentieth century.

Ellen Chadwick, a privileged young woman from New England, is visiting Miami with her invalid cousin when she meets, falls in love with, and rather precipitously marries Jason Horne, a man she barely knows. He has bought recently drained land in the Everglades to grow vegetables and rice. The second chapter moves back in time to recount the world of servants, French lessons, trips to Boston for symphony concerts, fine clothes, and proper behavior that were part of Ellen's upbringing.

In the opening scene of the novel Ellen is walking alone on the "grassy spillbank" that parallels the canal. Enjoying "a rising pulse of delight and exultation," she feels that she is "at the very center of the world." Surveying the 360-degree horizon, Ellen marvels at the light, the water, and most of all at the "marvelous flights of the birds" (p. 4). She revels in the wonder of being alone in the dazzling light looking out at the "rippling sawgrass wilderness." The experience is similar to that described in "An Early Morning Paddle," Douglas' first publication. Once again a figure alone in nature is awed by the water, the light, and the birds. Like the boy in that early piece, Ellen Chadwick is called away from all this beauty by the need for food: "Now it was time to get back and cut the ham for his noon dinner and start the potatoes boiling" (p. 8). Cooking for her new husband brings almost as much pleasure to Ellen as enjoying the beauty of the landscape. For a brief time she and Jason are absorbed with elemental pleasures of a simple life. They live in a tent, eat abundant meals, laugh and make love often, sleep soundly, and talk of their favorite novels and poetry. The black servants who help Jason with the farm do so willingly and with good humor.

But there is more than one serpent in this short-lived paradise. The fertile soil in which Jason is growing vegetables and plans to grow the rice that will make him rich is soon flooded by unexpected rains that bring more water than the canals can carry away. In the middle of the night, their nearest neighbor, Hemp Yandell, dynamites the dike he believes Jason has built over his property line. Part 1 of this five-part novel ends as Jason shoots and kills Yandell.

Parts 2 and 3 include detailed accounts of the three trials that finally end in Jason's acquittal. While he is in jail, Jason carefully follows the news of the war in Europe, which he believes is "the end of civilization." Meanwhile, Ellen supports herself at a variety of menial jobs. By the time he is released from jail, Ellen has just begun selling real estate and has made enough money for them to live comfortably. Jason, however, is restless and unable to settle into a job. He finally confesses to his wife that he is "as guilty as hell," and after much inner struggle he decides to join the army.

When Part 4 opens, the time of the trials, appeals, and the final acquittal is long past. Having moved "through the war's confusion like a sleepwalker," Jason has become a wanderer, unsure whether it is 1922 or 1923. Drawn back to the Everglades, he lives alone on an island in the river of grass, in an abandoned house once inhabited by a man who killed several people. There he is haunted by the ghost of a murdered woman and by the faces of his disapproving mother, of Ellen, and of Hemp Yandell.

In this country "empty of everything but water and air and the land distant like a shadow," he begins the "long, musing self-questionings" (p. 194) that eventually lead him back to life and society. Jason's encounters with wild creatures contribute to his recovery. He goes out in his boat to stare at "the secret heart of a secret country" and startles a flock of great white pelicans. He watches them rise in a "lifting spray of whiteness" that carries his own heart up as they soar "in vast white drifting spirals" (p. 192). He responds to the "whirring and humming sense of unquenchable life" when he hears "the tiny cheeping of new quail coveys" (p. 207). He watches night hawks diving to the river "on black sharp wings," hears fish flapping "loud and sudden in the watery murmuring," looks "out over that infinite leafy continent," and feels "the wideness seeping into his heart" (p. 203).

Jason's movement back into human society begins when Frank Carr arrives at his isolated outpost to solicit his help in building the Tamiami Trail. Later, when Carr's baby becomes fatally ill, Jason helps him get back to Miami by cutting through thirty-six miles of the glades, carrying nothing but food, a rifle, a pan, and a machete. As he emerges from this seemingly impenetrable wilderness, Jason is ready once again to be part of the human community.

Part 5 focuses on Ellen, who in Jason's absence has become a successful real estate agent. Buying low and selling high, she is one of the high rollers of the real estate boom. Douglas brings historical reality to Ellen's story by interweaving it with tales of real people—Carl Fisher, the developer of Miami Beach, and George Merrick, who founded Coral Gables. Publicly known as a "Woman of Vision," Ellen has limitless credit, her picture in the paper, invitations to all the desirable social events, and lines of people waiting to see her. Jason, now working for a seed and fertilizer company, watches Ellen and the real estate boom from afar, and concludes that "it can't last." And when the market collapses and she loses everything, he summons her.

In the final chapter of the novel, Ellen goes to Jason's house in a driving rain, which turns out to be the initial phase of the great hurricane of 1926. Jason has been injured; both know, but do not admit, that he may be dying. Then comes the hurricane.

Road to the Sun begins with a peaceful scene in which the elements of nature—wind, water, earth, and sky—seem to form a harmonious whole. It ends with a storm so violent that it leaves everything ruined. Dedicated to the memory of her mother, who knew the "beauty and the terror," *Road to the Sun* explores the light and the dark of the human psyche as well as the benevolent and destructive sides of raw nature.

FREEDOM RIVER: 1845
AND *ALLIGATOR CROSSING*

Douglas has written three books that the publishers intended for a young audience: two novels, *Freedom River: 1845* (1953) and *Alligator Crossing* (1959), and *The Key to Paris* (1961), an illustrated introduction to the history of the city. As one who was an avid reader of Dickens at the age of eight, Douglas does not distinguish between serious literature and children's literature. When I asked Douglas about writing for young people, she responded unequivocally: "I don't write for young people. I write for anybody. I don't believe in writing down to people." In *Voice of the River*, Douglas explains that she agreed to write this book that would be targeted for young people only when the editor at Scribner's assured her that she could write as she always had, as long as she omitted the "sex and swearing" (p. 202). And that is precisely what she did.

Adult readers might read *Freedom River: 1945* without ever thinking that they are reading children's literature in the same way they might read Mark Twain's *Adventures of Huckleberry Finn*. There are in fact similarities between the two books. Both are set in the 1840s and feature an escaped slave, a white boy who tries to save him, adventures with Indians, encounters with criminals, and a river journey. Both books end with a slave set free and a white boy about to take off for new territory. Douglas, however, does not attempt to use the humor that characterizes Twain's tale; in its place is a straightforward historical realism. Among the characters are members of the household of Richard Fitzpatrick, one of the leaders responsible for Florida's achieving statehood in March 1845.

Freedom River was one of a series of books about the contributions of individual states to the Union. Published in 1953, shortly before *Brown* v. *Board of Education* (1954), this novel about slavery speaks as well to the legalized racism of the mid-twentieth century. Though it is set more than a century before its publication date, *Freedom River* addresses the racial matters of the early civil rights movement as well as those of abolitionist times.

Almost all of the action takes place outside. The opening scene of the novel is set on a sun-dazzled beach where Eben, an escaped slave, has just been washed ashore. On this isolated place with no human habitation, he finds coconuts to assuage both his thirst and his hunger and builds himself a shelter. Across the bay a white boy, Richard Robinson, plans to have a solitary adventure, to sail across the water and to explore and camp out on this very beach. There the two boys meet when Richard rescues Eben from a slave catcher, Lopez y Garcia, and claims him as his own property. Back at the Robinson home, Eben is treated well, but he is still at risk of being reclaimed by unscrupulous slavers. Richard's mother, an abolitionist, teaches Eben to read; his father tries to convince Richard to sell his new property and use the money to go to college.

During their time together, the boys journey upriver, where they join Billy Micco, an Indian boy their age. The three teenagers have a series of adventures. Richard kills his first deer, Billy kills a wildcat, and Eben shoots a possum that they cook for dinner. Their experiences serve to bond the three boys in a way that cannot easily be broken; but when they return home, Eben and Richard have no way to recapture the privacy and feeling of safety they had on their wilderness adventures. History and forces from the outside world soon bring an end to this short-lived innocence.

After they return, news arrives that Florida has been awarded statehood—as a slave state—and the slavers are determined to have Eben. One night Billy Micco steals into the Robinson house to get Eben and take him deep in the Everglades to live with his people, the Mikasuki Indians. Eventually Richard joins his friends in the glades, and the three of them restore an old seagoing boat so that Eben can escape. In the final scene of the novel Billy and Richard are sitting on the shore, watching Eben sail into the rising sun toward the Bahamas, islands "where no man was a slave."

Of all her books, Douglas told me, she is particularly fond of *Freedom River*. Looking back over her career as a writer in *Voice of the River*, Douglas is sometimes quite critical of her own work. She observes that most of her poetry written for "The Galley" "wasn't any good," and that *Road to the Sun* "didn't sell too well" because "it wasn't very good" (p. 202). But of *Freedom River* she says, "There's nothing in it I would change, and I like it still" (p. 203).

Alligator Crossing, a book of which Douglas says, in her characteristic modesty, she is "not ashamed," is part of a series of novels, each set in a national park and intended by the publisher John Day for young readers. But, like *Freedom River*, this novel would be compelling reading for almost anyone interested in the natural history of the Everglades. It is also a good story. A coming-of-age novel, *Alligator Crossing* tells of a young boy's struggle to grow up in a world where the lives of most of the adults he knows are tainted by poverty, ignorance, alcoholism, or greed. Henry Albert Bunks is running away from seven older boys who are chasing him down an alley in a bad neighborhood in Miami. He succeeds in eluding the vicious gang of boys and stows away on the boat of an alligator poacher and former plume hunter, Arlie Dillon.

Dillon thinks nothing of killing large numbers of animals illegally and for profit, but he has a surprising soft side that leads him to cook for Henry and to show him the wonders of the Everglades. In the course of their adventures together, Dillon teaches Henry about the many different species of birds and snakes they see, and about the habits of crocodiles and alligators. He takes him to Flamingo, a tiny community that was his home before the residents were thrown out when it was incorporated into the Everglades National Park. There Henry stays in a trailer with people who are kind to him.

An alligator basks in the sun in Douglas' beloved Florida Everglades.

When he learns that Dillon plans to send him back to his family in Miami, Henry is determined not to go.

Once again Henry hides out on Dillon's boat; this time he ends up deep in the glades, where Dillon has gone to kill alligators. Dillon resumes his paternal role with the boy, feeding him and teaching him about the birds, snakes, and other creatures they encounter. He also teaches about killing alligators, an activity Henry despises. But he goes along and even helps in the slaughter, feeling that there is nothing he can do to stop Dillon, and that if he does not help, Dillon may "half-kill him." Finally, however, the boy has enough and tries to stop him from killing a deer. They scuffle, and Dillon falls, losing consciousness.

Henry, thinking he has killed Dillon, takes off in the dinghy through the labyrinth of the mangroves. In the days that follow, he meets people in this vast wilderness who are willing to help him: a research botanist who offers him food and a job for the coming summer, and park rangers who help him locate the man he has left for dead. In the end, Henry not only finds Dillon but saves him from jail and prosecution by burying the poached alligator skins before the rangers see them.

The main thrust of the story is Henry's initiation into adult understanding about how "to get along in any man's world." There are no "good guys" and "bad guys" in this book; rather, there are flawed and fallible human beings, each capable of good and evil, and often lacking in the knowledge necessary to understand the consequences of their actions. Henry learns that it is possible to "admire a man and hate him at the same time" (p. 55). Dillon regularly defies the law and kills large numbers of animals for profit; he also exhibits great knowledge about the Everglades wilderness and its plants and wildlife. Mr. Ward, a photographer whom Henry greatly admires, causes the deaths of many young birds by invading their rookery to take pictures and provoking the adults to abandon their nests.

The historical context is in the background of this novel. Published in 1959, it must be set in the mid-to-late fifties because the Everglades National Park has been established for some time and the apartments in the tenement where Henry lives have blaring television sets, which would not have become common until the middle of the decade. Woven into the story of Henry's adventure are highlights in the history of Florida—the development of southern Florida, the building of the overseas railway to Key West in 1904–1912, the war against plume hunters and the murder of the warden Guy Bradley in 1905, the establishment of the national park in 1947, and the uprooting of the families who had lived there for generations. Douglas introduces these events into the narrative indirectly and in small doses. There are no specific dates mentioned in the novel.

Natural history, however, is very much in the forefront of the novel. From the beginning to the end, Henry is intensely aware of the natural world. In the opening scene, after escaping from the city streets, he sits on the banks of a canal. He dreams of the river the canal must flow into and of the sea beyond. He sees an alligator, finds its hole, and names it George. Sitting on a rock in the sun, he looks down at the water: "The sound of birds, the quiet, the safeness, the aloneness, sink into all the places that had ached" (p. 23). In the days that follow, Henry observes not only the wondrous birds and reptiles of the glades, but also the large mammals that were still common in the 1950s, when the story is set. He sees a doe with twin fawns, adopts a motherless baby raccoon, and, after watching loggerhead turtles lay their eggs on a deserted beach in the moonlight, sees a black panther attempt to dig up the eggs. As the novel progresses, these encounters with the natural world inspire and eventually transform this wounded boy. The threats to this seemingly pristine world come in the form of poachers, illegal fishermen, and ignorance, like that of Mr. Ward, that results in unintended destruction.

In the final scene Henry strikes out across an island of high land deep in the Everglades to rescue Dillon. Imagining that he is walking where "no man had ever gone before," he sees himself in a "trackless wilderness, a small boy with knobby knees, sunburned, sun bleached, hatless, insignificant, alone," and "tall with pride" (p. 184).

Douglas knows how to tell a story. *Alligator Crossing* is a compelling and satisfying narrative that pulls the reader forward in eager anticipation of what will happen next. In the process of telling this story, she also creates a strong visual image of the geography, wildlife, and plants of the Everglades. Following Henry on boat rides through the canals, rivers, saltwater bays, and mangrove swamps; walking with him across the hammocks and tree islands; and soaring above the whole scene in the tiny surveillance plane used by the park rangers, readers acquire a detailed panorama of the region.

At the end of the narrative is an "Author's Note" in which Douglas provides basic information about the history and features of the Everglades National Park. Although she does include stories about poachers and others who carelessly destroy wildlife, there is no reference here or elsewhere in the book to the outside forces that threaten the Everglades. By focusing on the wonders of this vast wilderness and how they affect young Henry, Douglas wrote a book about the discovery of paradise rather than its loss.

HURRICANE

In 1958, the year before *Alligator Crossing* appeared, Douglas published a very different kind of book. Written at the request of Stanley Rinehart, whose company had published *River of Grass* and *Road to the Sun*, *Hurricane* considers virtually everything that was then known about these powerful storms that had periodically devastated many parts of Florida. Before she sat down to write, Douglas did extensive research that included reading historical accounts of hurricanes, gathering material from the weather bureau, and traveling to places in the Caribbean and on the east coast of North America that are frequently hit by these storms. As she had done for her book on the Everglades, she interviewed researchers as well as countless ordinary people who had lived through hurricanes.

Divided into eight books, each containing from three to eight short chapters, *Hurricane* gives the facts about hurricanes and the history of people's experience of them, going back to the days of early explorers. Douglas relates both folklore and stories about the actual experiences of those who have survived hurricanes in modern times. In addition, she discusses the science of predicting storms, the economics of the damage they cause, and the need for more research. The book tells of the various ways people have tried to protect themselves from loss of property, injury, and death due to these fearsome storms. As she does in almost everything she writes, Douglas combines a comprehensive overview of her subject with a look at specific details, in this case particular hurricanes. The most memorable writing in the book is in the stories of the specific individuals whose lives were lost, interrupted, or permanently changed by a hurricane.

The hardback first edition of this book sold well, but when a paperback edition was brought out, sales declined considerably. The new publisher cut out most of the parts about particular storms and retained the scientific parts. In *Voice of the River*, Douglas attributes the poor sales of *Hurricane* to the fact that the editor "cut out all the hurricanes." Those who want to receive the full force of Douglas' work on hurricanes would do well to read the first edition.

FLORIDA: THE LONG FRONTIER

Except for *The Key to Paris*, a general, illustrated overview of the history of Paris for young readers, Douglas did not publish another book until 1967 when *Florida: The Long Frontier* came out. Similar in format to the fifteen-chapter *River of Grass*, *Florida* has twelve chapters, a twenty-page personal prologue, and a lengthy epilogue. The two books contain some of the same information about the geology and early Indian inhabitants of Florida, stories of the early explorers like John Cabot and Ponce de Leon, and tales of people responsible for the twentieth-century development of the state. Both books have a huge cast of characters. The index of *River of Grass* lists names of more than 400 people; the index of *Florida*, a shorter book, contains almost 250. Many names appear in both. Douglas' first book focuses on south Florida with special emphasis on the Everglades.

Florida explores the whole state, with equal attention to the development of the north and the south.

Florida is mostly about the history of the peninsula before the twentieth century. Only in the prologue and the epilogue does Douglas describe the events and development projects that have created modern Florida—the building of roads and causeways, the real estate boom that lasted from 1923 to 1926, the drainage projects, the growth of the cattle industry and truck farming, the fishing industry, and the development of myriad tourist attractions. Douglas applauds what is good about many of the projects that have helped Florida grow, but always with an eye to what success is costing, particularly to the "ancient Everglades" that she first saw when they were "almost untouched."

In the final paragraphs of the book, she recalls, in the days before the national park, seeing "thousands upon thousands of white plumed birds, egrets and ibis, covering the sunset sky and the enormous rising moon with their silent wings," only to learn the next day that plume hunters had attacked "all those beautiful rustling winged things," turning them into "dead, torn, bloody heaps" (p. 282). The image of a multitude of birds in flight appears repeatedly in her writings, as does the heap of bloody birds.

Underlying much of Douglas' work is the impulse to achieve balance, to counter the power of destruction with at least equally powerful creative forces. In the final paragraphs of *The Everglades: River of Grass*, she observes that in spite of all the damage that people have done to that unique ecosystem, there is still a balance "between the forces of life and of death." Such equilibrium, she concludes, must be maintained by balancing the opposing forces of the human psyche: greed, inertia, and foolishness with courage, will, and the ability to cooperate with others. Twenty years later in *Florida*, she is still concerned with balance. Arguing that cities should be "in a balanced and preserved natural background," she concludes that the future may lie in such communities and "in the strength with which man himself can set his powers of creation against his impulses for destruction"

(p. 283). Perhaps, she writes, this struggle for balance is "the unending frontier."

Conclusion

Douglas never succumbs to simplistic solutions, nor does she lapse into sentimentality or despair. It is far too late for her to expect to see permanent solutions in her lifetime, and she knows that her "unending" work must be carried through by others. Having lived more than a century, she has continued to adjust her efforts and expectations to meet real life challenges. In her younger days, whether she was lobbying the state legislature or relating the subtleties of a love relationship, she did so with a determination to see things as they are and in the broadest possible context. She has brought to her writing the many and varied experiences of her long and fruitful life. When I asked her whether she thought writing for newspapers affected the way she wrote short stories, she said, "Everything affects your writing. Everything. Your whole life affects it."

At 104, Marjory Stoneman Douglas knows her limitations, that she "is not as useful as she used to be"; but she also knows full well that when a woman of her stature and age speaks, people listen. And speak she does.

Selected Bibliography

WORKS OF MARJORY STONEMAN DOUGLAS

NONFICTION

The Everglades: River of Grass (New York: Rinehart, 1947; repr., Atlanta: Mockingbird Books, 1974; rev. ed., Englewood, Fla.: Pineapple, 1988); *Hurricane* (New York: Rinehart, 1958; rev. ed., Atlanta: Mockingbird Books, 1976); *The Key to Paris* (Philadelphia: Lippincott, 1961); *Florida: The Long Frontier* (New York: Harper & Row, 1967); *The Joys of Bird Watching in Florida* (Miami: Hurricane House, 1969).

NOVELS

Road to the Sun (New York: Rinehart, 1951); *Freedom River: Florida 1845* (New York: Scribners, 1953); *Alligator Crossing* (New York: John Day, 1959).

AUTOBIOGRAPHY

Voice of the River (Englewood, Fla.: Pineapple, 1987), written with John Rothchild.

COLLECTED STORIES

Nine Florida Stories by Marjory Stoneman Douglas, ed. and with an intro. by Kevin M. McCarthy (Jacksonville: Univ. of North Florida Press, 1990).

SELECTED SHORT STORIES

"At Home on the Marcel Waves," in *Saturday Evening Post* (14 June 1924); "Solid Mahogany," in *Saturday Evening Post* (20 June 1925); "Goodness Gracious, Agnes," in *Saturday Evening Post* (17 October 1925); "The Woman of It," in *Saturday Evening Post* (21 November 1925); "A River in Flood," in *Saturday Evening Post* (3 April 1926); "The Mayor of Flamingo," in *Saturday Evening Post* (24 April 1926); "Guinevere," in *Saturday Evening Post* (1 January 1927); "The Beautiful and Beloved," in *Saturday Evening Post* (2 April 1927); "Stepmother," in *Saturday Evening Post* (4 June 1927); "The Third Woman," in *Boston Herald* (5 June 1927); "You Can Have Three Wishes," in *Woman's Home Companion* (June 1927); "The Peculiar Treasure of Kings," in *Saturday Evening Post* (26 November 1927); "Daphne and the Delicious Monster," in *Woman's Home Companion* (May 1928); "Second Marriage," in *Chicago Sunday Tribune* (6 January 1929); "The Man Who Was Homesick," in *Household Magazine* (October 1929); "Charcoal," in *Saturday Evening Post* (11 January 1930); "The Thirty," in *Sunrise* (May 1932); "Reunion at Forty," in *Saturday Evening Post* (7 January 1933); "Adventuress," in *Household Magazine* (February 1933); "Hey, Waiter!," in *Woman's Home Companion* (April 1933); "You Got to Go— But You Don't," in *Saturday Evening Post* (26 August 1933); "Noon," in *Saturday Evening Post* (21 July 1934); "Solo Flight," in *Cosmopolitan* (August 1934); "High Goal Man," in *Saturday Evening Post* (9 March 1935); "Wind Before Morning," in *Saturday Evening Post* (8 June 1935); "Barnstormer," in *Saturday Evening Post* (7 September 1935); "A Flight of Ibis," in *Saturday Evening Post* (21 December 1935); "From the Terror by Night," in *Saturday Evening Post* (1 August 1936); "The Sun and the Stars," in *McCall's* (January 1937); "A Thing Apart," in *Delineator* (March 1937); "Volcano," in *Saturday Evening Post* (14 August 1937); "A Mountain in the Sea," in *Saturday Evening Post* (30 October 1937); "The Hand Is Quicker," in *Saturday Evening Post* (5 March 1938); "Athens to Marseilles," in *Saturday Evening Post* (3 September 1938); "A Hill in Haiti," in *Cosmopolitan* (July 1939); "Earthquake," in *Saturday Evening Post* (3 August 1940); "Moment of Magic," in *Woman's Home Companion* (March 1943).

SELECTED ARTICLES

"Wings," in *Saturday Evening Post* (14 March 1931); "The Cars Pass, But the Everglades Remain," in *Sunrise* (November 1931); "He Talks with Volcanoes," in *Saturday Evening Post* (25 December 1937); "Communities Face Their Slums," in *Ladies Home Journal* (October 1950); "The Forgotten Man Who Saved the Everglades," in *Audubon* (September 1971).

BIOGRAPHICAL AND CRITICAL STUDIES

Charles Flowers, "Starting Over in the Everglades: A Look to Restore This Precious Wild Land Through the Eyes of Four Uncommon People," in *National Wildlife* 33 (April/May 1985); Valerie Gladstone, "Woman of the Year," in *Ms.* (January/February 1989); James LeMoyne, "Everglades Sentinel on Watch at 100," in *New York Times* (8 April 1990), sec. A; Dava Sobel, "Marjory Stoneman Douglas: Still Fighting the Good Fight for the Everglades," in *Audubon* 93 (July/August 1991); Steve Yates, "Marjory Stoneman Douglas and the Glades Crusade," *Audubon* 85 (March 1983).

GRETEL EHRLICH
(b. 1946)

STEPHANIE KAZA

IN JUNE 1976, Gretel Ehrlich journeyed to Wyoming to film a documentary on sheepherding for the Public Broadcasting System. Her assignment was to capture the solitary lives of the herders as they traversed the open landscape with their sheep. She had left her dying lover, David, in New York City. Every two or three days she drove down the mountain to call David, whose condition was growing worse. By late September the filming was done, and Ehrlich made plans to fly east and rejoin David. But she was too late. He died that morning, on the heels of a powerful storm.

After David's death, Ehrlich traveled for two years, beset by grief and emptiness. Her New York life fell away as she tried to find comfort and relief. The tears came in waves, blurring earlier reference points, as she drifted across the continent. When John, the sheep foreman in Wyoming, invited her to come back, she accepted. She joined the crew herding sheep, finding her way through the loneliness by immersing herself in open space. By winter, she had settled in a small cabin for a season of solitude.

Winter in Wyoming is a palpable force. The winter of 1978 was the third worst on record. Ehrlich started writing letters; the stories were too dramatic to keep to herself. Under extreme temperatures of forty, fifty, and sixty degrees below zero, her attention was necessarily riveted on survival. The elements that shaped the land-scape crept under her skin, penetrating to the bare bones of her life. In a matter of months, New York was a distant reality, displaced by the powerful presence of the Big Horn Mountains.

Ehrlich was no stranger to the West. Though she had gone east to Bennington College in Vermont, she was a native of California, born 21 January 1946 in Santa Barbara. At twelve, she wanted to be a painter, but by her early twenties her creative urge turned to filmmaking. She returned to California and enrolled in the film school at the University of California, Los Angeles. Later she moved to New York City, where she worked for PBS and attended the New School for Social Research.

Wyoming, the land she fell in love with, shaped much of Ehrlich's work. The Big Horn Mountains rise 10,000 feet above the valley floor. From her ranch in Shell where she lived with her husband, Press Stephens, the view to the east, west, and south is one unbroken landscape for one hundred miles in all directions. The steep mountains rise to the north—layers of rock holding the shallow seas that once covered the regions. Mudstones, sandstones, limestone—a collage of brown, red, orange, and white—press against gray granite upthrusts. The place is rich with fossils—marine sponges as well as saber-tooth tigers. The American Museum of Natural History found twenty-five complete dinosaur skeletons in the ranch's lower meadow.

Feeder creeks to the Big Horn River flow out of the mountains behind the ranch. Waterfalls of meltwater tumble to the valley floor each spring. Ranchers depend on the snow runoff for irrigating the hay fields. Rainfall is sparse in Wyoming—an average of less than eight inches per year. Sometimes the creeks stay frozen until June. In most years water is available only through August; by September all but the major rivers have dried up.

Wyoming is big sky country, like Montana and Colorado. The endless cerulean sky of summer can be the source of wild and dangerous weather in winter: sudden blizzards bury the land under six feet of snow; stunning hailstorms flatten corn crops in a day. In winter, cold fronts can plunge temperatures to thirty below zero overnight. It is not uncommon for weeks to go by with temperatures never rising above zero. People adapt by taking it all in stride. In her essay "Landscape" (in *Legacy of Light*, 1987), Ehrlich comments, "What can seem like a hard shell veneer on the people here is really a necessary spirited resilience."

Like other writers of place, Ehrlich speaks from the irrefutable power of her experience on the land, the particular piece of land she calls home. Like Henry David Thoreau and John Muir before her, she is a walker and wanderer: In "Landscape," she says, "I like to think of landscape not as a fixed place but as a path that is unwinding before my eyes, under my feet." Ehrlich feels that "to see and to know a place is a contemplative act. It means emptying our minds and letting what is there, in all its multiplicity and endless variety, come in." For her, sense of place is a matter of sensory knowledge accumulated over time in the mind and body. "We rise with the landforms. We feel the upper altitudes of thin air, sharp stings of snow and ultraviolet on our flesh." To empty out is to let go of preconceived ideas of the landscape, to meet directly the "otherness" of a place. For Ehrlich this is an act of surrender. "Surrendering means stripping down, taking away every veil, every obstacle between ourselves and the earth.... It is to allow ourselves to be touched from above and below and within, to let a place leave its watermark on us" ("Landscape").

First Essays

Ehrlich's first major book, *The Solace of Open Spaces* (1985), is the story of her surrender to the landscape of Wyoming. She describes the book as "a celebration of everything here." The book was written from 1979 to 1984, when she was learning to herd cattle and sheep. She helped neighbors and filled in frequently as a ranch hand during calving season, pulling stuck babies out of mothers and doctoring weak calves in cold weather. The essays grew out of journal entries kept during this time and sent as letters to a friend in Hawaii. In 1986 the book won the Harold D. Vursell Memorial Award of the American Academy and Institute of Arts and Letters.

In twelve essays, Ehrlich offers sketches of ranch life in Wyoming, shown through the lens of her own personal journey into the land. The title piece, "The Solace of Open Spaces," sets the stage for the human dramas to follow. She describes Wyoming as "the doing of a mad architect—tumbled and twisted, ribboned with faded, deathbed colors. Thrust up and pulled down as if the place had been startled out of a deep sleep and thrown into pure light" (p. 3). Great arid valleys stretch out across the center of the state, sheltered on the horizon by great mountain ranges: the Big Horns, the Absarokas, and the Tetons.

The wilderness of the landscape is matched by the unruliness of the seasons. "Winter lasts six months here. . . . At twenty, thirty, and forty degrees below zero, not only does your car not work, but neither do your mind and body" (p. 1). The end of winter does not necessarily mean an end of the harshness. "Spring weather is capricious and mean. It snows, then blisters with heat.... Melting snowbanks hiss and rot, viperous, then drip into calm pools" (p. 7). And through all the seasons of cold, heat, snow, and rain, there is always the wind. "If anything is endemic to Wyoming, it is wind. This big room of space is swept out daily, leaving a bone yard of fossils, agates, and carcasses in every stage of decay" (p. 8).

In this vastness, people conserve words. Solitude is a way of life for many of the ranchers and herders Ehrlich describes. Language is compressed, almost metaphorical. "Sentence structure is shortened to the skin and bones of a thought" (p. 6). Ehrlich comes to reflect this style of communicating in her own lean voice and carefully chosen words. A poet first, in her writing she reveals a keen ear for pacing, weight and understatement. In the introduction to *Words from the Land* (1988), Ehrlich is quoted as saying, "I'm very particular about language, as are most people who started out writing poetry. I think about every word. I care a lot about how it sounds" (p. 18).

Despite the laconic mode of speaking, Ehrlich feels warmed by the "coziness" of the state. Ranchers know each other from one valley to another, and people travel long distances to see each other. "Friendliness is a tradition" (p. 5). It mitigates loneliness and isolation, and provides essential help in emergencies. In this emptiness, people do not waste words; they value truth over etiquette, "believing honesty is stronger medicine than sympathy, which may console but often conceals" (p. 11). Though Ehrlich admits she originally returned to Wyoming to lose herself in the unpopulated vastness, instead "life on the sheep ranch woke me up. The vitality of the people . . . flushed out what had become a hallucinatory rawness inside me. . . . The arid country was a clean slate. Its absolute indifference steadied me" (p. 4).

In this waking up Ehrlich encounters the complexities of human history on this land, the wilderness stained by battles for territory. Crow, Shoshone, Arapaho, Cheyenne, Sioux once roamed the land without seeing a single barbed wire fence. White settlers carved the region into large ranch holdings dominated by cattle barons. Instead of emptiness, the land is full of stories that she tells in the rest of the book.

In "Obituary," the reader meets the odd characters who herd sheep for a living and have

Gretel Ehrlich

done so for most of their lives. There is Grady, the once-a-year binge drinker; Fred, the junk hoarder; and Albert, who tries to seduce her. She visits Bob Ayers, who is in jail for shooting six cows in a minor range war: "even if we are underpaid, I'd rather herd sheep than have some flat-footed prick telling me what I can and can't do" (p. 28). Each has a story born during long cold nights watching sheep, alone with the silent stars.

In "Other Lives" we meet Mary Francis "Mike," a third-generation rancher of "seamless loyalty" who taught Ehrlich to rope, and two other women "cowboys" who are frequent partners on the range. In "About Men," we meet the cowboys, who turn out not to be as tough as the men in the Marlboro ads. Ehrlich explodes the romanticized stereotypes, speaking in plain talk about how these men do their jobs. One old-timer told her, "Cowboys are just like a pile of rocks—everything happens to them. They get climbed on, kicked, rained and snowed on, scuffed up by the wind. Their job is 'just to take it'" (p. 50). Cowboy courage is based less on chasing outlaws and more on helping a stuck cow, a drowning horse, or someone in trouble. "Because these men work with animals... because they live outside in landscapes of torrential beauty... and awesome variables, because calves die in the arms that pulled others into life... their strength is also a softness, their toughness, a rare delicacy" (pp. 52–53).

Herding cows and sheep means working with animals at all times of day and night and in all seasons. In "From a Sheepherder's Notebook," Ehrlich describes riding for three days on horseback, tracking sheep through summer pastures. She deals with sun, wind, dust, and sheep ticks in the company of a trusty Kelpie sheepdog. "To herd sheep is to discover a new human gear somewhere between second and reverse—a slow steady trot of keenness" (p. 59). In "Friends, Foes, and Working Animals," Ehrlich experiences the "stripped-down compassion" of dealing with birth and death, and the "sacrament of nurturing" ailing animals. In contrast to "outsiders"—townspeople and city slickers with their patronizing attitudes—she sees in an animal's wordlessness "the cleansing qualities of space." She writes of horses as mischievous, intelligent, "chummy," telling stories of horse outlaws with ominous names—Bonecrusher and Widowmaker. Animals become meditation teachers, holding Ehrlich "to what is present; to who we are at the time, not who we've been." Wild animals make up for a lack of human contact out on the cattle range. In her terse style, she describes encounters with Big Horn rams, coyotes, and rattlesnakes. "I tried nude sunbathing once: I fell asleep and woke just in time to see the grim, flat head of a snake angling toward me" (p. 69).

In "On Water," Ehrlich traces the peculiarly Western preoccupation with water—when it will come, how much there will be, and whether it will be enough for crops and cattle. "Dryness is a common denominator in Wyoming. We're drenched more often in dust than in water" (p. 78). One hopes for spring rains in April, but in drought years there may be only thin runoff from the high peaks. As Ehrlich puts it, "Waiting for water is just one of the ways Wyoming ranchers find themselves at the mercy of weather" (p. 76). Wars over water rights have plagued the West since the first white settlers grabbed up the territories along the watercourses. Ehrlich is also drawn to water for "what is unconscious, instinctive, and sexual in us." She compares people to rivers, fearing the "dry spells," feeling the potency of water for healing, for creativity.

Ehrlich's long-standing heartache is finally resolved when she meets a local rancher at a film festival in nearby Cody. He serenades her with sandhill crane calls and they are married ten months later, in the middle of winter. They move soon after to what used to be the town of Cloverly. Their plan is to rescue an old ranch from neglect, though the price is surrender of their bachelor lives on "the bunkhouse-bedroll-barroom circuit." After a honeymoon in Oklahoma City at the National Finals Rodeo, they return to the ranch to follow "the narrative thread of birth, death, chores, and seasons," marked by everyday rituals and easy familiarities.

The Solace of Open Spaces was received with praise by reviewers. In the *Los Angeles Times Book Review*, Kristiana Gregory called the book "a tender, poetic salute to the West." Janet Cannon, in *Western American Literature Review*, described Ehrlich's writing as "hard, lean, yet feminine prose." In the *Sewaneee Review*, Pat C. Hoy II recognized Ehrlich's "fine ear for the western voice, local sayings, and local color" and her ability to become the earth itself—"at once full, barren, contradictory; acted upon, changed, and charged." In this first volume of essays, Ehrlich defines her voice: pithy, strong, terse, and vivid. She establishes her relationship as a writer to the land of Wyoming, to "landscape as sacramental... perfect, irrational, semiotic." She learns the hard lessons of impermanence: "loss constitutes an odd kind of fullness; despair empties out into an unquenchable appetite for life" (p. lxxxvi). She tells her life story as a story of place and context, inseparable from the changing weather and raw landscape she comes to know as home.

Stories of Heart Mountain

Before *The Solace of Open Spaces*, Ehrlich had written two volumes of poetry; afterward, she began experimenting with short stories. *Wyoming Stories*, published in 1986, were sketches of characters who later appeared in her first novel, *Heart Mountain* (1988). The collage of stories takes place during World War II, following President Roosevelt's executive order authorizing the establishment of Japanese internment camps. Heart Mountain, across the valley to the west of the Big Horns, was one of ten camps in which more than 110,000 Japanese immigrants and Japanese Americans were detained for over three years. The novel combines fact and fiction to present a view of camp life, the imposition of military rule on the Japanese, and the problematic juxtaposition with ranchers and rural values. Ehrlich was moved to expose this undertold history as an example of the complex tangle of people and cultures on this land she called home. She drew material from library archives at University of California at Berkeley and at Los Angeles, the Smithsonian, local libraries, personal interviews, and a trip to Japan to investigate Noh theater and maskmaking, Shinto, and Zen.

Heart Mountain is not nature writing, yet it reflects Ehrlich's sense of the land and the people who live there. Her curiosity and quest for understanding are personally motivated. As a resident of the Big Horn River valley, she has made Heart Mountain part of her landscape. Its history is her history, acquired in the act of taking up tenancy. The stories from wartime are still alive in the families of her wider neighborhood. She feels their weight and poignant lack of resolution. In telling the story of Heart Mountain, she honors those who were profoundly affected by the landscape by no choice of their own. By the end of the book, we see, as reviewer Marian Blue noted in *Twentieth Century Western Writers* (1991), that "there are no winners of a war, but only survivors left in various stages of healing" (p. 206). Thus *Heart Mountain* becomes a sequence to Ehrlich's own healing in *Solace*, opening her experience of compassion to those who suffered before her on the same land.

The drama of *Heart Mountain* turns around rancher McKay Allison and internee and painter Mariko Okubo. Though he has "more brains and common sense, good looks, and more natural ability than anyone in the valley" (p. 4), McKay is melancholy. McKay's brothers have gone off to war; he is left to manage the cattle ranch because he has a gimp leg. In an odd hunting accident, McKay injures Abe-san, Mariko's grandfather; he goes to the camp to make amends. At a time when most Americans viewed the Japanese as archenemies, McKay acts more like a neighbor than a patriot. After several visits, he finds himself drawn to Mariko. They fall in love, but it is a compromised love, torn by differences in culture and situation. Mariko is married, McKay is lonely. Yet he is close to Madeleine Heaney, a woman he has known since childhood. Madeleine is lonely, too, for her husband is missing in action. Ehrlich tells the story of life inside the camp through the journal voice of Kai, a Berkeley student who helps organize a draft resistance campaign.

The emotional tone throughout most of the story is one of longing—longing for the war to be over, longing to be with the one you love, longing for a window of openness in the midst of tension, strain, and uncertainty. Madeleine "came to think waiting was one of the things that go with being a woman, and she hated it. But during a war everyone is waiting, everyone is powerless, everyone is offering himself up to become dead in some way" (p. 142). She passes the months herding and calving, working long nights in the cold. McKay's response to longing is to seek solace in the landscape, paralleling Ehrlich's own journey into the open spaces for healing. "Under the clipped top of Heart Mountain...he imagined there was an eye that saw him, sometimes the only eye, and a beacon light which led his grasping, solitary thoughts home" (pp. 5–6). Like her, he cannot forget the powerful presence of the one he loves but can never really have. Kai, who also yearns for Mariko, finds stability in the practice of Zen Buddhism, which he learns from Abe-san. Abe addresses the point directly. "If you are enlightened, does not mean there is no pain, no confusion in your life. To Ikkuyu [a Japanese poet], desire and letting go of desire—same thing" (p. 181).

When the war is over, Mariko leaves Heart Mountain. On one of their last walks together, she and McKay climb the ridge and look down into a small canyon. "How different we are, Mariko thought. I look at all this but he is made of it. He is not separate from it as I am" (p. 345). Here Ehrlich shows the fruits of her own embrace of the land. In the character of McKay, she portrays the power of the land to possess those who live there. It is the land, after all, that remains constant through the war. Kai and Abe-san take a day of their new freedom to climb Heart Mountain. This pilgrimage represents the high point of the Zen teachings for Kai; Abe becomes one with the mountain that has cast its shadow on the camp throughout the internment. As if his task is complete, Abe dies soon after, while sitting in McKay's car.

Critics recognized the effort Ehrlich made to reveal the dark side of the American war years. Marian Blue writes, "Rarely has World War II literature successfully reached into the rural West and created a microcosm; Ehrlich has done so" (p. 206). Garrett Hongo in the *New York Times Book Review* complemented her for her "immense poetic feeling for the internal lives of [the book's] varied characters and the sublime high plains landscape that is its backdrop." Her portrayal of Japanese culture tends toward the "exotic Other," but at the same time it reveals her own growing fascination with Buddhism, a theme that surfaces repeatedly in her next volume.

Before Ehrlich returned to nature writing, she retrieved four of the earlier pieces from *Wyoming Stories* and added ten postscript stories. The new collection was published in 1991 as *Drinking Dry Clouds*. In each postscript she writes in first person, allowing herself to walk into the experience of the characters from *Heart Mountain* she knows so well. She speaks as Kai's mother, as Madeleine, as McKay. It is as if she is still haunted by these voices and cannot let them go until they have become part of her. All the people bear the scars of loneliness and loss. And all the stories take place in the empty benchlands that can drive people mad. "God, there's nothing here," says one of the relocation camp residents. But he is stating the view of a stranger; for Ehrlich, the fullness of the landscape shapes everything. Christopher Tilghman wrote for the *New York Times Book Review*, "The people in Ms. Ehrlich's stories seem compelled to bear witness to their times, to their land and the lives they have lived upon it" (p. 6). These themes are consistent in all of Ehrlich's work: she uses personal testimony to investigate, struggle, and ultimately accept the relative scales of life and death, love and loss, and the impermanent nature of it all.

"Home Is How Many Places"

In *Islands, the Universe, Home* (1991), Ehrlich returns to nature essays, based both at home in Wyoming and farther afield. This work was supported by a Guggenheim fellowship awarded in 1989. For wider perspectives on her own sense of place, she travels to Hawaii, Japan, and the Channel Islands off the Santa Barbara coast, collecting insights from physicists and astronomers as well as her Japanese hosts. True to the tradition of Thoreau, the book uses walking as a way to follow the landscape and the mind simultaneously. Ehrlich sets the frame for her journeys in the first essay, "Looking for a Lost Dog." She struggles with perspective, with distance and intimacy, with "impulse and reason, passion and logic." Walking over trails and washes, she is filled with longing. "Some days...this one place isn't enough.... Those days, like today, I walk with a purpose but no destination. Only then do I see, at least momentarily, that most everything is here" (p. 7).

Stories of Wyoming alternate with accounts of her journeys. "Spring," "Summer," and "This Autumn Morning" take the reader into the extremes of Wyoming weather. Winter is about not only cold but also about ice, "movement betrayed, water seized in the moment of falling" (p. 13). Spring is about restlessness, the return of movement. "Sap rises in trees and in me, and the hard knot of perseverance I cultivated to meet winter dissipates; I walk away from the obsidian of bitter nights" (p. 13). The mountain moves below her feet, a continent adrift. The wind blusters. "Its fat underbelly scrapes uneven ground, twisting toward me like taffy" (p. 17). The season brings on waves of doubt, deliberation, resistance. Questions of time and space blur over the face of the landscape, consuming the mind with questions. Meanwhile, Ehrlich "sit[s] cross-legged on old blankets" (p. 24).

Summer is not just any summer; it is the driest summer since the Dust Bowl, and Yellowstone is on fire. Ehrlich chronicles the storms of heat, the rainless thunderclouds, temperatures over 100 degrees, and the combination of dust and smoke darkening the sky. "A big hand is dropping matches all over the West. Like winged seeds, sparks are propelled into the sky, scratching and scarring its skin" (p. 47). On Black Saturday, 20 August, over 160,000 acres burn in a single day. Despite massive deployment of troops and helicopters, the West keeps burning. On 6 September, Ehrlich meditates on higher ground in the mountains, and ash lands on her tongue. "What have I eaten? A piece of tree, of fire; a piece of this island universe...?" (p. 55). The endless, weighty smoke becomes metaphor for obstacle, delusion, barrier to inner clarity. Almost the entire summer is obscured.

In autumn the nights turn cold. It is a year later, and Ehrlich flashes back to the previous spring when she and her husband visited Yellowstone to survey the damage: dead bison, dead elk, the charred ruins of the forest. At home death comes to a heifer and then to a good friend. She writes, "I knew how death is made—not why, but where in the body it begins, its lurking presence before the fact, its strangled music as if the neck of a violin were being

choked.... I know how easily existence is squandered, how noiselessly love is dropped to the ground" (p. 75). She sits, holding the Zen posture of stillness, seeking relief from the mind's chatter. A small island in her ranch pond is her refuge, her point of reference as time passes and the seasons shift. By November the lake is frozen and covered with snow.

This winter she escapes to Japan, following her desire to know more about the culture and spirituality she encountered when writing *Heart Mountain*. Ehrlich's attraction to Japan and Zen go back to an early love for Japanese poetry, especially that of Basho. Ehrlich identifies the tenth-century *The Kokinshu* as a favorite collection of poems. She came in her words,

> to sniff out *shizen*... spontaneous, self-renewing, inherently sacred natural world of which humans are an inextricable part. I wanted to see how and where holiness revealed itself, to search for those "thin spots" on the ground where divinity rises as if religion were a function of geology itself: the molten mantle of sacredness cutting through earth like an acetylene torch, erupting as temple sites, sacred mountains, plains, and seas, places where inward power is spawned. (*Islands, The Universe, Home*, p. 90)

Where does one find *shizen*? Ehrlich travels back before Buddhism to the animist traditions of Shinto, established through oral tradition before there was a written language in Japan. She watches the wild *kagura* play at midnight on New Year's Eve, where beating drums call down the *kami* (spirit-gods). *Kami* live everywhere: in pines, birds, rain clouds, fish, and waterfalls. Some have special temples built for them, especially on the sacred mountains like Fujiyama. Her pilgrimage leads her to the trail taken by Matsuo Basho, a Zen poet famous for his witty haikus. In June 1689 he climbed Mount Haguro in straw sandals; three hundred years and six months later, Ehrlich takes a car to the top, which now holds five or six temples, a huge parking lot, and many souvenir and noodle shops. She is in northern Honshu, the coldest part of Japan, where Basho wrote his well-known

Narrow Road to the Deep North. The spirits of the dead are said to live in the far northeastern corner. This is also the home of the *itako*, the women who speak with the dead.

Ehrlich meets several *itako*, all of whom are blind; blind women are thought to be especially receptive to the spirits. The third woman catches her by surprise, recognizing her need to speak with a dead one. Ehrlich is still haunted by the loss of her lover David. She makes a pilgrimage up Osorezon, the mountain of spirits—a twenty-six-mile round-trip in falling snow. This physical challenge in "seeking the Way" brings her to the heart of Buddhism—compassion. With insight born on the dark winter night, she finds compassion for her own suffering as well as for the suffering of others. In the end, this is the only true relief for the depth of her loss.

Her journey continues off the coast of southern California, in a boat trip to San Miguel, the northernmost of the Channel Islands. In "Home Is How Many Places," Ehrlich links islands to family, to history, to the native people who have gone before her, the Chumash. A friend of Chumash ancestry tells her, " 'If you want to know who you are and where you are, you have to know who lived here first' " (*Islands*, p. 143). Ehrlich speaks of islands as places of "birth and arousal of consciousness," as "reminders of arrival and departures," as "refuge and sanctuary." As a child living in Santa Barbara, she had often dreamed of swimming to San Miguel. Now she was going to San Miguel, finding a fresh view on her childhood reference point. As she lies on the wet boat deck, the ocean spray blots out the stars. "I lick darkness from my mouth. It's said that at the bottom of the gravest doubt there is satori [Zen enlightenment]" (p. 131). Stories of geologic and cultural origins establish her place in the much longer history of her life. The ocean, too, is home. In *Legacy of Light* (1987), she writes, "No matter where we live as adults, the landscape... in which we grew up stains us with its indelible ink" (p. 20).

All the themes of *Islands, the Universe, Home* come together in "The Fasting Heart," the last essay of the book: walking, landscape, season, water, quest, spirit, journey. The fasting heart is the one that is empty and open to receive the "knowledge that cannot know anything." Ehrlich engages fully with "the way material reality is unobservable and implicit order can be found in paradox." She draws on quantum physics, astronomy, and Taoism to grasp the illusion of separateness. Her lake island refuge is flooded by spring runoff; once again she sees that "the origin of life is always found in death; death is life's constant companion." She is haunted by questions, *"What is this wild embrace?... Who is holding me?"* (p. 192). "Pale clouds unfold... the mountain moves like a river" (p. 196). The embrace is infinite, delicious, aching. She asks, "Where do I break off and where does water begin?" (p. 196). Now the words of the thirteenth-century Zen master Dogen define her walking: " 'Walking beyond and walking within are both done on water' " (p. 196). Thus her journeys take her from island to island, and across all the expanses between.

Lightning Strike

On 6 August 1991, Ehrlich was struck by lightning. Her walk under blue skies ended abruptly when she was thrown to the ground unconscious. *A Match to the Heart: One Woman's Story of Being Struck by Lightning* (1994) is the astonishing story of her near death, her quest for help and understanding, and her eventual recovery. That she lived to tell the story is a miracle. Throughout her various hospital stays and blackout episodes, she chronicles her states of mind near the dark fog of death. Into this personal account Ehrlich weaves information on the nature of the heart and nervous system, the nature of thunder and lightning, and the complex long-term effects of lightning strikes on the human mind and body.

The book begins with Ehrlich's agonizing return to consciousness: "A single heartbeat stirs gray waters. Blue trickles in, just a tiny stream. Then a long silence" (p. 3). Awakening in a pool of blood and flung far off the path, Ehrlich considers Buddhist instructions for the dying.

Her chest numb and her heart beating wildly, she manages to walk the quarter mile back to her ranch house in Wyoming. "The earth felt like a peach that had split open in the middle; . . . the sky was tattered book pages waving in different directions" (p. 8–9). The emergency medical team brought her to the nearest hospital, thirty-five miles away, where the only doctor in town recorded her ailments: cardiac arrest, broken ribs, concussion, lacerations, and kerauno-paralysis from waist to throat. Alone in the hospital that night she felt "like an ancient, mummified child . . . bound tightly, unable to move, my dead face tipped backwards toward the moon" (p. 18).

When her condition worsened to the point where she could barely remain conscious, Ehrlich's father flew to Wyoming to bring her home to Santa Barbara. There she received proper medical care under the hands of compassionate cardiologist Blaine Braniff. Excruciating tests showed her sympathetic nervous system had been "fried," leaving the vagus nerve constantly telling everything to slow down, including her heart and blood pressure. "Clamminess turned to a drenching sweat; my breathing came fast and the terrible, elephantine heaviness invaded my body again" (p. 47). Between doctor visits Ehrlich tries to understand the landscape of human neuroanatomy. She compares the brain to a globe on a spindle, she sees the body as "a separate continent, a whole ecosystem, a secret spinning planet" (p. 51). Earlier she muses, "If I held a match to my heart, would I be able to see its workings, would I know my body the way I know a city, . . . would I know where this passion to live and love comes from" (p. 27)? In the course of her painstaking recovery she concludes "the mind-body split is a meaningless, laughable idea" (p. 88), and further, that neglect of the natural world outside the body reflects an equally serious neglect of the world within. Thus Ehrlich extends her curiosity and passion for the land to the inner wilderness of the human body—an equally complex system worthy of marvel.

The setting for much of *A Match to the Heart* is the Santa Barbara coast, where Ehrlich lets the healing power of water restore her strength. Here she "would surrender to whatever swam through me" (p. 65). She encounters grebes, kelp, pelicans, and fog, windswept beaches, and winter storms. Aching for a friend, she flies her beloved sheepherding dog Sam to town a week before Christmas. "Now one of my saviors was here at my side, we had both been struck, we had both survived, and I knew that if during the night I fell unconscious, he would bring me back alive" (p. 82).

In Sam's company and with the help of loving neighbors and Dr. Braniff, Ehrlich regains enough strength to visit Wyoming to ease her homesickness for the land she has known for seventeen years. But in the year away her marriage had failed and the ranch had changed noticeably. She could see this was no longer home, that she had to leave. "I felt like a river moving inside a river . . . the rivers were layers of grief sliding, the love of open spaces being nudged under fallen logs, pressed flat against cut banks and point bars" (p. 140). To soothe her soul from the loss of so much intimacy, she travels to Alaska where "thundering amputations" of calving glaciers made it seem like "the universe was falling apart" (p. 146). Here finally she could see the illuminating face of death: "Night came . . . and the face of the glacier turned bright as if a huge slab of moon had been cut off and laid against the mountains" (p. 150).

In this unusual natural history of body, place, and mind, Ehrlich again draws on scientific expertise to enrich her narrative. Two cardiologists show her the world of the beating heart by allowing her to observe open heart surgery. A neuropsychologist describes the "postelectrocution syndrome," confessing most doctors do not know to look for tiny damaged nerves. A lightning expert explains that winter is the most dangerous time of year because of the increased moisture in the atmosphere. Ehrlich attends the Third Annual Lightning Strike and Electric Shock conference and encounters strange and terrible stories of seizures, amnesia, night terrors, numbness, impotence, chronic pain. With startling richness, she communicates the alien inner landscape of those who have been irreversibly transformed by their experience with electricity.

Back in California after the conference, Ehrlich finally breaks through her long *bardo*, the Tibetan word for the "wandering state between life and death, confession and enlightenment, neurosis and sanity" (p. 40). Joining friends for a diving expedition off Santa Cruz Island, she jumps into the ocean for the first time in thirty years and "the shell of my body lifted off and was destroyed as cool water flowed in over new skin" (p. 189). This primordial plunge takes Ehrlich back to her home waters, revealing the dimension of healing in her experience of sense of place.

Yellowstone Country

Having survived this dramatic encounter with lightning, Ehrlich went on to write a vivid narrative for *Yellowstone: Land of Fire and Ice* (1995), a photo-essay of the wider Yellowstone bioregion. Beautifully produced, with exquisite full-page color photographs and double-page diagrammatic foldouts, the book is one in a series celebrating the epic geologic processes of America's national parks. Brilliant photos by Willard and Kathy Clay introduce the diverse landforms and habitats of Yellowstone—the grand mountains, valleys, canyons, the aspens, pines, and grasses.

Ehrlich is at her best returning to the land she knows so well. Though the book is a broad natural history of place, Ehrlich especially entices the reader to experience the grandeur of its geologic activity. "Standing in the midst of hot pots, wild gorges, and white capped mountains, it seemed that heaven, earth, and hell were all here in this one place, bound by the vertical stitchery of rain, snow, fire, and steam" (p. 17). She speaks of Yellowstone as an ecosystem, not as a single park with limited boundaries, but rather "an embarassment of riches" (p. 11)—"six plateaus, a grand canyon, ... ten thousand thermal features, ... dozens of rivers and creeks, several mountain ranges and ... huge glaciated valleys" (p. 17). She traces the development of a land ethic for the area, advocating agency management based on biological understanding.

As in all her writing, Ehrlich illuminates the vastness of landscape through her own personal experience. She monitors the recovery from the 1988 fires that burned over one million acres, she walks the rim of the Grand Canyon of the Yellowstone, she offers close-up views of grizzlies and coyotes, peregrine falcons, and deer mice. Returning from a weeklong pack trip in the high country, she comes to understand Yellowstone as "truly a living organism" (p. 129). The book's beautiful journey through this vital and remarkable place concludes with her concern for shrinking fragments of habitat. She urges, "we must do what we can to help restore the broken and defiled lands between these beautiful islands and understand that, when we travel through this fine wilderness, we are walking on the back of a living being" (p. 129).

Among Modern Writers

Like other nature writers, Ehrlich speaks from her experiences of landscape and pilgrimage, the quest of a mystic, rancher, naturalist, woman. Her work fits Peter Fritzell's description of nature writing (in *Nature Writing in America*, 1990) as part spiritual autobiography and part natural history. Fritzell suggests this is a literature of extreme positions, from celebrations of self to modest self-effacement and humility, from radical doubts to strong affirmations. In seeking to locate themselves, nature writers, Fritzell suggests, echo the elementary experience of early Americans. The New World, in effect, is an epistemological problem still being worked out on the Western frontier. Ehrlich's writing about Wyoming—its people, weather, seasons—is an explication of place, a way of "settling the country" by composing it into stories. She likewise explores her own story by going back to her California origins and learning about some of the original people there. In the journey to Japan, she gathers seeds of insight that will nourish her stories of the future.

Ehrlich typifies the type of nature writer John P. O'Grady describes (in *Pilgrims of the Wild*,

1993) as one "who documents the crossing of thresholds." These are the thresholds of perception and psychological transformation, where self and other blur in the experience of the larger whole. Walking is a way to prepare to receive the Other, to settle the mind and open the senses. O'Grady focuses on desire as the personal driving force behind powerful nature writing. He defines desire for the wild as an "objectless desire," a passion spread over the landscape, charging the space with erotic potency. Ehrlich expresses this desire again and again in her longing, her roaming, her questioning, her "obsession with origins." *What is this wild embrace?* She asks the question as a koan, seeking answers in dreams, rock formations, the physicality of life and death, in the pulsing, changing shape of the seasons and their consummation in her.

Ehrlich stands out among modern nature writers for her poetic voice, her intimacy with the Wyoming landscape, and her inclination to Buddhism. Her writing is marked by its attention to nuance expressed in haiku-like metaphor and simile. Speaking of an injured eagle, she writes, "How big she was, how each time she spread her wings it was like a thought stretching between two seasons" *(Islands,* p. 18). She intersperses poetic imagery of the landscape with terse philosophical insights. For example, in *The Solace of Open Spaces,* "There is nothing in nature that can't be taken as a sign of both mortality and invigoration" (p. 83). As a writer of place, she makes a particular effort to capture the people shaped by the place; in her time, these are ranchers, herders, outdoor people. She recognizes in them an evolutionary truth of character. A rancher's life "is not a series of dramatic events for which he or she is applauded or exiled but a slow accumulation of days, seasons, years, fleshed out by the generational weight of one's family and anchored by a land-bound sense of place" (p. 5). Her sketches of sheepherders and cowboys in *Solace* bring other voices than her own to comment on ranching life. For contrast she seeks out physicists, astronomers, and botanists to offer a scientific perspective on the larger scale of place.

Ehrlich places herself in the literary tradition of Emerson and Thoreau, quoting their works in her essays. She refers to Dante, Robinson Jeffers, and Walt Whitman—poets who inform her work. Basho is a special favorite, though she cites poetry by other Japanese writers as well. She is equally drawn by the spiritual writings of Lao-tzu, the Buddha, and the Zen teacher Dogen. These provide an Eastern counterpoint for her Western literary heritage. They offer guideposts of inspiration as she deals with the ephemeral nature of the universe.

To these East–West influences Ehrlich brings her sensibilities as a woman. She is one of a handful of women nature writers in the 1990s who are infusing their work with sensitivity and emotion that reveal the erotic. Her work is an effort to embody the power and attraction of the land. The wild is alive in her—in her body, in her feet, in her heart—and she cannot rest while this vitality stirs in her. Her work rings with the richness of lived experience, a depth that cannot be plumbed in a quick reading.

In Ehrlich's work we have the gifts of one who is willing to struggle with the questions of life and meaning. She invites readers to travel with her to the lands of paradox, beauty, intimacy, and spirit. She offers no final answers, but through her exploring, readers see a way to settle with the earth and find their way home. "To see means to stop, to breathe in and out," she writes in "Landscape." "If we go out in order to find, not to impose, the landscape touches us and we it. Only then is a sense of place born."

Selected Bibliography

WORKS OF GRETEL EHRLICH

ESSAYS

The Solace of Open Spaces (New York: Viking, 1985); "On Water" and "The Smooth Skull of Winter," in *Words from the Land,* ed. by Stephen Trimble (Salt Lake City: Peregrine Smith Books, 1989); "Spring," in *On Nature: Nature, Landscape, and Natural History* (San Francisco: North Point, 1986); "Landscape," in *Legacy of Light,* ed. by Constance Sullivan (New

York: Knopf, 1987); "A River's Route," *Harper's* 277 (December 1988); *Islands, the Universe, Home* (New York: Viking, 1991); "Time on Ice," *Harper's* 284 (March 1992); *A Match to the Heart: One Woman's Story of Being Struck by Lightning* (New York: Penguin, 1994), autobiography; *Yellowstone: Land of Fire and Ice* (New York: Harper Collins, 1995), photo-essays.

FICTION

Wyoming Stories (Santa Barbara, Calif.: Capra, 1986), short stories, bound with Edward Hoagland, *City Tales*; *Heart Mountain* (New York: Viking, 1988), novel; *Drinking Dry Clouds: Stories from Wyoming* (Santa Barbara, Calif.: Capra, 1991), short stories.

POETRY

Geode/Rock Body (Santa Barbara, Calif.: Capricorn, 1970); *To Touch the Water*, ed. by Tom Trusky (Boise, Idaho: Ahsahta, 1981); *Arctic Heart: A Poem Cycle* (Santa Barbara, Calif.: Capra, 1992).

BIOGRAPHICAL AND CRITICAL STUDIES

Marian Blue, "Ehrlich, Gretel," in *Twentieth Century Western Writers*, ed. by Geoff Sadler (2d ed., Chicago: St. James, 1991); Rosellen Brown, "Bolt from the Blue," in *Women's Review of Books* (November 1994); Janet Cannon, review of *The Solace of Open Spaces*, in *Western American Literature Review* 21, no. 3 (1986); Pico Eyer, "Buddhist at the Edge of the Earth," in *Tricycle* 5, no. 3 (spring 1996); Kristiana Gregory, review of *The Solace of Open Spaces*, in *Los Angeles Times Book Review* (5 January 1986); Daniel Halpern, ed., "Natural History: An Annotated Booklist," in *On Nature: Nature, Landscape, and Natural History* (San Francisco: North Point, 1986); Garrett Hongo, "Love Beyond the Fences," in *New York Times Book Review* (6 November 1988); Pat C. Hoy, "The Language of Natural Life," in *Sewanee Review* 95, no. 4 (1987); Paul Krza, "Life in the Empty Quarter," in *National Review* (4 July 1986); Edward Lueders, "The Solace of Open Spaces," in *Western Humanities Review* 40, no. 4 (1986); Christopher Merrill, "Voyages to the Immediate: Recent Nature Writings," in *New England Review and Breadloaf Quarterly* 10, no. 3 (1988); Judith Moore, "What a Mountain Is," in *New York Times Book Review* (1 December 1985); Christopher Tilghman, "A Man Who Barked and Chased Cars," in *New York Times Book Review* (26 May 1991); Stephen Trimble, ed., *Words from the Land* (Salt Lake City: Peregrine Smith Books, 1989); Roger M. Valade III, "Ehrlich, Gretel," in *Contemporary Authors*, vol. 140, ed. by Donna Olendorf (Detroit: Gale Research Inc., 1993); Louis Werner, "A Shared Passion for Nature," in *Christian Science Monitor* (14 November 1991).

VIRGINIA EIFERT
(1911–1966)

KAREN KNOWLES

VIRGINIA EIFERT'S work as a naturalist and writer of nature essays began when she was a young camp counselor for the YWCA in Springfield, Illinois. One of her responsibilities was to lead local groups on nature walks near the Sangamon River. Soon she was writing descriptive essays about the "birds, beasts and blossoms" she observed on these walks and publishing them in a four-page nature paper, which she mimeographed and distributed to interested readers in her neighborhood for a nickel a paper. One subscriber was her next-door neighbor, J. Emil Smith, the editor of the *Illinois State Journal*; he was impressed with Eifert's writing and observation skills and asked her to write a series of nature articles for publication in the newspaper. From that moment on, Eifert devoted her life to writing about the natural world. She was particularly inspired by the woods, fields, and rivers around her home of Springfield, Illinois, where she was born Virginia Louise Snider on 23 January 1911 to Ernest B(aldwin) and Felicie (Cottet) Snider. Except for a year studying at Eastern Illinois State College in 1934–1935 when she was twenty-three, Eifert made her home in Springfield, marrying Herman D. Eifert in 1936 and later having a son, Laurence Noel.

Early Essays

A few years after Eifert married, her career as a writer and editor of nature essays began when her articles for the *Illinois State Journal* caught the attention of Dr. Thorne Duel, Director of the Illinois State Museum, who invited her to become the editor of a new museum publication that would connect the stories of the museum's exhibits and activities with the world of nature. In 1939 Eifert began editing *The Living Museum* and remained its editor until her death twenty-seven years later, on 17 June 1966.

The Living Museum began as a four-page mimeographed leaflet sent to a thousand "subscribers" Eifert had selected from the local telephone directory. The immediate success of this first issue led to a six-page issue and then to state funding that allowed for the publication of a professionally printed version with illustrations. By 1966, *The Living Museum* had grown from its original thousand subscribers to twenty-five thousand. As a tribute to her editorship of almost three decades, in 1967 the museum published a posthumous collection of Eifert's essays in an anthology titled *Essays on Nature*. Each of these essays is dated and categorized by subject, so reading through the section titled "Spring,"

Eifert sketching by a deer habitat group at the Illinois State Museum

for instance, reveals pieces written as early as 1942 and as late as 1964.

Her *Living Museum* essays cover a diverse range of topics: the seasons, birds, trees, animal stories, rivers, plants and flowers, and the night sky. They tend to be short essays, five hundred- to six hundred-word sketches that capture a moment or a feeling: the silence of a marsh just before dawn awakens the birds; the thrill of watching a wild animal in the woods. In tone and purpose, they also tend to be instructive and conservation-minded, as is evident in a piece about the destruction of Illinois prairies and the need to preserve those still in existence; in this essay she recognized a problem that would become a major environmental issue in Illinois. Eifert's identification of such preservation issues began early in her work as a writer and editor, and continued to be a central theme in all her writing.

During the 1940s and 1950s Eifert was also establishing her reputation as a naturalist by writing for *Audubon, Nature Magazine,* and *Natural History.* These essays, in-depth discussions of wildlife or careful studies of plants and flowers in a particular landscape, established her reputation as a botanist and ornithologist. Often she wrote essays related to the material she was researching for her books, such as "Lincoln's Woods," which appeared in *Nature Magazine* before she published her children's novels on Lincoln's life.

A milestone essay for Eifert at this time was the publication of "These Birds Are American" in *Audubon,* a persuasive essay that chronicles the unwitting as well as willful destruction of birds before "men woke suddenly to what was happening" and conservation laws began to be enacted. She grimly describes such nineteenth- and early-twentieth-century attitudes as "shoot the birds—they're fair game," which caused a significant decrease in East Coast cormorants, gulls, and terns. Such attitudes were the basic reason that "rose-breasted grosbeaks and waxwings and many more were shot because they ate fruit. . . . Everywhere, small boys were permitted to shoot birds; it was what small boys were expected to do."

In spite of such devastation, Eifert's tone is hopeful: "Today, more people than ever before realize the significance of the bird in the landscape and derive from it a very real spiritual and intellectual pleasure. . . . Our rescued birds are the symbol of a growing America." But she also points out that the "battle is far from being won even now." As a tribute to the timelessness of her words, *Audubon* reprinted this article in 1973, with a caption that read: "The next time someone belittles your concern for birds, remember these thoughts from the 1945 pages of Audubon." Unfortunately, Eifert's pleas for preservation are just as necessary today as they were in 1945 and 1973.

Early Books: The Lincoln Series

At the same time Eifert was editing and writing for the museum publication and publishing essays in distinguished nature magazines, she was also writing books. The books that she published in her lifetime, whether they were forays into American history, juvenile literature, or natural history, all dealt with the natural world. The subject matter she first chose to write about in a novel was Abraham Lincoln's life, a topic she was undoubtedly familiar with since she grew up in Springfield, where Lincoln first began his political career. Her manuscript on Lincoln's young life was written for an adult readership, but it was rejected by several publishing houses. Then Dodd, Mead & Company—the eventual publisher of all her books—agreed to publish the work if she revised it for a younger audience. She reworked her manuscript in three days. The publication of *Three Rivers South: A Story of Young Abe Lincoln* in 1953 was a success that led to four other books on Lincoln's life.

Eifert presented her Lincoln series as fiction based on fact, embellishing on his thoughts and activities when factual material was unavailable. In addition to *Three Rivers South*, the series includes *Buffalo Trace: The Story of Lincoln's Ancestors* (1955), based on the life of Abraham Lincoln's grandfather and Lincoln's childhood; *Out of the Wilderness: Young Lincoln Grows Up* (1956), his young years to manhood; *With a Task Before Me: Abraham Lincoln Leaves Springfield* (1958), Lincoln's last years in Illinois before he departed for Washington as president; and *New Birth of Freedom: Abraham Lincoln in the White House* (1959).

Eifert used her knowledge of the natural world to describe the setting of Lincoln's life, in which nature had played an important role. In *Three Rivers South* she suggests that if Lincoln had not had the opportunity to guide a flatboat down the Mississippi when he was twenty-one, he might never have found the courage to leave his wilderness home and begin the arduous journey of self-education that ended in the highest position of leadership in his country.

River Books

The great rivers of the Midwest play an important part in all of Eifert's books. Her personal love of and enthusiasm for the Mississippi and Missouri Rivers influenced her writing and her decision to explore midwestern landscapes. She published nature essays and several books of history about the rivers, including *Mississippi Calling* (1957), *River World: Wildlife of the Mississippi* (1959), *Delta Queen: The Story of a Steamboat* (1960), *Wonders of the Rivers* (1962), and *Of Men and Rivers: Adventures and Discoveries Along American Waterways* (1966).

River World emphasizes her firsthand experiences exploring the shores, woods, and bogs of the Mississippi. To research *River World* she traveled over six thousand miles, from the sea marshes of the Louisiana gulf coast to the forests of Minnesota, by way of towboat and passenger steamer. She found the slow pace of the boats a perfect way to watch the wilderness of the river. Although she had often explored the river's shores, it was not until she had journeyed the length of the navigable Mississippi that she felt she had begun to understand this waterway. "For the river is a world apart," she writes in the introduction. "It is a liquid avenue endlessly in motion, a restless pathway which is never the same from one minute to the next or from one mile to another, uniting a stretch of the North American continent by means of 2,552 miles of running water."

Eifert was drawn to the river because of its diversity, and was attracted by the river's unique plants and wildlife, which she believed gave the river its "true personality, characterizing it as much as the color, the clarity or the potent murkiness of the waters, or the shores of its several life zones" (p. xi). Each chapter in *River World* is a study of a particular animal, bird, fish, or plant. She organizes the book by first looking at the plants found at each part of the river, then focusing on bird life, and ending with a close examination of the water itself, finding in it both the smallest of creatures, such as mayflies and water bugs, and the largest, such as alligator, gar, and sturgeon.

She is careful to show the connections between the various plants and animals that she observes. She describes the sight and smell of willow trees along the river in summer, a "sweet, slightly pungent, tantalizing aroma produced by sunshine on resin ducts in the leaves . . . a haunting, honeysuckle-like fragrance" (p. 101), then discusses the important role these willows play in the lives of wildlife. Birds and other creatures make their homes or find protection in the willows, and even crayfish benefit from the shaded waters surrounding the willow trees, finding in this protective environment a "cool, dark pool" (p. 120).

In her explorations, Eifert sometimes travels with companions, including her young son. In addition to watching the wilderness from the deck of a towboat or steamboat, she also disembarks to explore on foot the inland lakes close to the Mississippi. At Reelfoot Lake, a protected area in Tennessee that is an "offshoot, an outpouring, a child of the Mississippi" (p. 43), she goes in search of a bird colony known as Cranetown. With a guide from the Tennessee Fish and Game Commission, she and her son travel by canoe into the marshes; the "route, if it was one, seemed scarcely more than a paddling-path for coots and turtles" (p. 49). At Cranetown, she finds great blue herons and cormorants, as well as American egrets, which almost fifty years before had been "all but wiped out" until they were protected by legislation lobbied for by the National Audubon Society.

Although *River World* does not reflect the strong opinions Eifert later came to have on conservation, it does highlight the Mississippi as a refuge and resting place for migrating birds. Close to the river, at the Horseshoe Lake Wild Life Refuge in southwestern Illinois, Eifert reported that in 1959, two hundred thousand Canada geese and half a million ducks wintered there, "more than at any time in the past" (p. 74). She also noted that wood ducks, which had all but become extinct, were on the increase since federal law had prohibited shooting them. "The protection came in time," she writes. "Like the egrets, the wood duck has returned in numbers to haunt the shadowed glades of river forests" (p. 185). In *River World*, Eifert sets the tone for her later natural history books, particularly her last, *Of Men and Rivers*, in which she

writes more forcefully about conservation issues regarding the rivers.

In all of Eifert's writing, history is an important ingredient, and *River World* is no exception. Rather than isolating the Mississippi as a wonder separate from human existence, she demonstrates its powerful influence on human history, drawing examples from its earliest exploration, when people made many false starts in attempting to travel the length of the river and discover its source. Eifert herself went in search of the source at Lake Itasca in Minnesota, and found "a pearl set among forests of grandeur and unforgettable significance" (pp. 12–13).

The Land of the Snowshoe Hare

After *River World* and her next river book, *Delta Queen*, Eifert moved away from sweeping views of vast ecological areas to write instead about a specific place in *Land of the Snowshoe Hare* (1960). The landscape she describes includes the coniferous forests and aspen woods of northern Wisconsin, near the Canadian border, where she and her husband and son spent vacations. Followers of her work would have recognized some of the places she describes here from earlier essays published in *Nature Magazine*, *Natural History*, and the *Living Museum*.

Because she focuses on one particular place, *Land of the Snowshoe Hare* provides a detailed view of her discoveries as well as her reflections on the land's significance in her own life. It is the most personal of the books she had published up to this point, primarily because she writes in the first-person rather than in the impersonal voice she often adopted for her nonfiction prose. Although this style might appeal to modern readers, at the time reviewers for the *New York Times* considered Eifert's "inconspicuous I" in every chapter a drawback, although they also noted that she kept "people out of nature almost as much as she did in *River World*."

She is thorough in her treatment of the landscape and gives detailed accounts of the diverse plants, trees, flowers, birds, and other wildlife found there, ranging from one season to the next. Each chapter spotlights a specific subject, whether it is the snowshoe hare, a spruce bog, or the nighttime world. What links these essays is Eifert's deep love and reverence for this landscape, so full of mystery and endless discoveries.

One essay in particular reveals Eifert's lyrical writing style as well as her connection to this wilderness area. "The Hour of the Bear," a part of which was first published in *The Living Museum*, describes several different scenarios involving the same yearling bear. While she could drive to the local dump to watch the bears congregate to scrounge for scraps, she prefers to see them in the wild. "I can never really admire a bear in a garbage dump," she writes, but she can find plenty to admire in a bear coming down the ridge at twilight, "when the sugar maples had turned to pure gold and a most lovely daffodil light at sunset bathed everything with a supreme glow. Through it walked the bear, as black as the trunks of the maples, while highlights of gold struck the tips of his fur, his black nose, his eyes" (p. 201).

As Eifert stands outside her cabin, the bear seems to her "grace itself, a smooth black shape among the blacker trees, his alert ears and senses keyed to any breath of danger. He stood still for so long that he might have been a stump rooted there for a hundred years" (p. 198). When the bear finally notices her, he moves closer to investigate, puzzled because he cannot catch her scent and is unused to humans who stand so still (she reports that it was quite common to hear the sound of buckshot echoing off the lake when people panicked upon seeing a bear around their cabins). As soon as he was close enough to recognize her scent as human, he "whirled and tore for the high country. The crackling of branches and the snapping of hazel bushes... told where he went. His great soft feet carried him racing for the safe and distant darkness of the Big Woods" (p. 199).

Eifert is not just an observer in these woods in which she lives; she is also a participant, sometimes a slightly reluctant one. One night she experiences the thrill of meeting the bear when she is out foraging for a bedtime snack in the icebox, which is located outside the cabin. On her way back indoors, while holding a full tray of food and a flashlight, she and the bear meet, only eight feet apart; but the bear is more frightened than she is, and bolts. Eifert herself is delighted, and ends the essay with this reflection:

> To live so close to so many of [the animals], to feel their way of life, to hear them breathe, to know their footsteps, whether the thumping of a rabbit or the thudding of a startled deer, of the bear running, or his grunting alarm, and to know that my child was growing up with a happy kinship and knowledge that animals were friends, not enemies — this was good, a very special way of life. (p. 205)

Eifert's vivid prose allows readers a glimpse into a landscape they might never see. Her reflection on the personal meaning of this landscape establishes her work on a deeper level, one that unites the human and the natural world.

Journeys in Green Places

Journeys in Green Places: The Shores and Woods of Wisconsin's Door Peninsula, published in 1963, is similar in style to *Land of the Snowshoe Hare* in that it focuses on a specific landscape. This time Eifert writes about the Door Peninsula in Door County, Wisconsin, a place she clearly loves and knows well; her detailed treatment of the varied landscape reveals her long personal connection. It differs from *Land of the Snowshoe Hare* in that it is less personal; she approaches her subject as a study of the natural world. Eifert knew Door County well because she led nature classes there at The Clearing, an adult nature study program founded by Jens Jensen. Eifert was known for her skills as a guide to and teacher about the natural world, roles that are clearly evident in her writings.

As in many of her books, she begins with a discussion of the history of the land. In this first chapter she outlines the events that shaped the peninsula over eleven thousand years ago. Exploring the Ice Age and its influence is essential to her understanding of contemporary nature. She felt she must first learn all she could about "the long-gone yesterdays" before she could understand what she discovered in the wild. Thus, rather than "finding only a chaotic, temporary arrangement of plants and animals and their reactions to situations in which everything might seem to come and go as if in a static landscape, [she] recognized some of the real meanings in their associations with each other" (p. 5).

The scope of the book is provided by Eifert's quest to understand what she observes, the places she explores, and the connections between them. She divides her book into sections based on landscapes: the peninsula, the ridges, the pine dunes, the bog, the forest and woods, the water gardens. Then, with a series of questions in mind, Eifert roams the wild places to find answers. To do so means depending on science — geology, botany, ornithology — as well as her own observations. *Journeys in Green Places* can be characterized as a botanical guide as well as a book of ecology; anyone interested in wandering the woods and bogs of Door County would find it a valuable resource.

Eifert uses the language of botany to assist in her decriptions. Woven in with this Latin terminology is a history of the study of botany, which is especially helpful for readers unfamiliar with this science and its linguistic roots. She remarks that the tiny twinflower was named *Linnaea borealis* by the original namer of plants and flowers, the Swedish botanist Carolus Linnaeus, because it was his favorite. American botanists gave the twinflower another botanical name, hoping to distinguish it from the twinflowers growing in other countries. The name it is given by American botanists — *Linnaea borealis. var. longifolia* — is, Eifert comments rather wryly, "a ponderous title which stretches out longer than many a twinflower stalk itself" (p. 52). She also notes that the North American twinflower varies little from others around the world, and that the twinflower found in North America, "growing over mossy slopes and old logs and around tree trunks and among the ferns, opening hundreds of pendant pink bells on a June day, is the very same twinflower which Linnaeus chose as his favorite" (p. 53).

When she comes across a tiny white flower known as the goldthread, she describes its complex arrangement and explains that it was discovered in 1758 by Jane Colden, America's first recognized woman botanist. Eifert suggests that it should have been named "Coldenella," after Jane Colden herself, an idea to which Jane Colden's friends also subscribed. Instead, the flower was named *Copis trifolia*; the word *copis*, meaning "cut," refers to the flower's three-part leaves. In concluding her discussion of Colden and the reason the flower was not named after her, Eifert simply remarks, "Perhaps there was an aversion to women botanists at that time" (p. 133). A few years later, when she was researching the lives of botanists for her historical work *Tall Trees and Far Horizons: Adventures and Discoveries of Early Botanists in America* (1965), Eifert studied Jane Colden's life more fully and discovered that she was much respected by her fellow botanists; in fact, a friend of Colden's family, John Ellis, wrote Linnaeus to request that the flower be named after her, but he was too late; Linnaeus had already named it.

Eifert's limited discussion of this material in *Journeys in Green Places* raises a criticism of her work in general: she spent little time researching the contributions of women, choosing instead to concentrate on well-known men — from Abraham Lincoln to the most public of explorers, botanists, and ornithologists. She uses "man" and "men" to define humans in general, a choice that is also reflected in the titles of her books. Though such gender-specific language might disconcert the modern reader, it was consistent with the general usage of the time. Eifert was conservative in her views, and her choice of subjects also reflected mainstream views in an era when women's contributions to history and literature were not emphasized.

Although Eifert learned from botanists and used the language of botany to write her books, she also created her own system for describing the natural world. At times, her language is florid. In a moment when she is struck by the beauty of bog laurel, she writes: "The sunshine glitters through their bright, silken, wine-pink cups, and the wind causes them to dance all across the rosy-painted bogs of June" (p. 94). For the most part, however, she prefers a more straightforward style: "In the bud, the laurel is beautifully and crisply fluted in ten ridges to make a double cone which is broad around the middle and tapered at either end. On opening, the five points of the flower are held in a shallow cup, and in each of the ten ridges a stamen is pressed back as taut as a bowstring" (p. 94).

This descriptive style reflects Eifert's view that there are nine designs or patterns in the natural world. As she explains in her final chapter, "The Anatomy of Nature," these patterns include the sphere and spheroid; the circle and ellipse; the cube; the cylinder; the spiral; the undulate; the pyramid and triangle, which make up the star, pentagon, or hexagon; the lattice; and the frond. For Eifert, attempting to identify these designs is a "fascinating game in which no landscape or object will ever appear monotonous or uninteresting" (p. 201). By noting and reflecting on these designs she comes to understand the connections between all living things. She points out that the star design in both the world of nature and of humans is a "magical and often mystic figure" (p. 204). The five points are evident in the hands of a lizard, the arms of a starfish, and the top of a sand dollar; five has also been a favored number in human systems: the Five Classics of Confucius, Napoleon's Five Codes, the Five Nations of the Iroquois. The number has had a special significance since antiquity.

Eifert was passionate about her quest to locate rare plants. She first became interested in these flowers during her youth, when she was inspired by reading two books, *Bog-Trotting for Orchids* (1904), by Grace Greylock Niles, and *Our Wild Orchids* (1929), by Frank Morris and Edward A. Eames. Since there were few wild orchids in her part of the Midwest, the desire to locate one became a treasure hunt of sorts, "as much for the flowers as for the wilderness itself" (p. 101).

As an adult she spent years looking for lady's slipper and other orchids, finding only a few every now and then. In *Journeys in Green Places* she laments the fact that the thousands of white lady's slippers that once thrived in the marshes

outside Chicago have been replaced by the steel mills and railroad yards of South Chicago and Gary, Indiana, "conceal[ing] all traces of clean earth and bog" (p. 107). Even in the comparatively wild landscape of Door County, a good six hours from Chicago, orchids are scarce. And that is why, coming across over three hundred of them in some maple woods one May day, she is filled with "wonder, delight, and disbelief" (p. 107). She attributes this find to the fact that these particular woods had been "protected from fire, cutting, and grazing for more than a quarter of a century, so that a nucleus of orchids had had a chance to multiply freely, unhindered and undestroyed" (p. 108). She suggests that it is "the challenge of personal search and discovery, the mystery and the lure which send some of us on long hunts simply for the sight of a particular orchid." And she reminds her readers that "we are not like the plant hunters of the jungles who must collect their prey. We need not pick a flower in order to enjoy it, and we specifically do *not* pick orchids, those rarities which may perish as a species if collected too much" (p. 101).

While exploring and writing about the woods of Door Peninsula, Eifert muses on the nature writings of Henry David Thoreau and John Burroughs. Eifert quotes a John Burroughs poem, "Bird and Bush," which reminds her that he must have been familiar with the woods that she walks through. In her previous books Eifert had seldom looked to other literary sources to inspire her writing, relying instead on her own observations. In *Journeys in Green Places*, she establishes a strong literary theme that underscores her description of place and her discussion of the conservation issues of her day. This includes citing two of her contemporaries in the field of nature writing: Wendell Berry, author of the novel *Nathan Coulter* (1960), and Sigurd Olsen, a Minnesota naturalist and author of *Runes of the North* (1963), which was published the same year as Eifert's *Journeys in Green Places*.

Like Thoreau, Eifert makes a plea for preserving wild places. "Our land," she writes, "is surely broad enough and has enough elbowroom in which to expand cities, build steel mills, and lay out superhighways, so that we may at the same time still hold to and cherish the wild places, the invigorating atmosphere of swamp and forest and lake and bog" (p. 36). Thoreau, writing over a hundred years before Eifert's work was published, was also outspoken in his belief that the wild places should be safeguarded. Nevertheless, it is doubtful that he would have agreed with Eifert's "elbowroom" concept—the idea that this country has enough space for both conservation of natural areas and expansion of industry. For even though the air over cities was much clearer during his day, Thoreau advocated that the morning air should be bottled up and sold, "for the benefit of those who have lost their subscription ticket to the morning time of the world" (cited in *Journeys*, p. 187).

Eifert's concessions to the growing urbanization of America are balanced by her support of efforts to preserve wild landscapes, particularly those far from cities. For example, she describes the conservation history of the Range Light Forty, a natural area of forests, cold bogs, and cedar swamps near Bailey's Harbor in Door Peninsula. Originally the forty acres were federal land and housed a lighthouse and range light to signal passing ships and guide them into the harbor. The surrounding area was privately held, but most of the land remained unchanged. In 1936 the federal government gave the land to Door County. The county's plan was to turn it into a camping area by draining and clearing the land. A group of women from Bailey's Harbor stood in the way of the bulldozers long enough to get the Park Commission to change its plans. The Range Light Forty became a wildflower sanctuary and eventually a corporation was formed to preserve it. With each new opportunity to buy the surrounding land, the forty acres were expanded. In 1962, with the help of the Nature Conservancy, ten acres were purchased to prevent commercial development.

Eifert's commitment to conservation, so clearly in evidence in *Journeys in Green Places*, along with her knowledge of botany, drew positive reviews. She was compared with other contemporary writers of her day, including John Hay, author of *The Great Beach* (1963), and Hal Borland, a *New York Times* writer whose nature editorials were collected in *Sundial of the Seasons* (1964). Borland would later include an essay from Eifert's *Land of the Snowshoe Hare* in his anthology of nature writing, *Our Natural World* (1965). In a review of these writers in *Natural History*, nature writer Pieter Fosburgh described Eifert as a "competent geologist and botanist," and said that she and John Hay were "rarities" among the modern writers of that time.

Historical Works

As a competent geologist and botanist, Eifert was interested in what others had done before her. To that end, Eifert wrote three books during the 1960s that compiled the stories and achievements of historical figures in these fields. The books share a similar organization, and at times the same historical material. *Men, Birds, and Adventure: The Thrilling Story of the Discovery of American Birds* (1962) and *Of Men and Rivers: Adventures and Discoveries Along American Waterways* (1966) each begin with a chapter on one of the earliest river communities, a Hopewellian site in southern Illinois, located on the Ohio River. She discusses the carvings the people made and their use of the rivers as waterways for trade.

Men, Birds, and Adventure goes on to chronicle the history of ornithology, beginning with Columbus and then leaping two hundred and fifty years into the early eighteenth century, when people began "to search out the birds of America in quest of knowledge, not meat" (p. 21). The book ends with a chapter on birding in the United States in the 1950s. While the scope of the book is wide and could be characterized as an overview, Eifert does include excerpts from original journals, making fascinating primary source material available to her readers.

Tall Trees and Far Horizons: Adventures and Discoveries of Early Botanists in America (1965), the second book in this series, recounts the stories of botanists, and is organized in much the same fashion as *Men, Birds, and Adventure*, moving from the earliest explorers in the field to chapters on Henry David Thoreau and John Muir. The book concludes with a personal essay, in which Eifert discusses the importance of botany and its influence on people. "This interest in what grows is what gives incentive to many a vacation and motor trip, to the walk in the woods or the climb up the mountain. . . . As long as trees grow and flowers bloom, [botany] remains one of the natural assets of America and the living world" (p. 285).

The last book in this series, *Of Men and Rivers*, was in the process of being published when Eifert died of a heart attack at the age of fifty-five. Her final book is a historical depiction of major American rivers from the time of the earliest travelers to about 1946. The closing chapter is worthy of attention because it provides Eifert's personal and environmental views on the state of the rivers as they were in 1966. Her reaction to public use and abuse of the river system is both critical and hopeful. "America," she writes, "is noted for its possession of a conscience. That conscience may take a while to stir, but it seems to awaken before it is everlastingly too late." Criticizing Americans for polluting rivers by using them as a "dumping place" for the "carcasses of old motor cars, refrigerators . . . and other offal from that untidy creature, man," Eifert is saddened that "many of our once beautiful, clear, clean, glorious rivers that were the water routes for the explorers [are] being lost because of careless use." She blames this tardy awakening on Americans' complacent belief in the "endlessness of our wilderness and the abundance of our natural resources" (pp. 311–312). Still, she believes that Americans are aware of their folly in such thinking, although for many this realization has come "as a growing shock." While she notes the slowness of reform, she is hopeful that this awakening of a national conscience will expand as more public figures support conservancy efforts.

To that end, she includes a portion of President Lyndon Johnson's 1965 address to Congress, his "Message on the Natural Beauty of Our Country," which preceded the introduction of legislation to establish a National Wild Rivers System. The bill gave wild river status to six rivers around the country, including the Salmon in Idaho, the Rio Grande in New Mexico, and the Suwannee in Georgia and Florida. With this kind of federal support, Eifert was hopeful that the rivers of America would be preserved well into the future. In his speech to Congress, Johnson said:

> To deal with these new problems will require a new conservation. We must not only protect the countryside and save it from destruction, we must restore what has been destroyed. . . . [The] concern is not with nature alone, but with the total relation beween man and the world around him. . . . The time has also come to identify and preserve free-flowing stretches of our great scenic rivers before growth and development make the beauty of the unspoiled waterway a memory. (p. 314)

For Eifert, this important political support and the introduction of legislation was a positive step toward river protection, offering an "immediate hope that the rivers which made America great will be saved in their beauty and usefulness" (p. 315).

Conclusion

These final pages of Eifert's work were her strongest political effort toward conservancy during her lifetime, and the power of her voice is persuasive even today. After decades of exploring the natural world and sharing her discoveries with her reading public, Eifert's hope for a nationwide conservation effort is understandable. She had dedicated her life to observing the natural world and educating others about the wilderness she loved: the great rivers and forests of the Midwest, its plants and wild creatures. Her wide-ranging knowledge of botany, ornithology, geology, and American history, reflected in the many essays, articles, and books she published, established her as an authority on its natural landscape. Above all, her persistent commitment to a national awareness of preservation and respect for wildlife and wild places must be recognized as a significant contribution to the natural history of America.

Selected Bibliography

WORKS OF VIRGINIA EIFERT

NONFICTION BOOKS

Mississippi Calling (New York: Dodd, Mead, 1957); *River World: Wildlife of the Mississippi* (New York: Dodd, Mead, 1959); *Delta Queen: The Story of a Steamboat* (New York: Dodd, Mead, 1960); *Land of the Snowshoe Hare* (New York: Dodd, Mead, 1960); *Louis Jolliet, Explorer of Rivers* (New York: Dodd, Mead, 1961); *Men, Birds, and Adventure: The Thrilling Story of the Discovery of American Birds* (New York: Dodd, Mead, 1962); *Journeys in Green Places: The Shores and Woods of Wisconsin's Door Peninsula* (New York: Dodd, Mead, 1963); *Tall Trees and Far Horizons: Adventures and Discoveries of Early Botanists in America* (New York: Dodd, Mead, 1965); *Of Men and Rivers: Adventures and Discoveries Along American Waterways* (New York: Dodd, Mead, 1966).

JUVENILE LITERATURE

Three Rivers South: A Story of Young Abe Lincoln (New York: Dodd, Mead, 1953); *Buffalo Trace: The Story of Lincoln's Ancestors* (New York: Dodd, Mead, 1955); *Out of the Wilderness: Young Lincoln Grows Up* (New York: Dodd, Mead, 1956); *With a Task Before Me: Abraham Lincoln Leaves Springfield* (New York: Dodd, Mead, 1958); *New Birth of Freedom: Abraham Lincoln in the White House* (New York: Dodd, Mead, 1959); *Wonders of the Rivers* (New York: Dodd, Mead, 1962); *George Shannon: Young Explorer with Lewis and Clark* (New York: Dodd, Mead, 1963).

ANTHOLOGIES

Milton D. Thompson, ed., *Essays on Nature* (Springfield: Illinois State Museum, 1967).

ARTICLES

"Grand Mesa Birding," in *Audubon* 45 (July 1943); "These Birds Are America," in *Audubon* 47 (September 1945), repr. in *Audubon* 75 (January 1973); "Bird Explorers," in *Nature Magazine* 39 (November 1946); "Lincoln on a Totem Pole," in *Natural History* 56 (February 1947); "Lincoln's Woods," in *Nature Magazine* 40 (February 1947); "Lake for Lincoln's Country," in *Audubon* 51 (July 1949); "Listen for a Crying Loon," in *Nature Magazine* 42 (October 1949); "Glacier's Return," in *Nature Magazine* 43 (December 1950); "Piasa Country," in *Nature Magazine* 44 (August 1951); "Wilderness Piece," in *Nature Magazine* 45 (April 1952); "Place of the Golden-Breasted Woodpecker," in *Nature Magazine* 45 (May 1952); "Land of the Snowshoe Hare," in *Nature Magazine* 45 (October 1952); "Twenty Dollar Pine," in *Nature Magazine* 45 (October 1952); "Sangamon Springtime," in *Nature Magazine* 46 (March 1953); "Road to the Top of the World," in *Nature Magazine* 46 (June 1953); "World of the Waterway," in *Nature Magazine* 47 (October 1954); "One Night in Arizona," in *Nature Magazine* 47 (December 1954); "Buffalo Trace," in *Nature Magazine* 48 (February 1955); "Columbus and the Birds," in *Nature Magazine* 48 (October 1955); "Canadian Carpet," in *Nature Magazine* 49 (May 1956); "Lone Road Up," in *Nature Magazine* 49 (June 1956); "Continuity on Bayou Contraband," in *Nature Magazine* 49 (October 1956); "Men and Animals of Modoc Rock Shelter," in *Nature Magazine* 50 (February 1957); "Jens Jensen and the Clearing," in *Nature Magazine* 51 (January 1958); "North Woods Winter," in *Natural History* 70 (February 1961).

BIOGRAPHICAL AND CRITICAL STUDIES

Silence Buck Bellows, "Northwoods Cycle," review of *Land of the Snowshoe Hare*, in *Christian Science Monitor* (29 December 1960); Hal Borland, *Our Natural World: The Land and Wildlife of America as Seen and Described by Writers Since the Country's Discovery* (Garden City, N.Y.: Doubleday, 1965); Pieter Fosburgh, "A Naturalist's Book List," in *Natural History* 73 (August 1964); Richard M. Klein, review of *Tall Trees and Far Horizons*, in *Natural History* 74 (October 1965); Lorus and Margery Milne, review of *Land of the Snowshoe Hare*, in *New York Times Book Review* (20 November 1960).

LOREN EISELEY
(1907–1977)

FRED TAYLOR

WHEN LOREN EISELEY was in eighth grade, he wrote an essay for school about why he wanted to be a nature writer. "I feel it is my duty to do what I can to make people realize that the wild creature has just as much right to live as you or I. . . . As in human life, there are tragedy, and humor, and pathos; in the life of the wild, there are facts of tremendous interest, real lives, and real happenings, to be written about." Those prophetic words, quoted by Kenneth Heuer in *The Lost Notebooks of Loren Eiseley* (1987), his collection of Eiseley's unpublished writing (p. 14), marked the beginning of Eiseley's long and circuitous journey to become one of the twentieth century's great nature writers.

Not until almost forty years later, after turns in many directions, would the greatness of his gift for nature writing become apparent. The length and character of that wandering are characteristic of Eiseley, for the sense of a long journey runs throughout his life and work. And it is not surprising that his emergence as a writer brought him back to this childhood vision, for the seeds of much of his writing were planted in his early years. In his journal he noted that "every one of us is a hidden child. We are hidden in our beginnings" (p. 136). By turning to Eiseley's own beginnings, we find clues not only to his developing vision as a writer, but to the life journey revealed in his works. "Every man tracks himself through life," he once quoted

Thoreau, in *The Invisible Pyramid* (1970). "Thoreau meant that the individual in all his reading, his traveling, his observations, would follow only his own footprints through the snows of this world" (p. 103). Let us begin by tracking his path.

Life and Work

Before examining his life, it is important to note an issue that has surfaced in recent critical studies of Eiseley's life and work. Some critics and biographers have called attention to the way Eiseley "fictionalized" his accounts of his life in his autobiography and nature essays: elaborating, rearranging, even changing important details for dramatic effect. Critics have differed in their assessment of the extent to which he engaged in this, and to what degree it matters. This is to some extent an aspect of any autobiographical or personal narrative writing, and does not necessarily affect its literary significance. But as we approach the events of his life, it is important to keep in mind that Eiseley wrote of himself as employing "the ruse of the fox," so that the tracks we will be following may be elusive.

The image of a fugitive haunts Eiseley's reflections on his childhood and youth, where he describes himself as fox, fugitive, "running man," and "a refugee at heart." He was born

269

into a family that was never quite a home for him, and into a landscape that offered both vast solitudes for escape and a sense of wildness that became for him both refuge and home. In his complex and difficult family life, and in the vast and lonesome landscapes of the Nebraska plains, we find the seeds of Eiseley's gifts as a nature writer.

Loren Eiseley was born on 3 September 1907 in Lincoln, Nebraska, the son of Clyde Eiseley, a one-time itinerant actor turned hard luck hardware salesman, and Daisy Eiseley, an "ill-taught prairie artist" who had been deaf since childhood and "all her life...had walked the precipice of mental breakdown" (*The Unexpected Universe*, 1969, p. 86). In *All the Strange Hours* (1975), Eiseley remembered his home as a "silenced household of the stone age—a house of gestures, of daylong facial contortion" (repr. ed., p. 22). In that home, "dead silence was broken only by the harsh, discordant jangling of a voice that could not hear itself" (*The Night Country*, 1971, p. 197). Though the home was an abode of the grotesque, and the source of an abiding loneliness, it nurtured in its silences a sense of the interior life that was to become one of his greatest gifts as a writer. Eiseley later acknowledged important qualities he gained from each parent that became significant in his writing: from his mother a "capacity for tremendous visual impressions," and from his father the gift of eloquent speech.

Eiseley's relationship with his mother was characterized by a mutual lack of understanding and a vast unbridgeable gulf of silence. A story from his autobiography, *All the Strange Hours* (1975), captures the tone of that tortured relationship. Out roaming the fields with a group of new friends, at age ten, he was pursued by his mother, who demanded that he return home. Torn between his need for acceptance from his peers and his father's injunction never to cross his mother, because she "is not responsible" for her afflictions, he finally refused to obey. "I was humiliated. My mother was behaving in the manner of a witch. She could not hear, she was violently gesticulating without dignity, and her dress was somehow appropriate to the occasion."

He turned and ran with his buddies, "chuckling, with the witch, her hair flying, her clothing disarrayed, stumbling after. Escape, escape, the first stirrings of the running man. Miles of escape" (p. 34). Thus began the life of the fugitive.

His father was one of the only stabilizing influences in his childhood, and it is to him that he attributes the gifts of language and love. In *The Night Country* (1971) he recalls his "beautiful resonant speaking voice," in which he would "declaim long rolling Elizabethan passages that caused shivers to run up my back" (p. 198). He also provided Loren the few instances of caring and love he remembered from his childhood, such as the evening when his father took him out at age three to watch Halley's comet, a poignant incident he recalled all his life.

Yet his father also played a role in shaping the fugitive identity of the young Eiseley. Unsuccessful in his work as a hardware salesman, Clyde had to move numerous times, and the family lived in poverty as outcasts on the fringes of society. He too must have felt the urge to escape. Loren remembered his father's empathy for a group of escaped convicts as they struggled to make their way through a howling blizzard: "I could see by his eyes he was out there in the snow." Reflecting back on this as a seminal moment in his development as a writer, he adds: "The memory of that night stayed on. . . . Long after those fleeing men were dead I would re-enter that year to seek them out. I would dream once more about them. I would be—Never mind, I would be myself a fugitive. When once, just once, through sympathy, one enters the cold, one is always there" (*All the Strange Hours*, p. 174).

As his place of escape, the Nebraska plains had a profound effect on the young Eiseley's imagination. He describes it as a landscape of silence, infused with the restlessness that came with the end of the frontier era. "The bison had perished...the Sioux no longer rode," and "the one great western road no longer crawled with wagons" (repr. ed., p. 25). His early childhood explorations carried him into these dimensions of space and time, shaping his sense of place with the harsh expansiveness of the prairie, to which he was drawn all his life. From Lincoln, he found ways to escape to the surrounding country, or to the mysterious darkness beneath the city streets, which he explored with "the Rat," a friend who had an uncanny affinity for exploring the city's sewer system. Eiseley was fascinated with these "places below," a fascination he later pursued in his career as an archaeologist.

The haunting presence of time began to speak to Eiseley along with the vast sense of space on the prairie. He recalls building a small cemetery as a young child, where he buried dead birds and newspaper clippings telling of tragic or heroic deaths. When a thoughtless mower carried away his crosses, Eiseley cried over the futility of his attempt to preserve against time "the memory of what always in the end perishes: life and great deeds." W. H. Auden observed to Eiseley that "it was a child's effort against time. . . . And perhaps the archaeologist is just that child grown up" (*All the Strange Hours*, p. 29).

Out of his loneliness as a child and his fondness for outdoor exploration grew an unusual sense of companionship and compassion toward animal life. In high school he wrote an essay about his fondness for an adopted stray dog, and his autobiography tells of another stray he befriended as a young man while drifting across the plains in the company of hoboes. "If anyone taught me anything about love, it was that dog." His reflections show Eiseley's growing ethical sensitivity toward animals: "Let men beat men, if they will, but why do they have to beat and starve small things? Why? — why? I will never forget that dog's eyes. . . . This is why I am a wanderer forever in the streets of men, a wanderer in mind, and, in these matters, a creature of desperate impulse" (pp. 62–63). Such animal companions, and the reflections inspired by them, are a prominent feature of Eiseley's mature nature essays, marked by compassion, this reaching out across the boundaries between species, and haunted by the loneliness of, in Auden's words, "a solitary who feels more easily at home with animals than with his fellow human beings" (p. 19).

During Eiseley's college years, the metaphor of the fugitive became a way of life. He entered the University of Nebraska in 1925, and was in and out of school for eight years until he finally graduated in 1933. These were restless, painful years for him, and he dropped out of school a number of times and hopped freights back and forth across the West in the company of hoboes. These were his "days of a drifter," which he wrote about in stories poignantly celebrating the freedom and companionship, the hard times and the loss, of this era of wandering amid the vast landscapes of the American West.

Several traumatic events were especially disruptive for him. In 1928, his father died of cancer, leaving him bereft of the one parent who had given him the only love he had known as a child. The loss of his father was a devastating experience, and he entered a period of profound disorientation, marked by the onset of insomnia that plagued him for the rest of his life. His health deteriorated rapidly, and in 1929 he was diagnosed with tuberculosis, which forced him to take a year's leave from college to convalesce on a turkey farm in the Mojave Desert.

His early college years were formative for his developing interest in literature. He wrote poetry, essays, and reviews, some of which were published in the university's literary magazine, the *Prairie Schooner*, which he served as board member and contributing editor. But even as his interest was drawn to literature, he also recognized that it would not give him the stable livelihood that, as a child of poverty, he felt he needed. He began to take courses in anthropology, developed an interest in field studies, and during his last three years of college joined the South Party, an expedition to investigate vertebrate fossil beds on the Great Plains. These expeditions gave him a chance to develop his experience in the fields of paleontology and archaeology, and also ample opportunity to explore the wild spaces of the plains in solitude. On free weekends he would seek out the company of hoboes and exchange stories, and whenever he could he would ride the rails. After three summers of experience as a bone hunter, he had a wealth of stories and vivid sense impressions that he later drew on in many of his essays.

At the urging of his professors, he applied to graduate school and entered the University of Pennsylvania department of anthropology in the fall of 1933. During his years of graduate study, he worked closely with the chair of the department, Frank Speck, an unconventional professor who became a major influence in Eiseley's life. A specialist in the culture and language of the Native American peoples of the northern forest, and "a genuine, if belated shaman," Speck gave Eiseley a deep appreciation for the qualities of Native American thought and culture.

Eiseley received his doctorate in 1937, marking the passage from the fugitive life of his childhood and youth into the stability and reputation of his adult profession. The following year, after taking his first teaching position with the University of Kansas, he married Mabel Langdon, whom he had known during his student years at the University of Nebraska. During these early years of his teaching career, he began experimenting with the personal essay as a literary form, returning to his love of literature from early college days. Most of these pieces were based on his youthful experiences of fossil hunting in the West, and capture the spirit of his adventures in a vivid, dramatic style reminiscent of the Western tall tale.

After ten years of successful teaching, research, and well-received scholarly publications, Eiseley was invited to return to the University of Pennsylvania to take on Speck's position as chair of the anthropology department, where he remained for the rest of his professional life. Shortly after taking the new position at Penn, a dramatic series of incidents marked a turning point in his life as a writer. In the fall and winter of 1948, he suffered the trauma of an extended period of deafness. Plagued by memories of his deaf mother, haunted by fears that he would inherit her deafness and insanity, and desperate to hold on to his new position, he withdrew into a "winter silence" of intense introspection. During that period, he was devastated by the rejection of a scholarly article he had submitted for publication. In the midst of this silence and loss,

a new vision emerged that changed the course of his life:

> Sitting alone at the little kitchen table I tried to put into perspective the fears that still welled up frantically from my long ordeal. I had done a lot of work on this article, but since my market was gone, why not attempt a more literary venture? Why not turn it — here I was thinking consciously at last about something I had done unconsciously before — into what I now term the concealed essay, in which personal anecdote was allowed gently to bring under observation thoughts of a more purely scientific nature? (*All the Strange Hours*, p. 182)

Though he had already published several literary articles, this awakening marked a profound shift in his values and orientation. "Out of the ghost world of my journeys through the silent station arose by degrees the prose world. . . . I had lived so long in a winter silence that from then on I would do and think as I chose" (p. 183). After recovering his hearing, he went on to have a successful career as a teacher, but published few scholarly articles and focused his attention almost exclusively on the essay form. In his autobiography, he describes his first and most popular book of essays, *The Immense Journey* (1957), as born "on that little kitchen table where my wife had to write me notes to save her voice" (p. 183).

As Eiseley advanced in his career as an academic, he became increasingly wrapped up in the public sphere. He was promoted to university provost, then to Benjamin Franklin and University Professor of Anthropology and History of Science, a position created especially to give him the freedom to write; he was active with the Sierra Club as book editor and influential thinker; highly sought out as a lecturer and visiting scholar; the recipient of dozens of honorary degrees. Yet these more public events seem to have been less important for his writing than were the incidents from his childhood and youth. The events he writes about from his adult life are generally quite private moments, set apart in time and space: a solitary encounter with a fox on a beach, a chance meeting with a vagrant in an airport late at night, a return to the hometown of his childhood to search for the tree he planted with his father. It is as if the real work that nourished his writing, the inner process of recollection and reflection, was going on in a sphere quite apart from the growing recognition of his public life.

The publication of *The Immense Journey* in 1957 was greeted with enthusiasm by literary critics and the popular press, but many of Eiseley's scientific colleagues were skeptical of this new departure in his work, criticizing the book for its lack of scientific rigor. In the following years, Eiseley wrote a steady stream of books that won him growing recognition as a writer. In 1958, he published *Darwin's Century: Evolution and the Men Who Discovered It*, a major study of the history of evolutionary thought on which he had been working for years. In 1960, he adapted a series of lectures into *The Firmament of Time*, which won several prestigious honors, including the John Burroughs Medal for nature writing. In this book he surveys the history of thought about the natural world, showing how time, evolution, life, and human existence each came to be seen as the result of natural processes rather than supernatural influence. He concludes by questioning this notion, and suggesting that the "natural" may not be as natural as we think. By trying to understand everything as the outgrowth of an ordered "natural" universe, we may overlook the miraculous. Though most of the book is more expository in style than his other natural history narratives, this final chapter is a fine example of Eiseley's developing gifts as an essayist.

Francis Bacon and the Modern Dilemma (1962) expressed an important shift in Eiseley's developing thoughts about science. Having struggled for years with the reductionist assumptions and implications of contemporary science, he had been increasingly drawn to Bacon, whom he saw as a model of a visionary scientist, less concerned with the techniques of research than with its goals, and the ethics by which it should be guided. These questions were central to two subsequent books, *The Unexpected Universe*

(1969) and *The Invisible Pyramid* (1970). In the latter he considers the space program as an example of modern technology attempting to transcend human limits without the necessary guiding spiritual insight. He also develops the ecological implications of his thought, by suggesting humanity's need to learn to live within limits, both on the planet as well as in space.

During the final years of his life, Eiseley increasingly turned his attention as a writer to the poetic and the personal. Returning more actively to an interest in poetry that he had pursued quietly over the years since his *Prairie Schooner* days, he published two volumes of poems in the early 1970s, and two additional collections were issued posthumously.

The two final prose works published before his death, *The Night Country* (1971) and *All the Strange Hours* (1975), were the most personal of all his writing. In *The Night Country*, Eiseley the archaeologist focused his attention on uncovering his personal past. As he explained in an unpublished introduction included in the collection edited by Kenneth Heuer, the book's purpose was "to claim a time and to make it my own forever" (p. 214). The majority of these essays are anecdotal narratives, their depth coming from the power of the stories themselves, rather than through the scientific and philosophical questions woven into much of the rest of his writing. Many of these stories were written much earlier, based on events from his childhood and fossil-hunting days, and told with a flair for the tall tale, often interspersed with bizarre, unbelievable characters and touches of humor. Gathered together near the end of his life, they stand as evocative portraits, testifying to the power of memory and the word against the passage of time.

Eisley's autobiographical impulse found its fullest expression in *All the Strange Hours*, which was hailed by Gerber and McFadden in *Loren Eiseley* as a masterpiece of autobiographical writing. Here he links the task of the autobiographer with that of the archaeologist: instead of layers of sediment, the inner explorer digs through layers of memory, seeking fragments of meaning to weave together into a story.

Eiseley's intricate, nonlinear narrative gives a sense of the complex process of personal excavation, and the mysterious discoveries to which it leads.

Eiseley died of cancer on 9 July 1977. At the time of his death, he was at work on an additional prose work, a collection of his favorite pieces drawn from the full range of his previous writing. *The Star Thrower*, published in 1978, gives the reader a fine sampling of some of Eiseley's favorite and best essays, and the introduction of W. H. Auden is one of the most insightful short commentaries on Eiseley's achievement.

Eiseley as a Nature Writer

Eiseley has been praised as one of the great nature writers of the twentieth century. "If our manic century has produced an heir apparent to Henry David Thoreau," claims Kenneth Heuer, "Loren is it" (p. 159). Edward Hoagland is reported to have spoken of him as "a writer so good he can stop you in your tracks for a day or a week" (quoted in Cohen, p. 199). The power of Eiseley's writing is in part the result of several distinctive features that are unusual for a nature writer, and therefore worth a brief examination.

Perhaps most immediately apparent is the quality of his decriptions of landscape, which are pervaded by a sense of mystery. Nature writers use descriptions to convey a sense of place in their landscapes: Aldo Leopold gives us the minute particulars of a patch of Wisconsin prairie ground; Barry Lopez details the interrelationships between organisms in the arctic tundra, giving us a rich sense of the life of a particular ecosystem. But with Eiseley, we often do not even know where we are. Consider, for example, his description of the location of the climactic episode in "The Judgment of the Birds" from *The Immense Journey*:

> It comes from far away out of my past, in a place of pouring waters and green leaves. . . . You may put it that I had come over a mountain, that I had slogged through fern and pine needles for half a long day, and that on the edge of a little glade with one long, crooked branch extending across it, I had sat down to rest with my back against a stump. (pp. 173–174)

Eiseley sets his scene with a few vivid details but leaves the place deliberately obscure. His disclaimer, "you may say," accommodates the reader's desire to feel located, but his purpose in telling the story is quite different. Each detail serves to dislocate us, until we feel we are more in the world of myth or folktale than natural history.

Perhaps the most striking instance of a purposefully mystified landscape is in the title essay in *The Star Thrower*, where Eiseley describes one of the most memorable encounters in all his writing. He identifies the location as the seaside town of Costabel, which he describes as a place where "nothing . . . made sense," but where "all men are destined at some time to arrive." The mythic resonances of this elusive description are further heightened by his description of the beach itself, "an endless wave-beaten coast at dawn," "littered with the debris of life," a coast "set apart for shipwreck." I wondered for years about the location of this beach: Eiseley's landscapes have a way of haunting you like that. So I was recently surprised to discover that no such place exists. When asked about the name Costabel, Eiseley explained in a letter quoted by Angyal that he "picked it up by listening to a seashell many years ago . . . on what has sometimes been called the coast of illusion" (p. 81). It seems we are in a landscape as much mythic as actual, where description points beyond the outer landscapes of a particular place to the inner landscapes of myth and meaning, and to the universals of human experience.

Eiseley's mystified landscapes lead us to a second distinctive quality in his writing. In directing our attention away from the specificity of a given setting, he seems more interested in engaging us in the feel of a particular moment of awareness or encounter. Such epiphanies are frequent in Eiseley's writing, often coming at the climax of a long search that prepares him for a revelation. One of the most powerful of such

Loren Eiseley

ecstatic moment" (p. 210). At the end of the essay he describes this as the "gravest, most meaningful act I shall ever accomplish," the "miracle" he had been searching for all his adult life.

Spoken in the language of the soul, such moments reverberate in the imagination, inviting us to enter a world of haunting animal presences. Eiseley saw his encounters, like those of a shaman, as expansions of his identity to "contain more than himself." In the conclusion of *The Firmament of Time*, he agrees with the Renaissance idea that "man, the Microcosm, contains the Macrocosm." In touching the lives of other creatures, he saw himself as embracing them in his "own substance" and trying to give birth to a "greater, more comprehensive version" of himself. Some have criticized this tendency in his writing as anthropomorphizing. He responded to that charge in a journal entry included in Heuer's volume. "*Anthropomorphizing*: the charge of my critics. My countercharge: There is a sense in which when we cease to anthropomorphize, we cease to be men, for when we cease to have human contact with animals and deny them all relation to ourselves, we tend in the end to cease to anthropomorphize ourselves—to deny our own humanity" (p. 200).

Eiseley's miraculous moments were usually solitary, and often left him feeling painfully isolated from humans. While tumbling with the fox, he thinks of the callous words of a fox poacher, and drops "even further and painfully away from human stature." Such poignant moments in Eiseley's writing are legacies of the loneliness of one who learned about love from a homeless mongrel. They also serve as reminders of our connections, and as invitations into a deeper level of communion with all life.

Another notable quality of Eiseley's work is the manner in which he weaves these anecdotes together with scientific and philosophical reflections into a tapestry of image and idea that reveals the inner drama of one who has explored the meanings of things. Stories set in motion a series of developing ideas, which seem to emerge almost effortlessly as the narrator tells the story.

moments is his romp with "The Innocent Fox" in *The Unexpected Universe*, which he describes as the culmination of a long search for a miracle. As in "The Star Thrower," the climactic episode is set on a beach, "an unengaging and unfrequented shore." Eiseley describes how a fox pup picked up a chicken bone and began shaking it at him. His description heightens the sense of dramatic, even cosmic, significance of the encounter, with words of strong religious connotation: "It was not a time for human dignity. It was a time only for the careful observance of the amenities written behind the stars. Gravely I arranged my forepaws while the puppy whimpered with ill-concealed excitement." He then picked up his own bone and shook it "in teeth that had not entirely forgotten their original purpose. Round and round we tumbled for one

In the most complex of these essays, Eiseley portrays himself as on a search, the hero of a quest, sharing with the reader his process of discovery. Here the essay as a whole becomes the story of Eiseley's thought as it develops out of his experience. This structure of weaving together anecdotes and reflections enables Eiseley to explore scientific and philosophical questions of considerable complexity, while at the same time preserving the immediacy of the moment of encounter in nature. While this complexity makes many of Eiseley's essays difficult to interpret, they can be more easily understood and appreciated by following the process by which insights unfold from his stories.

In this interplay between experiences and ideas, we sense the mind of a person who is on a quest for meaning, and this is another distinguishing characteristic of his work. Eiseley believed that "all existence is a medium of revelation," the words of William Temple, which he used as an epigraph to *The Immense Journey*. The book's second epigraph, from Thoreau, suggests the influence on Eiseley of the transcendentalist idea of nature as a medium of revelation. "Man can not afford to be a naturalist, to look at Nature directly, but only with the side of his eye. He must look through and beyond her." Eiseley saw this movement beyond natural facts to deeper symbolic meanings as distinguishing the transcendentalists from what he called "mere 'nature writing' in the ordinary sense" (quoted in Paul, p. 183).

In Eiseley's writing, we see this search for the hidden meanings behind natural events as a prominent theme. In *The Unexpected Universe*, Eiseley reflects on the human need for symbols and meanings: "Man, since the beginning of his symbol-making mind, has sought to read the map of that same universe. . . . Bereft of instinct, he must search constantly for meanings. . . . He hungers for messages, and when he ceases to seek and interpret them, he will be no longer man" (pp. 144–146).

Yet in counterpoint with this urge to find meanings and messages hidden in experience, Eiseley often expresses a sense of tentativeness or caution about the attempt to interpret them.

In "The Judgment of the Birds," he describes a series of vivid moments and then begins to speculate on their meaning. But here, in a characteristic narrative of Eiseley's thought, his urge to assign meaning is interrupted by another, contradictory one.

> But as I hesitated, it became plain that something was wrong. The marvel was escaping— a sense of bigness beyond man's power to grasp, the essence of life in its great dealings with the universe. It was better, I decided, for the emissaries returning from the wilderness . . . to record their marvel, not to define its meaning. In that way it would go echoing on through the minds of men, each grasping at that beyond out of which the miracles emerge, and which, once defined, ceases to satisfy the human need for symbols. (*The Immense Journey*, p. 178)

Here he articulates one of his major themes: the mystery of life and the importance of not reducing it to any particular meaning. In this account he maintains a subtle balance between the two impulses. He suggests powerful meanings, and even attempts to give them form, but at the same time acknowledges the unnameable quality at the heart of human experience.

This paradoxical art of naming and not naming, of seeking to understand the mystery and at the same time letting it remain, is one of Eiseley's greatest gifts as a writer. His stories "go echoing on" through our minds, resonating with meanings we cannot fully grasp. When reading Eiseley's essays it is important to keep in mind this dynamic tension between meaning and mystery. Whenever he articulates a particular meaning for an experience, it is important to remember that the unknown and unknowable lurks in the shadows. And whenever his meanings appear hopelessly elusive, one can take comfort in the fact that Eiseley probably meant to leave it that way, and that it is better not to try too hard to figure it out.

As we proceed to examine in depth some of his most influential works, it will be important to keep these qualities in mind: the mythical landscapes; the visionary moments of encounter and incorporation; the use of the "concealed essay" as a narrative of experiences and ideas; and the dynamic tension between the search for meaning and its elusive character. Through understanding Eiseley's skilled balancing of these elements his essays can be appreciated as masterpieces of the natural history genre.

The Immense Journey

The Immense Journey, Eiseley's first book of essays, is still considered by many to be his most important and influential. In it we see the fruits of his renunciation of the scholarly essay as his major vehicle of communication, and his developing skill in the art of the personal, or "concealed" essay, characterized by the weaving together of scientific fact and personal story. By integrating more scientific material than had previously been customary in the genre, Eiseley is now credited with having expanded the range of the personal essay. Fred Carlisle emphasizes that Eiseley's achievement goes beyond the artful integration of science and human values in the science essay, to what he calls the development of a "new idiom" that weaves together science, autobiography, metaphor, and metaphysics, through complex rhythms of movement between inner and outer, fact and myth, past and present.

The essays of *The Immense Journey* fall into three groups, each one considering a different aspect of evolutionary thought. Chapters 1–5 focus on the broad theme of the evolution of life before humans, introducing several key evolutionary concepts. Chapters 6–10 consider human evolution and the factors that led to the emergence of the human brain. The final three chapters are more autobiographical, and explore in depth Eiseley's personal connections with the natural world.

The first essay in the book, "The Slit," begins with an account of Eiseley's descent into a deep fissure in a bed of sandstone, introducing both the theme of evolution and his style of interweaving story and idea. The essay unfolds as a fine example of the concealed essay, with a series of incidents leading us to consider more complex evolutionary and philosophical aspects of this descent into time. His description captures a sense of movement into another dimension: the slit is "a little sinister—like an open grave," and the sky overhead recedes "as far off as some future century I would never see" (p. 4). Coming upon the skull of a small primitive mammal embedded in the sandstone, he reflects that he, too, is embedded in a vast progression of time, "staring upward at that strip of sky which the ages were carrying farther away from me." As he chisels away, he reflects on the dexterity of his hands and their long evolution through "fin and scaly reptile foot and furry paw." This narrative of Eiseley's thought process invites us to discover along with him the deepening of experience into symbol, leading us to the central metaphor of the book, the journey: "Perhaps there is no meaning in it at all, the thought went on inside me, save that of journey itself" (p. 6). While pausing to smoke a pipe, he thinks back to a prairie dog town he used to wander through as a boy, and reflects on a surprising fact of evolutionary history: that our early primate ancestors were once dwellers of the plains, competing with rodents for their home there, and being displaced by them. The image of this world "we were driven out of," a lost home never to be regained, introduces a sense of nostalgia, of the loneliness of our "long wandering," which develops throughout the book as an emotional undertone of melancholy. His return to the surface is also disorienting, and leads Eiseley to reflect on time as a "dimension denied to man," which can, however, be entered through the power of the imagination. "Forward and backward I have gone, and for me it has been an immense journey."

In his concluding reflections, he alerts us to several important qualities of the book as a whole. Though it will contain science, it will not be "science in the usual sense," but a doubting, questioning science, a science that admits its limitations, even its ignorance, and celebrates what is unknown and mysterious. But even more dramatically, the book is to explore not only science but personal story, a "bit of my personal universe," a "somewhat unconventional record of the prowlings of one mind." Eiseley suggests that his weaving together of science and personal story is more than a stylistic device. It reflects an essential quality of the journey: both scientific and personal, it can only be evoked by a narrative style that includes them both. As the book unfolds, there are actually three levels of the journey for Eiseley: the long evolutionary path by which he, as a representative of all humanity, has come to the present; the quest of science for knowledge about evolution, which he also embodies as scientist; and the personal wandering of Eiseley's own search for his place, his home, in the cosmos.

In the third essay in the book, "The Great Deeps," Eiseley weaves together these three levels of the journey by considering the origins of life in the ocean, the quest of scientists to understand those origins, and Eiseley's own sense of mystery as he contemplates his own relation to other life. The movement of this essay is opposite to that of "The Slit," beginning with a discussion of evolutionary research, and moving to a personal anecdote at the end. He explains the nineteenth-century theory that the deeper levels of the ocean were like evolutionary strata, where one encountered, by descending, creatures further back in evolutionary time, until at the bottom one found the *urschleim*, the primordial ooze that was the first living matter. As Eiseley tells of the attempts of scientists to find these living fossils and to recreate life from the ooze on the ocean floor, he captures their "fascination with lost worlds," making the errors of an earlier era seem almost credible. This picture of the fallibility of science contributes to Eiseley's larger theme of human ignorance, and the need for humility in the search for truth.

Eiseley then shows how science discovered that "the abyss . . . was not the original abode of life," but rather a place where life demonstrated one of its "strangest qualities—its eternal dissatisfaction with what is, its persistent habit of reaching out into new environments." The image of "reaching out" leads Eiseley to his concluding personal reflections. After considering the great "eyes" with which science now searches out the deeps of outer space—another example of "life reaching out, groping for a billion years, life desperate to go home"—he turns his vision earthward to consider the eye of a frog. Standing still to keep from frightening it, he senses in his response "that this is the most enormous extension of vision of which life is capable: the projection of itself into other lives. This is the lonely, magnificent power of humanity. It is, far more than any spatial adventure, the supreme epitome of the reaching out" (p. 46). The metaphor of "extension" unifies the journeys of evolution, scientific search, and personal quest. It was the process by which life came to reside in the ocean depths, by which scientists went there to try to understand life's origins, and through which Eiseley felt a connection with, and responsibility for, the life of a frog. The journey is ultimately a search for finding our place in the natural world, a quest for belonging.

Other essays in *The Immense Journey* expand on the idea of extension, adding to both its personal and evolutionary meaning. "The Flow of the River" tells of a dramatic moment of merging with water, an "extension of shape by osmosis," as he floats down the Platte River. Mystical union with water leads to an imaginative leap into his evolutionary past, as he remembers "my green extensions, my catfish nuzzlings and minnow wrigglings, my gelatinous materializations out of the mother ooze" (p. 26). Evolution itself is full of such leaps, such dramatic movements from one form to another, like the fish venturing out onto dry land, those "things coming ashore" he describes in "The Snout," and the "explosion" of the flowering plants he evokes so colorfully in "How Flowers Changed the World." Each image of evolutionary change adds to the sense of the miraculous capacity of life to leap across boundaries and project itself into new forms.

The essays in the middle portion of the book focus on the extensions and leaps that brought humans into existence, and the evolution of the human brain, that "peculiar leap, unlike anything else we know in the animal world" (p. 109). Again, he tells the story of science's search for the truth of our origins, including some of its dramatic errors along the way and his own changing opinions in the face of new evidence. These essays expand some of the central themes of the book: scientific research about the development of life; the reaching out of life into new forms; and the need for humility before the baffling complexity of life. But their style is different from the other essays in *The Immense Journey*, lacking the careful balance between anecdote and idea which distinguishes his most successful work. Primarily expository in style, they lack the flavor of immediate experience found in the "concealed" essay.

In the last three essays of the book, Eiseley returns to a narrative style as he attempts to "put down such miracles as can be evoked from the common earth" (p. 13). Here he focuses on the personal quest for meaning, criticizing the reductionistic attempts of modern science to solve the mystery of life, and emphasizing the limitations of science in the face of the unknown.

"The Bird and the Machine" confronts the dangers and limitations of the mechanistic worldview by contrasting human-created machines with the vitality of living beings. Eiseley begins by describing his state of puzzlement one morning while reading the paper. He is troubled by an article about miraculous new machines that are as smart as humans, but cannot quite figure out "why I should be thinking of birds over the *New York Times* at breakfast" (p. 179). In this fine moment of thought narrative, he reveals the rough edges of his thinking as he tries to understand the connections that come to him, and suggests a contrast between the proud certainties of science and his own humility before the mysterious workings of the human mind. His puzzlement sets his memory to work, and he attempts to trace the connections his mind has made by digging back into his past.

He acknowledges the mechanistic view, for the reader who may not "believe there is any difference" between machines and animals, and gives a brief survey of the development of mechanistic thinking: Thomas Hobbes ("what is the heart but a spring?"), the world as a clock, the human as a puppet.

Then he begins to reconstruct his memory of the birds he encountered on a research expedition during one of his college summers. His description of the setting is a classic Eiseley landscape: indistinct, mysterious, mythic; shrouded in "the trailing mists of a spring night," a place "that looked as though it might never have known the foot of man" (p. 186). Given the task of capturing some birds to take back to a zoo, he goes to an abandoned cabin that has been taken over by birds and prepares to capture them.

Here the narrative becomes more complex through Eiseley's dual role as narrator and subject of the story. His attitude has changed dramatically since the time of the incident, and he skillfully renders this double aspect of his consciousness. He confesses that he was an "assassin": arrogant, ignorant, and set on following orders. In his self-assuredness he had been totally unaware of one important detail: the birds that waited in the dark corner of the cabin were a pair of small hawks ready to do battle. Eiseley describes the encounter in which the male attacks his hand, leaving it wounded and bloody, allowing the female's escape. His narration further reveals his cynical, uncaring attitude as a young man: "In the morning that bird would be just another episode," shipped along with a truck full of bones back to a city. "And a good thing, too. I sucked my aching thumb and spat out some blood. An assassin has to get used to these things. I had a professional reputation to keep up" (p. 190).

The next morning, a change in the weather reveals a transformed landscape and foreshadows a transformation in the young Eiseley. He decides, secretively, to "have a look at my last night's capture." He takes the bird out of the box, feeling its beating heart, and watches it look up into the clear sky. Then, unexpectedly, almost unconsciously, he reaches out and sets the hawk on the grass, and after a few moments the bird takes to the air. Eiseley hears a cry from far up in the sky, far above the bird he has just released. It is the hawk's mate. "I was young then and had seen little of the world, but when I heard that cry my heart turned over." The confession becomes a conversion story, depicting a fundamental change of heart. In a lyrical passage, he describes the dance of the two hawks in the morning light, and brings us back to the present moment with their cry "of such unutterable and ecstatic joy that it sounds down across the years and tingles among the cups on my quiet breakfast table" (p. 192).

As he returns to the present, he completes the circle of memory and suggests how much he has changed. He ponders again the machines, whose connection to the birds has now become clear. "Ah, my mind takes up, on the other hand the machine does not bleed, ache, hang for hours in the empty sky in a torment of hope to learn the fate of another machine, nor does it cry out with joy nor dance in the air with the fierce passion of a bird" (p. 193). Haunted by "that remote cry from the heart of heaven," he now understands his distress over the *New York Times* and its confident prediction of progress. By taking us through the story of his own thinking, back to this vivid moment of conversion, he invites us to rethink our own presuppositions, implying by his example that this shift in thinking must start with a transformation of the heart. The danger Eiseley sees in the pride of science is that it closes down our ability to be receptive to the miracle of life, more a matter of the heart and soul than of the mind.

In the final essay of the book, "The Secret of Life," Eiseley pursues these questions further by considering the attempts of science to re-create life. After surveying early attitudes toward the origins of life, he reflects skeptically on the optimistic predictions of scientists who are attempting to create it in the laboratory. If the time comes when humans are able to re-create life, he asserts, "we shall have great need of humbleness." He fears our pride will keep us from recognizing that "the secret of life has slipped through our fingers and eludes us still." He concludes that "so deep is the mind-set of an age" that our "desire to link life to matter" may "have blinded us to the more remarkable characteristics of both," a blindness that was to preoccupy Eiseley all his life and be a major theme in much of his later work.

As a scientist who has gone on an immense journey, he has discovered as the ultimate gift of his quest not knowledge, but wonder, humility, and the capacity to extend oneself across the boundary to other forms of life. But he also has learned from experience the capacity of science to diminish consciousness, put us in the thrall of machines, and blind us to the miracle of life. This dual vision of science that emerges at the end of *The Immense Journey* was to become even more central in *The Unexpected Universe*.

The Unexpected Universe

The Unexpected Universe, published in 1969, more than a decade after *The Immense Journey*, is another of Eiseley's landmark books: praised by both humanists and scientists, it was nominated for the National Book Award. It explores some of the same themes as his first book, such as evolution, the scientific quest for knowledge, and the personal quest for meaning, and also develops more fully his critique of the goals of modern science and its impact on the human spirit. But the book is different from its predecessor, and needs to be read with a very different eye. Lacking *The Immense Journey*'s carefully orchestrated progression following the central theme of evolution, it has been seen by some critics as a less integrated or fully realized work. But a close reading reveals another kind of unity: that of an interconnecting web of images and ideas. While it contains some of Eiseley's most powerful essays, each of which can be read for its own gifts, the book can best be appreciated as a network of associated images and ideas that reverberate throughout the whole. Let us call it an ecosystem of a book.

As in an ecosystem, no one image or idea dominates the whole, so the task of teasing them all out from their network of relationships is a delicate one. One could pick any thread and begin pulling on it to see where it leads, and eventually end up encompassing the whole.

Perhaps the best place to begin is with the familiar Eiseley metaphor of the journey, appearing here as the voyage of discovery. The opening essay introduces the figure of Odysseus as the archetypal wanderer, in words reminiscent of the introduction to *The Immense Journey*: "Let it be understood that I claim no discoveries. I claim only the events of a life in science as they were transformed inwardly into something that was whispered to Odysseus long ago" (p. 3). Modern science itself is an "epic journey," a "story at once of tremendous achievement, loneliness, and terror." Different chapters consider the geographical voyages of Cook and Darwin, the metaphorical voyages of Thoreau, and Eiseley's own quests, both literal and metaphorical: once again the fugitive and wanderer, but now in the company of other explorers in search of new truth.

A theme that ties together all of these voyages is the encounters with the "unexpected universe": that which is unpredictable and mutable, which challenges our assumptions about the nature of reality. Odysseus' encounter with the shape-changing magic of the goddess Circe is analogous to Darwin's discovery of "the whole Circean labyrinth of organic change. . . . What had appeared to Odysseus as the trick of a goddess was, in actuality, the shape shifting of the incomprehensible universe itself" (p. 15). In the title essay, Eiseley elaborates on the "ill-concealed heresy" that he originally discussed in the last chapter of *The Firmament of Time*. While science attempted to bring increasing order to the "natural" universe and our understanding of it, increasingly it found the indeterminate and the "unnatural." "However strung with connecting threads," his universe is "endowed with an open-ended and perverse quality we shall never completely master" (p. 45). Here Eiseley sets himself apart from the leading figures of modern science, noting that Darwin himself, who ushered in our awareness of this unexpected dimension, never fully grasped its implications. A variety of metaphors play upon the contrast between the "connecting threads of the universe" and its "open-ended and perverse quality." The spider web appears several times as a metaphor for the orderly aspect of the universe, each being self-contained in its network of inter-

connecting threads. Eiseley applies this metaphor to evolution. "The strands of the living web" serve to keep in check "the riotous extremes of variation," but sometimes "the tight-drawn strands" snap, allowing for "the advancement of life" (p. 155). This rent or rift in the apparently ordered fabric of life appears variously in these essays as "the roiling unrest of a tornado"; the trickster of native mythologies; a hidden doorway or "mysterious hole in the hedge" (p. 195); *Alice in Wonderland*'s rabbit hole; even islands, which can, because of their seclusion, "offer doorways to the unexpected, rents in the living web" (p. 159), through which new forms of life have evolved.

The rift that seems to fascinate Eiseley the most is that mysterious leap by which humans came into being, when "the net of life was once more wrenched aside so that an impalpable shadow quickly wriggled through its strands into a new, unheard-of dimension of existence" (p. 162). Unlike the chapters in *The Immense Journey* that deal with human emergence, Eiseley's treatment of this theme here is firmly rooted in personal narrative. In "The Angry Winter," a moment of encounter on a winter's night with a dog named Wolf evokes the memory of "the other time," of wolf and tribal hunter, which leads to a series of reflections about how the glacial ages of the past shaped the development of human consciousness.

The weaving together of personal past and evolutionary history is the central focus of "The Last Neanderthal." A series of memories takes him back to a young woman he once met on an anthropological expedition, whose face had the features of a Neanderthal. He longs for the era she represents to him, feeling an "agonizing, lifelong nostalgia, both personal and, in another sense, transcending the personal" (p. 225). This "endurance in a single mind" of two stages of human evolution stirs in him a deep restlessness that sends him searching back through the past for home. Perhaps he once had one, he reflects, but now he would never find it. "It lay somewhere in the past down that hundred-thousand-year road on which travel was impossible" (p. 226).

Sometimes this sense of nostalgia draws him even further back into the past, seeking, like Thoreau, a way back "through the leafy curtain that has swung behind us, never to open again," separating humanity from the rest of the natural world (p. 165). While human emergence was a liberation, a breaking "through that network of strangling vines," it was also, for Eiseley, a loss of our connections with the rest of life, our "kindred" (p. 165). While this sense of loss leaves Eiseley lonely in his isolation, it also leads him back "through the mysterious hole in the hedge that a child would know at once led to some other dimension at the world's end" (p. 195). Through the power of the imagination, Eiseley found the "return" that he sought. He describes the recognition of Odysseus by his dog Argos as "nature's cry to homeless, far-wandering, insatiable man: 'Do not forget your brethren, nor the green wood from which you sprang'" (p. 23). Eiseley sees such moments as opportunities to "correct time's arrow" (p. 211) by running it backward to a time before we broke away from our secure place in the natural order. As attempts to return home, they evoke again the image of Eiseley the fugitive, the cosmic wanderer in exile from a home to which he can never fully return.

Yet the way backward and the way forward are one, for Eiseley's leaps are not only nostalgia, but also leaps forward into the new, the unfolding potential for humanity to shape its own future through the power of the imagination. Eiseley describes Thoreau as one such "dweller along the edge of the known, a place where the new begins" (p. 137).

Eiseley's quest leads him into this new vision as well. Through his encounters with the "unexpected universe" and its revelations of the miraculous, he moves beyond the realm of the known and challenges the scientific dogma of the day and its power to stifle human wonder. Sensing that the path of science leads potentially to our own destruction, Eiseley sees this larger quest as a crucial one for our age. Facing awesome challenges and responsibilities, "we have learned to ask terrible questions," he says, quoting Emerson. "Perhaps it is just for this that the Unseen Player in the void has rolled his equally terrible dice. Out of the self-knowledge gained by putting dreadful questions man achieves his final dignity" (p. 47). So Eiseley the scientist, by exploring the boundaries of the world of science, confronts essential questions of human values about the future and our role in shaping it.

"The Star Thrower" embodies more than any other essay this leap into a new dimension of awareness. One of his most complex and difficult essays, and considered by many his finest, it deserves special attention. Here we see him confronting the "terrible question," wrestling with the darkness of both his own life and of modern science, and translating that question "into an even more terrifying freedom," which becomes a life-transforming choice. "If there is any meaning to this book," he says in the opening, "it began on the beaches of Costabel, with just such a leap across an unknown abyss" (p. 67).

Several stylistic features of the essay are helpful in understanding its power. Here, Eiseley's characteristic weaving together of threads and themes to create imaginative resonances is enhanced by his beginning with a series of allusions to earlier essays. The opening sentences recall the previous essay, "The Hidden Teacher": though himself a teacher, he has been "taught surely by none," suggesting that his teachers are not of the usual sort, but are manifestations of the "hidden teacher" of which he has been speaking. The glimpse "of what man may be" picks up directly from that essay's closing lines, and sounds the larger theme of emerging human consciousness. The "rift" in nature anticipates Eiseley's own "leap across an unknown abyss," a theme that gathers meaning as the essay proceeds, and gradually develops into a central metaphor of the book. And finally, the "terrible question" translating itself into an "even more terrifying freedom," alludes back to the Emerson quote from the conclusion of "The Unexpected Universe," and prepares the way for the dark crucible of Eiseley's struggle to create new meaning in the midst of despair. By reading the essay in its context we become aware of these overtones to Eiseley's words, enhancing our sense of their resonance in the book as a whole.

As a "concealed essay," much of the power of "The Star Thrower" grows out of its manner of unfolding from a series of anecdotes "thoughts of a more purely scientific nature." But here the process of the essay is his own inner struggle and discovery, in which both ideas and experiences are essential parts of the drama. Since the essay is the story of the transformation of both his scientific worldview and his personal stance toward life, we need to grasp the essay on both levels at once in order to see its meaning.

The role of metaphor is also central to understanding the unfolding of Eiseley's story. Many writers have analyzed the cognitive function of metaphors, showing how they not only express our view of reality, but actually help to create and embody it. Eiseley's metaphors function in this way, providing an avenue for exploring, and eventually transforming, his identity as a scientist, his understanding of evolution, and his experience of the power of compassion. As metaphors shift during the course of the essay, they do more than signal a change in Eiseley's view: the images themselves are integral to the process of transformation.

The essay begins with a series of metaphors that portray a bleak reductionistic view of the world. Eiseley speaks of himself as an eye looking out at the world from a dead skull, "like a pharos light, a beacon, a search beam revolving endlessly in sunless noonday or black night." He acknowledges that "with such an eye, some have said, science looks upon the world." He walks through a stark landscape of death and struggle, a beach where death takes many forms: small creatures cast up by the surf to die; human scavengers who collect from among the remains. Over it all hangs death, "the only successful collector." Here he meets the star thrower, a man who opposes death by flinging stranded starfish back out into the sea where they can live again: in Eiseley's eyes a futile gesture, the result of an absurd desire to find meaning in a bleak world of struggle and survival.

Eiseley then leads us through a series of reflections about science, describing two different ways it has seen the world. While envisioning a more orderly world, like the landscape of the plains, "where one step reasonably leads to another," science has in fact taken us into the mountainous world of precipice and abyss, a trickster world of chance and indeterminacy. The ordered world of Newton gave way to the dark mysterious depths revealed by Darwin and Freud, and "things, in the words of G. K. Chesterton, were to grow incalculable by being calculated." Now, "the dance of contingency, of the indeterminable, outwits us all." The implications of Darwin's view are quite complex here, for though the theory of evolution opened up this "trickster world," it also was founded on the reductionistic image of life as selfish struggle. No species ever changes for the benefit of another, without also benefiting itself. If this were not true, Darwin contended, " 'it would annihilate my theory.' " In this harsh, mechanistic view of life, only the strong survive, and the failures, those who cannot successfully compete, disappear. This aspect of the Darwinian view sets the context for Eiseley's personal transformation.

Now the metaphors of Eiseley's personal life reenter the story. He is haunted by the eye of a dead cephalopod he has seen on the beach, which brings to mind another eye he cannot quite place at first. He realizes it was the eye of his mother he recalled from a photograph of her as a child: here was where "it began, her pain and mine . . . the long crucifixion of life." Now, with the eye of his mother replacing the menacing lighthouse eye of science, he sees with compassion: " 'I *do* love the world. . . . I love its small ones, the things beaten in the strangling surf.' . . . I choked and said, with the torn eye still upon me, 'I love the lost ones, the failures of the world.' It was like the renunciation of my scientific heritage" (p. 86). In this grace-filled moment of return to the wounds of his childhood, he embraces in love all that has been lost or that has failed: the creatures cast up by the surf; his mother, toward whom he had remained bitter all his life; and all of the losses and failures in his own life.

Eiseley frames this "leap" into compassion in evolutionary terms, calling it a leap across "one of the last great rifts in nature." "With it, I flung myself as forfeit, for the first time, into some unknown dimension of existence. From Darwin's tangled bank of unceasing struggle, selfishness, and death, had arisen, incomprehensibly, the thrower who loved not man, but life. It was the subtle cleft in nature before which biological thinking had faltered." This leap into compassion carries him beyond the scientific "eye" that led to his despair, into a new kind of vision. As he joins the star thrower in his act, he feels its more far-reaching implications. "Somewhere far off . . . I felt as though another world was flung more joyfully . . . somewhere the Thrower knew." Here he casts his imagery on a grand, cosmic scale, suggesting more mythic, even supernatural resonances. His actions are no longer confined by the restrictive individualism implied in the Darwinian view, but join him to a larger life-affirming process that binds all life together.

Conclusion

With "The Star Thrower," Eiseley moves into the terrain of religious values: compassion, transformation, and the alignment of one's self with a life-affirming process beyond the individual. To speak of religion in relation to Eiseley is a leap, but not an inappropriate one. He once wrote that although he professed no formal religious affiliation, all his life had been a religious journey. W. H. Auden identifies his sensibility quite accurately when he calls Eiseley "a man unusually well trained in the habit of prayer, by which I mean the habit of listening." This kind of listening means hearing "something new and unpredictable—an unexpected demand, obedience to which involves a change of self, however painful" (p. 20).

Listening and transformation: these are perhaps two of the greatest gifts of this writer whose work is filled with gifts. By writing of encounters by which he has learned to listen, he engages us in our own deep listening, a receptivity to the voices of lives beyond our own. And by writing of the inner changes to which his journey of

listening has brought him, he suggests the transformations to which we as individuals, and as a culture, need to be open. He wrote of these necessary changes with a passion that could be called prophetic, recognizing as he did the external consequences of our inward life, and the dangerous directions in which modern culture and science are leading us. As he wrote in the conclusion of "The Chresmologue" in *The Night Country*: "If we banish this act of contemplation and contrition from our midst, then even now we are dead men and the future dead with us. For the endurable future is a product not solely of the experimental method, or of outward knowledge alone. It is born of compassion. It is born of inward seeing" (p. 74).

Few nature writers carry us to such soulful depths, leading us, as Thoreau would say, "through and beyond" nature deep into the interior life. To read Eiseley is to let yourself be changed, to grow into a deeper capacity for seeing, for listening, for wonder. And for reverence and gratitude. Eiseley is a writer for whom such words are not too strong: reverence and gratitude for the sense of life to which he leads us and for the life and words of this fugitive, questing soul, who leads us by his immense journeys.

Selected Bibliography

WORKS OF LOREN EISELEY

PROSE

The Immense Journey (New York: Random House, 1957); *Darwin's Century: Evolution and the Men Who Discovered It* (New York: Doubleday, 1958); *The Firmament of Time* (New York: Atheneum, 1960); *Francis Bacon and the Modern Dilemma* (Lincoln: Univ. of Nebraska Press, 1962); *The Mind as Nature* (New York: Harper and Row, 1962); *The Unexpected Universe* (New York: Harcourt, Brace & World, 1969); *The Invisible Pyramid* (New York: Scribners, 1970); *The Night Country* (New York: Scribners, 1971); *The Man Who Saw Through Time* (New York: Scribners, 1973), rev. and enl. ed. of *Francis Bacon and the Modern Dilemma*; *All the Strange Hours: The Excavation of a Life* (New York: Scribners, 1975; repr., 1975); *The Star Thrower* (New York: Times Books, 1978), intro. by W. H. Auden; *The Lost Notebooks of Loren*

Eiseley, ed. by Kenneth Heuer (Boston: Little, Brown, 1987).

POETRY

Notes of an Alchemist (New York: Scribners, 1972); *The Innocent Assassins* (New York: Scribners, 1973); *Another Kind of Autumn* (New York: Scribners, 1977); *All the Night Wings* (New York: Times Books, 1980).

BIOGRAPHICAL AND CRITICAL STUDIES

BOOKS

Andrew J. Angyal, *Loren Eiseley* (Boston: Twayne, 1983); E. Fred Carlisle, *Loren Eiseley: The Development of a Writer* (Urbana: Univ. of Illinois Press, 1983); Gale E. Christianson, *Fox at the Wood's Edge: A Biography of Loren Eiseley* (New York: Henry Holt, 1990); Leslie Gerber and Margaret McFadden, *Loren Eiseley* (New York: Ungar, 1983).

ARTICLES

W. H. Auden, "Concerning the Unpredictable," intro. to *The Star Thrower* (New York: Times Books, 1978); E. Fred Carlisle, "The Heretical Science of Loren Eiseley," in *Centennial Review* 18 (fall 1974) and "The Literary Achievement of Loren Eiseley," in *Prairie Schooner* 61, no. 3 (fall 1987); Erleen Christensen, "Loren Eiseley, Student of Time," in *Prairie Schooner* 61, no. 3 (fall 1987); Michael Peter Cohen, "The Leap: Loren Eiseley's Uses of Life," in *North Dakota Quarterly* 59, no. 2 (spring 1991); Robert E. Franke, "Blue Plums and Smoke: Loren Eiseley's Perception of Time," in *Western American Literature* 24, no. 2 (1989) and "Loren Eiseley and the Transcendentalist Tradition," in *Mosaic* 20, no. 3 (1987); Peter Heidtmann, "An Artist of Autumn: An Essay," in *Prairie Schooner* 61, no. 3 (fall 1987); Ben Howard, "Loren Eiseley and the State of Grace," in *Prairie Schooner* 61, no. 3 (fall 1987); Sherman Paul, "Back and Down: Loren Eiseley's Immense Journey," in his *For Love of the World: Essays on Nature Writers* (Iowa City: Univ. of Iowa Press, 1992); James M. Schwartz, "Loren Eiseley: The Scientist as Literary Artist," in *Georgia Review* 31 (winter 1977).

RALPH WALDO EMERSON
(1803–1882)

MICHAEL P. BRANCH

RALPH WALDO EMERSON, essayist, lecturer, and poet, is one of the most influential figures in American literary history. His call for an end to imitation of European cultural forms helped to inspire the rise of a distinctive national literature during the nineteenth century, and his work directly influenced Henry David Thoreau, Herman Melville, Emily Dickinson, Walt Whitman, and many other writers of the American Romantic period. Famous on both sides of the Atlantic in his own lifetime, Emerson put forth a radical philosophy of optimism and individualism that galvanized the transcendentalist movement and served to define the possibilities for American culture and character. His resonant concept of "self-reliance" helped to shape American ideas about the relationship of the individual to society, to God, and to nature. Emerson's assertion of the divinity of the self and nature challenged the ecclesiastical authority of the church, the secular authority of the government, and the intellectual authority of the academy, and thus encouraged the relocation of divinity from institutions to the individual soul and the natural world.

Throughout his career, Emerson maintained an enduring fascination with natural history; under the rubric of natural history, natural philosophy, or natural science, he repeatedly praised the study of nature as a means to the ultimate end of understanding the soul. Even a glance at some titles suggests Emerson's enduring interest in this subject: "The Uses of Natural History" (1833); "The Naturalist" (1834); *Nature* (1836); "The Method of Nature" (1841); "Nature" (1844); "Natural History of Intellect" (1870). Emerson's earliest addresses are on natural history, and the final lectures of his life once again attempt to demonstrate that the conceptual methods of natural history may be used to access truths about the human spirit.

Because Emerson's writing is often abstract and metaphysical—and therefore lacks the detailed naturalistic description usually associated with nature writing—his important contributions to the development of the genre are sometimes overlooked. First, Emerson was among the most outspoken critics of nineteenth-century America's dominant view of nature as "mere commodity." During an age in which the myth of inexhaustible natural resources fueled American expansion and industrialization, he reminded his audience that the material use of nature, though legitimate, was simply one use among many. He objected that a strictly economic interpretation of nature's gifts too often precluded the aesthetic, intellectual, symbolic, and spiritual enjoyments that he identified as "higher uses."

Emerson also argued that "nature is the symbol of spirit"—that all elements of the natural world exist as indications of divine truths. In addition to asserting the divinity of nature—an assertion that forms the basis of a great deal of subsequent nature writing—Emerson also endorsed the notion that study of the natural world may lead to moral illumination. In effect, his contention that the *liber naturae* (book of nature) should be carefully read and interpreted actually calls the nature writer into being. By insisting that the natural world be seen as a repository of beauty, divinity, and moral truth—and not simply as a larder of material wealth—Emerson helped to set the agenda for nature writing down to the present day.

It is little wonder, then, that Emerson's ideas directly inspired the work of many of America's greatest nature writers. Henry Thoreau, who was Emerson's close friend and literary protégé, proclaimed that "[Emerson's] personal influence upon young persons [is] greater than any man's," and much of Thoreau's work may be seen as a consequence and application of Emerson's ideas about nature. John Burroughs, whose earliest essays were mistaken for the work of Emerson, declared that Emerson's writing had "an immediate and stimulating effect upon all the best minds of the country." John Muir—who carried and annotated the 1870 edition of Emerson's *Prose Works* while exploring in the Sierras—also cited Emerson as a primary influence; Muir read and corresponded with Emerson enthusiastically, and he later described their 1871 meeting as among the most "memorable and impressive" of his life. Although Emerson's tremendous influence is felt throughout American literature and especially within the nature writing tradition, it is important to note that his ideas of individual and natural divinity have inspired a wide variety of literary responses to nature. As Walt Whitman recognized, "The best part of Emersonianism is, it breeds the giant that destroys itself. . . . No teacher ever taught, that has so provided for his pupil's setting up independently."[1]

[1]Quoted in *Columbia Literary History of the United States*, ed. by Emory Elliot (New York: Columbia Univ. Press, 1988) p. 382.

Before *Nature* (1803–1835)

Emerson was born in Boston on 25 May 1803. His father, Reverend William Emerson, a Harvard-educated Unitarian minister, died in 1811, leaving the family in serious financial difficulties. Although the Emersons were forced to take in boarders and to accept charity in order to escape poverty, Ruth Haskins Emerson saw to it that all of her six sons went to Harvard College. Ralph Waldo entered Harvard in 1817; although he won several prizes for his oratory and essays, his academic career was largely undistinguished, and he graduated in the middle of his class in 1821.

In retrospect, one of Emerson's most significant accomplishments at Harvard was to begin keeping a journal. It became his confidante, his practice field, and the source for a great deal of his published work. Inspirited by his Aunt Mary Moody Emerson, who had encouraged his poetry as early as 1812, Emerson began to use the journal to record his evolving ideas concerning self, society, and nature. Ultimately filling 182 notebooks covering the period from 1820 to 1882, the journal often provides the clearest sense of Emerson's enduring fascination with nature and natural history.

After graduating from Harvard, Emerson began teaching in his brother William's school for young ladies in Boston. Unenthusiastic about teaching, he returned to Harvard in 1825 to prepare for the ministry, but his course of study was repeatedly interrupted by health problems. Finally approbated to preach in October 1826, he traveled to South Carolina and Florida to restore his uncertain health before serving as a supply preacher in Massachusetts and New Hampshire. In 1828 he became engaged to Ellen Louisa Tucker, a frail young woman he had met while preaching in Concord, New Hampshire.

In 1829 Emerson's professional life seemed to have begun. He was ordained junior pastor of Boston's Second Church, a historic institution that had been the church of Increase and Cotton Mather; he became chaplain of the state senate, as his father had been before him; and he married Ellen Tucker on 30 September. Despite these outward signs of success and stability, Emerson's future was less secure than it seemed. He soon became dissatisfied with what he increasingly came to view as the limitations of his ministerial duties, and he began to question the very foundations of institutionalized Christianity. Although Unitarianism was a liberal sect that had attempted to purge New England Congregationalism of its legacy of strict Calvinist forms, Emerson began to feel that his Unitarian pastorate interfered excessively with the sort of highly individualized worship he was coming to prefer.

Although his readings in Platonism, European Romanticism, and reformist theology influenced his move away from the ministry, a decisive factor in Emerson's eventual break from the church was his blossoming interest in natural history. On 27 May 1832, just five months before he officially resigned the pastorate of the Second Church of Boston, Emerson preached a sermon with the unlikely title "Astronomy." The journals confirm that natural science was very much on his mind during the critical period preceding his break with the ministry, and the records of his book borrowings show that he was reading the works of Copernicus, Johannes Kepler, Pierre-Simon Laplace, Alexander von Humboldt, Mary Somerville, and William Herschel. What was the young preacher searching for in the work of scientists who studied the heavens? The universal order revealed in the stars encouraged him in his own search for a moral order—for ecumenical laws of ethics as firm and systematic as the laws that bound the motion of planets. Emerson also valued astronomy's power to modify assumptions about human centrality in the cosmic order.

As the facts of astronomy began to challenge the anthropocentric emphasis of the Christian paradigm, Emerson realized that developments in natural science would have profound theological implications: "And men take man of course for the type of the highest beings & suppose whatever is intelligent & great must be like him in nature. Astronomy gives the lie to all this. . . .

Well then it irresistibly modifies all theology" (*Journals and Miscellaneous Notebooks*, vol. 4, p. 26). What Emerson particularly welcomed about this decentering "modification" was that it shifted emphasis from particular doctrinal institutionalizations toward the spiritual laws he believed were the essence of true religion. As a natural philosopher Emerson picked up where his eighteenth-century deist predecessors had left off, with the assertion that increased knowledge of the physical world would testify to the glory of God even as it exposed the sciolism perpetuated by the observance of specific religious rituals. "Calvinism suited Ptolemaism. The irresistible effect of Copernican Astronomy has been to make the great scheme for the salvation of man absolutely incredible. . . . Thus astronomy proves theism but disproves dogmatic theology. . . . It operates steadily to establish the moral laws, to disconcert & evaporate temporary systems" (*Journals and Miscellaneous Notebooks*, vol. 4, pp. 26–27).

Emerson clearly recognized in natural science an emphasis upon universal law that might transcend the exigencies of institutionalized forms. As science enlarged his notion of the Creator, however, it also reduced the value of the traditional methods of worship to which the ministry bound him. In "Astronomy" he told his congregation that natural science would "correct and exalt our view of God"; like the Bible, nature was to be seen as a conduit to divinity, and the facts of science were to be read as a "sequel to the revelation." In short, Emerson's turn away from the ministry was simultaneous with his turn toward the spiritual possibilities of nature. If he objected to institutionalized Christianity's perpetuation of "dead forms" of worship, he embraced natural history's pursuit of the dynamic perfection of the natural world. Having decided that he could better pursue the ministry's highest functions outside the church, he therefore resigned his pastorate in October 1832. His wife, Ellen, long ill, had died of tuberculosis the previous year; Emerson now found himself without a companion, a vocation, or a direction in life.

In the wake of this series of difficult changes, and seeking improvement in his physical and emotional health, Emerson sailed for Europe on Christmas Day, 1832. Although he was extremely active during his nine months abroad, it is remarkable how rarely he was impressed by the cultural monuments he was visiting for the first time. He even records his disappointment with William Wordsworth, Samuel Taylor Coleridge, Walter Savage Landor, and other literary luminaries whom he met while abroad; interestingly, one of his complaints against them was their lack of interest in contemporary natural science. Emerson used his trip to continue his readings in natural history, and to expand them to include the treatises on hydrostatics, geology, optics, chemistry, and botany that were appearing in cabinet libraries and being disseminated through the publications of societies for the diffusion of useful knowledge.

More important than Emerson's reading, however, was his interest in the men of science whom he met or whose lectures he attended, and the museums of natural history he visited with so much enthusiasm. Although his travel journal enthusiastically documents a great many such meetings and visits, the zenith of his European tour clearly occurred in Paris, at the Muséum d'Histoire Naturelle's Jardin des Plantes. It was here, on 13 July 1833, that Emerson had the moving experience he recorded in several lengthy journal entries, and to which he appealed in "The Uses of Natural History," "The Naturalist," the "Prospects" chapter of *Nature*, and in even "Powers and Laws of Thought" in *Natural History of Intellect*, which was not written until thirty-six years later. Why was Emerson's visit to the cabinet of natural history and the botanical garden so powerfully resonant? How could a carefully organized showcase of plant and animal species be so memorable and important? Following is an excerpt from the account recorded in the journal, which has greater immediacy than the versions written for publication:

Ah said I this is philanthropy, wisdom, taste—to form a Cabinet of natural history.

... Here we are impressed with the inexhaustible riches of nature. The universe is a more amazing puzzle than ever as you glance along this bewildering series of animated forms,—the hazy butterflies, the carved shells, the birds, beasts, fishes, insects, snakes,—& the upheaving principle of life everywhere incipient in the very rock aping organized forms. Not a form so grotesque, so savage, nor so beautiful but is an expression of some property inherent in man the observer,—an occult relation between the very scorpions and man. I feel the centipede in me—cayman, carp, eagle & fox. I am moved by strange sympathies, I say continually "I will be a naturalist." (*Journals and Miscellaneous Notebooks*, vol. 4, pp. 199–200)

Emerson's experience in the cabinet of natural history was important to his understanding of nature because, through its juxtaposition of an otherwise bewildering array of natural forms, the cabinet emphasized the whole rather than the parts, the unifying principle rather than the constituent elements. Just as the pieces of a jigsaw puzzle cease to resemble fragments once the puzzle is properly assembled, so the conceptual order of the cabinet de-emphasizes the "facts" of science and insists instead upon the "theory" or "law" that describes their interrelationship. In effect, the pieces of the collection, as pieces, disappear, suddenly revealing how all pieces are universally bound by what Emerson called "the elemental law, the *causa causans*, the supernatural force." Like the elements of the cabinet, which are transformed from individual entities into interrelated members of a single family of nature, the ecstatic observer transcends the limitations of individual identity and becomes poignantly aware of an intimate relationship with all other incarnations of the "upheaving principle of life." By feeling "the cayman, carp, eagle & fox" in him, Emerson repudiates his own status as observer and is momentarily subsumed by the cabinet itself; he is initiated as a member of a vital corpus that is animated by the higher principle of life.

Emerson had once asked, "Is there not a secret sympathy which connects man to all the animals and to all the inanimate beings around him?" (*Early Lecturers*, vol. 1, p. 24). Now his experience in the Jardin des Plantes had suggested that a dizzying plethora of natural forms could be comprehended by a theory of interrelationship. Antoine-Laurent de Jussieu's garden and the cabinet of natural history, like Coleridge's *Essays on the Principles of Method*, possessed Emerson with "a conviction that Nature means something, that the flower, the animals, the sea, the rock have some relation to us not understood which if known would make them more significant" (*Early Lectures*, vol. 1, p. 78). It is not surprising, then, that he appropriated the cabinet of natural history as an epistemological model; by constellating "refractory facts" around the protoecological idea of familial interrelationship, he believed, the truth of essential relations could be revealed. So ardent was Emerson's enthusiasm for the method of natural history and for the natural world inscribed by that method, that he concludes: "I will be a naturalist."

As early as 1832 Emerson had invoked the notion of *liber naturae* to tell his congregation, in the sermon "Astronomy," that "religion will become purer and truer by the progress of science. This consideration ought to secure our interest in the book of nature" (*Young Emerson*, p. 171). By the time he returned from Europe, he was prepared to be even more explicit about the composition and interpretation of nature as a central text:

> I look then to the progress of Natural Science as to that which is to develop new and great lessons of which good men shall understand the moral. Nature is a language and every new fact we learn is a new word; but it is not a language taken to pieces and dead in the dictionary, but the language put together into a most significant and universal sense. I wish to learn this language—not that I may know a new grammar but that I may read the great book which is written in that tongue. A man should feel that the time is not lost and the efforts not misspent that are devoted to the elucidation of these laws; for herein is writ by

the Creator his own history. (*Early Lectures*, vol. 1, p. 26)

Emerson views nature as a form of divine communication that assumes the status of Scripture, thus becoming "the sequel of the revelation which our Creator is giving us of himself." To face nature and assert that "herein is writ by the Creator his own history" is not only to cast God in the traditional role of father or first cause but also to insist upon his being an artist and the author of the book of nature. As an author who writes his own history in the language of natural facts, God in effect composes a "natural history" that, according to Emerson, functions as a kind of spiritual autobiography of the Creation. "In geology," he declares, "we have a book of Genesis, wherein we read when and how the worlds were made, and are introduced to periods as portentous as the distances of the sky" (*Early Lectures*, vol. 2, p. 32).

If Emerson conceived of nature as a "language" composed of the "words" of natural facts, it was the challenge of natural history to provide a "grammar" or "dictionary" by which the sacred text could be understood. Emerson had described his memorable visit to the Jardin des Plantes precisely in terms of this semiotic analogy when he called the garden a "grammar of botany." "If you have read Decandolle with engravings," he exclaims, "conceive how much more exciting and intelligible is this natural alphabet, this green and yellow and crimson dictionary, on which the sun shines and the winds blow" (*Early Lectures*, vol. 1, p. 8). Emerson hoped that natural history would provide a "universal" language by which the scriptural text of nature could be interpreted. Thus, the Emersonian literary naturalist is not principally an empiricist or an aesthete, but rather is an inspired exegete, an agent of revelation who elucidates the "concurrent test" that is "authorized" by God.

On 7 October 1833, Emerson returned from Europe with great enthusiasm for natural history but no vocational prospects whatsoever. However, he soon secured a golden opportunity to present a lyceum lecture to the Natural History

Society in Boston on 5 November. The first lecture became a series of four addresses on natural history, and his initial success in the lyceum helped to establish him in the career that would last a lifetime: he became a prophetic orator who addressed his American audience from the secular pulpit of the lyceum. By 1833, the lyceum movement was well organized, and regular lecture series were in place in towns as well as cities. Along with societies for the diffusion of useful knowledge, the lyceum programs catalyzed the popularization of specialized branches of knowledge, especially in the sciences. Emerson seems to have been uniquely fitted for the role of lyceum lecturer. He had vowed to follow his conscience by studying only what suited his own temperament; he wished to speak as a "man to men," and never as a mouthpiece of institutionalized discourse; his fundamentally egalitarian belief in the potential of every individual found a ready audience in the heterogeneous assemblage of the lyceum hall; he always retained his ministerial proclivity for attempting to convert people to the truth; and, although he lacked the credentials of a specialist, Emerson possessed the oratorical eloquence that eclipsed expertise as a qualification for success in the lyceum.

Emerson's four lectures were titled "The Uses of Natural History," "The Relation of Man to the Globe," "Water," and "The Naturalist"; it is highly significant that he chose to begin his career by speaking on natural science. In light of his earlier claim that he wished to become a naturalist, Emerson may have been obliquely referring to his own inchoate sense of vocation when he told his first audience that "it seems to have been designed, if anything was, that men should study Natural History." Indeed, this first lecture, "The Uses of Natural History," reiterates the epiphany he had experienced in the Jardin: "I am moved by strange sympathies. I say I will listen to this invitation. I will be a naturalist" (*Early Lecturers*, vol. 1, p. 10).

It is difficult to know how literally we should take Emerson's stated plan to become a naturalist. We do know that during the period of the early lectures, he read enthusiastically in natural history and that he maintained a buoyant confidence in the prospects for scientific inquiry. In a letter to his brother William he asked, "Is it not a good symptom for society, this decided & growing taste for natural science which has appeared though yet in its first gropings?" (*The Letters of Ralph Waldo Emerson*, vol. 1, p. 404). Emerson's own "first gropings" led him infallibly to the subject of natural history, and the fact that his first four performances as a lyceum lecturer took natural science as their occasion reflects his personal faith in the spiritual potential of natural history. In a rarely noted journal entry Emerson addresses himself as follows:

> Well, my friend, are you not yet convinced that you should study plants & animals? . . . Say then that I will study Natural history . . . that I may never lose my temper nor be without soothing uplifting occupation. . . . Or again say that I am ever haunted by the conviction that I have an interest in all that goes on around me, that I would overhear the powers what they say.—No knowledge can be spared, or any advantage we can give ourselves. And this is the knowledge of the laws by which I live. But finally say frankly, that all the reasons seem to me to fall far short of my faith upon the subject, therefore—boldly press the cause as its own evidence; say that you love nature, & would know her mysteries, & that you believe in your power by patient contemplation & docile experiment to learn them. (*Journals and Miscellaneous Notebooks*, vol. 4, pp. 290–291)

Emerson's devotion to natural history persuaded him that "the axioms of geometry and of mechanics only translate the laws of ethics. . . . it will probably be found to hold of all the facts revealed by chemistry or astronomy that they have the same harmony with the human mind" (*Early Lectures*, vol. 1, p. 25). Just as he interprets nature as a manifestation of spirit, so he conceives of natural science as an ethical system whose goal is the tuition of the individual soul via the inexorable laws of the universe; thus, Emerson understood the moral law that spiritually empowers the individual to be a direct transliteration of the natural law as revealed by natural history.

If Emerson was attracted to nature as an "unlocking [of] the spiritual sight," he was ultimately disappointed in the failure of natural science to realize its visionary potential. He later complained, "Tis too plain that with the material power the moral progress has not kept pace." By the time he delivered "The Humanity of Science" in 1836, Emerson had tempered his annunciation of the value of natural science with an admonition that scientific reification of nature was "leav[ing] spirit out of the reckoning." Both in heralding science and in warning against the misapplication of its methods, Emerson insisted that the naturalist "be a poet in his severest analysis": "Shall the problems never be assayed in a feeling of their beauty? Is not the poetic side of science entitled to be felt and presented by its investigators? Is it quite impossible to unite severe science with a poetic vision? Nature's laws are as charming to Taste and as pregnant with moral meaning as they are geometrically exact" (*Early Lectures*, vol. 2, p. 36).

Emerson attempted to heal the rift between religion and science even into the age of Darwin, but when technology irreversibly propelled natural science toward what he considered to be profane ends, he warned his culture against the rebarbative influences of rampant scientific materialism. In a caveat that means more now than when originally published, he admonished that "Many facts concur to show that we must look deeper for our salvation than to steam, photographs, balloons, or astronomy. . . . Machinery is aggressive. The weaver becomes a web, the machinist a machine. If you do not use the tools, they use you. All tools are in one sense edge-tools, and dangerous" (*Complete Works*, vol. 7, p. 164).

Emerson's early natural history lectures were a decisive turning point in his life because they showed him a way of effectively communicating his highly spiritualized enthusiasm for nature. His initial success in the lyceum launched his secular career, and indirectly encouraged him to stabilize his life by relocating and remarrying; in 1835 he bought a house in Concord and married

Lydia Jackson of Plymouth. Furthermore, the lectures taught him that although nature is a source of divinity, the scientific method can obstruct as well as facilitate spiritual illumination. Despite his avowed desire to "be a naturalist," Emerson ultimately became a critic of science rather than a scientist, a philosopher of nature rather than a naturalist. Just as he had resigned the ministry because he felt that he could pursue its highest functions elsewhere, so he declined the vocation of natural scientist because he felt that he could better proclaim the spiritual value of nature through the lyceum and through literary efforts. These early natural history lectures contained the seeds of Emerson's most distinctive ideas, and they functioned as a rehearsal for the more fully developed discussion of nature that characterizes his most famous works. By 1835 Emerson's idiosyncratic natural philosophy had begun to mature, and the stage was set for his remarkable literary debut.

Nature and the Early Harvard Addresses (1836–1840)

Published anonymously in September 1836, but widely known to be the work of Ralph Waldo Emerson, *Nature* was a very small book destined to have a very large influence. Considered as a whole, *Nature* is Emerson's attempt to answer the ambitious question he puts forth on the book's first page: "Let us inquire, to what end is nature?" The question of nature's proper purpose, use, or destiny—a question that necessarily engages the imagination of any nature writer—receives in *Nature* a remarkably provocative and complex exploration. In a series of chapters organized in ascending levels of importance and abstraction, Emerson articulates a natural philosophy nearly cosmological in scope. After introducing the book and providing an operational definition of "nature," Emerson's chapters titled "Commodity," "Beauty," "Language," "Discipline," "Idealism," "Spirit," and "Prospects" consider the economic, aesthetic, symbolic, educational, philosophical, spiritual, and prophetic "uses" of nature, respectively.

Although terse, abstract, and often elliptical, *Nature* is an intellectual tour de force that attempts to articulate a comprehensive theory of nature. Emerson begins the "Language" chapter of *Nature* thus:

> 1. Words are signs of natural facts. 2. Particular natural facts are symbols of particular spiritual facts. 3. Nature is the symbol of spirit. The use of natural history is to give us aid in supernatural history: the use of the outer creation, to give us language for the beings and changes of the inward creation.

In this opening statement we find the seed of Emerson's thesis in *Nature*, for the logic of the book depends upon the Emersonian doctrine of correspondence. Derived from Neoplatonism through Coleridge and Emanuel Swedenborg, this doctrine asserts that the natural world exists as a template or cipher of the spiritual world. As Emerson put it in *Nature*, "The laws of moral nature answer to those of matter as face to face in a glass" ("Language"). Although the idea is clearly an outgrowth of Emerson's earlier intuition that nature exists as a "parallel scripture," *Nature* brings the principle of correspondence to the center of the Emersonian program. By asserting that "words are signs of natural facts," Emerson grants privileged status to the literary naturalist. To craft words about nature, if we follow Emerson's syllogistic reasoning, is to engage in the spiritual education of the reader.

The concept of "supernatural history" clarifies the unusual way in which Emerson may be considered a nature writer. Although he helped to introduce to American literature the idea that nature is a repository of divinity and a correlative of spirit, he also understood nature's value as thoroughly mediate—as a means to the end of recognizing and developing spiritual strength. Rightly studied, natural history describes a kind of transcendental ascension from fact to theory, from material to spiritual, from temporal to eternal, from natural to supernatural. If Emersonian self-reliance depends upon the paradox that descent into the individual soul reveals the greatest universal truths, Emersonian natural philosophy, conversely, is predicated upon the assumption that study of the laws of nature will infallibly reveal the highest truths of the soul.

Emerson's concept of "supernatural history" likewise insists upon the limitations of pure empiricism. In the "Prospects" chapter of *Nature* he warns that "Empirical science is apt to cloud the sight. . . . But the best-read naturalist who lends an entire and devout attention to truth, will see that . . . a dream may lead us deeper into the secret of nature than a hundred concerted experiments." This "best read naturalist" might be seen as an ideal type of the nature writer. Emerson's imaginative revision of natural history as a heuristic means to the higher end of supernatural history caused him to identify with the inspired figure whom Coleridge had called the "enlightened naturalist," and it was in this role that Emerson made his literary debut in *Nature*. As a proponent of supernatural history Emerson asserted, in "Humanity of Science," "[that] science is bankrupt which attempts to cut the knot which always spirit must untie" (*Early Lectures*, vol. 2, p. 30).

Because it insisted so vehemently upon nature as a substitute for more orthodox means of revelation, *Nature* was a controversial book that polarized critics the moment it appeared. Unsympathetic readers rightly perceived Emerson's theory of nature as an attack upon the ecclesiastical authority of institutionalized Christianity. Among another group of readers, which consisted largely of liberal Unitarian ministers under the influence of European Romanticism, the book was so well received that it became the gospel of American transcendentalism.

Although the transcendentalist movement remained fractured, fluid, and ill-defined during its relatively short heyday, it may be described as a form of romantic idealism that attempted to reform the institutions of church and state by shifting the locus of power toward the self and nature. Transcendentalists were often involved in movements to reform education, abolish slavery, nurture American art and literature, challenge the orthodoxy of the church, and establish experimental utopian communities. Although never an official organization with an established platform or membership, the transcendental movement grew from a group of liberal theologians and intellectuals (later referred to as the "Transcendental Club") that often met at Emerson's house in Concord. In its various incarnations, transcendentalism had been encouraged by *Nature*, the slim volume afterward called the "Bible" of the movement.

In the two years following the publication of *Nature*, Emerson delivered his most famous and controversial addresses. The occasion for the first was the 1837 meeting of Harvard's Phi Beta Kappa Society, to whom Emerson addressed an oration with the rather predictable subject "The American Scholar." Though conventional in its call for a revivification of the scholar and a move toward distinctive American arts and letters, Emerson's address is extremely radical both in its assertion of the scholar's need for absolute self-reliance and in its suggestion that the true scholar must be a student of nature. Emerson gives nature the premier position in his survey of the proper influences upon the mind of the scholar: "1. The first in time and the first in importance of the influences upon the mind is that of nature. . . . The scholar . . . must settle its value in his mind. What is nature to him?" (*Collected Works*, vol. 1, p. 54). In effect, he asks the scholar to undertake exactly the inquiry he had attempted in *Nature*.

As in the earlier book, Emerson appeals to the correspondential idea that "nature is the opposite of the soul, answering to it part for part. One is seal, and one is print" (p. 55). Because he believes the true scholar must recognize the correspondence between the individual soul and the natural world, Emerson conflates the scholar's duties to introspection and natural history. When the American scholar is at last freed from excessive convention and from puerile dependence upon the "courtly muses of Europe," he will recognize that "the ancient precept 'Know thyself,' and the modern precept, 'Study nature,' become at last one maxim" (p. 55).

Oliver Wendell Holmes called "The American Scholar" America's "intellectual Declaration of Independence" because the address so powerfully demanded that American genius turn from European literary models to the cultural resources of the American continent. In an earlier lecture Emerson had explained the role of natural history in the shift away from the unhealthy mimicry of European cultural forms:

> [Natural history studies] restrain Imitation— Imitation, the vice of overcivilized communities. To take an example. Imitation is the vice eminently of our times, of our literature, of our manners and social action. All American manners, language, and writing are derivative. We do not write from facts, but we wish to state facts after the English manner. . . . It is the tax we pay for the splendid inheritance of the English literature. We are exonerated by the sea and the revolution from the national debt but we pay this which is rather the worst part. Time will certainly cure us, probably through the prevalence of a bad party ignorant of all literature and of all but selfish, gross pursuits. But a better cure would be the study of Natural History. (*Early Lectures*, vol. 1, pp. 74–75)

By embracing natural history as a means to both literary and spiritual ends, Emerson's work suggested that the greatness of American nature could inspire great American literature and scholarship.

In 1838 Emerson gave the shocking oration that prevented him from being invited back to Harvard College for nearly thirty years. Addressing the faculty and graduating class of Harvard's Divinity School, he blasted institutionalized religion as ossified and vitiated. He insisted that the adherence of historical Christianity to ritualistic forms had sapped it of the life-giving force of individual inspiration, and he called upon the next generation of ministers to cast off conformity and convention, and instead trust their own experience and vision. Emerson lamented that "the church seems to totter to its fall, almost all life extinct."

Although "The Divinity School Address" focuses more upon religion than upon nature, it does implicitly appeal to the relationship between the individual soul and the natural world. After beginning the address with a paean to the "mystery of nature," Emerson chose to end with a call for "the new Teacher, that shall follow so far those shining laws, that he shall see them come full circle; shall see their rounding complete grace; shall see the world to be the mirror of the soul; shall see the identity of the law of gravitation with purity of heart" (*Complete Works*, vol. 1, p. 93). Although it was considered heretical by many in his audience, Emerson's assertion of the divinity of the soul and nature was consistent with the individualistic natural philosophy he had been developing since his break with the church six years earlier.

The Prolific Decade (1840–1850)

The 1840s was a remarkably productive period for Emerson. The decade began with the publication of the first number of *The Dial: A Magazine for Literature, Philosophy, and Religion* in July 1840. A journal edited first by Margaret Fuller and later by Emerson, Thoreau, and other members of the "Transcendental Club," *The Dial* was the unofficial publication of New England transcendentalism; as such, it functioned as an outlet for Emerson, Thoreau, Fuller, Jones Very, George Ripley, Bronson Alcott, William Ellery Channing, Theodore Parker, and other figures important in the movement. Thanks largely to Emerson's influence and support, *The Dial* survived from 1840 to 1844, long enough to publish the sixteen issues that gave transcendentalism visibility as a potent movement for intellectual and social reform.

Although Emerson had published very little before the 1840s, *Nature*, "The American Scholar," "The Divinity School Address," and his activities with *The Dial* had already brought him notoriety by the time his first book of essays appeared in 1841. Controversial for the same reasons *Nature* had been, *Essays: First Series* (as the book was later called) gained a substantial readership both at home and in Europe, and helped secure Emerson's fame. In twelve essays on morals and metaphysics, Emerson applied his individualistic philosophy to subjects such as

"History," "Spiritual Laws," "Love," "Heroism," and "Intellect." These disparate topics are connected by the central theme of power, and are devoted to exploring various means by which the individual may develop or access personal strength.

The most famous and most aggressive essay in the collection is "Self-Reliance," Emerson's consummate statement on behalf of individual power. In this piece Emerson strikes repeated blows against conformity and consistency, which he identifies as the two primary obstructions to the empowering realization of self-trust. In exhorting his readers to follow impulse and intuition at all costs, he mounts a scathing attack upon church, state, society, philanthropy, one's own past beliefs—in short, upon anything that may be identified as an impediment to absolute self-reliance. Recapitulating in a more direct way the heretical message of "The Divinity School Address," Emerson frankly claims that "God is here within."

"Self-Reliance" further suggests that humans have become "timid and apologetic" by their refusal to live within the spontaneous power of nature. According to Emerson, the person who lacks self-trust

is ashamed before the blade of grass or the blowing rose. These roses under my window make no reference to former roses or to better ones; they are for what they are; they exist with God to-day. . . . [the rose's] nature is satisfied, and it satisfies nature, in all moments alike. But man postpones or remembers; he does not live in the present, but with reverted eye laments the past, or, heedless of the riches that surround him, stands on tiptoe to foresee the future. He cannot be happy and strong until he too lives with nature in the present, above time. (*Complete Works*, vol. 2, p. 67)

By attempting to confront and conquer a number of likely obstacles to the attainment of self-trust, Emerson wished to redeem his readers from the fallen state in which they are alienated from a sense of their own inner divinity. Throughout much of his work, realization of that divinity is contingent upon an awareness of the intimate relationship between the individual soul and the natural world.

Essays: First Series also established the literary form and style Emerson employed for the remainder of his career. His usual form was a book-length collection of six to twelve loosely connected lectures and/or essays. His standard writing process involved recording thoughts and ideas in the journal, culling from journal entries to create lectures, then augmenting lectures with new material in order to produce finished essays. Thus, the Emersonian essay is usually a tissue of prose created through redaction and interpolation. As such, it tends to be compressed, intense, rich in powerful moments of illumination, but also somewhat elliptical and discontinuous. The same may be said of Emerson's sentences, which are periodic, aphoristic, epigrammatic, but often unconnected. John Burroughs accurately noted that Emerson's work "yields the reader so many strongly stamped medallion like sayings," but Matthew Arnold was also right to complain that "[Emerson's] style has not the wholeness of good tissue." Throughout his career, Emerson's style retained the oracular, homiletic quality he had developed while composing so many sermons.

Throughout this remarkably productive decade, Emerson continued to revisit and refine the theory of nature he had begun to develop in his early lectures on natural history and in *Nature*. As he continued to aspire to a synthesis of the facts of science and the truths of religion, he became especially enamored of the concept of organic growth. His passion for the principle of dynamic growth in nature and its potential for catalyzing commensurate growth in the human spirit is evident in his revival of the medieval theologians' distinction between *natura naturata* and *natura naturans*. The former describes the stuff of nature, the material world of natural facts that is in some sense "*scoriae* of the substantial thoughts of the Creator"; the latter is the creative force of nature, the active principle or divine inspiration in which all forms have their genesis.

Like the *First Series* essay "Circles," Emerson's 1841 address "The Method of Nature" is devoted to a theory of development and is his most complete exploration of organic growth, *natura naturans*. Emerson concludes that "nature's method" is not properly a method; rather, it is a divinely impelled tendency for organic growth:

> The method of nature: who could ever analyze it? That rushing stream will not stop to be observed. We can never surprise nature in a corner; never find the end of a thread; never tell where to set the first stone. The bird hastens to lay her egg: the egg hastens to be a bird. The wholeness we admire in the order of the world, is the result of infinite distribution. Its smoothness is the smoothness of the pitch of the cataract. Its permanence is a perpetual inchoation. . . . It will not be dissected, nor unravelled, nor shown. Away profane philosopher! seekest thou in nature the cause? This refers to that, and that to the next, and the next to the third, and everything refers. Thou must ask in another mood, thou must feel it and love it, thou must behold it in a spirit as grand as that by which it exists, ere thou canst know the law. Known it will not be, but gladly beloved and enjoyed. (*Complete Works*, vol. 1, pp. 199–200)

Emerson conveys beautifully the vital dynamism of *natura naturans*, the "method" or "way" of nature. "Perpetual inchoation" aptly describes the beneficent tendency to "become," upon which he believed the growth of the soul must be modeled. He emphasizes the integrity and "wholeness" of the natural world, and articulates a profound suspicion of the positivist epistemology of "analysis" and "dissection." Emerson further emphasizes nature's indissociable web of ecological interrelationships, and he insists that "another mood" is necessary for participation in the "dance" of organic growth. We can know nature's power only through love and immersion and wonder, through the adoption of what a late-twentieth-century nature writer might call "ecological consciousness": a spirit of universal affiliation by which the principle of growth is enacted. The "profane philosopher," then, is the naturalist who fails to realize that in order to comprehend nature, he must study it as a "Brother"—as a coextensive manifestation of the same divine principle of life.

By the time *Essays: Second Series* was published in 1844, Emerson's distinctive optimism had taken on a subtle tone of skepticism. Although critics have usually overdramatized Emerson's move from endorsing a transcendental "freedom" to embracing a stoical "fate," *Second Series* clearly shows signs of an individual coming to terms with the inscrutable and inescapable limitations of life. The nine essays comprising *Second Series* continue to advocate a program of spiritual empowerment through self-reliance and nature, but do so in a more cautious and mature way than does the earlier work. In "The Poet," Emerson imaginatively constructs the prophetic hero who—like the Emersonian "American scholar" or "best-read naturalist"—enlightens us by interpreting the symbols of spirit that are found in the natural world. Although his identification of the poet as "a liberating God" is characteristically sanguine, Emerson must finally admit: "I look in vain for the poet whom I describe." In "Experience," his most courageous confrontation with the limitations and disappointments of life, he attempts to catalog the "lords of life" that frustrate human aspirations to enlightenment and power. Although tenacious claims on behalf of the moral sentiment may be found even in "Experience," the essay differs from earlier pieces in its frank admission that "The results of life are uncalculated and uncalculable."

As its title suggests, "Nature" is the *Second Series* essay that most explicitly engages the natural philosophy Emerson had been crafting for over a decade. In a particularly beautiful passage (which John Muir later marked in his own copy of the essays) Emerson claims that "the day was not wholly profane, in which we have given heed to some natural object" (*Complete Works*, vol. 3, p. 172). Picking up where "The Method of Nature" left off, he also asserts the importance of *natura naturans*, the dynamic, organic principle of natural growth. Where "Na-

ture" deviates from earlier efforts is in its healthy skepticism about exactly how much of nature's book humans can actually interpret. "It is an odd jealousy," laments Emerson, "but the poet finds himself not near enough to his object. The pine-tree, the river, the bank of flowers before him, does not seem to be nature. Nature is still elsewhere" (*Complete Works*, vol. 3, p. 192). The Heraclitean "flowing" that Emerson had celebrated in "The Method of Nature" now serves to emphasize the elusiveness of nature's truth in the essay "Nature." "To the intelligent, nature converts itself into a vast promise, and will not be rashly explained. Her secret is untold" (*Complete Works*, vol. 3, p. 193). Although Emerson's faith in nature remains firm, the Godlike powers of the Emersonian literary naturalist are now tempered by the acknowledgment that nature's "method" often remains inscrutable.

As "The Poet" makes clear, Emerson accorded poetry a status akin to prophecy, and he imagined the poet as a kind of redeemer who would lead American culture out of the bondage of imitation and into the freedom of original genius. Emerson had written poetry since childhood, and in 1846 he published *Poems*, his first volume of verse. Critics from Emerson's day forward have generally agreed that his poetry is rarely exceptional, despite the fact that his prose is often remarkably poetic. Although he is sometimes credited with helping to direct American prosody toward the experimental verse forms that were used so effectively by Walt Whitman and Emily Dickinson, Emerson's awkward and frequently unmetrical tetrameter seldom matches the lyricism of his prose. Among the notable exceptions to the mediocrity of his verse is "Each and All," a poem in which students of nature writing will easily recognize a proto-ecological emphasis upon the ecosystemic "context" of habitat:

All are needed by each one;
Nothing is fair or good alone.
I thought the sparrow's note from heaven,
Singing at dawn on the alder bough;
I brought him home, in his nest, at even;

He sings the song, but it cheers not now,
For I did not bring home the river and the
sky . . .
> (*Complete Works*, vol. 9, pp. 4–5)

Despite such better moments, early critics of Emerson's verse were relatively unforgiving, and even his growing fame could not secure *Poems* a very warm reception. Emerson's successes and failures as "The Poet" are perhaps best explained by his own conviction that "it is not metres, but a metre-making argument, that makes a poem."

In 1850 Emerson published *Representative Men*, a series of biographical lectures devoted to "The Uses of Great Men," and to the accomplishments and symbolic importance of Plato, Emanuel Swedenborg, Michel de Montaigne, Shakespeare, Napoleon, and Goethe. This book demonstrates Emerson's lifelong interest in the notion of individual genius, which he often referred to simply as "character." His inclusion of "Swedenborg; or, the Mystic" suggests that the doctrine of correspondence was still of vital importance to his natural philosophy, and he compliments Swedenborg's work as "written with the highest end,—to put science and the soul, long estranged from each other, at one again." In "Goethe; or, the Writer" Emerson praises Goethe as a literary natural historian who "drew his strength from nature, with which he lived in full communion."

Nevertheless, *Representative Men* shifts Emerson's focus away from the natural world and toward hero types who often have little contact with it. The inclusion of "Montaigne; or, the Skeptic" suggests Emerson's increasing willingness to entertain a "noble doubt" about the pantheistic possibilities he had proclaimed in his earlier work, and his discussion of "Napoleon; or, the Man of the World" is a celebration of an individual power quite apart from nature.

Later Writings (1851–1882)

Although his literary career was devoted largely to an attack upon institutions, by 1850 Emerson

seems almost to have become an institution himself. He was now famous in Europe as well as America, and his books were being republished in new editions, translated into other languages, and even pirated. His opportunities for lecture engagements and occasional addresses had become virtually endless, and he was increasingly revered as one of America's foremost men of letters. As he moved toward the pantheon of literary luminaries that eventually included Henry Wadsworth Longfellow, Oliver Wendell Holmes, James Russell Lowell, John Greenleaf Whittier, and others, Emerson attained a respectability that seemed—at least to his friend Henry Thoreau—to compromise the transcendentalist rebellion upon which his fame was, paradoxically, predicated.

In 1847–1848 Emerson returned to Europe, not as a wandering ex-minister searching for

Ralph Waldo Emerson

direction in life but as a beloved writer traveling as unofficial ambassador of American culture. The literary product of this tour, *English Traits*, was published in 1856. Based upon the lecture series he presented during his travels, but organized as a relatively cohesive whole rather than simply a collection of orations, the book was extremely successful in its own day. Because Emerson seemed the ideal figure to appraise the virtues of English culture as implicitly compared with American culture, partisan readers on both sides of the Atlantic had an immediate appetite for his pronouncements on the subject. Despite its popularity, the book is remarkably genteel, rarely striking the radical chords that resonate through *Nature* and the early essays. Considered in light of Emerson's earlier attempt to articulate a comprehensive natural philosophy, *English Traits* may be seen as an absolute departure from previous efforts. Rather than exploring the ways in which cultural differences between Britain and America may be explained by differences in natural environment, Emerson concentrates primarily on such subjects as "Manners," "Wealth," and "Aristocracy."

If Emerson had become more urbane during the 1850s, he had lost neither his intellectual energy nor his loyalty to the moral sentiment. Although he often remained aloof from the ongoing political reform efforts of other transcendentalists, his anger at the unconscionable strengthening of the Fugitive Slave Law in 1850 drew Emerson into twelve years of lecturing in support of the abolitionist cause. He had earlier spoken out against displacement of Native Americans and against the Mexican War, but now he joined Thoreau and others in denouncing the institution of slavery, defying the unjust law that supported it, defending John Brown, and attempting to make "self-reliance" a genuine possibility for all Americans.

During the 1850s Emerson saw *English Traits* through press, spoke frequently in support of abolition, continued a demanding lecture schedule, helped edit the *Memoirs* of Margaret Fuller (who had died in a shipwreck in 1850), and prepared a new book for publication. *The Conduct of Life*, a collection of nine essays published

in 1860, is less terse and dynamic than the earlier collections, but is Emerson's most intrepid effort honestly to confront limitations to individual freedom and power. In the book's lead essay, "Fate," Emerson clearly revises his earlier view of nature as existing only to the end of human salvation: "Nature is, what you may do. There is much you may not. We have two things,—the circumstance, and the life. Once we thought, positive power was all. Now we learn, that negative power, or circumstance, is half. Nature is the tyrannous circumstance. . . . The book of Nature is the book of Fate" (*Complete Works*, vol. 6, p. 15). In "Beauty" Emerson reaffirms that "All the facts in nature are nouns of the intellect, and make the grammar of the eternal language," but he is more willing to acknowledge that every word in the language "has a double, treble or centuple use and meaning" (*Complete Works*, vol. 6, p. 304). In "Illusions" he admits that the world baffles us with "showers of deceptions," and he concludes with only a qualified optimism about the prospects for individual enlightenment. Emerson still believes in the spiritual potential of the *liber naturae*, but his later work increasingly recognizes the rich and elusive ambiguities that inhere in nature's text. The achievement of *The Conduct of Life* is the unblinking tenacity with which Emerson considers nature from all angles, as a form of limitation as well as liberation.

Although Emerson remained active during the 1860s—for example, he lectured seventy-seven times in 1865 alone—his faculties had clearly begun to wane by the middle of the decade, and his postbellum writing is largely desultory. He published a second volume of poetry, *May-Day and Other Pieces*, in 1867, and another volume of essays, *Society and Solitude*, in 1870. Both books contain fine moments, but are for the most part diffuse redactions of earlier material. It was only with the help of his literary executor, James Elliot Cabot, and his daughter Ellen that he was able to publish *Letters and Social Aims* in 1875.

Emerson continued his freethinking writing and lecturing as long as he possibly could. In

1867 he was invited to Harvard to give the Phi Beta Kappa address once again, and although he was almost too ill to read the piece, its content confirmed that Emerson's faith in the divine power of nature and the self had not changed substantially in the nearly three decades since "The American Scholar." Even as late as the 1860s Emerson's pantheistic rejection of institutionalized Christianity could win him condemnation as "a specimen of miserable, mutilated morality" from a Boston minister. In addition to awarding him the honorary LL.D. and appointing him to the Board of Overseers in 1866, Harvard invited Emerson to give a course of lectures on philosophy in 1870. It is highly significant that even at this late hour of life, he chose to speak on "The Natural History of Intellect." Emerson had always been interested in studying the intimate relationship between the natural world and the individual mind. He had delivered a lecture titled "The Relation of Intellect to Natural Science" as part of his 1847–1848 course in England and Scotland, and at that time he had begun generating ideas for a book on the subject. Now, more than twenty years later, Emerson welcomed the opportunity to use the Harvard lectures to revisit the inchoate book that he seems at times to have considered his potential magnum opus.

Near the beginning of his first lecture in the series, Emerson makes a claim that might as easily have been written in the early 1830s as in the late 1860s: "I believe in the existence of the material world as the expression of the spiritual or the real, and in the impenetrable mystery which hides (and hides through absolute transparency) the mental nature, I await the insight which our advancing knowledge of material laws shall furnish" (*Complete Works*, vol. 12, p. 5). Because he believed so firmly in the correspondence between nature and soul, Emerson still looked to natural history to elucidate spiritual laws. Unfortunately, his approach in the Harvard lectures was labored and unsystematic, and he was forced to content himself with "dotting a fragmentary curve." Problems of fatigue and memory forced him to cut the series short, though the rich fragments of it were posthumously published as *Natural History of the Intellect* in 1893.

Although the impediments of old age had prevented Emerson from using the Harvard lectures to substantially extend or refine his natural philosophy, his return to the subject at so difficult a time is evidence of his continued commitment to exploring what he would have referred to as the literary, intellectual, aesthetic, moral, and spiritual "uses" of nature. As late as the lectures "Natural History of Intellect," Emerson had continued to maintain that "Who we are, and what is nature, have one answer in the life that rushes into us." From the early 1870s on, his health and creative productivity continued to decline, and the last decade of his life was spent quietly among family and friends. Emerson died in Concord, at the age of seventy-nine, on 27 April 1882.

Conclusion: Emerson's Legacy to American Nature Writing

Emerson's critical reputation remained extremely favorable for at least forty years after his death. He was considered foremost among the men of letters who had helped to inspire American culture and shape American character; his influence was celebrated by luminaries in a variety of disciplines including literature, philosophy, theology, and the visual arts. The skepticism and disaffection that followed World War I caused his reputation to suffer in the 1920s and 1930s, when his untempered optimism and inadequate confrontation of the problem of evil made him appear unacceptably naive to a generation disillusioned by war. Since the mid-twentieth century, however, scholars of American intellectual history and Romantic aesthetics have reaffirmed Emerson's status as one of the most influential authors and philosophers American culture has produced. Even those who find his work elliptical and unsystematic acknowledge that his legacy is distinguished by remarkable contributions to American transcendentalism, pragmatism, and Romanticism. Emerson's uncompromising insistence upon the divinity of the individual soul, the spiritual value of nature, and the correspondential relationship between the two is widely recognized as his unique gift to American literature and culture.

Despite his well-established credentials as a literary proponent of nature, Emerson's critical reputation has not always fared well among scholars of American nature writing. First, many critics object that Emerson is fundamentally anthropocentric—that his writing exists not to celebrate nature but to proclaim the advent of what he once called "the kingdom of man over nature." A second complaint is that Emerson was a natural philosopher but never a natural man—that, unlike Henry Thoreau or John Muir, for example, he saw the wilderness from a pulpit or a lectern but refused to dirty his metaphysical hands in the fecund soil of the American wilderness. A third factor is that scholars sometimes assume Thoreau to be the progenitor of the American nature writing tradition and are therefore hesitant to accord Emerson real status in the lineage. Studies that do not omit Emerson entirely are often hostile toward his view of nature. In *The Idea of Wilderness* (1991), for example, Max Oelschlaeger claims that "Emerson's orientation toward the natural world . . . is conventionally anthropocentric and androcentric, enframed by a Baconian–Cartesian perspective: nature is mere putty in human hands, bestowed by God upon his most favored creation, Man" (p. 135).[2] Oelschlaeger further argues that Emerson viewed natural entities only as "commodities," and that he "never experienced a fundamental kinship with the organic realm."

Unfortunately, Emerson's reputation has suffered from a critical rebellion against the "transcendental bias" that has so long privileged highly speculative or philosophical nature writing over more explicitly factual natural history writing. It is undoubtedly true that Emerson is anthropocentric in the sense that he believes nature exists to be subject to human use. What sharply separates him from his contemporaries, though, is his influential insistence that such

"use" be spiritual rather than material. According to Emerson, nature is created for humankind but is intended for human moral edification, not for profligate waste nor for the provision of material luxury. Although the Emersonian concepts of "power" and "self-reliance" were interpreted by the likes of J. Paul Getty and Henry Ford as justification for nineteenth-century industrialism and its attendant environmental degradation, Emerson clearly did not view natural entities only as commodities. On the contrary, he was consistently critical of his culture's "mere commodity" orientation, on the grounds that it "left spirit out of the reckoning"; even a glance at the subordinate position of the "Commodity" chapter of *Nature* suggests that his view of nature is much less circumscribed than many critics have suggested.

It is of course true that Emerson did not share Thoreau's or Muir's physical contact with wilderness; he was a romantic "natural supernaturalist" who ultimately pursued his own transcendental agenda. However, there are several mitigating factors in the view of Emerson as hopelessly alienated from corporeal nature. First, his contention that nature is a primary agent of revelation contradicted American antipathy toward wilderness, and it established the emotional framework for the attitude of respect and reverence for nature that readers clearly recognize in subsequent nature writing. It is telling that Thoreau, Muir, and Burroughs (among many others) were personally inspired by Emerson, and each documented the experience of feeling his own love of nature confirmed in the work of his mentor. If Emerson never went deliberately to live in the woods, his work certainly made it possible for others to do so.

Emerson's contact with the "facts" of nature has also been underestimated because critics have largely ignored his early work—the sermons, lectures, and journals that document his passionate attraction to natural history. As we have seen, Emerson began his secular career lecturing on natural science, and he very nearly became a naturalist. He was remarkably well read in a variety of scientific fields; he initiated and maintained friendships with scientific lu-

[2] New Haven, Conn.: Yale Univ. Press.

minaries of his day; and his love of natural history is visible in the tenets of his mature philosophy, many of which were derived from organic models. Unfortunately, critics unfamiliar with this early work have often written as if *Nature* had been born ex nihilo, without the rich context of natural history studies that inspired it.

To be sure, Emerson was not Thoreau. He was not fully immersed in nature, let alone being fully immersed in a swamp. His vision of nature was mediated both by his idealism and by the spiritual imperatives that were the legacy of his religious training and inclinations. Although it is impossible to claim for him the status of an ecocentric literary ecologist, we should not, therefore, underestimate the importance of his place in the lineage of American nature writers. Unlike earlier American writers, Emerson brought the idea of nature to the very center of his literary and philosophical program. Although he is sometimes faulted for his abstraction, it was Emerson who legitimized the aesthetic and spiritual "uses" of nature, and thus opened the way for the generations of nature writers who followed him. Without the literary theory of natural history that Emerson articulated, the practice of American nature writing would not have flourished as it did.

How far, then, does Emerson finally move us toward the ecocentric environmental consciousness of such nature writers as Henry Thoreau, John Muir, Mary Austin, and Aldo Leopold? First, Emerson's fascination with natural science was genuine, and his knowledge of natural history was surprisingly broad. Second, Emerson was clearly moved by nature in the aesthetic, intellectual, and spiritual senses; he appreciated nature's beauty and complexity, and he believed in nature as a repository of divinity and as the consummate expression of moral law. Third, Emerson's transcendental moments—such as the one he experienced in the Jardin des Plantes—were usually epiphanies involving a profound recognition of the interrelationship with nature. Finally, the prominent holistic and organic elements of Emerson's metaphysics suggest a protoecological sensitivity to systemic integrity and the generative power of natural context.

Emerson is separated from later nature writers primarily by his penchant for abstraction in describing his relationship to nature. His writing is not distinguished by the physical immersion that characterizes the wilderness adventures of many of his literary descendants. Whereas Thoreau participated in a natural community at Walden, Muir vanished into his "family" of mountains in the Sierras, Leopold explored the ecological ramifications of his own presence in the Sand County ecosystem, and Austin claimed as neighbors the piñon pines and vultures of the American desert, Emerson often represented nature as a metaphysical construct rather than a place to live and die—as a book rather than a home.

Emerson is also distanced from such descendants by his ultimate unwillingness to exchange an instrumentalist environmental ethic for an assertion of the intrinsic value of natural entities; he typically subjects nature to the "higher use" of human enlightenment. Importantly, his assertion of nature as a moral resource did expose the limitations of his culture's dominant view of nature as "mere commodity"; but although Emerson's spiritualized nature made Thoreau's experiment at Walden and Muir's pantheistic naturalism possible, it also blocked his capacity to value nature for its own sake. Unlike many of the literary naturalists who followed him, Emerson's exegesis of the *liber naturae* ultimately follows anthropocentric lines.

Despite these objections, Emerson is clearly an important member of the lineage of American nature writers whose work is celebrated today. An American Antaeus who derived strength from what his contemporaries often viewed as a heretical faith in nature, he demonstrated that humans might locate more of their spiritual, aesthetic, and ethical values in the natural world. He argued that America's ideological inheritance of antipathy toward nature should be replaced with a spiritual sense of humankind's relationship to nature, and he suggested that the narrow perception of nature as material commodity should be exchanged for a richer sense of nature as moral community. In "The Young American," Emerson wrote:

> The land is the appointed remedy for whatever is false and fantastic in our culture. The continent we inhabit is to be physic and food for our mind, as well as our body. The land, with its tranquillizing, sanative influences, is to repair the errors of a scholastic and traditional education, and bring us into just relations with men and things. . . . I think we must regard the *land* as a commanding and increasing power on the citizen, the sanative and Americanizing influence, which promises to disclose new virtues for ages to come. (*Complete Works*, vol. 1, pp. 365–366, 370)

In the concluding chapter of *Nature*, Emerson had used the "axis of vision" formula to illustrate the ruptured, but recoverable, relationship between human and nonhuman nature:

> The problem of restoring to the world original and eternal beauty is solved by the redemption of the soul. The ruin or the blank that we see when we look at nature, is in our own eye. The axis of vision is not coincident with the axis of things, and so they appear not transparent but opaque. The reason why the world lacks unity, and lies broken and in heaps, is because man is disunited with himself. He cannot be a naturalist, until he satisfies all the demands of the spirit. (*Complete Works*, vol. 1, pp. 73–74)

Emerson characteristically asserts that only a spiritual vision in harmony with the natural system can redeem humans from the disunity and fragmentation of their condition; his desire to restore "original and eternal beauty" through "redemption of the soul" is an overtly religious mission. If natural science has provided Emerson with half his conceptual terms, theology has provided the other half; and in his eyes the imperative of each is a species of salvation. The human challenge, he asserts, is to integrate the functions of what Coleridge called the understanding and the reason, to "unite severe science with a poetic vision," to hear in harmony the song of nature and the "undersong" of spirit that

sings it. The "strange sympathies" that had germinated in him at the Jardin des Plantes came to fruition in a unique metaphysic that united the facts of science, the method of nature, and the imperatives of religion. Because Emerson viewed the nature writer as a natural historian of the soul, the "axis of vision" formula in *Nature* provides his clearest description of the conditions necessary for naturalism, literary or otherwise: "[Man] cannot be a naturalist until he satisfies all the demands of the spirit" (*Complete Works*, vol. 1, p. 74).

Selected Bibliography

WORKS OF RALPH WALDO EMERSON

PROSE

Nature (Boston: James Munroe, 1836); *An Oration, Delivered Before the Phi Beta Kappa Society, at Cambridge* (Boston: James Munroe, 1837), "The American Scholar"; *An Address Delivered Before the Senior Class in Divinity College, Cambridge* (Boston: James Munroe, 1838), "The Divinity School Address"; *Essays* (Boston: James Munroe, 1841); *Essays: Second Series* (Boston: James Munroe, 1844); *Nature; Addresses and Lectures* (Boston: James Munroe, 1849); *Representative Men* (Boston: Phillips, Sampson, 1850); *Memoirs of Margaret Fuller Ossoli*, ed. with James Freeman Clarke and William Henry Channing, 2 vols. (Boston: Phillips, Sampson, 1852); *English Traits* (Boston: Phillips, Sampson, 1856); *The Conduct of Life* (Boston: Ticknor & Fields, 1860); *Society and Solitude* (Boston: Fields, Osgood, 1870); *Letters and Social Aims* (Boston: Osgood, 1876).

POETRY

Poems (Boston: James Munroe, 1847); *May-Day and Other Pieces* (Boston: Ticknor & Fields, 1867); *Parnassus*, ed. by Emerson (Boston: James R. Osgood, 1875), an anthology; *Selected Poems* (Boston: Osgood, 1876); *Poems* (Boston: Houghton, Osgood, 1876).

POSTHUMOUSLY PUBLISHED WORKS

Lectures and Biographical Sketches, ed. by James Elliot Cabot (Boston: Houghton Mifflin, 1884); *Miscellanies*, ed. by James Elliot Cabot and Edward Waldo Emerson (Boston: Houghton Mifflin, 1884); *The Natural History of Intellect and Other Papers*, ed. by Edward Waldo Emerson (Boston: Houghton Mifflin, 1893); *Two Unpublished Essays: The Character of Socrates; The Present State of Ethical Philosophy* (Bos-

RALPH WALDO EMERSON

ton: Lamson, Wolffe, 1896); *Uncollected Writings: Essays, Addresses, Poems, Reviews and Letters by Ralph Waldo Emerson*, ed. by Charles C. Bigelow (New York: Lamb, 1912); "Emerson's Phi Beta Kappa Poem," ed. by Carl F. Strauch, in *New England Quarterly* 23 (March 1950); *The Early Lectures of Ralph Waldo Emerson*, ed. by Stephen E. Whicher, Robert E. Spiller, and Wallace E. Williams, 3 vols. (Cambridge, Mass.: Harvard Univ. Press, 1959–1972).

COLLECTED WORKS

The Complete Works of Ralph Waldo Emerson, ed. by Edward Waldo Emerson, 12 vols. (Boston: Houghton Mifflin, 1903–1904), the "Centenary Edition"; *The Collected Works of Ralph Waldo Emerson*, ed. by Alfred R. Ferguson et al., 5 vols. to date (Cambridge, Mass.: Harvard Univ. Press, 1971–   ).

JOURNALS

The Journals of Ralph Waldo Emerson, ed. by Edward Waldo Emerson and Waldo Emerson Forbes, 10 vols. (Cambridge, Mass.: Riverside, 1909–1914); *The Journals and Miscellaneous Notebooks of Ralph Waldo Emerson*, ed. by William Gilman et al., 16 vols. (Cambridge, Mass.: Harvard Univ. Press, 1960–1982); *The Topical Notebooks of Ralph Waldo Emerson*, ed. by Susan Sutton Smith, 3 vols. (Columbia: Univ. of Missouri Press, 1990–1995).

LETTERS

A Correspondence Between John Sterling and Ralph Waldo Emerson, ed. by Edward Waldo Emerson (Boston: Houghton Mifflin, 1897); *Letters from Ralph Waldo Emerson to a Friend*, ed. by Charles Eliot Norton (Boston: Houghton Mifflin, 1899), the friend is Samuel Gray Ward; *Correspondence Between Ralph Waldo Emerson and Herman Grimm*, ed. by Frederick William Holls (Boston: Houghton Mifflin, 1903); *Records of a Lifelong Friendship 1807–1882*, ed. by H. H. Furness (Boston: Houghton Mifflin, 1910), the friendship was between Emerson and W. H. Furness; *Emerson–Clough Letters*, ed. by Howard F. Lowry and Ralph Leslie Rusk (Cleveland: Rowfant Club, 1934; repr., Hamden, Conn.: Archon, 1968); *The Letters of Ralph Waldo Emerson*, ed. by Ralph L. Rusk, 6 vols. (New York: Columbia Univ. Press, 1939); *One First Love: The Letters of Ellen Louisa Tucker to Ralph Waldo Emerson*, ed. by Edith W. Gregg (Cambridge, Mass.: Harvard Univ. Press, 1962); *The Correspondence of Emerson and Carlyle*, ed. by Joseph Slater (New York: Columbia Univ. Press, 1964); *Carlyle and Emerson, Their Long Debate*, ed. by Kenneth Marc Harris (Cambridge, Mass.: Harvard Univ. Press, 1978); "The Philosopher and the Activist: New Letters from Emerson to Wendell Phillips," ed. by Irving H. Bartlett, in *New England Quarterly* 62 (June 1989).

SERMONS

Young Emerson Speaks: Unpublished Discourses on Many Subjects, ed. by Arthur C. McGiffert (Boston: Houghton Mifflin, 1938); *The Complete Sermons of Ralph Waldo Emerson*, ed. by David M. Robinson et al., 3 vols. (Columbia: Univ. of Missouri Press, 1989–1991).

MANUSCRIPTS AND PAPERS

Although there are small collections of papers at a number of libraries, the majority of Emerson's literary manuscripts and papers are in the Ralph Waldo Emerson Memorial Association collection at Houghton Library, Harvard University.

BIBLIOGRAPHIES

Jacob Blanck, *The Bibliography of American Literature*, vol. 3 (New Haven: Yale Univ. Press, 1959); Jackson R. Bryer and Robert A. Rees, *A Checklist of Emerson Criticism, 1951–1961* (Hartford, Conn.: Transcendental Books, 1964); Robert E. Burkholder and Joel Myerson, *Emerson: An Annotated Secondary Bibliography* (Pittsburgh: Univ. of Pittsburgh Press, 1985); Frederick Ives Carpenter, *Emerson Handbook* (New York: Hendricks House, 1953); William Charvat, *Emerson's American Lecture Engagements* (New York: New York Public Library, 1961); George Willis Cooke, *A Bibliography of Ralph Waldo Emerson* (Boston: Houghton Mifflin, 1908); *Emerson Society Papers*, annual bibliography of Emerson criticism; Alfred Riggs Ferguson, *Checklist of Ralph Waldo Emerson* (Columbus, Ohio: Merrill, 1970); Walter Harding, *Emerson's Library* (Charlottesville: Univ. Press of Virginia, 1967); Joel Myerson, *Ralph Waldo Emerson: A Descriptive Bibliography* (Pittsburgh: Univ. of Pittsburgh Press, 1982); Manfred Putz, J. K. Adams, and J. Boeck, eds., *Ralph Waldo Emerson: A Bibliography of Twentieth-Century Criticism* (Frankfort, Ky.: Peter Lang, 1986); Floyd Stovall, "Ralph Waldo Emerson," in James Woodress, ed., *Eight American Authors*, rev. ed. (New York: Norton, 1971); Albert J. von Frank, "Emerson Bibliography: History and Audience," in *Review* 9 (1987).

INDEXES AND CONCORDANCES

Kenneth Walter Cameron, *An Emerson Index; or, Names, Exempla, Sententiae, Symbols, Words, and Motifs in Selected Notebooks of Ralph Waldo Emerson* (Hartford, Conn.: Transcendental Books, 1958), *A Commentary on Emerson's Early Lectures with an Index-Concordance* (Hartford, Conn.: Transcendental Books, 1962), *Index-Concordance to Emerson's Sermons; with Homiletical Papers* (Hartford, Conn.: Transcendental Books, 1963), *Emerson's Workshop: An Analysis of His Reading in Periodicals Through*

1836 (Hartford, Conn.: Transcendental Books, 1964), and *The Emerson Tertiary Bibliography with Researcher's Index* (Hartford, Conn.: Transcendental Books, 1986); G. S. Hubbell, *A Concordance to the Poems of Ralph Waldo Emerson* (New York: H. W. Wilson, 1932); Mary Alice Ihrig, *Emerson's Transcendental Vocabulary: A Concordance* (New York: Garland, 1982); Eugene F. Irey, *A Concordance to Five Essays of Ralph Waldo Emerson:* Nature, *"The American Scholar," "The Divinity School Address," "Self-Reliance," "Fate"* (New York: Garland, 1981); William J. Sowder, *Emerson's Reviewers and Commentators: A Biographical and Bibliographical Analysis of Nineteenth-Century Periodical Criticism with a Detailed Index* (Hartford, Conn.: Transcendental Books, 1968).

BIOGRAPHIES

Gay Wilson Allen, *Waldo Emerson: A Biography* (New York: Viking, 1981); Van Wyck Brooks, *The Life of Emerson* (New York: Literary Guild, 1932); James Elliot Cabot, *A Memoir of Ralph Waldo Emerson*, 2 vols. (Boston: Houghton Mifflin, 1887); Kenneth Cameron, *Emerson the Essayist*, 2 vols. (Raleigh, N.C.: Thistle, 1945); Moncure Daniel Conway, *Emerson at Home and Abroad* (Boston: James R. Osgood, 1882); Edward Waldo Emerson, *Emerson in Concord: A Memoir* (Boston: Houghton Mifflin, 1889); Oscar W. Firkins, *Ralph Waldo Emerson* (Boston: Houghton Mifflin, 1915); Richard Garnett, *Life of Ralph Waldo Emerson* (London: W. Scott, 1888); Len Gougeon, *Virtue's Hero: Emerson, Antislavery, and Reform* (Athens: Univ. of Georgia Press, 1990); Hubert Hoeltje, *Sheltering Tree* (Durham, N.C.: Duke Univ. Press, 1943); John J. McAleer, *Ralph Waldo Emerson: Days of Encounter* (Boston: Little, Brown, 1984); Bliss Perry, *Emerson Today* (Princeton: Princeton Univ. Press, 1931); Henry F. Pommer, *Emerson's First Marriage* (Carbondale: Southern Illinois Univ. Press, 1967); Robert D. Richardson, *Emerson: The Mind on Fire, A Biography* (Berkeley: Univ of California Press, 1995); Ralph L. Rusk, *The Life of Ralph Waldo Emerson* (New York: Scribners, 1949); Townsend Scudder, *The Lonely Wayfaring Man: Emerson and Some Englishmen* (New York: Oxford Univ. Press, 1936); Denton J. Snider, *A Biography of Ralph Waldo Emerson* (St. Louis: William Harvey Miner, 1921); Charles J. Woodbury, *Talks with Emerson* (New York: Horizons, 1970).

CRITICAL STUDIES

There is a vast body of criticism on Emerson. The following list includes only a few studies that have been particularly important or representative, or that have a particular bearing upon Emerson as a nature writer.

Evelyn Barish, *Emerson: The Role of Prophecy* (Princeton: Princeton Univ. Press, 1989); Sacvan Bercovich, *The Puritan Origins of the American Self* (New Haven: Yale Univ. Press, 1975); Harold Bloom, ed., *Modern Critical Views on Ralph Waldo Emerson* (New York: Chelsea House, 1985); Lawrence Buell, *Literary Transcendentalism* (Ithaca, N.Y.: Cornell Univ. Press, 1973), and, as ed., *Ralph Waldo Emerson: A Collection of Critical Essays* (Englewood Cliffs, N.J.: Prentice-Hall, 1993); Robert E. Burkholder and Joel Myerson, eds., *Critical Essays on Ralph Waldo Emerson* (Boston: G. K. Hall, 1983); Kenneth Walter Cameron, ed., *Emerson Among His Contemporaries* (Hartford, Conn.: Transcendental Books, 1967); A. J. Cascardi, "Emerson on Nature: Philosophy Beyond Kant," in *ESQ* 30, no 4 (1984); Mary K. Cayton, *Emerson's Emergence: Self and Society in the Transformation of New England, 1800–1845* (Chapel Hill: Univ. of North Carolina Press, 1989); Harry Hayden Clark, "Emerson and Science," in *Philological Quarterly* 10 (July 1931); Michael H. Cowan, *City of the West: Emerson, America, and Urban Metaphor* (New Haven: Yale Univ. Press, 1967).

Elizabeth A. Dant, "Composing the World: Emerson and the Cabinet of Natural History," in *Nineteenth-Century Literature* 44 (June 1989); Jeffrey L. Duncan, *The Power and Form of Emerson's Thought* (Charlottesville: Univ. Press of Virginia, 1973); Alan D. Hodder, *Emerson's Rhetoric of Revelation: Nature, the Reader, and the Apocalypse Within* (University Park: Pennsylvania State Univ. Press, 1986); Vivian Hopkins, *Spires of Form: A Study of Emerson's Aesthetic Theory* (Cambridge, Mass.: Harvard Univ. Press, 1951); Irving Howe, *The American Newness: Culture and Politics in the Age of Emerson* (Cambridge, Mass.: Harvard Univ. Press, 1986); Milton Konvitz and Stephen Whicher, eds., *Emerson: A Collection of Critical Essays* (Englewood Cliffs, N.J.: Prentice-Hall, 1962); David Levin, ed., *Emerson—Prophecy, Metamorphosis, Influence* (New York: Columbia Univ. Press, 1975); F. O. Mathiessen, *American Renaissance: Art and Expression in the Age of Emerson and Whitman* (New York: Oxford Univ. Press, 1941); Joel Myerson, ed., *Emerson Centenary Essays* (Carbondale: Southern Illinois Univ. Press, 1982).

Leonard N. Neufeldt, "The Science of Power: Emerson's Views on Science and Technology in America," in *Journal of the History of Ideas* 38 (April–June 1977); Barbara Packer, *Emerson's Fall: A New Interpretation of the Major Essays* (New York: Continuum, 1982); Sherman Paul, *Emerson's Angle of Vision: Man and Nature in American Experience* (Cambridge, Mass.: Harvard Univ. Press, 1952); Richard Poirier,

The Renewal of Literature: Emersonian Reflections (New York: Random House, 1987); Joel Porte, *Representative Man: Ralph Waldo Emerson in His Time* (New York: Oxford Univ. Press, 1979), and, as ed., *Emerson: Prospect and Retrospect* (Cambridge: Harvard Univ. Press, 1982); Susan L. Roberson, *Emerson in His Sermons: A Man-Made Self* (Columbia: Univ. of Missouri Press, 1995); David Robinson, *Apostle of Culture: Emerson as Preacher and Lecturer* (Philadelphia: Univ. of Pennsylvania Press, 1949), "Fields of Investigation: Emerson and Natural History," in Robert J. Scholnick, ed., *American Literature and Science* (Lexington: Univ. Press of Kentucky, 1992), and *Emerson and the Conduct of Life: Pragmatism and Ethical Purpose in the Later Work* (New York: Cambridge Univ. Press, 1993); Merton M. Sealts, Jr., *Emerson on the Scholar* (Columbia: Univ. of Missouri Press, 1992); Merton M. Sealts, Jr., and Alfred R. Ferguson, eds., *Emerson's Nature: Origin, Growth, Meaning* (New York: Dodd, Mead, 1969); David van Leer, *Emerson's Epistemology: The Argument of the Essays* (New York: Cambridge Univ. Press, 1986); Stephen E. Whicher, *Freedom and Fate: An Inner Life of Ralph Waldo Emerson* (Philadelphia: Univ. of Pennsylvania Press, 1953); Donald Yannella, *Ralph Waldo Emerson* (Boston: Twayne, 1982).

ROBERT FINCH
(b. 1943)

J. PARKER HUBER

THE LIFEWORK of Robert Finch represents an honoring of the locales, personalities, and stories of "the bare and bended arm of Massachusetts," to use Henry David Thoreau's image, thirty miles at sea. His devotion to Cape Cod is an inextricable weave. This is the landscape—particularly its eastern portion, the Lower Cape—that has fostered his bond with the natural world. More than three decades of exploring the meaning and value of nature in this place has brought him closer to his community, his family and friends, and his own heart and spirit. His gift is his clear and vivid, even poetic, expression of that weave of the world.

Beginnings and *Common Ground*

Robert Charles Finch first came to Cape Cod in 1962, at age nineteen, after he had finished his first year at Harvard University. His roommate's father owned Camp Viking, one of several sailing camps dotting the shores of Pleasant Bay on the Atlantic. That summer, Finch worked at Camp Viking as cabin counselor and maintenance man. The impact of Cape Cod on him was immediate and profound: "I had never been in any place that reached me, that touched me the way this did. It was magic" (personal interview, 25 January 1994).

Until then, Finch's environs had been urban. His roots were industrial New Jersey. He was born 16 June 1943 in North Arlington, on the Passaic River—not far from New York City and Newark—and lived there for twelve years. In 1955 his family moved to Parkersburg, West Virginia, on the Ohio River, where his father, Charles Wesley, supervised a plant division for Dupont, while his mother, Fritzi Wasserburger, managed the Parkersburg Community College Bookstore. After graduating from Parkersburg High School, Finch was the first in his family to go to college.

The summer of 1962 changed Finch's life. In order to become more familiar with Cape Cod, he took a year's leave from Harvard and went to Provincetown, a seafaring village across Massachusetts Bay from Boston. There he worked for a weekly newspaper—"I was the reporting staff for local events"—and began keeping a journal and investigating his surroundings.

"Night in a Dune Shack," the first essay of his first book, *Common Ground: A Naturalist's Cape Cod* (1981), tells of these beginnings. At December's end, he walks out of Provincetown into the dunes, "totally ignorant of their geography . . . their origin or their behavior" (pp. 4–5). Traveling without map or compass, he feels secure that the Pilgrim Monument will guide him home. He discovers a dune shack, where he lingers over lunch. "Fascinated by this solitary and quirky outpost" (pp. 5–6), he decides to spend the night. After collecting driftwood, he starts a fire in the stove, closing a hole in the flue collar with rags: "In those days I was innocent not only of natural history but of wood stoves as well" (p. 6). While attempting to dislodge the soon-smoldering rags, Finch dismantles the stovepipe: "Within seconds the entire shack was filled with black smoke belching from the top of the chimneyless stove, and I was forced out into the night, stumbling, choking and blind, up onto the dune beside it" (p. 6). Fortunately, the shack does not catch fire, and Finch spends the night inside, warm under a bearskin. The next day, a northeaster thrashes the coast with wind and snow, so Finch settles back into the shack for another twenty-four hours, nourished only by a can of anchovies. The morning is clear, and he is able to return.

Though this story presents the novice reporter, the signature of the mature writer is evident. Here Finch uses the method that he still employs: one man walks alone through the landscape, discovering nature, culture, himself, and their interdependencies—a traditional pattern of nature writers such as Thoreau. Absent in Finch, however, is any portrayal of the author as professional–authority, hero–scientist, or romantic–idealist. These roles never fit him. Instead, Finch emerges as an amateur–inquirer, a persona he cultivates assiduously, showing its immense fertility, and never abandons. This infuses all his excursions with freshness. He rehearses an adage by A. R. Ammons: "tomorrow a new walk is a new walk." Leaving behind prescriptive intellectual baggage, Finch aproaches Cape Cod each time with an open, receptive attentive mind. It is his sense of enthusiastic engagement that enlivens his encounters and enlightens him and his readers.

"Night in a Dune Shack" is an initiation, a rite of passage into new territory. The sandy country acts as mentor to the untutored Finch, steering him through predicaments and perils, pleasures and possibilities. He weathers the interior and exterior weather. He returns recreated.

Though Finch went back to Harvard the next September, he now knew where he belonged. And he did not want to be there alone. On 19 September 1964, he and Elizabeth Ann Wolford, a Radcliffe College student, were married. Leaving their studies, they spent a year in Orleans, on Cape Cod. Finch worked as a carpenter, a skill learned on the job.

A fortuitous event happened that autumn. On 11 October 1964, Finch saw Henry Beston, then seventy-six. The occasion was the dedication of Beston's Cape Cod cottage as a national literary landmark. Beston had lived in a two-room dwelling of his own design on the dunes between Nauset Marsh and the Atlantic Ocean, and he had written about the round of seasons in his journal, passages he shaped into *The Outermost House* (1928). This book, place, and author became woven into the very fabric of Finch. Fifty years after the publication of *The Outermost House*, Finch watched a furious storm devour Beston's retreat, the effects of which he describes in "After the Storm" in *Common Ground*. In 1988 he prefaced an edition of *The Outermost House*, eloquently expressing his admiration of Beston. Finch applauds Beston's "extraordinary sense of natural drama," "his ability to reconnect us emotionally and imaginatively to these primal, natural sources of our being," and "his belief that any full understanding of nature requires the full engagement of the observer with what he observes, with all senses healthy and receptive." Finch included selections from *The Outermost House* in his two anthologies of nature writing.

In September 1965, after his second Cape Cod year, Finch was again a Harvard student. This time he stayed until he graduated cum laude in English in 1967, the year his wife finished at Radcliffe. With their son, Christopher, born that July (Katherine was born 26 August 1973), they headed west, first to Indiana University, where he earned an M.A. in English in 1969, and then to Oregon State University, where he taught English for two years. He medicated his homesickness for Cape Cod with infrequent visits.

Although the separation was long, it was fruitful. Finch found new literary mentors: moving

310

Robert Finch

on from his college models of Hemingway, Faulkner, and Fitzgerald, he discovered Beston and John Hay. Along with *The Outermost House*, Hay's *The Run* (1959), *Nature's Year* (1961), and *The Great Beach* (1963) were touchstones for Finch's artistic development. They expanded his awareness of the capacities of language and of nature writing. In the autumn of 1971, Finch responded to the call of Cape Cod, going home with his family for good.

His return was graced with good fortune. Seeking writing work, Finch met the author who had been so influential on him, John Hay. Hay, also a Harvard graduate (1938), came to Cape Cod in 1942 to study with the poet Conrad Aiken, who lived in Brewster from 1940 until his death in 1973. In 1947, Hay settled in Brewster on Red Top Road, where he still resides. Hay sold Finch some of his secluded parcel of glacial moraine, pitch pines, and oaks; there Finch built his home, an octagonal wood structure with wide overhangs, large glass windows, and a used brick chimney. For over twenty years, these two out-

standing nature writers have lived and worked side by side.

For the first four years, Finch supported the family with his carpentry. In "Roofing," an early essay from *Common Ground*, he describes the "sense of space and freedom and separateness in a magnificent setting" (p. 35) he shares with a community of carpenters. While happily engaged in "a noisy business . . . ripping off the old shingles, pounding on the new," Finch is distracted by an ever-increasing flock of flying terns: "the front rank of terns dropping down and diving beneath the water, then rising up to the rear, followed in turn by the next rank" (p. 36). The rhythm of his prose follows their metaphorical moves: "They were *reaping* the inlet, like some vast watery combine" (p. 36). Their mutual harvest—"epochs and cycles of light and cloud racing and scudding and mixing overhead" (p. 37)—yields guidance: "Sometimes I think our business is to put ourselves in such favorable positions . . . where . . . the poetry of life can catch us unawares" (p. 37).

311

Finch's body of work grew. He began each day writing in his journal, a practice he still pursues. "I always wanted to be a writer," Finch admits, "The question was the direction that the writing would take," Beginning in 1975, Finch focused on Cape Cod's natural history, producing articles for local newspapers: "It was a fortuitous format . . . a modest scale, not many words were required each week; and the feedback was immediate and appreciative." His audience affirmed his inner desire: "I was not happy creating a traditional nature column; I received encouragement for making it personal" (personal interview, 25 January 1994).

One of Finch's supporters was Deanne Urmy, then an editor at the publishing firm of David R. Godine in Boston. Her family owned a summer home in Brewster. Admiring Finch's writing in the *Cape Codder* newspaper, she asked him to submit a collection of his essays for Godine to publish. Gladly, Finch obliged. The result was *Common Ground*, which included many of his weekly pieces. Finch also wrote introductions for two Beacon Press rereleases edited by Urmy, *Tarka the Otter*, by Henry Williamson (1990), and *A Land*, by Jacquetta Hawkes (1991).

A major contributor to Finch's career has been the Cape Cod Museum of Natural History which is close to his home. Finch has made himself familiar with its conservation land on Cape Cod Bay, its fine library, and its staff. Particularly helpful have been its former director, Donald Schall; its former education director, Robert Prescott; and its founder and first president, John Hay. Until he was twenty-five, Finch confessed, he could not tell a maple from an oak. His formal science education had been minimal. Besides filling this gap, the museum cosponsored his newspaper column. Finch served as editor of *The Cape Naturalist* (1973–1982), their quarterly (now annual) publication; as director of publications (1982–1986); and since 1986 as a member of their publication committee. He also contributed to *The Cape Naturalist*: "Taxes, Restrictions and Open Space" (December 1973); "Hyla Crucifer, the Voice of Spring" (spring 1974); "A Sense of Place" (winter 1975);

"Meeting the Alewives of Stony Brook" (summer 1984); "Migrating South with the Birds" (summer 1985); and others.

Two of Finch's themes are contained in his title *Common Ground*. In one sense, "common" signifies "ordinary." It is the familiar that stimulates his imagination. Like Thoreau, Finch values the vernacular life. Almost all of his personal essays originate from an immersion in the local landscape and evoke its great diversity. Even the two exceptions in *Common Ground* lead him to a greater appreciation of his home turf. While waiting for a flight out of Pittsburgh, Finch admires a magnificent black oak, one of the "Local Gods," on a golf course, astonished by its size in comparison to trees of Cape Cod. And while visiting friends on Kezar Lake, Maine, he reflects, "Loons are one of the regrets I have about living on Cape Cod. . . . The birds that come south to us are dull and silent, leaving their essence in the north woods" (p. 29).

"Common" also refers to land held in trust for the welfare of the community. Finch wants his community to be composed of all sentient beings, not merely humans, an "intermingling of man and his environment, a land held truly in common, that produces the truest, richest natural history" (p. 126). His paradigm blends culture with nature: "I crave the feeling of men *having been* in a place, of having experimented repeatedly and earnestly with it in a biodegradable way, and of having had the grace and good sense to abandon it, when it was no go, leaving no permanent scars, only good ghosts and a fine wildlife habitat" (p. 126). Such an ethic echoes Aldo Leopold's; it requires a consciousness that reveres all plants, animals, soil, and air. What Finch says of whales is representative of his general belief: They have "an inalienable right to exist, not because they resemble man or because they are useful to him, but simply because they do exist" (p. 102). They are our common wealth. In his concluding essay, "Common Ground," Finch realizes both the value of "human intercourse, without which none of us survives for long," and the importance of feeling "a kinship with the hawk that might last the rest of my days here" (p. 142).

Centering on Cape Cod

In the next decades, Finch stood his common ground. He was situated advantageously to experience the poetry of place. His learning was perpetual and keeping pace with Cape Cod's constantly changing countenance. After all his study, after centuries of human use, he still found Cape Cod magical and mysterious. It is a land for "expeditions for the feet and mind, unending voyages for the spirit."

The Primal Place

Finch's second book, *The Primal Place* (1983) — the title is Conrad Aiken's designation of Brewster — is, in his words, "my attempt to study, in depth, the particular neighborhood in which I lived." These thirteen connected personal essays, fewer and longer than those of *Common Ground*, are divided by modes of being, "Digging In" and "Going Out." The first section begins in Finch's house and then passes "Through the Glass Doors" to the cemetery, his garden, the road, and the community. "Going Out" visits diverse wet habitats in town — Berry's Hole, Stony Brook, Lower Mill Pond, tidal flats, winter beach, and frozen bay — before "the landing."

"The first step must be to see clearly what is there," Finch announces (p. 5). This is to be a sight-step, step-sight journey. He tries not to get in his own way. Although he can enter almost anywhere — "and entrance is what I crave" — he finds himself everywhere, "a part of what I behold." Once there, other complications arise. "Change is the coin of this sandy realm," Finch asserts, aware of its mixed blessing (p. 3). Nature does not hold still for the artist. While watching animals, Finch posits some criteria: "a deliberate change of perspective, a loosening of focus, and a bending of your lines of sight to what it is you would see" (p. 10). Even then, his sense of his surroundings is not instant: "It is only by living in a place for a time that we begin to learn where we are" (p. 102).

But Finch does not sacrifice the specific to the general, the present to the past. His wide-ranging

eye takes in every detail and movement. He catches a female merlin (pigeon hawk) "preening herself, spreading out her richly colored tail and wings, scratching her head with one leg like a dog, then, catlike, stretching out each leg and claw separately, shaking them as though to fluff up her feather leggings" (p. 13). His is a lambent language, devoid of understatement and hyperbole, but sprinkled with figures of speech, such as similes. He describes oaks at dusk: their "thin limbs cut and weave across one another in a flat plane like a thousand shears, snipping apart the plaited continuities of the day" (p. 27).

Like Virginia Woolf, Finch strives "to give the moment whole." This entails an honest assessment of his interactions with nature. His virtue is his ability to express these interactions, as varied, layered, and limited as they may be.

For example, Finch discovers his own ferocity when he plants broccoli, peas, beans, and lettuce only to have a woodchuck plunder what he calls "the fruits of *my* labor." For two weeks, he searches for solutions, such as stringing chicken wire under his fence, but to no avail. The first glimpse of the predator provokes retaliation. Grabbing a baseball bat, Finch races to the garden and beats the beast into oblivion. This is surprising behavior for a calm, mild-mannered naturalist who serves on his town's conservation commission (though Thoreau did slaughter a woodchuck in his Walden beanpatch). Even Finch is alarmed that, in defense of his food, he would strike a lethal blow. Would his response have been the same to a human intruder? This episode awakens him to his own unpredictability, to his own and nature's ambiguities.

Death abounds on Cape Cod. The winter beach is strewn with casualties — squid, sea turtles, seals, whales, porpoises. Seeking understanding at a seminar, Finch receives a toxic dose — "seal bodies covered with viral eruptions and bacterial lesions" — that upsets his assumptions. He concludes that we cannot "afford to look nakedly at life in the wild for very long. . . . We dare not examine our belief in the sacredness of life too closely. . . . So we hide death" (p. 214).

But he finds there is no escape from suffering, not even at the Cape Cod Museum of Natural

History, where he goes one February Sunday for a book. In the hall, he hears noises coming from a garbage container. Looking inside, he sees a wasted scaup unable to eat its grain. "Poor, ravaged bird!" Finch kneels, "stroking its bony, exhausted body and staring back at those cold, yellow eyes." He flees the premises without the desired text, but with a story to tell.

Life and death are not in opposition for Finch, but in cooperation in the process of creation. On a June walk along Red Top Road, he encounters a decaying homestead and black locusts. These images fuse with sensual birth: "large, soft, pendulous clusters of white, fragrant blossoms ... such sweet, drooping abundance" (p. 40). A July saunter offers ruin in the form of an aborted development project. Disturbed, Finch is not misanthropic; he does not chastise his own kind. Instead, he looks at the meaning of speculation for homesteaders and realtors. For the former, it is "to guess the weather, the cranberry harvest, the scallop crop, the flounder runs, the rain, and the frost" (p. 76). For the latter, it involves investing cash for profit. The one responds to human needs, and the other attempts to create them. Even amid "the landscape with cut-and-fill construction," Finch hears music, "a hidden prairie warbler trilling out its ascending chromatic song."

Learning about our world by involvement is for Finch not just an intellectual exercise, but a physical and emotional one as well. The annual spring migration of alewives from Cape Cod Bay up Paine's Creek and Stony Brook for a mile to freshwater ponds to spawn has happened since time immemorial. Finch watches this spectacle with his townspeople. Like them, he uses the fish for garden fertilizer. At first he killed them; then he realized that the dead, plentiful from gulls having had their fill, served just as well. His switch is occasioned not by any change of attitude about killing—they "suffered crueler treatment than mine from nature"—but by a respect for this passionate stage of life. He finds that he relishes "the bloody, undisguised candor and natural appetite of this place ... that seems to excite raw emotion and primitive response in the midst of this pastoral setting" (p. 154).

His investigation reveals to him that "[s]anitary observation" of nature causes separation from nature. His wish is "not to learn about the fish but to *join* them": "Life demands participation" (pp. 155–156).

Participation includes, according to Finch, attachment to human neighbors, past and present. Eighty-year-old Lillian Scott tells Finch of Brewster's early residents, the Punkhorners. Conrad Aiken, whom Finch never met, "peopled and storied the neighborhood with his dreams, his poems, and his marvelous letters" (p. 86). Nathan Black cut hair in his barn for seventy years. Twice a week, he walked two miles to barber in East Dennis. Once, two of his customers passed him en route; he sat them down on a rock and gave them a trim. Between world wars, Charlie Ellis served in the Coast Guard. One February, answering an SOS, he and his crew rowed twelve miles "over bitter wintry seas" to reach the stranded vessel. Ellis, forgetting his gloves, went the distance barehanded.

Involvement may be passive. Rowing his boat across Lower Mill Pond, Finch notices algae, water mites, bullfrogs, tree swallows, gulls, damselflies, leeches on a musk turtle ("beautiful butterscotch patterns on a richly brown body with tints of red and green scattered throughout" [p. 171]), geese, black-crowned night herons (abundant until 1952 when a local colony was eradicated as a public nuisance by state game officers), and Bill Lazarus, a resident since 1937, whose personality Finch celebrates in two pages. His image of a kingfisher's "harsh clattering softened, elasticized by the coming of dusk," helps us become aware of the many moods of this moment and others.

Finch loves raking quahogs from tidal flats. Though "scratching" is "a satisfying, self-absorbed, introspective activity," he feels its limitations. Transfixed by the splendor of sunset across wet plains, he realizes that scratching makes him "more receptive to outer beauty." What good is that? he asks. His response is insightful: "Our sense of wonder and beauty is locked at the very deepest levels into the knotted reality and texture of the physical world from which we wrest a daily living" (p. 198). Walking back with his quota of quahogs, he is struck by the light upon his fellow rakers and by his intimate connection to the world: "We love not so much what we have acquired as what we have made and whom we have made it with" (p. 201). One of the blessings of taking our food from the land and sea is the contact it gives us with what is primary.

Outlands

Though still writing of eastern Cape Cod, in *Outlands* (1986) Finch extends his quest beyond his hometown. These are longer excursions: a canoe trip to Monomoy Island: a four-mile walk to Jeremy Point: a week of insular privacy—conducted in his preferred mode of travel, self-powered solos, and with his clear, concise integrity.

The themes of these peregrinations resonate with those of Finch's earlier works. Foremost is his search for how to be with nature. Though he is ambivalent about giving himself totally to nature, he realizes that the investment of his whole self is crucial to attaining a "present, living tactile memory" of the landscape.

Contact, Finch argues, is our birthright. He wants Cape Cod to be forever "a place where we can engage in earnest play with the earth." Ironically, our sheer numbers dictate discretion: "as the need for this kind of free encounter grows more urgent, the opportunities for it decrease daily" (p. 62). He must restrain himself and the children from touching the alewives, from tumbling down the dunes, from giving in to impulses in "the manner and scale on which we have chosen to express them" (p. 62).

Nonetheless, Finch presses his engagement with his surroundings. He is compelled to experience a February storm on Coast Guard Beach. His metaphor-rich wish "to be out there riding the bare dune ridge into the foamy teeth of destruction" (p. 9) propels him into danger. Momentarily his wish is granted. Even a leaky wader does not prevent his progress. Then a shot of "cold primal power" (p. 12) engulfs him, and "the overwhelming and undeniable authority of . . . time and tide" (p. 13) causes his retreat. His heroic vision crashes against reality. Our desire to be with nature, especially at its most tumultuous, must be tempered. We cannot be engaged all the time and survive.

Finch's proceedings with the primal test him and his limits. In February, he walks four miles to Jeremy Point, the remote sandspit between Wellfleet Harbor and Cape Cod Bay. His purpose is to observe seals. Along the way he sees a rolling pin, which he takes along. Land's end is "heavily encrusted with stranded ice floes" until "one of the pale ice slabs suddenly moved and rolled over, revealing the darker, spotted back of a large harbor seal" (p. 47). This is not an occasion for, as he says, "observing at close range large, wild animals . . . completely unaware of my presence" (p. 47). Detected, he runs, not away, but into the center of activity. The seals head for water: "Some were already splashing in, others were rowing energetically across the sand with their front flippers" (p. 48). Panicked by his place in the pack, Finch doesn't move. Seals pass by. On his way back, Finch notices "a primitive outline," the shadow of the rolling pin he could have used in his defense, "suggesting possibilities I had not expected to contemplate." Unconsciously, the hunter, as symbolized by the surrogate club, traveled with him.

His longest journey deepens him. Finch lives alone for a week in a friend's cottage on North Beach, arriving on Sunday; he writes in journal form. Though his is not the elaboration of inner terrain of an Alice Koller, who wintered on Nantucket and charted her growth in *An Unknown Woman* (1981), it is a genuine effort to commune with nature and self through the medium of solitude. Finch distinguishes himself from Thomas Merton and desert monks: "I do not live alone easily." Isolated he becomes introspective, "thinking of my daughter's irrepressible, continual engagement with life, my father's quiet, strong, indirect love" (p. 97). He settles into a daily routine of walking, writing, eating, painting, napping. His dwelling pleases him—"bright, spare," like his prose. He fantasizes staying for a year; not writing for a week. After two days he hauls up a trap, removes a lobster, and hurries to boil it. Thursday is disquieting; he can't work: "It is hard writing about the life one is actually living" (p. 107). He misses music. He eats dinner cold. "Oh, we are all such horrible mixtures," he confesses, including us for company. His gift of expression remains: "Any writer's honest journal is at once a revelation and an enigma" (p. 108). "The ocean shows no inordinate ambition tonight" (p. 110). Saturday's departure is welcome. Civilization is greeted with augmented appreciation. After a silent week, the first person he speaks to is his wife on the phone. While waiting for her, he walks into Chatham Center. The "easy motions and simple signs of our occupation of the earth" (p. 114) delight him. He buys flowers for his wife and toys for his children, happy to be a consumer and tourist again.

One purpose of such a retreat is renewal, a heightened awareness of what we most value. For Finch, this is clearly family and social relationships. He is not withdrawing in order to achieve greater insight into himself and his world. Such an ascetic discipline deprives him of his most cherished connections.

An August canoe trip to Monomoy Island, a National Wildlife Refuge and Wilderness Area, further defines his relationship with nature. On the island, Finch walks through the former breeding grounds of roseate and arctic terns. The beauty of a dune hollow "laced with lovely lavender mats of seaside spurge" summons his lyricism. Blackberries please his palate: "The largest, sweetest I've ever tasted." "Half a dozen large white egrets, four snowies and two common, standing still as cardboard cut-outs on stalked legs in the shallow water" (p. 132) attract him. Then, noticing a young herring gull caught in a fishing lure, he plunges into the water and rescues it. He reflects on what he has done and objectively addresses human efforts to minister to nature. His act of altruism had been driven by years of pain. He had seen too much of Cape Cod "mangled and wrenched by human greed, blindness, and indifference." Here had been an opportunity to relieve his "chronic helplessness" with a gallant deed "to restore the proportion of grace and shape and line, to put things aright

again" (p. 134). The next scene restores to him his sense of nature's vitality. Finch walks without clothes, reminiscent of Thoreau along the Concord, amid flocks of shorebirds—sandpipers, sanderlings, plovers, knots, turnstones, dowitchers, godwits, whimbrels, yellowlegs—who "formed an electric band of life, so intense, so intent on their probing, running, stalking, dipping, diving and flitting that I was only minimally regarded" (p. 137).

At a Labor Day clambake on Cape Cod Bay, Finch is sanguine about nature's resiliency. People have used this beach again and again without harming it. After leaving the party, he drifts through a deserted summer camp, pondering his once-held belief "that such places would always be what they were simply because they should be." Now summer camps are "endangered species." What is really lost? He locates the camp's value in its seasonal use of the land, which places it in accord with natural rhythms. Until the advent of condominiums here, "human enterprises on these shores . . . have all left the possibility of something replacing them, the potential of a new rendezvous with the land" (p. 161).

Even purposeless meetings nurture Finch. He watches a sunset over autumn tidal flats for the very reason that it is familiar. He is content to sit and observe, and not record. When it comes—"a thin, fading reddish light over near things, over the weathered wooden railing . . . over the yellowing dune grass, igniting it, over the white eroding sand of the bluff—he is overwhelmed (p. 169). In nature, the ordinary is forever extraordinary: "God oh God are we ever prepared for this? It is like nothing I have ever seen before" (p. 168).

The Cape Itself

"The Human Scale," the first of the nine sections of *The Cape Itself* (1991), opens with an engaging photograph by Ralph Mackenzie. We look down on Bound Brook Island in Wellfleet, a gray-green expanse of vegetated dunes elongated southward, its eastern edge scalloped by a white-capped, blue-green Cape Cod Bay, beyond which the continent is barely visible. The sky is dense with clouds washed white, gray, blue, and blue-green. It is a desert devoid of humans, except one. In the lower center, his south-bound footsteps bisecting a clear, cream crater, is a slim figure clad in black pants and red hooded slicker: Robert Finch.

This image addresses Finch's belief that human beings have a place in nature: "The Cape 'scene' calls for more than passive visual appreciation. It asks for active tactile exploration and recognition" (p. 9). His familiar theme resonates with its countertheme: involvement "is both its promise and our problem; for as more and more of us accept its promise, the less each of us will be able to touch it" (p. 9). Finch positions himself in between the horns of this dilemma. He decides that the Cape is not a place for "permanent habitation, sheltered lives or final answers."

The image is also symbolic of the book's purpose. The photographer and the writer enter into a dialogue with each other over the land. One medium illuminates the other's messages. There are sentences to savor, pictures to ponder. Together, they do not present a single impression of this volatile land, but offer our imaginations the freedom of choosing among and creating from many interactive representations.

Finch's prose complements the photographs with its literary power. For example, he captures the contrariness of the sea on two New Year's Days. On one day, after a northeaster, "the mighty surf . . . dashed itself in magnificent chaos. . . . No longer a series of breakers, it had become a shattering wall of green and white, crest breaking upon crest, wave receding crashing into wave oncoming" (p. 132). The turbulence is caught in a net of gerunds. The subdued pace of the sea on the other day is musical: "The sea was calm and flat gray, a sheet of shimmering metal. The tide was low and rising with small breakers purling and curling in, spreading out from the middle in both directions like the final, quiet repeated chords of Barber's Adagio for

Strings" (p. 173). Finch's three adjectives mirror the dissipating breakers.

In all seasons, both artists are attuned to the drama of color and light. Summer's end is signaled by purple-flowering sea lavender, "the earliest of the fall flowers and the loveliest of marsh plants" (p. 55). Finch does not overlook their brown and dark-red leaves hidden in beach grass ("The sprays form lavender veils through which I gaze") nor does MacKenzie, who frames the plant in deep-blue-to-black sky whitened with clouds. In November, Finch sees "wine and vermilion on the huckleberry and blueberry bushes, and the viburnum leaves illuminate the woods with a pale almost trembling light" (p. 60). Cord grass stems are "wetted and glint like strands of polished copper" (p. 60). Pale yellow butterflies dance with wine-red and purple cranberry plants in sandy bogs.

The atmosphere they explore is both human and nonhuman. The lead essay, "Local Color," concerns a cranberry bog and its owner, an old man with a "weathered-clean appearance, lean and tall, spare . . . refined by the years" (p. 91). Finch watches the old man through the seasons, caring for his bog, harvesting its crop. Finch does not talk with him because Finch is interested in his interpretation of the old man, in his own myth-making ability and need. Yet he is careful not to misrepresent this man. He warns his readers that his vision may be incomplete. We know how the owner treats his land, but not his family, if he has one, or his neighbors. Finch, however, is happy with his harvest of the old man's spiritual attributes: "an inner peace," "an affinity for his surroundings," "possession by long and loving acquaintance" (p. 92).

A discussion of Provincetown closes "Local Color." Finch praises it as an exemplary commercial community because it has retained its original identity, writ large in architecture, in open space, and in the sea and sand, pitch pines and pounds that encircle the town. MacKenzie complements this appraisal with a sunset over Long Point, parallel reflections of light over the rippled water of the harbor. The sun's reflection is a yellow-orange wand that resembles stacks of books piled askew one atop another, an anchored schooner's bare mast appears as a black corkscrew. Light and shadow, nature and culture rest calmly together in Provincetown.

"The Inner Cape" is about the curious pull of agrarian landscapes. Passing by on a bicycle, Finch feels a "deep connection" (p. 69) to a quintessential New England farm. Though in a hurry to avoid rain, Finch stops and pokes about the place. His attentive eye notes a kestrel catching a yellow butterfly, a pond feeding massive tupelos, a meadowlark hovering over pink clover and white composites, a rusted car by a stone wall. The smell of sweet hay and ammonia in the barn brings back memories of a summer on another Cape farm. That experience had given him contact with animals and earth, indelible memories, and a belief in that farm's eternity. That belief, however, was bulldozed away. He leaves this farm waiting "to weather out another storm." "Weather" is the perfect verb to convey the force and endurance required for people to remain at Cape Cod.

In the longest essay—four pages of text interlaced with four photographs—Finch is flounder fishing with a friend on a Boston Whaler in Nauset Harbor. Fishing is an excuse for idling on a quiet October day: absent are summering crowds and migrating shorebirds; anticipated are eiders and seals. Finch's mood of optimism, boosted by the knowledge that humans have fished these waters for centuries, is tempered by the flounder's not being "inexhaustible or indestructible" (p. 123). Finch's view contrasts with that of his friend, who grieves for the passing of so much nature. Finch feels "an almost constant sense of undeserved richness and unexpected beauty" (p. 123), a persistent attitude that contends with his consciousness of Cape Cod's vulnerability.

MacKenzie ruminates with Finch on the subject of fishing. He pictures two anglers sitting in a powerboat; one waits for a bite on his lines, and the other sets his lures. They are silhouetted against horizontally brush-stroked water of the faintest tan, lavender, lime, and gray, flecked with white and dark shadows. The impression-istic shoreline gives the merest suggestion of inhabitants—rooflines and chimneys in the forest. Except for the gasoline motor, this is a timeless image bearing testimony to Finch's ideas. The next photograph is equally serene: a rowboat, empty except for a black bird on its starboard gunnel, is centered in marsh grass and blue water. The boaters are nowhere in sight. Nor are there any humans in the third photo: two great blue herons stand erect, casting shadows over a still sheet of water at sunset. A more modern fisher is the subject of the last portrait. A lone man in fishing paraphernalia stands mid-calf in Scorton Creek; over his tan hat, beyond water and marsh, the horizon is clotted with contemporary houses built without regard to style or space, their march to the sea halted only by the marsh. Despite their intrusion, MacKenzie agrees with Finch that the ancient pastime will endure.

A Place Apart

Pick up any of the leading collections of nature writing today, and you will find Robert Finch. Two of them bear his name. He collaborated with John Elder on *The Norton Book of Nature Writing* (1990). It is a monumental work of over nine hundred pages of selections from ninety-four literary artists writing in English (the exception is French entomologist Jean Henri Fabre), from the work of the originator of the genre, the eighteenth-century English curate-gardener Gilbert White, to that of one of its youngest lights, Terry Tempest Williams, a Mormon from the Great Basin and Colorado Plateau.

Finch's *A Place Apart: A Cape Cod Reader* (1993) is remarkable in part for what its author list suggests about Cape Cod. This small headland has generated such a vast and superior literature that Finch cannot accommodate everyone. Omitted, for example, is the popular twentieth-century naturalist Edwin Way Teale, who began his *Autumn Across America* (1956) on Monomoy Island, birding with his wife, Nellie, and Rachel Carson. Finch's choices are based on affinity; he knows several of the writers personally: Annie Dillard, Marge Piercy, Mary Oliver, Brendan Galvin, Mark Doty, and John Hay. Such a community is important to Finch. Since 1986, he has met annually with a group of nature writers at Glen Brook in Marlborough, New Hampshire. (Finch was instrumental in organizing this group into a symposium in October 1991 that celebrated the life and writing of John Hay).

A Place Apart is deftly arranged by theme to show consistency and variety. "Natural Mystery" examines Cape Cod's stellar reputation in nature literature. Here are "the Cape's great triumvirate of nature writers"—Henry Thoreau, Henry Beston, John Hay—diary entries of Edmund Wilson, poems of Mary Oliver, and an essay of Cynthia Hungtington (a poet and Dartmouth English professor) depicting life with her husband in a rented dune shack "on the outermost, outward-reaching shore of Cape Cod, at no fixed address" (p. 235), where "each day is a slice of eternity—each day is the whole thing" (p. 244). In the category "How They Lived" is Finch's "The Legend of Screaming Island," which is about a story he heard from counselors at Camp Viking in 1962. His "The S.S. Longstreet: 1964"—the name of a former battleship used by the air force for bombing practice—joins other "Summer Rituals," such as memoirs of Alfred Kazin observing Edmund Wilson on the beach and of Helen Keller wondering who put the salt in the water.

"Extending My Range": Current Work and Beyond

Finch has completed the Southern New England volume of the Smithsonian Guide to Natural America series, to be published in mid-1996. Though Cape Cod is featured, he has been forced into new geography: the rest of Massachusetts, Rhode Island, and Connecticut. Wanting to consult an authority on this region's

natural history, Finch asked his editor, who thought for a moment and replied, "*You* will be when the book is done."

Finch's field research includes making audio and visual notes with a microcassette recorder and a video camera, respectively. The challenge is to put all of his material into the guide's format, into forty-four thousand words, into introductions for each section, and into narratives for each site.

Finch has sifted mounds of material collected from conservation organizations and individuals. His choice of landscapes represent diversity of ecology and ownership: the Berkshires; Martha's Vineyard; Rhode Island's coast; the Audubon sanctuary, Trail Wood, in Hampton, Connecticut; the former home of Edwin and Nellie Teale; and Rock House, a new Trustees of Reservations acquisition in West Brookfield, Massachusetts.

Finch's interest in a regional landscape is in how it has been subjected to human activity and reclaimed by natural processes. For example, the South River State Forest in Conway, Massachusetts, has a three-hundred-foot-deep gorge and a wetland created by a dam. The original intent of the dam was to generate power for the town and a trolley line. Interurban trolley lines, Finch learns, flourished practically everywhere from 1900 to 1920, when Model Ts replaced them as people's primary conveyance. Finch's description of this site will merge natural, technological, and cultural history.

His next project? "Perhaps another book or two might come from this guide." Or perhaps personal essays or a photo essay on Massachusetts with Tony King: "I like working with a photographer." Finch is also considering a book on Cape Cod's Native Americans. In *A Place Apart* he wrote of Nosapocket (Ramona Peters), a member of the Mashpee Wampanoag tribe, who introduced him to the tribe's oral tradition. Finch feels that if he can gain the tribe's confidence, he may be able to tell their story. He is excited to see what happens to narratives when they are translated from the spoken to the written word. At the moment, he is writing poetry, something he has not done for a long while but which he enjoys for "the non-linear leaps" of mind it allows.

In the summer of 1995, Finch traveled to Newfoundland, where he conducted research for a book to be published by Beacon Press. This idea came from Finch's first trip there in July 1987, a visit to a high school friend. He went on assignment for *Diversion*, a New York magazine on leisure pursuits for physicians. For a week, he lived in Trinity, strolling "the village's narrow tree-lined lanes that meander through clusters of neat, white and yellow wooden houses with bright green, blue, and red trim" (June 1989, p. 260); eating cod and blueberries at the Village Inn; marveling at how trawlers are made of native fir and spruce; and watching whales, moose, caribou, eagles, and gannets galore on Cape St. Mary's Bird Rock.

He returned to Newfoundland in the summer of 1988 and the fall of 1989. For two weeks in August 1991, he sailed from Cape Cod aboard *Voyager*, a 50-foot, gaff-rigged wooden schooner. He served as scribe and sailor, "literally learning the ropes" (*Sail*, January 1993, p. 59). Though he spent only a few hours in a few of the small fishing villages along Newfoundland's south coast, Finch appreciated their beauty and austerity. On a midnight anchorage deep in White Bear Bay fjord, Finch slept on deck, the moon "flecking the surface of the black water with a trillion silver minnows" (p. 61). Yet Finch is leery about writing a book of a land he knowns so little: "Look at how long it has taken me to say anything about Cape Cod." Nonetheless, Finch's enthusiasm for Newfoundland as literary subject is promising.

Although his books give the impression that Finch has seen only Cape Cod, it is a false one. Besides his four Newfoundland trips, Finch has led a Cape Cod Museum of Natural History tour of the Canadian Maritime Provinces. He has crossed the United States, camped in Wyoming with authors Gretel Ehrlich and Annie Dillard, discussed writing natural history with Terry Tempest Williams at the University of Utah in Salt Lake City, and explored Baja California. He has sailed the Intracoastal Waterway between Charleston, South Carolina, and Fernandina Beach, Florida, He has toured the Canary Islands, Europe, and Kenya, the latter's central mountains by horseback and its Tana River by dugout canoe.

Besides traveling and writing, Finch has devoted time to conservation. He served the Brewster Conservation Commission for fifteen years (1974–1989) and cochaired the Brewster Land Acquisition Committee from 1984 to 1988, during which time they preserved over one thousand acres, including Punkhorn Parklands, a project that originated from Finch's experience there, which he described in his "Good Ghosts" essay of *Common Ground*: "It gave me great satisfaction to be able to give something so substantial and tangible back to the town that has nourished me for so long" (personal letter, 22 April 1984). In 1987, the Brewster Conservation Trust honored him as Conservationist of the Year.

Finch has also concerned himself with the education of others. He was the first person to teach Cape Cod literature at Cape Cod Community College. He has served on the staff of the Breadloaf Writer's Conference at Middlebury College. He has held discussions on nature writers at the Cape Cod Museum of Natural History. And he has been a member of the January term faculty of Williams College, completing his third session in 1994. His students spend time with him on Cape Cod.

His guidance has encouraged new authors. When Erma J. Fisk finished her first manuscript in her seventies, she asked Finch to read it. He did, and after discussing it with her at her home in South Orleans, he sent it to his editor at Norton with a letter of endorsement. In 1983, Norton published Fisk's *Peacocks of Baboquivari*, and has since published three more books. In the last, *A Cape Cod Journal* (1990), published after her death, she acknowledged Finch's support.

Although it is premature to talk of Finch's legacy, it is clear that the great trio of Cape Cod nature writers—Thoreau, Beston, and Hay—has been expanded to a quartet. It is also certain that his skills are still flowering, that he is still asking to be taken to new places, toward new involvement.

Selected Bibliography

WORKS OF ROBERT FINCH

BOOKS

Common Ground: A Naturalist's Cape Cod (Boston: Godine, 1981); *The Primal Place* (New York: Norton, 1983); *Outlands: Journeys to the Outer Edges of Cape Cod* (Boston: Godine, 1986); *The Cape Itself* (New York: Norton, 1991); *Cape Cod National Seashore Handbook* (Washington, D.C.: National Park Service, 1992).

EDITED WORKS

The Norton Book of Nature Writing, ed. with John Elder (New York: Norton, 1990); *A Place Apart: A Cape Cod Reader* (New York: Norton, 1993).

INTERVIEW

"Dialogue Two: Landscape, People, and Place — Robert Finch and Terry Tempest Williams, 8 February 1988," in *Writing Natural History: Dialogues with Authors*, ed. by Edward Lueders (Salt Lake City: Univ. of Utah Press, 1989).

ARTICLES

"The Old World of Newfoundland," in *Diversion* (June 1989); "Being at Two with Nature," in *Georgia Review* 45 (spring 1991); "To Touch the Earth," in *New Choices for the Best Years* (April 1991), an assessment of ecotravel.

BIOGRAPHICAL AND CRITICAL STUDIES

Christopher Lehmann-Haupt, "Books of the Times," in *New York Times* (17 July 1981), review of *Common Ground*, and (27 June 1986), review of *Outlands*; Shaun O'Connell, *Imagining Boston: A Literary Landscape* (Boston: Beacon, 1990), includes treatment of Finch's literary themes in the chapter "Boston's Sphere of Influence"; Alec Wilkinson, "Of Bog and Beach," in *New York Times Book Review* (31 July 1983), review of *The Primal Place*.

JOHN GRAVES
(b. 1920)

MARK BUSBY

READING TEXAS WRITER John Graves's three major works, *Goodbye to a River*, *Hard Scrabble*, and *From a Limestone Ledge*, makes you feel as though you have made a friend. After riding down the river in his canoe and listening to him ruminate about the virtues of hardscrabble farming or the disappearance of his dog Blue, you have spent a substantial amount of time with a writer who gets inside you and who speaks with a clear personal voice. When you are through with one of his books you know you have met a man who understands the light and the dark of his world and a writer who helps you see the grays of it, too.

In his best-known work, *Goodbye to a River*, Graves sums up the dichotomy reflected in his life and work:

> If a man couldn't escape what he came from, we would most of us still be peasants in Old World hovels. But if, having escaped or not, he wants in some way to know himself, define himself, and tries to do it without taking into account the thing he came from, he is writing without any ink in his pen. The provincial who cultivates only his roots is in peril, potato-like, of becoming more root than plant. The man who cuts his roots away and denies that they were ever connected with him withers into half a man. (p. 145)

Graves uses the masculine language of his time,

and his work indeed concerns the traditionally masculine worlds of canoeing, camping, and building fences, but the double vision of this quote indicates that Graves has resisted narrowness, particularly the provincial jingoism that Texas regionalism has sometimes encouraged. Throughout his life Graves has looked clearly at where he came from, digging deeply into the roots sunk into Texas soil, and has also traveled widely. As a result, his work reveals his strong sense of the integral relationship between the particular and the universal.

Youth and Education

His keen sense of place resulted from Graves's growing up in two distinct environments, the newly urban Fort Worth, Texas, and the richly varied South Texas town of Cuero, where his grandparents lived. Born in Fort Worth on 6 August 1920, he explored the Trinity River bottom before it became layered with Coors cans. Fort Worth had evolved from a cattle town on the forks of the Trinity River along the Chisholm Trail into a city with a central downtown business district and a ring of homes circling it. As a boy Graves would take the streetcar down Camp Bowie Boulevard to visit the men's store his father operated, "where oilmen in tan gabardine suits and Borsalino hats would gather

323

around a big table in the rear and tell good profane stories about oil towns with names like Desdemona and Ranger and McCamey, and muse about the big-money game they played and the personalities of those with whom they played it" ("Recollections of Childhood," pp. 66–67).

The city life was complemented by the boy's venturing out into the nearby Trinity River bottom, where deer, quail, rabbits, and squirrels still abounded, and he and his friends took their scrappy hounds out to hunt. Back in the city, he hung around at drugstores and hamburger joints with other lanky-haired adolescents in a typical youth during the Depression. But this average life was marked by several influences that affected the young Graves, who was vaguely aware that he wanted to know more about the wider world. As a result of his varied reading, some good teachers, and an educated, cosmopolitan neighbor, Graves was led to imagine life outside his surroundings.

> I went through the melange of best-sellers and classics and leftover 19th-century sentimentality that was on the shelves at home, and stuff dragged down out of the attic of my grandfather's house in Cuero or sought out at the public library downtown. It made for a fine stew in the head, that mingling of Conrad and Fielding and Scott with the Southern soupiness of authors like F. Hopkinson Smith and the Reconstruction virulence of Thomas Dixon and the British Empire heroics of G. A. Henty and the farflung enthusiasm of roving Richard Halliburton. It was further flavored by reading on special subjects that seized me from time to time—Texas and Western lore, the Civil War, flyfishing, horses, how to make buckskin out of rabbit hides and brew tea out of sumac. . . .
>
> But I remember also three or four first-rate teachers along the way who cut through my hangdog dislike of school and showed me what poetry consisted of, and a few other people like the bachelor surgeon who lived with his brother-in-law and sister a couple of doors from our house. He smoked Edgeworth tobacco in the finest-smelling pipes I have ever been around, and had a Yale education and the literate feel for language that many of

> the old-time Texas Methodists used to have. During long summer-evening lawn conversations he could dip up out of memory, without self-consciousness, tags from Shakespeare or the Authorized Version or the whole long lovely flow of English poetry to suit almost any point, ironically more often than not. So despite all the hodgepodge reading I did, I had an early chance to see that good books were sense and language woven together, and that the weaving mattered greatly. ("Recollections of Childhood", pp. 69–70)

Reading books and listening to stories of the world beyond Fort Worth led him to think about the variety in the world, and this awareness was enhanced by a second major life influence: regular trips to visit his father's family in South Texas. Graves's grandfather had run away from his Missouri home in his teens. He settled in Cuero, Texas, along the Guadalupe River, shortly after the Civil War, and married into a ranching family. Although Cuero is only 250 miles from Fort Worth (a short distance in Texas terms), it seemed like a different world from the growing commercial city dotted with elm, sycamore, and bois d'arc. In Cuero "big dark liveoaks hung with Spanish moss stood around the houses and sometimes in the middle of the streets, the soft Gulf air working through them and beneath, with always somewhere the frenzy of mockingbirds and the sad low fluting of doves" (p. 72). South Texas also offered a variety of cultures and languages, as Germans, Czechs, and Mexicans lived, worked, and spoke among themselves and interacted with the English-speaking Texans from British and Scotch-Irish stock.

> South Texas was more than Grandpa and that house, even if the memory of them sums it up for me. It was friends I still have, when I see them, and camping and trotlining with them on the slow green Guadalupe, and racing ponies down dusty roads, and quail-hunting at Christmas with uncles to whom shooting and fishing and good dogs were a big part of what life was about, and Mexicans from whom I first got the taste of soft Spanish on

the tongue, and elders' bloody tales of Reconstruction days and the Sutton-Taylor feud. It was a lot of things that Fort Worth was not, but mainly for me, I think, it was the past. Not as you find the past in books, even good books, but as you find it to touch. South Texas was where I could reach back to the things, good or bad, that my own people had been, and comprehend a little bit about what other people had been in relation to them. Like all human pasts—and all human presents and all human futures—it had vast imperfections, but I am glad I got to touch it.

Because if you are a backward looker, you need something to look back to. ("Recollections of Childhood," p. 75)

So it was that these two areas of Texas profoundly influenced him, and he continued to carry with him the sense of place and history he had learned from them. He took these influences to Rice Institute (now Rice University) in Houston, graduating Phi Beta Kappa in the class of 1942. At Rice he studied with George Williams, who would also teach William Goyen and Larry McMurtry. When his graduating class went directly into the war, Graves entered the Marine Corps. After completing Marine Officer Candidate School, he served in the Pacific as a first lieutenant. Seriously wounded on Saipan, he was waiting to be evacuated from an army field hospital when a wounded young soldier next to him asked where he was from. When Graves told him Texas, the young Marine asked Graves to hold his hand, saying that he was glad to have a Marine from the South next to him who would understand what he said. And then the boy "clenched my hand harder still, and died" (*Hard Scrabble*, p. 92). As a result of his wounds, Graves lost the sight in one eye and received a Purple Heart. Later he was promoted to captain and served as a Marine reserve officer for many years.

Early Writings

After the war, Graves lived for a while in Mexico. Then, on the GI bill, he began graduate work at Columbia University in New York City. He took a writing class from Martha Foley, who edited *The Best American Short Stories* and *Story Magazine* for many years. He sold one of the stories he wrote for her class, "Quarry," to the *New Yorker* in 1947. His master's thesis subject was William Faulkner. After receiving his M.A. from Columbia in 1948, he taught at the University of Texas in Austin for two years. Then wanderlust seized him. He left the country and traveled to France and Spain, where he lived for a while, and then to Tenerife in the Canary Islands, and to New Mexico, before he came back home to Texas in 1957, prompted by his father's illness. He took a canoe trip down the Brazos River that fall and wrote an article about the experience, which was published in *Holiday* that year. After joining the English faculty at Texas Christian University in Fort Worth in 1958, he expanded his river article into his first book, *Goodbye to a River*.

With some of the money he had made from the book, Graves purchased a plot of land in Somervell County, Texas, near Glen Rose, about an hour southwest of Fort Worth, beginning a relationship with the land that eventually inspired his second major book, *Hard Scrabble*. He received a Guggenheim Fellowship in 1964 and then left TCU in the mid-1960s to work for Stewart Udall, who was then secretary of the interior. He concentrated on water issues in Washington, D.C., and wrote "A River and a Piece of Country: A Potomac Essay" for the *Potomac Interim Report to the President*, a collection of essays by a task force to which Graves was assigned. The report was eventually published as *The Nation's River* in 1968.

His interest in water issues led to his being one of three contributors to *The Water Hustlers*, an analysis of water issues in specific parts of the United States published by Sierra Club Books in 1971. Graves's essay, "Texas: You Ain't Seen Nothing Yet," provides an analysis of what he saw as the ill-conceived Texas Water Plan of 1968. The book demonstrates Graves's careful research and clear understanding of ecological issues. Nevertheless, Graves has dismissed the work, saying:

I guess I undertook it because I had so recently been doing that work for the Interior Department. I was really up on hydrology and the ins and outs of the water bureaucracy at the time. Up in Washington I had worked with some of the best people in the country in those fields, so I had already done a great deal of groundwork. What I did was all right, I guess, but the state water plan collapsed. Essentially any polemical writing is devoted to an evanescent problem. If it's solved, it disappears, and if it's not solved, it goes away. Polemics are self-destructive in that sense. They're not very satisfying. (quoted in Bennett, p. 71)

On his return to Texas in 1970, when the house he had spent ten years building was finished, Graves moved with his wife Jane (whom he had married in 1958) and daughters Helen and Sally to the 380 acres of land he called Hard Scrabble. Working on the land also led to Graves's becoming a regular contributor to *Texas Monthly* and to his third book, *From a Limestone Ledge*, a collection of these articles. He contributed the text to accompany photographs for a coffee-table book, *Texas Heartland: A Hill Country Year*, and has written prefaces, forewords, and introductions for a number of books. He has also lectured and commented widely, especially on Texas literature and the environment.

Two of Graves's books *The Last Running* (1974) and *Blue and Some Other Dogs* (1981), are short pieces expanded with photographs and drawings and published by William Wittliff's Encino Press. Wittliff, who is also a screenwriter and film director, has been one of Graves's closest friends and supporters over the years. *The Last Running* was originally a short story published in *Atlantic Monthly* in 1959 and included in *The Best American Short Stories* in 1960. *Blue and Some Other Dogs* was one of his *Texas Monthly* pieces and was included in *From a Limestone Ledge*. It is a poignant story about the disappearance of Graves's ten-year-old crossbreed sheepdog, described as the best dog he ever had. A third finely printed, small press book,

Self-Portrait with Birds: Some Semi-Ornithological Recollections (Chama Press, 1991) was first published as part of *Of Birds and Texas* in 1986.

Goodbye to a River

Graves's most significant work is *Goodbye to a River, a Narrative* (1960), based on his canoe trip down the Brazos River in 1957. Graves had written articles for a number of magazines by this time, and had a contract with *Sports Illustrated* to do a piece on the canoe trip. The essay turned out to be more concerned with philosophy than sports, and was published in *Holiday* instead. He knew that if the project for five dams to be built along the Brazos were completed, the area would be irreparably changed. The Brazos is the third largest river in Texas and the largest between the Red River and the Rio Grande. Called *el Rio de los Brazos de Dios* (the River of the Arms of God) by the early Spanish explorers, it flows for 840 miles from its source until it empties into the Gulf of Mexico near Freeport, just south of Galveston Island.

Drawing from a long tradition of nature writing about rivers, from Henry David Thoreau's *A Week on the Concord and Merrimack Rivers* (1849) to Paul Horgan's *Great River: The Rio Grande in North American History* (1954), as well as from the elegiac pastoral tradition, Graves brings his own unique approach and concerns to writing. He often reveals a deep ambivalence about being identified as a nature writer in the tradition of Thoreau, or about being perceived as an ideologue single-mindedly pursuing a temporal agenda. In a 1963 essay, "On the Desirable Reluctance of Trumpets," Graves articulates his concerns about hard-nosed persuasion. He writes that polemical writing "is preachment, a trumpet-note for good action, an exhortation boiling up out of a vision of present wrong and possible right. It arises from a belief that something can be done about almost anything" and from "the principle of action that will produce change" (p. 210). He asks if it follows that writers should "tootle our built-in trumpets frankly in favor of whatever cavalry charges against evil we see as desirable, encourage the conscripts to do the same" and then answers his own rhetorical question:

> No, sir, not for a good many of us, it doesn't. Those who like to tootle are going to keep on tootling; their number is legion and they will be with us always, and bless their good hearts one and all. But the fact that even those who don't want to are forced by their own humanness into reluctant or unconscious music of this sort does not invalidate detachment as an ideal, any more than democracy as a concept is invalidated by the fact that it has nowhere ever quite worked, and never will.
>
> The fact is that detachment is in spite of everything probably the best general ideal that a writer can hold to. First rank writing whatever its form is concerned with expressing human truth. All-out tootlers are apt to confuse truth with facts. . . . The facts of human existence are mostly obvious, and if they are evil facts that can often be changed; they are susceptible to cavalry charges. The truths the facts add up to, though, are neither obvious nor very susceptible. (p. 212)

These comments clarify some of Graves's basic assumptions about writing persuasively. Both his desire for detached rather than polemical persuasion and his acute awareness of the complexity of human truth make his approach to writing more subtle. His trumpeting is muted, a reluctant persuasion that takes the form of presenting human truths that are attached to the history of places and objects, thus demonstrating their value beyond and beneath the surface.

The detached position Graves stakes out leads to subtle persuasion in *Goodbye to a River.* He adopts a rhetorical stance similar to that of Shakespeare's Mark Antony in his famous eulogy for Caesar, who claims that he has "come to bury Caesar, not to praise him," and then sets out to move his audience with subtle praise. Graves's similar strategy in his piece on the Brazos is profoundly persuasive. As the book begins, Graves disarms a reluctant reader by saying that he holds no bitterness about the proposed series of dams:

> In a region like the Southwest, scorched to begin with, alternating between floods and drouths, its absorbent cities quadrupling their censuses every few years, electrical power and flood control and moisture conservation and water skiing are praiseworthy projects. More than that, they are essential. We river-minded ones can't say much against them—nor, probably, should we want to. (p. 8)

The clue to his real position here is the emphatic placement of waterskiing last, and his saying, tongue firmly in cheek, that it is "essential." He then goes on to announce that this is not his fight; he is just going down the Brazos to "wrap it up" before the river and "Satanta the White Bear and Mr. Charlie Goodnight," figures from Texas history, disappear under the "Criss-Crafts and the tinkle of portable radios." This ironic contrast between the weighty significance of Texas history and the brittle inconsequence of skiing to the sound of portable radios heightens his appeal and allows him to achieve the detached position he seeks.

Goodbye to a River, like many Texas narratives, uses a journey for structure, a journey that takes on symbolic significance as well. This journey is a personal process, a trip to recover a wanderer's sense of history and place. By returning to places that have meaning, Graves demonstrates how one regains a rootedness that gives life meaning. Although he does not mention Ishmael's water journey in *Moby Dick*, which was undertaken during a "damp, drizzly November in my soul," Graves also has his narrator set out on a gray, threatening November day. He thus connects *Goodbye to a River* to Melville's novel, which also uses the water journey of escape and return to suggest powerful personal insights. *Goodbye to a River* enacts this pattern of escape and return on a small scale, with the narrator leaving on 11 November for a 175-mile journey that ends with a return to civilized life on December 2, but Graves's return to Texas after a decade as a sojourner abroad also underpins the book.

The particular and the general pulse like systolic and diastolic in Graves's work, intertwining into a whole. The story of one man's experience on the river represents the possibility of understanding available to everyone, because "one river, seen right, may well be all rivers that flow to the sea" (p. 254). Still, it is the vividness and intensity of Graves's particulars that make the book memorable. His casual and folksy yet philosophical and literate canoeist, with his dachshund pup, Passenger, spins out stories connected to the history of places like Poke Stalk Bend, Old Painted Campground, Thorp Spring, and Mitchell Bend. By revisiting these places and recovering the stories that the locals tell, and by examining the natural history of the area, Graves dramatizes the process of achieving awareness of self through valuing a place.

With the river journey providing the structure, Graves moves back and forth beween the river and the larger world with references to his own wandering past and through epigraphs and allusions to Sir Gawain, King Arthur, Lawrence Sterne, William Butler Yeats, Thomas Hardy, Henry David Thoreau, Thorstein Veblen, T. S. Eliot, and one of Graves's favorite writers, the Spanish poet and philosopher Juan Ramón Jiménez, who provides a quotation that sums up the book: "Foot in one's accidental or elected homeland: heart, head in the world's air" (p. 254). From these and other references to "the world's air," Graves shifts to stories of the homeland. He recalls the times he and his friend Hale and their massive companion Bill Briggs spent on the river in their youth (with echoes of Huck Finn), tells stories about the Comanches and about the Mitchell-Truitt feud, which ended with Cooney Mitchell's hanging in Granbury. He recalls the time the hermit Sam Sowell was almost burned up by thoughtless kids and was saved by Graves's friend Davis Birdsong, and the time Birdsong tried to impress a French ambassador by putting his leg behind his head. This human history is complemented by careful examination of natural history, as Graves observes the plants and animals along the route and reproduces in hieroglyphics the calls of redbirds and Carolina wrens.

Along the way Graves returns to several important concerns, including his relationship to Thoreau, hunting, and the persistent puritanism of the people who live along the river. Anticipating that critics would note Thoreau's influence, Graves attempts to distance himself from his strong predecessor. Graves make it clear that he finds Thoreau too rooted in the world's air, too transcendently "ascetic," and consistently refers to him as "Saint Henry." The Texan's distance from his literary precursor is especially clear when it comes to hunting. Graves notes that even though "Saint Henry had impulses to gobble woodchucks raw," Thoreau eventually concluded that "blood sports were for juveniles" (p. 54). Although Graves wavers along the way, he ultimately aligns himself with "Prince Ernest Hemingway" and asserts that

> killing itself can be reverent. To see and kill and pluck and gut and cook and eat a wild creature, all with some knowledge and the pleasure that knowledge gives, implies a closeness to the creature that is to me more honorable than the candle-lit consumption of rare prime steaks from a steer bludgeoned to death in a packing-house chute while tranquilizers course his veins. (p. 167)

At one point late in the book the narrator seemingly decides to hunt no more—only to grab his gun when a good shot presents itself, suggesting that the persona the writer has created is inconsistent. Yet such wavering is itself significant. Repeated references to the country's puritanism reinforce Graves's emphasis on his shifting awareness of varying positions. Nature itself confirms his point:

> Sunshine and warm water seem to me to have full meaning only when they come after winter's bite; green is not so green if it doesn't follow the months of brown and gray. And the scheduled inevitable death of green carries its own exhilaration; in that change is the promise of all the rebirths to come, and the deaths,

too. . . . Without the year's changes, for me, there is little morality. (p. 119)

Later, while considering the puritan outlook of the people who live along the river, Graves makes a similar point, noting that if "wrong is sharply wrong enough, its edge digs deeper down into the core of that sweet fruit, pleasure, than hedonism ever thought to go" (p. 191). Still later he makes the same point symbolically, when Davis Birdsong tells a story about following Sam Sowell through the shin oak one day and finding a coiled diamondback rattlesnake. As Birdsong raises his axe to dispatch the snake, Sowell stops him and acknowledges the human connection to the snake's symbolic evil. Good and evil intertwine in Graves's world, and his trip down the river reinforces this knowledge for him in personal, historical, and natural ways.

This awareness suggests how Graves differs from some other Western nature writers. Graves's world is ultimtely a "fallen," Manichaean world with good and evil intertwined, unlike the innocent world that Thomas Lyon describes as the terrain of other Western nature writers in "The Nature Essay in the West." The function of the nature writer, Lyon suggests, is "to reforge a fundamental continuity between inner and outer, so that for the reader the world is alive again, seen precisely for what it is, and the mind is alive to it." Lyon continues:

> To have known the beauty of the world, seen with unclouded eyes the sheer wonder of a clear river or a mesa or a cottonwood tree, is to be in some sense and for that time, psychologically whole. The deepest attraction of the nature essay, probably, is this basic rightness of gestalt. Good nature writing is a recapturing of the child's world, the world before fragmentation, the world as poets and artists can see it. (p. 221)

Although the elegiac tone of *Goodbye to a River* suggests nostalgia, Graves does not look back to an innocent world devoid of evil. Rather, his piece of the Brazos reinforces and becomes the vehicle for his understanding of human complexity.

Goodbye to a River: Critical Reflections

In an insightful observation of Graves's style in 1981, Larry McMurtry, who taught with Graves at TCU in the early 1960s, points out that "one of his most frequent rhetorical devices . . . is to undercut himself: questioning a story he has just retold, doubting an observation he has just made, twisting out from under a position. Often he simply reverses his field and abandons whatever line of thought he has been pursuing." This technique highlights the complexity and mystery of human truth rather than clarifying it. McMurtry continues:

> He is popularly thought to be a kind of country explainer, when in fact he seems more interested in increasing our store of mysteries than our store of knowledge. He loves the obscure, indeterminate nature of rural legend and likes nothing better than to retell stories the full truth of which can never be known. If nature continues to stimulate him it may be because it too is elusive, feminine, never completely knowable.
>
> Certainly he is not looking forward to becoming the Sage of Glen Rose. His best writing is based on doubt and ambivalence—or at least two-sidedness; he is not eager to arrive at too many certainties, or any certainty too quickly. The persona he adopts most frequently is that of the man who *considers*. He may choose to consider a goat, a book, an anecdote, or some vagary of nature, but the process of considering is more important to the texture of his books than any conclusions that may get drawn. (pp. 29–30)

Goodbye to a River clearly demonstrates the reluctant trumpeter considering, in this case the human and natural history of a small piece of the Brazos River. Through his emphasis on using the natural world to consider both the human history associated with it and his own consciousness, Graves provides an example of the process Scott Slovic describes in *Seeking Awareness in American Nature Writing*. Slovic notes that the tradition of nature writing from

Thoreau through Annie Dillard, Edward Abbey, Wendell Berry, and Barry Lopez reveals an emphasis on the relationship between nature and the writer's mental state: "Nature writers are constantly probing, traumatizing, thrilling, and soothing their own minds—and by extension those of their readers—in quest not only of consciousness itself, but of an understanding of consciousness" (p. 3).

Graves's consciousness arises from a combination of personal experience, history, folklore, nature, and philosophy—a unique mixture that led to numerous positive reviews. Paul Horgan in the *New York Herald Tribune Book Review* hailed Graves as a new talent: "This highly original book bears witness to the appearance of an excellent literary talent not previously seen in book form." Wayne Gard in the *New York Times Book Review* called it "a memorable saga . . . a warm, moving book with many rewards for the reader." And Edward Weeks in the *Atlantic Monthly* pointed out the connection between the specific and the general, saying that "as you read, you have the feeling that the whole colorful, brutal tapestry of the Lone-Star State is being unrolled for you out of the biography of this one stream." The book was selected as a finalist for the National Book Award for 1960 and won the Texas Institute of Letters Carr Collins Award for nonfiction that year.

Hard Scrabble

Graves uses numerous themes and techniques that demonstrate his sense of the complexity of human experience. Those same concerns recur in his second book, which follows logically from *Goodbye to a River*. *Hard Scrabble: Observations on a Patch of Land* (1974) takes the commitment to place further by dramatizing Graves's attempts to recapture a worn-out piece of land. But this seemingly simple purpose takes on layers of meaning and demonstrates Graves's awareness of "simple" complexity. He adopts several terms that on the surface seem simple and clear. One is the term "Tonk Nation," which initially seems to refer to the Tonkawa

Indians who lived in central Texas at the time of first contact with European explorers, but whose numbers decreased until they disappeared from the state. Graves soon broadens the term to refer generally to a band of native people, explaining that it can be applied "to the hard-bitten whites who settled and lingered there." He then adopts it as a generic term that is "quite descriptive of the country itself," noting that "as erosion and agricultural ruin spread down through the lower hills, Tonkishness spread with them, and in later days the name came to fit the whole hill zone, including Hard Scrabble. I use it that way in my mind. The Tonk Nation wherein we dwell . . ." (p. 27).

Another term that contains layers of meaning is the "Ownership Syndrome," shortened usually to "the Syndrome." Initially negative, it refers at first to the narrow vision of people who own and work land; later, it comes to indicate the kind of concern for land and property that ownership instills. The Syndrome is usually in conflict with "the Way," shortened from the natural or "Sacred Way" of preserving nature for wild things. Together, both terms achieve a creative tension that adds complexity to seemingly simple ideas.

Yet another term that seems uncomplicated but achieves complexity is "O.F.," which Graves applies humorously to the Old Farts like himself who putter around "reading magazines about making compost and how to build things out of hunks of busted concrete," as his lawyer friend comments (p. 8). But Graves quickly tells the lawyer that the O.F. is a "friend of mine—kinfolks, sort of" and makes it clear that he identifies with the O.F. In chapter 10 the O.F. becomes the major character, as Graves traces his leaving home, coming to the area, marrying, and having children. The O.F., in his dealings with his wife and daughter, becomes a young and later an old father. Although Graves never translates O.F. as "Old Father," by focusing on the fictional character's problematic relationship with his daughter Midge, the story emphasizes his identity as a father, and the O.F.'s connection with husbanding the land gains more emphasis throughout the rest of the book. Finally,

Graves asserts:

> If much of a future remains to mankind on this planet—a good moot point, of course, it probably rests largely in the hands of Old Farts, of whatever age or size or color or sex or wealth or class or profession or level of educational bliss. For the mark and sign of a true hydrogen-sulfide Old Fart is this: that while he knows men must use the earth, he knows too that it matters for its own sake and that it must stay alive, and therefore according to such understanding as he may have he tries to keep his dealings with it right and gentle, and only thereafter reflects on fiscal gain. (p. 230)

This reconciliation with the land is the underlying subject of *Hard Scrabble*, for Graves takes as his major theme the process of recovery. Ostensibly, working this hardscrabble farmland is an attempt to recover the land itself from the unproductive state it has reached because of relentless cotton farming and mindless overgrazing by his thoughtless predecessors in the Tonk Nation. But the book is also about recovering a sense of balance between human and natural worlds, which the seemingly warring camps of nature lovers and economic Darwinians obscure. Just as *Goodbye to a River* examines the balance between a concern for the particular and an understanding of the general, larger world, *Hard Scrabble* emphasizes that both "the Way" and the "Ownership Syndrome" have competing truths.

The book's structure derives largely from the pull of these opposite positions, as thesis and antithesis, and then points toward the synthesis that the writer—the O.F., the Head Varmint—ultimately achieves:

> So that he can no longer truly find the dividing line between his more or less useful country self, who plows and sows and builds and fences . . . and that other less pragmatic self, older in time but younger in spirit, who sips with bees and envies trumpeting cranes, and is restless when the plover flute from beneath low clouds on their way . . . and runs in his mind with Evetts Gilliver's hounds and with the fox they chase as well as with all honest chasers and all chased beasts now and in all times past. . . .
>
> Queerly, they are the same man. (p. 248)

John Graves at work in the barn at Hard Scrabble, his ranch near Glen Rose, Texas, 1977

Throughout the book, Graves moves easily from one position to another as he heads toward a final reconciliation. In the first part of the book, Graves traces the history of the region, explains how he came to buy his 380-acre plot in Somervell County, and considers the trees, shrubs, grasses, and creatures (deer, wolves, foxes, and bobcats, among others) that are native to the region. This material is interspersed with "irrelevancies": his story about the marine's death in the bunk next to his on Saipan, stories about bootleggers and lawmen, a story about an Arab father with three retarded children, and the fictional story of the O.F. This last story creates a break between the book's initial concern with natural creatures and its consideration, in its second half, of farming, building fences, setting stones, and other aspects of "the war with Nature."

Like *Goodbye to a River*, *Hard Scrabble* generally received good reviews in such publications as the *New York Times Book Review*, *Atlantic Monthly*, the *New Yorker*, and *Sewanee Review*. Edward Hoagland, in a review for the *New York Times*, concluded that the "exceptional staying power is a tone that suits the book." *Hard Scrabble* was also criticized for lacking the structure of Graves's first book. Hoagland called it a "homemade book—clumsy once in a while in the way it's put together or rhetorically empurpled," but he further described it as "imperfect like a handmade thing, a prize." Timothy Dow Adams, in an analysis in the *Dictionary of Literary Biography Yearbook*, noted:

> For some readers the disjointed structure of *Hard Scrabble*, the agricultural details, and the author's occasional crotchetiness on some topics might be irritating at times, more jarring in the relative civilization of the author's farm than similar eccentricities were out on the river in his first book. But for scope and detail, for the harsh juxtaposition of nature at its worst with a sweet afternoon rain in early autumn, *Hard Scrabble* is nearly equal to *Goodbye to a River* in its power to make the reader stop reading and consider moving to the countryside. (p. 236)

Like his first book, *Hard Scrabble* won the Texas Institute of Letters Carr Collins Award for nonfiction, in 1974.

From a Limestone Ledge

Graves's third book, *From a Limestone Ledge: Some Essays and Other Ruminations About Country Life in Texas* (1980), is a collection of essays, all initially published in *Texas Monthly* between 1977 and 1980. In the preface, Graves calls many of them "footnotes" to *Hard Scrabble*, noting that they "are expansions or variations on themes found there." *From a Limestone Ledge* returns to several of Graves's concerns and amplifies ideas introduced in the earlier books. The book is divided into three parts. The first, "Coping," covers various topics related to working the land, with essays on fences, preparing meat, growing grapes and making wine, collecting trash, and sensing the spirits surrounding the accumulating things. The second part, "Creatures," considers the rancher-farmer's domesticated natural creatures—cows, goats, bees, dogs, and chickens. Part 3, "Ponderings, People, and Other Oddments," is something of a miscellany, with essays on noticing things, the weather, treasure hunting, snuff, chewing tobacco, country ownership, and a farm auction.

From a Limestone Ledge lacks the unity and metaphysical analysis of Graves's previous books, primarily because the essays were written with space and time constraints, and for a specific audience. As Graves explained candidly to Patrick Bennett: "You do edit yourself to some extent when you're writing for any publication; you know what their slant is, what their readership is largely like. Those pieces, even though they're fairly honest, don't for the most part have a lot of depth to them" (p. 68). Nevertheless, the same persona appears, the cosmopolitan wanderer who has chosen to settle in a hardscrabble world he observes with clarity. In "Noticing," for example, Graves begins by recalling the time he lived in New York City and observed the trivial events in the rooms of a department store across from his apartment. He then contrasts the level of observation in the city with that required in the country, what he calls the "noticingness" of rural life:

> It comes from having a personal stake in the landscape that envelops you, in the various beasts and fowls and crops and objects it contains whose ownership you claim, and in the activities of many wild things that own themselves. To take stock of all this daily, to exercise surveillance, is about as much as requisite for survival as was my Fifteenth Street indifference—survival for your chattels alive or inert and therefore for you as a countryman. (p. 155)

It is this quality of "noticingness" that typifies the essays in *From a Limestone Ledge*, and Graves becomes a kind of country Boswell to the valuable and possibly soon-to-disappear country life that is his subject.

Graves reinforces the elegiac quality of the book in the last essay, "A Loser,'" which tells of Graves's attending a foreclosure auction at a 125-acre farm in another county, drawn there by an advertisement for a grain combine. Graves captures the sights and sounds of the auction and the auctioneer's snappy, garbled patter: " 'Urba durba dibba rubba hurty-fie,' said the auctioneer in abandonment of the subject. 'Hurty-fie hurty-fie, who say fitty? Fitty, fitty, fitty, fitty, durba dubba ibba dibby who say forty-fie? Forty-fie, forty-forty-fie, come on, folks'" (p. 226). Ultimately, Graves makes the "pinched waxy" man losing his farm a representative figure: "The Loser had made us view the fragility of all we had been working toward, had opened our ears to the hollow low-pitched mirth of the land against mere human effort" (p. 228). This is one of Graves's continuing themes: those who work with the earth possess and understand its value; the more we lose this ability, the more diminished our humanity. But again, Graves achieves his purpose in a subtle, understated way, by allowing the narrative and the details to carry the point.

Literary Style and Fiction Writing

What makes Graves a memorable writer is both his subtlety and his distinctive style, an amalgam of fiction, folklore, philosophy, history, nature, personal experience, anecdotes, and allusions presented with repeated use of sentence fragments, ellipses, dashes, parenthetical remarks, and dialogue. Graves achieves a balance between high and popular culture, moving from a quotation by Shakespeare or Thorstein Veblen to regional dialect to sounds such as the auctioneer's chant. He is also fond of shifting from the formal third person "one" to the informal second person, with "you" referring both to the narrator and the audience. His style reflects his theme of assimilation:

> Neither a land nor a people ever starts over clean. Country is compact of all its past disasters and strokes of luck—of flood and drouth, of the caprices of glaciers and sea winds, of misuse and disuse and greed and ignorance and wisdom—and though you may doze away the cedar and coax back bluestem and mesquite grass and side-oats grama, you're not going to manhandle it into anything entirely new. It's limited by what it has been, by what's happened to it. And a people, until that time when it's uprooted and scattered and so mixed with other peoples that it has in fact perished, is much the same in this as land. It inherits. (*Goodbye to a River*, p. 237)

An important aspect of Graves's style is his merging of personal experience and fiction. The persona he creates in his three major books is ostensibly the writer himself. But Graves makes it clear in a note at the beginning of *Goodbye to a River* that although this is a work of nonfiction, "it has some fictionalizing in it," including the dramatic presentation of historical events and the transposition of places and incidents. He also states that some "of the characters, including at times the one I call myself, are composite," but he concludes that "even those parts are true in a fictional sense. As true as I could make them." This tendency to fictionalize reflects Graves's early interest in Faulkner, and the fact that his first published work was a story in the *New Yorker*. He told Patrick Bennett that having his first story accepted by a major magazine was "far too auspicious a beginning" and that he "couldn't duplicate it" (p. 67). Still, he has worked hard at fiction over the years; he has written two unpublished novels, one finished and one unfinished, and has used his talent as a fiction writer to create his persona and to merge fictional elements, such as the story of the O.F. in *Hard Scrabble*, into his nonfiction works.

The subject matter of his published stories is as varied as Graves's wanderings. "Quarry" concerns New York apartment dwellers who capture a mouse and keep it overnight, debating whether to kill it or set it free; finally, they release it, only to see it fall from the fire escape and die. Several stories are set in Mexico. "The Aztec Dog," selected for *Prize Stories for 1962: The O. Henry Awards*, examines a Mexican aristocrat and a feckless American who spar over the old man's dog. "The Green Fly" concerns a young American completing a Ph.D. in English literature who goes to Mexico to fish and relax and ends up in a complicated relationship with an old doctor. "The Off-Season" focuses on two veterans who visit Acapulco after the war to escape from the complications of life, only to find a different reality when two women arrive.

The passing western frontier is the subject of two stories. "The Dreamer" involves a former hunter, trapper, and mountain man who marries and then loses a Ute woman. After he returns to civilization, he is often lost in "dreams," times of despondence during which he recalls his experiences. The end of the frontier is the subject of what is probably Graves's best story, "The Last Running," called by former *Texas Monthly* editor William Broyles "the best short story in the English language." Gordon Lish describes it as "one of the great stories in American writing." A. C. Greene says it is "a classic . . . American short story"; William Kittredge calls it "the great father of stories written about the American West" (quoted in Bass). And in a 1990 review of the story, Rick Bass asserts that it

should be "required reading" because the "story and the emotions are as real and honest and important as the land across which they drift: the land having been developed, and the emotions fading too."

Based on an anecdote originally recounted in *Goodbye to a River*, about Comanches coming to beg a buffalo from rancher Charles Goodnight long after the Indians had been confined to a reservation in Oklahoma, the story fictionalizes these events. Goodnight is transformed into Tom Bird, who in 1923 is an aging rancher who lovingly keeps fourteen buffalo on his caprock ranch. A ragtag group of Comanches from the Oklahoma reservation, led by a crippled chief named Starlight, come to get a buffalo so that they can perform a ritualistic buffalo hunt one last time. The old rancher initially refuses, but Starlight, who had once fought against Bird after a horse-stealing raid, persists, and eventually gets Bird to give them not only a buffalo, but the prize bull, Shakespeare. The group then performs the ritualistic last running, kills the buffalo, and leaves.

In this story, as in all of his writing, Graves demonstrates how a writer with a clear sense of purpose, a respect for the bounty of the natural world, an understanding of the depth of simplicity, and a strong grip on language can step forth and move people in ways that last. It is the work of a masterful writer. One final irony remains about John Graves. Near Hard Scrabble is a small historic site called Comanche Peak; the construction of a nuclear power plant near the hill began shortly after Graves finished *Hard Scrabble*. A troubled nuclear plant in the shadow of a historic place seems a fittingly complex image for a writer who has attempted to dramatize his own awareness of the world's multilayered and paradoxical realities.

Selected Bibliography

WORKS OF JOHN GRAVES

BOOKS

Home Place: A Background Sketch in Support of a Proposed Restoration of Pioneer Buildings in Fort

Worth, Texas (Fort Worth: Pioneer Texas Heritage Committee, 1958); *Goodbye to a River, A Narrative* (New York: Knopf, 1960; repr., Sierra Club/Ballantine, 1971; Lincoln: Univ. of Nebraska Press, 1977; Austin, Tex.: Texas Monthly Press, 1985); *The Nation's River* (Washington, D.C.: G.P.O., 1968); *Hard Scrabble: Observation on a Patch of Land* (New York: Knopf, 1974; Austin, Tex.: Texas Monthly Press, 1985); *The Last Running* (Austin, Tex.: Encino, 1974; repr., New York: Lyons and Burford, 1990); *Texas Heartland: A Hill Country Year*, with photographs by Jim Bones, Jr. (College Station: Texas A&M Univ. Press, 1975); *From a Limestone Ledge: Some Essays and Other Ruminations About Country Life in Texas* (New York: Knopf, 1980; repr., Austin: Texas Monthly Press, 1985); *Blue and Some Other Dogs* (Austin: Encino Press, 1981).

SHORT FICTION

"Quarry," in *New Yorker* (8 November 1947); "The Off Season," in *Stateside* (11 November 1947); "The Green Fly," *Town and Country* 108, no. 4379 (1954), repr. in *Prize Stories of 1955: The O. Henry Awards* (Garden City, N.Y.: Doubleday, 1955); "The Laughter from the Western Islands," in *Colorado Quarterly* 2, no. 3 (1954); "The Last Running," in *Atlantic Monthly* 203, no. 6 (1959), repr. in *The Best American Short Stories 1960* (Boston: Houghton Mifflin, 1960; Austin: Encino, 1974; New York: Lyons and Burford, 1990); "The Aztec Dog," in *Colorado Quarterly* 9, no. 1 (1960), repr. in *Prize Stories of 1962: The O. Henry Awards* (Garden City, N.Y.: Doubleday, 1963), repr. in *A Part of Space: Ten Texas Writers*, ed. by Betsy Feagan Colquitt (Fort Worth: Texas Christian Univ. Press, 1969); "In the Absence of Horses," in *Escapade* 6, no. 4 (1961); "The Dreamer," in *Readers and Writers* (May/June 1966).

ESSAYS AND INTRODUCTIONS

"Carlsbad, the Incredible," in *Holiday* (September 1951); "The Lost Americans," in *Holiday* (February 1954); "U.S. Go Home," in *Colorado Quarterly* 4, no. 2 (1955); "Drifting Down the Brazos," in *Holiday* (November 1959); "On the Desirable Reluctance of Trumpets," in *College Composition and Communication* 14 (December 1963); "The Overlap Land, Gringo and Mexican Meet in the Rio Grande Valley," in *Holiday* 35 (March 1964); "Rice University: The Pangs of Change," in *Holiday* (June 1964); "The Bright New Waters," in *Ford Times* (November 1964); "A River and a Piece of Country: A Potomac Essay," in *Potomac Interim Report to the President* (Washington, D.C.: Dept. of Interior, 1966); "The Thirty Year Fence," in *Why Work* (Palo Alto, Calif.: Behavioral Research Laboratories, 1966); "The Brazos of the Northwest Texas Frontier, Today," in *West Texas

Historical Association Yearbook 34 (1968); "Aunt Clara's Luminous World," in *American Heritage* 21, no. 5 (1970); "Texas: You Ain't Seen Nothing Yet," in *The Water Hustlers*, with Robert H. Boyle and T. H. Watkins (New York and San Francisco: Sierra Club, 1971); "Recollections of Childhood," in *Growing Up in Texas: Reflections of Childhood* (Austin: Encino, 1972), essays by Graves and other Texans; "The Hard Used Land," in *Atlantic* 35 (March 1975); Introduction, *Landscapes of Texas: Photographs from Texas Highways Magazine* (College Station: Texas A&M Univ. Press, 1980); Preface, *Digging into South Texas Prehistory: A Guide for Amateur Archaeologists*, by Thomas R. Hester (San Antonio, Tex., Corona, 1980); "The Southwest as the Cradle of the Writer," in *The American Southwest: Cradle of Literary Art*, ed. by Robert W. Walts (San Marcos: Southwest Texas State Univ. Press, 1981); "The Old Guard: Dobie, Webb, and Bedichek," in *The Texas Literary Tradition: Fiction, Folklore, History*, ed. by Don Graham, James W. Lee, and William T. Pilkington (Austin: College of Liberal Arts of the University of Texas and the Texas State Historical Association, 1983); "Folklore and Me," in *Sonovagun Stew: A Folklore Miscellany*, ed. by Frances Edward Abernethy (Dallas: Southern Methodist Univ. Press, 1985); "Recollections of a Texas Bird Glimpser," in *Of Birds and Texas*, with Scott Gentling and Stuart Gentling (Fort Worth: Gentling Editions, 1986), pub. separately as *Self Portrait with Birds: Some Semi-Ornithological Recollections*, with wood engravings by John Depol (Dallas: Chama, 1991); Foreword, *Gringos in Mexico: One Hundred Years of Mexico in the American Short Story*, ed. by Edward Simmen (Fort Worth: Texas Christian Univ. Press, 1988); "State of Nature: A 50th Anniversary Celebration," *Texas Parks and Wildlife* 50 (December 1992).

BIOGRAPHICAL AND CRITICAL STUDIES

Timothy Dow Adams, "John Graves," in *Dictionary of Literary Biography Yearbook: 1983*, ed. by Mary Bruccoli and Jean W. Ross (Detroit, Mich.: Gale, 1984); Rick Bass, review of *The Last Running*, in *Dallas Morning News* (8 April 1990), sec. J; Patrick Bennett, "John Graves: A Hard Scrabble World," in his *Talking with Texas Writers: Twelve Interviews* (College Station: Texas A&M Univ. Press, 1980); M. E. Bradford, "Arden Up the Brazos: John Graves and the Uses of the Pastoral," in *Southern Review* 57 (1972), "In Keeping with the Way: John Graves' *Hard Scrabble*," in *Southwest Review* 60 (1975), and "John Graves," in *Fifty Western Writers: A Bio-Bibliographical Sourcebook*, ed. by Fred Erisman and Richard W. Etulain (Westport, Conn.: Greenwood, 1982); Clifford Endress, "Texas Literature: The Twists and Turns of an Enigmatic Tradition," in *The Texas Humanist*

(1983); Fred Erisman, "Western Writers and the Literary Historian," in *North Dakota Review* (autumn 1979).

Wayne Gard, "A World of Its Own," in *New York Times Book Review* (9 October 1960); A. C. Greene, *The Fifty Best Books on Texas* (Dallas: Pressworks, 1982); Dorys Crow Grover, *John Graves* (Boise, Idaho: Boise State Univ., 1989); Edward Hoagland, review of *Hard Scrabble: Observations on a Patch of Land*, in *New York Times Book Review* (19 May 1974); Joe Holley, "John Graves: A Master of Details and Ruminations," in *The Texas Humanist* (1984); Paul Horgan, "A Sort of Love Letter to the Brazos," in *New York Herald Tribune Book Review* (9 October 1960), and *Great River: The Rio Grande in North American History* (New York: Holt, 1954); Thomas J. Lyon, "The Nature Essay in the West," in *A Literary History of the American West*, ed. by J. Golden Taylor et al. (Fort Worth: Texas Christian Univ. Press, 1987); Larry McMurtry, "Ever a Bridegroom: Reflections of the Failure of Texas Literature," in *Texas Observer* (23 October 1981), repr. in *Range Wars: Heated Debates, Sober Reflections, and Other Assessments of Texas Writing*, ed. by Craig Clifford and Tom Pilkington (Dallas: SMU Press, 1989); David D. Medina, "When the Work Comes Right," *Sallyport: The Magazine of Rice University* (spring 1955); Noel Perrin, "Rediscovering *Goodbye to a River* by John Graves," in *The Georgia Review* (winter 1993); William T. Pilkington, *Imagining Texas: The Literature of the Lone Star State* (Boston: American Press, 1981); Scott Slovic, *Seeking Awareness in American Nature Writing* (Salt Lake City: Univ. of Utah Press, 1992); Edward Weeks, "Biography of a River," review of *Goodbye to a River, A Narrative*, in *Atlantic Monthly* (April 1961).

TELEVISION DOCUMENTARY

Bill Moyers, "John Graves, the Head Varmint of Hard Scrabble," in *Bill Moyers Journal*, transcript PBS Special (23 July 1979).

LINDA HASSELSTROM
(b. 1943)

KATHLEEN DANKER

LINDA HASSELSTROM'S WRITINGS are based on her experiences living and working on a small family ranch on the high plains of western South Dakota near the Black Hills. In her works, she details the duties of ranch life, the beauties and hazards of the natural world, the importance of protecting the prairie environment, and the joys, griefs, humor, and courage of those who make a living on the land by working to care for its soil and water, grass and animals.

Hasselstrom has written that her most important professional achievement is her "increasing ability to write and publish informal essays evaluating our environmental future, with particular attention to the future of ranch agriculture" (autobiographical statement). Her convictions about the environmental and social issues that affect her life and region come through clearly in her work. But the power of her writing also derives from her storytelling skill, her poetic voice, her lively sense of humor, and the precision and clarity of her style.

Hasselstrom has published one book-length journal and several collections of essays and poetry. Her work has appeared in over seventy journals and anthologies. Taken together, these writings paint a broad yet detailed portrait of the author's life and thought as a rancher, writer, and environmentalist, as well as a publisher, neighbor, daughter, wife, stepmother, widow, feminist, and seeker of spiritual truth in nature.

It is Hasselstrom's conviction that the goals of environmentalism and family (noncorporate) ranching are compatible. The ranchers she knows are neighborly, hardworking people who conserve their resources to protect their land and livelihoods. In the introduction to *Windbreak: A Woman Rancher on the Northern Plains* (1987), she says:

> A ranch may operate in several ways. Some ranchers buy yearling cattle, fatten them in summer, sell them in fall, and go south for the winter. We run a cow-calf operation, raising cows to breed and selling their calves; such an operation demands almost constant attention. Our 365-day-a-year-job is raising those calves to become beef.
>
> What we're really selling is grass packaged inside a cow. Ranchers have a close relationship with grass, learning which kinds provide the best grazing, how to recognize overgrazed land, and what to do about it. The old ranchers in the area would hesitate to call themselves environmentalists—or even take offense at the idea—but they take good care of the land so it will continue to support their cattle. (p. xiv)

Life and Work

Born in Texas on 14 July 1943, Hasselstrom moved to South Dakota in 1947 with her mother Mildred Bovard following the divorce of her parents. In 1952, the author was adopted by her mother's second husband, John Hasselstrom, whose family had ranched in the Black Hills area since his father had come over from Sweden in the late nineteenth century.

The author writes in the introduction to *Going Over East: Reflections of a Woman Rancher* (1987) that she did not realize at the time of her adoption that it meant "I had pledged my soul to a ranch, to acres of tawny grass and dry creeks that would absorb my blood and sweat, as they had my father's, and still look parched" (p. 3). Nonetheless, she soon developed a passionate attachment to a land and climate she found beautiful as well as exacting and to a lifestyle she describes as satisfying in spite of its physical rigors and dangers.

An only child who preferred working outdoors, Hasselstrom embarked on a long apprenticeship to her father in the art of ranching. At the age of nine, while learning how to herd cattle, close gates, and roam the prairies on her first horse, she began writing a novel and keeping the near-daily journals that have ever since provided the ideas and raw material for her writing. She published a few stories and poems in local magazines in high school and while obtaining undergraduate and graduate degrees: a B.A. in English and Journalism from the University of South Dakota in 1965 and an M.A. in American Literature from the University of Missouri in 1969.

As an undergraduate, Hasselstrom was editor of the student newspaper at the University of South Dakota. In 1965, she produced her own first chapbook of poetry on a handfed press and was employed on the night staff of the *Sioux City Journal*. In 1966, she married Daniel Lusk, becoming a part-time stepmother to his three children, and moved with him to Missouri to attend graduate school. She served as director of student publications at Christian (now Columbia) College in Columbia, Missouri, from 1966 to 1969 and taught classes as a Ph.D. candidate at the University of Missouri at Columbia from 1969 to 1971.

In 1971, Hasselstrom and her husband returned to the family ranch in South Dakota in an attempt to save their shaky marriage. With the support of the South Dakota Arts Council, they began a journal of arts and literature entitled *Sunday Clothes: A Magazine of the Arts* and an independent publishing company called Lame Johnny Press, named after a local horse thief. In addition to helping her father operate the ranch, Hasselstrom continued to write and teach in area colleges.

The marriage ended in 1973, but Hasselstrom went on to publish *Sunday Clothes* for a total of eleven years, going broke three times in the process. Though financially risky, the magazine was an important way, she felt, to promote the arts in South Dakota and provide a forum for regional writers and artists. Eventually, she published work by some three hundred individuals, and was the first to print several authors, including novelist and short story writer Dan O'Brien. Through Lame Johnny Press, she also put out twenty-three books from or about the Great Plains region.

In 1984, a small San Francisco press published a collection of Hasselstrom's poems entitled *Caught by One Wing*, and at the end of the year she received a fellowship in poetry from the National Endowment for the Arts. In 1985, Hasselstrom suspended the Lame Johnny Press in order to devote more time to her own writing. Though no longer in the publishing business, she continued to eke out the time to write from around the edges of ranch work, household responsibilities, a number of temporary jobs, and environmental activism.

"I was adopted by the land," the author writes in *Land Circle: Writings Collected from the Land* (1991), "and began developing a personal land ethic the first time I looked out on the empty, rolling prairie around my home" (p. 240). With her return to the ranch after college, she became increasingly interested in the environmental movement and began reading the work of nature essayists, including Loren Eiseley, John McPhee, Wendell Berry, Annie Dillard, and Edward Abbey. Hasselstrom developed the conviction that

338

not enough attention was being given to threats to the ecology of the Great Plains. In *Going Over East* she writes:

> Today . . . more populous areas seem to regard the plains as an "empty quarter," fit only for the disposal of garbage, as if it were the country's back alley. Within the past five years, we've entertained proposals for the placement here of: uranium mines and mills, a national hazardous waste disposal site, a national radioactive waste disposal site, a processing and disposal site for sewage ash, several strip mining and heap leach processing operations, a superconducting supercollider, a site for incineration and/or landfilling of PCBs (polychlorinated biphenyls), a sulfide mine, and several sites for the building, testing and disposal of ammunition and other explosive devices. Low population, a crippled agricultural industry, a body of potential employees who used to be farmers, and a lack of factory industry apparently make the area a target for promoters of such plans. (pp. 5–6)

When a mining company filed uranium claims close to her grandmother's ranch in the Black Hills in 1979, Hasselstrom joined the Black Hills Energy Coalition, a group that sponsored a voter initiative to ban nuclear power plants and waste dumps as well as uranium mines and mills. That initiative failed, but a few years later she served the coalition as newsletter editor, policy writer, and spokesperson when they spearheaded another, successful, voter initiative to prohibit the opening of a large nuclear waste dump in western South Dakota. She also served, until its disbanding, as the president and on the board of directors of the Technical Information Project, a research group organized to provide data concerning environmental issues.

To supplement the always meager income of the ranch, Hasselstrom has taught at area colleges and done editing work. She has served as a writer-in-the-schools for the South Dakota Arts Council and taught at the Prairie Winds Young Writers' Conference for many years. She has served as a juror for writing contests, conducted many writing workshops, and given numerous lectures and readings.

In 1979, the same year she was named South Dakota Press Woman of Achievement, Hasselstrom married George R. Snell. An avid outdoorsman with an interest in the nineteenth-century mountain men, he introduced Hasselstrom to rendezvous camping, while she and her father instructed him in the intricacies of running a cow-calf operation. The couple lived in a small apartment added on to her parents' house until they built their own home on a buffalo-grass-covered hillside on the ranch in the early 1980s.

Snell figures prominently in *Windbreak*, *Going Over East*, and *Land Circle*, as does Michael, his son from a previous marriage, who lived with them part of each summer. In *Land Circle*, Hasselstrom has written of her husband:

> Sometimes people who saw George for the first time were intimidated by his size, the fierceness of his face in repose, perhaps the knife. But once they saw those deep blue eyes, no one ever failed to trust him—or tried to make him mad.
>
> . . . He worked hard on the family ranch because I love it; often cooked so I had more time to write, and urged me to say no to demands that took me away from my writing. (p. 138)

In the fall of 1988, George Snell died of the side effects of radiation treatment he had received earlier for Hodgkin's disease. Hasselstrom was devastated. She planted his grave with prairie flowers, and with the help of friends, moved a large stone from the Black Hills to serve as its marker. Of his death, she writes, "I believe anyone who wants to die as George died, smiling and talking of the love he felt for us, must live as he lived: enjoying what each day gives us, wasting nothing. He truly knew that death could take him at any moment of half his young life; that knowledge gave his days more meaning than most of us ever taste" (*Land Circle*, p. 251).

Hasselstrom's writing career began to take off in 1987. In that year, she published three books: the journal *Windbreak: A Woman Rancher on the Northern Plains*, which was reviewed in the *New York Times Book Review* and selected as an alternate for a book club; *Going Over East: Reflections of a Woman Rancher*, a volume of essays that won the Fulcrum American Writing Award; and a collection of poems entitled *Roadkill*.

In 1989, Hasselstrom was named author of the year by the South Dakota Hall of Fame and was awarded a literary fellowship by the South Dakota Arts Council. She also received the 1989 Governor's Award for Distinction in Creative Achievement, and used her acceptance speech in the capitol rotunda to encourage the governor and other state officials to protect South Dakota's natural resources. In 1990, she became the first woman to receive the Western American Writer award from the Center for Western Studies in Sioux Falls, South Dakota.

In 1991, Hasselstrom published *Land Circle: Writings Collected from the Land*. For it, she won the Elkhorn Prize, a trophy belt buckle awarded for poetry by *Nebraska Territory* of Wayne, Nebraska. *Dakota Bones: The Collected Poems of Linda Hasselstrom* appeared in 1992, the year Mountains and Plains Booksellers selected Hasselstrom for one of its four awards. In addition, the *Rapid City Journal* listed her as one of ten West River Notables for 1992 for her books about ranching, women, families, community, and preserving the environment.

In the summer of 1991, Hasselstrom asked her father, then in his mid-eighties, to make her a partner in the family ranch because she knew that many sons and daughters of ranchers were having to sell their land to pay inheritance taxes after their parents' deaths. He refused and demanded as well that she quit writing to ranch full time.

In the spring of 1992, when he had not changed his mind, Hasselstrom moved away to a small city in a neighboring state. She says, "I missed the ranch so much that I could hardly stand it. But also I knew I could not live without

writing. . . . So I decided, 'O.K., if that's the choice I have to make, that's the choice I'm making.' And I gave it up" (personal interview).

John Hasselstrom died in August of 1992, and left his estate to his widow Mildred who moved to a nursing home in Rapid City, South Dakota. The Hasselstroms sold their cattle to pay probate expenses and leased their land to a neighbor. Along with the problems of taxes and the costs of overdue maintenance and repairs, parts of the ranch are threatened with condemnation for proposed highway construction.

Although Hasselstrom has had some difficulty adapting to the noise and pace of city life, she appreciates having more time to devote to her writing. She says she is "seeing myself writing better, and therefore my chances of achieving my potential as a writer are greater now than they have been. . . . Every book I'd written . . . had been written around the edges of my life, had been written at night and in snatches between pulling calves and jobs. I have never sat down and said, 'I'm not going to do anything for the next year but write'" (personal interview).

Caught by One Wing, Roadkill, and *Dakota Bones*

Hasselstrom began writing poetry as a child of nine and put out her "first *real* publication," *Caught by One Wing*, thirty-two years later in 1984 (Prairie Winds interview). It was published in a delicate handset letterpress edition of five hundred copies by Julie Holcomb in San Francisco. In 1990, the volume was reprinted in a sturdier and less expensive form by David Pichaske of the Spoon River Poetry Press, which had also published *Roadkill*, in 1987. *Dakota Bones: Collected Poems of Linda Hasselstrom*, which Pichaske published in 1992, consists of the complete texts of both previous collections and twenty-six newer poems. The most recent of these later poems were composed at Vallecitos, New Mexico, in 1990.

In the preface to *Dakota Bones*, Hasselstrom explains that she resisted the urge to delete weaker poems from *Caught by One Wing*, choosing not "to edit the self and the writer I was then in the light of what I know now." While some of the earlier pieces are awkward in places, others are as strong as anything she has written since.

"Mulch," written in the early 1970s, published in *Caught by One Wing*, *Windbreak*, and *Dakota Bones*, and separately handset on parchment by Holcomb, has proven to be the most popular of Hasselstrom's poems, the one most often requested at readings. She says, "People keep asking me to read 'Mulch.' And I keep analyzing 'Mulch' and trying to figure out how to write another poem that's as good as 'Mulch,' that will have that kind of cult following, and I don't think you can do it. It either happens or it doesn't" (personal interview).

The narrator of this tongue-in-cheek treatment of the theme of loss begins by defining the term used for the poem's title:

> A mulch is a layer of organic matter
> used to control weeds,
> preserve moisture,
> and improve the fertility of the soil.
> You will not find naked soil
> in the wilderness.

She goes on to explain how one day she realized that she could mulch old love letters and give "undying love to the tomatoes,/the memory of your gentle hands to the squash." This taught her "a whole new style/of gardening" so that

> Now my garden is the best in the
>   wilderness,
> and I mulch everything:
> bills; check stubs;
> dead kittens and baby chicks.
> I seldom answer letters; I mulch them
> with the plans I made for children of my
>   own,
> photographs of places I've been
> and a husband I had once;
> as well as old bouquets
> and an occasional unsatisfactory lover.

> Nothing is wasted.

> Strange plants push up among the corn,
> leaves heavy with dark water,
> but there are
> no weeds.

At the time it was composed, "Mulch" represented "a real breakthrough in freedom in writing" for the author. During the period that her first marriage was coming apart, she took a visiting cousin to see her garden. As he looked down at her new six-by-three-foot tulip bed, he scratched his head and asked, "Where did you say Dan went?" Hasselstrom says that the minute her cousin left:

> I sat on the back porch of the apartment and started writing this poem. Started right out. And this is one of the few poems that I hardly revised at all. When I wrote that line down about "and a husband I had once," ... I recognized as I wrote it down that it isn't clear in the poem whether I'm mulching the photographs or the husband. And I laughed— and left it that way.
> And I felt like all of a sudden I'd learned something new about poetry—how much fun it could be. . . . You can lie in poems, you can fantasize in poems, you can have all this fun from them. . . . I've learned a lot more about humor now and how to use it and where to put it in a reading. And I think that has a lot to do with why people do enjoy my readings. (personal interview)

"Butchering the Crippled Heifer," a fine, graphic work published in *Roadkill*, *Dakota Bones*, and *Land Circle*, is not as popular at readings as "Mulch." Yet one member of the Pipestone (Minnesota) Meat Cutters Local enjoyed hearing it so much that he gave the author his cap. Hasselstrom thinks that, like herself, this man must have been tired of being called cruel by people who would rather not know how their packages of steak get to the supermarket. The poem does not permit such ignorance when it instructs:

Make meat:

> worship at a bloody altar, knives singing
>   praises
> for the heifer's health, for flesh she made
> of hay pitched at forty below zero last
>   winter.
> Your hands are red with her blood,
>   slick with her fat.

> You know
>   where your next meal is coming from.

Hasselstrom says that when she writes she attempts to keep in mind as her intended audience specific people like this meat cutter and the many people who have written her letters or talked with her about her writing. There are times when she can see them frowning at ideas they do not agree with. But she tries to talk them into at least listening to what she has to say.

Few listeners or readers can fail to relate to the common situation so felicitously described in "Walking the Dog," one of the new pieces appearing in *Dakota Bones*. Following her husband's death, the author must take his dog with her on her travels to meetings and workshops, even though "Walking a dog in the city humbles me;/we're used to acres of prairie privacy." She goes on to say:

> You've seen us, or a similar pair:
> the human studies the sky, historical
>   plaques, treetops,
> apparently unaware of and not responsible
>   for
> what the dog at the other end of the leash is
>   doing.
> The dog plays his part: stares at bicycles,
> challenges windowed cats,
> barks at children on a merry-go-round.
> He lifts his leg as a cardinal
> might lift a hand over a crowd of pilgrims,
> with immense dignity, a modicum of grace,
> and an expression of concentrated
>   rectitude.

> He's a short dog, but his eyes
> focus on higher things: the heavens and
> flying squirrels which he—and I—
> believe to be ghosts of those caught by
>   larger dogs
> whose mark he senses when he stands
>   beside a tree.

Back in the car, the dog curls up on his blanket
and dreams of catching rabbits in a place

> where George tosses chunks of fresh
>   venison
> over the campfire's coals at night,
> and in the morning leads him beside still
>   waters
> waiting for a dry fly to land, a trout to rise.
> I keep awake, read maps, watch the gas
>   gauge,
> try to determine where we go from here.

Poems such as this make it clear that Hasselstrom is one of those rare writers whose hand is as sure at poetry as it is at nonfiction.

Windbreak

> A windbreak is a precious thing.
>   It is a promise in fall,
> a lifesaver and a place of warmth in
>   winter, a sign of hope in spring, and
> a place of loveliness in the dry heat of
>   summer.

> We all need a windbreak.
>   (*Windbreak*, p. v)

Windbreak: A Woman Rancher on the Northern Plains is a journal representing a year in Hasselstrom's life on the family ranch. She compiled it by combining journal entries she had kept over two or three years in the mid 1980s and adding explanatory material to give the finished journal continuity. Though combined and reworked in this fashion, all of the events in the volume did occur.

Hasselstrom sent the manuscript to twenty-four publishers before it was accepted in 1987 by

Linda Hasselstrom checking the moisture level under the mulch (junk mail, catalogs, and discarded carpet) around a windbreak tree on her ranch near the Black Hills

Barn Owl Books, a one-woman press then located in Berkeley, California. A biographical sketch of the author and her family is presented in the book's preface, while its introduction describes the region and the ranch, and includes a map of the ranch property in relation to a nearby town and highway. Hasselstrom later regretted publishing so detailed a map after strangers began dropping in to visit.

The body of *Windbreak* is organized into four main parts according to the seasons, starting with fall. A poem is printed at the beginning of each season and the end of each month, and the volume concludes with a glossary of ranching terms. Entries appear for most days of the year, each beginning with a record of the day's high and low temperature and, often, a description of the weather.

The ranch work connected with each season of the year is the main subject of the entries in *Windbreak*. In the fall, the author, her husband, and her father prepare the ranch for the rigors of the coming winter:

> At that time we are fixing fences, moving hay, cutting firewood and stocking up on winter feed for the cattle and ourselves. In winter, while my parents vacation in Texas, my husband George and I move the cattle closer to home, and our main daily job is providing them with feed. In spring we calve the cows out, often during the worst of the spring blizzards. During summer we maintain the cow-calf herd, fix fences, and put up hay for winter. (p. ix)

Any danger that the repetitive nature of these labors might make for tedious reading is countered by the vividness of Hasselstrom's writing. She lets us see what is unique about the circumstances of each birth of a calf or each journey by horse to another pasture. Moreover, by combining several years into one, the author succeeds in incorporating a large variety of activities and events into her journal. The first entry erupts with a sudden wind-driven grass fire that all the neighbors must fight to protect their property and lives. Another tells of the author's experiences teaching poetry to children on a nearby Indian reservation.

Hasselstrom relates stories about the two weeks in July that she and her husband spend with friends at a rendezvous camp in the mountains of Utah, living like the mountain men of the 1840s. She tells how her horse comes to leave hoofprints up the side of her leg during an accident in a January snowstorm and of the meadowlarks she finds frozen on the ground in a late April blizzard. The weather, ranging from drought to hailstorms to deep drifting snow, remains a constant force to be reckoned with throughout the year.

The poems in *Windbreak* do not relate directly to the events in the journal since most were written, and first published, earlier. They do correspond to the season of the section in which they appear and concern the everyday aspects of ranch life reflected in their titles: "Drying Onions," "Late March Blizzard," "Calving Time," "Haying: A Four-Part Definition." They are also rooted in the author's life and emotions; "Digging Potatoes," for instance, concerns the legacy left by her grandmother's death. It ends,

> Wearing her shoes, I'm digging potatoes.
> The sweet, rotten earth smell reaches up;
> soil clings to my fingers, to the red
> potatoes I drop in the bucket. I expect
> to see her face at the bottom of each hole,
> hear her voice answering the question
> I've barely begun to ask. (p. 23)

The cumulative detail in *Windbreak* about the lives of its main characters gives readers the sense that they know Hasselstrom, her husband, her stepson Michael, her neighbor and best friend Margaret, her father, and her uncle Harold—even the horses and dog. In the four years following the volume's publication, this sense of personal involvement prompted readers to send Hasselstrom over six hundred letters, most of which she answered.

Such letters have often given a lift to the author's spirits, and she is pleased by the popularity of this record of a period in her life that she cherishes. She says:

> My favorite is still the book *Windbreak*, about my life on the ranch before my husband died, because I put so much about our lives into it, and that helps me remember how wonderful he was. Also, a lot of other people who live on ranches have written to tell me that what I wrote in that book described their lives too, and that makes me happy. (Prairie Winds interview)

A brief sequel to *Windbreak* was published in the July 1989 issue of *Life* under the title "Journal of a Woman Rancher." Consisting of a poem "for George" entitled "Windbreak Now" and eight days of journal entries from the spring following his death, it stresses the nurturing strength and endurance of women who choose to live in the country—women like Hasselstrom's neighbor Margaret, who plants and mulches five hundred pine trees in a day despite a fused back. After describing the death of a cow injured in calving, the author closes the last day's entry by saying:

> Spring always brings this tart mixture of life and death, and I am oddly heartened to see it again, to know I am part of the cycle. When Margaret and I talked of ranch women the other day, we were thinking of women through the ages. Even in primitive societies, while the men sharpened spears and hunted, the women tended to growing things—to the birth of humans and the animals living with them and to death. From this awareness and love of the work we do comes a sense of responsibility to the earth. The country women I know are responsible in the best sense—they understand how everything they do affects their world. Perhaps knowing deep darkness helps us open ourselves to the joys of greening grass to feed new calves that will feed our families, as well as to the "useless" loveliness of herons sweeping overhead. When Margaret plants trees and I plant flowers on my husband's grave, we are making a joyful promise to life and to the earth that supports it. (p. 94)

Most of Hasselstrom's published work is not in the journal format of *Windbreak* and "Journal of a Woman Rancher," yet virtually everything she publishes has its inception in the notebooks in which she writes down what she observes or thinks of during a day. She copies down conversations overheard in cafés and collects pithy quotations from many sources. Sometimes she will write an outline or start a draft of an essay or poem. Caught without her notebooks and pen while doing ranch work, she has even been known to jot down observations on scraps of paper with the nose of a bullet.

Going Over East

Going Over East: Reflections of a Woman Rancher was published by Fulcrum in 1987. These meditations on what the home pastures and prairie hills mean to the author take place as she and her husband and stepson travel by pickup across the eleven or so miles from their ranch house to their easternmost pasture, known as "over east." Each gate they open and close on their trip starts another chapter. The volume begins with an introduction to some of the difficulties of sustaining ranch agriculture and protecting the plains environment, and it ends with a list of suggested readings about ranching.

Going Over East covers roughly the same time period as *Windbreak*, but repeats little from that journal. Its structure allows for more sustained storytelling, fuller description, lengthier digressions. All are triggered by the grasses, deserted homesteads, watering tanks, prairie dog holes, and other features of the landscape that the travelers pass on their way over east.

Hasselstrom tells stories about the people who used to live in the fallen-down buildings, reviews what her father taught her about ranching, recalls the hours she spent trying to tame a wild filly, tells her stepson why he should not kill bull snakes, describes what she and her husband look for when they inspect their cows, and explains her fears about threats to her way of life: perilously small profit margins, inheritance taxes, uranium prospectors who drill into precarious aquifers, managers of large corporate ranches who let their cattle overgraze pastures, and misinformed activists who think that *all* ranchers abuse the land and kill off the wildlife. In the book's last chapter, she poses a question:

> What will I inherit? Perhaps nothing that I don't already have: the knowledge and love of the land I have gained from my father and from my own absorption in this unique world. . . .
>
> Sometimes watching a hunting hawk cruise air currents, I experience . . . a moment of clear vision that stuns me with its simplicity and promise. Then it is gone, and I am uncertain again—but the memory sustains me: a solution is possible. The answer might not save this ranch or me—but it can be found. (pp. 199–200)

Hasselstrom has found readers' responses to *Going Over East* to be positive and helpful:

> I started getting real thoughtful letters from English teachers and ranchers and people who had read that book and who said, "That's your best book. It's the most coherent. It all flows together: everything's tied together. That's the best writing you have done—period." And I'm starting to believe that they were on to something, and I really studied that book in writing the one that I've just finished to try to aim for that kind of coherence in about quadruple the length.
>
> Part of it is that device that I hit on for structuring it—first gate, second gate. It wasn't a fake device; it was strictly dictated by the physical geography of the land. Here's the first gate and here's what this suggests to me. Trying to come up with something else like that is a nightmare. (personal interview)

Land Circle

Land Circle: Writings Collected from the Land (1991) lacks the cohesion of *Going Over East*, but it is a rich and ambitious work containing many of the best essays and poems Hasselstrom has written. She calls it

> the most serious, the most extended, the most complex book I've tried, and it evolved considerably during the time I worked on it. I began with the idea of doing a series of short "word portraits" of people, places, and ideas that are part of prairie life, but the issues facing us—even in the middle of what many people consider to be an underpopulated wasteland—were so complex the book kept growing. My husband died after I had begun working on the book, so that changed the focus considerably as I learned to live with his dying. (Prairie Winds interview)

In the introduction to *Land Circle*, Hasselstrom lays out her belief that the West faces a third frontier of exploitation as outside populations attempt to appropriate its resources and use it as a dump for their unwanted trash. She says: "Residents know their mineral wealth is sometimes hidden under beautiful mountains, trout streams, pasture land, or just simply 'purty country,' and they're not convinced it's beneficial to send it all to the city, and get waste dumps and federal aid in return" (p. xviii). To provide more information on the environmental issues it raises, the volume concludes with footnotes and a list of books, periodicals, catalogs and regional organizations.

The alternating thirty-six poems and thirty-nine essays that make up the body of *Land Circle* are arranged in three sections. Among the many excellent pieces in "Part I: Where Neighbor Is a Verb," the poem "Chant for the Rain" (" 'I'm dry clear to the bone,'/ranchers say/'Dry clear to the bone.' ") is paired with the essay "Finding Buffalo Berries," a meditation that likens the tart and thorny fruits of the parched prairies to the character of the "prickly" people who live there. Perhaps even better are the myth-debunking poem "The Wild and Woolly West" (Wild Bill never cared for Jane/and he was married anyway/Calamity/died broke.") and a fine saga of a trial ride through the mountains told in "The Cowboy and the Ride."

The second part of *Land Circle*, "George: In Beauty Walk," is the heart of the collection. "George's Poem" ("Even dying, he kept it simple:/'Be happy. Watch the sunsets.' ") leads into the essay "George R. Snell, 1946–1988," which combines a eulogy on Snell's life with a moving description of his death. Other essays such as "Rolling up the Hoses" document the author's attempts to come to terms with her loss and find solace in work and nature. Pieces including the poem "What the Falcon Said" ("I kill to eat./So do the cats./So do you.") and "Vultures," an essay in praise of turkey buzzards, examine the role of death in the natural world.

Circumstances rushed the editing of *Land Circle*'s last section, "A Woman's Covenant," so that Hasselstrom ended up deleting two poems and the last three essays with which she had intended to sum up the volume. Along with its abrupt ending, the author is dissatisfied with what she now considers its didactic tone. If there is didacticism in "A Woman's Covenant," it comes from Hasselstrom's desire to pass on to others lessons that she has learned from her life on the land. In the essay "Land Circle: Lessons," she writes:

I have been a student all my years on the ranch; I might have learned the same lessons elsewhere, but I learned well where the tests were life or death for my animals and myself. The lessons of the ranch can be summarized in a way that is almost absurdly simple, yet they cover the larger work of my life as a rancher and a writer, as well as my politics and religion. Succinctly, they give me hope for the simplest and most difficult job I face: survival. The lessons I have learned concern birth, death, and responsibility for the life between. (p. 242)

The theme of taking responsibility for life, death, and the environment runs through essays like "Work Boots and the Sustainable Universe," "The Cow Versus the Animal Rights Activist," and "Why One Peaceful Woman Carries a Pistol." It appears as well in poems including "Beef Eater," "Drought Year," and "My Last Will and Testament." In this last piece, Hasselstrom addresses those who will follow her tenure on the ranch:

You earn the land
after your name is on the title.
The sacraments of inheritance
require payment in blood and sweat.
If you only accept, you lose everything.

Recording the Details

The attention Hasselstrom gives to the details of her environment is a hallmark of her writing. She chooses to describe the less conspicuous forms of wildlife on the plains, not the buffalo, but the bull snakes, coyotes, nighthawks and other creatures she has come to know by observing their habits all her life. She believes that such intimate knowledge is central to understanding her region. In *Going Over East* she says:

> It's easy to romanticize and distort the West; our history invites it, being filled with gunmen, cattle rustlers, conflicts over land, bawdy houses and madams with hearts of gold. People who visit the West briefly and then write about it tend to do so in sweeping generalities: purple mountains have majesty above fruited plains, good-hearted if occasionally profane people ride noble horses into the sunset. The longer I live here, the more I fear such generalities, and study details in my lifelong attempt to understand my surroundings more completely. . . .
>
> . . . Reality hinges on practicality, on knowledge that has daily use. (pp. 104–105)

By presenting the reality of the West as she knows it, Hasselstrom combats the stereotypes and polarities she sees standing in the way of solutions to its problems. Her life and writings expose the ignorance of those who would say that the interests of ranchers and environmentalists are necessarily opposed, that wildlife and cattle cannot exist side by side, or that it is not possible to both love animals and kill them.

Hasselstrom is pleased that more Western women are beginning to write about their connections with other women and the earth, and their love of its animals. In *Land Circle* she writes, "Women and country people, each existing in informal communities, circles formed around stewardship of the earth, should lead the attempt to rethink our relationship to it" (p. 279). Yet she distrusts generalities which maintain that women, because of their nurturing natures, will never do anything violent. As a rancher, she has had to kill animals that were suffering or that posed too high a danger to other life, and she knows that she is not the only woman to have done this.

Hasselstrom's correspondence indicates that her readers are diverse: not just ranchers and farmers, but teachers, students, professionals, and people living in metropolitan areas. They have all been touched in some way by her stories, her humor, and her plainspoken convictions about life on the plains.

Selected Bibliography

WORKS OF LINDA HASSELSTROM

POETRY

Caught by One Wing (San Francisco: Julie D. Holcomb, 1984; repr., Granite Falls, Minn.: Spoon River, 1990); *Roadkill* (Peoria, Ill.: Spoon River, 1987); *Dakota Bones: Collected Poems of Linda Hasselstrom* (Granite Falls, Minn.: Spoon River, 1992).

PROSE

The Book Book: A Publishing Handbook (Hermosa, S.Dak.: Lame Johnny, 1979); *Going Over East: Reflections of a Woman Rancher* (Golden, Colo.: Fulcrum, 1987); *A Roadside History of South Dakota* (Missoula, Mont.: Mountain, 1994).

PROSE AND POETRY

Windbreak: A Woman Rancher on the Northern Plains (Berkeley, Calif.: Barn Owl Books, 1987); *Land Circle: Writings Collected from the Land* (Golden, Colo.: Fulcrum, 1991).

EDITED WORKS

Next-Year Country: One Woman's View (Hermosa, S.Dak.: Lame Johnny, 1978); *A Bird Begins to Sing: Northwest Poetry and Prose* (Hermosa, S.Dak.: Lame Johnny, 1979); *Horizons: The South Dakota Writers' Anthology* (Hermosa, S.Dak.: Lame Johnny, 1983); *Journal of a Mountain Man: James Clyman* (Missoula, Mont.: Mountain, 1984).

SELECTED ARTICLES

"Educating Young Publishers," in *Design* (January/February 1980); "Ranching for Fun and Profit," in *North Country Anvil* (spring 1988); "Camping with a 'Possibles' Bag," in *Christian Science Monitor* (11 January 1989); "What's Black and White and Odorous?" in *Christian Science Monitor* (10 March 1989); "Heat Wave on the Highway," in *Christian Science Monitor* (23 June 1989); "Journal of a Woman Rancher," in *Life* (July 1989); "O Holy Night on the Prairie," in *Christian Science Monitor* (21 December 1989); "Ignoring the Windchill Factor," in *Christian Science Monitor* (23 June 1990); "The Pot of Hospitality," in *Christian Science Monitor* (18 October 1990); "The Land Circle: Lessons," in *North American Review* (December 1990); "A Peaceful Woman Explains Why She Carries a Gun," in *Utne Reader* (May/June 1991); "Bullsnake," in *Northern Lights* (summer 1991); "Finding Buffalo Berries," in *South Dakota Magazine* (July/August 1991); "The Cow Versus the Animal Rights Activist," in *Northern Lights* (fall 1991); "Rock Lover," in *Whole Earth Review* (fall 1991); "Who Cares for the Land?" in

South Dakota Magazine (September/October 1991); "Addicted to Work," in *The North American Review* (December 1991); "Night of the Bells," in *Reader's Digest* (April 1992); "Learning from the Land," in *Partners* (May/June 1992); "A Real Workout," in *Utne Reader* (May/June 1992); "The Covenant of the Holy Monkey Wrench," in *Hembra* (December 1992/January 1993); "When January Thaw Strikes," in *Christian Science Monitor* (17 February 1993); "Winterlude: Human Hibernation" in *Utne Reader* (January/February 1994).

AUTOBIOGRAPHY

Biographical statement by Linda Hasselstrom, undated typescript.

UNPUBLISHED INTERVIEWS

Interview by students at Prairie Winds Writers' Conference, 1987, with answers edited and updated by Linda Hasselstrom, 1993, typescript. Personal interview by Kathleen Danker, 27 May 1994, tape recording.

BIOGRAPHICAL AND CRITICAL STUDIES

Kathleen Danker, "Reimagining the West for the Twenty-First Century: Linda Hasselstrom's View from the Plains," Western Literature Association paper (Wichita, Kans., October 1993), a discussion of Hasselstrom's advocacy of ecological responsibility and sustainability on the plains; Paul Higbee, "At Home on the Range," in *South Dakota Magazine* (September/October 1992), an article on Hasselstrom's life and work that features excerpts from letters written to her by readers and a description of how *Windbreak* was plagiarized in a Harlequin romance; John Murray, "Of Ranching and Writing: A Talk with Linda Hasselstrom," in *the Bloomsbury Review* 12 (1992), relates the healing power of nature discussed in *Land Circle* to similar themes in the writing of Thoreau and others; Geraldine Sanford, "The Dichotomy Pulse: The Beating Heart of Hasselstrom Country," in *South Dakota Review* 30 (1992), explores ways in which Hasselstrom's writing reconciles oppositions and contradictions, including the beauty and harshness of nature, the role of death in life, and the desire for privacy and self-revelation; Kathleen Wallace, "Hey, Minnesota, Come Celebrate with Us, but Leave Your Cigarette Butts at Home. Tourism and Native Appreciation of Place in Linda Hasselstrom's *Windbreak: A Woman Rancher on the Northern Plains*," Western Literature Association paper (Coeur d'Alene, Idaho, October 1989), a comparison of the subtlety and detail of Hasselstrom's descriptions of the prairie in *Windbreak* to the monumentalism of tourist attractions such as Mount Rushmore.

JOHN HAY
(b. 1915)

CYNTHIA HUNTINGTON

JOHN HAY has deep roots in New England, but it was only as an adult that he came to Cape Cod to explore and claim the home ground that would inspire so much of his best writing. This late arrival is significant, since so much of Hay's work centers on the process of discovery, of learning to be in a place fully, and on the ethos and practice of reinhabitation. Though he has ventured further afield in many of his later writings to explore a wider geographic and philosophic terrain, he remains most closely identified with the streams, beaches, dunes, woods, and marshes of the Cape, whose landscape he has wandered over, described, and defended for more than half a century.

The Cape is "a place of great circulation," Hay noted in *The Great Beach* (1963). Perched on the edge of the continent, it represents an outpost, linked to global currents and to the planetary movements of birds and fishes. It is also a symbol of the fragility of these currents and their susceptibility to human incursions. Here where the Puritan settlers made their first landfall in the new world, we can read the beginning of the continent's exploitation.

"These Cape Cod shores are migratory. They are sandy, fragile, temporary, subject to storm tides and constant erosion; they are subject to migrant hordes of people, to the onslaughts of a national, a world economy, but at the same time they are right in the middle of the kinds of migrations that make up the living world," Hay said in an address to the Cape Cod Museum of Natural History's annual meeting on 7 September 1978. These themes of exploration and exploitation are inextricably linked in Hay's writings about the Cape and beyond, drawing him into an ethical as well as philosophical relationship to the natural world.

Regarded by many as a distinguished elder and pioneer in the field of modern nature writing (Robert Finch has called him "the nature writer's writer") John Hay has published books of natural history, nature essays, poetry, and memoir. All his work shows the imprint of a writer who somewhat reluctantly accepts the title of naturalist, and who repeatedly affirms the primacy of universal processes. Hay's writing focuses again and again on the awakening of perception, curiosity, an enthusiasm for the living world, and for all life. A central theme in his work is his unshakable faith in the individual's ability to apprehend nature directly, and to understand through direct experience and careful attention the kinds of patterns in nature that inevitably include the human observer. In his concern with preserving a primary sense of nature, he has constantly argued for the humanist over the technocrat, urging an attitude of inquiry and interdependence and not one of mastery. "Civilized life has never replaced its origins in wilderness, meaning all of nature, the integral life of the earth, and has never risen above our dependence on it," he says in *The Immortal Wilderness* (1987). "There is, finally, nothing but the wild, in its rhythmic timing with the sun and stars, no aspiration lives without it" (p. 26).

John Hay was born on 31 August 1915 in Ipswich, Massachusetts, the son of Clarence Leonard and Alice Appleton Hay, and grew up in New York City and Lake Sunapee, New Hampshire. He was born into a distinguished family; both his father and grandfather were known as men of action and accomplishment. His father was a curator of archaeology for the American Museum of Natural History in New York who undertook several exploring expeditions to Mexico and the Yucatán in the early part of this century. His paternal grandfather, John Milton Hay, was Abraham Lincoln's private secretary, and later served as secretary of state under Presidents William McKinley and Theodore Roosevelt. A writer as well as a diplomat, he was a coauthor of the definitive ten-volume biography of Lincoln and also published several volumes of poems and essays. A statesman, novelist, editor, and poet, the elder Hay's varied career included years as an editorial writer for the *New York Tribune* and an appointment as U.S. ambassador to Great Britain.

It was the elder John Hay, who died ten years before John Hay was born, who first built the family's summer home, the Fells, in New Hampshire in 1891. With over one thousand acres of lakeshore pastureland on a hillside overlooking Lake Sunapee, the landscape and open country around the Fells proved an important influence on Hay's boyhood summers, providing space to roam, as well as offering a space for his imagination to grow. Lake Sunapee is eleven miles long, and as a boy Hay sailed up and down the lake on a fourteen-foot houseboat he built himself of white pine, modeled after a plan from *The American Boy's Handybook*. The boat was a flat-bottomed scow with an uptilted bow and stern and a cabin; fitting it out with a Johnson outboard, the young Hay wandered up and down the lake, fishing for sunfish and black bass,

exploring inlets and coves, climbing local mountains and spending nights on the boat.

His interest in writing and in the natural world grew together, and he dates the beginnings of his identity as a writer from those early summers. He read Whitman, Robinson Jeffers, James Fenimore Cooper, Tolstoy, and took particular pleasure in the descriptive passages in D. H. Lawrence's *Mornings in Mexico*. Thoreau he discovered early, and read with great excitement. This discovery of landscape and natural space coincided with an opening of the imagination for Hay. Though both his father and grandfather had strong literary interests, and both wrote poetry, Hay felt that his family was governed by a civility and restraint that prevented any extravagant or wayward impulses from ever taking hold. They seemed to him afraid of ideas, and he felt early on a need to break out. Later years would find him seeking a wider scope, away from the expectations of his family, serving as an enlisted man in World War II, studying with an eccentric poet on Cape Cod, and finally moving to the Cape after the war to begin a new, independent life.

Hay was educated at St. Paul's school in Concord, New Hampshire, under Master Henry Kittredge, and at Harvard, where he graduated a member of Phi Beta Kappa in 1938. After graduating, Hay moved to Washington, D.C., where he worked as the Washington correspondent for the Charleston, South Carolina, *News and Courier*. A turning point came in 1940, when, while waiting to be called to the army, he spent two months living with the poet Conrad Aiken in Brewster, Massachusetts. It was a life structured around work, talk, and, in Aiken's case, a long cocktail hour. In the mornings, the young apprentice was set to work writing sonnets and clearing woods. His time with Aiken provided an introduction to the landscape that has been central to his life and work, and also offered him an example of a different way to live, the life of a writer. The effect of this brief period was to be lifelong, instilling in him a new idea of independence, of breaking away from established ideas of how he should live, and of taking risks. While living in Brewster, Hay conceived another notion of independence: he found a piece of land for twenty-five dollars an acre and bought ten acres, intending to return.

Hay married Kristi Putnam on 14 February 1942, and moved to Cape Cod when the war ended. John and Kristi Hay live in a house off Red Top Road in Brewster, Massachusetts, on a 110-foot hill that runs across the glacial moraine about a mile back from Cape Cod Bay, known as Dry Hill. He has described the house, in *Nature's Year*, as "a ship above the trees." They spend summers in Maine, in a seaside cottage on Broad Cove where Hay devotes his time to gardening, boating between islands, watching seabirds, and writing in the mornings in a converted horse stall inside an old barn.

Early Work: Defining a Landscape

John Hay published his first book, a collection of poems entitled *A Private History*, in 1947. These early poems are most interesting (and perhaps most accurately predict Hay's later career) not for their approach or subject matter, but for the strength and complexity of their language, with its vigorous syntax and precise vocabulary. The tone of the poems is formal, controlled, the voice of a young man preoccupied with private concerns and seeing in nature primarily a reflection of or a backdrop to the human drama. Though the settings and subject matter vary, from the title poem, which recounts a soldier's (presumably Hay's) war experiences, to some poems that seem clearly to describe the Cape, Hay's language and imagery have not here achieved the immediacy for which he is known in his later writings. In "The Gull," which appears early in the book, Hay describes the bird in elevated terms that stress its separateness from the poet, seeing it as "feathers / Aflame in the cruciform of blood and sky." An even earlier poem, "The Herring-Run," describes seagulls "like vultures hunting high air of dying." (The mature writer will not confuse gulls with vultures.) Most of the poems in the collection find themselves, how-

ever, in a conventional literary world replete with images of "velvet shoes," "pale heliotrope," alleys and beggars, "and clowns with painted cheeks." It is clear from these poems that Hay is first a writer, drawn to natural history, and not a naturalist who has learned to write.

It was not until 1959, twelve years after *A Private History* was published, that *The Run*, Hay's classic Cape Cod book, appeared. In the meantime he had spent several years trying to live as a freelance writer, writing articles, reviews, and whatever else came to hand. His time with Aiken had provided a model of independent living that the aspiring writer tried to emulate, making use of his experience writing for the Charleston *News and Courier*, as well as a wartime stint as associate editor of *Yank*, the army newspaper.

The Run is considered a groundbreaking book, not only for its intense and detailed investigation of its subject, the annual migration of the alewives from the sea to freshwater to spawn and then back again, but for its invention of a contemporary sensibility for writing about nature. In David Miller's foreword to *The Run*, he describes "a more meaningful balance being developed between descriptive and experimental work." Blending personal observation with scientific inquiry and research, the book circles around to a realization of the uncertainty built into the quest for knowledge, and a sense of the abiding mystery within nature.

Each spring, close to the vernal equinox, the alewives, a type of herring, begin to enter streams, river mouths, and estuaries all along the Atlantic coast, migrating upstream to spawn in freshwater ponds, and finally returning once more to the sea. In Brewster, thousands of them travel from Cape Cod Bay and up Stony Brook, choking the brook for weeks on end. Tracing one migratory season, beginning in earliest spring with what Hay calls March's "waiting weather," through the fishes' journey inland through streams to the quiet freshwater of Walker's and Upper and Lower Mill Ponds, and back again to the ocean, Hay sets out to investigate every aspect of the fishes' lives and to try to understand the meaning of their extravagant journey.

Hay begins with his own questions: Why, and how? Why do the fish undertake such a hazardous journey, from salt water to fresh, in order to spawn? How do they know when to come in, and where? How do they find the "parent stream" where they were spawned? And why do the young stay behind in the ponds after their parents return downstream, finding their ways to the ocean without any adult direction? His attempt to answer these questions merely draws him deeper into the mystery. No one he asks can tell him what he wants to know, and everything he learns raises new questions.

Organized in an alternating sequence of personal observations and factual knowledge garnered from his research, *The Run* proceeds through the season, Hay's initiation paralleling the adventure of the fishes. He visits the brook and sees the run beginning as a trickle in April and escalating to a torrent as the fish work their way upstream through a salt marsh and against the current into brook water and into the ponds. He sees them traveling up the narrow channel, the colors of their scales changing to match the colors of the stream bed, hundreds of gulls crying overhead. He describes what he sees and then pulls away from the scene to offer scientific, historical, and anecdotal information, cutting across disciplines to create the widest possible focus. This includes a chapter on fishing and the use of alewives, incorporating bits of local history and recounting how townspeople once depended on the alewives for food and eagerly awaited their run each spring. Now just the fishes' roe is used, or the fish are sold as bait. Other lore of alewives, their various names, and details of their biology and life cycle help to weave the fishes' story into the human story.

It is a book begun in wonder, and carried forward through close observation and inquiry. Throughout, Hay positions himself as novice and seeker, a pilgrim in search of knowledge. The alewife itself serves as a totem in the search for initiation, an embodiment of mystery and meaning. He sees the first one in early spring as a "whole deep image in the air" and again as a

"radiant clarity in the water" (1965 ed., p. 15). Later he finds himself looking at "a professional from an old water world . . . deserving profound respect" (p. 15).

In his preface, Hay characterizes the book as an attempt to go farther from his own center. He is excited by the scope and extravagance of the fishes' journey. The mystery of migration is a universal phenomenon, linking the local to the vast oceans beyond. The alewives' commitment to return to a single brook, a certain pond, out of the whole world in which they wander, represents to him an example of the life force itself, allied with planetary rhythms. His attempt to follow them in his imagination has the effect of opening the world along new and mysterious lines as he exhausts all ways of knowing to arrive at another kind of intimacy through a shared wonder with his subject.

Nature's Year: The Seasons of Cape Cod (1961) is Hay's second Cape Cod book. *Nature's Year* follows the calendar, beginning in July, in "the full, crowded height of life," and ending the following June with a meditation during a late spring rain. This book comprises very short essays of three or four pages each, focusing on such close-to-home topics as insects, birds, the weather, chipmunks, mushrooms, clouds, and the change of seasons. Hay deliberately confines his explorations to the local and mundane, stating that "In a small country field is all existence and its hazards" (p. 197). In doing so he offers an account of the course of one man's observations and discoveries throughout a single year and recounts his deepening sense of connection to the place where he lives.

Nature's Year begins with a brief description of driving to Cape Cod in heavy summer traffic, over "blistering, insatiable roads," and witnessing a terrible accident along the way. Hay observes the human migration of "cars, and casualties" with some disquiet, remarking that "We come in with speed and we go away with speed, and we are both afraid and desirous of it." Thus the book begins with questions of dislocation and alienation, as Hay survives the migration and returns home to ask himself where he is. "To answer the question 'where am I?' seems

John Hay at the Brewster, Massachusetts, Herring Run

not to be an easy thing" (p. 19). The book unfolds as a series of approaches to that question, locating itself in time and space by exploring the seasons of the land. As Hay steps off the road and begins to look around himself more closely, he discovers how little he knows about what is around him, finding surprises everywhere, from the cool climate of the woods just off the road to the beetle under the bark of a tree, or the flight of a wood peewee chasing insects through the air.

Hay's conscious reclaiming of an intimate relationship with the land where he dwells leads him to define the idea of home as more than the known world around us. He says: "Just the other side of us is not only a bewildering variety but a space, which we still have to find, filled with an unfamiliar silence, or random sounds, seemingly disconnected motions, sudden flights that we witness out of the corner of an eye" (p. 19). In essays on the tenacity of lichens, wintering birds, and the reawakenings of spring, including one particularly haunting passage about the wreck of a fishing boat, the *Paulmino*, off of South Wellfleet in an April fog, Hay proceeds to underscore his point that "this is not just 'natural history' I have found, unless you are also willing to call it 'natural mystery'" (p. 196).

A major phase of John Hay's exploration of Cape Cod and its mysteries finds its culmination in his much-praised fifth book, *The Great Beach* (1963). Winner of the Burroughs Medal for Best Nature Writing of the Year in 1964, *The Great Beach* is encyclopedic in approach, cataloging every aspect of Cape Cod's vast outer coast, from its geology to its fish, dunes, beach, and wildlife. The book is also a personal account of the feelings and revelations that the land and sea awaken in him and of his search to find the true essence of Cape Cod.

Taking its title from Thoreau, who first named the forty-mile-long outer coast of Cape Cod "the Great Beach," this book of natural history and celebration of place has clear, and acknowledged, literary antecedents. In his foreword to the first printing, Hay recognizes debts to Conrad Aiken, as well as to Henry Kittredge, Henry Thoreau, and Henry Beston. ("The three Henrys," he calls them, and to each belongs a share of the credit for mapping the literary and literal territory Hay will retrace in this ambitious work.) But it is Beston's classic, *The Outermost House: A Year of Life on the Great Beach of Cape Cod* (1928), which provides the most significant influence, even appearing to serve as a structural model for *The Great Beach*. The book's organization recapitulates much of the design of Beston's great work, beginning with an overview of the Cape's geology, history, and prehistory, and proceeding to focus more closely on individual elements of the landscape. Early on, each author attempts to place himself physically in the scene, positioning himself as subject as well as interpreter. Beston accomplished this by moving into the Fo'castle, his two-room house atop a dune on Nauset Spit, where he would spend a year recording the rhythms of beach, tides, and seabirds. For Hay, his move into the landscape involves a three-day hike from Race Point to Nauset Light one June, a distance of some twenty-five miles, walking between the dunes and the sea and recounting the feelings and thoughts evoked by the experience.

He spends two nights sleeping on the beach (this was before the establishment of the Cape Cod National Seashore, whose regulations forbid camping) and finds there a landscape that is virtually unchanged since the Pilgrim's first arrival more than three centuries before. The elemental presence of the sun, sand, and sea, experienced in solitude, overwhelm his personal concerns, placing him in a timeless expanse and isolation, seemingly outside of history. Here plovers, terns, and tree swallows outnumber people; he passes the remains of two old shipwrecks, reminders of vulnerability and loss, and reflects on the human inability to ever master this landscape. The emptiness of the beach, enormous and raw, even the brilliance of the sun, unmediated, induces in him a feeling of helplessness in the face of the unimagined frontier of the sea. Though only a few miles from the nearest road, never very far from home, he feels at an enormous remove from the life he has known. Returning from this experience, Hay proceeds in the next chapters to explore the landscape with renewed curiosity, with chapters on the sea and fishes, the rhythms of the shore through erosion and wave action, and the country of the dunes, presenting these as timeless realms untouched by human experience.

Another touchstone with *The Outermost House* comes in the central chapters of *The Great Beach*. Both books, after establishing the setting and the character of the narrator, turn to grapple with the demands of the human presence in the landscape. What wider meaning, what impact do we find from our history of inhabitation here? This fruitful question raises a different set of responses for each author. A peculiar strength of Beston's book is his ability to situate a human drama directly in the heart of a meditation on aloneness in nature. Real life and death drive Beston's chapters about the Coast Guard, compelling the reader's attention with urgent, authentic stories of shipwreck and rescue at sea. Similarly, Hay turns, halfway through *The Great Beach*, to human concerns, discussing the Cape's recent population growth, settlement patterns, deforestation, and its history of fishing and sailing.

Where Beston, writing in 1928, found a remote and heroic outpost of coastguardsmen risking their lives against the sea to save wrecked sailors, Hay, writing thirty-five years later, encounters a more twisted history. Increasing pressures of growth and development, pollution, deforestation, and the impact of tourism conspire to lay waste to old ways. In chapter 6, "A Change in History," Hay contrasts "quaint" or charming images of Cape Cod with the reality of a changing population in a gradually urbanized landscape. New houses dot the hillsides, fishing fleets have declined, and the Coast Guard monitors the shore by radar. "Barren Grounds" is a melancholy chapter in which Hay visits a recently disbanded army antiaircraft post at Camp Wellfleet. Wandering among deserted buildings and lookout towers, barbed wire and firing ranges, he surveys a wasteland, flattened under reminders of war and technology. Cape Cod has been a military as well as a geographic outpost, subject to worldwide forces. The dire consequences of war are reflected for him in the denuded landscape, now bare and silent. Finally, it is an outpost not of lifesaving, but of war, that defines this human landscape.

The book returns to the beach in a more sober mood. Seen in this context, the sea, with its long vistas and reflections, its endless crash and moan, seems to hold all possibilities, a constantly changing, inexhaustible presence to which we can turn as a release from human concerns. The beach is, finally, uninhabitable, an original space of freedom and expanse, swept by nonhuman tides, connecting to greater rhythms than one individual life can encompass. The various lives which exist on this shore share a space and time that is contingent, constantly renegotiated, and mysterious. Hay's interest in the lives, both animal and vegetable, which manage to exist in this zone is imbued with a feeling of wonder in the face of an inexhaustible life force, "completely new, with a freshness made of a million years" (1980 ed., p. 86).

Middle Work: Description and Argument

The Great Beach appeared in 1963, and offered a closely rendered synthesis of natural history and philosophical inquiry. Three books of collaboration and one field guide written in the 1960s and early 1970s have a much different appeal, showing the naturalist as teacher, reaching out to the general reader with information and advice. Where the early books show John Hay as an amateur, finding his way by trial and error, and trusting his powers of observation, in these works—*A Sense of Nature* (with Arline Strong), *The Atlantic Shore* (with Peter Farb), *The Primal Alliance* (Kenneth Brower, editor), and *The Sandy Shore*—he speaks as an expert, helping to celebrate and interpret the natural world. Less strongly focused on Cape Cod, in these books Hay explores a wider geographical range and a range of more general issues, especially his growing awareness of danger to the environment and the need for conservation and protection of natural areas.

The Atlantic Shore: Human and Natural History from Long Island to Labrador (1966) is a handbook for exploring the North Atlantic coast, offering an overview of the geology, botany, and zoology of the region, including birds, animals, fish, crustaceans, plants, and insects. Hay and Farb also recount the history of the discovery and inhabitation of the coast, from the earliest explorers to the population pressures, pollution, and development of the present. The book's final chapter, "The Shore in Human Hands," is a detailed argument for conservation, concluding with a suggested list of supplemental reading and an appendix listing some fifty coastal areas worth exploring along the North Atlantic coast.

The Sandy Shore (1968) is a field guide to the beach, illustrated and full of factual information to enable the reader to recognize the residents of the beach, from the lowly sand flea to the graceful shorebirds. It is a book addressed to the beachgoer and vacationer, encouraging the reader to stop and look again, to discover the delicate balance between animal and environment.

Hay's purpose here, clearly, is to educate, not only by providing facts, but by challenging assumptions and encouraging, even chastising, the reader to show a greater respect for nature. He is relentless in his insistence on the effects of human use and misuse of the shore and oceans. Reviewing *The Atlantic Shore* for the *New York Times* (16 August 1966), Bosley Crowther remarked: "No one could dare toss a beer can on the beach after he has read this book." (This was in 1966—when not tossing the beer can might actually have seemed like a new idea!)

In the midst of this descriptive, educational period, in 1969, Hay published a book in an entirely new tone, a credo and call to arms, the environmental manifesto *In Defense of Nature*. Here Hay argues passionately: "Our livelihood, even our sanity, depends on a natural environment which is allowed its own proper growth and functions" (p. 35). He stresses that our survival as a species hangs in the balance: "Man against the natural world is man against himself" (p. 208).

In Defense of Nature is a sermon of particulars. Hay recounts more than twenty years of exploration along the Atlantic seashore, mostly in Maine and on Cape Cod, watching tides and seasonal migrations, investigating the lives of clams, shore birds, and fish. The cumulative effect of his travels yields a realization of the human impact on all these systems. Noting the effects of pollution on animal and plant life, he catalogs losses, describing an encounter with a dovekie coated with oil, and giving a long description of the history of DDT and the near destruction of the osprey. He concludes that our destruction of the natural world springs directly from our own alienation from nature and our inability to perceive our absolute reliance on it. He argues the need for a change in attitudes: we need to slow down and reconnect, to learn again to look and listen to what is around us, to learn lessons in codependence with all of creation.

When it appeared in 1969, during the early years of the environmental movement (a term Hay himself distrusts), *In Defense of Nature* marked a departure from his earlier work. More cry of alarm than pastoral idyll, more argument than description, *In Defense of Nature* can be read in the light of its time, when much new information about damage to the environment through pollution and destruction of habitats was coming to light. Though some of the problems Hay discusses have since been addressed, in most cases they have been supplanted by more complex ones, so his central points remain unfortunately relevant today, while the list of our offenses has grown much longer.

Spirit of Survival: A Natural and Personal History of Terns (1974) is a gentler book than *In Defense of Nature*, a narrative celebrating the life history of the tern, but it is still written out of a deep sense of unease. "So I found that one wild bird's egg, shaped like the globe itself, lying out in open territory, was a sign of the supreme risk in which all life engages" (p. 2). Many species of terns are now endangered; even in the best of times they are a species that lives in a delicate balance with their environment, subject to storms and predators, displaced by gulls and humans, threatened by development. They represent for Hay the struggle of nature to continue against heavy odds and the spirit and will to survive on the brink of existence.

Hay follows the terns' nesting season, their migrations, their courtships and care of the young, gathering information on various species, including the least, arctic, common, and roseate terns. Terns are migratory water birds with a vast range, and to understand them requires an extension of the imagination to take in a global point of view. Hay travels to several continents to observe the relationships within tern colonies and describe their various habitats, rituals, and behavior.

Hay's evident admiration for these birds lends a subjective aspect to the information he presents, resulting in a highly personal and philosophic narrative. He identifies with their struggle and tenacity, aware of what he believes to be a superiority of adaptation and spirit in these fragile birds. They are lifelong travelers, graceful and quick, vulnerable and filled with the hunger of life. For Hay they represent a call out of himself, offering a regenerative association with a dynamic nature, and an invitation to understand the "common planetary existence" of all things.

Later Work: Primal Affinities

The later phase of John Hay's career begins in 1981 with *The Undiscovered Country*, which looks back to his early years on Cape Cod following World War II. More than twenty years after *The Run* documented the young writer's discovery of the energy and passion of the fishes' migration and his own excitement in the face of that phenomenon, the author, by now in his mid-sixties, recalls his beginnings on the Cape, revealing the sense of disillusionment and uprootedness he felt then, which fired his search for a home in nature.

In a series of nineteen connected essays, *The Undiscovered Country* ranges from Massachusetts to New Hampshire and Maine, but

its center remains the home ground of Cape Cod. Of all Hay's books, this one seems most intimate with human weakness, even at times veering close to despair as he recalls his own youthful confusion and fears in an unsettled time. Feeling permanently uprooted, a stranger in the land of his birth, he lays the blame for this dislocation on the war's violence and on the march of technology. He senses that the world is moving too fast and bypassing natural rhythms. Feeling stranded by history, "part of the tidal wrack" (p. 16), he struggles to find connections and to forge a way to identify with the place he has come to.

In a telling and memorable passage, he recounts a dream of seeing his house, newly built overlooking Cape Cod Bay, floating in the ocean like a raft, with waves breaking over it, the floor leaking. This image crystallizes his precarious sense of self at the time, the feeling of being engulfed by immense and indifferent forces. Nothing he can think or imagine leads him anywhere and he asks how he can hope to start again with no guidance.

Looping back to the past, Hay distills his years of experiences as he looked for ways to ground himself in this new place. He tells of his joy at finding unexpected links that help him to understand the intricate relationships between people and nature. The calm fecundity of the tidal flats, changing light on water, the run of the alewives in March and April, all these lead him closer to a reach of consciousness that is able to interpenetrate the living world. He also looks back to the prehistory of the land, subsuming his personal history in the ancient round of tides and waves and thousand-year migrations. He finds release and perspective in contemplating "the oldest place on earth," the tidal flats where barnacles and plankton live and die, where shells and fish eggs wash up on shore and life continues unchanged for millions of years. These links with the past lead him out of himself and enable him to develop a wider identification with the world around him.

The Undiscovered Country falls into two main sections: "Dimensions of the Past," which unearths a personal as well as a primal past, and "Live with Me," which Hay sees as nature's deepest invitation. When we change the face of the earth through our power and progress, when we redefine its mysteries and regard scientific intelligence as the sole way of knowing the world, we risk forgetting nature. Hay quotes Henry James to say that nature's appeal is not "Do something kind for me," but "Live with me" and make a commitment to knowing and sharing the world as it is.

Hay discovers two kinds of commitment in "Live with Me." He praises things that go and things that stay, both offering lessons on how to get your bearings. The chapter "Homing" extends his inquiry into the magical logic of migrations; he celebrates the seasonal movements of alewives, geese, and swallows, amazed by all the birds and fishes and turtles that move around an invisible axis to points of origin and departure. Their ability to sense their place in time and space and to time their arrivals and departures with the calendar show an intimate familiarity with the earth. He has an equal respect for life that is rooted within its own particular circumstance. In "Living with Trees" he looks at the rough, woody substantiality of trees that hang on to the earth with real roots, growing "out of life's original sources" (pp. 109–110). Trees "identify their ground," lose and grow leaves; wind and moonlight move through their branches: they bend, "braced against the wobbling, racing planet" (p. 115). The trees move with us all as the planet moves; they move in time and into time; they lift into the sky. Hay's identification with trees joins them with wider currents. "We wait, and we move out at the same time. It is not only the long-distance migrants who make daring leaps into the unknown" (p. 115).

The kinds of connections Hay is seeking, such as those between trees and birds, must be arrived at intuitively, not through research, experiment, or any collection of facts. If they are "true," it is a truth to be recognized and felt, rather than proven. In his foreword to *The Undiscovered Country*, Hay broaches this idea of truth and sets out to define it beyond the purely factual,

objective level. He argues the necessity of a subjective, inner, even a spiritual truth, and he will find this truth for himself. He writes that "science, though our major explorer, is not enough," fearing estrangement through over-definition as much as through ignorance. Hay objects to mere scientific designation as an end in itself, distrusting the tendency of its language to appropriate rather than enter experience. He seeks instead a "supreme innocence"—the innocence in which all beings were nurtured. We were born into the great democracy of nature . . . and more and more people are looking for ways to be its citizens again" (p. 12). A key word in his writing, which appears again and again in various contexts, is "primal." This is, for Hay, a word of highest praise, signaling the presence of what is most essential, nourishing, valuable in its own right.

The undiscovered country of the title refers to two things: the landscape of Cape Cod that Hay comes to as a young man and a stranger, and, more important, to the sense of connectedness and interchange that we may miss even as we think we have the countryside "known." Without it we remain newcomers to these shores, still unable to see what is around us, feeling cut off and out of favor with creation.

Summoning an extreme example of estrangement from place, Hay begins his thirteenth book, *The Immortal Wilderness* (1987), with a visit to Los Alamos in 1950. Calling it "Main Street on the Moon," he evokes a town cloistered behind security checkpoints in the middle of the desert, its mysteries carefully disguised behind the facade of a compact new community. Bright, clean, and bare, this is an abstract place, steeped in an air of unreality. There is a high school, but no graveyard (people are shipped home to be buried), community clubs and organizations, but no real friendships, only acquaintances, since everyone must keep secrets in their jobs. No one owns real estate. Hay depicts this scene in some detail, letting it serve as an allegory for our culture's disengagement from the land in pursuit of science. Of course, all the secrecy and deliberate unreality of Los Alamos is supposed to be for a "greater good"—in the name of national security and weapons control—an argument Hay distrusts almost as much as he distrusts the neat, regulated exterior behind which these laboratories have cultivated enough power to blow up the world.

This unsettling glimpse of the nuclear fifties is immediately followed by a quick overview of American history, which Hay portrays as a story of violent settlement and land grabs, of legal rights construed as open season on both wildlife and wilderness. The settlers' conquest has gone hand in hand with an idea of "taming" nature, an idea Hay sees as completely discredited and the cause of much harm. He describes our society as "a force of natural energy gone out of bounds" and concludes that "we have not tamed ourselves" (p. 32).

In twenty essays discussing such subjects as phalaropes at Hudson's Bay, oil spills, sea pollution, trees, rocks, fish and turtles, encounters with wildlife, birds and their behavior, Hay argues that no creature is greater or lesser than another and that all are part of one system. All participate in the same life; all inhabit the same world. Later in the book he ventures farther afield, from coastal Maine to Florida, New Hampshire, Texas, and Mexico, to the rain forests of Costa Rica and to the edges of the great ice cap covering Greenland, exploring the unseen links between geographically separate regions. Terns and alewives continue to be important touchstones as he struggles to express his sense of interconnection and codependence, his belief that "the whole genius of the earth is to contain multitudes of distinct communities, each of which expresses the profound capacities of life in its own way" (p. 62).

The dark side of this interconnection, of course, is universal vulnerability. Recognizing how one thing affects another, how all systems are tied together, we cannot help but be aware of our dependence on the earth. In the face of continued environmental destruction, none of our discoveries is a substitute for nature. And though our willful disengagement from nature encourages the illusion that we are not obligated,

as a species, to anything beyond ourselves, this sense of isolation does not release us, and we remain subject to natural law.

While many of Hay's earlier natural histories depict the workings of nature in sensitive detail and challenge us to search for a more appropriate relationship to it, in *The Immortal Wilderness* Hay addresses the underlying idea of wilderness itself. Wilderness, he says, is not outside us—even if we want it to be. Instead it is the fundamental ground of our being, the very texture of our life and death. Wilderness is not vanishing, absent, or past; it is the ground beneath our feet, where the roots of our human nature are laid. Its primal laws are everywhere seen, whether in the branching arrangement of a tree or the flight of a bird. Wilderness remains for Hay the "great container of life and death, the earth's immortal genius" (p. 14).

The Immortal Wilderness is much more closely argued than *In Defense of Nature* (1969), which it resembles in many ways, as an attempt to articulate the inner coherence of the natural world. Similarly, *The Bird of Light* (1991) revisits familiar territory, with a second look at Hay's beloved terns. In this book Hay is less focused on the birds' struggle for survival and more on their spirit, represented here as an affinity for the sun, an observation that is at once abstract and actual. "They rise up, dip, turn, and swing like a casting of silver facets into the air, or dancing flowers, alternating the dark shading of their backs and the white of their bellies. When they flip over on their sides, reflecting the sunlight, it is as if they were deliberately courting it" (p. 18).

Loosely structured around a year in the life of Gray's Beach, a large sand dune on the edge of a salt marsh near his home, *The Bird of Light* mixes personal observations with facts about terns, horseshoe crabs, humpback whales, and other marine life. Hay watches terns through the nesting season, marking their mating and brooding rituals, their competition for food, their relation to the environment. He also revisits the grim facts brought up in *Spirit of Survival*: how terns are threatened by development, off-road vehicles, other birds. Though he collects facts in order to arrive at a clear view of the birds, he is aware that facts alone are not enough. He wants, as well, a mental union with nature, seeking to connect with what the terns represent to him as well as with their literal presence. This tension between his use of scientific information and his distrust of the objective approach is, interestingly, never quite resolved. Instead he achieves a lyrical poise in contradiction, balancing the two in opposition. The birds represent a poetic longing for him, a sense of home and homing as well as a sense of flight and release, a sense of vulnerability and of tough survival. All this is present before his gaze, and constantly unreachable, and since he cannot follow the birds along their journey across thousands of miles of water, he learns to wait for them to return to his shore. "The season gradually delivers them and they come," harbingers of continuity, risk, and survival.

A Beginner's Faith in Things Unseen (1994) is John Hay's fourteenth book, a collection of rememberance and observation. Here he returns to his boyhood summers in New Hampshire, recalling his childhood intuitions and initiation into nature. He speaks of a boy's education, and also, miseducation. His childhood memory paints a family picture of order and post-Victorian restraint that he was able to overcome partly through his experiences of nature during his summers in New Hampshire.

Other essays in the book discuss more recent experiences, such as the annual return of the swallows to the barn where he writes during the summers in Maine. Whether discussing the past or the present, Hay's focus here is on the lifelong process of opening himself to his surroundings, the challenge of responding to nature and a readiness to admit the unexpected. Writing in a gentle, contemplative tone, he seems more interested in discovering how he knows than what he knows. He remembers how as a child he gradually came to notice and interpret the world around him; interspersed with more recent observations, the past and present are played off one another to produce a picture of lifelong questioning, learning, and increased sensitivity to the given world.

Conclusion

From his beginnings as a poet, John Hay came to natural history out of his curiosity and love for the landscape he had adopted. Hay's first love is language, a lens he uses to focus on the world in order to yield him his observations of detail, pattern, and resemblance. Where his early books convey a sense of the mystery of nature and a willingness to approach the natural world again and again as an initiate, the works of the late 1960s and 1970s seem to grow more urgent, and even fierce. Their mood is darker, with a growing feeling of loss, as Hay confronts the continuing damage done to the natural world by humankind's so-called progress and our society's endless mobility. The early works rely heavily on a faith in his ability to describe nature, and with description to point beyond the perceived world. What the later work accomplishes is to bring together these feelings of wonder with those of loss, excitement along with fear, and to achieve a personal synthesis, a psychologizing of nature that brings it home to the self. These recent works seem to unite the factual with a search for greater intimacy and personal connection to the life force in nature. What is recovered through grief in *The Undiscovered Country* is brought more deeply into the self in *The Immortal Wilderness*. *The Bird of Light* is a triumph of the imagination in which identification with the birds releases the writer's spirit to soar toward the unreachable from a centrifugal point, while *A Beginner's Faith in Things Unseen* looks back to gather a sense of wholeness from past and present observations.

"You might think, after many years of teaching a class called 'Nature Writers,' that I would know what nature meant, but I do not," he writes in "The Nature Writer's Dilemma," an essay that leads off the natural history essay collection *On Nature* (1986). "The word comes from the Latin 'to be born,' which is fundamental enough, and puts it under the heading of abiding mystery." Mystery, for Hay, is an intimation of greatness, of primal capacity, beyond the limited understanding and control of human beings.

Though lauded as an accomplished naturalist, with a wide command of factual information, and praised as a skilled interpreter of facts, Hay seems to have grown to distrust the scientific worldview. Taken in isolation, or over and above the evidence of the senses and intuition, this view tends to alienate us from our original response to the environment. He finds difficulty with terms such as "ecology," "the environment," or "conservation," which, while they may be politically useful in defending the natural world, "hardly guarantee an intimacy with its sources" (pp. 7–8). He distrusts science when it separates the perceived and the perceiver or colonizes other disciplines, when the naming of a thing, its classification and label, begins to stand in for the thing itself, substituting an attitude of ownership and mastery for one of inquiry.

This insistence on a personal experience of nature has ethical as well as philosophical applications for Hay. As writer, naturalist, conservationist, teacher, and local citizen, he has affirmed the importance of the local through service and action. A founder and former president of the Cape Cod Museum of Natural History, he has seen that institution grow under his direction from its beginnings as a small children's museum housed in the Brewster town hall to a major regional center for environmental education. President of the museum for twenty-five years, he has continued to serve as a senior fellow on its board of trustees. As chairman of the Brewster Conservation Commission (1964–1971), Hay led many fights against overdevelopment on the Cape, particularly the battle to preserve local salt marshes and other critical habitats. He was named Conservationist of the Year in 1970 by the Massachusetts Wildlife Federation and was a member of the standing committee of the Massachusetts Trustees of Reservations from 1975 through 1980.

Hay has also worked closely with the New Hampshire Division of Parks and Recreation and with the U.S. Fish and Wildlife Service to establish a land studies center at the John Hay Wildlife Refuge at the Fells, the family's former estate on Lake Sunapee. The stately country house and its surrounding formal gardens passed to the Fish and Wildlife Service at Alice Hay's death in 1987. Earlier, in 1960, Clarence and Alice Hay had deeded most of the estate's one thousand acres to the Society for the Protection of New Hampshire Forests. Restored and managed by the New Hampshire Division of Parks and Recreation as a center for the study of interactions between individuals and the land, the Fells will host conferences and seminars and serve as a resource center for land studies in New England.

His teaching is of a piece with his conservation work. Hay served as visiting professor of environmental studies at Dartmouth College for fifteen years, teaching courses called "Nature Writing," and "Nature and Human Values." This is in keeping with his aim of uniting disciplines, educating consciousness. He spent fall terms of those years in New Hampshire and divided the rest of the year between Cape Cod and his summer home in Bremen, Maine. Since his retirement from regular teaching, he visits and speaks regularly at writing conferences across the country.

In 1964, Hay received the prestigious Burroughs Medal for Best Nature Writing of the Year for *The Great Beach*, his fifth book. Established in 1926 by the American Museum of Natural History, the Burroughs Medal was described by John Wilkes in the *Los Angeles Times Book Review* as "the equivalent of a Nobel Prize in the little world of nature writing." He has been Phi Beta Kappa poet at Harvard, and in 1978 was named the first recipient of the Richard D. Perkins Award given by the Henry David Thoreau School of Wilderness Studies at Eastern Connecticut State College. This award is presented to "people who have absorbed the natural and human history of a particular place, found its essence, and expressed it in some form."

Admired by other nature writers and honored alike for his writings and his conservation work, Hay seems nonetheless not to have received the broader critical or popular attention that might be expected, given his long and prolific career. His writing has been termed sensitive and poetic, while also being commended for its sound scientific observation and its balance between descriptive and experimental work. Rare criticisms have found his comparisons and parallels with the human condition to be strained, though thoughtful, but for the most part he remains respected though somewhat obscure to the general public in spite of his wide history of publication.

As the genre of nature writing has grown more visible, however, a greater recognition seems to be accruing to Hay as a pioneer of the genre, whose approach to nature has been both radical and sustained. In October of 1992, the Myrin Foundation and *Orion* magazine sponsored a three-day colloquium on Cape Cod to honor John Hay and his contributions to conservation and to the field of nature writing. Held in a Coast Guard station on the glacial bluffs above the great beach of Cape Cod, the colloquium was attended by more than forty writers, teachers, students, editors, and conservationists from across the country who met to honor Hay and to inaugurate the foundation's John Hay Award. This award honors individuals whose life's work has demonstrated significant achievement in at least two of the three areas in which Hay has excelled: nature writing, conservation, and environmental education. The John Hay Award bears an inscription from *The Bird of Light*: "The world begins and ends in love and unexplored affinities."

Selected Bibliography

WORKS OF JOHN HAY

A Private History, poems (New York: Duell, Sloan and Pearce, 1947); *The Run* (Doubleday, 1959; rev. ed., 1965; repr., New York: Norton, 1979); *Nature's Year: The Seasons of Cape Cod* (Garden City, N.Y.: Doubleday, 1961); *A Sense of Nature*, with Arline Strong (Garden City, N.Y.: Doubleday, 1962); *The Great Beach* (Garden City, N.Y.: Doubleday, 1963; repr., New York: Norton, 1980); *The Atlantic Shore: Human and Natural History from Long Island to Labrador*, with Peter Farb (New York: Harper & Row, 1966; repr., Parnassus Imprints, 1982); *The Sandy Shore* (Chatham, Mass.: Chatham, 1968); *Six Poems* (privately printed, n.p., 1969); *In Defense of Nature* (Boston: Atlantic Monthly Press, 1969); *The Primal Alliance: Earth and Ocean*, photos by Richard Kauffman, ed. by Kenneth Brower (San Francisco: Friends of the Earth, 1971); *Spirit of Survival: A Natural and Personal History of Terns* (New York: Dutton, 1974); *The Undiscovered Country* (New York: Norton, 1981); "The Nature Writer's Dilemma," in *On Nature: Essays on Nature, Landscape, and Natural History*, ed. by Daniel Halpern (San Francisco: North Point, 1986); *The Immortal Wilderness* (New York: Norton, 1987); *The Bird of Light* (New York: Norton, 1991); *A Beginner's Faith in Things Unseen* (Boston: Beacon, 1994).

BIOGRAPHICAL AND CRITICAL STUDIES

Hal Borland, review of *The Atlantic Shore*, in *Natural History* 75 (October 1966); Bosley Crowther, review of *The Atlantic Shore*, in *New York Times* (18 August 1966); Robert Finch, "A Place of Wide Circulation, A View of the John Hay Colloquium October 3–5, 1992," in *Orion* 11 (summer 1992); Thomas Foster, review of *In Defense of Nature*, in *New York Times Book Review* (21 December 1969); Donald Gropman, review of *In Defense of Nature*, in *Christian Science Monitor* (28 November 1969); Laurie Lane-Zucker, "The John Hay Award," *Orion* 11 (summer 1992); Thomas J. Lyon, *This Incomperable Lande* (Boston: Houghton Mifflin, 1989); Jake Page, "Closely Watched Terns," *Oceans* 20 (November/December 1987); Stephan Salisbury, review of *The Immortal Wilderness*, in *New York Times Book Review* (8 February 1987); Stephen Trimble, *Words from the Land, Encounters with Natural History Writing* (Salt Lake City: Gibbs M. Smith, 1988); Frederick Turner, *Spirit of Place* (San Francisco: Sierra Club Books, 1989); John Wilkes, *Los Angeles Times*, "A Walk Through Nature—With a Poet," in *Los Angeles Times Book Review* (November 1991), review of *Bird of Light*.

EDWARD HOAGLAND
(b. 1932)

DAVID W. TEAGUE

EDWARD HOAGLAND is the author of five novels, a collection of short stories, six collections of nonfiction prose, and two travel narratives. His more than one hundred essays have been published in such periodicals as *Esquire*, the *Paris Review*, the *Village Voice*, and the *New Yorker*. Hoagland has taken as his subject the disappearing wilderness, the Golden Rule, the circus, boxing, bears, marriage, moose, tigers, tugboat captains, turtles, and a host of other things, many of which are drawn from the natural world.

Because he so often treats the nonhuman world in his work, Hoagland is usually characterized as a "nature writer." Nevertheless, while two of his novels, *Cat Man* (1955) and *Seven Rivers West* (1986) are, in his own words, "full of nature," and while his essay collections abound in treatments of the natural world, he is, paradoxically, an avowed "city rat" who returns to New York after visits to wild places with a sign of relief and a great deal of enthusiasm for the people he encounters there. His readers thus find that Hoagland is a unique kind of nature writer, one whose attention is always at least partially directed at his own desires as a human being, even while he immerses himself in the nonhuman world.

Edward Hoagland was born on 21 December 1932, in New York City, the son of an oil company attorney. He holds the A.B. degree from Harvard University (1955) and has taught writing at the New School for Social Research, Rutgers University, Sarah Lawrence College, Columbia University, Bennington College, Brown University, and the University of California at Davis.

Essays

The essay has a special place in Edward Hoagland's heart; his most striking nature writing is in this genre. As Hoagland posits in "What I Think, What I Am," collected in *The Tugman's Passage* (1982), "the extraordinary flexibility of essays is what has enabled them to ride out rough weather and hybridize into forms that suit the times" (p. 27). One of the characteristics of the times to which Hoagland has suited his essays is the increasingly conflicted relationship between human beings and the natural world.

Hoagland's essays, even those concerned with exploring wild natural places, are seldom exclusively about nonhuman concerns. Hoagland's is a perspective that makes specific demands on humans in the natural world. One of his best-known reflections on a wild place, for instance, "Walking the Dead Diamond River," collected in the 1973 book of the same name, includes a digression on "the American brand of walking," which Hoagland contrasts with Coleridge's, Car-

Edward Hoagland

lyle's, and Wordsworth's mode of perambulation. As Hoagland explores the relationship between the human and the natural worlds, he makes diversions to explore ways in which the relationship might be improved. Here, he suggests that Americans simply learn to walk through nature more gracefully. In Hoagland's nature essays, then, wild things provide one of his subjects, but people invariably provide the other, and their relationship becomes a *tertium quid* that is in many cases the most intriguing subject of all.

The complex prose style Hoagland employs to accommodate his multiplicity of subjects has proven difficult to characterize. Its organization is associative, allusive, and highly personal. His essays avoid traditional hierarchical structures and, instead, follow Hoagland's imagination as it moves from subject to subject. Hoagland rarely subordinates one idea to another, rarely indicates directly to the reader which points are more important than others. Rather, he often leaves readers to draw their own conclusions about his intentions.

Thus, readers who have a commitment to the tradition of linear narrative have been uncertain what to make of his style. Critics have complained, for instance, that at times Hoagland's prose can "risk organizational chaos" (Edwards, p. 7), or that Hoagland is in fact "sometimes . . . a clumsy writer" (Hall, p. 669). Certainly it is the case that reading Edward Hoagland's prose requires strict concentration, lest one become stranded somewhere along a digression, but it is not the case that his prose lacks organization. As Geoffrey Wolff, Alfred Kazin, and other critics have discerned, readers must learn to recognize nonlinear organizational strategies in order to reap the rewards of Hoagland's prose. Kazin writes enthusiastically in his review of *Walking the Dead Diamond River* of Hoagland's "reader-capsizing sentence[s]," which comprise an apt vehicle for expressing observations of "city street, circus lot, go-go girls, freight trains, juries in the jury room plus, and especially, any and every surviving patch of North American wild he can get to moon around in" (p. 31). Wolff, in his introduction to *The Edward Hoagland Reader* (1979), notes that "the most radical quality of [Hoagland's] architecture...is the detour" (p. xxiv), which takes him away, but never too far away, from the central design of the piece at hand.

Both Hoagland's fiction and his nonfiction exhibit this digressive style, but his "detours" are most striking when they arise in his nonfiction essays. As Hoagland himself has said, "essays presuppose a certain standard of education in the reader, a world ruled by some sort of order...where people seek not fragmentation but a common bond" (quoted in the introduction to *The Edward Hoagland Reader*, p. xxv). Thus, Hoagland's style seems more transgressive of traditional boundaries of genre in his essays, because it is there that he most directly challenges the notion of order; improvisation is his organizing principle.

Hoagland has in fact questioned the existence of some genre boundaries. The distinction between the nonfiction essay and other literary categories, most notably fiction, may, he suspects, be a specious one. He claims that "prose

EDWARD HOAGLAND

has no partitions now. . . . No forms exist anymore, except that to work as a single observer, using the resources of only one mind, and to work with words—that is being a writer" (quoted in Wakefield, p. 8). In Hoagland's hands, the traditional, strictly ordered structure of the nonfiction essay gives way to the digressive, discursive, associative structures of fiction; Hoagland's essay style can be said to represent a genre innovation.

As the natural world recedes in the face of modern culture, such a wide-ranging literary approach to the natural world is not only appropriate, it is in fact necessary. Wild nature is becoming more difficult to locate, literally, and Hoagland's discursive style goes after it—pursues it.

In discussing Hoagland's style and subject matter, Alfred Kazin has concluded that "only fiction writers now seem capable of satisfying our demand for 'facts'" (p. 31). Hoagland feels as well that a fictive imagination must be part of writing about nature, simply because nature is disappearing, becoming inaccessible both to modern readers and to modern writers. In his essay "Writing Wild," collected in *Red Wolves and Black Bears* (1976), Hoagland describes the difficulties inherent in contemporary nature writing: "It's becoming impossible for any writer to depict from firsthand experience a real wilderness. From now on an act of imagination will be required, equivalent to the effort of a man who is not a war veteran writing a war novel: even if the writer be Stephen Crane, some of the richness of reality is going to be lost" (p. 106). Hoagland's reaction to this loss of the "richness of reality" is to modify the literary form in which he treats the natural world, the better to capture what is left of it. Thus, in Hoagland's nature writing, style and subject matter become functions of one another.

Hoagland, then, does not compose pastoral idylls; to find a straightforward paean to the beauties of nature in his writing is uncommon. Nor is his approach to the nonhuman world in any way a "biocentric" or "deep ecology" approach. Edward Hoagland's experience of nature is always a human's experience of the nonhuman world, and the human at the center of the experience is usually Edward Hoagland.

Hoagland often expresses amusement at finding himself an arbiter of nature for his culture: "How long," he asks in "Writing Wild," "will these readers continue to miss walking in the woods enough to employ oddballs like me and Edward Abbey and Peter Matthiessen and John McPhee to do it for them?" (p. 107). His answer is, "Not long, I suspect," for he sees that wilderness is becoming a dead issue for Americans—it "no longer exists at all except in the terms the public allows it to" (p. 106).

Surprisingly enough, however, Hoagland sympathizes with this "public" to an extent. He admits that at times he contemplates "embarking upon still another trip to some bleak national swamp or public forest, and I think, Good God, who needs it? Like anybody else, I'm lonely enough right in the bosom of family and friends" (p. 108). Hoagland insists upon the importance of the wild as "excitement, the hope of visions and some further understanding—that old, old boondoggle perpetrated by the wilderness—draws [him] on" (p. 108). But, as attractive as the wilderness is, it still represents something whose influence ought to be examined with a certain amount of circumspection—it does, after all, perpetrate a "boondoggle" upon those who embrace it.

But humans perpetrate various acts upon nature, as well, and humans are consistently actors in Hoagland's nature writing. Humanist and realist that he is, Hoagland constructs nature as intricately related to human activity. This is why, in his view, humans have made such a brutal impact on the nonhuman world. "We don't know enough about what has been destroyed of the natural world even to take inventory," he laments in his essay "Other Lives," from *Red Wolves and Black Bears*, and he goes on to conclude that "though there should be other reasons besides what we call nature to believe in the permanence of the world, if nature in health and wealth and variety is to be permitted to exist only for its recreational value to man, then we must base our convictions about the world's permanence in the meanwhile, on the permanence of him" (p. 268). Unlike many American nature writers, Hoagland does seem to feel that the fate of the nonhuman world is predicated on the permanence of humankind. Still, although he expresses serious doubts about the ultimate survival of both the human and the nonhuman worlds, his doubts do not dampen his enthusiasm for either.

Especially his enthusiasm for the human world. It's remarkable, given the critic Robert Jones's comment that "the next best thing to a walk in the woods . . . is to read Ted Hoagland on the subject" (p. 10), that Hoagland demonstrates in his work such a keen interest in what people do. He makes claims for cities that seem not in keeping, perhaps, with someone consistently characterized as a "nature writer." He insists, for example, in his essay "Thoughts on Returning to the City After Five Months on a Mountain where the Wolves Howled," that "city people are more supple than country people, and the sanest city people, being more tested and more broadly based in the world of men, are the sanest people on earth" (*Red Wolves and Black Bears*, p. 3). This is an unlikely sentiment for a nature writer who more than once has been called a modern-day Thoreau. But in Hoagland's world, there is no wilderness unless there are people to appreciate it. R. Z. Sheppard has felicitously described this complexly rendered nonhuman world, Hoagland's wilderness, as a "bewilderness, an inexhaustible human resource that Hoagland exploits while scarcely leaving a track on the forest floor" (p. 88). Sheppard's is an astute assessment of Hoagland's world, a world in which wild nature is indeed a resource that will continue to exist as long as there are humans interested in imagining it.

Although, as noted, Hoagland has imagined this world in nearly one hundred essays addressing widely varied subjects and employing numerous prose strategies, there is in fact a central style to his essays, familiarity with which can be a great deal of help in approaching his work. "Fred King on the Allagash," which appears in *Walking the Dead Diamond River*, provides an opportunity to get at this style, to see Hoagland

construct his "bewilderness" in the literary space where the nonhuman world and human language converge. As with most of Edward Hoagland's essays, "Fred King on the Allagash" does not proceed along one line of thought. The title indicates that what follows will be a descriptive essay about a man on a river in Maine, but instead of discussing either the man or the river, the essay's opening paragraph articulates the two sides most commonly taken in wilderness debates.

Hoagland tells us in this introduction that the logging industry counters arguments for preserving wilderness areas by claiming that there is no longer any "tract of forest that hasn't already been logged, no river drainage that hasn't been dammed." Conservationists nevertheless reply, "It's all we have." "And so the battle is joined," Hoagland writes (p. 79). Initially, then, Hoagland sets up in his piece the sort of objective conflict one expects to see worked out in a traditional nonfiction essay. Despite the obvious importance of the debate in the author's mind, however, this is the last direct mention of it in the essay.

Hoagland next introduces the title characters of the essay. The second paragraph describes the Allagash River, the river's official designation as "wild," and it puts Hoagland in a canoe on the Allagash with his guide, Fred King, and a middle-aged couple who has also secured King's service as a guide. From this point in the narrative, Fred King and the Allagash will remain somewhere in the narrator's consciousness, but they will move aside often to make way for the essay's various digressions.

Because "Fred King on the Allagash" develops in discursive patterns representative of most of Hoagland's essays, labels for it such as "descriptive," "informative," or "persuasive" are unsatisfactory. Although the essay does describe, inform, and persuade, Hoagland never devotes himself explicitly to any one purpose. On the surface the essay seems to be, apart from its odd first paragraph, a chronological narrative of Hoagland's trip down the Allagash, interspersed with digressions into personal history, natural history, and imaginative fancy. But close attention reveals that the narrative is driven by subtle questioning. The essay implicitly poses a series of questions about how people define the term "wilderness" — is this river in fact "wild," as the state has designated it? How do humans treat such a place? In the end, is it possible to adjudicate the conflict between the logging companies and the conservationists of the essay's introduction?

By appearing simply to observe as he canoes, Hoagland manages not only to imply such questions without asking them directly, he also manages to overcome the impulse to give unequivocal answers to them, and instead supplies his readers with material from which they may generate their own answers. As he describes Fred King, for instance, Hoagland not only develops him as a character in his essay, but he also forces his readers to confront some hard facts about the myths surrounding humans in the wilderness. King seems like a modern-day mountain man, a strong soul who quit college and lived in the Maine woods during the Depression to support himself through trapping. He seems to thrive on isolation in the wild woods: "he still likes to be by himself. His ideas sound as if they had been worked out in isolation in the woods and perhaps spoken first in a loud voice all alone" (p. 81).

Yet King has spent most of his life, as do most Americans, in civilization. He has worked on highway crews and, ironically, was once a real estate developer. Hoagland describes him as insisting that he is only a " 'fake woodsman,' and that although occasionally he spoke for some of the old fellows who couldn't go on TV themselves and spout off, if we wanted to meet the real thing we'd have to go farther afield" (p. 91).

But no one in the narrative, no Hoagland, not his companions on the trip, and certainly not Fred King, shows any inclination to "go farther afield." The "wild"-designated river, even though it is at times choked with tourists, provides enough of the challenges of the wilderness, as Hoagland shows in page after page of description of the difficulties involved in navigating it. No one in the narrative has the desire to penetrate any deeper.

Thus, Hoagland is careful to demonstrate the ambivalence with which he and his companions regard even this much state-designated "wilderness," and to demonstrate how, even though it is domesticated to a large degree by canoeists, it still compromises the humans who encounter it. Fred King believes, with Hoagland's endorsement, that the current crop of canoeists on the river are a paradoxical band of wilderness travelers. King calls them "pilgrims" in nature who are "groping for something" (p. 84). The people on the wild river are products of civilization compelled to make the journey to the marginal wilderness to find what is lacking in their ordinary lives. Hoagland and the other "pilgrims" "believe . . . that even in its protected status the Allagash River is being altered irrevocably, and so they have rushed to experience it before the herds finish it off." But the difference between rushing pilgrims and finishing herds is not large. And these pilgrims do not entirely like what nature holds for them, however much they seek it: "they think that a rainy day on a canoe trip is a disaster and therefore to be wet and uncomfortable on a rainy day is natural" (p. 84). For these people, experiencing nature involves experiencing a level of discomfort that one rarely encounters in civilization. In their association of the natural world with pain, they express a highly civilized masochism.

Nevertheless, Hoagland exhibits in his prose a genuine investment in the beauty of his experience on the Allagash. Lyrical and perfectly balanced descriptions of his river passage abound:

> We passed bits of islands covered with drift-piles, saw a doe and a fawn, a sheldrake with seven ducklings, a squirrel swimming the river, its tail like a rudder. A heron flew up and stood for a minute atop a fir tree. The river curved gently in a stretch sweet as honey, softening its watery sounds so that we could hear the white-throated sparrows. (p. 100)

But in the end, Hoagland has to admit that even "going into the rips," the most exciting parts of this river, when Fred King calls out jubilantly, "Everybody for himself and God for us all," he cannot escape the conviction that this is in many ways a futile endeavor, one that "has all somehow ossified now that the wilderness is gone" (p. 101).

And so the original question, posed so objectively by "the logging industry" and "the conservationists" in the first paragraph of the essay, is answered during the essay's course, a process that brings home the futility of trying to answer such a question in terms any less careful, and subtle, than Hoagland's. "Fred King on the Allagash" undercuts naive assumptions about the distinction between "wilderness" and "civilization" as it explores the convoluted ways in which humans construct the two terms and the conflicted ways in which they experience wilderness.

Humans, the lesson goes, can never be completely happy on one side or the other of the stark distinction they make between the wilderness and civilization. As if to prove his point finally, Hoagland concludes his trip to the wilderness by consuming one of the staples of American civilization, ice cream. Bidding the backcountry adieu, he orders not only a butterscotch sundae when he emerges, but also a strawberry milkshake. Fred King, his guide, "depart[s] like a boy let out of school," relieved that the trip is over, and the couple that has accompanied them is last seen changing a tire on their new Chrysler, "putting gas into the empty tank from a one-gallon can and reminding each other that no minor mishap should spoil such a fine trip" (p. 106). Certainly, most or all of the wilderness is gone, as the logging company claims, and certainly whatever versions of it that survive must be preserved, as the conservationists insist. But as the debate, framed in such irreducible terms, continues to rage, writers such as Edward Hoagland will eat ice cream and imagine the natural world in new ways.

Thus, the complexity of Hoagland's nature essays mirrors the complexity of the human/ nature relationships they explore. His style, especially the discursive structures he typically employs, serves to complicate and recast traditional questions about nature so that humans can get away from rigid distinctions, such as the logging companies' definition of "wilderness" in "Fred King on the Allagash."

Quite often, Hoagland's essays offer an even less clearly discernible thematic center than the implied "wilderness"/"civilization" distinction in "Fred King on the Allagash." "Hailing the Elusory Mountain Lion," from *Walking the Dead Diamond River*, one of Hoagland's best-known pieces, is representative of such essays. It, too, is a subtly articulated treatise on human beings in the wilderness. "Hailing the Elusory Mountain Lion," however, demonstrates the extremely personal focus that Hoagland's essays often take. Hoagland's is the central consciousness in the narrative, so that the essay becomes a public exploration of his private relationship to the wild. "Hailing the Elusory Mountain Lion" is characteristically, then, only marginally "about" anything at all — about wilderness, about mountain lions — yet it represents some of Hoagland's most focused prose.

The essay begins with two remarkable sentences that are both an evocation of and a eulogy for the American wilderness. "The swan song sounded by the wilderness," Hoagland laments, "grows fainter, ever more constricted, until only sharp ears can catch it at all. It fades to a nearly inaudible level, and yet there never is going to be any one time when we can say right *now* it is gone" (p. 46). He then supplies a litany of wild animal species that have either disappeared with the wilderness or come to uneasy terms with its absence: wolves, woodland caribou, and bighorn sheep disappear, while coyotes and moose persist, at least temporarily.

Supplying no transition and no introduction, Hoagland next presents the reader with a description of the cat known "in the Rockies" as the mountain lion. In a breathless four-hundred-word paragraph, he describes its range, habits, diet, and various names, and he claims that the mountain lion in its several incarnations is "the most versatile land mammal in the New World" (p. 46). By devoting such a disproportionately large passage to the mountain lion's description, Hoagland implies that it is a supremely important creature. The elusory mountain lion serves him as an emblem for wilderness.

Nevertheless, mountain lions and wilderness do not remain the center of attention for long. The name "mountain lion," along with another of the animal's names, "Mexican lion," suggests to Hoagland the cat's relationship to other cats, and so his discussion turns to African lions. After describing African lions, he supplies a paragraph on leopards and one on jaguars. Thus mountain lions become, even in the essay devoted to them, elusory. Not until past the midway point of the essay does Hoagland begin describing his actual experience of seeing a mountain lion.

Once the narrative does turn to the quest for the lion, a pattern begins to emerge from Hoagland's digressions. This essay is about desire, desire for the beauty and spectacle of wild things. The detailed descriptions of wild cats Hoagland gives comprise an exploration of the fascination they hold for him. The essay up to this point has been a personal explication of the attraction of cats. Near the middle of the essay, Hoagland turns to other people's experiences of the animals; he catalogs their stories of mountain lion sightings and recounts his "seeking out people who have claimed at one time or another to have seen a mountain lion" (p. 56). These excursions within the essay, which often depart widely from its central narrative, the quest for the lion, nevertheless remain close to its central question — what is it that attracts humans to such wild creatures?

Hoagland finally addresses this question by describing his own experience with the animal. The climactic passage of the essay (though Hoagland's essays seldom have linear narrative structures such as plots, they frequently have climaxes) involves Hoagland's own possible sighting of a mountain lion. He punctuates the beginning of this section of the essay with a declarative sentence that stands out in his prose because of its simplicity. "I, too, cherish the notion that I may have seen a lion" (p. 61), he relates, and then spins a "perfect-day" narrative of wilderness and wildness in which he walks in

the Alberta Rockies, following a particularly majestic bighorn sheep higher and higher into the mountains.

His pursuit of the ram ends when he encounters what he imagines to be a mountain lion "skulking among some outcroppings" on the mountain where "a pair of hawks or eagles were swooping at him by turns" (p. 66). The animal is too far away from Hoagland to be unequivocally identified as a mountain lion, but Hoagland can see that there "are creatures he wasn't: he wasn't a marmot, a goat or other grass-eater, a badger, a wolf or coyote or fisher." And because of what mountain lions symbolize to him, he engages in a bit of wish fulfillment—he reports simply, "Anyway, I believed him to be a mountain lion" (p. 66). In his desire to make contact with the animal, he moves toward it, "as clumsy as anyone who is trying to attract attention," and the mountain lion flees. Still, Hoagland walks home from the encounter "Foolish, triumphant and disappointed" (p. 67), exclaiming in closing that "the forest's night beauty was supreme in its promise, and I didn't hurry" (p. 68). He finds himself suitably content with even the illusion that he has seen a mountain lion in the wild.

Fiction

Of Edward Hoagland's six works of fiction, *Cat Man* and *Seven Rivers West* are directly concerned with relationships between humans and the natural world, as is the title story of the collection *The Final Fate of the Alligators* (1992). *Seven Rivers West* is a frontier "nature story"; it relates the passage of a group of travelers through western Canada in the 1880s. *Cat Man*, the story of a circus lion handler, depicts human interaction with a more circumscribed version of nature—wild cats in captivity. "The Final Fate of the Alligators," written in 1960, describes the relationship between an aging New York City resident and his pet, a large alligator that lives in his bathtub.

Of these three fictions, "The Final Fate of the Alligators" is perhaps the most traditional. On its simplest level, it is a pet story. Hoagland, however, endows his short narrative with many of the sensibilities of his nature essays. During the course of the story, the alligator comes to symbolize in his owner's eyes the entire experience of nature: "having it in the apartment, he found a great many of his seaman's memories springing alive with a clarity even surpassing the clarity of life. The smoldering waves, the sharks and whales, the dull-colored, impassive seas on a smoky day—these sailors' sights and many more churned in the roil along with the alligator" (p. 23). In order to learn more about his alligator, the protagonist of the story, Bush, begins reading up on the species, and so he finds himself in the paradoxical position of studying a wild animal by visiting a library.

The close relationship Bush develops with the animal is typical of Hoagland's characters. He "got it out onto the floor every couple of days for a walk and to let it dry thoroughly—let it lie flat, sprawling its arms, while he cleaned the interstices of its skin where fungi might gather. The logistics were not ideal, but the business was very brotherly" (p. 27). The closeness of the relationship is expressed as physical affection; Bush discovers that the alligator "liked to feel its throat rubbed, including the gums of its eighty teeth" (p. 24), and Bush himself "didn't get tired of rubbing his hands across the rich hide" (p. 27).

As is often the case in Hoagland's world, however, the relationship between humanity and wildness, between Bush and the alligator, is a conflicted one. Not surprisingly, the alligator sickens and begins to die in the bathtub, and Bush can think of nothing to do for it but watch: "besides the problems of fresh air and space" in the New York City apartment where he lives, "there was the elaborate question of diet. How could he duplicate the crunchy, glittery nutrients of a jungle river?" Bush realizes that the answer is "of course finally he couldn't." He observes that "whereas before when he watched the beast's clumsy galumphing he had imagined the alligators in the swamps in their glory, now he began to see his friend just trying to stay alive" (p. 27). Bush is incapable of saving the wild animal, and so he watches it die.

The story ends with an image typical of the ambivalence with which Hoagland's fictional characters treat their allotments of nature. After the alligator's death, Bush and his neighbor put it on "the street late Sunday night, leaving it stretched in solitary magnificence across the sidewalk for the city to figure out what to do with" (p. 28). Bush has the grace not to sell the animal for a handbag, but, because he lives in the city, he cannot arrange for its final fate to be any more attractive than the garbage dump. Only in life was the creature capable of showing him the sort of wildness that thrilled him. It has nothing to show him in death.

Hoagland's first novel, *Cat Man*, published five years before "The Final Fate of the Alligators," develops a similar fictional relationship between humans and wild animals. The prose style of the novel is much less direct, however, much more discursive: it exhibits striking similarities to the style of Hoagland's essays. *Cat Man* displays Hoagland's unmistakable associative, improvisational, and digressive organizational strategies as it explores the relationship between a young circus hand and the wild caged cats he tends.

Significantly, there is no sense in the novel that wild cats—or elephants, or snakes, or any other animal, for that matter—should not be in cages, or that they should not be utilized in the circus for the entertainment of human beings. Although Hoagland's characters, especially his protagonist, Fiddler, demonstrate a deep and abiding respect for the wildness of the creatures in the cages, wild nature is nevertheless a spectacle in this novel—a pageant that human beings are privileged to appreciate, but a pageant nonetheless. The portion of the natural world that the novel focuses on is an unusual one for Hoagland.

Fiddler's attachment to the cats he tends, his attachment to their wildness, is a profound, visceral, and sometimes physical one, much like Bush's attachment to his alligator. Fiddler knows, for instance, the individual personalities of the five leopards in his charge, Rajah, Sweetheart, Taboo, Minny, and Rita. Not surprisingly, it is Rita, because she is "wilder than the day

EDWARD HOAGLAND

she'd been caught" (p. 60), whom Fiddler is most enamored of.

> Rita was the nuisance, lightning Rita always flattened in a corner, watching her chance. Her eyes were deep gray-blue and her spots were navy blue, not black. What should be white on a leopard was gray on Rita. . . . But now and then the blue would mingle with the gray and make her very beautiful, misty blue, loose-muscled, small and slim and gray. Fiddler would ache to touch her. (p. 61)

He does touch her, often, and the other cats, as well. As his badly scarred hands attest, he touches the cats far too often.

Apart from his own attraction to the cats, Fiddler realizes the effect their wildness has on other people. He employs this effect to his advantage at circus stops such as Winona, Minnesota, where he and his companion Red use the leopards to impress two local girls. One of the girls is indeed duly taken with Sweetheart's tail, for when Fiddler put the tail in her hand, "she squealed, just barely touched it — then suddenly she bent and kissed the tip, frantic, clutching Fiddler round the waist. . . . Cupping her fingers, Fiddler's girl stroked the tail and kissed it with tiny mouse squeaks. He held the leopard still by massaging the fur along her ribs" (p. 43). These animals provoke profound physical, almost sexual, responses in the humans who encounter them.

Nevertheless, the attraction of the wild animals is more than physical. Their wildness also instills a respect that is manifested as a titillating fear in the humans of the novel, and at one point Fiddler contemplates releasing Joe the lion from his cage so that he will no longer be a contained wildness, an entertainment for humans, but instead wildness at large, a terror to them. "Joe, Joe," he asks,

> what would you do if I let you out? . . . You'd go and catch a cow and chase the farmer's daughter and ramble all around, and they'd shoot you. You wouldn't be easy to shoot, but they'd have to shoot you. I'd like to see you charge. Maybe their aim might not be so good

> on you as on a pheasant or whatever they have here. They'd be talking about you for the rest of their lives around here. (p. 126)

The terror they instill is one of the wildcats' most attractive attributes.

But as his life among the complex and confusing human society of the circus becomes increasingly unstable, as his friends get into fights, descend into alcoholism, and simply disappear, his relationship to the animals that both attract him and terrify him becomes more reckless. His difficulty negotiating the human world pushes him toward the wild one in the cages, and Fiddler begins to demand more of the cats' wildness while respecting its danger less. He engages in more of the sort of behavior that has scarred his hands so badly. Finally, Fiddler ceases to acknowledge the distinction between himself and the wild animals at all. The book ends in a final, deadly union of human and wild life, suggesting perhaps that humans cannot survive in both worlds at the same time.

The second of Hoagland's novels addressing questions of humans and nature is *Seven Rivers West*, published in 1986. Although it is set in the Canadian Rockies in the 1880s, *Seven Rivers West* extends the nature-as-pageant theme Hoagland had explored in *Cat Man*. The book, like *Cat Man*, is imbued with the spirit of the circus, the perception of wild-nature-as-spectacle, even when its protagonists are high in the northern Rockies, thousands of miles from civilization.

To a large extent, this is because the characters of *Seven Rivers West* bring the circus with them into the backcountry. The prospector Sutton is an ex-circus showman. The novel's central character, Cecil Roop, is a patent-medicine salesman and would-be vaudevillian who has come west to capture a grizzly bear for the act he hopes to develop after he returns East.

Hoagland actually transplants acts he has seen and written essays about into the novel. Sutton is a trick diver who looks remarkably like the eponym of Hoagland's essay "A Low-Water Man" from *Red Wolves and Black Bears*. "On his seventieth birthday," this man, Henri

371

LaMothe, "dove from a forty-foot ladder into a play pool of water 12 inches deep," something that he had regularly done for the entertainment of people in cities and towns around the United States for over forty years. LaMothe's fictional counterpart in *Seven Rivers West*, Sutton, dives off the scaffolding of a new frontier town's water tower for the entertainment of the new townspeople; he jumps off a rock ledge into a pool of river water in order to impress a group of Native Americans, and he jumps into a pool at the bottom of a ravine to catch the attention of a magical animal in the wilderness, a Sasquatch. Sutton not only brings the circus to the wilderness, he brings Edward Hoagland's specific experience of showmanship to the wilderness.

Thus, the spectacular larger-than-life element of the human-animal relationships of *Cat Man* arises in *Seven Rivers West* as well, although the relationships are structured inversely in the two books. The wild animals of *Cat Man* are kept in cages; in that novel, humans must literally reach inside containment structures to make contact with them. The wildness that Sutton and Cecil Roop encounter in *Seven Rivers West* is unbounded, uncontrollable, and they are uncomfortable before it. In order to make sense of their experience, they must assert themselves. The two make their presence known in the wilderness in spectacular ways.

Cecil Roop intends to contain the wildness, like the leopards of Fiddler's circus, in cages. Cecil expresses Hoagland's conviction that humans will always stand in line and pay money to see evidence that wildness exists somewhere in the world. He has set out across the Canadian frontier not to find gold, build a railroad, or even stake out a farm, as most of his peers do, but instead to catch a grizzly bear, or perhaps a Sasquatch and take whatever he catches back east with him as a vaudeville act. The wilderness to Cecil is something to be experienced, to be respected, and even to be treasured, but it is also something to be boxed up and transported back for the entertainment of the civilized world.

As in *Cat Man* and "The Final Fate of the Alligators," however, the wild world is too unstable to coexist with the human world. The characters of *Seven Rivers West* meet various unhappy fates in the Canadian wilderness. Cecil fails to capture either of the animals after which he set out, and he also loses his friends, his lover, and all his material goods in the wilderness. Sutton loses his very life there; he dies of injuries sustained while attempting to perform his low-water diving trick in front of the hoped-for Sasquatch. Except for Cecil and Sutton's companion Margaret, the characters of the narrative all are subsumed into the wild.

Cecil ends exactly where the title of the book suggests he might end, seven rivers west of where he started. But he has not lost his impulse to see the wilderness as a show. In the last scene of the book he observes a fish so large that it seems possible, according to his companion, that he might "paint him up and sell him to P. T. Barnum" to be exhibited under the title "The Bigfoot of the River" (p. 319).

In Hoagland's fiction, then, as in his nonfiction, human motives for approaching wild things devolve from human desires. However, the desires people exhibit in *Cat Man*, *Seven Rivers West*, and even "The Final Fate of the Alligators" are more pointed and ultimately less likely to be fulfilled than, for instance, the desire, expressed in "Hailing the Elusory Mountain Lion," simply to see a wild animal. Hoagland's fictions about nature depict humans who want both to identify with and control wild nature, a desire that, according to Hoagland, can never be met.

Travel

Hoagland has published two travel narratives, *Notes from the Century Before: A Journal from British Columbia* (1969) and *African Calliope: A Journey to the Sudan* (1979). *Notes from the Century Before* is an edited diary that chronicles Hoagland's experiences in the wild backcountry of western Canada. The structure of *African Calliope* is similar, but slightly more sophisticated. It too began as a daily diary, this time of the author's travels in the Sudan, but as Hoagland indicates in an author's note, he has in *African Calliope* "given emphasis to what [he] saw by rearranging certain experiences, putting them a little earlier or later than they chanced to occur, or narrating them so that they are not beads on a string." "Beads on a string" is a somewhat pejorative characterization of chronological organization—but then Hoagland very seldom has use for chronological organization in his essays. The essays of *African Calliope*, and to a large extent the individual chapters of *Notes from the Century Before* as well admit his characteristic literary detours.

The premise of *Notes from the Century Before* is that the landscape of British Columbia looks the way the landscape of the western United States must have looked in 1885. By visiting the place and chronicling it, Hoagland hopes to encounter the sort of frontiersmen who first came to it from the East. He also hopes to experience the wild country itself before it disappears, bringing his readers along with him through a sort of literary time warp to "the century before." As he embarked on his journey, it appeared to Hoagland that "except for the draw-and-shoot business, which didn't concern me, it seemed that the life would be the same. I would be talking to the doers themselves, the men whom no one pays any attention to until they are dead, who give the mountains their names and who pick the passes that become the freeways" (pp. 13–14). But despite Hoagland's enthusiasm for these people and for the land, the book has a somber tone: it is due to these people that "there is a frank new air of rapine" across the land. According to Hoagland, "the problem everywhere nowadays turns on how we shall decide to live" (p. 15). Through most of the book, this concern of Hoagland's is, as his concerns often are, implied rather than stated.

Although the chronicle is presented in the form of a journal, its style is not the style of a typical travel narrative, a straightforward account of sights and places encountered. This is a chronicle composed by a writer who characterizes himself as "a novelist, not a historian, but at best . . . a rhapsodist too—that old-fashioned, almost anachronist form" (p. 14). Woven into his factual, chronological, and geographical account of Canada is Hoagland's joy at what the land is like, and his sadness that it will not survive the humans who have come to inhabit it. Thus, the individual essays of *Notes from the Century Before* tend often to resemble the freely structured essays of his other collections.

"In Hazelton and Flying North," for example, is about many things besides flying north. At first, the essay seems to be something of a "local color" piece providing impressionistically rendered details of the British Columbian countryside. But the essay is in fact a sophisticated lesson in perception. It has an odd first paragraph, as do many of Hoagland's pieces, one that seems at first not to fit the essay. The paragraph's syntax indicates that it was indeed drawn from a journal: "July 6, Wednesday: Am reading *Pickwick Papers*, which I once thought egregiously trivial. One is always a fool disliking a classic. Like disliking a nation one visits, it's the result of a blind spot, which goes away and leaves one embarrassed" (p. 138). With that strange cautionary note, Hoagland begins describing what he calls an "elbow-grease country," an unsophisticated place that may at first seem "egregiously trivial" to readers who have not overcome their "blind spots."

Hoagland sets out to do this visionary work for his readers, to help them overcome any limits in perception they may have. He begins the essay with the image of a "plaster-and-plastic motel" in which he sits recuperating from a knee injury, goes on to describe a bisexual woman with whom he consorted while visiting the province, and then depicts the confluence of the Skeena and Kispiox rivers where Hazleton sits. He also discusses logging, cows, sawmills, fishing, and finally a giant paper fish flying above the house of a Chinese man in Smithers, Canada, a fish that is "more of a fish than all these caught salmon" he's seen in the country (p. 152). He thus demonstrates that the countryside around Hazelton, and presumably any other countryside, will reward those who look closely enough at it. This is an especially trenchant lesson in light of the subtext of *Notes from the Century Before*, the fact that the face of the landscape around Hazelton is being irrevocably changed by humans.

African Calliope brings Hoagland's improvisational style to the endeavor of travel writing to an even greater degree than *Notes from the Century Before*. *African Calliope* is perhaps more oriented around personal observation and less dependent on objective organizing factors than *Notes from the Century Before*, because, as noted, Hoagland has "rearranged" the events it recreates to better represent the Africa he has experienced. This Africa "can be wonderfully bewildering," so bewildering, in fact, that strict chronological reconstructions of observation may not provide the most accurate descriptions of it.

Thus, in developing his essay "Sugar and Cotton," he supplies different sorts of information. Much of it is the customary sort. "Sugarcane," he writes, "is a perennial grass which itself improves the structure of the soil, just as fallow-field grasses will do." It grows in the

> famous dark "cotton soil" of this stretch of the Nile [which] is a viscid, self-mulching clay, ideal for irrigating because it cracks and becomes friable when dry, so that water quickly penetrates to the roots of the cane. But as soon as the ground is sufficiently wet, it seals itself in lovely fashion . . . as impermeable as a sheet of plastic, and cannot be overirrigated. (p. 81)

This is the kind of detailed relation of the objective facts about a region's soil one would expect to find in a discussion of cotton and sugar farming.

But again, Hoagland the traveler complicates the picture. Besides indicating what kind of soil covers this cotton and sugar region, he also reports that to get a travel permit to see it, one must wade through the bureaucratic red tape of police stations where

> homely Bari girls in military uniforms with waddly buttocks moved from office to office . . . each with a sheaf of papers, although already thousands and thousands of papers were stacked right to the ceiling in pyramidal heaps in several of the rooms the clerks were

working in. . . . The thought occurred that this was the stage set for some existentialist play. (p. 72)

Hoagland also includes descriptions of the slowness of the trains and the Kenana Sugar Corporation's "gap-ridden planning" (p. 79).

In the end, the region provides an opportunity for Hoagland to reveal his motive for coming to Africa. Graham Lestro, a "cane specialist" he meets, demands to know that motive. Hoagland replies that he is "forty-four, and was after experiences and writing matter [he] had not tried before" (p. 81). The African landscape becomes to him what North American landscapes have been: a place in which he will, through his prose, construct a unique experience of the land. His African experience is the result of places he visits, people he meets, and stories he hears and tells. It includes company towns, Texans installing cotton-ginning equipment, the infant African agribusiness, as well as John McWhorter, a "peanut specialist from Rochelle, Georgia," with whom, at the close of the essay, Hoagland takes in the African night, considering "how lucky we were to be underneath the glittering stars, all expenses paid, so far from New York City and Georgia" (p. 89). The Sudan must, in the end, be a function of the civilized landscape he knows.

Edward Hoagland's travel essays provide a useful paradigm for his nature writing in general, for his experience of the natural world takes the form of an excursion. Hoagland rarely travels so far that he leaves behind human civilization. In the end, in both Hoagland's fiction and nonfiction, it is his investment in the world of human beings that ultimately marks the beginning and the end of his experience in the wild world.

Selected Bibliography

WORKS OF EDWARD HOAGLAND

NOVELS

Cat Man (Boston: Houghton Mifflin, 1955); *The Circle Home* (New York: Thomas Y. Crowell, 1960); *The Peacock's Tail* (New York: McGraw-Hill, 1965);

City Tales (Santa Barbara, Calif.: Capra, 1986); *Seven Rivers West* (New York: Summit Books, 1986).

SHORT STORY COLLECTION

The Final Fate of the Alligators: Stories from the City (Santa Barbara, Calif.: Capra, 1992).

ESSAY COLLECTIONS

The Courage of Turtles (New York: Random House, 1971); *Walking the Dead Diamond River* (New York: Random House, 1973); *Red Wolves and Black Bears* (New York: Random House, 1976); *The Edward Hoagland Reader*, ed. by Geoffrey Wolff (New York: Random House, 1979); *The Tugman's Passage* (New York: Random House, 1982); *Heart's Desire: The Best of Edward Hoagland* (New York: Summit Books, 1988); *Balancing Acts* (New York: Simon and Schuster, 1992).

TRAVEL

Notes from the Century Before: A Journal from British Columbia (New York: Random House, 1969); *African Calliope: A Journey to the Sudan* (New York: Random House, 1979).

BIOGRAPHICAL AND CRITICAL STUDIES

Spencer Brown, "Four Essayists," in *Sewanee Review* 88 (1980); Thomas Edwards, "Serious Games, Tasty Crabs and a Natural Writer: 'Red Wolves and Black Bears,'" in *New York Times Book Review* (13 June 1976); Donald Hall, "Hoagland Was There!" in *National Review* 32 (30 May 1980), review of *African Calliope* and *The Edward Hoagland Reader*; Dennis Drabelle, "Edward Hoagland on the Loose in the Sudan and at Large in the World of Letters," in *Book World* (23 September 1979), review of *African Calliope* and *The Edward Hoagland Reader*; Robert Jones, "Love and Loss, Delight and Dolor," in *Book World* (25 March 1973), review of *Walking the Dead Diamond River*; Diane Johnson, "One of the Best in a Tricky Business," in *New York Times Book Review* (16 September 1979), repr. as "The Traveling Self: Edward Hoagland," in her *Terrorists and Novelists* (New York: Knopf, 1982), review of *African Calliope* and *The Edward Hoagland Reader*; Alfred Kazin, "Walking the Dead Diamond River," in *New York Times Book Review* (25 March 1973), review; Carl Klaus, Chris Anderson, and Rebecca Faery, "Edward Hoagland," in their *In Depth: Essayists for Our Time* (New York: Harcourt Brace Jovanovich, 1990); Margaret Bonner Lowry, "Frontier," in *Commentary* 48, no. 3 (September 1969), review of *Notes from the Century Before*; Peter Prescott, "Endangered Species," in *Newsweek* (10 May 1976), review of *Red Wolves and Black Bears*; R. Z. Sheppard, "The Inner Outback," in *Time* (2 April 1973), review of *Walking the Dead Diamond River*; William Smart, "Edward Hoagland," in *Eight Modern Essayists* (New York: Saint Martin's, 1985); Dan Wakefield, "Turtles? Birds with the Governor Turned Down," in *New York Times Book Review* (7 February 1971), review of *The Courage of Turtles*; Geoffrey Wolff, "A Very Busy Life," in *Newsweek* (18 January 1971), review of *The Courage of Turtles*.

LINDA HOGAN
(b. 1947)

HERTHA D. WONG

LINDA HOGAN is an award-winning writer of great flexibility and expansive vision, having published numerous books of poetry, a collection of short stories, a play, two novels, and a book of essays. Influenced by the storytelling of her Chickasaw father, uncle, and grandmother and by the work of such diverse writers as Paula Gunn Allen, Elizabeth Bishop, Louise Erdrich, Carolyn Forche, Joy Harjo, Meridel Le Sueur, Audre Lorde, Pablo Neruda, and Tillie Olsen, Hogan combines Native American oral narratives and values with a highly trained literary sensibility. With an acute consciousness of class, gender, and ethnicity, Hogan writes about twentieth-century Native American life, women, nature, and global survival.

Linda Hogan was born to Charles and Cleona (Bower) Henderson in Denver, Colorado, on 16 July 1947. As a child, she traveled between Denver and southern Oklahoma, spending vast stretches of time playing alone outdoors. "Outside," she explained in an interview with Joseph Bruchac, "was my church, my place of vision and dreaming" (p. 129). An unlikely candidate to become a writer due to her family's rural poverty and disinterest in books, Hogan nonetheless began writing poetry in her late twenties. After her marriage to Pat Hogan (she was later divorced), she moved to the East Coast where she worked with physically challenged students. During her lunch breaks, she says, she would write poetry.

It became a way for her to explore her inner life, including her Oklahoma past, and a way for her to reconcile the two parts of her background, Chickasaw and white. Feeling out of place in Washington, D.C., she returned to Colorado where she enrolled at the University of Colorado at Boulder. In 1978, after considerable soul-searching about her contested position as a working-class, Native woman in a graduate program, Hogan received her M.A. degree in creative writing. Later, she adopted two daughters, both Oglala Lakota—Sandra Dawn Protector and Tanya Thunder Horse—to whom she has dedicated many poems; and she now has a young granddaughter, Vivian.

Hogan's electric publications have received several prestigious awards. Her play, a three-act work titled *A Piece of Moon*, won the Five Civilized Tribes Playwriting Award in 1980. Her book of poems *Seeing Through the Sun* (1985) received an American Book Award from the Before Columbus Foundation; and *The Book of Medicines*, her 1993 poetry book, received a Colorado Book Award and was a finalist for the National Book Critics Circle Award. Her novel *Mean Spirit* (1990) garnered wide critical acclaim and was given the 1990 Oklahoma Book Award for Fiction and the Mountains and Plains Booksellers Award. *Mean Spirit* was also one of three finalists for the 1991 Pulitzer Prize. Hogan has been the recipient of a National Endowment for the Arts grant, a Guggenheim Fellowship, a Minnesota State Arts Board grant, a Colorado Independent Writers Fellowship, a Yaddo Artists Colony Residence Fellowship, a D'Arcy McNickle Memorial Fellowship, and a Lannan Fellowship in Poetry. She has taught creative writing classes and workshops at numerous universities and in Native American communities. From 1984 to 1989, she was an associate professor of American and American Indian studies at the University of Minnesota–Twin Cities; in 1989, she accepted a professorship in the English department at the University of Colorado in Boulder. In addition to her writing and teaching, she has worked for many years as a volunteer for wildlife rehabilitation centers; in 1994 she began organizing a tribal elders' conference on endangered species. In September 1995 the conference, a traditional gathering organized as a Talk Circle and funded by the Flintridge Foundation, was held in Colorado. Native people gathered to discuss the traditional relationship between animals and indigenous people, the meaning of the loss of species that have sustained physical, spiritual, and cultural survival, and the human responsibility to the many animals central to Native ceremonies, mythology, and lives.

Much of Hogan's work is inspired by her deep connection to southern Oklahoma, specifically her family's home on Chickasaw relocation land to which, as a child, she traveled regularly from her birthplace in Colorado. "I know, in my mind, that the air and earth and my body are all really home, but my *heart* home is there, in Chickasaw country" (p. 145), Hogan explained in her interview with Patricia Clark Smith. "A champion of small existences," as Bo Schöler has described her (p. 107), Hogan often focuses on the small but significant details of daily life. Each moment and each creature is important to Hogan, in part because of her sense of the sacredness and interconnectedness of all life and, in part, because of her awareness of how perilously close we have come to planetary destruction. Over the twenty years that she has been publishing, her work has increasingly linked contemporary environmental problems with the historical treatment of American

Indians, who, as Paula Gunn Allen reminds us, "daily, for five hundred years, have lived in the face of imminent destruction" (p. 2). The environment has been similarly jeopardized by a short-term way of thinking that does not, as many Native traditions instruct, take into consideration the effects of human action for seven generations. In all her work, Hogan attempts to reconcile ancient Native systems of knowledge and contemporary life and language.

Poetry

Linda Hogan has been publishing poetry since 1975. "Poetry," she explains in her essay "The Two Lives," in *I Tell You Now: Autobiographical Essays by Native American Writers* (1987), "is a large spiritual undertaking" and, as such, often demands a political vision, "a vision of equality and freedom" (p. 247). For Hogan, as for many Native American writers, writing is not merely description or reflection or narration. Rather, language is an active force for change, for transformation, for personal, cultural, and global survival. Seeing poetry as "a process of uncovering our real knowledge" (Bruchac interview, p. 125), Hogan uses language to strip away superficial boundaries, to tap subterranean sources of understanding and vision.

Arising out of her experiences in Oklahoma, Hogan's first book of poems, not surprisingly, is titled *Calling Myself Home* (1978). As a mixed-blood woman from the country working in a large city populated by European Americans, she experienced a keen sense of alienation. The "split between the two cultures in my life became a growing abyss," she explained to Joseph Bruchac, and writing poems was "what I did to heal it" (Bruchac interview, p. 122). Hogan's experience is not unique. In her essay "Relocations," Inés Hernández-Ávila points out, "For many activist native women of this hemisphere, the concern with 'home' involves a concern with 'homeland'" (p. 3). But what and where is home to a relocated people? Where is the home*land* for a displaced nation? Because of their history of forced and multiple displacements, the Chickasaws have a precarious sense of home, or at least of a permanent landbase. The Chickasaw people are "always leaving" ("Blessing"), writes Hogan. But "like the spider/we weave new beds around us/when old ones are swept away" ("Man in the Moon"). The images of stolen or appropriated Indian land paved over by a money-hungry society—images so dominant in her poetry—arise out of personal and historical experience. Hogan's grandfather's allotment land in southern Oklahoma was, according to Hogan, "foreclosed . . . during the thirties by the government, by the banks" (Smith interview, p. 146). Now it is the site of the nonfunctional Ardmore Airport. She remembers her father pointing out to her the expanse of asphalt, concrete, and buildings that was once family land. For Hogan to call herself home, then, is to remember her Chickasaw homeland; it is also to articulate a suppressed history and to acknowledge a way of thinking that is often in opposition to the dominant society.

Like many other Native American writers, Hogan must reconstitute herself as writer, woman, and Chickasaw through an imaginative act of language. One way she does this is by situating herself in relation to the entire natural world. Unlike Western humanist assumptions of biological hierarchy, Native American philosophies do not see humans as the pinnacle of life on earth. "We share the planet with plants and animals equal to ourselves," Hogan explains, "and we are small in the universe" (Bruchac interview, p. 125). As emblematic of this vision of the world, she associates her poetic persona with an assortment of animals. In the following example, she identifies herself with the turtle. "Wake up, we are women," she writes in "turtle," a poem addressed to her sister, "The shells are on our backs." And once she has imagined herself (and her sister) in this form, she sees "the years/back through his eyes." Although she does not describe what it is like to see with turtle eyes, she suggests that the vision of another species communicated through anthropomorphism and myth—might enrich human perception. Hogan also suggests that this

kind of identification could complement human self-perception.

In a reciprocal relationship with humans, the natural world, according to Hogan, has its own view of humanity. Insects, for instance, perceive the women as part of the land: "The insects walk over our warm skin./They think we are the earth" ("hackberry trees"). Even "the red earth/passes like light into us [the two women]/and stays" ("red clay"). But Hogan's linkage of women and earth is made most explicitly in the title poem of *Calling Myself Home*:

> This land is the house
> we have always lived in.
> The women,
> their bones are holding up the earth.

Calling herself home, then, is remembering her intimate connection to the earth and her place in the interrelatedness of all living things. Positioning herself as part of the natural world also reaffirms her connection to her Chickasaw family and land and the stories which link them.

Hogan's connections can be critical as well as affirming. For example, in a move reminiscent of Thoreau's detailed description of the process of a tree in the forest being felled and manufactured into toothpicks or pencils, Hogan retells her family's story of how their "black walnut trees" were "stolen during the night" ("Going to Town") and the dark wood was transformed "into the sleek handles of rifles" ("Stolen Trees"). With such an image, she criticizes not only the greed and corruption of thieves in general, but the entire economic system that sees the natural world as valuable only as a potential resource—in this case, as material with which to manufacture a violent and destructive product, one that helped to dispossess indigenous people of their land.

While Thoreau focuses on the human time and energy used to make wood products and their subsequent circulation and use, Hogan emphasizes what is left behind. What remains is absence—"vacant places" ("Stolen Trees") where the lovely, shady walnut trees once stood. The vacancies suggest not only stolen resources, but stolen land and the palpable absence of native people who were killed or removed to make way for the colonizers.

Like the walnut trees cut down for their wood and the native people murdered for their land, the animals have disappeared also. In "Blessing," a poem in which Hogan's language ironically echoes Psalm 23, the persona walks "in the valley/of the shadow of Elk/who aren't there." The abstract "shadow of death" in the psalm has been replaced by the more concrete shadow of disappeared elk. In a subtle way, Hogan's poems suggest that European American culture is haunted by the ghosts of Native America—plants, animals, and people—who linger beneath the colonizer's temporary dominance.

But even though Hogan acknowledges loss, she insists on the possibility of renewal and celebration. As Kenneth Lincoln points out in the foreword to Hogan's book of poems *Eclipse* (1983), her poetry "looks to reconciliations for the survival of family, community, and the natural world" (p. v). Such optimism is made possible by her intimate relationship with earth and by her animism: "Everything speaks," she insists. "Put your ear to the earth/and hear it" ("Left Hand Canyon," in *Calling Myself Home*). Similarly, the speaker of "Song for My Name" (in *Calling Myself Home*) describes herself as

> a woman living
> between the white moon
> and the red sun, waiting to leave.
> It's the name that goes with me
> back to earth
> no on[e] else can touch.

Not only is the duality of "white moon" and "red sun" an appropriate metaphor for a mixed-blood woman living in both white and Indian worlds, it is a precise temporal positioning, suggesting the cycles of night and day on earth as well as the inevitable human return to earth in death. Death, though, is not perceived as loss, but rather as reconnection. The name, along with the woman, will be reunited with mother earth.

Her next two books consider the earth from two different perspectives. Whereas *Daughters, I Love You* (1981) denounces the destructive capacities of nuclear weapons, *Eclipse* (1983), as Kenneth Lincoln has noted, is "in six sections, honoring the four winds, father sky, and mother earth" (p. vi). In both collections, Hogan continues her articulation of Native American beliefs and her insistence on, as she referred to it in one interview, "caretaking [as] the basic work of living on earth" (Smith, p. 148).

Just two years later, Hogan's lyrical voice and political vision had deepened significantly. In *Seeing Through the Sun* (1985), she bares the violence at the heart of the world and demands a confrontation, a truthtelling. In this collection, the earth is paradoxically a source of both sustenance and destruction. "One way or another," the speaker of "Porcupine on the Road to the River" says,

> the earth is after us.
> Let's lie down together
> before it stops us in our tracks.
> Let's lie down on the bank of the river
> and listen to water's pulse.

In a Whitmanesque moment, she is mad to be in contact with the natural world as an affirmation of life.

Hogan also sees the human body as the conduit of a larger affirmation. In "Heartland" the speaker asks that we listen to our own pulse, "the underground language/of the wrist":

> Through the old leather of our feet
> city earth with fossils and roots
> breathes the heart of soil upward,
> the voice of our gods beneath concrete.

For Hogan, listening to our human pulses means necessarily connecting to or becoming aware of our connection to the earth. We must become aware, she suggests, of the subterranean sounds of roots and fossils and the buried voices of indigenous gods.

In her poem "Evolution in Light and Water," Hogan compares herself to the natural world and its evolutionary processes:

> Dark amphibians
> live in my skin.
> I am their country.
> They swim in the old quiet seas
> of this woman.
> Salamander and toad
> waiting to emerge and fall again
> from the radiant vault of myself,
> this full and broken continent of living.

The watery, interior worlds of women and earth are portrayed as originative and life-giving.

At times, her political message is stated explicitly. In poems such as "To Light," she states, "Even the trees . . . /have kept track/of the crimes that live within/and against us." Hogan suggests that the earth has a voice, suppressed like much of Native American history, that will inevitably break forth into utterance:

> At the spring
> we hear the great seas traveling
> underground,
> giving themselves up
> with tongues of water
> that sing the earth open.
>
> They have journeyed through the
>   graveyards
> of our loved ones,
> turning in their graves
> to carry the stories of life to air.
>   . . .
> We remember it all.
>   . . .
> We have stories
> as old as the great seas
> breaking through the chest,
> flying out the mouth,
> noisy tongues that once were silenced,
> all the oceans we contain
> coming to light.
>
> ("To Light")

The earth holds the memory of all life and all violence against life. Like the earth's narrative geography, native people (or perhaps all people), "have stories/as old as the great seas" breaking

out of silence, "coming to light." These stories must break through barriers—the earth's crust or the body's skin—to emerge from silence. Her final poem in *Seeing Through the Sun*, titled "Wall Songs," asserts that the artificial divisions of class, race, geography, and nationality can be spanned if we "turn our flesh to bridges," showing "that boundaries are all lies."

In *Savings* (1988), a poetic critique of rampant capitalism and what one unidentified reviewer calls a "modern book of revelations," Hogan again illustrates that "the conjunction of truth and poetry just might make something happen" (Krupat, p. 23). The title of the collection can be sen as referring not only to saving money or memory or culture or earth, but also to being saved from danger or destruction or silence, and, in a spiritual sense, to being saved.

The image of earth emerging from its technological tomb, a dominant aspect of *Seeing Through the Sun*, continues here. Hogan's sense of the buried or suppressed connections to earth are reiterated and refined in this collection. She envisions "earth pecking her way out" through cracks in the sidewalk ("The House"). Even things as mundane as potholes become symbols of a tired and crumbling civilization:

> these holes are not just holes
> but a million years of history
> opening up, all our beautiful failures
> and gains. The earth is breathing
> through the streets.
>
> ("Potholes")

She expands the idea of breaking through, this time into speech, in "The Other Voices" when she describes how "other voices"—of pine needles and night crawlers—speak "and even police can't stop earth telling."

In *The Book of Medicines* (1993), a visionary book of promise and hope, Hogan offers the ritual language of healing, a literary path to balance and wholeness, the goal of most ceremonies. "The closed bundles of healing," she writes, "are beginning to open" ("Other, Sister, Twin"). The cure allows each individual to "reach through time/and find the bare earth/

within your living hand" (p. 84); it also fosters the recognition of earth as mother and of the natural world as sisters and kin.

As always, Hogan's awareness of her relation to animals and ancestors continues. Linking animals, women, and ancestors is part of Hogan's strategy to reveal the undercurrent of thinking that is common to destructive behavior against all life: "women and Indians are often equated with animals, in ways that have negative connotations...and allow for the perpetuation of violence on all three" (Smith interview, p. 148). Her aim is to reclaim and restore interrelationships between them and between them and the earth. "The grandmothers were my tribal gods," begins her poem entitled "The Grandmother Songs" (p. 57). The grandmothers exist prior to the speaker's birth, and they accompany her out of life back to her origin; along the way, they lay out a pathway of song upon which members of the community meet and travel. Throughout her poetry, Hogan focuses on the extended kinship of women — grandmothers, mothers, daughters, and mother earth from whom all arise and to whom all return.

Linda Hogan

Novels

Although for years Linda Hogan has been regarded as a preeminent Native American poet, noted particularly for her luminous language and incisive political vision, the publication of her novel *Mean Spirit* in 1990 proved she was a gifted novelist as well. It is not surprising that Hogan associates the Western world's plundering of the earth with the domination and murder of indigenous people in the United States. Based on historic events, *Mean Spirit* is one chapter of this story. When oil was discovered on the land of relocated Oklahoma Indians in the 1920s, the formerly "barren" land, allotted to Indians because it was deemed worthless property, became extremely valuable. Greedy non-Indians used every means possible to exploit Indian land and "the dark wealth" within it: marriage to Indian women to acquire title to their land; "legal" proclamations that conveniently found full-

bloods "incompetent" to handle their own affairs and mixed-bloods "competent" but disqualified from federal compensation because of their mixed blood; intimidation; coercion; deception; and outright murder.

The novel opens in Watona, Oklahoma, in 1922, and the action focuses on the Grayclouds, an Osage family. Although the Grayclouds live near town, they have contact with the Hill People who, warned by the Blue River of the dangers of white encroachment, removed themselves to the relative safety of the hills above Watona in the 1860s. Over sixty years later, a river prophet of the Hill People, Lila Blanket, receives another warning from the river: Everything may be lost. Lila tells the Indians, "Some of our children have to learn about the white world if we're going to ward off our downfall" (p. 5). Unbeknownst to the Hill People, one of the dangers that awaits them is the threat that their sacred river will be dammed up by the U.S. Army Corps of Engineers. Lila ends up sending her own daughter, appropriately named Grace, on the mission of participating in "the quick and wobbly world of mixed-blood Indians, white loggers, cattle ranchers, and . . . oil barons" (p. 5). An unlikely savior, Grace, who takes to white ways all too readily, is welcomed into the family of Belle and Moses Graycloud.

Years later, because oil is discovered on Grace's land, the damming of the Blue River is postponed so that the black gold can be accessed: "the sacrifice of Grace to the town of Watona had indeed been the salvation of the Hill Indians" (p. 9). But shortly after, Grace is murdered, one of a series of Indians murdered by oil-hungry whites. As Joanna Hurley notes, "The Whites don't regard the Indians as fellow human beings so much as objects to be exploited, like nature herself." The young Creek Indian preacher, Joe Billy, explains, "It's more than a race war. They are waging a war with earth. Our forest and cornfields are burned by them" (p. 13). Billy prays that God will "speak to the greedy hearts of men and move them" (p. 13), but he receives no response. The "greedy hearts of men" continue to inspire unholy actions.

Unlike the European American characters — primarily John Hale, the elusive but powerful oilman behind the murders — who are generally linked to the violent exploitation of people and land, many of the Native American characters are associated with a harmonious relationship with the natural world. The story opens with a beautiful image of Indians sleeping in their beds outdoors, escaping the summer heat. Amidst vines, leaves, mosquitoes, and blossoms lie the sleeping people, as if nature herself is embracing and claiming them. As Luci Tapahonso points out, "Land, plants, animals and people continue to intertwine as the story unfolds." Belle keeps bees; Moses learns about bat medicine; and many of the native characters can understand the earth's language. It is the earth herself who saves Grace's daughter, Nola, from being murdered along with her mother: to hide from the white men, she goes into the pond among the cattails, all but her face submerged in the muddy red water.

Illustrating multiple points of view about the land, Hogan presents three perspectives of an explosion at an oil refinery. China, a European American woman from Arkansas, decides "that the earth had a mind of its own," compared to which "the wills and whims of men were empty desires" (p. 183). Father Dunne, a Catholic priest longing for a divine connection, is surprised to discover that divinity might be found in a relationship with the earth; he hears "the sound of earth speaking. It was the deep and dreaming voice of land" (p. 186). He feels "as if he had wakened for the first time" and assumes he has heard the "real words of God." But nearby, Michael Horse, an Indian healer and seer the reader has come to trust, "knew the words the land spoke were words of breaking, moans of pain" (p. 186). What they were hearing "wasn't the voice of God," concludes Horse, but "the rage of mother earth" (p. 187). Although China and the priest are in the process of reevaluating their ideas about human sovereignty over the earth, they still do not understand the earth's language.

With so much fear and violence at hand, Lionel Tall, an Indian man visiting from South Dakota, prepares to "perform a sing, a ceremony for healing everyone, even the injured earth tht had been wounded and bruised by the oil boom" (p. 211). Some time later, Horse locates the Sorrow Cave with its bat medicine and decides, "The medicines were coming alive" (p. 237). Like Hogan herself, he also uses writing as a kind of medicine; he writes the Gospel of Horse as a corrective to the Bible's mistakes. "For instance," he asks, "where does it say that all living things are equal?" (p. 270). But, like Reverend Billy's prayers earlier, ceremonies and medicines and biblical revisions are not enough to save Oklahoma Indian lands and lives from greedy non-Indians. In the middle of the night, the Grayclouds' home is blown apart. One of the final surviving native families, they too decide to leave.

The conclusion is tragically optimistic, as survivor tales often are. The Graycloud family loses everything but their lives and their memories. As the family watches, "they could see the fireline begin to move outward, like blood of the wounded earth" (p. 371). They look back to see "the life they had lived, nothing more than a distant burning. No one spoke. But they were alive. They carried generations along with them, into the prairie and through it, to places where no road had been cut before them. . . . The night was on fire with their pasts and they were alive" (p. 371). Hogan's insistent repetition of "they were alive" emphasizes how life is all they have (and barely so), just as it was all they had when they were forced out of their southern homelands years before. As Hogan describes so vividly in *Dwellings*, "what happens to people and what happens to the land is the same thing" (p. 89).

In her second novel, *Solar Storms* (1995), Hogan continues to link the fate of humans and the natural world, this time five generations of strong Native American women living in the Boundary Waters area linking Canada and Minnesota. Told primarily by Angel Jensen, the abused and abandoned daughter of Hannah Wing and a survivor of a series of foster homes, the story is about Angel's return home. As a tough and scarred seventeen-year-old, Angel returns to her birthplace searching for clues to her story—her home, her birth mother, her relatives, and her community. " 'What happened to you started long ago,' " Angel's great-grandmother Agnes tells her. " 'It began around the time of the killing of the wolves. When people were starving' " (p. 37). Just as human greed led to the misuse of the natural world and the destruction of human life in *Mean Spirit*, in *Solar Storms* it is what causes the disappearance of the wolves, the starvation of the people, and the soul-scarring of a family. Hogan suggests that Hannah's brutal abuse of Angel arises not merely from personally aberrant behavior, but social and eco-political trauma. When Angel finally confronts her birth mother, looking into her face, she sees Hannah as "more ruined than the land" (p. 231). Poignantly, Angel's face has been scarred by her mother's abuse, literally mapping the legacy of violent disrespect for life on Angel's facial topography.

When Angela, along with Bush (a mother figure), her great-grandmother, and great-great-grandmother, set out by canoe on a quest through the waters bordering the United States and Canada, she discovers developers' plans to build a hydroelectric dam. Resisting "plans for dams and drowned rivers" (p. 224), Angela joins the struggle to save the Cree and Inuit land she is visiting from European American developers. Fittingly, the novel does not conclude with the dramatic, although diffused, act of indigenous eco-resistance, but with Angel's new sense of wholeness and connection that arises from her search, her resistance, and her love.

Hogan's explicit connection between the animals, the land, and the mother suggests the betrayal of an indigenous natural order, a violation of the pacts linking animal and human, land and community, and mother and daughter. Angel tells the reader: "Our lives, the old people say, are witnessed by the birds, by dragonflies, by trees and spiders. We are seen, our measure taken, not only by the animals and spiders but even by the alive galaxy in deep space and the windblown ice of the north" (p. 80). It is returning home to a place, a family, a people, and a history and finding herself at home as a member of the diverse, fecund, and beautiful natural world that finally heals Angel. In Hogan's presentation of a dynamic and intricate web of life, no strand can be destroyed without threatening the whole, a theme she elaborates more fully in her collection of essays on the natural world.

Essays

After her success as a poet and novelist, Linda Hogan proved herself a powerful essayist. Her collection of essays, *Dwellings: A Spiritual History of the Living World* (1995), demonstrates her skills as a writer on nature in the traditional form of the essay. Hogan brings to her essays her dual background and her experiences in poetry and fiction. It is important to point out that Hogan, like many Native American writers, does not choose to identify herself as a nature writer. For some, to do so emphasizes the Western assumption of separation between humans and the natural world; for others, to do so risks their being sentimentalized as "authentic indigenous voices of the earth" and considered part of an environmental movement perceived as white and middle class; and for still others, to do so would gloss over a very real antagonism (about fishing and hunting practices, for instance) between their communities and certain environmental groups. The fact that Linda Hogan speaks to, through, and beyond these conflicts sets her apart.

Her essays can be read in the Western tradition of nature essay writing. They bear the Thoreauvian hallmarks of close observation and precise description of the natural world, express a desire for a return to a simpler life, and call the reader to awaken to the wonder and beauty of nature. Like other late-twentieth-century writers with an environmentalist vision, she sounds the alarm for humans to reevaluate our relationship with the natural world. Yet her vision of human beings as part of (not separate from) and equal to (not superior to) the natural world associates her with the intellectual traditions of Native Americans, particularly, but not only, her Chickasaw people.

Throughout her work Hogan calls for a "new" relationship with the natural world, but, of course, as she points out, this idea is not "new" to many indigenous people. Rather it is a return to an older way of apprehending that world, one that sees connections rather than divisions; one that understands, values, and respects dream, vision, and intuition — not only rational analysis — as valid modes of knowing the world. As Inés Hernández-Ávila notes in her essay "Land Base and Native American Religions," "it is humans who must be reinvented, especially humans who consider themselves civilized" (p. 403). Native elders, writes Hogan, believe "that it is possible to wind a way backward to the start of things, and in so doing find a form of sacred reason, different from ordinary reason, that is linked to forces of nature" (p. 19). This is a way of thinking "older than measured time" (p. 19), one reflected in indigenous ceremonies meant to assist such a return.

The title of Hogan's collection of essays is itself evocative. "Dwellings" might be defined as habitations or homes, places where we reside or linger. The fact that the term is plural suggests that we inhabit many such dwellings. Also, dwellings may be associated with a thinking process, such as when one "dwells" upon a particular idea. Hogan, of course, is concerned with both places and thought processes. Hogan's notion of a place of power, for instance, is not merely a physical location for spiritual connection, but a mode of perception — a position — "a still place, a gap between worlds," "the place of spirit, and mystery" (p. 20), a physical and mental place to dwell and dwell upon.

Hogan plays with the idea of dwellings in the title chapter when she suggests that we arise from "the first red house of our mothers' bodies" (p. 128) and finally return to our most basic dwelling: earth. Hogan as always insists on the interconnectedness of the dwellings of all life forms. She describes swallows who built an elaborate nest from "mud's earth and water" (p. 121). Sounding like Walt Whitman, who, in "Song of Myself," delineates the unity of all beings through a description of the food chain (how the dead bodies in the earth nourish the plants we eat), Hogan imagines how the "bodies of prophets and crazy men were broken down" in the mud nests of swallows (p. 121), uniting past and present, seers and seekers, human and animal people. She reiterates this point later in the chapter, when she finds a blue thread from one of her skirts and a dark strand of her daughter's hair in a bird's nest. "The whole world was a nest" (p. 124), she concludes, the whole earth a single, intimate dwelling place capacious enough for all.

Perhaps Hogan's interest in the multiplicity of a unified dwelling helps to explain why she is so drawn to humble, even (to many) terrifying, animals like the bat and snake. Unlike the bear and mountain lion (animals usually portrayed as noble, fearsome, and powerful) or the deer and rabbit (animals typically depicted as gentle, cuddly, and benign), bats are the stuff of human fantasy and nightmare. They reside in the dark, travel at night, and navigate by entirely

385

different senses than our own, hearing "the sounds that exist at the edges of our lives" (p. 25). A "key element in the medicine bundles of some southern tribes" (p. 26), bats, according to Hogan, "live in double worlds of many kinds. They are two animals merged into one, a milk-producing rodent that bears live young, and a flying bird. They are creatures of the dusk, which is the time between times, people of the threshold, dwelling at the open mouth of inner earth like guardians at the womb of creation" (p. 27). Given this description, bats are perfect metaphors for mixed-blood Indian experience such as Hogan's, and they are appropriate as mediators between our everyday world and the spiritual world. Although, in most native contexts, these worlds are interlinked and interpenetrating, mediators, like spiritual specialists or writers, still may be necessary or helpful. Hogan concludes her essay on bats with a series of questions: "How can we get there from here, I wonder, to the center of the world, to the place where the universe carries down the song of night to our human lives? . . . How do we learn to trust ourselves enough to hear the chanting of earth? To know what's alive or absent around us, and penetrate the void behind our eyes, the old, slow pulse of things, until a wild flying wakes up in us, a new mercy climbs out and takes wing in the sky?" (p. 28).

For Hogan, natural hot springs, ceremonial sweat baths, wells, and caves are "places of healing" (p. 29), sites of spiritual reconnection and power. All of these are hidden, interior places into which one enters and out of which one emerges transformed. In the old days, for many indigenous people, such sites were "neutral ground, a sanctuary outside the reign of human differences, law, and trouble" (p. 30). Hogan describes caves as "a feminine world, a womb of earth, a germinal place of brooding" (p. 31). "Brooding," in this instance, means not only thinking deeply, but also the process of bringing to life or nurturing, such as when a hen "broods" over her eggs. Caves, then, are places to think deeply and to nurture life, to link—like bats and snakes—what only appear to be disparate worlds. Many indigenous people have crea-

tion stories that describe emergence from a world or worlds below this one; often birth is considered a type of emergence, as are shifts in consciousness throughout life.

In her essay "All My Relations," Hogan continues this line of thought when she describes in detail some of the symbolism of the sweat lodge ceremony, in whicnh "the entire world is brought inside the enclosure" (p. 39)—plants, animals, water, wind, earth—reminding humans of their connection to all things. Like all ceremony, the sweat lodge experience is meant to reshape a person "by restructuring the human mind" (p. 40). "By the end of the ceremony, it is as if skin contains land and birds" and all life (p. 41); and people, reminded of their rightful status as part of everything, are reconnected to the natural world.

Unlike some other native writers, Hogan is not necessarily interested in redefining terminology. She is more concerned with reshaping how we think. She points out, "Even wilderness is seen as having value only as it enhances and serves our human lives, our human world" (p. 45). What we need instead, she says, is a new way of seeing the world and a language with which to articulate that vision: "to say that wilderness and water, blue herons and orange newts are invaluable not just to us, but in themselves, in the workings of the natural world that rule us whether we acknowledge it or not" (p. 46).

Because English, a "language of commerce and trade" (p. 45), is insufficient to describe the "magical strength and power" of the earth, Hogan asks that "we make our own songs to contain these things, make ceremonies and poems, searching for a new way to speak, to say we want a new way to live in the world," a way that reflects the intimate interconnectedness and sacredness of all life (p. 46). "We need new stories," Hogan insists, "new terms and conditions that are relevant to the love of land, a new narrative that would imagine another way, to learn the infinite mystery and movement at work in the world" (p. 94).

But in addition to a new language and new stories, we need a return to old languages, ancient narratives and the epistemology contained within them. Indigenous myths, "a high form of truth" (p. 51), are "cultural stories of our human journeys toward spiritual and psychological growth" and hearing and telling them allows us to "return to... a mythic time" (p. 51), a time of creation and possibility. "We are looking for a tongue that speaks with reverence for life," says Hogan, "searching for an ecology of mind" (p. 60). Linda Hogan's work, with its ancient vision and new voice, serves, like the bat, as one of the mediators who help humans emerge from their sense of separation into an awareness of relationship with all living things.

With the idea of emergence in mind, Hogan cites Vickie Hearne's description of Western culture as undergoing an "intellectual emergency" (p. 54). Hogan reenvisions this "crisis of the mind" as "a potential act of emergence, of liberation" (p. 54). To see the possibility in necessity, to focus on the liberatory potential in what seems to some to be the danger of intellectual extinction, is typical of Hogan. She is a writer whose family history of surviving the worst the world has to offer — poverty, relocation, attempted genocide — has allowed her to focus on the fundamental act of survival, rejoicing in each delicious moment of awareness.

Selected Bibliography

WORKS OF LINDA HOGAN

POETRY

Calling Myself Home (Greenfield Center, N.Y.: Greenfield Review, 1978), repr. in *Red Clay: Poems and Stories* (Greenfield Center, N.Y.: Greenfield Review, 1991); *Daughters, I Love You* (Denver, Colo.: Loretto Heights College, Research Center on Women, 1981); *Eclipse* (Los Angeles: American Indian Studies Center, Univ. of California at Los Angeles, 1983); *Seeing Through the Sun* (Amherst: Univ. of Massachusetts Press, 1985); *Savings* (Minneapolis, Minn.: Coffee House, 1988); *Red Clay: Poems and Stories* (Greenfield Center, N.Y.: Greenfield Review, 1991); *The Book of Medicines* (Minneapolis, Minn.: Coffee House, 1993).

SHORT STORY COLLECTIONS

That Horse (Acoma Pueblo, N.Mex.: Pueblo of Acoma Press, 1985, repr. in *Red Clay: Poems and Stories*); *Red Clay: Poems and Stories* (Greenfield Center, N.Y.: Greenfield Review, 1991).

ANTHOLOGIZED SHORT STORIES

"New Shoes," in *That's What She Said: Contemporary Poetry and Fiction by Native American Women*, ed. by Rayna Green (Bloomington: Indiana Univ. Press, 1984), also in *A Gathering of Spirit: A Collection by North American Indian Women*, ed. by Beth Brant (Rockland, Maine, 1984; repr., New York: Firebrand Books, 1988); "Making Do," in *Spider Woman's Granddaughters: Traditional Tales and Contemporary Writing by Native American Women*, ed. by Paula Gunn Allen (Boston: Beacon, 1989); "Aunt Moon's Young Man," in *Talking Leaves: Contemporary Native American Short Stories*, ed. by Craig Lesley (New York: Laurel, 1991); "Bush's Morning Feast," in *Returning the Gift: Poetry and Prose from the First North American Native Writers' Festival*, ed. by Joseph Bruchac (Tucson: Univ. of Arizona Press, 1994).

NOVELS

Mean Spirit: A Novel (New York: Atheneum, 1990); *Solar Storms* (New York: Scribners, 1995).

ESSAYS

Dwellings: A Spiritual History of the Living World (New York: Norton, 1995).

PLAYS

A Piece of Moon (self-published in Ideldale, Colo., 1980; first produced at Oklahoma State University, Stillwater, Okla., October 1981).

AUTOBIOGRAPHY

"The Two Lives," in *I Tell You Now: Autobiographical Essays by Native American Writers*, ed. by Arnold Krupat and Brian Swann (Lincoln: Univ. of Nebraska Press, 1987).

DOCUMENTARY

Everything Has a Spirit, coproduced and codirected with Ava Hamilton, Gabriele Dech, and Johnny Bear Cub Stiffarm (Denver, Colo.: Front Range Educational Media Corp., 1993).

WORK EDITED BY HOGAN

The Stories We Hold Secret: Tales of Women's Spiritual Development, coedited with Carol Bruchac and Judith McDaniel (Greenfield Center, N.Y.: Greenfield Review, 1986).

INTERVIEWS

Joseph Bruchac, "To Take Care of Life: An Interview with Linda Hogan," in *Survival This Way: Interviews with American Indian Poets*, ed. by Joseph Bruchac (Tucson: Univ. Arizona Press, 1987); Bo Schöler, "A Heart Made Out of Crickets: An Interview with Linda Hogan," in *Journal of Ethnic Studies* 16 (spring 1988); Laura Coltelli, *Winged Words: American Indian Writers Speak*, ed. by Laura Coltelli (Lincoln: Univ. of Nebraska Press, 1990); Carol Miller, "The Story Is Brimming Around: An Interview with Linda Hogan," in *Studies in American Indian Literature* 2 (winter 1990); Patricia Clark Smith, "Interview with Linda Hogan," in *This Is About Vision: Interviews with Southwestern Writers*, ed. by William Balassi, John F. Crawford, and Annie O. Eysturoy (Albuquerque: Univ. of New Mexico Press, 1990).

BIOGRAPHICAL AND CRITICAL STUDIES

Paula Gunn Allen, intro. to *Daughters, I Love You*, by Linda Hogan (Denver, Colo.: Loretto Heights College, Research Center on Women, 1981), and "Answering the Deer: Genocide and Continuance in the Poetry of American Indian Women" and "Let Us Hold Fierce: Linda Hogan," in *The Sacred Hoop: Recovering the Feminine in American Indian Traditions* (Boston: Beacon Press, 1986); Carl L. Bankston III, review of *The Book of Medicines*, in *Bloomsbury Review* 13 (November/December 1993); Betty Louise Bell, ed., *Studies in American Indian Literature* 6, no. 2 (1994), special issue on Linda Hogan; Laura Coltelli, "Linda Hogan," in *Native American Women: A Biographical Dictionary*, ed. by Gretchen Bataille (New York: Garland, 1993); Inés Hernández-Ávila, "Land Base and Native American Religions," in *Our Voices: Four Centuries of American Women's Religious Writing*, ed. by Rosemary Skinner Keller and Rosemary Radford Ruether (San Francisco: HarperSanFrancisco, 1995), and "Relocations," in *American Indian Quarterly* (fall 1995); Joanna T. Hurley, "A Dark Vision of Hope," in *Bloomsbury Review* 11 (January/February 1991); Kenneth Lincoln, foreword to *Eclipse*, by Linda Hogan (Los Angeles: UCLA American Indian Studies Center, 1983); Denise Low, review of *Seeing Through the Sun*, in *American Indian Culture and Research Journal* 9, no. 4 (1985); Arnold Krupat, "Facing the Page," in *American Book Review* 12 (July/August 1990); Kathleen Norris, "Linda Hogan and How We Came to Be," in *North Dakota Quarterly* 59 (fall 1991), review of *Mean Spirit* and *Savings*; A. LaVonne Brown Ruoff, *American Indian Literatures: An Introduction, Bibliographic Review, and Selected Bibliography* (New York: Modern Language Association, 1990); Kathryn Shanley, "Linda Hogan," in *Dictionary of Native American Literature*, ed. by Andrew Wiget (New York: Garland, 1994); Luci Tapahonso, "Vital Connections," in *Women's Review of Books* 8 (April 1991); Gerald Vizenor, review of *Mean Spirit*, in *World Literature Today* 65 (winter 1991); Janet Witalec, ed., "Linda Hogan," in *Native North American Literature: Biographical and Critical Information on Native Writers and Orators from the United States and Canada from Historical Times to the Present* (New York: Gale, 1994).

HELEN HOOVER
(1910–1984)

NANCY FREEHAFER

IN APRIL 1954, Helen Hoover traveled to northern Minnesota with her husband, Adrian ("Ade"), for an early spring vacation. The Hoovers had long searched for a piece of wilderness property, and this time they found what they were looking for: a cabin on the lake accessible only by a dirt road, forty-five miles from the nearest town. Later that same year, they decided to quit their Chicago jobs—Helen as a metallurgist at International Harvester, Ade as a textbook illustrator—to build a new life in the north woods. They were forty-four years old.

Ade, a former electrician in the navy, was a fix-it man, and Helen had done her share of "nature study" as a child. But neither had ever lived in the wilds. Their friends and coworkers and the people in the village all doubted that the Hoovers would make it through the first winter. But they persevered, and the woods became their home for more than thirteen years. Their adventures and misadventures of wilderness survival and the relationships they developed with the forest animals provided Helen with material for numerous stories and articles and for four books.

Helen Hoover was born on 20 January 1910 in the small town of Greenfield, Ohio, a town she once described as "full of Victorian houses, great trees from the original forest, and people with circumscribed minds" (Commire, p. 101). She was an only child, the daughter of Hannah Gomersall and Thomas F. Blackburn. Her father was a factory manager.

As a child, Helen was an avid reader of mystery and adventure stories. She described herself as having been "older mentally" than her classmates and "very near-sighted": "I was constantly scribbling and my mother was as constantly chasing me out to play" (Commire, p. 101). After graduating from high school, Hoover studied classical languages and the physical sciences at Ohio University (1927–1929), but she left school without a degree because of family financial problems during the Depression.

After her father died of a heart attack, Hoover went to Chicago, seeking to support herself and her mother. She worked as a proofreader, before making a career as a metallurgist, eventually taking out patents and winning an award for the development of agricultural implement disks. In 1937 Helen married Adrian Everett Hoover. In her free time, she took science courses at DePaul University and the University of Chicago. She also began freelancing around 1948, writing mostly romance and mystery stories under the pen names Drusilla Blackburn and Jennifer Price.

Hoover never stated the exact reason for her and her husband's move to the north woods. In explaining their decision, she sometimes emphasized Ade's health problems and the "flu-and-cold atmosphere of the city" (Commire, p. 102).

In *A Place in the Woods* (1969), she writes that they wanted to make the move before they were "too old to leave a desk job and undertake the hard and even dangerous living the winter woods might bring" (p. 76). Certainly they wanted to live close to nature, although neither seemed to have a very clear idea of what their new life would be like.

Once at home in the wilderness, the Hoovers were faced with the question of how to make a living. Although Ade made a little money with a line of illustrated notepaper, Helen was bringing in no income. In the spring of 1955, she tried unsuccessfully to sell an article about the challenge of making a home in the wilderness; she had not thought of writing about nature. Then she chanced on a copy of *Audubon* magazine and guessed that *Audubon* might be interested in her experiences with animals. Within months, her writing career was launched.

The Long-Shadowed Forest

It was six years after her magazine work had begun that Hoover signed a contract for her first book, *The Long-Shadowed Forest* (1963). This, like her following works, was illustrated by Adrian Hoover. In it she documents her and her husband's involvement with the wilderness, with chapters on fungi, insects, amphibians, the surrounding rocks and soil, as well as local trees, birds, and large mammals. Hoover was interested in everything about her environment and responded to everything. Nothing was too small to attract her attention; she regularly fed and observed frogs and toads, for example, and a house spider learned to accept live flies from her fingers.

But Hoover's primary subjects are the birds and mammals that she and her husband fed in the open area near their cabin. The visiting creatures regularly included several deer, two woodchucks, a weasel, mice of various kinds, squirrels, chipmunks, and birds. The smaller animals would sit on the Hoovers' shoes or climb up their legs; the birds would perch on their shoulders and head.

Hoover provides a list of their feed supplies for the animals in a typical year: eight hundred pounds of cracked corn, sixty-five pounds of suet, seventy-five pounds of graham crackers, and twenty-one pounds of ground beef, "along with assorted leftovers like macaroni and boiled potatoes . . . pancakes, bread, cookies, fudge crumbs . . . bacon rind and grease . . . [for] ninety-one birds and eighty mammals as regular guests, and more than two hundred birds and ten mammals as occasional visitors" (pp. 112–113).

Though most of Hoover's first book is devoted to a fairly systematic nature study, it also contains several of the kind of stories that came to characterize her work. One of these stories concerns an ermine, or short-tailed weasel, that the Hoovers named Walter. The ermine learned to run up and down the screen door to alert the Hoovers to its presence and then would take meat from Helen's fingers. This routine changed with the arrival of a fisher, a weasel-like animal more than three times the size of the foot-long ermine. The fisher also came to the Hoovers to be fed, and subsequently it raided the ermine's storing places and even destroyed the ermine's living hole in an apparent effort to catch it.

One night Hoover awoke, the ermine "trembling pitifully, crouched on my eiderdown, his face gashed from brow to nosetip and his right eye black and swollen shut" (pp. 152–153). The ermine had found a way into the Hoovers' cabin, having narrowly escaped the fisher's attack. With Helen's aid, the ermine recovered from its wounds and learned to time its feeding visits to the darkest parts of the night, when the fisher could not see it. Although the ermine remained "wild," it stayed in the area, returning often for food, while the fisher eventually disappeared.

The Long-Shadowed Forest contains some beautiful descriptive passages. Here is one in which Hoover expresses awe at the beauty and mystery of the ermine's nemesis:

By night the fisher is as fearfully exquisite as a creature out of dreams. Moving about in the cold light of the stars, moon, or aurora borealis, it is a mysterious, fluid part of the half-dark. The frosty hairs that give it daytime fluffiness are invisible and, smooth and sleek and sinuous, it flows and poses, a shadow darker than all other shadows, its eyes like emeralds exploding into flame. It glides in the unearthly beauty that belongs to the untamed land and its children. (p. 154)

In *The Long-Shadowed Forest*, Hoover discusses several issues that recur in her later books. One theme is the relationship between humans and the rest of nature. Because the Hoovers knew they were modifying their environment, they developed what they considered to be a responsible philosophy toward the creatures they encountered. Even though they fed the animals (and sometimes left things like newspapers and old pillow feathers out for the creatures to use in their nests), they never tried to tame them. The Hoovers claimed that they let the animals show *them* how to act, that they simply made food available and then observed the results.

Occasionally, the Hoovers would rescue a wounded bird or animal if they thought the recovery period would be short and the creature could be returned to the wild. In addition, some animals—a family of mice for example—lived *with* the Hoovers in their cabin, and other animals frequently ran in and out. In all these situations, the Hoovers believed that they were not interfering with the animals' natural lives.

Some readers today may differ with the Hoovers' view, believing that naturalists should remain invisible, unobtrusive, that they should observe the animals in their "pure" environment. But the Hoovers lived in a different time. At least in the early years, they believed that they could exist in the wilderness and relate to the animals on human terms without disturbing the overall ecology of the area. They could not have guessed the speed with which later residents would destroy the wilderness.

Hoover saw her role as that of teacher about ecology and about the relationships between humans and nature. In *The Long-Shadowed Forest* she stresses the importance of the balance of nature, explaining the roles of little-understood creatures such as bats in maintaining this balance. She warns against feeding bears and against taking orphaned animals out of the wild. Hoover also writes about the destruction of nature caused by modern life, especially the dangers of pesticides and the steady expansion of roads and civilized amenities into the wilderness.

Another set of issues that Hoover raises in this work has to do with how humans in general, and nature writers in particular, talk and think about wild animals. Anticipating her critics, she discusses the issue of sentimentality:

Although "sentimental" may imply emotionalism so excessive or affected that it is silly, any thought influenced by feeling is sentimental in some degree. Every time I remember the trust of some departed wild friend, I feel its loss and hope that its end was quick and not too filled with terror and pain. There is nothing maudlin about this; I am simply not calloused to the suffering of other living things. Nor do I want to be. (pp. 98–99)

Hoover also criticizes the tendency of humans to judge wild animals by human moral or aesthetic standards. Animals, she says, "are guided much by instinct and little by learning, and human standards of behavior and esthetics do not apply to them in any way. It is thus completely false representation to seriously say that any wild thing is cruel, immoral, kind, or the like" (p. 214). And she stresses the important roles that predator animals have in controlling the populations of their prey.

Hoover points out the tendency of animal studies to test for what human beings know or do: "The experiments do not measure the native abilities of the animal that man lacks, has in unimportant measure, or in different form" (p. 218). Animals, she believes, should be seen for what they are, not for what humans wish them to be.

Yet Hoover also acknowledges that animal behavior must be interpreted from a human perspective, since "we have no terms except human ones to apply to other species" (p. 215). In her own writing, Hoover does not hesitate to interpret animal behavior. Here is how she describes a squirrel that had dropped some building material: "She sits up . . . and, stamping her hind feet, complains vigorously about such undeserved harassment" (p. 20). Observing flying squirrels that were fighting over a cracker, Hoover touched them with her hands: "They froze, then . . . like chastened children, they politely accepted crackers that I offered to both simultaneously" (p. 119).

Hoover's human view of animal behavior is also reflected in the pet names she uses: the squirrels are called "The Outfielder," "The Butler," "The Little Old Lady." The groundhog is named Gregory, the weasel, Walter, two ravens become Mr. E. A. Poe and Annabelle Lee, and so forth. Naming is a human tendency, of course, and readers might consider the use of such names a domestication, a violation of the animals' wildness.

In his review of *The Long-Shadowed Forest*, Pieter Fosburgh comments on what he sees as Hoover's projecting of human values and motivations onto animals: "I regret, even resent, the coziness and the interpolation, whereby an author undertakes to move into the minds of his natural subjects and speak for them with the voice of authority." Yet he calls *The Long-Shadowed Forest* a "good and readable book," and it sold well enough to encourage Hoover and her editors to complete another.

The Gift of the Deer

By the time *The Long-Shadowed Forest* appeared, Hoover was publishing a regular column in *Defenders of Wildlife News* (called "Wilderness Chat," 1963–1973), and a regular feature, "Nature Story," in *Humpty Dumpty*, a children's magazine. She was also working on her second, most successful, book, *The Gift of the Deer* (1966). In this work Hoover does what she loved to do: tell stories. *The Gift of the Deer* is the history of the Hoovers' relationship with a family of deer, woven together with accounts of life in the woods. The story begins on Christmas Day of 1959, when a starving buck appears in the snow outside the Hoovers' cabin. The Hoovers fed the buck and named it Peter. By spring Peter had recovered. He continued to visit the cabin regularly and was joined by a doe the Hoovers called Mama and a fawn, Snowboots.

The deer family eventually grew to eight. During the next few years, however, two young bucks were killed by hunters, who were beginning to penetrate the woods near the Hoovers' cabin; a young doe was hit and killed by a passing car; and Peter himself was killed by a wolf as he tried to protect his son. Yet the deer family as a whole survived. In an epilogue reflecting the passage of more years, Hoover describes how Mama, now old but with new family members, continued to visit.

The book tells of a magical world: of a time before deer became known as carriers of Lyme disease and as nuisances to suburban gardens, of a time before hunting season made life outdoors risky for humans as well as for other animals. *The Gift of the Deer* is full of ecstatic admiration of nature in general and of the deer in particular. Here is how Hoover describes the two young bucks in spring:

> They glided, curved, circled, raced, with first one, then the other leading. They flashed across the yard in front of me, their leaps so long and effortless that their hoofs seemed hardly to skim the ground. They cleared a brush pile as though riding a wave. They flowed like liquid, soared like winged creatures, seemed to hover in mid-leap as their lithe young bodies stretched through the exciting air of spring. (p. 109)

The narrative also accommodates a kind of internal dialogue concerning the impact of Hoover's involvement with the wildlife around the cabin. She examines the danger to the deer of becoming overly dependent, and considers the possibility of eventual overpopulation because of the unnatural quantity of food: "Out of our fondness for them . . . our interest in their behavior, Ade and I were contributing to a change in the natural sequence of events in our part of the forest. Were we doing the right thing or were we wrong?" (p. 87).

The book contains abundant animal lore. One of the most fascinating sections of the text relates the three-month visit of a bobcat and lynx that were hunting and traveling together. But most of the animal study is about the deer, including information about biology, feeding preferences, diseases, and behavior.

Hoover describes how the deer train their young. By the third year of observation by the couple, the animals had become "tame" enough to carry on much of their family life in the Hoovers' yard. In one passage, the author tells how Mama disciplined a young buck the Hoovers called Pig because he was so greedy. Hoover watched Mama with Pig and his brother as they were beginning to feed. When the brother moved in to feed with Pig, Pig struck him with a hoof, slashing his cheek. Here is what followed:

> Mama crossed the yard in one leap and Pig guiltily jerked back from the corn. She, however, went to Brother, so Pig began to guzzle again.
>
> Mama, after licking Brother's cheek and moving her nose gently along his side as though checking for injury, saw him settled to eat at a corn pile. . . . Then she approached Pig and bumped him away from the corn with her lowered head. He reared, forefeet ready to strike. Mama, looking as though she could not believe he had shown such disrespect, brought her hoof smartly down on his head. . . . Pig backed off, shaking his head, then tried to approach the corn again, but Mama blocked his way with raised hoof. (pp. 76–77)

A few months later, Hoover observed Peter training the two bucks to "stand guard." When Pig failed to stay alert during his turn, Peter struck the young buck with both hoofs and reared threateningly, after which Pig stood at the alert until he was relieved (pp. 92–93).

Other passages bring the Disney film scenes from *Bambi* to mind. For example, in describing one of the fawns, Hoover writes, "Starface's weakness was butterflies. He tried his best to catch every one he saw by flicking at it with his tongue. . . . When a cloud of migrating Monarchs fluttered into the yard, he . . . scattered them

with his antics and they drifted on, leaving him to stare foolishly after them" (p. 177). Though this image, and others like it, is engaging, skeptical readers might maintain that Hoover embellished what she saw. In addition, readers might think that writing about "Starface's weakness" and saying that he stared "foolishly" reduce the behavior of wild animals to "human size" or to pet status.

The Gift of the Deer was very popular with juvenile readers, and it was widely read in schools. Though the book was intended for an adult audience, adults and children alike could appreciate its sence of mystery and wonder, however. In a review of the book, Hal Borland praises Hoover's emotional attachment: "Good naturalist though she is, she participates emotionally. The personal involvement was inevitable. Without it the book would be cold and colorless." He concludes his review, "I can name on the fingers of one hand the wild-animal stories that fulfill the ideal—true, credible, warm and unsentimental. *Gift of the Deer* stands close beside those few" (p. 16).

Hoover had already been receiving mail and visitors as a result of her first book, but *The Gift of the Deer* made her even more well-known. Ironically, Hoover's writing success coincided with the steady destruction of the idyllic wilderness life she was attempting to portray.

A Place in the Woods

Hoover dedicated her next book, *A Place in the Woods* (1969), to "all the people who asked the questions I have tried to answer here." The book traces the Hoovers' efforts to create a life in northern Minnesota; it tells of their early forays into nature study and their attempts to make a living. Except for a foreword in which Hoover responds to criticism of her work as sentimental, *A Place in the Woods* is written almost entirely in a light tone and is full of dialogue. The book opens with an incredible string of misadventures recounted with a dramatic flair that no doubt characterizes the mystery stories Hoover wrote in Chicago.

The misadventures, which began during two vacation weeks the Hoovers took in 1954, resulted in the near collapse of their cabin and the total loss of their car. Hoover describes how, during a thunderstorm, she felt the cabin shift: "I felt the floor sag and saw a crack between the floor-boards and the bottom log of the north wall under the desk" (p. 29). Water rushed into the open cellar, destroying the cabin's foundation.

A few minutes later, a tree fell on the house, but not before a bear tried to enter the cabin through the cellar. Helen watched in terror as the animal tried to force its way through a trap door that Ade had just nailed down: "Black claws were splintering the edge of a broken board and a paw groped through, all of five inches broad and covered with black hair" (p. 31). Just after Helen had pushed a three-hundred-pound barrel over the trap door, the tree fell, the bear ran away, and she weakly waited out the rest of the storm.

The next major mishap involved an auto collision on a snowy day in early winter. Both Helen and Ade were injured in the accident and could barely walk for weeks. After they were patched up by a doctor, distant neighbors who had come to their assistance took them back home and the Hoovers were left to fend for themselves. They had no transportation and only eighty-three dollars. The only way for them to get to town was to hike three miles and then hitch a ride with the mailman. And to make matters worse, Ade missed out on a ten-thousand-dollar illustrating contract because he couldn't call Duluth to accept the offer.

The book covers a period of almost two years, describing the Hoovers' ingenious methods of overcoming these and other hardships.

Somewhat surprising, given the apparent speed with which the Hoovers made the decision to move from Chicago, is Helen's apparent lack of preparation for life in the wilderness. Despite the fact that she had been a successful metallurgist, a traditionally male occupation, she presents herself in *A Place in the Woods* as somewhat ill-suited to the challenges of the wild—she expresses surprise at being able to help move furniture, lift a fifty-pound can of kerosene, and carry logs, for example, and she has to ask Ade how to make a fire in the cookstove.

Possibly Hoover thought that presenting herself this way—contrasting herself with her wiser, more able husband—would make the book more amusing. Certainly the stereotype of the weak, helpless woman was popular in the 1950s. But it is also possible that Hoover really saw herself this way. It is consistent with her description of herself as a child: near-sighted and introverted. People who knew her in Minnesota said that she rarely went far from the cabin. In addition to reading mystery and adventure stories, her hobbies were needlework, playing the piano, and learning foreign languages.

But for both Helen and Ade, just to survive in the wilderness during the first few months required tremendous effort, and *A Place in the Woods* does not skimp on the details. The two remained on the edge financially. They did not need much money, only a little to buy food (they refused to hunt or fish). But there were times when they lived for days on oatmeal and canned vegetables.

The focus of *A Place in the Woods* shifts gradually from survival to the Hoovers' experiences of the natural world. Their first encounters with wild animals were with the mice that lived in the cabin. Hoover writes of an early decision to coexist with the mice rather than trap them; she left crumbs specifically *for* the mice and kept all other food tightly covered. And she tells the story of helping a partially paralyzed mouse rear its four babies. Because she "got acquainted" with individual animals, she soon stopped seeing them as mere members of species and began to see them as individuals with different personalities. Thus, she recalls, she decided not to try to study them scientifically.

After the first big snow, the Hoovers put suet out for the birds, making wire cages to keep the suet from being carried away whole, and they developed a system of arranging piles of corn and other dry foods in different spots around the yard so that animals could feed without disturbing or competing with one another. It was during this first winter that the weasel and the fisher described in *The Long-Shadowed Forest* appeared, and Hoover retells their story here. She also tells about her discovery that she could write and sell nature stories. Her first sale was an article about Walter the weasel; her second, a story about Mrs. Mouse.

Although most of *A Place in the Woods* is devoted to stories, there are passages which show how her new life was changing her: "My eyes and mind and heart had turned to the forest dwellers and slipped into their kind of time. Time that measured itself by light and dark, by moons and seasons, by sunshine and rain and snow" (p. 205). She often lost track of calendar time—she and Ade would have missed Thanksgiving if a friend hadn't stopped in to remind them.

Hoover recalls loving the total isolation of winter during those early years, and she describes natural phenomena beautifully, as in this description of an early winter frost:

Unfamiliar voices sang around us—the snap of a whip, the whine of a ricochet, the cry of strained thin steel. We followed these sounds to the shore where rime clung to the trees and rocks, dense and of the whiteness of sand-blasted marble. The lake had closed during the night and was an unbroken plane, smooth and sparkling white with the frost, its thickening ice creaking and snapping as it fitted itself around the rocks and into the bays. (p. 152).

The Years of the Forest

A Place in the Woods was followed in 1973 by *The Years of the Forest*, which continues the saga of the Hoovers' north woods adventures. But the Hoovers had already left their cabin home when Helen wrote this book. In the fall of 1967 they began looking for a new home in the West. In 1971, they moved to Taos, New Mexico, where Helen completed her last book.

The Years of the Forest covers a much longer period than the previous book—sixteen years—and in a foreword, Hoover compares her experiences in writing the two, indicating that *A Place*

in the Woods had been written almost directly from notes, but that she had stopped keeping detailed notes for the more recent book after the first year and a half.

The overall plan of *The Years of the Forest* is different as well. Although her approach is chronological, Hoover creates a thematic emphasis, using, in her words, "in both text and table of contents the items from a list of things-to-do, scribbled by my husband shortly after we bought our log cabin." The book is also divided into two parts, "The Innocent Years" and "The Years of Change." The second half of the book reflects the changes that resulted from the steadily increasing human presence in the area.

Like *A Place in the Woods*, this book opens with mishaps and reflections on the rigors of wilderness living. In the earlier book Hoover had commented on her and her husband's diet, lightly dismissing the monotony, almost bragging about their ability to subsist on cornmeal, canned goods, and occasional meat. But they weakened physically. After four years, Helen was severely anemic. She relates how she fainted one forty-degree-below-zero morning, but luckily revived before she froze. She also developed scurvy, suffering from loose teeth and bruised skin until some lemons could be sent from town.

People living in the wilderness usually establish patterns of mutual help, and Hoover indicates that she and her husband did have contact with neighbors. But in general, the Hoovers kept to themselves and solved their own problems. Helen dismissed the suffering and isolation they endured as unimportant. She believed that she and her husband would have missed many priceless experiences if they had lived a more conventional lifestyle. As she writes, "The wild creatures were our friends and companions, our teachers, our entertainers, the source of the material for our livelihood. . . . The forest offered us such beautiful experiences that hope never vanished, not even in our darkest hours" (p. 83).

In *The Years of the Forest* Hoover again describes the animals that came regularly to her and her husband's yard. Some of the stories from her earlier works are retold here; she of course

Drawing by Adrian Hoover, Helen Hoover's husband, from her book *The Years of the Forest*

includes a few new ones. Hoover also continues some of the themes from her earlier books, including a discussion of the dangers of DDT. DDT had been used in some areas of northern Minnesota to combat a budworm infestation that had attacked the balsam and spruce trees beginning in the mid-1950s. Hoover opposed its use, arguing that most budworm damage is temporary and that nature always repairs imbalances, whereas the long-term dangers of DDT were impossible to predict. She waged a campaign through the local newspapers against the spraying, a campaign that won her a number of enemies as well as friends.

Hoover concludes the passage about DDT with a general statement about the arrogance of modern civilization in trying to meddle with natural processes: "The earth and its life are not static, and man is only one among its many life forms, none of which is valueless to the whole. . . . The efforts of man to 'conquer nature' and so prove himself greater than the unity of which he is a part . . . seem not only dangerous and presumptuous, but stupid and silly" (p. 185).

By the mid-1960s the inroads of civilization in the north woods were increasingly evident; in fact, the wilderness was no more. *The Years of the Forest* details many of the changes. Summer cottages were converted to year-round dwellings, the lake was polluted, and telephone cables and power lines were laid (although the Hoovers refused electricity because it would give the power company authority to cut their trees). Hunters killed several of the animals that frequented the Hoover cabin. In addition to the deer described in *The Gift of the Deer*, these animals included a small bear and a groundhog. In 1965, a hunter fired directly at Hoover, missing her by inches.

The Hoovers began to vacate their cabin during hunting season. On one of their returns in 1966, they found the cabin and yard littered with footprints, food containers, broken glass, and cartridge shells; and someone had left poisoned grain in the house to kill the mice the Hoovers had befriended.

The forest had been infiltrated. The Hoovers left their cabin on an extended vacation in 1967.

The Years of the Forest ends with the Hoovers visiting their north woods home for the last time in 1971. Despite her sadness, Hoover ends the book on a positive note. The wilderness cabin had been their fulfillment. And once you find fulfillment, Hoover writes, "you never leave it entirely and you never lose it, because it has become a part of you" (p. 318).

Conclusion

After *The Years of the Forest*, Hoover wrote little. In an interview in the mid-1970s, she indicated that she was considering a book "on the whys and wherefores of life-style changes" (Commire, p. 101), but such a work never appeared. Hoover even stopped writing stories and articles, which she had published steadily in nature and children's magazines. In the wilderness, she had written out of necessity and inspiration; now the challenge and adventure were gone.

With the income from Helen's books, the Hoovers had a comfortable living. But Helen was in poor health, and although they often wrote to their friends about returning to the north woods for a visit, they never did so. In 1977, they moved from Taos to Laramie, Wyoming, and in 1980 they sold their north woods property. Helen died of peritonitis on 30 June 1984.

Hoover's books were very popular throughout the 1970s. *The Gift of the Deer* was especially successful, and was translated into numerous languages. By the 1990s, however, Hoover's books, like those of many other nature writers of note, were out of print. Certainly her writing is uneven. Her books include a variety of material: passages of natural history; discussions of ecology and of the ethics of life in nature; descriptions of natural beauty; pictures of the Hoovers' daily activities; stories of their efforts to survive and of their interactions with animals. Some passages are marred by cliché, some by sentimentality, some by a chatty tone. But for the most part, the passages about natural history are illuminating and interesting; the discussions of ecology are concrete and lively; the stories of the

Hoovers' life in the woods are entertaining; the descriptive passages are inspired and evocative; and the observations of animal behavior are fascinating. The books are always good reading.

Helen Hoover was not a trained writer. Nor was she trained as a naturalist or a philosopher. Yet she was not afraid to enter all these fields. In the 1960s, when her agricultural disk was making money for International Harvester, an article about Hoover in the farm magazine *Implement and Tractor* commented on her lack of training in metallurgy, comparing her to the "inspired barnyard engineers who made this industry what it is today" (p. 64). Hoover used this same common sense and self-confidence when she trained herself to be a nature writer. She entered into the life of nature and wrote about what delighted and fascinated her. She wrote about her life and about the relationships between humans and other animals. And she tried to influence her readers to take responsibility for the natural environment.

Hoover can be compared to many other nature writers of her generation. Like Sigurd Olson, she wrote about the boundary waters. Like Stanwell-Fletcher, she wrote about the experience of creating a home in the wilderness. Like Rachel Carson, she tried to raise public consciousness about ecology. Like Sally Carrighar and Wallace Byron Grange, she studied closely the behavior of the animals she wrote about. Like all these writers, she regarded nature with awe and wonder.

Hoover's experience was, however, unique. Few writers have spent as long a time studying and coexisting with a community of animals, much less one that included not only deer and groundhogs but wildcats and bears. Her experience of animal behavior informs her most memorable passages.

In his review of *The Gift of the Deer*, Hal Borland claims "The naturalist who writes about his animal friends has three choices. He can be scientifically detached and write a flat, factual report as impersonal as a column of statistics. He can personalize the animals, write "from the heart" and risk the charge of sentimentality, which probably will be justified. Or he can reach for the almost impossible ideal, factual truth warmed with compassion and understanding but untinged with romance" (p. 14).

Hoover's feeling for nature was her greatest strength—and possibly her greatest weakness. Here is her conclusion to *The Gift of the Deer*. Let the reader decide whether it is sentimental:

> Moonlight flooded between the trees. . . . I thought of cities and forests, of man and his brothers in fur, of the stars—and of Peter. I felt the snow melting on my hand and knew that to touch a snowflake, to feed Peter, was to touch them all.
>
> If we had not brought Peter back from the edge of death, he would not have led Mama to stay with us. Starface would not have been born. Most of the things—the personal things—I have been writing about would never have happened. . . . When these deer have gone on the long road that Peter, and so many others, have taken, there will be deer still.
>
> Peter brought them to us, he left them for us, a gift priceless beyond all accounting. What can I say of him?
>
> He was Peter, our buck with the generous heart. (pp. 208, 210)

Selected Bibliography

WORKS OF HELEN HOOVER

NONFICTION

The Long-Shadowed Forest (New York: Crowell, 1963); *The Gift of the Deer* (New York: Knopf, 1966); *A Place in the Woods* (New York: Knopf, 1969); *The Years of the Forest* (New York: Heinemann and Knopf, 1973).

CHILDREN'S BOOKS

Animals at My Doorstep (New York: Parents' Magazine, 1966); *The Great Wolf and the Good Woodsman* (New York: Parents' Magazine, 1967); *Animals Near and Far* (New York: Parents' Magazine, 1970).

BIOGRAPHICAL AND CRITICAL STUDIES

Hal Borland, "Wilderness Friends," in *New York Times Book Review* (13 November 1966), review of

The Gift of the Deer; Hal Borland, *"A Place in the Woods,"* in *Natural History* 78 (November 1969), review; Gerald Carson, "The Joy of Life to Be Found in a Wilderness: *The Years of the Forest,"* in *New York Times Book Review* (20 May 1973), review; Anne Commire, "Hoover, Helen (Drusilla Blackburn) 1910– (Jennifer Price)," *Something About the Author,* vol. 12 (Detroit: Gale, 1977); L. R. Dries, *"The Gift of the Deer,"* in *Library Journal* 91 (1 November 1966), review; "Better Discs . . . or a Woman's Influence, in *Farm and Implement News"* (10 March 1958); Pieter Fosburgh, "A Naturalist's Booklist," in *Natural History* 73 (August 1964), review of *The Long-Shadowed Forest;* "Disks and the Unspoiled North," in *Implement and Tractor* (20 May 1964); Anita Nygard, *"A Place in the Woods,"* in *Library Journal* 69 (1 July 1969), review, and *"The Years of the Forest,"* in *Library Journal* 73 (15 February 1973), review.

SUE HUBBELL
(b. 1935)

MARILYN CHANDLER MCENTYRE

SUE HUBBELL WAS a librarian before she became a beekeeper. It was not just a profession but a way of life she took with her on her great migration from Brown University to her farm in the Missouri Ozarks in 1973. The habit of fishing around in remote volumes for elusive bits of information and the voracious curiosity that are the librarian's most endearing qualities have surely made her one of the most entertaining and widely informed farmers and bug watchers in the Midwest. Not all the information she unearths might seem equally useful to the budding entomologist or apiarist: an eighteenth-century nursery rhyme about daddy longlegs; statistics on how much one can make harvesting ladybugs for sale on a good day (at seventy-five thousand ladybugs to a gallon, up to one thousand dollars if you know where to look); and a passage from Virgil's Fourth Georgic relaying Aristaeus' theory that bees are spawned in the fermenting blood of dead cattle (her *Book of Bees* includes a recipe for honey apple pie).

Born on 28 January 1935 in Kalamazoo, Michigan, to a landscape architect and a homemaker, LeRoy and Marjorie Gilbert, Hubbell attended Swarthmore College and the University of Michigan before receiving her A.B. from the University of Southern California in 1956. She received an M.S. from Drexel Institute in 1963. Hubbell worked as acquisitions librarian at Trenton State College until 1967, as an elementary school librarian in Peacedale, Rhode Island, from 1967 to 1968, and as serials librarian at Brown University in Providence, Rhode Island, from 1968 to 1972. In 1973 she and her husband since 1955, Paul Hubbell, moved to a farm in the Ozarks in southern Missouri and embarked on the country life well known to her readers. In addition to five books, Hubbell has written a wide range of articles and essays for the *New Yorker, Smithsonian, New York Times Magazine, Time, Harper's, Sports Illustrated,* and *Discover.* She now divides her time between her farm in the Ozarks and Washington, D.C., where she lives with her second husband, Arne Sieverts.

I came across Sue Hubbell's work in a way she would appreciate. I was looking for something else. Discovery as a fruit of digression seems to be a method of research for which she has a certain affinity. *On This Hilltop* (1991) caught my eye—a small book that looked as if it might rest easily on top of the pile by my bedside, might yield a new vein in the rich mine of nature writing, a new woman's voice, and could provide a modest feast in bite-sized essays suitable for reading during late night hours. As it turns out, they are suitable for prime daytime hours as well, and for sharing with any friend who likes to read. Within the week I bought her other three volumes: *A Country Year: Living the Questions* (1983), a similar collection of essays on subjects related to farming and beekeeping; *A Book of Bees* (1988), an unorthodox and informative conversation about life with bees that is far more than a manual on beekeeping (it's a compendium of entomological fact and lore, personal reflections, and parables of rural life); and *Broadsides from the Other Orders* (1993), a lively, affectionate, and digressive tour of the insect world guaranteed to dispel bug phobia and instill a certain respect for bugs in even the most hardened mosquito smasher. Now a confirmed Hubbell fan, I spent several happy afternoons hunting down her numerous articles, many of them in the *New Yorker* and the *Smithsonian*. These range from elegant essays on loons, ladybugs, magpies, and of course bees, to a survey of truck-stop culture on U.S. interstates, a report from a magicians' conference, and a biographical sketch of Polly Pry, an early and infamous female journalist.

Hubbell's essays on farming and practical ecology are liberally interlarded with advice (as on how to keep an old truck running), reflections (as on the loneliness of winter and the goodness of loneliness), and an occasional Thoreauvian homily (as on human folly). She pauses in the midst of informative disquisitions on hive construction or current controversies over requeening to regale her readers with small adventure stories about life on the farm that seem to have occurred to her in midthought. With their odd bits of literature and poetry about bees and bugs, her essays move freely from the scientific to the poetic in a way that gracefully reunites these typically estranged worlds of discourse.

Science and poetry are, for Hubbell, complementary ways of seeing that, like binary vision, enable a kind of depth perception. Thus a comical poem by E. B. White about mating queens precedes several pages of detailed instructions about the commercial handling and mailing of queen bees. And another chapter includes passages from a nineteenth-century Swiss naturalist and popular writer; a passage from Columella, a Roman agriculturalist; and a recommendation that her readers seek out a children's tale about bees, Frank R. Stockton's *The Bee-Man of Orn*, illustrated by Maurice Sendak. Such digressions widen the focus of her work and invite imaginative reflection, but take nothing from its value to the general reader as a guide to some of the smaller corners of the natural world.

Hubbell's bibliographic enthusiasm surfaces frequently; she recommends books in the way one friend does to another, eager to share what she has discovered and learned from. In *A Book of Bees* she digresses at one point from the topic at hand to provide short summaries of three books she regards as "basic texts" for beekeeping, adding by way of friendly advice that the novice beekeeper "shouldn't read them as an introduction to beekeeping, because they will overwhelm him, but he should buy them and save them for his second winter's reading" (p. 58).

It was once said fondly of Ralph Waldo Emerson that when he appeared as a lecturer, he seemed to think his listeners were as good as he was. It might similarly be said of Hubbell that she seems to think her readers are every bit as avid, persistent, eager, eclectic, and enthusiastic as she is, and will, in their turn, read everything they can find when questions come to mind. Such trust can generate unwonted enthusiasm in even the casual reader, and her intellectual delight is infectious. She loves to remind us how one thing leads to another, how learning continues in an enlarging spiral. Her interest in bees' habitats, for instance, leads her to conclude that "a beekeeper must be something of a botanist in order to learn the blossoming patterns of flowers that represent significant nectar flows for the bees" (*A Book of Bees*, p. 71). Apparently, he or she must also be something of a carpenter, mechanic, local diplomat, politician, and, in a Thoreauvian or Whitmanesque way, a loafer. In her more meandering essays—patterned perhaps on the rambling conversations of village life—she seems, like Whitman, to invite the reader to "lean and loaf with me."

Hubbell is certainly no purist. She gives herself permission to change plans, linger over a second cup of coffee, spend an afternoon picnicking, and stop and watch rather than move on in the midst of work when curiosity overrides plan. For her, all rules are rules of thumb, dispensable if something else works better. Her most consistent advice about beekeeping, as about any other skill, is to learn from the bees themselves. "After a person learns something of bee biology and behavior," she assures us, "he can make up his own rules—and then can have the fun of defending them passionately to other beekeepers" (*A Book of Bees*, p. 53).

But for all her happy eclecticism, Hubbell is no dilettante. *A Book of Bees* and *Broadsides* are two of the best introductions to bees and bugs available both to the general reader and to those with professional or academic entomological interests. She generously bears in mind the problems of the novice beekeeper or rookie naturalist, often writing as though to encourage (and sometimes amuse) those starting out on a perilous and frustrating path toward a promised land of vocational or avocational delights. Hard upon a lengthy discussion of certain problematic issues in techniques of beekeeping, she wryly cites an obscure manual giving advice to woman beekeepers, written by one Cyiula Linswik in 1875, warning the female apiarist to buy rather than make her own frames, so as to "spare her gentle fingers for finer uses" and in recognition of her "lack of natural or acquired ability to drive a nail straight." This intrepid but orthodox Victorian goes on to claim that "the woman who begins to keep bees without having her attention directed to this matter is in danger of suffering from vexation of spirit and wounded fingers many times during the course of her novitiate" (*A Book of Bees*, pp. 24–25). Hubbell believes in a hardier breed of women, but allows freely for vexations.

One of the recurrent problems in beekeeping for newcomers to the trade is technical language. Hubbell loves language and classification, though she shuns jargon. To her, the scaffolding of any discipline is vocabulary, and she stops frequently in the middle of a discussion to explain terms, lest readers stumble on an unfamiliar word—"supersedure," for instance, which is the process by which worker bees detect a queen's failing health and set about raising a new queen. "People new to beekeeping tell me," she writes, "that one of the most confusing aspects of the craft is the vocabulary beekeepers

Sue Hubbell

use" (*A Book of Bees*, pp. 8–9). She savors the "lovely Latin name that slips easily over the tongue," such as *Anemonella thalictroides* or *Sanguinaria canadensis*, the way one savors color with the eye or the hand lingers over certain textures. The great orderly system of language has a beauty of its own, related to, but not entirely contiguous with, nature's order. To love order and also delight in the exception, the anomaly, the unpredictable is the "negative capability" that belongs to the true naturalist just as Keats claimed it for the poet: the capacity to dwell "in uncertainties, mysteries, doubts, without any irritable reaching after fact and reason."

Hubbell loves the irregular, the unclassifiable, the unpredictable in nature—those phenomena that foil all attempts at the ultimate taxonomy, the definitive method, the final word. She questions categories and conventions, and holds all method with an open hand. She's comfortable with exceptions and oddities and the general messiness of life; she neither feels embarrassed by the inevitable limitations of human systems nor daunted by their pretentious claims to comprehensiveness. She points out, for instance, how odd a phenomenon the drones are. They "have grandfathers but no father, and . . . produce grandsons but no sons"; their only function is to mate with nubile queens; they cannot collect nectar or pollen or defend the hive; and they "are not very bright"—not only are their brains small, but "they have been known to try to mate with a swallow flying by or an artificial queen trailed on a helium balloon by entomologists" (*A Book of Bees*, p. 93). She tells a story culled from a 1932 treatise about a cockney beekeeper who, deploring the death by negligence of a fellow keeper's bees, observed, "You can't do just as you like with bees. They be wonderfully chancy things; you can't ever get to the bottom of they" (p. 76). Hence, perhaps, her own observation that beekeeping is "farming for intellectuals" (p. 53).

A Book of Bees, though not her first book, may provide the best introduction to the richness of Hubbell's work. Organized in four sections that detail the seasonal occupations of the beekeeper, it is clearly a book written to share a passion. She recalls of her first year as beekeeper: "I bought my first beehives in the autumn, and then spent the following winter trying to figure out what to do with them. I read everything I could find in print about bees. I talked to as many beekeepers as would stand still for my questions. I joined the state beekeeping association and heard talks by the experts at its meetings. I found there are as many ways to keep bees as there are people to tell about it" (p. 52). Hubbell purveys information with the delight a scavenger takes in his trophies, often recounting the conversation in which some question sent her to read "all I could find" about some insect disease, climatic variables in honey production, or the distinguishing habits of a rare subspecies. Her voracious curiosity seems born of, or perhaps the source of, compassion for all living beings. She tells how on some bright days in midwinter, between storms, she will pack a lunch and "drive around to my beeyards to see how the bees are wintering" (p. 46). Candidly, she admits to more than entrepreneurial interest: "It is good to assure myself that all the telescoping covers are tightly in place, and to check whether cows have knocked over any hives. But the truth is I just miss the bees and I want to see them" (p. 46). Hubbell's occasional anthropomorphisms are affectionate; her imagination tends toward empathy, not fantasy, to bring her closer to an accurate reading of plan and purpose in lives and designs so alien to our own. She leaves the question open of what is an anthropomorphism and what may be an accurate description of the ontology of animal and insect behavior. Can bees, for instance, have a morale problem (p. 18)?

Dedicated to "the Sweet Bee, Apis Mellifera," *A Book of Bees* offers practical, unpretentious instruction in beekeeping, including some of the controversies about method that enliven the conversation among the large club of apiarists. "Beekeepers are an opinionated lot," Hubbell tells us, "each sure his methods and his methods alone are the proper ones" (p. 52). She goes on to account for this diversity by recognizing that the variables are countless. For example, some beeyards, only a few miles apart, may be in different climate zones and thus need different kinds of care (p. 53). Her passion for research is thus balanced by a certain good-humored disrespect for textbook knowledge: "The textbooks say bees cannot fly unless it is 10 C or more. The bees have not read the textbooks and often fly out for their cleansing flights on days like today" (pp. 47–48). She also dispels numerous myths and misconceptions about bees, generously taking into account the reasons why they have taken hold:

> "I had some bees once," I hear from now-and-again beekeepers, "but the moths got 'em." This is confusing the sign with its cause. Wax moths are everywhere. A strong bee colony can defend itself from their damage, but once there is a drop in strength and morale the balance will tip in favor of the wax moths. (p. 18)

The book sometimes reads like an almanac, sometimes like an advice column. Sometimes the advice takes the homey tone of "Hints from

Heloise": "I prefer this method..." she frequently begins, after explaining the alternatives, and always says why. In places, her detailing of the paraphernalia of beekeeping is reminiscent of Herman Melville's whaling chapters in *Moby-Dick*, where it is assumed that a reader interested in the metaphysics of the Pequod's voyage will also be interested in the technology. For her, the technical questions are just as interesting as the metaphysical questions—and not entirely separable. As she details the processes, she stops along the way to explain, reflect, entertain.

The teaching function of the book is enhanced by Hubbell's capacity to imagine the problems of the novice making his or her first forays into beekeeping or, for that matter, into nature observation. (After assuring "those new to bees" that the best way to avoid being stung is to "move easily and confidently" among the bees, she adds compassionately, "There is nothing that gives a person more confidence in the presence of bees than to be zipped snugly inside a bee suit" [p. 7].) She seems refreshingly able to keep what is sometimes called a "beginner's mind," looking not with false naïveté but with renewed wonder at the natural world in her own backyard. Her side trips into history, in particular, widen the canvas and put beekeeping into a long and noble and sometimes eccentric tradition. Like Henry David Thoreau, she sees as a natural historian: always aware that ideas and practices and the very form of natural things come to us in the midst of their long course of development; that nothing is final and fixed; and that we are heirs of both the knowledge and the illusions of the past: It is in this spirit that she calls our attention to the ancient Greek tales of the god of beekeeping, Aristaeus, to Pliny's writings on bees, to Aristotle's observations, and Virgil's poems, and to Columella's practical advice about bees, noting that for centuries bees have been a focus of attention for "able and literate observers" of all stripes (p. 55). She writes of Lorenzo Langstroth, inventor of the modern beehive, with particular admiration not only because of his considerable contributions in writing and invention to beekeeping, but also because he was by his own account mentally

unbalanced for half his life, afflicted with melancholia, hysteria, depression, and various compulsions (pp. 11–12). These sad facts seem to add a note of poignancy and humanity to what he sees in the world of bees.

To see like a beekeeper is to see a landscape anew; in the foreground are the flowers that attract and the animals that threaten bees. "Snow asters are so common," for instance, "that they are seldom noticed except by bees and beekeepers, to whom they are among the most cheerful of flowers" (p. 6). Hubbell's maxim that the way to informed beekeeping is to learn from the bees comes from the humility of the real learner: "The only time I ever believed that I knew all there was to know about beekeeping was the first year I was keeping them. Every year since I've known less and less and have accepted the humbling truth that bees know more about making honey than I do" (p. 47). She adds, "The less I disrupt and fiddle with the bees, the more they can concentrate on making honey" (p. 68). But Hubbell's laissez-faire philosophy is organic rather than capitalistic. She concludes, "the best beekeepers I know are those who let the bees themselves, not equipment manufacturers, be their teachers" (p. 38).

Hubbell details patiently and never dully the various meticulous processes of caring for the bees and the hives. She describes signs of sickness or irregular conditions and explains equipment, likely problems, and alternative methods as she goes along. In doing so, she demonstrates what flexibility and imagination may be brought to the enterprise. Hubbell shows how knowledge of process can allow one to reinterpret sense experience. If all we know about bees is that they sting, we are most likely to think of them as always preparing to sting. The more we know about the intricate purposes of bees' productive lives, the more we realize how little we matter to them—and what does matter to them. Recognizing, for instance, that the rank odor that struck her the first autumn of her beekeeping as a possible sign of American foulbrood, a dread disease for bees, was actually the smell of aster honey, Hubbell experienced a change in her sense of smell: "Now that I know better, the smell of aster honey does not seem bad; it is a strong, fine scent, a sign that the bees will winter well" (p. 7). T. S. Eliot's observation from *Four Quartets* (1943) about the quality of much human experience certainly applies to the novice observer of nature who sees but does not see because he or she doesn't know how to interpret what is seen: "We had the experience but missed the meaning; an approach to the experience restores the meaning in a different form."[1]

Interpretation is part of the art of beekeeping: reading signs, often subtle ones; learning, as in any relationship, how to read new ones. When the entrance to a hive is "scattered with small dirty-white and blue flakes," the beekeeper should recognize chalk brood, a serious hive disease. When the beekeeper notices that the bees' abdomens are in the air after the hive is opened, he or she should recognize that they have been disturbed and are fight-ready. In her sensitivity to the complex sign systems of bee life, Hubbell leaves room for the anomalous and the inscrutable. Seeing bees hover in an unusual pattern around the hive, she considers possible explanations for their behavior before concluding, "Perhaps they were doing no work at all. Bees look terribly busy. An opened hive is the stuff of platitude, but the truth is that bees, like other animals (including humans), spend a lot of time doing nothing at all" (p. 78). She quotes one apiarist's conclusion, founded upon extended observation: " 'No single bee that I watched ever worked more than three and one-half hours a day' " (p. 78). Hubbell is comfortable with exceptions and skeptical of generalities; she values inconsistencies and anomalies because they keep us on our toes.

One of the more endearing and amusing moments in *A Book of Bees* is an account of Hubbell's occasional conversations with her insect friends. Like gardeners who talk to their plants, she allows for the possibility of communication with beings unlike us — a practice that might be efficacious in some mysterious way for us, if not for them:

It is silly to talk to bees — for one thing, they can't hear — but I often do anyway. I tell them encouraging things, ask them for help and always thank them for doing good work. It is said that when a beekeeper dies someone must go and tell his bees about his death or they will fly away. . . . In the West Country of England, the custom also requires tapping on the hive three times and giving the news with each tap. If this ritual is not observed, someone else in the beekeeper's family may die within a year. It all sounds very superstitious, but I like the courtesy toward bees implied by the custom; I hope someone remembers to tell my bees when I die. (p. 82)

This sometimes whimsical habit of empathy adds a personal quality to Hubbell's strong ethical sense about dealing with the animal world. She is unsentimental, clear, and respectful. Her essential principles are to watch and learn: don't disrupt; don't exploit; understand what they need; be grateful. She objects to commercial methods that increase honey production at the expense of the bees' own elaborate ways of organizing and maintaining themselves as a working colony, and recalls with some satisfaction a professional meeting at which a speaker, advocating such exploitative methods, was critcized by "a tough ex-marine, a shrewd businessman and no sentimentalist" who objected that these methods were cruel and "an ungrateful way to keep bees" (p. 52). Reflecting on her own methods, Hubbell unevasively states that trade-offs are involved for both beekeepers and bees in domestication. She believes that all living creatures evolve their life strategies in an environment of compromise. "More harm than good" is a formula that occurs repeatedly in her assessments of certain methods of honey production. Winter feeding of bees, for instance, "may do more harm than good. Chilled, they will drown in the liquid honey or sugar syrup in a feeder. It is possible to give them a frame of honey from another hive, which they can use directly, but in order to do so the donor hive, too, must be opened and the seals that the bees have so carefully made against the cold must be broken. This stresses both colonies" (p. 51). Hub-

1. "The Dry Salvager," in *T. S. Eliot: The Complete Poems and Plays, 1909–1950* (New York: Harcourt, Brace, and World, 1952), p. 133.

bell reminds herself again and again that the bees do not need her to do their work in the world; she needs them. Hers is a healthy recognition of reciprocity, based on respect.

Without preaching, she communicates how anthropocentrism can blind us to the lives and needs of other species:

> I long ago gave up a number of beekeeping practices conceived with the notion of making bees do certain things that seemed good from a human standpoint but which usually involved radically disrupting the hive. Instead, I watch the bees more, try to understand what they are doing and then see if I can work in a way that will be in keeping with their biology and behavior. I try to create conditions that will make them happy, and then leave them alone as much as possible. (p. 30)

Hubbell regards "watching" as a vital part of her work, sometimes taking her lunch or coffee out to the hives and settling in for the express purpose of witnessing the bees "attending to their wintertime chores" (p. 51).

The difference between work and play for her is not large. "It took me several years to convince myself that I was doing genuine productive work when I walked out into wild places with field guides to the wildflowers and shrubs, a notebook and picnic lunch (and, if I could persuade a friend to come along, a bottle of wine) in a knapsack. It seemed like too much fun" (p. 71). Hubbell seems since then to have reconciled herself to fun. The playful tone that infuses all her writing testifies to a fundamental delight in life in all its forms. Such playfulness is quite the opposite of the frivolous, glib, or trivial. It is a profound recognition of the goodness of the world and a wish to participate gratefully in life.

Nevertheless, Hubbell chuckles at, and sometimes deplores, the naive, romantic pieties of "back to the landers" who come to the country seeking spiritual refuge from urban wastelands. She generously reminds us that she herself left the city for the country, the East for the Midwest, seeking just such refuge. However, she was able to survive country life only by replacing utopianism with pragmatism. She stayed

through the disenchantment of broken machinery, crop failures, repeated lessons on the cost of ignorance, and ultimately a broken marriage. Instead of romantic myths, she offers a practical guide to a truly alternative life.

Yet she might utter Thoreau's own caveat— that those who want to live such a life must carve out their own. Even farming is a matter of style, philosophy, and metaphysical imagination. She accepts with wry humor her own more or less permanent status as novice and outsider to the generations-old natives. She writes as an amateur in the best sense, admitting, "None of us is making much money, but we stay with farming because we enjoy it and like to mess around with animals" (p. 26).

Hubbell sometimes appreciates, sometimes laughs good-naturedly at popularized versions of rural folk culture that make large claims for homespun wisdom. The inaccuracy of some bee lore is entirely compensated for by its charm. Thus, Hubbell claims that the advice of Columella, a Roman writer on agriculture, "still bears consideration":

> If thou wilt have the favor of thy bees, that they sting thee not, thou must avoid such things as offend them: thou must not be unchaste or uncleanly; for impurity and sluttiness (themselves being most chaste and neat) they utterly abhor; . . . thou must be no stranger to them. In a word, thou must be chaste, cleanly, sweet, sober, quiet, and familiar, so they will love thee. (p. 55)

Similar cited are factual oddities like the discovery of Karl von Frisch, a Nobel laureate and zoologist, that "it helped bees to find their own hives if those placed in a row were painted different colors; in addition, he found that they rather fancied blue" (p. 42).

But Hubbell carefully distinguishes lore from fact and is quick to label "anecdotal" some of the many claims for various bee products of commercial value to health-food stores and the alternative medical establishment, such as the alleged value of bee pollen and royal jelly. She never casts aspersions but, like any conscientious scientist, puts warning labels on speculative information:

> In recent years, vendors of nostrums to the health-food industry have been delighted by Ronald Reagan's public consumption of pollen, and pollen has become a hot item in health-food stores. Claims are made that humans who eat pollen are stronger, sexier, livelier and more cheerful, but there is no good medical evidence to back up these claims so far. (pp. 64–65)

Hubbell modifies her criticisms with an affirmation that she maintains an open mind as an empiricist, that bee venom does help her arthritis for whatever reason, and that her cautions are not condemnations but attempts to restore common sense to a discussion where it is easily lost. After some discussion of diseases that affect bees, she cautions the beekeeper to maintain a sense of balance. "Young medical students," she reminds us, "often decide they have each fatal condition they learn to diagnose, and new beekeepers sometimes fall into a similar habit, believing their bees have every disease they read about. Most strong colonies of bees never sicken. Most well-kept bees are healthy" (p. 73).

Hubbell, like Annie Dillard, David Quammen, and Edward Abbey, among others, is clearly aware of the importance of entertainment in science writing. Frequently quoting from favorite writers on scientific subjects, she admits to style as a serious criterion of judgment even in science. "Unfortunately," she laments, "elegance and vivid style is no longer the fashion in entomological writing" If that is true, her own book on entomology stands as a notable exception. She lists others: J. L. Gould, Roger Morse, E. H. Erickson. But the place of story and the importance of style remain significant pedagogical issues in nature writing. If we know what we know most deeply through stories, as some narratologists and psychologists maintain, then information without some context that might be grasped as story is sterile stuff.

The short essays in *A Country Year* and *On This Hilltop*, collected from columns contributed to newspapers, allow Hubbell a wider canvas on which to address a variety of issues in country living: machine maintenance, village politics, seasonal occupations, single observations of natural phenomena—the behavior of dogs, wild animals, and a variety of insects. In the opening chapter of *A Country Year* she recalls a research project years earlier where her job was "to dig up a cube of earth from each place every week, sift it, count and rough-classify the inhabitants visible to the naked eye, and then plot the population growth." She has never since forgotten, when she looks at the land, "what is going on down there: Millions of little bodies are fiercely metabolizing and using the land" (p. 6). The story sets the tone for the ensuing essays; underlying the observations of a naturalist, the advice of a farmer, and the human interest stories of a good journalist is a deep ecology of the heart: husbandry, stewardship, sound agriculture begin in respect for the beings with which we share resources and upon which we depend in more ways than we know. To live a fully human and fully conscious life is, to follow her model, to recognize the presence of the nonhuman and to honor our interdependencies. "It begins to make me dizzy," she writes, "even trying to think of taking a census of everybody who lives here; and all of them seem to have certain claims to the place that are every bit as good as and perhaps better than mine" (p. 7).

The various and overlapping rubrics used by biologists over the centuries testify to the wild intricacy of life. Hubbell takes a certain perverse pleasure in exposing the inadequacies of classifying schemes—our ways of getting comfortable with what's out there by imposing our ideas of "structure, framework, schemata, system, classification and order" (p. 9). She never lets us forget that our schemata, including Linnaeus' elegant system of Latin binomials, are merely tools to help us get a handle on the incredible diversity of the world. She is grateful for them and wary of them. They are traps as well as tools. The impulse to order must always be tempered by a willingness to take into account what doesn't fit the paradigm—the oddities and monstrosities and surprises that keep us thoughtful and wondering.

Hubbell looks back and forth from animals and plants to humans, seeking to discern what may be learned from the animal world, recognizing common ground, but unwilling to romanticize or to push analogy too far. Reverence is tempered with common sense, and she retains a firm grip on her own and her readers' humanness even as she exposes the limitations of the human point of view. Her own experience of motherhood thus becomes matter for reflection both as something shared with all animals and something apart from and immensely more complicated than animal bonds:

> In order to become an adequate mother, I had to learn to keep the old sow bear under control. Sow-bear love is a dark, hairy sort of thing. It wants to hold, to protect; it is all emotion and conservatism. Raising up a man child in the middle of twentieth-century America to be independent, strong, capable and free to use his wit, intellect and abilities required other kinds of love. Keeping the sow bear from making a nuisance of herself may be the hardest thing there is to being a mother. (p. 90)

This book, more than the others, combines autobiography with nature writing. In itself this does not distinguish Hubbell from many other nature writers who routinely include self-reflection in their repertoire of observational habits. Questions become important, she posits, when they become personal.

Her attention to her own needs and impulses, long-term and momentary, is visible in the range and design of the essays: something catches Hubbell's notice in an unsuspecting moment, and she follows it like a dog sniffing out a scent, always alert to the possibility of new sources of nourishment for her ravenous curiosity. Thus a sudden appearance of frogs on her windows produces a chapter on frogs that begins with the acknowledgement "I had not known before that they were attracted to light" (p. 13). Typically the chapter ranges a bit afield—from the plague of frogs in ancient Egypt ("a fussy man, that Pharaoh, and one easily unnerved" [p. 16]) to a fleeting speculation about the frog-prince,

to a story about a summer-long relationship with a frog who took up residence in her barn. "I came to regard him," she reminisces, "as a tutelary sprite, the guardian of the honey house, the Penate Melissus" (p. 17).

One notable chapter takes up chicken farming, an aspect of agricultural life Hubbell seems to regard with somewhat less fascination than beekeeping. It's less complicated and more frustrating:

> My chicken operation, I like to believe, is one of the few straightforward bits of farming that goes on at my place. But during the past weeks I have been trying to get the chickens organized to sleep inside the coop, and in doing so I've been forced to think like a chicken, which is not very straightforward at all. (p. 111)

She seems to manage the emphatic leap successfully enough to train the chicks to recognize home by devising ingenious ways to get them there, and is able in the final paragraph to report. "Chickens' tiny brains do not remember much, and when I let them out a few days ago they had lost all memory of roosting anywhere but in the coop, and tidily returned to it each evening" (p. 116). Some years ago John Seed wrote a book called *Thinking Like a Mountain* (1988). When Hubbell seeks understanding of nature by thinking like a chicken, a bee, a dog, a caterpillar—reasoning from their necessities, curiosities, and capacities—she notices not only what is predictable in their behavior but, perhaps as important, what is quirky, odd, or unique. She returns repeatedly to the mystery of animal organization. Even Henri Fabre, she notes, "never discovered what it was that could turn one [pine processionary] caterpillar into a leader as soon as he was at the head of the line" (p. 220). A fellow naturalist, a friend named Asher Treat, sharing her curiosity about this particular unexplained phenomenon, speculated, " 'Maybe it's the same thing that makes people drive in Sunday traffic or watch TV or vote Republican" (p. 221). No creature, she concludes, lives by rule or rote.

Despite the fact that her two major books are about insects, "higher" forms of animal life interest Hubbell as well. Human beings are among the life forms investigated in these essays, though they by no means receive top billing. Hubbell treats the customs, mores, and lore of country life with a delicate combination of amusement and respect. In a small town where everyone's business provides material for gossip at the feed store and any unusual occurrence is a news item, the patterns of human communication, judgment, prejudice, and superstition become as fascinating to her naturalist's eye as the mating and gathering behavior of bees. "Here in the country," she writes, "Listening to the police scanner vies with television as an evening's entertainment" (p. 31). When news thus circulates one night of a strange death at the Veterans of Foreign Wars campground down by the river, she spends a night letting herself be aware of the proximity and mystery of death, and the following day responds to an urgent invitation to a party at that same campground: "I said I would come. . . . The campground had been taken over by death; it had to be returned to life and parties before it grew a ghost." And so the neighbors gathered and partied: "We all ate something or other. I sat with the circle of wives and daughters, and we talked of something or other. The men sat by themselves, drinking" (p. 32). These acts she recognizes not as banalities but as the rituals of communal life that bind individuals to each other in necessary mutual loyalties. Her outsider's amusement at such things never trivializes. The importance of community life surfaces again and again as a theme for this urbanite-turned-countrywoman, whose process of acculturation has called forth both humor and humility. Thus, when she gets help roofing her barn, she learns that her role in the process is to bake pies. "It took six pies to finish the roof," she recalls. "I had not known that pies were such an important part of construction" (p. 89).

A recipe finds its way into *On This Hilltop*. Hubbell points out that her "Richard Nixon artichokes," which we can all enjoy for the cost of her small book, are "the only benefit I've ever received from Richard Nixon." It appears in a chapter whose opening line is "I'm a lousy cook" (p. 127). This book often intersperses Hubbell's observations of other creatures with brief forays into self-scrutiny. Frequently, a confessional opener—"I worried a lot when I was a kid" (p. 137); "I'll never be an Ozarker" (p. 114); "Some years back when Paul and I found ourselves with a bad case of jitters, we swore off coffee and threw out our coffee pot" (p. 62)— provides a point of departure for anecdotes that become parables of country life, often winding their way through the byways of human comedy to a startling or sobering insight of much larger dimensions than the short essay seemed to promise. Less exclusively focused on plants, animals, and insects than her other books, this one shows that "nature writing" can be a habit of mind as well as a topical focus. These essays are often Montaigne-like excursions into topics that seem to arise out of what Virginia Woolf would have called "an ordinary moment on an ordinary day." They suggest that, looked at in a particular light, any experience becomes matter for philosophical and scientific reflection.

Broadsides from the Other Orders continues in the idiom of the personal essay—a woman who can get personal about beetles and daddy longlegs is someone who has much to teach even the most casual reader, who, doubtful of his or her own entomological interest, most often sees the insect world through the frame of a fly swatter or from behind a can of bug spray. Here, once again, Hubbell tries to see what a bug sees, to appreciate what these tiny creatures respond to in mating, in their various attractions to particular flowering plants, in their resistances to what humans might believe are congenial artificial environments.

In *Broadsides* Hubbell's interest in systems of organization and classification comes to the foreground. The book is very simply organized: each chapter focuses on a particular insect as representative of its order, beginning with "Order Lepidoptera: Butterflies," making its slow journey through the microcosms of midges, gnats, blackflies, silverfish, katydids, and gypsy moths, among others, to the final chapter, "Order Orthoptera: Camel Crickets." She explains her preoccupation with insects in an introduction in which she reports having learned that "for every pound of us there are 300 pounds of bugs" (p. xvii). Realizing, however, that interest in bug life is not a passion shared by the common man, she tells the story of her cousin, an entomologist, who got that way more or less by accident. "He is a modest man," she writes, "startled to be the world authority on moth ear mites," which specialty he began to pursue when he discovered mites "tucked away in a moth's ear." The little creatures prove to have a large impact on moths' survival patterns, which in turn affect their ecosystems . . . and so it goes on. This same cousin, Hubbell hastens to tell us, is a French horn player, learned to play the viola after the age of eighty, and "had not intended to be an entomologist . . . his ambition had always been to be a horn player in a circus" (p. xix). It is a moral tale about how we are often surprised into our vocations by something noticed from the corner of the eye that finds its way to the center of our vision and reorients us in the world.

To be a scientist seems for Hubbell a discipline of the heart that combines a willingness to be amazed with the patient pursuit of truth in its humbler forms: facts, statistics, data. The chapter on butterflies recounts a trip Hubbell took to the Beartooth Mountains of Wyoming to join the Xerces Society's annual Fourth of July butterfly count. Its opening line communicates something of the joy of lepidoptery to those who may doubt its excitement value: " 'Hot damn!' said Ernest Williams. 'It's *ursadentis*!' " Her love of the entertaining anecdote never buries the deeper purpose of this book, which is to turn our attention to the small creatures whose delicate ecosystems interface with our own in more consequential ways than most of us imagine. Hubbell reports, for instance, what she learned from a researcher on that trip: "the most important research problem in lepidoptery is to figure out 'the subtle and elusive character we call "habitat fit" ' "—what causes butterflies to

be happy in some areas and not in others. The larger importance of such studies is made clear: " 'The ability to manage habitats in ways that preserve biological diversity depends upon a clear understanding of the limiting factors, and we generally lack that knowledge,' Bob told me. The Butterfly Count is helping to fill that lack" (p. 6).

The breadth of Hubbell's attention span is perhaps most evident in her chapter on blackflies, which states the obvious at the outset: "It is hard to find any human being who has a good word to say about black flies" (p. 74). She acknowledges how hard it may be to believe that they are reluctant to take human blood (especially for someone "walking along a stream in Maine on a Memorial Day weekend" [p. 77]). She also acknowledges their high ranking on the world's list of "pests." Nevertheless, the chapter presents a persuasive argument against waging a pesticide war on blackflies. Hubbell sides with a researcher at the Beneficial Insects Lab who insists that research should not be concentrated on killing blackflies, which among other inconveniences, carry onchocerciasis, or riverblindness, but on preventing those diseases. The blackfly becomes a case study in the futility of most attempts to eliminate pestiferous species; such efforts frequently result in disruptions that produce larger and more complex problems in environmental management. She includes a reminder that appears throughout her work like a leitmotif: "One hundred and eighty million years of survival, apparently, gives the insects a formidable edge in their competition with us" (p. 88). Her own final solution to the blackfly problem is a full outfit of killer-bee regalia: a nylon suit, zippered veil, and cowhide gloves. And that, she concludes, "is a good, Maine-like solution."

In a rare metaphysical digression midway through her reflections in "The Beekeeper's Spring," in *The Book of Bees*, Hubbell tells a story about the widow from whom she bought her farm. The former owner explained the unusually straight, long rows of daffodils on one of the hills. She had bought a sack of bulbs and given them to her husband to plant. " 'He tried digging holes for 'em by hand,' she said, 'but after a few he decided he weren't going to bother that hard, so he just hitched the cultivator to the mule and made him some long straight furrows and dropped in them daffodils. I thought they looked pretty funny, but I never did say anything, and now they make me think of him and his mule and that day and wish it were all now'" (pp. 70–71). Hubbell thinks of him and his mule, too, when she roams her farm in spring, with gratitude for "the good things they did to establish this farm where I have had bees and been happy" (pp. 69–70). She adds, "I've come to the belief that we manufacture whatever immortal souls we have out of the bits of difference we make by living in this world. It seems no bad thing to have a soul of yellow daffodils in lines cross an Ozark hilltop" (p. 70). It seems no bad thing, either, to have a row of books and essays as variegated and delightful as hers, rich with color, making their bit of difference in this world.

Selected Bibliography

WORKS OF SUE HUBBELL

BOOKS

A Country Year: Living the Questions (New York: Harper & Row, 1983; New York: Random House, 1986); *A Book of Bees* (New York: Ballantine, 1988); *On This Hilltop* (New York: Ballantine, 1991); *Broadsides from the Other Orders* (New York: Random House, 1993); *Far-Flung Hubbell* (New York: Random House, 1995).

ARTICLES AND ESSAYS

"The Sweet Bees," in *New Yorker* 64 (9 May 1988); "Be It Ever So Glitzy, There's No Place Like the New Truck Stop," in *Smithsonian* 20 (November 1989); "Bee Lines," in *New York Times Magazine* (24 March 1991); "Ladybugs," in *New Yorker* 67 (7 October 1991); "Polly Pry Did Not Just Report the News; She Made It," in *Smithsonian* 21 (January 1991).

JOHN JANOVY, JR.
(b. 1937)

STEPHEN B. SHIVELY

THE WORKS OF John Janovy, Jr., a parasitologist, are about the intricacies of relationships and the dependencies that sustain them. As the relationship between parasite and host is the most intimate of relationships, Janovy is intimate with his readers, writing of his life, his family, his desires, his fears. Author of numerous scholarly articles in scientific journals, Janovy is best known for his collections of nature essays. These books, which draw heavily on his experiences with students as the Paula and D. B. Varner Distinguished Professor of Biological Sciences at the University of Nebraska, and on his growing-up years in Oklahoma, read like entries from a personal diary. But rather than keep his observations to himself as most diary writers do, Janovy desperately wants his words to be read, because despite his casual, often folksy style, his subject is nothing less important than how human beings should live their lives.

The son of John Janovy, Sr., a petroleum geologist, and Lillian Bernice Locke, Janovy was born in Houma, Louisiana, on 27 December 1937. The family moved to Oklahoma—first Tulsa, then Oklahoma City—before he started school, and ever since, his life and work have been rooted in the Great Plains. Though his researches have taken him far afield, Janovy has brought something of the plains landscape with

him, wherever he has gone, and he has always returned home to the plains. In *Yellowlegs* he follows the migration of a sandpiper, a bird he first saw in Nebraska, from the Canadian prairies across the Gulf of Mexico and the Yucatán to Argentina. In *Vermilion Sea* he travels with fellow Nebraskans to Baja California to see a whale. But the center of John Janovy's literary world is Keith County, in western Nebraska, site of the Cedar Point Biological Station. Here is the laboratory where Janovy and his students return summer after summer to dissect the plains killifish; here too is the base where they begin their forays into the cattail marshes of Lake Ogallala, the weedy pothole called Dunwoody Pond, the grasshopper-infested hayfields of the Ackley Valley Ranch, and the dozens of other natural laboratories where they collect their specimens and learn about life.

The centrality of Keith County and the unusual stability of Janovy's academic career—he earned all three of his degrees at the University of Oklahoma (B.S., 1959; M.S., 1962; Ph.D., 1965), and except for a postdoctoral year at Rutgers University in 1965–1966, his teaching and research have been conducted solely at the University of Nebraska—might make him appear provincial; indeed, critics have suggested that his writing can be monotonous. Most observers, however, do not consider Janovy limited by the geographic peculiarities of western Nebraska or the political boundaries of Keith County. Instead, they suggest that like Henry David Thoreau and Lewis Thomas and Annie Dillard, he finds the universal in the particular. The lessons of Cedar Point don't fade away when their architect crosses the border of Keith County, because they are about so much more than snails and termites and cliff swallows; they are about the power of the human imagination to make sense of the world.

For Janovy, writing about nature is an imperative response to a life lived in nature. In his books, we find him emersed in the sunset, tramping through muddy marsh bottoms in pursuit of the snail *Stagnicola elodes*, and getting out of his car to watch cliff swallows weave in and out of nests plastered on a highway overpass. This is one scientist who doesn't just send his students into the muck to seine for specimens; he crawls into the river with them. Janovy's affinity for the natural world in all its grubby wonder grew out of a boyhood in Oklahoma spent hunting and fishing and running a trapline for muskrat.

Janovy is a cynic and proud of it. He explains why his fascination is with animal creatures, rather than humans, by suggesting that it would be ridiculous to be overly impressed by a creature bent on self-destruction. Janovy's cynicism is expressed in a certain disappointment for the choices people have made, choices that have destroyed special environments, harmed educational institutions, and threatened the survival of the human race. Janovy is direct in revealing his disgust at what people have done to the world and his fears for the future, but his cynicism leaves room to celebrate natural wonders. He claims he is not particularly romantic or sentimental about the creatures he studies, but such a statement is incompatible with the reality of *Yellowlegs*, ostensibly the celebration of the life of a single sandpiper, a life that gripped the curiosity of the author with an intensity that demanded a full sabbatical's study. In the end of that book Janovy concedes a "kind of

faith in unknown workings [that] went well beyond the classic and into the romantic" (p. 191).

Janovy's cynicism is also tempered by a clear admiration for a wide range of human achievement: music, teaching, sculpture, painting, literature. He is a scientist who places John Barth, Somerset Maugham, and Gore Vidal alongside Thoreau and Stephen J. Gould on his list of favorite authors, and who peppers his works with literary quotations. Janovy rues the transformation of universities into trade schools, yet he celebrates individual professors, in particular his own mentors, Leslie A. Stauber at Rutgers and J. Teague Self and Harley P. Brown at Oklahoma, and he praises individual students. There is no denying that Janovy is deeply troubled by what the world has become, but a die-hard cynic would not have his vital concern for preparing future generations to live in a distressed world. If enough bright minds can study the right questions and spend a little time following sandpipers or seining the South Platte River, he writes in *Yellowlegs*, there will be enough true artists to "provide the eternal framework upon which to hang and arrange the thoughts which would guarantee the survivals of species" (p. 191).

In many ways Janovy is more a philosopher and a teacher than a writer. When he discusses the relationship of host and parasite in *Yellowlegs*, he acknowledges that often there is little difference between sharing and stealing. Host and parasite both give and take, and the two actions are neither distinct nor separate. Similarly, Janovy blurs the distinctions between teacher and student; just as he gives his students the benefit of his own years of study, he takes from them their energy, their questions, their insights. Janovy shares with his readers his stories, his diaries, the journals of his observations, and his conclusions. He is also alert to what he can take from others in the way of learning, appreciation of beauty, and community. The result is a series of books in which the author builds a highly personal relationship with his readers, a relationship that demands lively, critical engagement and returns provocative ideas about the natural world.

Keith County Journal

Keith County Journal (1978), Janovy's first published book and a manuscript he claims was rejected twenty-two times before being published in virtually unedited form, is a rather eclectic collection of essays that come together as an intellectual journey through the animal kingdom. More than this, however, the book is about a place. Keith County, Nebraska, is known to students of American history as an interval along the Oregon Trail; it is known to everyone else, if it is known to them at all, as a place one passes through on the seemingly interminable journey across the middle of the country. For almost no one is it a destination, though it became that for John Janovy as the home of the University of Nebraska's Cedar Point Biological Station, which Janovy directed for several years. Characteristically philosophical in his analysis, Janovy relishes the difficulties Keith County throws at those who try to study it: "Live in a place where you are not tested, and you are living in a place of inferior quality" (p. 48). Janovy finds that Keith County is not the desolate Nebraska grassland of its reputation; there, he and his students examine a dazzling variety of life. This is a place where humans are inundated with nature rather than the other way around. Janovy feels the electricity of Keith County while "standing knee-deep in the muck of the prairie cattail marsh":

> There is a force in this place, a force that communicates with every living thing, that establishes the psychic environment encompassing snail and curlew and human alike. . . . It is a force that gives you strength, and although it is a force that puts you on a level with the snails, it is also a force that puts the snails on a very high level indeed. (p. 88)

Such a passage takes readers to the high plane of mysticism, but Janovy also writes about the locale with an earthy commonness: "The Ackley Valley Ranch is the girl next door; Arthur Bay is your high-school girl friend, the first real one; Keystone Lake is your sister's friend; Big Mac [Lake McConaughy] is your sister; and the South Platte River is the town putout" (p. 112). Keith County exerts a strong pull on Janovy, becoming the power at the heart of each of his books on biology.

John Janovy is a man capable of deep feeling, and his fondness for the geography of Keith County does not take away from his affection for the people and creatures who inhabit it. The communities those inhabitants form, made up of species that depend on one another for their very existence, are the most significant subject of this book. For example, the first chapter tells of the tiny parasitic protozoa that live in the intestines of termites, doing the work of digestion for the termites, which eat cellulose-laden dung dropped by cows. Neither termite nor protozoa could survive without the other, and both are dependent on a supply of cows dropping dung in a pasture. The discussion is slightly irreverent, but the lesson is clear: what these creatures know by instinct about their interdependence is what people with all their powers of thought have yet to understand.

People who let themselves be touched by the Keith County experience are forever altered by it. Those who live there, like Waldo Haythorn, principal owner of the Ackley Valley Ranch, earn Janovy's respect because they know the rhythms of nature better than any college professor ensconced in a well-equipped university laboratory. And a few students are enthralled by the place and its creatures, finding themselves suddenly burdened with the compulsion to seek answers to questions that can be answered, if at all, only after years of studying *Fundulus kansae* in the South Platte River. Those who accept the challenge, Janovy believes, are better fit to live in human communities: "We now try to see the artists and laborers, ballerinas and boors, classics and romantics in our human friends, and because we do we feel we are able to fight off the dehumanizing conformity pressed upon us by today's world of pride and money and power and poverty" (p. 131).

Ritual is important in Keith County, both for the animals who live there and for the people who study them. Learning from nature is hard work, and Janovy suggests that by repeating tasks and investing them with a certain sacredness, people can touch the past and each other in ways that make the lessons easier:

> The mist net is the basic tool, and there is a ritual that accompanies the setting of the net for the first time each year. Tribesmen have been setting nets for untold centuries; tribesmen have ritualized their hunting techniques in thanks to various deities and in dances, and we are not very different standing in the canyon with nylon mist net. The ritual is about to begin. The air is charged. (pp. 68–69)

Janovy in western Nebraska preparing to seine for specimens

The power in such a ritual lies not only in its connection to heritage; it lies in the implication that performing a ritual represents a commitment. Janovy writes of his commitment to perform his own rituals year after year, to pack up his microscopes and test tubes and turn his van toward the west, to dig the seines out of winter storage and repair them, to explore a new pond, to collect a new crop of specimens and examine them with fresh eyes. The cumulative effect—the reassurance each year that the plains killifish continues to swim in the Platte River, and that its gills continue to support a population of the protozoan *Myxosoma funduli*—means that there is hope for human survival. Ritual, moreover, is not a burden; rather, it is liberating: "I wash, almost every day, what seems like an awful lot of glassware. . . . There is something about washing glassware that is very soothing, that occupies the hands but frees the mind" (p. 164).

Keith County Journal finds value in mundane tasks, but it also celebrates beauty, both in the natural world and in the world of fine art. Janovy finds beauty in the undulations of protozoan parasites and in the buzzing song of the marsh wren, in the swift flight of a barn swallow and in the wild and rugged headwaters of Whitetail Creek. He is also impressed by a series of massive abstract sculptures erected along Nebraska's Interstate 80, the road to Keith County, as part of the state's celebration of the nation's bicentennial. One of these, John Raimondi's *Erma's Desire*, "may be one of the most dramatic pieces of public sculpture ever created," Janovy writes. Some observers would say that a group of angled steel spires set in concrete is not a piece of art compatible with the natural world, but they lack Janovy's power of imagination; noting the sculpture's setting near the Platte River and its reflections in a nearby lake, Janovy concludes, "There may not be another piece of art in the entire world that works with nature the way *Erma's Desire* does, that can tell the story of a whole section of the world as one drives past, going east, at fifty-five miles per hour" (p. 178). An accomplished watercolor painter himself, Janovy dedicates a chapter of *Keith County Journal* to his inspiration and mentor, George M. Sutton, and to explaining his own painting method. Janovy's paintings decorate the covers of three of his books—*Keith County Journal, Yellowlegs,* and *Back in Keith County*—and some sixteen black-and-white reproductions illustrate *Keith County Journal.* Watercolor painting, the man-created art, and biology, the study of art in nature, come together in Janovy's books, and as usual, the world of man and the world of nature depend on each other.

John Janovy celebrates beauty wherever he finds it, in the tangible—natural places, wild creatures, and artistic creations—and in the intangible—knowledge and imagination and curiosity. Foremost among the things of beauty in Keith County are the lessons to be learned from nature. Unabashedly didactic, Janovy fills his book with lessons of science and morality, and readers are never quite sure if there is any distinction between them. "A minute . . . in a marsh is never wasted" (p. 87); "We have never met an animal that has been reduced to a place in the same way some humans have been reduced to places" (p. 92); "A world with a magpie in the hand is not dull" (p. 151); "If we are ever going to place the kind of value on our world that is required to preclude its total destruction as a planet, then we must be able to find the love and joy in a dickcissel" (p. 157); "Keith County has taught us we are not so very different after all from snails and swallows" (p. 207). The lesson of Janovy's book is that our concern must be with "what there is to learn *from* nature rather than *about* nature" (p. ix).

Yellowlegs

The first sentence of Janovy's second book, *Yellowlegs* (1980), announces that this will be an expansive book: "One of these days I'm going to leave Nebraska, cut all those strings and ties and travel to the other prairies of this earth." While *Keith County Journal* is about a place, a small universe that deserves to be studied and loved, *Yellowlegs* is about travel, about joining the timeless migration of the sandpiper, about leav-

ing the classroom and the laboratory and the research station for a journey that Janovy describes with the hyperbole characteristic of this book as a journey "across oceans of ignorance to exotic islands of insight" (p. 20). But *Yellowlegs* is no armchair travelogue for its readers. This is a book of strong, active verbs, words of power and force; it is a book that does not shy away from challenging the scientific community, that attacks the research process as often resulting in "the prostitution of . . . ideas for Federal money" (p. 23). Janovy doesn't stop with criticizing his own profession; he takes on the petrochemical industry, a farm economy that is overly reliant on machinery, dam builders, and all those who have ripped apart the planet in the name of progress. *Yellowlegs* is a more purposeful book than *Keith County Journal,* more aggressive and political.

The book's subtitle, "A Migration of the Mind," comes from a passage that extends literal experience to the symbolic: "And I can tell you now . . . that stomping through the mud after sandpipers in August is sure to launch you into a migration of the mind from which you may never return to what we often call 'civilization'" (p. 15). This is a book about two journeys and two journeyers—the migratory journey of a single female sandpiper and the author's journey in pursuit. Their stories, their trials and tribulations, are compelling enough, particularly because both bird and man often represent their respective species and the successes and failures of those species. But more than an interesting story of travel and travelers, this is a book about ideas, about the values and practices people must adopt if they are to survive.

Janovy argues that the biggest enemy of human survival is technology. Unimpressed by the modern technological explosion, he nevertheless acknowledges that technology can be seductive. Most scientists, unfortunately, listen to the voices of computers and machinery—the same voices responsible for the proliferation of irrigation systems that "are sucking us dry, sapping the very lifeblood of the prairie" (p. 17)—instead of to the voices of nature and naturalists, which call for the preservation of wilderness and the conservation of resources. Janovy realizes that he must abandon the technological state and act like an animal if he is to learn the lessons the yellowlegs has to offer; ironically, it is only by attempting to leave technology behind him that he learns of its prevalence: "The lesser yellowlegs has to face almost every minute of its life the manifestations of our technological age" (pp. 19–20). By the end of the book, having followed his sandpiper for thousands of miles in a second-hand automobile with little more than a pair of binoculars for his research tools, Janovy can recite a litany of the sins of an industrial society:

> Industries that dumped thousands of *new* kinds of compounds into water supplies every year, that spread oil upon mud that looked from the air like water, that raised towers for the projection of energy, towers that snapped the necks of warblers and robins alike, that placed guns in the hands of little boys at early ages . . . that drained prairie wetlands, that shot random birds when ducks or doves weren't flying, that built dams across rivers with broken rock beds beneath, that drove used cars and filled the air with more fumes and chemicals, and that in the final analysis would always be modified to support as a first, and usually only, priority a species other than the yellowlegs. (pp. 168–169)

Technology, however, is more than destructive—it has ultimately failed in giving people what they want and need. Unable to follow the sandpiper across the Gulf of Mexico, Janovy realizes that even in the most technologically advanced society, "wild things can do stuff no human can do or can ever hope to do" (p. 147).

Appropriately enough in a book about travel and technology, there is much in *Yellowlegs* about cars and what it takes to keep them running. Janovy gives an affectionate portrait of his father-in-law, a small-town Ford mechanic named Glenn Oneth, who at his death was eulogized as a master mechanic. Glenn was one of the finest teachers Janovy ever knew, and the most valuable lesson he taught was the importance of being a romantic, someone who values imagination and intuition, the *sense* and *feel* for

things, over "objective reductionist machine-age analytical thinking" (p. 30). Glenn made his living because people didn't know how to take care of their cars, a fact that led to the wry observation he passed on to his son-in-law: "The world [is] a complicated machine driven by a species that doesn't know how to take care of it" (p. 32). What the world needs is a master mechanic with vision, intuition, and a romantic's touch.

The master mechanic is one of Janovy's favorite symbols; another is the river. Janovy is fascinated by the river because it is ever changing yet always constant. Indeed, the same can be said about the migration of birds; the instinct to travel and the migratory paths are constants, but the individual birds always change and there are new challenges along the way each year. The river of John Janovy's world is usually the Platte, the river of the Oregon and Mormon Trails, the river of human migration. The Platte River of *Yellowlegs* is a living thing, even a sensual creature, the object of desire for the people of every state that it passes through. But Janovy believes the Platte has been loved too much; it has been manipulated and used, its lifeblood borrowed or stolen, and now it is in danger of dying. Janovy points out that an abused river is a tamed and servile river, which no longer has the power to carry people into the future and no longer has the potential to inspire and teach young minds. Of course, Janovy is writing metaphorically as well as literally; whenever a technological society takes the wildness out of a natural thing, whether it is the Platte River or a lesser yellowlegs or the Gulf of Mexico or a beginning graduate student in biology, the cost is high.

While tracking the migration of his sandpiper and berating human destruction of the planet, Janovy creates several memorable characters in *Yellowlegs*. One of them is Pops, the elderly, folksy proprietor of Merl's Bar and Grill/Auto Shop/Whore House/Used-Car Sales, the single store in a one-store town in the middle of Kansas. Pops is a bartender who can look at the single feather offered by Janovy and name the species of bird and the part of the body from which it came. The intimacy of his knowledge comes, however, not from a relationship built on respect but rather from shooting hundreds of birds in a single day, from repeated acts of "consumption and wanton waste" (p. 78). Lingering over Pops' story, Janovy moves readers beyond the horror of the slaughter to lessons about people and nature. Pops learns that the birds he destroyed were valuable and comes to regret his actions. Janovy learns to appreciate the larger-than-life memories Pops has of the old hunts, the stories of time spent with friends and family, the natural lore embedded in the old hunter. The scene is typically complex, first because it communicates real affection for a human being in a book that rails at human behavior, then also because it demonstrates the intricacies of teaching and learning—the best lessons often occur outside of the classroom, the roles of teacher and student are interchangeable, and lessons often cannot be planned.

Early in *Yellowlegs* Janovy calls the book his "Report to the American Public of my last year's research upon the natural history of *Tringa flavipes* (Gmelin) 1789, the lesser yellowlegs" (p. 20). Indeed, much in this book can be called a justification—justification for biology as a profession, justification for leaving home and family to follow a bird, justification for writing about the experience. But in no way is *Yellowlegs* simply a "report." It is an intriguing blend of experience and imagination. Readers are never quite sure when Janovy narrates from fact and when he travels in his mind, when he describes the present and when he recalls the past.

Janovy is still angry at the end of the book, angry at people who use technology to destroy the earth and angry at those who place so little value on the life of a bird. When the migration is over, and the banded yellowlegs he has followed is dead, his anger comes out in a passage colored with violent words:

I kicked the Mercury into life, punched in the cassette with the five-string banjo exploding inside, spilling out over the Kansas pasture and plowed fields for hundreds of yards, and threw the bird on the seat. The pedal jammed into the rubber floormat, spitting gravel up into fender wells and out over the driveway, clattering against a wooden shed, sending cats scurrying, wrenching the wheel; and still with the pedal jammed, I turned north back home, back home with a dead banded yellowlegs lying on a front car seat. (p. 190)

But the human journeyer in this book has learned perspective and the ability to synthesize ideas, and he has strengthened his own commitment to the world. While he knows there is no master mechanic who can fix all that is wrong with the Earth, there are people who can lend the master mechanic's touch, who can offer the sense of a romantic to the task of improving the world. The yellowlegs is dead, but Janovy offers hope that the carbon and nitrogen into which she will decay might some day find its way into her descendant. The greatest hope for the future, however, lies in the resolve that Janovy carries back to his teaching: "I had to go back now, go back and teach some biology lessons and tell of the value of some experiences and attitudes I'd learned along the way" (p. 192).

Back in Keith County

In his third book, *Back in Keith County* (1981), Janovy returns to the place he knows best. The theme of this book is intellectual freedom, and one wonders what prompted the choice of topic. Early in the book he relates the story of his work with the World Health Organization, his subsequent discovery that scientists in the rest of the world face unacceptable constraints on intellectual freedom, and finally the realization that few American scientists appreciate their good fortune. Janovy uses this story to explain why he wrote the book, but the anger that sometimes surfaces here makes it apparent that his concern for intellectual freedom is not confined to a single incident. How many colleagues at the University of Nebraska, complacent in their safety net of tenure, had he seen refusing to exercise their freedom to explore new ideas? How many students had he looked upon morning after morning who were afraid to have an original thought? How many narrow, close-minded people had inspired the writing of this book? Such people, who are bright and capable but too stubborn or too lazy or too afraid to think, are Janovy's target.

Keith County is a place conducive to the opening of minds. The expansive vistas, the low, spread-out architecture all promote a broad view of the world. Janovy knows that Keith County is where he does his best thinking:

> My best place *is* along the Platte where in spring the wildest call of all the world, the guttural resonance of sandhill cranes, takes me back to the freedom of primeval times, where in the winter my fish nets freeze solid and bald eagles watch from trees near the interstate, where only my obligations to my own thoughts and ideas guide my eyes and feet. (p. 4)

In the first paragraph of his book, Janovy affirms the phrase that is the motto of Nebraska tourism and the cocky slogan for the cowboy families of Keith County: "the good life" (p. 1). But he immediately counters the boast by warning that the good life is easily taken for granted. That is something Janovy can't tolerate; he intends to wake up those who fail to appreciate the special value of what seems routine and ordinary: the annual return of the sandhill cranes, the call of the bullfrogs, and the freedom to ask questions and seek answers.

Back in Keith County celebrates disorder, the confusion that encourages creativity. The sandhills of western Nebraska, changing their contours with every windstorm, represent a kind of disorder, a small universe of infinite possible arrangement. Unfortunately, human society follows a different pattern in its communities, trying to create a harmonious world, a world with a time and place for everything, a world where predictability is valued. Such a world may be comfortable, but it limits creativity and narrows the range of possibilities. Janovy calls for a world that isn't afraid to mess things up: "Disturbed areas represent opportunity. Too much order represents the opposite" (p. 167).

Janovy uses the cliff swallow to introduce an indictment of higher education. When it is time for them to fledge, nestling swallows leave the interiors of their nests, which offer a comfortable "tunnel-vision view of the world," and perch on the edge of a world "where a panorama of choices awaits" (p. 104). Some birds perish, of course, but others earn the reward of free flight. All too often, colleges and universities encourage the tunnel-vision approach, limiting student choices, packing students into lecture halls that simply don't allow for good teaching, and preventing controversial speakers (Janovy gives the example of Jane Fonda) from lecturing on campus. Janovy rebels against such a system, which takes excitement and anticipation out of learning and deemphasizes the imagination. He suggests that the most worthwhile thing he does as a teacher is "to get college students to . . . go off by themselves and study something they choose out of personal interest" (p. 135).

The major metaphors of *Back in Keith County*—birds in flight and a sailboat named *Lido*—encourage thoughts of freedom. As with all of his books, Janovy supplements the nature-based symbolism with stories of people, the angry tears shed by Janovy's daughter Cindy when she taps the power of her free spirit and challenges a Nebraska congresswoman's opinions about the protection of the snail darter; the incommunicable isolation of Millie and Erle Corfield, who quietly affirm their choice to live on their sandhills ranch; the bumbling eccentricity of Lonnie Paul Dinkle, the oaf who wins Janovy's heart by missing dinner to sit on a bluff and watch the prairies.

In *Back in Keith County* Janovy strays from his usual concern with *inter*dependence to focus on *in*dependence; he is not so much interested in the quality of people's choices as he is in celebrating the freedom in which those choices are made. Keith County reminds Janovy—and all who seek a Keith County experience—of the value of wilderness: "Wilderness is the freedom to think your own thoughts, to put them into practice, to have them judged with the same impartiality that greets the fledgling swallow" (p. 178). Getting away from the population centers, living with and like the animals, pondering the rhythms of nature, provides a way to recover what is truly human: "An awareness of *freedom*, of *independence*, is that not the ultimate essence also of being a human, of realizing all the potential contained in that word 'human'? Yes it is" (p. 19).

On Becoming a Biologist and *Fields of Friendly Strife*

The potential contained in the biological sciences profession is the subject of Janovy's next book, *On Becoming a Biologist* (1986). This book calls on student biologists to take an active role in every aspect of their preparation for the field, as well as in helping to define the profession. Janovy's book is not a lab manual or a career guidebook, nor is it a handbook on course or school selection; rather it is a straightforward intellectual discussion of the characteristics and practices Janovy feels should define the modern biologist.

Foremost among the fundamental characteristics Janovy feels a biologist must have is a belief in the connections between people and other forms of life, a belief that humans "share a common bond with even the most bizarre beetle of the Peruvian rain forest" (p. 2). This worldview suggests an integrated approach to life that links not only people and beetles but also the past and the present, scientist and philosopher, writer and artist. But it is a worldview that differs from that of most other professions in that it perceives humans as late intruders on the planet, at present the most effective competitors for the world's resources but without any inherent claim to permanence.

Janovy argues in this book that values—a reverence for organisms, for example, and a sense of wonder—are more important to a developing biologist than high-tech tools like the electron microscope and the gas chromatograph. He also calls for a broad and tolerant view of the field of biology, and he insists that a biologist be educated in the social sciences and in the arts. Several times in his book Janovy marks distinc-

tions between a biologist and a technologist. Technologists, who often have tremendous biological knowledge of the structures of life forms, operate complicated machinery, collect data, and record observations. But a biologist applies values to information and then formulates hypotheses and theories, bringing a unique and individualized mind-set to the effort of solving problems.

Janovy sets down in *On Becoming a Biologist* the theoretical principles that have guided his work in the natural sciences. He brings biological study out of the world of scientific journals and specialization into a world that values creativity and risk-taking and that counts ethical considerations among the requirements of the profession. This is a noncommercial approach to biology, which sees natural resources not with a view toward utilitarianism and exploitation but as essential contributors to a developing understanding of the complexities of life. Nature is the best teacher of one of the most important lessons for a biologist: "Patience with, tolerance for, and courage in the face of complexity" (pp. 84–85).

Janovy's next book, *Fields of Friendly Strife* (1987), deals with courage of a different sort. The book is a study of the basketball career of Janovy's daughter Jena. It is of limited value to the naturalist, but it shows how the same scientific principles that guide his work in Keith County, the same curiosity, careful observation, and analytical reasoning are brought to bear on a different kind of scientific problem, the question of why Jena plays basketball, why she made the choice to play the sport she was least prepared for physically.

Vermilion Sea and *Dunwoody Pond*

After this interlude in the world of sports, Janovy returns to the natural world and to the method of his first book. In *Vermilion Sea* (1992), the story of two trips to Baja California, Janovy is out to expand his horizons—he wants to see a whale, and to put his hand in the waters made famous to ecologists by John Steinbeck and Edward Ricketts in their book *The Sea of Cortez* (1941). As Janovy explored Nebraska's Keith County by studying its components and seeking to understand the relationships between them, so he explores this new locale; the *Smithsonian* reviewer noted, "What he's after here is the essence of Baja through a series of meditations on its parts—cactus and mountains, whales and intertidal critters, and more" (p. 136).

Vermilion Sea has the same concern about the high-tech mind-set of society and of scientists that Janovy expressed in *Yellowlegs*, but with an important difference; he was confronted by technology at nearly every turn on his *Yellowlegs* journey, whereas in Mexico he finds a landscape that is less permeated by industry. If not quite escapist, the journey of *Vermilion Sea* is more purposeful in recognizing the need to get away: "I am on my way to Mexico to gather ideas and repair the damage of too comfortable an existence" (p. 1). This book is more objective than *Yellowlegs*, and there is less wandering, less questioning of self, less searching for identity.

Janovy is impressed with the pre–World War II attitudes of *The Sea of Cortez*, with the book's "combination of childlike wonder, anticipation, and discovery" (p. vii), qualities sorely lacking in modern scientists. Janovy is not in charge of the Vermilion Sea Field Station; here he can "be a child—a student—again, in a blissful haze of wonder, in the company of grownups who tell me it's okay to stay that way" (p. 6).

When Janovy argues that "the most fundamental activity of science [is] the recovery of a pattern" (p. 12), he is advocating for the activity that has guided his professional life. The recovery of patterns is essential to all his books: what is learned about snails and whales, about pelicans and barn swallows, about oysters and protozoa, can teach much about human beings. If Keith County can be understood, other places can be understood as well. In *Vermilion Sea* Janovy states the fact that validates all of his work: "Of all the traits that separate us from other animals, the ability to detect a pattern of symbolic events and then construct metaphors and allegories must be the most distinctive" (p. 6). The Baja offers its own patterns in such things as sand dollars, pelicans, and the hummingbird sculptures of a twelve-year-old street artist.

Janovy often connects the new wonders of Mexico to those of Keith County, thus demonstrating again the value of patterns. For example, in *Keith County Journal* Janovy vests in the marsh wren the power of the "keeper of the keys"; he sees this bird as the proprietor of Keystone Marsh, whose permission must be solicited by anyone wanting to explore the natural area. He discovers in the Baja a similar creature: "I have found my keeper of the keys, the one responsible for Bahía de los Ángeles. It is a hermit crab named *Clibanarius digueti*" (p. 88). One realizes that the keeper—an "element of nature claiming possession of and responsibility for" a place (p. 82), a being that is so nondescript, so crucial, so pervasive that its absence is unthinkable—exists in all special places for those willing to look for it. The natural world is fascinating for its own sake, but it is valuable because of its patterns, its repeated tendencies that enable scientists to make predictions as they bring beauty and order out of chaos.

The availability of natural patterns to explain the world is not a notion as simplistic as it may sound, however. Janovy acknowledges the "monumental ignorance that characterizes our intellectual relationship with the planet" (p. 121), an ignorance that often precludes the discovery of patterns, which is an act requiring observation, study, and identification. More specifically, he finds that "Baja California appeared different, in some fundamental way, from other lands" (p. 18); uniqueness and difference, particularly apparent in the awe-filled moments of new discovery, are often more obvious than patterns. Back home, after months spent researching in the library and pondering trip notes and photographs, Janovy discovers what it is that explains the Baja California mystique: the answer is a new analogy—the mosaic, that unified work of art made up of individual pieces, each one only partly subordinate to the whole.

This new model, unique parts coming together in meaningful completeness, augments the metaphor of the pattern:

> From a study of art and desert, I learn to build mosaics whose pieces are chips of experience, a skill that is not consumed by such use, but rather is honed and polished, maybe even replicated, in those I teach. Thus by analogy, I think, there is a time to do your daily job and a time to go exploring in places you've never been before, and both must be present and in their proper context before the mural can be considered complete. (p. 23)

For John Janovy, completing his own mural depends on a developing understanding of the patterns and mosaics of the natural world.

Despite his emphasis on making sense of the world, Janovy celebrates the mystical and sacred in nature, which resists categorization. In *Vermilion Sea* he wonders at the sounds of the gray whale:

> We all sit in silence and listen. The morning is dead calm. From far across the glassy surface comes a sound, a deep and mighty sigh—the sound of a gray whale breathing, a sound of great exhalation that is thirty million years old. How far the earth has come, I think, from the Cambrian seas, how much has changed, how many forms have lived for millions of years, then disappeared forever. And how little most of us understand where we truly fit in that parade of success and failure. (p. 189)

One of the places that John Janovy understands better than most people is Keith County, Nebraska, and he returns there in *Dunwoody Pond* (1994). The title comes from an unnatural place that is filled with nature; named for its owner and creator, Dunwoody Pond is an ecosystem consisting of a dug-out hole, a blocked spring, and an overflow pipe that work together to make a pond, water a hay meadow, and create a habitat for thousands of natural species. Despite the title, place is incidental to this book; *Dunwoody Pond* is really about a teaching scientist and his students, and about how they use the natural world to explore answers to their questions about life. More specifically, this book is about the transformation of students into professional scientists, a change that occurs all too infrequently for those, like Janovy, who believe that a threatened species requires the attention of many bright, well-trained minds.

Dunwoody Pond is full of vignettes describing individual students and their discoveries about such things as intestinal parasites in the damselfly or the prairie darkling beetle. In all of his books, Janovy writes about birds and fish and sculptures; in *Dunwoody Pond* he confirms that what he's *most* interested in are his students. The species that houses the parasite may change, and the body of water that is his subject may vary from Lake McConaughy to the Sea of Cortez, but the basic lesson of his books remains: get away from civilization, spend some time grubbing around in the natural world, and you'll learn important lessons from creatures and their environments. Janovy has been doing it for so long that he knows his "system" works. What he discovers in this book is that the greatest variety, the highest forms of stimulation, the most original questions, come from his students, and they are new each year. By seeing Keith County through his students' eyes, Janovy continually uncovers a wealth of new information and insights.

For the most part, the tone of *Dunwoody Pond* is upbeat, even warm—there's the homespun humor of Duane Dunwoody and the smelly beetle named Herkimer, and most of all there are the success stories of the dozen or so students that Janovy suggests can make a difference in their professions. But the book is also disturbing. Janovy tells of students who walk out of class or drop out of school because they disagree with some scientific fact or with something Janovy says; these are students who have been failed by human authority, by the parents, ministers, teachers, and counselors who exert power over intellectual development. Even more disturbing are the stories of the best and brightest students, those who Janovy believes have the potential to become university presidents but settle for careers as athletic trainers. Janovy is particularly angry at a system that teaches students, especially women and minorities, with horrifying success, to say, "I don't believe in the power of the mind I was born with" (p. 104). Janovy is forward-looking in his anticipation of the next class of young scientists, but his hope is blunted by the realization that not all deserving young people will even undertake to look for their Dunwoody Pond, let alone find it.

Janovy's writing, for all its unity of purpose and method, contains its paradoxes, and they reflect the paradoxes of the author. In one moment Janovy expresses hope for the future, in the next he subjects his readers to apocalyptic warnings. He is as much at home drinking beer at the Sip 'n Sizzle in Ogallala as he is at a World Health Organization conference in Geneva, Switzerland. But wherever he is, or however he communicates a new insight or discovery, concern for humanity and respect for the scientific process permeate his work. Janovy developed his methods of inquiry and teaching in a quiet corner of Nebraska, but it turns out that the particular place doesn't really matter, for there are many like it—natural places that contain answers to questions about human survivability on the planet Earth.

Selected Bibliography

WORKS OF JOHN JANOVY, JR.

Keith County Journal (New York: St. Martin's, 1978); *Yellowlegs* (New York: St. Martin's, 1980); *Back in Keith County* (New York: St. Martin's, 1981); *On Becoming a Biologist* (New York: Harper & Row, 1986); *Friends of Friendly Strife* (New York: Viking, 1987); *Vermilion Sea: A Naturalist's Journey in Baja California* (Boston: Houghton Mifflin, 1992); *Dunwoody Pond* (New York: St. Martin's, 1994).

BIOGRAPHICAL AND CRITICAL STUDIES

David Holmstrom, "Salt and Spice Travel Tales," in *Christian Science Monitor* 7 (February 1992), review of *Vermilion Sea*; Donald Dale Jackson, review of *Vermilion Sea*, in *Smithsonian* 23 (September 1992); Diane Casselberry Manuel, "Taking a New Look at Nature," in *Christian Science Monitor Monthly Book Review* 14 (April 1980), review of *Keith County Journal*; Clem Rawlins, *Western American Literature* 17 (August 1982), review of *Back in Keith County*; Matthew Schudel, "The Biologist's Lens and the Life of Nebraska," in *Washington Post* (4 December 1981); Elizabeth Stark, *Psychology Today* 21 (June 1987), review of *Fields of Friendly Strife*; Peter Stoler, "Natural Philosopher," in *Time* (February 1979), review of *Keith County Journal*.

CATHY JOHNSON
(b. 1942)

ALISON R. BYERLY

IT IS DIFFICULT TO SAY whether Cathy Johnson is more accurately described as an artist who writes, or as a writer who draws. The two forms of expression seem equally important in Cathy Johnson's studies of nature, which are texts that she illustrates herself. The collaboration of words and pictures allows her to present her subjects in an intensely realistic manner. At the same time, she retains the imaginative artistry of both media. She sees no conflict between the claims of science and of art in her drawings: "While as an artist I am of course interested in creating a pleasing design on the page, accuracy and clear observation are always most important to me" (personal interview, 11 April 1994). Her verbal descriptions maintain this same fidelity to the actual appearance of things.

Cathy Johnson has lived all of her life in Missouri, and many of her works explore the beauties of that midwestern state. Cathy Ann Hattey was born on 2 October 1942 in Independence, the second daughter of a steel-plant bricklayer and a mother whom she describes in *On Becoming Lost* (1990) as an "artist-poet." Johnson attributes her love of nature not only to her early explorations in the woods, but also to her childhood reading of some of her mother's favorite authors, early nature writers like Gene Stratton Porter and Mrs. William Star Dana. Johnson has said that she feels lucky to have actually become what she wanted to be when she grew up—a naturalist—and her commitment to the role of the amateur naturalist is reflected in the accessibility of her books. They are not daunting displays of expertise; they are educational tools designed to teach the reader how to become what she is herself: an informed lover of nature.

Johnson's training for her chosen vocation has been a continual process. She began her artistic studies at the Kansas City Art Institute in the 1960s, continuing on and off for many years, and she has also taken courses in geology and other subjects at the University of Missouri at Kansas City. She married Harris Johnson in 1963, and they eventually settled in Excelsior Springs. They have no children; in *On Becoming Lost*, Johnson says that her "books and field journals and paintings" are her "progeny," "children of the mind and heart" (p. 130). In addition to her work as an artist and writer, she has taught workshops on watercolor and field sketching in Missouri and elsewhere.

Cathy Johnson's method of self-education is clear in her work, which frequently refers to the authorities whom Johnson has consulted on a variety of subjects. When she is confronted by an unfamiliar plant, she calls a local botanist; when she is interested in a rock formation, she visits a university geology professor. Entomologists, meteorologists, astronomers, and even herbalists become characters in her books, answering questions in dialogues that are recounted verbatim. Many of her books also include bibliographies that encourage the reader to learn more. The tone and structure of her works are perhaps best characterized as "investigative." They are records of her own wanderings, musings, and discoveries.

The popular appeal of Cathy Johnson's work is evident in the wide variety of magazines that have published her articles and sketches. She is a contributing editor and staff naturalist for *Country Living* magazine, and she writes a regular monthly column for *The Artist's Magazine*. Her work has appeared in such publications as *Country Journal, Harrowsmith, Science Digest, Early American Life, Muzzleloader, Sports Afield*, and *Sierra*. In addition to the books about nature listed in the bibliography of this essay, she has written several books on art as well as a wild-foods cookbook. Her book *A Naturalist's Cabin: Building a Home in the Woods* (1991) received a Thorpe Menn Award, and in 1987 Johnson was chosen Conservation Communicator of the Year by the Burroughs Audubon Society.

The Naturalist's Path

The foreword to Cathy Johnson's introduction to nature study is by Ann Zwinger, herself a well-known artist and writer. Zwinger explains how the visual and verbal elements of experience complement each other: "Drawing what you see makes you see more to write about, and writing about what you see makes you see more to draw" (p. ix). *The Naturalist's Path: Beginning the Study of Nature* (1987) is illustrated with full-page excerpts from Johnson's field journals that exemplify this reciprocity. Each picture is a narrative in itself. The casual sketches of plants and creatures are accompanied by jotted notes that give life to the drawings: "a cardinal silently inspects the mossy rocks" (p. 38); "*huge* cup fungus in the dry, rocky creekbed. It's been there most of the summer" (p. 26); "ground is very soft and mushy—did the water get up this high? Looks as if it did—grass is bent" (p. 18). *The*

Naturalist's Path establishes the warm, personal tone that is characteristic of Cathy Johnson's writing. Johnson's books are all written in the same genuine, conversational voice. She speaks to her audience in the manner of a friend sharing an important source of pleasure—casually, but with an intensity that conveys her deep love of her subject matter.

Zwinger calls *The Naturalist's Path* a "guidebook to competent observation" (p. ix), and Johnson distinguishes her book from the many other field guides available to the nature lover by saying that "this book encourages you to write your own field guide" (p. xiii). She feels that reading about nature is not enough; you must go out and experience it. Anyone can be a naturalist, and anyplace can be a rewarding area of study. We tend, she points out, to expect a naturalist to study subjects that are "exotic, removed, remote, unique" (p. xv). But this book demonstrates that you can become a naturalist in your own backyard—"even a city backyard" (p. xviii).

Johnson first advises the reader to discover his or her own special place, pointing out that local parks, museum courtyards, and terrariums can all be "accessible islands of natural history" (p. 5). The important thing, she says, is to free yourself from distractions and learn how to wait quietly for whatever is offered. This will allow your natural, "childlike" curiosity to assert itself (p. 19). Johnson gives examples of questions to ask about the things around you, and recommends attentiveness to "anomalies" such as movement or differences in color (p. 28). She encourages her reader to look for what may be hidden under a rock or behind a strip of bark, and to consider experiencing the outdoor world in unusual conditions—in the winter, at night, during storms—in order to see nature's variety more clearly.

The Naturalist's Path reminds us that we have other senses in addition to vision to draw upon. For example, sitting on a rock in a stream, a listener can hear a symphony of sound: "a rock raised above the others lifts the water into a hollow curl; an oboelike sound, low and rich, results. A shallower riffle, like liquid lace, makes a rapid rustle like brushes on a snare drum" (p. 37). By likening these natural sounds to an orchestra, Johnson suggests that there is a pleasing harmony to the environment, but also that each specific noise has its own part to play. As when listening to music, separating out the individual parts enhances appreciation of the whole. Johnson also recommends lying in the grass, brushing your lips with a leaf, putting your hand through the ice at the edge of a puddle. These things may help to reawaken the "primeval sensitivity" that we have lost (p. 34).

Johnson advocates recording one's observations both verbally and pictorially in a field journal. Although a professional artist, she is not jealous of her craft's prestige; she insists that we all can draw well enough to focus our observations and stimulate our memory. Her practical advice about equipment and technique is balanced by her emphasis on the informal, spontaneous nature of the field journal, which is meant to function as a private learning aid. In order to identify and understand living things, Johnson suggests, we must be alert to the differences in one organism from place to place and from season to season. Familiarity—*practice* in looking at a particular place—is the key to observing such changes, and a journal enables you to record and compare what you see.

In order to help the reader learn to identify some of the plants he or she might encounter, Johnson devotes a section of *The Naturalist's Path* to descriptions of common wildflowers, trees, lichens, and mosses. In a chapter titled "Wildflowers and Weeds," Johnson makes a persuasive case for learning to tolerate and even respect the weeds you may find in your lawn and garden, calling them "nothing more than flowers we haven't yet come to appreciate" (p. 64). Although Johnson refers the reader to botanical guides that will give precise scientific information on plants, her own descriptions are nontechnical and vivid. Here, for example, is wild ginger:

... this plant is unique. With its nearly triangular red-brown petals and a fuzzy white back, it looks as if it couldn't quite decide whether to be a flower or a small, furry animal. It is a member of the birthwort family (Aristolochiaceae). You may miss this little flower altogether; like the shy forest creature it resembles, it tends to hide beneath the cover of its large, hairy leaves that may measure six inches wide. It's earned its name: The strong, gingerlike flavor works well as a substitute for imported ginger when sweetened with sugar. Look under those broad green umbrellas in April and May, where small beetles aid in pollination. (p. 69)

This presents a clear picture of the plant by conveying a sense of its personality. The image of a small animal hiding shyly in the leaves allows Johnson to give pertinent information about the flower's appearance (fuzzy), structure (flower located beneath leaves), genesis (beetles pollinate), season (early spring) and use to humans (edible) by creating a kind of miniature

Cathy Johnson sketching near her home in Excelsior Springs, Missouri

narrative that makes these facts more interesting and memorable. Johnson's frequent addresses to the reader ("You may miss this little flower. . . . Look under those broad green umbrellas") help to bring us into the scene with her, reinforcing the participatory agenda of the book as a whole. She does not want us to just sit at home reading her descriptions; she wants us to go out and look for ourselves.

All of Johnson's descriptions are geared toward understanding how a particular organism functions within an ecosystem. The chapter on trees stresses their longevity and adaptability, describing the different environments in which particular species are found and the kinds of wildlife that surround them. Johnson suggests collecting leaf samples in order to identify local trees and briefly summarizes the commonest leaf structures. As in the discussion of wildflowers and weeds, however, Johnson sees these plants not as passive objects of study, but as living presences. In a section called "Defensive Measures," she describes the protective devices that allow trees to repel dangerous insects. They do more than exist; they change and adapt. Like animals, trees have a distinctive behavior.

Of course, animals are more dramatic, but their mobility makes them harder to observe. In a section on zoological field observation, Johnson talks about the places where particular birds and animals can typically be found, and explains how to determine what lives in your area. Tracking, for example, is an easily acquired skill: "Fresh snow is a *tabula rasa*, a blank slate upon which the day's (or night's) activity is written clearly. You can even judge the time elapsed since the tracks were made—are they crisp and sharp? Has the blowing snow begun to fill them in? Has alternate thawing and refreezing softened the contours or enlarged them out of all proportion?" (p. 134). By calling the snow a blank slate, Johnson reinforces her contention that nature presents many signs that we can learn to read. The Book of Nature is a familiar image in nature writing; Ralph Waldo Emerson, for example, wrote in a famous entry to his *Journal* on 2 November 1833:

Nature is a language, and every new fact that we learn is a new word; but rightly seen, taken all together, it is not merely a language, but the language put together into a most significant and universal book. I wish to learn the language, not that I may learn a new set of nouns and verbs, but that I may read the great book which is written in that tongue.

While Emerson's language has a religious resonance that is missing from Cathy Johnson's words, Johnson's adoption of this metaphor gives her otherwise practical, literally down-to-earth advice a wider applicability. She seems to suggest that learning to read individual signs will allow you eventually to put your pieces of knowledge together into a coherent reading of the whole.

Johnson, like Emerson and other nature writers who have preceded her, sees grandeur in the most mundane aspects of existence. Some of the most common creatures on the planet, Johnson points out, are the least appreciated. Reptiles, amphibians, and fish are plentiful in most climates. Insects and worms are available in gardens and compost heaps. All of these things are worthy objects of interest, Johnson insists, and present a manageable place to begin one's study of nature. Johnson makes her subject accessible to the reader by removing nature from the realm of the exotic. Nature is the familar, everyday life that surrounds us. A "naturalist," then, need not be a highly trained scientist. A naturalist is anyone who takes the time to look carefully at the world.

The Nocturnal Naturalist

The Nocturnal Naturalist: Exploring the Outdoors at Night (1989) exemplifies many of the precepts outlined in *The Naturalist's Path*. Written in journal form, it presents four seasons of change in Johnson's hometown of Excelsior Springs, Missouri. Johnson's experiences and observations are presented through a day-to-day (or rather night-to-night) account. This diary format creates an intimate tone, but the material is in a sense quite impersonal. Johnson certainly records her own reactions to the things that she sees, but she does not lapse into a confessional mode. Her journal contains no digressions about her personal life or feelings on subjects other than nature. And yet, after following Johnson's explorations over the course of the year, the reader develops a strong sense of her distinctive personality and viewpoint.

By focusing exclusively on nighttime observation, Johnson is able, paradoxically, both to narrow her scope and to open up new possibilities. Introducing an unexpected variable—night—to familiar scenes makes them fresh to her eyes. The book's illustrations are more formal than those of *The Naturalist's Path*; rather than on-the-spot sketches, it contains a number of woodcuts, including full-page frontispieces for each of the book's chapters. Their stark black-and-white contrasts are well suited to the book's nocturnal subjects.

Each stage of the night, Johnson finds, has its own special beauty. Dusk is a time of transition: "A small rim of blue light hangs suspended in the west. All the rest of the sky is rich cobalt—glistening, trembling, transparent" (p. 79). It seems to herald the end of possible discoveries, with "night . . . just tipping over the last of the day like the cover on a rolltop desk" (p. 79). But it is still possible to read what seems hidden under cover of darkness. The world takes on a new dimension as the sky fills with lights. Johnson tracks the movement of stars and anxiously awaits the Perseid meteor showers in late summer. Comets can be seen on most clear nights, and the larger pieces, consisting of ice, iron and rock, "flare like a lit match in the darkness at the rate of twenty per hour" (p. 101).

Small details seem to be magnified by partial light and quiet. The entry "January 25—Pre-dawn" memorializes the formation of frost on the windows in the early morning—not an uncommon occurrence, but one that Johnson describes with microscopic care:

This fugitive mycelium of frost marks the passage of warmth and moisture from my house into the night air. It is the breath of the building itself. It gathers along the bottoms of the windows where there is the least turbulence and where heavy, moisture-laden, colder air collects, molecule by molecule. Like snowflakes, these lovely patterns are geometrical, following the immutable laws of freezing water, and they are formed by water melting and recrystallizing over and over through the night. (p. 204)

She characterizes the pattern as "Mondrian gone as mad as Van Gogh" (p. 204), an image that suggests her professional respect for nature's artistry. At the same time, she casually provides an explanation for how, physically, these patterns are produced.

The night is a surprisingly active time. Many things take place that seem mysterious to us because they are so seldom observed, and Johnson is able to discern the ongoing processes and larger patterns. Watching a fat garden spider building a new web every night, she is in awe of its careful architecture. The web consists of eighteen central spokes that are connected by seven hundred and fifty-six "stitches"—which Johnson calculates from the spider's forty-two revolutions around the web (p. 121). As in the description of frost, Johnson balances aesthetic appreciation with scientific accuracy.

The small dramas that unfold during the night seem to take on a theatrical dimension with Johnson in the audience. She watches helplessly as a black rat snake overhead in a tree devours a nest full of robin eggs. While in theory, she likes rat snakes and does not begrudge them the food they need to survive, in practice, she feels "desolate" at the sight of the mother robin chirping disconsolately by the nest (p. 78). One night, an amber bug's divestiture of his carapace becomes a heroic metamorphosis; he "steps out of it like a forgotten life and flexes the promise of his new self, testing his boundaries" (pp. 64–65). When he finally "take[s] his place in the loud alleluia chorus" (p. 65), Johnson is ready to applaud his performance.

During these nocturnal prowls, her reduced vision seems to make Johnson more reliant on her other senses. The noises of the evening ring out clearly in the stillness. She describes a chorus of frogs, "crawling out at once from muddy hibernation . . . jubilant as sleigh bell [sic] at their sudden freedom." Johnson notes with amazement that "one tiny frog sounds like many, not only in his astonishing volume—*impossible* coming from that thumbnail-sized body, that miniscule, vibrating throat—but by a kind of trick of the notes themselves. They seem to overlap, weave in on themselves, magnify themselves." These voices sound like a choir, but are even more entrancing by virtue of their difference: they are "*other*. Not us. Not human. Wild" (p. 13). The combination of familiarity and unfamiliarity evoked by the frogs' noises, the fact that these nonhuman creatures seem to mimic human sounds, gives the scene a kind of uncanniness.

Smells, too, take on a new power. Johnson describes the scents of a late summer night as "sweet and evocative":

> I sink into them as into a cool, northern lake. To tread on bergamot or gill-over-the-ground in the darkness is to be instantly enveloped in spicy sweetness. The heady smell of ozone from a nearby lightning strike is almost tangible on a hot summer night. . . . The odd fungal smell of mushrooms shouldering up through the soil prickles in our nostrils, unmistakable and indescribable. We sniff like bears. (pp. 87–88)

As the final image suggests, the sensuousness of the experience gives it a primal intensity that makes Johnson feel at one with the wild.

The darkness seems to erase all differences between this observer and the creatures that she studies. Even a hornet is a welcome companion. When it lands on her, she watches it calmly: "A hornet explores me like strange terrain—tastes my salt, cools my flesh with the small breeze of his wings. . . . I feel his scratchy insect feet on my arm. They move slowly toward my wrist where the skin is thin and transparent" (p. 117).

Undisturbed by the fear of being stung, she simply feels "at home with him and his apparent curiosity," admitting: "I share that need to explore, to taste, to feel, to know" (p. 117).

This exploratory impulse provides the impetus for an otherwise unstructured narrative. *The Nocturnal Naturalist* has no particular theme or agenda; it is simply a series of observations and meditations, propelled by Cathy Johnson's inquiring mind. Freed from the distractions of her daytime existence, she allows herself to become absorbed in the alternate reality that springs into existence when most of us are asleep. Her record of that world reminds us that nature is not a static picture but an ongoing process, whether we take the time to observe it or not.

On Becoming Lost

In the most philosophical of her works, *On Becoming Lost: A Naturalist's Search for Meaning* (1990), Johnson considers the implications of her own desire to lose herself in nature. She uses her observations of the natural world as a springboard to reflection about subjects as abstract as time and space, and as specific as chaos theory, seasonal affective disorder, and Alzheimer's disease. *On Becoming Lost* is also among Johnson's most autobiographical works, as she uses some of her own life choices to illustrate her central premise, that being lost is a necessary prelude to discovery.

Johnson describes her own methodology as a naturalist: "I unravel a tread left by nature, follow it through labyrinths and long, slow loops, and bring home treasures I never could have planned: the pale, coral tubers of a wildflower uncovered by a hard night's rain . . . a piece of crinoid's fossilized flower in a place unexpected—and unlikely—telling me the great inland sea once licked at all the corners of my territory" (p. 22). Images of weaving recur throughout the text, as she discovers that such threads make up "the weft of the universe, the web of life" (p. 8). She traces her love of "serendipity," the discovery of unexpected treasures in life, to her father, who was also a wanderer.

One important aspect of wandering is the way in which it tests one's own capacity to adjust to the unexpected. Johnson wonders how she will react to the stress of being lost, then thinks back to moments of emotional "lostness" in her life.

Who else lurks within my skin? If I surprise her, plunk her down unaware in a new situation, she may surprise me yet. She already has. Who would have recognized the person I've become, five, ten, fifteen years ago? Smartly-dressed businesswoman, ad exec, hippie farmer, church secretary, artist, writer—ditch them all and see who happens. If I can lose my physical self, perhaps I can learn more about the strengths and weaknesses and abilities of the one who lives inside. (pp. 34–35)

She understands the human alternation between the desire for security and the love of "a tiny spark of danger" (p. 108), and finds that wandering can satisfy these opposing impulses. This book chronicles many such moments of self-abandonment. When Johnson has watched a muskrat in the creek for so long that she has begun to feel his movement in the water, she realizes gratefully: "I have what I have come for; I have lost myself—if only for an instant—and become something wholly other" (p. 86). Her ability to feel a kind of kinship with living creatures while still respecting their otherness makes her descriptions empathetic without being anthropomorphic. She has a fellow-feeling, too, for the strange "breed" of humans known as "hermits" or "solitaries," like the early naturalist Thomas Nuttall, or Henry David Thoreau at Walden Pond (pp. 11–13). Although she admits that she is only a "part-time" solitary, she says: "this is the kind of hermit I can feel within my bones" (p. 13).

Johnson's allusion to Robert Frost's "road less traveled" (p. 17) makes explicit her debt to a long tradition of using outdoor exploration as a metaphor for an inner journey. Frost's poem "Directive" shares her emphasis on the need to retreat from one world in order to discover another, and Johnson may well have expected that the reader of her work would hear echoes of Frost's advice in that poem:

And if you're lost enough to find yourself
By now, pull in your ladder road behind
    you . . .
Then make yourself at home.

By organizing her book around the idea of becoming lost, Johnson actually creates a tighter narrative structure for this work than for most of her other essay collections. This book reads more like a story; rather than presenting discrete descriptive passages, insights, and chunks of research, as her journal-style works do, *On Becoming Lost* follows the author step by step, sharing the thoughts that arise at each sight or occurrence. These thoughts often become an independent stream of digressive mediation, but always return to their starting point: the natural scenes that inspired them.

The chapter entitled "Lost in the Cold" provides one example of Johnson's skillful interweaving of natural events and human fortunes. She illustrates the effect of the Ice Age on northern Missouri by describing the geologic evidence near her home: the shape of the landscape, the glacial erratics (boulders deposited by glacial movement) that are strewn across the fields, the specific rocks found in a local lake (pp. 93–95). She then goes on to recount her own experience of some particularly harsh midwestern winters in the 1970s. The effect of the snow on her own environment seems a microcosm of the larger geologic forces she had previously described:

We awoke to a world scoured smooth by wind—scoured smooth or sculpted into fantastic shapes. The drifts rose like breakers frozen in time, always but not quite falling. Our driveway was as level as a beach; the blown snow had filled it from bank to bank, packed hard and glistening in the thin, predawn light. (p. 95)

The impact of such forces even on modern life is not negligible; the inconvenience of blocked roads and downed power lines eventually forced Johnson and her husband to abandon their farm and move into town, where they could "take winter on a less elemental level" (p. 96).

Each section of the book contains leaps from the literal to the metaphoric and back again. "Lost on the Edge" talks about Johnson's feeling of being "pushed to the edge" (p. 136), then goes on to discuss other kinds of edges: transition zones that mark the blending of one habitat into another; the edges of tectonic plates that grind away beneath the earth's surface; and, finally, the thin edge that separates faith from belief. "Lost Time" connects the human life span with a larger sense of time. It begins with a personal memoir of deaths that Johnson has herself witnessed, examines different kinds of deaths in nature, and finally compares different ways of measuring time: sundials, Stonehenge, Newtonian physics.

Johnson's formulation of the common theme to be derived from these comparisons, "change is the only constant" (p. 114), applies to the entire book. Johnson sees life as a continual alternation between forces. "We find; we lose; we find again. We are ourselves lost and found" (p. 67). In her frequent discussions of contemporary social, political, and environmental problems, she oscillates between fear and hope. She describes the members of her generation as "the first to have lost forever a childhood sense of security" (p. 60). The threat of nuclear war led them to hide their fear in a "marijuana haze" of idealism that was shattered by the triple assassinations that heralded the fall of Kennedy's Camelot. They "wandered, dazed, in disbelief," then turned to environmentalism as a way to build hope for the future (p. 62). But the environmental movement, too, seemed a naive dream during the Reagan years, when that administration's disastrous environmental policies and a general ethic of greed led to serious reverses for environmentalists. More recently, however, Johnson sees reason for renewed hope, as more Americans have become concerned about overcrowded landfills, acid rain, and endangered species. This pattern of setbacks and victories seems to suggest that even human society participates in what Johnson calls the "continuing creation" of nature (p. 67).

The Sierra Club Guide to Sketching in Nature

While *The Sierra Club Guide to Sketching in Nature* (1991) is not, strictly speaking, an example of "nature writing," it is one of Johnson's better-known works and an important contribution to nature studies. She sees field sketching not as the province of professional artists like herself, but rather as an essential tool for scientists and nature enthusiasts of all kinds. "Field sketching," she says, "is learning, period. About the world and our sometimes precarious place in it. About the creatures, large and small, that share this island earth with us. About life in general—and in delightful, intimate particular" (p. 83). Johnson belongs to a distinguished tradition of artist-naturalists like Thomas Bewick, the engraver whose *History of British Birds* (1797) was famous for its tiny, dramatic vignettes (it is remembered today as the favorite picture book of Charlotte Bronte's young Jane Eyre); John James Audubon, the ninteenth-century naturalist whose monumental *The Birds of America* (1838) consisted of 435 colored plates, containing 1,055 life-sized bird figures; and John Muir, founding president of the Sierra Club, who made sketches to help record the observations that culminated in his book *The Mountains of California* (1894). Among contemporary influences, Johnson most often mentions artist-naturalists Ann Zwinger and Clare Walker Leslie.

The Sierra Club Guide to Sketching in Nature provides advice about the different media and techniques Johnson has found useful in her own artistic renderings of nature. Johnson outlines basic principles of composition, perspective, lighting, and color as they relate to outdoor sketching. Individual chapters on landscape, plants and flowers, trees, and animals provide detailed explanations of how these subjects are best approached.

Cathy Johnson's discussion of drawing and painting and technique in this guidebook, like her writing elsewhere, reveals her appreciation for the details of nature. The book is especially useful in its emphasis on rendering a wide variety of textures. In order to reproduce petro-glyphs in a watercolor painting of the Southwest desert, for example, Johnson draws them into the painting with a wax candle to protect them from color; to create realistic rock formations she scrapes her damp wash with a paper towel and applies plastic wrap to the wash, giving the color a subtly uneven look.

A section titled "Sketching in the Animal Kingdom" includes such headings as: Careful Observation, Gesture Drawings, Blocking In Forms, Skulls and Bones, Value and Form, Capturing Life in the Eyes, Rendering Fur, Catching the Shine, and Life in Landscape. Her advice on drawing animals has as much to do with observation as with sketching. "To compensate for the propensity of animal life to *move*," she says, you must quickly note salient details by asking yourself questions as: "What is the animal doing? What is it feeding on? How large is it in relation to the family cat—or a cow? How large are its ears in relation to its head? How are its wings shaped—long and bent like scimitars or stubby and powerful. . . . What is its basic stance? Can we guess at mood (alert, sleepy, angry, nervous)?" (p. 194). Johnson demonstrates that describing nature through pictures, like describing nature through words, requires a combination of attention to minutiae and a feeling for the life of the whole.

One Square Mile

One Square Mile: An Artist's Journal of America's Heartland (1993) inaugurated a series published by Walker and Company called America in Microcosm, which consists of sketchbooks by artists in different regions of the United States. Each book is intended to bring out the unique qualities of a single mile, and Johnson's book set the standard for achieving a detailed sense of place.

Cathy Johnson's procedure in developing this book was the reverse of her usual practice. Instead of choosing field sketches or creating new drawings to illustrate a text, in *One Square Mile* she collated her existing sketches and added

Johnson's illustrations bring to life the animals she describes. These views of a baby starling are from *One Square Mile*.

descriptive text to the drawings. As a result, the interplay between words and pictures is more dynamic than in her other works. The end result is both more disjointed and more spontaneous.

Every page of the book is a combination of image and text, and the two are so carefully intertwined that the illustrations seem to leap off the page at exactly the right moment. When Johnson begins to describe a heron, a deer mouse, or a bullfrog, the animal steps forward into the blank space next to a column or at the bottom of the page. The drawings animate her already vivid descriptions. This is especially true of her many sequential drawings, quick sketches that portray the same animal in numerous poses. A squirrel is depicted in the act of leaping from tree to tree, with four tiny, connected sketches captioned: "checking me out / getting ready to jump / sizing up his leap /airborne!" (p. 17) A green heron is shown fishing in a strip of sketches that are so closely sequential that they resemble early stop-action photographs, or cartoon flip-books that create the illusion of movement as you riffle through the pages (p. 91). Sometimes, these drawings are half-finished gesture sketches that are begun and abandoned as the animal moves around. By showing the process of capturing the animal on paper, Johnson gives a powerful sense of motion to her depictions.

The book is divided into sections that each focus on one of the habitats that are represented within the square mile of land that surrounds Johnson's cabin-studio: "The Woods," "The Meadows," "The Pond," and "The Creek," finally narrowing to the area of human presence: "The Cabin and the Walnut Grove—and Other Signs of Life." Johnson seems to be particularly interested in the fact that such a small area can offer such a variety of life, commenting that "the meadows are a markedly different ecosystem from the forest on this square mile near the muddy Missouri River. But the meadows themselves are varied, unlike each other by virtue of soil and location and microclime" (p. 37). Alert to the minor differences that can have a major effect on the particular plants and animals that inhabit a region, she pays close attention to the transition zones between these major areas. These transition zones offer clear evidence of the changes that have taken place. "Nothing is static," she points out. "All moves slowly, glacierlike, toward that inevitability of transmutation, meadow-becoming-forest on the hill" (p. 39). The organization of her book into separate habitats, she realizes, is approximate at best.

Johnson writes convincingly of her own attachment to this small plot of land, saying that "interaction between the human and wild alters both" (p. 149). But she is also painfully aware of the potentially damaging effects of human presence on the land, writing indignantly: "I've discovered limbs hacked from the oaks on the dam for no better reason than to allow someone a better cast, without thought of ownership, or the tree's health or beauty—cut and tossed in a tangled pile behind the dam" (p. 86). She even includes a full-page still life titled "Tree and Trash Midden," depicting a pile of cans and bottles left at the foot of a tree. In her concluding description of her own cabin, she is careful to point out that she never cuts live wood for her woodstove. Ultimately, she does not question the necessity for humans to share living space with other creatures. While an ardent supporter of the environmental movement, she recognizes that most people's experience of nature occurs not in wildlife preserves, but in local settings that are so familar that they are taken for granted. The project of *One Square Mile* is not really to educate the reader about a particular plot of land in Missouri. It is to teach the reader to respect his or her own special place, and become aware of its unique beauties.

Nature Walks

Cathy Johnson's most recent book, *Nature Walks* (1994), is not centered on a single place; it is organized instead around the idea of a journey. Its subtitle, *Insight and Advice for Observant Ramblers*, summarizes its guiding premise: that a casual ramble through a landscape can yield valuable insights if the rambler is sufficiently observant. Johnson wanders through the prairies of her native Missouri, the deserts of the Southwest, and the New England seacoast, describing the native plants and wildlife of each region. Like her earlier works, this collection of essays seeks to teach the skill of observation, as Johnson examines the minute details of each scene as well as the larger issues raised by its relationship to the people who inhabit it.

In her preface to this collection of essays, Johnson explains how walking enhances her appreciation of the world around her. On the one hand, the landscape itself seems more variable, as "perceptions alter with the changing perspective" (p. 10): "Habitat modifications are immediate, as edges give way to open savannas, and forests close in again a few yards down the path" (p. 11). Walking "at a snail's pace" allows her to "see what's what," as she moves in a "rhythm more synchronous with the slow turning of the earth" (p.12). Not only the slower pace, but the activity itself is an aid to reflection. She calls it a form of therapy that relieves the tension and pressure of modern existence, a "way to enter the equation, to rejoice in life" (p. 12).

Johnson's emphasis on walking, with its inevitable evocation of Henry David Thoreau's classic essay "Walking" (1862), places her squarely within the tradition of American nature writing. Thoreau makes an eloquent case for "the noble art" of walking, claiming that a true walker is a kind of crusader for whom wilderness is the Holy Land. Walking is not a mundane mode of transportation, but a sacred journey on which to re-create oneself. Many writers have since combined the careful observation afforded by a leisurely walk with the metaphoric implications of a quest.

Walking was also a characteristic activity of Romantic poets. The popularity of walking tours, an early form of sight-seeing, in the eighteenth century enhanced the popularity of a literary genre known as "topographical poetry." Topographical poems described specific scenes and landscapes in a way that rendered them vivid to the reader, functioning almost as travelogues in an age when only the wealthy could afford travel. Romantic poets like William Wordsworth appropriated and transformed this minor genre by combining philosophic meditation with detailed description. Wordsworth's earliest published poems, *An Evening Walk* and *Descriptive Sketches* (1793), might have served as models for Johnson's project. Like Wordsworth, who sought to memorialize simple yet meaningful events and perceptions through his poetry, Johnson uses her notes and sketches

in order to ensure that "*this* walk, *this* day, will stand out among all the others" (p. 15).

Nature Walks is organized around activities as well as places. In "Walking Through Time," Johnson tries to make sense of bones that she has discovered, giving life to the dead animals through her descriptions of what their bones, skulls, and teeth reveal about their habits. She sees these bones as a gift that must be properly used, "an ivory endowment to teach me the names of my neighbors" (p. 46). Johnson's examination of fossils and artifacts leads to a discussion of the archaeological value of waste. From abandoned seventeenth- and eighteenth-century pits to modern-day landfills, humans leave evidence that can be read just as fossils are read: "I can discover what type of creature has used the den by what is left there, and speculate on our resemblance to these other animals" (p. 53).

In "Walking Through Weather," Johnson re-creates her experience of a thunderstorm in terms that evoke the Romantic ideal of the sublime: an experience that creates aesthetic pleasure through a combination of wonder and fear. Johnson writes, "To say it was exciting to be there purposely and alone in the heart of the storm would be understating the case. It was terrifying, wonderful—outside of anything I'd ever done before" (p. 58). Johnson nonetheless then retreats from this elevated tone with some practical advice on how to dress for wet, cold, or extremely hot weather. She notes the advantages of winter walking, when snow allows for easy tracking of animals. Tracking, like the extreme experience of the thunderstorm, seems to put her in touch with a more elemental self.

It's a return to a different time, not just on the linear scale that arrows backward a hundred years or so (or a thousand, or a million) to a time when we were *all* more closely attuned—and less calloused by the blitz of sensory stimuli that surrounds us. It's parallel time as well; we could as easily step sideways to enter. It's that side door I look for today, walking slowly in the snow. (p. 69)

Unlike most people, Johnson does not prefer one kind of weather to another, but simply appreciates the *difference* in experience that weather provides, a point she emphasizes laconically: "I like weather; always have" (p. 73). Weather, like walking, creates the variation that is necessary to see clearly.

The aesthetic value Johnson attributes to nature is evident in the kinds of metaphors that she applies to animals, plants, and landscape. Two hawks seem "powerful and graceful as young Nureyevs" as they dance a *"pas de deux"* overhead (p. 76). Wind and water are described as "dramatic actors, working with broad Shakespearean gestures" as they cut and shape a rock face (p. 197). Johnson's sense of nature as a kind of performer, and herself as an audience, is made explicit in her description of the climactic moment in a storm: "When the wind finally reached the bluff where I stood, leaves blew straight up in front of my face like a curtain rising on an ancient Greek drama" (p. 60).

Johnson is especially fond of metaphors that evoke the idea of artistic *writing*. She describes the prairie as "a graph of wind direction written in the sweeping, elegant calligraphy of stems" (p. 130); "calligraphic" is a favorite adjective, applied several times to meandering streams. Calligraphy, as a form of decorative writing that both communicates and pleases, is a perfect model of what Johnson sees in nature: an expression of spirit that uses the landscape itself as a writing tablet, conveying its message through sheer beauty of form. She extends this metaphor even further in her description of tidal flats on a New England seacoast:

> I was fascinated by the patterns drawn by the water, intricately interwoven lines etched in silver like an illuminated manuscript—trying to capture their sense on paper. The long perspective of the tide flats and the braided lines of the water were a complex Book of Kells and more beautiful by far, transiently scribed with earth and light, gull feathers and moving water. (p. 219)

The Book of Kells, a Hiberno-Saxon manuscript produced in southeastern Ireland in the period 760–820, is a classic example of Early Christian illuminated art in which the words of the Gospels are transcribed with enormous initial letters that are individual masterpieces of abstract design. The elaborate interlacing and geometric ornamentation that embellish the words glorify their meaning, just as, in Johnson's view, the rivulets of water that play across the tidal flats have a pure beauty that enhances her perception of an underlying "sense" to it all.

The pictorial quality of Johnson's descriptions evince her artistic training. Her delicate adumbration of two red-tailed hawks gives a vivid impression of the texture of the scene:

> Time and again the two light-phase red-tails circle, as if held on an invisible tether. Sunlight finds the undersides of their wings, rendering them opaque, then, as they reach the apogee of their orbit, shines through feathers suddenly translucent. Each primary feather is clearly delineated, outspread to catch the wind; each overlaps the next at the base, sketching a dark outline. (p. 76)

The composition of the scene, the play of light on the surface of the feathers, and the outline of the birds' shapes combine to create the effect of a work of art.

In recalling her visit to the desert Southwest, Johnson says, "The predominant color that remains in my memory is red" (p. 183), and she emphasizes the bold colors of the landscape throughout her account of it. As if painting a picture in words, she adds other colors to her canvas: "Much of this red sandstone is marked with the long spill lines of dark-colored desert varnish . . . as though someone had poured buckets of ebony stain over the cliffs. . . . At certain angles in the strong slant of desert light, whole cliffs gleam in the sun, reflecting the intense blue of the desert sky" (p. 185). She notes self-consciously that the scene presents "a challenge to the artist"; she herself has "painted the landscape in bright striations of blue sky, blue-black cliff, and redstone, and it recalls a specific place and time" to her (p. 186). The visual painting, like the verbal one, acts as an aid to her memory, fixing the scene's details in her mind. Looking at the Anasazi petroglyphs that are etched into the rocks, Johnson is reminded that "ancient artists have preceded [her] by many hundreds of years" (p. 186). By placing herself within that historic continuum, she affirms the importance of art as a record of a particular moment and point of view.

Johnson's account of the plant and animal life she encounters in the regions she visits is interspersed with historical background on the changing face of each landscape and the people who have inhabited it. She describes early settlers' impressions of the prairie and the eventual consequences of their decision to turn grasslands into farmlands. She gives a history of medicinal uses of sumac from the Indians through modern herbalists. She narrates the rise and fall of rail travel in Missouri, and explains how the Rails-to-Trails movement is attempting to take advantage of the abandoned rail tracks. And she gives a detailed portrait of the life of Excelsior Springs, Missouri, her current home, and the way its fortunes have been tied to water: to the mineral-water deposits that were the source of a booming tourist trade before their health benefits were questioned in the 1950s and to the floodwater that has several times engulfed the town.

In a detailed account of the flood of 1993, Johnson emphasizes the problematic relationship between humanity and wetlands. She points out that "The concept of 'flood' is a human one; the fluctuations of water levels in spring and fall are essential for the life and health of the biosystem. It is our tendency to build or farm in the floodplains that raises the question of flood damage" (p. 176). Thus, while she sympathizes with the human loss that flooding imposes, she does not see water itself as the enemy. "Life and water are one" (p. 178), she insists, and we must recognize that water is an elemental force beyond our control.

Cathy Johnson moves unapologetically from the historical to the political in her discussions of such current issues as wetlands and waste-water treatment, endangered-species preservation, and the reintroduction of wolves to Yellowstone. She has always been an active member of environmental organizations like the Sierra Club, the Audubon Society, the Wilderness Society, and Greenpeace, and her books have become more explicitly political over the years. Johnson's books are themselves proof of what she writes over and over, that humans can be "at home" in nature. They are testimony to the possibility of peaceful coexistence between humankind and other living creatures. The necessary prelude to such coexistence, she believes, is the kind of observation and understanding of nature that will inevitably lead to love.

Current Interests

Cathy Johnson has said that through most of her career she felt no need to emphasize the idea of women as naturalists. But an experience several years ago of being told, in her words, "that I couldn't do something because I was a woman" (personal interview), led her to consider the subject of women naturalists more specifically. This has led to a series of pieces in *Early American Life* magazine on early women nature writers—including some of the same little-known writers that she enjoyed as a child. She has also established her own imprint, the Graphics/Fine Arts Press, in order to bring out her new book herself. *Living History: Drawing on the Past* (1994) is written, illustrated, and published by Cathy Johnson.

Johnson's latest venture again demonstrates the range of talents and interests that makes her work unique. Her books illustrate the beauty of nature in every possible way: verbally, using description, scientific research, and historical background; and visually, using a watercolor brush to capture the broad sweep of nature's patterns and a sharpened pencil to render its wondrous details. She thus lives up to the deceptively simple goal she set for herself in *The Naturalist's Path*: to help us see.

Selected Bibliography

WORKS OF CATHY JOHNSON

BOOKS

The Local Wilderness (New York: Prentice Hall, 1987); *The Naturalist's Path: Beginning the Study of Nature* (New York: Walker, 1987); *The Nocturnal Naturalist: Exploring the Outdoors at Night* (Old Saybrook, Conn.: Globe Pequot, 1989); *On Becoming Lost: A Naturalist's Search for Meaning* (Salt Lake City: Gibbs-Smith, 1990); *Missouri: Off the Beaten Path*, with Patti DeLano (Chester, Conn.: Globe Pequot, 1990; 2d ed., 1993); *A Naturalist's Cabin: Building a Home in the Woods* (New York: NAL-Dutton, 1991); *The Sierra Club Guide to Sketching in Nature* (San Francisco: Sierra Club Books, 1991); *Kansas: Off the Beaten Path*, with Patti Delano (Chester, Conn.: Globe Pequot, 1991); *One Square Mile: An Artist's Journal of America's Heartland* (New York: Walker, 1993); *Living History: Drawing on the Past* (Excelsior Springs, Mo.: Graphics/Fine Arts Press, 1994); *Nature Walks: Insight and Advice for Observant Ramblers* (Mechanicsburg, Pa.: Stackpole, 1994).

JOSEPHINE JOHNSON
(1910–1990)

VERA NORWOOD

I have had a love of the land all my life, and today when all life is a life against nature, against man's whole being, there is a sense of urgency, a need to record and cherish, and to share this love before it is too late. Time passes—mine and the land's.
—*The Inland Island*

IN 1967, in the midst of the Vietnam War, as the inner cities of America were burning with the fires of racial anger, and concerns about the pollution of the country's air, water, and soil mounted, Josephine Johnson began writing *The Inland Island*, a chronicle of one year on her farm outside Cincinnati, Ohio. When it appeared in 1969, the book was widely and positively reviewed. The apocalyptic undercurrent to her nature journal mirrored the broad-based social malaise of the times, expressed in films like *Dr. Strangelove*, in fiction like James Baldwin's *The Fire Next Time*, and in environmental exposés, most notably Rachel Carson's *Silent Spring*. That Johnson, a middle-aged, middle-class, Midwestern wife and mother who so clearly had lost faith in the future, found a ready audience for her concerns revealed the depth and breadth of popular disaffection with the nation's social and political trajectory.

As much as it was a product of the immediate moment, *The Inland Island* also served as the coda for Johnson's life. Vietnam was the third

war that had challenged her pacifist beliefs. The race and class inequities expressed in inner-city turmoil were the latest in a series of social injustices that she first spoke out against during the Great Depression of the 1930s. Even fears of environmental degradation were not new in her life—growing up in the farming country of Missouri and Ohio, she had witnessed and recorded the terrible droughts of the Dust Bowl years. *The Inland Island* culminated Johnson's lifelong struggle against forces destroying the land and people she loved. Its apocalyptic tone captures her own sense of desperation and determination in the sixth decade of her life. Her only hope was, at last, to preserve and record the lessons she had learned from long tenancy on her thirty-seven-acre sanctuary in the middle of the continent.

Life

Josephine Winslow Johnson was born on 20 June 1910 in Kirkwood, Missouri, a small community outside St. Louis. She was the second of four daughters. Her father, Benjamin H. Johnson, owned a prosperous wholesale coffee business in St. Louis. In her memoirs, *Seven Houses* (1973), Johnson notes that her father had few relatives. Thus, it is Ethel Franklin

Johnson's large family and their various houses and farms that Johnson mentions most in *Seven Houses*. Her maternal grandfather, Joseph Franklin, was born in 1836 in County Cork, Ireland, and immigrated to the United States as a servant indentured to a St. Louis merchant. By 1883 he was a wealthy businessman who, like many men in his class, built a spacious home in the country. His home, Oakland, sat on ten acres in Kirkwood, outside of St. Louis. It became the family home to his six daughters and one son.

When Ethel Franklin married Benjamin Johnson, they bought a fine house in Kirkwood. Although not as large as Oakland, it had spacious grounds, large trees, and a barn. Nearby, Ethel's unmarried sisters built a house with lovely gardens. They also had a small farm, Rose Cottage, on the outskirts of Columbia, Missouri, across from their brother's dairy farm. Here Josephine and her sisters spent each summer. Among the grounds and gardens of the Kirkwood homes and in the farmland around Rose Cottage, the girls were to free to roam. In *Seven Houses* Johnson recounts the love of nature that this childhood engendered. Her time at Rose Cottage was particularly affecting—she called the place Arcadia and contrasted the security she felt there, as a child, with contemporary life: "There is no sense now of the future, of returning rhythm, as in those days. No sense of both the now and the future now. Again and again and again we knew the same marvelous things would happen. Again the purple clematis would bloom . . . again the dew on the grass, again the moonflowers opening white in the evening" (p. 70).

Like most privileged children, Johnson unthinkingly accepted her life. Looking back in *Seven Houses*, a more socially conscious Johnson remembers that although the members of her family espoused liberal ideas and "felt sorry for the Poor in General" (p. 64), they did not treat their domestic staff very well, or question the class and race divisions in Kirkwood. The African-American service workers lived separately, in poor housing with few amenities, and their children went to segregated schools.

Johnson's family was deeply religious. She remembers being trained never to place other books on top of the Bible. But, unlike her more slowly emerging sensitivies to the privileges of her class, her struggles with religion seemed to begin at an early age, and were connected to her gender and her life among her sisters and aunts. In *Seven Houses*, she remembers her resistance to the image of Jesus as "comforter" and God's "heir." Part of her reluctance came, she argues, from being a Franklin—from growing up in a family of daughters who had no experience with the father-son relationship or the status of male heirs. Also, the concept of "God the Father" as a figure to fear was uncomfortably intertwined with her relationship with her own father, who inspired fear in the girls and showed them little love. Nancy Hoffman's biographical afterword to *Now in November* reports that Johnson's mother was a Quaker who was deeply opposed to World War I and joined the religious, pacifist Fellowship of Reconciliation. Although Johnson does not speak directly of her mother's influence on this issue in *Seven Houses*, she does note that her life among women led to her "wanderings from masculine convention" on the issue of war (pp. 60–61).

Yet Johnson knew that she had internalized many messages from her father—messages that she struggled to overcome as an adult. Just as it was difficult to slough off the masculinized religion he represented in her mind, so she found it hard to recover from his "mock endearingness" when he dubbed her "old slow" because of her appearance and habits. In her memoirs, Johnson turns this childhood denigration into an explanation of the divided self that she felt all her life. Noting that she was "born within the margin of the Gemini's power and doomed already to a dual soul," she accepted her birthstone, the "muddy ferrous" and "dumb" agate, as an appropriate talisman for the woman she grew to be: "one who is continuously a cloudy mass of the dead and the living, the trivial and the great . . . the faint and the strong. . . . In whose kitchen the breakfast dishes mingle with the thoughts of the dying in Vietnam, ghosts, pain" (*Seven Houses*, pp. 35–38). This feeling of being un-

Josephine Johnson at twenty, writing under her dormer window at Hillbrook house

retirement for only a few years. His death left Ethel and their four adolescent daughters to run the farm. Josephine lived with her family at Hillbrook for the next twenty years. At eighteen she enrolled at Washington University in St. Louis as an art student. She dropped out of college in 1932 to pursue a career as a writer.

Setting up a study in the top of the house, Johnson wrote "if not endlessly, then enormously, fulsomely" (*Seven Houses*, p. 87). By 1934 she had published a number of poems and short stories, and in the fall of the year her most acclaimed novel appeared. *Now in November*, the story of a young farm girl's adolescent struggles with her father and her love of the land during the Great Depression and Dust Bowl of the 1930s, was a popular success and brought Johnson the 1935 Pulitzer Prize for fiction. Her collected short stories appeared in 1935 as *Winter Orchard*, and her poems came out in *Year's End* (1937). Also in 1937 she published another novel, *Jordanstown*, whose protagonist, a small-town journalist, struggles against capitalists and for workers. In all this work, social issues and concerns mingle with vibrant descriptions of the natural settings in which her characters live. Some of the poems and short stories were harbingers of the nature essayist and environmentalist she became in later life.

By her mid-twenties Johnson was developing a personal ethic synthesized from her religious training, her liberal background, her elite education, and her life in small towns and economically fragile farm communities in a Midwest wracked by drought. Committed to acting on her beliefs, she joined other American intellectuals who fought for the rights of the poor and of ethnic and racial minorities. Much of Johnson's fiction espoused leftist ideals and goals; thus she began "a desperate search for reform and change" that led her to write for *The New Masses* and to work as an activist when "unions were young and revolutionary and a force for change" (*Seven Houses*, pp. 87–88). It was even reported in the *New York Times* (6 September 1936) that she had been arrested in Arkansas "under suspicion of encouraging cotton field workers to strike" (Hoffman, p. 270).

worthy to the larger tasks at hand dogged her throughout her life and represented a form of self-doubt that the female adolescents in her fiction also often suffer.

Except to note that "growing up is a terrible time" (p. 86), Johnson chose to skip over her adolescence and young womanhood in *Seven Houses*. Many of her personal feelings at the time are contained in the fiction and poetry she published in her early twenties. In 1922, her father sold his coffee business and the house in Kirkwood. He retired to a two-hundred-acre farm fifteen miles outside St. Louis to grow "grapevines and cows and corn and horses" with the help of "a good man to do the work" (p. 86). Here the family built a new house, Hillbrook. Benjamin Johnson enjoyed his dream of country

In 1939 Johnson married Thurlow Smoot, a National Labor Relations Board lawyer. They divorced in 1941. Johnson makes no mention of her first marriage in *Seven Houses*, stating only that despite her social activism and literary fame, she "seemed to be waiting to begin to live" (pp. 87–88) until she met Grant Cannon in a St. Louis courtroom. Cannon had grown up in Salt Lake City, the grandson of Mormon pioneers. Like Johnson, he struggled with his family's religious beliefs and left the Mormon church at eighteen. When they met, he was working for the National Labor Relations Board as a field examiner. They were married on Easter of 1942. Johnson remembered her wedding day as "literally my birthday" (p. 88). Their son, Terence, was a toddler, and Johnson was pregnant with their daughter Ann when Cannon was drafted to serve in World War II. She spent the next several years living with her mother while Cannon was in the army. By 1947, the family was reunited and had bought a house of their own in Newtown, Ohio. The Old House, the first home either had owned, had been built in 1810 and was surrounded by three acres containing old maples, a swamp, and a view of surrounding fields of alfalfa and corn. Here their last child, Carol, was born, and Johnson settled into the life of a 1950s middle-class wife and mother. She and Cannon attended the (Quaker) Friends meetings; he became the editor of *The Farm Quarterly* and worked on his book, *Great Men of Modern Agriculture*.

The Old House is the last of the homes Johnson describes in *Seven Houses*. She remembers the family's ten years there as "the high noon and summer of our lives" (p. 152). Her memoirs recount many adventures trying to maintain and repair a 150-year-old house and the times she and the children explored the green spaces in their yard and neighborhood. Here she was able to give her children the love for plants and animals she learned as a child. And, just as she and her sisters had retreated each summer to their aunts' farm, so she sent her children to spend summers with their grandmother at Hillbrook.

During this period, Johnson continued to write. Another novel of a young girl's adolescence, *Wildwood*, appeared in 1946. Her short stories written during the 1940s and 1950s are collected in *The Sorcerer's Son* (1965). Although *Wildwood* continued to mine the market for fiction about adolescent love—its heroine's one true love abandons her just when she is finally free to marry him—her short stories documented the lives and experiences of young wives whose lives were disrupted by the war, of struggling artists, and of men and women trapped in middle and old age. Throughout her writing, the constant themes are nature, how humans live in it, and what lessons it has to offer men and women trying to find answers to family problems and social inequities.

By 1956 the quarries and suburbs that surrounded the Old House had so encroached on the property that the family no longer felt separate from urban life. The struggle to maintain the huge house weighed on Johnson: "There were times when I was so tired I wondered if the other end of the room would ever be reached, and the spider webs on the ceiling seemed up among the stars" (*Seven Houses*, p. 152). The family moved ten miles outside Cincinnati to the thirty-seven-acre former farm that would be Johnson's last home and the subject of her finest nature writing in *The Inland Island*. They moved in search of "land and living things and greenness and silence" (p. 152).

Cannon and Johnson were not following in her father's footsteps, searching for the gentleman farmer's life. Having lived through the droughts of the 1930s, aware of the economic and environmental changes corporate farming was bringing to vast areas of the Midwest, and concerned about environmental degradation of America's last green spaces, they planned to allow the land to regain its natural state. They lived there as protectors of the plants and animals that began returning. For ten years, Johnson traipsed her acreage as trees took over artificial clearings and snapping turtles returned to ponds.

During the same period, she witnessed yet another war, this time in Vietnam. Very much opposed to all wars, she supported her son's decision to be a conscientious objector. She continued writing fiction; her last novel, *The Dark Traveler*, was published in 1963.

At the beginning of 1967, Johnson sat down at her desk and began a journal of the nature preserve the farm had become. At the end of the year, she had finished the manuscript of *The Inland Island*, which was published in 1969. Her seasonal journal earned high praise from other environmental writers, and she gained a place among the environmental activists of the late 1960s and 1970s. In 1969, on the verge of her second wave of literary fame, her husband died of cancer. Johnson felt that her life had truly begun when she married Grant Cannon: "He made me into a human being. . . . Out of something more sea grass and sand" (*Seven Houses*, pp. 98–99). In her marriage, she had finally found a way past the self-hatred instilled in her youth. She seemed most taken with Grant's optimism, his hopeful outlook on life, which she contrasted to her own pessimism. Unlike herself, she believed that he never "made a truce with despair" (*Seven Houses*, p. 92).

After Cannon died, Johnson stayed on alone at the farm, writing articles for *McCalls*, *Country Journal*, and *Ohio Magazine*. She published two other books: *Seven Houses* (1973) and *Circle of Seasons* (1974), a series of essays that accompanied Dennis Stock's nature photographs. Much of her writing in her later years echoes the fears about the future that permeate *The Inland Island*, but she never gave up on her nature preserve or her social causes. She lived on her beloved property until her death from pneumonia at Batavia, Ohio, on 27 February 1990.

Fiction and Poetry

The nature essayist Robert Finch argues that nature writers have closer connections to the humanities than to the sciences. Nature writing shares an affinity with lyric poems and short stories rather than with scientific reports. Recounting his own training in English, Finch describes nature writers as "conscious literary craftsmen, shapers of experience" (p. 100). Certainly, a number of twentieth-century nature essayists also have produced excellent fiction: John Steinbeck, Mary Austin, Gene Stratton Porter, and Edward Abbey are among those who achieved a popular following in both arenas. Although Johnson's early writings include a few pure nature essays, she was initially drawn to poetry and fiction as the best media for expressing her feelings about nature.

These media offer writers the opportunity not only to create a scene in which all the correct plants and animals are rendered in their proper relationships, but also, as Finch says, to "restore nature to its central place in individual, personal experience" (p. 101). Although Johnson's poems in *Year's End* (1937) cover many facets of her early life—from her arguments with Christianity ("The Snow-Blind") to her pacifism ("The White Spring") and her support for workers' rights ("Under the Sound of Voices")—one constant theme is the universal human struggle to survive the forces of nature. Many of these poems came out of her life at Hillbrook, where she remembered "sky and wind" most vividly (*Seven Houses*, pp. 86–87). The mixed relief and discouragement farming Midwesterners feel when the prairie winds settle is the subject of one of her best poems, "The Great Wind": "And so, knowing the great wind quiet, / Hearing no sound of storm / . . . We are now free to go / About our business, free to creep / Salvaging broken ash and elm, / Piling the scattered bark to burn" (*Year's End*, p. 49). Alternating with these poems of struggle are those in which nature offers moments of peaceful retreat, both from its own destruction and from the forms of destruction, such as war and class struggles, wrought by human societies. "The Quiet Flower" is representative of Johnson's lifelong search for a home in nature: "But there is need of silence, deep, undying, / The need to be still, to turn and go / Back to a quiet acre in the hills" (p. 58).

The short stories collected in *Winter Orchard, and Other Stories* (1935) reflect the many social and philosophical concerns of Johnson's twenties; but here, too, her central interest in the meanings of nature in human life is well developed. One story that seems closest to Johnson's life at Hillbrook in the 1930s is "The Quiet Day." The story's setting, reminiscent of Hillbrook, is a house built on a hill surrounded by a mixed agricultural and native landscape. The narrator has come across a moment of peace in a place that is usually crowded with family. Seeking to prolong the quiet, she goes for a solitary walk through the early spring orchards and into a field of milkweeds and asters. Here, she finds escape from the "poverty and insanity" of a country in economic depression and her own need to come to "decision, arbitration, denial or acquiescence" about life's challenges (p. 35).

In nature, the narrator finds herself able to acknowledge the struggle of life without having always to feel responsible for it. Examining the galls on various plants, she finds that "the tortured symbolism of these plants seems only foolish and unimportant here in the sun—cruelty and disease are homely things, not sinister, and their deformity only another shape of life" (pp. 36–37). In the course of her walk, she moves downhill, a progression symbolizing her release from the family and social responsibilities connected to the house on the hill. Arriving, at last, in a secluded valley she feels protected from both the wind and the "great views" that sometimes let one see too much (p. 38). Here, she sleeps beneath an oak tree and discovers that "Your life is your own . . . each of us finds his own healing" (p. 39). The moment gives her the strength to return to the pressures ("old fears and obsessions and causes") of life, secure in the knowledge that "there will be always these intervals of peace" (p. 40).

This heroine, able to see clearly beyond the demands of culture and to locate peace in all the forms of nature, is a key figure in most of Johnson's fiction. Her most popular representation of such a woman is Marget, who narrates *Now in November* (1934). The novel recounts Marget's adolescence and young womanhood. She lives with her parents and two sisters, Kerrin and Merle, on a Midwestern farm in the 1930s, during a period of economic depression and severe drought. The father takes on a mortgaged farm after failing in business in the city. Although they are well aware of the financial insecurity the farm represents, Marget and Merle are entranced: "From the beginning we had felt rooted and born here, like the twin scrub-oak trees that grew together in the north pasture and turned lacquer-red in fall" (p. 58).

Nature provides a place of escape from various family crises—their father's increasing violence as the farm fails, the girls' rivalry over the handsome ranch hand, Grant. In the throes of unrequited love for Grant, Marget looks to nature: "if anything could fortify me . . . it would have to be the small and eternal things—the whip-poor-wills' long liquid howling near the cave . . . the chorus of cicadas, and the ponds stained red in the evenings" (p. 119). Like the heroine of "The Quiet Day," who understands that galls do not necessarily symbolize evil, Marget finds beauty in the drought-stricken landscape while understanding that, for nature, lack of rain is simply a part of the cycle: "even in this year . . . The earth was overwhelmed with beauty and indifferent to it, and I went with a heart ready to crack for its unbearable loveliness" (pp. 113–114).

Johnson's women in *Now in November* distinguish themselves from the farm men in their appreciation of the land in its original state and in their willingness to let nature win, to take human lessons from defeat. They find little to celebrate when fields of phlox are plowed under, pin oaks and sycamores are sacrificed to cornfields, or roads are widened to get dwindling crops to market. Finally Marget's mother, losing faith in the lies they keep telling themselves about the future, counsels her husband to give up trying to meet the market demands—"Let'm have pig-weed and cockle! That'll grow wild" (p. 224).

But seeing nature clearly and finding some solace in the view is never enough for humans—a fact with which Johnson struggled all her life. The contradictions in human behavior toward nature (demanding separation, requiring sustenance) are the source of many naturalist narratives. Literary critics Jacqueline Johnson Cason and Scott Slovic have commented on the ways in which nature writers probe the disjunctions between human culture and the natural world—often focusing on those human endeavors that separate us from nature. The key message in so much of the European–American tradition of naturalism is that we expect the green world to respond to our demands—and it does not, cannot.

In *Now in November*, Marget's sensitivity to the beauties of the natural world is at times overwhelmed by her allegiance to human culture. Much of the novel documents the divided self that Cason and Slovic argue is central to naturalism. On one hand, Marget knows that nature simply exists, that the green world was not created to meet human needs; she finds great beauty in its separate existence. On the other hand, she is a child of Christianity and capitalism. At times she shares her mother's religious faith in the future; at other times, she respects her father's way of providing for his family. At one point, the family believes that God and nature have finally answered their prayers in the form of a coming rainstorm: "We all looked at each other and felt burst free, poured out like rain" (p. 153). However, the clouds dissipate, and they are left looking up, "hating and helpless . . . [at] enormous stretches of sky . . . clean as glass" (p. 155).

The way human belief systems function to separate us from nature is Johnson's bridge between her calling as a nature writer and her social and political activism. Not only do institutionalized religion and economic capitalism separate us from nature, they help destroy nonhuman nature and whatever is left of natural goodness in humans. Johnson was one of the few writers in the 1930s who understood that Midwestern lands were being pushed beyond their limits by the food demands of World War I and its affluent aftermath. As Donald Worster has documented in his history of the Dust Bowl, economic pressures collided with cyclical dry spells on the plains to create the tragedy of the black storms that blew across the country in the 1930s. Johnson's *Now in November* offers a prescient study of the pressures on farmers that led them to destroy the land. Her critique is not of the farmers themselves but of a system be-

yond individual control that rendered it impossible for Midwesterners to live on reasonable terms with the land.

Similarly, Johnson found much in Christianity that separates humans from nature. In *Now in November*, Johnson's heroine understands that it is her mother's faith that God will provide that keeps her on the farm. But Marget struggles to believe in a religion that seems to have no answers for the real challenges of life, offering instead only a "stupid, earnest little" minister who rants vaguely about sin and guilt. She hears this man on the one Sunday the family is able to leave the farm and attend the community service. She also experiences religious hypocrisy when her family is denied communion and is asked to leave the service because they are not regular members of the church. That inhumanity, that denial of natural community, moves the eldest sister, Kerrin, to tear up a clump of grass and leave a cross-shaped stain on the church door. This experience, coupled with her understanding that faith alone will not bring rain, leads Marget on a search for a "faith that would *fit* life, not just hide it" (p. 142).

Women torn between nature and culture, who struggle with this divided self, predominate in Johnson's fiction. *Winter Orchard* includes the humorous old woman in "Matilda" who decides to become a hermit so that she will quit meddling in her family's lives, but succeeds only in meddling in the lives of the animals around her solitary cabin. *The Sorcerer's Son* contains many of the stories written while Johnson raised her family in the 1950s. In "Penelope's Web" she sympathetically portrays a middle-class housewife who finally overcomes the social pressures to create a perfectly clean home by acknowledging that "in the nature of life there was no finishing" (p. 66). One of Johnson's most powerfully conceived heroines appears in *Wildwood*. In this novel she probes the damage that is done to the female child who is unable, finally, to find her own way back to the natural world.

Perhaps as a reflection of her own feelings that her father's disdain had damaged her self-esteem, Johnson created a heroine in *Wildwood* who is the victim of social expectations about female roles. Reminiscent of the way Johnson would describe herself as a child with connections to "oakum and wet muskrat" (p. 35) in *Seven Houses*, she imagines twelve-year-old Edith Pierre as an animal with eyes "sometimes vacant, as though gone blind and stupid and the little marmotish thing inside asleep" (*Wildwood*, p. 6). But Edith never awakens to the natural woman she might have been. Instead, she lives her life defined through other people's projections. Like all Johnson heroines, Edith finds her happiest moments in nature, but is often divided from nature by human culture. She is first depicted as a member of nature's community. Her repression symbolizes the problem of being a member of the human community as well.

Edith was adopted at age twelve by Matthew and Valerie Pierre. Matthew is an ornithologist who anthropomorphizes birds, a mistake Edith does not make. Valerie is an extremely religious woman whose passion is her domesticated garden. Before Edith arrives, they assume she will be a sweet, beautiful child, much younger than twelve. Matthew imagines her as a "tiny gold-finch" whose existence, like that of all "his" birds, is to make his life "pleasant" (p. 10). What the Pierres get is a dark-haired, awkward, adolescent girl—their dismay begins Edith's history of self-hatred, her sense of never being able to live up to their expectations.

Johnson uses bird imagery throughout to develop her message about how human projections onto nature (including our own nature, here represented in Edith) hide and destroy the green world. Matthew buries his "little cheeping gold-finch" and takes to thinking of Edith as a "cuckoo's offspring" unfairly placed in his nest (p. 126). Internalizing their projections, Edith becomes a divided self and participates in this perversion—at one point imagining that when she speaks "toads plunked out, gross, awkward bodies with a soft, ridiculous sound" (p. 60). When she reaches adulthood, the Pierres hold onto her—refusing her freedom, keeping her with them as their companion. Her one hope of escape rests in a young doctor she loves. Yet finally he deserts her, using bird imagery to justify his actions. As he leaves town, just at the

moment they are free to marry, he imagines himself taking the "kindest way" by killing their love, wringing its neck as he would a sick sparrow's (p. 157). Edith dies young, unable to find a way to live in the world.

One of the key themes in Johnson's poetry and fiction is that humans are in danger of forfeiting the solace, the intervals of distance from social striving, that nonhuman nature sometimes provides. Such is the case with Edith in *Wildwood*, but not with Marget in *Now in November*. Although the drought and the human need for rain threaten her sensitivity to nature, in the end Marget is saved because she is able to move beyond her parents' misplaced faith in capitalism and religion. She comes to understand the drought as a part of the ecological cycle in the Midwest. Determined to stay on the farm after her mother's death, she finds a new faith to fit life, a faith located in "the cold fire of the oak trees, not fallen yet, and a kind of icy red along the woods" (p. 231).

Of course, such an experience requires that nature still be available to women like Marget in spite of all the mistakes humanity makes in trying to make nature fit human needs and desires. The other primary concern Johnson expressed in her fiction is for the future of the green world. She shared the insecurities of her generation. Raised during severe economic depression, environmental catastrophe, and a series of wars, she produced writing that always had an apocalyptic edge. Apocalypse meant the end of nature and could be caused by too much success as well as too much failure. Each remove her grandparents and parents made as the city usurped the green landscapes of suburb and farm represented the destruction of yet more nature, threatening the one place she felt secure. From a young age, she was fearful that such landscapes would disappear altogether.

One of the short stories Johnson wrote in her twenties eerily foretold the battle she would wage in her old age. In "The Old Lady Returns," a woman has been dead and in hell for fifty years, but she refuses to forget her previous life on an idyllic farm. She regales the other inhabitants of hell with tales of this farm to such an extent that they refuse to go about the duties assigned by the Devil; they will only sit in their rockers and listen to her. Finally, the Devil is so fed up that he sends her back to earth. She finds, however, that her farm is gone: "earth was thronged and plastered, crossed and counter-crossed with great white roads that led into each other until not even the thickness of a spider-web could come between. . . . And there was no green spot on earth. Not one" (*Winter Orchard*, p. 280).

Nature Essays

In her middle forties, Johnson attempted to return to the natural landscape of her youth. The house that in 1946 had seemed close to the country had become hemmed in by roads and other houses. In 1956, she and her family moved, for the last time, to a thirty-seven-acre farm with the humble goal of restoring and preserving one green spot on earth. In January 1967, Johnson sat down to tell what she had learned on her return to the earth. *The Inland Island* is a chronicle of her attempt to stave off forces of human destruction by retreating to nature—to find, as she had imagined so many of her heroines doing, a momentary peace and to send some news from nature to a populace in dire need of a new faith in the world.

Organized as a monthly journal that reflects the changing seasons, *The Inland Island* follows Johnson's daily hikes in 1967 as she searches for indicators that a more balanced ecosystem is taking over the once-domesticated land. Her decision to try to keep her hand out of the making of the landscape is mirrored in her attempt to keep her symbol-making about nature at bay as well. Like her fictional character in the short story "Matilda" (*Winter Orchard*), who could not stop meddling in the life around her even when she became a hermit, Johnson struggles to overcome the human tendency to make nature fit human desires. Waxing sentimental over a woodchuck's den, for example, she first imagines him "coming out and contemplating this fresh April world, the smell of broken mint, the violets

moving in the morning breeze, the trilling sounds of wrens." She realizes, however, that she is projecting her experiences onto his life: "But in good truth he is not emerging that early, and if it is a cold day, he is not emerging at all. . . . The smell of woodchuck holes on warm days drives out our old dream of dozing through winter in dark woodchuck dens" (p. 51). This meditation on the woodchuck's resistance to human mythmaking is charming, but it also carries a very important lesson: nature contains much that humans do not like but must accept.

The danger in trying to form nature to human needs and desires is that in the process we destroy it. Although Johnson likes to imagine her farm as an island in the midst of a world gone insane, she knows that its isolation is tenuous and constantly under attack. The Vietnam war invades in February, when she realizes that she "can't keep the horror of the burned children away" because of the taxes she will be paying in April. There are two creeks on her place, one running pure and the other polluted with waste from surrounding suburbs: "I can't separate the beauty of this place from the destruction of this place. . . . The target practice of the neighbors, the pollution of the air from sewers and burning garbage, from factories in the valley and even dust from Oklahoma. A world of war and waste" (p. 26). She casts this destruction as the physical manifestation of beliefs that are morally wrong. The Vietnam war is fought in Christ's name and is fueled by the military-industrial complex, which, in the form of the Pentagon, "sits . . . squat on top of our lives," draining and polluting the world (p. 153). She argues that we mask our villainy in sugared sentiments. One that she found particularly troubling was the appeal to motherhood (and the need to protect "our" women and children) as justification for "killing and making money" (p. 92).

Johnson tries in *The Inland Island* to counter these destructive and immoral actions by vividly recounting her own struggles to throw off values and beliefs acquired from family, friends, and teachers concerning gender roles and religion. At one point, feeling trapped in the assumption that as wife and mother she is an "unfailing spring" of "maternal wisdom and patience," Johnson reports that she seeks relief from gender role pressures by fantasizing about the life of a "wild free fox" who lives on the farm. The fox is a vixen, and after months of trying to see her at her den, Johnson is finally rewarded with a view into fox life. Once close to her mythical creature, Johnson discovers that the vixen is tick-ridden and ragged around the edges. She and the fox look each other in the eye and, in that moment, she confronts a very different maternity—neither the sentimental Mom nor the free spirit—but a vixen who is "small, thin, harried, heavily burdened—not really free at all. Bound around by instinct, as I am bound by custom and concern" (p. 90). The experience puts an end to her "heart's fox." The real fox is killed that winter by a hunter.

Johnson makes a double-edged point here. One part of the message is aimed at readers who wax sentimental over nature, using it as an escape from their problems and as a screen for projected desires. Johnson reveals how difficult, yet how important, it is to step outside our own skins and accept those aspects of nature we do not like. The other part of the message is directed at the ways we construct human "nature." Johnson posits that we are just as apt to misrepresent our own lives in our mythmaking. Deeply offended that wars are fought in the name of a sentimentalized "motherhood," Johnson moves directly from the story of the vixen into her own (and other women's) alienation from the Vietnam war: "I am sick of war. Every woman of my generation is sick of war. Fifty years of war" (p. 91). One of the truths Americans had to face in the late 1960s was the disaffection of so many citizens with the powerful machinations of the military-industrial complex. Johnson here argues that if we can learn to look clearly, unsentimentally, at women's lives, as she looked at her "heart's fox," we can look at the face of America and denounce its makeup of war.

Much of *The Inland Island* considers the differences between men and women. Sometimes these differences are a cause for humor, as in Johnson's intimate and enriching personal relationship with Grant Cannon. But the men who dominate American social and political life seem to wield a power that is destroying nature—both human life and all other life on the earth. One key pressure here is the masculinized need to control nature through forms of dominance. For example, Johnson applies her distinction between male and female values to male scientists, who take control of nature by naming and categorizing in such a way that ordinary people (particularly women) are denied access to both science and nature. She notices differences even in the ways that men and women write about nature (and why they pursue nature writing). At one point she refers to her youthful attempt to "be a great writer at all costs," in part by copying the self-absorbed focus and "hard masculine" style that was approved by literary tastemakers. But, by middle age, she felt unable to slough off "the undisciplined, poorly organized pack of women and children that live inside" her and make it impossible to sacrifice her daily round to a desk in an attic (p. 117).

Johnson's most caustic critique of men in power is reserved for those who staged the Vietnam war—which she casts as the ultimate form of dominance over all of nature. In her meditations on the masculine meanings of war, Johnson makes strong connections between the men in power and the "fatherhood of God." Although pacifism in America has roots in certain religious groups (among them the Quakers, whose faith Johnson learned from her mother), Johnson casts most of Christianity as a warmongering religion driven in part by a male God, in whose name war was waged and peaceful resisters were brutalized by the "club on the skull" (p. 135). Johnson had grown up in a household in which the Bible was so sacred that no other book could be placed on top of it. She also had struggled throughout her youth with the hypocrisies of organized religion—and imagined her heroine in *Now in November* finding a new, more honest faith. *The Inland Island* explicitly states Johnson's fear that, by separating humans from nature, Christianity helps create a social climate that accepts the necessity of war. She therefore presents her struggle against God as a literal shedding of the skin that protects her from the elements: "The state of my soul reminds me of a spring camel. My agnostic soul. Half-raw pink skin. . . . The old shedding beliefs itch. The raw new skin exposed . . . is cold, cold" (p. 26).

At times when she is able to walk through her preserve in this new skin, Johnson finds an interval of peace in nature that she imagined for her fictional heroines. These intervals tend to occur on the sections of the farm that are still free of pollution. At the end of the year, for example, she walks past the sewage-polluted stream and its dying trees to the healthy world around the pure creek. Here she comes to a "rose-crystal" granite rock that she often rests against. On the rock she finds a blacksnake sunning: "Two old reptiles, we doze in silence. . . . The sunlight falls. . . . It is a free and mindless benediction over the wider world. . . . The heart is a warm and humming hollow. I live. I am. This is not holy, this is not heaven. This is the ancient pagan hollow of the hand that holds the sun" (p. 156).

Sadly, however, the hopes of her youth for a more permanent faith arising from such moments in nature have been blasted by intervening wars. *Now in November*, written when Johnson was twenty-four, created a heroine able to look back and make sense of her life: "Now in November I can see our years as a whole" (p. 3). Johnson returned to this phrase, and her youthful hopes, when her journal took up a November some thirty years later: "Now, in November, I do not see our lives as a whole. I see a great breaking up and out" (*The Inland Island*, p. 138). The problem is that communion with nature, as on that December day at rest on the granite rock, only contributed to Johnson's sense of alienation, her feeling that she was being split down the middle—torn between her love of nature and her unwilling citizenship in a society that was destroying the world. Blessed in winter by one of those "perfect" snows "that is almost too beautiful to be borne," she can understand

why people may believe in God and appeal to him to stop humans from destroying themselves and the earth. But the only solutions come from ourselves, and the problems seemed so enormous to her at the end of 1967 that the daily round on the preserve could offer no escape: "How can I hold such bitterness in this white snow on this lovely darkening land? Because there is nothing in all of nature that can compare to this enormous dying of the nation's soul" (p. 159).

Robert Finch argues that the primary job of the nature writer is "not to limit or encompass nature, nor even necessarily to explain or interpret it, but to show it in all its scope . . . its immeasurable providence and (more terrifying than any malice) its indifference to human aspirations—and in so doing to extend our own humanity" (p. 104). Although Johnson would have agreed with Finch that such was one task of the naturalist, she was too much of a social activist to accept his corollary premise: that nature writers "have no agenda . . . for salvation" (p. 101). She well understood that although nature is indeed indifferent to human aspirations, it is not secure from them. She felt very strongly that it was her responsibility as a writer to call her readers to action, action that would serve both humans and the earth.

It was this activist stance throughout *The Inland Island* that garnered it a good deal of attention in 1969—an era of increased activism against war, against racism and sexism, and against environmental destruction. Johnson, who had first achieved fame as a novelist in the 1930s, was rediscovered and recast as an important voice of resistance. In following years she pursued her environmental agenda in essays and articles. John Fleischman, who visited the inland island and interviewed Johnson for a biographical article (published in 1986) about her thirty-year tenancy on the farm, found that she had continued to support many causes, "particularly conservation and alternative energy organizations" (p. 113). One of Johnson's last published essays, "Journal of a Drought Year," continued her chronicle of human-created natural disasters and posed her neighbor, who farmed his land only for sustainable yields, as one of our "real patriots" (p. 73). She remained committed as well to the goals of social justice. In one of the last essays she wrote before her death, she called attention to the toxic working conditions of many laborers—including the man who cleaned her furnace and then *"crawled* up the cellar stairs, pausing on each step to regain his breath. . . . He had been breathing the cleaning fumes too many years of his life" ("Shoring up the House," p. 22).

Close to her eightieth birthday when she wrote "Shoring Up the House," Johnson had turned her attention to the shrinking realm of nature that was easily accessible to her—the green world immediately around and inside her home. Many scholars of naturalism would, however, see such a subject as trivial to the great narratives of nature writing, which are assumed to arise from challenge in the wilderness. Feminist historian Mary V. Davidson has charted the argument afloat among influential male critics that women are not capable of writing great studies of nature because they are relegated to the landscapes of home. Davidson and Vera Norwood (in her study of female nature writers from Susan Fenimore Cooper to Josephine Johnson) find that women who have written about nature around home and neighborhood have, indeed, found an audience and made an impact on the wider culture. Johnson's most important contribution to nature writing may be her fifty-year defense of the green landscapes of home — whether farm, country place, or suburban plot. In merging social justice issues with a call for the protection of the natural world, she presaged the environmental justice movement of the 1990s. The grassroots organizations that have sprung up across America seeking to protect homes, neighborhoods, and workplaces from pollution and development have often been led by women—women who, like Josephine Johnson, know that their family's future depends on their own and their society's ability to find a faith that fits the world, and then to act on that faith.

Selected Bibliography

WORKS OF JOSEPHINE JOHNSON

FICTION

Now in November (New York: Simon and Schuster, 1934; repr., New York: Feminist, 1991); *Winter Orchard, and Other Stories* (New York: Simon and Schuster, 1935); *Jordanstown* (New York: Simon and Schuster, 1937; repr., New York: Ames, 1976); *Paulina: The Story of an Apple-Butter Pot* (New York: Simon and Schuster, 1939); *Wildwood* (New York: Harper & Bros., 1946); *The Dark Traveler* (New York: Simon and Schuster, 1963); *The Sorcerer's Son* (New York: Simon and Schuster, 1965).

POETRY

Year's End (New York: Simon and Schuster, 1937).

PROSE

The Inland Island (New York: Simon and Schuster, 1969; repr., Columbus: Ohio State Univ. Press, 1987); *Circle of Seasons* (New York: Viking, 1974), photographs by Dennis Stock.

MEMOIR

Seven Houses (New York: Simon and Schuster, 1973).

SELECTED ARTICLES

"Winter Morning," in *Country Journal* 7 (February 1980); "Secrets of a Summer Garden," in *Ohio Magazine* 6 (August 1983); "A Journal of the Drought Year," in *Ohio Magazine* 12 (August 1989); "Shoring Up the House," in *Ohio Magazine* 14 (October 1991).

BIOGRAPHICAL AND CRITICAL STUDIES

Jacqueline Johnson Cason, "Nature Writer as Storyteller: The Nature Essay as Literary Genre," in *CEA Critic* 54 (fall 1991); Mary V. Davidson, "What We've Missed: Female Romantic Poets and the American Nature Writing Tradition," in *CEA Critic* 54 (fall 1991); Robert Finch, "Being at Two with Nature," in *Georgia Review* 45 (spring 1991); John Fleischman, "News from the Inland Island," in *Audubon* 88 (March 1986); Todd Gitlin, *The 60s: Years of Hope, Days of Rage* (New York: Bantam, 1987); Nancy Hoffman, "Afterword," in Josephine Johnson, *Now in November* (New York: Feminist, 1991); Margaret McFadden-Gerber, "Josephine Winslow Johnson," in *American Women Writers: A Critical Reference Guide from Colonial Times to the Present*, ed. by Lina Mainiero (New York: Ungar, 1980); Vera Norwood, *Made from This Earth: American Women and Nature*

(Chapel Hill: Univ. of North Carolina Press, 1993); Scott Slovic, *Seeking Awareness in American Nature Writing* (Salt Lake City: Univ. of Utah Press, 1992); Lawrence Wittner, *Rebels Against War: The American Peace Movement, 1933–1983* (Philadelphia: Temple Univ. Press, 1984); Donald Worster, *Dust Bowl: The Southern Plains in the 1930s* (New York: Oxford Univ. Press, 1979).

DIANA KAPPEL-SMITH
(b. 1951)

KAREN KNOWLES

IN THE EARLY 1970s, Diana Kappel-Smith was working toward a degree in biology at the University of Vermont and spending long afternoons studying the effects of gamma radiation on the growth of seeds. One day in late March she looked up from her lab work and saw through the window the beautiful mist-drenched Vermont hills. The sight of the wet, reddened tree branches and the vapor from the snow that "trailed among the hills like the veils of dancing girls" transformed her so that her "sensible casing...cracked and fell to the floor" (*Wintering*, p. 216). Suddenly, her research made little sense. She packed up her slides and never took them out again to finish her research. Instead, she preferred to present inconclusive findings to her science seminar because "a lab with a view can be a dangerous thing. To do good science you aren't supposed to see the forest. You aren't even encouraged to see the trees" (p. 217). For Kappel-Smith, it was time to balance the lab work and its attention to microscopic detail with visits to those forests to discover for herself a broader ecological relationship.

Kappel-Smith was born in Connecticut on 9 September 1951 to Albert David and Victoria (Stuart) Kappel. She grew up in New Canaan, Connecticut, where she learned about the natural world by playing in the woods, building terrariums, and identifying birds. She was "the

type of kid who always had a frog in her pocket" (Rierden, p. 3).

In 1972, Kappel-Smith and her sister bought an old farmhouse on six acres in Wolcott, Vermont, with an inheritance they received from an uncle. They intended to farm this land and raise sheep, and Kappel-Smith wanted to become more knowledgeable as a naturalist. At the same time she finished up her college course work. In 1976 she earned a bachelor of science degree in biology from the University of Vermont, and began working as a reporter for a rural newspaper.

The same year she graduated, she married Shapleigh Smith, a neighbor, and had a son, Coulter David. For eight years they farmed in Vermont, expanding the original six acres to 275. During this time she learned about the natural history of the land around her as well as the practical side of working a farm for her livelihood. She described her experiences living on a farm in several essays that were published in 1979 and 1980 in *Country Journal*. These essays eventually inspired her to begin a collection of natural history essays, a portion of which *Vermont Life* published in 1983. The following year her first book, *Wintering*, was published.

Throughout the early 1980s, Kappel-Smith was also writing articles for *Country Journal* that instructed readers on the intricacies of growing Christmas trees, tapping sugar maples for sap, or making hay. Her knowledge came from experience: at various points during her eight years of farming she grew 15,000 Christmas trees, made 289 gallons of maple syrup, and put up 5,600 bales of hay.

The articles provide practical instructions along with a good dose of reassurance for people just learning these skills. In a February 1982 *Country Journal* article on installing pipeline between sugar maples as an updated method for collecting sap, she offers specific information ("pipeline hardware costs less than buckets: mainline, tubing, and fittings cost less than $1.75 per tap for most installations; a new bucket, spout, and cover now cost $4.83" [p. 67]) and advice ("try to avoid the mistake we made in setting up our mainlines over the deepest snowpack recorded in three decades [p. 69]). And she gives these instructions in an engaging, conversational style. When she is discussing why most people prefer pipeline over buckets, she describes how difficult it is to haul buckets around, especially during the best sap run in ten years: "It's getting dark; and you find a drowned mouse in one bucket; then you trip and spill sap into your boots; and as you're hefting a full pail up into the sap tank, you slip and spill more sap down your front" (p. 66).

With the publication of *Wintering* (1984), Kappel-Smith joined a growing group of naturalists who explored, contemplated, and wrote about the wilderness of their "backyards," a tradition long since established by Henry David Thoreau. She shares this tradition with modern naturalists such as Wendell Berry, also a farmer; Edward Hoagland, a fellow Vermont resident; and Sue Hubbell, who wrote about her farm in the Ozark hills in *A Country Year* (1983) with much the same regard for science, particularly botany, that lends itself to Kappel-Smith's detailed examination of a landscape.

Wintering

Kappel-Smith chose an unusual subject for her first book—northern Vermont in the winter months when to most eyes the land is frozen and the animals are hidden. It is in *Wintering* that she best demonstrates that her years of lab experiments were not in vain. When she wants to enter a world hidden from her she turns to scientific methods for insight; science is her "chief tool." She might use a thermocouple and a microvolt meter to measure cold or peel the bark away from a twig and study it under the dissecting microscope, peeling away each layer until she comes to the inner membrane, "the living stuff, milky with tiny organs; the part of the tree that mustn't be allowed to freeze" (p. 68). Such scrutiny reveals the secretive inner workings of the natural world, a view of winter that Kappel-Smith consistently seeks out. Inspecting her subject with a scientist's logic and an artist's critical eye, she explains her scientific observations by using nonscientific images: looking at the twig under the microscope she notes that "one of these layers, which poked out farther than the others, had the texture of the gridlike glass walls of a city office building. The centers of the 'windowpanes' were translucent, the 'windowframes' a solid green" (p. 68).

As she delves more deeply into this hidden world, her imagery becomes more expressive. During a week of extremely cold weather, when the temperature rises only slightly above zero, she makes a hole in a pond by chipping away at the ice with an ice spud, a pole made of heavy metal with a chisel at the end. Inside this four-foot hole the water is a balmy thirty-five degrees Fahrenheit. She drags her net through the water until she comes up with "brilliant green plants—leafy *Elodea*, *Myriophyllum*—and things squiggling, the tip of a worm, a beetle all glossy" (p. 148) and dumps them in a pail of the warm pond water to examine under a microscope what her naked eye cannot see. Her descriptions blend the language of biology with that of a skilled writer: "round *Diaptomus* like spinning jewels, ruby, citron, sapphire"; "jar-shaped *Cyclops* with a kind of mustache of tentacles flowing from their round front ends"; and *Daphnia*, or water fleas, "with treelike tentacle arms flailing over their heads, doomed to a mad life of whisking their whole selves around in backward circles" (p. 151). Her

DIANA KAPPEL-SMITH

Branch Dancer

Pencil drawing by Kappel-Smith of an owl with rabbit prey, from *Wintering*

imagery is the stuff of motion; it enhances the picture of a winter that is indeed full of lively creatures, even though they are hidden under layers of ice.

This penchant for collecting and creating images—whether through language or in her illustrations, which appear in all of her natural history books—reveals a naturalist's curiosity. In *Wintering*, she comments that she has taken to wearing pants with deep pockets so she can collect at will for later examination and sketching. She fills a bag with the last living remnants of autumn's plant life to pore over and use for the illustrations she includes in *Wintering*. Her line drawings catch the wintering animals in motion. She shows an owl, just returned from its hunt, perched on a thick tree limb with a rabbit slung over the branch; she expresses the changes in plant life with a drawing of the metamorphosis of a maple twig from late April to early May. Each illustration complements her verbal imagery and shows her keen attention to the world around her, particularly to those animals whose activities are the most difficult to witness.

She collects information as easily and thoroughly as she does the evidence of winter life. She owns a gray box she has labeled "Wonders," in which she keeps notes, articles, and scientific papers about her subject that have astonished her. This box becomes "a kind of archive of enchantment" (p. 155) that leads her searching for one thing after another in the world of nature. Such desire for intellectual understanding about the natural world underscores all of her forays into woods, fields, and forests.

One of the things Kappel-Smith looks for as autumn turns to winter is the changing patterns of the birds. The first section of *Wintering* explores the bird life around her, and she ponders their migratory patterns and the lives of those that stay during the harsh winter months. These observations lead her to more philosophical musings about the connections between all living things on the planet. She suggests that a hummingbird's "dual nationality" in her Vermont hay meadow and in a garden in Mexico is a metaphor for the "gulfs" humans need to cross to realize that their treatment of ecosystems in

one place will eventually affect the entire world. She recognizes that "we too have our dual citizenships, our gulfs to cross," particularly when it comes to oil spills, the depletion of the Brazilian rain forest, and industries that "bankrupt the economies of lakes, streams, whole soil systems, acidifying them to shadows" (p. 10).

Wintering is dedicated to her father, Albert David Kappel, who founded the New Canaan, Connecticut, Audubon Society. In an interview with Andi Rierden in the *New York Times*, Kappel-Smith commented that her father was "never a great birder or naturalist, nor did he have a science background. But he understood very well that people were making a mess of the environment" (p 3). It is clear that he influenced her own vision of the world, both the human-made and the natural.

In her intellectual pursuit of winter and its hidden world, Kappel-Smith also contemplates the environmental issues relating to both the wildlife and farm life around her as she raises sheep and competes with deer and other wildlife for her harvests. She is concerned with living in harmony with the land and its animals. To that end, she makes careful decisions about her impact on the woods she lives in. While she confesses that her "lust for hefty dry firewood has always bordered on the intemperate" (p. 61), she follows a practical and conservative line of thinking in her husbandry of the woods. Acknowledging that "most foresters think of gray birches as worthless trees, best cut and left to rot to make room for maples and ash and spruce" (p. 115), she prefers to make a deal with her birches; she will not cut them down unnecessarily; in return, she asks that they be there when she needs them. This arrangement was inspired by the contrasting practices of local foresters, who shoot porcupines on sight because they eat the bark of trees, and of the Native Americans of the eastern woodlands, who spared the porcupines in times of plenty so they would be there when needed during difficult times.

Harmony with the land, she discovers, happens when she is least expecting it. When she comes face to face with a coyote, she freezes and forgets that she is holding her sketch pad in her hand. She and the coyote stare at each other for a while, contemplating their options, until the coyote turns and disappears into the woods. She is left with the "euphoria of knowing that I was an animal, here, whole, and very much alive" (p. 264).

Night Life

In 1984, Kappel-Smith divorced her husband, but stayed in Vermont to farm and write. Two years later, around the time of her father's death, she moved to Connecticut, the state where she had grown up. By the late 1980s she was at work on her second natural history book, *Night Life: Nature from Dusk to Dawn*, which was published in 1990. In her research for this book, Kappel-Smith switched from an in-depth exploration of the land where she lived to an exploration of parts of the country she was unfamiliar with. *Night Life* is a combination of natural history and travel writing, a combination that she built upon in her third book, *Desert Time*.

Night Life received favorable critical attention, with reviews appearing in such national newspapers as *Wall Street Journal* and the *Christian Science Monitor*, and an interview in the *New York Times*. Her writing was compared with Annie Dillard's and with Aldo Leopold's *A Sand County Almanac* (1949), an indication that she was beginning to gain more solid recognition as a nature writer, at least in the popular press.

Night Life describes her five-month journey to five quite different places in the United States. She visits Arizona in August, North Dakota in December, Hawaii in January, Connecticut in April, and Louisiana in June. Before she began her field research she created a list of night animals and the places they could be found, the names of experts who observe these animals, and their methods of observation. Then she cut out each item on her list and put it into a bowl that was formerly used to hold scented herbs. As she visited these five places over the next two years, she would remove each word from the bowl after she had encountered that animal, person, or technology. By the time she wrote the book, the bowl was empty. This unusual

organizational style reflects Kappel-Smith's approach to her subject; rather than drawing conclusions before setting off to study these nocturnal animals, she uses the discoveries of her fieldwork to shape her ideas.

In the introduction to *Night Life*, Kappel-Smith describes herself as a "translator of science and nature," a job she thinks can "never be done, only attempted" (p. 5). She considers herself an "old-fashioned naturalist... a job requiring that you keep your eyes wide open. Trouble is, you can never keep them open wide enough" (Rierden, p. 15).

Keeping her eyes open, or being as fully aware as possible, is a consistent theme in *Night Life* and a full-time occupation for a naturalist wandering around in the dark. Kappel-Smith emphasizes in the *New York Times* interview that the night world is a foreign place for humans:

> What happens in the dark is that we feel lost, out of it. Our vision doesn't work well. We can't walk as well. You take an animal out of its natural environment, and it's going to be scared. And night is not our natural environment, so we get scared in it and invariably find some demon. Feeling scared at night is nature's way of saying that you don't belong here. (p. 14)

Even though she knows she does not belong, she works hard at overcoming this obstacle because she finds studying the night and the animals it conceals an intriguing challenge. This is evident in her determination to "see" in the figurative sense — to step beyond mere sight and use other senses as a way to comprehend the world of nighttime creatures.

Kappel-Smith's research for *Night Life* takes her first to Arizona where she stays at the Southwestern Research Station of the American Museum of Natural History in the Peloncillo Mountains. After settling in, she goes in search of a campsite where she will camp alone for several days to test her skills as a nighttime observer of wildlife. She chooses a canyon that offers a broad botanical variety. Initially, the landscape seems foreign and full of ominous shadows. She worries about missing things because her eyes "aren't made to make sense of moonless shadow"; she lacks the animals' "keen equipment" (p. 19). She describes herself as blind and deaf in comparison to the night life around her, and this inability to see plays havoc with her imagination and drums up her fears.

She is particularly afraid of snakes, a fear that is "like a wave, like an ague, a fever" (p. 22). Every sound makes her suspicious and her brain begins to tell her lies, so that she hears "*writhe rattle gape creep crunch* and other things, all unpleasant in the extreme" (p. 19). Kappel-Smith admits that she has done everything possible to ward off her terror—she has studied snakes, hoping that education will relieve her anxieties, and also confesses her "snake-shakes" to another naturalist. In the dark of night, though, "each shadow-shift here still has the sliding-stone color of a diamondback" (p. 23). But she stays at her camp. In the end, her curiosity outweighs her fear.

Gradually, in spite of her fear of snakes, she finds herself growing more at ease in the canyon. Soon the darkness comforts her and she sleeps through the stifling heat of daylight, finding that she has transformed into a "dawn/dusk creature" (p. 20). These first few nights camping alone in the canyon prepare her for the rest of her journey. She has sharpened her nighttime observation skills by developing her senses, casting off her overreliance on sight. She becomes more aware.

Her night blindness never disappears entirely, and with each new landscape she explores in her research, darkness presents new challenges. In the Badlands of North Dakota near the Killdeer Mountains, where she has gone to educate herself about predators, she realizes she will never see at night the way these animals do. So she does the next best thing; she travels with the humans who know the habits of these animals well: hunters and trappers, men whom she believes "are learning to speak the predators' languages themselves" (p. 84). A trapper teaches her to read the landscape, to interpret the language of coyotes, and to use scent lures. What he is really teaching her is how to sense the presence of the animal, to "see" by intuition, perception, and experience. Eventually, she begins to feel she can "read the landscape, haltingly," as if she had "half learned the alphabet in Greek" (p. 93).

Learning from a trapper raises some interesting questions for a naturalist such as Kappel-Smith who is quite aware of the contradiction between her work—observing and sharing her knowledge and discoveries—and that of a trapper who hunts these animals for a living. It is an unusual combination, and both parties are sensitive to the other's worlds and ideologies. Although they differ in objective, they share a reverence for the animal. "We're after the coyotes and foxes and bobcats for different reasons," the author comments, "but these do not seem so different as they did before I came. I know this sounds odd; it seems odd to me" (p. 87). It is precisely this quality of searching out and understanding the "other side" of a management issue that distinguishes her writing; without judging she offers her readers an informed view of the diverse ways people interact with the natural world. In the end, her own beliefs have not changed, but they have been expanded by the complexities of the issues she investigates.

In order to achieve a balance in her perspective, Kappel-Smith seeks out a scientist to educate her about coyote habits and behavior. "There is more than one way of knowing things and more than one way to approach the finding out," she writes, while noting that she has read many research studies about coyotes, and "garnered only crumbs" (pp. 88–89). Once she has spoken with a wildlife biologist who spent eight years researching and observing a family of coyotes, she receives a fuller picture. The biologist's research, combined with the lessons she has learned from the trapper, not only inform her but enhance her appreciation of this animal. When she sees a coyote at dusk on one of her last nights in North Dakota, it is this sheer appreciation brought on by all that she has learned that colors her description:

The coyote stops and looks at us and dips his neck to smell the warm smells that rise along the ground. His eyes never leave us and his ears never leave their forward aim. At last he spins and goes through a fence as if it weren't there and he is over the rise and gone. He leaves a track of weightless grace, like a ballerina whose work in life is defying gravity, or in giving the illusion of defiance. (p. 113)

Learning from the specialists is a consistent element in her study of nature. In each new landscape she explores, Kappel-Smith consults the experts. In Hawaii, she spends time with scientists in diverse fields—exploring the Ala Moana reef with an ichthyologist, watching the mysterious mating dance of melon flies with an entomologist. She eagerly accepts invitations to join the scientists in the field; she is a curious observer who relishes looking over their shoulders and sharing their discoveries while at the same time offering her own insights.

Even when she is not in the field, her descriptions are vivid. She wanted to visit a lava tube, a cave formed from volcanic lava, but when she discovered how delicate that ecosystem is, she spoke instead to Frank Howarth, a leading entomologist who had discovered that the caves, once thought to be lifeless, were teeming with strange and mysterious insect life. He showed Kappel-Smith his collection of cave life—blind hunting spiders; wingless, blind crickets; and three-legged bugs—and his discoveries feed her own poetic musings on the eternal, ephemeral nature of caves.

One of the finest qualities of Kappel-Smith's writing is her ability to draw on diverse images to capture the visual appeal of a wild creature. In *Night Life*, where she is describing disparate things, she finds it useful to compare them. Who would see similarities between a crustacean and a coyote? Kappel-Smith does. In Hawaii she observes the night walking of crabs and lobsters, and thinks the "forked antennules between their eyes jerk and flutter like semaphore arms, waving the bushlike ends that are furred with esthetasc [sic] hairs. These are the sensory hairs with which they taste the water, like coyotes scenting the wind" (p. 130). Such imagery uncovers patterns of behavior and physical make-up, no matter how small, among the various

creatures she encounters. An octopus has eyes like the slit eyes of goats; its mottled, warty skin is like a toad's. The octopus brings to mind other images, as well. When an ichthyologist holds an octopus for her to get a close-up view, she sees a black body the "size of a large plum" with tentacles "fine as spaghetti wriggling into everything, twining in his fingers like runnels of brown sauce" (p. 143). This expressiveness of thought and vision reveals Kappel-Smith's style and personality in an evocative, engaging voice, a trademark of all her nature writing.

Though Kappel-Smith's method of research always encompasses working in the field, whether alone or with others, there are times when she must deal with prejudice against her as a woman encountering dangerous situations. She herself never comments on the perception that a woman exploring the wilderness at night is a rarity; in fact, she does not consider it a rarity at all. Through persistence and determination to accomplish her goal, she breaks down barriers thrown up by those who are unsettled by her work. When she wants to accompany game wardens into the Louisiana bayou one night, they are wary at first, especially because the party is likely to encounter poachers. One of them tells her he "doesn't like the idea of having a reporter along, and a reporter from the East . . . and a *lady* reporter from the East; and then he grins and pulls his hat down and spits out of the window" (p. 272).

Their attitude does not dissuade her from accompanying them. During the course of that night, however, she is aware of the danger they face and questions herself about why she felt compelled to join them. Soon enough, she has an answer: she is there because she can learn something important not only about an ecosystem, but also about the way humans use and abuse it. By the end of a long night of searching out poachers and other unsavory characters, she has earned the respect of these game wardens— by not complaining about the heat and the mosquitoes that plague them, by staying on the alert, and by cleverly extricating herself from a potentially dangerous situation when the game wardens board a boat from Texas whose occupants might be running drugs. More important, she has picked up a good deal of information about an ecosystem that would have been difficult to access on her own.

Kappel-Smith is matter-of-fact about her successes and her failures. When she joins biologists for a day of tagging young alligators, she hauls her first alligator over the side of the boat and then realizes she is holding the alligator by the tail rather than the neck; since she is in danger of getting bitten, she drops it onto the deck of the boat; the biologists have to grab it and band it before anyone gets hurt. Still, she keeps working at hauling in the alligators and gets better with each new try. Such tenacity is the essence of her encounters in these unfamiliar landscapes: she faces her fears, learns the details, and searches out and writes about the little known.

Kappel-Smith's night-life encounters yield some unusual and intriguing observations: alligators, she is surprised to learn, court by blowing bubbles at each other; in Hawaii, she discovers that corals turn aggressive at night, "carrying stinging cells that are as lethal as those of a Portuguese man-of-war" (p. 118). Even in the tamer landscape of Connecticut, in the fields and woods behind her mother's backyard that bring back memories of her childhood explorations, the wildlife is just as appealing and mysterious; here she finds a place that is "richer in wildlife than many a chunk of virgin wilderness" (p. 203). In these suburban fields and woods, she relies on her own knowledge and experience to discover the nighttime world. She livetraps shrews and meadow voles, talks to owls, and hunts out peeper ponds. She moves easily from observation and description to insights that leave her readers contemplating the significance of her encounters. On her last night wandering in the back meadow, she hears the "trilling" of toads and the "belling" of peepers. Her "ears are full of music, music backed by silence—or stillness ... by a deep and lucid dark against which more than music sounds" (p. 258). It is a moment of simplicity and truth, the ultimate destination in Kappel-Smith's journeys in the dark of night.

Desert Time

Just two years after the publication of *Night Life*, Kappel-Smith published her third book of natural history, *Desert Time: A Journey Through the American Southwest* (1992). Critical attention to this book was more widespread, with favorable reviews in several major newspapers and environmental magazines, including *Audubon*. The *New York Times Book Review* described *Desert Time* as a "thoroughly instructive and interesting account of the history and character of desert life and geology" that provides "a sense of the grand scale, both in space and time, of a living earth" (Cone, p. 7).

To research *Desert Time* Kappel-Smith spent over a year and a half trekking some twenty-five thousand miles by car across the Southwest to capture "verbal and visual" sketches of the immense land she crisscrossed. Each season she visited a particular section of the desert. Her choices were practical: in the winter she traveled to the southern deserts of California and Arizona; in the summer she moved farther north, to the deserts of Idaho and Nevada.

Desert Time is quite different from her previous books because she approaches her subject both as a traveler and as a naturalist. Kappel-Smith did little preparatory work for *Desert Time*, in contrast to the detailed research she did before the journeys described in *Night Life*. This lack of preparation does not detract from the depth of her experience; instead, it lends her observations a sense of freshness that comes with seeing a place for the first time. Before leaving for the Southwest, she simply consulted an oversized map, abandoning preliminary investigation in favor of firsthand experience. This reflects a certain level of self-confidence in her knowledge and skills as a naturalist, a confidence that undoubtedly emerged as a result of the time spent researching and writing her first two books.

Of her own role, she says she is "a naturalist, which means that I tend to approach plants, animals, and rocks in the same way that I approach people. I like to know their names and where they live and what they do. I like to find out what is important to them. I like to discover their relationships to the land and to each other" (p. xv). With *Desert Time* she redefines her role as a nature writer, by describing "landscapes with people in them, and animals and plants, too" (p. xiii).

The people she first writes about are Native Americans, both ancient and modern. The early chapters of the book discuss the landscape of Mesa Verde (Spanish for "green table") and the fact that it was once farmed by people we now call the Anasazi. While documenting the agricultural and geological changes this area underwent, she imagines the lives of the families who migrated from place to place as conditions grew colder and drier and less food was available. She visits their ancient homes in the caves that are still part of Mesa Verde's canyon walls, and conjures up their lives.

This visit to Mesa Verde at the beginning of her journey establishes her vision and comprehension of the land, its people, and its history. Thus, when she stays on the Navajo and Hopi reservations in Arizona, she possesses a sense of the Native Americans' spiritual connection to the land. Ultimately, these spiritual beliefs are beyond her grasp; she is an outsider, a foreigner who gets only a fleeting glimpse of another culture. Still, for a moment at the end of her stay she experiences harmony with the land and a people not her own, and this moment erases her feeling that she is an "odd unrooted stranger with a frail hold on life" (p. 43).

When she is not on the reservations, she most often travels alone, although twice her eleven-year-old son, Coulter, joins her. But whether alone or with a companion, Kappel-Smith confronts the physical challenges of camping out in the desert: extreme temperatures, rattlesnakes, getting lost and feeling alone—all worth enduring so that she can locate an infrequently sighted plant or animal. Fear, she writes, goes hand in hand with having the freedom to explore these wild places; she is willing to risk danger to satisfy her curiosity.

Her search is more than "mere naturalist's curiosity" (p. 91); it is also about endangered species and sinking water tables and other de-

struction caused by humans. She confronts these environmental issues by focusing on a number of endangered species, as well as other ecological problems. She takes note of the damage humans have wrought on the desert, first by urbanizing central locations and then by causing "havoc with creatures most like ourselves, the largest predators and the most long-lived and social of beasts" (p. 99). Among them is the tortoise. In an article entitled "Something About Turtles," published in *Country Journal* in 1991, Kappel-Smith documents the many different types of turtles and their population status, noting that "we seem to have done great damage to turtles in a short time. . . . If we want to live with them we have to make an effort to protect them and conserve their habitats, and we have to stop collecting them under any pretext" (p. 35). In *Desert Time*, she describes the similar predicament of wild tortoises that are put at risk by people collecting them to take home, or from the gunfire of "plinkers"— those people, often from urban areas, who shoot at almost anything. Even pet-store tortoises let loose in the desert infect these wild tortoises with deadly flu-like diseases.

She also takes a look at cattle ranching, one of the more environmentally unpopular desert livelihoods, and its influence on desert ecology. She interviews an Arizona rancher who has established a family-run outfit and is spokesman for the Arizona Cattle Growers' Association. The rancher impresses on her the difficulties of raising cattle—from the environmentalists who want all cattle off public lands to the urban visitors who damage and destroy ranch property in search of their own pleasure. His description of cattle ranching leads her to compare it to an endangered species, an analogy that some environmentalists would criticize as an apology by a naturalist or the wrong side of a sensitive issue. Kappel-Smith, however, as a scientist and journalist, is curious, and, as she demonstrates in both *Night Life* and *Desert Time*, wants to understand what it is like to be the unpopular trapper, hunter, or rancher. Most important, she seeks to become more fully educated. In the case of the cattle rancher, she discovers what actions he is taking to help solve the ecological problems

AMERICAN NATURE WRITERS

caused by overgrazing and by the growth of mesquite and scrub that is overwhelming desert grasslands. She learns about arid lands ecology, which involves the use of alternate grazing sites, and the theories about why mesquite has overtaken grass (one is that the deserts are drying out and mesquite can better handle the drought). Still, she is clear-sighted about the larger problems: "Nowadays, the cattle-raising industry is under fire, and no amount of cowboy romance—or reality—can change that" (p. 108).

Like the environmental politics of raising cattle, there exist political issues regarding wild animals, as well, even for those whose job it is to protect them. Kappel-Smith tags along with Nevada Department of Wildlife biologists to Lake Mead to scout out desert bighorn sheep. The biologists trap some of the animals in highly populated areas and place them in areas where none, or very few, exist. The program is funded by taxes on guns and ammunition and by hunting-permit sales. Though the Department of Fish and Wildlife's program helps keep the animals from extinction and cuts down significantly on hunting and poaching, their method of obtaining funding is criticized by some environmental groups.

Kappel-Smith's exploration of desert ecology and its problems marks *Desert Time* as an important contribution to the natural history literature of the American Southwest. As she points out, the study of this landscape cannot be an isolated exercise; the influence of humans—both positive and negative—must be taken into account. "Our sins against nature are sins against ourselves. This is certain," she writes in her closing lines. In *Desert Time* she relates some of these "sins" while at the same time investigating the way the natural world works. The result of her investigation is a broad array of knowledge and insight about a vast expanse of land.

In the years between the publication of *Wintering* and *Desert Time*, Kappel-Smith traveled from the Vermont hills to diverse and ecologically complex landscapes around the country. As her work evolves and as she finds new ways to explore and write about wild places, we can be

assured that her skilled use of scientific detail, creative imagery, and ecological reportage will continue to establish her as an insightful, engaging voice in the world of modern American nature writers.

Selected Bibliography

WORKS OF DIANA KAPPEL-SMITH

BOOKS

Wintering (Boston: Little, Brown, 1984); *Night Life: Nature from Dusk to Dawn* (Boston: Little, Brown, 1990); *Desert Time: A Journey Through the American Southwest* (Boston: Little, Brown, 1992).

SELECTED ARTICLES

"On Painting the Hills," in *Vermont Life* 34 (winter 1979); "Honeymoon of the Owl," in *Country Journal* 6 (March 1979); "Camp Followers of the Ice: New England Flora," in *Country Journal* 6 (July 1979); "Fall Migrations," in *Country Journal* 6 (September 1979); "The Granite Quarry," in *Vermont Life* 34 (autumn 1979); "Journey into Winter," in *Country Journal* 7 (November 1980); "Christmas Business," in *Country Journal* 7 (December 1980); "The Best Sugar Place," in *Vermont Life* 35 (summer 1981); "Pipeline in the Sugarbush," in *Country Journal* 9 (February 1982); "Making Hay," in *Country Journal* 9 (June 1982); "Best Time to Put Longjohns On," in *Vermont Life* 37 (autumn 1982); "Where the Birds Are," in *Vermont Life* 38 (winter 1983); "Prospecting for Goldeneyes" in *Vermont Life* 39 (winter 1984); "Locking Time: Life at the Edge of Winter," in *Country Journal* 16 (November/December 1989); "At the Fringes of Light," in *Country Journal* 17 (May/June 1990); "Something About Turtles," in *Country Journal* 18 (July/August 1991); "Salt," in *Orion* 13 (summer 1994); "Fickle Desert Blooms: Opulent One Year, No-Shows the Next," in *Smithsonian* 25 (March 1995).

BIOGRAPHICAL AND CRITICAL STUDIES

Jim Bencivenga, "Twilight Worlds for Nature Explorers," review of *Night Life*, in *Christian Science Monitor* (20 February 1990); Kathy Cone, "The Biggest Place There Is," review of *Desert Time*, in *New York Times Book Review* (28 February 1993); Stanley Crawford, "The Secret Life of Emptiness," review of

Desert Time, in Los Angeles Times Book Review (10 January 1993); Stephen MacDonald, "Midnight Rambles with Rattlers and Gators," review of Night Life, in Wall Street Journal (21 February 1990), sec. A; Mary Warner Marien, "Tales of the Desert, Hot and Cold," review of Desert Time, in Christian Science Monitor (8 January 1993); Harry Middleton, "A Place in the Sun," in Audubon 95 (March/April 1993); Andi Rierden, "Naturalist Illuminates World of the Night," in New York Times (11 March 1990), sec. CN.

JOSEPH WOOD KRUTCH
(1893–1970)

STUART C. BROWN

NEAR THE CENTER of the University of Arizona campus, in Tucson, is a small cactus garden named for a longtime resident, literary and cultural critic, naturalist and nature writer. The garden contains nearly every major plant species found in the Sonoran Desert, the region celebrated in some of Joseph Wood Krutch's better-known nature writings. A cynic might observe that the garden sits amid sidewalks and a large, grassy mall watered from Tucson's diminishing wells and is overlooked by the university's central administration building. A further irony is that the crowded proximity and unnatural juxtaposition of plant species too readily shows human intervention in the garden's design. Yet Krutch himself would likely have been optimistic as well as critical about this development, seeing the garden as a haven, a monument to the diversity and rich complexity of the desert, that offers residents and visitors an opportunity for a brief and necessary solitude amid bustling city life.

On sabbatical from Columbia University in 1950, Krutch was attracted to Arizona's Sonoran Desert for its remoteness from his urban and academic life on the East Coast. After moving to Arizona in 1952, he increasingly came to hold a nearly mystic appreciation for the strange world he found in the arid landscapes of the American Southwest. He began raising issues that would increasingly draw public attention to the uses and misuses of these lands, urging that the human-centered conservation efforts of the time needed rethinking.

Krutch acknowledged that the destructive effects of human intervention in a natural environment can be mitigated by efforts to save individual plant and animal species or parcels of land. But he also believed that, as conservation, such efforts were not enough. Krutch emphasized the development of a conservation *ethic*, one grounded in a striving for coexistence with the natural world. The more humans meddle with the intricacy of the natural environment, he argued, the more difficult it is to maintain a safe ecological balance. Roderick Frazier Nash, in *The Rights of Nature* (1989), notes that Krutch became one of the leading spokesmen for Aldo Leopold's ideas of extending ethical considerations to the environment.

"Ethic," for both Leopold and Krutch, is an encompassing term. Leopold provides a definition in *The Sand County Almanac* (1970): "An ethic, ecologically, is a limitation on freedom of action in the struggle for existence" (p. 238). That is, an ecological ethic evaluates human actions in terms of the environment in which they take place. To the extent that such actions are detrimental to the environment, they are considered unethical.

Krutch clearly understood the irony of modern humanity's successes in altering the natural world. The survival and welfare of a society, he argued, depend upon a genuine regard for the environment. Materialist culture and its reliance on technology represent what he perceived as human tyranny over nature. This tyranny, if unchecked, would lead to fatal ends: "All living things stand or fall together. Or rather man is of all such creatures one of those least able to stand alone" (*The Voice of the Desert*, p. 205). The problem, however, is that this awareness implies a restriction on human ambition: "How can he learn to value and delight in a natural order larger than his own order? How can he come to accept, not sullenly but gladly, the necessity of sharing the earth?" (p. 205).

Particularly within the Judeo-Christian tradition, human superiority to animals, for example, has been long accepted as an established fact. Man is to nature as God is to man. Within this rationale, the natural world becomes a possession, an object to be manipulated for human gain. A conservation ethic, however, establishes that humans are an intrinsic part of nature. Krutch claims that in order to live healthily and successfully on the land, humans must practice restraint and learn to function as members of the biotic community: "Ours is not only 'one world' in the sense usually implied by that term. It is also 'one Earth'" (*The Voice of the Desert*, p. 194).

The founding of Earth Day in 1970, the year of Krutch's death, signaled a growing public concern about environmental issues and the implications of human disregard for "one Earth." Americans began to acknowledge the ecological responsibilities Krutch had strongly advocated in his essays written in the 1950s and 1960s. There was a shift in public attitudes, a movement toward greater environmental responsibility and awareness, a recognition that the well-being of individuals depends upon the well-being of the natural environment in which they live.

Krutch is rightly regarded as having predicted, if not prompted, some of this change. Some twenty years after his death, his writings seem extremely prescient, laced with concepts and issues that are now commonplace: the crucialness of biodiversity, the relevance of ecology as a science, the need for wilderness areas, the misuse of public lands by special interest groups, the failings of wildlife management, the development of what now might be called "deep ecology" and what he would call "conservation ethics," and the irreparable damage caused by human populations that exceed their biological limits.

In 1949, Krutch's first writings as an amateur naturalist and advocate for nature, *The Twelve Seasons*, appeared. He writes near the end of this collection of essays:

> If I choose to live as much of my life as possible just beyond the city's outermost limits, if I observe my woods and cultivate the friendship of my pets, even if I think sometimes that I have established some sort of communication with life itself, I hardly suppose that I am thereby going to reverse a trend or point the way to salvation for the human race. (pp. 186–187)

Given his subsequent writings, one can assume that he attempted to prove himself wrong, that he would at least propose a model for salvation—quixotic or not.

Early Life and Career: The Seeding

Krutch's autobiography, *More Lives Than One* (1962), is aptly titled. His first career provided little indication of the tack he would take in his later years. Born on 25 November 1893 in Knoxville, Tennessee, Krutch (pronounced "Krootch") was the youngest of the three sons of Edward Waldemore and Adelaid (Wood) Krutch. His paternal grandmother, known as "Grossmother" (née) Von Wiersing, was influential in shaping his interest in plants and animals, an interest he never really abandoned but put in abeyance as he pursued studies in drama, literature, and social conditions.

In 1915, having graduated from the University of Tennessee with a B.A., Krutch entered Columbia University to pursue graduate work in English literature. After completing his doctoral coursework in 1917, he taught composition at Columbia. In the spring of 1918 he enlisted in the Psychological Corps of the U.S. Army; he served there until the end of the First World War, primarily administering psychometric tests and developing an enduring skepticism toward the social sciences and their reliance on empirical methodology. Krutch spent much of the rest of his career criticizing those sciences that, in pursuit of "objectivity," attempt to leave humans out of their methodologies.

In 1921 Krutch completed his dissertation, on the transformation of drama during the Restoration, and received the Ph.D. In 1923, he married Marcelle Leguia and settled into a career as an essayist and drama critic for the *Nation*. Before joining the English faculty at Columbia University full-time in 1937, he attended the Scopes trial as a correspondent for the *Nation*, wrote a critical biography of Edgar Allan Poe (1926), and produced one of the germinal works of social criticism, *The Modern Temper: A Study and a Confession* (1929).

The Modern Temper outlines Krutch's notion that culture follows the dictates of organicism from greening to fruition to decay. Rejecting the optimism of the 1920s, which was founded on perceptions of the miraculous capabilities of science and a repudiation of historical understanding, Krutch argues in *The Modern Temper* that these elements ultimately lead to despair rather than to hope for the human condition. "Ours is a lost cause," he concludes, "and there is no place for us in the natural universe" (p. 169).

William Holtz summarizes Krutch's vision as one of loss: "the loss of sustaining values that had been the price of modern knowledge; the loss of religious faith and of an earth-centered cosmology; the diminished stature of man in the natural order; and the diminished range of his freedom in the face of deterministic forces" (p. 269). In the chapter titled "The Paradox of Humanism," Krutch considers humanity's contemporary problems in relation to the state of nature: "Nature reveals herself as extraordinarily fertile and ingenious in devising *means*, but she has no *ends* which the human mind has

been able to discover or comprehend. Perhaps, indeed, the very conception of an end or ultimate purpose is exclusively human" (*The Modern Temper*, p. 27). Echoes of this observation appear again and again in his works.

In *More Lives Than One*, Krutch notes that his criticism in *The Modern Temper* "left man too bleakly and hopelessly alone in an alien universe" (p. 210), a position he would eventually redress. But in the years that immediately followed *The Modern Temper*, Krutch wrote drama and literary criticism and critical biographies, notably one of Samuel Johnson (1944) and, perhaps most important in setting the stage for his future endeavors, his highly acclaimed study *Henry David Thoreau* (1948).

Transformative Years: The Greening

Already interested in nature as a subject, Krutch agreed just after World War II to contribute to the American Men of Letters series, provided he could do a biographical-critical study of Thoreau. In *Thoreau*, he recognizes the presence of an individualist: "Thoreau's principal achievement was not the creation of a system but the creation of himself, and his principal literary work was, therefore, the presentation of that self" (p. 11). Thoreau became a model and a mirror for Krutch as a writer and thinker, a critic of society, and a celebrant of nature. In later years he returned again and again to Thoreau's maxim "Simplify," examining the concept carefully, as if it were a spadefoot toad on his windowsill, knowing its importance but fully aware that here was a complexity not easily or lightly grasped. Careful study of Thoreau's work led Krutch to conclude, "On the one hand, nature is a moral hieroglyphic; but on the other, morality is merely a jaundice reflected from man. The human race is no more important to the universe than a mushroom is to a forest, but the lover of nature is inevitably a lover of man" (p. 179).

Krutch's next book, *The Twelve Seasons: A Perpetual Calendar for the Country* (1949), is a series of brief nature essays drawn from observations of his garden and the land around his Connecticut summer home. It is a book of reflections on the natural order, reflections based on close scrutiny of creatures ranging from protozoa to katydids to frogs to owls. As the title implies, *Twelve Seasons* is also a cyclical work, beginning in April and ending in March. Writing the book led Krutch to "a kind of pantheism which was gradually coming to be an essential part of the faith—if you can call it that—which would form the basis of an escape from the pessimism of *The Modern Temper*" (*More Lives Than One*, p. 295).

In his prologue to the collection *Great American Nature Writing* (1950), which he edited, Krutch reflects on the rich and varied history of nature writing. He both critiques and celebrates humanity's self-conscious relation to nature: "it may be assumed that primitive man was not interested in nature. But it would also appear that he had hardly got himself urbanized before he began, in imagination at least, to return to it" (p. 3). This realization also informs *The Twelve Seasons* and was part of Krutch's next phase of development as social critic and naturalist writer.

By the late 1940s various forces were pushing Krutch away from the life of an urban academic and New York City drama critic. Increasingly, he described his home in Connecticut as offering an escape from the travails and impositions of city life. Given the "excuse" of his allergies, he took a sabbatical in Tucson, Arizona, where he wrote *The Desert Year* (1952), a series of essays that reflect on the experiences of a newcomer discovering the Sonoran Desert and its life. Before the sabbatical was over, Krutch determined that he would make a radical break from his previous life and move permanently to Tucson.

The Naturalist and Nature Writer: The Maturing

Krutch's reexamination of the views he espoused in *The Modern Temper* led him to write *The Measure of Man: On Freedom, Human Values,* *Survival, and the Modern Temper* (1954), which won the National Book Award for nonfiction that year. In this book he elaborates on what he sees as the consequences of separating human culture from its natural world. In *The Measure of Man* and his subsequent social critiques, as well as his nature essays, Krutch adopts a more and more strident stance: humans are essentially a part of nature, and whatever hope is possible for humankind resides in recognizing that humans must develop moral values congruent with living in a world where "man's ingenuity has outrun his intelligence." As he observes in *More Lives Than One* (1962), "other living things are fellow creatures in ways not always recognized" (p. 335).

In *The Great Chain of Life* (1956), Krutch criticizes the mechanistic and behaviorist views of the human condition that privilege science and technology over more humanistic concerns. A deterministic evolutionary mechanism, he argues, suggests that humans are essentially incapable of escaping predetermined biological dictates—a dangerously limiting self-conception. He cautions, "Whenever man's thinking starts with himself rather than with his possible origins in lower forms of life he usually comes to the conclusion that consciousness is the primary fact" (p. 123).

Further, the scientific and positivist tendency to regard humans as machines leaves certain questions unanswered. In his critique of Darwin, Krutch points out that "Man's willingness, sometimes at least, not only to sacrifice himself but to sacrifice himself and others for an ideal" contradicts "the inviolable rule of nature that no organism can develop what is not biologically useful," especially the inherent impulse for self-preservation (p. 121). Krutch proposes a more inclusive position that acknowledges the metaphysical: "Unless there is some emotion outside our own in which we can participate or from which we may draw comfort and joy then there is no universe beyond our own to which we can in any sense belong" (p. 223).

In *Human Nature and the Human Condition* (1959), Krutch argues that prevailing opinion based on Darwin, Marx, and Freud has concluded the following:

> (1) that man is an animal; (2) that animals originated mechanically as the result of a mechanical or chemical accident; (3) that "the struggle for existence" and "natural selection" have made man the kind of animal he is; (4) that once he became man, his evolving social institutions gave him his wants, convictions, and standards of value; and (5) that his consciousness is not the self-awareness of a unified, autonomous *persona* but only a secondary phenomenon which half reveals and half conceals a psychic nature partly determined by society, partly by the experiences and traumas to which his organism has been exposed. (p. 99)

Biology and psychology, via the scientific method, have come "to explain away whatever used to seem unique or even in any way mysterious" (p. 100). Science has blinded humans from inquiry into the *"concept of what ought to be"* through its demand for "a *description of what is*" (p. 94). Scientific explanation, in effect, limits awareness of consequences and abnegates responsibility.

As a warning against this shortsightedness, Krutch concludes the book with a Sanskrit parable in which three great magicians set out on a journey to demonstrate their powers to the world. They reluctantly allow a simpleton to join them. Before they have traveled very far, they come upon a pile of bones. Each of the magicians, eager to demonstrate his particular skill, performs a magic feat. The first causes the bones to assemble themselves into a skeleton; the second clothes the skeleton in flesh; the third endows the whole with life. Just before this last feat, the simpleton asks the three men whether they realize that their re-creation is a tiger. They are scornful, however, caught up in their abilities to perform these feats. The simpleton then climbs a tree, the tiger is brought to life, and the magicians are eaten. Technological know-how, suggests Krutch, is not enough to assure the continued survival of humankind. He makes a similar point at the end of *The Voice of the Desert: A Naturalist's Interpretation* (1955):

"We have three tigers—the economic, the physical and the biological—by the tail and three tigers are more than three times as dangerous as one" (p. 203).

Krutch's critiques of economics, the physical and social sciences, and culture took place alongside his development of a biological awareness. This awareness was situated in his newly adopted natural world, the Sonoran Desert. *The Desert Year* (1952), winner of the John Burroughs Medal, presents the observations of a person encountering an alien landscape in which the commonplace natural phenomena follow rules distinctly different from what he has been used to. Instead of resisting the unfamiliar or attempting to introduce through alteration the known and the comfortable, Krutch closely observed his new environment, paying attention to detail. This, in turn, allowed him to reconsider his own position in that world:

> What I learned from my desert year was, first and most generally, to be "more sure of all I thought was true." Specifically, I re-learned many platitudes . . .—such as, for instance, that courage is admirable even in a cactus; that an abundance of some good things is perfectly compatible with a scarcity of others; that life is everywhere precarious, man everywhere small. (pp. 269–270)

It is the contemplative toad, the saguaro, the roadrunner, the scorpion, the creosote that know the ways of living in the desert.

The Voice of the Desert (1955) continues Krutch's attention to living in the desert, an inquiry that becomes increasingly a proposal as Krutch moves himself and his readers from observation to realization that "Man can change things as no other animal can. But by way of compensation he can change himself much less" (p. 27). The central issues are both simple and complex: "How to get water, how to keep it when you have got it, and how to get along with the minimum gettable and keepable" (pp. 133–134). As Krutch comments, "It is not easy to live in that continuous awareness of things which alone is true living" (p. 37).

For Krutch, the intangible values of silence, a flower, solitude, a bird's song, a place without roads are human requirements, too. Echoing Aldo Leopold, Krutch proposes in *The Voice of the Desert* that a new ethic be developed to address these needs, an ethic that would provide a "moral framework" within which humans can redefine their relationship to the environment. In practical terms, this conservation ethic would set standards by which environmental policies could be judged. It would provide a unity of purpose and direction for the entire conservation movement.

Krutch's polemic becomes apparent in the chapter "Conservation Is Not Enough." First published as an essay in *American Scholar* in the summer of 1954, the chapter sounds the alarm that "enlightened selfishness cannot be enough because enlightened selfishness cannot possibly be extended to include remote posterity" (p. 194). Krutch believes that, with the tools of science and technology, humans too easily overcome the limitations inherent in nature. He identifies a paradox at the heart of the struggle for existence: "Neither man nor any other animal can afford to triumph in that struggle too completely" (p. 197). As too-successful predators, humans will ultimately succumb to their own successes.

Krutch argues for necessary and self-imposed restriction of action, by humans, on humans, for the sake of the entire biosphere. As unopposed victors in the struggle for existence, humans already live among ghosts. Threatening the natural order, humankind has become "the tyrant of the earth, the waster of its resources, the creator of the most prodigious imbalance in the natural order which has ever existed" (pp. 201–202). Technological intervention creates the need for more and more sophisticated and complicated methods to hold off the inevitable collapse.

Existing efforts at "conservation" have been misguided at best, limited by ignorance of the complexity of the natural order. Krutch points to predator control and failed deer management approaches on the Kaibab Plateau in the Grand Canyon area. He notes that after near extermination of mountain lions, wolves, and coyotes in

the 1920s, 4,000 deer became 100,000, of which 60,000 died of disease and starvation in one year. Predator and prey have a natural relationship with which humans interfere at their own risk. "Conservation" is not really conservation, in Krutch's view, because behind it is "only a more knowledgeable variation of the old idea of a world for man's use only" (p. 199).

In *Grand Canyon: Today and All Its Yesterdays* (1958), Krutch "brings to the Canyon the perspective of the dramatic critic, the essayist and the biographer," writes Charles Bogert in his foreword to the American Museum of Natural History edition (p. xviii). Adds Bogert, "he also brings the perspective of the philosopher, the naturalist, and the conservationist" (p. xviii). A rich and detailed chronology of both human history and geological time, *Grand Canyon* is also an argument for wild places where humans can encounter their humanness by separating themselves from one another. Krutch fears that "when the time comes that there is no more silence and no more aloneness, there will also be no longer anyone who wants to be alone" (p. 9). Only through solitude, Krutch suggests, is it possible to see nature as it is, rather than what human intervention makes it.

Most telling in *Grand Canyon* are the concluding chapters, in which Krutch furthers ideas such as "multiple use" policies. In "What Men? What Needs?" he observes that those who cut timber, slaughter animals as game, turn cattle loose to graze, build dams, and open lands indiscriminately to real estate development are the first to claim that "human needs come first." The question of policy, according to Krutch, is a question of preference: "Of the material needs (or rather profits) of a few ranchers and lumbermen, or of the mental and physical health, the education and the spiritual experiences, of a whole population?" (p. 225).

In conflicts of special interests over the use of public lands, Krutch notes that no one opposes "conservation." Rather, it is the competing interests who promote their own particular uses that create the problems. To compound the abuses that inevitably occur on public lands, the prevailing view usually emphasizes material and immediate use; profitability is the most powerful determination of rightful use. Both optimism and despair are apparent in Krutch's observations about the Canyon and its environs. Once again, he raises an argument for the immaterial, spiritual value of such places: "Unless we think of intangible values as no less important than material resources, unless we are willing to say that man's need of and right to what the parks and wildernesses provide are [sic] as fundamental as any of his material needs, they are lost" (pp. 224–225). Echoing Thoreau, he concludes, "The wilderness and the idea of the wilderness is one of the permanent homes of the human spirit" (p. 243). That spirit is greatly in danger of being lost, Krutch muses, and the consequence will be the loss of that which makes humans human.

The Forgotten Peninsula: A Naturalist in Baja California (1961) records Krutch's travels into the interior of another little-understood landscape. Krutch found a land out of time: "Because it has stood still the conservation of wild life and of unspoiled natural grandeur was, until recently, no problem at all. . . . Here is a land pretty much out of this world; and that, for certain people, is one of its charms" (p. 14). The book chronicles the land and its exotic flora and fauna, such as the boojum, the Heerman gull, and the elephant seal.

As a travel book, it also contrasts the human condition of the Baja inhabitants with those among whom Krutch lives. Although he comes "to Baja less to study society than to get away from it; to see less of man and more of nature," he recognizes he cannot do so and therefore seeks lessons from a comparison of "an economy of almost unqualified scarcity" with the economy of the United States and its "almost unqualified abundance" (p. 260). As he reflects on writing about the Baja in *More Lives Than One*, desperate scarcity marks the economy of the Baja, where food and water are hard to come by and manufactured goods no longer able to "serve their original purpose are made to serve some other" (p. 345). People just north of the border, however, worry more about obtaining the second car and a TV for the bedroom.

The recognition that Baja is changing, that progress in human terms is close at hand, does not escape Krutch. Technology has made the Baja not only more accessible, but more desirable. Krutch sees the "forgotten peninsula" becoming a destination for tourists looking for the offbeat, but not the primitive. And with the coming of the tourists and their accompanying resorts and roads and airstrips, the people of Baja discover their own desires for the things that others have.

Six years later, the Sierra Club brought out Krutch's *Baja California and the Geography of Hope* (1967) with photographs by Eliot Porter and a foreword by David Brower. In the introduction, Krutch is ever more attentive to the changes wrought on the land. Baja is being lost to development and the encroachment of "civilization." What is lost is irreplaceable: "Nature gave to Baja nearly all of the beauties possible in a dry, warm climate" (p. 10). It is a land that exists as it does because its "resources" remained hidden, "because very little of what we call progress has marred it" (p. 10). He celebrates the time when only a few, bad roads crossed the Baja: "Bad roads act as filters. They separate those who are sufficiently appreciative of what lies beyond the blacktop to be willing to undergo mild inconvenience from that much larger number of travelers which is not willing. The rougher the road, the finer the filter" (p. 11). Krutch warns that there are fewer and fewer such places each year, that wilderness is possible only without roads.

Krutch's careful and close observations of the intimate details of the land and its creatures, whether in Connecticut or the desert Southwest, hardly interfered with his prolific output. In addition to nearly thirty books and collections, he wrote for national periodicals, including *American Scholar, Audubon, Harper's, House and Garden, Saturday Review, Nation,* and the *New York Times*. He also wrote and narrated several hour-long TV nature documentaries for NBC that appeared in the 1960s.

The essays and occasional pieces collected in *If You Don't Mind My Saying So: Essays on Man and Nature* (1964) and *And Even If You Do:*

Essays on Man, Manners, and Machines (1967) reflect Krutch's dual role as naturalist and social critic. They also suggest the increasing inseparableness of these two positions. *If You Don't Mind My Saying So*, divided into four sections that cover his various careers, gathers materials published from 1936 to 1964, including "Thoreau on Madison Avenue," "On Being an Amateur Naturalist," "Man's Ancient, Powerful Link to Nature—A Source of Fear and Joy," "Now the Animal World Goes to Sleep," "Man's Mark on the Desert," and "Wilderness as More Than Tonic." Erudite and thoughtful reflections on humans and their place in the world, these essays brought sensitive and little-considered issues to large contemporary audiences.

And Even If You Do collects essays and occasional pieces Krutch published between 1931 and 1967. Although they are more weighted toward social critique, Krutch's naturalist ethic is still apparent in essays such as "Men, Apes, and Termites," "Green Thumb, Green Heart," "The Delights of Unnatural History," "What Are Flowers For?" and "Dam Grand Canyon?" *The Best Nature Writing of Joseph Wood Krutch* (1969) and *A Krutch Omnibus: Forty Years of Social and Literary Criticism* (1970), Krutch's final compilations, reflect his interests in nature, social critique, and literary studies, and his evaluation of his own works.

Krutch's range as a writer and thinker is demonstrated in the variety of texts he produced, including an odd little book meant for children, *The Most Wonderful Animals That Never Were* (1969). Invoking wide-ranging sources from the classics, literature, and historical accounts of fabled beasts, Krutch celebrates the imagination that has led to the invention of such creatures as unicorns, mermaids, werewolves, and the Loch Ness Monster, suggesting that perhaps their origin is to be found in misunderstandings of nature.

Krutch avidly collected and edited for anthologies the writings of others. These anthologies include *The Gardener's World* (1959), *The World of Animals: A Treasury of Lore, Legend, and Literature by Great Writers and Naturalists from 5th Century B.C. to the Present* (1961), *Thoreau: Walden and Other Writings* (1962), and *A Treasury of Birdlore* (co-edited by Paul S. Eriksson, 1962).

Of special note among Krutch's writings is the coffee-table book *Herbal* (1965), in which he includes information from old herbals and provides illustrations drawn from Pierandrea Mattioli's *Commentaries on the Six Books of Dioscorides*, first published in 1544. Krutch's interest in this project is a familiar one:

> Closely regarded, every one of the individual plants will be found useful, beautiful, or wonderful—and not infrequently all three. Perhaps the chief charm of the Herbalists (and certainly the one this book would like especially to suggest) is that they are more likely than the modern scientist to impart a sense of beauty and wonder—both of which the scientist may feel, but considers it no part of his function to communicate. (p. 34)

Drawing attention to the decline of biodiversity and the loss of unique plants, Krutch urges the reader to recognize that "nothing grows in vain."

Krutch's Ethical Challenge: Decay and Renewal

Challenges to accepted scientific method and authority have led to sounder assessments of resource exploitation, energy use, and technological development. Awareness of biological limits has become a public as well as a scientific issue, and the problems of population growth and the capabilities of ecosystems to survive human involvement are receiving increasing attention. Arguments for ecologically sound lifestyles have proliferated as these have become more acceptable and their benefits more widely known. And political actions by conservationists have involved citizenry in the decision-making processes of government and industry.

Joseph Wood Krutch

For Krutch, attempting to solve the conflict of interests by simply declaring all interests to be of equal value ultimately solves nothing at all. Implicit in his conservation views is the acknowledgement that human dependence on nature is not easily or simply addressed. Determining natural resources policy solely on the basis of material considerations, for example, leads to neglect of less obvious, less discernible uses that are equally necessary.

In a plea for recognition of the value of "intangible needs," Krutch concluded that if parks and other public lands are to be saved only until someone can determine a "use" for them, they will not last much longer. Recognition that such lands are put to the best use by being left alone allows for the fulfillment of some of our intangible needs. And these needs will last a long time, says Krutch, much longer than their easily stripped "natural resources," or at least until "overpopulation has reached the point where the struggle for mere survival is so brutal that no school or theater, no concert hall or church, can be permitted to 'waste' the land on which it stands" (*Grand Canyon*, p. 225).

Krutch proposed that a true conservation must provide for a fundamental shift in orientation toward the natural world. This reorientation will not come out of logic, he insisted, but out of attitudes that are in essence emotional and perhaps mystical. Krutch reoriented himself in the deserts of the Southwest. As he notes at the end of *The Voice of the Desert*, it is in places of scarcity that the contemplative meets the conservationist. The desert is the last frontier in more than obvious ways:

Krutch was a strong and vocal advocate for these issues, perhaps an originator of some of them. Following Thoreau and Leopold, he brought to the public's attention difficult and sensitive matters that question common assumptions, notably the propriety of "multiple use" of wild lands, especially federally owned public lands on which ranchers, miners, and recreation seekers are allowed equal access. Krutch indicts the power and the materialism of these special interest groups: "The pressure to allow the hunter, the rancher or the woodcutter to invade the public domain is constant, and the plea is always that we should 'use' what is assumed to be useless unless it is adding to material welfare" (*The Voice of the Desert*, p. 201). Reading the future with startling clarity, he observed in the 1950s that the great majority of these public lands, found in the western states, would experience increased multiple use as more and more of the country's population moved into these states.

It is the last because it was the latest reached, but it is the last also because it is, in many ways, a frontier which *cannot* be crossed. It brings man up against his limitations, turns him in upon himself and suggests values which more indulgent regions minimize. Sometimes it inclines to contemplation men who have never contemplated before. (p. 221)

Krutch's ethic reaches toward the mystical.

To understand Krutch's valuation of the natural order, his near mysticism, one must first turn to his notion of "metabiology." The term, coined by George Bernard Shaw, suggests that since life itself is not completely explainable in merely physical terms, moral and aesthetic questions should be discussed in connection with what we know about living creatures without any attempt to reduce such questions to merely physical terms" (*The Voice of the Desert*, p. 209).

James McClintock convincingly argues that Krutch developed his definition of the term from his readings of the American entomologist William Morton Wheeler, a scholar Krutch cites frequently. In the introduction to *The Best Nature Writing of Joseph Wood Krutch* (1969), Krutch uses a quote from Wheeler to summarize the need for the concept of metabiology: "apart from the members of our own species, they [animals and plants] are our only companions in an infinite and unsympathetic waste of electrons, planets, nebulae and stars" (p. 23). With its methodology rooted in observation and speculation rather than experimentation, metabiology questions all potentialities and limitations of living matter and seeks to determine, as far as possible, the "intentions" and "standards of value" found in nature. It is biology that goes beyond the purely scientific or technological.

Purely scientific biology seeks to describe solely the interrelationships of living organisms. Technological biology seeks to apply this knowledge—to determine, for instance, how farms can be kept fertile. Because the consideration of value is metaphysical in itself, biology becomes "metabiological" when it concerns itself with notions of natural value. Within metabiology, the realm of emotion is seen as having value equal to the realm of fact or the realm of speculative reason.

Yet metabiology does not explain the origin of emotion, according to Krutch: "The reason for my deepest caring does not lie within the scope of biology or even metabiology. One cannot recognize it without being to that extent a mystic" (*The Voice of the Desert*, p. 214).

Krutch did not use the term "mystic" lightly. The concluding chapter of *The Voice of the Desert* is titled "The Mystique of the Desert." Here his own involvement with nature is extrapolated into an argument for the "momentary acceptance of values not definable in terms of that common sense to which we ordinarily accord our first loyalty" (p. 215). There is a sense of satisfaction, he observes, that is impersonal: "One no longer asks 'What's in it for me?' because one is no longer a separate selfish individual but part of the welfare and joy of the whole" (p. 215).

A better proposal for the mystic experience could hardly be imagined. But Krutch neither called himself a true mystic nor claimed that one must be a mystic in order to experience a transcendental relation with the universe. Likewise, he understood that no sensible ethic requires all those who espouse it to spend forty days and forty nights in the desert, although he thought such an experience would be to many people's advantage. What an appropriate ethic does require, Krutch believed, is learning to forsake technological and scientific detachment and to value emotional responses to nature.

This is the end toward which all of Krutch's writing on the subject of man and nature necessarily leads. If human regard for the natural world has splintered and weakened, it is because the full realm of human response has never been taken seriously. In his reasoning on this point, Krutch relied heavily on Leopold, who argued that the solution to the problem of conservation cannot be simply "more conservation." It is not only the volume of education and of action that needs to be stepped up; it is attention to what is lacking in the content of what is called conservation.

Love, admiration, and respect are key to what Krutch identified as emotional. Scientists, particularly in the modern age, avoid placing a high value on emotion. Separating human consciousness from the workings of the natural world, Krutch contended, leads to rigidly objective, nonemotional responses to nature. A conservation ethic must affirm the intrinsic value of the human subjective response. To be subjective is to place human consciousness within the bounds of the natural world, to perceive nature not as "out there" but as "in here."

An ethic of conservation, therefore, is much more than a contemporary statement of old ideals. It advocates a complete restructuring of traditional assumptions regarding the natural environment. Krutch affirmed, with Leopold, that more conservation is an inadequate solution because the focus is still on use. He asks that we learn other ways of appreciation:

> But how can man be persuaded to cherish any other ideal unless he can learn to take some interest and some delight in the beauty and variety of the world for its own sake, unless he can see a "value" in a flower blooming or an animal at play, unless he can see some use in things not useful? (*The Voice of the Desert*, p. 199)

What he saw missing in debates on conservation "is love, some feeling for, as well as understanding of, the inclusive community of rocks and soils, plants and animals, of which we are a part" (*The Voice of the Desert*, p. 193). An ecologically aware value system is the necessary first step in a widespread shift in attitude. The emotion of love must be behind the effort to change what is now incomplete, rigid, and destructive.

The process requires reevaluation of human desire as well as of human material needs. Krutch questioned hunting for sport: Can it be ethical to destroy the natural predators of deer, such as the cougar and the wolf, thus allowing the deer population to increase out of all proportion to its natural habitat, and then declare an open season on that population? Invoking the natural order, Krutch pointed out that natural predators tend to strike down the old and the weak, whereas human hunters destroy the strong and the healthy. Humans, not nature, are responsible for the excessive deer populations in many areas that have threatened or destroyed many species of forage plants, and for the mil-

lions of deer that die of starvation during a harsh winter.

Agriculture, too, is guilty. Krutch observed that all agriculture is an interference with the state of nature, and that increasing human population means increasing dependence on such interference. It makes little sense to ask whether agriculture is necessary. But it makes eminent sense to ask which lands should be cultivated, and by what methods. Should arid lands, for instance, be irrigated for the production of cash crops? Krutch warned that the scale of agriculture is perhaps already too complicated and technologically dependent to be restricted or to accommodate alternative, ecologically sensitive procedures. The ethical approach to agriculture would first examine what is good for the land, in full awareness that what is good for the land cannot, in the long run, be detrimental to humans.

Krutch questioned the construction of access roads into parks and wilderness areas. Some Americans assume that it is their right to reach any area of interest on a well-built road. Ethically, this right has to be weighed against the disruption of the balance of nature set off by the presence of motorized vehicles and too many humans. Krutch sees this as an area for compromise: "It is not unreasonable to protect both wilderness areas and nature reserves by keeping them for those who are willing to take a certain amount of trouble to get there" (*Grand Canyon*, p. 232). For those who want to see the wilderness, but are unwilling to leave their cars and motorcycles behind, many areas would necessarily be off-limits. "When roads are too good, too wide, and too fast, they not only become eyesores themselves but are, at the same time, invitations to those who have no real interest in what they lead to," he cautions in *Baja California* (p. 11).

Krutch did not favor any compromise on the question of opening parks and wilderness areas to exploitation of their material resources. He advocated the formulation of a definite policy of protection from both the would-be exploiters and the increasing numbers of recreation seekers.

Such a policy also would need to judge "improvements" and "facilities," such as good roads, as indirect exploitation and closely monitor their implementation.

According to Krutch, the articulation and application of an ethic of ecology should not be a one-time effort but a process, a continuous reevaluation. Time and dedication are necessary in order for the effects of thousands of years of history to be revised. Human sovereignty over the natural world has traditionally carried with it the assumption that nature exists primarily for human benefit, and in particular for human material benefit. With civilization came the control of nature, and greater civilization means greater control. Land that cannot be planted and harvested for human consumption has thus been defined as valueless. When a certain species has been domesticated, species that prey upon it have become the enemy, destined to extermination. These definitions and manipulations, and their consequences, are found everywhere.

Krutch maintained that any real management of resources entails a willingness to sacrifice, to some extent, the immediate interests not only of certain individuals or groups but also of the human species. As the battle for limited resources intensifies under increasing population pressures, the need for such a system of values becomes greater. At stake is the survival of millions of plant and animal species, as well as that of humans.

The future, wrote Krutch in 1954, holds two distinct possibilities. If humans continue to disregard love for the world, nature may someday "violently reassert herself," bringing about a series of catastrophes that will demonstrate to man "the hollowness of his supposed success" (*The Voice of the Desert*, p. 204). On the other hand, if humans set reasonable limits to their ambitions and recognize that being the most highly evolved of living creatures is not an easily carried entitlement, then life on this planet may continue, may prosper. Some forty years later, Krutch's proposals have become more necessary, his warnings more alarming with the ring of truth they carry. "Don't forget," Krutch whispers to both his readers and the spring peepers in *The Twelve Seasons*, "we are all in this together" (p. 13).

Selected Bibliography

WORKS OF JOSEPH WOOD KRUTCH

BOOKS

The Modern Temper: A Study and a Confession (New York: Harcourt Brace, 1929; repr., 1956); *Samuel Johnson* (New York: Henry Holt, 1944); *Henry David Thoreau* (New York: Sloane, 1948; repr., New York: Morrow, 1974); *The Twelve Seasons: A Perpetual Calendar for the Country* (New York: Sloane, 1949); *The Desert Year* (New York: Sloane, 1952; repr., New York: Viking, 1963); *The Best of Two Worlds* (New York: Sloane, 1953); *The Measure of Man: On Freedom, Human Values, Survival, and the Modern Temper* (New York: Bobbs-Merrill, 1954); *The Voice of the Desert: A Naturalist's Interpretation* (New York: Sloane, 1955; repr., 1969; repr., New York: Morrow, 1980); *The Great Chain of Life* (Boston: Houghton Mifflin, 1956; repr., 1978); *Grand Canyon: Today and All Its Yesterdays* (New York: Sloane, 1958; repr., Garden City, N.Y.: Doubleday and American Museum of Natural History, 1962); *Human Nature and the Human Condition* (New York: Random House, 1959; repr., New York: Morrow, 1968).

The Forgotten Peninsula: A Naturalist in Baja California (New York: Sloane, 1961); *More Lives Than One* (New York: Sloane, 1962); *If You Don't Mind My Saying So: Essays on Man and Nature* (New York: Sloane, 1964); *Herbal* (New York: Putnam, 1965); *And Even If You Do: Essays on Man, Manners, and Machines* (New York: Morrow, 1967); *Baja California and the Geography of Hope*, ed. by Kenneth Brower (San Francisco: Sierra Club, 1967; repr. 1969); *The Best Nature Writing of Joseph Wood Krutch* (New York: Morrow, 1969); *The Most Wonderful Animals That Never Were* (Boston: Houghton Mifflin, 1969); *A Krutch Omnibus: Forty Years of Social and Literary Criticism* (New York: Morrow, 1970).

WORKS EDITED BY KRUTCH

Great American Nature Writing (New York: Sloane, 1950); *The Gardener's World* (New York: Putnam, 1959); *The World of Animals: A Treasury of Lore, Legend, and Literature by Great Writers and Naturalists from 5th Century B.C. to the Present* (New York: Simon and Schuster, 1961); *Thoreau: Walden and Other Writings* (New York: Bantam, 1962); *A Treasury of Birdlore*, with Paul S. Eriksson (Garden City, N.Y.: Doubleday, 1962).

JOSEPH WOOD KRUTCH

INTERVIEW

Edward Abbey, "On Nature, *The Modern Temper*, and the Southwest: An Interview with Joseph Wood Krutch," in *Sage* 2 (1968), excerpts repr. in Abbey's intro. to the 1978 ed. of *Great Chain of Life*.

MANUSCRIPTS AND PAPERS

Many of Krutch's papers were destroyed in a fire at his Connecticut home in 1952. Most of his typescripts, published copies of essays, notes and clippings, book reviews, and correspondence are in the Manuscript Division of the Library of Congress. John Margolis has assembled and indexed several thousand of Krutch's writings; these are deposited in the Special Collections Department of the Northwestern University Library.

BIOGRAPHICAL AND CRITICAL STUDIES

Durant da Ponte, "Quest for Values: The Pilgrimage of Joseph Wood Krutch," in *Tennessee Studies in Literature* spec. no. (1961); René Dubos, "The Despairing Optimist," in *American Scholar* 40 (1971); Charles I. Glicksberg, "Joseph Wood Krutch: Critic of Despair," in *Sewanee Review* 44 (1936); John Gorman, "Joseph Wood Krutch: A Cactus Walden," in *MELUS* 11 (winter 1984); William Holtz, "Homage to Joseph Wood Krutch: Tragedy and the Ecological Imperative," in *American Scholar* 43 (spring 1974); James Kilgo, "Krutch's Sonoran Pastoral: The Aesthetic Integrity of *The Desert Year*," in *Southwestern American Literature* 7 (fall 1981); John D. Margolis, "Joseph Wood Krutch: A Writer's Passage Beyond the Modern Temper," in George Bornstein, ed., *Romantic and Modern: Revaluations of Literary Tradition* (Pittsburgh: Univ. of Pittsburgh Press, 1977), and *Joseph Wood Krutch: A Writer's Life* (Knoxville: Univ. of Tennessee Press, 1980).

James I. McClintock, "Krutch, Joseph Wood, and Wheeler, William Morton—Metabiologists," in *Journal of American Culture* 10, no. 4 (1987), and *Nature's Kindred Spirits: Aldo Leopold, Joseph Wood Krutch, Edward Abbey, Annie Dillard, Gary Snyder* (Madison: Univ. of Wisconsin Press, 1994); Paul N. Pavich, "Joseph Wood Krutch: Persistent Champion of Man and Nature," in *Western American Literature* 13 (summer 1978), and *Joseph Wood Krutch* (Boise, Idaho: Boise State Univ., 1989); Peter Gregg Slater, "The Negative Secularism of *The Modern Temper:* Joseph Wood Krutch," in *American Quarterly* 33 (summer 1981); Peter Wild, "Joseph Wood Krutch: Quiet Voice for the 'Devil's Domain,'" in *Pioneer Conservationists of Western America* (Missoula, Mont.: Mountain Press, 1979).

MAXINE KUMIN
(b. 1925)

HILDA RAZ

A "Swedish doctor . . . weighed the deathbeds of his terminal patients just before and after they lost their vital signs. There was a twenty-one gram difference." (Maxine Kumin, *The Designated Heir*, 1974)

"On the outside all the life of the earth is expressed in the animal or vegetable, but make a deep cut in it and you find it vital. . . . The earth is pregnant with law." (Henry David Thoreau, *Journal*, March 1854)

WHAT THOREAU NOTICED in the mid-nineteenth century, the steady replication of forms throughout nature, New England writer Maxine Kumin describes in language wrought to its uttermost. Her nature essays include serviceable accounts of life on the farm—how to find and keep a horse, tell a mule from an ass, or identify a puffball ("Mushrooms are not a fast food," she reminds foragers)—rendered in words of surprising immediacy. In "Jicama Without Expectations," collected in *Women, Animals, and Vegetables* (1994), she provides a lyrical catalog of seeds for a sustenance garden: "the little cobbles of beet seeds that separate when rolled between your fingers, the flat, feathery parsnip ones that want to drift on air en route to the furrow, the round black dots that will be Kelsae onions, fat and sweet by September, the exasperatingly tiny lettuce flecks

that descend in a cluster, and the even harder-to-channel carrot seeds" (p. 95). This descriptive passage characteristically evolves into a speculative fabrication: "consider the lotus seeds found under an ancient lake bed in Manchuria. Carbon-dated at 800 years old, they grew into lotus plants of a sort that had never been seen in that particular area. Such extravagant longevity makes me hopeful that we humans too will ever so gradually advance into new forms, a higher level of lotus, as it were." Her nature writing demonstrates that the human mind in its intricate workings is both animal and vegetable, and is everywhere governed in its perceptions by the possibilities of language. Kumin's work invites literary and cultural analysis as a part of a gathering international concern with the preservation of the earth and the methods to be used. What she brings to the discourse is art made from a woman's life.

Maxine Kumin is best known in the literary world as a poet, but she has written in almost every genre, twenty-seven books in all as of 1994 (excluding limited editions and broadsheets). A sense of place in nature, underwritten by private and public history, has been her ground for three decades and more. Bearing witness to the Holocaust, Korean and Vietnam wars, civil rights and women's movements, the Kennedy and King assassinations, the factionalizing of the geo-political world, and the increasingly dire ecology news, she has made her reputation in a profession that has little honored the work of women.

In 1952, the critic Edmund Wilson wrote of his friend the poet Edna St. Vincent Millay:

> There is always a certain incommensurability between men and women writers. But . . . she was able to identify herself with more general human experience and stand forth as a spokesman for the human spirit . . . putting herself beyond common embarrassments, common oppressions and panics. This is man who surveys himself and the world in which he moves, not the beast that scurries and suffers; and the name of the poet comes no longer to indicate a mere individual with a birthplace and a legal residence, but to figure as one of the pseudonyms assumed by that spirit itself. (*The Shores of Light*, p. 752)

Wilson's assumptions that men and women writers have no common attributes to compare, that spirit and body are gender, one male and the other here female, and that a successful woman writer must divide herself from her body and her life are representative of the time in which Maxine Kumin began to write.

Although Kumin won the Pulitzer Prize for poetry in 1993 and numerous other honors throughout her career, some critics have said of her nature essays that they "dote" on "minute particulars" and are "charming." Her poems have been called "pastoral," a term that commonly connotes simplicity and charm and a lack of depth. When Kumin herself ascribes the term to her country poems, she is acknowledging her use of the literary conventions of the pastoral to critique the dominant society. Sixteenth-century English poets had taken Virgil's Latin Eclogues as models for tales of happy shepherds and shepherdesses in an idealized countryside. They evoked the prelapsarian garden where urban materialism, moral expediency, and favoritism at court were absent. These representations •of "natural" and virtuous human lives in the peaceable kingdom, where the lion lay down with the lamb, criticized by contrast the corruptions of government and society. Edmund Spenser's *The Shepheardes Calender* (1579), for

example, considers the moral nature of poetry as well as the responsibilities of the poet in the life of the state. Kumin's contemporary pastorals mention natural impediments to farming (earwigs, weasels, acid rain, thrip), commercial reasons for the failure of the small farm, and the role of the writer in an international community. Her moral vision is implacable. In the essay "Kumin on Kumin: The Tribal Poems," she meets critical dismissal with irony: "although I [am] . . . concerned with the smallest particulars in the natural world, I too have a thesis to advance" (*To Make a Prairie*, 1979, p. 107). In a later essay, "A Sense of Place," collected in *In Deep: Country Essays* (1987), she elaborates: "Now I must face the issues of survival, of hunger and genocide, of natural (or unnatural) human depravity" (p. 178).

The 1992 *Bloomsbury Guide to Women's Literature* notes that Kumin has been increasingly concerned with "humanity's troubled relationship with the natural world, and nature's domination and exploitation by humans" (p. 709). Susan Ludvigson in the *Dictionary of Literary Biography* (1980) agrees: In the late twentieth century, Kumin "shows man now asserting his sometimes irresponsible dominance over the natural world" (vol. 5, p. 421).

Kumin's short story "Other Nations" (collected in *Why Can't We Live Together Like Civilized Human Beings?* [1982]) introduces Martha Carpenter, a veterinarian who prefers to be called an "ethologist." She lectures and writes books on "conservation, behavioral adaptation, and the ethics of man/animal relationships" but "does not begrudge the current spate of folksy tales by veterinarians . . . [since] they promote empathy." Martha Carpenter "flies from conference to symposium raising the issue the Judeo-Christian tradition dismissed when it separated man from the natural world. She illustrates her thesis with colored slides" of animal atrocities. "In a world that divides out between the tortured and the torturers," Kumin writes, "Martha Carpenter knows it is difficult to sustain that sense of outrage necessary for change" (p. 59). She also knows "that animals are neither our spiritual brothers nor our slaves. As Henry Beston has said, *they are other nations, caught with ourselves in the net of life and time*" (p. 73, emphasis in original).

Maxine Kumin is a writer who teaches, an expert rider, trainer, and breeder of horses, and a farmer. She is a poet, not an ethologist. She reminds us in interviews that poets write because they must, out of "an inner need to sing." Kumin is a Jewish woman writer who claims the natural and literary landscape of the Puritan fathers as well as the wild and non- or prelingual sides of existence. She writes to honor and preserve the continuum of a small and particular tribe of family, friends, and other poets, yet she attempts to breach large boundaries of culture, gender, and species. Emphatic blurring is her most powerful literary effect, but she sees herself at work as solitary, androgynous, and alert. She is a critic who writes in many genres — stories, essays, poems, journals, children's books — yet she refers to herself in the third person as "the poet." Although she is committed to the radical formulations of women, she often cites male authority. She honors androgynous values yet writes of women's experience and elaborates new conceptions of the maternal. A champion of wilderness, she has a consuming passion for cultivation. The woman poet with semipermeable boundaries is balanced by the separate and solitary, nongendered worker. In her poem "The Bangkok Gong" (in *Nurture*, 1989), she describes her survival as depending both on the resonant sounding of a gong made from industrial castoffs in Thailand, and on the fact that, though it is the gift of a loved but absent daughter, "Some days I/barely touch it."

Poetry of Resistance

Born 6 June 1925 in the predominantly Protestant suburb of Germantown in Philadelphia, Pennsylvania, Maxine Winokur was the youngest and only daughter in a Jewish family of four children whose father, Peter Winokur, a stern patriarch, owned one of the largest pawn shops in the city. Her mother, Doll Simon Winokur, referred to him as "a broker." Kumin

grew up in a Victorian house next door to the convent of the Sisters of Saint Joseph, where she attended nursery school and the first years of elementary school. Providing material for her early poems were the tension between the Jewish and Catholic elements of her background, as well as the stories that her German nurse, whom she called Fräulein, read aloud to her — original stories from the Brothers Grimm, with their vivid details of abuse and violence, and Heinrich Hoffman's moral tales for children, *Der Struwelpeter*. ("Mind me, says Fräulein. God stands up in Heaven. / See how He watches? He snatches the bad ones," are lines from "Fräulein Reads Instructive Rhymes," in Kumin's first book, *Halfway*, 1961.) When Kumin was eight, Hitler came to power in Germany and soon thereafter the European Holocaust began. As she wrote in her novel *The Abduction* (1971), "the terrible unexpungeable fate of the six million sat like an iceberg" in Jewish consciousness. The title poem of her third collection of poetry, *The Nightmare Factory* (1970), introduces images of blight:

> blind sockets
> of subways and mine pits
> . . .
> nazis and cossacks ride
> klansmen and judases
> . . .
> and for east asians
> battalions of giants
> dressed in g i fatigues.

These oppressions of nature and peoples weigh heavily in all of her work. Her early memories include the tradesmen's skinny horses laboring uphill, to which she responded with compassionate gifts of her brothers' camp blankets. In an essay describing her own creative process, Kumin writes, "animals in general and horses in particular represent [for me] a kind of lost innocence in our technological society and they often stand as a symbol for mute suffering" (*To Make a Prairie*, p. 101). Horses join images of water as redemptive, first in her life, then in her work.

Kumin began to write as a child to work out feelings of "isolation and solitude." Her poem

"Life's Work" (in *House, Bridge, Fountain, Gate,* 1975) blends the story of her mother's training as a concert pianist with Kumin's as a competitive swimmer. Although they thrived under the rigors of practice, both were dissuaded from their goals. Her mother got married after her parents forbade her to go on tour. Kumin, who aspired to be an Olympic swimmer, was not allowed to join Billy Rose's Aquacade when she was offered the job the summer she was eighteen. The family thought it was an improper occupation for a young woman. Still, the strong body—"I was all muscle and seven doors"—is a measure of health in her work and the site of "the little ball-bearing soul" ("Body and Soul: A Meditation," a poem in *The Retrieval System,* 1978). (Her family neither encouraged nor discouraged her writing.) "A Hundred Nights," an early poem reprinted in *Our Ground Time Here Will Be Brief* (1982), evokes her father chasing bats with a carpet beater: "My father had his principles./He smacked to stun them, not to kill." Kumin describes herself as looking on:

> Frozen underneath the sheets,
> I heard the bats mew when he hit.
> I heard them drop like squashing fruit.
> I heard him test them with his foot.

The family says the bats came only twice, but quantity had little to do with the effect on Kumin: "Once before my father died,/I meant to ask him why he chose/to loose those furies at my bed." Her mother—whose reserved presence in Kumin's work is most vivid in the stories she told Kumin of barnyard and kitchen girls' and women's work from her southwest Virginia childhood at the turn of the century—was especially pleased by her daughter's later success. She set a standard of ambition and productivity for Kumin, who reminds us that her mother couldn't escape housekeeping chores for the "dramas of field and barn" that she imagined ("Enough Jam for a Lifetime," in *Women, Animals, and Vegetables,* p. 65). In 1942 Kumin entered Radcliffe College. She wrote in "Breaking the Mold" (collected in *Where We Stand:*

Women Poets on Literary Tradition, edited by Sharon Bryan, 1993) that during her undergraduate years she never found "a female instructor, assistant, associate, or, heaven forfend, full professor in any discipline" (p. 101). In 1946 she received her A.B. degree and married Victor Kumin, an engineer to whom she is still married. In 1948 she received the A.M. from Radcliffe and gave birth to their first child. In her essay "The Care-Givers," Kumin reflects on the early years of her marriage: "I was housebound, dutiful, and diligent . . . pacifying and feeding three youngsters born between October of 1948 and June of 1953." She began ghostwriting articles for medical journals and writing rhymed fillers for magazines, earning money at home: "Luckily, we were poor and the money I earned was significant, which gave my work some stature" (*The Writer on Her Work,* vol. 2, pp. 61–62).

In the late 1950s, Kumin joined a writing workshop taught by poet and Tufts University English professor John Holmes at the Boston Center for Adult Education. There she met Anne Sexton and their much documented friendship began. As Kumin writes in *To Make a Prairie,* they were suburban neighbors, "two shy housewives, a pair of closet poets" (p. 78), with two husbands and five children between them. Together they heard George Starbuck read at the New England Poetry Club in 1958, and he and Samuel Albert, Kumin, Sexton, and Holmes met as a biweekly workshop for three years, writing and revising the poems that went into their books. Kumin's and Sexton's first books were an initiating part of the watershed of women's poetry that marked the 1960s. Each was to win a Pulitzer Prize in their years of intense collaboration, and each was to write prose as well as poetry. As "intimate friends and professional allies" (p. 83), they worked together every day, wrote children's books to make money, provided company and instruction for one another's children, and contributed critical response, titles, lines, dialogue, and ideas for each other's work. In the essay "A Sense of Place," collected in *In Deep: Country Essays* (1987), she writes, "As one another's most immediate and sympathetic audience, I suppose it was inevitable that we take on some of the same subjects. But I like to think that our voices are distinctively separate, even as critics shuffle our poems today in search of overlapping images" (p. 176). "My focus was always more in the natural world, Anne's focus was always more on human relationships," she said in an interview with Diana Hume George (1985).

Kumin's own speculations on human relationships appear most convincingly, and perhaps most despairingly, in her short stories about middle-class white parents and children, heterosexual lovers and friends. The formal restraints of the poems give way to narratives more broadly placed in the world. Nature as explored in these stories is human and political, and the news is not good. Only friendship and memory endure, and often because of a survivor's determination. The title of Kumin's collection of stories, *Why Can't We Live Together Like Human Beings?*, suggests that though civility is the measure of human behavior, it is also often the problem to be addressed.

John Holmes supported Kumin, she said in an interview with Martha George Meek (in *To Make a Prairie*), for a teaching job at Tufts, "where I was a part-time English instructor, equipped, in the eyes of the university, only to teach freshman composition to physical education majors and dental technicians" (p. 30). From 1961 to 1963 she and Sexton were scholars of the Radcliffe Institute for Independent Study in an experiment for married, educated women carefully selected for their promise and/or achievements. Although most of the women were privileged by their middle-class status, Tillie Olsen, also a scholar, brought socialist, working-class perceptions, as well as the makings of her important book *Silences* (1978), to the mix. With stipends, rooms, and some Harvard University resources, they were encouraged to make up time spent taking care of a family instead of pursuing careers.

When Kumin and Sexton were raising small children, white middle-class women in America were valued as homemakers, mothers, and moral guardians: "We were second-class citizens, the repository of all goodness and truth in the home and seldom welcome outside it" ("Breaking the Mold," in *Where We Stand*, p. 104). Closed off from the world of economic power and isolated by the demands of family and household, some protested with a new literature of their own. Diane Wood Middlebrook in *Anne Sexton: A Biography* (1991) writes, "women's poetry was to provide a very important form of resistance" during the 1960s and 1970s, "and much of the most influential was to be written by Sexton, . . . Kumin, Denise Levertov, Sylvia Plath, and Adrienne Rich," who were Boston friends (p. 40).

Kumin's first book, *Halfway* (1961), was published when she was thirty-six (she remembers she was forty: "I never had any early publications") in an edition of one thousand copies, seven hundred of which were remaindered or destroyed. Her style may have been marked by skill in the traditional prosody favored by male poets of her generation, but the subjects of her poems were radical. With what Alicia Ostriker in *Stealing the Language* calls "tender bawdiness" (p. 117), Kumin presented examples of female discourse and culture in and outside the family as well as talk of the female body and women's sexuality. In "Kumin on Kumin: The Tribal Poems" (in *To Make a Prairie*), she says, "it was not popular . . . to speak of the uterus or the birth canal" (p. 107); nevertheless her work made aspects of women's experience a primary subject. Sexton's work developed more flamboyantly under Kumin's tutelage than Kumin's own, but both writers, with the support of their daily collaboration that continued for seventeen years until Sexton's suicide in 1974, provided a keenly interested audience with, in Ezra Pound's definition of art, news that stayed news. They were poets, each said, whose business was words; yet they thought differently about them. Sexton synecdochically called her work "language." Kumin's work discloses a conviction that words are only part of the equipment of human beings, whose presence in nature is not remarkable and whose ways of communicating are not superior.

Life on the Farm

A poem in *Halfway* addressed to Henry David Thoreau, "My Quotable Friend," shows the speaker's disappointment with Thoreau for staying in his rowboat on Walden, "as if that pond were meant for oars/and plumb-line measurements." She eschews Thoreau's desire to observe and measure, to separate himself from the natural world of the pond. She would prefer he swamp the boat to drift and lose himself "until the lake soaked you in two and only/your head was real or dry." Thoreau chooses to measure; Kumin to commingle. The better use of mind is to describe the body's reunion with water.

In 1963, Kumin and her husband, Victor, bought a neglected two-hundred-plus-acre dairy farm in Warner, New Hampshire. In the previous year Rachel Carson had brought ecology to the attention of the general public with her book *Silent Spring*, which Kumin remembered twenty-six years later in a book review (titled "Farm") for the *New York Times Book Review* (24 September 1989): Carson "warned us . . . nature does not operate in isolation, and that pollution of ground water is total pollution." Kumin's desire for an expanded domestic environment where words are commodities could be considered ecological: "Ecology" comes from the Greek *oikos* (house) and *logos* (word). The Kumins moved their family and her increasingly successful "cottage industry" of writing from the suburbs to rural New Hampshire each summer, whereas Sylvia Plath moved from Boston to London, Adrienne Rich to New York, and Anne Sexton to a larger suburban house near Boston. These writers took refuge in urban centers; Kumin's removal was another kind of resistance to the sexism of the 1950s. "I . . . have settled into a hillside farm out of sight or sound of neighbors. All this chaos is of my own devising" (the essay "Two Foals," in *In Deep*, p. 53). She chose this site as her necessary home: "If I am

to write . . . words arranged in their natural work order in the conversational tone of voice used between consenting adults, I need the centrality of the natural world to draw on" ("A Sense of Place," in *In Deep*, p. 162).

Kumin's move to the farm on Joppa Road in the Mink Hills signaled a change in her books, which now began to document life in a particular place, where all creatures are esteemed and all work—physical and intellectual—is done for the renewal of life. *The Privilege* (1965), her second book of poems, took its title from something Joseph Conrad wrote in a letter to his aunt: "One must drag the ball and chain of one's selfhood to the end. It is the price one pays for the devilish and divine privilege of thought." The first mention of the farm appears in "Joppa Diary," a group of dated poems about the rigors and seasonal resurrections of country life, which follows the poem "Despair," the last poem in a series of conceits. Despair "is a mildewed tent" that the camper must kneel to enter "blind end first." After introducing a woolen blanket roll, a brown moth, a weasel, and toadstools, the poet asks, "what makes you think that rattling your ribs here will/save you?" The poem ends, "Yank up the pegs and come back! Come back in the house." The camper, come from the city or suburbia for a holiday out of doors, brings along despair. Better the disappointments of a life in the house. Kumin in "Joppa Diary" finds an alternative life in nature, where the human self is no longer the thinking center of the world and the house of the body takes up a wider residence.

In a blurb that appeared on the back cover of *The Privilege*, Babette Deutsch echoes Montaigne's comment on his own essays: "Elsewhere you can commend or condemn a work independently of its author; but not here: touch one and you touch the other." Deutsch writes "Who touches this book touches a woman, as candid as she is compassionate, and deeply aware of what her forebears gave her to pass on to her children. . . . There is a person behind the poems." The tone of this remark suggests that it is touch that invites intimacy rather than text, and it lists the requirements for female inscription: candor, compassion, motherhood and the twin burden of memory and tradition.

Through Dooms of Love, her first novel, about her father, was published in 1965, followed by a second, *The Passions of Uxport,* called *The Keeper of His Beasts* in paperback (1968). In 1966, Kumin won a National Endowment for the Arts grant; in 1968 she won the Poetry Society of America's William Marion Reedy Award and was invited to teach at the Bread Loaf Writers' Conference in Vermont, which she continued to do for seven seasons. There she was called "the witch of fungi" for her mushroom hunts, her acerbic wit, and the power of her writing and her presence. *The Nightmare Factory* (1970), poems, was followed by a novel about the depredations of life in the inner city, *The Abduction* (1971). *Up Country: Poems of New England* (1972) begins with poems of retreat from urban society into country solitude, poems Kumin said, in an interview conducted on 6 January 1977 (in *To Make a Prairie*), were "written in a male persona" because "when I was writing them I did not think that anyone could take a female hermit seriously, so I invented the hermit who, of course, is me" (p. 40). In 1972 she won *Poetry* magazine's Eunice Tietjens Memorial Prize; in 1973 she was awarded the Pulitzer Prize for poetry for *Up Country* and in 1995 she was elected a member of the Board of Chancellors of the Academy of American Poets.

Present in this early work are signs of a familiar attachment to creatures as relief. Consider "Quarry, Pigeon Cove" from *The Privilege,* where, in a mined-out stone pit filled with water, "The dead city waited,/hung upside down in the quarry." In this landscape, "Badlands the color of doeskin/lay open like ancient Egypt." The poet dives into this water—whose images yoke the destruction of nature with culture—and into danger: "I might have swum down looking/soundlessly into nothing,/down stairways and alleys of nothing/until the city took notice/and made me its citizen." But she is saved by a vision of life:

A dog was swimming and splashing.
Air eggs nested in his fur.
The hairless parts of him bobbled like toys
and the silk of his tail blew past like
      milkweed
The licorice pads of his paws
sucked in and out,
making the shapes of kisses.

The image draws the swimmer back to the surface: "Coming up, my own face seemed beautiful./The sun broke on my back." The poem recalls Muriel Rukeyser's "Sand Quarry with Moving Figures," published in 1935, and anticipates Adrienne Rich's "Diving into the Wreck," published in 1973, almost a decade after "Quarry, Pigeon Cove," which appeared in 1965.

The Designated Heir (1974) shows Kumin establishing a careful distinction between the healing properties of nature and our anthropomorphic appropriation. The novel's protagonist, Robin, becomes a vegetarian after adopting a vealer, a baby calf raised for the table, whom she refuses to see sent to the knacker. Warned off by a farmer, she nonetheless raises the calf as a pet. Grown into a bull, the animal gores and kills the farmer's puppy—and is sent to slaughter. This novel about family, town and country, and continuance, dedicated to Kumin's daughter Jane, was published the year of Anne Sexton's suicide. Now Kumin begins the labor of mourning Sexton's daily absence in poems of great range and power. "Splitting Wood at Six Above," one of Kumin's first elegies to Sexton, begins, "I open a tree./In the stupefying cold/—ice on bare flesh a scald—." "How It Goes On," another in a series of poems for Sexton (it was gathered in *The Retrieval System* [1978]), was "initiated by a fact: I had a pair of lambs (Southdown ewes, named Gertrude Stein and Alice B. Toklas)," she explains in *To Make a Prairie* (p. 101). One of the lambs strangled by accident; the survivor was traded for hardwood for the stove. The ewes' namesakes, those two devoted partners, suggest the magnitude of Kumin's loss. But the lamb's death is not privileged in the poem; the animal that goes to be slaughtered in trade for "two cords of stove-length oak" is unnamed. The loss is catastrophic but must be transmuted for the sake of survival. The most recent of the series, "On Being Asked to Write a Poem in Memory of Anne Sexton," collected in *Nurture* (1989), conflates and transforms Sexton and her reputation into an elk burdened by antlers "destined to ossify," destined to be sloughed off.

> What a heavy candelabrum to be borne
> forth, each year more elaborately turned:
>
> the special issues, the prizes in her name.
> Above the mantel the late elk's antlers
>   gleam.

The poem conjures up the image of Cernunnos—the elk-antlered figure out of Celtic and other mythologies. This guardian of wild creatures presides over sacrifice to insure continuance; his companion gives birth to humans and other animals and plants, and protects the dwelling places of the dead. Myth begins to resonate in Kumin's poetry.

What began as the hard labor of exorcism, ghosts laid out and examined, informs the poems in *House, Bridge, Fountain, Gate* (1975). "History Lesson" shows her emphatic connection to her stepson, Steven Burgess, "a bi-racial product of the Korean War who lived with us from age 14 thru high school, followed by 2 years at the U of Chicago," Kumin wrote in a 7 November 1994 letter to Hilda Raz (unpublished).

> That a man may be free of his ghosts
> he must return to them like a garden
> He must put his hands in the sweet rot
> uprooting the turnips, washing them
> tying them into bundles
> and shouldering the whole load to market.

Images of the natural world evoke, then fix, then bleed off particular loss—of the familial, tribal, and gendered—in order to address the subject of continuance. The price of human thought—an egocentric world—invoked in the epigraph to *The Privilege* is refunded: "Christ on the lake was not thinking/where the next heel-toe went./ God did him a dangerous favor/whereas Peter, the thinker, sank" ("To Swim, to Believe"). A sense of the self both as mortal, sentient, and individual and as generic and anonymous (an important part of the life force) is essential for survival. The book's title comes from the German poet Rilke, in whose work language is given the moral charge to witness: Kumin's poems in *House, Bridge, Fountain, Gate* name and recall departed parents, uncles and aunts, cousins, grandparents, lovers, children, and their stories. Her own stories are of traveling to teaching and speaking engagements, of "changing houses like sneakers and socks." After winning the Pulitzer Prize, Kumin began to teach at an accelerated pace, to convey her particular gloss on traditional texts and introduce new ones. Readings and teaching trips to Washington University, Brandeis, Columbia, and Princeton, among others, helped support the animals and the growing expenses of the farm's renovation. In the Amanda poems, written about her horse and collected in *House, Bridge, Fountain, Gate*, we see the bud of the nature essays and poems that lessen the distinctions between human and animal, woman and nature.

By 1975, she had "let go of the large children." Jane, the eldest, graduated from Radcliffe in 1970, Judith in 1971; Daniel followed, from Bennington. In 1976, in what may have begun for Kumin as a "pervading desire to be totally self-sufficient," to "be really outside the mainstream" she and her husband made a permanent move to the farm. She had "equine compensations" for the empty nest, along with the pleasures of raising Scotch Highland heifers, sheep, and goats: "As if in search of sainthood, [they] anointed themselves daily hauling water, mucking stalls, paring hoof abscesses till they bled, poulticing sore ligaments, and keeping up a soothing banter with their herd of home-raised [horses]" (the short story "Jack," collected in *Women, Animals, and Vegetables* [p. 186]). One hundred taps a year ran from their sugar bush, leading to this ecstatic description in "Journal—Later Winter-Spring 1978" in *To Make a Prairie*:

Putting in the spiles I lean on the brace and bit, having to use all my weight to keep the metal spiral angling upward into the tough tree. How astonishing, after the hole is bored, that the sap glistens, quivers, begins to run freely. To think that I have never seen or done this before! I am as captivated as the city child finding out where milk comes from." (p. 182)

The poems in *The Retrieval System* (1978) link explicitly the eulogizing power of language with the evocative power of the daily round. Life on the farm, with its repetitive and labor-intensive service to animal and land, invites Kumin's "androgynous, pagan muse." In these poems, the organizing principle is resemblance. As Ostriker writes, "For Kumin there is no hierarchy: humans, animals, and plants uncannily resemble each other, are often metaphorically interchangeable, enjoy the same energies, and suffer the same downfalls" (p. 116). At the time, this pattern of association and the resulting poems seemed final to the poet: "I just don't see where I can go after *The Retrieval System*," she said in a 1980 interview with Shelley Armitage. But she was learning a new culture and language of care—for horses. In the barn, where men traditionally have held sway, Kumin had taken up residence.

Blurring Boundaries

In *To Make a Prairie: Essays on Poets, Poetry, and Country Living* (1979) Kumin continues to express her growing concern about human damage to the environment. "Where there are questions of survival, the poet belongs on the battlements," she has said. She names as her progenitor Henry David Thoreau, the nineteenth-century nature writer and inveterate New England iconoclast. Kumin may well have chosen Thoreau in part because her choices were limited. Female nature writers such as Susan Fenimore Cooper, Thoreau's contemporary and the first woman nature writer in America, have been neglected and their works often out of print. Cooper, whose journal of the seasons, *Rural Hours*, was published in 1850, four years

before *Walden*, grew up "when many northeastern, middle-class, Euro-American women were confined to the home and domesticity." Cooper's work, widely read during her lifetime, was unavailable to most readers until Syracuse University Press reprinted it in 1995; also long out of print was the work of her contemporaries Mary Treat, Olive Thorne Miller, and Florence Merriam Bailey. Their writings about home and garden became less popular as the public turned to stories of wilderness written by Edgar Rice Burroughs, Teddy Roosevelt, and Jack London. According to Vera Norwood, both men and women had written nature essays, but men's exploration of uncharted wilderness was judged heroic while women's accounts of home-based experience were ignored. Thoreau was praised for the aspects of his writing deemed heroic.

But Thoreau's delineated perspective and graceful prose also appeal to Kumin. As she explains in "The Unhandselled Globe" (in *In Deep*),

> All of us who write, however tangentially, about the human place in nature hold a legacy from Thoreau. His language of specificity, from its soaring allusions to mythology to its startling metaphors, goes beyond the clinical measurements of the laboratory biologist, with whom he shares a passion for accuracy. Thoreau makes us see ourselves as part of the picture, standing somewhere in the middle ground, looking in both directions, to the mountains, and into the moss at our feet." (p. 156)

Whereas Cooper avoids Latin taxonomies in order to make more readily available to interested readers the things named, Thoreau and Kumin love the Latin names. Kumin's language of specificity includes, most importantly, "heterosis" or hybrid vigor, a geneticist's term she applies particularly to the bloodline of her horse, who has been so badly abused it was unrestrainable: the animal's feisty nature, its refusal to surrender, replicated itself in its descendants. We also encounter "anthelmintic" (having deworming properties), "decurrent, adnexed, and adnate" (mushroom gills), "cryptobiosis" (suspended animation), "defalcated" (embezzling, more or less), and more colloquial terms such as "bummer lamb" (rejected by the ewe, so bottle-fed), "slickensides" (the slick sides of granite), and "snowball poppers" (winter pads for horses' hooves).

Thoreau's nonhierarchical respect for nature appeals to Kumin as well. "Shall I not rejoice also at the abundance of the weeds whose seeds are the granary of the birds?" asks Thoreau, who seems to take equal delight in the workings of the mind as in the workings of nature.

Culture (represented in *Walden* by the use of Latin and Greek) and nature are one to Thoreau, as Kumin notes in a passage she cut from the essay "Jicama Without Expectations": "His daily record is delightfully discursive, ranging from 'I put in a little Greek now and then, partly because it sounds so much like the ocean,' a good example of naturalizing culture, to noting that he found some broccoli growing in a Wellfleet garden [which] . . . is possibly the earliest reference to broccoli in North America."

But in the same essay Kumin points out Thoreau's gendered attitudes toward the wild forest and the civil garden: "Even Thoreau, who wanted to break with the past and start over as a sort of new Adam, an innocent in Paradise on the shores of Walden Pond, was susceptible to the blandishments of growing things. He narrowly escaped enslavement by hoe when he 'made the earth say beans instead of grass.' In *A Week on the Concord and Merrimack Rivers*, he pronounced gardening 'civil and social, but it wants [lacks] the vigor and freedom of the forest and the outlaw'" (p. 75, brackets in original). The new Adam prefers the vigorous, free, and uncivilized (male) forest to the seductive (female) domestic garden, a preference that is as judgmental and moralistic as it is sexist.

In general, however, Thoreau's nonhierarchical perspective, along with his ability to naturalize culture, has served (if not mirrored) Kumin's literary ambitions, one of which has been to blur and breach boundaries. The mixed genres of *To Make a Prairie*, for example, defy traditional arrangements: interviews and essays on poetry and nature mingle with journal entries and poems. A similar blurring appears in Kumin's use of certain phrases and sounds. For example, in an essay about her mare, Taboo, and Taboo's foal, Boomerang, she repeats *o* sounds familiar from her earlier work, but to new effect. In early poems, *o* rises as the sleep sounds of an infant and later as the single howl protest against chaos, against the boundless forces of dissolution. Most movingly, the *o* is apostrophe. "O to turn away," she says at the end of "Journal — Late Winter–Spring, 1978," an essay about the horses and one of her most eloquent, describing the moment when all the forces of burgeoning spring in human, animal, and vegetative life come to climax not in birth, as expected, but in an eleven-month, full-term, stillborn foal Kumin buries in hard soil "behind the old chicken coop." "I got down beside Boomerang and folded the long legs in, tucking them back into fetal position, and then we shoveled the earth back over it and finally packed the top with stones so that nothing would disturb the grave" (p. 192). At the time of burying, woman and foal enter the grave together. The maternal horse already has turned away. But human imperatives demand a recapitulation before boundaries between child and mother will stand again. What it taboo, forbidden, is inscribed as news of the body giving birth, and dying, and in an emphatic merging of species.

Boundaries between species are again blurred in her story "The Match" (in *Women, Animals, and Vegetables*), where the slogan of a radical environmentalist group called Animals All is "A rat is a cat is a dog is a pig is a boy." The embodiment of the slogan is a tapestry whose border is interlocking animals: "an oversized mouse . . . linked to a cat, in turn hanging on to a dog that seemed to be chasing a pig. At the front of the little parade, a child. The pattern repeated all the way around" (p. 262).

Another example of Kumin's empathic identification is in the short story "Beginning with Gussie" (collected in *Women, Animals, and Vegetables*) about attending the birth of a grandchild. A woman experiences simultaneously her daughter's labor and her own years before. Only when the new child crowns does she return to herself, in time to deliver him to his mother, her grown child. Kumin's poem "After Love," in *The Nightmare Factory*, recognizes the fluidity of selves: "Afterwards, the compromise./Bodies resume their boundaries." In her short story, Kumin extends that understanding to childbirth, where maternal empathy works its magic blur.

Genre boundaries and perspectives may mix and blur in Kumin's work, but they rarely lead to the collapse of an image, a narrative, a life. In the poems, rhyme and rhythm govern emotionally chaotic subjects; in her novels obsessive rhyming signals emotional breakdown, and too regular rhythm a heartbeat-like insistence on unavailable infant comforts. Kumin has marked Thoreau's careful observations of difference in the natural world. She maintains "a working distance" in her own work.

Writing about Kumin's relation to Thoreau, Joyce Carol Oates praises Kumin's acceptance of her individuality:

> Maxine Kumin's book [*Up Country*] acknowledges its debt to Thoreau, though in my opinion Kumin's poetry gives us a sharp-edged, unflinching and occasionally nightmarish subjectivity exasperatingly absent in Thoreau. The most valuable, because most powerful, statements of the transcendental experience are those rooted firmly in existence, however private or eccentric. We are ready to believe Miss Kumin's energetic praises of nature, her insistence upon her own place in it—"we teem, we overgrow . . . we are making a run for it"—because we have suffered along with her the contraction of the universe . . . her occasional despair, her speculations upon forms of mortality in an old burying ground.

Gender in Art and Nature

In 1981, Maxine Kumin was named consultant to the Library of Congress. She presented her lecture at the library on 5 May 1981. "Rather than bring it out as a separate pamphlet—the usual custom—the L[ibrary] of C[ongress] sequestered it in their quarterly bulletin," Kumin

wrote in a 7 November 1994 letter (unpublished) to Hilda Raz. The lecture appeared in the winter issue of *The Quarterly Journal of the Library of Congress.* "Stamping a Tiny Foot Against God: Some American Women Poets Writing Between the Two Wars" discusses the poetry of seven women poets whose work had attracted a broad audience but little serious critical attention: Amy Lowell, Hilda Doolittle (H.D.), Sara Teasdale, Edna St. Vincent Millay, Marianne Moore, Muriel Rukeyser, and Louise Bogan. Kumin took her title from the poet Theodore Roethke's description of the "aesthetic and moral shortcomings" of women poets that appears in his review of his friend and once lover Louise Bogan's work. His list includes "a concern with the mere surfaces of life . . . hiding from the real agonies of the spirit . . . running between the boudoir and the altar; caterwauling; writing the same poem about fifty times." Kumin's evaluation of the women poets exposes Roethke's supercilious sexism. She praises Millay's use of images from nature to comment on public events, and points out that Muriel Rukeyser's *Wake Island* (1942), by "linking the struggle in Spain with the war in the Pacific[,] connects all antifascist struggles into a whole." She also introduces evidence of difference to challenge the idea that women writers are essentially bonded by mutuality, sisterhood, and nurturance. Kumin reveals the powerful Louise Bogan's enmity for Rukeyser to suggest one reason for Bogan's public neglect during her most productive years, and she notes the difference in voice between lifelong friends Marianne Moore and H.D., who were classmates at Bryn Mawr. At the same time Kumin uses her own visibility to discuss both the critical neglect and misreading and the work of some uncanonized women poets. Kumin's lecture includes literary gossip—she describes how the influential critic and poet Ezra Pound put "an old-fashioned tin washtub on his head like a helmet" during one of Amy Lowell's dinner parties, a disrespectful gesture Horace Gregory reports as one indication of Pound's "coolness" toward the lesbian poet. Acknowledging the difficulties inherent in a single category for the range of difference in their work, Kumin nevertheless constitutes women's poetry as worthy of sustained inquiry.

Our Ground Time Here Will Be Brief: New and Selected Poems was published in 1982. In the diction of the recycling citizen, Kumin had written in *To Make a Prairie* that art should "create something natural out of all the used-up sticks and bureaus of our lives, the detritus of our lives" (p. 25). Recycler and artist meet in the poem "Retrospect in the Kitchen," an elegy for her brother:

> After the funeral I pick
> forty pounds of plums from your tree
>   . . .
> and carry them by DC 10
> three thousand miles to my kitchen
>
> and stand at midnight—nine o'clock
> your time—on the fourth day of your
>   death
> putting some raveled things
> unsaid between us into the boiling pot
> of cloves, cinnamon, sugar.

In 1985, Kumin won an Academy of American Poets fellowship and published *The Long Approach* (poems). *In Deep: Country Essays* followed in 1987. This book closes with the essay "A Sense of Place," an *ars poetica* with a central tenet: "Without religious faith and without any sense of primal certitude that faith brings, I must take my only comfort from the natural order of things" (p. 162). Kumin echoed and revised Thomas Hobbes, the seventeenth-century British political philosopher, when she said in an interview with Martha George Meek published in *To Make a Prairie*, "I don't put terribly much store by human nature. . . . I think we're infinitely depraved, and brutish, and nasty" (p. 20). Hobbes's much-quoted observation on nature places humanity without government in the center of the natural morass: "No arts; no letters; no society; and which is worst of all, continual fear and danger of violent death; and the life of man, solitary, poor, nasty, brutish, and short." Human beings as part of nature must contract to form a society, Hobbes thought, for the sake of survival. Kumin invokes not social contracts but "the saving nature" of family and friends, the tribe. In time, her sense of the tribe comes to include not only creatures of her species and in her care, but nature itself. And her vision increasingly incorporates myths from other cultures to account for what is apparently not patterned in nature, the unpredictable and chaotic. *In Deep* gathers vision in service to traditional ways of working the land. Her longtime commitment to a "tribe" of family, poets, and a few friends loosens to admit others—horse people and farmers, and a family of species. What she has called "the tribal notion of succession" modulates to admit the place where succession happens. Sentience is redefined, as is nurture. In later collections such as *Looking for Luck* (poems, 1992) and *Women, Animals, and Vegetables* (essays and stories, 1994), she considers nonhuman systems of communication to better understand nonverbal behavior between genders, generations, and nationalities. "Sleeping with Animals," in *Nurture* (1989), explicates the effort:

> Nightly I choose to keep this covenant
> with a wheezing broodmare who, ten days
>   past due,
> grunts in her sleep in the vocables
> of the vastly pregnant. She lies down
> on sawdust of white pine, its turp smell
>   blending
> with the rich scent of ammonia and
>   manure.
> I in my mummy bag just outside her stall
> observe the silence . . .

The poem continues,

> What we say to each other in the cold black
> of April, conveyed in a wordless yet perfect
> language of touch and tremor, connects
> us most surely to the wet cave we all
> once burst from gasping, naked or furred,
> into our separate species.

While the same sensibility informs Kumin's poems and essays, the essays show her as a moralist; her outrage can be palpable and contagious. What she calls "the extra long taproot of the transplant" holds her fast to the farm, fourteen acres of which became pasture after annual applications of manure and ashes from wood stoves, as well as "lime annually, and as little commercial fertilizer as possible (every few years)." "Acid rain is not helping the situation," Kumin remarked to Raz. In "Menial Labor and the Muse" (*Women, Animals, and Vegetables*), we learn they "probably won't be setting any taps this March. Acid rain and the depredations of the pear thrip that followed have so weakened the trees that they need a rest period" (p. 18). In "A Sense of Place" she speaks of "the old Hebraic Puritan inside me, equating tranquillity with hard physical labor" (*In Deep*, p. 170). Her sense that freedom exists only within rigorous discipline is equally visible in her poems, where the most deeply personal narratives are expressed within a strict formal prosody: "rigors of form" are "a forcing agent" (*To Make a Prairie*, p. 85). Although she expresses reservations about "any kind of didacticism" in poetry, which is "too fragile a vessel to bear the weight of polemic," she notes that some of her poems are angry. But it is in the nature essay that she takes up battle. Speaking in "Jicama Without Expectations" of the treatment of animals raised for slaughter, she asks, "Does it matter how they live, since they are all going to die to feed us? I think it matters mightily . . . because how we treat the animals in our keeping defines us as human beings" (*Women, Animals, and Vegetables*, p. 106).

Kumin has said that in poetry everything is metaphor. Yet as an essayist she refuses to claim the poet's trick of seeing the natural world with a "master eye," that is, in a metaphorical sense. In an interview with Virginia Elson and Beverlee Hughes collected in *To Make a Prairie*, she said, "It's true that minutiae fascinate me [but] . . . I don't think I see objects in a multiple way at all." She wants to know everything particular, even "the Latin names of things after I find out what they properly are" (p. 5). As an amateur naturalist ("amateur" is from the Latin *amator*, lover), she is true to the task of recording information,

Maxine Kumin

true to the task of naming and particularizing. Her large collection of reference texts attests to her profession: "Since, as a writer, my business is words, I tend to put my faith in the printed page. . . . Much of what I have learned about the natural world came to me from handbooks" (the essay "Children of Darkness," in *Women, Animals, and Vegetables*, p. 76). These texts also provide a continuity of women's perceptions of nature. She admires Nina Marshall's 1904 study of mushrooms, for example: "published as Volume 10 of a very ambitious Nature Library, this text is rich in hand-colored or -tinted photographic illustrations . . . and represents what must have been an enormous undertaking at that time" (p. 83). At the turn of the century, women's nature writing had been eclipsed by a public taste for heroic undertakings in the conquest of wilderness as noted earlier, but at the same time, women with artistic ability were being employed as scientific illustrators by the government. Their precise and often beautiful drawings brought knowledge about the natural world to the public. The artful reproductions of minute particulars neither roused the competitive anxiety of the male-dominated art world nor raised suspicions concerning the painters' modesty and their role as keepers of garden and home. Kumin refers to these images and conveys her pleasure in the knowledge they bring. This generous urgency to extend knowledge informs the essays. Whereas the poems invite empathic deciphering, the essays offer information and suggest action. Whereas the formal poems cinch up at the end, the essays sprawl, held together by the urgencies of observation and Kumin's particular vision.

A superb collection of poems, *Nurture*, was published in 1989. Given Kumin's well-established interest in nature, its title begs for a weighing of the old dualities, nature and nurture: which is the more important influence on human beings? The motive for "Nurture" in the book's title poem, according to Constance Merritt, "seems less a compulsion to exercise an ethic of care than a deep yearning for the embrace of all things wild. The [feral] child imagined in the last moments of the poem comes from and brings access to a pre-linguistic, pre-social realm." "Nurture" comes from the Latin word to nurse. Language is the milk, the mode of exchange—not English or even necessarily human, but a language reciprocal and constructed. The poem ends,

> Think of the language we two, same and
>   not-same,
> might have constructed from sign,
> scratch, grimace, grunt, vowel:
>
> Laughter our first noun, and our long verb,
>   howl.

Kumin tends to be dismissive of dualities and other categorical impositions on the world. Another old duality, nature and culture, however, is important to ecofeminism, a late-twentieth-century international discourse that unites ecology with feminism. Any discussion of women writing about nature must take this development into account. According to Karen J. Warren, the term "ecological feminism" appeared first in 1974 in the work of Françoise d'Eaubonne, who showed the theoretical and practical connections between "the oppression of women and the domination of nature, . . . conceptual frameworks and practices which sanction the subordination of both women and nature . . . by feminizing nature and then assuming that both women and nature are inferior to men and men's culture" ("Toward an Ecofeminist Ethic," *Studies in the Humanities* 15 [December 1988]: 140–156). The American poet Susan Griffin's mixed-genre *Women and Nature: The Roaring Inside Her* (1979) found in Western thought a distinction between teeming nature, of which woman is a part, and a taming masculine culture. For example, Edward Abbey in 1968 wrote of Arches National Park, "I want to know it all, possess it all, embrace the entire scene intimately, deeply, totally, as a man desires a beautiful woman." James Galvin's much praised and more recent *The Meadow* (1993) continues to sexualize landscape from a familiar male perspective: "all summer long flotillas of sheepish clouds sailed in and tried to look like rain. They turned dark and sexual. They let down their hair, like brushstrokes on the air, like feathers of water, like the principle [*Virga*] it was named for, sublime indifference its gesture, its lovely signature over us." Some contemporary ecofeminists have turned to quantum physics in order to argue against active/passive, male/female, culture/nature dualities. They see "a complicated web of relations between the various parts of a unified whole" and point to "the shifting boundaries between matter and energy to argue with any sort of duality, particularly the assertion that nature is merely the passive subject of objective scrutiny" (Fritjof Capra, *The Tao of Physics*, quoted in Norwood, p. 269). Ariel Salleh, an Australian ecofeminist writer and activist, writes in "Second Thoughts on Rethinking Ecofeminist Politics: A Dialectical Critique" (in *Isle: Interdisciplinary Studies in Literature and Environment*, 1 [fall 1993]: pp. 93–106) that ecofeminism "is concerned about the oppression of all life forms . . . [and posits] that the same patriarchal attitudes which degrade nature are responsible for the exploitation and abuse of women." But, she notes, "a *real* political shift means letting go of the culture versus nature polarity all together." The changing issues of ecofeminism are apparent in Kumin's work. In "Estivating — 1973," she repeats that nature is neither moral nor immoral — "Nature pays me no attention, but announces the autonomy of everything. Here nothing is good or bad, but *is*, in spite of" (*To Make a Prairie*, p. 162).

Whereas Euro-American women in nature are rarely depicted as working — the gardens in which they rest seem to flower because of the work of others — Kumin's work on the farm is never hidden. Unlike the static Edna St. Vincent Millay, framed by a blooming magnolia, of Arnold Genthe's familiar photograph, which appears in the publication of Kumin's Library of Congress address, Kumin has never allowed herself to be a passive recipient of scrutiny. She describes herself often in athletic terms. As a child, she found escape from the restrictions of family and gender in long-distance competitive swimming; as an adult, she is an expert and competitive long-distance rider, at home in the breeding barn or working the two- and three-year-old horses on the longe line. The work of the body is a central subject of her essays. She and her husband have carved fourteen hard-won acres of pasture for the horses from granite outcroppings. They regularly take hundreds of pounds of produce from the garden and split twelve cords of wood for the winter stoves in their effort to make order from "rampant growth." She assigns value to diligence and productivity, not gendered roles. While Kumin's life honors androgynous values of performance and training, in her writing, the farm seems an extension of a sensual subjectivity, part of what she calls "the moi."

Plowed fields, to Kumin, "release a sweet rancidness / warm as sperm" ("Relearning the Language of April"). In "Peeling Fence Posts" she writes, "hard as it is, / ash splits its skin clean, / . . . / comes away like a glove. / I finger the torso under, / pale, wet alive." Or she dis-

covers "In the Pea Patch" plants "saying dance with me, / saying do me, dangle their intricate / nuggety scrota." In the final stanza of this poem, she sees "under the polishing thumb / in the interior / sweet for the taking, nine little fetuses / nod their cloned heads." In the green world of the vegetable garden every sexuality bends to her trope. In the poem "Surprises," collected in *Nurture*, the aging poet/farmer finds red peppers in her garden for the first time in fifteen years, which

> hang
> in clustered pairs like newly hatched sex
> organs
>
> Doubtless this means I am approaching
> the victory of poetry over death
> where art wins, chaos retreats, and beauty
> . . .
> rises again, shiny with roses, no thorns.
> No earwigs, cutworms, leaf miners either.

The pastoral tradition's idealization of nature is linked here with sexual generation in a wry reunion of culture and nature.

Nurture continues Kumin's valorization of both empathic merging and the careful preservation of a respectful "working distance." The poem "Distance" compares the poet as she drives a powerful tractor with two bear cubs and their mother the poet had seen on her birthday the previous week. She notes that old age is androgynous, as is the skill necessary to drive the heavy mower, itself androgynous in detail — "with two forward speeds and a wheel clutch, nippled hand grips, / a lever to engage the cutting blade." She salutes in her mind (both hands are occupied with driving) the wild mother and cubs, a vision of sexual continuance she no longer identifies as her own, with the poet's trick of rhyming:

> Androgyny. Another birthday. And all the
> while
> the muted roar of satisfactory machinery.
> May we flourish and keep our working
> distance.

Language of Transformation

But even as she notes their differences, she enacts an important similarity: she is fostering the land as the female bear is fostering her cubs.

In *Looking for Luck* (1992), poems about travel, Kumin seems to emphasize distance in the form of hard boundaries and insoluble differences: between "paid-up overfed" Americans and "People who/cannot come in from place of origin/and steadfastly refuse to go back to" (Fat Pets On"); between herself and her careless and impoverished neighbors, the Schutzes; between Japanese immigrants and Southern Californians; in the local jail, between representatives of Alaska's native peoples and their colonizers; between herself and the barn cats, whom she ironically thanks for "doing God's work—fledglings, field mice, shrews/moles, baby rabbits—else why would He/have made so many? I bury what I deplore"; even between herself and Anne Sexton, her "suicided long-term friend .../All these years I've fought somehow to bless/her drinking in of the killer car exhaust/but a coal of anger sat and winked its live/orange eye undimmed in my chest/while the world buzzed gossiping in the hive" ("The Green Well"). This book is filled with anger, contained though it is within the poems' tight form. How to reconcile these compelling differences with a sense of common identity? The artist's answer here is an athletic leap into faith by remaking Kiowa legend, so that blurring between species is made real and eternal—at least in the text. Kumin also remakes the Tlingit legend of encounter between bear and woman. In the legend, the woman is counseled to undress, since a male bear feels shame before a naked woman and will run away. In "The Rendezvous," the epilogue of *Looking for Luck*, the woman undresses. The bear takes out its teeth, shucks its skin and drops it for a pallet.

> He smells of honey
> and garlic. I am wet
> with human fear. How

> can he run away, unfurred?
> How can I, without my clothes?

> How we prepare a new legend.

The legend Kumin uses in "The Rendezvous" and others about bears—the Navaho story for example, where Bear Woman transforms herself from woman into bear by thrusting her weaving spindles, which recall the bewitching of Sleeping Beauty, into her gums for teeth—reveal the bear as one of the great symbols of transformation. Channeling potentially destructive power into less malevolent forms, Kumin is shaping myth to her liking.

In the poem "The Envelope," collected in *The Retrieval System*, she writes, "I carry the ghost of my mother under my navel . . . /a miracle/folded in lotus position." As she told Diana Hume George in 1985, "A transformation has taken place in the childbearing process. Now it is our mothers, as well as our children, whom we carry about with us, internalized lares and penates." Kumin's mother, who lived a long life and died easily in her sleep, reappears in dreams, poems, essays, and in the kitchen, helping with the jam making, performing essential chores. Kumin's own daughters live far from her New Hampshire farm: Jane is a lawyer in San Francisco; Judith, who attended the Fletcher School of Law and Diplomacy at Tufts, lives with her son Yann in Bonn, Germany, where she runs an agency of the United Nations for Eastern Europe. Daniel, whose name appears in *Readers' Guide to Periodical Literature* as the author of thirty-two articles published between April 1991 and July 1995, lives twenty minutes away from his parents with his wife, a lawyer, and their son Noah. The dedication to *Looking for Luck* is "For Yann and Noah, lucky cousins." Kumin's passionate sense of family/tribe is informed by intimacy and separation, as Ostriker writes, by "the need to possess and the need to release." Listening to her visiting daughter play the cello, "fierce now in the half light/at her harmonics," the poet tells another mother, a barn swallow, about her daughter's imminent move to Germany, where "she will raise her children/in a language that rusts in my mouth, / in a language that locks up my jaw." Her companion in another poem, "We Stood There Singing," in *Nurture*, is a Swiss stranger who takes in the touring family of mother, daughter, and grandson, and sings and rocks the cranky child: "We stood there singing. / I remember / that moment of civility among women."

Kumin added "women" to Thoreau's catalog —"the life of the earth is expressed in the animal or vegetable"—for the title of *Women, Animals, and Vegetables*. In these essays, Kumin is still mucking out the stalls, tapping the sugar bush, planting and sowing and preserving the earth's plenty. Now when she travels, her saddle goes, too. Riding in different landscapes she sounds a less distanced, more crotchety voice. Her connection with animal presence appears in complaints about absentee farm owners; Kumin believes that the keepers of animals should be licensed as drivers are. Time now has a full measure: the last of the dalmatians, puppy Gus who appeared as one of a lively pair in the early essays, becomes in *Women, Animals, and Vegetables* an arthritic old denizen unable to climb the stairs. A new puppy, Josh, surrenders his hard-won place at the foot of the bed to sleep in company with the old geezer by the stove. These creature stories, as much exempla of her later life as *Der Struwelpeter* was of her youth, evoke not nostalgia but an appropriate introspection.

Kumin's vegetable garden is the locus of one of her best essays, "Jicama Without Expectation." It leans on the cultural irony of using the *New York Times*, one of the world's most admired newspapers, for mulch. If civilization poisons, then news of civilization not only does not stay news but can best be used to keep the weeds at bay. In the late twentieth century, Maxine Kumin mixes the garden with the farm and extends domestic space for the making of art. Her pleasure is not identified so much with fecundity as with the usefulness and beauty of provender. She views landscape with the farmer's eye, preferring, as she says, pasture to forest. Kumin laments that "there is not one full-time farmer left in my community." And

indeed, her own domestic economy depends on money earned from what she calls "po-biz" — teaching, readings, writer-in-residence semesters in academia, the royalties and payments for published work, and the prizes (which pay for the horse business). Kumin affirms, however, that her farm work and her writing are both one business, a "very expensive one." In the spring of 1994, she was looking for "the right stallion for Boomer"; she wants to have another foal coming.

In Kumin's work the sounds of life carry in echoing vowels and slant rhymes, the rhythms—the *feel*—of the English language on the tongue. With an accretion of living detail, she works to inscribe the contract human beings make with death; and she connects life with text. "I think there wouldn't be any art whatsoever if we were immortal," she has written.

In her essay "Enough Jam for a Lifetime," in *Women, Animals, and Vegetables*, Kumin's subject may be blackberry jam, but this passage points also to her craft: "There is no quality control in my method. Every batch is a kind of revisionism. It makes its own laws. But the result is pure, deeply colored, uncomplicated, and unadulterated blackberry jam, veritably seedless, suitable for every occasion" (p. 66).

In her catalog of women, animals, and vegetables, where "human" takes up but one entry, language and memory are used in service to all. Few writers have taken up residency in the world better than Kumin, recording similarities and celebrating differences in the rich sensory imagery of flesh. And who but Maxine Kumin can conjure "blue and dainty, the souls. / They are thin as an eyelash. / They flap once, going up"— and then, in another context, remind us of the exact weight of each one.

Selected Bibliography

WORKS OF MAXINE KUMIN

POETRY

Halfway (New York: Holt, Rinehart and Winston, 1961); *The Privilege* (New York: Harper & Row,

1965); *The Nightmare Factory* (New York: Harper & Row, 1970); *Up Country: Poems of New England* (New York: Harper & Row, 1972); *House, Bridge, Fountain, Gate* (New York: Viking, 1975); *The Retrieval System* (New York: Viking, 1978); *Our Ground Time Here Will Be Brief: New and Selected Poems* (New York: Viking, 1982); *The Long Approach* (New York: Viking, 1985); *Nurture* (New York: Viking, 1989); *Looking for Luck* (New York and London: Norton, 1992).

COLLECTIONS

To Make a Prairie: Essays on Poets, Poetry, and Country Living (Ann Arbor: Univ. of Michigan Press, 1979); *In Deep: Country Essays* (New York: Viking, 1987); *Women, Animals, and Vegetables: Essays and Stories* (New York: Norton, 1994).

SELECTED UNCOLLECTED ESSAYS

"The Place of Poetry: A Symposium," in *The Georgia Review* 35 (winter 1981); "How It Was," foreword to the Complete Poems of Anne Sexton (Boston: Houghton Mifflin, 1981); "Stamping a Tiny Foot Against God," in *The Quarterly Journal of the Library of Congress* 39 (winter 1982); "Custom, Birth, Food, Nature: A Perspective on Some Women Poets," in *Georgia Review* 39 (spring 1985); Introduction to *Rain*, by William Carpenter, ed. by Maxine Kumin (Boston: Northeastern Univ. Press, 1985); "John Ciardi and the 'Witch of Fungi,'" in *John Ciardi: Measure of the Man*, ed. by Vince Clemente (Fayetteville: Univ. of Arkansas Press, 1987); "On 'North Winter,'" in *In the Act: Essays on the Poetry of Hayden Carruth* (Geneva, N.Y.: H. and W. Smith Colleges Press, 1990); Foreword to *Marianne Moore: The Art of a Modernist*, ed. by Joseph Parisi (Ann Arbor, Mich.: UMI Research Press, 1990); "The Care-Givers," in *The Writer on Her Work*, vol. 2, ed. by Janet Sternburg (New York: Norton, 1991); "Who and Where We Are," in *Miller Williams and the Poetry of the Particular*, ed. by Michael Burns (Columbia: Univ. of Missouri Press, 1991); "Breaking the Mold," in *Where We Stand: Women Poets on Literary Tradition*, ed. by Sharon Bryan (New York: Norton, 1993).

NOVELS

Through Dooms of Love (New York: Harper & Row, 1965), repub. as *A Daughter and Her Loves* (London: Gollancz/Hamilton, 1965); *The Passions of Uxport* (New York: Harper & Row, 1968), also pub. as *The Keeper of His Beasts* (New York: Harper & Row, 1968); *The Abduction* (New York: Harper & Row, 1971); *The Designated Heir* (New York: Viking, 1974).

SHORT STORIES

Why Can't We Live Together Like Civilized Human Beings? (New York: Viking, 1982).

SELECTED CHILDREN'S BOOKS

Sebastian and the Dragon (Eau Claire, Wis.: E. M. Hale, 1960); *Follow the Fall* (New York: Putnam's, 1961); *A Winter Friend* (New York: Putnam's, 1961); *Spring Things* (New York: Putnam's, 1961); *Summer Story* (New York: Putnam's, 1961); *Mittens in May* (New York: Putnam's, 1962); *No One Writes a Letter to the Snail* (New York: Putnam's, 1962); *Eggs of Things*, with Anne Sexton (New York: Putnam's, 1963); *The Beach Before Breakfast* (New York: Putnam's, 1964); *More Eggs of Things*, with Anne Sexton (New York: Putnam's, 1964); *Speedy Digs Downside Up* (New York: Putnam's, 1964); *Paul Bunyan* (New York: Putnam's, 1966); *The Wonderful Babies of 1809 and Other Years* (New York: Putnam's, 1968); *When Grandmother Was Young* (New York: Putnam's, 1969); *When Mother Was Young* (New York: Putnam's, 1970); *Joey and the Birthday Present*, with Anne Sexton (New York: McGraw-Hill, 1971); *When Great-Grandmother Was Young* (New York: Putnam's, 1971); *The Wizard's Tears*, with Anne Sexton (New York: McGraw-Hill, 1975); *What Color Is Caesar?* (New York: McGraw-Hill, 1978); *Faraway Farm* (New York: Norton, 1967).

SELECTED INTERVIEWS

Elaine Showalter and Carol Smith, "A Nurturing Relationship: A Conversation with Anne Sexton and Maxine Kumin, April 14, 1974," in *Women's Studies* 4 (1976); Georgia Litwack, "A Conversation with Maxine Kumin, Poet," in *Harvard Magazine* (January/February 1977); Shelley Armitage, "An Interview with Maxine Kumin," in *Paintbrush* 7–8 (1980–1981); Diana Hume George, "Kumin on Kumin and Sexton: An Interview," in *Poesis: A Journal of Criticism* 6, no. 2 (1985); Jo-Ann Mapson, "An Interview with Maxine Kumin," in *High Plains Literary Review* 7 (fall 1992); Diana Hume George, "An Interview with Maxine Kumin," in *Associated Writing Programs Chronicle* (March/April 1993).

CRITICAL STUDIES

Philip Booth, "Maxine Kumin's Survival," in *American Poetry Review* (November/December 1978); Sybil P. Estess, "Past Halfway: *The Retrieval System* by Maxine Kumin," in *Iowa Review* 10, no. 4 (1979); Diana Hume George, " 'Keeping Our Working Distance': Maxine Kumin's Poetry of Loss and Survival," in *Aging and Gender in Literature: Studies in Creativ-*

ity, ed. by Anne M. Wyatt-Brown and Janice Rossen (Charlottesville: Univ. Press of Virginia, 1993); Karen Knowles, ed., *Celebrating the Land: Women's Nature Writings, 1850–1991* (Flagstaff, Ariz.: Northland Publishing, 1992); Vera Norwood, *Made from This Earth: American Women and Nature* (Chapel Hill: Univ. of North Carolina Press, 1993); Joyce Carol Oates, "One for Life, One for Death," in *New York Times* (19 November 1972), review of *Up Country* and Sylvia Plath's *Winter Trees*; Alicia Ostriker, *Stealing the Language: The Emergence of Women's Poetry in America* (Boston: Beacon Press, 1986).

ANNE LABASTILLE
(b. 1938)

KATE H. WINTER

ANNE LABASTILLE begins her fourth book, *Women and Wilderness* (1980), with Louise Bogan's poem "Women," its opening lines presenting as oppositional two concepts, women and wilderness, that LaBastille sought to reconcile in her life and work: "Women have no wilderness in them,/They are provident instead." LaBastille's life has been a constant struggle between the imperatives of the wilderness in her and the need to accommodate civilization and its attendant constraints.

Born on 20 November 1938 in New York City and raised in Montclair, New Jersey, LaBastille found herself at a young age pressing against the limits of suburban life, seeking a more essential experience of landscape. With no encouragement for her wilderness interests, she camped out in the yard and supported the S.P.C.A., the National Audubon Society, and the Wilderness Society. She reveled in the few green spaces left in the sprawl of New Jersey—backyards and golf courses—and immersed herself in the literature of adventure and wilderness as though anticipating the nickname her husband would later give her, "Daniel Boone." Her mother, Irma Goebel, was a writer and concert pianist; her father, Ferdinand Meyer LaBastille, was a professor of languages.

As a child of six or seven, LaBastille wrote poetry and little books, and although she later found that she excelled in English classes, she chose to pursue her interest in nature and attended college at the University of Miami in Coral Gables, Florida, intending to study marine biology in spite of her lack of experience in water skills. In her book *Beyond Black Bear Lake* (1987), she suggests that her love for the outdoors was based in a revolt against the constraints of middle-class suburban living and a repressive culture manifest in the protectiveness of her mother. In her search for the sources of her passion for wild things and places, she focuses on her male ancestors, a "bunch of rascals," including an "English-Yankee grandfather who made his fortune treasure-hunting in the Caribbean," an early governor of Massachusetts, and an "intrepid paternal French forebear who pioneered a plantation in the West Indies." "I like to think their blood courses more vigorously through my veins," LaBastille writes, "than that of the plump, homey Dutch and German grandmothers on the other side of the family" (p. 16). LaBastille claims a strong male-identified persona for herself, rejecting identification with the domestic and defying the feminist enterprise of women reclaiming connection with their foremothers and valorizing their lives and accomplishments.

Yet her own writing is essentially about domestic life as she conducted it in the wild. Her second book, *Woodswoman* (1976), details the building of a cabin in the Adirondack Mountains

499

of New York State, where LaBastille established a home for herself after her divorce; *Mama Poc* (1990) chronicles her valiant but doomed campaign to save the giant grebe or "poc" of Lake Atitlan, Guatemala, and her life in a rural Indian village; *Women and Wilderness* records the attempts of women who lived intimately with the wild to create domestic arrangements for themselves; and *Beyond Black Bear Lake* describes LaBastille's second wilderness home in a more remote and serene part of the mountains. All of these books tell of her lovers and friends, the deaths and disasters, and the triumphs and pleasures that make up her emotional as well as professional life. There is always an ironic tension between her desire for privacy and her impulse to share the intimate details of her experience. The criticism that her writing foregrounds the author and diminishes the importance of her subject, wildlife, issues from a discourse model that values the traditionally masculine strategies of dissection, analysis, and seeming objectivity. LaBastille's work in fact represents a feminist rhetoric that emerged in the women's movement of the 1970s. In that mode, the visceral, emotional, and relational are emphasized along with the "scientific."

After earning a teaching certificate in biology from the University of Miami, LaBastille entered Cornell University, majoring in conservation. She imagined life as a cowboy wrangler or a woodswoman, and her first job, at an Adirondack Mountain lodge, opened the wilderness world to her. Marriage to the owner of the inn led her deeper into the wilderness experience. With her husband's support, she completed a master's degree in wildlife management at Colorado State University, the only program that would allow her to do fieldwork. Summers were spent running the inn; winters the couple led wildlife tours in Florida, the Caribbean, Mexico, and Central America. It was during one such trip that LaBastille first encountered the flightless pied-billed giant grebe, a species that had not been widely studied, and this bird became the focus of her wildlife work for the next twenty-four years. In 1964, she wrote and illustrated her first book, a seventy-seven-page collection of folktales, natural history, and birding information, *Birds of the Mayas*, and thus began her career-long work to combine her naturalist's knowledge with her cultural and literary insights in order to make science accessible and interesting to nonscientists. The bird stories that make up much of this slim volume are renderings of oral tales told in Mayan. With the help of a guide who accompanied LaBastille on wildlife tours, she retold these tales in ways that preserve their social, moral, and ethical values while engaging birders in the fantastic web of Mayan bird life and native art, history, and myth. The second part of the book functions as a field guide, offering illustrations, a bibliography, and an English-Mayan glossary. The volume appeals to the specialist while engaging the lay reader with the universal elements of story. Over the next ten years, LaBastille wrote natural history into popular articles and stories for children, perhaps remembering the comfort and inspiration that such works were to her as a child.

The end of her seven-year marriage sent LaBastille in search of a safe place to live and recover from the pain of divorce. Knowing that the peace and comfort of the mountains was important to her well-being, and having no family to turn to, she searched until she found a piece of land she could afford, twenty-two acres on the edge of a body of water she called "Black Bear Lake" in her writings in order to protect its sanctity and her privacy. She was not reclaiming inherited land. The landscape had no connection to her family history; hers was a "found" home, which became part of her private history of the self; a self redefined and constructed outside the biological family. Shunning the chalets and camps that others had built on the land, she set up the cabin that came to be called "West of the Wind." With the help of two local carpenters and assorted friends, she had the cabin ready to occupy in a month's time.

Twenty-five years later her detractors would still be arguing about whether she could rightfully call herself a woodswoman, but the controversy arose more from her mystique — the cult of personality that the public and her publishers helped create around her — than from anything

LaBastille wrote or did. The image of the woman hermit became a cultural icon during the feminist revolution of the 1970s, and LaBastille was the unwitting embodiment of that icon. Quick to acknowledge the importance to her of her friendships and of her kinship with other professionals and Adirondackers, LaBastille challenged the nineteenth-century idea of the bachelor adventurer abandoning domesticity and personal relationships for the embrace of a feminine Nature. In her work, the land is generally ungendered, and her world is well-populated with men — game wardens, police officers, guides, adventurers, and other naturalists and scientists. Yet the main effort of her life and work has been to narrate a woman's wilderness experience, with its concern for housekeeping, cooking, caretaking, the health of the body, and the nourishment of the soul. Her story has done at least as much as feminist theorizing to bring women into the wilderness movement, by modeling how the wild can be a safe and sacred place to work out one's perspective and identity free of the limits and expectations of culture. Her quest combines the search for adventure and meaningful work and, almost incidentally, a partner. LaBastille's story conveys both the risks and the rewards of liberation from culturally defined feminine roles.

Woodswoman and *Assignment Wildlife*

In *Woodswoman* LaBastille artfully describes her first camping trip as a comical near disaster, in which she brought the wrong equipment and had little knowledge of the woods. That first experience, largely devoid of human contact or support, centered her attention on her fears of accidental injury and male predation that surface frequently in the remainder of her work. Preparing to hike the Northville–Lake Placid Trail, she asks a male police officer to both see her off and meet her. After adding a gun to her gear, he advises her to tell suspicious persons she encounters on the trail that her husband is nearby. Without commenting on the assumptions underlying this subterfuge, LaBastille begins her

trek. The diversions of the wild push her concerns away, but this continuing awareness of a lone woman's vulnerability to assault haunts her as it does her readers. Years later the writer concluded that in fact the wilderness is likely to be the place where a woman is safest from male violence, though persistent concerns about victimization are never far from her consciousness and recur often in the later books.

Several other of LaBastille's recurring motifs emerged first in *Woodswoman*. She typically begins a narrative with a descriptive passage that locates the reader in a landscape, mood, and moment. Her images are both accurate and suggestive, often domestic — that is, she uses words related to the realm of the kitchen, hearth, and closet to describe the world she experiences. Navigating the lake at freeze-up time, for example, she notes that "the propeller seems to be churning syrup" (p. 1). Christmas snow is "decorated with wedding cake frillery" (p. 124). Her cat "dashed around the cabin as if it was a mixing bowl and she was the electric beater" (p. 58); her dog's paws are described as being like spatulas. After noting that the lake water is brown as tea, she explains that it is colored by tannic acid from the tamaracks and cedars that line the shore. As though to make the wild more accessible and friendly to women, she describes it in terms familiar to them. Occasionally she resorts to the mercantile imagery of some nineteenth-century writers, finding "jade" and "amber" under water, but these images also have domestic implications.

LaBastille's images of wilderness also have religious connotations. Raised as a Congregationalist, participating in choir and attending Sunday school, LaBastille later became an agnostic, but her diction reveals a reverence for the sacred. She refers to the "magnificent baptism of spring sun on bare skin" (p. 160) and describes a September dusk as bringing a hush deeper than that in an old European cathedral, bathing her in "holy incandescence" (p. 239). The white blossoms of witch hobble are "as guiltless as any church flower" (p. 161), and the silence at the lake affects her "like a benediction" (p. 5). Her spirituality is not sky-centered and transcendent but grounded, literally earth-honoring. At the lake, she is gradually filled with a sense of ordered goodness, a persistent movement "toward balance, regularity, homeostasis" (p. 276), and the conviction that the universe operates harmoniously. For some readers, the mystical mingling of LaBastille's spirituality with her naturalist impulses obscures both her science and her call to arms on ecological issues. The oft-cited episode in which she describes herself hugging a beloved white pine tree and feeling its life force pour into her—a scene depicted on *Woodswoman* T-shirts—has somewhat undercut her credibility as a scientist/naturalist. Embracing the giant tree, she describes it as pouring its life-force into her. She cites Carlos Castaneda's *The Teachings of Don Juan* and Michael Serano's *Serpent of Serpico,* and refers to energy points in the body, Kerlian photography, and plant polygraphs—phenomena suggesting a pervasive force at work, which the author believes she can tap into through the trees. She resists the separation of emotion and reason, feeling and thought, self and other, finding instead holistic truth in the fusion of heart and brain in her work.

LaBastille moves along a continuum of engagement with the natural world, from scientific detachment to sensuous intimacy to internalization and unity. She makes unscientific imaginative leaps, trying to feel and see what it would be like to be a migrating Canada goose, for example, and in a time of crisis over a lover, trying to merge in her mind with a mating magnolia warbler who had only hormones and instincts to operate from instead of conflicting human concerns. This blending of science and mysticism is a constant in LaBastille's work, and a calculated choice about which she expresses some ambivalence. She is disturbed by the possibility that some of the public and certain members of the scientific community will not respect her work.

The Adirondacks offer her succor, solitude, and the security of a family where she is unconditionally loved and the wilderness within her is honored. At her cabin at sunset, she experiences the mountains as nurturing guardians: "I could

plainly 'feel' them, their '*Gestalt,*' their ancientness, solidarity, reliability. They were very comfortable mountains, deep-rooted, well-preserved. They were not given to sudden outbursts of lava flows, landslides, earthquakes, hurricanes, floods, droughts, or erosion. It was like living with a grandparent who could always be counted on" (p. 239). Within this wilderness family she claims almost a patriarchal ownership of the land and its inhabitants. Coming upon a family of beavers gnawing a young birch, she watches and records their responses to her presence. She concludes that in a few days, when they are finished eating the bark and tender branches, she will return to claim the rest for firewood because it is, after all, "my tree" (p. 31). In the larger context of her works, this proprietorship seems an essentially maternal, feminine response to nature that falls just short of the claim to sisterhood that ecofeminists make. Yet there are epiphanic moments of unity between herself and the wild and a consciousness that the health of both are interdependent.

Almost entirely without sentimentality and resisting the urge to draw moral conclusions from what she observes, LaBastille melds personal anecdote, local history, and natural science. Her works are as much about human nature as they are about nature. Human stories, sometimes melodramatic, always intensely personal, mingle with the recounting of seasonal events and animal habits: guiding lost hunters over the lake by torchlight, helping a neighbor whose husband has had a heart attack, dealing with her own injuries and emotional crises, and reveling in her adventures.

Her life, as well as her prose, demonstrates the competing impulses of the soul for communion and solitude. Having acquired a doctorate in wildlife ecology from Cornell University in 1969 and established herself as a woodswoman, ecological consultant, and freelance photojournalist, her work outside the mountains increased during the 1970s, bringing her public acclaim and honors but drawing her away from the refuge she had created there. Lured by the "mystique and prestige" (*Woodswoman,* p. 93) she became one of roughly 250 registered guides (and one of the first women) certified by the Department of Environmental Conservation to take people into the woods for recreation or rescue. In 1974 she was awarded the World Wildlife Fund Conservation Gold Medal and the next year named a juror for the John Paul Getty wildlife conservation award. The success of *Woodswoman* and her widespread publications drew the attention of the New York State Outdoor Education Association, and in 1977 she was named that organization's writer of the year. In 1976 she became a commissioner of the Adirondack Park Agency. In 1980 she received an honorary doctorate from Union College, and the start of that decade saw the sales of *Woodswoman* on the way to over 100,000 copies.

Assignment Wildlife (1980) is a companion volume to *Woodswoman*, focusing on LaBastille's professional life outside her mountain retreat, her various environmental and ecological missions and experiences. Here she begins her account of the sun and spectacle of Lake Atitlán in Guatemala, where she commits herself to documenting the plight of the giant grebe and saving it from extinction. In Guatemala she encounters profound challenges to her intellectual and spiritual background. In the alien culture of Panajachel, she meets a shaman who tests her Anglo-American experience of spirituality and expands her thinking about spirits and magic. The shaman, LaBastille writes,

> began to recite the Lord's Prayer, mixed up with Indian and Latin words. . . . Gradually a curious sensation of peace stole through my body. I also had the sense of a force in that room—something vibrant and harmonious. My scientific training was making me coolly observe, classify, analyze the entire ceremony; at the same time, my emotional being was thrilling to what was happening. . . . I slipped into a trancelike lethargy, barely moving. (p. 38)

She suspends judgment and surrenders to the experience, integrating head and heart, and acknowledges that the more she travels in "primitive" cultures, the more she learns about the occult and the extrasensory, things that her training in Western sciences does not explain. Ecology thus becomes for her a discipline that incorporates anthropology, ethnography, and archaeology. Dismayed to find that a college education and grounding in science are not the only or even the most appropriate tools for working in the world, she risks the disdain of her colleagues in the scientific community by insisting that witch doctors, shamans, extrasensory perception, superstition—an assortment of nonscientific phenomena—operate in the world and deserve investigation. Humbled by her experience, she has a new perspective on science's place in Western culture and becomes aware that indigenous peoples are as endangered as grebes and rainforests.

In this book, LaBastille's discussions of her fieldwork are strung together with intimate, personal stories about people: a boy who has fallen in love with the *gringa*; a widowed Guaymi Indian who miraculously finds a wife and child; a gravely injured workman whom the author accompanies out of the rainforest and over the Andes to aid; and others. In *Assignment Wildlife*, her conservation ethics are more clearly articulated and more urgent than in earlier works. Because she places human beings at the center of nature, naming them the "dominant force in the natural world," (p. xii) she can confidently claim, "Triage came as the most sobering thought of my entire conservation career" (p. 151). Echoing Rachel Carson's message of global housekeeping, she insists that humankind is dependent on the health of the ecosystem for physical and spiritual well-being; ultimately, the reason to save the earth's environment is to save humans.

In her own work to establish conservation programs, LaBastille sees herself as "playing God" (p. 141) by virtue of her education and powerful connections. Gradually she came to believe that only the privileged can afford to concern themselves with conservation, that it is an effort available exclusively to those who do not have to wrest a living from the environment. As a scientist and environmentalist, LaBastille expressed no qualms about a West Indian government's policy of moving native peoples off land they claim as squatters and resettling them in new homes, finding them jobs, and integrating them into a different lifestyle, effectively obliterating their traditional connectedness to the environment. While conducting a survey in the Dominican Republic, she found a solitary woman living next to the sea. Without self-consciousness, LaBastille speculates on how hard, tedious, and lonely her life must be, seemingly unaware that the woman has chosen a life similar to her own, a life of solitude, independence, and harmony with her surroundings. The author's concern with forms of exploitation does not extend to the sanctioned presence of prostitutes at oil exploration camps or to the women in the brothel of an Amazon port city—because she insists that prostitution affirms the erotic and therefore life—but implicitly she compares the trade in women's bodies with the outlaw trade in the skins of big cats and animal contraband, aligning man's oldest profession, dealing death, with woman's oldest profession.

As an early interloper in the masculine domain of science, LaBastille inevitably and of necessity adopted some of the values informing the discipline. Unlike later feminists and ecofeminists, she does not explicitly connect the rape of wilderness with other atrocities of patriarchy. Aware that she has been criticized as being an elitist, she stands by her belief in the centrality of humankind in nature. Although she insists on ecological awareness, she also seems to believe in the nature/culture dualism that some ecologists feel is at the heart of environmental destruction. Critics of her politics focus on her insistence on balancing the preservation of wilderness areas with the interests of economic sustenance and growth.

In *Assignment Wildlife*, LaBastille explores the choices she had made in her life. She recalls a professor's misogynist warning that if she pursued a career in science, she would end up a spinster. She confronts sexism in the professional realm and struggles with an evolving identity, searching for a balance between the wilderness woman and the educated, cultivated female. Her deep separation from her mother is mirrored in the conflict she sees inside of her between the socially constructed feminine and her own traditionally masculine qualities of analytical thinking, independence, self-reflexiveness, athleticism. Noting the absence in herself of the typical markers of femininity, she questions her attractiveness as a woman, wanting to claim an erotic female self, but she also demands to be taken seriously as a professional. She deliberately details her dress and hair as though insisting that the reader see her as a whole person; it is an attempt at obliterating the artificial boundary between the personal and the professional and challenging the boundary between masculinist science and feminist consciousness. In *Assignment Wildlife*, she acknowledges failure as well as success. After a brief shipboard romance, she assumes her lover would prefer the company of elegantly groomed, cosmopolitan women rather than that of a pigtailed ecologist with muddy boots, and she seems to regret some of the loss incurred in choosing to be a wilderness woman without challenging the cultural assumptions that set up such a choice.

Yet she never doubts the wilderness in herself, and her representation in *Assignment Wildlife* of the landscape and her work in it reflects her deepening identification. She depicts Amazonia as a woman who adapts to shifts in the environment with powerful survival mechanisms. This landscape is eroticized, celebrated as an autonomous female whose ecosystem has enormous powers of resilience and regeneration. As in her previous works, LaBastille uses images that draw on women's experience more than on men's: water is "clear as champagne" (p. 103); the deer tracks "embroider" (p. 109) the edges of a pool; orchids are as fancy as flowers worn to a prom; geese in "skeins" (p. 149) mount the sky; and aquatic creatures are likened to ingredients in an overboiled soup. In writing about her doctoral work at Cornell, she describes her writing process through the image of a torn tapestry; ideas and data are woven in thread by thread, until the damaged original has been reworked into a new pattern.

Assignment Wildlife ends in a pragmatic stance, with suggestions for effecting change for conservation worldwide. LaBastille not only exhorts her readers to environmental activism but explains how the natural world has deteriorated to its current state; she stops just short of theorizing about the political and social causes. She suggests that the ethic of competition prevents conservation and compromise. The author believes she knows which arguments work and is prepared to set aside the youthful enthusiasm of her early efforts as an ecologist for a more deliberate, sophisticated assault. In her closing thoughts and predictions she returns to the spiritual, hoping that whatever form God takes, the deity is watching over the wild spaces of the world. Having visited and studied much of the one percent of the earth's surface set aside as wilderness preserves, she recognizes the impediments to conservation that make God's attention so necessary: politics, economics, overpopulation, corporate greed, tourism, military activity and civil unrest, poaching, and commercial exploitation of land and water.

Women and Wilderness

Also appearing in 1980 was LaBastille's *Women and Wilderness*, which introduces her readers to another narrative style—scholarly, objective, political, aggressive. LaBastille is engaged in the feminist enterprise of reclaiming connection with her professional foremothers and celebrating their work, and here she opens up the work of feminist scholars, such as Annette Kolodny and Dawn Lander, to women who were thus far aware only of the popular ideas of the women's movement. The book itself breaks barriers of genre by including a historical overview of women and the American frontier, several case studies of women who traveled through the western wilderness, a survey of frontier women as characters in fiction, and a brief chapter addressing professional issues facing women in science and academia. The second part of the book profiles fifteen women pioneers of science and conservation, women who have challenged the traditionally "male bastions of wilderness work and life" (p. 1). Defining wilderness as a state of mind as well as an ecological entity, she

sees it as a construct of shifting meanings that reflect the changing relationships among men and women and the natural world. Her goals in this amalgam of history, biography, and natural science are to examine women whose lives were grounded in an interaction with the outdoors; to discover how that essential relationship affected other aspects of their lives; to assess how women's involvement differs from that of men in similar circumstances; and finally to demonstrate how exposure to the wilderness changes women and permits the wilderness within them to emerge. Certain assumptions underlie her research: that childbearing and wilderness living are incompatible for most women and that women and men are psychologically and biologically equal.

Her discussion of frontier women focuses on homesteaders, gold seekers, military wives, teachers, and female adventurers, and includes the story of Sacajawea. Aware of the importance of adventure fiction as a source of role models, she turns to literary representations—Conrad Richter's trilogy *The Trees*, *The Fields*, and *The Town*; A. B. Guthrie's *The Way West*; Ole Rölvaag's *Giants in the Earth*; and Willa Cather's *My Ántonia* and *O, Pioneers!* Her readings of these texts reflect the feminist concerns of her contemporaries and engages a readership that might not otherwise be familiar with the literary heritage of wilderness stories centering on women. A quick summary of legal and social changes precedes her analysis of changing views of wilderness and nature, and she lists women writers alongside the canonical Ralph Waldo Emerson, Henry David Thoreau, John Burroughs, Henry Wadsworth Longfellow, and John Muir, including not only Emily Dickinson, Cather, Sarah Orne Jewett, Mary Austin, Anne Morrow Lindbergh, and Rachel Carson but also lesser-known women, like cowgirl Lucille Mulhall and entomologist Anna Botsford Comstock. Having thus established a line of foremothers as a cultural context for herself, LaBastille slips again into the autobiographical, narrating her own development as a naturalist and the increasing resistance she met with, from the conflicts with her mother to the guidance she received

505

from men in her life. Male professors warned her of the cost to a woman of choosing a career in science. When she discovered that her deepest interest lay in fieldwork, barriers of gender slammed down. Though she had a bachelor's degree from Cornell University, and applied for a job in wildlife management with every state conservation department in the United States, only one offered her any kind of position, and that was as a volunteer. Tough-minded, insisting on equal rights within the system without critiquing the values informing the system itself, LaBastille confronted the obstacles women face in building careers as naturalists—inequities in salary and promotion, the perpetual struggle to be better than their male coworkers just to keep even with them, the subtle prejudices that undermine women's confidence as professionals, and the need to continually create an identity that embraces all the aspects of the woman's being. It is a story told again and again by the women profiled: confronted by prejudice and danger, frustrated and gratified by the work that they fight to do, negotiating the dangers of the natural world as well as the career path, tending marriages and children as well as the denizens of woodlands and seas.

Throughout her intimate sketches of these wilderness women, LaBastille includes detailed material on the wildlife they study and defend, demonstrating the belief they share: that human beings must learn to exist in nature without abusing it and pursue their stewardship conscientiously, enacting an ethic of reciprocity that preserves natural diversity. She typically begins a profile by locating herself, her subject, and her reader in the terrain with clear, precise, almost photographic, images. As always, the author works in the imagery of kitchen and home—a floodtide covers a salt marsh "with silver plate" (p. 209), and water is described as "tea-brown" (p. 263)—but there is less description than interpretation here. She deliberately asks women about their relationship to feminism and concludes that while most wilderness women she has met would identify themselves as feminists, they "lack the militancy and hostility toward men" (p. 290) that has often been assumed to be

part of the women's movement. She explores the complicated relationships they have with men in the field, how women establish their authority, how female peers treat them, and the strategy of adopting a gender-neutral persona. LaBastille's naive feminism surfaces again in her assumption that if a woman knows as much as her male peers and presents herself "well"—she does not question what that might mean or who defines it—the woman will be accepted as a professional. She clings to the belief that men will treat a woman with respect if she behaves correctly—"professional, competent, and polite" (p. 294)—without questioning why it is the woman's responsibility to control male behavior by acting in ways that will not threaten or challenge male beliefs about women and their work.

In telling these women's lives, LaBastille comments on their physical strength, the energy and efficiency of their bodies; she notes the astrological sign of each woman and how it is manifest in her being; she honors intellect, spirit, and body, and demonstrates that women have the power to change the circumstances that destroy habitat and humanity as well as creatures. She anticipates the work of Carol Gilligan, Nancy Chodorow, and other feminist philosophers and psychologists in explaining why women have more invested in saving the environment than men: women have more compassion for the individual; they respond more to detail than to the panorama of life; for them the death of a single animal is important and the death of a population intolerable; being more intuitive, they respond to the world around them intimately, viscerally. The feminization of environmentalism is illustrated best in the story of one activist who provides a space in her home where conservationists and anticonservationists could meet—a place more intimate than a public meeting hall, thus more conducive to compromise and consensus than contention. Sitting by the hearth, sharing simple refreshments and negotiating change, the activist concludes, "This is where and how it happens. It all depends on tea and cookies" (p. 249). LaBastille shows that the personal is political as women attempt to rebalance the masculine and feminine in the push to environmentalism.

The social change effected by feminism not only brought women into the wild but freed the wild in them. Success in the wilderness empowered women to believe they could fight male violence and made them less apt to be victims. The ever present danger that impinges on the life choices of every woman provides an important point of contrast for women of the wilderness. The wild is a place where they are not afraid to be alone, because they have the skills to protect themselves as well as their environment. It is no longer the male frontier code that protects them but their own power and integrity.

Earlier in her career LaBastille had lamented the passing of the frontier code. In Latin countries where she worked, she had originally found a welcome contrast to the repressive sexism of her own culture and colleagues: in response to her, men were chivalrous, attentive, appreciative. At this point in her career, however, the author identifies the underbelly of such chivalry: women are accorded respect if they conform to the rules imposed by the dominant culture, that they be passive and domestic, working within their own spheres of influence—the classroom (but rarely the college classroom), laboratories, and hospitals—and not encroaching on men's domain. LaBastille found herself in graduate school during the heyday of women's liberation when the prejudices against women in formerly male-dominated fields were being challenged if not entirely undone. Her experience of herself as a young, eager but inexperienced woman who is taken up by a man as a protégé, reinforced the perceived dominance of the male professional, and contributed to the conflict she felt between her girlish self and the competent, independent adult who had jettisoned the femininity that was inextricably linked to passivity. Her experiences at home and abroad lead LaBastille to conclude that encounters between women and men in the wilderness have changed since the eighteenth and nineteenth centuries, that the resentment, competition, discourtesy, and brutality in men's behavior toward women in the outdoors is a "natural" reaction to women's "invasion"

(p. 293) in professions and lifestyles that had previously been uncontestably masculine.

Beyond Black Bear Lake and Mama Poc

Beyond Black Bear Lake, published in 1987, serves as a sequel to *Woodswoman* in its summary of LaBastille's twenty years of living as a naturalist and the changes that she, the environment, and the world have undergone. Her ethics have shifted somewhat, and she has come to understand nature as a force that has its own pace and order, balance and agenda. In the book, she expresses her belief that human beings should only intervene when there is an ecological malfunction and a threat of biological impoverishment. LaBastille acknowledges changes in her position/philosophy: as a result of her experiences, she is more concerned than ever about the fate of nature and at the same time more cynical; she is less of a romantic idealist than before; and she has overcome her upbringing, the rules about being a "nice girl" who doesn't talk loudly or question authority. The intrusions and interruptions that the success of *Woodswoman* brought and the shift in her career to more lecturing and writing necessitated changes in her lifestyle. Acid rain and the encroachments of civilization into the mountains increased her anguish and ultimately led to her decision to move deeper into the wilderness to reclaim some of the solitude and serenity she had lost to intrusive fans, boat motors and airplane engines, people, and pollution.

In 1984, the Explorers Club made LaBastille the first woman to receive the Jade Chiefs Award. In 1986 she was honored as distinguished alumna of Cornell University; the following year Colorado State University repeated the honor. Public recognition of her work was welcome, but it also eroded the security and serenity of her wilderness life. She retreated to a more remote spot on her property and constructed a new cabin, resolved to live like Thoreau. Her enterprise became a conscious parallel to his: to live as economically as possible with as little dependence on the world as possible, in a place where she could return to the most essential elements—the creation of a dwelling place for her soul.

In this book LaBastille confronts the imperatives of conservation, this time from the position of local people who want to use their land as they choose—in her case, to build a ten-by-ten-foot cabin with no utilities or nearby road. Her frustration and bitterness over the legal obstacles she faces is exaggerated by her belief that her sensitivity to the issues and passion for the mountains entitles her to some freedom from the usual constraints imposed on landowners in the Adirondack Park. She feels that this wilderness area has become an extension of herself, and as in *Woodswoman* she takes a proprietary interest in it: "my woods" and "my ponds." Her dogs and her land are the family she always needed, and she struggles to hold onto the peace and communion that the Adirondacks provide.

Her struggles and triumphs in building the tiny rustic cabin she calls "half a haven" make up the heart of this book, but it is also about evanescence and loss—the death of her mentor Rob, who became the grandfather she never knew, the end of a love affair, and the sudden death of a beloved dog. Her professional life—deadlines, travel, research, the business that surrounds writing—conspires to erode the peace of her wilderness life. Her concerns about the scope of environmental distress are heightened after a trip to Scandinavia to study acid rain; she realizes that it is an international rather than a regional problem. She sees the fighter planes practicing their maneuvers over the Adirondacks as part of a network of destruction connected to the horror of Vietnam. *Beyond Black Bear Lake* is not just about a place but also about an understanding of the scope of environmental crisis: the world's ecosystems are in danger, and the threats are deeply rooted in modern culture. When she discovers that the federal government is considering the Adirondack Park as a repository for nuclear waste, she is awakened to the values and institutions that permit such murderous acts against landscape and people: she is "suddenly catapulted into space age worries.

Anne LaBastille at the dock with Condor and the new puppy, Chekika

How could this happen to a simple woodswoman?" (p. 140). The immensity and complexity of the value system that destroys wilderness and the enormity of saving the world and its inhabitants weighs on her. Facing the possibility of environmental cataclysm, she also ponders her choices and the life they have left her with: loneliness, aging, childlessness and matelessness.

Her search for certainty in the face of personal crises leads her to the religious images and affirmations that appeared in her earlier books—she compares her walks around the lake to Thoreau's "sauntering" (with its echo of the pilgrimages of the Middle Ages), envisions her morning dip as a religious exercise, and sees her tiny cabin lit like a shrine in the woods. Though she recognizes that Thoreau II has "diluted and disturbed" the wilderness, she believes that it was "such a small and loving intrusion, done with such a gentle, careful touch" that "the forest gods won't mind" (p. 242). She speculates about whether all is chaos or if there is a pattern to life. She searches nature's ways for moral and cosmic truth and comfort. Finally, she retreats to a view of the natural world as "utterly mechanistic, regulated, unchangeable": "It operates in great, fixed, implacable laws of physics" (p. 250). Yet she still holds that humans are at the center of creation and have power and self-determination that can work with or against nature. Her familiar mix of science and mysticism is still there: she pauses to offer prayers to the trees she cuts, thanking them and asking their blessing on her home.

Beyond Black Bear Lake demonstrates LaBastille's growth as a writer. To her imagery and narrative style she brings a surer sense of thematic architecture. A chapter entitled "The Ponds" begins with a quotation from Thoreau, in which he refers to a lake as "the earth's eye." LaBastille then relates an incident wherein her eyes were injured in a mishap at the cabin. She tells of her fear of blindness before describing her recovery and the regaining of her sight. As though responding to the criticism aimed at her because of *Woodswoman*, she re-creates the camaraderie and network of caring friends and neighbors who helped her raise the second cabin and supported her through her injuries and hard times. At the close of the book, she again makes one of her imaginative leaps into the avian world, flying with a string of geese headed south for the winter, seeing through their eyes the changes in and threats to the landscape, the pollution and poachers, until only a quarter of the original flock lands on the barrier islands of Georgia, facing loss but holding on against terrible odds. She portrays her nurturing environment with her dogs as an alternative to marriage and family.

Mama Poc reveals the politicized environmentalist at work on old material. Here LaBastille surveys her twenty-four-year mission to save a species from extinction, and names the forces that doomed the attempt. The title of this work derives from the sobriquets given to LaBastille by the Mayans around Lake Atitlan. For her efforts to create a refuge for the grebes, or "pocs," she was called "Lady Anne of the Pocs," with its connotations of aristocratic and economic privilege, and "Mama Poc," suggesting the caring mother who had come to clean up the mess and rescue the helpless. LaBastille's preoccupation with the domestic details of native inhabitants—fish, bird, and human—suggests again her belief that conservation work is really global housekeeping. Once again the author is concerned with creating a home—a reliable habitat for the endangered giant grebe and an appropriate dwelling for herself, this time named "The Little House with Green Shutters." LaBastille's familiar themes recur here: finding and losing love, the domestic details of cooking and eating, the impulse to create more than a mere shelter for herself. Characteristically, her assessing gaze takes in the domestic terrain:

> Sun was pouring through the glass window of the *ranchito* now and highlighting the new white rug I'd purchased. It lay before the fireplace, and its red, blue, and yellow birds made a cheery splash against the stone floor. The rustic wooden dining room table, desk, and chairs looked drab. Tonight I would sew red cotton curtains for the windows and make tablecloths to match. With a pair of candlesticks, red tapers, and flowers in a pot, my new home would look better." (p. 285)

And LaBastille's unquestioned ownership of the environment—"my grebes" and "my jacaranda"—continues in this work.

Unlike contemporary ecofeminists who claim sisterhood and female identification with the wild, LaBastille has always experienced it in more than one way: scientifically, emotionally, politically, environmentally. In one scene, for example, she sees it as separate from her, something against which she tests herself. After a particularly difficult crossing of the lake, she ascribes intent and assigns a feminine character to the lake: "You tried *again* Atitlan. You don't want me to forget you, lovely lady" (p. 292). While her conception of nature and landscape as female here approaches the connotations of conquest and penetration that the traditional masculine view has promulgated, it maintains the distance between human and environment that defining nature as "other" engenders.

In *Mama Poc*, the author again confronts the political issues embedded in environmental activism, beginning with her experience as a warden at the Guatemalan game refuge, feeling the authority and power of that male-identified role. The crux of the conflict for LaBastille remains in the culture's definition of wilderness as a masculine domain. She can reconcile her love of the wild with her identity as a female by identifying with her male forebears, shunning the domesticated and cultivated domain of her female ancestors. This explains a deeply ingrained bias against the feminine that pervades her work and creates ironic tension, forcing her to create a self that subverts the masculine/feminine dichotomy, replacing it with an enriched definition of the self as a human creature in nature.

The first part of this book, detailing LaBastille's early discovery of the grebes and initial attempts to establish a system of protection for them, is recycled from *Assignment Wildlife*. The story here is not only the death of a species but the education and evolution of an ecologist. This book is both angry and resigned. The grebes are doomed, their population below the minimum number to insure breeding and survival. The visitors' center at the refuge has been commandeered as a rebel outpost. LaBastille confronts the political violence that killed her comrade at the refuge and even the local priest, neither of whom was engaged in the revolution. Without elaborate theorizing about the fundamental causes of environmental ills, she treats the tangle of natural and manmade events that plague the natural world by focusing on and responding to the values that permit the abuse of animals, that prevent women from controlling their childbearing, that propel the destruction of sea and land. LaBastille tries to save an injured dog; she also offers help to a pregnant Mayan woman. Overarching both of these dramatic moments is her fight to save the grebes and the lake. Finally, her consciousness of interconnectedness prevails. She accepts the necessity of political compromise, of balancing wildlife and human needs in conservation initiatives. Her choice to be an environmental activist puts her in jeopardy, as it has others—Dian Fossey and Chico Mendez, for example, and the game warden at Lake Atitlan, Edgar Bauer. The natural dangers of wilderness work pale beside the human vio-

lence this ecologist has endured, from native Mayan witchery to slashed fuel lines to threats and sabotage at home. As early as the 1960s she was threatened with arson, what she called in *Woodswoman* "the time-honored revenge in our mountains" (p. 183). LaBastille knows well that defining the self as separate from and superior to nature can lead to violence and vigilantism by those willing to fight for their dominion and domination over it.

Conclusion

The book LaBastille published in 1992 begins and ends with explicit references to Thomas Merton's vision of monastic serenity, to be found in a church's "caves of silence" (p. 12). For her, the only places for people to find solitude and silence are churches and wildlands, and she chooses the latter. In this collection of poetry, reminiscences, and nature essays, the author reveals her most self-consciously literary work, much of it completed during the 1980s. Publication of *The Wilderness World of Anne LaBastille* coincided with the Adirondack Park centennial celebration. With this book, the writer/naturalist portrays herself in a distinctly new way, revealing her private poetry alongside the comfortable prose of her earlier work, both illuminated by her own photographs. Quoting Merton, she declares again one of the primary reasons for the necessity of wilderness: "I live in the woods, as a reminder that I am free" (p. 118). The corollary is that LaBastille found freedom in honoring the wilderness in herself. Still living in the Adirondack Mountains, she finds that the world has become a more threatening and threatened place since she made her first trip into the woods, and the value of the wilderness increases as its integrity diminishes. Like the philosophers, naturalists, and clergy of the nineteenth century, she sees the wild as a place where humans can be made whole and healthy:

I predict that the Adirondack Park's greatest value to humankind in the future will be the healing of psychological wounds. The mountains, lakes, and forests will become our psychiatrists. Stress therapy will consist of solitude and silence scheduled at regular intervals. Rather than seeking city churches and counselor's couches, come seek sanctuary in this Park. . . . The sacred spaces will soothe and gentle your soul, nourish and toughen your body, clarify your mind, and empower your life. (p. 13)

For LaBastille, such grace comes for women in touching the wilderness within them, thereby proving that they are wild as well as provident.

Selected Bibliography

WORKS OF ANNE LABASTILLE

BOOKS

Birds of the Mayas (Big Moose, N.Y.: West of the Wind Publications, 1964; repr., 1993); *Woodswoman* (New York: Dutton, 1976); *Assignment Wildlife* (New York: Dutton, 1980); *Women and Wilderness* (San Francisco: Sierra Club Books, 1980); *Beyond Black Bear Lake* (New York: Norton, 1987); *Mama Poc* (New York: Norton, 1990); *The Wilderness World of Anne LaBastille* (Westport, N.Y.: West of the Wind Publications, 1992).

ESSAYS

"Conservation Careers for Women," in *The Conservationist* 24 (June 1970); "How Fares the Poc?" in *Audubon* 74 (March 1972); "Panama Practices the Art of the Possible," in *Audubon* 75 (September 1973); "My Backyard—The Adirondacks," in *National Geographic* 147 (May 1975); "A Delicate Balance," in *National Wildlife* 14 (June 1976); "On the Trail of Wisconsin's Ice Age," in *National Geographic* 152 (August 1977); "Heaven, Not Hell," in *Audubon* 81 (November 1979); "Acid Rain: How Great a Menace?" in *National Geographic* 160 (November 1981); "Goodbye, Giant Grebe?" in *Natural History* 92 (February 1983); "The Adirondacks—Forever Wild and Wondrous," in *Reader's Digest* 129 (November 1986); "And Now They Are Gone," in *International Wildlife* 20 (July/August 1990).

PAPERS AND MANUSCRIPTS

LaBastille Reference Collection, Old Forge Library, Old Forge, N.Y.

BIOGRAPHICAL AND CRITICAL STUDIES

James Howard Kunstler, "Wild Thing," in *Adirondack Life* (July/August 1989); Kate H. Winter, "Anne LaBastille," in *The Woman in the Mountain: Reconstructions of Self and Land by Adirondack Women Writers* (Albany, N.Y.: State Univ. of New York Press, 1989).

WILLIAM LEAST HEAT-MOON
(b. 1939)

DAVID W. TEAGUE

WILLIAM LEAST HEAT-MOON is known primarily for his two books about the landscape of the United States: *Blue Highways: A Journey into America*, published in 1982, and *PrairyErth (a deep map)*, published in 1991. The name under which he publishes, "Least Heat-Moon," provides a helpful way by which to approach these books, for it signifies his unique perspective on American landscapes. Born William Trogdon to Ralph G. and Maurine Trogdon of Kansas City, Missouri, on 27 August 1939, he did not take "Least Heat-Moon" until more than forty years later, in 1981. During that year, Trogdon was working on a loading dock in order to support himself while he sought a publisher for *Blue Highways*. As he was standing on the dock one night, suddenly and unexpectedly the recollection of a paternal Osage ancestor came vividly to him. This memory, along with the Native American persona that it led him to embrace, enabled him to endow his manuscript with a depth it had previously lacked. As he told Alvin Sanoff, "it flashed into my mind that the hollowness in my writing came from drawing only on the Anglo-Irish side of my existence" (p. 58). This "hollowness" had been a very real concern for him, because he had for years been unsuccessful in publishing *Blue Highways*, even after rewriting the book six times.

What he added to his manuscript when he became William Least Heat-Moon were the sali-

ent characteristics of what he calls "Indian storytelling." This form of storytelling has a unique depth to it, because, as he tells Margot Boyer, in practicing it you "circle your topic. You go into [it] and back out again . . . and then round again, and back" (p. 9). His Native American name, recalled from his days as a Boy Scout, suggests the origin of his multiperspective, nonlinear approach to landscape. Significantly, after taking the new name he was able to revise *Blue Highways* into its highly successful present form.

Because of his concern with the landscape of the United States and the innovative perspectives from which he approaches that landscape, Least Heat-Moon is usually considered a nature writer, although his books are based on structures that clearly arise from human civilization. *Blue Highways* relates his experience of thirteen thousand miles and three months of automobile travel on the back roads of the United States; its underlying structure is the U.S. secondary highway system. His second book, *PrairyErth*, takes its shape from the U.S. Geological Survey's topographical grid. Least Heat-Moon's subject matter does not seem overwhelmingly "natural" either; his books are pointedly concerned with the human beings and the human artifacts he encounters as he explores the country. But the nonhuman with which Least Heat-Moon insists humans must eventually come to terms—the streams, the trees, the land itself—always exists in his work alongside the domesticated world reproduced on highway maps and in government surveys.

Maps and mapmaking are a major theme in Least Heat-Moon's work. He is what might be called a revisionist mapmaker, one who augments traditional flat representations of the earth's surface with the dimension of depth. Bill McKibben, for instance, has called *PrairyErth* "the deepest map anyone ever made of an American place" because in it Least Heat-Moon meticulously renders not only the surface of Chase County, Kansas, but also a myriad of phenomena both above and below the county's surface (p. 47).

The settings of *Blue Highways* and *PrairyErth*, the maps on which they are structured, are remarkably different, although they overlap. *Blue Highways* explores specific places Least Heat-Moon has encountered in the lower forty-eight states, while *PrairyErth* is a careful exploration of one single county within Kansas. Nevertheless, his books are very similar to one another in their deep or "thick" descriptions of the landscapes they treat. "Thick description" is a term Least Heat-Moon borrowed from the field of anthropology. According to Anatole Broyard, whom he quotes on page eight of *PrairyErth*, " 'thick description' refers to a dense accumulation of ordinary information about a culture, as opposed to abstract or theoretical analysis. It means observing the details of life until they begin to coagulate or cohere into an interpretation."

Thus, what both books share, and what constitutes one of Least Heat-Moon's most important contributions to contemporary landscape description, is what he has called in an interview with Daniel Bourne his technique of constructing "verticalities" or "excavations" that go deep into the history of a place. These "verticalities" are constructed somewhat differently in the two books: *Blue Highways* comprises many small ones, while *PrairyErth* is a single extended collection.

His "verticalities" shed light on the connections between Americans and their landscapes. They are lines drawn between humans and the land across whose face they move. Thus, objective representations of the landscape provide the structure for Least Heat-Moon's books, while his explorations of what people do as they live on the land provide the substance. As Peter Gilmour has noted, the reader is left to construct a "psychic topography" in this intersection between form and content, to construct the new face of the landscape as it is transformed through Least Heat-Moon's painstaking description.

Blue Highways

William Least Heat-Moon tells Daniel Bourne that, as a child, he traveled the United States with his father, developing "a sense of what could happen on American highways: the excitement in those days of finding little cafes, the pleasure of seeing the country, seeing the landscape change." Years later, aged twenty-three and "locked up in an aircraft carrier," he read John Steinbeck's *Travels with Charley in Search of America* (1962), and for sixteen years after that the idea of writing a book about travel in the United States "worked on" him (p. 93). In 1974, four years before he would embark on the journey he had dreamed of, it occurred to him that crossing the nation by traveling only on country roads might be feasible. It turned out that extended travel on unimproved country roads would not in fact prove possible, but the next best thing would: travel on the secondary highways denoted by blue lines on Rand McNally road maps.

Apart from a letter published in the *Kansas City Star* when he was a child, which he had written to protest Ted Williams' excessive spitting toward the press box after each of his home runs, and a life history of an acorn he had written as a model essay for his composition students, the book about that trip down the United States' blue highways was William Least Heat-Moon's first published work.

His travels along the blue highways, however, were only a small part of his preparation to write the book. According to Least Heat-Moon, the journey recorded in *Blue Highways* was actually

Least Heat-Moon surveying the Ancient Bluff Ruins along the Oregon Trail, near Broadwater, Nebraska

two journeys, one that took place over three months in a Ford van nicknamed "Ghost Dancing," and one that took place over the next four years in the library, as he pieced together the information that takes his readers deep into the landscapes he visited. This is a crucial fact about *Blue Highways*: its landscapes are William Least Heat-Moon's landscapes. Least Heat-Moon is no passive recorder of scenery. He tells Bourne that "the entire book is a fiction," and that there are times in the book where he "let the tale take over"—the tale of himself abroad on the land, the "traveler-in-search-of-whatever" (pp. 96, 97).

Thus, *Blue Highways* is not the work of a moment, nor is it even the work of the three months Least Heat-Moon spent traveling the country's back roads. It is the realization of an idea he had carried with him for sixteen years. It is also the record of his endeavor to organize a life that had begun unraveling. Immediately before the journey, Least Heat-Moon had endured the loss of a job, and was enduring a failing marriage. The book of travel-writing records his attempt to reorient himself in American society.

Early reviewers of his book were quick to note the figure of William Least Heat-Moon standing squarely in the foreground of his American landscape, and often they objected to it. Jonathan Yardley, for instance, finds his recurrent use of the word "I" to be obtrusive. Still, as readers have come to see, "I" is part of the book—a character—because William Least Heat-Moon, the "I" who discursively explores the back roads of the United States, is not merely a person behind a pen name. He is a character in the narrative, a character on a quest to locate himself somewhere on the map of his country.

His quest is complicated, and his description of the quest is enriched, by the fact that he identifies himself with a Native American name. In fact, William Least Heat-Moon says that as William Trogdon he could not have written either *Blue Highways* or *PrairyErth*, because the author's "core as a writer comes from the Osage" part of his heritage. In adding the name William Least Heat-Moon to his title page, along with the name William Trogdon, he tells Bourne in the *Artful Dodge* interview, he also added "another connection with the American land" (p. 111).

This other connection, the depth or "verticality" of his writing, involves reconceiving some of the most basic ways in which contemporary

Americans approach their landscape. *Blue Highways* is a paean to slow, meandering, sometimes destinationless travel. Part of Least Heat-Moon's attraction to the blue highways arises out of a disdain for highways marked in red—interstate highways—which separate people from each other and from the ground over which they travel, sacrificing contact with the land to accommodate high-speed travel over it. Recalling his drive through Indiana, where he chose for a short time to drive on a major highway, he reports that the "interstate afforded easy passage over the Hoosierland, so easy it gave no sense of the up and down of the country; worse, it hid away the people." And he goes on to scoff at the superhighway concept, insisting that "life doesn't happen along interstates. It's against the law" (p. 9). Ease of passage through a landscape contributes to alienation from that landscape, from other people, and, finally, Least Heat-Moon concludes, from oneself.

The journey he recreates in *Blue Highways* is, then, purposely a difficult, complicated, and sometimes complex one. It takes place on crooked, seldom-traveled roads. It involves encounters with strange people. It causes the author to pose difficult questions to himself. William Least Heat-Moon, the persona who travels America before his readers' eyes for the space of 412 pages, feels—because of his mixed heritage, his failing marriage, his lost job, his age—as if he is changing into an alien in his own land, and he has had enough of alienation. He takes to the back roads "in search of places where change did not mean ruin and where time and men and deeds connected" (p. 5). His journey is intended to be an affirmation of a new way of life, but not a condemnation of the old way, for his Native American heritage, his "red way of thinking," tells him that "a man who makes peace with the new by destroying the old is not to be honored" (p. 4). Thus, by celebrating the land as he finds it, he sets out to locate himself anew.

Least Heat-Moon supplies two maps of this journey. One map, reproduced on the last page of the book, represents the continental United States, and on it appears the route Least Heat-

Moon took as he explored the blue highways. The other map appears on the first page of the book, and continues to appear at the beginning of each section. It is the Hopi symbol for emergence. Least Heat-Moon describes it in the text of *Blue Highways*:

> Its lines represent the course a person follows on his "road of life" as he passes through birth, death, rebirth ... a kind of map of the wandering soul, an image of a process; but it is also, like most Hopi symbols and ceremonies, a reminder of cosmic patterns that all human beings move in. (p. 185)

Blue Highways is the conjunction of the two maps. Over the map of the physical shape of the continental United States is superimposed the map of William Least Heat-Moon's psychic journey of reemergence into the human society that occupies that physical space.

His "verticalities," or explorations of what he finds during the journey, serve to illuminate the relationship between the two maps. The explorations are generally fairly short, ranging from one paragraph to about ten pages, but they are vividly detailed. An early example of such a vertically structured description comes immediately after Least Heat-Moon turns off that regrettable stretch of Indiana interstate. Leaving the superhighway, Least Heat-Moon follows Indiana 66, "a road so crooked it could run for the legislature" (p. 9). He stops under the bluffs of the Ohio River to see the periwinkle growing there, and at the edge of a field, sees Sulphur Spring as it bubbles up "beneath a cover of dead leaves." He tells the reader that "Shawnees once believed in the curative power of the water, and settlers even bottled it. I cleared the small spring for a taste. Bad enough to curve something."

In the course of two paragraphs, Least Heat-Moon takes the reader from riding along in the bland, efficient insularity of an interstate highway, where stopping by the roadside is illegal except in cases of emergency, to tasting a bitter spring beside a small road in a field under the bluffs of the Ohio River. Here the landscape becomes, literally, as he drinks it, part of the author, and his relation of the history of its contact with the Shawnees and with early settlers makes the spring accessible to his readers.

Such explorations of place, part immediate experience and part historical research, provide the substance of the book. Not all are so brief, and not all the landscapes are as neatly contained as a spring and the field at whose edge it rises. The book is divided into ten geographical sections that combine to circle the lower forty-eight states, and so Least Heat-Moon must often explore landscapes on a larger scale. Still, because of the particularity with which he approaches his subjects, even though his book's ten demarcations sometimes necessitate fairly general descriptions of the landforms and ecosystems they comprise, Least Heat-Moon manages to maintain strong connections to the landscape he is exploring.

The section entitled "South by Southwest," to take one example, is a treatment of the somewhat generically delineated American "deserts." It begins with a workable, if broad, definition of desert. Least Heat-Moon explains that deserts are usually "a high land (two thousand feet and up), commonly arid (less than twenty inches rainfall), with mountains, evergreen forests, prairie grasses, and even some sand" (p. 132). Here, it seems as if Least Heat-Moon's map, as do most maps when their scale is increased drastically, loses its detail. In the next paragraph, Least Heat-Moon states the obvious when he tells the reader that "the true West differs from the East in one great, pervasive, influential, and awesome way: space" (p. 132).

But his strategy is quickly to go beyond such generalizations in order to develop more thorough descriptions of particular parts of this landscape. He relates that blue highway 21, which carries him into the southwest by way of Texas, started as a buffalo trail, which Indians began to follow in order to hunt. The Spanish made the trail part of their *camino real*, and after that

> adventurers, padres, traders, smugglers, armies, settlers . . . laid down a route that a nation whose explorers steer tangents past the planetary arcs still follow. And all travelers

coming in season see the orange and red nobs of Indian paintbrush blow in the spring winds. (pp. 132–133)

The descendants of these adventurers, padres, traders, and so on, the people who now inhabit the landscape, are inextricably part of it, as well, for Least Heat-Moon consistently peoples his landscape. In Dime Box, Texas, Claud Tyler represents a commonly encountered character type in the book, a local resident who can provide the author (and therefore the reader) a detailed anecdotal history of the area. Tyler, as Least Heat-Moon's characters often do, engages in colorful work while he talks. He gives the author a $1.50 haircut.

During the course of the haircut, Tyler tells Least Heat-Moon that he built the barbershop in which they sit in the 1940s, and he shows Least Heat-Moon a cottonwood tree that grew up under the corner of the shop from a seed hidden in river sand he had used to level the ground before he built. Prompted by the sight of the tree, Tyler goes on to consider the things that have happened in the town as he has watched the tree grow. "Barbering" has fallen off as economic and ecological factors have caused the cotton business to fall off; the village has shrunk, and now people "get out to the bigger towns anymore" for haircuts (p. 139). Tyler's business now comes from people stopping off at his shop on the way to another environmental development, an artificial lake near Dime Box. Least Heat-Moon Endows this passage with a typically fine image of a human engaging his landscape. This description of barber, haircut, shop, tree, town, provides an environmental history of the small part of the West called Dime Box.

As they do in Dime Box, Least Heat-Moon's connections to places almost always come through people, and consistently his most compelling experiences of the land arise as he learns to see places through the eyes of their inhabitants. His skill at achieving this sort of vision develops considerably over the course of the book. The discomfort, unease, condescension, or downright distaste with which he treats many of his early contacts—the Boss of the Plains to whom he condescends in chapter 13 of "South by Southwest," for example—gives way toward the end of the book to genuine interest on his part. This interest in turn inspires more and more compellingly rendered conversations in his later explorations.

His experience on Smith Island, Maryland, with Alice Venable Middleton is the last such extended exploration in the book. It is the culmination of his experience on the blue highways. Middleton, Least Heat-Moon's guide to the island, is someone whose voice he seems truly to respect. Hers is perhaps the only voice in the book that he accords more authority than his own. The Smith Island section is as much celebration as description, and it is as much a celebration of Alice Venable Middleton as it is of Smith Island.

Alice Middleton has already in fact beaten Least Heat-Moon to the punch in a small way: she has written about Smith Island. As he learns when he meets her, she is the town historian: she composed the text of the historical marker by the Ewell town church. In that text, she was unfortunately limited to forty-two words, but as Least Heat-Moon learns, she has many more than forty-two words for her place. She has descriptions of events on the island that go back to John Smith, the first white man to visit the island, and descriptions that go back farther than that, for among the historical artifacts in her attic is a "Nanticoke spearpoint as long as [her] palm" (p. 391).

The island, she informs Least Heat-Moon, was named after John Smith, and in Middleton's mind, John Smith may have understood it, and the country of which it later became a part, better than any Anglo-American who came after him. She tells Least Heat-Moon that Smith came to the island in 1608 looking for harbors and salt for the Jamestown Colony. "In his log," she remembers,

> he mentions the island and says the waters teemed so with fish that when he dipped a ship's skillet overboard it filled with several species. . . . He thought heaven and earth had never agreed better in framing a place

for man. He said it best in four words, "The land is kind." Somewhere in America they should cast those words in bronze. Cast them big. THE LAND, MY FRIENDS, IS KIND. (p. 389)

This passage constitutes a significant innovation in the heretofore strictly "vertical" structure of the book. In addition to the connections Least Heat-Moon forges with the landscape under his feet, he also makes a "horizontal" connection with another human, Alice Venable Middleton, which is something he has not done with his previous subjects. Her experience with writing about the landscape, and her impulse to write it in bronze so the correct words will not be lost, becomes an emblem for Least Heat-Moon's desire to find the correct description of the United States he has seen from the blue highways, and he identifies with her.

Middleton has been a teacher on the island for "more years than the bottom's got oysters" (p. 388). She had taught her students the island's ecology before it was called ecology—her name for what she taught was "the system of things" (p. 389). As she speaks about this system, she articulates Least Heat-Moon's own theme of connection to place as connection to the natural world. Middleton laments that the inhabitants of the island have an attitude

> that God will take care of it all—oystering, crabbing, water, the geese. "I'll get as many crabs today as getting can get," that's the way we talk. "Then I'll get more tomorrow." Now we've caught the bottom and haven't bothered much to put it back. Fished out the babies for years. But, as I hope to fly, a man's deeds count. Everything counts. We live in dependence, not independently. (p. 390)

During this conversation arises one of the crucial images of the book. Middleton motions as she speaks to a network of waterways in the island's flats. She sees them as a symbol. "They go every direction you can point," she tells Least Heat-Moon, but they never stop going to the sea. A thousand directions inside a grand direction. Going forward by going sideways—like the crab. That's how they get the feeling of the territory. Narrow at the head, wider at the shore. A picture of a life lived well, I deem. (p. 393)

Going forward by going sideways is, of course, the premise of the travels Least Heat-Moon documents in *Blue Highways*. This is his emergence; this is how he gets the feel of the United States of which he intends to be a part, by going "a thousand directions inside a grand direction" as he moves across it.

PrairyErth

PrairyErth has less of "going sideways" to it than *Blue Highways*; although Least Heat-Moon's second book is also an account of his peregrinations, in *PrairyErth* he confines his movement to one American county. The book is, in essence, one of the small "verticalities" of *Blue Highways* writ large. It comprises seventy-six chapters, over six hundred pages of "thick description" of the physical features of Chase County, Kansas, and of the people who move among them.

The idea of writing *PrairyErth* arose in his mind at the same time as the idea for *Blue Highways*. The title comes from a quote by John Madson, cited on page three: "In a stroke of scientific shorthand, the soils of our central grasslands are sometimes called simply 'prairyerths.'" Least Heat-Moon told Daniel Bourne that, intrigued by a particularly large empty space on the Rand McNally road map of the United States, he felt compelled "to write something about this little blank spot in east central Kansas" (p. 93).

Despite Least Heat-Moon's bland assessment, this blank spot on the map provides considerably more than an empty space to be filled with words. The place named Chase County, Kansas, acts as a conceptual space in which Least Heat-Moon refines the project he had started in *Blue Highways*, the project of viewing the American landscape from a broader perspective than

Americans traditionally employ. In writing *PrairyErth*, he "was interested in looking at a land that was minimal . . . a land that was lean, where there didn't seem to be much material for a writer to take up" (Bourne, p. 103). Such a land enables him to escape many conventions of Anglo-American narrative writing. Confronting the place, Least Heat-Moon finds himself challenged to create a plot from this "minimal," "plotless land." As he meets this challenge during the course of the book, he suggests the implications a "plotless" American landscape might hold.

Rather than present a chronological or hierarchically logical argument, Least Heat-Moon presents, as Margot Boyer has suggested, a "visual and spatial" narrative. Just as the Hopi maze of emergence symbolically defines the structure of *Blue Highways*, the grid imposed on Chase County by the United States Geological Survey in order to map it defines the structure of *PrairyErth*. A symbolic grid appears on the title page, and on the first page of every chapter of the book. As a chapter heading it serves as more than mere decoration; on it Least Heat-Moon marks the section of the grid to be discussed in the chapter at hand with a black dot.

Because it took twelve USGS maps laid together, each showing six square-mile sections, to cover the bulk of the county, Least Heat-Moon includes twelve sub-divisions in his book, each named after a corresponding USGS quadrangle. Each of these sub-divisions in turn contains six sections, thus emphasizing the book's cartographic structure. The first chapter of each sub-division is a "commonplace book," a collection of relevant quotations by various authors. The following five sections describe the landscape and the people of the quadrangle. The structure of *PrairyErth*, then according to its author's plan, includes seventy-two central sections, and Least Heat-Moon was so committed to this structure that he concludes one section he cannot finish with a black page, simply to fulfill his structural projection. Without this unwritable chapter, his deep map would have had only seventy-one sections. Alluding to Laurence Sterne's famous black page in *Tristram Shandy*

(1760), Least Heat-Moon leaves readers to interpret his "Tristramian" strategy and write the chapter themselves. In a very literal way, the structure of the book is linked in instances like this one to the map of the landscape it describes.

The land and the people on the land actually seem to grow up through this potentially restrictive structure, for from under the grid that Least Heat-Moon imposes on his work arises a truly organic literary endeavor, one that, in the end, challenges the assumptions on which rest grids, plots, and hierarchical logic in general. Onto the strict, spatial organization of his grid, Least Heat-Moon pours out newspaper articles, farm inventories, personal histories, personal interviews, botanical, biological, and geological investigations, weather reports, and the loosely, associatively organized collections of quotations he calls "Commonplace Books."

Out of the various items Least Heat-Moon assembles, patterns emerge, but they are not linear patterns. In view of the book's organic structure, Least Heat-Moon himself surmises that there may be as many ways of organizing *PrairyErth* as there are readers of *PrairyErth*. He tells Peter Gilmour that the book is built "upon a notion of the way that Native Americans often tell stories" (p. 10). The story has a central kernel around which the author wants to work, but it is then related through a series of "ramblings that appear to be about other things." The ultimate "assemblage of the book depends upon the reader being able to put these pieces together to make sense of the tale."

Least Heat-Moon thus intends explicitly to set his "Indian" sensibility against a more "Anglo" one, to move away from what he perceives as the linearity of Anglo-American language to a more holistic Native American perspective. Margaret Boyer sees his use of language as an attempt to show his readers "how to be reborn as natives of this continent, this planet." *PrairyErth* is a "major effort to use language, that delimiter of our imaginations which so often has been used to cut us off from the earth and from our bodies, to bring us back into the circle of life" (p. 9). Truly, to approach a landscape with as much care as Least Heat-Moon has approached Chase

County, Kansas, is to accord it a level of respect that the land has seldom commanded in the literature of the United States.

As part of its holistic approach to the landscape of Chase County, *PrairyErth* presents the reader with an imposing collection of raw data to process. Least Heat-Moon's treatment of the county is in fact, as Bill McKibben has noted, remarkably similar to Herman Melville's treatment of whales: "*PrairyErth*" is, he holds, "the *Moby Dick* of American history," and the two books, in their insistence on the importance of exhaustive, factual description, certainly do resemble each other.

PrairyErth is, among other things, a book about names. As part of his characterization of the state of Kansas, for instance, Least Heat-Moon provides a chapter entitled "By Way of Spelling Kansas." In the chapter, he supplies "the 140 variations" of the name "Kansas" in order to demonstrate the arbitrariness of names, especially landscape names; but more than anything, one suspects, he supplies them—"Cah" ... "Cau" ... "Kansais" ... "Kathagi" ... "Quonzai"—simply to encourage his reader to look at the state in 140 different ways.

His characterizations of the people in the landscape are equally exhaustive. They range from broad abstractions to rusty and bent specifics. The description of Gabriel Jacobs is typical of Least Heat-Moon's treatment of Chase Countians. Jacobs' life is cataloged in great detail. He was a Dunkard preacher who came to the county in 1856, and he is represented in the book not only by a chapter of objective description, but also by his estate inventory, which Least Heat-Moon found in a third-floor room of the county courthouse, and which he reproduces in his text exactly, all 125 items, complete with the clerk's misspellings. Least Heat-Moon presents the plows, hammers, tin cups, pincers, and the "monkey wrentch" recorded in the inventory as the entire objective manifestation of Gabriel Jacobs' life on the land.

The diary kept by Elizabeth Mardin, another Chase County resident, from May to Christmas, 1862, is excerpted in the chapter "Within Her Pages." Elizabeth Mardin's quickly sketched reading days, washing days, unpleasant days, berrying days, and baking days appear in *PrairyErth* just as she preserved them.

Complementing such intimate descriptions of particular lives in particular places are more general descriptions painted in broader strokes. "At the Diamond of the Plain" is a series of firsthand travelers' accounts of a once pure and once famous spring just north of the Chase County line—the Diamond of the Plain, "the most famous oasis on the Santa Fe Trail" (p. 448). "According to the *Leader*" illustrates a similar descriptive strategy on Least Heat-Moon's part. It, too, reproduces verbatim the original accounts of events in and around the county. The chapter consists of sixteen pages of newspaper articles from the *Leader*, a Chase County newspaper, presented with minimal editorial comment. The chapter "On the Town: A Night at Darla's" catalogs primary sources in yet a third way as they describe life in the county. "On the Town" contains a nearly verbatim account of conversations Least Heat-Moon has heard in Darla's Fun Center, a brief but precise record of the few hours he shares in several Chase Countians' lives.

Not surprisingly, during the course of his exploration of Chase County, William Least Heat-Moon himself becomes part of the life of the place. His "deep map" draws him into the landscape. Recounting a particularly affecting experience that becomes a paradigm for his other experiences with the Chase County landscape, he explores Jacobs' Mound, a "truncated cone sitting close to the center of the Gladstone quadrangle." Jacobs' Mound is one of the geographical highlights of the county, and one of its tallest features, a "most obvious old travelers' marker" plainly visible from "two of the three highways," yet Least Heat-Moon reports that he had been in the county several days before he saw the "frustum so distinct." Significantly, he had missed seeing it because he had been looking "to closely and narrowly" at the land around him (p. 81).

Once the existence of Jacobs' Mound dawns on him, however, he sets out to look at it from as broad a perspective as he can create for himself. On the morning he sets out to climb the mound, he first collects from four Chase County residents four narratives describing it.

> That morning four people told me four things, one of them, the last, accurate: the regular sides and flattened top of the knob prove Indians built it for a burial mound; Colorado prospectors hid gold in it; an oil dome lay beneath it; and, none of those notions was true. (p. 81)

Before he actually sets out on his journey to experience the landscape of the mound personally, physically, by walking it, he sits and observes the mound in order to form an impression of it. Then he begins walking toward it. Curiously, though, while he walks, there is little mention of the mound in the text, even though it is the object of his hike. Least Heat-Moon describes the grasses he sees, the terrain he covers, the flowers, insects, and prairie chickens he encounters, but as he walks, he does not fix his attention on the landform. Instead, he is only vaguely aware of "the mound drawing [him] as if it were a stone vortex in a petrified sea" (p. 82).

The prairie across which he walks is a lesson to him. Because of its scarcity of landmarks, certifiers of genuine forward progress, the prairie turns "movement to stasis and openness to a wall." Least Heat-Moon as explorer is thus left only with what is near him. He is left to concentrate on his immediate surroundings in order not to feel lost, literally, in the huge prairie distances, or figuratively, by becoming a "complacent cartoon" in the vastness.

When he attains the top of the mound, Least Heat-Moon realizes that this goal, the physical end to the linear path he has cut across the prairie, is much different, much smaller, than he had imagined. He realizes that "its power lay not in size but rather in shape and dominion and its thrust into the imagination" (p. 83).

And so it is imagination, he concludes, that connects humans to this landscape, and in the closing paragraphs of the chapter he recounts some of the things humans have imagined about it. Least Heat-Moon reports that a particular human who had been abroad in this place, John Buckingham, a nineteenth-century farmer, once ploughed up what he imagined to be a treasure map near the mound. Buckingham looked for gold around its base. But other people, in whom Least Heat-Moon seems much more interested, experienced the mound through imaginations "more calligraphic than auricular." While picnicking on the summit of the mound, these others scratched their names on the flat rocks that Least Heat-Moon finds there.

He turns the stones over, reading the names etched upon them, until he finds a stone that, as he says, freezes him. On it, he sees the name WAKONDA, which is a Plains Indian name for the "Great Mysterious, the Four-Winds-Source-of-All." Thrilled, he continues to see the name WAKONDA etched in the stone until the realization hits him that Plains Indian names are not likely to be written in Roman characters. Upon closer examination, the rock turns out to bear the legend "W KENDA," perhaps, the author guesses, once "W. KENDALL," as he replaces the stone again face down so that it can continue transferring its figures into the earth beneath it.

The stone, despite its disappointing inscription, has evoked a pointed imaginative response in Least Heat-Moon. It is the response to landscape that ultimately informs both *PrairyErth* and *Blue Highways*. Jacobs' Mound, this "lone rising," brings him back to his symbolic evocation of the vortex earlier in the passage, and as he closes his discussion of the mound, he juxtaposes the holistic, nonlinear thought patterns represented by that symbol, which he associates with Native Americans, with linear thought, which he associates with European settlers. He concludes that

> across America, lone risings have been sacred places to tribal Americans, places to reach out for the infinite. Where whites saw this knob and dreamed gold, aboriginal peoples (it's my guess) found it and dreamed God, and it must have belonged to their legends and gramarye, and they surely came to this erosional ellipse as leaves to the eddy. (p. 84)

This eddy or vortex, a part of the natural world that draws humans and their artifacts toward it in an indirect, almost circular path, provides a helpful image for readers of William Least Heat-Moon's first two books. He is a writer invested in circumspect, careful, and cautious approaches to the landscapes he treats. He provides compelling description of literally hundreds of American places, and in the end, his methods of description and his strategies for seeing places in both their environmental and human contexts prove to be as compelling as the places themselves. The lesson William Least Heat-Moon's readers stand to learn from observing his careful and unhurried treatment of American places is that to drive, to run, or even to walk in a straight line across the face of the landscape is an impoverished experience, one to be avoided in favor of explorations, either metaphorical or actual, of winding paths along which lie many stops.

Selected Bibliography

WORKS OF WILLIAM LEAST HEAT-MOON

BOOKS

Blue Highways: A Journey into America (Boston: Little, Brown, 1982); *The Red Couch*, with photography by Kevin Clarke and Horst Wackerbarth, text and interviews by William Least Heat-Moon (New York: Alfred Van der Marck Editions, 1984); *PrairyErth (a deep map)* (Boston: Houghton Mifflin, 1991); *Three Essays*, ed. by Bill McKibben (Arlington, Va.: Nature Conservancy, 1993), essays by William Least Heat-Moon, Bill McKibben, and Terry Tempest Williams.

INTRODUCTIONS

American Roads, by Winston Swift Boyer (Boston: Little, Brown, 1984; repr. Bullfinch, 1989); *Old Indian Trails*, by Walter McClintock (Boston: Houghton Mifflin, 1992).

ARTICLES

"Blue Highways," in *Atlantic* 250 (September 1982); "A Place Called Nameless," in *Reader's Digest* (June 1983); "Up Among the Roadside Gods," in *Time* (1 August 1983); "The Native Son," in *Esquire* (December 1984); "Travel and Nature," in *New York Times Book Review* (8 December 1985); "A Glass of Handmade," in *Atlantic* 260 (November 1987); "Prairy-Erth: Portraits from Chase County, Kansas," in *Atlantic* 268 (September 1991).

BIOGRAPHICAL AND CRITICAL STUDIES

Daniel Bourne, "*Artful Dodge* Interviews William Least Heat-Moon," in *Artful Dodge* 20/21 (1991); Margot Boyer, "PrairyErth," in *Heartland Journal* (March/April 1992); Peter Gilmour, "The Heartland Interview: William Least Heat-Moon," in *Heartland Journal* (March/April 1992); Bill McKibben, "The Deepest Map," in *Hungry Mind Review* (spring 1992); Noel Perrin, "Blue Highways," in *New York Times Book Review* (6 February 1983); Alvin P. Sanoff, "Whispers from the Kansas Tallgrass," in *U.S. News and World Report* (11 November 1991); Paul Theroux, "The Wizard of Kansas," in *New York Times Book Review* (27 October 1991); Jonathan Yardley, "Seeing America from the Roads Less Traveled," in *Book World—The Washington Post* (26 December 1982).

ALDO LEOPOLD
(1887–1948)

PETER A. FRITZELL

ALDO LEOPOLD did not consider himself a nature writer, and he did not live to know his reputation as such. Although he certainly knew himself as nature writing, as an organism seeking composure through language and logic, through parable and metaphor, through phenological study and official report, he did not live to experience or respond to our attempts to classify him and his writings; and he almost certainly would have smiled a bit at our efforts. Neither, while he was alive, did Leopold's contemporaries consider him a nature writer. His closest associates certainly knew that he could write with persuasive and entertaining fluency, and they took frequent advantage of his talents; but they saw him less as writer than as statesmanlike tactician with wide-ranging experience and deep commitments to resource management, as nationally and internationally known student and professor of wildlife and watershed, of forestry and fisheries, of wilderness and wetlands.

In a manner, and after a fashion, that he doubtless would have appreciated, Leopold became a living, recognized nature writer only in dying. Although he wrote over one thousand essays, articles, reviews, handbooks, newsletters, reports, and position papers over the course of his life—and although he saw to publication some five hundred of these, along with two books—his stature as an American nature writer rests almost solely on the reputation and fate, the style and the form, of one seemingly slight volume that appeared in the fall of 1949, a year and a half after his death—*A Sand County Almanac and Sketches Here and There*, a collection of brief narratives and essays that, in less than forty years, became—after Thoreau's *Walden*—the best known, most widely read, and most frequently cited work of American nature writing.

The case of Aldo Leopold, then, is an unusual case among major American nature writers; and *Sand County* is an unusual work of nature writing, both in its reception and in some of its most notable stylistic and formal traits. By 1987, the centenary year of Leopold's birth, *Sand County* had sold over a million copies in five editions and well over forty printings. In a way that no other work of American nature writing can yet be said to have matched, it had proven to be a resounding commercial success; and in a manner that only *Walden* can, as yet, be said to have equaled or surpassed, it had had a wide-ranging impact upon American culture—upon politics, law, and education; upon the ways in which we conceive and manage what we still too easily call "natural resources"; upon the ways in which we see and treat our home places; and, indeed, upon the styles and tones as well as the functions of nature writing.

In fact, few works of American literature of any kind have had the practical and programmatic impact of *Sand County*. It has become the essential scripture of the so-called environmental movement, and of so-called environmental education. It has been primarily responsible for the development of a professional subfield in philosophy, "environmental ethics." It has been read, reread, and cited at length not only by students of nature writing, but by those engaged in wildlife and fisheries management and in landscape and regional planning. It has been adopted as a text in countless university and college courses, and parts of it have been anthologized in still other textbooks and readers. It has been read and appreciated by conservationists and by preservationists—by devotees of "wilderness" and by those who know, however unhappily, that, in Leopold's words, "all conservation of wildness is self-defeating" (*A Sand County Almanac*, p. 101). Particular propositions—indeed, specific clauses and sentences—from *Sand County*'s concluding section, "The Land Ethic," have been the subjects of exhaustive conceptual and logical analysis, in at least one monograph and in untold numbers of articles, essays, and chapters. Indeed, "The Land Ethic" has been extolled both by those who find in it a hopeful resolution and by those who see in it irresolvable ambiguity, irony, and paradox. It has been commended, on the one hand, by those who find in it a lasting solution to environmental problems, an evolutionary extension of ethics to land and its component species (if not its individuals), a sustainable harmony among self, society, and nonhuman surroundings. It has been reverenced, on the other hand, by those who find in its ethics, however laudable and necessary, another in what Leopold called a series of "excursions from a single starting point" to which we humans return "again and again to organize yet another search for a durable scale of values" (*Sand County*, p. 200).

Early Life

Aldo Leopold was born into a historic watershed, in Burlington, Iowa, on 11 January 1887. The American frontier, still officially open, was rapidly closing. In 1890, a report from the superintendent of the census of the United States announced that the line marking the frontier of American settlement had all but vanished; and three years later, in July 1893, a young historian from the central sand counties of Wisconsin delivered to the American Historical Association a landmark paper in which he simultaneously commemorated "The Significance of the Frontier in American History" and lamented its passing. "And now," said Frederick Jackson Turner, "four centuries from the discovery of America, at the end of one hundred years of life under the Constitution, the frontier has gone, and with its going has closed the first period of American history."

Although three decades would pass before Turner and Leopold would become neighbors in Madison, Wisconsin, the essential terms of Turner's address would reverberate in the life and writings of the then six-year-old in Burlington, whose rather palatial family home looked east (back across the river, as some Americans might yet be inclined to say) from the western bluffs of the Mississippi, and whose personal and familial welfare depended in substantial part upon the exploitation of northern forests and the building of the prairies and plains. In and upon the grounds of that eastward-facing home, the young Aldo Leopold would play Daniel Boone or Kit Carson. Inside, while his mother played the piano, he might entertain himself with the cadences of "Hiawatha." While his father and maternal grandfather were shooting teal and mallards at the Crystal Lake Hunt Club across the river, he would absorb himself in hunting adventures of the West in magazines like *Forest and Stream* and *Outing*. While his mother spoke of the opera or read to him poetry in German, he might think of skating on the river. While his grandfather was organizing and promoting yet another civic cause, perhaps the Burlington opera house, he might recall his father's hunting stories or yearn to go trapping with his brother.

For Aldo Leopold, as for other of his generation, the alternate slopes and antipodal motives of the historic watershed were there in the beginning—the rememberances of frontiers and wilderness that were supposed to be open, the highly styled closures of his mother's readings. While he was learning and practicing the essential mythology of the American frontier, the freedom of the wild imagined from a dependable home, Frederick Jackson Turner was lamenting (even fearing) the disappearance of what he called "free land" and, with it, the impending disappearance of what he saw as the original causes of American character, culture, and institutions.

In half-conscious echoes of James Fenimore Cooper and Davy Crockett, among many others—and echoes upon those echoes that Leopold found in his preferred youthful reading (of Stuart Edward White, Jack London, and Ernest Thompson Seton)—Turner's original American had advanced across a "simple, inert continent," leaving behind him a "complex" and distinctly American "nervous system," a continent as organism come to its own uniquely, civilized life. The experience of that continent, the frontier experience, had provided for the American "a gate of escape from the bondage of the past," a gate that opened on a land where "waters ran clear" and "free grass waved a carpet over the fence of the earth," a truly liberating place, an Eden without a serpent, where "America's man on horseback . . . rode over the rim with all the abandon, energy, insolence, pride, carelessness, and confidence epitomizing the becoming West." As Turner saw it, the frontier experience had enabled Americans to free themselves from the currupt and constraining complexities of previous history and society, and to start anew. And now, said Turner, it was gone; and the consequences of its going were troublesome and unpredictable. If the frontier experience survived, it would survive only in the annals of history, or in the short-lived memories of those who had known "free land" in fact.

As the life of Aldo Leopold, among many others, would demonstrate, the legacy of the frontier would prove far more powerful than Turner suggested in 1893, and the wilderness memories of his Americans far deeper and far more extensive. The history and mythology of that "gate of escape from the bondage of the past" would prove to be far more binding, especially, perhaps, for the generation of Aldo Leopold.

Although neither Turner nor Leopold could have known it at the time, what was taking shape in Burlington during the 1890s was a part of a historic reenvisioning of Turner's "free land." Ultimately, it would be a vision considerably more tragic and less romantic than Turner's, more "existential" and less "transcendental," more aware of limits and limitations, and less inclined to seek to escape them. But it would be no less dependent upon, nor any less dedicated to, the legacy of the frontier or the originally wild. Its authors, including Leopold, would share Turner's lament—indeed, would depend upon it, perhaps even feel it more deeply than he did—but they would consider and understand the lament in contexts that Turner either ignored or underestimated. They would view the legacy of the frontier not only as a deep-seated historical phenomenon—not only as an expression of age-old psychic and social habits, customs, and needs—but as a virtually inescapable cultural form, a formative and definitive typos and mythos, and occasionally, then, even as an expression of a kind of biocultural need. In fact, the inheritance of that "gate of escape," and the legacy of that "free grass" would lend a particular and ongoing poignancy—a difficult, if also motivating, melancholy—to several notable works of the next and ensuing generations, including *A Sand County Almanac*—to Willa Cather's *My Ántonia*, F. Scott Fitzgerald's *The Great Gatsby*, William Faulkner's "The Bear," James Baldwin's *Notes of a Native Son*. For Turner, "free land" had been far too much fact, and not nearly enough metaphor, story, image, and idea—not nearly enough historical or historic. He had underestimated his Americans' capacities to discern the costs of conceiving free land solely as fact. He had underestimated not only the extent of their memories, but the formative years, especially, of their imaginations.

Like many Americans of his time and many more of later times—like Cather and Fitzgerald and Faulkner and Baldwin—Aldo Leopold drank

AMERICAN NATURE WRITERS

early, deeply, and inescapably at the inherited well of America's frontier freedoms, at the legacy of that "gate of escape from the bondage of the past." But, like his compatriots, Leopold also drank deeply, inescapably, and just as early at the inherited well of historic and civilized discipline, including especially, perhaps, the kinds of discipline necessary to frontiers, the kinds of discipline that may provide a sense of continuity and stability in the face of the new, the uncertain, or the unknown. These kinds of discipline the young Leopold found not only in the architectural and aesthetic forms of his family's rather Italianate home in the then burgeoning city of Burlington, not only in the verbal and stylistic discipline of his mother's readings—but in his maternal grandfather's efforts at picturesque landscape gardening or collecting tropical plants—and even in such less conspicuously provincial disciplines as the family's efforts to outline and cultivate productive vegetable and flower gardens in unproductive soil.

Along with the family's greenhouse, the Leopold Desk Company, and the legally incorporated hunting clubs, each of these signs of discipline might suggest to a Turnerian the closed or closing frontier—the lost opportunities of an essentially romantic and Jeremiadic vision. But these and other signs of discipline should also suggest the more comprehensive and tragic vision of Leopold's and ensuing generations. They should suggest, in other words, that from the imagined frontiers of childhood may well come the advocate of legislated wilderness areas, that from the trappings and huntings and gardenings of youth may well come the broadly-read scientist deeply engaged in the commerce and politics of conservation, that in the early and powerful experience of wildness and wilderness is the author of "The Land Ethic," the analyst, the critic, and the appreciator of the customs of the country.

Put alongside the playings at Daniel Boone and the readings of "Hiawatha"—indeed, embedded in them—these signs of familial and societal discipline may evoke the Aldo Leopold who, by age eleven, was already trying his hand at some of the conventional enclosures of nature writing, at what might be called ornithological science and appreciation. "I like to study birds," he wrote in a notebook, thus announcing that among a plethora of options that seemed available for this composition, birds might work, since he knew something about them: "I like the wren best of all birds. We had thirteen nests of wrens in our yard last summer. We hatched one hundred and twenty young wrens last summer. Here are a few of our birds." He then listed thirty-nine different kinds (they were not yet quite species) in a list that is less a demonstration of precocity than it is an effort to begin to try to fit some of the signal elements of his life into a working pattern—in short, to begin composing himself in relation to his surroundings—to try to fit the vocabulary of pretty birds and slight, sweet songs together with the vocabulary of nest-counts and reproductive success—to try to fit together what one could make of mother's art and father's science, perhaps, and all in a manner that would meet the often difficult demands of conventional spelling and grammar: "I like wrens because they do more good than almost any other bird, they sing sweetly, they are very pretty, and very tame. I could have caught them many a time if I wanted to" (Meine, p. 17). His youthful voices were divided, of course, as they would be for some time to come; but the pattern of Leopold's life had been set—the birds (the nonhuman other), the self, the "we," the science, and the language of valued appreciation, both ethical and aesthetic. The effort to blend them in a coherent vision would continue for the remainder of his life.

By the time he was thirteen, Leopold's parents had given him a copy of Frank Chapman's *Handbook of Birds of Eastern North America*; and by the summer of his sixteenth year, he was keeping a more elaborate ornithological notebook, in the manner of Mark Catesby or John James Audubon. He was still pretending, of course, still trying things on; but, as his catalogue of "Visitants," his notations, and his corrections indicate, he was continuing to learn parts of the vocabulary, learning to discriminate among types and kinds, learning something about the business of dates and dating, and also

528

something, apparently, about legitimate and il-legitimate sightings:

Winter Visitants (~~17~~)

Saw-whet Owl
~~Bald Eagle~~
~~Marsh Hawk~~
Tree Sparrow—Rare 1902–3
Junco—Apl. 1–22–24–25
Brown Creeper—Apl 19–24
Northern Shrike
Horned Lark
Mallard—Ad. ♀ ~~May 9, may have had nest, acted strangely).~~
Goose, Canada
Pintail
Golden-Eye
Dusky Mallard (1901–02)
Ringbill—Apl 11
Rusty Blackbird—Apl 11
Green Winged Teal (1901–2)
Bluebill—Apl 11
American Crossbill
Red Breasted Nuthatch
("Journal 1903," p. 1)

Although he could not have known it at the time, in this youthful notebook, Aldo Leopold was trying out conventional ways of answering two of the most fundamental questions that confront anyone facing the unknown—"What is it?" and, in relation to it, "What (or who) am I?" He was reenacting a substantial part of the experience of many an early American who encountered the frontier—noting things, then naming (or trying to name) them, then trying to organize them into conventionally acceptable types. He was trying to sort out and stabilize the elements of his experience. In fundamental psychic terms, he was practicing a kind of morphology and the beginnings of a phenology, and through them, taking some of his first, tentative steps toward a disciplined sense of who and what he might be.

In other sections of this notebook—kept mainly in the spring and summer before he left for the Lawrenceville School in New Jersey—Leopold sought to fix the elements of his surroundings in basic taxonomic and methodological terms, as well as to elaborate those terms, and to add to them elements of the then conventional vocabularies and styles of appreciation.

3. Black-Throated Blue Warbler. May 7– On first seeing the ♀ of this species, I was at a loss to identify her. The breast had a dirty tinge, and the throat a metallic reflection. When joined by her handsome mate however, I was relieved of my suspence [*sic*]. In their movements, the pair was very leisurely, and practiced flycatching to some extent, the ♂ even descending to the ground. Their haunts seemed to be the lower branches, although they afterwards ascended to the treetops. The song was very peculiar, and delivered in the manner of a Vireo. It might be written $\overline{swee}$-$\overline{ee}$-$\overline{ee}$, and somewhat resembled the quaint lisp of the Black-throated Green, but there was something about it which suggested the sputtering of "Vireo bells." That of the ♀ seemed longer and more full than that of her mate. ("Journal 1903," p. 32)

As this notebook entry and others reveal, for Leopold there was more to the business of identifying and accounting for things than meets the usual eye. Like other entries, this one is more than a record of the sometimes awkward efforts of a youth to learn the methods and language of ornithology, of accurate description and appropriate appreciation—more than a record of efforts to learn to spell or punctuate correctly, or to avoid "embarrassing" dangling modifiers ("When joined by her handsome mate however, I was relieved of my suspense"). Important as such things are, the entry is not simply a record of a youth learning to distinguish (by color, habit, habitat, or song) what we call the black-throated blue from the black-throated green from the vireo. Read closely, it is a part of a complex record, the record of a self gradually taking shape. Read with empathy, it is a reminder that, despite handbooks and fieldguides, distinctions among the black-throated blue, the black-throated green, and the vireo do not come ready made, that they are not given in what we sometimes call original experience, no more than is the distinction between ♀ and ♂, or between human self and the "bird" whose breast had "a dirty tinge" and "throat a metallic reflection." Even if unintentional, as we say—indeed, perhaps, because it is—this notebook entry is a reminder that the "mis-taken," "grammatical" affinity between "her handsome mate" and "I" is likewise not given in experience, and cannot be taken too much for granted—no more than either of the distinctions that would have been provided by correct usage—either "When she was joined by her handsome mate, I . . ." or "When we were joined by her handsome mate, I. . . ." Perhaps there is even something to be learned here from the final reflection on the song of the female—"longer and more full than that of her mate"—something, perhaps, of a sixteen-year-old boy about to leave home.

As he prepared to head east, then—or, rather, as he continued to—Leopold was trying on both the vocabularies and methods of disciplined science and the vocabularies and styles of disciplined ethical and aesthetic appreciation. He was learning—at times no doubt even against his own wishes—something of the differences between "flew" and "ascended," between "haunts" and "habitat," between "resembled" and "somewhat resembled," between "that of" and "the song of"—and something as well of relationships among "quaint," "strange," "old-fashioned," and "artful."

From Midwest to East

Early in his time at Lawrenceville, Leopold became known among his peers as "the naturalist," for his inclination to set off alone into the surrounding countryside; and his many letters home corroborated his increasingly public identity. He wrote of discovering Charles Darwin, particularly *A Naturalist's Voyage Around the World* ("It is very instructive and interesting."); he described, often at some length, what he called "new species" of birds, and announced the addition of 13 to his life-list (by now 274), at the same time reminding (or trying to remind) himself that the count, although "rather inter-

esting to note," was "not by any means the end or object of my study of Ornithology" (Meine, pp. 35–36).

By the time he was nearing the end of his second and final year at Lawrenceville, Leopold had all but confirmed the childhood promise and youthful prospect of his early notes and notebooks. He was still trying out the conventional vocabulary of nature appreciation. His "Sweet Violets" were still "a beautiful flower . . . unsurpassed for the delicacy of their perfume"; his swallows still skimmed "merrily over the pond all day long"; and a towhee continued to be "handsome." But the relationships among his figures and his vocabularies were becoming more complex—his metaphors more extended, more conscious, and occasionally even self-conscious. By the spring of his eighteenth year (1905), "the most eloquent of all Easter-day sermons" was "to breathe the Spring-breeze laden with the warmth of sunny skies, the essence of April flowers and the joy of a thousand bird-songs, and then to realize that countless centuries would not have prepared such an abode for us if we terminated our existence in the grave" (Meine, p. 42). The classical and clichéd "abodes," and "essences" were still much present; but the poses he struck were more openly poses, and the tones more various. He was trying on adaptations, both syntactic and tonal, of the clichéd and conventional; and he was already displaying a disposition to mix conventional idioms, including the pointedly colloquial:

Perfectly motionless, a bird with spread tail and greenish back perches on the trunk of a sapling. He turns! a flash of black and gold! and Ye Gods!—A Hooded Warbler! He regards you still motionless, but on the alert for your slightest movement. Nervously you fumble for glasses, get them focussed successfully, and look and look and look. A Hooded sure enough, and O what a beauty! (Meine, p. 43).

In letters home, at least he was now worrying openly, if nonetheless conventionally, that his efforts were "too frequently narrow and dry."

"Who can write the great things," he asked, "the deep changes, the wonderful nameless things, which are the real object of study of any kind" (Meine, pp. 42–43).

In a sense, Leopold was already thinking, at age eighteen, of what would become *A Sand County Almanac.* Even in the face of the more ordinary business of making a living, of changing careers and routine assignments, he would keep in mind "the great things," "the deep changes"; and barring some major disappointment or failure, some convincing and utterly disappointing evidence of misdirection, some economic accident or exigency, he would be a naturalist and a writer, whatever his professional label of the moment.

After graduating from Lawrenceville, Leopold went to Yale to prepare for a career in forestry. He studied first at the Sheffield Scientific School, taking a two-year preparatory program that included chemistry, physics, German, English, mechanical drawing, and analytic geometry. He then entered the Yale Forest School, where he continued his study of German, composition, and mechanics; added French; and began taking the subjects then associated with what would be his first profession—among them surveying, mineralogy, physical geography, hydraulics, plant taxonomy, forest botany, silviculture, dendrology, plant morphology, and something called timber construction. His sense of professional discipline continued to grow, as did his vocabularies and his ways of understanding; but what finally distinguished his time at Yale was a kind of psycho-social coming out, a coming out that included an elaboration of his reading, of course, but more important, the first significant signs of the kinds of organizational and societal commitments that would characterize the vast majority of his writing and his adult life. His letters home continued, as did his outdoor expeditions, though both became less frequent and generally more pointed than they had been at Lawrenceville. The letters were now as often wry or sardonic as descriptive or meditative; and their subjects were more frequently human and institutional—the collegiate culture of a football game or the impracticality of latinate binomials

in plant morphology. His parents, who had earlier been concerned about what seemed to be his tendency to a lonely earnestness, now became concerned about the temptations of his several extracurricular engagements. He was taking in concerts and public lectures, too many of them; and he was missing too many classes; but he was also extending his conceptions of nature and "the great things," his views of the writing of nature, and not least his views of himself.

From East to West and Midwest Home Again

In 1909, Leopold literally lit out for the territory, with other newly minted disciples of conservationist Gifford Pinchot. Traveling by ship (the SS *Comus*) to New Orleans, he made his way to the territories of New Mexico and Arizona, to the headquarters of District 3 of the U.S. Forest Service in Albuquerque, and soon to his assigned post in the year-old Apache National Forest in east-central Arizona. After Yale and the East, after silviculture and the Latin binomials of plant morphology, the experience of some of the least settled lands remaining in the continental United States naturally created in him a clear sense of relief and release, a renewed acquaintance with, and a reaffirmation of, the landscape mythology of his childhood and youth. The apparently perpetual, clear running waters and the seemingly free grass of the territories (which did not become states until 1912) immediately replenished his youthful allegiances to the frontier and the wilderness. With but little stretching of the tone of his letters home, one might even say of his early days in the Apache that he often rode over its rims and ridges "with all the abandon, energy . . . and confidence epitomizing the becoming West."

He made rather egregious and embarrassing mistakes in his first efforts at forest reconnaissance. He misrepresented transits, misstated latitudes, miscalculated baselines, and in general continued to take lessons in locating himself. Only much later would he write in *Sand County* with an appreciative sense of irony for his time in the Apache: "We cruised timber there, converting the tall pines, forty by forty, into notebook figures representing hypothetical lumber piles. Panting up a canyon, the cruiser felt a curious incongruity between the remoteness of his notebook symbols and the immediacy of sweaty fingers, locust thorns, deer-fly bites, and scolding squirrels" (*Sand County*, pp. 133–134). In the meantime, he found—at a ranger station called Iris—"the most beautiful single place" he had ever seen in his life:

> From Iris one sees 100 miles into the Datils of New Mexico, and in the early morning a silvery veil hangs over the far away mesas and mountains—too delicate to be called a mist, too vast to be merely beautiful—it isn't describable, it has to be seen. And all framed in a little Iris-dotted meadow bordered by the tall orange-colored shafts and dark green foliage of the pines, with a little rippling, bubbling spring, half buried in the new green grass, flowing by the door. (Meine, p. 97)

Gradually, even without knowing it, he was coming to terms with the sciences and the aesthetics of wilderness, with the wild and the civilization of the wild, with the value of calculated prospects and perspectives ("one sees 100 miles"), with the names of nature ("the Datils of New Mexico") without which lasting appreciation is impossible, and with the limitations of the "merely beautiful."

From the Apache to the Carson National Forest of New Mexico (his next and longest set of assignments with the Forest Service), to his year (1918) as secretary of the Albuquerque Chamber of Commerce, through his years of affiliation with the New Mexico Game Protective Association and his increasingly complex work on erosion, grazing, wildlife, and recreation in the forests and watersheds of the Southwest, the underlying elements of Leopold's development as a nature writer remained rather constant. And more or less the same can be said of the years of his associations with the U.S. Forest Products Laboratory in Madison, Wisconsin (1924–1928), with the Sporting Arms and Ammunition Manufacturers' Institute (1928–

1931), with the Game Policy Committee of the American Game Conference, with the conservation agencies of Iowa and Wisconsin, with the Civilian Conservation Corps, the Wilderness Society, the Wildlife Society, and, finally, the Ecological Society of America. On the one hand, he maintained—even against steadily increasing evidence of insurmountable odds—his original and ongoing commitment to the idea and imagery of uncharted lands. On the other hand, he maintained and steadily extended his manifest countercommitment to the methods and institutions of the historic and the civilized, including, especially, those that sought to underwrite the meaning and value of uncharted lands, lands which viewed wisely, as he increasingly came to see, were the only hope for the truly civilized and civilizing.

Perhaps no single work of the years between the Apache and his final adjustments to *A Sand County Almanac* (1910–1948) is as clear a herald of what was to come—or, for that matter, of what lived on—as the unfinished manuscript essay entitled "The River of the Mother of God," dating roughly from 1924. Leopold began this essay, as he did so many others, with a characteristically simple and much-loaded statement. "I am conscious of a considerable personal debt to the continent of South America," he wrote; and listed, before getting to the big debt, some little ones—tires, coffee, rare woods, leather, medicines, and books about exotic animals and "ancient peoples," among others. But more than all of these, he explained, he was indebted to South America for "The River of the Mother of God":

> The river has been in my mind so long that I cannot recall just when or how I first heard of it. All that I remember is that long ago a Spanish Captain, wandering in some far Andean height, sent back word that he had found where a mighty river falls into the trackless Amazonian forest, and disappears. He had named it *el Rio Madre de Dios*. The Spanish Captain never came back. Like the river, he disappeared. But ever since some maps of South America have shown a short heavy line

running eastward beyond the Andes, a river without beginning and without end. (*River of the Mother of God*, p. 123)

As an expression of its author's ongoing concerns for the civilization of wilderness, the passage is so powerful and poignant that one is reluctant to elaborate or explicate. "That short heavy line," wrote Leopold, "flung down upon the blank vastness of tropical wilderness has always seemed the perfect symbol of the Unknown Places of the earth. And its name, resonant of the clank of silver armor and the cruel progress of the Cross, yet carrying a hush of reverence and a murmur of the prows of galleons on the seven seas, has always seemed the symbol of Conquest, the Conquest that has reduced those Unknown Places, one by one, until now there are none left" (pp. 123–124).

Begun, as far as we can tell, as Leopold left the national forests of the Southwest and took his position with the Forest Products Laboratory in Madison—begun, in other words, in the immediate aftermath of his own participation in the mapping and measuring of one of the last "unknown" places on the North America continent—the essay is a meditation of sorts, however unfinished, upon a time, all too immediate, when history, as previously learned and conceived, will virtually have ceased to be history, a time when history will have to be turned around, as it were, headed back east, perhaps. Written (or begun) in the same year in which, after five years of hard work in design and advocacy, Leopold saw the Gila National Forest officially designated as "wilderness," the essay is a torn and tellingly human piece of resigned advocacy and reluctant explanation, not a confession exactly, but an attempted acceptance of an inevitable closure. It represents the beginnings, at least, of a recognition of the historic and epistemological ironies in the designating and labeling of the unknown, the "Unknown" when it is clearly known as such. In it, Leopold recasts his understanding of "Unknown Places," of the concept and imagery of wildness and wilderness, and of the place of illusion in human endeavor. Having participated actively in the design and designation of a "wil-

derness," of an administrative wild and scenic area—and having committed himself to continue doing so—he doubts the efficacy of such designed "wild" areas. Like Frederick Jackson Turner, he worries about those less open times already upon us, and even more about those times to come, when designated surrogates for the wild and uncharted will have to suffice, when what will have to suffice will be "that capacity for illusion which enables little boys to fish happily in wash tubs," a capacity that, "if not overworked," is "a precious thing." At the same time, he worries openly about overworking that capacity—"To artificially create wilderness areas would overwork the capacity for illusion of even little boys with wash-tubs" (pp. 125, 127).

All in all, this essay—still much too little known, and even less studied—marks a turning point in the life of Aldo Leopold, both the so-called literal and cartographic turning point that brought him back to the midwest, but a turning point as well in his thinking and in his view of writing, in his understanding of illusions, in his manner of handling them, and in his appreciation of ambiguity and irony.

In the years between the Apache and *Sand County*—the years that encompassed "The River of the Mother of God"—when he was not writing, and often when he was, Leopold estimated timber sales and negotiated compromises between competing users of public lands. He developed the proposal for the Gila National Forest to be administered as a wilderness area, the first such administrative wilderness area in the nation. He undertook and completed systematic state- and regionwide surveys of wildlife populations (most particularly in the Southwest and Midwest). He designed and implemented model projects to bring together landowners and sportsmen to control erosion, restore soils, and reestablish indigenous vegetation. He completed *Game Management* (1933), and also in 1933 accepted an appointment as the nation's first professor of game management at the University of Wisconsin. In that position, and later as chairman of its successor, the Department of Wildlife Management, Leopold and his students counted, charted and otherwise sought to characterize and manage species after species (including the human) in situ, as it were, both in their relations to each other and in their relations to their inorganic surroundings. In short, he informed his senses of the vanishing unknown places with systematic and technical knowledge, and with hard-nosed experience of the politics and commerce of American land use.

As he came to comprehend the significance of transits and transects, of baselines and hypothetical lumber piles, of measures and methods without which his original loves could neither be counted nor accounted for, much less operatively valued, he became one of the nation's and the world's first ecologists. From hard experience in the arid Southwest and the dust bowl of the 1930s, he learned both that the waters were less perpetually clear and running than he had originally imagined or hoped, and that the grass, however green, was far from free. And he came to understand as well that transits and transects, and even short heavy lines on the map, needed to be viewed much more frequently than they were as hominid and hominoid habits and tools, not only of the twentieth-century but of the pleistocene or holocene. He came to understand, in other words, that the models, methods and measures of biological surveys and phenological studies were rather late developing means by which the modern Western branch of homo sapiens attempted to come to terms with want and fear. Like many so-called applied scientists, whose daily and seasonal actions directly (and often visibly) affect the distribution of what we call species, as well as the lives and deaths of particular individual organisms, he came to see himself as a human and hominid predator, however scientific, however caring. In part, at least, because of his continuing experiences as a hunter, he came to see himself as a scientific organism, competing and cooperating in the systems of which he was a part. He came to see (as he taught his students to see) that his and their phenological studies, chartings, and estimates of populations—their manipulations of the elements of what we too easily call land—were considerably less the disinterested accounts of disembodied and disconnected intellects than

they were the peregrinational mind-tracks of interested organisms. Like the field biologist who cannot help but think of destroying homes as he or she digs up the dens of foxes to account for the predatory impacts of one species upon others, he came increasingly to see himself and others of his biotic kind as organisms, however conscious, verbal, cultured, or literary.

Over the years between his reflections on that Spanish captain and his final adjustments to *Sand County*, Leopold gave varying and increasingly complex voice to this modern point of view. For some audiences, his voice was as direct and plain as he could make it, as it was, for example, in 1932, when he responded in *Condor* to what he called a "protectionist" critic of his recently published *Report on a Game Survey of the North Central States*. "Have we not already compromised ourselves?" Leopold asked, in a manner that echoed the Old Testament:

> I realize that every time I turn on an electric light, or ride on a Pullman, or pocket the unearned increment on a stock, or a bond, or a piece of real estate, I am "selling out" to the enemies of conservation. When I submit these thoughts to a printing press, I am helping cut down the woods. When I pour cream in my coffee, I am helping to drain a marsh for cows to graze, and to exterminate the birds of Brazil. When I go birding or hunting in my Ford, I am devastating an oil field, and re-electing an imperialist to get me rubber. Nay more: when I father more than two children I am creating an insatiable need for more printing presses, more cows, more coffee, more oil, and more rubber, to supply which more birds, more trees, and more flowers will either be killed, or what is just as destructive, evicted from their several environments.
>
> What to do? I see only two courses open to the likes of us. One is to go live on locusts in the wilderness, if there is any wilderness left. The other is surreptitiously to set up within the economic Juggernaut certain new cogs and wheels whereby the residual love of nature, inherent even in Rotarians, may be made to recreate at least a fraction of those values which their love of "progress" is destroying. (*River of the Mother of God*, pp. 165–166)

To other audiences, he would wax openly nostalgic and sentimental, or plainly programmatic and practical. To still others, more often than not professional, he came increasingly to emphasize and underscore the rather classical competing allegiances, ironies, and even paradoxes of his own and our Occidental condition. Thus, in the essay entitled "The Conservation Ethic," first published in *Journal of Forestry* (1933)—and parts of which he later reworked into "The Land Ethic" of *Sand County*—he asked, "Do I overdraw this paradox?" and then answered himself with "I think not," and went on to speak of "the welter of conflicting forces, facts, and opinions which so far compromise the result of the effort to harmonize our machine civilization with the land whence comes its sustenance." In that essay as in cognate phrasings elsewhere, he called attention to "conflicting conceptions of the end toward which we are working," spoke openly of the oxymoronic "idea of controlled wild culture or 'management,'" and called for readjustments in the "tensions" of what he called "the human medium"—the point being, of course, not to think of eliminating the tensions (they had long since become inescapable), but of adjusting them. In a companion piece to "The Conservation Ethic" entitled "Conservation Economics," and likewise published in *Journal of Forestry* (1934), he turned to a metaphor of "crossed wires" in yet another attempt to get at "the horns of this dilemma." In "Means and Ends in Wild Life Management," a lecture delivered to the Chamberlain Science Club at Beloit College in 1936, he went so far as to say that "the wild life manager is perforce a dual personality" (*River of the Mother of God*, p. 236); and in a book review published in *Bird-Lore* in 1937, he pressed the point even further, in speaking of a textbook entitled *Our Natural Resources and Their Conservation*. "Conservation," he wrote, "without a keen realization of its vital conflicts, fails to rate as authentic human drama; it falls to the level of a mere Utopian dream. Paradox is the earmark of valid truth. . . ."

In "Engineering and Conservation," a talk he gave to the University of Wisconsin College of Engineering in 1938, Leopold elaborated this notion of the truth of paradox, in speaking, as only a few ecologists even today would speak, of "ecological evils," thus revealing his by now seasoned understanding that both the good and the evil, both the beautiful and the ugly, both the ethical and the unethical, abide in ecosystems; and he concluded in what was becoming an increasingly characteristic two-sided manner, with a statement that might at once satisfy the part of his audience that sought a clear, conventional resolution and, yet, satisfy as well both his own sense of being an inseparable part of the processes of which he spoke (even as he spoke) and the senses of that part of his audience, however small, who saw as deeply as he did:

> We end, I think, at what might be called the standard paradox of the twentieth century: our tools are better than we are, and grow better faster than we do. They suffice to crack the atom, to command the tides. But they do not suffice for the oldest task in human history: to live on a piece of land without spoiling it. (*River of the Mother of God*, p. 254)

In a 1939 address to a joint meeting of the Society of American Foresters and the Ecological Society of America (later published in *Journal of Forestry*), Leopold spoke of "a peculiar dilemma" in which "the emergence of ecology has placed the economic biologist":

> With one hand he points out the accumulated findings of his search for utility, or lack of utility, in this or that species; with the other he lifts the veil from a biota so complex, so conditioned by interwoven cooperations and competitions, that no man can say where utility begins or ends. No species can be "rated" without the tongue in the cheek; the old categories of "useful" and "harmful" have validity only as conditioned by time, place, and circumstance. The only sure conclusion is that the biota as a whole is useful, and biota includes not only plants and animals, but soils and waters as well.

In short, economic biology assumed that the biotic function and economic utility of a species was partly known and the rest could shortly be found out. That assumption no longer holds good; the process of finding out added new questions faster than new answers. The function of species is largely inscrutable, and may remain so. (*River of the Mother of God*, pp. 266–267)

In the last analysis, as Leopold now knew, the dilemma of the "economic biologist" was far less "peculiar," and rather more classical, than he might otherwise have seemed to imply; for, as he also knew by now, there really were no noneconomic biologists, and despite the centrality of species to biology, ecology, and wildlife management, no one had ever seen one. All science was, by ecologic definition, applied science.

Throughout the years during which he wrote the first elements of what would become *Sand County*, Leopold became more and more a self-conscious writer of nature, and his figures of thought and speech increasingly reflected the fact. "To him who reads fencerows, thickets, and fields as the letters of a great and tragic history," he said, "the direction to go is clear" (*River of the Mother of God*, p. 162). "There is hardly an acre," he wrote, "that does not tell its own story to those who understand the speech of hills and rivers" (*River of the Mother of God*, p. 175). He spoke of "the alphabet of conservation" or "the alphabet devised by taxonomy and natural history," and then of the process of building "ecological words or sentences" ("Teaching Wildlife Conservation in the Public Schools," 1937). He spoke of the "language" of flora and fauna—and of the very "few lines here and there" that even he was able to understand (in "The Farmer as a Conservationist," 1939). A year before he died, he spoke to his students of trying to teach them that "this alphabet of 'natural objects' (soils and rivers, birds and beasts) spells out a story, which he who runs may read—if he knows how" (*River of the Mother of God*, p. 337). In short, he took on fully the classic metaphor of reading the book of nature, and added to it the more modern consciousness of participating in the writing of it.

Like any sensitive writer trying simultaneously to satisfy himself as well as his audience, Leopold seldom, if ever, overplayed the self-reflexive elements of his prose and his understanding. In fact, he so subdued his self-reflexive voice that many readers and critics refuse to accept its evidence even today; yet one strongly suspects that it is just this subdued self-consciousness, this sense of himself as organism, even as he writes, this sense of himself as a product of history, and the humility that sense expresses, that have made *Sand County* much more than a short-lived work of environmental advocacy— or, rather, that have made it amenable both to environmental advocacy and to the deeper, more tragic visions of self-conscious nature writing.

The Final Statement

The story of the gestation and publication of *A Sand County Almanac* is a story both of the maturation of a nature writer and of what has proved to be a new form of American nature writing. Through the mid 1930s, Leopold had confined the vast majority of what most of us would call his nature writing to letters and journals, to illustrative segments of lectures and speeches, and to an occasional embryonic essay. Even if he had tried his hand from time to time at an essay such as "The River of the Mother of God," generally he had been far too busy with professional activities and engagements, with reports to agencies and talks to organizations, to give much extended time to amplifying and refining the belletristic prose which had been his original inclination, if not his first love.

By the late 1930s, however, he had begun to turn a greater proportion of his writing time and attention toward the meditatively descriptive and narratively reflective. Encouraged, perhaps, by a growing sense that his audiences most valued his illustrative vignettes, his parabolic tales, and aphoristic phrasings, he turned increasingly toward nature writing—to "The Thick-billed Parrot in Chihuahua," for example (published in *Condor* in 1937 and reprinted in

Sand County as "Guacamaja"); to "Marshland Elegy" (first published in *American Forests* in 1937); and, no doubt as important to the eventual development of *Sand County*, to a long series of brief, highly popular articles in *Wisconsin Agriculturalist and Farmer* (1938–1942). In the spring of 1940 he wrote the first draft of what would become *Sand County*'s "The Geese Return," and that summer he published "Song of the Gavilan" (*Journal of Wildlife Management*) and produced a draft version of "Escudilla," each of which eventually found a place in *Sand County*.

By early 1941, at least, Leopold was thinking of putting together an illustrated book of essays, although by no means yet of the particular configuration that would become his final and classic statement—rather, of the kinds of essays he had been writing recently. By midsummer, he had written two more essays that would eventually appear in the second section of *Sand County*. The first was a celebration of a Manitoba marsh named "Clandeboye"; the second, "Cheat Takes Over," was the result of summer work throughout the West with the U.S. Fish and Wildlife Service. By September, Leopold was reworking "The Geese Return" and had published a version of another sketch that would appear in the first section of *Sand County*, a piece entitled "Sky Dance of Spring" (part of a booklet produced by the *Wisconsin Agriculturalist and Farmer*). By later fall, he was thinking even more seriously about "the book," and had begun tinkering with additional essays that derived from his own and his family's experiences at the old farm shack/renovated chicken coop in central Wisconsin that he had purchased in 1935, and upon which he and the family had been working steadily over the intervening years. Among these essays was a touching piece about a particular banded chickadee that had returned to the farm for five winters, the patriarch, at last, of his generation.

November 1941 brought an unsolicited inquiry from an editor at Alfred A. Knopf, about the prospect of a book that would capture the personal field experiences of professionals in wildlife management, a book Leopold thought could only be written by several hands. He was working on what he envisioned as an illustrated Christmas book of "ecological essays" for the following year. The editor at Knopf was immediately interested, and requested whatever of the manuscript Leopold had in hand. And then the United States entered full force into World War II.

Well over a year passed before correspondence with Knopf resumed, and Leopold was by then deep into the politics, commerce, and science of Wisconsin's deer herds, among several other matters of state, national, and continental resource management. The book of essays was slow in developing because Leopold was a busy and painstaking writer. Still, in the intervening time, he had managed to write or draft seven additional essays that ultimately appeared in *Sand County*; and between April 1943 and April 1944, he wrote or drafted at least six more. Eight of these thirteen essays would ultimately appear among the personal reminiscences in Part I of *Sand County*, two in the more broadly ranging essays of Part II, and one in the abstract and philosophical Part III. Seven of the thirteen were published in 1942 and 1943.

In response to the comments and criticisms of those with whom he shared the essays he had so far drafted, written, and published—in reponse, particularly, to one of his most talented students, Albert H. Hochbaum—Leopold set out, in the spring of 1944, to write an essay in which he faced directly his own early role in the extermination of predators in the ecosystems of the American Southwest. Hochbaum had complained to Leopold that he too often seemed to convey an air of unwarranted superiority—unwarranted largely because nowhere in his essays thus far did he seem forthrightly to confront his own early efforts to do the very things for which he now so often seemed to be disparaging others. The developing book of essays demanded a kind of forthright confession, Hochbaum thought—preferably a confession of its author's early role in the killing of southwestern wolves, or, at the very least an acknowledgment—that would underscore his mentor's essential humility, and would put his and others' early actions and attitudes into historical and ecological perspective.

We will probably never know just how much impact Hochbaum's comments and criticisms had upon the tonal refinements of *Sand County* as a whole, but we do know that Leopold's famous essay "Thinking Like a Mountain" was a direct result of his suggestions. In it, Leopold spoke not only of a trigger-happy youth, or of the terribly limited views and methods of the early days of wildlife management, but also, if less directly, of the differently limited views of his own later years:

> We all strive for safety, prosperity, comfort, long life, and dullness. The deer strives with his supple legs, the cowman with trap and poison, the statesman with pen, the most of us with machines, votes, and dollars, but it all comes to the same thing: peace in our time. A measure of success in this is all well enough, and perhaps is a requisite to objective thinking, but too much safety seems to yield only danger in the long run. . . . Perhaps this is the hidden meaning in the howl of the wolf, long known among mountains, but seldom perceived among men. (*Sand County*, p. 133)

In the last analysis, Leopold did not so much confess in "Thinking Like a Mountain." Or if he did, he confessed to much more than later understandings of wildlife management, of biomes and biota, were empowered to forgive. He did not so much drop his "superior," ironic voice as extend and deepen it, and with it, the sweeping, almost metaphysical humility that went with it. "We all strive for safety . . . and dullness," he wrote in April 1944, the deer among us; and "it all comes to the same thing: peace in our time." The statement, famous as it is, is far more, and far more deeply, ironic than it may appear to be. Indeed, it is most probably doubly or triply ironic, as a kind of statement, certainly, about his own early conceptions, but also as a statement about the light cast by World War II upon his own and his students' endeavors, and, finally, as a statement upon the peace that inevitably accompanies each of us at the end of our time. There is even, perhaps, a

shadow of the aging, but still competitive organism about it. Deeply humble as it is — self- and ultimately even species-effacing — it retains a characteristic and critical feistiness no doubt because "too much safety seems to yield only danger in the long run."

Albert Hochbaum to the contrary, there were many essays in what would become *Sand County* that entertained and dramatized the underlying perspective of "Thinking Like a Mountain." Still, Leopold was practical enough to realize that if he had not been speaking fully to one of his best students, he certainly would not speak to other prospective readers or to the editors at Knopf, or to the editor of "outdoor" books for Macmillan, whom he met at a conference in late spring of 1944, and who also was much interested in Leopold's "books," in part, at least, because Leopold was by this time the elder and respected statesman in an increasingly significant field of study.

In June 1944, Leopold pulled together for both Macmillan and Knopf not what he had of his book-to-be but the kinds of things with which he was most clearly satisfied and in which he thought the editors were most interested. The result was a blend of eight essays that would eventually appear in Part II of *Sand County* and five essays that would ultimately appear in Part I: "Marshland Elegy," "Song of the Gavilan," "Guacamaja," "Escudilla," "Smoky Gold," "Odyssey," "Draba," "Great Possessions," "The Green Lagoons," "Illinois Bus Ride," "Pines Above the Snow," "Thinking Like a Mountain," and "The Geese Return." Of the thirteen essays he selected, five had been published; and his preferred title of the moment was "Thinking Like a Mountain and Other Essays." "The object" of the essays, he wrote to both editors, "is to convey an ecological view of land and conservation" (Meine, p. 460).

As the responses of both Knopf and Macmillan indicate, in several fundamental ways Leopold was ahead of his time. Macmillan rejected his manuscript more or less outright, and probably for some of the same reasons that Knopf sent him a highly qualified review. Both publishers were obviously looking for a more

Leopold at his shack in central Wisconsin, 1947

conventionally sanguine kind of nature writing than Leopold had provided, something more in what they no doubt thought of as the tradition of *Walden*, or of John Burroughs' reflections at Slabsides, or of Henry Beston's on Cape Cod; and Knopf elaborated its concerns, even while appreciating Leopold's stylistic talents. Knopf's editor found the essays too various in subject, length, style, and point of view, and urged Leopold to find either a unifying theme or a single setting for the book, and preferably both. In either way, Knopf wanted Leopold to undertake more elemental narrative and descriptive essays, more intimate, local, and conventionally appreciative observations of "nature," and to dissuade him from his inclination to "ecological" ideas and theories, as well as his tendencies to criticize the course of American history and land-use.

The issues were essentially the same in November 1947, when Knopf rejected a substantially revised version of the book. By then,

Leopold had rethought and rearranged almost the entirety of his manuscript. He had written additional essays of the Sand County shack, and he had adopted the notion of an almanac as a means of organizing them. He had gotten Knopf's initially positive response to some of his more philosophic writings and, tentatively, to his suggestion that they might be included in the book. He had written an autobiographical and introductory foreword, and he had organized the manuscript into three parts: the first the almanac of the shack, the second a collection of reflective essays that ranged over a good part of the North American continent (to which he had added two in the last year and a half), and the third an arrangement of wholes and parts of his more abstract writings, some of which he had written much earlier and others of which he had written recently. He had been encouraged particularly by complimentary responses to a rather aggressive speech he had delivered in Minneapolis in June to the Conservation Committee of the Garden Club of America, a speech entitled "The Ecological Conscience," which had immediately been printed, then reprinted and excerpted in several periodicals. Clearly, he was reading a good part of his audience well, even in his most aggressive voice—far better, it would turn out, than were the editors at Knopf. Sometime in late summer, buoyed by his successes in Minneapolis, he had put together the essay for which he is now best known, "The Land Ethic."

When he received his response from Knopf in early November of 1947, Leopold was plain angry. The manuscript would neither work nor sell as a book, he had been told; and the editors and readers of the manuscript seemed clearly to have missed not only his many fine-tunings, but also and far more, most of the basic argument of the work: "What we like best is the nature observations, and the more objective narratives and essays. We like less the subjective parts— that is, the philosophical reflections, which are less fresh, and which one reader finds sometimes 'fatuous.' The ecological argument everyone finds unconvincing; and as in previous drafts, it is not tied up with the rest of the book" (Meine, p. 509). Just so, in what was very close to its final phrasing, and the essence of its final form, Aldo Leopold's manuscript was written off. The editors and readers of Knopf had proven to be less advanced thinkers and less precise observers or listeners than had the members of the Garden Club of America. With their straitjacketed "nature observations" and their stereotypical distinctions between "the more objective" and "the subjective," the editors had apparently missed out on a good deal of the intellectual history of the first half of the twentieth century; and they no doubt seemed to Leopold as much a part of the problem he was attempting to address as they seemed readers capable of comprehending it. They apparently had missed the not-so-implicit ecological arguments in the several episodes of Part I, the rather obvious ecological arguments of Part II, and the ultimately much personal voice of Part III. They were looking for an uncritical appreciation of nature, as we say, and no doubt for some sanguine celebration of "the wilderness experience," in the aftermath

not only of the dust bowl and World War II, but also of the establishment of administrative wilderness areas and refuges for wildlife. They seemed to know next to nothing of the historic ironies in "controlled wild culture," next to nothing of that Spanish captain, and not even much of little boys in washtubs. They wanted a pleasant narrative of activities at the sand-county shack, a narrative, they said, that would provide "a natural continuity that the present book lacks" (Meine, p. 509). The phrase "natural continuity" by itself must have been enough to provoke anger.

Leopold almost gave up on his book in November 1947; but his second son, Luna, kept him going, told him that he simply was not tough enough to negotiate with editors and publishers, and more or less insisted that his father put the manuscript and the negotiations in his son's hands. The father agreed, and by late November Oxford University Press was interested in reading his manuscript. He recovered his energy in corresponding with Oxford, wrote a notable meditation entitled "Axe-in-Hand" for the "November" chapter of the almanac, and in early December, rewrote and shortened the foreword to the manuscript, took out its autobiographical elements, and tied it rather closely to the ideas and commitments of "The Land Ethic." In mid December he sent the manuscript, augmented and further refined, both to Oxford and to William Sloane Associates.

Compliments for "The Ecological Conscience" continued to arrive; and although his eyes were troubling him, in early 1948 Leopold wrote another essay that would appear in the first section of the book, the "Good Oak" that would become "February." In late winter, he revised his recently rewritten foreword; and in April—on the same day he recommended to other members of the Wisconsin Conservation Commission that the homestead farm of John Muir's family be treated as a kind of ecological history of central Wisconsin—he got a call from Oxford University Press informing him that his book had been accepted for publication. All he had to do was to reserve time in the upcoming summer for recommended adjustments and adaptations to the manuscript. Within a day, he had all but signed the contract; and within six additional days, he died (on 21 April), fighting, at age sixty-one, a grass fire on a neighbor's farm that threatened to jump to the old farm shack/ renovated chicken coop. He was buried in the Western, eastward-looking bluffs of his childhood Burlington.

After Leopold died, his son Luna shepherded the manuscript of the book to publication. He did a bit of retitling and rearranging in which his father's last "Good Oak" played a role; and he moved "The Land Ethic" to the end of Part III, so it became the capstone of "The Upshot." Otherwise, Luna made few changes in the manuscript, although he and the editors at Oxford spent considerable time trying to come up with a title that might be more explicitly indicative than Leopold's "Great Possessions" seemed to be. The editors at Oxford, unlike those at Knopf, were searching for a title that would establish the book's kinship to such works as Fairfield Osborn's *Our Plundered Planet* and William Vogt's *Road to Survival*, both published in 1948. Several suggested titles rightly spoke of a sense of loss; but none of them was simultaneously adequate to Leopold's sustaining sense of great possessions, including especially his sense of the ongoing inheritance of the wild and frontiered. In the end, Luna and the editors at Oxford settled on *A Sand County Almanac and Sketches Here and There*.

In 1949, *A Sand County Almanac and Sketches Here and There* was an unusual work, as it still is in many ways, certainly as unusual as the editors of Macmillan and Knopf had thought it to be. In combining elements of the practical and philosophically programmatic with the highly personal and historically critical, it marked a turning point in the history of American nature writing. It was as if elements of Henry Thoreau's personal and individualistic protests had been put together with the active, professionally informed social criticism of Fairfield Osborn's *Our Plundered Planet*. It was as if Thoreau's intense self-examination had somehow come together with what, in little more than another decade, would be the sadly sharp

scientific criticism of Rachel Carson's *Silent Spring* (1962). It was as if the rhetorical stances of the meditative and appreciative John Muir had coalesced in one work with the rhetoric of Muir the political and programmatic activist.

Certainly *Sand County*'s combination of these traits explains a good deal of its growing renown in the late 1960s and beyond, when it finally came into its own, when—like Edward Abbey's *Desert Solitaire* (1968) or Josephine Johnson's *The Inland Island* (1969)—it was far more widely appreciated than it was in the late 1940s. By the late 1960s, clearly increasing numbers of Americans were finding in *Sand County* a style of thinking that enabled them to begin, at least, to come to terms with closed frontiers and the attitudes of closed systems, with legislated wilderness areas, with wildlife management and wildlife refuges, with "controlled wild culture." Difficult as the underlying message may have been to accept—almost "un-American" though it may occasionally have seemed—the style that carried it seemed almost entirely reassuring—even hopeful, perhaps. Some anger and bitterness may have been behind it, but if so, they seemed well enough behind it. Little, if any, serious distress or anxiety seemed apparent on the surface; and what one might have noticed of ambiguity, irony, and paradox could apparently be skipped without losing much if anything of its author's major statement. If the book seemed to say, finally, that a love of wild things simply is not consonant, and never really has been, either with a sanguine appreciation of nature or with an uncritical and naively Jeremiadic lament of its loss or passing (in the manner of Frederick Jackson Turner), it did so in subdued and comforting tones. Its narrator and expositor, and even its scientific and ethical critic, seemed at home with ambiguity and paradox, resigned to them in a way that, far from being fatalistic, was purposeful and ultimately content. The complexities of his episodes, critiques, and commentaries, if one noticed them, were like the complexities and momentary puzzlements of ancient parables. He embodied his comments and criticisms of the historic geography of the continent in personal vignettes of particular locales and biomes, of particular mountains and watersheds, of a particular dying wolf and even of a particular chickadee. All in all, it was a subtle way of seeing and speaking, occasionally puzzling, perhaps, but if deceptive or paradoxical, then pleasantly so.

Many readers of the late 1960s and beyond thus experienced in *Sand County* a new form of American nature writing; but it was new, finally, more in its vocabulary and its concepts, its modern articulations, than it was in its underlying issues or dramas. There was much of *Walden* and Thoreau's *Journals* in it, as much certainly as there was of *Our Plundered Planet*. In two brief paragraphs of *Sand County*'s very first chapter, for example — two brief paragraphs ostensibly about the narrator-speaker, a meadow mouse, and a "January" thaw — one might find the man of Sand County seeming almost to satirize both the organized economic systems of humankind and the analogous systems of the mouse:

> A meadow mouse, startled by my approach, darts damply across the skunk track. Why is he abroad in daylight? Probably because he feels grieved about the thaw. Today his maze of secret tunnels, laboriously chewed through the matted grass under the snow, are tunnels no more, but only paths exposed to public view and ridicule. Indeed the thawing sun has mocked the basic premises of the microtine economic system!
>
> The mouse is a sober citizen who knows that grass grows in order that mice may store it as underground haystacks, and that snow falls in order that mice may build subways from stack to stack; supply, demand, and transport all neatly organized. To the mouse, snow means freedom from want and fear. (*Sand County*, p. 4)

If one's first instinct is to label such a passage "satiric," one's second instinct, informed by the underlying and rather obvious similarities of need and attitude between human and nonhuman species, is to query one's first instinct, to look further for the basic premises of the pas-

sage, to label it "ironic," perhaps. But why render ironic the tunnels and paths of an obviously "unthinking" meadow mouse, of which (or is it "of whom" by now?) one clearly expects so little by way of consciousness, much less of self-consciousness? One's first instinct again (or is it by now a thought?) — that it simply will not do to expose, ironically or otherwise, the sober, anthropomorphic citizenship of a being which clearly does not have the capacity to be a citizen, or to formulate and promulgate what we call "premises," much less to discern meaning. Just whose quest for "freedom" from want and fear are we dealing with here? Just whose tunnels and paths are being exposed to "public view and ridicule"? Is the speaker, the narrator and expositor (and, for that matter, the reader), not aware of the exposure which this thaw has affected upon his own now-not-so-secret paths and tunnels, the basic premises of his microtine system? Just who is abroad in daylight here? Just who is grieved about what thaw?

This is the way of *Sand County*. As it repeatedly demonstrates, an uncritical appreciation of what we call "nonhuman nature" misrepresents the ecosystem in which it abides and, coincidentally, the uncritical appreciator. The narrator and expositor of *Sand County* knows from the beginning, as it were (if sometimes more deeply than he would like to), that an uncritical appreciation of wilderness and wild things — an appreciation that attempts to divorce the human from the nonhuman, and most of all, perhaps, to separate our personal quests for freedom from want and fear from our accounts, scientific or otherwise, of meadow mice — is just as misleading and destructive in the long haul as an uncritical and comparably unself-conscious "use" of "our natural resources" — indeed, that the two views are two sides of the same historic coin.

Thus, the human figure of Sand County presses upon us both the seemingly pleasant narrative details of thinning his woodlot in "November" and the fundamental philosophical issues and understandings that are parts of it (whether we know it or not), all by way of arguing that we ought to be more aware of them, that our actions and our judgments ought to be far more querying, analytic, and self-reflexive than they conventionally are. Just after having spoken of the conservationist as "one who is humbly aware that with each stroke he is writing his signature on the face of his land," just after having said that "signatures of course differ, whether written with axe or pen," he brings to mind one of those questions that underlie all our differing signatures (*Sand County*, p. 68). He finds it "disconcerting" to analyze his own "axe-in-hand decisions," but he goes on immediately to do so, and in the process, finds further, with characteristic touches of irony, that "not all trees are created free and equal," that where white pines and red birch are crowding each other, he has "an *a priori* bias," that he always cuts "the birch to favor the pine." But why, he wonders, does he do so? It may be that he himself planted the pine, whereas the birch moved in on its own; or it may be simply that the birch is more common in his locale; or it may be that the pine will eventually bring more dollars per board-foot than will the birch. But none of these conventionally comparative evaluations seems sufficient to account for his prejudice. So he tries again, thinking that now he may have found something more promising by way of an answer or explanation:

> Under this pine will ultimately grow a trailing arbutus, an Indian pipe, a pyrola, or a twin flower, whereas under the birch a bottle gentian is about the best to be hoped for. In this pine a pileated woodpecker will ultimately chisel out a nest; in the birch a hairy will have to suffice. In this pine the wind will sing for me in April, at which time the birch is only rattling naked twigs. These possible reasons for my bias carry weight, but why? Does the pine stimulate my imagination and my hopes more deeply than the birch does? If so, is the difference in the trees, or in me? (*Sand County*, pp. 69–70)

Thus, the man in Sand County poses, virtually between strokes of his "Axe-in-Hand," one of the classical questions of Western philosophy, a question integral to thinning a woodlot or to formulating a management plan or to advocating an ethic. In just this way, he brings home to particular personal decisions the basics of what philosophers call value theory. He does not find an answer, of course; but in the process of raising such age-old questions, both his cuttings and his writing become more conscious, more self-conscious, and conscientious than they might otherwise have been.

In an essentially similar fashion, his "Marshland Elegy" (the first subchapter of "Wisconsin," which, in turn, is the first chapter of Part II of *Sand County*) begins (or seems to begin) as an elegiac and present-tense meditation upon sandhill cranes and their pleistoscenic marshes. It then moves into a past-tense critique of the Civilian Conservation Corps of the 1930s, and ends with a set of statements that lead one to question one's initial impressions, to wonder just for whom or what this elegy is being sung:

> Solitude, the one natural resource still undowered of alphabets, is so far recognized as valuable only by ornithologists and cranes.
>
> Thus always does history, whether of marsh or market place, end in paradox. The ultimate value in these marshes is wildness, and the crane is wildness incarnate. But all conservation of wildness is self-defeating, for to cherish we must see and fondle, and when enough have seen and fondled, there is no wilderness left to cherish. (*Sand County*, p. 101)

Some of the paradoxes are subtle: "The one natural resource still undowered of alphabets." Others are painful and deeply poignant, like the self-defeating cherishment of wildness to which the statement itself and the book are dedicated. Still others, apparently, are a good deal less paradoxical. "Thus always does history . . . end in paradox."

All appearances to the contrary, the same kinds of thing can be said of the more abstract, less narrative and imagistic, and more pointedly philosophical Part III of *Sand County*, the section entitled "The Upshot." In the paragraph immediately preceding the introduction of the by-now-famous, final chapter of the book, the chapter entitled "The Land Ethic," the man of Sand County presents what may have been his own preferred last word both upon that ethic and upon the legacy of wilderness and wild things that it seeks to address and conserve:

> Ability to see the cultural value of wilderness boils down, in the last analysis, to a question of intellectual humility. The shallow-minded modern who has lost his rootage in the land assumes that he has already discovered what is important; it is such who prate of empires, political or economic, that will last a thousand years. It is only the scholar who appreciates that all history consists of successive excursions from a single starting-point, to which man returns again and again to organize yet another search for a durable scale of values. It is only the scholar who understands why the raw wilderness gives definition and meaning to the human enterprise. (*Sand County*, pp. 200–201)

"The raw wilderness" thus "gives definition and meaning to the human enterprise," because it represents that single starting-point—that historical and, so far as what we call hominids are concerned, that evolutionary ground zero—"to which man returns again and again to organize yet another search for a durable scale of values." That, if one may so phrase the matter, is "the cultural value of wilderness," the definition and meaning it gives to all elements of "the human enterprise," including that last phrase, and including as well "The Land Ethic" soon to follow. Without "raw wilderness"—without a mental image of it, without memory of it, without experience of it—its opposite, "the human enterprise," neither has nor can have meaning. And the opposite is also true. Without "the human enterprise," "raw wilderness" neither has nor can have meaning.

Although "the shallow-minded modern" may have lost sight of the fact, he has not lost his rootage in the land. He could not lose it if he tried. As long as "the shallow-minded modern" continues to live—and, for that matter, even when he dies—he cannot lose his rootage in the

land, not even when he thinks he has. The proof of his shallow-minded modernity lies in his manner of speaking as if he has lost touch with the land, lost touch with nature, as some people are still inclined to say, or, conversely, as if he has somehow subdued it or otherwise triumphed over it. Far from being the co-equal of nature or the land, much less some especially alienated beast, he is the co-equal of far less than he thinks he is, and no more alienated, despite his pride, than any other organism. He is, in fact, neither more nor less than "one of thousands of accretions to the height and complexity" of "the biotic pyramid," a "biotic pyramid" which itself is neither more nor less than one of the "mental images" he creates and uses in seeking, like the meadow mouse, to be free of want and fear, determined as all get out not to be exposed by the revelations of some "January" thaw (*Sand County Almanac*, pp. 215–216). So much for the shallow-minded modern.

The deep-minded modern knows his own inescapably anthropomorphic limitations, including the limitations of his ethics and aesthetics, his science and his almanacs. He knows that his ethics, including here his land ethic, presume "the existence of some mental image of land as a biotic mechanism"—"the biotic pyramid"—and that likewise his metaethics, his views of the history and functions of ethics, presume some concept of some presumed mental image of land as biotic mechanism. Although intellectual humility in no way demands or devalues his critique of the shallow-minded modern, it does demand an awareness of his bioethical interests in making the critique. It demands precisely the awareness which he criticizes the shallow-minded modern for lacking. It demands an awareness of the rather simple biotic fact that one's critiques, like one's ethics, are functions of one's place or places in ecosystems—precisely the awareness that the deep-minded man of Sand County regularly extends to himself and his composition, in order to follow and account for his own tracks, as it were.

In the last analysis, it is this capacity to acknowledge and account for his own ecosystemic tracks that makes Leopold's land ethic so compelling. It is not, finally, his pithy, quotable, aphoristic propositions—"A thing is right when it tends to preserve the integrity, stability, and beauty of the biotic community. It is wrong when it tends otherwise" (*Sand County*, pp. 224–225)—and certainly not their prospects of formal validation, but his disposition to put and keep those propositions, like his reflections on crane marshes and meadow mice, in historical, evolutionary, and ecological perspective. It is his capacity to say with clearly apparent conviction, for example, that "An ethic, ecologically, is a limitation on freedom of action in the struggle for existence" (*Sand County*, p. 202), at the same time that he otherwise reminds both himself and his audience that no organism, human or non-human, has ever known "freedom of action in the struggle for existence"—in short that there is no such thing as ecological or energetic freedom. What finally distinguishes Leopold's work, then—his "Upshot" and his "Land Ethic," no less than his almanac and his sketches—is his capacity to appeal to a modern, Western, and American understanding of social and political contracts—and, at the same time, to remind us of what we know of the ongoing "struggle" for existence.

"The Land Ethic," then, is no salvation or justification, not even if it could be fully adopted and implemented; and the man of Sand County knows that it is not. It is, however, an attempted adaptation, neither more nor less than another in the series of successive excursions from that "single starting-point, to which man returns again and again to organize yet another search for a durable scale of values." As Leopold said to his students in Wildlife Ecology 118 in the spring of 1941:

Every living thing represents an equation of give and take. Man or mouse, oak or orchid, we take a livelihood from our land and our fellows, and give in return an endless succession of acts and thoughts, each of which changes us, our fellows, our land, and its capacity to yield us a further living. Ultimately we give ourselves. (Meine, pp. 413–414; *River of the Mother of God*, p. 281)

Selected Bibliography

WORKS OF ALDO LEOPOLD

BOOKS

Report on a Game Survey of the North Central States (Madison, Wis.: Sporting Arms and Ammunition Manufacturers' Institute, 1931); *Game Management* (New York: Scribners, 1933; repr., Madison: Univ. of Wisconsin Press, 1986); *A Sand County Almanac and Sketches Here and There* (New York: Oxford Univ. Press, 1949; 1968; 1987); *Round River: From the Journals of Aldo Leopold*, ed. by Luna B. Leopold (New York: Oxford Univ. Press, 1953, 1972; repr., Minocqua, Wis.: NorthWord, 1991); *A Sand County Almanac with Other Essays on Conservation from* Round River (New York: Oxford Univ. Press, 1966), repr. as *A Sand County Almanac with Essays on Conservation from* Round River (New York: Ballantine Books, 1970); *The River of the Mother of God and Other Essays by Aldo Leopold*, ed. by Susan L. Flader and J. Baird Callicott (Madison: Univ. of Wisconsin Press, 1991).

Except for his *Report on a Game Survey* and *Game Management*, no book listed or published under Aldo Leopold's name may be said to be his because its final composition and publication were not overseen by its author. Each of the books identified and associated with Aldo Leopold is a posthumous publication, published without the author's counsel. The inclusion and arrangements of the parts are generally not his, except in the original (1949) edition of *A Sand County Almanac*, the edition quoted herein. In fact, even the arrangement of the original edition of *Sand County* is in significant part the work of others—in the placement of its final, famous chapter, "The Land Ethic," for example.

If even the original edition of *Sand County* is thus something less than Leopold's own book, both *Round River* and two later editions of *Sand County* are even less so. As fate would have it, several of the parts of *Round River*, several of Leopold's manuscript essays first published in *Round River*, have for many readers become entangled (if not identified) with *A Sand County Almanac*. In 1966, eight of those essays from *Round River* were incorporated into a substantially modified, hardbound "Enlarged Edition" of *A Sand County Almanac*, the edition entitled *A Sand County Almanac with Other Essays on Conservation from* Round River, arranged (or rearranged) and slightly edited by Leopold's son, Luna, and his wife, Carolyn Clugston Leopold. In 1970, this enlarged edition was reproduced in a popular, paperback edition by Ballantine Books, two years after Oxford University Press itself had reprinted the original edition of *Sand County* in paperback. Both that original edition in paperback and the enlarged Ballantine edition, different as they are, were in print throughout the 1970s, 1980s, and early 1990s. From the early 1970s onward, then, members of *Sand County*'s increasing and increasingly appreciative audience have been able to quote accurately from what they took to be *Sand County*, and yet to find themselves quoting from two quite different books.

To further complicate the matter of what readers mean when they speak of Aldo Leopold's *Sand County Almanac*, Oxford University Press "replaced" its enlarged, hardbound edition of 1966 with a hardbound, commemorative edition of the original *Sand County* (1949) in the centenary year (1987) of Aldo Leopold's birth. In view of these rather radically varying editions of *A Sand County Almanac*, it is best to quote either from the original edition (1949) or from one of its two reprintings (the Oxford Press paperback of 1968 or the commemorative hardbound edition of 1987). Except for slight variations in the table of contents, the printing and pagination of the primary text in each of these later Oxford editions is identical to the original.

ESSAYS, ARTICLES, REVIEWS

The most complete and convenient guides to the five hundred or more articles, essays, reviews, handbooks, newsletters, and reports that Leopold published in his lifetime are the extensive bibliographies in Curt Meine, *Aldo Leopold: His Life and Work* (Madison: Univ. of Wisconsin Press, 1988), and Susan L. Flader and J. Baird Callicott, eds., *The River of the Mother of God and Other Essays by Aldo Leopold* (Madison: Univ. of Wisconsin Press, 1991). Many of Leopold's most important published articles and essays, including several mentioned and quoted herein, are reprinted in *The River of the Mother of God*. Several of the articles and essays reprinted in *The River of the Mother of God* are reprinted as well—along with several others devoted to land and game management in the American Southwest—in David E. Brown and Neil B. Carmony, eds., *Aldo Leopold's Wilderness: Selected Early Writings by the Author of* A Sand County Almanac (Harrisburg, Pa: Stackpole Books, 1990). Leopold's published writings—many other essays, articles, reports, reviews, and even poems—played a significant role in his development as a nature writer. The following are mentioned or quoted herein: "The Conservation Ethic," in *Journal of Forestry* 31 (October 1933); Review of A. E. Parkins and J. R. Whitaker, *Our Natural Resources and Their Conservation*, in *Bird-Lore* 39 (January/February, 1937); "Teaching Wildlife Conservation in Public Schools," in *Transactions of the Wisconsin Academy of Sciences, Arts, and Letters* 30 (1937); "The Thick-billed Parrot in Chihuahua," in *Condor* 39 (January/February 1937); "Marshland Elegy," in *American For-*

ests 43 (October 1937); "The Farmer as Conservationist," in *American Forests* 45 (June 1939); "When Geese Return Spring Is Here," in *Wisconsin Agriculturalist and Farmer* 67 (April 1940); "Song of the Gavilan," in *Journal of Wildlife Management* 4 (July 1940); "Escudilla," in *American Forests* 46 (December 1940); "Cheat Takes Over," in *The Land* 1 (autumn 1941); "The Ecological Conscience," in *Bulletin of the Garden Club of America* (September 1947).

MANUSCRIPTS

Well over half of what Leopold wrote, including an immense amount germane to his development as a nature writer, remains unpublished, much of it in the University of Wisconsin–Madison Archives, but significant amounts as well in several other collections and repositories. For guides to these unpublished works and for cues to their locations, see Meine's biography, *Aldo Leopold: His Life and Work*, as well as Flader and Callicott's *The River of the Mother of God*. In building his portrait of Leopold, Meine quotes from many of these manuscript sources; and several of the most influential and revealing of these manuscripts (manuscripts of Leopold's professional and public lectures, for example) are published in their entirety for the first time in *The River of the Mother of God*. The specific and youthful notebook, "Journal 1903," that plays an early and exemplary role near the beginning of the present essay, is among the hundreds of unpublished manuscripts in the Leopold papers at the University of Wisconsin–Madison Archives. The entirety of "Journal 1903" can be found in box no. 1, series 9/25/10-7 of the Leopold papers. Papers 1 and 32 are quoted here through the aid of Bernard Schermetzler (of the Archives) and with the generous permission of Nina Leopold Bradley, on behalf of the Leopold family.

BIOGRAPHICAL AND CRITICAL STUDIES

J. Baird Callicott, *In Defense of the Land Ethic: Essays in Environmental Philosophy* (Albany: State Univ. of New York Press, 1989) and, as ed., *Companion to* A Sand County Almanac: *Interpretive and Critical Essays* (Madison: Univ. of Wisconsin Press, 1987); Susan L. Flader, "The Person and the Place," in *The Sand County of Aldo Leopold* (San Francisco: Sierra Club, 1973), ed. by Anthony Wolff, and *Thinking Like a Mountain: Aldo Leopold and the Evolution of an Ecological Attitude Toward Deer, Wolves, and Forests* (Columbia: Univ. of Missouri Press, 1974); Peter A. Fritzell, "*A Sand County Almanac* and the Conflicts of Ecological Conscience," in his *Nature Writing and America: Essays upon a Cultural Type* (Ames: Iowa State Univ. Press, 1980); James I. McClintock, "Aldo Leopold: Mythmaker," in his *Nature's Kindred Spirits: Aldo Leopold, Joseph Wood Krutch, Edward Abbey,*

Annie Dillard, and Gary Snyder (Madison: Univ. of Wisconsin Press, 1994); Curt Meine, *Aldo Leopold: His Life and Work* (Madison: Univ. of Wisconsin Press, 1988) and "The Utility of Preservation and the Preservation of Utility: Leopold's Fine Line," in *The Wilderness Condition: Essays on Environment and Civilization* (San Francisco: Sierra Club, 1992), ed. by Max Oelschlaeger; Roderick Nash, "Aldo Leopold: Prophet," in his *Wilderness and the American Mind*, 3d ed. (New Haven, Conn.: Yale Univ. Press, 1982), and *The Rights of Nature: A History of Environmental Ethics* (Madison: Univ. of Wisconsin Press, 1989); Max Oelschlaeger, "Aldo Leopold and the Age of Ecology," in his *Idea of Wilderness: From Prehistory to the Age of Ecology* (New Haven, Conn.: Yale Univ. Press, 1991); Sherman Paul, "The Husbandry of the Wild" and "Aldo Leopold's Counter-Friction," in his *For Love of the World: Essays on Nature Writers* (Iowa City: Univ. of Iowa Press, 1992); Dennis Ribbens, "The Making of *A Sand County Almanac*," in *Companion to* A Sand County Almanac: *Interpretive and Critical Essays* (Madison: Univ. of Wisconsin Press, 1987), ed. by J. Baird Callicott; Robert Sayre, "Aldo Leopold's Sentimentalism: 'A Refined Taste in Natural Objects,'" in *North Dakota Quarterly* 59 (spring 1991); Don Scheese, " 'Something More Than Wood': Aldo Leopold and the Language of Landscape," in *North Dakota Quarterly* 58 (winter 1990); John Tallmadge, "Anatomy of a Classic," in *Companion to* A Sand County Almanac: *Interpretive and Critical Essays* (Madison: Univ. of Wisconsin Press, 1987), ed. by J. Baird Callicott; Thomas Tanner, ed., *Aldo Leopold: The Man and His Legacy* (Ankeny, Iowa: Soil Conservation Society of America, 1987).

BARRY LOPEZ
(b. 1945)

JOHN TALLMADGE

DURING ONE OF HIS sojourns in the Far North, Barry Lopez asked an Eskimo hunter what he did when entering unfamiliar country. The man replied, "I listen." When questioned about his own work, Lopez often replies, "I am a writer who travels." Indeed, few authors have traveled as widely or listened as deeply to the voices of North America's landscapes and native peoples. In a distinguished body of work comprising dozens of essays and stories as well as two prizewinning books of natural history, Lopez has searchingly criticized Western ways of knowing and valuing the land. His writing achieves an extraordinary power through its combination of moral vision and immense learning with an intimate narrative voice and a lapidary precision of style. It amply fulfills Henry David Thoreau's vision of natural history as a catalyst for personal and social transformation while exploring its loftiest literary possibilities.

Barry Holstun Lopez was born on 6 January 1945 in Port Chester, New York, a town on Long Island Sound, to John Edward Brennan and Mary Frances (Holstun) Brennan, both of whom worked in journalism and advertising. Some of Lopez's earliest landscape memories involve wading into Long Island Sound as a three-year-old, drawn by the light and space out on the water. In 1948 his brother Dennis was born, and the family moved to southern California, settling in the semirural San Fernando Valley, where Lopez developed a strong feeling for the desert. In 1950 his mother divorced John Brennan and in 1955 she married Adrian Bernard Lopez, a businessman who adopted her sons and whom Barry considers to be his father.

In 1956 the Lopez family moved to Manhattan, where Barry continued his Catholic education at the Jesuit-run Loyola School. After the wild California desert New York City came as a shock, but it also provided an infusion of high culture and intellection. Lopez traveled to Europe in the summer of 1962 after graduating from the twelfth grade, and that fall he enrolled at the University of Notre Dame, intending to major in aeronautical engineering but soon switching to communication arts, a program that combined writing and theater with American studies. He traveled widely during his undergraduate years, driving through nearly every state, working on a classmate's Wyoming ranch for two summers, and paying extended visits to a West Virginia farmer who nurtured his interest in local geography and storytelling.

Lopez had also been impressed by Roman Catholic spiritual traditions, especially those exemplified by the Jesuits and the Desert Fathers. He had considered entering seminary before enrolling at Notre Dame, and after receiving his B.A. in 1966 he visited the Trappist Abbey of Gethsemane in Kentucky, where Thomas

Merton lived, thinking that he might become a monk. As Lopez explained to interviewer Alice Evans, he was attracted by the idea of realizing a life of service through work and prayer and so becoming an "instrument of grace." But he concluded that the monastic life would be "too easy," and resolved to teach instead.

In 1967 Lopez married Sandra Landers, a book artist, and enrolled in the Master of Arts in Teaching program at Notre Dame. After completing that degree in 1968 he entered the M.F.A. program in creative writing at the University of Oregon, where, under the guidance of folklorist Barre Toelken, he began the study of Native American cultures that led him to write his first book, *Giving Birth to Thunder, Sleeping with His Daughter: Coyote Builds North America*. Midway through the program at Oregon, Lopez decided that teaching was not for him. He had begun publishing stories and book reviews while he was still an undergraduate, and he decided that he might be able to make a living as a photographer and a writer. So he withdrew from the M.F.A. program and began contributing articles and pictures to newspapers and magazines. In 1970 he and Sandra settled on the upper Mackenzie River, in the rain forest of the Cascade Mountains east of the university. It is there that Lopez still does almost all his writing, in the intervals between journeys.

Lopez began his literary career with journalism, features, and short fiction. Although his early articles strike a reader as serviceable but undistinguished, the stories reveal a bold and visionary imagination already preoccupied with mature themes. Lopez's first published book was *Desert Notes: Reflections in the Eye of a Raven* (1976), a collection of short stories grounded in the austere, mysterious landscapes of the Great Basin and Mojave deserts. Next came *Giving Birth to Thunder* (1977), which had been composed seven years earlier, and *Of Wolves and Men* (1978), a passionate natural history informed by Western science and literature, the wisdom of Native American hunters, and Lopez's own travels and observations. *Of Wolves and Men* became a best-seller, won the Bur-

roughs Medal, and established its author as a major nature writer.

Meanwhile, Lopez continued to publish essays and short stories. *River Notes: The Dance of Herons* followed *Desert Notes* in 1979 as the second volume of a projected short fiction trilogy. In contrast to *Desert Notes*, which treats the landscape as a setting or occasion for spiritual discovery, *River Notes* treats nature as a character in the action. It is a work of dazzling experimentation, informed equally by Lopez's Native American studies and his reading of Western writers such as Herman Melville, John Steinbeck, and Ernest Hemingway. Cultural conflicts also inform Lopez's next collection of stories, *Winter Count* (1981), which explores the wonder and suffering that can follow from glimpsing a nature that does not conform to Western expectations.

By the 1980s Lopez was writing for an array of national magazines that would eventually include not only *Harper's*, *Outside*, and the *North American Review*, but also *Orion*, *Audubon*, *Sierra*, the *Georgia Review*, and *National Geographic*. He had given up photography in 1981 because of doubts about how the medium was affecting his perceptions, although his fiction and natural history show a persistent interest in visual aesthetics. Themes of light, space, and perspective figure prominently in *Arctic Dreams: Imagination and Desire in a Northern Landscape* (1986), a meditative natural history of North America's polar regions that grew out of Lopez's experiences in Alaska while researching *Of Wolves and Men*. "I was obsessed with the incredible beauty of that landscape," Lopez explained to interviewer Trish Todd. "I had the same quickness of heart and very intense feelings that human beings have when, in an utterly uncalculated way, they fall in love. *Arctic Dreams* is about that experience—what happens between the heart and a piece of land, what happens between the mind and a piece of land." Lopez's paean to the Far North unfolds on an operatic scale while maintaining a resonant lyricism and an intimate, personal tone. It brings a wealth of learning and firsthand experience to

BARRY LOPEZ

bear on some of the most vexing universal questions: How does one live an honorable life? What constitutes authentic wealth? How do we achieve a dignified relationship with the land? Lopez's inquiries lead to a harsh critique of Western culture, but he finds hope in the ecological integrity of northern landscapes and the skilled wisdom of the Eskimos. *Arctic Dreams* became a Book of the Month Club Main Selection and Lopez's second best-seller, winning several literary prizes, including a National Book Award.

After *Arctic Dreams* Lopez began work on another large-scale book, intending to explore "the scale of human time in remote landscapes . . . and the relationship between landscape and emotion, particularly the emotion of hope" (*Current Biography*, July 1995). Portions are set in such diverse places as Ellesmere Island, northern Kenya, the Tanami Desert of Australia, the Galápagos Islands, and Antarctica. Meanwhile, Lopez has continued to turn out shorter works. A collection of essays, *Crossing Open Ground*, appeared in 1988. Uncollected articles include "Life and Death in Galápagos" (*North American Review*, 1989), "The American Geographics" (*Orion Nature Quarterly*, 1989), "Who Are These Animals We Kill?" (*Witness*, 1989), reprinted with corrections in as "Apologia" (*Harper's*, 1990), and "The Rediscovery of North America" (*Orion*, 1992). A trend toward autobiography is evident in "Replacing Memory" (*Georgia Review*, 1993) and "Caring for the Woods" (*Audubon*, 1995).

Lopez has also continued to write fiction. The novella *Crow and Weasel* (1990) describes how two mythical North American youths reach manhood and wisdom by traveling farther north than any of their people have gone. Designed for juvenile and adult readers, the book treats many of Lopez's favorite themes: the sacredness of friendship and community, the spiritual dimensions of nature, the importance of attentiveness, and the obligations of the storyteller. Another collection of stories, *Field Notes: The Grace Note of the Canyon Wren*, completed his short fiction trilogy in 1994. Uncollected short stories

include "The Interior of North Dakota" (*Paris Review*, 1992) and "Thomas Lowdermilk's Generosity" (*American Short Fiction*, 1993).

Besides the Burroughs Medal and the National Book Award, Lopez has received numerous other prizes and honors, including a Guggenheim Fellowship (1987), a Governor's Award for Arts (1990), a Lannan Foundation Award (1990), the Pushcart Prize (1993), and an hororary doctorate from the University of Portland (1994). Both his fiction and his nonfiction have been widely anthologized.

Lopez's working habits accord in interesting ways with the themes and materials of his art. "My life is divided," he told interviewer Kay Bonetti. "I deeply enjoy the time that I spend with animals. . . . And at the same time, I have a deep and abiding love for libraries and for books and for scholarship." When he goes to an unfamiliar place, Lopez tries to "pick a good companion," meaning either a good book or a local guide. Paying attention is his essential discipline; it means reading, listening, and observing as closely as possible. Although Lopez travels assiduously and keeps extensive field notes, he does most of his reading and composition at his home in Oregon, where he often works outside under the giant firs or indoors in a study whose window is always open. He keeps a daily journal whose entries are "just like physical exercises." His practice seems to embody the rhythmic alteration between movement and rest, experience and thought, remoteness and home that pervades both his fiction and his natural history.

While working on books, Lopez continues to write stories and essays, which offer convenient vehicles for exploring tangential possibilities suggested by his material. He tends to compose a draft at one sitting, then revises extensively. "I think it is always imperative to be mindful of the reader's position," he told Kay Bonetti. "Writing is not something to fool around with; the course of history is changed by language. . . . The language has a power to heal and to elevate and to instill hope in the bleakest of circumstances." Fine distinctions between fiction and nonfiction do not trouble him; the object of both is to "create a coherent ecosystem," even though the latter must answer to an outside authority as well as to the writer's own mind. Lopez believes that all genuine stories aim to "create an atmosphere of grace within apparent contradiction," and that effective writers can "bring about an atmosphere in which truth can reveal itself." In so doing, modern Western writers can teach or heal after the fashion of aboriginal storytellers. "I think if you can really see the land," Lopez told interviewer Jim Aton, "if you can lose your sense of wishing it to be what you want it to be, if you can strip yourself of the desire to order and to name and see the land entirely for itself, you see in the relationship of all its elements the face of God. . . . If you pay close attention you can discern patterns, and perhaps subconsciously those are the patterns of story."

Giving Birth to Thunder, Sleeping with His Daughter

Lopez's collection of Coyote stories, *Giving Birth to Thunder, Sleeping with His Daughter*, shows his respect for Native American worldviews and narrative techniques. Although the stories are identified by culture of origin, Lopez chose mimesis over transcription in the retelling. He created a uniform narrative voice to suggest the intimate, laconic manner of a tribal elder, and he omitted notes and commentary in order to focus upon Coyote's universality while highlighting the distinctive and contradictory aspects of his character. The book unfolds as a series of picaresque adventures in which Coyote appears by turns as demiurge, victim, swindler, hero, or buffoon. He is always traveling, always snooping around, a meddler driven by appetite, full of bravado and self-importance. At the same time, however, he exercises important powers of shape-shifting and resuscitation. Above all, he is a protagonist, someone who makes things happen.

These stories are very short, often no more than two or three pages long. Pared to the essentials of action and character, they seem ad-dressed to an audience already familiar with both. The players are all "representative animals" who maintain both social and ecological relations with one another, and the stories unfold with almost no exposition or commentary, compelling the reader to flesh out and interpret the events and thereby engage the moral issues they raise. Upon reflection, the stories prove rich and provocative; correct interpretation requires close attention to detail and extensive knowledge of both culture and landscape.

As an example, consider the Yokuts story, "Prairie Falcon Loses." It begins as follows:

> There was a village where Eagle was chief. Coyote was there too. He was a good talker and knew everything. Prairie Falcon was there. He was fierce. The large owl and the small ground owl were medicine men and they lived there too. Panther was there. He was a good hunter. Weasel, Fox and Magpie lived there also. They were gamblers. Many others lived there.
>
> Every day the hunters, Eagle and Prairie Falcon and Panther, went out for rabbits. Coyote brought wood to every house, but he never went hunting. When the hunters came back they gave Coyote the entrails. He took them home and breathed on them and they became rabbits again.
>
> The gamblers played every day at the gambling ground with the hoop and stick.

The narrator establishes setting, characters, and tension with a few bold strokes, assuming a knowledge of both social and natural systems on the reader's part. The village is dominated by hunters who despise Coyote because he scavenges. Apparently ignorant of his magic powers, they toss him the leftovers which he converts back into living rabbits, thereby sustaining both the ecosystem and the culture on which the hunters depend. Moreover, because Coyote delivers wood (another servile occupation) he knows what is going on in every household. His work seems to be the maintenance of both social and natural relationships.

One day a small, black-eared rabbit approaches the village and is greeted by Coyote, who takes him directly to Eagle's lodge. This is an act of extraordinary bravery on Rabbit's part, but he also demonstrates diplomatic skill by presenting gifts to the chief, which gains him protection from being hunted. The next morning he humiliates his enemies by winning everything they own; his success appears linked to his exercise of virtue the day before. But Rabbit overreaches the following day by taking on Prairie Falcon, his natural enemy, and so he begins to lose until he has nothing left to bet. Prairie Falcon tempts him to wager his ear, and Rabbit, desperate to save face, agrees. But without his ears, Rabbit (and the class of creatures he represents) would be defenseless against fierce predators like Prairie Falcon; therefore, this wager threatens to upset the ecosystem.

At this point, Coyote calls for a time-out and runs off to Prairie Falcon's lodge, where, having changed himself to look like Prairie Falcon, he tricks the latter's wife into a compromising position and copulates with her. This burlesque reveals the sad state of Prairie Falcon's home life while changing his luck for the worse. By the time Coyote returns to the gambling ground, Rabbit has won everything back. Apparently, Prairie Falcon has been spending too much time hunting and gambling to pay attention either to his wife or to Coyote. Now he loses at home as well as at gambling: he and his wife will surely argue whether he came home during the game and had intercourse with her, and he will realize he has been cuckolded without knowing who to blame. Prairie Falcon loses because of his pride and cruelty (at least Rabbit never tried to kill anyone). As for Coyote, his trickery both safeguards the ecosystem and punishes misconduct. In this story, the natural and social orders are one.

From a literary point of view, Lopez's Coyote stories are noteworthy in several respects. As fables, they go far beyond the simple allegories of an Aesop or a La Fontaine. Although Coyote and his neighbors are treated as persons, they are not just humans dressed up as animals. Rather, their characters and behavior make sense only when interpreted ecologically as well as culturally. In this respect, Coyote himself appears as the char-

acter most resembling humans, but humans as seen from the perspective of other animals. As written imitations of oral narrative, the stories also reveal the rich literary possibilities that Native American plots, characters, and themes can open for Western readers; they honor indigenous thought while inviting a creative synthesis of traditions. And finally, as mythic narratives grounded in social as well as physical landscapes, they show how story can work to harmonize the individual psyche with the community and the sustaining earth.

Desert Notes

The twelve stories of *Desert Notes* explore the spiritual meaning of landscape by combining a Native American understanding of animal powers, ecological contracts, and initiatory transformation with a Western devotion to science, learning, and ascetic practice. Many of Lopez's mature themes appear: the dignity and order of nature, the search for identity and atonement, the danger of broken contracts, and the power of close observation to reveal wonders and portents in the landscape. Lopez's desert is a country of alkaline lake beds and treeless mountains, of vast perspectives, silence, and unrelenting light. It is the central fact with which the characters in these stories must come to terms.

Opening allusions to Thomas Merton and the Desert Fathers establish the theme of ascetic practice. In "Introduction," a seasoned narrator offers advice on perseverance to a novice reader about to embark on a contemplative journey. Ritual practice and observation are keyed to self-discovery in "Conversation" and "Directions," and to cleansing and renewal in "The Hot Spring" and "The Wind." "The Blue Mound People," a fictive scholarly article, describes a sect whose archaeological remains indicate that all their food and clothing were supplied by neighboring tribes. The narrator speculates that by devoting themselves so completely to contemplation of the desert, these people were somehow holding the world together; their disappearance suggests that the order of things may have changed, perhaps because humans have begun to overlook something vital.

The theme of broken contracts and disconnection from nature reverberates through this book, though the destructive human presence remains below the horizon. In "Coyote and Rattlesnake," Coyote complains to the Creator and is told to have patience: the human juggernaut will grind to a halt, and things will grow back. In other stories, the critique of humanity remains implicit. Lopez's desert seekers have all sensed the spiritual dimension in nature and recognized the desert's strangeness as a sign of its capacity for revelation. Having accepted their need for cleansing, they are already "in recovery." The reader, in contrast, is depicted as ignorant of desert truth, someone like the interlocutor in "Conversation," to whom the narrator's earnest, cryptic statements appear tinged with madness. These stories deal centrally with ways of knowing and valuing the landscape; they imply that the desert's apparent strangeness and emptiness are actually symptoms of the reader's own moral and cultural poverty.

According to critic Sherman Paul, the landscapes of *Desert Notes* (and of Lopez's other short-story collections) all involve "sacred space: not just the landscape of desert, river, or plains, but the deep interior landscapes of self and imagination, landscapes at times undifferentiated, surreal" (p. 74). The preeminent character type in these stories is a person who lives in two worlds, that of profane Western society (the reader's world) and the visionary world of the desert. This person is "one who knows," someone who has seen both sides of reality. The stories explore variations ranging from the ascetic narrator to the woman in "The Wind" who lies naked on the sand to the old man, Leon, in "Directions," who has visited the secret desert and carries a mental map of its spiritual landscape. Many stories deal with a process of growth or initiation whereby a person becomes "one who knows." And the narrative act itself emerges as a process of crossing between ordinary and nonordinary reality, a revelatory process analogous to initiation itself.

River Notes

River Notes, the second volume in Lopez's short fiction trilogy, continues the intercultural experimentation of *Desert Notes* but achieves greater symbolic resonance and lyric intensity. It is Lopez's most challenging and original book, the work of a master. Themes of contemplative devotion, animal power, broken ecological contracts, and longing for intimacy with the land weave powerfully through these stories. The landscape itself, represented by the river, becomes a key player as the human world and its depredations move to center stage. The human characters are richly varied, their interactions with the land often violent and dramatic. Although the stories run for only a few pages each, their abundance of precisely limned metaphors gives them the density and radiance of poems.

The preeminent character type in *River Notes* is a "visionary naturalist," someone whose obsessive, meticulous devotion to nature leads to clairvoyant insight. As critic William Rueckert observes, the narrator wants to "know and understand this natural world without trespassing upon it or causing it any harm" (p. 289), including reducing it to formulas or abstractions. Thus, in "Introduction," the narrator confesses, "I have spent nights with my palms flat on the sand, tracing the grains for hours like braille until I had the pattern precisely, could go anywhere—the coast of Africa—and recreate the same strip of beach" (p. x). And in "The Shallows," surely the most astonishing nature walk in all literature, the narrator asks the reader to "imagine what might be learned in a place like this if one took the time":

> If you lie out flat on the stones—it seems odd to try, I know—you will feel—here, that's it—the warmth of the sunlight emanating from the stones. Turn your head to the side, ear to rock, and you will hear the earth revolving on its axis and an adjustment of stones in the riverbed. The heartbeats of salmon roe. (p. 40)

Sometimes the figure even appears in the third person, for example as Gene Thompson, the boy in "The Log Jam," who, "when he listened with his forehead against a tree . . . heard the thinking of woodpeckers asleep inside. He heard the flow of sap which sounded like stratospheric winds to him" (p. 18).

Written from the point of view of such characters, Lopez's vivid, precise descriptions create a sense that even the most trivial detail is highly significant. The landscape is both real and revelatory—that is, apocalyptic—like the landscapes of Dante's *Paradiso* but with no otherworldly accoutrements. To approach such a landscape requires an attentiveness devoid of projection or self-serving motives. Lopez's naturalists go out alone, seeking to be "tutored by the land." Their quests often begin with some kind of call: a dream, an illness, an encounter with a totemic animal. The end result is personal transformation as they cross the line between ordinary and nonordinary reality.

"The Bend" offers a telling example. The narrator (reminiscent of the obsessed scholars in stories by Edgar Allan Poe and Jorge Luis Borges) begins with illness, a back pain and accompanying depression that he imagines would disappear if he could just understand the river bend outside his window. Why he should make such a connection remains unclear, but he is rich enough to hire a team of scientists who spend years reducing the bend to measurements and equations. Their work fails to cure him, yet such is its precision that, as years pass, their pile of notes begins to resemble rocks, grow moss, and emit river sounds. One day the narrator comes to "a dead space in my depression, a sudden horizontal view, which I seized" (p. 25). One might say he has "hit bottom," or, in the story's own terms, aligned himself finally with the position of water. Paralyzed for years, he gets up and walks, calling for help. At that moment the line between ordinary and nonordinary reality dissolves: "Bears heard me (or were already waiting at the door). I told them I needed to be near the river. They carried me through the trees (growling, for they are not used to working together), throwing their shoulders to the alders until we stood at the outer bank" (p. 26). Then the narrator becomes a participant: "The first thing

I did was to feel, raccoonlike, with the tips of my fingers the soil of the bank just below the water's edge" (p. 26). There is no aesthetic or philosophical distance here: it is an image of extraordinary intimacy. He has given up trying to interpret, to "wrestle meaning from this spot," as he described his initial efforts. Now he is ready to be tutored by the land, and he experiences atonement and healing.

In terms of its plot, this powerful, compressed story—it is three pages long—follows the conversion paradigm of Saint Augustine's *Confession*: illness and restlessness, a search by trial and error, despair, a call, a response, and, as denouement, entry into an effortful new life. In terms of characterization and theme, "The Bend" resembles other stories in the collection. Lopez's narrators and protagonists appear crazy at first: meticulous, obsessed, extravagant and cryptic in their actions. Yet they compel attention by the seriousness and eloquence of their speech. It soon becomes clear that although they speak the reader's language, they see the world quite differently. This is most evident in the ways Lopez manipulates the conventions of realism. "The Bend" climaxes at the moment when bears appear. It is hardly normal (in Western experience) for wild animals to address, befriend, or aid human beings, yet the event is told as if it were unexceptional: there is no change in the narrator's language or tone. We may be shocked by the bears, but the narrator is not, and that only compounds our surprise. The story has entered a domain of "magical realism" similar to myth (where the marvelous and the quotidian occupy the same space) or the work of South American writers like Jorge Luis Borges or Gabriel García Márquez, whose kinship Lopez has acknowledged.

As William Rueckert has justly said, "these stories and notes flow into you and you can't get rid of them" (p. 294). In fact they invite interpretation in the manner of parables or koans, and the key to their understanding lies in the framework of ecocentric values within which they unfold. They propose relations of dignity, courtesy, respect, honor, and mutual obligation between humans and other beings in nature. When agreements based on this ethic are broken, droughts, storms, floods, or accidents follow. Harmony is restored when individual humans act toward the land with abnegation or self-sacrifice, transforming both themselves and the world in the process.

This process is vividly portrayed in a pair of stories dealing with salmon. In "The Salmon," an artist aspires to honor the fish by creating a perfect, monumental image. After years of research and labor, he completes his masterpiece and sets it up in the river. But the migrating salmon respond by turning back, and he realizes with horror how he has insulted them by omitting the ravages of their upstream journey. In "The Falls," an itinerant laborer with shamanic powers pursues the river's call to the point where he turns eventually into a salmon. The narrator, an older man who also lives on the edge of society, understands the hero's vocation and the spiritual side of nature, though he cannot cross back and forth as the hero does ("I am not a man of great power"). He tells the story so that no one will think that the hero wasted his life, but he describes both the ordinary details (where they worked, what they ate) and the hero's extraordinary acts (changing bodies with his dog, vision quests, ritual self-mutilations) in the same matter-of-fact tone. Although he refrains—strikingly—from interpreting the hero's final plunge over the falls, the context provided by the other stories invites us to see it both as an ultimate, mystic atonement and a heroic sacrifice to pay for all the times and ways that humans have broken their covenants with the river.

This image of a man turning into a salmon at the climax of a devotional practice requiring many years, much suffering, and total dedication to the land represents a kind of ecocentric transfiguration, an apotheosis of the visionary naturalist. It is an intensely spiritual image but also a violent one, like that of Christ on the cross. For humans have violated their contracts, and the land has responded with violence of its own. These stories are full of grief and loss. But Lopez ends on a note of hope. In the final story, "Drought," the narrator dreams of a fish dying in an upstream pool. He exhausts himself in the climb to reach the fish, carries it to the last trickle of moving water, then tries clumsily to dance. Eventually the animals gather around, and Blue Heron teaches him the rain dance. This final image of grace, of humans and animals dancing together, suffuses the reader's mind like light. One gives thanks for the narrator's gentle heroism. It is something within the reach of anyone.

Winter Count

Lopez's next collection of short fiction, *Winter Count*, broadens the range of landscapes and characters while continuing his interest in natural history, indigenous culture, and visionary transformation. These nine stories take place in regions of North America with archetypal significance: the Arizona desert, the Great Plains of North Dakota, the Gulf Coast of Florida, the foothills of the Rocky Mountains, even the concrete canyons of Manhattan. The protagonists suffer alienation from families, lovers, professional life, or mainstream society. Their search for intimacy and self-knowledge often leads to a deeper consideration of the landscape and the views of Native American people. A confessional mode predominates: many stories are told in the first person or from the point of view of a sentient character. Often, they culminate in the portentous appearance of animals.

In "Restoration," the narrator happens upon an incongruous French château while driving through North Dakota; he discovers its remarkable collection of early natural history books, which is being restored by a learned European craftsman. Fascinated by the old man and his esoteric craft, the narrator soon learns how the collection was assembled by an eccentric Frenchman, René de Crenir, a devotee of Montaigne whose studies led him to conclude that in North America animals were theologically equivalent to humans. Astonished to realize that de Crenir reached these conclusions without reference to Native American culture, the narrator presses questions upon the old restorer but can learn nothing of de Crenir's subsequent work or history. His insights apparently disappeared with him. At this point the narrator suddenly notices a group of antelope staring at him from the plains that open beyond the library windows. After a moment of eye contact, they vanish, leaving him struck by the "excessive neatness" of his own notes. The story invites the reader to ponder both the promise and the insularity of Western scholarship as a way of discovering the landscape's deepest truths.

Lopez's characters have a scholarly bent; they tend to be learned and sober, careful with facts and dates. In "Buffalo," the narrator describes his research into incidents that took place on the Laramie Plains in the mid-1800s, beginning with an ice storm that killed a herd of buffalo and concluding with Indian reports of mysterious white buffalo moving up into the Medicine Bow Mountains while singing a death song. The Indians became convinced that the buffalo had known of the coming exterminations and were trying to show the Indians how to climb out through a hole in the sky. Articles in the *Journal of Mammalogy* report discoveries of buffalo skeletons found at unusual altitudes. But the narrator's suspicions are not confirmed until the very end, when direct experience replaces scholarly investigation: "I recently slept among weathered cottonwoods on the Laramie Plains in the vicinity of the Medicine Bow Mountains. I awoke in the morning to find my legs broken" (p. 35). Here the place acts as a scene of instruction where a magical reality breaks through. But knowledge of this sort exacts a price. The narrator's epiphany brings him suffering of the kind endured by both the buffalo and the Indians. The story expresses both the necessity and the peril of rewriting history.

"The Orrery" also turns upon place as a scene of instruction, though with a less drastic outcome. The narrator becomes fascinated by the feel of the wind in a nondescript Arizona valley. After several visits he meets a hermit sweeping the desert floor, "an impossible task," the man explains, "at which to work each day, as one might meditate or pray" (p. 42). This image seizes the narrator's imagination, compelling

him to return a few years later. This time the hermit invites him to his home, where they enjoy good food, learned conversation, and classical music; the man seems completely centered and at peace in his solitary life. As their conversation becomes more intimate, the man displays an antique mechanical model of the solar system that he has restored, then takes the narrator outside. As they approach the swept area, a breeze arises; the narrator waits as the hermit walks forward into "hurricane winds, that . . . snapped all round him" (p. 47). The man moves a few stones on the ground, and the wind begins lifting them into the sky, where they eventually constellate with thousands of others into a perfect, glowing replica of the Milky Way. "If one is patient," the hermit explains to the dumbstruck narrator, "if you are careful, I think there is probably nothing that cannot be retrieved" (p. 49). Here the scene of instruction incarnates an ancient mystical doctrine of correspondence, "As above, so below." It resembles the Aleph in Borges' eponymous story — a point from which all other points are visible — and it reveals the transcendent significance concealed by mundane appearance. For the restlessly seeking narrator, this epiphany holds a promise of overcoming loss, resanctifying the world, and achieving a healthy and centered life through devotional practice.

A fierce sense of longing permeates these stories. Sometimes it is fulfilled, as in "The Woman Who Had Shells," where the narrator discovers a soul mate, and sometimes it remains unrequited, as in "Winter Herons," where the narrator's love for the Far North costs him the loyalty and affection of a dancer who finds that she cannot abandon the city. The characters in these stories yearn for intimacy and truth, for an authentic life. Their researches and encounters with landscape show them the way but also divide them from their contemporaries. Like Roger Callahan, the historian in "Winter Count 1973" whose paper on Native American stories is spurned by his peers, they become "cognitive renegades" at odds with the values and epistemology of their culture. But hope lies in the fact that their stories are told, for, as Callahan realizes, "Everything is held together with stories. . . . That is all that is holding us together, stories and compassion" (p. 62).

Field Notes

Field Notes ostensibly completes Lopez's "Notes" trilogy, but except for "Introduction," where a visionary naturalist is aided by animals as he attempts to walk across the Mojave Desert, the book follows the trajectory of *Winter Count*. Its geography widens beyond North America to include Australia, Mexico, and Greenland, and its central characters are monastic personalities, artists, scientists, or contemplatives whose odd inquiries take them to the borders of Western understanding. The stories turn on "threshold experiences," where a momentary glimpse of alternative reality offers hope for redemption or atonement. The narrative voice is less oracular than that of *River Notes*, the mode more consistently realistic, the plots and relationships more complex, the dialogue extensive and revealing. An air of vividness and mystery emanates from the situations, the people, and the language.

The characters in *Field Notes* manifest the same eccentric intensity as the naturalists of *River Notes* or the scholars of *Winter Count*. "The Open Lot" concerns Jane Weddell, a paleontologist whose extraordinary perception and imagination enable her to discern in nondescript rocks the fossils of soft-bodied Precambrian organisms. Her gift for detecting such "phantoms" of vanished life begins to operate in another way when she looks into a vacant lot on her way to work and begins to see birds and animals from the native ecosystem. When the museum cuts back her hours, the lot becomes her study. Its organisms multiply with the changing seasons, and she fills several notebooks with observations before the lot is tragically bulldozed. By then, however, she has gained the strength to return to her work, recognizing that she and the land have both suffered from the ignorance of the powerful.

Other stories imagine avenues of atonement with animals. In "Pearyland," the narrator hears an explorer's story of finding an Arctic oasis where the souls of dead animals go to await rebirth. The caretaker, a ghostly Eskimo, explains that fewer animals come now because they are being killed without prayer; a renewed sense of their spirituality is needed to save them. In "Lessons from the Wolverine," a man born in the Caribbean but drawn to the Far North eventually migrates to an Alaskan village, where he hears of a family of wolverines that have turned against the Eskimos after being disrespectfully hunted. Fascinated, he goes in search of them. His tact and earnestness win their trust, and they grant him a vision that makes sense of all his previous encounters with animals and landscapes.

Several stories deal with prejudice and turn on the revelation of unexpected value. In "The Entreaty of the Wiideema," an undiscovered Australian tribe instructs an ambitious anthropologist in the mystery of human violence and the healing power of story. In "Teal Creek," the narrator discovers that a hermit living up in the hills has achieved a congruent relation to nature that has enabled him, through years of meditative practice, to wrestle successfully with evil and so protect the community below. In "The Negro in the Kitchen," a self-satisfied investment counselor awakens one morning to find a mysterious black man at his breakfast table. Eloquent, courteous, and apparently rich, the man explains over toast and yogurt how he has reached Sun Valley, Idaho, by walking from his home in Greenwich, Connecticut. He explains that he intends to walk to the Pacific: "I wanted to become an African-American indigene . . . a black man who identifies with the American landscape, who fractures the immortality of his heritage in this country so completely that he finally gains a consoling intimacy with the place, the very place that for so long had been unapproachable" (pp. 81–82). The man's story reveals both humility and success, confronting the narrator with the shallowness of his own life.

Family and love relationships are also explored. In "The Runner," a smug lawyer learns from a college student that his older sister, to whom he had long condescended for her apparent lack of ambition, has in fact spent years running obscure trails in the Grand Canyon. By devoting herself so completely to the place, she has not only made important archaeological discoveries, but achieved a spiritual integrity and physical grace that inspire the young. In "Homecoming," a workaholic botanist at the peak of his academic career realizes that he must reconnect with his home landscape or risk losing his wife and daughter. And in "Sonora," one of the most haunting stories, a deaf scientist is engaged by a Mexican philanthropist to study the dunes on his remote desert estate. Excited and grateful, the young man devotes himself wholeheartedly to this esoteric task, but loneliness, brought on by the isolation and by the final loss of his hearing, threatens to cripple him. Salvation comes in the form of a glamorous call girl, imported by his patron, who turns out to share his deep sense of freedom and his profound feeling for wind, sand, and movement.

In these stories, as in Lopez's short fiction generally, the action turns on a search for identity, intimacy, and reconciliation. The landscape and its creatures play catalytic and often therapeutic roles. Epistemologically, the stories deal with approaching or crossing the threshold that divides Western and non-Western views of the world, bringing the reader to a point where nature and culture can be seen as parts of one reality. To reach such atonement the main characters have to do extraordinary things that often involve acts of research, imagination, or devotion carried on at a remove from society. No matter how fantastic these actions or their consequences may seem, the stories compel belief. Lopez's writing has a crystalline, almost molecular precision, a sense of flawless congruence between observation, word, and idea. One thinks of the "bold, piercing glass" of Jane Weddell's microscope that reveals the unobtrusive lineaments of fossils. The same could be said of Lopez's own narrative eye. Reading his stories, one experiences the same unexpected wonder one feels on looking through a microscope at a section of tissue brilliantly illuminated and magnified to reveal the geometric elegance of its structures.

Crow and Weasel

Lopez's longest work of fiction, a novella intended for both juvenile and adult readers, reflects his ongoing concern with travel, indigenous cultures, storytelling, and social responsibility. Crow and Weasel are adolescent males from a Northern Plains culture, living in myth time and sharing both human and animal features. When they propose to journey farther north than anyone in their tribe has gone, their parents object, but Mountain Lion, an elder guided by a powerful dream, gives them his blessing and encouragement. On the way north the two friends meet various challenges and encounter helpers and companions from whom their courtesy and good sense elicit valuable gifts. Eventually they reach the tundra and meet a party of Inuit who, after a dangerous but comical first encounter, accept them as emissaries and exchange both stories and gifts with them. On the return journey, racing against winter, they meet Badger, who instructs them in the techniques and responsibilities of storytelling, and Grizzly Bear, who saves them from starvation and reminds them of the hunter's sacred obligations and the sustaining power of what is beautiful in the world. They return to their people, ready to assume the responsibilities of fatherhood and leadership.

Crow and Weasel is a coming-of-age story in which travel serves as the vehicle for initiation. Character, wisdom, and woodcraft are all needed for success. Crow and Weasel have likable personalities; they are earnest, courageous, loyal, honest, and sensible. They seem to have no self-serving motives or hidden agendas, no intractable family conflicts, deep anxieties, or smoldering resentments. Their self-esteem appears intact, their hormones under control. Though challenged at key moments, they make good decisions. They pay attention to their elders and to the landscape. They generally do the right thing, and when they do not, they quickly make amends. Although this image of adolescent behavior might strike some adults as unrealistic, Crow and Weasel appeal as characters because they embody the hopes of both kinds of readers. They achieve early success, and they act the way all parents wish that their teenagers would.

The dialogue in this story yields some of the most succinct and memorable expressions of Lopez's favorite ideas. When Crow and Weasel meet Mouse, a young warrior on a vision quest, their exchange sounds like a conversation between sages:

> "It's very difficult to lead a good life," said Crow, finally. "What you have set out to do," he said, turning to Mouse, "is hard. But our older people tell us that without a dream you do not know what to do with your life. So it is a good thing, I think, what you do, what your people believe."
>
> "Yes. To be a good hunter," said Mouse, "to be a good family man, to be truthful instead of clever with people, to live in a community where there is much wisdom — that is what all of us want."

> "Ah," said Crow. "But it takes your life to learn to do these things."
>
> "Hah!" said Mouse, and they all laughed. (p. 16)

Later on, Badger, the good editor, affirms the power and responsibility of storytelling:

> "I would ask you to remember only this one thing," said Badger. "The stories people tell have a way of taking care of them. If stories come to you, care for them. And learn to give them away where they are needed. Sometimes a person needs a story more than food to stay alive. That is why we put these stories in each other's memory. This is how people care for themselves. One day you will be good storytellers. Never forget these obligations." (p. 48)

That they have not forgotten is evident in their last conversation, as they stand on the edge of the village before going up to Mountain Lion's lodge to tell their stories:

> "I wonder if in the country where Grizzly Bear lives the sun is setting like this," said Crow. "I hope it is. I hope as we speak that this light, this color, is streaming down on him."
>
> In the silence that followed, Weasel said very softly, "It is good to be alive. To have friends, to have a family, to have children, to live in a particular place. These relationships are sacred."
>
> "Yes," said Crow. "Yes, this is the way it should be." (p. 63)

The story thus ends with a ringing affirmation of the values with which Crow and Weasel embarked. Their journey has not been a quest or exploration in the Western sense — not a colonial enterprise, that is — but rather a testing of their own culture, which is not found wanting. Their experiences extend the boundaries of their world but not their view of it. They are heroes, not prophets. Once they have accomplished their self-appointed mission, they give up traveling. If they lived in today's world, they would sit down and write a book.

Essays

Lopez has published numerous essays in periodicals ranging from newspapers to literary quarterlies to national magazines. Apart from *Crossing Open Ground*, a small but representative sample of fourteen pieces, his essays remain uncollected. They fall into four general categories: journalism and travel pieces, programmatic essays, profiles, and autobiography. He has also written occasional criticism, including commentary for art exhibition catalogs, and infrequent book reviews.

The journalism and travel pieces describe encounters with landscapes, animals, or indigenous cultures that follow the same narrative and thematic modes as his natural history books. The programmatic essays argue a position or set forth an agenda. The profiles describe people who love what they do and exemplify skills that Lopez admires, such as mentoring, woodcraft, knowledge of place, or storytelling. The autobiographical pieces reflect on Lopez's home and family. Space does not permit a full-scale commentary on this diverse and extensive body of work, but two of the programmatic essays are especially pertinent to an understanding of Lopez's fiction and natural history. They are "Landscape and Narrative" (from *Crossing Open Ground*) and "The Rediscovery of North America."

"Landscape and Narrative" opens with a framing story: Lopez is sitting in a cabin near Anaktuvuk Pass in the Brooks Range of northern Alaska, listening to Nunamiut hunters talk about wolverines. One story reflecting the animal's courage and resourcefulness impresses him deeply, and, as he walks out into the Arctic evening, he feels refreshed by the congruency between the story and the landscape. For a story to work this way, he realizes, "intimacy is indispensable—a feeling that derives from the listener's trust and a storyteller's certain knowledge of his subject and regard for his audience" (p. 64). Within this intimate relationship, narrative can function as a metaphor that brings the listener's "interior landscape" of character, memory, and desire—everything that we call "mind"—into accord with the external landscape, whose "unimpeachable" integrity derives from relationships that have been shaped by evolution. Hence the importance of storytelling as an "elevated experience among aboriginal peoples" (p. 66). "Inherent in story," Lopez writes, "is the power to reorder a state of psychological confusion through contact with the pervasive truth of those relationships we call 'the land'" (p. 68).

From this perspective, distinctions between myth and legend or between fiction and nonfiction are less important than those between authentic and inauthentic stories. The former are both ingenuous and verifiable, with an allowance for honest mistakes. We are accustomed, Lopez explains, to think of truth in terms of propositions, but in fact truth is "something alive and unpronounceable." "Story creates an atmosphere in which it becomes discernible as a pattern," Lopez continues. "For a storyteller to insist on relationships that do not exist is to lie. Lying is the opposite of story" (p. 69). This theory of narrative—concise, provocative, and ecocentric—expresses Lopez's loftiest expectations for his craft and illuminates both the construction and the appeal of his own work. Mutual dignity and courtesy are essential in the transaction between writer and reader. Lopez warns: "Beyond this—that the interior landscape is a metaphorical representation of the exterior landscape, that the truth reveals itself most fully not in dogma but in the paradox, irony, and contradictions that distinguish compelling narratives—beyond this there are only failures of imagination: reductionism in science; fundamentalism in religion; fascism in politics" (p. 71).

"The Rediscovery of North America" develops this final set of themes in a critical reappraisal of the Spanish encounter with the New World. After describing the violence and corruption of the first incursions (whose habits of mind persist to this day), Lopez concludes that such horrors arose from an assumption of superiority based upon ignorance and a misguided conception of wealth. Because we imposed our conceptions and agendas instead of "listening" to the New

World and its peoples, we lost the best things it had to offer, "the elements of true wealth [that] come with the maintenance of a home" (p. 12). Lopez acknowledges this deplorable history but asserts that we need not let it define us. "What we need," he says, "is to discover the continent again" (p. 15). This will involve searching out and cultivating local knowledge, learning from indigenous peoples, and practicing natural history. If we can learn to do this we may eventually gain a true sense of home, a place "in which we know exactly who we are" and "from which we speak our deepest beliefs" (p. 14). It is a question of practicing attentiveness and courtesy, of accepting people and land as parts of one community, of broadening our concept of literacy and accepting limits to our own understanding. From this perspective, travel and natural history become serious political undertakings designed to transform the ways in which we think and live. Combined with storytelling, they constitute a prophetic endeavor.

Of Wolves and Men

Lopez's radical critique of culture emerges vividly in his first natural history book, a comprehensive account of relations between humans and wolves. It is a work of deep passion and wide-ranging scholarship, a carefully orchestrated presentation of narrative, lore, and reflection that builds toward a challenging moral vision. Lopez not only reinvents natural history as a science and as a mode of writing; he shows why we need it in order to rediscover the continent.

The book opens with Lopez writing in a cabin near Fairbanks, Alaska, on a winter night with the outside temperature dropping toward forty below. He thinks of wolves surviving in the woods. "Go out there," he says, launching the reader on the book's imaginative journey. Opening vignettes suggest the mystery and power of wolves, the fascination and fear they still elicit. Lopez describes his methods, a combination of travel, research, personal observation, and expert testimony, but he cautions the reader that no animal can ever be fully known.

Part I presents a digest of what Western science knows about wolves. It is a succinct, comprehensive, and fascinating exposition from which the wolf emerges as a resourceful and well-adapted animal with an admirable gift for survival. Lopez begins with evolution and anatomy, proceeds through social structure and communication, and concludes with territorial and hunting behavior. He dwells on the mysterious "conversation of death" that occurs when wolf and prey lock eyes at the culmination of the attack. By opening with scientific exposition, Lopez gains the reader's confidence even as he begins to undermine whatever simplistic or prejudicial notions the latter may harbor concerning wolves. He also honors the prestige of science while preparing to expose its limitations, and he sets the reader up to realize, ultimately, that unthinking trust in science is ethnocentric.

This process begins in Part II, where Lopez presents the perspectives of native peoples like the Nunamiut, who share both environment and prey with the wolf. In such cultures "a correspondence begins to emerge" between people and wolves (p. 85). One can learn about how wolves think and act by talking with such people, who need the same skills to survive. Hunting peoples recognize the conversation of death as "a ceremonial exchange, the flesh of the hunted in exchange for respect for its spirit" (p. 94). A death of this sort is not tragic but full of dignity. Hunting becomes a holy activity: "the life of a hunting people is regarded as a sacred way of living because it grows out of this powerful, fundamental covenant" (p. 91). Lopez describes the rich variety of myths, rituals, games, shamanic practices, and forms of social organization that such cultures have developed to express their sense of correspondence with wolves. By the book's midpoint the reader has come to appreciate native and Western views of the wolf as complementary but still incomplete understandings.

Part III describes how people in Western culture have hunted and persecuted wolves since medieval times. It is a horrifying catalog of violence, cruelty, and obsession. Wolves have not only been trapped, shot, and poisoned by the millions; they have been mutilated and tortured as well. Lopez characterizes this centuries-long campaign as a holocaust. "When a man cocked a rifle and aimed at a wolf's head," he asks, "what was he trying to kill?" (p. 138). And why did so many people look the other way? In Europe wolves were killed out of fear, superstition, retribution, and contempt. They symbolized wilderness, scavenged corpses from battlefields, and, according to Descartes, possessed no souls. Wolves have been hunted using dogs, eagles, and airplanes in the belief that killing them was morally right. Lopez comes down hard on sport hunting. The alienated modern hunter, he says, actually envies the wolf his courage, endurance, and skill; to aspire to such qualities is admirable, but to kill the wolf for them is not. Lopez brings similar passion and detail to his account of the "pogrom" unleashed against wolves by government and the cattle industry following the Civil War. Wolves were associated with Indians and treated in much the same way. Thousands were shot, trapped, or poisoned with strychnine, and millions of other animals died in the process. Lopez concludes that "the scope, the casual irresponsibility, and the cruelty of wolf killing" arose from a defect in Western character: "I think it is that we simply do not understand our place in the universe and have not the courage to admit it" (p. 196).

Recognizing that this assault was directed against an animal that was imagined rather than intimately known, Lopez turns in Part IV to a cultural archaeology of the wolf, beginning with classical natural historians such as Aristotle and Pliny and medieval encyclopedists such as Isidore of Seville. He shows that the West's enduring wolf imagery originated during the Middle Ages, and he examines mythology, folklore, fables, and literature to reveal the limited and negative range of our vision. He concludes that "the possibility has yet to be realized of a synthesis between the benevolent wolf of many native American stories and the malcontented wolf of most European fairy tales" (p. 270).

Such a synthesis would require people to entertain a worldview that did not place humanity at the center of things, a prospect more terrifying than any imagined wolf. But Lopez affirms the possibility of such a wider view in an epilogue that describes his and his wife's experience of raising two wolves. Poignant, intimate, and tinged with tragedy, this final section tells that story of Lopez's own conversion to the enlightened view of animals elaborated in his preceding chapters. The book as a whole thus appears as a confession, following the model of spiritual autobiography established by Saint Augustine but shifting the emphasis from the conversion process itself to the new life of belief and practice that follows. The book enacts the values it preaches by realizing a synthesis of Western and indigenous perspectives. And the narrator, who listens to native people, who resists easy categories, and who observes wolves himself, exemplifies the qualities of character that are needed for honorable relations with the land. The narrator sets an example for the reader, completing the book's conscious design of personal, and eventually social, transformation.

As a work of natural history, *Of Wolves and Men* invites comparison with other books that incorporate native perspectives, notably Richard Nelson's *Make Prayers to the Raven* (1983) and the poems of Gary Snyder. It also revives pre-Cartesian models of natural history, which considered behavior, folklore, literature, and mythology as important as anatomy and morphology. Finally, it offers this inclusive, multidisciplinary approach not only as a form of inquiry but also as a spiritual discipline. In these respects it embodies Lopez's own expectation that natural history will "not only produce a major and lasting body of American literature but . . . also provide the foundation for a reorganization of American political thought" (*Antaeus* 57, autumn 1986, p. 297).

Arctic Dreams

Lopez's longest and most ambitious work of natural history broadens his focus from a single species to an entire region and deepens the inquiry to embrace the most profound moral and spiritual questions. Like *Of Wolves and Men,*

Arctic Dreams is a work of breathtaking scholarship and trenchant analysis, but it also brings the narrator's own journeys to the fore as framing devices and sources of insight. Lopez begins by describing a walk on the tundra. Impressed by the fierce expressions of ground-nesting birds, he finds himself bowing out of respect for their wildness and resolve. He also recalls passing the grave of a young American sailor who died on a polar expedition and wondering what dreams had inspired him. These encounters spark an inquiry that addresses three main themes: how the Arctic has affected the imagination, how utilitarian desires shape one's view of landscape, and how we might understand the true meaning of wealth. These opening sections are framed in the excursion mode of classic natural history but conclude with a profession of faith that coming to know some different place can lead to "a lasting security of the soul and heart" (p. 14). The book therefore presents itself as a spiritual autobiography in which natural history becomes a species of pilgrimage.

The first chapter, "Arktikós," attempts to define the "northern landscape" of the book's subtitle, no easy task, it proves. Lopez takes the reader on an imaginary journey from equator to pole along a single meridian, demonstrating how changes in the quality and quantity of solar radiation affect the character of terrestrial ecosystems. One way or another, he concludes, everything in the landscape depends upon light.

The next three chapters, "Banks Island," "Tôrnârssuk," and "Lancaster Sound," present close views of three celebrity species, the musk ox, the polar bear, and the narwhal. Watching musk oxen graze in an arctic oasis on Banks Island, Lopez marvels at their perfect adaptation to the climate and the terrain. "There is something," he muses, "of the original creation here" (p. 44). Discussions of musk ox anatomy, nutrition, temperature control mechanisms, behavior, and population cycles lead Lopez back to his initial impression of Edenic innocence: "They were so intensely good at being precisely what they were" (p. 75).

If the musk oxen exemplify innocence and harmony, the polar bear exemplifies intelligence and restless power. A solitary and indefatigable traveler, equally at home on sea, ice, or land, the bear lives by its wits and is much respected by the Eskimos, though for Europeans it symbolized "the implacable indifference of an inhospitable landscape" (p. 113). Lopez describes its marvelous fur, whose hollow guard hairs conduct ultraviolet light to the dark skin below, the bare foot pads that dispel excess heat, the extraordinary senses that enable it to locate a ringed seal surfacing in its breathing cave under the snow. Eskimo hunters and research biologists share their findings with Lopez, but all agree that the bear's life can never be fully known, nor broken conveniently into pieces: "Like the skater's long, graceful arc, it is a statement about life, the full exercise of which is beautiful" (p. 89).

Narwhals, which are even more elusive, embody for Lopez the Arctic's abiding mystery. "We know more about the rings of Saturn than we know about the narwhal," he writes (p. 128). Standing on the ice edge in Admiralty Inlet with a party of Eskimo hunters, Lopez ponders narwhal anatomy and behavior, which includes synchronous swimming, and wonders how they conceive of space in their dark, three-dimensional world: "perhaps only musicians have some inkling of the formal shape of emotions and motivation that might define such a sensibility" (p. 138). The narwhal's strange tusk, still a puzzle to science, became entwined during the Middle Ages with the legend of the unicorn, a fact that leads Lopez to speculate on the economic and moral consequences of projecting our dreams upon animals. He thinks of a mythical Chinese creature, the *ki-lin*, which possessed the "compassion of the unicorn but also the air of a spiritual warrior, or monk" (p. 150) and which, therefore, was never hunted or sold. Lopez does not propose the narwhal as a *ki-lin* but hopes that "in the simple appreciation of a world not our own to define, that poised arctic landscape, we might find some solace by discovering the *ki-lin* hidden within ourselves, like a shaft of light" (p. 151).

The fifth chapter, "Migration," moves from the species level to that of the landscape. The interwoven movements of different animals form patterns older than human nations, "a calming reminder of a more fundamental order" (p. 155). Vast and complex, they make Lopez think of "the land breathing" (p. 162). He considers tundra birds such as the snow geese, the profusion of fish and marine mammals that move through Bering Strait, the exemplary caribou. He concludes that time passes differently in the Arctic than it does in the temperate zones, and that animals may be understood better using the metaphors of quantum physics than those of Cartesian mechanism. "Animals confound us not because they are deceptively simple but because they are finally inseparable from the complexities of life . . . the relationships that bind forms of energy into recognizable patterns" (p. 178).

Because human movements are inextricably linked to those of animals in the Arctic, Lopez turns next to a sustained examination of Eskimo culture, concentrating on prehistory and traditional hunting techniques. He recounts with admiration explorer Robert Flaherty's story of Comock, an Eskimo man whose family, fleeing starvation, lost all their belongings when the ice split open beneath their camp. Excaping to a distant island, Comock, his wife, and his children survived for years by improvising tools and clothing; eventually, they saved enough driftwood and sealskins to build a boat and sail to the mainland. In effect, says Lopez, they recreated their entire material culture.

Such accomplishments require a knowledge, dexterity, and strength of character fostered by hunting, which Lopez experiences as a "state of mind [in which] all of one's faculties are brought to bear in an effort to become fully incorporated into the landscape" (p. 199). Lamentably, Western culture has separated us from the animals' world and taught us to treat them as objects, thus closing us off from the sacred transaction of the gift. Lopez enjoys traveling with Eskimos because they "know something about surviving":

At their best they are resilient, practical, and enthusiastic. They pay close attention in realms where they feel a capacity for understanding. They have a quality of *nuannaarpoq*, of taking extravagant pleasure in being alive; and they delight in finding it in other people. Facing as we do our various Armageddons, they are a good people to know. (p. 202)

As Sherman Paul observes, Lopez does not hunt, and his acquaintance with Eskimos is that of a traveler or journalist, not an ethnographer or apprentice in the manner of a Franz Boas or a Richard Nelson. He does not try to learn Eskimo arts or work them into his own life. For all the dignity and respect he accords them, he is interested only in aspects of their culture that cast light on issues raised by his own. He does not dwell, for example, on acculturation (such as the use of rifles or exploding harpoons) nor on religion, family life, or the role of women, though he nods toward the latter in passing. His interest centers less on contemporary social realities than on traditional lifeways. In this respect his portrayal of Eskimos carries a romantic tinge of the "noble savage," though nobility is now defined in ecocentric terms.

In the sixth chapter, "Ice and Light," Lopez turns back toward his own culture with an examination of the Arctic's physical elements as they affect perception and imagination. Icebergs fascinate him, as do the character and movement of sea ice, and remarkable bodies of open water called polynyas, and the complex ecologies of ice and snow. He describes stunning optical phenomena such as the aurora borealis, solar rings, and the mirage known as a fata morgana, which caused early explorers to report coasts and mountain ranges in the midst of the open sea. Wondering at how the imagination can deal with such splendor, Lopez considers paintings of arctic landscapes as a "conversation with the land" and concludes by comparing icebergs to cathedrals, both of which engage "our passion for light" (p. 248).

The next chapter, "The Country of the Mind," takes Lopez to the flat tundra shore of a barrier island. After the foregoing sublimities, such a place might seem "impoverished" to a Western eye, but it provides rich opportunities for speculation about how aboriginal peoples construe their landscapes. As they live in a region, people accumulate "small bits of knowledge" that eventually constellate to form a spiritual view of landscape. Lopez cites the Lakota, who sensed a "correspondence" between the natural order and a higher, sacred order that occasionally revealed itself in natural phenomena. "The land is like poetry," he writes, "it is inexplicably coherent, it is transcendent in its meaning, and it has the power to elevate a consideration of human life" (p. 274). A comparison of two fundamental symbolic forms, language and maps, sharpens the contrast between Western and indigenous ways of thinking in the Arctic. Following anthropologists such as Benjamin Whorf, Franz Boas, and Claude Lévi-Strauss, Lopez sees language evolving out of a people's conversation with the land. English is good for describing historical sequences and causal relationships; Eskimo language is good for describing the land and human activity in it. Eskimo maps, startlingly accurate by Western standards, reflect intimate, firsthand knowledge of the terrain keyed to survival needs, rather than the distant, homogeneous perspective of aerial photography and universal coordinates. Lopez follows geographer Yi-Fu Tuan in recognizing stories as the principal means that human beings have used throughout time to connect themselves to the landscape and thereby to preserve both their wisdom and their sense of identity:

> The aspiration of aboriginal people throughout the world has been to achieve a congruent relationship with the land, to fit well in it. To achieve occasionally a state of high harmony or reverberation. The dream of this transcendent congruency included the evolution of a hunting and gathering relationship with the earth, in which a mutual regard was understood to prevail; but it also meant a conservation of the stories that bind people into the land. (p. 297)

Such a vision includes both individual and collective stories, for "the undisturbed landscape verifies both" (p. 298). And it highlights the social and therapeutic role of the storyteller, whom the Eskimos call *isumataq*, "a person who can create the atmosphere in which wisdom shows itself" (p. 298).

Lopez rounds out the book with two long chapters dealing with European exploration. Although he surveys more than a thousand years of expeditions, his aim is critical rather than comprehensive. "The Intent of Monks," which covers the early voyages from Saint Brendan through Sir John Barrow, focuses on a critique of motive. Lopez sees Arctic history as a "legacy of desire" (p. 309). It is "the record of human longing to achieve something significant, to be free of some of the grim weight of life" (p. 310). Wealth was one focus of desire, albeit a distorted one: first the search for a northwest passage to Asia, later the hunt for whale oil and furs, and finally the quest for geographic knowledge that would perpetuate naval power. These limited ideas of wealth restricted the imaginations of most early explorers, although a few did glimpse the land's other dimensions. To Elizabethan navigator John Davis, for instance, the Arctic's suffusion of light made it "the place of greatest dignitie" on earth (p. 333).

The next chapter, "A Northern Passage," brings a critique of character to more recent explorations. Nineteenth-century expeditions such as those of Sir John Franklin and Adolphus Greely met with disaster through a combination of ethnocentrism and poor leadership. Few appreciated the knowledge and skills of the Eskimo, and those who did, like Robert Peary and Vilhjalmur Stefansson, put it to the service of personal ambition or distorted utilitarian goals. Lopez concludes with a visit to an oil camp on Prudhoe Bay, where the "muscular equipment" and the lonely workers medicating their boredom with thick steaks and pornography offer a hellish contrast to the dignity of traditional Eskimos. The utopian dreams of its managers notwithstanding, the oil camp reveals a colonial mentality that cannot insure peace or security in the long run. "For a relationship with landscape to be lasting, it must be reciprocal," Lopez concludes. "In approaching the land with an attitude of obligation . . . one establishes a regard from which dignity can emerge. From that dignified relationship with the land, it is possible to imagine an extension of dignified relationships throughout one's life" (pp. 404–405).

This hope is, indeed, a lofty one, counter to so many of the signs of modern times. Lopez does not attempt to refute these signs. Instead, he offers an epilogue linking his hope once again to its sources: travel with Eskimos and the contemplation of Arctic landscapes. His last gesture, a bow toward the north from the shores of the Bering Sea, reflects the ceremonial act with which he began, now deepened by years of travel and learning:

> When I stood I thought I glimpsed my own desire. The landscape and the animals were like something found at the end of a dream. The edges of the real landscape became one with the edges of something I had dreamed. But what I had dreamed was only a pattern, some beautiful pattern of light. The continuous work of the imagination, I thought, to bring what is actual together with what is dreamed is an expression of human evolution. The conscious desire is to achieve a state, even momentarily, that like light is unbounded, nurturing, suffused with wisdom and creation, a state in which one has absorbed that very darkness which before was the perpetual sign of defeat. (p. 414)

These beautiful images both sum up the book's moral vision and signal its literary achievement. *Arctic Dreams* is an epic work, but more in the Dantean than in the Homeric or Virgilian sense. Like all epics it unfolds on a grand scale, moralizing the landscape, detailing feats of heroism, engaging the deepest spiritual, political, and historical questions, and propounding a view of the noblest possibilities for human life. But it departs from the classical model of epic in the same manner as Dante's *Divine Comedy*, by placing the narrator at the center and focusing on his own journey toward understanding. In Dante, the warfare that was central to classical epic is sublimated into the pilgrim's struggle with sin; in Lopez, the pilgrim struggles with his own culture. Both works end

with a beatific vision, a glimpse of transcendent meaning and universal harmony. Indeed, Lopez's aspiration to achieve a state like that of light vividly recalls Dante's Empyrean, the highest heaven of pure light reached at the end of the *Paradiso*.

Sherman Paul has justly called Lopez a "legatee of the transcendentalists" because of his moral explorations of nature and his love of light (p. 107). But it would also be fair to call him an heir of that medieval Catholicism which viewed all things as meaningfully connected and aspired to a state of contemplative resonance with that divine order as the ultimate spiritual goal. It might seem strange that someone as ecologically minded as Lopez would identify beatitude with something as abstract as light, instead of with something more fecund and earthly, like grazing musk oxen. But for Aquinas and for Dante, who relegated his earthly paradise to the top of Purgatory, heaven itself was a matter of character. For them, as for Lopez, it was truly a country of the mind. Similarly, for both Lopez and his precursors in spiritual autobiography, the pilgrimage must eventuate in a story. By casting the experience into a form that can be shared, the pilgrim not only makes return for the wisdom he has received, but also realizes the prophetic vocation for which his experiences have prepared him. And the story itself, when fully realized, enacts a method for attaining wisdom: the narrator's art becomes a demonstration, a form of spiritual exercise.

In his examination of the search for awareness in American nature writing, critic Scott Slovic observes that part of the appeal of *Arctic Dreams* comes from its message that anyone can achieve a personal and "particularized" understanding of the land through "imaginative scrutiny but not necessarily mystical vision" (p. 153). The book takes the reader through a learning process that mirrors "the hopefulnesses of the narrator's ongoing conversion" (p. 165). That conversion, as we have seen, involves a distinctive practice combining the research and observations of a naturalist with the attentiveness of a hunter and the devotion of a monk. This practice, enacted in writing as well as in life, leads not only to a deeper appreciation of the landscape and its inhabitants, but to a rediscovery of one's own culture. A large part of the joy and affection one feels on reading Lopez comes from the manner in which his most exotic journeys confirm the noblest insights of Western civilization.

Selected Bibliography

WORKS OF BARRY LOPEZ

FICTION

Desert Notes: Reflections in the Eye of a Raven (Kansas City, Mo.: Sheed Andrews and McMeel, 1976); *Giving Birth to Thunder, Sleeping with His Daughter: Coyote Builds North America* (Kansas City, Mo.: Sheed Andrews and McMeel, 1977); *River Notes: The Dance of Herons* (Kansas City, Mo.: Sheed Andrews and McMeel, 1979); *Winter Count* (New York: Scribners, 1981); *Crow and Weasel* (San Francisco: North Point, 1990); "Remembering Orchards," in *American Short Fiction* 1 (winter 1991); "Benjamin Claire, North Dakota Tradesman, Writes to the President of the United States," in *North American Review* 277 (September/October 1992); "The Interior of North Dakota," in *Paris Review* 34 (winter 1992); "Thomas Lowdermilk's Generosity," in *American Short Fiction* 3 (winter 1993); *Field Notes: The Grace Note of the Canyon Wren* (New York: Knopf, 1994); "Ruben Mendoza Vega, Suzuki Professor of Early Caribbean History, University of Florida at Gainesville, Offers a History of the United States Based on Personal Experience," in *Manoa* 6 (summer 1994).

ESSAYS

"Renegotiating the Contracts," in *Parabola* 8 (spring 1983), corrected version repr. in Thomas J. Lyon, ed., *This Incomperable Lande: A Book of American Nature Writing* (Boston: Houghton Mifflin, 1989); "California Desert: A Worldly Wilderness," in *National Geographic* 171 (January 1987); "Landscapes Open and Closed," in *Harper's* 275 (July 1987); *Crossing Open Ground* (New York: Scribners, 1988); "Informed by Indifference," in *Harper's* 276 (May 1988); "Life and Death in Galápagos (A Journalist's Perspective)," in *North American Review* 274 (June 1989); "The American Geographies," in *Orion Nature Quarterly* 8 (autumn 1989); "Who Are These Animals We Kill?" in *Witness* 3 (winter 1989), repr. with corrections as "Apologia," in *Harper's* 281 (July 1990); *The Rediscovery of North America* (Lexington: Univ. of Kentucky Press, 1990), repr. in *Orion* 11 (summer 1992); "Replacing Memory," in *Georgia Review* 47 (spring 1993); "Offshore: A Journey to the Weddell Sea," in *Orion* 13 (winter 1994); "Caring for the Woods," in *Audubon* 97 (March/April 1995).

NATURAL HISTORY

Of Wolves and Men (New York: Scribners, 1978); *Arctic Dreams: Imagination and Desire in a Northern Landscape* (New York: Scribners, 1986).

INTERVIEWS

Jim Aton, "An Interview with Barry Lopez," in *Western American Literature* 21 (spring 1986); Kay Bonetti, "An Interview with Barry Lopez," in *Missouri Review* 11, no. 3 (1988); Alice Evans, "Leaning into the Light: An Interview with Barry Lopez," in *Poets and Writers* 22 (March/April 1994); Edward Lueders, *Writing Natural History: Dialogues with Authors* (Salt Lake City: Univ. of Utah Press, 1989); Douglas Marx, "Barry Lopez: 'I Am a Writer Who Travels,'" in *Publishers Weekly* (26 September 1994); Nicholas O'Connell, *At the Field's End: Interviews with Twenty Pacific Northwest Writers* (Seattle: Madrona, 1987); Trish Todd, "Barry Lopez Recalls His Arctic Dreams," in *Publishers Weekly* (11 October 1985).

BIOGRAPHICAL AND CRITICAL STUDIES

Sherman Paul, "Making the Turn: Rereading Barry Lopez," in his *For Love of the World: Essays on Nature Writers* (Iowa City: Univ. of Iowa Press, 1992); Daniel W. Ross, "Barry Lopez's *Arctic Dreams:* Looking into a New Heart of Darkness," in *CEA Critic* 54 (fall 1991); William H. Rueckert, "Barry Lopez and the Search for a Dignified and Honorable Relation with Nature," in *North Dakota Quarterly* 59 (spring 1991); Scott Slovic, " 'A More Particularized Understanding': Seeking Qualitative Awareness in Barry Lopez's *Arctic Dreams,*" in his *Seeking Awareness in American Nature Writing* (Salt Lake City: University of Utah Press, 1992); Peter Wild, *Barry Lopez* (Boise, Idaho: Boise State University Western Writers Series, 1984).

FAITH MCNULTY
(b. 1918)

AINA NIEMELA

IN THE AUTUMN of 1963, Faith McNulty, a writer on the staff of the *New Yorker*, clipped a short item she happened to read in the *New York Times*. She recalls the moment in "The Whooping Crane," in her collected wildlife stories (1980). The article reported that forty-two whooping cranes had migrated from their nesting grounds in Canada and arrived at their wintering grounds on the Gulf Coast of Texas. It added that despite many years of effort by the Fish and Wildlife Service to protect the tiny population, the cranes were threatened with extinction. McNulty was intrigued. She loved animals but had never studied them or written about them. The birds she saw on her Rhode Island farm "seemed to come and go as interchangeably as windblown leaves." How could anyone know that there were just forty-two of one kind? And how was it possible that the Fish and Wildlife Service wanted to protect them but was not able to do so? Her instincts as a journalist told her she was on the scent of a good story.

The questions she asked were less naive in 1963 than they might be today, when wildlife issues are staples for writers and filmmakers, and the term "endangered species" appears in the media again and again. But in the early 1960s, this was not so. The efforts of conservation organizations received little attention outside the pages of their own publications, and many of the magazines that plead the cause of wild animals today did not exist. Nor had television yet discovered wildlife as a nearly inexhaustible source of film footage. In 1963, Secretary of the Interior Stewart Udall was just about to draw up a list of animals that were "rare and endangered," and the first endangered species legislation was still three years away. Despite the lesson of the passenger pigeon, the meaning of extinction had not yet begun to dawn on the public consciousness. Few people outside of conservation circles had ever heard of a whooping crane.

Faith McNulty worked on the whooping crane story for more than two years. She read everything that scientists and conservationists had written about the bird and the problems of its survival. She went to the offices of the Fish and Wildlife Service in Washington and made her way through the relevant files, starting from the late 1930s and the founding of the Texas wildlife refuge that had become the winter home of the last remaining whooping cranes. The story appeared in the *New Yorker* (6 August 1966) as a "Reporter at Large" feature. The subtitle, "The Thread Remains Very Thin"—quoting biologist Robert Porter Allen, the crane's tireless defender—referred to the slender margin between the bird's survival and its extinction. Later that year the story was published as a book by E. P. Dutton and received Dutton's annual Animal Book Award.

The Whooping Crane: The Bird That Defies Extinction is an unusual work, excellent by several standards. A beautifully written portrait of a rare animal, it is also an engrossing piece of investigative journalism and a revealing history of a significant conservation effort—all in less than two hundred pages. Reviewers were full of praise. "A rare book on a rare bird," said *Time*. Franklin Russell, reviewing in *Life*, thought it read "like a tragicomic play." Faith McNulty had found the theme that would occupy the next twenty years of her writing life.

Being on the staff of the *New Yorker* during the 1960s and 1970s was a fortunate position for a writer with an interest in wildlife. Starting in 1959, E. B. White issued continuous "bulletins tracing Man's progress in making the planet uninhabitable" in the magazine. At White's urging, Rachel Carson wrote about the devastating effects of DDT on animals and humans in three articles that were published in the *New Yorker* in 1962 and appeared in her book *Silent Spring* the same year. On the first Earth Day, in 1970, the *New Yorker* took a full-page ad in the *New York Times* that cited Carson's articles as marking the beginning of a new era of environmental awareness and that pledged the magazine to publishing ongoing "authoritative reports in this limitless field." It was a good time, and a good place, to be a writer on wildlife subjects. And by virtue of her upbringing and training as a journalist, Faith McNulty brought unique skills and sympathies to the task.

The Education of a Wildlife Reporter

She was born Faith Corrigan, the daughter of Joseph Eugene Corrigan, a highly regarded judge in New York City, and Faith Robinson Corrigan, on 28 November 1918. The family, which included Faith and her younger sister Elisabeth, lived in a brownstone on East Tenth Street. "Split Level Living" (1955), an early story she wrote for the *New Yorker*, depicts the stable and orderly life in the Corrigan household of the

1920s, in which each generation lived on a separate floor: "the family existed in depth, built tier upon tier, with a chain of command protectively linking all its members."

Summers were spent at the Victorian home built by Mrs. Corrigan's parents in southern Rhode Island, where members of her family had lived since the seventeenth century. In those days the place was still a working farm. Faith followed the resident farmer as he tended the horses, cows, and chickens, and cared for the garden. Animals were her closest companions, and animal stories were her favorite reading. She describes the kinship with animals she felt as a child in "Woodchuck," one of her collected wildlife stories: "Any creature I encountered was an individual, as distinct, as worthy of life as myself and much more marvelous" (p. 373). In the introduction to the collection, she tells of her longing for closer acquaintance: "I wanted so much to know what it is like to be an animal; how it would feel to be part of their world, to see *our* world through their eyes" (p. 3). Her parents did not object when she brought home frogs, snakes, birds, and turtles or tried to raise orphaned creatures in the bathroom.

Her mother had strong feelings about the humane treatment of animals and was the founder of the town's animal shelter. As an adult, Faith McNulty recalled her mother's distress when she saw the farmer carry the chickens by their feet on the way to the chopping block. Mrs. Corrigan ordered him to hold the birds upright. (This anecdote and others that follow are taken from an interview with the author in Wakefield, Rhode Island, in 1994.)

Faith could also be outspoken in the defense of animals. When her father reminisced about hunting frogs during his youth in Florida, she reproached him. "I don't want you to hunt frogs. They are nice animals and want to live."

As the elder daughter, Faith had a special rapport with her father. From the time she was small, he encouraged her to think that she would one day be part of the working world. The glimpses she got as a girl made it seem an exciting place, and she always imagined that her role there would be that of a writer. Judge Corrigan's involvement in the politics of liberal reform meant that the family's New York home was frequented by writers and journalists, among them several prominent newswomen. Occasionally Faith would visit the courtroom where her father presided and witness the drama of criminal justice and the legal system. Her father was heading for a career in national politics when he died in 1935, at the age of sixty.

At the time of her father's death, Faith Corrigan was sixteen and completing the education appropriate for a daughter of a well-to-do family, at Miss Porter's School in Connecticut. She went on to Miss Hewitt's in New York and Barnard College, where she studied for a year. She left to marry Charles Fair in September 1938, returned to Barnard briefly when the marriage ended, and then left for good to look for work in publishing.

In 1941, her mother moved back to Rhode Island, and Faith Fair was on her own in New York. She soon learned that magazines were unwilling to hire a young woman with no experience. *Life* turned her down flat. After many months of rejection, one of her late father's journalist friends opened a door for her at the *New York Daily News*, which, because of the war and a shortage of men, was hiring its first copygirls. Faith joined two other young women in the city room. When *Time* magazine ran a story on the new faces in the traditionally male workplace with her name included, *Life* called and offered her a job. Without mentioning that they had just turned her down, she told them that she would let them know when she was ready.

As a copygirl at a New York daily, Faith learned how news is turned into print—news that included world-shaking events like the Japanese attack on Pearl Harbor, as well as the day-to-day happenings of a major city. But two years at the *Daily News* was enough time to show her that the paper gave female reporters little scope outside the women's pages. She called *Life* to say she would accept their offer and was immediately welcomed aboard. At *Life* she researched picture stories, acted as a factotum for the magazine's well-known photographers, and did some reporting, thereby gaining the confidence and enjoying the excitement that

comes with being part of an influential national publication during a time of war.

A short story Faith wrote in the early 1940s, "No Flowers," deftly conveys people's sense of priorities during the war. In it a woman returns to her country home in early spring and tries to persuade the gardener to take out the perennial beds and plant "things to eat" instead. "Everything's got to be different," she explains. In the author's life as well, the natural world was being preempted by human affairs.

She had been encouraged to write the story by a friend she had met at the *Daily News*, an experienced newspaperman. When she told him about the conversation between the woman and her gardener, which she had heard in the Rhode Island country town where her mother lived, he suggested she write it down exactly as she had spoken it. He would send it to the *New Yorker*, which published his own short fiction. She wrote it, he sent it, and on 10 April 1943 the *New Yorker* published it, the first story she ever wrote for a magazine.

The war that had given Faith her first job opportunity gave her the next as well. In 1944 she went to London to work for the U.S. Office of War Information, where amid the sound of buzz bombs and sirens, she helped to produce propaganda magazines to be dropped from planes over occupied Europe. The ship on which she came home in the summer of 1945 sailed into Portland, Maine, just as the dropping of the atomic bomb on Hiroshima was being announced.

A month after her return, in September 1945, Faith married the helpful newspaperman. John McNulty, some twenty years her senior, was well known for his stories of life on New York's Third Avenue. Over the course of two decades, the *New Yorker* published more than sixty of them, with titles like "Man like Grady, You Got to Know Him First," "Two Bums Here Would Spend Freely Except for Poverty," "Labor Dispute Starts on Account Everybody Got Rights."

John McNulty's direct, vernacular style was greatly admired by his colleagues at the *New Yorker*, especially James Thurber and E. B. White. In a letter to Faith, White wrote that John

McNulty's ear was "better . . . than anybody's I can think of." Faith often said she had learned much from his work. The deceptive simplicity of her writing may owe something to John McNulty's stories, "so off-hand, so modest-seeming," as Brendan Gill characterized them.

Faith and John McNulty's son, John Jr., was born in 1950. In *My Son Johnny*, the senior McNulty describes their family life in New York City, father writing at home and looking after Johnny with the help of a wonderful woman named Josephine, while Faith goes to the office. She worked at *Collier's* and *Cosmopolitan* until 1953, when she joined the staff of the *New Yorker* as a "Talk of the Town" writer.

"Talk of the Town" pieces, the short, often anecdotal pieces at the front of the magazine, are meant to entertain and surprise—"interesting information found in unusual places" is the assignment. Faith McNulty wrote about everything from the king of Togoland to the number of pneumatic drills being used on a given day in New York City. When she started, "Talk of the Town" writers more or less dashed off the stories, which Brendan Gill polished and edited. They were published unsigned. The experience was a liberating one for a writer who tended to worry about every word.

The McNulty family spent holidays at an old farm they had bought in Wakefield, Rhode Island, not far from Faith's mother's family property. It was in South County, as the area is called, that John McNulty died of a heart attack in 1956, at the age of sixty, the same age at which Faith's father had died. *Time* magazine paid him tribute as the "gentle troubadour of cabbies, rummies, and $2 bettors in Manhattan . . . and other places where elbows are bent."

At the end of the following year, Faith McNulty married Richard Martin, a theatrical director. In 1958, together with young Johnny, they left the city to settle in Wakefield. The life of an urban journalist was behind her, and the skills it had provided her were about to find new employment.

At Bittersweet Farm, now her home in South County, McNulty could keep horses and ride, as she had in her girlhood, through farmland just

beginning to reveal the inroads of development. Gradually she began to rediscover, as a writer, the interests of her childhood. In 1962 she wrote the first of her children's books about animals, this one about a fish called Arty the Smarty. With her sister, Elisabeth Keiffer, who lived nearby, she collaborated in the writing of *Wholly Cats* (1964), an informative volume on felines. When her husband brought in a baby mouse from the barn, she raised it in a cage in the kitchen. It quickly became full grown and wonderfully tame. After observing it closely for many months, she wrote "Notes from a Mouse-keeper's Diary," which was published in *Audubon Magazine* in 1964.

Mousie, as she describes her, is a beguiling creature, and the writer's fondness for her is evident. McNulty was beginning to allow her readers into the intimate relationship she enjoyed with animals. But it was a while before she introduced familiar creatures into the pages of the *New Yorker*. Her first wildlife reports there were about animals she saw from a distance.

The Whooping Crane

Her two years of research and study on the whooping crane yielded a rich lode of information about the rare bird and the people who became involved in its fate. The report McNulty wrote is heavily freighted with facts, names, and numbers—numbers of birds returning each fall, numbers of eggs hatched, dates of administrative changes in the agencies responsible for the bird's protection, and a large cast of characters, human and avian. Through her artful presentation, a sizable body of information tells a moving story. In a letter congratulating her, Katharine White (the wife of E. B. White and the *New Yorker* editor who had handled her fiction) wrote that "the writing is so good that the reader hardly realizes how many facts he is absorbing."

The writing was undeniably excellent, and the material itself abounded in suspense and human interest. The life history of the whooping crane and the history of the efforts to save it included dramatic elements that were necessarily missing from McNulty's later reports, such as the ones on the black-footed ferret and the numinous whale.

First, there was the numerability of the birds, which had struck her when she first read about them—the fact that the entire species could be counted in figures that were humanly imaginable. The number of whoopers arriving at the Aransas Refuge in Texas from their nesting ground had been recorded year after year, and the figures were there in the files of the Fish and Wildlife Service—fourteen birds in 1938, increasing slowly and uncertainly to forty-four in 1966. But no one had given those figures wings, so to speak. As the story unfolds, the number of birds that manage to reach the refuge each October becomes a heart-pounding cadence in the narrative.

Then there were the detailed records that told the stories of individual birds. The lives of the flock at Aransas had been chronicled by Robert Porter Allen, the biologist assigned by the National Audubon Society to study the bird, and McNulty quotes generously from his well-written accounts. The reader comes to know certain crane families and individuals by name. For example, there is Josephine, the imperturbable heroine of the story, who perseveres in laying and hatching eggs despite all her guardians do to make her a tragic example of human error and fecklessness. In the book, the number of eggs she lays each year—two, one, none, in her small cage at the New Orleans Zoo—and the resulting offspring form a numerical counterpoint to the numbers of migrants that return each fall to the refuge.

The whooping crane's twenty-five-hundred-mile migratory flight is a further source of dramatic tension. The whereabouts of the bird's last remaining nesting grounds, somewhere in Canada's Northwest Territories, was unknown for many years. Into her finely braided narrative McNulty weaves the story of Allen's repeated searches for the bird's mysterious summer home.

Such is McNulty's art that we not only absorb without effort the amount of information she relates, as Katharine White remarked, but we must make an effort to notice what is missing in the account. In *The Whooping Crane*, we glimpse the bird almost entirely through the eyes of Allen and a few others. The only time we see author and crane in the same frame, both are in a museum, and the bird is stuffed. Yet a passage like the following, near the end of the book, seems as though it must describe McNulty's own experience.

> For some of us there is a strange magic in knowing that once again the flock has completed another extraordinary journey. Somehow, mysteriously, from high in the air the birds sense the nearness beneath them of the small patches of sand and water that are theirs. They brake their flight, and descend, floating down in narrower and narrower spirals. For an instant before a whooping crane touches the ground, its huge wings seem to hold it in the air. Its legs stretch out, reaching for the earth, and then it settles. Its great tapered, shining white body comes down so softly it seems as though it could light upon an egg and not break it. It is a marvelous thing. (p. 186)

In the original *New Yorker* story and in the version that appears in her collected wildlife stories, the last sentence reads, "Those who have seen this say it is a marvelous thing." The added phrase destroys the illusion of immediacy created in the preceding passage but gives the bird a still greater sense of rarity and mystery.

Passages of lyrical description like this one are a rarity themselves in a narrative dense with information. But the same simplicity and directness of expression and the same sensitivity to rhythm inform her writing throughout. They became McNulty's signature as a nature writer. In *The Whooping Crane*, they give a fact-laden narrative the weightless grace of the great bird's landing flight. For a reader with even a moderate interest in wild animals, the intertwined stories of the birds' fortunes at the beleaguered refuge, their perilous migration to and from the unknown breeding grounds, and the pathetic struggle of the captive queen Josephine to continue the species form a narrative with the gripping power of a thriller. McNulty never again wrote anything quite like it. But then, as she was at pains to explain, in all the species on earth, there is just one whooping crane.

In the course of writing about the whooping crane, McNulty was made aware of the imperiled state of other wildlife. As she sought to answer her own question about why it was so difficult to save the cranes, a creature many people thought deserved to be saved, she learned that the fate of some less-favored species hung in the balance. She wrote, with a sharp sense of the historic moment, "This [extinction of a species] is a death quite different from the death of an individual . . . it has a different finality. This extinction of something that will never, in all eternity, be duplicated, is an occurrence that seems to break a strand of time itself" (*The Whooping Crane*, p. 23).

Within months of writing the above, McNulty passed a display of furs in a Saks Fifth Avenue shopwindow in New York City. She visited the store's fur salon, and in "Talk of the Town" (17 December 1966) she reported on what she saw there, including "a zebra that lay on the floor as though it had been run over by a steam roller. . . . tigerskins . . . draped over tables and couches." But the salon's pièce de résistance, proudly brought from the vault by an obliging salesperson, was the pelt of a river otter: " 'Very, very rare,' she said. 'Very, very expensive. . . . Of course, this fur is too heavy to wear. It will be used as trimming.' " In the next sentence, the writer quotes the World Wildlife Fund on the same giant Brazilian river otter, now "believed to be confined to a few rivers." "Fun Furs," a "Talk of the Town" story she published soon thereafter (20 May 1967), focuses on her interviews with New York merchants who sell the skins of leopards, cheetahs, and other spotted cats, doomed to extinction "because of [their] ill luck in being beautiful." The tone of both pieces is cool and controlled, with thrusts of dark humor (Fun for whom? the author asks).

Some years later, in a talk about her work given at the Peacedale Library at South Kingston, Rhode Island, McNulty voiced her faith in information to evoke a moral response: "I have tried to present facts, uncluttered by sentimentality, so that the deeper ethical and emotional problems implicit in our relationship to animals could manifest themselves" (13 July 1978). Of course, the success of such a strategy depends on the artistry with which the facts are delivered; and in these short pieces on the fur trade, as in *The Whooping Crane*, McNulty proved to be a virtuoso performer. Her next extended report again relied on researched information, tellingly presented, to make its case.

Must They Die?

While she was conducting her research on the crane, McNulty learned that the U.S. Fish and Wildlife Service was busy destroying wildlife in vast areas of rangeland in the Midwest. In 1964, the listing of the black-footed ferret as an endangered species placed the agency in an awkward position. The agency was now responsible for protecting an animal that for years it had been decimating, through its highly successful program aimed at eradicating prairie dogs. Ferrets depend on prairie dogs as food and live in their burrows. The new charge to save the ferret produced "a crisis in what was already a bad case of governmental schizophrenia" (*Must They Die?*, p. 8).

"The Prairie Dog and the Black-Footed Ferret" came out as a "Reporter at Large" story in the *New Yorker* in 1970 and a year later was expanded into a book, which the publisher titled *Must They Die? The Strange Case of the Prairie Dog and the Black-Footed Ferret*.

As background to the ferret-prairie dog story, McNulty documents the history of how the federal government got into the business of killing wildlife. She exposes the economic and political forces that maintained an army of government agents who "had gone about the West pressing their services as though they were peddling vacuum cleaners. Killing was their business, and dead animals were their product" (p. 24). Her thorough research made *Must They Die?*, like her preceding wildlife book, a valuable source for conservationists and wildlife biologists.

Though the threat of the ferret's extinction provides the occasion for the book, the *They* in the book's title could as easily refer to the many other animals—coyotes, foxes, eagles—killed when they fed on the victims of 1080, the potent poison used to kill the prairie dogs. In the microcosm of a prairie dog town, she says, the poisoning was "a Hiroshima-like disaster." (Thanks in part to negative publicity, 1080 was banned the year following the book's publication; it was later reinstated for limited use.) But on a wider scale still, *Must They Die?* refers to all the hundreds of thousands of animals killed deliberately or indirectly in the name of Animal Damage Control, as the program was then called.

With her book on the ferret, McNulty entered the lists against all those who believe that animals that infringe on human freedom of action—whether in farming, raising livestock, hunting, or building houses—deserve extermination. The "varmint" mentality dates back to the settlement of the country and was even shared by early conservationists. McNulty's challenge to this viewpoint is part of the shift in thinking about the value of wildlife that has been taking place since the 1940s.

Aldo Leopold had stepped into this arena more than thirty years earlier, after his conversion from a killer of wolves to a defender of wolves and other predators. He described the reversal in the often-quoted passage in *A Sand County Almanac* (1949) in which he watches the "green fire" die in the eyes of a wolf he has just shot. Throughout much of his later career in the U.S. Forest Service, Leopold argued strenuously for the importance of predators to the "land community." (His son, biologist A. Starker Leopold, figures prominently in *Must They Die?* as the head of the advisory board that in 1964 attempted to limit the abuses of animal control.) Olaus Murie, a biologist with the Fish and Wildlife Service and Aldo Leopold's contemporary, would have extended protection to rodents as well as predators. And in *Silent Spring* (1962) Rachel Carson had shown the costs of pouring DDT into the air and water in order to control a few insect species. These and other scientists helped shape the new ecological understanding of animal life that validated the existence of varmints and other inconvenient creatures and cautioned against large-scale extermination of any species. In a letter to McNulty, E. B. White neatly expressed the idea in its contemporary application when he wrote, "No animal is unimportant, and I'm glad you are sticking up for the Black-footed ferret."

In the 1980s and 1990s, the federal program McNulty spotlighted in *Must They Die?* has continued to generate heated political debate in the West over the rights of wildlife versus the rights of livestock owners on public land. Those who would answer the question of the book's title in the affirmative are often sheep ranchers who claim losses to coyotes. The naysayers include a number of humane organizations, environmentalists, and legal experts who argue that the country's wildlife is a national resource that should not be sacrificed to the economic interests of a small group of citizens.

McNulty stated the philosophical position of the opponents of "animal damage control," from Leopold to the present, with characteristic directness when she said, in writing about the whooping crane, that the birds' survival "represents the wishes of those who feel strongly that mankind should not take over the earth at the expense of all other creatures" (*The Whooping Crane*, p. 15). Her later researches on the prairie dog informed her how far the takeover had gone in the case of this creature and others, and in *Must They Die?* she writes in anger.

While taking aim most directly at the bureaucrats and politicians behind the poisoning program, McNulty scatters shot at all who sanction or participate in the wanton killing of wildlife, as in the passage below, which begins as an idyllic description of the South Dakota landscape where the ferret was thought to be making its last stand.

> Everywhere, the land stretching to the horizon seemed prosperous and undisturbed, offering everything needed to sustain countless forms of animal life. . . . Perhaps as many animals survive there as anywhere else in the United States. They are important to the human

population. Killing them provides almost every man and boy in the region with his greatest source of excitement and entertainment. (p. 82)

This is not so much the statement of an environmentalist concerned with the loss of a species as the outburst of a lover and defender of all animals, rare or not.

The Great Whales

In 1973, when Congress enacted a third Endangered Species Act, Faith McNulty's readers were already familiar with several of the imperiled animals and would shortly learn about more, as she continued to make new efforts to interest people in the lives of animals. In her *New Yorker* piece "The Falcons of Morro Rock" (23 December 1972), she takes the reader with her to join the vigil of a couple keeping watch over a nest repeatedly robbed by falconers off the coast of California. In "Kill the Pupfish? Save the Pupfish!," a piece published in *Audubon* (November 1973) she describes her travels to the Mojave Desert to peer into the ponds that hold what was then the smallest endangered animal species, the desert pupfish. Her next long report, on whales, balances researched information with her own impressions of the animal.

McNulty wrote "Lord of the Fish" for the *New Yorker* (6 August 1973) when Greenpeacers had not yet gone out in their Zodiacs to challenge whaling vessels and "Save the Whales" bumper stickers had not been printed. Few people knew a humpback from any other kind of whale, much less how many were left and where to find them. McNulty's profile of the whale explains what was then known about the different kinds of whales; gives a short history of whaling, drawing on the vivid, often horrific, accounts by the American whaling captain Charles Scammon; and describes her own whale-watching experiences. To publish such a piece in a major national publication was a deed on behalf of the whales and the nascent movement to protect them. It

was published in book form in 1974, as *The Great Whales.*

In it McNulty joins researcher Roger Payne in a sailboat off Bermuda to listen through a hydrophone to the songs of humpback whales, goes whale watching in the lagoons where the gray whales breed along the coast of Baja California, and visits the whale Gigi at Sea World in San Diego before Gigi is set free. For the first time in her longer reports, McNulty describes her own experiences as a researcher. In language carefully calibrated to the scenes she records, she conveys a mood of rapt attention. For a while, the world in which the animal has its being becomes more real than the human one around it. In one scene, she is alone on the deck of a boat, listening through earphones to the whales singing below.

The cold, empty world of the surface dropped away as I slipped into the populated depths. Far from being empty, the great chamber below was filled with life. I relaxed as I listened to its lively hum. It was like looking through a pane of glass . . . yet not being quite able to enter. I thought about the various speculations as to why whales make their strange sounds, and the answer suddenly seemed clear: they sing their songs so that they won't be alone. (p. 63)

In such passages, the quality of her attention approaches the state of immersion that biologist E. O. Wilson calls the naturalist's trance.

While the trance lasts, the person participates in the lives of other creatures. When it is over, there is a sense of loss. She describes her feelings after long listening to the songs of whales: "I . . . hear groans, bleats, moos, even motorcycles starting up and receding into the distance. . . . We feel left alone, like watchers when a parade has turned the corner" (p. 56). Later, when she walks along the shore of Scammon's Lagoon and hears the gray whales' soft breathing, she finds it "a companionable sound." The author's empathy with the living world makes her a participant in the scenes she describes, as well as their witness.

Other Reports on Animals

McNulty's use of her platform at the *New Yorker* to champion endangered wildlife drew the admiration of many conservationists, among them Edward Steele, a director of Defenders of Wildlife. Defenders had been furiously protesting the Fish and Wildlife Service's poisoning of animals on rangeland, and Steele counted McNulty's *New Yorker* exposé a coup for wildlife protection. He telephoned to tell her so and to enlist her aid in another urgent project.

Steele's attention was focused on Madagascar, the island nation that had evolved plants and animals found nowhere else on earth. At the time, in 1974, Madagascar, an emerging country beset with problems of poverty and a growing population, and bent on rapid development, showed little intention of taking the necessary measures to protect its dwindling wildlife. Defenders of Wildlife hoped to alert the world conservation community by devoting an entire issue of its magazine to the mounting tragedy.

Steele identified McNulty as the writer to tell Madagascar's story. He sent her and her husband, a good amateur photographer who often helped in her research travels, to the island nation. McNulty and Richard Martin spent six weeks in primitive countryside, guided by a native Malagasy. The April 1975 issue of *Defenders of Wildlife* carried her report.

In "Madagascar's Endangered Wildlife," McNulty shares her fascination with the island's exotic animals as she tallies up the forces arrayed against their survival. As on the whale excursion, after long concentration on the world of wild nature, she finds the return to human surroundings disconcerting. At the end of a day spent in the forests, she stands outdoors for a few moments, listening to "the sounds of small, unseen beings—unidentifiable squeaks and chirps and rustlings—birds, bats, insects, lemurs. . . . We left the lively dark and went into the house and the harsh, steady glare of the electric bulb. For a time it seemed very silent and dead inside the cement walls of the small room" (p. 131). Such contrasts between the fullness of

the living world and the emptiness of the spaces we create in its despite are again reminiscent of E. O. Wilson, who coined the term "biophilia" to account for the pleasure we take in other forms of life.

McNulty was often drawn to animals by their sheer beauty, and she was greatly taken by lemurs, those strange early ancestors of the monkey ("it seems," she notes in the version of the story that appears in her collected wildlife stories, "that primate looks have been going downhill ever since the monkeys took over from the lemurs" [p. 362]). In the final paragraph of the article, she lets the image of a particular lemur, a tame animal named Chico that she met at a refuge at Berenty and that had rested on her arm while she groomed its soft fur, bring home the enormity of the impending loss. She describes a visit to a museum:

> In the center was a glass case containing stuffed lemurs of a number of species. . . . Then I saw my little friend from Berenty—a brown *fulvus* just like Chico. . . . The lemur was posed so that it seemed to peer into the empty shadows behind me. I had the sudden notion that it was staring into the future, its glass eyes forever open in a tearless gaze. (p. 134)

McNulty's next wildlife assignment came when *Audubon* asked her to write a report on the California condor, whose numbers in the wild had fallen to fifty or sixty birds, perhaps even fewer. McNulty found herself entangled in the dispute over how best to preserve the small population. She disagreed with the biologists who favored capture. Perhaps as a result of the editorial tussle over how to represent both sides of the controversy, the two-part article that appeared in *Audubon* in 1978 lacks the clarity and force of the author's other reports on endangered animals. The condor story was a deeply frustrating experience for McNulty; and the condor's history since its removal from the wild has been equally full of frustration for conservationists.

Most of her experiences as a wildlife reporter were enjoyable ones, and she writes appreciatively of the biologists who shared their knowledge with her. In "Manatees" (*New Yorker*, 26 February 1979), she notes that "until recently few scientists bothered to study in depth creatures whose lives appeared to have no direct relation to human welfare." One of these few is biologist Daniel Hartman, who takes her for a swim in the Crystal River in Florida and introduces her to "what may be the gentlest creature on earth." "Manatees" ends on a philosophical note, as she considers the placid mammal's chances for survival in a society where many people "believe that every animal must serve a human purpose." She does not attempt to refute this belief; instead, she ventures to say what the manatee's purpose might be:

> It can be answered that the manatee serves a very high purpose indeed, although it is an abstract one. The manatee is, as far as I know at the moment, the only example of a higher mammal that lives its life virtually without aggression toward its own species or any other species. . . . Surely there is some use in contemplating this uniquely blameless life. (p. 89)

McNulty's fears about the future of all animals increased as she learned more about their struggles to survive in a world more and more dominated by human self-interest. In children she found some ground for hope. The growing awareness of the animal world that she observed among young people held out the possibility that animals might fare better at the hands of a new generation.

By 1995 McNulty had published more than fifteen books for children, most of them about animals and the natural world. In these stories she calls on the empathy she believes all children feel for living things. Some stories are spin-offs from her other books and articles about endangered species—*Whales: Their Life in the Sea* (1975), *Peeping in the Shell: A Whooping Crane Is Hatched* (1986). Others are about familiar creatures, like a woodchuck (*Orphan: The Story of a Baby Woodchuck*, 1992), and the spider she brought in from the garden on a leaf of lettuce (*The Lady and the Spider*, 1986).

From 1979 through 1991, McNulty wrote the *New Yorker*'s annual essay on and review of children's literature, a feature that Katharine White initiated and that McNulty took over from Jean Stafford. Among the recommended books were always a number about animals and the natural world. From time to time she reviewed children's books for the *New York Times* and other publications.

The Wildlife Stories

In 1980, *The Wildlife Stories of Faith McNulty* brought together many of her previously published stories about animals and added several new ones. The wildlife represented in the 470-page collection includes all the endangered animals she wrote about for the *New Yorker* (except for the ferret) plus the pupfish and the lemurs, which appeared elsewhere, and the gorilla Koko; *The Whooping Crane* and *The Great Whales* are reprinted in revised versions. The book also gives significant attention to South County wildlife, in stories first published in "Talk of the Town" and in *Audubon*.

By placing her anecdotal stories about local wildlife alongside her rigorous research reports, *Wildlife Stories* encompasses the full range of McNulty's repertoire and illumines her identity as a nature writer. Without this collection, her more personal writing about animals might have gone unrecognized a generation later, because most of it was published in magazines and some pieces were unsigned. In addition, the introductions to some of the stories, telling how and why McNulty wrote them, furnish autobiographical material that appears nowhere else. One reviewer commented that *Wildlife Stories* permitted her finally to meet an author whose work she had been reading for years.

Taken together, the twelve stories reveal the depth of McNulty's involvement with animals, as well as her self-awareness as a writer on animal subjects. In the introduction to one of

McNulty with Koko in Stanford, California, 1975

the essays, for instance, she identifies a critical difference between her reports on endangered species and her South County pieces when she says that there are "those who see individual animals as interchangeable digits in a very large number and point out that . . . only the existence of the species need concern us. This view has its validity. . . . and yet I have never divorced myself from the idea that individual worth in the animal kingdom is not restricted to human beings" (p. 374). She is aware that "this is a feeling that may be attacked as sentimental." Certainly neither *The Whooping Crane* nor her other long pieces are open to criticism on that score. Even though McNulty often dwells on individual animals—one of the compelling motifs in the crane narrative is the handful of birds whose lives we follow, and the pet lemur lends poignancy to her

vision of the species' future—there is never any doubt that the individual represents its kind.

By contrast, in several of her South County stories (and in the piece on the gorilla Koko) the individual animal is presented very much for its own sake. In these stories about a woodchuck, a starling, a mouse, McNulty returns to the theme of her childhood fascination with animals: the wish somehow to penetrate the world of another creature. As she explains in the introduction to *The Wildlife Stories*, that wish led to her adult interest in what scientists have been learning about the inner life of animals. Beginning with Robert Allen, McNulty developed a great respect for those biologists and ethologists who shared her curiosity about the animal mind: Francine Patterson, the keeper and mother figure for the gorilla Koko; George Archibald, who personally wooed a whooping crane that would respond only to human suitors. McNulty closely followed the work of scientists studying primate intelligence, and read with satisfaction Donald R. Griffins' books positing the mental experience of nonhuman creatures. The same interest inspired her careful observation of the animals that entered her own life.

Among the assembled wildlife stories are accounts of close encounters with animals, recorded in the lapidary prose she had refined over decades. Her first impression of "snakeness" is rendered as "a being neither cold nor warm, hostile nor friendly, and supple from tip of tongue to tip of tail." Coming face to face with the gorilla Koko, she says, "gave me a confusing sensation of looking into the eyes of someone almost, but not quite, like me." She contrasts the experience to that of looking into the eyes of a cat, "who looks out but doesn't allow us to look in." In one rare instance, that urge to look in, to make contact, seems to have come close to fulfillment.

In the story of the pet mouse as it appears in this collection, Mouse has died, and the mouse-keeper reflects on their life together:

> There had been moments, elusive of description, when I had felt a contact between her tiny being and my own. Sometimes when I

touched her lovingly and she nibbled my fingers in return, I felt as though an affectionate message were passing between us. The enormous distance between us seemed to be bridged momentarily by faint but perceptible signals. (p. 21)

The passage provides the most intimate picture of her own relationship to an animal of any McNulty wrote. Of all her wildlife reports, "Mouse" may come closest to being a true "animal story," with all the risks of sentimentality the term implies. Perhaps conscious of the liability, in the next paragraph McNulty tells how she threw Mouse's body into the grass behind the house, with the comment, "I knew that there may be as many mice as there are visible stars" (p. 21). And in *Wildlife Stories*, Mouse's story is followed by a bemused investigation of the British mouse fancy—the society of Englishmen who breed mice to show in competitions—in which the detached tone is unmistakably *New Yorker*.

The focus in the South County pieces on individual local animals does more than illuminate McNulty's affinity for animals. It avoids or at least reduces the scale of some of the problems she examines in her researched articles and allows for more hopeful endings. "The Ever-Hungry Jay" lightly sketches the possibility of sharing the planet with nonhuman inhabitants, as McNulty makes a study of the daily cost of provisioning the twenty-five blue jays that crowd her bird feeder. One jay, it turns out, eats twenty-five seeds a day. "At 15/100 of a penny," she concludes, the spectacle of the jays at her feeder "is a real bargain. It gives me a feeling that is rare these days. It makes me feel terribly rich" (p. 318). She makes the point yet more whimsically when she writes of Mouse's fondness for melon seeds: "To this day, when I throw melon seeds in the garbage I feel sad to waste them and wish I had a mouse to give them to" (p. 14).

Wildlife Stories received good reviews but little publicity. It was easily eclipsed in terms of sales and media attention by another of the author's books published in the same year.

Other Writings

In 1978, Faith McNulty began two years of research and writing for a book about an abused wife charged with murdering her husband by setting fire to the bed where he slept. *The Burning Bed* (1980) sold over five hundred thousand copies and was turned into a television drama. The vivid recounting of the woman's story drew praise from reviewers and professionals, and the book became a text in some sociology courses.

The wildlife writer's shift of focus might seem abrupt to readers of her other books and articles, but McNulty explained that this story, too, was about an underdog. In *Wildlife Stories*, she likens the fate of animals to that of "other inarticulate minorities—they are cheated, exploited, abused." When the Milwaukee School of Engineering awarded her an honorary doctorate in humane letters in 1992, it cited her book on domestic violence as well as her writing on wildlife as evidence of "her devotion to educating for understanding, sensitivity and compassion."

After *Wildlife Stories* came out, McNulty wrote several more stories about animals for the *New Yorker*: a charming one about the hatching of a whooping crane chick, two about her horses. She was working on a long piece about parrots in 1984 when Richard Martin died. The article was left unfinished while she reordered her life and tried to keep pace with the stacks of children's books sent for review. Her last *New Yorker* essay on children's literature, in 1991, was on E. B. White as a writer for children.

Although she wrote for other publications, it is probably as a *New Yorker* writer that McNulty made her signal contribution as a nature writer. The magazine allowed her to put her seemingly artless literary style at the service of her love for animals, and it offered her message of compassion and concern an influential readership. In 1992 the magazine that had published her first story and had been her literary home for almost forty years was under new management and indicated a new editorial direction. McNulty viewed the change as the end of the magazine as she had known it and wrote an epitaph, which she circulated among friends. Below a tombstone with the inscription "R.I.P. Eustace Tilley" (the bemonocled gentleman who had graced the first cover) she wrote, "During its long life it embodied truth and honor in journalism, precision and beauty in the use of language, and gave artists and writers freedom and dignity in the practice of their profession."

Her tribute names some of the qualities she herself brought to the magazine's pages. McNulty wanted to tell people the truth about the many "simple, beautiful, and defenseless living things, vanishing before the relentless forces of human expansion." And she told it in words that were painfully precise and beautiful.

Selected Bibliography

WORKS OF FAITH McNULTY

BOOKS

Wholly Cats (Indianapolis: Bobbs-Merrill, 1962), with Elisabeth Keiffer; *The Whooping Crane: The Bird That Defies Extinction* (New York: Dutton, 1966); *Must They Die? The Strange Case of the Prairie Dog and the Black-footed Ferret* (Garden City, N.Y.: Doubleday, 1971); *The Great Whales* (Garden City, N.Y.: Doubleday, 1974); *The Wildlife Stories of Faith McNulty* (Garden City, N.Y.: Doubleday, 1980); *The Burning Bed* (New York: Harcourt Brace Jovanovich, 1980).

ARTICLES

"No Flowers," in *New Yorker* (10 April 1943), written under the name Faith Fair; "Split-Level Living," in *New Yorker* (1 October 1955); "Notes and Comment," in "Talk of the Town," *New Yorker* (17 December 1966); "Fun Furs," in "Talk of the Town," *New Yorker* (20 May 1967); "Notes from a Mousekeeper's Diary," in *Audubon* 66 (November 1964); "The Thread Remains Very Thin," in "A Reporter at Large," *New Yorker* (6 August 1966); "The Silent Shore," in *Audubon* 73 (November 1971); "The Falcons of Morro Rock," in "Our Far-Flung Correspondents," *New Yorker* (23 December 1972); "Lord of the Fish," in "Profiles," *New Yorker* (6 August 1973); "Kill the Pupfish? Save the Pupfish!," in *Audubon* 75 (November 1973); "Madagascar's Endangered Wildlife," in *Defenders of Wildlife* 50 (April 1975); "Peruvian Conservationist," in "Talk of the Town," *New Yorker* (4 October 1976); "Last Days of the Condor?," in *Audubon* 80 (March–May 1978); "Manatees," in "Our Far-Flung Correspondents," *New Yorker* (26 February 1979); "Notes and Comment," in "Talk of the Town," *New Yorker* (10 November 1980); "Notes and Comment," in "Talk of the Town," *New Yorker* (19 April 1982); "Crane Man," in "Talk of the Town," *New Yorker* (24 May 1982); "Peeping in the Shell," in "Our Far-Flung Correspondents," *New Yorker* (17 January 1983); "Children's Books for Christmas," in *New Yorker* (25 November 1991).

CHILDREN'S BOOKS

Whales: Their Life in the Sea (New York: Harper & Row, 1975); *Peeping in the Shell: A Whooping Crane Is Hatched* (New York: Harper & Row, 1976); *The Lady and the Spider* (New York: Harper & Row, 1987); *A Hug from Koko* (New York: Scholastic, 1990); *Orphan: The Story of a Baby Woodchuck* (New York: Scholastic, 1992); *Dancing with Manatees* (New York: Scholastic, 1994); *A Snake in the House* (New York: Scholastic, 1994).

INTERVIEW

Interview with McNulty by Aina Niemela, Wakefield, R.I., 15 February 1994.

BIOGRAPHICAL AND CRITICAL STUDIES

Roy Bongartz, "The Many Worlds of Faith McNulty," in *Sunday Journal Magazine* [*Providence Journal*] (6 September 1981); John McNulty, *My Son Johnny* (New York: Simon and Schuster, 1955); Stanwyn G. Shelter, review of *The Wildlife Stories of Faith McNulty*, in *Smithsonian* (April 1981); Ben Tyler, "A Journalist Joins the War Effort from London," in *What Did You Do in the War, Grandma?*, oral history project at South Kensington (R.I.) High School (1989); Carol Van Strum, "All God's Creatures," review of *The Wildlife Stories of Faith McNulty*, in *Washington Post Book World* (2 November 1980); Peter Wild, "Keeping Faith with Wildlife," review of *The Wildlife Stories of Faith McNulty*, in *Orion Nature Book Review* (May 1981).

JOHN MCPHEE
(b. 1931)

MICHAEL PEARSON

JOHN MCPHEE, the author of more than twenty books of nonfiction over the years, is a nature writer in spite of himself. He says, "I've written about nature, and it is terribly important to me," but he bristles at being defined simply as a nature writer. Although not all nature writers are environmentalists, it is as if he associates such a title with the polemicist, and if there is one thing McPhee clearly is not, it is a writer of angry doctrinal disputations. He calls himself a reporter, and when he is linked to the "new journalists," he smiles ironically and says he is an "old journalist." If anything, though, he is a literary journalist, a writer of creative nonfiction, closer to novelist than editorialist. He does not write about issues but about people. Often they are people like David Brower, the former director of the Sierra Club, or Dick Cook, an Alaskan pioneer, who have strong opinions about the natural world and humanity's place in it. But McPhee's interest is in letting the issues come to life through the individual drama. The rib of theory stays securely attached to the human subjects he observes. McPhee's interest is in showing his readers the world through the people who live in it, not in crafting political arguments. He lets his characters speak for themselves, and he allows his readers to draw their own conclusions.

McPhee, the naturalist, is also a sports writer, a cultural reporter, a travel writer. He reports on science and technology. He writes adventure stories. It is fair, however, to say that a majority of his books focus on nature, on the most serious questions of preservation and development, on human expectation and responsibility in the natural world. Many of his stories are centered in wilderness areas, and quite a few of his profiles recount the lives of naturalists, environmentalists, and rural dwellers.

McPhee is a stern-eyed romantic, a transcendentalist with a wry sense of humor, a careful reporter whose journeys into the world are reminiscent of Henry David Thoreau's, whose descriptions of representative men and women echo Ralph Waldo Emerson's. McPhee's subjects, whether they are Euell Gibbons, the famous wild-food forager; Ted Taylor, the nuclear physicist; or Ed Gelvin, an Alaskan gold miner, are all knotty individualists. Like Thoreau and Walt Whitman, McPhee celebrates the individual life, and like them he focuses on the "knit of identity" between the individual and the larger world. If McPhee is a preservationist, he is one in a very special sense, a rebellious thinker like Thoreau but perhaps a bit more moderate. McPhee makes this clear in *Coming into the Country* (1977), a book that, among other things, traces the Alaskan search for a new capital city and describes some of its recent settlers in the wilderness areas. In describing the Gelvins, a family able to live exclusively on its own intelligence, strength, and acquired resources, McPhee says, "Their kind is more endangered every year. . . . For myself, I am closer to the preserving side—that is, the side that would preserve the Gelvins. To be sure, I would preserve plenty of land as well" (p. 430). If McPhee had to choose between preserving huge tracts of the wilderness and destroying the unique men and women who forcefully confront the world on their own terms, men and women who often seem to be living in a way that is admirably at odds with their own times and cultures, he would choose, it seems, to stand with people like the Gelvins. In their mining ventures they make their nick in the mountain, certainly, but in their lives and their relationship to the natural world they make a more important nick, perhaps in time. McPhee stands with the developers and the conservationists, those who would conserve the individual soul, those who would continue to develop a way to live freely within the confines of our complex civilizations.

He also stands as a soft-spoken advocate for the land itself. Behind much of his dialogue, his carefully wrought scenes, and his scrupulously constructed stories is a question: what kind of natural world do we need for a certain brand of independence to survive, or even thrive? Although McPhee's books elude glib classification, the common thread that holds them together is his vision of the world, his sense of where he belongs and where he comes from. The title of his book on the former basketball star Bill Bradley, *A Sense of Where You Are* (1965), might serve as a resounding theme in his work. Many of his characters seem to have a sense of their place in the world. In a subtle respect these portraits offer a composite of the writer himself—his interests, his values, his principal concerns, most of which had their source in his early years in New Jersey and Vermont.

Life

John Angus McPhee was born in Princeton, New Jersey, on 8 March 1931, in the heart of the Great Depression, in a state that was already on its way to becoming noted for soot and suburbs. The town of Princeton, however, always seemed exempt from economic shifts and safe from the twisting lanes of traffic and carbon monoxide. Princeton is only a few minutes from Trenton and a brief train ride from Philadelphia or New York City, but despite its proximity to urban blight and interstate roadways, it is a bucolic town with a population of about twenty-five thousand, mainly students, professors, and affluent exurbanites who amble along leaf-dappled paths and sycamore-lined streets, past quaint shops and inspiring stone buildings. McPhee went to high school there, learning a great deal about writing from Olive Mckee, an English teacher who required that her students write three essays each week, and learning almost as much about basketball from Irwin Weiss, one of his grammar-school coaches. He learned enough to become an excellent student, a disciplined writer, and the captain of the Princeton High School basketball team.

After graduating from high school, McPhee spent a year at Deerfield Academy in Massachusetts, studying under the general guidance of Frank L. Boyden, a man he later immortalized in *The Headmaster* (1966). In that book he described Boyden as "an educator by intuition . . . one of the great headmasters in history, and for many years he has stood alone as, in all probability, the last man of his kind" (p. 7). With his profile of Boyden, McPhee may have found his true subject—that is, the iconoclast, the expert, the man or woman engaged in an activity in the world, at times even obsessed by it. The McPhee protagonist can be cantankerous, eccentric, arrogant, or reserved, man or woman, field zoologist, woodsman, crofter, or tennis player. They all have one thing in common, however. Their vocations are truly callings, summoning them into the world. McPhee, the writer, seems always fascinated by the skills of others, especially by others who take those skills seriously, who play their games with devotion and intensity. At Deerfield, McPhee met some of his most influential teachers and mentors—Frank Conklin in geology, Helen Boyden in chemistry, and Robert McGlynn in English.

In 1949 McPhee entered Princeton University, where he played basketball on the freshman team, wrote for the college literary magazines, and eventually convinced the rather conservative English department to accept his unpublished novel, "Skimmer Burns," for the required senior thesis. During those four years in college he was also a regular contestant on the weekly radio and television program *Twenty Questions*, a show in which an individual must guess a mystery item by asking yes-or-no questions. Clearly, this experience was groundwork for a man who became famous for writing on all manner of animals, vegetables, and minerals.

After receiving his B.A. in English from Princeton in 1953, he spent a year at Cambridge University in England, studying literature and in his spare time touring the Midlands to play basketball against teams from Oxford or the London School of Economics. His first essay to be accepted by the *New Yorker*, "Basketball and Beefeaters," published in 1963 and later collected in *Pieces of the Frame* (1975), recounts his experience playing on the Cambridge team against the Royal Fusiliers in a game that was scheduled to be played in the Tower of London.

At five feet seven inches tall, McPhee may have sensed the limits of his basketball career, but his aspirations as a writer were another story. McPhee was eighteen years old when he decided he wanted to one day write for the *New Yorker*. His dream was to write a long fact piece. It took fourteen years and an imposing collection of rejection slips before the magazine published "Basketball and Beefeaters" when he was thirty-two. But during those fourteen years he had not merely waited for the *New Yorker* to answer his call. As an apprentice writer, he tried his hand at all aspects of the craft. In an interview he said, "I didn't rule out anything as a younger writer. I tried everything, sometimes with hilarious results. I think that young writers have to roll around like oranges on a conveyor belt. They have to try it all" (personal interview, 1992).

A short stint in the business world writing speeches for executives at W. R. Grace and Company, a Wall Street firm, and producing articles for the organization's magazine taught him that he was not cut out to be a corporate man. In his short story "Eucalyptus Trees," published in 1967, he may have been making this point dramatically. In the story the main character, Ian Gibbons, resigns his position in a company because the managers refuse to give him a transfer that would make it possible for him to see the eucalyptus trees that he has been writing about for them. "It's nothing personal," they tell him, but for Gibbons, and McPhee as well, the "individual case" is really the important thing.

He tried unsuccessfully to get his novel "Skimmer Burns" published, and he continued to write fiction, although his interest in fiction waned as his fascination with nonfiction swelled. As late as 1968, however, he was still writing short stories, publishing "Ruth, the Sun Is Shining" in *Playboy*. The story begins with the description of a man named Bobby Norton lecturing his wife that there is no such thing as heat lightning; soon after, the narrator explains that Norton "never needed much of an occasion for one of these lectures. If he had the information, it would eventually come out; and he was full of information" (p. 114). At the end of the story Norton disappears in a burst of smoke and sound, the victim of his own misinterpretation of the facts. This may have been McPhee's parabolic warning to himself. During the course of the next twenty-five years McPhee would become a master of telling a story filled with information without ever appearing to lecture to his readers. And he is always precise with the facts. In an interview with Douglas Vipond and Russell Hunt in 1991, McPhee said, "That's the common denominator of all the work I've done and that's what attracts me to it. I'm describing people engaged in their thing, their activity, whatever it is. . . . I find myself disappointed when I read something like 'This writer is really interested in *facts*, he just loves *facts*.' It's like saying that somebody who is a painter really loves *paint*, he just can't get enough of it, he eats it in the morning" (p. 207). By the early 1960s McPhee was already revising the fiction writer's dictum of "Show, don't tell" into "Show *and* tell." Pamela Marsh recognized this skill when she wrote in the *Christian Science Monitor*: "John McPhee ought to be a bore. He has all the

585

qualifications. With a bore's persistence he seizes a subject, shakes loose a cloud of more detail than we ever imagined we could care to hear on any subject—yet somehow he makes the whole procedure curiously fascinating" (p. 9).

For a few years as a freelance writer McPhee wrote, among other things, television scripts for *Robert Montgomery Presents*. He wrote five scripts; NBC bought three and two of them, based on *New Yorker* stories written by Robert Coates, were produced. In 1957 he became a reporter for *Time*, writing the Show Business section with profiles of such celebrities as Jackie Gleason, Sophia Loren, Richard Burton, and Joan Baez. Eventually he was promoted to associate editor. None of these successes, however, made him forget his first dream: to become a writer for the *New Yorker*. In 1965, two years after his brief essay on basketball at the Tower of London had been published by the magazine, he wrote on speculation a seventeen-thousand-word profile of the Princeton all-American basketball player Bill Bradley. "A Sense of Where You Are" became his first long *New Yorker* fact piece. The article led to an essentially freelance position as a staff writer at the *New Yorker*, and also became McPhee's first book.

As a *New Yorker* staff writer, a position that William Howarth describes in his introduction to *The John McPhee Reader* as "one of the most liberated jobs in modern journalism," McPhee has picked his topics, determined his own deadlines, and immersed himself fully in any subject he writes about. McPhee likes to make it clear, however, that he is a freelance writer. "I don't have a job at the *New Yorker*," he said to me in a 1992 interview. "I have a 1099 form. It's not a salaried job. I have no income if I don't produce."

The vast majority of the topics he chooses are a reflection of his early life, and also a reflection of his roots in Princeton. Although those roots stretch out to Philadelphia, where his mother's father was a publisher; and to Youngstown, Ohio, where his paternal grandfather was a steelworker; or even to Colonsay, a rugged island off the craggy western coast of Scotland, from which his ancestors emigrated, the "epicenter of his cartography," as William Howarth phrases it, is still Princeton. Its character, according to Howarth, is varied and particularly American, but even more significant is the town's elegant stability, reflected in the calm, ordered prose that is the hallmark of McPhee's stories. He has remained in Princeton since his days as a *Time* reporter, father to four daughters from his first marriage, to Pryde Brown, and stepfather to four more children in his second marriage, to his present wife, Yolanda Whitman. His sense of place and family are the steady ground from which he has been able to see the rest of the world clearly.

Except for a year at Deerfield, another at Cambridge, and a few years living in New York City, McPhee has spent his whole life in Princeton. His father, Harry Roemer McPhee, a general practitioner with an interest in sports medicine, was a physician for U.S. Olympic teams and Princeton athletic squads for more than a quarter of a century. McPhee's mother, Mary Ziegler, gave up teaching French when she moved from Cleveland to Iowa and finally to Princeton and concentrated on raising her children, Roemer, Laura Anne, and John. It was his mother's idea that John should attend Deerfield Academy after he graduated from Princeton High. He had already been acccepted into Princeton University, but his mother thought he needed some time to mature. He had skipped a grade in his schooling and had just turned seventeen before he graduated from high school. He wanted to go straight to college, but as he said in a 1992 interview, "She was firm, and in that sort of situation you *listened* to her."

One of the most significant influences in McPhee's life was the New England camp where his father worked as a physician for half a dozen summers. Camp Keewaydin, eight miles south of Middlebury, not far from the trails that Robert Frost used to explore during his days in the state, is the place where the young McPhee spent his summers and eventually worked as a counselor. Much of his inspiration for the subjects he chooses to write about has its source in that youthful experience. He says, "A few years back I was giving a talk at Vassar and a young man raised his hand and asked me what academic institution had influenced me the most. Well, I had gone to Princeton High School and Princeton University and Cambridge, but I didn't hesitate for a second. I said Keewaydin. It was a real educational institution." At Keewaydin his days were focused on canoeing, sports, and learning about the natural world. Most of his adult life has been spent writing about just those topics.

Early Works

McPhee's first book, *A Sense of Where You Are*, was dedicated to his father, who in the winter of 1962 called him on the telephone to say, "There's a freshman basketball player down here who is the best basketball player who has ever been near here and may be one of the best ever" (personal interview). Dr. McPhee had once been a college basketball player himself, and John had been a freshman player at Princeton a dozen years before Bill Bradley. With these incentives, McPhee began to write about "the most graceful and classical basketball player who had ever been near Princeton."

A Sense of Where You Are is an elegant treatise on the game itself, but finally it is about more than just basketball or even a great player. It is about a Renaissance man, an American hero. For a few critics this marred the book—the fact that McPhee presents his main character in too flattering a light, that he does not work his way into the darker corners of Bradley's life. This criticism has been made of McPhee's work in general. Edward Hoagland objected to McPhee's not being "aloof enough about some of the subjects of his pieces, over-admiring them, taking them just at their word" (p. 49). But this objection does not take into account characters like Henri Vaillancourt in *The Survival of the Bark Canoe* (1975) or Clark Graebner in *Levels of the Game* (1969). It also fails to acknowledge the variety and subtlety of McPhee's "heroes." His heroes are not all rich or famous or blessed with talents that our society clearly reveres. Rather, they are men and women like Fred Brown in the Pine Barrens, living in a shack on the edge of civilization; or Frank L. Boyden quietly doing his work at Deerfield Academy; or Carol Ruckdeschel of Georgia, a field zoologist and preserver of nature. McPhee's first female central character, Ruckdeschel is not unlike many of the other characters he writes about— independent, resourceful, observant, fascinated by the world around her. If McPhee's subjects are heroes, they are comic ones—like us, ordinary people, vulnerable and human, men and women who are admirable despite their foibles and idiosyncrasies, not because they are free from them.

With *A Sense of Where You Are* McPhee's career was smoothly launched. Rex Lardner said in the *New York Times Book Review* that it was "immensely well-written, inspiring without being preachy" (p. 71). The same could be said of McPhee's second book, *The Headmaster*, published in 1966. Both Bradley and Boyden are representative men, who reach the highest level of expertise in their respective careers. Both have a sense of where they are, a clear idea of their place in the world. In *A Sense of Where You Are*, McPhee says of Bradley: "[His] play was integral. There was nothing missing. . . . He did all kinds of things he didn't have to do simply because those were the dimensions of the game" (pp. 7–8). Boyden, he says in *The Headmaster*, is "a simple man with the gift of authority," who has "spent his life building a school according to elemental ideas, but only a complicated man could bring off what he has done" (p. 13). Bradley, the perfectionist who practices just one more shot, always one more shot, draws his teammates up to their best performances. Boyden does the same for his students at Deerfield, with his unflagging energy, his humanity, and his scrupulous awareness of everything that is going on around him. At one point McPhee says of Boyden: "He is lost in the school, and there is nothing of him but the school" (p. 13).

Both Bradley and Boyden are men of enormous drive and talent, men who are able to focus that energy precisely in terms of their lifework. Their passions, to a certain extent, make them "isolatoes," separating them from the mass of men in their discipline, skill, and craftsmanship.

Like McPhee as a writer, these men concentrate on even the smallest details, but finally it is the larger story that each is interested in. Bradley is not only the complete basketball player; he is the complete human being. He receives many honors at Princeton, but only as an afterthought, it seems, is he named best athlete. Boyden, the benevolent despot of Deerfield, is attentive to minute details, but finally his motto is taken from Robert E. Lee: "A boy is more important than any rule" (p. 19). McPhee, too, is interested in more than pedagogy or sports in these profiles. He is interested in a portrait of the *individual*, for he knows that such a picture will always be unique.

In his third book, *Oranges*, published in 1967, McPhee's naturalistic sensibility begins to emerge. In one hundred and forty-nine pages, he offers history, botany, and anecdote. Some, like the *New York Times* reviewer, thought the book unsuccessful, an unintentional parody of trivial *New Yorker* subject matter. Others, like the reviewer for *Harper's*, thought it was a surprising accomplishment, "more absorbing than many a novel." In *Oranges*, McPhee the careful craftsman merges with the naturalist-reporter. The precise descriptions of the natural world that become a hallmark of his style in the later books begin here, often coming, as they do in later books as well, from the mouth of an expert-guide:

Citrus is monoecious—both sexes are in the same blossom—but in some varieties the pollen and the ovules are always imperfect and fertilization seldom occurs. Oranges can set fruit parthenocarpically—that means "by virgin development"—so they can develop a fruit even if the flower isn't fertilized. The fruit, however, will be essentially seedless. If an orange has five seeds or less, it is called seedless. People write in and complain about the seeds they find in seedless oranges. On the other hand, if an orange likes its own pollen, as the Parson Brown and the Pineapple do, it will have dozens of incestuous seeds. The sex life of citrus is something fantastic. (p. 34)

As interested as McPhee can get in esoterica, none of his books are written for experts. Even *Oranges*, accented as it is with botanical tidbits, is written in a voice that is clear and dramatic. McPhee offers a fascinating description of orange pickers and in particular of Doyle Waid, a twenty-nine-year-old master of the trade. For McPhee, these pickers in general, like John Steinbeck's migrant workers in *The Grapes of Wrath*, are an "admirable group," with a toughness and strength of spirit necessary for the task. The best of them, like Doyle Waid, are craftsmen like Bradley or Boyden. In explaining his job to McPhee, Waid says, "That tree is good picking. . . . It's got big fruit. It's easy to ladder. You can set your ladder in there and get your inside fruit good. That's a bad tree next to it, with the branches close together. It's a hard set. A good, average tree, it oughtn't to take over seven sets to get it" (p. 57). A bit less polished in his speech than Bradley or Boyden, Waid nevertheless speaks articulately and with a similar enthusiasm and acumen about his vocation. Hook shots, education, or the intricacies of fruit picking—finally, McPhee suggests, individuals may find their humanity by engaging wholeheartedly in some activity.

The Pine Barrens

In 1968, with the publication of *The Pine Barrens*, McPhee widened his naturalistic circle from the orange to the encircled piece of wilderness near his home in Princeton, 650,000 acres of wild land that "constitute the geographical center of the developing megalopolis between Boston and Richmond" (Lounsberry, p. 102) and that seemed to McPhee "to be headed slowly toward extinction."

The book is a portrait of both a people and a place. The Pine Barrens are a separate world, another country, alien and distinct, but also typically American, representative of our culture. McPhee says that this sandy-soiled wilderness between Philadelphia and Atlantic City is a place "where attitudes and ambitions are at variance with the American norm" (p. 55). The locals, known as Pineys, seem to have a muted sense of ambition and a spiritual connection to the land that make them more closely akin to Navajos than to natives of nearby New York City. The Pineys, although they are far from the typical modern American, actually seem to be archetypal Americans—proud, prickly individualists and self-reliant survivors. The Pine Barrens is the perfect dramatic location for McPhee to explore his concerns about endangered species and environments—the individual and the wilderness. It is the ideal setting to dramatize the debate between the voices of conservation and development. The paradoxical relationship between the individualistic spirit and the opposing forces of preservation and development, which McPhee begins to explore in *The Pine Barrens*, becomes a central theme in many of his later books. He offers no simple solutions, no blueprint to follow that will allow us to save both the self-reliant spirit and the wilderness as well. Logically, it would seem, the two should be compatible, but often preserving a tract of land means forcing off it the most adventurous, independent individuals.

In *The Pine Barrens* this drama is enacted within the perimeter of a contracting circle. The seventy-nine-year-old Fred Brown is all for development and the opportunities it will bring, but the twenty-six-year-old Bill Wasovwich feels, "It'd be the end of these woods" (p. 12). In describing this unique world, McPhee writes of the vanished towns, the history and legends, the strange language and exotic plants, but he does not omit the developer's perspective. He allows Herbert Smith, a local planner, to speak his mind: "I will predict that if nothing at all is done in terms of planned development here, within twenty years the area will be so spotted with exploitative development that it will be impossible to assemble the land into something that is sensibly planned" (p. 153). McPhee seems to have similar fears for the area, and he closes on a pessimistic note, suggesting that the Pine Barrens will soon be extinct, that there is a noose

tightening around the wilderness at the rate of "a mile or so each year."

Clearly, the Pine Barrens is one of the most controversial areas in the state—a botanist's wonderland, a developer's dream, and a naturalist's last stand. Politicians discussed building a jetport larger than LaGuardia and Kennedy airports combined. Others greedily eyed the pure aquifer, a potable subsurface water supply that could readily satisfy New York City's thirst. All of this threatened a slow strangulation of the area and a steady corruption of the wilderness. However, in 1978 the National Parks and Recreation Act established the Pinelands National Reserve and called for the preparation of a comprehensive management plan. In 1979 New Jersey passed the Pinelands Protection Act, resulting in the designation of more than one million acres as land in which development was strictly controlled. The "preservation area" is the heart of the Pine Barrens, and within those approximately four hundred thousand acres development is virtually prohibited. The "protection area" also carefully regulates growth, but the restrictions within its roughly one million acres are less severe. Finally, there is the Pinelands National Reserve, slightly more than one million acres with broader and fewer restrictions on development. Most of the reserve lands are on the periphery of the Pine Barrens, leaving the thousand-square-mile heart remarkably pristine. Many people feel that McPhee's book, whose readers and admirers included Governor Brendan Byrne, was the catalyst for change—that although McPhee ended his book with the bleak image of the extinction of the Pine Barrens, his story has played a large part in keeping the area unchanged in the decades since 1968.

Encounters with the Archdruid

McPhee's next important nature book came three years later, in 1971. *Encounters with the Archdruid* is a recounting of three separate confrontations between David Brower, former director of the Sierra Club, and, respectively, an exploration geologist, a developer, and a dam builder. Between 1968 and 1971 McPhee had published three other books. *The Crofter and the Laird* (1970) is a rich account of the legends, history, and landscape of Colonsay, McPhee's ancestral home off the coast of Scotland. For him, Colonsay is "a small continent," and like the Pine Barrens or Alaska, it is a separate world. As McPhee says, "There are great men here, within their context—masters, for a few pounds' rent a year, of considerable domains, with an independence that must go beyond any usual sense of that word elsewhere, except on another remote island" (p. 58). In addition, he had published *A Roomful of Hovings and Other Profiles* (1968), a collection of shorter pieces that includes one on Euell Gibbons, titled "A Forager," and another on the Massachusetts Institute of Technology Fellows in Africa Program. In the story about MIT fellows in Africa, McPhee's principal narrative focuses on Carroll Brewster. One of his descriptions of Brewster could aptly serve as a self-portrait: "Brewster, for his part, is frank and unselfconscious, open, full of humor, more than a little romantic, and always ready to move with enthusiasm into something new. He is the kind of person who sees the stories in the lives around him" (p. 159). During this period McPhee had also written *Levels of the Game* (1969), an intricate narrative that works within the minds and court play of Clark Graebner and Arthur Ashe in a 1968 U.S. Open semifinal match. *Levels of the Game* was McPhee's first attempt at a double profile, a contrapuntal arrangement structured to the serve-and-volley rhythm of the game itself.

In *Encounters with the Archdruid* the structure becomes even more complex. It was the challenge of structure even more than the subject, McPhee claims, that led him to write about the environmental visionary David Brower. Joan Hamilton says that McPhee decided on an "A-B-C over D" configuration for a story and then looked for a fitting subject—an architect and three clients, a choreographer and three dancers, or a director and three actors? A deep interest in the natural world may have finally led him to write about Brower—the "archdruid" of the environmental movement—and three prodevelopment people.

Encounters with the Archdruid is divided into three parts—"A Mountain," "An Island," and "A River"—and each part positions Brower against one of his philosophical adversaries in a natural setting that is an environmental battleground. McPhee's position as the literary reporter is one of firm impartiality, allowing each speaker to show and tell his own story. Joan Didion has argued that every cut and every choice changes a story, that perhaps the experience of writing nonfiction is more "electrical than ethical"; finally, however, McPhee seems honestly open to all sides. He is not an acolyte for the archdruid or a spokesman for developers. He comes to no conclusions but lets the reader weigh the facts of the narrative. "A well-written editorial is a good thing," he said in an interview, "but it's not what I'm out to do."

Even Brower, the ostensible hero of the story, is shown to have many facets to his character. In the first section, "A Mountain," in which Brower hikes with Charles Park, a geologist and mineralogist, in the mountains of the Glacier Peak Wilderness, there appears to be no simple villain or hero. Park wants to mine the mountains. He is a man who believes "that if copper were to be found under the White House, the White House should be moved" (p. 5). But he is also a geologist who goes into the field "because of love of the earth and the out-of-doors" (p. 55). He is a man, McPhee says, "who knows what he is looking at in the wild country. I have never spent time with anyone who was more aware of the natural world" (p. 67). As opposed to Brower, though, Park thinks principally in terms of practicality, not aesthetics. He is pragmatic, not spiritual. It is Brower who is linked symbolically with the mountain, a man who could be set down at night anywhere in the Sierra Nevada and in the morning light know exactly where he was. It is Park who gets satisfaction chipping away at the mountain, swinging at outcroppings with his pick. When McPhee asks him what he is looking for, Park grins and says, "Nothing . . . I just haven't hit one in a long time" (p. 18). He is a man who loves the outdoors, but he also wants the wilderness to supply people's needs. "We need to lumber," he says. "We need to mine" (p. 67).

Even though McPhee takes no editorial stance on the environmental issues in *Encounters with the Archdruid*, he does take a position as a dramatist. His sympathies are with Brower in the first encounter, which ends as Brower, Park, and McPhee sit resting on Miner's Ridge, Park eating blueberries straight from the bush and Brower gathering his in a cup.

Brower's cup was up to its brim, and before he ate himself he passed them among the rest of us. It was a curious and surpassingly generous gesture, since we were surrounded by bushes that were loaded with berries. We all accepted.

"I just feel sorry for all you people who don't know what these mountains are good for," Brower said.

"What are they good for?" I said.

"Berries," said Brower.

And Park said, "Copper." (p. 75)

Park may have the last word, and he may be an attractive person, but it is Brower who, to use the words of one of McPhee's other characters, gives us a view of the possibilities of our "companionship with the earth." He is a man whose "love of beauty is so powerful it leaps ... [and] lands in unexpected places" (p. 198).

The next two sections of *Encounters with the Archdruid* narrate the story of Brower's meeting with Charles Fraser, a real-estate entrepreneur famed for the development of Sea Pines Plantation on Hilton Head, and of Brower's encounter with Floyd Dominy, Commissioner of the U.S. Bureau of Reclamation and arch-builder of dams, on a rafting trip through the Grand Canyon. Fraser, although a real-estate developer, is something of a druid himself, a builder with a concern for the environment, and Brower wishes to take him into the fold. Brower's final words to this potential apostle are, "I have seen evidence of what you can do. Now make others do it" (p. 144).

More philosophical distance separates Floyd Dominy and Brower. Dominy is an imposing figure, a scourge to conservationists, a man whose initials, F. E. D., seem more profoundly appropriate than coincidence would allow. Brower is determined to see the rivers in the United States run their natural course. Dominy, who grew up in dry western country and began his career building dams seven feet high, eventually built dams more than seven hundred feet high. He would like to see "the Colorado River become a series of large pools, one stepped above another, from the Mexican border to the Rocky Mountains, with the headwaters of each succeeding lake lapping against the tailrace of a dam" (p. 162).

The trip they take down the Colorado River is a confrontation between giants, the archdruid and the devil, but McPhee presents them as strong, well-meaning individuals who disagree about the wisdom, morality, and practicality of attempting to control nature. Dominy, the "devil" from the point of view of conservationists, is portrayed as a heroic and undaunted, if at times arrogant, figure. Brower, the religious leader of the conservation movement, is depicted as enigmatically human. At one point in their journey down the river, Brower decides not to run a rapid with the group. Dominy snarls contemptuously, "The great outdoorsman!" When the raft glides to the shore at the other end of the rapid, Dominy asks Brower why he did not ride with them. "Because I'm chicken," Brower replies (pp. 231–232).

McPhee never analyzes Brower's fear or explains his actions. Rather, he allows the structure of the narrative to make the comment. Immediately after Brower declares that he is "chicken," McPhee offers a biographical section describing Brower's scaling thirty-three peaks in the Sierra Nevada. Then he depicts Brower's and Dominy's conversation, a dialogue by turns mocking, collegial, and angry. McPhee concludes the story with a description of the group's negotiating the fearsome Lava Falls. Right before they hit the drop, McPhee notices that Brower is in the raft, hands tight on the safety rope, tendons taut in his neck. But he is there. The narrative ends with admiration for Brower's courage and character, but it ends with no clear winner, for the battle will continue beyond this encounter:

> For a moment, we sat quietly in the calm, looking back. Then Brower said, "The foot of Lava Falls would be two hundred and twenty-five feet beneath the surface of Lake Dominy."
> Dominy said nothing. He just sat there, drawing on a wet, dead cigar. Ten minutes later, however, in the dry and baking Arizona air, he struck a match and lighted the cigar again. (p. 245)

Later Works

McPhee's next two books, *The Deltoid Pumpkin Seed* (1973) and *The Curve of Binding Energy* (1974), are ventures into science and technology. In the first, he details the building of Aereon, a new form of rigid airship, but it is not so much a story of a modern dirigible as it is of the idealists and dreamers who imagine it. *The Curve of Binding Energy* is a profile of Ted Taylor, a theoretical physicist who helped miniaturize the atomic bomb and design the largest-yield fission bomb. It is a profile of his genius, a tracing of his evolution of thought, and through Taylor a plea for the control of nuclear material that could be stolen or misappropriated and made into terrorist devices. In a sense, the book becomes a vehicle for Taylor's plaintive warning: "a deadline is on us; it is almost too late" (p. 227).

In 1975, with *Pieces of the Frame*, McPhee collected eleven stories that had been published in the *New Yorker* and other magazines, and returned in a few of the pieces, like "Travels in Georgia," "Reading the River," and "Ranger," to a focus on the natural world. In that same year he published *The Survival of the Bark Canoe*, a profile of Henri Vaillancourt, an artisan who builds birch-bark canoes by hand in the manner that the Malecite Indians once did. Vaillancourt, in his mid-twenties, lives and works in the small town of Greenville, New Hampshire. He has built thirty-three birch-bark canoes, "with a singleness of purpose that defeats distraction"

John McPhee

(p. 5). He is an artist by style and temperament and in obvious ways he is a typical McPhee hero—obsessed by his work, a dedicated craftsman, skillful. However, Vaillancourt turns out to be the obverse of the usual McPhee protagonist; he is the expert in extremis. McPhee says, "Nothing much enters his time, his thought, or his conversation that does not have to do with the making and use of birch-bark canoes" (p. 7). Whereas most of McPhee's subjects are led into the wider world through their specialized skills, Vaillancourt's obsession permits him "to be interested in almost nothing else" (p. 7).

Early in the profile McPhee hits at Vaillancourt's principal flaw, his arrogance: "He has visited almost all of the other living bark-canoe makers, and he has learned certain things from the Indians. He has returned home believing, though, that he is the most skilful of them all" (p. 5). Besides being arrogant, Vaillancourt turns out to be selfish, opinionated, inconsiderate, and bullying. Worst of all, perhaps, for McPhee—a

592

man who has spent his life canoeing—is that Henri is not really a skilled canoeist. His skill at making canoes has not, it seems, led to an interest in learning how to maneuver them. Most significantly, though, his love of his craft has not enhanced his humanity or his good humor.

As McPhee narrates his story of the 150-mile canoe trip he took with Vaillancourt and three other men into the Penobscot-Allagash wilderness of northern Maine, the reader's estimate of Vaillancourt's character declines even as admiration for the builder's artistry rises. McPhee, however, never loses his sense of perspective or his sense of the humor in the story, even when the journey comes to its most wretched point: "The long carry has about every obstacle a carry can have, short of German shepherds trained to kill. It has quagmires, slicks of rock, small hills, down trees, low branches, and, primarily, distance" (p. 109).

Throughout the story, McPhee invokes the image of Thoreau and his nineteenth-century travels through the same Maine woods. Both Thoreau and McPhee serve as implicit contrasts to Vaillancourt and his narrow vision of the world. It is McPhee, not Vaillancourt, who sees the world around him. McPhee, like Thoreau, shows his love of nature by observing it with care:

> We had hoped to see a moose even by now, but none has yet appeared in lake, stream, or river. Meanwhile, the loon will do. He is out there cruising still, in the spiralling morning mist, looking for fish, trolling. He trolls with his eyes. Water streams across his forehead as he moves along, and he holds his eyes just below the surface, watching the interior of the lake. He is gone. . . . When he dives, he just disappears. . . . Now his body is up again, and he laughs. If the laugh were human, it would be a laugh of the deeply insane. (pp. 29–30)

Coming into the Country

Coming into the Country (1977) is perhaps McPhee's most popular nature book, what Ed-

ward Hoagland in the *New York Times* called "a big, long, permanent book . . . a species of masterpiece." Robert Coles saw it as "an evocation of a kind of life once the norm in the nation." Alaska, an Aleut word that means "the great land," becomes McPhee's symbol of what America once was, still is in certain corners, and can continue to be, possibly, if bureaucracies do not destroy both the wilderness and the rebellious individual spirit. Alaska may be the appropriate locale for the environmental Armageddon; it has been called the last frontier. As McPhee envisions it, the state "runs off the edge of the imagination, with its tracklessness, its beyond-the-ridge-line surprises, its hundreds of millions of acres of wilderness" (p. 133). Amidst such vast and untrammeled beauty, places like Anchorage, which to McPhee are like the northern rim of Trenton, the ocean-blind precincts of Daytona, or the center of Oxnard, are mere "pustules." A city like Anchorage is an insignificant dot on the map in the vastness of Alaska, "virtually unrelated to its environment" (p. 130).

Initially, the line of plot in the multistructured *Coming into the Country* appears to be the search for a new capital site to replace Juneau. But, ultimately, it seems that no city would fit well within the breathtaking and unapproachable landscape of the state. The question "Where will we locate the new capital" soon expands to "What will be the fate of this land?" And finally, the question becomes, "What is to be the fate of its people?" Such questions—dramatized in the portraits of Dick Cook and Donna Kneeland, Brad Snow and Mike Potts, and even in the mysterious River Wind—are actually questions about the American character, about a brand of self-confidence, skill, independence of thought and spirit, a blend of idealism and common sense that are becoming increasingly rare. The question, then, becomes, "Will this survive, especially if the wild country is lost or even tamed into more civilized parks?"

Alaska is the great land, reminiscent of what America once was. How much do we preserve, and how much do we use? Where is the balance?

As in his other books, McPhee lets his expert guides speak. He allows them to debate the questions, to dramatize the issues in their own lives. John Kauffmann, a National Park Service planner, is one spokesperson in the story for the conservation viewpoint: "We must protect it, even if artificially. The day will come when people will want to visit such a wilderness.... We're talking fifty and more years hence, when there may be nowhere else to go to a place that is wild and unexplored" (p. 28). But two-thirds of the book—in the long final section titled "Coming into the Country"—depicts the stories of those adventurers who have come into the wild land, as Thoreau did, to live deliberately and freely. Preserving the land might mean destroying them. As Joe Vogler, an advocate of independence for the state, said about a family he considers archetypal Alaskans, "The Gelvins would be misfits somewhere else. They're doers. They don't destroy. They build. They preserve. They are conservationists in the true sense of the word. They have killed wolves right and left," Volger says. But as he sees it, "They are responsible for many moose being alive today" (pp. 317–318).

As in *The Pine Barrens* and *Encounters with the Archdruid*, in *Coming into the Country* McPhee presents no simple resolutions. He offers no easy answers, but he does clearly admire the Thoreauvian spirit in many of the residents of Eagle and Circle, Alaska. In his admiration of them and his love of the land, he seems to call for a balance, a preservation of both the environment and the American character. The tough spirit and the ruggedly beautiful landscape are inextricably linked.

In the final image of *Coming into the Country*, McPhee describes his meeting with a young man who has just come into the country, stocked up with supplies from the Eagle General Store, and is off into the woods. The reader is left to decide whether the newcomer has what it will take to survive in the wild land.

> I asked him where he meant to go.
> "Down the river," he said. "I'll be living on the Yukon and getting my skills together."

I wished him heartfelt luck and felt in my heart he would need it. I said my name, and shook his hand, and he said his. He said, "My name is River Wind." (p. 438)

The Control of Nature

Since *Coming into the Country*, McPhee has published two collections, *Giving Good Weight* (1979) and *Table of Contents* (1985), a book on the Swiss army (*La Place de la Concorde Suisse*, 1984), and another on the U.S. merchant marine (*Looking for a Ship*, 1990). He has also published more books that specifically focus on nature. *The Control of Nature*, published in 1989, sounds one of the main themes of his work in general: that as persistent and imaginative as humankind may be in the struggle against the forces of water, fire, and earth, nature will prove to be more uncontrolled and stubborn, more imaginative. McPhee's three separate milieus in the book—the deltaic shifts of the Mississippi River, the surges of molten rock from an Icelandic volcano, and the intermittent debris flows in the San Gabriel Mountains near Los Angeles—serve up some interesting battles that dramatize both nature's awesome power and human beings' amazing ingenuity. In these battles, as in the battle between Ahab and Moby Dick, the victor seems predetermined, but the contest is a chance to view both the spectacle of nature and the endurance of the individual. For instance, in the section titled "Los Angeles Against the Mountains," he describes the undaunted Genofiles, a family who survived the nightmare of a debris flow, as heroes, of sorts. After their house is inundated with mud and rock up to their chins, leaving them inches away from suffocation, they decide to rebuild and remain where they are on the mountain. There is something laudable about their courage, about their standing up to ultimate forces, about their skillful creation of their "fortress," but, overall, McPhee notes the irony in the human warfare with the mountain. Reservoirs and debris basins, artificial craters cut into the sides of the mountain to contain streams of debris that flow across homes and cars, can take in well over a million cubic yards in a season. Clear-out costs can exceed sixty million dollars each year. Much of the rock is returned to the mountains, where it becomes fodder for the next debris flow. In this Sisyphean situation, nature always wins, even if people look heroic in their refusal to quit trying. "If Los Angeles hangs on long enough," McPhee says, "it will cart the mountains entirely away, but already it is having difficulty figuring out where to put them" (p. 265).

Annals of the Former World

In McPhee's largest effort, *Annals of the Former World*, his quartet on geology written between 1978 and 1993, he chooses his most impressive hero—the earth itself. The four books—*Basin and Range* (1981), *In Suspect Terrain* (1983), *Rising from the Plains* (1986), and *Assembling California* (1993)—describe his journeys across America with professional geologists. He travels mainly along Interstate 80, the spine that connects all four of the books, allowing him to cover huge portions of the country but also to cut deeply into the meaning of the new geology. William Howarth has written that texts are journeys, and in that sense travel provides the structure for *Annals of the Former World*, a journey into deep time, into a more profound and humbling perspective on our companionship with the earth. In a certain respect, as David Espey points out in an article on John McPhee as travel writer, the journeys in *Annals of the Former World* are a form of time travel, roadcuts that offer a view of the geologic past.

McPhee never explicitly accounts for his fascination with geology, and although his observation of the natural world at Camp Keewaydin may shed some light on his interest, there may be another explanation. One of the geologists in *In Suspect Terrain* declares that geology is something like scientifically approved tourism. And McPhee, like Thoreau, is a traveler in the deepest sense of the term, as David Espey says, a person who "subordinates travel to the task of studying the disciplines and the characters with whom he journeys" (p. 174).

In *Annals of the Former World*, the earth may be the enduring hero, but the main characters are the geologist-guides like Anita Harris and David Love, and the conflict centers on the revolutionary theory of plate tectonics. In the first book in the series, *Basin and Range*, McPhee focuses on the mystery of the earth and the science that studies it. Geology is laced with the humanities. According to geologist Karen Kleinspehn: "You can't prove things as rigorously as physicists or chemists do" (p. 12). It is a picture with, as McPhee says, 99 percent of it in darkness, melted or broken to bits. Therefore, theory, based upon the available knowledge, brings the rest of the picture into a flickering light. Plate-tectonic theory offers the most recent "consensual biography of the earth." The theory has it that some twenty crustal plates, thin and rigid as pieces of eggshell, divide the earth. These plates move, drift together, and gradually separate, collide, or slide past one another. The motions are expressed in earthquakes, a climactic moment for humans where, in a sense, two time scales coincide. In the movement of the plates the continents are assembled and disassembled over geologic time. McPhee describes this process as "structure on the move," a phrase that could describe his narratives as well. The lesson in all this, McPhee suggests, is that the earth is ever-changing and shifting.

In his next book on geology, *In Suspect Terrain*, McPhee presents an opposing view, that of Anita Harris, a paleontologist working for the U.S. Geological Survey. Anita, like her late husband Leonard Harris, is an iconoclast. She believes that plate-tectonic theory has been overapplied, that geologists often claim to see details that simply cannot be accounted for by the theory.

In *Rising from the Plains*, the third book in the series, McPhee drifts from theory to its personification in a portrait of field geologist David Love of Wyoming. Love is a firm individualist, a man cut from the same American cloth as David Brower in *Encounters with the Archdruid* or Mike Potts, a trapper in *Coming into the Country*. Like those men, he leaves at a young age to go off into the mountains, a Thoreau sounding the depths of his own character and connection to the world. David Love is the embodiment of the field geologist, a man who becomes for McPhee the focus of three time periods. There is the present: Love's exploration of Wyoming; the frontier past: Love's mother's witty and beautifully written diary; and the geologic past: the story of the geological history of the area.

In *Assembling California*, the final volume in the tetralogy, McPhee's guide is Eldridge Moores, a University of California at Davis geologist. This is the climactic volume, the story of, among other things, earthquakes, one of the most dramatic aspects of plate tectonics. In this book, McPhee moves to the western end of the continent to focus on the point where human and geological time intersect. The final effect of these four volumes is to place our often arrogant sense of time and of our individual importance in the broader geological perspective, where human history is a blink of the giant's eye and the earth abideth forever. Tony Hillerman has said that he switched from journalism to fiction because he wanted to work with clay rather than marble. McPhee has proven, specifically in his tetralogy, that he can structure narrative out of the most unyielding materials. A statement in an essay by the novelist Alice Walker sums up many of McPhee's themes, especially those that converge in *Annals of the Former World*: "I couldn't live without the earth. Those who speak of living in outer space are crazy. The earth gives me everything."

Conclusion

In the spirit of nature writers like Henry David Thoreau, essayists like E. B. White, and reporters like Joseph Mitchell, John McPhee has a secure position in American literary history. Even if the debate about how to define his work continues, he will be acclaimed for the breadth and consistency of his achievement. In his eclectic topics and crisply defined subjects, he never strays from his one true course of study: nature, human nature, in a variety of contexts from the city to the wilderness. His expert-guides are his subjects

and his teachers at the same time. Often, they seem to be his alter egos, as when he describes his encounter with a northwoods game warden named John McPhee in the essay "North of the C.P. Line."

> Whenever I think about him, however, I feel such a strong sense of identification and I wonder if it is not a touch of envy—an ancestral form of envy, a benign and wistful envy, innocent of chagrin. As anyone might, I wish I knew what he knows—and wish not merely for his knowledge but for his compatibility with the backcountry and everything that lives there. I envy him his world, I suppose, in the way that one is sometimes drawn to be another person or live the life of a character in a fiction. Time and again, when I think of him, and such thoughts start running through my mind, I invariably find myself wishing that I were John McPhee. (*Table of Contents*, pp. 292–293)

Indeed, many of his readers find themselves wishing to be John McPhee, wanting to be travelers through time and place, into the heart of the American wilderness, seeking the true and individual American heart.

Selected Bibliography

WORKS OF JOHN McPHEE

BOOKS

A Sense of Where You Are (New York: Farrar, Straus, and Giroux, 1965); *The Headmaster* (New York: Farrar, Straus, and Giroux, 1966); *Oranges* (New York: Farrar, Straus, and Giroux, 1967); *The Pine Barrens* (New York: Farrar, Straus, and Giroux, 1968); *A Roomful of Hovings and Other Profiles* (New York: Farrar, Straus, and Giroux, 1968); *Levels of the Game* (New York: Farrar, Straus, and Giroux, 1969); *The Crofter and the Laird* (New York: Farrar, Straus, and Giroux, 1970); *Encounters with the Archdruid* (New York: Farrar, Straus, and Giroux, 1971); *The Deltoid Pumpkin Seed* (New York: Farrar, Straus, and Giroux, 1973); *The Curve of Binding Energy* (New York: Farrar, Straus, and Giroux, 1974); *Pieces of the Frame* (New York: Farrar, Straus, and Giroux, 1975); *The Survival of the Bark Canoe* (New York: Farrar, Straus, and Giroux, 1975); *Coming into the Country* (New York: Farrar, Straus, and Giroux, 1977); *Giving Good Weight* (New York: Farrar, Straus, and Giroux, 1979).

Basin and Range (New York: Farrar, Straus, and Giroux, 1981); *In Suspect Terrain* (New York: Farrar, Straus, and Giroux, 1983); *La Place de la Concorde Suisse* (New York: Farrar, Straus, and Giroux, 1984); *Table of Contents* (New York: Farrar, Straus, and Giroux, 1985); *Rising from the Plains* (New York: Farrar, Straus, and Giroux, 1986); *The Control of Nature* (New York: Farrar, Straus, and Giroux, 1989); *Looking for a Ship* (New York: Farrar, Straus, and Giroux, 1990); *Assembling California* (New York: Farrar, Straus, and Giroux, 1993); *The Ransom of Russian Art* (New York: Farrar, Straus, and Giroux, 1994).

SELECTED UNCOLLECTED FICTION

"The Fair of San Gennaro," in *TransAtlantic Review* 8 (winter 1961); "Eucalyptus Trees," in *Reporter* (19 October 1967); "Ruth, the Sun Is Shining," in *Playboy* (April 1968).

SELECTED NONFICTION FROM *NEW YORKER*

"Big Plane" (19 February 1966); "Two Commissioners" (5 March 1966); "Coliseum Hour" (12 March 1966); "Beauty and Horror" (28 May 1966); "Girl in a Paper Dress" (25 June 1966); "On the Way to Gladstone" (9 July 1966); "Ms and FeMs at the Biltmore" (12 July 1966); "The License Plates of Burning Tree" (30 January 1971); "Three Gatherings" (25 December 1971); "The Conching Rooms" (13 May 1972).

"Sullen Gold" (25 March 1974); "Flavors & Fragrances" (8 April 1974); "Police Story" (15 July 1974); "'Time' Covers, NR" (28 October 1974); "The P-1800" (10 February 1975); "In Virgin Forest" (6 July 1987); "Release" (28 September 1987); "Altimeter Man" (25 September 1989); "Travels of the Rock" (26 February 1990); "Irons in the Fire" (20 December 1993).

ARTICLES IN *TIME* AND SELECTED MAGAZINES

Time cover stories on Mort Sahl (15 August 1960); Jean Kerr (14 April 1961); Jackie Gleason (29 December 1961); Sophia Loren (6 April 1962); Joan Baez (23 November 1962); Richard Burton (26 April 1963); Barbra Streisand (10 April 1964); and the New York World's Fair (5 June 1964).

" . . . Josie's Well," in *Holiday* (January 1970); "Pieces of the Frame," in *Atlantic* (January 1970); "Centre Court," in *Playboy* (June 1971); "Tennis," in *New York Times Book Review* (10 June 1973), p. 1; "The People of New Jersey's Pine Barrens," in *National Geographic* 145 (January 1974), with photographs by W. R. Curtsinger.

INTERVIEWS

Interview with the author, 1992, Princeton, New Jersey; Douglas Vipond and Russell A. Hunt, "The Strange Case of the Queen-Post Trust: John McPhee on Writing and Reading," in *College Composition and Communication* 42 (May 1991).

BIOGRAPHICAL AND CRITICAL STUDIES

Joanne K. Clark, "The Writings of John Angus McPhee: A Selected Bibliography," in *Bulletin of Bibliography* (January/March 1981); Robert Coles, "Alaska, the State That Came in from the Cold," in *Book World–Washington Post* (22 January 1978); Roderick Cook, review of *Oranges*, in *Harper's* (March 1967); John F. Baker, "John McPhee," in *Publishers Weekly* (3 January 1977); Edgar Allen Beem, "John McPhee on Maine: Conversation with the Archjournalist," in *Maine Times* (1 November 1985); Spencer Brown, "The Odor of Durability," in *Sewanee Review* (winter 1978); Benjamin DeMott, "Two Reporters: At Peace and War," in *Atlantic* (January 1978); "Devouring a Small Country Inn," in *Time* (12 March 1979); Dennis Drabelle, "Conversations with John McPhee," in *Sierra* (October/November/December 1978); Tom Dunkel, "Pieces of McPhee," in *New Jersey Monthly* (August 1986); David Eason, "The New Journalism and the Image-World," in *Literary Journalism in the Twentieth Century*, ed. by Norman Sims (New York: Oxford Univ. Press, 1990); David Espey, "The Wilds of New Jersey: John McPhee as Travel Writer," in *Temperamental Journeys: Essays on the Modern Literature of Travel*, ed. by Michael Kowalewski (Athens: Univ. of Georgia Press, 1992).

Donald Hall, "Johnny Can Write," in *National Review* (31 March 1978); Joan Hamilton, "An Encounter with John McPhee," in *Sierra* (May/June 1990); Edward Hoagland, "Where Life Begins Over," in *New York Times Book Review* (27 November 1977); William Howarth, intro. to *The John McPhee Reader* (New York: Farrar, Straus, and Giroux, 1976), and "Itinerant Passages: Recent American Essays," in *Sewanee Review* (fall 1988); Rex Lardner, "Shoot That Ball," in *New York Times Book Review* (28 November 1965); John Leonard, "Books of the Times," in *New York Times* (25 November 1977), sec. 3; Barbara Lounsberry, "John McPhee's Levels of the Earth," in her *The Art of Fact: Contemporary Artists of Nonfiction* (Westport, Conn.: Greenwood, 1990); Pamela Marsh, "The Lively Snippet, the Appetizing Trifle," in *Christian Science Monitor* (1 February 1969); Leslie Moore, "The Architectonics of the Personal Essay," in *English Journal* 81 (October 1992); Michael Pearson, "Twenty Questions: A Conversation with John McPhee," in *Creative Nonfiction* 1 (fall 1993).

Tony Schwartz, "Establishing the Levels of the Game," in *More* (July/August 1976); Israel Shenker, "The Annals of McPhee," in *New York Times* (11 January 1976), sec. 11; Norman Sims, "The Literary Journalist," in his *The Literary Journalists* (New York: Ballantine, 1984); Stephen Singular, "Talk with John McPhee," in *New York Times Book Review* (27 November 1977); Kathy Smith, "John McPhee Balances the Act," in *Literary Journalism in the Twentieth Century*, ed. by Norman Sims (New York: Oxford Univ. Press, 1990); Jeannette Smyth, "John McPhee of the *New Yorker*," in *Washington Post* (19 March 1978), sec. L; Phillip Terrie, "The River of Paradox," in *Western American Literature* 23 (May 1988); Ronald Weber, "Letting Subjects Grow: Literary Non-fiction from the *New Yorker*," in *Antioch Review* (fall 1978), repr. in Roland Weber, *The Literature of Fact: Literary Nonfiction in American Writing* (Athens: Ohio Univ. Press, 1980).